GUN TRADER'S GUIDE™

Thirty-Eighth Edition

A Comprehensive, Fully Illustrated Guide to Modern Collectible Firearms with Current Market Values

Edited by Robert A. Sadowski

Skyhorse Publishing

Skyhorse Publishing books may be purchased in bulk at special discounts for sales promotion, corporate gifts, fund-raising, or educational purposes. Special editions can also be created to specifications. For details, contact the Special Sales Department, Skyhorse Publishing, 307 West 36th Street, 11th Floor, New York, NY 10018 or info@skyhorsepublishing.com.

Skyhorse® and Skyhorse Publishing® are registered trademarks of Skyhorse Publishing, Inc.®, a Delaware corporation.

Visit our website at www.skyhorsepublishing.com.

10 9 8 7 6 5 4 3 2 1

Library of Congress Cataloging-in-Publication Data is available on file.

Cover design by Brian Peterson
Cover photographs courtesy Browning and Barrett

Print ISBN: 978-1-5107-1092-4
Ebook ISBN: 978-1-5107-1094-8

Printed in Canada

Contents

Introduction

Welcome to the 38th Edition of *Gun Trader's Guide* (*GTG*), the most comprehensive reference for identifying and determining the value of modern firearms. Each year we update this magnificent tome so you can be sure you are getting the most current values on all modern firearms. In fact, for more than half a century, *GTG* has been the standard reference for collectors, curators, dealers, shooters, hunters, and gun enthusiasts. Because *GTG* is updated annually, it remains the definitive source for making informed decisions on selling and purchasing used firearms. Over 2 million copies have been sold. We at *GTG* take buying and selling firearms as serious business. Whether you are buying a used gun for duck hunting, trading in your old concealed carry pistol for something better, or trying to figure out the value of a wall hanger you've come into possession of, *GTG* is a valuable resource used by both professional and amateur firearms enthusiasts.

CURRENT AND UP-TO-DATE

GTG offers detailed firearms specifications as well as photographs so you can be more confident when identifying a firearm and its value.

The *GTG* is revised annually to ensure information is both current and detailed. In the past fifty years, *GTG* has grown to over six hundred pages and more than six thousand standard firearms and their variations, evolving into one of the most complete catalogs of modern smokeless-powder rifles, shotguns, and handguns from the very late 19th century, through the 20th century, to the 21st century. Every effort is made to ensure the information is current and up-to-date. Not every gun ever manufactured can be listed in a catalog of this size, but every effort has been made to include the makes and models that are most popular with collectors. Please note *GTG* does not include antique or recently manufactured blackpowder firearms.

EASY-TO-USE FORMAT

GTG's reference guide format is simple and straightforward. Three tabbed sections—handguns, rifles, and shotguns—make it fast and easy to find the model in question. Entries are alphabetized by manufacturer and model with specifications that include:

- Manufacturer
- Model Name
- Model Number
- Caliber or Gauge
- Barrel Length
- Overall Length
- Weight
- Distinguishing features
- Variations of different models
- Dates of manufacture (when they can be accurately determined)
- Date of discontinuation (if applicable)
- Current value for condition
- Photos (or illustrations)

EXTENSIVE PHOTOGRAPHS

Unique to *GTG* are photographs to help identify and compare firearms. The exclusive and extensive pictorial format, along with comprehensive specifications, provide a complete resource for identifying firearms and their current value.

ACCURATE FIREARM VALUES

Values shown are based on national averages obtained by conferring with knowledgeable gun dealers, traders, collectors, online auction sites, and auctioneers around the country, not by applying an arbitrary mathematical formula that could produce unrealistic figures. The listed values accurately reflect the nationwide average at the time of publication and are updated annually. Keep in mind that the stated values are averages based on a wide spectrum of variables. No price given in any such catalog should be considered the one and only value for a particular firearm. Value is ultimately determined by the buyer and seller. Supply and demand also dictate price.

In the case of rare or one-of-a-kind items, such as the Winchester Model 1873 One of One Thousand rifle or the Parker AA1 Special shotgun in 28 gauge, where little trading takes place, active gun collectors were consulted to obtain current market values.

In researching data, some manufacturers' records were unavailable and at times information was unobtainable. Some early firearms manufacturers' production records have been destroyed in fires, lost, or were simply not maintained accurately. These circumstances resulted in some minor deviations in the presentation format of certain model listings. For example, production dates may not be listed when manufacturing records are unclear or unavailable. As an alternative, approximate dates of manufacture may be listed to reflect the availability of guns from a manufacturer or distributor. These figures may represent disposition dates indicating when that particular model was shipped to a distributor or importer. Frequently, and especially with foreign manufacturers, production records are unavailable. Therefore, availability information is often based on importation records that reflect domestic distribution only.

This is meant to explain the procedure and policy used regarding these published dates and to establish the distinction between production dates, which are based on manufacturers' records, and availability dates, which are based on distribution records in the absence of recorded production data.

To ensure *GTG* has the most accurate information available, we encourage and request users contact our research staff at Skyhorse Publishing, especially in relation to older out-of-production models.

ACKNOWLEDGMENTS

The publisher wishes to express special thanks to the many collectors, dealers, manufacturers, shooting editors, firearm firms and distributors' public relations and production personnel, research personnel, and other industry professionals who provide us with updates throughout the year. We are especially grateful for their assistance and cooperation in compiling information for this edition, as well as allowing *GTG* to reproduce photographs and illustrations of their collectible firearms. Special thanks to James D. Julia Auctioneers, Fairfield, Maine, (www.jamesdjulia.com) and Rock Island Auctions (www.rockislandauction.com) for the use of photos.

Finally, *GTG* thanks all the dedicated readers who take the time to email us with comments, suggestions, and queries about collectible firearms. We appreciate and value your input.

Readers may send comments or suggestions to: info@skyhorsepublishing.com

Sales of Note: Winchester 1886 — Serial No. 1
The new world record for a single firearm sold at auction is now $1.265 million, which was paid for a Winchester Model 1886 Sporting Rifle—serial number 1—auctioned through Rock Island Auction Company (rockislandauction.com) in March 2016. The Model 1886 is a popular rifle with Winchester collectors. The condition was graded as excellent and showed little wear and relatively minor handling marks. Not only is this rifle serial number

one, which makes it extremely rare, the provenance of this rifle it made it even more valuable.

This Winchester Model 1886 rifle was presented to Congressional Medal of Honor Recipient Capt. Henry W. Lawton on September 27, 1866. Lawton was the individual who captured Geronimo. With a long service record of valor during the Civil War, Lawton made the Army his career and with the 4th Cavalry fought in campaigns against the Kiowa and Comanche nations. It was in the summer of 1886, under direct orders of Gen. Nelson A. Miles, that Capt. Lawton, along with Capt. Charles Gatewood, led a small force of soldiers and Apache scouts into Mexico. Their mission was to hunt down and capture hostile Chiricahua Apaches led by Geronimo. Lawton was relentless, chasing Geronimo and his band over 1,300 miles through Mexico and Arizona territory. In September 1886, Gatewood and Lawton caught up with Geronimo and negotiated a surrender. Geronimo and his people were the last of the hostile Apaches to surrender to the U.S. Army and ended over two decades of bloody conflict in the Southwest.

According to Rock Island Auction's catalogue, "the Model 1886 Sporting Rifle has a 26-inch full octagon barrel and full length magazine . . . and was presented to Lawton along with a gold pocket watch made by C. Howard & Company, Boston."

This is a truly one-of-a-kind rifle, owned by a well-known and decorated soldier responsible for ending one of the bloody eras in our country's history. Special thanks for Rock Island Auction for providing information and photographs.—Robert A. Sadowski, ed.

POPULAR SALES IN 2015

Online auction sites like Gunbroker.com publish a "Best Sellers" list. Here is a look at what used firearms sold best on Gunbroker.com in 2015.

Semiauto Pistols
1: Colt 1911
2: Glock G22
3: Heckler & Koch USP

Revolvers
1: Colt Python
2: Ruger Blackhawk
3: Smith & Wesson 10

Semiauto Rifles   1: Ruger Mini-14
2: Springfield M1 Garand
3: Ruger 10/22

Bolt-Action Rifles
1: Remington 700
2: Winchester 70
3: Ruger M77 Hawkeye

Lever-Action Rifles
1: Winchester 94

2: Marlin 336
3: Marlin 1894

Semiauto Shotguns
1: Remington 1100
2: Browning A5
3: Remington 11-87

Pump-Action Shotguns
1: Mossberg 500
2: Remington 870
3: Remington 870 Wingmaster

Over/Under Shotguns
1: Browning Citori
2: Ruger Red Label
3: Winchester 101

Single-Shot Rifles
1: H&R Handi-Rifle
2: Ruger No. 1

3: Winchester 1885

Pump-Action Rifles
1: Remington 760
2: Remington 7600
3: Winchester 61

Single-Shot Shotguns
1: Winchester 37
2: H&R Topper
3: Browning BT-99

Side-by-Side Shotguns
1: Stoeger Coach Gun
2: Stoeger Uplander
3: CZ-USA Bobwhite

How to Use *GTG*

Are you planning on buying or selling a used rifle, shotgun, or handgun? Perhaps you just want to establish the value of a favorite rifle, shotgun, or handgun in your collection. No matter what your interest in collectible modern, smokless-powder firearms, today's enthusiast inevitably turns to the *Gun Trader's Guide (GTG)* to determine specifications, date of manufacture, and the average value (in the United States) of a specific modern firearm.

Opening the book, the collector asks him- or herself the first obvious question: "How much is my used gun worth?" Values contained in this book should be considered retail; that is, the average price a collector anywhere in the United States may expect to pay for a firearm in similar condition. Don't leap to the conclusion that your firearm will bring top dollar! There is no right or wrong price for any collectible firearm. The listings shown here are based on national averages and may be higher or lower depending on where you live and the strength of the market in your area. There is a market for everything from folk art to Star Wars action

figures, but the range of values can be extreme and only items in perfect condition will bring top dollar.

Many variables must be considered when buying or selling a used gun. Scarcity, demand, geographic location, and the buyer's position. The condition of the gun ultimately governs the selling price. Sentiment often shades the value of a particular gun in the seller's mind, but the market value of Grandpa's old .30-30 cannot be logically cataloged nor effectively marketed—except possibly to someone else in the family!

GRANDPA'S DEER GUN

To illustrate how the price of a particular gun may fluctuate, let us consider the popular Winchester Model 94 (it was discontinued in 2006, after 110 years of continuous production, then reintroduced in 2010) and see what its value might be.

The Model 1894 (or Model 94) is a lever-action, solid-frame repeater. Round or octagon barrels of twenty-six inches were standard when the rifle was first introduced in 1894. However, half-octagon barrels were offered for a slight increase in price. Various magazine lengths were also available.

Many firearms are inherited from avid hunters or shooters. Since such firearms were used, they will not have as high a value as firearms in new or mint condition.

Fancy grade versions in all calibers were available featuring a checkered walnut pistol grip stock and forearm.

In addition, Winchester produced this model in a carbine style with a saddle ring on the left side of the receiver. The carbine had a twenty inch round barrel and a full or half magazine. Some carbines were supplied with standard-grade barrels while others were made of nickel steel. Trapper models were also available with shorter fourteen-, sixteen-, or eighteen-inch barrels.

In later years, the Rifle and Trapper models were discontinued, and only the carbine remained. Eventually, the saddle ring was eliminated from this model and the carbine butt stock was replaced with a shotgun-type butt stock and shortened forend.

After World War II, the finish on Winchester Model 94 carbines changed to strictly hot caustic bluing; thus, prewar models usually demand a premium over postwar models.

In 1964 (a turning point for many American firearms manufacturers), beginning with serial number 2,700,000, the action on the Winchester Model 94 was redesigned for easier manufacture. Many collectors and firearms enthusiasts considered this and other design changes to be inferior to former models. Therefore, the term pre-'64 has become the watchword for collectors when it comes to setting values on Winchester-made firearms. This will likely be the case in the future, as the now-discontinued models 70, 94, and 1300 Winchester reach the collectible market.

Whether this evaluation is correct or not is unimportant. The justification for an immediate increase in the value of pre-'64 models was that they were no longer available. This diminished availability placed them in the scarce class, making them more desirable to collectors.

Shortly after the 1964 transition, Winchester began producing Model 94 com-memorative models in great numbers, which added confusion to the concept of limited production. Increased availability adversely affected the annual appreciation and price stability of these commemorative models. The negative response generated by this marketing practice was increased when Winchester was sold in the 1980s. The name of this long-established American firearms manufacturer was changed to U.S. Repeating Arms Company, which manufactured the Model 94 in standard, carbine, and big-bore models until 2006. Later, the Angle-Eject model was introduced, a design change that allowed for the mounting of scope sights directly above the action. Currently the Model 94 in various configurations are in production in Japan; originals were built in New Haven, Connecticut.

With the above facts in mind, let's explore *GTG* to establish the approximate value of your particular Model

Winchester Model 94 Lever Action Saddle Ring Carbine with 20-inch round barrel, walnut stock, chambered in .32 W.S. (Winchester Special), and manufactured in 1927. This example rates GOOD (Gd). Courtesy of Rock Island Auctions.

94. We will assume that you recently inherited the rifle, which has "Winchester Model 94" inscribed on the barrel. Turn to the "Rifle" section of the book and look under "Winchester." The index at the back of the book is another way to locate your rifle.

The listings in the *GTG* are arranged within each manufacturer's entry, first by model numbers in consecutive order followed by model names in alphabetical order. At first glance, you see that there are two model designations that may apply: the original designation (Model 1894) or the revised, shorter designation (Model 94). Which of these designations applies to your recently acquired Winchester?

The next step in the process is to try to match the appearance of your model with an illustration in the book. The photos may all look alike at first glance, but close evaluation and careful attention to detail will enable you to eliminate models that are not applicable. Further examination of your gun might reveal a curved or crescent-shaped butt plate. By careful observation of your gun's characteristics and close visual comparison of the photographic examples, you may logically conclude that your gun is the Winchester Model 94 Lever-Action Carbine. (Please note that the guns shown in the *GTG* are not always shown in proportion to one another; that is, a carbine barrel might not appear to be shorter than a rifle barrel.)

You have now tentatively determined your model, but to be sure, you should read through the specifications for that model and establish that the barrel on the pictured rifle is twenty-six inches long and round, octagonal, or half-octagonal.

Upon measuring you find that the barrel on your rifle is approximately twenty inches, and it is round. Additionally, your rifle is marked .32 W.S. The caliber offerings listed in the specifications include .32 W.S., so you are further convinced that this is your gun. You may read on to determine that this rifle was manufactured from 1894 to 1937. After that date, only the shorter-barreled carbine was offered by Winchester, and then only in .25-35, .30-30, and .38-55.

At this point, you know you have a Winchester Model 94 manufactured before World War II. You read the value and take the rifle to your dealer to initiate a sale.

Here is a look at some of the trades you may encounter for Grandpa's deer rifle:

WHAT TO EXPECT
Since the rifle rates Gd, this means there are/may be some minor replacement parts, the metal is smoothly rusted or lightly pitted in places, and the stock is lightly scratched, bruised or minor cracks repaired. It is also in good working order. However, keep in mind that the dealer is in business to make a profit. If he pays you the full value of the gun, he will have to charge more than this when he sells it to make a reasonable profit.

Therefore, expect a reputable dealer to offer you less than the published value for the gun in its present condition. The exact amount will vary for a variety of reasons. For example, if the dealer already has a dozen or so of the same model on his shelf and they do not sell well, his offer will be considerably lower. On the other hand, if the dealer does not have any of this model in stock and knows several collectors who want it, chances are his offer will be considerably higher.

Maybe you think refinishing the rifle will increase the value. Even when a collectible firearm has been expertly refinished to excellent condition, it is no longer original, and a rule of thumb is to deduct 50 percent from the value listed in this book. If the job is poorly done, deduct 80 percent or more.

TOP-DOLLAR OPTIONS
One alternative for getting top dollar for your gun is to go online and list it with one

of several online gun auction websites, and sell the firearm directly to a private collector. Many collectors have a special interest in certain models, manufacturers, or product lines and will happily pay full price and sometimes more for a hard-to-find piece. However, this approach may prove time-consuming, frustrating, and expensive. Online auction websites charge fees, and you have to package and ship the firearm to your buyer's FFL dealer. In addition, there may be federal and local restrictions on the sale of firearms in your area, so be sure to check with the local police chief or sheriff before you proceed with a private sale.

STANDARDS OF CONDITION
The condition of a firearm is an important factor in determining its value. In some rare and unusual models, a variation in condition from excellent to very good can mean a value difference of 50 percent or more. Therefore, you must be able to determine the gun's condition before you can accurately evaluate the value of the firearm.

Several sets of value standards have been used in gun trading, but the National Rifle Association Standards of Condition of Modern Firearms is the most popular, with the condition established as a percentage of original finish remaining on the wood and metal of the firearm.

Here's a look at how these standards are applied:

EXCELLENT
For the purpose of assigning comparative values as a basis for trading, firearms listed in this book are assumed to be in excellent (Ex) condition if they have 95 percent or more remaining original finish, no noticeable marring of wood or metal, and the bore has no pits or rust.

To the novice, this translates to meaning a practically new gun, almost as though it had just been removed from its shipping box. The trained eye, however, will see the difference between new in the box (NiB) or mint condition and merely excellent.

VERY GOOD
Any other defects, no matter how minor, diminish the value. For example, if more than 5 percent of the original finish is gone and there are minor surface dents or scratches, regardless of how small, the gun is no longer in excellent condition. Instead, it is considered to be in very good condition, provided the gun is in perfect working order. Despite the minor defects, the gun will still look relatively new to the untrained buyer.

GOOD
If the gun is in perfect working condition and functions properly but has minor wear on working surfaces (perhaps some deep scratches on the

wood or metal), the gun is considered to be in good (Gd) condition, one grade below very good according to NRA standards. Again, the price shown in this book for that particular firearm must be reduced to reflect its true value.

The two remaining NRA conditions fall under the headings of fair and poor. These guns normally have little value unless they are of historical importance or an aficionado simply must have them to complete his collection. The value of such guns is then determined by the price the buyer is willing to pay.

In any case, do not sell any gun until you have researched its history and value. Many plain-looking guns have sold for thousands of dollars for a variety of reasons. Many an innocent widow has given away her deceased husband's guns without knowing that they were of extremely high value. Avoid buyers who are in a hurry to make a purchase or who quickly offer what seems to be more money than the gun is worth. Not every gun is priceless, but many of them are nearly so!

GTG offers multiplication factors to use for firearms in other than excellent condition. These factors are listed below. Be aware that the figures given are simply another rough means of establishing value.

For guns in other-than-excellent condition, multiply the price shown in this book for the model in question by the following factors:

Multiplication Factors:

Condition	X	Factor
Mint or New (NiB)		1.25
Excellent (Ex)		1.00
Very Good (VG)		.85
Good (Gd)		.68
Fair		.45
Poor		.15

UNIQUE SERIAL NUMBERS

The serial number on a firearm can increase the value if it is unique, and consecutive serial numbers can boost value to a set of firearms.

PROVENANCE

Provenance means place or source of origin. In gun trading, it means who owned the gun and to a certain extent, when or where the gun was used. Beware of Jesse James six-shooters or else I may want to sell you the Brooklyn Bridge. Make sure the gun has documentation stating prior ownership. It can mean the difference between a really valuable firearm or a really expensive fake.

PARTING THOUGHTS

Remember, the word "guide" in *GTG* should be taken literally. This book is meant to be a reference only and is not the gospel of the collectible trade. We sincerely hope, however, that you find this publication useful when you decide to buy or sell a used collectible modern firearm.

Also, keep in mind that gun values vary from region to region. For example, lever-action deer rifles are more popular among collectors and hunters in the east, while bolt-action bean field rifles bring higher prices in the south and west. For this reason, we recommend that you attend regional gun shows, auctions, and look online to develop a better understanding of local gun values and pricing. And, whenever you travel, check the prices of guns you're familiar with to compare their values in other parts of the country. The difference can be surprising!

Finally, beware of guns that have been refinished or refurbished by amateurs or even expert gunsmiths. A century-old gun that looks brand new has probably been refinished and will actually be worth far less than a time-worn original. Every new screw, pin, or spring added to an original firearm diminishes its value—the worn, pitted original parts of a firearm enhance its value far more than modern replacements. Refinishing a gun may improve its looks and satisfy the final owner, but it will lose collectible value that will never be recovered.

ABBREVIATIONS:

ACP = Automatic Colt Pistol	lbs. = Pounds	SL = Self Loading
Adj. = Adjustable	LC = Long Colt	Spl. = Special
AE = Action Express	LR = Long Rifle	STW = Shooting Times Westerner
Auto. = Automatic	M = Modified choke	Syn. = Synthetic
Avail. = Available	M&P = Military & Police	TH = Target Hammer
Bbl. = Barrel	Mag. = Magnum	TT = Target Trigger
C = Cylinder choke	Mfg. = Manufactured	UCC = Usel Caseless Cartridge
c. = Circa	mm = Millimeter	Vent. = Ventilated
DA = Double Action	NiB = New in Box	VR = Vent rib
Disc. = Discontinued	NM = National Match	w/ = with
Eject. = Ejector	O/U = Over-and-under	w/o = without
F = Full choke	Reintro. = Reintroduced	Wby. = Weatherby
FN = Fabrique Nationale	Rem. = Remington	Win = Winchester
Ga. = Gauge	Rnd. = Round	WMR = Winchester Magnum Rimfire
H&H = Holland & Holland	S/N = serial number	WRF = Winchester Rimfire
IC = Improved Cylinder choke	S/S = side-by-side	
in. = inch	SA = Single Action	
L.H. = Left hand	SK = Skeet choke	

Colt Model 1911 Semi-Automatic Pistol

Adopted by the U.S. Ordnance Department in 1911, the Colt semi-automatic pistol was originally manufactured by Colt and the government's Springfield Armory. In 1917, with the US entry into World War I, the government contracted with Colt for one million pistols and contracts were signed for the production of a total of two million more pistols with Remington-UMC, North American Arms, Savage, Winchester, National Cash Register Co., Burroughs Adding Machine, Lamston Monotype, and Caron Bros. A total of 629,000 pistols were completed by the war's end in1918. Production was resumed in 1924 with a series of design modifications introduced during the inter-war period resulting in the Model 1911 A1. From the onset of World War II until its end in 1945 Colt, Remington UMC, Remington-Rand, Ithaca, Singer, and Union Switch and Signal Company manufactured nearly 2 million M1911A1s.

NRA Perfect Condition is 100 percent original condition. This Colt 1911 has all original parts and commands the same price with or without the box. The frame and receiver are in perfect condition with no wear or damage. The checkering on the grip is in "as new" condition and the wood shows no wear, scratches, or stains.

NRA Good Condition ranges from 60 to 80 percent original condition. There are no replacement parts. This 1911 has worn, rounded edges on the frame with slight pitting and scratches. The bluing is thinning on the working surfaces and stampings show minor wear in areas. The checkering on the grips is slightly rounded with minor nicks. The wood is in good condition, not cracked or stained. A good condition pistol must be in safe working condition.

NRA Fair Condition ranges from 20 to 60 percent original condition. This Model 1911 is in well-worn condition with the frame retaining only 40 percent of its original finish. Some major and minor parts have been replaced and scratches and pitting from rust and corrosion are evident on the frame and slide. Serial numbers and other markings are shallow and difficult to identify. While the grips on this pistol are not badly scratched or soiled, they show worn checkering and several large and small dents. The gun must function and shoot properly.

Winchester Model 94

Winchester produced approximately 2,550,000 Model 94 lever action rifles between 1894 and 1962. The Model 94 was manufactured in both rifle and carbine versions with several configurations that included pistol- and straight-grip stocks, various grades of wood, and several different barrel lengths and magazine capacities. Crescent and shotgun style buttstocks and takedown barrels were also offered. The Model 94 was produced in 25-35, 30, 30-30, 32-40 and 38-55 calibers.

NRA Perfect Condition ranges from 95 to 100 percent original condition. This Model 94 shows very little use and looks in new condition with 96 percent of its original finish remaining. All parts are original and in excellent condition. There is no noticeable wear with the wood and metal showing no stains, scratches or nicks. The bluing is in near-perfect condition. The action functions smoothly and the rifle is in perfect working condition.

NRA Good Condition ranges from 60 to 80 percent original condition. There are no replacement parts. The gun has all original parts and shows no corrosive rusting or pitting. The edges of the action are slightly rounded and the bluing is beginning to wear thin on the working surfaces. The stampings show minor wear in areas. There are no broken parts and the stock fits smoothly to the metal with only minor nicking. The gun must be in safe working condition.

NRA Fair Condition ranges from 20 to 60 percent original condition. This Model 94 is in well-worn condition with some minor parts replaced or requiring restoration or adjustment. The serial numbers and descriptive stampings are shallow and hard to read. The wood is badly scratched and dented with evident repairs. There is corrosive pitting and scratches but the gun remains in safe firing condition.

Winchester Model 12

When introduced in 1912, the hammerless Model 12 slide-action shotgun was offered only in 20-gauge with a 2½-inch chamber. In 1914 12- and 16-gauge versions were introduced followed by a 28-gauge in 1937. The Model 12 was available with various chokes and with walnut, straight or pistol grip stock and forearm. Winchester sold more than 1,900,000 Model 1912s during the shotgun's 51-year history.

NRA Perfect Condition is 100 percent original condition. This Model 12 is in NIB condition and has not been previously sold at retail. The shotgun shows no signs of use and retains 100 percent of its original finish. All parts are original and in new condition.

NRA Good Condition ranges from 60 to 80 percent original condition. This gun has all original parts in good condition. There is no corrosive pitting or rusting and the action displays only slightly rounded edges. The gun retains 70 percent of its original finish with bluing beginning to wear on the working surfaces. The stock fits smoothly to the metal and has only minor nicking. The shotgun must be in good working order.

NRA Fair Condition ranges from 20 to 60 percent original condition. Showing a well-worn condition, this gun may require minor parts to be replaced or adjusted. The serial numbers and descriptive stamping are shallow and difficult to read. The wood is badly scratched and dented with evident repairs. Corrosive pitting and scratches in the metal, while considerable, do not render the gun unsafe.

The Art of Gun Trading

No matter if you are trading baseball cards, action figures, or fine firearms, there is an art and a science to the process that beginners often fail to realize and seasoned experts rely on. In other words, if you do not know what you are doing, you can expect to be burned—badly, in some cases.

GUN TRADING BASICS

As is the case when selling any collectible item, there is no substitute for research.

The first step in shrewd gun trading is to know your firearm, its condition, and its value in your market—meaning your part of the country. A Marlin .30/30 lever-action rifle, for example, will not carry as high a value in California, Georgia, or Texas as it will in Pennsylvania, Maine, New York, or elsewhere in the east, where short-range brush-country guns are most popular.

Next, study the NRA Standards of Condition (see pages xii-xiv) and get a feel for such terms as New In Box, Excellent, and Good and what they mean to a collector.

DICKERING HOW-TO

When it comes to "horse trading" there are no rules, but the conflict is always the same: Each party wants to come out a winner.

Below are a few tips for the new gun trader to consider.

DON'T SAY TOO MUCH

Present the gun to the prospective buyer and let him or her make all the comments and ask all the questions.

DECIDE ON A PRICE

This requires a little of the poker player's panache. If you name a price and the buyer pounces on it, then you came in too low. But set the price too high and he or she might walk away.

The right price will keep a buyer interested, which is why knowing your gun and its value is important.

DON'T LIE OR EMBELLISH

Gun collectors generally know their guns as well as anyone and are quick to spot a fraud. If your gun is not in its original condition, has been refurbished, or is not what it appears to be, be honest and say so. If you don't know the answer to an important question, take the time to find out.

KNOW WHEN TO QUIT

Trust your instincts when a buyer seems overeager to buy your gun, tells you its value is much less than you know it is worth, or tries to tell you the gun is illegal, a fake, or otherwise not what you say it is. If you feel that you are being tricked—while either buying or selling—back away, do more research, and come back with new knowledge and a different offer.

LEARN AS YOU GO

If you spend time buying and selling guns, or any collectible for that matter, you are going to make some great sales and unfortunately, you are also going to be beaten in price by a buyer or dealer who has been in the game longer than you have. Generally, the best advice is to never sell a gun for less than you paid for it. Good research will keep you from selling a $10,000 gun for $100—it happens!—or from paying thousands more than a gun is worth, which also happens.

The ultimate value of a firearm depends on the rarity of the model, the region, and the buyer's needs; rare, unusual, or one-of-a-kind guns can be worth substantially more than the standard model. It's in your best interest to find out what kind of gun you have and what it is worth before you offer it for sale.

Courtesy of NSSF.org.

Gun Shows

The best classroom for learning about the value and condition of used firearms is the weekend gun show. Dealers from the region and often across the country will attend to show, sell, buy, trade, and talk about new and used guns of every make and model. Some dealers specialize in firearms made by a specific manufacturer while some deal in just one model of firearm. Others may offer custom guns while others offer a variety of collectibles including swords, knives, and ancient weaponry.

Attending gun shows is a chance to see a wide variety of firearms, their condition, and their value at the local level. This is the place to really learn about guns and how their value is determined. Most dealers will gladly explain the nuances of gun condition, why perfectly refurbished firearms are worth so much less than a rusted, beat-up original, and what makes one firearm worth so much while another seemingly similar model is worth so much less.

GUN SHOW ETIQUETTE
Unless otherwise noted, all gun shows in the United States are open to the public. There are security requirements that must be met and procedures that must be followed. In general, anyone attending a gun show may bring guns for appraisal, sale, or trade. Laws vary from state to state, so be sure to check with show promoters or local law enforcement before bringing a gun.

Most guns shows are well attended, often crowded, and sales can be brisk. If a particular dealer or booth is overrun with customers, come back later to talk. There are always slow periods at gun shows, such as early in the day, lunchtime, and just before closing.

In general, do not bring a gun to a show and expect to get top dollar for it. Show dealers often work in volume sales and may have a dozen or more of your model on the table.

Specialty guns, of course, will draw any dealer's attention, and once in a while you will get far more than you expected from a particular firearm. However, it is best to see what the dealer is willing to give you and compare that to the prices listed in the *GTG* and other collectible gun books. If he or she is offering you a higher price than you expected, then conduct some more research because you may have a unique and valuable model.

In most cases, there will be too much diversion to allow you to make a serious sale or trade. If you are feeling rushed or pressured, move on to another dealer. Don't be rushed into a sale.

WORK THE CROWD
While huge crowds at gun shows can be a hindrance, you can use the crowd to your advantage by carrying your locked and tagged for-sale gun with you as you move around the booths. There will be gun buyers, dealers, and fans in the crowd who may stop you to discuss your firearm. A buyer who needs a particular piece to complete his collection could easily offer you more than the gun is listed for, more than the dealer offered, and more than you ever expected to get for it.

Even if you do not make a sale, you can make valuable contacts for future transactions.

Gun shows are ongoing events that occur weekly, monthly, or annually in towns and cities around the country. Some shows are sponsored by the same organizations in the same location each time, so it is easy to keep track of them.

For a complete, updated list of gun shows near you, go to gunshows-usa.com for a listing of all the gun shows scheduled in every state. Google "gun shows" and you will find both local and national shows.

Online Buying and Selling

There is not a facet of our lives that isn't touched by technology. Auction websites such as gunbroker.com, gunsamerica.com, and others offer a vast selection of firearms you can buy and sell using your computer.

Online auction websites enable sellers to reach buyers they might not have normally reached. If you are a private individual with a gun to sell, all you need to do is create an account, type in a description, take a few digital pictures of the item, and list it. It's that simple and that easy.

All the same federal, state, and local gun laws apply when selling and purchasing a gun online as when purchasing a gun at a brick-and-mortar retailer. In fact, the transfer of the firearm is the same. When a buyer purchases a firearm the buyer must provide the seller with a copy of their gun shop's FFL (Federal Firearms License) or arrange to have the seller ship the firearm to one of the FFL located near the buyer that is listed on the website. The seller then ships the gun to the gun shop with the FFL holder—not directly to the buyer—and the buyer then fills out the necessary state and local paperwork to take transfer of the gun. Gun shops usually charge the buyer a fee to transfer the gun. It is up to the buyer to be aware of state and local laws.

Auction sites charge a small percentage of the sale to all sellers. The fee is only charged if the seller actually sells the gun through an auction. There is no charge to list a firearm. When setting up an account with online auction websites, a seller needs to provide a credit card. Once an auction closes with a sale, the fee is automatically charged to the seller's credit card.

Finding a specific firearm is easy for buyers because of search functionality built into auction websites. Once a user has an account, they can click off search options to zero in on a specific manufacturer, model, caliber, barrel length, magazine capacity, and other criteria. The user then has the ability to save the search and have e-mail alerts sent to their e-mail inbox with search results.

Most sellers and buyers online strive to ensure all parties are satisfied with the transaction. Like any aspect in a buying and selling situation, there are some who will try to take advantage. Do your due diligence and contact the seller prior to making a bid, get as much information as you can about the item, and finally look at the seller's rating. Most sellers do their best to keep their rating high, and most will be willing to go the distance to satisfy a customer.

The auction websites have a system in place to deal with buyer and seller protection. Like in anything, the old dictum "buyer beware" applies. If the deal seems too good to be true, then it probably is. Move on.

With online auctions, there is an excitement about bidding against other buyers—remember your budget, and remember what the firearm is worth. You do not want to get caught up in a bidding frenzy and overpay. On the other hand, you may be inclined to pay slightly more for an item that is rare in your geographic area or for an item that is no longer manufactured. Technology has opened up gun trading 24/7/365.

TYPES OF ONLINE AUCTIONS

Basic: The seller's starting price is the amount the seller is willing to take for the item.

Dutch: A seller is auctioning two or more identical items, and a buyer bids on the per-item cost. If you bid $1 and there are ten items, the total price is $10.

Absolute or Penny: Starts out at $.01 with no reserve with the item selling for the last bid after the auction closes.

Reserve: A seller has a minimum reserve price set for the item. This amount is hidden.

38th Edition
GUN TRADER'S GUIDE TO
Handguns

A.A. (Azanza y Arrizabalaga) — Eibar, Spain

M1916 PISTOL . . . . **NiB $240 Ex $140 Gd $100**
Semiautomatic blowback-operated pistol. Caliber: 7.65mm, 9-rnd. magazine. 3.25-in. bbl. Wood grip, blued finish. Made 1916.

REIMS PISTOL. . . . . **NiB $190 Ex $120 Gd $95**
Semiautomatic blowback-operated pistol. Caliber: 6.25mm or 7.65mm. Similar to M1906 Browning pistol. Made 1914.

A.A. ARMS — Monroe, North Carolina

AP-9 SERIES
Semiautomatic recoil-operated pistol w/polymer integral grip/frame design. Fires from a closed bolt. Caliber: 9mm Parabellum. 10- or 20-round magazine, 3- , 5- or 11-inch bbl., 11.8 inches overall w/5-inch bbl., Weight: 3.5 lbs. Fixed blade, protected post front sight adjustable for elevation, winged square notched rear. Matte phosphate/blue or nickel finish. Checkered polymer grip/frame. Made from 1988-99.
AP9 model (pre-94 w/ventilated bbl.,
  shroud) . . . . **NiB $445 Ex $369 Gd $267**
AP9 Mini model
  (post-94 w/o bbl., shroud) . . . . . . **NiB $265 Ex $250 Gd $195**
AP9 Target model
  (pre-94 w/11-inch bbl.) . . . . **NiB $550 Ex $425 Gd $315**
Nickel finish, add **$40**

ACCU-TEK — Ontario, California

MODEL AT-9 AUTO PISTOL
Caliber: 9mm Para. 8-round magazine, Double action only. 3.2-inch bbl., 6.25 inches overall. Weight: 28 oz. Fixed blade front sight, adj. rear w/3-dot system. Firing pin block with no External safety. Stainless or black over stainless finish. Checkered black nylon grips. Announced 1992, but made from 1995-99.
Satin stainless model . . . . **NiB $347 Ex $275 Gd $210**
Matte black stainless . . . . **NiB $311 Ex $250 Gd $200**

MODEL AT-25 AUTO PISTOL
Similar to Model AT380 except chambered .25 ACP, 7-round magazine. Made from 1992-96.

Arrizabalaga Hijos De C
1916

Lightweight w/aluminum frame . . . **NiB $164 Ex $135 Gd $115**
Bright stainless (disc. 1991) . . . . . . **NiB $164 Ex $135 Gd $115**
Satin stainless model . . . . **NiB $164 Ex $135 Gd $115**
Matte black stainless . . . . **NiB $164 Ex $135 Gd $115**

MODEL AT-32 AUTO PISTOL
Similar to AT-380 except chambered .32 ACP. Made from 1990-2003.
Lightweight w/aluminum
  Frame (disc. 1991) . . . . **NiB $215 Ex $160 Gd $110**
Satin stainless model . . . . **NiB $215 Ex $160 Gd $110**
Matte black stainless . . . . **NiB $225 Ex $170 Gd $120**

MODEL AT-40 DA AUTO PISTOL
Caliber: .40 S&W. 7-round magazine, 3.2-inch bbl., 6.25 inches overall. Weight: 28 oz. Fixed blade front sight, adj. rear w/3-dot system. Firing pin block with no External safety. Stainless or black over stainless finish. Checkered black nylon grips. Announced 1992, but made from 1995-96.
Satin stainless model . . . . **NiB $290 Ex $166 Gd $129**
Matte black stainless . . . . **NiB $295 Ex $177 Gd $140**

MODEL AT-380 AUTO PISTOL
Caliber: .380 ACP. Five-round magazine, 2.75-inch bbl., 5.6 inches overall. Weight: 20 oz. External hammer w/slide safety. Grooved

Accu-Tek Model AT .380

Accu-Tek Model BL-9

Accu-Tek HC-380SS

Action Arms AT-84 with Prototype of Model AT-84P in background

black composition grips. Alloy or stainless frame w/steel slide. Black, satin aluminum or stainless finish. Made from 1992-2003.

Standard alloy frame (disc. 1992) . . . . . . NiB $291 Ex $165 Gd $145
AT-380II Satin stainless (Avail. 1990) . . . . NiB $291 Ex $165 Gd $145
Matte black stainless . . . . NiB $279 Ex $188 Gd $129

MODELS BL-9, BL 380 . . . . NiB $200 Ex $155 Gd $130
Ultra compact DAO semiautomatic pistols. Calibers: .380 ACP, 9mm Para. 5-round magazine, 3-inch bbl., 5.6 inches overall. Weight: 24 oz. Fixed sights. Carbon steel frame and slide w/black finish. Polymer grips. Made 1997 to 1999.

MODELS CP-9, CP-40, CP-45
Compact, double action only, semiautomatic pistols. Calibers: 9mm Parabellum, .40 S&W, .45 ACP, 8-, 7- or 6-round magazine, 3.2-inch bbl., 6.25 inches overall. Weight: 28 oz. Fixed blade front sight, adj. rear w/3-dot system. Firing-pin block with no External safety. Stainless or black/stainless finish. Checkered black nylon grips. Made 1997-2002 (CP-9), 1999 (CP-40), 1996 (CP-45).

Black stainless model . . . . NiB $255 Ex $190 Gd $140
Satin stainless model . . . . NiB $255 Ex $190 Gd $140

MODEL HC-380 AUTO PISTOL . . . . . NiB $280 Ex $235 Gd $220
Caliber: .380 ACP. 13-round magazine, 2.75-inch bbl., 6 inches overall. Weight: 28 oz. External hammer w/slide safety. Checkered black composition grips. Stainless finish. Made 1993 to 2003, Reintro. 2007.

ACTION ARMS — Philadelphia, PA

See also listings under CZ pistols. Action Arms stopped importing firearms in 1994.

AT-84S DA AUTOMATIC PISTOL . . NiB $530 Ex $380 Gd $320
Caliber: 9mm Para. 15-round magazine, 4.75-inch bbl., 8 inches overall. Weight: 35 oz. Fixed front sight, drift-adj. rear. Checkered walnut grips. Blued finish. Made in Switzerland from 1988 to 1989.

AT-84P DA AUTO PISTOL . . . . . . NiB $510 Ex $365 Gd $320
Compact version of the Model AT-84. Only a few prototypes were manufactured in 1985.

AT-88P DA AUTO PISTOL . . . . . . NiB $530 Ex $479 Gd $377
Compact version of the AT-88S w/3.7-inch bbl. Only a few prototypes of this model were manufactured in 1985. Note: The AT-88 pistol series was later manufactured by Sphinx-Muller as the AT-2000 series.

AT-88S DA AUTOMATIC PISTOL . . NiB $550 Ex $479 Gd $377
Calibers: 9mm Para. or .41 AE, 10-round magazine, 4.6-inch bbl., 8.1 inches overall. Weight: 35.3 oz. Fixed blade front sight, adj. rear. Checkered walnut grips. Imported 1989 to 1991.

ADVANTAGE ARMS — St. Paul, Minnesota

MODEL 422 DERRINGER . . . . NiB $175 Ex $115 Gd $110
Hammerless, top-break, 4-bbl., derringer w/rotating firing pin. Calibers: .22 LR and .22 Mag., 4-round capacity, 2.5 inch bbl., 4.5 inches overall. Weight: 15 oz. Fixed sights. Walnut grips. Blued, nickel or PDQ matte black finish. Made from 1985 to 1987.

S. A. ALKARTASUNA FABRICA DE ARMAS — Guernica, Spain

"RUBY" AUTOMATIC PISTOL . . . . NiB $355 Ex $283 Gd $225
Caliber: .32 Automatic (7.65mm), 9-round magazine, 3.63-inch bbl., 6.38 inches overall. Weight: About 34 oz. Fixed sights. Blued finish. Checkered wood or hard rubber grips. Made from 1917-22. Note: Mfd. by a number of Spanish firms, the Ruby was a secondary standard service pistol of the French Army in World Wars I and II. Specimens made by Alkartasuna bear the "Alkar" trademark.

AMERICAN ARMS — Kansas City, Missouri

Importer of Spanish and Italian shotguns, pistols, and rifles. Acquired by TriStar Sporting Arms, Ltd., in 2000.

BISLEY SA REVOLVER . . . . NiB $490 Ex $400 Gd $315
Uberti reproduction of Colt's Bisley. Caliber: .45 LC, 6-round cylinder, 4.75-, 5.5- or 7.7-inch bbl., Case-hardened steel frame. Fixed blade front sight, grooved top strap rear. Hammer block safety. Imported from 1997 to 1998

CX-22 CLASSIC DA AUTOMATIC PISTOL
Similar to Model PX-22 except w/8-round magazine, 3.33-inch bbl., 6.5 inches overall. Weight: 22 oz. Made from 1990 to 1995.

CX-22 Classic . . . . NiB $200 Ex $145 Gd $125
CXC-22 w/chrome
  Slide (disc. 1990) . . . . NiB $195 Ex $140 Gd $120

EP-380 DA AUTOMATIC PISTOL NiB $410 Ex $299 Gd $160
Caliber: .380 Automatic. 7-round magazine, 3.5-inch bbl., 6.5 inches overall. Weight: 25 oz. Fixed front sight, square notch adj. rear. Stainless finish. Checkered wood grips. Made 1989 to 1991.

ESCORT DA AUTO PISTOL. . . . NiB $315 Ex $225 Gd $155
Caliber: .380 ACP, 7-rnd. magazine, 3.38-inch bbl., 6.13 inches overall. Weight: 19 oz. Fixed, low-profile sights. Stainless steel frame, slide, and trigger. Nickel-steel bbl., Soft polymer grips. Loaded chamber indicator. Made 1995 to 1997.

MATEBA AUTO REVOLVER
Unique combination action design allows both slide and cylinder to recoil together causing cylinder to rotate. Single or double action. Caliber: .357 Mag, 6-round cylinder, 4- or 6-inch bbl., 8.77 inches overall w/4-inch bbl., Weight: 2.75 lbs. Steel/alloy frame. Ramped blade front sight, adjustable rear. Blue finish. Smooth walnut grips. Imported from 1997-99.
Mateba model (w/4-inch bbl.) NiB $1630 Ex $1130 Gd $775
Mateba model (w/6-inch bbl.) NiB $1695 Ex $1195 Gd $870

P-98 Classic DA Automatic NiB $215 Ex $140 Gd $105
Caliber: .22 LR, 8-round magazine, 5-inch bbl., 8.25 inches overall. Weight: 25 oz. Fixed front sight, square notch adj. rear. Blued finish. Serrated black polymer grips. Made 1989 to 1996.

PK-22 Classic DA
AUTOMATIC PISTOL . . . . NiB $190 Ex $145 Gd $120
Caliber: .22 LR. 8-round magazine, 3.33-inch bbl., 6.33 inches overall. Weight: 22 oz. Fixed front sight, V-notch rear. Blued finish. Checkered black polymer grips. Made 1989 to 1996.

PX-22 DA AUTOMATIC PISTOL NiB $245 Ex $177 Gd $155
Caliber: .22 LR. 7-round magazine, 2.75-inch bbl., 5.33 inches overall. Weight: 15 oz. Fixed front sight, V-notch rear. Blued finish. Checkered black polymer grips. Made from 1989-96.

PX-25 DA AUTOMATIC PISTOL NiB $255 Ex $220 Gd $190
Same general specifications as the Model PX-22 except chambered for .25 ACP. Made from 1991-92.

REGULATOR SA REVOLVER
Similar in appearance to the Colt Single-Action Army. Calibers: .357 Mag., .44-.40, .45 Long Colt. Six-round cylinder, 4.75- or 7.5-inch bbl., blade front sight, fixed rear. Brass trigger guard/backstrap on Standard model. Casehardened steel on Deluxe model. Made from 1992 to 2000.
Standard model. . . . . NiB $279 Ex $210 Gd $125
Standard combo set (45 LC/.45 ACP
  & .44-.40/.44 Spec.) . . . . NiB $445 Ex $375 Gd $275
Deluxe model . . . . NiB $375 Ex $315 Gd $225
Deluxe combo set (.45 LC/.45
  ACP & .44-40/.44 Spl.) . . . . . . NiB $445 Ex $389 Gd $260
Stainless steel . . . . NiB $425 Ex $355 Gd $250

BUCKHORN SA REVOLVER
Similar to Regulator model except chambered .44 Mag. w/4.75-, 6- or 7.7-inch bbl., Fixed or adjustable sights. Hammer block safety. Imported 1993 to 1996.
w/standard sights . . . . NiB $425 Ex $315 Gd $255
w/adjustable sights, add $40

SPECTRE DA AUTO PISTOL
Blowback action, fires closed bolt. Calibers: 9mm Para., .40 S&W, .45 ACP, 30-round magazine, 6-inch bbl., 13.75 inches overall.

Mateba Auto Revolver

American Arms Regulator Deluxe Model

American Derringer Model 1

Weight: 4 lbs. 8 oz. Adj. post front sight, fixed U-notch rear. Black nylon grips. Matte black finish. Imported 1990 to 1994.
9mm Para.. . . . . NiB $545 Ex $450 Gd $260
.40 S&W (disc. 1991) . . . . NiB $515 Ex $400 Gd $300
.45 ACP. . . . . NiB $560 Ex $445 Gd $315

WOODMASTER SA AUTO PISTOL. . NiB $300 Ex $250 Gd $195
Caliber: .22 LR. 10-round magazine, 5.88-inch bbl., 10.5 inches overall. Weight: 31 oz. Fixed front sight, square-notch adj. rear. Blued finish. Checkered wood grips. Disc. 1989.

454 SSA REVOLVER . . . . NiB $795 Ex $680 Gd $530
SSA chambered 454. 6-round cylinder, 6-inch solid raised rib or 7.7-inch top-ported bbl., satin nickel finish, adj. rear sight. Hammer block safety. Imported from 1996 to 1997.

AMERICAN DERRINGER CORPORATION — Waco, Texas

MODEL 1 STAINLESS
Single-action similar to the Remington O/U derringer, 2-shot capacity. More than 60 calibers from .22 LR to .45-70, 3-inch bbl., 4.82 inches overall, weight: 15 oz. Automatic bbl., selection. Satin or high-polished stainless steel. Rosewood grips. Made from 1980 to date.
.45 Colt, .44-40 Win., .44
  Special, .410. . . . . NiB $575 Ex $420 Gd $300
.45-70, .44 Mag., 41 Mag.,
  .30-30 Win., .223 Rem. . . . . . NiB $650 Ex $550 Gd $458
.357 Max., .357 Mag., .45 Win.
  Mag., 9mm Para. . . . . NiB $655 Ex $555 Gd $460
.38 Special, .38 Super, .32 Mag.,
  .22 LR, .22 WRM.. . . . . NiB $655 Ex $560 Gd $455

MODEL 2 STEEL "PEN" PISTOL
Calibers: .22 LR, .25 Auto, .32 Auto. Single-shot, 2-inch bbl., 5.6 inches overall (4.2 inches in pistol format). Weight: 5 oz. Stainless finish. Made from 1993 to 1994.
.22 LR . . . . NiB $500 Ex $430 Gd $337
.25 Auto . . . . NiB $600 Ex $530 Gd $430
.32 Auto . . . . NiB $650 Ex $580 Gd $480

www.skyhorsepublishing.com

American Derringer
Model 3

American Derringer
Model .38 DA

American Derringer
Lady Derringer

MODEL 3 STAINLESS STEEL . . . . . NiB $125 Ex $90 Gd $75
Single-shot. Calibers: .32 Mag. or .38 Special. 2.5-inch bbl., 4.9 inches overall. Weight: 8.5 oz. Rosewood grips. Made from 1984 to 1995.

MODEL 4 DOUBLE DERRINGER
Calibers: .357 Mag., .357 Max., .44 Mag., .45 LC, .45 ACP (upper bbl., and 3-inch .410 shotshell (lower bbl.). 4.1-inch bbl, 6 inches overall. Weight: 16.5 oz. Stainless steel. Staghorn grips. Made from 1984 to date. (.44 Mag.and .45-70 disc. 2003.)
.357 Mag., .357 Max. . . . . NiB $789 Ex $525 Gd $345
.44 Mag., .45 LC, .45 ACP . . . . NiB $899 Ex $555 Gd $489
Engraved, add $150

MODEL 4 ALASKAN SURVIVAL
MODEL. . . . . NiB $880 Ex $570 Gd $340
Similar specifications as Model 4 except upper bbl., chambered for .45-70 or 3-inch .410 and .45 LC lower bbl. Also available in .45 Auto, .45 LC, .44 Special, .357 Mag. and .357 Max. Made from 1985 to date.

MODEL 6. . . . . NiB $785 Ex $625 Gd $499
Caliber: .22 Mag., .357 Mag., .45 LC, .45 ACP or .45 LC/.410 or .45 Colt. Bbl.: 6 inches, 8.2 inches overall. Weight: .22 oz. Satin or high-polished stainless steel w/rosewood grips. Made 1986 to date.
Engraved, add $150

MODEL 7
Similar as Model 1 except w/high-strength aircraft aluminum used to reduce its weight to 7.5 oz. Made from 1986 to date. (.44 Special disc. then reintroduced in 2008.)
.22 LR, .22 WMR. . . . . NiB $575 Ex $440 Gd $280
.44 Special, add $150

MODEL 8 . . . . NiB $920 Ex $530 Gd $280
Calibers: .45 LC/.410, 8-inch bbl., 9.8 inches overall. Weight: 24 oz. Rosewood grips. New 1997.
Engraved (Made from 1997 to 1998), add $1000

MODEL 10
Similar as the Model 7 except chambered for .38 Special, .45 ACP or .45 LC with aluminum grip frame
.38 Special or .45 ACP . . . . NiB $559 Ex $365 Gd $295
.45 LC. . . . . NiB $500 Ex $395 Gd $279

Model 11 . . . . NiB $559 Ex $490 Gd $369
Same general specifications as Model 7 except with a matte gray finish only, weight: 11 oz. Made from 1980 to 2003.

25 AUTOMATIC PISTOL
Calibers: .25 ACP or .250 Mag. Bbl.: 2.1 inches, 4.4 inches overall. Weight: 15.5 oz. Smooth rosewood grips. Limited production.
.25 ACP blued
(est. production 50) . . . . NiB $650 Ex $540 Gd $385
.25 ACP stainless
(est. production 400) . . . . NiB $510 Ex $425 Gd $380
.250 Mag. stainless
(est. production 100) . . . . NiB $675 Ex $530 Gd $407

DA 38 DOUBLE ACTION DERRINGER
Hammerless, double action, double bbl (o/u). Calibers: .22LR, .357 Mag., .38 Special, 9mm Para., .40 S&W. 3-inch bbls., satin stainless with aluminum grip frame. DA trigger, hammer-block thumb safety. Weight: 14.5 oz. Made from 1990 to date.
.22LR (1996-03)
.38 Special, 9mm Para., ... NiB $615 Ex $415 Gd $230
.357 Mag. or .40 cal. (Disc. 2012). . NiB $710 Ex $445 Gd $265
Lady Derringer (faux ivory grips, made from 1992-94), add ..$40

COP DA DERRINGER . . . . NiB $660 Ex $510 Gd $291
Hammerless, double-action, 4-bbl., derringer. Caliber: .357 Mag. 3.15-inch bbl., 5.5 inches overall. Weight: 16 oz. Blade front sight, open notched rear. Rosewood grips. Intro. 1990, disc. 1994.

LM-5 AUTOMATIC PISTOL
Calibers: .25 ACP, .32 H&R Mag. or .380 Automatic. Bbl.: 2 inches, 3 inches overall. Weight: 15 oz. Stainless steel construction, smooth wood grips. Limited production.
.25 ACP or 32 H&R Mag. . . . . . NiB $650 Ex $540 Gd $385
.380 Automatic (Disc. 1999). . . NiB $425 Ex $380 Gd $300

LADY DERRINGER . . . . NiB $769 Ex $610 Gd $499
Similar specifications as Model 1 except w/custom-tuned action fitted w/scrimshawed synthetic ivory grips. Calibers: .32 H&R Mag., .32 Special, .38 Special (additional calibers on request). Deluxe Grade engraved and highly polished w/French fitted jewelry box. Made from 1991 to date.
Deluxe Engraved (Disc. 1994) . NiB $699 Ex $470 Gd $355
Gold Engraved (Disc. 1994) . . . . Rare
Lady II (aluminum frame,
made 1999-03). . . . . NiB $400 Ex $350 Gd $255

MINI-COP DA DERRINGER . . . NiB $325 Ex $200 Gd $145
Similar general specifications as the COP except chambered for .22 WMR. Made from 1990 to 1995.

SEMMERLING LM-4
Manually operated repeater. Calibers: .45 ACP or 9mm, 4-round (.45 ACP) or 6-round magazine (9mm), 3.6-inch bbl., 5.2 inches overall. Weight: 24 oz. Made from 1997 to date. Limited availability.
Blued or Stainless steel . . . NiB $4350 Ex $3200 Gd $2020

American Derringer Simmerling.LM-4

AMT .45 ACP Hardballer

AMT .45 ACP Hardballer Long Slide

TEXAS COMMEMORATIVE . . . NiB $380 Ex $350 Gd $300
Similar to Model 1 except w/solid brass frame, stainless bbls. and stag grips. Calibers: .22 LR, .32 Mag., .38 Special, .44-40 Win. or .45 LC. Made from 1991 to date.
.44-40 Win. or .45 LC . . . . NiB $800 Ex $750 Gd $695

125TH ANNIVERSARY
Same general specifications as Model 1 except w/solid brass frame, stainless bbls. and stag grips. Calibers: .38 Special, .44-40 Win. or .45 LC. Disc. 1993. Limited production.
.38 Special . . . . NiB $337 Ex $320 Gd $295
.44-40 Win. or .45 LC . . . . NiB $400 Ex $395 Gd $375

AMERICAN FIREARMS MFG. CO., INC. — San Antonio, Texas

25 AUTO PISTOL
Caliber: .25 Auto. 8-round magazine, 2.1-inch bbl., 4.4 inches overall. Weight: 14.5 oz. Fixed sights. Stainless or blued ordnance steel. Smooth walnut grips. Made from 1966 to 1974.
Stainless steel model . . . . NiB $215 Ex $190 Gd $110
Blued steel model . . . . NiB $200 Ex $145 Gd $110

380 AUTO PISTOL . . . . NiB $735 Ex $540 Gd $389
Caliber: .380 Auto. 8-round magazine, 3.5-inch bbl., 5.5 inches overall. Weight: 20 oz. Stainless steel. Smooth walnut grips. Made from 1972 to 1974.

AMT (ARCADIA MACHINE & TOOL) —Trademark owed by Crusader Gun Company Houston, TX
Previously Galena Industries, Strugis, SD; and Irwindale Arms, Inc., Irwindale, CA

NOTE: *The AMT Backup II automatic pistol was introduced in 1993 as a continuation of the original .380 Backup with a double action trigger and a redesigned double safety. AMT Backup and Automag II line of handguns is currently marketed by High Standard Manufacturing, Houston, TX.*

45 ACP HARDBALLER . . . . NiB $545 Ex $430 Gd $345
Colt 1991 style. Caliber: .45 ACP, 7-round magazine, 5-inch bbl., 8.5 inches overall. Weight: 39 oz. Adj. or fixed sights. Serrated matte slide rib w/loaded chamber indicator. Extended combat safety, adj. trigger and long grip safety. Wraparound Neoprene grips. Stainless steel. Made 1978-2001.
Long slide conversion kit (disc. 1997), add. $315

45 ACP HARDBALLER LONG SLIDE
Similar to the standard Hardballer except w/7-inch bbl. and slide. Also chambered for .400 Cor-Bon. Made from 1980-2001
.45 ACP long slide. . . . . NiB $529 Ex $435 Gd $320
**.400 Cor-Bon long
    slide (Intro.1998) . . . . NiB $535 Ex $425 Gd $300**
5-inch conversion kit (disc. 1997), add. $315

**45 ACP STANDARD GOVERNMENT MODEL
AUTO PISTOL . . . . NiB $460 Ex $395 Gd $339**
Caliber: .45 ACP, 7-round magazine, 5-inch bbl., 8.5 inches overall. Weight: 38 oz. Fixed sights. Wraparound Neoprene grip. Made from 1979 to date.

AUTOMAG II AUTOMATIC PISTOL . . . NiB $845 Ex $575 Gd $360
Caliber: .22 Mag., 7- or 9-round magazine, bbl. lengths: 3.38, 4.5-, 6-inch. Weight: 32 oz. Fully adj. Millett sights. Stainless finish. Smooth black composition grips. Made from 1986 to 2001, reintro. 2004.

AUTOMAG III AUTOMATIC PISTOL . . NiB $600 Ex $495 Gd $365
Calibers: .30 M1 or 9mm Win. Mag., 8-round magazine., 6.38-inch bbl., 10.5 inches overall. Weight: 43 oz. Millet adj. sights. Stainless finish. Carbon fiber grips. Made from 1992 to 2001.

AUTOMAG IV AUTOMATIC PISTOL . . NiB $610 Ex $520 Gd $395
Calibers: 10mm or .45 Win. Mag., 8- or 7-round magazine, 6.5- or 8.63-inch bbl., 10.5 inches overall. Weight: 46 oz. Millet adj. sights. Stainless finish. Carbon fiber grips. Made from 1992-2001.

AUTOMAG V AUTOMATIC PISTOL . . NiB $1000 Ex $855 Gd $775
Caliber: .50 A.E., 5-round magazine, 7-inch bbl., 10.5 inches overall. Weight: 46 oz. Custom adj. sights. Stainless finish. Carbon fiber grips. Made from 1994 to 1995.

BACKUP (SMALL FRAME) AUTOMATIC PISTOL
Caliber: .22 LR, .380 ACP, 8-round (.22LR) or 5-round (.380 ACP) magazine, 2.5-inch bbl., 5 inches overall. Weight: 18 oz. (.380 ACP). Open sights. Carbon fiber or walnut grips. Stainless steel finish. Made from 1990 to 1987.
.22 LR (disc. 1987) . . . . NiB $495 Ex $335 Gd $188
**.380 ACP (disc. 2000, reintro.
    2004, disc. 2010) . . . . NiB $450 Ex $305 Gd $171**

BACKUP II . . . . **NiB $300 Ex $260 Gd $200**
Caliber: .380 ACP, 5-round magazine, 2.5-inch bbl., 5 inches overall. Weight: 18 oz. Single action. Open sights. Stainless steel finish. Carbon-fiber grips. Made from 1993 to 1998.

BACKUP (LARGE FRAME) AUTO PISTOL
Calibers: .357 SIG, .38 Super, 9mm Para., .40 Cor-Bon, .40 S&W, .45 ACP. Six-round (.357 SIG, .38 Super 9mm) or 5-round (.40 Cor-Bon, .40 S&W, .45 ACP) magazine, 2.5-inch bbl., 5.75-inches overall. Weight: 23 oz. Double action only. Open fixed sights. Stainless steel finish. Carbon fiber grips. Made from 1992 to date.
.357 SIG, .38 Super, 9mm.40 S&W,
  .45 ACP . . . . **NiB $530 Ex $400 Gd $300**
.40 Cor-Bon (disc. 2010) . . . . . . **NiB $630 Ex $500 Gd $400**

BULL'S EYE TARGET MODEL . **NiB $695 Ex $550 Gd $415**
Similar to the standard Hardballer. Caliber: .40 S&W, 8-round magazine, 5-inch bbl., 8.5 inches overall. Weight: 38 oz. Millet adjustable sights. Wide adj. trigger. Wraparound Neoprene grips. Made from 1990 to 1991.

JAVELINA . . . . **NiB $695 Ex $550 Gd $420**
Caliber: 10mm, 8-round magazine, 7-inch bbl., 10.5 inches overall. Weight: 48 oz. Long grip safety, beveled magazine well, wide adj. trigger. Millet adj. sights. Wraparound Neoprene grips. Stainless finish. Made from 1991 to 1993.

LIGHTNING AUTO PISTOL
Caliber: .22 LR. 10-round magazine, 5-, 6.5-, 8.5-, 10-inch bbl., 10.75 inches overall (6.5-inch bbl.). Weight: 45 oz. (6.5-inch bbl.). Millett adj. sights. Checkered rubber grips. Stainless finish. Made from 1984 to 1987.
Standard model. . . . . **NiB $455 Ex $315 Gd $210**
Bull's-Eye model
  (6.5-inch bull bbl.) . . . . **NiB $520 Ex $355 Gd $240**

ON DUTY DA PISTOL
Calibers: .40 S&W, 9mm Para., .45 ACP. 15-round (9mm), 13-shot (.40 S&W) or 9-round (.45 ACP) magazine, 4.5-inch bbl., 7.75 inches overall. Weight: 32 oz. Hard anodized aluminum frame. Stainless steel slide and bbl., Carbon fiber grips. Made from 1991 to 1994.
9mm or .40 S&W . . . . **NiB $465 Ex $316 Gd $235**
.45 ACP. . . . . **NiB $515 Ex $400 Gd $265**

SKIPPER AUTO PISTOL. . . . . . . **NiB $465 Ex $359 Gd $325**
Calibers: .40 S&W or .45 ACP, 7-round magazine, 4.25-inch bbl., 7.5 inches overall. Weight: 33 oz. Millet adj. sights. Walnut grips. Matte finish stainless. Made from 1990 to 1992.

AMT Backup

AMT Backup DAO

AMT Bull's Eye Target

AMT Skipper

Anschutz Exemplar XIV

ANSCHUTZ — Ulm, Germany

Mfd. by J.G. Anschutz GmbH Jagd und Sportwaffenfabrik.
Currently imported by Champion's Choice, La Vergne, TN; previously imported by Accuracy International, Boseman, MT and AcuSport Corporation, Bellefontaine, OH

MODEL 64P
Calibers: .22 LR or .22 WMR, 5- or 4-round magazine, 10-inch bbl., 64MS action w/two-stage trigger. Target sights optional. Rynite black synthetic stock. Imported from 1998 to 2003.
.22 LR . . . . **NiB $490 Ex $305 Gd $225**
.22 WMR . . . . **NiB $515 Ex $249 Gd $195**
w/tangent sights, add **$100**

EXEMPLAR (1416P/1451P) BOLT-ACTION PISTOL
Caliber: .22 LR, single-shot or 5-round magazine, 7- or 10-inch bbl., 19 inches overall (10-inch bbl.). Weight: 3.33 lbs. Match 64 action. Slide safety. Hooded ramp post front sight, adjustable open notched rear. European walnut contoured grip. Exemplar made from 1987-95 and 1400 series made from 1997. Disc. 1997. Note: The .22 WMR chambering was advertised but never manufactured.
Exemplar w/7- or 10-inch bbl . . . **NiB $420 Ex $295 Gd $185**
Left-hand model (disc. 1997) . . **NiB $535 Ex $455 Gd $365**

Model 1451P (single-shot) .... NiB $450 Ex $365 Gd $285
Model 1416P (5-round repeater) NiB $1150 Ex $869 Gd $610

EXEMPLAR HORNET ...... NiB $1015 Ex $815 Gd $700
Based on the Anschutz Match 54 action, tapped and grooved for scope mounting with no open sights. Caliber: .22 Hornet, 5-round magazine, 10-inch bbl., 20 inches overall. Weight: 4.35 lbs. Checkered European walnut grip. Winged safety. Made from 1990 to 1995.

EXEMPLAR XIV .... NiB $875 Ex $560 Gd $465
Same general specifications as the standard Exemplar bolt-action pistol except with 14-inch bbl., weight: 4.15 lbs. Made from 1989 to 1995.

ARMALITE, INC. — Genesco, IL

Formerly Costa Mesa, CA.

AR-24 AUTOMATIC PISTOL ... NiB $550 Ex $380 Gd $300
Full size automatic, mfg. by Sarszilmaz in Turkey. Caliber: 9mm Para, 15-round magazine, 4.67-inch bbl., 8.3 inches overall. Parkerized finish, checkered synthetic grips. Imported from 2007 to 2013.
AR-24-15C Combat Custom
  (adj. rear sight) .... NiB $630 Ex $430 Gd $375
AR-24K-13 Compact
  (3.89-inch bbl.) .... NiB $560 Ex $400 Gd $380
AR-24K-13 Combat Custom Compact (adj. rear sight,
  3.89-inch bbl.) .... NiB $630 Ex $430 Gd $375

ARMSCOR (Arms Corp.)—Manila, Philippines

Currently imported by Armscor Precision Int'l. Pahrump, NV. Previously Imported by K.B.I., Harrisburg, PA., 1991–95 by Ruko Products, Inc., Buffalo NY., Armscor Precision, San Mateo, CA.

MODEL M1911-A1 .... NiB $400 Ex $320 Gd $275
Semi-automatic pistol. 1911 style. Caliber: .45 ACP. Eight-round magazine, 5-inch bbl., 8.75 inches overall. Weight: 38 oz. Blade front sight, drift adjustable rear w/3-dot system. Skeletonized tactical hammer and trigger. Extended slide release and beavertail grip safety. Parkerized finish. Checkered composition or wood stocks. Imported from 1996 to 1997. Reintro. 2001 to 2008.

MODEL M1911-A1 COMMANDER .. NiB $410 Ex $300 Gd $220
Caliber: .45 ACP. Similar to M1911-A-1 except with Commander configuration and 4-inch bbl. Rear slide serrations only. Disc. 1991.
Two-tone finish, add $50
Stainless, add $95

MODEL M1911-A1 OFFICER .. NiB $425 Ex $350 Gd $265
Caliber: .45 ACP. Similar to M1911-A-1 except with Combat configuration. Bbl.:3.5 inches. Checkered hardwood grips. Weight: 2.16 pounds. Disc. 1991.
Two-tone finish, add $50
Stainless, add $95

MODEL M1911-A1
MEDALLION SERIES .... NiB $495 Ex $360 Gd $285
Caliber: 9mm Para., .40 S&W, .45ACP. Standard or Tactical, blue finish standard. Bbl.: 5 inches. Custom model with match barrel, checkered wood Pachmayr grips. Disc. 1991.
Two-tone finish (Tactical), add $200
Chrome (Tactical), add $250

MODEL200 DC/TC
DA REVOLVER .... NiB $240 Ex $160 Gd $110
Caliber: .38 Special. Six-round cylinder, 2.5-, 4-, or 6-inch bbl.; 7.3, 8.8, or 11.3 inches overall. Weight: 22, 28, or 34 oz. Ramp front and fixed rear sights. Checkered mahogany or rubber grips. Disc. 1991.

MODEL 202A REVOLVER ..... NiB $165 Ex $110 Gd $95
Caliber: .38 Special. Similar to Model 200 (DC) revolver except does not have barrel shroud. Disc. 1991.

MODEL 206 REVOLVER .... NiB $250 Ex $203 Gd $170
Caliber: .38 Special. Similar to Model 200 (DC) revolver except has a 2.87-in. bbl. Weight: 24 oz. Disc. 1991.

MODEL 210 REVOLVER ...... NiB $219 Ex $170 Gd $135
Caliber: .38 Special. Similar to Model 200 (DC) except has a 4-inch ventilated rib bbl., adj. rear sight. Weight: 28 oz. Disc. 1991.

ASAI AG — Advanced Small Arms Industries Solothurn, Switzerland

Currently imported by Magnum Research Inc., Minneapolis, MN. See listings under Magnum Research Pistols

ASTRA — Guernica, Spain

Manufactured by Unceta y Compania.Currently not imported to U.S., previously imported by E.A.A. Corporation, Sharpes, FL.

MODEL 357 DA REVOLVER ... NiB $385 Ex $299 Gd $230
Caliber: .357 Magnum. Six-round cylinder. 3-, 4-, 6-, 8.5-inch bbl., 11.25 inches overall (with 6-inch bbl.). Weight: 42 oz. (with 6-inch bbl.). Ramp front sight, adj. rear sight. Blued finish. Checkered wood grips. Imported from 1972 to 1988.

MODEL 44 DA REVOLVER
Similar to Astra ..357 except chambered for .44 Magnum. Six- or 8.5-inch bbl., 11.5 inches overall (6-inch bbl.). Weight: 44 oz. (6-inch bbl.). Imported from 1980 to 1993.
Blued finish (disc. 1987) ...... NiB $375 Ex $290 Gd $245
Stainless finish (disc. 1993) .... NiB $395 Ex $320 Gd $255

MODEL 41 DA REVOLVER .... NiB $375 Ex $295 Gd $235
Same general specifications as Model 44 except in .41 Mag. Imported from 1980-85.

MODEL 45 DA REVOLVER .... NiB $366 Ex $275 Gd $215
Similar to Astra .357 except chambered for .45 LC or .45 ACP. Six- or 8.5-inch bbl., 11.5 inches overall (with 6-inch bbl.). Weight: 44 oz. (6-inch bbl.). Imported from 1980-87.

Astra Model .44 DA

MODEL 200 FIRECAT
VEST POCKET AUTO PISTOL . . NiB $320 Ex $260 Gd $205
Caliber: .25 Automatic (6.35mm). Six-round magazine, 2.25-inch bbl., 4.38 inches overall. Weight: 11.75 oz. Fixed sights. Blued finish. Plastic grips. Made 1920 to date. U.S. importation disc. in 1968.

MODEL 202 FIRECAT
VEST POCKET AUTO PISTOL . . NiB $590 Ex $475 Gd $400
Same general specifications as the Model 200 except chromed and engraved w/pearl grips. U.S. importation disc. 1968.

MODEL 400 AUTO PISTOL . . . NiB $725 Ex $595 Gd $350
Caliber: 9mm Bayard Long (.38 ACP, 9mm Browning Long, 9mm Glisenti, 9mm Para. and 9mm Steyr cartridges may be used interchangeably in this pistol because of its chamber design). Nine-round magazine., 6-inch bbl., 10 inches overall. Weight: 35 oz. Fixed sights. Blued finish. Plastic grips. Made 1922-45. Note: This pistol, as well as Astra Models 600 and 3000, is a modification of the Browning Model 1912.
Nazis Mfg. (S/N range 92,850-98,850), add 100%

MODEL 600 MIL./POLICE-TYPE
AUTO PISTOL . . . . NiB $565 Ex $425 Gd $300
Calibers: .32 Automatic (7.65mm), 9mm Para. Magazine: 10-round (.32 cal.) or 8-round (9mm)., 5.25-inch bbl., 8 inches overall. Weight: About 33 oz. Fixed sights. Blued finish. Checkered wood or plastic grips. Made from 1944 to 1945.
Nazis markings, add 100%

MODEL 800 CONDOR
MILITARY AUTO PISTOL . . NiB $2101 Ex $1754 Gd $1512
Similar to Models 400 and 600 except has an external hammer. Caliber: 9mm Para. Eight-round magazine, 5.25-inch bbl., 8.25 inches overall. Weight: 32.5 oz. Fixed sights. Blued finish. Plastic grips. Imported from 1958 to 1965.

MODEL 2000 CAMPER
AUTOMATIC PISTOL . . . . NiB $395 Ex $279 Gd $215
Same as Model 2000 Cub except chambered for .22 Short only, has 4-inch bbl., overall length, 6.25 inches, weight: 11.5 oz. Imported from 1955 to 1960.

MODEL 2000 CUB
POCKET AUTO PISTOL . . . . . . NiB $363 Ex $297 Gd $214
Calibers: .22 Short, .25 Auto. Six-round magazine, 2.25-inch bbl., 4.5 inches overall. Weight: About 11 oz. Fixed sights. Blued or chromed finish. Plastic grips. Made 1954 to date. U.S. importation disc. 1968.

MODEL 3000
POCKET AUTO PISTOL . . . . . NiB $1001 Ex $654 Gd $467
Calibers: .22 LR, .32 Automatic (7.65mm), .380 Auto (9mm Short). Ten-round magazine (.22 cal.), 7-round (.32 cal.), 6-round (.380 cal.). Four-inch bbl., 6.38 inches overall. Weight: About 22 oz. Fixed sights. Blued finish. Plastic grips. Made from 1947 to 1956.

MODEL 3003
POCKET AUTO PISTOL . . . . NiB $2420 Ex $1419 Gd $880
Same general specifications as the Model 3000 except chromed and engraved w/pearl grips. Disc. 1956.

MODEL 4000
FALCON AUTO PISTOL . . . . . . NiB $675 Ex $495 Gd $320
Similar to Model 3000 except has an External hammer. Calibers: .22 LR, .32 Automatic (7.65mm), .380 Auto (9mm

**Astra Model 3003
Pocket**

**Astra Model
4000 Falcon**

Short). Ten-round magazine (.22 LR), 8-round (.32 Auto), 7-round (.380 Auto), 3.66-inch bbl., 6.5-inches overall. Weight: 20 oz. (.22 cal.) or 24.75 oz. (.32 and .380). Fixed sights. Blued finish. Plastic grips. Made from 1956 to 1971.

CONSTABLE DA AUTO PISTOL
Calibers: .22 LR, .32 Automatic (7.65mm), .380 Auto (9mm Short). Magazine capacity: 10-round (.22 LR), 8-round (.32), 7-round (.380). 3.5-inch bbl., 6.5 inches overall. Weight: about 24 oz. Blade front sight, windage adj. rear. Blued or chromed finish. Imported from 1965 to 1992.
Stainless finish. . . . . NiB $395 Ex $290 Gd $229
Blued engraved finish . . . . NiB $605 Ex $419 Gd $297
Chrome finish (disc. 1990) . . . . NiB $500 Ex $335 Gd $234

MODEL A-60 . . . . NiB $415 Ex $285 Gd $210
Similar to the Constable except in .380 only, w/13-round magazine and slide-mounted ambidextrous safety. Blued finish only. Imported from 1980 to 1991.

MODEL A-70 COMPACT AUTO PISTOL
Calibers: 9mm Para., .40 S&W. Eight-round (9mm) or 7-round (.40 S&W) magazine., 3.5-inch bbl., 6.5 inches overall. Blued, nickel or stainless finish. Weight: 29.3 oz. Imported 1992–96.
Blued finish. . . . . NiB $414 Ex $295 Gd $210
Nickel finish . . . . NiB $424 Ex $345 Gd $229
Stainless finish. . . . . NiB $593 Ex $430 Gd $372

MODEL A-75 ULTRALIGHT . . . NiB $400 Ex $299 Gd $234
Similar to the standard Model 75 except 9mm only w/24-oz. aluminum alloy frame. Imported from 1994 to 1997.

Astra Cadix DA

Astra Constable DA

Auto-Ordnance 1927 A-1
Deluxe w/drum magazine

MODEL A-80 AUTO PISTOL. . . NiB $450 Ex $404 Gd $265
Calibers: 9mm Para., .38 Super, .45 ACP. 15-round or 9-round
(.45 ACP). magazine. Bbl.: 3.75 inches., 7 inches overall.
Weight: 36 oz. Imported from 1982 to 1989.

MODEL A-90 DA
AUTOMATIC PISTOL. . . . . . . NiB $505 Ex $400 Gd $245
Calibers: 9mm Para., .45 ACP. 15-round (9mm) or 9-round
(.45 ACP) magazine, 3.75-inch bbl., 7 inches overall. Weight:
about 40 oz. Fixed sights. Blued finish. Checkered plastic grips.
Imported 1985 to 1990.

MODEL A-100 DA AUTO PISTOL
Same general specifications as the Model A-90 except selective
double action chambered for 9mm Para., .40 S&W or .45 ACP.
Imported from 1991 to 1997.
Blued finish. . . . . NiB $470 Ex $310 Gd $249
Nickel finish . . . . NiB $495 Ex $340 Gd $287
For night sights, add $100

CADIX DA REVOLVER
Calibers: .22 LR, .38 Special. Nine-round (.22 LR) or 5-round (.38
cal.) cylinder. Four- or 6-inch bbl., Weight: About 27 oz. (6-inch
bbl.). Ramp front sight, adj. rear sight. Blued finish. Plastic grips.
Imported from 1960-68.

Standard model. . . . . NiB $275 Ex $229 Gd $160
Lightly engraved model. . . . . . . NiB $380 Ex $255 Gd $200
Heavily engraved model (shown) . . NiB $700 Ex $515 Gd $395

MODEL A-75 DECOCKER AUTO PISTOL
Similar to the Model 70 except in 9mm, .40 S&W and .45 ACP w/
decocking system and contoured pebble-tExtured grips. Imported
from 1993-97.
Blued finish, 9mm or .40 S&W . . . . NiB $395 Ex $320 Gd $235
Nickel finish, 9mm or .40 S&W . . . NiB $405 Ex $330 Gd $245
Stainless, 9mm or .40 S&W . . . . NiB $410 Ex $305 Gd $197
Blued finish, .45 ACP . . . . NiB $395 Ex $315 Gd $235
Nickel finish, .45 ACP. . . . . NiB $405 Ex $350 Gd $275
Stainless, .45 ACP. . . . . NiB $420 Ex $365 Gd $290

AUTAUGA ARMS — Prattville, Alabama

MODEL 32 (MK II)
DAO AUTOMATIC PISTOL. . . . NiB $367 Ex $309 Gd $267
Caliber: .32 ACP. Six-round magazine, 2-inch bbl., weight:
11.36 oz.. Double action only. Stainless steel. Black polymer
grips. Made from 1996 to 2000.

AUTO-ORDNANCE CORPORATION —
Division of Kahr Arms, Worchester, MA

Previously West Hurley, New York.

1911 A1 GOVERNMENT AUTO. . . NiB $515 Ex $375 Gd $300
Copy of Colt 1911 A1 semiautomatic pistol. Calibers: 9mm
Para., .38 Super, 10mm, .45 ACP. 9-round (9mm, .38 Super)
or 7-round 10mm, .45 ACP) magazine. 5-in. bbl., 8.5 inches
overall. Weight: 39 oz. Fixed blade front sight, rear adj. Blued,
satin nickel or Duo-Tone finish. Checkered plastic grips. Made
1983 to 1999.
1911 A1 WWII
  (parkerized finish) . . . . NiB $540 Ex $393 Gd $315
1911 A1 100th Anniversary (laser engraved), add 20%

1911A1 .40 S&W PISTOL. . . . . NiB $498 Ex $399 Gd $309
Similar to the Model 1911 A1 except has 4.5-inch
bbl., w/7.75-inch overall length. Eight-round magazine,
weight: 37 oz. Blade front and adj. rear sights w/3-dot
system. Checkered black rubber wraparound grips. Made
1991–99.

1911 A1 "THE GENERAL". . . . . NiB $441 Ex $351 Gd $253
Caliber: .45 ACP. Seven-round magazine, 4.5-inch bbl., 7.75
inches overall. Weight: 37 oz. Blued nonglare finish. Made
1992 to 1999.

1927 A-1 DELUXE SEMIAUTOMATIC PISTOL
Similar to Thompson Model 1928A submachine gun except
has no provision for automatic firing and does not have detachable buttstock. Caliber: .45 ACP, 5-, 15-, 20- and 30-round
detachable box magazines. 30-round drum also available.
13-inch finned bbl., 26 inches overall. Weight: About 6.75 lbs.
Adj. rear sight, blade front. Blued finish. Walnut grips. Made
from 1977 to 1994.
w/box magazine . . . . NiB $1412 Ex $1078 Gd $764
w/drum magazine, add $300

ZG-51 PIT BULL PISTOL. . . . . . NiB $435 Ex $325 Gd $288
Caliber: .45 ACP. Seven-round magazine, 3.5-inch bbl.,
7 inches overall. Weight: 32 oz. Fixed front sight, square-

notch rear. Blued finish. Checkered plastic grips. Made from 1991 to 1999.

LES BAER — Le Claire, Iowa
Previously Hilldale, Illinois.

1911 CONCEPT SERIES AUTOMATIC PISTOL
Similar to Government 1911 built on steel or alloy full-size or compact frame. Caliber: .45 ACP. Seven-round magazine, 4.25- or 5-inch bbl. Weight: 34 to 37 oz. Adjustable low mount combat or BoMar target sights. Blued, matte black, Two-Tone or stainless finish. Checkered wood grips. Made from 1996 to date.

Concept models I & II	NiB $1402	Ex $1116	Gd $797
Concept models III, IV & VII	NiB $1556	Ex $1414	Gd $1204
Concept models V, VI & VIII	NiB $1538	Ex $1369	Gd $863
Concept models IX & X	NiB $1529	Ex $1237	Gd $1045

1911 PREMIER SERIES AUTOMATIC PISTOL
Similar to the Concept series except also chambered for .38 Super, 9x23 Win., .400 Cor-Bon and .45 ACP. 5- or 6-inch bbl. Weight: 37 to .40 oz. Made from 1996 to date.

Premier II (9x23 w/5-inch bbl.)	NiB $1760	Ex $1479	Gd $1331
Premier II (.400 Cor-Bon w/5-inch bbl.)	NiB $1540	Ex $1369	Gd $1292
Premier II (.45 ACP w/5-inch bbl.)	NiB $1446	Ex $1314	Gd $1098
Premier II (.45 ACP S/S w/5-inch bbl.)	NiB $1531	Ex $1265	Gd $875
Premier II (.45/.400 combo w/5-inch bbl.)	NiB $1749	Ex $1457	Gd $1281
Premier II (.38 Super w/6-inch bbl.)	NiB $1996	Ex $1864	Gd $1490
Premier II (.400 Cor-Bon w/6-inch bbl.)	NiB $1798	Ex $1529	Gd $1364
Premier II (.45 ACP w/6-inch bbl.)	NiB $1672	Ex $1501	Gd $1408

S.R.P. AUTOMATIC PISTOL
Similar to F.B.I. Contract "Swift Response Pistol" built on a (customer- supplied) Para-Ordance over-sized frame or a 1911 full-size or compact frame. Caliber: .45 ACP. Seven-round magazine, 5-inch bbl., weight: 37 oz. Ramp front and fixed rear sights, w/Tritium Sight insert.

SRP 1911 Government or Commanche model	NiB $2295	Ex $2084	Gd $1905
SRP P-12 model	NiB $2619	Ex $2346	Gd $2199
SRP P-13 model	NiB $2404	Ex $2178	Gd $2021
SRP P-14 model	NiB $2320	Ex $2109	Gd $1317

1911 ULTIMATE MASTER COMBAT SERIES
Model 1911 in Combat Competition configuration. Calibers: .38 Super, 9x23 Win., .400 Cor-Bon and .45 ACP. Five- or 6-inch NM bbl., weight: 37 to 40 oz. Made from 1996 to date.

Ultimate MC (.38 or 9x23 w/5-inch bbl.)	NiB $2580	Ex $2010	Gd $1400
Ultimate MC (.400 Cor-Bon w/5-inch bbl.)	NiB $2480	Ex $1835	Gd $1300
Ultimate MC (.45 ACP w/5-inch bbl.)	NiB $2430	Ex $1910	Gd $1300
Ultimate MC (.38 or 9x23 w/6-inch bbl.)	NiB $2680	Ex $2025	Gd $1495
Ultimate MC (.400 Cor-Bon w/6-inch bbl.)	NiB $2630	Ex $2060	Gd $1450
Ultimate MC (.45 ACP w/6-inch bbl.)	NiB $2580	Ex $2010	Gd $1400

**Auto-Ordnance
ZG-51 Pit Bull**

Ultimate "Steel Special" (.38 Super Bianchi SPS)	NiB $2855	Ex $2310	Gd $1661
Ultimate "PARA" (.38, 9x23 or .45 IPSC comp)	NiB $2871	Ex $2326	Gd $1650
w/Triple-Port Compensator, add			$100

1911 CUSTOM CARRY SERIES AUTOMATIC PISTOL
Model 1911 in Combat Carry configuration built on steel or alloy full-size or compact frame. 4.5- or 5-inch NM bbl., chambered for .45 ACP. Weight: 34 to 37 oz.

Custom carry (steel frame w/4.24- or 5-inch bbl.)	NiB $1728	Ex $1555	Gd $1166
Custom carry (alloy frame w/4.24-inch bbl.)	NiB $2039	Ex $2029	Gd $1521

BAUER FIREARMS CORP. — Fraser, Michigan

.25 AUTOMATIC PISTOL . . . . . . NiB $175 Ex $125 Gd $95
Stainless steel. Caliber: .25 Automatic. Six-round magazine, 2.13-inch bbl., 4 inches overall. Weight: 10 oz. Fixed sights. Checkered walnut or simulated pearl grips. Made from 1972 to 1984.

BAYARD — Herstal, Belgium
Mfd. by Anciens Etablissements Pieper.

MODEL 1908
POCKET AUTOMATIC PISTOL . NiB $455 Ex $300 Gd $195
Calibers: .25 Automatic (6.35mm), .32 Automatic (7.65mm), .380 Automatic (9mm Short). Six-round magazine, 2.25-inch bbl., 4.88 inches overall. Weight: About 16 oz. Fixed sights. Blued finish. Hard rubber grips. Intro. 1908. Disc. 1923.

MODEL 1923 POCKET
.25 AUTOMATIC PISTOL . . . . . NiB $393 Ex $300 Gd $170
Caliber: .25 Automatic (6.35mm). 2.13-inch bbl., 4.31 inches overall. Weight: 12 oz. Fixed sights. Blued finish. Checkered hard-rubber grips. Intro. 1923. Disc. 1930.

MODEL 1923 POCKET
AUTOMATIC PISTOL . . . . NiB $429 Ex $313 Gd $218
Calibers: .32 Automatic (7.65mm), .380 Automatic (9mm Short). Six-round magazine, 3.31-inch bbl., 5.5 inches overall. Weight: About 19 oz. Fixed sights. Blued finish. Checkered hard-rubber grips. Intro. 1923. Disc. 1940.

MODEL 1930 POCKET
.25 AUTOMATIC PISTOL . . . . . NiB $395 Ex $255 Gd $195
This is a modification of the Model 1923, which it closely resembles.

Benelli MP90S

Benelli MP95E

BEEMAN PRECISION ARMS, INC. — Santa Rosa, California

P08 AUTOMATIC PISTOL . . . . . . NiB $420 Ex $335 Gd $245
Luger toggle action. Caliber: .22 LR. 10-round magazine, 3.8-inch bbl., 7.8 inches overall. Weight: 25 oz. Fixed sights. Blued finish. Checkered hardwood grips. Imported from 1969 to 1991.

MINI P08 AUTOMATIC PISTOL NiB $470 Ex $375 Gd $295
Caliber: Same general specifications as P08 except shorter 3.5-inch bbl., 7.4 inches overall. Weight: 20 oz. Imported 1986 to 1991.

SP METALLIC SILHOUETTE PISTOLS
Caliber: .22 LR. Single-shot. Bbl. lengths: 6-, 8-, 10- or 15-inches. Adj. rear sight. Receiver contoured for scope mount. Walnut target grips w/adj. palm rest. Models SP made 1985-86 and SPX 1993-94.

SP Standard w/8-or 10-inch bbl.	NiB $285	Ex $235	Gd $172
SP Standard w/12-inch bbl.	NiB $330	Ex $266	Gd $191
SP Standard w/15-inch bbl.	NiB $344	Ex $286	Gd $200
SP Deluxe w/8-or 10-inch bbl.	NiB $346	Ex $276	Gd $199
SP Deluxe w/12-inch bbl.	NiB $355	Ex $291	Gd $209
SP Deluxe w/15-inch bbl.	NiB $374	Ex $306	Gd $215
SPX Standard w/10-inch bbl.	NiB $679	Ex $548	Gd $387
SPX Deluxe w/10-inch bbl.	NiB $925	Ex $744	Gd $524

BEHOLLA — Suhl, Germany
Mfd. by both Becker and Holländer and Stenda-Werke GmbH.

POCKET AUTOMATIC PISTOL . NiB $272 Ex $227 Gd $191
Caliber: .32 Automatic (7.65mm). Seven-round magazine, 2.9-inch bbl., 5.5 inches overall. Weight: 22 oz. Fixed sights. Blued finish. Serrated wood or hard rubber grips. Made by Becker and Hollander 1915 to 1920, by Stenda-Werke circa 1920 to 1925. Note: Essentially the same pistol

was manufactured w/the Stenda version as the "Leonhardt" by H. M. Gering and as the "Menta" by August Menz.

BENELLI — Urbino, Italy
Imported by Larry's Guns in Gray, ME since 2003. Previously imported by EEA in Sharpes, FL; Sile Dist. New York, NY; Saco, Arlington, VA.

MP90S WORLD CUP TARGET PISTOL
Semiautomatic blowback action. Calibers: .22 Short, .22 LR, .32 W.C. Five-round magazine, 4.33-inch fixed bbl. 6.75 inches overall. Weight: 36 oz. Post front sight, adjustable rear. Blue finish. Anatomic shelf-style grip. Imported 1992 to 2001.
MP90S (.22 LR) . . . . NiB $1430 Ex $1221 Gd $1095
MP90S (.22 Short, disc. 1995) . . . NiB $1314 Ex $1155 Gd $984
MP90S (.32 S&W) . . . . NiB $1562 Ex $1364 Gd $1221
w/conversion kit, add $80

MODEL B-76 . . . . NiB $441 Ex $326 Gd $257
Semi-auto, SA/DA. Cal.: 9 mm Para. Bbl.: 4.25 inches. 8-round mag. Weight: 34 oz. Disc. 1990.

MODEL B-765 TARGET . . . . NiB $604 Ex $475 Gd $665
Cal.: 9 mm Para. Similar to B-76 model but w/5.5-inch bbl., target grips, adj. rear sight. Disc. 1990.

MODEL B-77 . . . . NiB $405 Ex $309 Gd $220
Semi-auto, SA/DA. Cal.: .32 ACP. Bbl.: Steel, 4.25 inches. 8-round mag. Disc. 1995.

MODEL B-80 . . . . NiB $425 Ex $315 Gd $245
Semi-auto, SA/DA. Cal.: .30 Luger. Bbl.: Steel, 4.25 inches. 8-round mag. Weight: 34 oz. Disc. 1995.
B-80s Target, add $126

MODEL B-82 . . . . NiB $813 Ex $551 Gd $414
Limited production Italian police model; serial no. with "D" suffix. Cal.: .30 Luger, .32 ACP, 9 mm Ultra.

MODEL MP3S . . . . NiB $603 Ex $467 Gd $336
Semi-auto, target model. Cal.: .32 S&W Long Wadcutter. Bbl.: 5.5 inches. High gloss blued finish, target grips. Adj. rear sight. Disc. 1995.

MP95E SPORT TARGET PISTOL
Similar to the MP90S except with 5- or 9-round magazine, 4.25-inch bbl., Blue or chrome finish. Checkered target grip. Imported from 1994 to date.
Blue MP95 (.22 LR) . . . . NiB $892 Ex $708 Gd $467
Blue MP95 (.32 WC) . . . . NiB $981 Ex $840 Gd $640
Chrome, add $80

BERETTA USA CORP. — Accokeek, Maryland
Beretta firearms are manufactured by Fabbrica D'Armi Pietro Beretta S. p. A. in Gardone Val Trompia (Brescia), Italy. This prestigious firm has been in business since 1526. In 1977, Beretta U.S.A. Corp., a manufacturing and importing facility, opened in Accokeek, MD. (Previously imported by Garcia Corp., J.L. Galef & Son, Inc. and Berben Corporation.) Note: Beretta holdings also owns additional firearms companies including: Benelli, Franchi, Sako, Stoeger, Tikka and Uberti.

MODEL 20 DA AUTO PISTOL . . . NiB $257 Ex $203 Gd $136
Caliber: .25 ACP. Eight-round magazine, 2.5-inch bbl., 4.9 inches overall. Weight: 10.9 oz. Plastic or walnut grips. Fixed sights. Made 1984 to 1985.

MODEL 21 DA AUTO PISTOL

Calibers: .22 LR and .25 ACP. Seven-round (.22 LR) or 8-round (..25 ACP) magazine, 2.5-inch bbl., 4.9 inches overall. Weight: About 12 oz. Blade front sight, V-notch rear. Walnut grips. Made from 1985 to date. Model 21EL disc. 2000.

Blued finish.................**NiB $285 Ex $210 Gd $165**
Nickel finish (.22 LR only) ....**NiB $300 Ex $225 Gd $177**
Model 21EL engraved model......**NiB $375 Ex $310 Gd $230**

MODEL 70 AUTOMATIC PISTOL.. NiB $278 Ex $199 Gd $131

Improved version of Model 1935. Steel or lightweight alloy. Calibers: .32 Auto (7.65mm), .380 Auto (9mm Short). Eight-round (.32) or 7-round (.380) magazine, 3.5-inch bbl., 6.5 inches overall. Weight: Steel, 22.25 oz.; alloy, 16 oz. Fixed sights. Blued finish. Checkered plastic grips. Made 1959–85. Note: Formerly marketed in U.S. as "Puma" (alloy model in .32) and "Cougar" (steel model in .380). Disc.

MODEL 70S .... NiB $420 Ex $288 Gd $210

Similar to Model 70T except chambered for .22 Auto and .380 Auto. Longer bbl. guide and safety lever blocking hammer. Front blade and rear sight fixed on breechblock. Weight: 1 lb., 7 oz. Made 1977 to 1985.

MODEL 70T AUTOMATIC PISTOL NiB $315 Ex $231 Gd $189

Similar to Model 70. Caliber: .32 Automatic (7.65mm). Nine-round magazine, 6-in. bbl., 9.5-in. overall. Weight: 19 oz. adj. rear sight, blade front sight. Blued finish. Checkered plastic grips. Intro. in 1959. Disc.

MODEL 71 AUTOMATIC PISTOL.. NiB $268 Ex $199 Gd $142

Similar to alloy Model 70. Caliber: .22 LR. Six-inch bbl., 8-round magazine, Adj. rear sight frame. Single action. Made 1959 to 1989. Note: Formerly marketed in U.S. as the "Jaguar Plinker."

MODEL 72 .... NiB $315 Ex $231 Gd $190

Same as Model 71 except has 6-inch bbl., weight: 18 oz. Intro. in 1959. Disc. Note: Formerly marketed in U.S as "Jaguar Plinker."

MODEL 76 AUTO TARGET PISTOL

Caliber: .22 LR. 10-round magazine, 6-inch bbl., 8.8 inches overall. Weight: 33 oz. adj. rear sight, front sight w/interchangeable blades. Blued finish. Checkered plastic or wood grips. Made from 1966-85. Note: Formerly marketed in the U.S. as the "Sable."
Model 76 w/plastic grips ....**NiB $393 Ex $315 Gd $257**
Model 76W w/wood grips ....**NiB $430 Ex $357 Gd $299**

MODEL 81 DA AUTO PISTOL .... NiB $341 Ex $247 Gd $199

Caliber: .32 Automatic (7.65mm). 12-round magazine, 3.8-inch bbl., 6.8 inches overall. Weight: 23.5 oz. Fixed sights. Blued finish. Plastic grips. Made principally for the European market 1975 to 1984, w/similar variations as the Model 84.

MODEL 82W DA AUTO PISTOL ... NiB $330 Ex $231 Gd $178

Caliber: .32 ACP. Similar to the Model 81 except with a slimmer-profile frame designed to accept a single column 9-round magazine. Matte black finish. Importation disc. 1984.

MODEL 84 DA AUTO PISTOL .... NiB $325 Ex $222 Gd $173

Same as Model 81 except made in caliber .380 Automatic w/13-round magazine, 3.82-inch bbl., 6.8 inches overall. Weight: 23 oz. Fixed front and rear sights. Made from 1975 to 1982.

MODEL 84B DA AUTO PISTOL ... NiB $335 Ex $230 Gd $184

Improved version of Model 84 w/strengthened frame and slide, and firing-pin block safety added. AmbidExtrous reversible magazine release. Blued or nickel finish. Checkered black plastic or wood grips. Other specifications same. Made circa 1982 to 1984.

Beretta Model 21

Beretta Model 71

Beretta Model 72

Beretta Model 84

MODEL 84(BB) DA AUTO PISTOL

Improved version of Model 84B w/further-strengthened slide, frame and recoil spring. Caliber: .380 ACP. 13-round magazine, 3.82-inch bbl., 6.8 inches overall. Weight: 23 oz. Checkered black plastic or wood grips. Blued or nickel finish. Notched rear and blade front sight. Made circa 1984-94.
Blued w/plastic grips ....**NiB $393 Ex $241 Gd $152**
Blued w/wood grips ....**NiB $446 Ex $372 Gd $270**
Nickel finish w/wood grips.......**NiB $630 Ex $493 Gd $383**

MODEL 84 CHEETAH SEMI-AUTO PISTOL

Similar to the Model 84 BB except with required design changes as mandated by regulation, including reduced magazine capacity (10-round magazine) and marked as 9mm short (.380) as a marketing strategy to counter increased availability of 9mm chamberings from other manufacturers. Made 1994–2002,, reintro. 2004.
Blued w/plastic grips ....**NiB $650 Ex $520 Gd $360**

Beretta Model 85

Beretta Model 85BB

Beretta Model 86 Cheetah

Blued w/wood grips . . . . NiB $667 Ex $551 Gd $367
Nickel finish w/wood grips . . . . NiB $735 Ex $498 Gd $372

MODEL 85 DA AUTO PISTOL . . . . NiB $660 Ex $460 Gd $330
Similar to the Model 84 except designed with a slimmer-profile frame to accept a single column 8-round magazine, no ambidextrous magazine release. Matte black finish. Weight: 21.8 oz. Introduced in 1977 following the Model 84.

MODEL 85B DA AUTO PISTOL . . . NiB $430 Ex $330 Gd $210
Improved version of the Model 85. Imported from 1982-85.

MODEL 85BB DA PISTOL
Improved version of the Model 85B w/strengthened frame and slide. Caliber: .380 ACP. Eight-round magazine, 3.82 inch bbl., 6.8 inches overall. Weight: 21.8 oz. Blued or nickel finish.

Checkered black plastic or wood grips. Imported from 1985 to 1994.
Blued finish w/plastic grips. . . . . . . NiB $520 Ex $395 Gd $280
Blued finish w/wood grips . . . . NiB $530 Ex $404 Gd $295
Nickel finish w/wood grips. . . . . . . NiB $582 Ex $430 Gd $315

MODEL 85 CHEETAH SEMI-AUTO PISTOL
Similar to the Model 85BB except with required design changes as mandated by regulation and marked as 9mm short (.380). Made from 1994 to date.
Blued finish w/plastic grips. . . . . . . NiB $656 Ex $470 Gd $310
Blued finish w/wood grips . . . . NiB $680 Ex $490 Gd $330
Nickel finish w/wood grips. . . . . . . NiB $719 Ex $525 Gd $393

MODEL 85F DA PISTOL
Similar to the Model 85BB except has re-contoured trigger guard and manual ambidextrous safety w/decocking device. Matte black Bruniton finish. Imported in 1990 only.
plastic grips. . . . . NiB $390 Ex $315 Gd $255
wood grips . . . . NiB $420 Ex $344 Gd $283

MODEL 86 CHEETAH . . . . NiB $628 Ex $493 Gd $278
Caliber: .380 auto. Eight-round magazine, 4.4- inch bbl., 7.3 inches overall. Weight: 23.3 oz. Bruniton finish w/wood grips. Made from 1986-89. (Reintroduced 1990 in the Cheetah series.)

MODEL 87 CHEETAH AUTOMATIC PISTOL
Similar to the Model 85 except in .22 LR w/8- or 10- round magazine (Target) and optional Extended 6-inch bbl. (Target in single action). Overall length: 6.8 to 8.8 inches. Weight: 20.1 oz. to 29.4 oz (Target). Checkered wood grips. Made from 1987 to date.
Blued finish
  (double-action) . . . . NiB $735 Ex $550 Gd $430
Target model
  (single action) . . . . NiB $765 Ex $580 Gd $467

MODEL 89 GOLD STANDARD TARGET
AUTOMATIC PISTOL . . . . NiB $703 Ex $556 Gd $467
Caliber: .22 LR. Eight-round magazine, 6-inch bbl., 9.5 inches overall. Weight: 41 oz. Adj. target sights. Blued finish. Target-style walnut grips. Made from 1988 to 2000.

MODEL 90 DA AUTO PISTOL . . . . NiB $325 Ex $235 Gd $195
Caliber: .32 Auto (7.65mm). Eight-round magazine, 3.63-inch bbl., 6.63 inches overall. Weight: 19.5 oz. Fixed sights. Blued finish. Checkered plastic grips. Made from 1969 to 1983.

MODEL 90-TWO TYPE F . . . . NiB $600 Ex $460 Gd $400
Similar to 92F. Caliber: 9mm Para or .40 S&W, DA/SA, 4.9-inch bbl., 8.5 inches overall. Weight: 32.5 oz. Fixed sights. Blued finish. Wrap around grip in two sizes. Accessory rail w/cover. Made from 2006-09.

MODEL 92 DA AUTO
PISTOL (1ST SERIES) . . . . NiB $824 Ex $640 Gd $445
Caliber: 9mm Para. 15-round magazine, 4.9-inch bbl., 8.5 inches overall. Weight: 33.5 oz. Fixed sights. Blued finish. Plastic grips. Initial production of 5,000 made in 1976.

MODEL 92S DA AUTO
PISTOL (2ND SERIES) . . . . NiB $645 Ex $520 Gd $370
Revised version of Model 92 w/ambidextrous slide-mounted safety modification intended for both commercial and military production. Evolved to Model 92S-1 for U.S. Military trials. Made 1980-85.

MODEL 92SB-P DA

AUTO PISTOL (3RD SERIES) . . . . . NiB $598 Ex $430 Gd $345
Same general specifications as standard Model 92 except has slide-mounted safety and repositioned magazine release. Made 1981 to 1985.

MODEL 92D DA AUTO PISTOL . . NiB $667 Ex $470 Gd $364
Same general specifications as Model 92F except DAO only w/ bobbed hammer and 3-dot sight. Made from 1992 to 1998.
w/Tritium sights, add $100

MODEL 92F COMPACT

DA AUTOMATIC PISTOL . . . . NiB $630 Ex $560 Gd $279
Caliber: 9mm Para. 12-round magazine, 4.3-inch bbl., 7.8 inches overall. Weight: 31.5 oz. Wood grips. Square-notched rear sight, blade front integral w/slide. Made from 1990-93.

MODEL 92F COMPACT L TYPE M DA AUTOMATIC PISTOL
Same general specifications as the original 92F Compact except 8-round magazine, Weight: 30.9 oz. Bruniton matte finish. Made 1998–2003.

MODEL 92F Compact L Type M . . . NiB $660 Ex $580 Gd $390
Inox finish . . . . NiB $656 Ex $583 Gd $393
w/Tritium sights, add $100

MODEL 92F DA AUTOMATIC PISTOL
Same general specifications as Model 92 except w/slide-mounted safety and repositioned magazine release. Replaced Model 92SB. Blued or stainless finish. Made from 1992 to 1998.
Blued finish . . . . NiB $630 Ex $493 Gd $341
Stainless finish . . . . NiB $619 Ex $477 Gd $325
Model 92F-EL gold, add $200

MODEL 92FS DA AUTOMATIC PISTOL
Calibers: 9mm, 9mmx19 and .40 S&W. 15- round magazine, 4.9- inch bbl., 8.5 inches overall. Weight: 34.4 to 35.3 oz. Ambidextrous safety/decock lever. Chrome-lined bore w/combat trigger guard. Bruniton finish w/plastic grips or Inox finish w/rubber grips. Made from 1999 to date. This model was adopted as the standard-issue sidearm by the U.S. Armed Forces in 1985 and renamed the M9.
matte black Bruniton finish . . . . NiB $630 Ex $520 Gd $325
olive drab finish (made 2004), add $30
Inox finish . . . . NiB $660 Ex $550 Gd $355
Inox Tacical . . . . NiB $690 Ex $470 Gd $380
w/ checkered wood grips, add $25
w/B-lok (made 2003), add $25
470th Anniversary (made 1999) . . . NiB $2205 Ex $1900 Gd $1690
"Desert Storm" edition (made 1991-92) . . NiB $630 Ex $500 Gd $450

MODEL 92FS BRIGADIER AUTOMATIC PISTOL
Similar to 92FS except w/heavier slide and rubber wrap around grips. Made from 1999-2005; reintro. 2015 to date.
Matte black Bruniton . . . . NiB $760 Ex $556 Gd $395
Inox . . . . NiB $766 Ex $630 Gd $477

MODEL 92FS CENTURION AUTOMATIC PISTOL
Similar to 92FS except w/compact barrel/slide and full size frame. Wood or plastic grips. Made from 1999-2005; reintro. 2015 to date.
Matte black Bruniton . . . . NiB $525 Ex $400 Gd $340

MODEL 92FS VERTEC . . . . NiB $640 Ex $450 Gd $400
Similar to 92FS except w/straight backstrap, thin grip panels, short-reach trigger, and accessory rail. Made from 2002 to 2005.

MODEL 92G-SD . . . . NiB $960 Ex $590 Gd $460
Similar to 92F except w/srping loaded decocking lever, accessory rail, 10-round magazine, Tritium sights. Made from 2003-05.

MODEL 92FS BORDER MARSHAL

AUTOMATIC PISTOL . . . . NiB $675 Ex $485 Gd $460
Similar to 92F except commericial equivilent of I.N.S. gov't. contract pistol. Made from 1999 to 2000.

Beretta Model 92F

**Beretta Model 92
Compact L Type M**

**Beretta Model 92FS
Brigadier Inox**

**Beretta Model 96
Stock**

**Beretta Model 949
Olimpionico**

**Beretta Model 950BS
Jetfire**

MODEL 92G ELITE IA . . . . NiB $730 Ex $500 Gd $360
Similar to 92FS Brigadier except w/4.7-in. stainless bbl. Made from 1999 to 2005.
Elite II (made 2000-2005) . . . . NiB $820 Ex $540 Gd $390

MODEL 96 DA AUTO PISTOL
Similar to Model 92F except in .40 S&W. 10-round magazine (9-round in Compact model). Made from 1992 to 1998.
Model 96 D (DA only) . . . . NiB $475 Ex $355 Gd $300
Model 96 Centurion (compact) . . . NiB $550 Ex $460 Gd $310
w/Tritium sights, add $110
w/Tritium sights system, add. $115

MODEL 96 STOCK . . . . NiB $1200 Ex $870 Gd $610
Similar to Model 96 except w/frame mounted safety. Set up for I.D.P.A. competion. Made from 1997 to 1999.

MODEL 101 . . . . NiB $270 Ex $200 Gd $155
Same as Model 70T except caliber .22 LR, has 10-round magazine, Intro. in 1959. Disc.

MODEL 318 AUTO PISTOL . . . . NiB $270 Ex $200 Gd $155
Caliber: .25 Automatic (6.35mm). Eight-round magazine, 2.5-inch bbl., 4.5 inches overall. Weight: 14 oz. Fixed sights. Blued finish. Plastic grips. Made from 1934 to c. 1939.

MODEL 418 AUTO PISTOL . . . . NiB $270 Ex $200 Gd $155
Similar to Model 318 but with loaded chamber indicator and grip safety. Made from 1937 to 1961.

MODEL 949 OLYMPIC TARGET . . . NiB $708 Ex $577 Gd $456
Calibers: .22 Short, .22 LR. Five-round magazine, 8.75-inch bbl., 12.5 inches overall. Weight: 38 oz. Target sights. Adj. bbl., weight. Muzzle brake. Checkered walnut grips w/thumbrest. Made from 1959 to 1964.

MODEL 950B AUTO PISTOL . . . . . NiB $225 Ex $168 Gd $115
Same general specifications as Model 950CC except caliber .25 Auto, has 7-round magazine, Made from 1959 to date. Note: Formerly marketed in the U.S. as "Jetfire."

MODEL 950B JETFIRE SA PISTOL
Calibers: .25 ACP or .22 Short (disc.1992). Seven- or 8-round magazine, 2.4- or 4- inch bbl. Weight: 9.9 oz. Fixed blade front and V-notch rear sights. Matte Blue or Inox (Stainless) finish. Checkered black plastic grips. Made from 1987 to 2002.
Blued finish . . . . NiB $168 Ex $99 Gd $84
Nickel finish . . . . NiB $225 Ex $173 Gd $147
Inox finish . . . . NiB $257 Ex $204 Gd $160
w/4-inch bbl., (.22 Short) . . . . NiB $256 Ex $207 Gd $157

MODEL 950CC AUTO PISTOL . . . . NiB $157 Ex $126 Gd $104
Caliber: .22 Short. Six-round magazine, hinged 2.38-inch bbl., 4.75 inches overall. Weight: 11 oz. Fixed sights. Blued finish. Plastic grips. Made from 1959 to date. Note: Formerly marketed in the U.S. as "Minx M2."

MODEL 950CC SPECIAL. . . . . NiB $155 Ex $103 Gd $88
Same general specifications as Model 950CC Auto except has 4-inch bbl. Made from 1959 to date. Note: Formerly marketed in the U.S. as "Minx M4."

**MODEL 951 (1951)
MILITARY AUTO PISTOL** . . . . NiB $330 Ex $251 Gd $200
Caliber: 9mm Para. Eight-round magazine, 4.5-inch bbl., 8 inches overall. Weight: 31 oz. Fixed sights. Blued finish. Plastic grips. Made from 1952 to date. Note: Was standard pistol of the Italian Armed Forces, also used by Egyptian and Israeli armies and by the police in Nigeria. Egyptian and Israeli models usually command a premium. Formerly marketed in the U.S. as the "Brigadier."

MODEL 1915 AUTO PISTOL . . NiB $1587 Ex $1386 Gd $1087
Calibers: 9mm Glisenti and .32 ACP (7.65mm). Eight-round magazine, 4-inch bbl., 6.7 inches overall (9mm), 5.7 inches (.32 ACP). Weight: 30 oz. (9mm), 20 oz. (.32 ACP). Fixed sights. Blued finish. Wood grips. Made 1915-1922. An improved postwar 1915/1919 version in caliber .32 ACP was later offered for sale in 1922 as the Model 1922.

MODEL 1923 AUTO PISTOL . . NiB $2136 Ex $2094 Gd $1669
Caliber: 9mm Glisenti (Luger). Eight-round magazine, 4-inch bbl., 6.5 inches overall. Weight: 30 oz. Fixed sights. Blued finish. Plastic grips. Made circa 1923 to 1936.

MODEL 1934 AUTO PISTOL

Caliber: .380 Automatic (9mm Short). Seven-round magazine, 3.38-inch bbl., 5.88 inches overall. Weight: 24 oz. Fixed sights. Blued finish. Plastic grips. Official pistol of the Italian Armed Forces. Wartime pieces not as well made and finished as commercial models. Made from 1934 to 1959.

Commercial model	NiB $2340	Ex $2100	Gd $1333
War model	NiB $598	Ex $383	Gd $299

MODEL 1935 AUTO PISTOL

Caliber: .32 ACP (7.65mm). Eight-round magazine, 3.5-inch bbl., 5.75 inches overall. Weight: 24 oz. Fixed sights. Blued finish. Plastic grips. A roughly-finished version of this pistol was produced during WW II. Made from 1935 to 1959.

Commercial model	NiB $1806	Ex $1465	Gd $1078
War model	NiB $598	Ex $383	Gd $299

**Beretta
Model 3032 Tomcat**

MODEL 3032 DA SEMIAUTOMATIC TOMCAT

Caliber: .32 ACP. Seven-round magazine, 2.45-inch bbl., 5 inches overall. Weight: 14.5 oz. Fixed sights. Blued or stainless finish. Made from 1996 to date.

Matte blue	NiB $329	Ex $262	Gd $180
Polished blue	NiB $386	Ex $329	Gd $252
Stainless	NiB $412	Ex $365	Gd $252

MODEL 8000/8040/8045 COUGAR DA PISTOL

Calibers: 9mm, .40 S&W and .45 Auto. Eight- or 10-shot magazine, 3.6 to 3.7-inch bbl., 7- to 7.2 inches overall. Weight: 32 to 32.6 oz. Short recoil action w/rotating barrel. Fixed sights w/3-dot Tritium system. Textured black grips. Matte black Bruniton w/alloy frame. Made 1995-2005.

8000 Cougar D (9mm DAO)	NiB $715	Ex $649	Gd $400
8000 Cougar F (9mm DA)	NiB $750	Ex $644	Gd $388
8040 Cougar D (.40 S&W DAO)	NiB $685	Ex $618	Gd $373
8040 Cougar F (.40 S&W DA)	NiB $685	Ex $618	Gd $373
8045 Cougar D (.45 Auto DAO)	NiB $736	Ex $637	Gd $400
8045 Cougar F (.357 Sig SA/DA)	NiB $685	Ex $536	Gd $386

**Beretta
Model 8000 Cougar D**

MODEL 8000/8040/8045 MINI COUGAR DA PISTOL

Calibers: 9mm, .40 S&W and .45 Auto. Six- 8- or 10-round magazine, 3.6- to 3.7-inch bbl., 7 inches overall. Weight: 27.4 to 30.4 oz. Fixed sights w/3-dot Tritium system. AmbidExtrous safety/decocker lever. Matte black Bruniton finish w/anodized aluminum alloy frame. Made from 1995 to 2008.

8000 Mini Cougar D (9mm DAO)	NiB $654	Ex $577	Gd $326
8000 Mini Cougar F (9mm DA)	NiB $654	Ex $577	Gd $326
8040 Mini Cougar D (.40 S&W DAO)	NiB $654	Ex $577	Gd $326
8040 Mini Cougar F (.40 S&W DA)	NiB $654	Ex $577	Gd $326
8045 Mini Cougar D (.45 Auto DAO)	NiB $654	Ex $577	Gd $326
8045 Mini Cougar F (.45 Auto DA)	NiB $654	Ex $577	Gd $326

**Beretta
Model 8000 Cougar F**

MODEL 9000S SUBCOMPACT PISTOL SERIES

Calibers: 9mm, .40 S&W. 10-round magazine, 3.5-inch bbl., 6.6 inches overall. Weight: 25.7 to 27.5 oz. Single/double and double-action only. Front and rear dovetail sights w/3-dot system. Chrome-plated barrel w/Techno-polymer frame. Geometric locking system w/tilt barrel. Made from 2000–05.

Type D (9mm)	NiB $432	Ex $366	Gd $304
Type D (.40 S&W)	NiB $432	Ex $366	Gd $304
Type F (9mm)	NiB $432	Ex $366	Gd $304
Type F (.40 S&W)	NiB $432	Ex $366	Gd $304

PX4 STORM	NiB $575	Ex $490	Gd $440

SA/DA semi-automatic pistol. Rotating barrel system. Polymer frame. Calibers: 9mm, .40 S&W or .45 ACP. 9-17 rnd. magazine. Bbl lengths: 3.2 or 4 inches. Finish: matte black, Pronox or Super Luminova. Made from 2005 to date.

Inox finish, add	90%

**Beretta
Model 8040 Mini Cougar D**

Beretta Stampede

Bernardelli Model 60 Pocket

Bernardelli Model 68

Bernardelli Model 80 Pocket

Storm Special Duty . . . . NiB $1145 Ex $980 Gd $830

LARAMIE SA REVOLVER . . . . NiB $1030 Ex $760 Gd $550
Reproduction of S&W Model 1870 Schofield. Calibers: .38 Special, .45 Long Colt. 6-round cylinder, Bbl length: 5, 6.5 inches. Blued finish. Built by Uberti from 2005 to 2008.

STAMPEDE SA REVOLVER
Calibers: .357 Magnum, .44-40, .45 Long Colt. 6-round cylinder, Bbl length: 4.75, 5.5, 7.5 inches. Built by Uberti from 2003-11.

Blued finish . . . . NiB $490 Ex $345 Gd $265
Brushed nickel finish. . . . . NiB $510 Ex $355 Gd $275
Deluxe finish. . . . . NiB $520 Ex $425 Gd $325
Old west finish . . . . NiB $515 Ex $405 Gd $305
Bisley model . . . . NiB $510 Ex $355 Gd $275

U22 NEOS . . . . NiB $295 Ex $240 Gd $210
SA semi-automatic pistol. .22 LR w/10-rnd. magazine. Bbl length: 4.5 or 6 in. Modular design. Finishes: aqua, black/blue or gray. Weight: 31.5-36 oz. made from 2002 to date.
DLX (adj. trigger, interchangable sights) add $40

BERNARDELLI, VINCENZO S.P.A. — Gardone V. T. (Brescia), Italy

MODEL 60 POCKET
AUTOMATIC PISTOL . . . . NiB $247 Ex $221 Gd $190
Calibers: .22 LR, .32 Auto (7.65mm), .380 Auto (9mm Short). Eight-round magazine (.22 and .32), 7-round (.380). 3.5-inch bbl., 6.5 inches overall. Weight: About 25 oz. Fixed sights. Blued finish. Bakelite grips. Made from 1959 to 1990.

MODEL 68 AUTOMATIC PISTOL . . . NiB $180 Ex $128 Gd $92
Caliber: 6.35. Five- and 8-round magazine, 2.13-inch bbl., 4.13 inches overall. Weight: 10 oz. Fixed sights. Blued or chrome finish. Bakelite or pearl grips. This model, like its .22-caliber counterpart, was known as the "Baby" Bernardelli. Disc. 1970.

MODEL 69 AUTOMATIC
TARGET PISTOL . . . . NiB $693 Ex $570 Gd $383
Caliber: .22 LR. 10-round magazine, 5.9-inch bbl., 9 inches overall. Weight: 2.2 lbs. Fully adj. target sights. Blued finish. Stippled right- or left-hand wraparound walnut grips. Made from 1987 to date. This was previously Model 100; not imported to the U.S.

MODEL 80 . . . . NiB $204 Ex $128 Gd $92
Calibers: .22 LR, .32 ACP (7.65mm), .380 Auto (9mm Short). Magazine capacity: 10-round (.22), 8-round (.32), 7-round (.380). 3.5-inch bbl., 6.5 inches overall. Weight: 25.6 oz. adj. rear sight, white dot front sight. Blued finish. Plastic thumbrest grips. Note: Model 80 is a modification of Model 60 designed to conform w/U.S. import regulations. Made from 1968 to 1988.

MODEL 90 SPORT TARGET . . . NiB $245 Ex $199 Gd $148
Same as Model 80 except has 6-inch bbl., 9 inches overall, weight: 26.8 oz. Made from 1968 1990.

MODEL 100 TARGET PISTOL . . NiB $428 Ex $362 Gd $291
Caliber: .22 LR. 10-round magazine, 5.9-inch bbl., 9 inches overall. Weight: 37.75 oz. Adj. rear sight, interchangeable front sights. Blued finish. Checkered walnut thumbrest grips. Made from 1969-86. Note: Formerly Model 69.

MODEL AMR AUTO PISTOL . . NiB $433 Ex $321 Gd $270
Simlar to Model USA except with 6-inch bbl. and target sights. Imported from 1992 to 1994.

"BABY" AUTOMATIC PISTOL . NiB $321 Ex $235 Gd $179
Calibers: .22 Short, .22 Long. Five-round magazine, 2.13-inch bbl., 4.13 inches overall. Weight: 9 oz. Fixed sights. Blued finish. Bakelite grips. Made from 1949 to 1968.

MODEL P010 . . . . **NiB $712 Ex $520 Gd $341**
Caliber: .22 LR. Five- and 10-round magazine, 5.9-inch bbl. w/7.5-inch sight radius. Weight: 40 oz. Interchangeable front sight, adj. rear. Blued finish. Textured walnut grips. Made from 1988 to 1992 and 1995 to 1997.

P018 COMPACT MODEL . . . . . **NiB $571 Ex $461 Gd $385**
Slightly smaller version of the Model P018 standard DA automatic except has 14-round magazine and 4-inch bbl., 7.68 inches overall. Weight: 33 oz. Walnut grips only. Imported from 1987 to 1996.

P018 DOUBLE-ACTION AUTOMATIC PISTOL
Caliber: 9mm Para. 16-round magazine, 4.75-inch bbl., 8.5 inches overall. Weight: 36 oz. Fixed combat sights. Blued finish. Checkered plastic or walnut grips. Imported from 1987 to 1996.
w/plastic grips . . . . **NiB $510 Ex $405 Gd $305**
w/walnut grips . . . . **NiB $551 Ex $428 Gd $342**

P-ONE DA AUTO PISTOL
Caliber: 9mm Para. or .40 S&W. 10- or 16-round magazine, 4.8-inch bbl., 8.35 inches overall. Weight: 34 oz. Blade front sight, adjustable rear w/3-dot system. Matte black or chrome finish. Checkered walnut or black plastic grips. Imported from 1993 to 1997.
Model P-One blue finish. . . . . . **NiB $622 Ex $525 Gd $357**
Model P-One chrome finish . . . **NiB $693 Ex $556 Gd $393**
w/walnut grips, add **$50**

P-ONE PRACTICAL VB AUTO PISTOL
Similar to Model P One except chambered for 9x21mm w/2-, 4- or 6-port compensating system for IPSC competition. Imported 1993 to 1997.
Model P One
  Practical (2 port) . . . . **NiB $1148 Ex $1068 Gd $785**
Model P One
  Practical (4 port) . . . . **NiB $1259 Ex $1054 Gd $782**
Model P One
  Practical (6 port) . . . . **NiB $1678 Ex $1393 Gd $995**
w/chrome finish, add **$75**

SPORTER AUTOMATIC PISTOL . **NiB $332 Ex $245 Gd $133**
Caliber .22 LR. Eight-round magazine, bbl., lengths: 6-, 8- and 10-inch, 13 inches overall (10-inch bbl.). weight: About 30 oz. (10-inch bbl.) Target sights. Blued finish. Walnut grips. Made 1949 to 1968.

MODEL USA AUTO PISTOL
Single-action, blowback. Calibers: .22 LR, .32 ACP, .380 ACP. Seven-round magazine or 10-round magazine (.22 LR). 3.5-inch bbl., 6.5 inches overall. Weight: 26.5 oz. Ramped front sight, adjustable rear. Blue or chrome finish. Checkered black bakelite grips w/thumbrest. Imported from 1991 to 1997.
Model USA blue finish . . . . **NiB $420 Ex $330 Gd $265**
Model USA chrome finish. . . . . **NiB $469 Ex $385 Gd $219**

VEST POCKET
AUTOMATIC PISTOL . . . . **NiB $275 Ex $199 Gd $148**
Caliber: .25 Auto (6.35mm). Five- or 8-round magazine, 2.13-inch bbl., 4.13 inches overall. Weight: 9 oz. Fixed sights. Blued finish. Bakelite grips. Made from 1945 to 1968.

BERSA — Argentina
Currently imported by Eagle Imports, Wanamassa, NJ.
Previously by Interarms & Outdoor Sports.

Bernardelli P010

Bernardelli P018

Bersa Model 85

MODEL 83 DA AUTO PISTOL
Similar to the Model 23 except for the following specifications: Caliber: .380 ACP. Seven-round magazine, 3.5-inch bbl., Front blade sight integral on slide, square-notch rear adj. for windage. Blued or satin nickel finish. Custom wood grips. Imported from 1988 to 1994.
Blued finish. . . . . **NiB $275 Ex $201 Gd $126**
Satin nickel . . . . **NiB $321 Ex $271 Gd $194**

MODEL 85 DA AUTO PISTOL
Same general specifications as Model 83 except 13-round magazine, Imported from 1988 to 1994.
Blued finish. . . . . **NiB $326 Ex $235 Gd $128**
Satin nickel . . . . **NiB $377 Ex $286 Gd $179**

Bersa Model 383

Bersa Thunder .380

MODEL 224
Caliber: .22 LR. 10-round magazine, 4-inch bbl., weight: 26 oz. Front blade sight, square-notched rear adj. for windage. Blued finish. Checkered nylon or custom wood grips. Made 1984. SA. disc. 1986.
Double-action . . . . NiB $240 Ex $204 Gd $143
Single-action . . . . NiB $204 Ex $179 Gd $122

MODEL 226
Similar as Model 224 but w/6-inch bbl. Disc. 1987.
Double-action . . . . NiB $240 Ex $204 Gd $143
Single-action . . . . NiB $204 Ex $179 Gd $122

MODEL 383 AUTO PISTOL
Caliber: .380 Auto. Seven-round magazine, 3.5-inch bbl. Front blade sight integral on slide, square-notched rear sight adj. for windage. Custom wood grips on double-action, nylon grips on single action. Blued or satin nickel finish. Made 1984. SA. disc. 1989.
Double-action . . . . NiB $235 Ex $150 Gd $102
Single-action . . . . NiB $219 Ex $158 Gd $122

MODEL 622 AUTO PISTOL . . . NiB $204 Ex $138 Gd $100
Caliber: .22 LR. Seven-round magazine, 4- or 6-inch bbl., 7 or 9 inches overall. Weight: 2.25 lbs. Blade front sight, square-notch rear adj. for windage. Blued finish. Nylon grips. Made from 1982 to 1987.

MODEL 644 AUTO PISTOL . . . NiB $286 Ex $240 Gd $168
Caliber: .22 LR. 10-round magazine, 3.5-inch bbl., weight: 26.5 oz. 6.5 inches overall. Adj. rear sight, blade front. Contoured black nylon grips. Made from 1980 to 1988.

THUNDER 9 AUTO PISTOL . . . NiB $408 Ex $272 Gd $168
Caliber: 9mm Para. 15-round magazine, 4-inch bbl., 7.38 inches overall. Weight: 30 oz. Blade front sight, adj. rear w/3-dot system. AmbidExtrous safety and decocking device. Matte blued finish. Checkered black polymer grips. Made from 1993 to 1996.

THUNDER .22 AUTO PISTOL (MODEL 23)
Caliber: .22 LR, 10-round magazine, 3.5-inch bbl., 6.63 inches overall. Weight: 24.5 oz. Notched-bar dovetailed rear, blade integral w/slide front. Black polymer grips. Made from 1988 to 1998.
Blued finish. . . . . NiB $254 Ex $214 Gd $168
Nickel finish . . . . NiB $260 Ex $220 Gd $177

THUNDER .380 AUTO PISTOL
Caliber: .380 ACP. Seven-round magazine, 3.5-inch bbl., 6.63 inches overall. Weight: 25.75 oz. Notched-bar dovetailed rear, blade integral w/slide front. Blued, satin nickel, or Duo-Tone finish. Made from 1995 to 1998.
Blued finish. . . . . NiB $306 Ex $230 Gd $183
Satin nickel finish . . . . NiB $333 Ex $255 Gd $204
Duo-Tone finish . . . . NiB $306 Ex $230 Gd $168

THUNDER .380 PLUS AUTO PISTOL
Same general specifications as standard Thunder .380 except has 10-round magazine and weight: 26 oz. Made 1995-97.
Matte finish. . . . . NiB $306 Ex $230 Gd $168
Satin nickel finish . . . . NiB $321 Ex $245 Gd $194
Duo-Tone finish, add. $40

MODEL 86 DA AUTO PISTOL
Same general specifications as Model 85 except available in matte blued finish and w/Neoprene grips. Imported from 1992 to 1994.
Matte blued finish. . . . . NiB $347 Ex $270 Gd $219
Nickel finish . . . . NiB $362 Ex $262 Gd $199

MODEL 95 DA AUTOMATIC PISTOL
Caliber: .380 ACP. Seven-round magazine, 3.5-inch bbl., weight: 23 oz. Wraparound rubber grips. Blade front and rear notch sights. Imported from 1995 to date.
Blued finish. . . . . NiB $329 Ex $214 Gd $158
Nickel finish . . . . NiB $318 Ex $204 Gd $143

MODEL 97 AUTO PISTOL . . . . NiB $389 Ex $332 Gd $219
Caliber: .380 ACP. Seven-round magazine, 3.3-inch bbl., 6.5 inches overall. Weight: 28 oz. Intro. 1982. Disc.

MODEL 223
Same general specifications as Model 383 except in .22 LR w/10-round magazine capacity. Disc. 1987.
Double-action . . . . NiB $243 Ex $213 Gd $143
Single-action . . . . NiB $224 Ex $168 Gd $125

BROLIN ARMS — La Verne, California

"LEGEND SERIES" SA AUTOMATIC PISTOL
Caliber: .45 ACP. Seven-round magazine, 4- or 5-inch bbl., weight: 32-36 oz. Walnut grips. Single action, full size, compact, or full size frame compact slide. Matte blued finish. Lowered and flared ejection port. Made from 1995 to 1998.

Model L45. . . . . NiB $469 Ex $398 Gd $306
Model L45C . . . . NiB $487 Ex $366 Gd $305
Model L45T. . . . . NiB $487 Ex $366 Gd $305

"PATRIOT SERIES" SA AUTOMATIC PISTOL
Caliber: .45 ACP. Seven-round magazine, 3.25- and 4-inch bbl., weight: 33-37 oz. Wood grips. Fixed rear sights. Made 1996 to 1997.

Model P45 . . . . NiB $627 Ex $469 Gd $301
Model P45C (disc. 1997) . . . . . NiB $638 Ex $479 Gd $311
Model P45T (disc. 1997). . . . . . NiB $658 Ex $551 Gd $372

"PRO-STOCK AND PRO-COMP" SA PISTOL
Caliber: .45 ACP. Eight-round magazine, 4- or 5-inch bbl., weight: 37 oz. Single action, blued or two-tone finish. Wood grips. Bomar adjustable sights. Made from 1996 to 1997.

Model Pro comp. . . . . NiB $872 Ex $663 Gd $566
Model Pro stock . . . . NiB $714 Ex $551 Gd $475

TAC SERIES
Caliber: .45 ACP. Eight-round magazine, 5-inch bbl., 8.5 inches overall. Weight: 37 oz. Low profile combat or Tritium sights. Beavertail grip safety. Matte blue, chrome or two-tone finish. Checkered wood or contoured black rubber grips. Made from 1997 to 1998.

Model TAC 11 service. . . . . . . NiB $643 Ex $510 Gd $398
Model TAC 11 compact . . . . . . NiB $653 Ex $531 Gd $419
w/Tritium sights, add $100

BANTAM MODEL . . . . NiB $403 Ex $283 Gd $ 204
Caliber: 9mmPara., .40 S&W. Single or double-action, super compact size, concealed hammer, all steel construction; 3-dot sights; royal blue or matte finish. Manufactured 1999 only.

BRONCO — Eibar, Spain
Manufactured by Echave y Arizmendi.

MODEL 1918 POCKET
AUTOMATIC PISTOL . . . . NiB $204 Ex $129 Gd $92
Caliber: .32 ACP (7.65mm). Six-round magazine 2.5-inch bbl., 5 inches overall. Weight: 20 oz. Fixed sights. Blued finish. Hard rubber grips. Made circa 1918- to 1925.

VEST POCKET AUTO PISTOL . . . NiB $203 Ex $128 Gd $66
Caliber: .25 ACP, 6-round magazine, 2.13-inch bbl., 4.13 inches overall. Weight: 11 oz. Fixed sights. Blued finish. Hard rubber grips. Made from 1919 to 1935.

BROWNING — Morgan, Utah

The following Browning pistols have been manufactured by Fabrique Nationale d'Armes de Guerre (now Fabrique Nationale Herstal) of Herstal, Belgium, by Arms Technology

Browning Model 25 Automatic

Inc. of Salt Lake City and by J. P. Sauer & Sohn of Eckernforde, W. Germany. See also FN Browning and J.P. Sauer & Sohn listings.

.25 AUTOMATIC PISTOL
Same general specifications as FN Browning Baby (see separate listing). Standard Model, blued finish, hard rubber grips. Light Model, nickel-plated, Nacrolac pearl grips. Renaissance Engraved Model, nickel-plated, Nacrolac pearl grips. Made by FN from 1955 to 1969.

Standard model. . . . . NiB $587 Ex $534 Gd $283
Lightweight model . . . . NiB $592 Ex $540 Gd $294
Renaissance model . . . . NiB $1121 Ex $867 Gd $539

.32 AND .380 AUTOMATIC PISTOL, 1955 TYPE
Same general specifications as FN Browning .32 (7.65mm) and .380 Pocket Auto. Standard Model, Renaissance Engraved Model as furnished in .25 Automatic. Made by FN from 1955 to 1969.

Standard model (.32 ACP). . . . NiB $507 Ex $386 Gd $291
Standard model (.380 ACP). . . . NiB $454 Ex $376 Gd $283
Renaissance model . . . . NiB $1121 Ex $918 Gd $740

.380 AUTOMATIC PISTOL, 1971 TYPE
Same as .380 Automatic, 1955 Type except has longer slide, 4.44-inch bbl., is 7.06 inches overall, weight: 23 oz. Rear sight adj. for windage and elevation, plastic thumbrest grips. Made 1971 to 1975.

Standard model. . . . . NiB $509 Ex $387 Gd $294
Renaissance model . . . . NiB $1132 Ex $913 Gd $616

BDA .380 DA AUTOMATIC PISTOL
Caliber: .380 Auto. 10- or 13-round magazine, bbl. length: 3.81 inches., 6.75 inches overall. Weight: 23 oz. Fixed blade front sight, square-notch drift-adj. rear sight. Blued or nickel finish. Smooth walnut grips. Made from 1982 to 1997 by Beretta.
Blued finish . . . . NiB $602 Ex $454 Gd $284

BDA DA AUTOMATIC PISTOL
Similar to SIG-Sauer P220. Calibers: 9mm Para., .38 Super Auto, .45 Auto. Nine-round magazine (9mm and .38), 7-round (.45 cal), 4.4-inch bbl., 7.8 inches overall. Weight: 29.3 oz. Fixed sights. Blued finish. Plastic grips. Made from 1977 to 1980 by J. P. Sauer.

**Browning
BDA .380 Nickel Finish**

**Browning
BDM 9mm DA**

**Browning
Buck Mark 5.5 Field**

**Browning
Buck Mark Bullseye**

**Browning
Buck Mark Plus**

9mm, .45 ACP . . . . NiB $611 Ex $464 Gd $326
.38 Super . . . . NiB $741 Ex $465 Gd $437
Nickel finish . . . . NiB $692 Ex $524 Gd $377

BDM SERIES AUTOMATIC PISTOLS
Calibers: 9mm Para., 10-round magazine, 4.73-inch bbl., 7.85 inches overall. Weight: 31 oz., windage adjustable sights w/3-dot system. Low profile removable blade front sights. Matte blued, Bi-Tone or silver chrome finish. Selectable shooting mode and decocking safety lever. Made from 1991 to 1997.
Standard . . . . NiB $622 Ex $499 Gd $333
Practical . . . . NiB $598 Ex $490 Gd $373
Silver Chrome finish . . . . NiB $693 Ex $509 Gd $384

BUCK MARK AUTOMATIC PISTOL
Caliber: .22 LR. 10-round magazine, 5.5-inch bbl., 9.5 inches overall. Weight: 32 oz. Black molded grips. Adj. rear sight. Blued or nickel finish. Made from 1985 to date.
Blued finish . . . . NiB $342 Ex $221 Gd $143
Nickel finish . . . . NiB $403 Ex $285 Gd $203

BUCK MARK BULLSEYE PISTOL
Same general specifications as the standard Buck Mark 22 except w/7.25-inch fluted barrel, 11.83 inches overall. Weight: 36 oz. Adjustable target trigger. Undercut post front sight, click-adjustable Pro-Target rear. Laminated, Rosewood, black rubber or composite grips. Made from 1996 to 2006.
Standard model (composite grips)...NiB $487 Ex $344 Gd $249
Target model . . . . NiB $475 Ex $316 Gd $219

BUCK MARK
BULLSEYE TARGET . . . . NiB $487 Ex $344 Gd $249
Caliber: .22 LR. 10-round magazine, 7.25-inch fluted bbl., 11.83 inches overall. Weight: 31 oz. Rosewood wrap-around finger groove grips w/matte blued finish. Made 1996-2005.

BUCK MARK CAMPER . . . . . . NiB $300 Ex $210 Gd $150
Similar to Buckmark except w/5.5-inch heavy bbl., matte blued or satin nickel finish. Black polymer grips. Made from 1999 to 2012.
Stainless . . . . NiB $320 Ex $230 Gd $17

BUCK MARK CHALLENGER . . NiB $345 Ex $220 Gd $165
Similar to Buckmark except w/smaller grip. 5.5-inch bbl., matte blued finish. Made from 1999 to 2010.
Micro Challenge (4-in. bbl.) . . . . NiB $300 Ex $210 Gd $155

BUCK MARK 5.5 FIELD . . . . . . NiB $487 Ex $344 Gd $249

**Browning
Buck Mark Silhouette**

**Browning
Buck Mark 5.5 Target**

Similar to Buck Mark 5.5 Target except w/standard sights. Made from 1991 to 2011.

BUCK MARK LITE SPLASH URX . . . NiB $375   Ex $235   Gd $200
Similar to Buck Mark except w/5.5- or 7.25-in. round aluminum bbl. sleeve. TruGlo fibrtr optic sights. Made from 2006 to 2009.

BUCK MARK MICRO AUTOMATIC PISTOL
Same general specifications as standard Buck Mark except w/4-inch bbl., 8 inches overall. Weight: 32 oz. Molded composite grips. Ramp front sight, Pro Target rear sight. URX grip introduced in 2007. Made from 1992 to 2013.
Blued finish . . . . NiB $367   Ex $271   Gd $181
Nickel finish . . . . NiB $418   Ex $321   Gd $244
Stainless finish . . . . NiB $367   Ex $271   Gd $181

BUCK MARK MICRO PLUS AUTO PISTOL
Same specifications as the Buck Mark Micro except ambidextrous, laminated wood grips. Made from 1996 to 2001.
Blued finish . . . . NiB $285   Ex $234   Gd $192
Nickel finish . . . . NiB $382   Ex $321   Gd $204

**Browning
Buck Mark Micro Plus**

BUCK MARK PLUS AUTO PISTOL
Same general specifications as standard Buck Mark except for black molded, impregnated hardwood grips. Made from 1987-2001.
Blued finish . . . . NiB $383   Ex $321   Gd $204
Nickel finish . . . . NiB $404   Ex $329   Gd $223

BUCK MARK 5.5 TARGET AUTO PISTOL
Caliber: .22 LR. 10-round magazine, 5.5-inch bbl., 9.6 inches overall. Weight: 35.5 oz. Pro target sights. Wrap-around walnut or contoured finger groove grips. Made from 1990 to 2009.
Matte blue finish . . . . NiB $455   Ex $374   Gd $223
Nickel finish (1994 to date) . . . NiB $499   Ex $395   Gd $245
Gold finish (1991-99) . . . . NiB $385   Ex $270   Gd $184

**Browning Challenger
Standard Model**

BUCK MARK SILHOUETTE . . . . NiB $544   Ex $372   Gd $220
Similar to standard Buck Mark except for 9.88-inch bbl. Weight: 53 oz. Target sights mounted on full-length scope base, and laminated hardwood grips and forend. Made from 1987 to 1999.

BUCK MARK UNLIMITED
SILHOUETTE . . . . NiB $547   Ex $431   Gd $285
Same general specifications as standard Buck Mark Silhouette except w/14-inch bbl., 18.69 inches overall. Weight: 64 oz. Interchangeable post front sight and Pro Target rear. Nickel finish. Made from 1991 to 1999.

BUCK MARK VARMINT
AUTO PISTOL . . . . NiB $346   Ex $282   Gd $230
Same general specifications as standard Buck Mark except for 9.88-inch bbl. Weight: 48 oz. No sights, full-length scope

**Browning Challenger
Renaissance Model**

**Browning
Challenger III Sporter**

**Browning
9mm Hi-Power w/Molded Grips**

**Browning
9mm Hi-Power AmbidExtrous Safety**

**Browning
Hi-Power Captain**

base, and laminated hardwood grips. Made from 1987 to 1999.

CHALLENGER AUTOMATIC PISTOL
Semi-automatic pistol. Caliber: .22 LR. 10-round magazine, bbl. lengths: 4.5 and 6.75-inches. 11.44 inches overall (with 6.75-inch bbl.). Weight: 38 oz. (6.75-inch bbl.). Removable blade front sight, screw adj. rear. Standard finish, blued, also furnished gold inlaid (Gold model) and engraved and chrome-plated (Renaissance model). Checkered walnut grips. Finely figured and carved grips on Gold and Renaissance models. Standard made by FN 1962-75, higher grades. Intro. 1971. Disc.

Standard model. . . . . NiB $590 Ex $427 Gd $285
Gold model. . . . . NiB $3172 Ex $2448 Gd $1742
Renaissance model . . . . NiB $3058 Ex $2445 Gd $1744

CHALLENGER II . . . . NiB $363 Ex $259 Gd $164
Same general specifications as Challenger Standard model w/6.75-inch bbl. except changed grip angle and impregnated hardwood grips. Original Challenger design modified for lower production costs. Made by ATI from 1976 to 1983.

CHALLENGER III . . . . NiB $266 Ex $217 Gd $153
Same general description as Challenger II except has 5.5 inch bull bbl., alloy frame and new sight system. Weight: 35 oz. Made from 1982-84. Sporter Model w/6.75-inch bbl.. Made from 1982-85.

HI-POWER AUTOMATIC PISTOL
Same general specifications as FN Browning Model 1935 except chambered for 9mm Para., .30 Luger or .40 S&W. 10- or 13-round magazine, 4.63-inch bbl., 7.75 inches overall. Weight: 32 oz. (9mm) or 35 oz. (.40 S&W). Fixed sights, also available w/rear sight adj. for windage and elevation, and ramp front sight. AmbidExtrous safety added after 1989. Standard model blued, chrome-plated or Bi-Tone finish. Checkered walnut, contour-molded Polyamide or wraparound rubber grips. Renaissance Engraved model chrome-plated, w/Nacrolac pearl grips. Made by FN from 1954 to 2002.

Standard model,
fixed sights, 9mm . . . . NiB $895 Ex $689 Gd $510
Standard model, fixed sights,
.40 S&W (intro. 1995). . . . . . NiB $784 Ex $683 Gd $582
Standard model,
.30 Luger (1986-89) . . . . NiB $942 Ex $702 Gd $489
Renaissance model,
fixed sights . . . . NiB $4098 Ex $3651 Gd $2688
w/adjustable rear sight, add $75
w/ambidextrous safety, add $110
w/moulded grips, deduct $50
w/tangent rear sight (1965-78), add* $315
w/T-Slot grip & tangent sight (1965-78), add* $620
*Check with FN to certify serial number.

HI-POWER CAPTAIN . . . . NiB $804 Ex $605 Gd $429
Similar to the standard Hi-Power except fitted w/adj. 500-meter tangent rear sight and rounded hammer. Made from 1993 to 2000.

HI-POWER MARK III
AUTOMATIC PISTOL . . . . NiB $793 Ex $498 Gd $398
Calibers: 9mm or .40 S&W. 10-round magazine, 4.75-inch bbl., 7.75 inches overall. Weight: 32 oz. Fixed sights with molded grips. Durable non-glare matte blue or black epoxy finish. Made from 1985 to 2000; reintro. 2002.

**Browning
Hi-Power Mark III**

**Browning
Hi-Power Practical**

**Browning
Hi-Power Silver Chrome**

**Browning
Hi-Power 9mm Classic**

**Browning
Medalist International**

HI-POWER PRACTICAL AUTOMATIC PISTOL

Similar to standard Hi-Power except has silver-chromed frame and blued slide w/Commander-style hammer. Made from 1991 to 2006.

w/fixed sights . . . . NiB $729 Ex $533 Gd $385
w/adj. sights, add $75

HI-POWER SILVER CHROME . . NiB $792 Ex $650 Gd $407

Calibers: 9mm or .40 S&W. 10-round magazine, 4.75-inch bbl., 7.75 inches overall. Weight: 36 oz. Adjustable sights with Pachmayer grips. Silver-chromed finish. Made from 1991 to 2000.

HI-POWER 9MM CLASSIC

Limited Edition 9mm Hi-Power, w/silver-gray finish, high-grade engraving and finely-checkered walnut grips w/double border. Proposed production of the Classic was 5000 w/less than half that number produced. Gold Classic limited to 500 w/two-thirds proposed production in circulation. Made 1985-86.

Gold classic . . . . NiB $5401 Ex $4999 Gd $3495
Standard classic . . . . NiB $895 Ex $657 Gd $542

INTERNATIONAL MEDALIST EARLY MODEL

TARGET PISTOL . . . . NiB $1197 Ex $992 Gd $804

Modification of Medalist to conform w/International Shooting Union rules. 5.9-inch bbl., Smaller grip with no forearm. Weight: 42 oz. Made from 1970-73. Subtract 30% for post 1974 models

MEDALIST AUTOMATIC TARGET PISTOL

Caliber: .22 LR. 10-round magazine, 6.75-inch bbl. w/ vent rib, 11.94 inches overall. Weight: 46 oz. Removable blade front sight, click-adj. micrometer rear. Standard finish, blued also furnished gold-inlaid (Gold Model) and engraved and chrome-plated (Renaissance Model). Checkered walnut grips w/thumbrest (for right- or left-handed shooter). Finely figured and carved grips on Gold and Renaissance Models. Made by FN from 1962 to 1975. Higher grades. Intro. 1971.

Standard model. . . . . NiB $1552 Ex $1333 Gd $1072
Gold model. . . . . NiB $3071 Ex $1835 Gd $1032
Renaissance model . . . . NiB $2631 Ex $2183 Gd $1426

**Browning
Medalist Automatic Target**

**Browning Medalist
Renaissance**

**NOMAD AUTOMATIC PISTOL.........NiB $486 Ex $328
Gd $227**
Caliber: .22 LR. 10-round magazine, bbl. lengths: 4.5 and 6.75-inches, 8.94 inches overall (4.5-inch bbl.). Weight: 34 oz. (with 4.5-inch bbl.). Removable blade front sight, screw adj. rear. Blued finish. Plastic grips. Made by FN from 1962 to 1974.

**RENAISSANCE 9MM, .25 AUTO AND .380 AUTO (1955)
ENGRAVED, CASED SET...NiB $4080 Ex $3565 Gd $3160**
One pistol of each of the three models in a special walnut carrying case, all chrome-plated w/Nacrolac pearl grips. Made by FN from 1964 to 1975. Options and engraving varies.

BRYCO ARMS INC. — Irvine, California
Distributed by Jennings Firearms. Inc. Carson City, NV.

MODELS J22, J25 AUTO PISTOL
Calibers: .22 LR, .25 ACP. Six-round magazine, 2.5-inch bbl., about 5 inches overall. Weight: 13 oz. Fixed sights. Chrome, satin nickel or black Teflon finish. Walnut, grooved black Cycolac or resin-impregnated wood grips. Made 1981-85.
Model J-22 (disc. 1985) ....NiB $73 Ex $56 Gd $45
Model J-25 (disc. 1995) ....NiB $123 Ex $90 Gd $75

MODELS M25, M32, M38 AUTO PISTOL
Calibers: .25 ACP, .32 ACP, .380 ACP. Six-round magazine, 2.81-inch bbl., 5.31 inches overall. Weight: 11oz. to 15 oz. Fixed sights. Chrome, satin nickel or black Teflon finish. Walnut, grooved, black Cycolac or resin-impregnated wood grips. Made from 1988 to 2000.
Model M25 (disc.)............NiB $119 Ex $92 Gd $74
Model M32.................NiB $143 Ex $102 Gd $77
Model M38.................NiB $147 Ex $108 Gd $91

MODEL M48 AUTO PISTOL.... NiB $128 Ex $102 Gd $81
Calibers: .22 LR, .32 ACP, .380 ACP. Seven-round magazine, 4-inch bbl., 6.69 inches overall. Weight: 20 oz. Fixed sights. Chrome, satin nickel or black Teflon finish. Smooth wood or black Teflon grips. Made from 1989 to 1995.

MODEL M58...............NiB $132 Ex $108 Gd $90
Caliber: .380 ACP. 10-round magazine, 3.75-inch bbl., 5.5 inches overall. Weight: 30 oz. Fixed sights. Chrome, satin nickel, blued or black Teflon finish. Smooth wood or black Teflon grips. Made 1993 to 1995.

MODEL M59 AUTO PISTOL.... NiB $128 Ex $102 Gd $82
Caliber: 9mm Para. 10-round magazine, 4-inch bbl., 6.5 inches overall. Weight: 33 oz. Fixed sights. Chrome, satin nickel, blued or black Teflon finish. Smooth wood or black Teflon grips. Made 1994 to 1996.

MODEL NINE............NiB $171 Ex $136 Gd $112
Similar to Bryco/Jennings Model M59 except w/redesigned slide w/loaded chamber indicator and frame mounted ejector. Weight: 30 oz. Made from 1997 to 2003.

MODEL 5 AUTO PISTOL ....NiB $102 Ex $69 Gd $46
Caliber: .380 ACP, 9mm Para.; 10- or 12-shot magazine. Bbl: 3.25 inches. Blue or nickel finish, black synthetic grips. Weight: 36 oz. Disc. 1995.

BUDISCHOWSKY — Mt. Clemens, Michigan
Mfd. by Norton Armament Corporation

TP-70 DA AUTOMATIC PISTOL
Calibers: .22 LR, .25 Auto. Six-round magazine, 2.6-inch bbl., 4.65 inches overall. Weight: 12.3 oz. Fixed sights. Stainless steel. Plastic grips. Made from 1973 to 1977.
.22 LR....................NiB $487 Ex $361 Gd $372
.25 ACP...................NiB $362 Ex $249 Gd $192

CALICO LIGHT WEAPONS SYSTEM — Hillsboro, Oregon

MODEL 110 AUTO PISTOL ...NiB $635 Ex $576 Gd $486
Caliber: .22 LR. 100-round magazine, 6-inch bbl., 17.9 inches overall. Weight: 3.75 lbs. Adj. post front sight, fixed U-notch rear. Black finish aluminum frame. Molded composition grip. Made from 1986 to 1994.

MODEL M-950 AUTO PISTOL .NiB $850 Ex $479 Gd $362
Caliber 9mm Para. 50- or 100-round magazine, 7.5-inch bbl., 14 inches overall. Weight: 2.25 lbs. Adj. post front sight, fixed U-notch rear. Glass-filled polymer grip. Made 1989-94.

CANIK — Turkey
See Century Arms.

CARACAL — Abu Dhabi, UAE

MODEL C ....NiB $560 Ex $460 Gd $340
Semi-automatic. Striker-fire. Glock style trigger safety. Caliber: 9mm, 15-rnd. magazine, 3.5-in. bbl., 6.6 inches

Charter Arms Bonnie

Charter Arms Clyde

Charter Arms Bulldog Police

TP9 (CANIK55) . . . . NiB $350 Ex $320 Gd $300
Similar to Walther P99 platform. Semi-automatic. DAO. Caliber: 9mm, 17-rnd. magazine, 4.07-in. bbl., 6.75 inches overall. Weight: 29 oz. Fixed sights. Finish: Matte black. Polymer frame. Made from 2013 to 2015.
TP9v2 (improved version) . . . . . NiB $350 Ex $320 Gd $300

PAP M85 NP . . . . NiB $630 Ex $560 Gd $370
Similar to AK-47 platform. Semi-automatic. Caliber: 5.56x45mm, 30-rnd. magazine, 10-in. bbl., 19.7 inches overall. Weight: 6.4 lbs. Fixed sights. Finish: blued. Krinkov style muzzle brake and hinged dust cover. Stamped receiver. Made in U.S. from 2013 to date.

PAP M92 PV . . . . NiB $530 Ex $550 Gd $350
Similar to AK-47 platform. Semi-automatic. Caliber: 7.62x39mm, 30-rnd. magazine, 10-in. bbl., 19.7 inches overall. Weight: 6.4 lbs. Fixed sights. Finish: blued. Krinkov style muzzle brake. Stamped receiver. Made in U.S. from 2013 to date.

CHARLES DALY — Dayton, Ohio

See Daly, Charles.

CHARTER ARMS — Shelton, CT

Formerly Charter 2000 and ChartArmsms Corp. (Ansonia, CT). Established in 1962 Charter Arms has gone through several names changes. Models name and features are similar; recent manufacture noted.

MODEL 40 AUTOMATIC PISTOL . NiB $283 Ex $224 Gd $171
Caliber: .22 LR. Eight-round magazine, 3.3-inch bbl., 6.3 inches overall. Weight: 21.5 oz. Fixed sights. Checkered walnut grips. Stainless steel finish. Made from 1985 to 1986.

**MODEL 79K DA
AUTOMATIC PISTOL** . . . . NiB $362 Ex $286 Gd $230
Calibers: .380 or .32 Auto. Seven-round magazine, 3.6-inch bbl., 6.5 inches overall. Weight: 24.5 oz. Fixed sights. Checkered walnut grips. Stainless steel finish. Made from 1985 to 1986.

BONNIE AND CLYDE SET . . . . NiB $454 Ex $342 Gd $297
Matching pair of shrouded 2.5-inch bbl., revolvers chambered for .32 Magnum (Bonnie) and .38 Special (Clyde). Blued finish w/scrolled name on bbls. Made 1989 to 1990 and 1999.

BULLDOG .44 DA REVOLVER
SA/DA revolver. Caliber: .44 Special. Five-round cylinder, 2.5- or 3-inch bbl., 7 or 7.5 inches overall. Weight: 19 or 19.5 oz. Fixed sights. Blued, nickel-plated or stainless finish. Checkered walnut Bulldog or square buttgrips. Made from 1973 to 1996.
**Blued finish/
    Pocket Hammer (2.5-inch)** . . . NiB $260 Ex $192 Gd $134
**Blued finish/Bulldog grips
    (3-inch disc. 1988)** . . . . NiB $244 Ex $206 Gd $147
Electroless nickel. . . . . NiB $274 Ex $223 Gd $146
**Stainless steel/
    Bulldog grips (disc. 1992).** . . . NiB $220 Ex $193 Gd $132
Neoprene grips/Pocket Hammer. . NiB $242 Ex $203 Gd $148

NOTE: *In 1999 the Bulldog was reintroduced. Simialr to other Bulldog models but with 2.5-inch barrel, shrouded ejector rod,*

overall. Weight: 24.6 oz. Fixed sights. Finish: Matte black. Polymer frame. Made from 2006 to date.
Model SC (subcompact version) NiB $560 Ex $460 Gd $340

MODEL F . . . . NiB $560 Ex $460 Gd $340
Semi-automatic. Striker-fire. Glock style trigger safety. Caliber: 9mm, 18-rnd. magazine, 4.1-in. bbl., 7 inches overall. Weight: 26 oz. Fixed sights. Finish: Matte black. Polymer frame. Made from 2006 to date.

CENTURY ARMS — Delray Beach, FL

Formerly Century Arms International, importer of military surplus firearms. In 2015 named changed to Century Arms with continued import of new firearms and U.S.-made AK-47 platform firearms.

**Charter Arms
Bulldog Pug**

**Charter Arms
Bulldog Target**

**Charter Arms
Explorer II**

blued finish, and checkered rubber grips. Other older model were also reintroduced as noted. Recent models offered in numerous color finishes and patterns.

- Recent Manufacture (1999 to date) -
Standard . . . . NiB $409 Ex $355 Gd $315
stainless finish, add. $20
Classic. NiB $436 Ex $400 Gd $395
DAO . . . . NiB $426 Ex $370 Gd $345
On Duty (shrouded hammer,
    stainless finish) . . . . NiB $432 Ex $380 Gd $355
Police (4.2-in. bbl., stainless) . . . . NiB $408 Ex $360 Gd $320
Target (4.2-in. bbl., adj. sights,
    stainless). . . . . NiB $475 Ex $420 Gd $370

BULLDOG .357 DA REVOLVER. . . NiB $214 Ex $169 Gd $129
Caliber: .357 Magnum. Five-round cylinder, 6-inch bbl., 11 inches overall. Weight: 25 oz. Fixed sights. Blued finish. Square, checkered walnut grips. Made from 1977 to 1996.

BULLDOG NEW POLICE DA REVOLVER
Same general specifications as Bulldog Police except chambered for .44 Special. Five-round cylinder, 2.5- or 3.5-inch bbl. Made from 1990 to 1992.
Blued finish. . . . . NiB $263 Ex $201 Gd $148
Stainless finish (2.5-inch bbl. only) NiB $202 Ex $166 Gd $114

BULLDOG POLICE DA REVOLVER
Caliber: .38 Special or .32 H&R Magnum. Six-round cylinder, 4-inch bbl., 8.5 inches overall. Weight: 20.5 oz. Adj. rear sight, ramp front. Blued or stainless finish. Square checkered walnut grips. Made from 1976-93. No shroud on new models.
Blued finish. . . . . NiB $272 Ex $204 Gd $158
Stainless finish. . . . . NiB $234 Ex $194 Gd $147
.32 H&R Magnum (disc.1992). . . NiB $270 Ex $204 Gd $142

BULLDOG PUG DA REVOLVER
Caliber: .44 Special. Five-round cylinder, 2.5 inch bbl., 7.25 inches overall. Weight: 20 oz. Blued or stainless finish. Fixed ramp front sight, fixed square-notch rear. Checkered Neoprene or walnut grips. Made from 1988 to 1993.
Blued finish. . . . . NiB $262 Ex $224 Gd $183
Stainless finish. . . . . NiB $224 Ex $172 Gd $121

BULLDOG TARGET. . . . . NiB $207 Ex $134 Gd $102
Calibers: .357 Magnum, .44 Special (latter intro. in 1977). Four-inch bbl., 8.5 inches overall. Weight: 20.5 oz. in .357. Adj. rear sight, ramp front. Blued finish. Square checkered walnut grips. Made 1976 to 1992.
Stainless steel . . . . NiB $271 Ex $203 Gd $147

BULLDOG TRACKER . . . . NiB $207 Ex $134 Gd $102
DA reviolver. Caliber: .357 Mag. Five-round cylinder, 2.5-, 4- or 6-inch bbl., 11 inches overall (6-inch bbl.). Weight: 21 oz. (2.5-inch bbl.). Adj. rear sight, ramp front. Checkered walnut grips. Blued finish. 4- or 6-inch bbl., Disc.1986. Reintro. 1989 to 1992.

EXPLORER II SEMIAUTO SURVIVAL PISTOL
Caliber: .22 LR, 8-round magazine, 6-, 8- or 10-inch bbl., 13.5 inchesoverall (6-inch bbl.). Weight: 28 oz. finishes: Black, heat cured, semigloss textured enamel or silvertone anticorrosion. Disc. 1987.
Standard model. . . . . NiB $158 Ex $100 Gd $66
Silvertone (w/optional
    6- or 10-inch bbl.). . . . . NiB $143 Ex $123 Gd $83

MAG PUG. . . . . NiB $397 Ex $345 Gd $305
SImilar to Bulldog .357 except w/2.5-in. bbl. w/ejector shroud and rubber grips. Made from 2001 to date.

OFF-DUTY DA REVOLVER
Calibers: .22 LR or .38 Special. Six-round (.22 LR) or 5-round (.38 Special) cylinder. Two-inch bbl., 6.25 inches overall. Weight: 16 oz. Fixed rear sight, Partridge-type front sight. Plain walnut grips. Matte black, nickel or stainless steel finish. Made from 1992 to 1996.
Matte black finish . . . . NiB $185 Ex $153 Gd $112
Nickel finish . . . . NiB $230 Ex $194 Gd $150
Stainless steel . . . . NiB $260 Ex $194 Gd $128
- Recent Manufacture (1999 to date) -
Standard (2-in. bbl., hammerless, aluminum frame, matte
    black finish). . . . . NiB $419 Ex $360 Gd $315
two-tone finish, add $20

ON DUTY. . . . . NiB $402 Ex $355 Gd $310
SImilar to Mag Pug or Undercover depending on caliber except w/shrouded hammer. Matte stainless finsih. Made 2009 to date.

PATHFINDER DA REVOLVER
Calibers: .22 LR, .22 WMR. Six-round cylinder, bbl. lengths: 2-, 3-, 6-inches, 7.13 inches overall (in 3-inch bbl.), and regular grips. Weight: 18.5 oz. (3-inch bbl.). Adj. rear sight, ramp

**Charter
Arms Pathfinder**

**Charter Arms Explorer II
Silvertone w/optional barrels**

**Charter Arms Police Undercover
.32 H&R Magnum**

**Charter Arms Undercover
.32 S&W Long**

PATRIOT . . . . NiB $345 Ex $305 Gd $255
SImilar to Bulldog .357 except in .327 Federal. Made 2009 to 2012.

PIT BULL DA REVOLVER
Calibers: 9mm, .357 Magnum, .38 Special. Five-round cylinder, 2.5-, 3.5- or 4-inch bbl., 7 inches overall (2.5-inch bbl.). Weight: 21.5 to 25 oz. All stainless steel frame. Fixed ramp front sight, fixed square-notch rear. Checkered Neoprene grips. Blued or stainless finish. Made from 1989 to 1991.
Blued finish . . . . NiB $261 Ex $223 Gd $137
Stainless finish . . . . NiB $270 Ex $ 230 Gd $143
- Recent Manufacture (2010 to date) -
Standard (2-in. bbl., 9mm, .40 S&W or .45 ACP, 5-shot cylinder, stainless finish) . . . . NiB $502 Ex $420 Gd $380
.40 S&W or .45 ACP, deduct $10

SOUTHPAW . . . . NiB $419 Ex $365 Gd $330
SImilar to Undercover except true left hand design. Made 2008 to date.

UNDERCOVER DA REVOLVER
Caliber: .38 Special. Five-round cylinder,. bbl., lengths: 2-, 3-, 4-inches, 6.25 inches overall (2-inch bbl.), and regular grips. Weight: 16 oz. (2-inch bbl.). Fixed sights. Plain walnut, checkered Bulldog or square buttgrips. Made from 1965 to 1996.
Blued or nickel-plated finish . . . NiB $216 Ex $120 Gd $101
Stainless finish . . . . NiB $281 Ex $230 Gd $148
- Recent Manufacture (1999 to date) -
Standard (2-in. bbl., blued finish) . . NiB $346 Ex $290 Gd $255
stainless finish, add $10
DAO (2-in. bbl., blued finish) . . NiB $352 Ex $300 Gd $265

UNDERCOVER DA REVOLVER
Same general specifications as standard Undercover except chambered for .32 H&R Magnum or .32 S&W Long, has 6-round cylinder and 2.5-inch bbl.
.32 H&R Magnum (blued) . . . . . NiB $316 Ex $253 Gd $170
.32 H&R Magnum nickel . . . . . . NiB $212 Ex $171 Gd $109
.32 H&R Magnum (stainless) . . NiB $332 Ex $268 Gd $187
.32 S&W Long (blued) disc. 1989 . . . NiB $303 Ex $225 Gd $179

UNDERCOVER LITE . . . . NiB $397 Ex $345 Gd $305
SImilar to Undercover except w/aluminum frame. Caliber: .38 Special. Five-round cylinder,. bbl., lengths: 2-in. Rubber grips. Weight: 12 oz. Fixed sights. Matte aluminum finsh. Made from 1991 to date.
colored finishes, add $20

UNDERCOVER POCKET POLICE DA REVOLVER
Same general specifications as standard Undercover except has 6-round cylinder and pocket-type hammer. Blued or stainless steel finish. Made from 1969 to 1981.
Blued finish . . . . NiB $342 Ex $283 Gd $ 214
Stainless steel . . . . NiB $356 Ex $290 Gd $219

UNDERCOVER POLICE DA REVOLVER
Same general specifications as standard Undercover except has 6-round cylinder. Made from 1984 to 1989. Reintroduced 1993.
Blued, .38 Special . . . . NiB $337 Ex $ 279 Gd $204
Stainless, .38 Special . . . . NiB $270 Ex $204 Gd $158
.32 H&R Magnum . . . . NiB $250 Ex $200 Gd $143

UNDERCOVERETTE
DA REVOLVER . . . . NiB $179 Ex $130 Gd $101
Same as Undercover except w/2-in. bbl., caliber .32 S&W Long, 6-round cylinder, blued finish only. Weight: 16.5 oz. Made 1972 to 1983.

front. Blued or stainless finish. Plain walnut regular, checkered Bulldog or square buttgrips. Made 1970 to date. Note: Originally designated "Pocket Target," name was changed in 1971 to "Pathfinder." Grips changed in 1984.
Blued finish . . . . NiB $203 Ex $148 Gd $112
Stainless finish . . . . NiB $240 Ex $192 Gd $128
- Recent Manufacture (1999 to date) -
Standard (2-in. bbl., .22 LR or .22 Mag., 6-shot cylinder, stainless finish) . . . . NiB $365 Ex $320 Gd $280
two-tone colores finish, add $20

**Charter Arms
Undercover Stainless**

**Colt
Model 1902 Military**

**Cimarron
El Pistolero**

- Recent Manufacture (1999 to date) -
Standard (2-in. bbl., .32 H&R Mag.,
    stainless finish) . . . . NiB $375 Ex $330 Gd $290
two-tone colores finish, add $20

CIMARRON F.A. CO. — Fredricksburg, Texas

*Currently imports, distrbutes and retails black powder and
cartridge firearms manufactured by Armi-Sport, Chiappa,
Pedersoli, Pietta, and Uberti.*

1872 OPEN-TOP SA REVOLVER...NiB $510 Ex $345 Gd $270
Reproduction of Colt Navy and Army open-top conversion revolv-
ers. Calibers: .38 Long Colt, .38 Spl., .44-40, .44 Spl., 44 Russian,
.45 Schofield or .45 Long Colt. Six-round cylinder, 4.75- 5.5- or
7.5-inch bbl., brass backstrap and triggerguard, blued finish.
Made from 1999 to date.
**Silver plated backstrap (2010)....NiB $550 Ex $385 Gd $310
Engraved, add $1000**

BADLAND SA REVOLVER.....NiB $280 Ex $210 Gd $180
Calibers: .357 Mag., .45 Colt. 6-round cylinder, 4.75-in.
bbl., brass backstrap and triggerguard, wood grip. Made
2005-07.

BADLAND SA REVOLVER.....NiB $400 Ex $315 Gd $200
Calibers: .44 Spl./.44 Mag. 6-round cylinder, 4.75-, 6- or 7.5-in.
bbl., brass or steel backstrap and triggerguard, wood grip. Made
from 1984 to 1993.
Buntline . . . . .NiB $415 Ex $330 Gd $220

EL PISTOLERO SA REVOLVER. . NiB $444 Ex $336 Gd $260
Calibers: .357 Mag., .45 Colt. Six-round cylinder, 4.75- 5.5-
or 7.5-inch bbl., polished brass backstrap and triggerguard.
Otherwise, same as Colt Single-Action Army revolver w/parts

being interchangeable. Made from 1997 to 1998; reitro. 2007
to 2013.

FRONTIER SIX SHOOTER. . . . . NiB $730 Ex $580 Gd $450
Calibers: .22 LR, .22 Mag., .38 Spl./.357 Mag., .38-40, .44 Spl.,
.44-40 or .45 Long Colt. 6-round cylinder, 4.75-, 5.5- or 7.5-
in. bbl., steel backstrap. Original Colt-like finish. Made from
2008 to 2010.
**Sheriff's model (3- or 4-in. bbl.). . .NiB $400 Ex $300 Gd $220
Target model (adj. rear sight) . .NiB $360 Ex $270 Gd $200**

COLT'S MANUFACTURING CO., INC. — Hartford, Connecticut

*Previously Colt Industries, Firearms Division. Production of
some Colt handguns spans the period before World War II
to the postwar years. Values shown for these models are for
earlier production. Those manufactured c. 1946 and later generally are less desirable to collectors and values are approximately 30 percent lower.*

NOTE: *For ease in finding a particular firearm, Colt handguns are
grouped into three sections: Automatic Pistols, Single-Shot Pistols &
Derringers, and Revolvers. For a complete listing, please refer to the
Index.*

- AUTOMATIC PISTOLS -

MODEL 1900 .38 AUTOMATIC PISTOL
Caliber: .38 ACP (modern high-velocity cartridges should not be
used in this pistol). Seven-round magazine, 6-inch bbl., 9 inches
overall. Weight: 35 oz. Fixed sights. Blued finish. Hard rubber and
plain or checkered walnut grips. Sharp-spur hammer. Combination
rear sight and safety unique to the Model 1900 (early production).
In mid-1901 a solid rear sight was dovetailed into the slide. (S/N
range 1-4274) Made 190003. Note: 250 models were sold to the
military (50 Navy and 200 Army).
**Early commercial model
    (w/sight/safety) . . . NiB $15,810 Ex $14,586 Gd $11,220
Late commercial model
    (w/dovetailed sight)... NiB $15,810 Ex $14,586 Gd $11,220
Army Model w/U.S. inspector marks (1st Series - S/N 90-150
    w/inspector mark J.T.T)... NiB $32,130 Ex $27,540 Gd $22,185
    (2nd Series - S/N 1600-1750
    w/inspector mark R.A.C.)...NiB $11,577 Ex $9736 Gd $6700
Navy model (Also marked
    w/USN-I.D. number)...NiB $18,967 Ex $13,107 Gd $10,200**

MODEL 1902 MILITARY .38 AUTOMATIC PISTOL
Caliber: .38 ACP (modern high-velocity cartridges should
not be used in this pistol). Eight-round magazine, 6-inch
bbl., 9 inches overall. Weight: 37 oz. Fixed sights w/blade

**Colt
1903 Early Hammer**

**Colt
Model 1903 Pocket Hammerless**

front and V-notch rear. Blued finish. Checkered hard rubber grips. Round back hammer, changed to spur type in 1908. No safety but fitted w/standard military swivel. About 18,000 produced with split S/N ranges. The government contract series (15,001-15,200) and the commercial sales series (15,000 receding to 11,000) and (30,200-47,266). Made from 1902 to 1929.

Early military model (w/front
slide serrations) . . . . . . NiB $6,120 Ex $3871 Gd $3528
Late military model (w/rear
slide serrations) . . . . NiB $6115 Ex $3732 Gd $2525
MARKED "U.S. ARMY"
(S/N 15,001-15,200) . . . NiB $19,635 Ex $17,340 Gd $15,402

MODEL 1902 SPORTING
.38 AUTOMATIC PISTOL . . NiB $5008 Ex $3213 Gd $2443
Caliber: .38 ACP (modern high-velocity cartridges should not be used in this pistol). Seven-round magazine, 6-inch bbl., 9 inches overall. Weight: 35 oz. Fixed sights w/blade front and V-notch rear. Blued finish. Checkered hard rubber grips. Round back hammer was standard but some spur hammers were installed during late production. No safety and w/o swivel as found on military model. Total production about 7,500 w/split S/N ranges (4275-10,999) and (30,000-30,190) Made from 1902 to 1908.

MODEL 1903 POCKET .32 AUTOMATIC PISTOL
FIRST ISSUE - COMMERCIAL SERIES
Caliber: .32 Auto. Eight-round magazine, 4-inch bbl., 7 inches overall. Weight: 23 oz. Fixed sights. Blued or nickel finish. Checkered hard rubber grips. Hammerless (concealed hammer). Slide lock and grip safeties. Fitted w/barrel bushing but early models have no magazine safety. Total production of the Model 1903 reached 572,215. The First Issue maded from 1903 to 1908 (S/N range 1-72,000).
Blued finish. . . . . NiB $1132 Ex $806 Gd $587
Nickel finish . . . . NiB $1153 Ex $826 Gd $602

MODEL 1903 POCKET .32 AUTOMATIC PISTOL
SECOND ISSUE - COMMERCIAL SERIES
Same as First Issue but with 3.75-inch bbl. and small Extractor. Made from 1908 to 1910 (S/N range 72,001 -105,050).
Blued finish. . . . . NiB $816 Ex $602 Gd $474
Nickel finish . . . . NiB $842 Ex $689 Gd $498

MODEL 1903 POCKET .32 AUTOMATIC PISTOL,
THIRD ISSUE - COMMERCIAL SERIES
Caliber: .32 Auto. Similar to Second Issue w/3.75-inch bbl. except with integral barrel bushing and locking lug at muzzle end of bbl. Production occurred 1910 to 1926 (S/N range 105,051-468,096).
Blued finish. . . . . NiB $1326 Ex $1030 Gd $813
Nickel finish . . . . NiB $1474 Ex $1234 Gd $918

MODEL 1903 POCKET .32 AUTOMATIC PISTOL
FOURTH ISSUE - COMMERCIAL SERIES
Caliber: .32 Auto. Similar to Third Issue except a slide lock safety change was made when a Tansley-style disconnector was added on all pistols above S/N 468,097, which prevents firing of cartridge in chamber when the magazine is removed. Blued or nickel finish. Checkered walnut grips. These design changes were initiated 1926 to 1945 (S/N range 105,051-554,446).
Blued finish . . . . NiB $1331 Ex $1020 Gd $804
Nickel finish . . . . NiB $1535 Ex $1132 Gd $945

MODEL 1903 POCKET (HAMMER) .38 AUTOMATIC PISTOL
Caliber: .38 ACP (modern high-velocity cartridges should not be used in this pistol). Similar to Model 1902 Sporting .38 but w/shorter frame, slide and 4.5-inch bbl. Overall dimension reduced to 7.5 inches. Weight: 31 oz. Fixed sights w/blade front and V-notch rear. Blued finish. Checkered hard rubber grips. Round back hammer, changed to spur type in 1908. No safety. (S/N range 16,001-47,226 with some numbers above 30,200 assigned to 1902 Military). Made from 1903 to 1929.
Early model
(round hammer) . . . . NiB $2030 Ex $1713 Gd $1418
Late model
(spur hammer) . . . . NiB $2254 Ex $1953 Gd $1641

MODEL 1903 POCKET HAMMERLESS (CONCEALED HAMMER)
.32 AUTOMATIC PISTOL - MILITARY
Caliber: .32 ACP. Eight-round magazine, Similar to Model 1903 Pocket .32 except concealed hammer and equipped w/ magazine safety. Parkerized or blued finish. (S/N range with "M" prefix M1-M200,000) Made from 1941 to 1945.
Blued service model (marked
"U.S. Property") . . . . NiB $1333 Ex $1179 Gd $852
Parkerized service model (marked
"U.S. Property") . . . . NiB $2162 Ex $1821 Gd $1520
Blued documented
Officer's model. . . . . NiB $3182 Ex $2880 Gd $1760
Parkerized documented
Officer's model. . . . . NiB $3182 Ex $2880 Gd $1760

MODEL 1905 .45 AUTOMATIC PISTOL
Caliber: .45 (Rimless) Automatic. Seven-round magazine, 5-inch bbl., 8 inches overall. Weight: 32.5 oz. Fixed sights w/ blade front and V-notch rear. Blued finish. Checkered walnut, hard rubber or pearl grips. Predecessor to Model 1911 Auto Pistol and contributory to the development of the .45 ACP cartridge. (S/N range 1-6100) Made from 1905 to 1911.
Commercial model . . . . NiB $7461 Ex $5579 Gd $3784
w/slotted backstrap
(500 produced) . . . . . . NiB $10,761 Ex $8966 Gd $7359
w/shoulder stock/holster, add. . . . . $7650 to $10,200

**Colt
Model 1905 Military**

**Colt
Model 1908 Pocket 25**

**Colt
Model 1911**

MODEL 1905 .45 (1907)
CONTRACT PISTOL . NiB $22,440 Ex $17,340 Gd $10,200
Variation of the Model 1905 produced to U.S. Military specifications, including loaded chamber indicator, grip safety and lanyard loop. Only 201 were produced, but 200 were delivered and may be identified by the chief inspector's initials "K.M." (S/N range 1-201) Made from 1907 to 1908.

MODEL 1908 POCKET .25 HAMMERLESS AUTO PISTOL
Caliber: .25 Auto. Six-round magazine, 2-inch bbl., 4.5 inches overall. Weight: 13 oz. Flat-top front, square-notch rear sight in groove. Blued, nickel or Parkerized finish. Checkered hard rubber grips on early models, checkered walnut on later type, special pearl grips illustrated. Both a grip safety and slide lock safety are included on all models. The Tansley-style safety

disconnector was added in 1916 at pistol No. 141000. (S/N range 1-409,061) Made 1908 to 1941.
Blued finish . . . . NiB $1734 Ex $1415 Gd $1137
Nickel finish, add $125
Marked "U.S. Property"
   (w/blued finish) . . . . NiB $3213 Ex $2861 Gd $2560

MODEL 1908 POCKET .380 AUTOMATIC PISTOL
Similar to Pocket .32 Auto w/3.75-inch bbl. except chambered for .380 Auto w/seven-round magazine. Weight: 23 oz. Blue, nickel or Parkerized finish. (S/N range 1-138,009) Made from 1908 to 1945.
First Issue (made 1908-11, w/bbl., lock and bushing,
   w/S/N 1-6,250) . . . . NiB $1734 Ex $1528 Gd $1312
Second Issue (made 1911-28,w/o bbl., lock and bushing,
   w/S/N 6,251-92,893) . . . NiB $2017 Ex $1693 Gd $1528
Third Issue (made 1928-45, w/safety disconnector,
   w/S/N 92,894-138,009). . . . NiB $1734 Ex $1528 Gd $1312
Parkerized service model (Marked "U.S. Property" made
   1942-45, w/S/N "M" prefix.) . . . NiB $2649 Ex $1972 Gd $1723
Documented officer's model (service model w/military
   assignment papers) . . . . . NiB $3162 Ex $2557 Gd $1804

NOTE: *During both World Wars, Colt licensed other firms to make these pistols under government contract, including Ithaca Gun Co., North American Arms Co., Ltd. (Canada), Remington-Rand Co., Remington-UMC, Singer Sewing Machine Co., and Union Switch & Signal Co. M1911 also produced at Springfield Armory.*

MODEL 1911 AUTOMATIC PISTOL (COMMERCIAL)
Caliber: .45 Auto. Seven-round magazine, 5-inch bbl., 8.5 inches overall. Weight: 39 oz. Fixed sights. Blued finish on Commercial model. Parkerized or similar finish on most military pistols. Checkered walnut grips (early production), plastic grips (later production). Checkered, arched mainspring housing and longer grip safety spur adopted in 1923 on M1911A1. C-series.
Model 1911 commercial (mfg. 1912-1925, S/N range:
   C1-C138532). . . . . NiB $15,300 Ex $13,255 Gd $11,424
Model 1911A1 commercial Pre-WWII ("C" prefix serial number,
   mfg. 1925-1942, S/N range: C138533-
   C215000) . . . . NiB $3886 Ex $3172 Gd $2240
Model 1911A1 commercial Post-WWII (changed to "C" suffix S/N
   in 1950, mfg. 1946-1970) NiB $3886 Ex $3172 Gd $2240

MODEL 1911 U.S. MILITARY GOVERNMENT
These are U.S. Military pistols made between 1912 through 1918 by a variety of manufacturers. Typical characteristics include: Straight mainspring housing, checkered wood grips, lanyard loop, and long trigger.
Colt manufacture
   (mfg. 1912) . . . . NiB $10,353 Ex $8975 Gd $6849
   (mfg. 1913-1915) . . . . . . NiB $5500 Ex $4800 Gd $4300
   (mfg. 1916) . . . . NiB $5700 Ex $5100 Gd $4300
   (mfg. 1917-1918, blue
   finish) . . . . NiB $4300 Ex $3300 Gd $2100
   (mfg. 1917-1918, black Army
   finish) . . . . NiB $4300 Ex $3300 Gd $2100
   (mfg. 1919-1925) . . . . . . NiB $4300 Ex $3300 Gd $2100
Marine Model M1911 type (stamped: "MODEL OF 1911
   U.S. ARMY" on r. of slide) NiB $8771 Ex $6654 Gd $4995
Navy Model M1911 type (stamped: "MODEL OF 1911 U.S.
   NAVY" on right of slide) . NiB $8771 Ex $6654 Gd $4995
North American Arms Co. manufacture (1918)
   under 100 produced. . . NiB $36,720 Ex $29,580 Gd $24,990

**Colt
1991 A1**

Colt Cadet .22

**Colt All American
Model 2000**

Remington-UMC manufacture (1918-1919)
  S/N range: 1-21676 ..... NiB $6120 Ex $4070 Gd $2458
Springfield manufacture (1914-1915)
  S/N ranges: 72751-83855, 102597-107596, 113497-120566,
  125567-133186.........NiB $6120 Ex $4070 Gd $2458

MODEL 1911 FOREIGN MILITARY CONTRACTS
Simialr to U.S. Military M1911s except exported to foreign goverments.
**Argentine type (Arg. seal stamped on top of slide, S/N w/"C"
  prefix, mfg. 1914-19) ... NiB $3900 Ex $3600 Gd $3200**
**British type (stamped: "CALIBRE 455",
  mfg. 1915-1919) ... NiB $5800 Ex $4800 Gd $3000**
**Norwegian 1914 type (w/extended slide release,
  mfg. 1918-1947) .... NiB $2400 Ex $1900 Gd $1600**
**Russian type (w/Cyrillis markings on left side of receiver,
  mfg. 1916-1917) .... NiB $8800 Ex $4600 Gd $4100**

M1911 SERIES 70 WWI MODEL 1918
REPRODUCTION..............NiB $1500 Ex $950 Gd $700
Reproduction of Model 1911 (see above) w/black finish, original WWI rollmarks. Made from 2008 to 2009.

M1911 MODEL O SERIES 70
REPRODUCTION..............NiB $1500 Ex $950 Gd $700
Reproduction of Model 1911 (see above) w/original 1911 U.S. Military rollmarks, carbonia blue finish. Made 2003-09.

MODEL 1911A1 U.S. MILITARY GOVERNMENT
These are U.S. Military pistols made between 1924 through 1945 by a variety of manufacturers. Simialr to M1911 except w/arched main spring housing, blued or parkerized (mot common) finsih, cheched plastic grips, short trigger, longer grip safety, finger groove cut out in frame.
Colt manufacture........ NiB $4600 Ex $3900 Gd $3000
Ithaca manufacture ...... NiB $2300 Ex $1900 Gd $1600
Remington-Rand manufacture. .NiB $2600 Ex $2200 Gd $200
Singer manufacture.. NiB $65,900 Ex $50,015 Gd $40,455
Union Switch &
  Signal manufacture..... NiB $6227 Ex $5247 Gd $4047

MODEL 1911A1 FOREIGN MILITARY CONTRACTS
Simialr to U.S. Military M1911A1s except exported to foreign goverments.
**Argentine contract (stamped w/Argentine crest and
  "Model 1927") ....NiB $1600 Ex $1400 Gd $1200**
**Argentine manufacture (stamped w/crest and two lines on r.
  side of slide: "EJERCITO ARGENTINO / SIST. COLT. CAL.
  11.25mm MOD. 1927") NiB $1500 Ex $1300 Gd $1100**
**Brazilian contract (stamped w/crest and two lines on
  right side of slide: "EXERCITO BRASILEIRIO / 1937", mfg.
  1937-1941)...........NiB $4900 Ex $4100 Gd $3800**
**Mexican contract (stamped w/seal and one line on right
  side of "EJERCITO NACIONAL", S/N w/"C" prefix
  mfg. 1921-1927).......NiB $3900 Ex $3000 Gd $2700**

M1911A1 MODEL O SERIES 70 WWII
REPRODUCTION..............NiB $1300 Ex $850 Gd $680
Reproduction of Model 1911A1 (see above) w/pakerized finish, original WWII rollmarks. Made from 2001 to 2004.

1991 SERIES GOVERNEMNT MODEL SERIES 70 MODEL O
Reissue of Series 70 action. Caliber: .38 Super, .45 ACP. Seven-round magazine, 5-inch bbl., 8.5 inches overall. Weight: 39 oz. Fixed blade front sight, square notch rear. Blued or stainless finish. Made from 2003 to date.
Blued.....................NiB $1080 Ex 900 Gd $600
Stainless ....NiB $1120 Ex $940 Gd $650
.38 Super (stainless) ....NiB $800 Ex $700 Gd $600
.38 Super (bright stainless) ...NiB $1200 Ex $900 Gd $600

1991 SERIES GOVERNMENT MODEL SERIES 80 MODEL O
Similar to Series 80 model except w/9mm or .45 ACP. Seven-round magazine, 5-inch bbl., 8.5 inches overall. Weight: 39 oz. Fixed sights. Rollmarked "Colt M1991A1" on slide. Blued, stainless or parkerized finish. Made from 1991 to date.
Blued.....................NiB $975 Ex $600 Gd $300
Parkerized.................NiB $975 Ex $600 Gd $300
Stainless ....NiB $1040 Ex $750 Gd $380
Commander model ....NiB $995 Ex $560 Gd $380
Officer's Compact model .....NiB $620 Ex $430 Gd $380

.22 CADET AUTOMATIC PISTOL . NiB $479 Ex $343 Gd $270
Caliber: 22 LR. 10-round magazine, 4.5-inch vent rib bbl., 8.63 inches overall. Weight: 33.5 oz. Blade front sight, dovetailed rear. Stainless finish. TExtured black polymer grips w/ Colt medallion. Made 1993 to 1995. Note: The Cadet Model name was disc. under litigation but the manufacturer continued to produce this pistol configuration as the Model "Colt

22". For this reason the "Cadet" model will command slight premiums.

.22 SPORT AUTOMATIC PISTOL . NiB $485 Ex $345 Gd $270
Same specifications as Cadet Model except renamed Colt .22 w/ composition monogrip or wraparound black rubber grip. Made 1994 to 1998.

.22 TARGET PISTOL . . . . NiB $464 Ex $321 Gd $204
Similar to Colt 22 Sport Model except w/6-inch vent rib bbl., 10.12 inches overall. Weight: 40.5 oz. Partridge style front sight, adjustable white outline rear on full length grooved rib. Made from 1995 to 1999.

ACE AUTOMATIC PISTOL
Caliber: .22 LR (regular or high speed). 10-round magazine. Built on the same frame as the Government Model .45 Auto w/ same safety features, etc. Hand-honed action, target bbl., adj. rear sight. 4.75-inch bbl., 8.25. inches overall. Weight: 38 oz. Made 1930 to 1940.Commercial model NiB $4650 Ex $3783 Gd $3264
Service model (1938-42). . . NiB $7710 Ex $5498 Gd $4769
Post-War model (1978-89) . . NiB $1500 Ex $1000 Gd $800

ALL AMERICAN
MODEL 2000 DA PISTOL. . . . . NiB $785 Ex $566 Gd $408
Hammerless semiautomatic w/blued slide and polymer or alloy receiver fitted w/roller-bearing trigger. Caliber: 9mm Para. 15-round magazine, 4.5-inch bbl., 7.5 inches overall. Weight: 29 oz. (Polymer) or 33 oz (Alloy). Fixed blade front sight, square-notch rear w/3-dot system. Matte blued slide w/ black polymer or anodized aluminum receiver. Made from 1992 to 1994.

AUTOMATIC .25 PISTOL
As a result of the 1968 Firearms Act restricting the importation of the Colt Pocket Junior that was produced in Spain, Firearms International was contracted by Colt to manufacture a similar blowback action with the same Exposed hammer configuration. Both the U.S. and Spanish-made .25 automatics were recalled to correct an action malfunction. Returned firearms were fitted with a rebounding firing pin to prevent accidental discharges. Caliber: .25 ACP. Six-round magazine, 2.25-inch bbl., 4.5 inches overall. Weight: 12.5 oz. Integral blade front, square-notch rear sight groove. Blued finish. Checkered wood grips w/Colt medallion. Made from 1970 to 1975.
Model as issued. . . . . NiB $386 Ex $316 Gd $198
Model recalled & refitted . . . . . NiB $386 Ex $316 Gd $198

COLT 22 . . . . NiB $430 Ex $260 Gd $200
Semi-automatic. SA. Caliber: .22 LR, 10-rnd. magazine. 4.5-in. vent rib bbl. Weight: 33.5 oz. Sights: fixed. Finish: stainless. Pachmayr rubber grips. Made from 1994 to 1998.

COLT 22 TARGET . . . . NiB $430 Ex $260 Gd $200
Similar to Colt 22 model except w/6-in. vent rib bbl. Weight: 40.5 oz. Sights: adj. rear. Made from 1995 to 1999.

CHALLENGER. . . . . NiB $1100 Ex $800 Gd $400
Similar as Second Series Woodsman Target model but 4.5- or 6-inch bbl., 9 to 10.5 inches overall. Weight: 30 oz. (4.5-inch bbl.) or 31.5 oz. (6-inch bbl.) Blued finish. Checkered plastic grips. Made from 1950 to 1955.

COMMANDER (pre-Series 70) AUTOMATIC PISTOL
Same basic design as Government Model except w/shorter 4.25-inch bbl., and a special lightweight "Coltalloy" receiver

and mainspring housing. Calibers: .45 Auto, .38 Super Auto, 9mm Para. Seven-round magazine (.45 cal.), nine-round (.38 Auto and 9mm), 8 inches overall. Weight: 26.5 oz. Fixed sights. Round spur hammer. Improved safety lock. Blued finish. Checkered plastic or walnut grips. Made from 1950 to 1969.
9mm Para. . . . . NiB $1350 Ex $1000 Gd $700
.38 Super, .45 ACP . . . . NiB $1450 Ex $1150 Gd $900

SERIES 70 COMBAT COMMANDER AUTOMATIC PISTOL
Similar to Lightweight Commander except w/steel frame, blued or nickel-plated finish. Made from 1971 to 1980.
9mm Para. . . . . NiB $736 Ex $590 Gd $444
.38 Super, .45 ACP . . . . NiB $852 Ex $691 Gd $486

SERIES 70 LIGHTWEIGHT COMMANDER AUTOMATIC PISTOL
Same as Commander except w/blued or nickel-plated finish. Made from 1970 to 1983.
9mm Para. . . . . NiB $1350 Ex $1000 Gd $700
.38 Super, .45 ACP . . . . NiB $1150 Ex $870 Gd $620

CONVERSION UNIT—.22-.45 . . . NiB $306 Ex $255 Gd $179
Converts Service Ace .22 to National Match .45 Auto. Unit consists of match-grade slide assembly and bbl., bushing, recoil spring, recoil spring guide and plug, magazine and slide stop. Made from 1938 to 1942.

CONVERSION UNIT — .45-.22 . . . NiB $617 Ex $489 Gd $362
Converts Government Model .45 Auto to a .22 LR target pistol. Unit consists of slide assembly, bbl., floating chamber (as in Service Ace), bushing, ejector, recoil spring, recoil spring guide and plug, magazine and slide stop. The component parts differ and are not interchangable between post war, series 70, series 80, ACE I and ACE II units. Made from 1938 to 1984.

DEFENDER. . . . . NiB $1100 Ex $700 Gd $480
Caliber: 9mm, .40 S&W or .45 ACP. 3-inch bbl. 7-round magazine, Three-dot, sights. rubber finger-groove wrap around grips. Matte stainless finish. Made from 1998 to date.
Defender Plus (2002-03). . . . . NiB $880 Ex $660 Gd $5801

DELTA ELITE SEMIAUTO PISTOL
Caliber: 10mm. Five-inch bbl., 8.5 inches overall. Eight-round magazine, Weight: 38 oz. Checkered Neoprene combat grips w/Delta medallion. Three-dot, high-profile front and rear combat sights. Blued or stainless finish. Made from 1987 to 1996.
First Edition
    (500 Ltd. edition) . . . . NiB $975 Ex $784 Gd $551
Blued finish. . . . . NiB $923 Ex $626 Gd $468
Matte stainless finish. . . . . NiB $975 Ex $784 Gd $551
Ultra bright stainless finish, add $100

DELTA ELITE (CURRENT MFG.)
SEMIAUTOMATIC PISTOL. . . NiB $1115 Ex $830 Gd $520
Updated model similar to earlier Delta Elite except stainless finish only. Made from 2008 to date.

DELTA GOLD CUP SEMIAUTO PISTOL
Same general specifications as Delta Elite except w/Accro adjustable rear sight. Made 1989 to 1993; 1995 to 1996.
Blued finish (disc. 1991). . . . . . NiB $997 Ex $693 Gd $474
Stainless steel finish . . . . NiB $1076 Ex $792 Gd $576

GOLD CUP TROPHY NATIONAL
MATCH .45 AUTO . . . . NiB $1250 Ex $900 Gd $640
Similar to MK IV Series 80 Gold Cup National Match except w/aluminum trigger, Bo-Mar raer adj. sight, black checkered

**Colt
National Match**

**Colt MK II/Series 90
Double Eagle**

**Colt MK IV/
Series 80 .380**

**Colt Series 70 Combat
Commander**

rubber wrap around grips, 7 or 8-round magazine. Weight: 39 oz. Made 1997 to 2010.

GOLD CUP

NATIONAL MATCH . . . . NiB $1220 Ex $880 Gd $700
Similar to Gold Cup Trophy National Match. Made 2010 to date.
Stainless steel finish . . . . NiB $1240 Ex $750 Gd $530

GOVERNMENT MODEL 1911/1911A1
See Colt Model 1911.

HUNTSMAN . . . . NiB $900 Ex $650 Gd $350
Similar to Third Series Woodsman Traget and Sport models, except 4.5- or 6-in. bbl., fixed rear sight, no automatic slide stop. Early versions had black plastic grips. Later versions, beginning in 1960, had walnut stocks. No thumbrest. Made from 1955 to 1977.

MK I & II/SERIES 90 DOUBLE EAGLE
COMBAT COMMANDER . . . . NiB $2080 Ex $1832 Gd $1433
SA/DA trigger. Calibers: .40 S&W, .45 ACP. Seven-round magazine, 4.25-inch bbl., 7.75 inches overall. Weight: 36 oz. Fixed blade front sight, square-notch rear. Checkered Xenoy grips. Stainless finish. Made from 1992 to 1996.

MK II/SERIES 90 DOUBLE EAGLE SEMIAUTO PISTOL
SA/DA trigger. Calibers: .38 Super, 9mm, .40 S&W, 10mm, .45 ACP. Seven-round magazine. Five-inch bbl., 8.5 inches overall. Weight: 39 oz. Fixed or Accro adj. sights. Matte stainless finish. Checkered Xenoy grips. Made from 1991 to 1996.
.38 Super, 9mm,
.40 S&W (fixed sights) . . . . NiB $760 Ex $581 Gd $425
.45 ACP (adjustable sights) . . . . NiB $729 Ex $577 Gd $428
.45 ACP (fixed sights) . . . . NiB $714 Ex $546 Gd $407
10mm (adjustable sights) . . . . . NiB $729 Ex $576 Gd $434
10mm (fixed sights) . . . . NiB $714 Ex $550 Gd $407

MK II/SERIES 90 DOUBLE EAGLE
OFFICER'S ACP . . . . NiB $2141 Ex $1641 Gd $1448
Same general specifications as Double Eagle Combat Commander except chambered for .45 ACP only, 3.5-inch bbl., 7.25 inches overall. Weight: 35 oz. Also available in lightweight (25 oz.) w/blued finish (same price). Made from 1990 to 1993.

MK II/MK III NATIONAL MATCH
MID-RANGE . . . . NiB $1241 Ex $1020 Gd $704
Similar to Gold Cup National Match .45 Auto except chambered for .38 Special Mid Range. Five-round magazine, Made 1961 to 1974.

MK IV/SERIES 70 COMBAT COMMANDER
Same general specifications as the Lightweight Commander except made from 1970 to 1983.
Blued finish . . . . NiB $1020 Ex $903 Gd $750
Nickel finish . . . . NiB $1193 Ex $974 Gd $815

MK IV/SERIES 70 GOLD CUP
NATIONAL MATCH . . . . NiB $1743 Ex $1356 Gd $1153
Match version of MK IV/Series '70 Government Model. Caliber: .45 Auto only. Flat mainspring housing. Accurizor bbl., and bushing. Solid rib, Colt-Elliason adj. rear sight undercut front sight. Adj. trigger, target hammer. 8.75 inches overall. Weight: 38.5 oz. Blued finish. Checkered walnut grips. Made from 1970 to 1984.

MK IV/SERIES 70
GOVERNMENT . . . . NiB $1120 Ex $815 Gd $570
Calibers: .45 Auto, .38 Super Auto, 9mm Para. Seven-round magazine in .45, 9-round in .38 and 9mm. Five-inch bbl., 8.38 inches overall. Weight: 38 oz., (.45); 39 oz. in .38 and 9mm. Fixed rear sight and ramp front sight. Blued or nickel-plated finish. Checkered walnut grips. Made from 1970 to 1984.

MK IV/SERIES 80 .380 GOVERNMENT AUTOMATIC PISTOL
Caliber: .380 ACP, 3.29-inch bbl., 6.15 inches overall. Weight: 21.8 oz. Composition grips. Fixed sights. Made since 1983 to 1996.

Colt MK IV/Series 80 Gold Cup National Match

Colt MK IV/Series 80 Government Model

Colt MK IV/Series 80 Mustang Plus II

Colt MK IV/Series 80 Mustang Pocketlite

Stainless finish. . . . . NiB $1173 Ex $974 Gd $755

MK IV/SERIES 80 COMBAT COMMANDER
Simialr specifications as MK IV/Series 80 Governemnt except w/ steel frame, 4.25-in. bbl. Made 1983 to 1993.

Blued finish (disc.1996) . . . . . . NiB $950 Ex $620 Gd $470
Satin nickel (disc.1987). . . . . . . NiB $975 Ex $650 Gd $580
Stainless finish (disc.1998) . . . . NiB $860 Ex $570 Gd $450
Two-tone finish (disc.1998). . . . NiB $810 Ex $600 Gd $450
Gold Cup (disc.1993) . . . . NiB $1200 Ex $930 Gd $830

MK IV/SERIES 80 COMBAT
GOVERNMENT . . . . NiB $960 Ex $670 Gd $480
Same general specifications as MK IV/Series 80 Government except w/matte black finish. Calibers: .45 ACP. Made from 1983 to 1998.

Combat Elite (.38 Super). . . . . . NiB $980 Ex $700 Gd $600
Combat Target (adj. sights) . . . . NiB $770 Ex $530 Gd $460

MK IV/SERIES 80 GOLD CUP NATIONAL MATCH
Same general specifications as Match Series 70 except w/ additional finishes and "pebbled" wraparound Neoprene grips. Made from 1983 to 1996.

Blued finish. . . . . NiB $1071 Ex $714 Gd $490
Bright blued finish . . . . NiB $1071 Ex $714 Gd $490
Stainless finish. . . . . NiB $1148 Ex $867 Gd $638

MK IV/SERIES 80 GOVERNMENT MODEL
Similar specifications as Government Model Series 70 except w/firing pin safety feature. Made 1983 to 1997.

Blued finish. . . . . NiB $1117 Ex $755 Gd $520
Nickel finish . . . . NiB $1150 Ex $800 Gd $570
Stain nickel/blue finish . . . . . . NiB $1150 Ex $800 Gd $570
Matte stainless finish. . . . . NiB $1100 Ex $730 Gd $490
Bright stainless finish . . . . . . NiB $1410 Ex $1010 Gd $580

MK IV/SERIES 80 LIGHT-
WEIGHT COMMANDER . . . . NiB $1071 Ex $714 Gd $490
Updated version of the MK IV/Series 70.

MK IV/SERIES 80
MUSTANG .380 AUTOMATIC
Caliber: .380 ACP. Five- or 6-round magazine, 2.75-inch bbl., 5.5 inches overall. Weight: 18.5 oz. Blued, nickel or stainless finish. Black composition grips. Made from 1983 to 1998.

Blued finish. . . . . NiB $638 Ex $437 Gd $296
Nickel finish (disc.1994). . . . . . NiB $770 Ex $479 Gd $308
Satin nickel
  Coltguard (disc.1988). . . . . . . NiB $740 Ex $474 Gd $306
Stainless finish. . . . . NiB $709 Ex $397 Gd $306

MK IV/SERIES 80 MUSTANG PLUS II
Caliber: .380 ACP, 7-round magazine, 2.75-inch bbl., 5.5 inches overall. Weight: 20 oz. Blued or stainless finish w/checkered black composition grips. Made from 1988 to 1996.

Blued finish. . . . . NiB $693 Ex $407 Gd $302
Stainless finish. . . . . NiB $693 Ex $407 Gd $302

MK IV/SERIES 80 MUSTANG POCKETLITE
Same general specifications as the Mustang 30 except weight: 12.5 oz. w/aluminum alloy receiver. Blued, chrome or stainless finish. Optional wood grain grips. Made since 1987.

Blued finish. . . . . NiB $683 Ex $405 Gd $305
Lady Elite (two-tone) finish. . . . NiB $683 Ex $405 Gd $305
Stainless finish. . . . . NiB $683 Ex $405 Gd $305
Teflon/stainless finish . . . . NiB $683 Ex $405 Gd $305

Blued finish (disc.1997) . . . . . NiB $1132 Ex $918 Gd $712
Bright nickel (disc.1995). . . . . NiB $1181 Ex $974 Gd $729
Satin nickel Coltguard (disc.1989) NiB $1219 Ex $1016 Gd $751

Colt MK IV/Series 80 Officer's ACP

Colt Pocket Junior

Colt Super Match .38

MK IV/SERIES 80 SPECIAL COMBAT GOVERNMENT SEMI-AUTOMATIC PISTOL...... NiB $2100 Ex $1450 Gd $800
Calibers: .38 Super or .45 ACP, 5-inch bbl., custom tuned for competition. Blued, hard crome or two-tone finsh. Made from 1992 to date.
Carry (1992-00, reintro. 1996) ... NiB $2095 Ex $1450 Gd $800
CMC Marine Pistol .... NiB $2160 Ex $1200 Gd $820

MK IV/SERIES 90 DEFENDER
SA LIGHTWEIGHT .... NiB $918 Ex $576 Gd $398
Caliber: .45 ACP. Seven-round magazine, 3-inch bbl., 6.75 inches over-all. Weight: 22.5 oz. Aluminum alloy receiver w/ stainless slide. Dovetailed low-profile sights w/3-dot system. Matte stainless finish w/Nickel-Teflon receiver. Wraparound black rubber grip w/finger grooves. Made since 1998.

MK IV/SERIES 90
PONY DAO PISTOL .... NiB $772 Ex $567 Gd $396
Caliber: .380 ACP. Six-round magazine, 2.75-inch bbl., 5.5 inches overall. Weight: 19 oz. Ramp front sight, dovetailed rear. Stainless finish. Checkered black composition grips. Made 1997 to 1998.

MK IV/SERIES 90
PONY POCKETLITE .... NiB $794 Ex $577 Gd $396
Similar to standard weight Pony Model except w/aluminum frame. Brushed stainless and Teflon finish. Made 1997-99.

NATIONAL MATCH (PRE-WWWII)
Identical to the Government Model .45 Auto but w/hand-honed action, match-grade bbl., adj. rear and ramp front sights or fixed sights. Made from 1932 to 1940.
w/adjustable sights ..... NiB $10,000 Ex $8000 Gd $4300
w/fixed sights .... NiB $8500 Ex $7000 Gd $4000

NATIONAL MATCH (WWII & POST-WWII)
AUTOMATIC PISTOL ..... NiB $2500 Ex $1600 Gd $900
Similar to Pre-WWII National Match except in .45 Auto only. Made from 1957 to 1970.

NEW AGENT .... NiB $1080 Ex $800 Gd $500
Series 80 system. Similar to Defender except in 9mm or .45 ACP w/trench style sights, hammerless. Made 2008 to date.

NRA CENTENNIAL .45 GOLD CUP
NATIONAL MATCH .... NiB $1321 Ex $1024 Gd $841
Only 2500 produced in 1971.

POCKET JUNIOR MODEL
AUTOMATIC PISTOL .... NiB $464 Ex $344 Gd $260
Made in Spain by Unceta y Cia (Astra). Calibers: .22 Short, .25 Auto. Six-round magazine, 2.25 inch bbl., 4.75 inches overall. Weight: 12 oz. Fixed sights. Checkered walnut grips. Note: In 1980, this model was subject to recall to correct an action malfunction. Returned firearms were fitted with a rebounding firing pin to prevent accidental discharges. Made from 1958 to 1968.

SUPER .38 AUTOMATIC PISTOL
Identical to Government Model .45 Auto except for caliber and magazine capacity. Caliber: .38 Automatic. Nine-round magazine, Made from 1928 to 1970.
Pre-war .... NiB $6125 Ex $4429 Gd $3010
Post-war .... NiB $2709 Ex $2199 Gd $2008

MK IV/SERIES 80 OFFICER'S ACP AUTOMATIC PISTOL
Caliber: .45 ACP, 3.63-inch bbl., 7.25 inches overall. 6-round magazine. Weight: 34 oz. Made from 1984 to 1998.
Blued finish (disc.1996) ...... NiB $605 Ex $500 Gd $357
Matte finish (disc.1991) ...... NiB $581 Ex $474 Gd $349
Satin nickel finish (disc.1985).. NiB $669 Ex $544 Gd $378
Stainless steel (disc.1997)..... NiB $630 Ex $514 Gd $367
Lightweight (disc.1997) ...... NiB $900 Ex $710 Gd $520
Conceal Carry (disc.1998) .... NiB $900 Ex $710 Gd $520
General's Officer (disc.1996) NiB $1350 Ex $1040 Gd $680

MK IV/SERIES 80 SA LIGHTWEIGHT CONCEALED
CARRY OFFICER............ NiB $741 Ex $581 Gd $415
Caliber: .45 ACP. Seven-round magazine, 4.25-inch bbl., 7.75 inches overall. Weight: 35 oz. Aluminum alloy receiver w/ stainless slide. Dovetailed low-profile sights w/3-dot system. Matte stainless finish w/blued receiver. Wraparound black rubber grip w/finger grooves. Made in 2000.

Colt Targetsman

Colt Woodsman Match Target First Series

Colt Woodsman Target Model First Series (pencil barrel 1915-1922)

Colt Woodsman Target Model Firts Series (straight taper barrel 1934-1937)

SUPER MATCH .38 AUTOMATIC PISTOL

Identical to Super .38 Auto but w/hand-honed action, match grade bbl., adjustable rear sight and ramp front sight or fixed sights. Made from 1933 to 1946.

w/adjustable sights ..... NiB $11,595 Ex $6125 Gd $3162
w/fixed sights .... NiB $10,125 Ex $5125 Gd $2125

TARGETSMAN MODEL....... NiB $950 Ex $700 Gd $400

Similar to Third Series Woodsman Target model except w/ 6-in. bbl. only, economy adj. rear sight, lacks automatic slide stop. Grip: Early versions had black plastic stocks, later versions, beginning in 1960, had walnut stocks, standard with left panel thumbrest. Made from 1959 to 1977.

USMC M45 CQBP .... NiB $1995 Ex $1500 Gd $1000

Caliber: .45 ACP. Same general specifications as MK IV/Series 80 Rail Gun except w/Cerakote desert tan finish, stainless barrel, G10 grips. Made from 2013 to date.

COLT AUTOMATIC TARGET PISTOL

(PRE-WOODSMAN) ...... NiB $3000 Ex $2000 Gd $700
Semi-automatic. SA. Caliber: .22 LR (reg. velocity). 10-rnd. magazine w/ bottom release. 6-5/8-in. bbl., 10.5 in. overall. Weight: 28 oz. Adj. front and rear sights. Blued finish. Checkered walnut grips. Serial number range: 1-54000. Made 1915 to 1922.

NOTE: The earliest model of what would come to be known as the Woodsman originally came in only one version and was known simply as "Colt Automatic Target Pistol." Usually called Pre-Woodsman by collectors today.Note: The mainspring housing of this model is not strong enough to permit safe use of high-speed cartridges. Change to a new heat-treated mainspring housing was made at pistol No. 83,790. Many of the old models were converted by installation of new housings. The new housing may be distinguished from the earlier type by the checkering in the curve under the breech. The new housing is grooved straight across, while the old type bears a diagonally-checkered oval.

FIRST SERIES WOODSMAN TARGET

MODEL.................. NiB $2600 Ex $1500 Gd $500
Similar to late pre-Woodsman except "THE WOODSMAN" is marked on side of receiver. Made from 1927 to 1947.

NOTE: There are three series of Woodsman pistols, corresponding to three basic frame designs. First Series refers to all those built on the S frame as it existed prior to and during World War Two. Second Series includes all versions built on the second S frame design from late 1947 until mid 1955, and Third Series means the third S frame design as used from 1955 to the end of regular production in 1977. Each series had a Sport Model with a 4-1/2 inch round barrel, a Target Model with a 6 or 6-5/8 inch round barrel, and a Match Target Model with a heavy, flat sided barrel. The very similar Challenger, Huntsman, and Targetsman were made during the post-WWII years only.

FIRST SERIES WOODSMAN MATCH TARGET

MODEL.................. NiB $4500 Ex $2600 Gd $1500
Same basic design as other First Series Woodsman Target model. Caliber: .22 LR. 10-rnd. magazine, 6-5/8-in. bbl. slightly tapered w/flat sides, 11 inches overall. Weight: 36 oz. Adjustable rear sight. Blued finish. Checkered walnut one-piece grip w/extended sides known as "Elephant Ear" grips. Made from 1938 to 1943.

FIRST SERIES WOODSMAN SPORT

MODEL .... NiB $2800 Ex $1700 Gd $600
Similar as Firts Series Woodsman Target model except has 4.5-inch bbl., fixed front sight. Weight: 27 oz., 8.5 inches overall. Note: Some of the early Sport Models had a lighter, medium weight barrel, and some of the later pre-WWII Sport Models had an optional elevation adjustable front sight. Made from 1933 to 1947.

NOTE: The Second Series Woodsmans are the only models that have a push button thumb magazine release, similar to Colt Government Model 1911 pistols.

SECOND SERIES WOODSMAN MATCH TARGET

MODEL.................. NiB $2400 Ex $1600 Gd $800
Same basic design as First Series Woodsman Target model except: Caliber: .22 LR (reg. or high speed). 10-round magazine. 4.5- or 6-in. bbl. Grips: plastic with left panel thumbrest. Made from 1947 to 1955.

**Colt Woodsman
Target Model Third Series**

**Colt Woodsman
Sport Model Third Series**

**Colt World War II
D-Day Invasion
Commemorative**

**Colt World
War II
50th Anniversary
Commemorative**

NOTE: The Third Series replaced the Second Series in mid 1955. The most obvious change was the replacement of the push button magazine release with a snap catch at the butt. The Challenger was replaced in the third series with the very similar Huntsman.

THIRD SERIES WOODSMAN TARGET
MODEL . . . . NiB $1400 Ex $950 Gd $500
Same basic design as Second Series Woodsman Target model but w/6-in. bbl. only. Grip: early versions had black plastic stocks, later versions, beginning in 1960, had walnut stocks. NOTE: All Second and Third Series Target models were standard with left panel thumbrest. Made from 1955 to 1977.

THIRD SERIES WOODSMAN SPORT
MODEL . . . . NiB $1450 Ex $1000 Gd $500
Same basic design as Third Series Woodsman Target model but w/4.5-in. bbl. only. Grip: standard with left panel thumbrest, early versions had black plastic stocks, later versions, beginning in 1960, had walnut stocks. Made from 1955 to 1977.

THIRD SERIES WOODSMAN MATCH TARGET
MODEL . . . . NiB $900 Ex $650 Gd $350
Same basic design as Third Series Woodsman Target model but w/4.5- or 6-in. bbl. Grip: early versions had black plastic stocks, later versions, beginning in 1960, had walnut stocks. NOTE: All Second and Third Series Target models were standard with left panel thumbrest. Made from 1955 to 1977.

WORLD WAR I 50TH ANNIVERSARY
COMMEMORATIVE SERIES
Limited production replica of Model 1911 .45 Auto engraved w/battle scenes, commemorating Battles at Chateau Thierry, Belleau Wood Second Battle of the Marne, Meuse Argonne. In special presentation display cases. Production: 7,400 Standard model, 75 Deluxe, 25 Special Deluxe grade. Match numbered sets offered. Made 1967 to 1969. Values indicated are for commemoratives in new condition.
Standard grade . . . . NiB $1046 Ex $780 Gd $638
Deluxe grade . . . . NiB $2152 Ex $1743 Gd $1220
Special Deluxe grade . . . . . NiB $4687 Ex $3890 Gd $2448

WORLD WAR II COMMEMORATIVE
.45 AUTO . . . . NiB $1047 Ex $774 Gd $562
Limited production replica of Model 1911A1 .45 Auto engraved w/respective names of locations where historic engagements occurred during WW II, as well as specific issue and theater identification. European model has oak leaf motif on slide, palm leaf design frames the Pacific issue. Cased. 11,500 of each model were produced. Made in 1970. Value listed is for gun in new condition.

WORLD WAR II 50TH ANNIVERSARY
COMMEMORATIVE . . . . . . NiB $2647 Ex $2064 Gd $1629
Same general specifications as the Colt World War II Commemorative .45 Auto except slightly different scroll engraving, 24-karat gold-plate trigger, hammer, slide stop, magazine catch, magazine catch lock, safety lock and four grip screws. Made in 1995 only.

WORLD WAR II D-DAY
INVASION COMMEMORATIVE . . NiB $1550 Ex $1436 Gd $1138
High-luster and highly decorated version of the Colt Model 1911A1. Caliber: .45 ACP. Same general specifications as the Colt Model 1911 except for 24-karat gold-plated hammer, trigger, slide stop, magazine catch, magazine catch screw, safety lock and four grip screws. Also has scrolls and inscription on slide. Made in 1991 only.

SECOND SERIES WOODSMAN SPORT
MODEL . . . . NiB $2100 Ex $453 Gd $316
Same as Second Series Match Target model except w/4.5-inch bbl., 9 inches overall. Weight: 36 oz. Grips: standard was plastic, before mid-1949 no thumbrest, after mid-1949 left panel thumbrest. Made from 1948 to 1955.

SECOND SERIES WOODSMAN TARGET
MODEL . . . . NiB $1900 Ex $800 Gd $750
Same as Second Series Woodsman Match Target model except 6-in. bbl. only, 9 inches overall. Weight: 30 oz. Grips: standard with plastic and left panel thumbrest. Made 1948-55.

**Colt
Camp Perry First Issue**

**Colt Agent
First Issue**

**Colt
Camp Perry Second Issue**

WORLD WAR II GOLDEN ANNIVERSARY V-J DAY
TRIBUTE .45 AUTO . . . . NiB $2662 Ex $2239 Gd $1658
Basic Colt Model 1911A1 design w/highly-polished bluing and decorated w/specialized tributes to honor V-J Day. Two 24-karat gold scenes highlight the slide. 24-karat gold-plated hammer. Checkered wood grips w/gold medallion on each side. Made 1995.

XSE SERIES MODEL O SEMI-AUTOMATIC PISTOL
Caliber: .45 Auto. 8-round magazine, 4.24- or 5-in. bbl. Novak sights, front/rear slide serrations, extanded ambi. thumb safety. Checkered rosewood grips. Made 2000 to date.

Combat Elite	NiB $1100	Ex $700	Gd $500
Commander	NiB $1200	Ex $730	Gd $530
Government	NiB $1100	Ex $700	Gd $500
Ligthweight Commander.	NiB $1100	Ex $700	Gd $500
Ligthweight Government	NiB $1100	Ex $700	Gd $500
Rail Gun	NiB $1200	Ex $730	Gd $530

- SINGLE-SHOT PISTOLS & DERRINGERS -

CAMP PERRY MODEL SINGLE-
SHOT PISTOL, FIRST ISSUE . . . NiB $2410 Ex $1960 Gd $1660
Built on Officers' Model frame. Caliber: .22 LR (embedded head chamber for high-speed cartridges after 1930). 10 inch bbl., 13.75 inches overall. Weight: 34.5 oz. Adj. target sights. Hand-finished action. Blued finish. Checkered walnut grips. Made 1926 to 1934.

CAMP PERRY MODEL
SECOND ISSUE . . . . NiB $3374 Ex $2744
Gd $2324
Same general specifications as First Issue except has shorter hammer fall and 8-inch bbl., 12 inches overall. Weight: 34 oz. Made from 1934 to 1941 (about 440 produced).

CIVIL WAR CENTENNIAL MODEL PISTOL
Single-shot replica of Colt Model 1860 Army Revolver. Caliber: .22 Short. Six-inch bbl., weight: 22 oz. Blued finish w/gold-plated frame, grip frame, and trigger guard, walnut grips. Cased. 24,114 were produced. Made in 1961.
Single pistol . . . . NiB $362 Ex $265 Gd $204
**Pair w/consecutive
  serial numbers** . . . . NiB $689 Ex $541 Gd $408

DERRINGER NO. 4
Replica of derringer No. 3 (1872 Thuer Model). Single-shot w/sideswing bbl., Caliber: .22 Short, 2.5-inch bbl., 4.9 inches overall. Weight: 7.75 oz. Fixed sights. Gold-plated frame w/blued bbl., and walnut grips or completely nickel- or gold-plated w/simulated ivory or pearl grips. Made 1959 to 1963. 112,000 total production. (S/N w/D or N suffix)
Single pistol (gun only) . . . . NiB $128 Ex $88 Gd $61
Single pistol (cased w/accessories). . . NiB $408 Ex $281 Gd $189

DERRINGER NO. 4 COMMEMORATIVE MODELS
Limited production version of .22 derringers issued, w/appropriate inscription, to commemorate historical events. Additionally, non-firing models (w/unnotched bbls.) were furnished in books, picture frames and encased in plExiglass as singles or in cased pairs.
**No. 4 Presentation Derringers
(Non-firing w/accessories)** . . . . NiB $408 Ex $281 Gd $189
**Ltd. Ed. Book Series(w/nickel-plated
  derringers)** . . . . NiB $388 Ex $255 Gd $143
**1st Presentation Series
  (Leatherette covered metal case)** . . NiB $408 Ex $281 Gd $189
**2nd Presentation Series
  (Single wooden case)** . . . . NiB $408 Ex $281 Gd $189
**2nd Presentation Series
  (Paired wooden case)** . . . . NiB $423 Ex $291 Gd $198
**1961 Issue Geneseo, Illinois,
  125th Anniversary (104 produced)** . . NiB $729 Ex $556 Gd $388
**1962 Issue Fort McPherson, Nebraska, Centennial
  (300 produced)**. . . . . NiB $729 Ex $556 Gd $388

LORD AND LADY DERRINGERS (NO. 5)
Same as Derringer No. 4. Lord model with blued bbl., w/gold-plated frame and walnut grips. Lady model is gold-plated w/simulated pearl grips. Sold in cased pairs. Made from 1970 to 1972. (S/N w/Der suffix)
Lord derringer, pair in case. . . . NiB $577 Ex $408 Gd $301
Lady derringer, pair in case. . . . NiB $577 Ex $408 Gd $301
**Lord and Lady derringers,
  one each, in case** . . . . NiB $577 Ex $408 Gd $301

ROCK ISLAND ARSENAL
CENTENNIAL PISTOL. . . . . NiB $520 Ex $489 Gd $332
Limited production (550 pieces) version of Civil War Centennial Model single-shot .22 pistol, made Exclusively for Cherry's Sporting Goods, Geneseo, Illinois, to commemorate the cen-

Colt Banker's Special

Colt Bisley

Colt Buntline Special .45

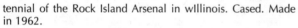

Colt Anaconda

tennial of the Rock Island Arsenal in wIllinois. Cased. Made in 1962.

NOTE: *This section of Colt handguns contains only revolvers (single action and double action) by model name in alphabetical order. For automatic pistols or single-shot pistols and derringers, please see the two sections that precede this. For a complete listing, refer to the Index.*

- REVOLVERS -

MODEL 1877 LIGHTNING NiB $4197 Ex $3264 Gd $2973
DA revolver w/fixed cyilnder. Also called Thunderer Model. Calibers: .38 and .41 centerfire. Six-round cylinder, bbl. lengths: 2.5-, 3.5-, 4.5- and 6-inch without ejector, 4.5- and 6-inch w/ejector, 8.5 inches overall (3.5-inch bbl.). Weight: 23 oz. (.38 cal., with 3.5-inch bbl.) Fixed sights. Blued or nickel finish. Hard rubber bird's-head grips. Made 1877 to 1909.

MODEL 1877 THUNDERER NiB $4210 Ex $3210 Gd $2260
Similar to Lightning except in .41 Colt only. Made 1877 to 1909.

MODEL 1878
DA REVOLVER . . . . NiB $5780 Ex $5260 Gd $3250
DA. Calibers: ..32-20, .38 Colt, .38-40, .41 LC, .44 Russian, .44 S&W, .44-40, .45 LC, .450 Eley, .455 Eley or .476 Eley. Six-round fixed cylinder. Bbl. Lengths: 2.5-, 3.5-, 4- w/o ejector rod and 4.75-, 5.5-, 7.5-, 8.5-, 9-, 10- or 12-in. w/ejctor rod. Fixed sights. Finish: blued, case hardened or nickel. Checkered hard rubber bird's-head grips. Made 1878 to 1905.

.357 MAGNUM . . . . NiB $910 Ex $810 Gd $735
DA. Simialr to Trooper model. Caliber: .357 Mag. Six-round cylinder, 4- or 6-in. bbl. Accro target sights. Finish: blued or nickel. Grips: checkered walnut. Made from 1953 to 1961.

.38 DS II REVOLVER . . . . NiB $660 Ex $560 Gd $430
Similar to Detective Special. Caliber: .38 Special or .357 Mag. Six-round cylinder, 2-inch bbl., 7 inches overall. Weight: 21 oz. Ramp front sight, fixed notch rear. Satin stainless finish. Black rubber combat grip w/finger grooves. Made from 1997 to 1998.

.38 SF-VI . . . . NiB $660 Ex $560 Gd $430
DA. Caliber: .38 Special only. Six-round cylinder, 2- or 4-in. bbl. Ramp front sight, fixed notch rear. Finish: Satin, polished or black. Grip: black rubber. Made from 1995 to 1996.

AGENT FIRST ISSUE . . . . NiB $800 Ex $710 Gd $510
Same as Cobra, first issue except has short-grip frame .38 Special only, weight: 14 oz. Made from 1955 to 1972.

AGENT (LW) SECOND ISSUE . . NiB $630 Ex $530 Gd $430
Same as Colt Agent, first issue except has shrouded ejector rod and alloy frame. Made from 1973 to 1986.

AIRCREWMAN . . . . NiB $4010 Ex $3510 Gd $2760
DA revolver made for U.S. Air Force. Caliber: .38 Special only. Six-round swing-out cylinder, 2-in. bbl. Aluminum frame. Weight: 11 oz. Fixed sights. Grip: checkered walnut that overlapped the frame above the grip w/silver U.S. Air Force medallions. Satmped "Property of U.S. Air Force" on back strap and an U.S. Air Force issue number on the butt. S/N range: 2,901LW to about 7,775LW. Made 1951.

ANACONDA DA REVOLVER
Calibers: .44 Mag., .45 Colt., bbl. lengths: 4, 6 or 8 inches; 11.63 inches overall (with 6-inch bbl.). Weight: 53 oz. (6-inch bbl.). Adj. white outline rear sight, red insert ramp-style front. Matte stainless or Realtree gray camo finish. Black Neoprene combat grips w/finger grooves. Made 1990 to 1999 and 2002 to 2006.
Matte stainless . . . . NiB $1000 Ex $714 Gd $487
Realtree gray camo
  finish (disc. 1996). . . . . . . NiB $1632 Ex $1357 Gd $1151
Custom model
  (.44 Mag. w/ported bbl.) . . . NiB $1510 Ex $816 Gd $587
First Edition model
  (Ltd. Edition 1000) . . . . . . NiB $1800 Ex $1460 Gd $1160
Hunter model
  (.44 Mag. w/2x scope) . . . NiB $1652 Ex $1357 Gd $1151

Colt Commando Special

**Colt Cobra
Round Butt First Issue**

.38 caliber . . . . NiB $2260 Ex $1860 Gd $1260
.22 caliber . . . . NiB $3210 Ex $2510 Gd $1860

BOA . . . . NiB $3860 Ex $3360 Gd $2810
DA. Uses Mark V action. Caliber: .357 Mag. 4- or 6-in. bbl.
w/full ejector shroud. Lew Horton distributor. Made 1985.
Two gun set . . . . NiB $7960 Ex $6885 Gd $5510

COBRA (ROUND BUTT)
FIRST ISSUE . . . . NiB $810 Ex $660 Gd $610
Similar to Detective Special model except w/Colt-alloy lightweight frame. Two-inch bbl., calibers: .22 LR, .38 Special,
.38 New Police, .32 New Police. Weight: 15 oz., (.38 cal.).
Blued finish. Checkered plastic or walnut grips. Made 1950
to 1972.
.22 LR, add 20%
nickel finish, add 20%

COBRA SECOND ISSUE . . . . . . NiB $960 Ex $835 Gd $735
Similar to Cobra First Issue except w/shrouded ejector rod.
Made from 1973 to 81.

COBRA (SQUARE BUTT)
FIRST ISSUE . . . . NiB $530 Ex $425 Gd $304
Similar to Cobra First Issue except w/4-inch bbl., Calibers: .38
Special, .38 New Police, .32 New Police. Weight: 17 oz. in
.38 caliber. Blued finish. Checkered plastic or walnut grips.
Early models.

COMMANDO SPECIAL . . . . . . NiB $546 Ex $423 Gd $329
Similar to Detective Special. Caliber: .38 Special. Six-round
cylinder, 2-inch bbl., 6.88 inches overall. Weight: 21.5 oz.
Fixed sights. Low-luster blued finish. Rubber grips. Made from
1984 to 1986.

COURIER . . . . NiB $1310 Ex $1110 Gd $960
Aluminum "D" frame, similar to Cobra. Caliber: .22 LR or .32
S&W. Six-round swing-out cylinder, 3-in. bbl. Fixed sights.

ANACONDA TITANIUM DA REVOLVER
Same general specifications as the standard Anaconda except
chambered .44 Mag. only w/titanium-plated finish, gold-plated
trigger, hammer and cylinder release. Limited edition of 1,000
distributed by American Historical Foundation w/personalized
inscription. Made in 1996.
One of 1000 . . . . NiB $2744 Ex $2242 Gd $1624
Presentation case, add $255

ARMY SPECIAL
DA REVOLVER . . . . NiB $1300 Ex $1000 Gd $760
.41-caliber frame. Calibers: .32-20, .38 Special (.41 Colt).
Six-round cylinder, right revolution. Bbl., lengths: 4-, 4.5, 5-,
and 6-inches, 9.25 inches overall (4-inch bbl.). Weight: 32 oz.
(4-inch bbl.). Fixed sights. Blued or nickel-plated finish. Hard
rubber grips. Made 1908-27. Note: This model has a somewhat
heavier frame than the New Navy, which it replaced. S/N begin
w/300,000. The heavy .38 Special High velocity loads should
not be used in .38 Special arms of this model. Made from 1908
to 1927.

BANKER'S SPECIAL DA REVOLVER
This is the Police Positive w/a 2-inch bbl., otherwise specifications
same as that model, rounded butt intro. in 1933. Calibers: .22 LR
(embedded head-cylinder for high speed cartridges intro. 1933), .38
New Police. 6.5 inches overall. Weight: 23 oz. (.22 LR), 19 oz. (.38).
Made from 1926 to 1940.

**Colt
Detective Special First Issue**

Bright blue-black anodized finish. Checkered wood grips. Made from 1953 to 1956.

DETECTIVE SPECIAL DA REVOLVER, FIRST ISSUE
Similar to Police Positive Special except w/2-inch bbl., otherwise specifications same as that model, rounded butt intro. 1933. .38 Special only in pre-war issue. Blued or nickel-plated finish. Weight: 17 oz. 6.75 inches overall. Made from 1927 to 46.
Blued finish . . . . **NiB $2155 Ex $1855 Gd $1630**
Nickel finish, add **20%**

DETECTIVE SPECIAL SECOND ISSUE
Similar to Detective special first issue except w/2- or 3-inch bbl., and also chambered .32 New Police, .38 New Police. Wood, plastic or over-sized grips. Post-WWII manufacture, made from 1947 to 1972.
Blued finish . . . . **NiB $1355 Ex $1155 Gd $955**
Nickel finish, add **20%**
w/three-inch bbl., add **15%**

**Colt
Detective Special Second Issue**

DETECTIVE SPECIAL THIRD ISSUE
"D" frame, shrouded ejector rod. Caliber: .38 Special. Six-round cylinder, 2-inch bbl., 6.88 inches overall. Weight: 21.5 oz. Fixed rear sight, ramp front. Blued or nickel-plated finish. Checkered walnut wraparound grips. Made from 1973 to 1986.
Blued finish . . . . **NiB $980 Ex $860 Gd $760**
Nickel finish . . . . **NiB $571 Ex $464 Gd $342**
w/three-inch bbl., add **$90**

DETECTIVE SPECIAL DA REVOLVER, FOURTH ISSUE
Similar to Detective Special, Third Issue except w/alloy frame. Blued or chrome finish. Wraparound black neoprene grips w/ Colt medallion. Made from 1993 to 1995.
Blued finish . . . . **NiB $700 Ex $662 Gd $596**
Chrome finish, add **10%**
DAO model (bobbed hammer) . . . **NiB $855 Ex $730 Gd $610**

DIAMONDBACK DA REVOLVER
"D" frame, shrouded ejector rod. Calibers: .22 LR, .22 WRF, .38 Special. Six-round cylinder, 2.5-, 4- or 6-inch bbl., w/vent rib, 9 inches overall (with 4-inch bbl). Weight: 31.75 oz. (.22 cal., 4-inch bbl.), 28.5 oz. (.38 cal.). Ramp front sight, adj. rear. Blued or nickel finish. Checkered walnut grips. Made from 1966 to 1984.
Blued finish . . . . **NiB $1336 Ex $1127 Gd $826**
Nickel finish . . . . **NiB $1545 Ex $1231 Gd $986**
.22 Mag. model . . . . **NiB $2118 Ex $1937 Gd $1754**
w/2.5-inch bbl., add **$100**

**Colt
Diamondback**

Blued finish, plastic grips . . . . . **NiB $464 Ex $395 Gd $272**
Nickel finish, wood grips . . . . . **NiB $499 Ex $407 Gd $286**
Buntline model, add **$75**
Extra interchangeable cylinder, add **$100**

FRONTIER SCOUT REVOLVER COMMEMORATIVE MODELS
Limited production versions of Frontier Scout issued, w/appropriate inscription, to commemorate historical events. Cased, in new condition.
1961 ISSUES
Kansas Statehood Centennial (6201 produced) . . . **NiB $536**
**Pony Express Centennial
    (1007 produced)** . . . . **NiB $638**

1962 ISSUES
**Columbus, Ohio, Sesquicentennial
    (200 produced)** . . . . **NiB $638**
**Fort Findlay, Ohio,
    Sesquicentennial (130 produced)** . . . . **NiB $913**
**Fort Findlay Cased Pair, .22 Long
    Rifle and .22 Magnum (20 produced)** . . . . **NiB $2627**
New MExico Golden Anniversary . . . . **NiB $638**
**West Virginia Statehood
    Centennial (3452 produced)** . . . . **NiB $6130**

DA ARMY (1878) . . . . **NiB $6140 Ex $4524 Gd $3177**
Also called DA Frontier. Similar in appearance to the smaller Lightning Model but has heavier frame of different shape, round disc on left side of frame, lanyard loop in butt. Calibers: .38-40, .44-40, .45 Colt. Six-round cylinder, bbl. lengths: 3.5- and 4-inches (w/o ejector), 4.75-, 5.5- and 7.5-inches w/ejector. 12.5 inches overall (7.5-inch bbl). Weight: 39 oz. (.45 cal., 7.5-inch bbl.). Fixed sights. Hard rubber bird's-head grips. Blued or nickel finish. Made from 1878 to 1905.

FRONTIER SCOUT REVOLVER
SA Army replica, smaller scale. Calibers: .22 Short, Long, LR or .22 WMR (interchangeable cylinder available). Six-round cylinder, 4.75-inch bbl., 9.9 inches overall. Weight: 24 oz. Fixed sights. Plastic grips. Originally made w/bright alloy frame. Since 1959 w/steel frame and blued finish or all-nickel finish w/composition, wood or Staglite grips. Made 1958 to 1971.

Colt Lightning/Thunderer
1877-1912

Colt Idaho Territorial
Centennial 1963 Issue

Colt New Jersey Tercentenary 1964 issue

Colt General Hood
Centennial 1964 issue

Colt Indiana
Sesquicentennial 1966 Issue

1963 ISSUES
Arizona Territorial Centennial
(5355 produced) . . . . NiB $638
Battle of Gettysburg Centennial
(1019 produced) . . . . NiB $638
Carolina Charter Tercentenary (300 produced) . . NiB $2270
Fort Stephenson, Ohio,
Sesquicentennial (200 produced) . . . . NiB $638
General John Hunt Morgan Indiana Raid . . . . NiB $689
Idaho Territorial Centennial (902 produced) . . . . . NiB $638

1964 ISSUES
California Gold Rush (500 produced) . . . . NiB $638
Chamizal Treaty (450 produced) . . . . NiB $638
General Hood Centennial (1503 produced) . . . . . NiB $638
Montana Territorial Centennial (2300 produced) . . NiB $638
Nevada "Battle Born" (981 produced) . . . . NiB $597
Nevada Statehood Centennial (3984 produced) . . NiB $2678
New Jersey Tercentenary (1001 produced) . . . . . . NiB $577
St. Louis Bicentennial (802 produced) . . . . NiB $638
Wyoming Diamond Jubilee (2357 produced) . . . . . NiB $638

1965 ISSUES
Appomattox Centennial (1001 produced) . . . . NiB $577
Forty-Niner Miner (500 produced) . . . . NiB $638
General Meade Campaign (1197 produced) . . . . . NiB $1647
Kansas Cowtown Series—Wichita (500 produced) . . . . . . NiB $577
Old Fort Des Moines Reconstruction (700 prod.) . NiB $2280
Oregon Trail (1995 produced) . . . . NiB $638
St. Augustine Quadricentennial (500 produced) . . . NiB $638

1966 ISSUES
Colorado Gold Rush (1350 produced) . . . . NiB $638
Dakota Territory (1000 produced) . . . . NiB $638
Indiana Sesquicentennial (1500 produced) . . . . . . NiB $638
Kansas Cowtown Series—Abilene (500 produced) . . NiB $577
Kansas Cowtown Series—Dodge City
(500 produced) . . . . NiB $577
Oklahoma Jubilee (1343 produced) . . . . NiB $638

1967 ISSUES
Alamo (4500 produced) . . . . NiB $577
Kansas Cowtown Series—Coffeyville
(500 produced) . . . . NiB $561
Kansas Trail Series—Chisholm Trail (500 produced) NiB $577
Lawman Series—Bat Masterson (3000 produced) . . NiB $570

1968 ISSUES
Kansas Cowtown Series—Santa Fe
Trail (501 produced) . . . . NiB $577
Kansas Trail Series—Pawnee Trail (501 produced) . NiB $577
Lawman Series—Pat Garrett (3000 produced) . . . . NiB $638
Nebraska Centennial (7001 produced) . . . . NiB $577

1969 ISSUES
Alabama Sesquicentennial (3001 produced) . . . . . NiB $577
Arkansas Territory Sesquicentennial
(3500 produced) . . . . NiB $561
California Bicentennial (5000 produced) . . . . NiB $577
General Nathan Bedford Forrest (3000 produced) . . NiB $577
Golden Spike (11,000 produced) . . . . NiB $577
Kansas Trail Series—Shawnee Trail
(501 produced) . . . . NiB $577
Lawman Series—Wild Bill Hickock
(3000 produced) . . . . NiB $638

Colt Golden Spike
Centennial 1969 Issue

Colt King Cobra

Colt Lawman
MK V

1970 ISSUES

Kansas Fort Series—Fort Larned (500 produced) . . . NiB $577
Kansas Fort Series—Fort Hays (500 produced) . . . NiB $577
Kansas Fort Series—Fort Riley (500 produced). . . . NiB $577
Lawman Series—Wyatt Earp (3000 produced) . . . NiB $780
Maine Sesquicentennial (3000 produced). . . . . NiB $577
Missouri Sesquicentennial (3000 produced) . . . . . NiB $577

1971 ISSUES

Kansas Fort Series—Fort Scott (500 produced) . . . . NiB $577

1972 ISSUES

Florida Territory Sesquicentennial
   (2001 produced) . . . . NiB $638

1973 ISSUES

Arizona ranger (3001 produced) . . . . NiB $638

KING COBRA REVOLVER

Caliber: .357 Mag., bbl. lengths: 2.5-, 4-, 6- or 8-inches, 9 inches overall (with 4-inch bbl.). Weight: 42 oz., average. Matte stainless steel or blued finish. Black Neoprene combat grips. Made 1986 to date. 2.5-inch bbl. and "Ultimate" bright or blued finish. Made from 1988 to 1992.
Blued. . . . . NiB $1260 Ex $1145 Gd $970
Matte stainless . . . . NiB $1210 Ex $1085 Gd $910
Ultimate bright stainless, add 15%
2.5-in. bbl., add 20%

LAWMAN MK III DA REVOLVER

Shrouded ejector rod on 2-inch bbl., only. Caliber: .357 Magnum. Six-round cylinder, bbl. lengths: 2-, 4-inch. 9.38 inches overall (w/4-inch bbl.), Weight: (with 4-inch bbl.), 35 oz. Fixed rear sight, ramp front. Service trigger and hammer or target trigger and wide-spur hammer. Blued or nickel-plated finish. Checkered walnut service or target grips. Made from 1969 to 1983.
Blued finish. . . . . NiB $560 Ex $465 Gd $380
Nickel finish . . . . NiB $660 Ex $565 Gd $480

LAWMAN MK V DA REVOLVER

Similar to Trooper MK V. Caliber: .357 Mag. Six-round cylinder, 2- or 4-inch bbl., 9.38 inches overall (4-inch bbl.). Weight: 35 oz. (4-inch bbl.). Fixed sights. Checkered walnut grips. Made 1984 and 1991.
Blued finish. . . . . NiB $655 Ex $555 Gd $455
Nickel finish . . . . NiB $680 Ex $580 Gd $480

MAGNUM CARRY

DA REVOLVER . . . . NiB $900 Ex $800 Gd $790
Similar to Model DS II except chambered for .357 Magnum. Made from 1998 to date.

MARINE CORPS MODEL (1905) DA REVOLVER

General specifications same as New Navy Second Issue except has round butt, was supplied only in .38 caliber (.38 Short & Long Colt, .38 Special) w/6-inch bbl. (S/N range 10,001-10,926) Made 1905 to 1909.
Marine Corps model . . . NiB $15,606 Ex $14,050 Gd $13,260
Marked "USMC". . . . . NiB $7803 Ex $5636 Gd $3886

METROPOLITAN MK III . . . . . . NiB $630 Ex $530 Gd $430
Same as Official Police MK III except has 4-inch bbl. w/service or target grips. Weight: 36 oz. Made from 1969 to 1972.

NEW FRONTIER BUNTLINE SPECIAL

Same as New Frontier SA Army except has 12-inch bbl.,
Second generation (1962-75). . . NiB $2570 Ex $2028 Gd $1392
Third generation (1976-92) . . . NiB $1352 Ex $1120 Gd $861

NEW FRONTIER SA ARMY REVOLVER

Same as SA Army except has flat-top frame, adj. target rear sight, ramp front sight, smooth walnut grips. 5.5- or 7.5-inch bbl., Calibers: .357 Magnum, .44 Special, .45 Colt. Made 1961 to 1992.
Second generation (1961-75). . . NiB $2902 Ex $2647 Gd $2458
Third generation (1976-92). . NiB $1362 Ex $1118 Gd $857

NEW FRONTIER

SA .22 REVOLVER. . . . . NiB $532 Ex $342 Gd $235
Same as Peacemaker .22 except has flat-top frame, adj. rear sight, ramp front sight. Made from 1971-76; reintro. 1982-86.

Colt Model 1877
Lightning

Colt New Navy

Colt New Service

NEW NAVY (1889) DA, FIRST ISSUE
Also called New Army. Calibers: .38 Short & Long Colt, .41 Short & Long Colt. Six-round cylinder, left revolution. Bbl. lengths: 3-, 4.5- and 6-inches, 11.25 inches overall (with 6-inch bbl.). Weight: 32 oz. with 6-inch bbl. Fixed sights, knife-blade and V-notch. Blued or nickel-plated finish. Walnut or hard rubber grips. Made 1889 to 1994. Note: This model, which was adopted by both the Army and Navy, was Colt's first revolver of the solid frame, swing-out cylinder type. It lacks the cylinder-locking notches found on later models made on this .41 frame; ratchet on the back of the cylinder is held in place by a double projection on the hand.
First issue . . . . NiB $2260 Ex $1860 Gd $1460
First issue w/3-inch bbl., add 40%
Navy contract (marked U.S.N. on butt,
  S/N range: 1-1500) . . . . . . NiB $3682 Ex $2981 Gd $2121

NEW NAVY (1892) DA, SECOND ISSUE
Also called New Army. General specifications same as First Issue except double cylinder notches and double locking bolt. Calibers: .38 Special added in 1904 and .32-20 in 1905. Made 1892 to 1907. Note: The heavy .38 Special High Velocity loads should not be used in .38 Special arms of this model.
Second issue . . . . NiB $1950 Ex $1446 Gd $1020

NEW POCKET
DA REVOLVER . . . . NiB $1360 Ex $1150 Gd $900
Caliber: .32 Short & Long Colt. Six-round cylinder. bbl. lengths: 2.5, 3.5- and 6-inches. 7.5 inches overall w/3.5-inch bbl., Weight: 16 oz., with 3.5-inch bbl. Fixed sights, knife-blade and V-notch. Blued or nickel finish. Rubber grips. Made from 1893 to 1905.

NEW POLICE
DA REVOLVER . . . . NiB $1260 Ex $960 Gd $760
Built on New Pocket frame but w/larger grip. Calibers: .32 Colt New Police, .32 Short & Long Colt. Bbl. lengths: 2.5-, 4- and 6-inches; 8.5 inches overall (with 4-inch bbl.). Weight: 17 oz., with 4-inch bbl. Fixed knife-blade front sight, V-notch rear. Blued or nickel finish. Rubber grips. Made from 1896 to 1907.

NEW POLICE TARGET
DA REVOLVER . . . . NiB $1860 Ex $1660 Gd $1110
Target version of the New Police except w/target sights. Six-inch bbl., blued finish only. Made 1896 to 1905.

NEW SERVICE DA REVOLVER
Calibers: .38 Special, .357 Magnum (intro. 1936), .38-40, .44-40, .44 Russian, .44 Special, .45 Auto, .45 Colt, .450 Eley, .455 Eley, .476 Eley. Six-round cylinder, bbl. lengths: 4-, 5- and 6-inch in .38 Special and .357 Magnum, 4.5-, 5.5- and 7.5 inches in other calibers; 9.75 inches overall (with 4.5-inch bbl.). Weight: 39 oz. (.45 cal. with 4.5-inch bbl.). Fixed sights. Blued or nickel finish. Checkered walnut grips. Made 1898-42. Note: More than 500,000 of this model in caliber .45 Auto (designated "Model 1917 Revolver") were purchased by the U.S. Gov't. during WW I. These arms were later sold as surplus to National Rifle Association members through the Director of Civilian Marksmanship. Price was $16.15 plus packing charge. Supply Exhausted during the early 1930s. Made from 1898 to 1927.
1909 Army . . . . NiB $3300 Ex $2900 Gd $2500
1909 Navy . . . . NiB $3600 Ex $3200 Gd $2700
1909 USMC . . . . NiB $4100 Ex $3700 Gd $3200
1917 Army . . . . NiB $2000 Ex $1680 Gd $1500
1917 Commercial . . . . NiB $1600 Ex $1300 Gd $1000
Commercial model . . . . NiB $2888 Ex $2483 Gd $2197
Magnum . . . . NiB $1223 Ex $1018 Gd $729
RNWMP/RCMP model . . . . NiB $2000 Ex $1483 Gd $1197
Shooting Master (various calibers, 6-in. bbl., round or square
  butt, checkered grips straps) . . . NiB $2000 Ex $1900 Gd $1700
Shooting Master (.357 Mag.), add $1000
Shooting Master (.45 ACP or .45 LC), add $2000
Shooting Master (.44 Spl.), add $3000

NEW SERVICE TARGET . . . . NiB $3500 Ex $3350 Gd $2800
Target version of the New Service. Calibers: Originally chambered for .44 Russian, .450 Eley, .455 Eley and .476 Eley, later models in .44 Special, .45 Colt and .45 Auto. Six- or 7.5-inch bbl., 12.75 inches overall (7.5-inch bbl.). Adj. target sights. Hand-finished action. With blued finish. Checkered walnut grips. Made 1900 to 1940.

OFFICER'S MODEL
FIRST ISSUE . . . . NiB $1860 Ex $1499 Gd $1260
DA/SA. Caliber: .38 Spl. or .38 LC. Six-inch bbl., flat top frame, hand-finished action, adj. target sights. Checkered with walnut grips w/o medalion. Made 1904 to 1908.

Colt Officers' Match

Colt Officers' Target Second Issue

Colt Official Police

Colt Peacekeeper

OFFICER'S MODEL SECOND

ISSUE . . . . NiB $1760 Ex $1550 Gd $1150
Similar to Officer's Modle First Issue except using improved Army Special action and more bbl. lengths: 4-, 4.5-, 5-, 6- and 7.5-inch. Made from 1908 to 1926.

OFFICER'S MODEL TARGET THIRD

ISSUE . . . . NiB $1460 Ex $1250 Gd $1000
Calibers: .22 LR (intro. 1930, embedded head-cylinder for high-speed cartridges after 1932), .32 Police Positive (made 1932-1942), .38 Special. Six-round cylinder, bbl. lengths: 4-, 4.5-, 5-, 6- and 7.5-inch (in .38 Special) or 6-inch only (.22 LR and .32 PP), 11.25 inches overall (6-inch bbl. in .38 Special). Adj. target sights. Blued finish. Checkered walnut grips. Hand-finished action. General features same as Army Special and Official Police of same date. Made from 1908 to 1949 (w/ exceptions noted).

.38 caliber . . . . NiB $1130 Ex $930 Gd $653
.32 caliber . . . . NiB $1744 Ex $1426 Gd $984
.22 caliber . . . . NiB $1232 Ex $1018 Gd $729
w/shorter bbls. (4-, 4.5- or 5-inches), add 50%

OFFICER'S MODEL SPECIAL

(FOURTH ISSUE) . . . . NiB $1030 Ex $930 Gd $830
Post WWII model. Similar Officers' Model Third Issue excpt w/ extra heavy, nontapered bbl. Redesigned hammer. Ramp front sight, "Coltmaster" rear sight adj. for windage and elevation. Blued finish. Checkered plastic reddish-brown "Coltwood" grips. Made from 1949 to 1952.

OFFICER'S MODEL MATCH

(FIFTH ISSUE) . . . . NiB $960 Ex $900 Gd $810
Same general design as Officers' Model Special except w/ tapered heavy bbl., wide hammer spur, Adjustable rear sight ramp front sight, large target grips of checkered walnut w/medalion. Calibers: .22 LR, .22 Mag., .38 Special. Six-inch bbl., 11.25 inches overall. Weight: 43 oz. (in .22 cal.), 39 oz. (.38 cal.). Blued finish. Made from 1953 to 1969.
.22 Mag., add $1000

OFFICER'S MODEL MATCH MK III

(SIXTH ISSUE) . . . . NiB $1900 Ex $1525 Gd $1400
Similar to Officers' Model Match Fifth Issue except .38 Special only. Made from 1969 to 1971.

OFFICIAL POLICE DA REVOLVER

Calibers: .22 LR (intro. 1930, embedded head-cylinder for high-speed cartridges after 1932), .32-20 (disc. 1942), .38 Special, .41 Long Colt (disc. 1930). Six-round cylinder, bbl. lengths: 4-, 5-, and 6-inch or 2-inch and 6-inch heavy bbl. in .38 Special only; .22 LR w/4- and 6-inch bbls. only; 11.25 inches overall. Weight: 36 oz. (standard 6-inch bbl.) in .38 Special. Fixed sights. Blued or nickel-plated finish. Checkered walnut grips on all revolvers of this model except some of postwar production had checkered plastic grips. Made 1927-69. Note: This model is a refined version of the Army Special, which it replaced in 1928 at about serial number 520,000. The Commando .38 Special was a wartime adaptation of the Official Police made to government specifications. Commando can be identified by its sandblasted blued finish and stamped "COLT COMMANDO". Serial numbers start w/number 1-50,000 (made 1942 to 1945). Marshal Model marked "COLT MARSHAL" has S/N w/"M" suffix (made 1954 to 1956).
Commercial model (pre-war) . . NiB $960 Ex $850 Gd $560
Commercial model (post-war) . . . NiB $860 Ex $700 Gd $550
Commando model . . . . NiB $1950 Ex $1700 Gd $1450
Marshal model . . . . NiB $2000 Ex $1750 Gd $1500

OFFICIAL POLICE MK III . . . . . NiB $560 Ex $510 Gd $460
"J" frame, without shrouded ejector rod. Caliber: .38 Special. Six-round cylinder. bbl., lengths: 4-, 5-, 6-inches, 9.25 inches overall w/4-inch bbl., weight: 34 oz. (4-inch bbl.). Fixed rear sight, ramp front. Service trigger and hammer or target trigger and wide-spur hammer. Blued or nickel-plated finish. Checkered walnut service grips. Made 1969 to 1975.

PEACEKEEPER DA REVOLVER . . . NiB $580 Ex $455 Gd $330
Caliber: .357 Mag. Six-round cylinder, 4- or 6-inch bbl., 11.25 inches overall (6-inch bbl.). Weight: 46 oz. (with 6-inch bbl.). Adj. white outline rear sight, red insert ramp-style front. Non-reflective matte blued finish. Made from 1985 to 1989.

**Colt
Pocket Positive**

**Colt
Police Positive First Issue**

Colt SA Army

PEACEMAKER .22 SECOND AMENDMENT
COMMEMORATIVE . . . . **NiB $660 Ex $544 Gd $286**
Caliber: .22, revolver w/7.5-inch bbl., nickel-plated frame, bbl. ejector rod assembly, hammer and trigger, blued cylinder, backstrap and trigger guard. Black pearlite grips. bbl., inscribed "The Right to Keep and Bear Arms." Presentation case. Limited edition of 3000 issued in 1977. Top value is for revolver in new condition.

PEACEMAKER .22
SA REVOLVER . . . . **NiB $423 Ex $332 Gd $275**
Calibers: .22 LR and .22 WMR. Furnished w/cylinder for each caliber, 6-round. Bbl.: 4.38-, 6- or 7.5-inches, 11.25 inches overall (with 6-inch bbl.). Weight: 30.5 oz. (with 6-inch bbl.). Fixed sights. Black composite grips. Made from 1971 to 1976.

POCKET POSITIVE DA REVOLVER FIRST & SECOND ISSUES
General specifications same as New Pocket except this model has positive lock feature (see Police Positive). Calibers: .32 Short & Long Colt (disc. 1914), .32 Colt New Police (.32 S&W Short & Long). Fixed sights, flat top and square notch. Blue or nickel finish. Made from 1905 to 1940.
Blue finish. . . . . **NiB $1300 Ex $1000 Gd $760**
Nickel finish, add **20%**

POLICE POSITIVE FIRST ISSUE
Improved version of the New Police w/the "Positive Lock," which prevents the firing pin coming in contact w/the cartridge except when the trigger is pulled. Calibers: .32 Short & Long Colt (disc. 1915), .32 Colt New Police (.32 S&W Short & Long), .38 New Police (.38 S&W). Six-round cylinder, bbl. lengths: 2.5- (.32 cal. only), 4- 5- and 6-inches; 8.5 inches overall (with 4-inch bbl.). Weight 20 oz. (with 4-inch bbl.). Fixed sights. Blued or nickel finish. Rubber or checkered walnut grips. Made from 1907 to 1927.

Blue finish. . . . . **NiB $800 Ex $660 Gd $560**
Nickel finish, add **20%**

POLICE POSITIVE SECOND ISSUE
Same as Detective Special second issue except has 4-inch bbl., 9 inches overall, weight: 26.5 oz. Intro. in 1977. Note: Original Police Positive (First Issue) has a shorter frame, is not chambered for .38 Special. Made   1928 to 1947.
Blue finish. . . . . **NiB $860 Ex $760 Gd $530**

POLICE POSITIVE SPECIAL FIRST & SECOND ISSUES
DA REVOLVER . . . . **NiB $810 Ex $660 Gd $460**
Based on the Police Positive w/frame lengthened to permit longer cylinder. Calibers: .32-20 (disc. 1942), .38 Special, .32 New Police and .38 New Police (intro. 1946). Six-round cylinder; bbl. lengths: 4-(only length in current production), 5- and 6-inch; 8.75 inches overall (with 4-inch bbl.). Weight: 23 oz. (with 4-inch bbl. in .38 Special). Fixed sights. Checkered grips of hard rubber, plastic or walnut. Made 1907 to 1927 (First Issue) and 1928 to 1946 (Second Issue).

POLICE POSITIVE SPECIAL THIRD & FOURTH ISSUES
Based on Detective Special Second Issue but w/4-, 5- or 6-in. bbl. in .38 Spl. only. Made from 1947 to 1976 (Third Issue), 1977 to 1978 (Fourth Issue).
Third Issue . . . . **NiB $560 Ex $460 Gd $360**
Fourth Issue, dedunct **10%**

POLICE POSITIVE MK V FIFTH ISSUE
DA REVOLVER . . . . **NiB $450 Ex $380 Gd $330**
.38 Spl. only. 4-in. bbl. w/ejector shroud. Finish: blued. Grips: rubber. Made from 1994 to 1995.

POLICE POSITIVE TARGET FIRST AND SECOND ISSUES
DA REVOLVER . . . . **NiB $1310 Ex $1110 Gd $860**
Target version of the Police Positive. Calibers: .22 LR (intro. 1910, embedded-head cylinder for high-speed cartridges after 1932), .22 WRF (1910-35), .32 Short & Long Colt, (1915), .32 New Police (.32 S&W Short & Long). Six-inch bbl., blued finish only, 10.5 inches overall. Weight: 26 oz. in .22 cal. Adj. target sights. Hard rubber grips until 1923 then checkered walnut grips. Second Issue had heavier fram. Made from 1907 to 1925 (First Issue), 1926 to 1941 (Second Issue).
Second Issue, deduct **10%**

PYTHON DA REVOLVER
"I" frame, shrouded ejector rod. Calibers: .357 Magnum, .38 Special. Six-round cylinder, 2.5-, 4-, 6- or 8-inch vent rib bbl., 11.25 inches overall (with 6-inch bbl.). Weight: 44 oz. (6-inch

Colt Police Positive Target

Colt Python

bbl.). Adj. rear sight, ramp front. Blued, nickel or stainless finish. Checkered walnut target grips. Made from 1955 to 1996. Ultimate stainless finish made in 1985.

Blued or Royal
Blued finish . . . . NiB $2100 Ex $1900 Gd $1500
Nickel finish . . . . NiB $1910 Ex $1510 Gd $1275
Stainless finish. . . . . NiB $2310 Ex $2010 Gd $1610
Ultimate stainless finish . . . NiB $2210 Ex $1960 Gd $1660
2.5-in. bbl., add 100%
Elite model (mfg. 2002-06). . NiB $2760 Ex $2410 Gd $2010
Grizzly model (ported bbl., non-fluted cylinder,
    Pachmayer grips) . . . . . . NiB $4000 Ex $3610 Gd $3260
Hunter model (w/2x scope) NiB $3500 Ex $3230 Gd $2960
Silhouette model (w/2x scope)NiB $3760 Ex $3360 Gd $3060
Ten Pointer model (w/3x scope, carrying case, two sets
    of grips, 8-in. bbl.) . . . . . NiB $3000 Ex $2810 Gd $2760
Whitetailer model (w/2x scope, 8-in. bbl., aluminum
    case). . . . . NiB $1860 Ex $1610 Gd $1385
Whitetailer II model (w/1.5-4x scope, 8-in. bbl., bright
    satinless finish) . . . . NiB $2210 Ex $2010 Gd $1960
Ultimate model (custom shop tuned, two sets of sights, two
    sets of grips, 1991-93) . . NiB $2310 Ex $2060 Gd $1935

SHOOTING MASTER DA REVOLVER
Deluxe target arm based on the New Service model. Calibers: Originally made only in .38 Special, .44 Special, .45 Auto and .45 Colt added in 1933, .357 Magnum in 1936. Six-inch bbl., 11.25 inches overall. Weight: 44 oz., in (.38 cal.), adj. target sights. Hand-finished action. Blued finish. Checkered walnut grips. Rounded butt. Made from 1932 to 1941.
Shooting Master
.38 Special . . . . NiB $1507 Ex $1344 Gd $915
Shooting Master
.357 Mag. . . . . NiB $1533 Ex $1269 Gd $908
Shooting Master
.44 Special, .45 ACP, .45LCNiB $4092 Ex $3773 Gd $2285

TROOPER MK III . . . . NiB $587 Ex $418 Gd $225
DA revolver. "J" frame, shrouded ejector rod. Calibers: .22 LR, .22 Magnum, .38 Special, .357 Magnum. Six-round cylinder. bbl. lengths: 4-, 6-inches. 9.5 inches overall (with 4-inch bbl.). Weight: 39 oz. (4-inch bbl.). Adj. rear sight, ramp front. Target trigger and hammer. Blued or nickel-plated finish. Checkered walnut target grips. Made 1969 to 1978.

Nickel finish . . . . NiB $643 Ex $452 Gd $224

TROOPER MK V REVOLVER
Re-engineered Mark III for smoother, faster action. Caliber: .357 Magnum. Six-round cylinder, bbl. lengths: 4-, 6-, 8-inch w/vent rib. Adj. rear sight, ramp front, red insert. Checkered walnut grips. Made from 1982 to 1986.
Blued finish. . . . . NiB $562 Ex $437 Gd $321
Nickel finish . . . . NiB $577 Ex $499 Gd $316

VIPER DA REVOLVER . . . . . NiB $1500 Ex $1400 Gd $1200
Same as Cobra, Second Issue except has 4-in. bbl., 9 in. over-all, weight: 20 oz. Made from 1977 to 1984.

SINGLE ACTION ARMY (SAA) REVOLVER
Also called Frontier Six-Shooter and Peacemaker. Available in more than 30 calibers including: .22 Rimfire (Short, Long, LR), .22 WRF, .32 Rimfire, .32 Colt, .32 S&W, .32-20, .38 Colt, .38 S&W, .38 Special, .357 Magnum, .38-40, .41 Colt, .44 Rimfire, .44 Russian, .44 Special, .44-40, .45 Colt, .45 Auto, .450 Boxer, 450 Eley, .455 Eley, .476 Eley. Six-round cylinder. Bbl. lengths: 4.75, 5 .5 and 7.5 inches w/ejector or 3 and 4 inches w/o ejector. 10.25 inches overall (with 4.75-inch bbl.). Weight: 36 oz. (.45 cal. w/4.75-inch bbl.). Fixed sights. Also made in Target Model w/flat top-strap and target sights. Blued finish w/casehardened frame or nickel-plated. One-piece smooth walnut or checkered black rubber grips. Note: S.A. Army Revolvers w/serial numbers above 165,000 (circa 1896) are adapted to smokeless powder and cylinder pin screw was changed to spring catch at about the same time. The "First Generation" of SA Colts included both blackpowder and smokeless configurations and were manu-factured from 1873 to 1940. Production resumed in 1955 w/ serial number 1001SA and continued through 1975 to com-plete the second series, which is referred to as the "Second Generation." In 1976, the "Third Generation" of production began and continues to to date. However, several serial num-ber rollovers occurred at 99,999. For Example, in 1978 the "SA" suffix became an "SA" prefix and again in 1993, when the serial number SA99,999 was reached, the serialization format was changed again to include both an "S" prefix and an "A" suffix. Although the term "Fourth Generation" is frequently associated with this rollover, no series change actually occurred, therefore, the current production is still a "Third Generation" series. Current calibers: .357 Magnum, .44 Special, .45 Long Colt.
Pinched frame
    (1873 only). . . . . .Ex $250,000 Gd $175,000
Early commercial
    (1873-77) . . . . .Ex $90,000 Gd $70,000
Early U.S. Military
    (1873-77) . . . . Ex $175,000-$87,000 Gd $80,000-$42,000
Large bore rimfire
    (1875-80) . . . . .Ex $75,000 Gd $60,000
Small bore
    rimfire (1875-80). . . . . Ex $40,000 Gd $25,000
Frontier six-shooter, .44-40
    (1878-82) . . . . . Ex $52,000-$42,000 Gd $26,000-$20,000
Storekeeper's model, no ejector
    (1883-98) . . . . . Ex $95,000-$75,000 Gd $35,000-$32,000
Sheriff's model
    (1883-98) . . . . . Ex $95,000-$75,000 Gd $35,000-$32,000
Target model, flat top strap,
    target sights . . . . .Ex $25,000 Gd $11,000
U.S. Artillery model, .45
    (1895-1903) . . . . .Ex $16,000 Gd $7,500

Colt SA Army — 125th Anniversary

Colt 150th Anniversary Deluxe

Colt 150th Anniversary Engraving Sampler

Note: *In the previous section the GTG deviates from the observed practice of listing only the value of firearms produced after 1900. This deliberate departure from the standard format is intended to provide a general reference and establish proper orientation for the reader, because the Colt SSA had its origins in the last quarter of the 19th century. Consequently, antique firearms produced prior to 1898 have been listed as a preface and introduction to the first series of production (what is now recognized as "1st Generation") in order to systematically demonstrate the progressive and sequential development of the multi-generation Colt SAA. Therefore, the previous general values have been provided to establish a point of reference to allow a more comprehensive Examination of the evolution of the Colt SAA. However, please note that the following values apply only to original models, not to similar S.A.A. revolvers of more recent manufacture.*

1st generation (mfg. 1873-1940)

SAA (COMMERICAL) . . . . **Ex $250,000 Gd $10,000**
Variation of the SAA military model developed for commercial market.

SAA (U.S. MILITARY) . . . . **Ex $175,000 Gd $11,000**
Original SAA revolver model developed for U.S. military. Mfg. 1873 to 1909.

SAA BISLEY . . . . **NiB $10,000 Ex $8600 Gd $7600**
Variation of the SAA commercial developed for target shooting w/modified grips, trigger and hammer. Made 1894 to 1915.
Flattop Target Bisley (w/flattop frame, adj. rear sight,

7.5-in. bbl., mfg. 1894-1913) . . . NiB $20,000 Ex $18,000 Gd $15,000

SAA FLATTOP
TARGET . . . . NiB $25,000 Ex $20,000 Gd $16,500
Similar to the SAA Commercial model developed for target shooting w/flattop frame w/adj. rear sight. 925 mfg. Made 1888 to 1896.

SAA LONG FLUTE . . . . . NiB $17,600 Ex $9,999 Gd $6,200
Similar to the SAA Commercial model except w/modified long fluted cylinders from 1878 DA revolvers. Made 1913 to 1915.

SAA SHERIFF . . . . EX $95,000 TO $25,500
Similar to the Single-Action Army except commercial model w/o an ejector rod.

2nd generation (mfg. 1956-1975)
SAA (STANDARD MODEL)
Variation of the 1st Gen. SAA commercial w/slight changes to mechanism. Calibers: .38 Spl., .357 Mag., .44 Spl. or .45 LC. Bbl. length: 4.75-, 5.5- or 7.5-in. Finish: blued or nickel.
.38 Spl. . . . . NiB $3000 Ex $2600 Gd $1800
.357 Mag. . . . . NiB $2600 Ex $2000 Gd $1250
.44 Spl. . . . . NiB $3260 Ex $2650 Gd $1900
.45 LC . . . . NiB $3200 Ex $2950 Gd $2600
4.75-in. bbl., add 15%
nickel finish, add. 10%
factory engraved w/ factory letter, add 75-100%

BUNTLINE SPECIAL . . . . . . NiB $2448 Ex $1960 Gd $1260
Same as standard 2nd Gen. SAA except w/12-in. bbl., caliber .45 Long Colt only. Made from 1957 to 1975.

NEW FRONTIER . . . . NiB $1420 Ex $1220 Gd $1120
Similar to 2nd Gen. SAA except w/adj. rear sight and ramp blade front sight. Calibers: .38 Spl., .357 Mag., .44 Spl. or .45 LC. Bbl. length: 4.75-, 5.5- or 7.5-in. Finish: blued or nickel. Grip: smooth walnut w/medalion. Made from 1961 to 1975.
.38 Spl., add 270%
4.75-in. bbl., add 50%
5.5-in. bbl., add 25%
Buntline (12-in. bbl.,
.45 LC) . . . . NiB $2520 Ex $2200 Gd $1895

SHERIFF MODEL . . . . NiB $2260 Ex $2060 Gd $1780
Same as standard 2nd Gen. SAA except w/3-in. bbl. w/o ejector rod. Caliber .45 Long Colt. Finish: blued and case hardened or nickel.
nickel finish, add. 350%
3rd Generation (1976 to date)

Colt New Frontier

SAA (STANDARD MODEL) . . . NiB $1420 Ex $1230 Gd $1000
Variation of the 2nd Gen. SAA standard w/slight changes to mechanism. Calibers: .32-20, .38-40, .38 Spl., .357 Mag., .44 Spl., .44-40 or .45 LC. Bbl. length: 4-, 4.75-, 5-, 5.5- or 7.5-in. Finish: blued or nickel. Grip: smooth wood or black plastic w/eagle.
.38 Spl., add 25%
nickel finish, add. 20%
black powder frame (pre-1996), add. 15%
factory ivory grip, add 70%
factory Class A engraving, add $1200
factory Class B engraving, add $2400
factory Class C engraving, add $3500
factory Class D engraving, add $4700

COWBOY SAA . . . . NiB $800 Ex $660 Gd $510
SA revolver with transfer-bar safety system. Caliber: .45 Long Colt only. Bbl.: 4.75-, 5.5- or 7.5-in. Blued and case hardened finish. Grip: checkered composite. Made 1999 to 2003.

BUNTLINE SPECIAL . . . . NiB $1300 Ex $1070 Gd $900
Same as standard 3rd Gen. SAA except w/12-in. bbl. Caliber: .44-40 or .45 Long Colt. Blued and case hardened finish. Grip: smooth walnut.

NEW FRONTIER . . . . NiB $1560 Ex $1120 Gd $900
Similar to 2nd Gen. New Frontier except w/adj. rear sight and ramp blade front sight. Calibers: .357 Mag., .44 Spl., .44-40 or .45 LC. Bbl. length: 4.75-, 5.5- or 7.5-in. Finish: blued. Grip: smooth walnut w/medalion. Made 1978 to 1981 and 2008 to 2010, reintro. 2011 to date.
Buntline (12-in. bbl.,
.45 LC) . . . . NiB $2520 Ex $2200 Gd $1895

SHERIFF MODEL . . . . NiB $1300 Ex $1060 Gd $900
Same as standard 2nd Gen. Sheriff except w/3-in. bbl. w/o ejector rod. Caliber .44 Spl., .44-40 or .45 LC. Finish: blued and case hardened, royal blue or nickel.
extra convertiable cylinder, add 10%
factory ivory grip, add 70%
nickel finish, add. 10%
Royal blue finish, deduct 15%

STOREKEEPERS MODEL . . . NiB $1810 Ex $1660 Gd $1510
Similar to 3rd Gen. Sheriff except w/4-in. bbl. w/o ejector rod. Caliber: .45 LC only. Finish: blued and case hardened or nickel. Grips: ivory. Made from 1984 to 1985 and 2008 to 2010.
nickel finish, add. 10%

SAA 125TH ANNIVERSARY . . . NiB $1668 Ex $1438 Gd $1239
Limited production deluxe version of SAA issued in commemoration of Colt's 125th Anniversary. Caliber: .45 Long Colt., 7.5-inch bbl., cold-plated frame trigger, hammer, cylinder pin, ejector rod tip, and grip medallion. Presentation case w/anniversary medallion. Serial numbers "50AM." 7368 were made in 1961.

SAA COMMEMORATIVE MODELS
Limited production versions of SAA .45 issued, w/appropriate inscription to commemorate historical events. Cased. Note: Values indicated are for commemorative revolvers in new condition.

Colt Trooper

Colt Trooper MK V

1963 ISSUES
Arizona Territorial Centennial (1280 produced) . . NiB $1663
West Virginia Statehood Centennial
(600 produced) . . . . NiB $1663

1964 ISSUES
Chamizal Treaty (50 produced) . . . . NiB $1867
Colonel Sam Colt Sesquicentennial
Presentation (4750 produced) . . . . NiB $1663
Deluxe Presentation (200 produced) . . . . NiB $3621
Special Deluxe Presentation (50 produced) . . . . . NiB $5687
Montana Territorial Centennial (851 produced) . . NiB $1724
Nevada "Battle Born" (100 produced) . . . . NiB $2672
Nevada Statehood Centennial (1877 produced) . . NiB $2275
New Jersey Tercentenary (250 produced) . . . . NiB $1663
Pony Express Presentation (1004 produced) . . . . . NiB $1836
St. Louis Bicentennial (450 produced) . . . . NiB $1663
Wyatt Earp Buntline (150 produced) . . . . NiB $2809

1965 ISSUES
Appomattox Centennial (500 produced) . . . . NiB $1454
Old Fort Des Moines Reconstruction
(200 produced) . . . . NiB $1454

1966 ISSUES
Abercrombie & Fitch Trailblazer—Chicago
(100 produced) . . . . NiB $1423
Abercrombie & Fitch Trailblazer—New York
(200 produced) . . . . NiB $1423
Abercrombie & Fitch Trailblazer—San Francisco
(100 produced) . . . . NiB $1423
California Gold Rush (130 produced) . . . . NiB $1423
General Meade (200 produced) . . . . NiB $1663
Pony Express Four Square (4 guns) . . . . NiB $7268

1967 ISSUES
Alamo (1000 produced) . . . . NiB $1663
Lawman Series—Bat Masterson
(500 produced) . . . . NiB $1760

1968 ISSUES
Lawman Series—Pat Garrett (500 produced) . . . . . . NiB $1663

1969 ISSUES
Lawman Series—Wild Bill Hickok
(500 produced) . . . . NiB $1663

1970 ISSUES
Lawman Series—Wyatt Earp (501 produced) . . . . . NiB $2907
Texas Ranger (1000 produced) . . . . NiB $2351

1971 ISSUES
NRA Centennial, .357 or .45 (5001 produced) . . . . NiB $1525

1975 ISSUES
Peacemaker Centennial .45 (1501 produced) . . . NiB $1872
Peacemaker Centennial .44-40
(1501 produced) . . . . NiB $1872
Peacemaker Centennial Cased Pair
(501 produced) . . . . NiB $1872
Missouri Sesquicentennial
(501 produced) . . . . NiB $1627

1975 ISSUES
Peacemaker Centennial .45 (1501 produced) . . . NiB $1872
Peacemaker Centennial .44-40 (1501 produced) . . . NiB $1872
Peacemaker Centennial Cased
Pair (501 produced) . . . . NiB $1872

1979 ISSUES
Ned Buntline .45 (3000 produced) . . . . NiB $1367

1986 ISSUES
Colt 150th Anniversary (standard) . . . . NiB $2064
Colt 150th Anniversay (engraved) . . . . NiB $3647

COLT COWBOY REVOLVER . . . NiB $632 Ex $468 Gd $363
SA variant designed for "Cowboy Action Shooting" w/ safety transfer bar system. Caliber: .45 Colt. Six-round cylinder, 5.5-inch bbl., 11 inches overall. Weight: 42 oz. Blade front sight, fixed V-notch rear. Blued finish w/color casehardened frame. Smooth walnut grips. Made from 1999 to 2003.

SA SHERIFF'S MODEL .45
Limited edition replica of Storekeeper's Model in caliber .45 Colt, made Exclusively for Centennial Arms Corp. Chicago, Illinois. Numbered "1SM." Blued finish w/casehardened frame or nickel-plated. Walnut grips. Made in 1961.
Blued finish
(478 produced) . . . . NiB $2152 Ex $1780 Gd $1454
Nickel finish
(25 produced) . . . . NiB $8155 Ex $5763 Gd $4024

THREE-FIFTY-SEVEN DA REVOLVER
Heavy frame. Caliber: .357 Magnum. Six-shot cylinder, 4 or 6-inch bbl. Quickdraw ramp front sight, Accro rear sight. Blued finish. Checkered walnut grips. 9.25 or 11.25 inches overall. Weight: 36 oz. (4-inch bbl.), 39 oz. (6 inch bbl.). Made from 1953 to 1961.
w/standard hammer and
service grips . . . . NiB $711 Ex $601 Gd $431
w/wide-spur hammer and
target grips . . . . NiB $733 Ex $612 Gd $444

Colt U.S. Bicentennial Commemorative Set

TROOPER DA REVOLVER
Similar specifications as Officers' Model Match except has 4-inch bbl. w/quick-draw ramp front sight, weight: 34 oz. Claiber: .22 LR, .38 Spl. or .357 Mag. Made from 1953 to 1969.
w/standard hammer and
  service grips . . . . NiB $810 Ex $710 Gd $635
w/wide-spur hammer and
  target grips . . . . NiB $835 Ex $735 Gd $660

U.S. BICENTENNIAL COMMEMORATIVE SET . . . NiB $3290
Replica Colt 3rd Model Dragoon revolver w/accessories, Colt SA Army revolver, and Colt Python revolver. Matching roll-engraved unfluted cylinders, blued finish and rosewood grips w/Great Seal of the United States silver medallion. Dragoon revolver has silver grip frame. Serial numbers 0001 to 1776. All revolvers in set have same number. Deluxe drawer-style presentation case of walnut w/book compartment containing a reproduction of "Armsmear." Issued in 1976. Value is for revolvers in new condition.

COONAN ARMS, INC. — Blaine, MN
Formerly Maplewood, Minnesota and St. Paul, Minnesota.

MODEL .357 MAGNUM SEMI-AUTO PISTOL
Caliber: .357 Mag. Seven-round magazine, 5- or 6-inch bbl., 8.3 inches overall (with 5-inch bbl.). Weight: 42 oz. Front ramp interchangeable sight, fixed rear sight, adj. for windage. Black walnut grips. Made from 1983 to 1999; reintro. 2010.
Model A Std. grade w/o grip
safety (disc. 1991) . . . . NiB $1221 Ex $1056 Gd $869
Model B Std. grade
  w/5-inch bbl., ... NiB $944 Ex $703 Gd $500
Model B Std. grade
  w/6-inch bbl., ... NiB $714 Ex $601 Gd $437

Model B w/5-inch compensated bbl.,
  (Classic) . . . . NiB $1336 Ex $1122 Gd $923
Model B w/6-inch
  compensated bbl . . . . NiB $1016 Ex $789 Gd $561

.357 MAGNUM CADET COMPACT
Similar to the standard .357 Magnum model except w/3.9-inch bbl., on compact frame. Six-round (Cadet), 7- or 8-round magazine (Cadet II). Weight: 39 oz., 7.8 inches overall. Made 1993 to 1999; reintro. 2010.
Cadet model . . . . NiB $897 Ex $653 Gd $497
Cadet II model . . . . NiB $897 Ex $653 Gd $497

CZ (CESKA ZBROJOVKA), INC. — Uhersky Brod Czechoslovakia
Formerly Strakonice, Czechoslovakia. Mfd. by Ceska Zbrojovka-Nardoni Podnik formerly Bohmische Waffenfabrik A. G. Currently imported by CZ-USA (cz-usa.com), Kansas City, KS. Previously by Magnum Research and Action Arms. Vintage importation is by Century International Arms. Also, see Dan Wesson Firearms listings.

CZ P-01 . . . . NiB $658 Ex $406 Gd $305
Caliber: 9mm Para. Based on CZ-75 design but with improved metals, aluminum alloy frame, hammer forged bbl. (3.8 inches), checkered rubber grips, matte black polycoat finish. Imported 2003.

CZ P-07 DUTY . . . . NiB $440 Ex $330 Gd $270
Caliber: 9mm Para. or .40 S&W. Polymer frame in black or OD green, 3.8-in. bbl. Made from 2009 to 2013.

CZ 2075 RAMI P. . . . . NiB $440 Ex $330 Gd $270
Caliber: 9mm Para. or .40 S&W. Polymer frame in black, 3-in. bbl. Made from 2006 to 2011.

CZ 40 . . . . NiB $530 Ex $372 Gd $321
Caliber: .40 S&W. M1911-style frame, CZ-75B operating mechanism; single or double-action; black polycoat finish. Fixed sights; 10-round mag.

MODEL 27 AUTO PISTOL . . . . NiB $653 Ex $555 Gd $385
Caliber: .32 Automatic (7.65mm). Eight-round magazine, 4-inch bbl., 6 inches overall. Weight: 23.5 oz. Fixed sights.

CZ 2075 Rami P shown w/ extended magazine

CZ Shadow

CZ Model 75 Compact

CZ Model 75 Kadet

CZ Model 83

Blued finish. Plastic grips. Made from 1927 to 1951. Note: After the German occupation (March 1939), Models 27 and 38 were marked w/manufacturer code "fnh." Designation of Model 38 was changed to "Pistole 39(t)."

MODEL 38 AUTO PISTOL (VZ SERIES)
Caliber: .380 Automatic (9mm). Nine-round magazine, 3.75-inch bbl., 7 inches overall. Weight: 26 oz. Fixed sights. Blued finish. Plastic grips. After 1939 designated as T39. Made 1938 to 1945.

CZ DAO model . . . . NiB $518 Ex $442 Gd $358
CZ SA/DA model . . . . NiB $1451 Ex $1144 Gd $825

MODEL 50 DA AUTO PISTOL . NiB $265 Ex $191 Gd $153
Similar to Walther Model PP except w/frame-mounted safety and trigger guard not hinged. Caliber: .32 ACP (7.65mm), 8-round magazine, 3.13-inch bbl., 6.5 inches overall. Weight: 24.5 oz. Fixed sights. Blued finished. Intro. in 1950. disc.
Note: "VZ50" is the official designation of this pistol used by the Czech National Police ("New Model .006" was the Export designation but very few were released).

MODEL 52
SA AUTO PISTOL . . . . NiB $248 Ex $202 Gd $137
Roller-locking breech system. Calibers: 7.62mm or 9mm Para. Eight-round magazine, 4.7-inch bbl., 8.1 inches overall. Weight: 31 oz. Fixed sights. Blued finish. Grooved composition grips. Made 1952 to 1956.

MODEL 70
DA AUTO PISTOL . . . . NiB $530 Ex $420 Gd $296
Similar to Model 50 but redesigned to improve function and dependability. Made from 1962 to 1983.

MODEL 75 DA/DAO AUTOMATIC PISTOL
Calibers: 9mm Para. or .40 S&W w/selective action mode. 10-, 13- or 15-round magazine, 3.9-inch bbl., (Compact) or 4.75-inch bbl., (Standard), 8 inches overall (Standard). Weight: 35 oz. Fixed sights. Blued, nickel, Two-Tone or black polymer finish. Checkered wood or high-impact plastic grips. Made from 1994 to date.
Black polymer finish . . . . NiB $459 Ex $385 Gd $284
High-polish blued finish . . . . . . NiB $526 Ex $453 Gd $347
Matte blued finish. . . . . NiB $499 Ex $398 Gd $295
Nickel finish . . . . NiB $541 Ex $442 Gd $330
Two-tone finish . . . . NiB $530 Ex $431 Gd $325
w/.22 Kadet conversion, add $281
Compact model, add. $65
Champion (1999-04,
    2006-09). . . . . NiB $1430 Ex $1055 Gd $610

MODEL 75 SHADOW AUTOMATIC PISTOL
Competition variant of the Model 75 except w/DA/SA or SAO trigger and Model 85 style trigger. Caliber: 9mm Para. Made from 2011 to 2013.
DA/SA. NiB $920 Ex $730 Gd $580
SAO . . . . NiB $850 Ex $660 Gd $460
CTS LS-P (long slide). . . . . . . NiB $1300 Ex $1030 Gd $780

MODEL 75 SP-01 PHANTOM. . NiB $530 Ex $380 Gd $280
Caliber: 9mm Para. Polymer black frame. Made from 2009 to 2013.

MODEL 75 B DA/DAO AUTOMATIC PISTOL
Similar to Model 75 except w/firing pin safety block. Made from 1998 to date.
Military (2000-02) . . . . NiB $370 Ex $275 Gd $230
Target SA (2010) . . . . NiB $1055 Ex $800 Gd $530

MODEL 82 DA AUTO PISTOL. . . NiB $407 Ex $306 Gd $221
Similar to the standard CZ 83 model except chambered in 9x18 Makarov. This model currently is the Czech military side-arm since 1983.

MODEL 83 DA AUTOMATIC PISTOL
Calibers: .32 ACP, .380 ACP. 15-round (.32 ACP) or 13-round (.380 ACP) magazine, 3.75-inch bbl., 6.75 inches overall.

CZ Model 85 Combat

CZ Model 97B

CZ Model 100

Daewoo DH40

CZ VZ 61 Skorpion

Weight: 26.5 oz. Fixed sights. Blued (standard); chrome and nickel (optional special edition) w/brushed, matte or polished finish. Checkered black plastic grips. Made 1985-2012.

Standard finish . . . . NiB $434 Ex $357 Gd $221
Special edition . . . . NiB $580 Ex $453 Gd $322
Engraved . . . . NiB $1234 Ex $1017 Gd $718

MODEL 85 AUTOMATIC DA PISTOL
Same as CZ 75 except w/ambidExtrous slide release and safety. Calibers: 9mm Para., 7.65mm. Made 1986 to date.

Black polymer finish . . . . NiB $478 Ex $388 Gd $274
High-polish blued finish . . . . NiB $576 Ex $477 Gd $319
Matte blued finish . . . . NiB $529 Ex $372 Gd $267

MODEL 85 COMBAT DA AUTOMATIC PISTOL
Similar to the standard CZ 85 model except w/13-round magazine, combat-style hammer, fully adj. rear sight and walnut grips. Made from 1986 to date.

Black polymer finish . . . . NiB $569 Ex $489 Gd $306
High-polished blued finish . . . . NiB $610 Ex $498 Gd $373
Matte blued finish. . . . . NiB $614 Ex $486 Gd $366

MODEL 97B DA . . . . NiB $629 Ex $540 Gd $344
Similar to the CZ Model 75 except chambered for the .45 ACP cartridge. 10-round magazine, Frame-mounted thumb safety that allows single-action, cocked-and-locked carry. Made from 1998 to date.

MODEL 100 DA . . . . NiB $488 Ex $398 Gd $265
DA semi-automatic. Caliber: 9mm, .40 S&W. 10-round magazine, 3.8-inch bbl., Weight: 25 oz. Polymer grips w/ fixed low-profile sights. Made from 1996 to 2007. Reintro. 2009.

MODEL 1945 DA POCKET . . . . NiB $328 Ex $241 Gd $183
Caliber: .25 Auto (6.35mm). Eight-round magazine, 2.5-inch bbl., 5 inches overall. Weight: 15 oz. Fixed sights. Blued finish. Plastic grips. Intro. 1945. disc.

CZ VZ 61 SKORPION . . . . NiB $599 Ex $340 Gd $300
Semi-automatic version of VZ 61 Skorpion submachine gun. Caliber: .32 ACP. 20-round magazine, 4.5-in. bbl. Made from 2009 to 2010.

DUO POCKET AUTO PISTOL . NiB $328 Ex $252 Gd $174
Caliber: .25 Automatic (6.35mm). Six-round magazine, 2.13 inch bbl., 4.5 inches overall. Weight: 14-.5 oz. Fixed sights. Blued or nickel finish. Plastic grips. Made circa 1926 to 1960.

DAEWOO — Seoul, Korea
Mfd. by Daewoo Precision Industries Ltd. Imported by Daewoo Precision Industries, Southhampton, PA, Previously by Nationwide Sports Distributors and KBI, Inc.

DH40 AUTO PISTOL . . . . NiB $357 Ex $255 Gd $172
Caliber: .40 S&W. 12-round magazine, 4.25-inch bbl., 7 inches overall. Weight: 28 oz. Blade front sight, dovetailed rear w/3-dot system. Blued finish. Checkered composition grips. DH/DP series feature a patented "fastfire" action w/5-6 lb. trigger pull. Made from 1994 to 1996.

DH45 AUTO PISTOL . . . . NiB $346 Ex $248 Gd $189
Caliber: .45 ACP. 13-round magazine, 5-inch bbl., 8.1 inches over all. Weight: 35 oz. Blade front sight, dovetailed rear w/3-dot

system. Blued finish. Checkered composition grips. Announced 1994, but not imported.

DP51 AUTO PISTOL . . . . **NiB $330 Ex $221 Gd $148**
Caliber: 9mm Para. 13-round magazine, 4.1-inch bbl., 7.5 inches overall. Weight: 28 oz. Blade front and square-notch rear sights. Matte black finish. Checkered composition grips. Made from 1991 to 1996.

DP52 AUTO PISTOL . . . . **NiB $358 Ex $255 Gd $172**
Caliber: .22 LR. 10-round magazine, 3.8-inch bbl., 6.7 inches overall. Weight: 23 oz. Blade front sight, dovetailed rear w/3-dot system. Blued finish. Checkered wood grips. Made from 1994 to 1996.

DAKOTA/E.M.F. CO. — Santa Ana, California

MODEL 1873 SA REVOLVER
Calibers: .22 LR, .22 Mag., .357 Mag., .45 Long Colt, .30 M1 carbine, .38-40, .32-20, .44-40. Bbl. lengths: 3.5, 4.75, 5.5, 7.5 inches. Blued or nickel finish. Engraved models avail.
Standard model . . . . NiB $347 Ex $305 Gd $229
Nickel finish, add 40%

MODEL 1875 OUTLAW . . . . . . NiB $525 Ex $420 Gd $293
Calibers: .45 Long Colt, .357 Mag., .44-40. 7.5-inch bbl. Casehardened frame, blued finish. Walnut grips. Exact replica of the Remington Number 3 SA revolver produced 1875 to 1889.

MODEL 1890 REMINGTON POLICE
Calibers: .357 Mag., .44-40, .45 Long Colt, 5.75-inch bbl., blued or nickel finish. Similar to 1875 Outlaw w/lanyard ring and no bbl. web.
Standard model . . . . NiB $560 Ex $441 Gd $332
Nickel model . . . . NiB $637 Ex $523 Gd $371
Engraved model . . . . NiB $780 Ex $603 Gd $444

BISLEY SA REVOLVER
Calibers: .44-40, .45 Long Colt, .357 Mag, 5.5- or 7.5-inch bbl., disc. 1992. Reintroduced 1994.
Standard model . . . . NiB $459 Ex $378 Gd $272
Engraved model . . . . NiB $638 Ex $509 Gd $283

HARTFORD SA REVOLVER
Calibers: .22 LR, .32-20, .357 Mag., .38-40, .44-40, .44 Special, .45 Long Colt. These are Exact replicas of the original Colts w/steel backstraps, trigger guards and forged frames. Blued or nickel finish. Imported from 1990 to 2008.
Standard model . . . . NiB $444 Ex $367 Gd $274
Engraved model . . . . NiB $734 Ex $546 Gd $499
Hartford Artillery, U.S. Cavalry
  models . . . . NiB $484 Ex $401 Gd $267

**Dakota Hartford
Engraved Model**

SHERIFF'S MODEL . . . . NiB $437 Ex $377 Gd $271
SA revolver. Calibers: .32-20, .357 Mag., .38-40, .44 Special, .44-40, .45 LC. 3.5-inch bbl. Reintroduced 1994.

TARGET SA REVOLVER . . . . . . NiB $478 Ex $351 Gd $279
SA revolver. Calibers: .45 Long Colt, .357 Mag., .22 LR; 5.5- or 7.5-inch bbl. Polished, blued finish, casehardened frame. Walnut grips. Ramp front, blade target sight, adj. rear sight.

DALY, CHARLES — Dayton, Ohio
Mfd. by Flli. Pietta (SAA models) Armscor (1911 series) and Bul Transmark (M-5 series).

MODEL 1873 CLASSIC SERIES NiB $520 Ex $370 Gd $315
SA revolver based on Colt SAA. Caliber: .357 Mag. or .45 LC. 6-rnd. cylinder. Bbbl. length: 4.75-, 5.5- or 7.5-in. Brass or steel backstrap/trigger guard. Imported from 2004 to 2007.
Birdshead model (birdshead grip, .45 LC only), add $30
Lightning model, add $30
Sonora model (matte blue finish), add $100

MODEL 1911-A1 SERIES . . . . . NiB $480 Ex $420 Gd $360
SA semi-auto. 1911 style. Various bbl. lenghts depending on model.Caliber: .38 Super, .40 S&W or .45 ACP. 8- or 10-rnd. magazine, 5-in. bbl. Weight: 39.5 oz. Blued finish. Imported from 1998 to 2008.
Satinless finish, add $100
Target model, add $80
Empire ECMT Custom Match model, add $275
Commander model . . . . NiB $480 Ex $420 Gd $360
Officer's model . . . . NiB $480 Ex $420 Gd $360
Polymer Frame PC model . . . . . NiB $470 Ex $410 Gd $350

MODEL M1911-A1 FIELD FS AUTOMATIC PISTOL
Caliber: .45 ACP. Eight- or 10-round magazine (Hi-Cap), 5-inch bbl., 8.75 inches overall. Weight: 38 oz. Blade front sight, drift adjustable rear w/3-dot system. Skeletonized tactical hammer and trigger. Extended slide release and beavertail grip safety. Matte blue, stainless or Duo finish. Checkered composition or wood stocks. Imported from 1999 to 2000.
Matte blue (Field FS) . . . . NiB $525 Ex $479 Gd $326
Stainless (Empire EFS) . . . . NiB $560 Ex $459 Gd $361
Duo (Superior FS) . . . . NiB $653 Ex $497 Gd $363
w/.22 conversion kit, add $204

MODEL DDA
10-45 FS PISTOL . . . . NiB $455 Ex $400 Gd $345
SA/DA semi-automatic polymer pistol. Calibers: .40 S&W or .45 ACP. 10-rnd. magazine. 4.3-in. bbl. Weight: 28.5 oz. Finish: matte black or two-tone. Imported from 2000 to 2002.

FIELD HP HI-POWER . . . . NiB $390 Ex $340 Gd $295
Similar to Browning HP pistol. 9mm. 10- or 13-rnd. magazine. 4.75-in. bbl. Finish: matte blued. Made in U.S. from 2003 to 2006.
Hard Chrome finish, add $100

M-5 FS
SEMI-AUTOMATIC PISTOL . . . . NiB $670 Ex $585 Gd $505
Based on 1911 pistol w/polymer frame. Caliber: 9mm, .40 S&W or .45 ACP. 10-, 14- or 17-rnd. magazine. 3.1-, 4.2- or 5-in. bbl. Finish: blued or chrome. Weight: 31-33 oz. Imported from 2004 to 2009.
IPSC model (2004-07) . . . . . . NiB $1255 Ex $1100 Gd $945

DAN WESSON — Kansas City, KS

Currently owned by CZ-USA. Listsing below are for recent production of pistols and revolvers. Also see Wesson Fireams Company for older production revolvers.

**MODEL 44-AGS (ALASKA GUIDE SPECIAL)
REVOLVER** . . . . **NiB $1295 Ex $1080 Gd $960**
Caliber: .445 Super Mag., 6-shot cylinder. 4-in. heavy w/VR bbl. Finish: black teflon. Grip: rubber finger groove. Made 2002-04, and 2006-07.

MODEL 715 SEREIS . . . . **NiB $710 Ex $630 Gd $560**
Small frame revolver. Caliber: .357 Mag., 6-shot cylinder. 2.5-, 4-, 6-, 8-, or 10-in. heavy w/VR interchangeable bbls. Finish: stainless. Grip: rubber finger groove. Made 2002 to 2004, and 2011 to 2012.
2011-2012 mfg. (6-in. bbl.).. NiB $1168 Ex $1030 Gd $910

MODEL 741 SEREIS . . . . **NiB $830 Ex $730 Gd $660**
Large frame revolver. Caliber: .44 Mag., 6-shot cylinder. 4-, 6-, 8-, or 10-in. heavy w/VR interchangeable bbls. Finish: stainless. Grip: rubber finger groove. Made 2002 to 2004.

MODEL 7445 SEREIS . . . . **NiB $830 Ex $730 Gd $660**
Supermag frame revolver. Caliber: .445 Super Mag., 6-shot cylinder. 4-, 6-, 8-, or 10-in. heavy w/VR interchangeable bbls. Finish: stainless. Grip: rubber finger groove. Made 2002 to 2004, and 2006 to 2007.

MODEL 7460 SEREIS . . . . **NiB $1070 Ex $810 Gd $730**
Supermag frame revolver. Caliber: .45 ACP, .45 Auto Rim, .445 Super Mag., .45 Win. Mag., or .450 Rowland, 6-shot cylinder. Made 1999.

**COMMANDER
CLASSIC BOBTAIL.** . . . . **NiB $1050 Ex $780 Gd $610**
1911 platform. Caliber: 10mm or .45 Auto. 4.25-in. bbl., bobbed frame. Series 70. Made 2005 to 2009.

GLOBAL . . . . **NiB $1000 Ex $790 Gd $610**
1911 platform. Caliber: 10mm or .45 Auto. 5- or 6-in. bbl., accessory rail or full length dust cover frame. Series 70. Made 2005.

PATRIOT . . . . **NiB $830 Ex $660 Gd $480**
1911 platform. Caliber: 10mm or .45 Auto. 4.25- or 5-in. bbl., blued or stainless. Series 70. Made 2001 to 2005.

POINTMAN SEVEN . . . . **NiB $1050 Ex $780 Gd $610**
1911 platform. Caliber: .40 S&W, 10mm or .45 Auto. 5-in. bbl., blued or stainless, adj. target sights. Series 70. Made 2005 to 2009.

DAVIS INDUSTRIES, INC. — Chino, CA

MODEL D DERRINGER
Single-action double derringer. Calibers: .22 LR, .22 Mag., .25 ACP, .32 Auto, .32 H&R Mag., 9mm, .38 Special. Two-round capacity, 2.4-inch or 2.75-inch bbl., 4 inches overall (2.4-inch bbl.). Weight: 9 to 11.5 oz.
Laminated wood grips. Black Teflon or chrome finish. Made from 1987 to 2001.
.22 LR or .25 ACP . . . . **NiB $192 Ex $109 Gd $88**
.22 Mag., .32 H&R
    Mag., .38 Spec. . . . . **NiB $204 Ex $128 Gd $91**
.32 Auto . . . . **NiB $214 Ex $115 Gd $91**
9mm Para.. . . . . **NiB $170 Ex $122 Gd $96**

LONG BORE DERRINGER . . . . . **NiB $219 Ex $122 Gd $97**
Similar to Model D except in calibers .22 Mag., .32 H&R Mag., .38 Special, 9mm Para. 3.75-inch bbl., weight: 16 oz. Made from 1995 to 2001.

MODEL P-.32 . . . . **NiB $152 Ex $101 Gd $78**
Caliber: .32 Auto. Six-round magazine, 2.8-inch bbl., 5.4 inches overall. Weight: 22 oz. Black Teflon or chrome finish. Laminated wood grips. Made from 1987 to 2001.

MODEL P-.380 . . . . **NiB $192 Ex $115 Gd $89**
Caliber: .380 Auto. Five-round magazine, 2.8-inch bbl., 5.4 inches overall. Weight: 22 oz. Black Teflon or chrome finish. Made from 1990 to 2001.

DESERT INDUSTRIES, INC. — Las Vegas, NV

Previously Steel City Arms, Inc.

DOUBLE DEUCE DA PISTOL . . **NiB $386 Ex $286 Gd $225**
Caliber: .22 LR. Six-round magazine, 2.5-inch bbl., 5.5 inches overall. Weight: 15 oz. Matte-finish stainless steel. Rosewood grips.

TWO-BIT SPECIAL PISTOL . . . . **NiB $431 Ex $326 Gd $237**
Similar to the Double Deuce model except chambered in .25 ACP w/5-shot magazine.

DETONICS FIREARMS IND. — Phoenix, AZ

Previously Detonics Firearms Industries, Bellevue, WA.

COMBATMASTER
Calibers: .45 ACP, .451 Detonics Mag. Six-round magazine, 3.5-inch bbl., 6.75 inches overall. Combat-type w/fixed or adjustable sights. Checkered walnut grip. Stainless steel. Disc. 1992.
**MK I, matte stainless,
    fixed sights (disc. 1981)** . . . . **NiB $1097 Ex $963 Gd $893**
**MK II polished finish,
    (disc. 1979).** . . . . **NiB $1494 Ex $1370 Gd $1133**
MK III chrome, (disc. 1980) . . . **NiB $551 Ex $443 Gd $328**
**MK IV polished blued,
    adj. sights, (disc. 1981).** . . . . . . **NiB $612 Ex $500 Gd $373**
**MK V matte stainless,
    fixed sights, (disc. 1985).** . . . . . **NiB $762 Ex $621 Gd $499**
**MK VI polished stainless, fixed
    sights, (disc. 1985)** . . . . **NiB $831 Ex $666 Gd $509**
**MK VI in .451 Magnum,
    (disc. 1986)** . . . . **NiB $1199 Ex $979 Gd $695**
**MK VII matte stainless steel,
    no sights, (disc. 1985)** . . . . . **NiB $1037 Ex $845 Gd $591**

Detonics Combatmaster

Detonics Scoremaster

Dreyse Model 1907

**Enfield
(British Service) No. 2 MK 1 Revolver**

**MK VII in .451 Magnum,
(disc. 1980)** . . . . **NiB $1380 Ex $1131 Gd $806**

POCKET 9 . . . . **NiB $668 Ex $541 Gd $426**
Calibers: 9mm Para., .380. Six-round magazine, three-inch bbl., 5.88 inches overall. Fixed sights. Double- and single-action trigger mechanism. Disc. 1986.

SCOREMASTER . . . . **NiB $1550 Ex $1257 Gd $1120**
Calibers: .45 ACP, .451 Detonics Mag. Seven-round magazine. Five- or 6-inch heavyweight match bbl., 8.75 inches overall. Weight: 47 oz. Stainless steel construction, self-centering bbl., system. Disc. 1992.

SERVICEMASTER . . . . **NiB $1117 Ex $780 Gd $530**
Caliber: .45 ACP. Seven-round magazine, 4.25-inch bbl., weight: 39 oz. Interchangeable front sight, Millett rear sight. Disc. 1986.

SERVICEMASTER II . . . . **NiB $1117 Ex $780 Gd $530**
Same general specifications as standard Service Master except comes in polished stainless steel w/self-centering bbl., system. Disc. 1992.

DOWNSIZER CORPORATION — Santee, CA

MODEL WSP DAO PISTOL . . . . **NiB $499 Ex $381 Gd $264**
Single-round, tip-up pistol. Calibers: .22 Mag., .32 Mag., .380 ACP. 9mm Parabellum, .357 Mag., .40 S&W, .45 ACP. Six-round cylinder, 2.10-inch bbl. w/o Extractor, 3.25 inches overall. Weight: 11 oz. No sights. Stainless finish. Synthetic grips. Made from 1994 to 2007.

DREYSE — Sommerda, Germany
Mfd. by Rheinische Metallwaren und Maschinenfabrik ("Rheinmetall").

**MODEL 1907
AUTOMATIC PISTOL** . . . . **NiB $273 Ex $224 Gd $179**
Caliber: .32 Auto (7.65mm). Eight-round magazine, 3.5-inch bbl., 6.25 inches overall. Weight: About 24 oz. Fixed sights. Blued finish. Hard rubber grips. Made circa 1907 to 1914.

**VEST POCKET
AUTOMATIC PISTOL** . . . . **NiB $357 Ex $293 Gd $204**
Conventional Browning type. Caliber: .25 Auto (6.35mm). Six-round magazine, 2-inch bbl., 4.5 inches overall. Weight: About 14 oz. Fixed sights. Blued finish. Hard rubber grips. Made 1909 to 1914.

DWM — Berlin, Germany
Mfd. by Deutsche Waffen-und-Munitionsfabriken.

POCKET AUTOMATIC PISTOL . . . **NiB $1050 Ex $918 Gd $713**
Similar to the FN Browning Model 1910. Caliber: .32 Automatic (7.65mm). 3.5-inch bbl., 6 inches overall. Weight: About 21 oz. Blued finish. Hard rubber grips. Made circa 1921 to 1931.

ED BROWN — Perry, Montana

Manufacturer of custom 1911 style pistols.

CLASS A LTD. . . . . **NiB $2312 Ex $2152 Gd $1041**
Caliber: .38 Super, 9mm, 9x23, .45 ACP. Seven-round magazine, 4.25- or 5-inch bbl., weight: 34-39 oz. Rubber checkered or optional Hogue Exotic wood grip. M1911 style single action pistol. Fixed front and rear Novak Lo-mount or fully adjustable sights.

CLASSIC CUSTOM . . . . **NiB $3231 Ex $2553 Gd $1527**
Caliber: .45 ACP. Seven-round magazine, 4.25- or 5-inch bbl., weight: 39 oz. Exotic Hogue wood grip w/modified ramp or post front and rear adjustable sights.

SPECIAL FORCES . . . . **NiB $2240 Ex $1918 Gd $1437**
Caliber: .45 ACP. Seven-round magazine, 4.25- or 5-inch bbl., weight: 34-39 oz. Rubber checkered, optional exotic wood grips. Single action M1911 style pistol.

E.M.F. Co., In. — Santa Anna, California
Importer, distrributor and retailer of numerous reproduction and new deisgn pistols and revolvers. See Davide Pedersoli & Co., F.A.P F.LLI. Pietta, and Uberti.

ENFIELD — Enfield Lock, Middlesex, England
Mfd. by Rheinische Metallwaren und Manufactured by Royal Small Arms Factory.

NO. 2 MK 1 DA REVOLVER . . . NiB $362 Ex $271 Gd $221
British Military Service. Webley pattern. Hinged frame. Double action. Caliber: .380 British Service (.38 S&W w/200-grain bullet). Six-round cylinder, 5-inch bbl., 10.5 inches overall. Weight: About 27.5 oz. Fixed sights. Blued finish. Vulcanite grips. First issued in 1932, this was the standard revolver of the British Army in WW II. Now obsolete. Note: This model also produced w/spurless hammer as No. 2 Mk 1* and Mk 1**.

ENTERPRISE ARMS — Irwindale, California

ELITE SERIES SA AUTO PISTOL. . . NiB $661 Ex $498 Gd $401
Single action M1911 style pistol. Caliber: .45 ACP. 10-round magazine, 3.25-, 4.25-, 5-inch bbl., (models P325, P425, P500). Weight: 36-40 oz. Ultraslim checkered grips, Tactical 2 high profile sights w/3-dot system. Lightweight adjustable trigger. Blued or matte black oxide finish. Made from 1997 to date.

MEDALIST SA AUTOMATIC PISTOL
Similar to Elite model except machined to match tolerances and target configuration. Caliber: .45 ACP, .40 S&W. 10-round magazine, 5-inch compensated bbl. w/dovetail front and fully adjustable rear Bo-Mar sights. Weight: 40 oz. Made from 1997 to date.
.40 S&W model. . . . . NiB $1015 Ex $862 Gd $689
.45 ACP model . . . . NiB $893 Ex $740 Gd $577

TACTICAL SA AUTOMATIC PISTOL
Similar to Elite model except in combat carry configuration. De-horned frame and slide w/ambidExtrous safety. Caliber: .45 ACP. 10-round magazine, 3.25-, 4.25-, 5-inch bbl., weight: 36-40 oz. Tactical 2 Ghost Ring or Novak Lo-mount sights.
Tactical 2 ghost
  ring sights. . . . . NiB $917 Ex $724 Gd $571
Novak Lo-Mount. . . . . NiB $917 Ex $724 Gd $571
Tactical plus model. . . . . NiB $917 Ex $724 Gd $571

BOXER . . . . NiB $1243 Ex $1122 Gd $831
Similar to Medalist model except w/profiled slide configuration and fully adjustable target sights. weight: 42 oz. Made from 1997 to date.

TOURNAMENT SHOOTER MODEL SA AUTOMATIC PISTOL
Similar to Elite model except in IPSC configuration. Caliber: .45 ACP, .40 S&W. 10-round magazine, 5-inch compensated bbl., w/dovetail front and fully adjustable rear Bo-Mar sights. Weight: 40 oz. Made from 1997 to date.
TSM I model. . . . . NiB $2145 Ex $1986 Gd $1637
TSM II model . . . . NiB $1834 Ex $1687 Gd $1331
TSM III model. . . . . NiB $2575 Ex $1403 Gd $1661

ERMA-WERKE — Dachau, Germany

MODEL ER-772. . . . . NiB $1132 Ex $1071 Gd $655
MODEL KGP68
Revolver. Caliber: .22 LR. Six-round cylinder, 6-inch bbl., 12 inches overall. Weight: 47.25 oz. Adjustable micrometer rear sight and front sight blade. Adjustable trigger. Interchangeable walnut sporter or match grips. Polished blued finish. Made from 1991 to 1994.

**Erma
Model ER-772 Match Revolver**

**Erma-Werke
Model KGP69**

**Model ESP-85A
Competition Pistol**

MODEL ER-773 MATCH. . . . . . NiB $957 Ex $831 Gd $587
Same general specifications as Model 772 except chambered for .32 S&W. Made from 1991 to 1995.

MODEL ER-777 MATCH. . . . . . NiB $923 Ex $785 Gd $623
Revolver. Caliber: .357 Magnum. Six-round cylinder. 4- or 5.5-inch bbl., 9.7 to 11.3 inches overall. Weight: 43.7 oz. (with 5.5-inch bbl.). Micrometer adj. rear sight. Checkered walnut sporter or match-style grip (interchangeable). Made from 1991 to 1995.

MODEL ESP-85A COMPETITION PISTOL
Calibers: .22 LR and .32 S&W Wadcutter. Eight- or 5-round magazine, 6-inch bbl., 10 inches overall. Weight: 40 oz. Adj. rear sight, blade front sight. Checkered walnut grip w/thumbrest. Made from 1991 to 1997.
Match model. . . . . NiB $1280 Ex $1128 Gd $716
Chrome match . . . . NiB $1540 Ex $1330 Gd $998
Sporting model . . . . NiB $1251 Ex $1049 Gd $735
Conversion unit .22 LR . . . . NiB $1566 Ex $1212 Gd $1030
Conversion unit .32 S&W . . NiB $1566 Ex $1212 Gd $1030

**European American Armory
Big Bore Bounty Hunter shown
w/optional scope**

MODEL KGP68
AUTOMATIC PISTOL . . . . **NiB $484 Ex $306 Gd $239**
Luger type. Calibers: .32 Auto (7.65mm), .380 Auto (9mm Short). Six-round magazine (.32 Auto), 5-round (.380 Auto), 4-inch bbl., 7.38 inches overall. Weight: 22.5 oz. Fixed sights. Blued finish. Checkered walnut grips. Made from 1968 to 1993.

MODEL KGP69
AUTOMATIC PISTOL . . . . **NiB $357 Ex $291 Gd $214**
Luger type. Caliber: .22 LR. Eight-round magazine, 4-inch bbl., 7.75 inches overall. Weight: 29 oz. fixed sights. Blued finish. Checkered walnut grips. Imported from 1969 to 1993.

EUROPEAN AMERICAN ARMORY —
Rockledge, Florida
See also listings under Astra Pistols.

EUROPEAN MODEL AUTO PISTOL
Calibers: .32 ACP (SA only), .380 ACP (SA or DA), 3.85-inch bbl., 7.38 overall, 7-round magazine, Weight: 26 oz. Blade front sight, drift-adj.
rear. Blued, chrome, blue/chrome, blue/gold, Duo-Tone or Wonder finish. Imported 1991 to date.
Blued .32 ACP (disc. 1995) . . . . **NiB $140 Ex $101 Gd $81**
**Blue/chrome .32 caliber
   (disc. 1995)** . . . . **NiB $204 Ex $117 Gd $81**
**Chrome .32 caliber
   (Disc. 1995)** . . . . **NiB $137 Ex $101 Gd $81**
Blued .380 caliber. . . . . **NiB $158 Ex $116 Gd $88**
**Blue/chrome .380 caliber
   (disc. 1993)** . . . . **NiB $204 Ex $136 Gd $91**
DA .380 caliber (disc. 1994). . . **NiB $398 Ex $267 Gd $167**
Lady .380 caliber (disc. 1995) . **NiB $270 Ex $203 Gd $143**
Wonder finish .380 caliber . . . . **NiB $275 Ex $186 Gd $131**

BIG BORE BOUNTY HUNTER SA REVOLVER
Calibers: .357 Mag., .41 Mag., .44-40, .44 Mag., .45 Colt. Bbl., lengths: 4.63, 5.5, 7.5 inches. Blade front and grooved topstrap rear sights. Blued or chrome finish w/color casehardened or gold-plated frame. Smooth walnut grips. Imported 1992.
Blued finish . . . . **NiB $377 Ex $255 Gd $189**
**Blued w/color-
   casehardened frame** . . . . **NiB $388 Ex $265 Gd $190**
Blued w/gold-plated frame . . . . **NiB $403 Ex $281 Gd $214**
Chrome finish . . . . **NiB $408 Ex $286 Gd $219**
Gold-plated frame, add. **$110**

BOUNTY HUNTER SA REVOLVER
Calibers: .22 LR, .22 Mag. Bbl. lengths: 4.75, 6 or 9 inches. Blade front and dovetailed rear sights. Blued finish or blued w/ gold-plated frame. European hardwood grips. Imported from 1997 to date.
Blued finish (4.75-inch bbl.) . . . **NiB $281 Ex $191 Gd $128**
**Blued .22 LR/.22 WRF combo
   (4.75-inch bbl.).** . . . . **NiB $281 Ex $191 Gd $128**
**Blued .22 LR/.22 WRF combo
   (6-inch bbl.)** . . . . **NiB $281 Ex $191 Gd $128**
**Blued .22 LR/.22 WRF combo
   (9-inch bbl.)** . . . . **NiB $281 Ex $191 Gd $128**

EA22 TARGET . . . . **NiB $398 Ex $281 Gd $214**
Caliber: .22 LR. 12-round magazine, 6-inch bbl., 9.10 inches overall. Weight: 40 oz. Ramp front sight, fully adj. rear. Blued finish. Checkered walnut grips w/thumbrest. Made from 1991 to 1994.

FAB 92 AUTO PISTOL
Similar to the Witness model except chambered in 9mm only w/slide-mounted safety and no cock-and-lock provision. Imported 1992 to 1995.
FAB 92 standard . . . . **NiB $437 Ex $342 Gd $223**
FAB 92 compact . . . . **NiB $437 Ex $342 Gd $223**

STANDARD GRADE REVOLVER
Calibers: .22 LR, .22 WRF, .32 H&R Mag., .38 Special. Two-, 4- or 6-inch bbl., blade front sight, fixed or adj. rear. Blued finish. European hardwood grips w/finger grooves. Imported 1991 to date.
.22 LR (4-inch bbl.) . . . . **NiB $215 Ex $171 Gd $128**
.22 LR (6-inch bbl.) . . . . **NiB $228 Ex $181 Gd $133**
.22 LR combo (4-inch bbl.) . . . . **NiB $301 Ex $237 Gd $171**
.22 LR combo (6-inch bbl.) . . . . **NiB $337 Ex $265 Gd $187**
**.32 H&R, .38 Special
   (2-inch bbl.)** . . . . **NiB $231 Ex $174 Gd $128**
.38 Special (4-inch bbl.) . . . . . . **NiB $235 Ex $187 Gd $132**
.357 Mag. . . . . **NiB $242 Ex $206 Gd $144**

TACTICAL GRADE REVOLVER
Similar to the Standard model except chambered in .38 Special only. Two- or 4-inch bbl., fixed sights. Available w/compensator. Imported from 1991-93.
Tactical revolver . . . . **NiB $229 Ex $185 Gd $109**
**Tactical revolver
   w/compensator** . . . . **NiB $316 Ex $270 Gd $192**

**European American Armory
Windicator Target**

European American Armory Witness

**WINDICATOR TARGET
REVOLVER** . . . . **NiB $444 Ex $381 Gd $255**
Calibers: .22 LR, .38 Special, .357 Magnum. Eight-round cylinder in .22 LR, 6-round in .38 Special and .357 Magnum. Six-inch bbl. w/bbl. weights. 11.8 inches overall. Weight: 50.2 oz. Interchangeable blade front sight, fully adj. rear. Walnut competition-style grips. Imported from 1991-93.

WITNESS DA AUTO PISTOL
Similar to the Brno CZ-75 w/a cocked-and-locked system. Double or single action. Calibers: 9mm Para. .38 Super, .40 S&W, 10mm; .41 AE and .45 ACP. 16-round magazine (9mm), 12 shot (.38 Super/.40 S&W), or 10-round (10mm/.45 ACP), 4.75-inch bbl., 8.10 inches overall. Weight: 35.33 oz. Blade front sight, rear sight adj. for windage w/3-dot sighting system. Steel or polymer frame. Blued, satin chrome, blue/chrome, stainless or Wonder finish. Checkered rubber grips. EA Series imported 1991 to date.
9mm blue . . . . **NiB $475 Ex $337 Gd $249**
9mm chrome or blue/chrome. . **NiB $475 Ex $337 Gd $249**
9mm stainless . . . . **NiB $469 Ex $337 Gd $283**
9mm Wonder finish . . . . **NiB $500 Ex $356 Gd $265**
.38 Super and .40 S&W blued . **NiB $475 Ex $337 Gd $237**
**.38 Super and .40 S&W chrome
   or blue/chrome** . . . . **NiB $469 Ex $388 Gd $273**
**.38 Super and .40 S&W
   stainless** . . . . **NiB $546 Ex $425 Gd $292**
.38 Super and .40 S&W Wonder finish. . . **NiB $577 Ex $340
   Gd $296**
**10mm, .41 AE and .45 ACP
   blued**. . . . . **NiB $474 Ex $346 Gd $235**
**10mm, .41 AE and .45 ACP
   chrome or blue/chrome** . . . . **NiB $546 Ex $437 Gd $316**
**10mm, .41 AE and .45 ACP
   stainless** . . . . **NiB $577 Ex $464 Gd $337**
**10mm, .41 AE and
   .45 ACP Wonder finish** . . . . . **NiB $562 Ex $439 Gd $321**

WITNESS COMPACT DA AUTO PISTOL (L SERIES)
Similar to the standard Witness series except more compact w/ 3.625-inch bbl., and polymer or steel frame. Weight: 30 oz. Matte blued or Wonder finish. Imported 1999 to date.
9mm blue . . . . **NiB $468 Ex $330 Gd $235**
9mm Wonder finish . . . . **NiB $468 Ex $330 Gd $235**
.38 Super and .40 S&W blued . **NiB $468 Ex $330 Gd $235**
**.38 Super and .40 S&W Wonder
   finish**. . . . . **NiB $468 Ex $330 Gd $235**

**10mm, .41 AE and .45 ACP
   blued**. . . . . **NiB $549 Ex $369 Gd $273**
**10mm, .41 AE and .45 ACP
   Wonder fin.** . . . . **NiB $549 Ex $369 Gd $273**
w/ported bbl., add $50

WITNESS CARRY COMP
Double/Single action. Calibers: .38 Super, 9mm Parabellum, .40 S&W, 10mm, .45 ACP. 10-, 12- or 16-round magazine, 4.25-inch bbl., w/1-inch compensator. Weight: 33 oz., 8.10 inches overall. Black rubber grips. Post front sight, drift adjustable rear w/3-dot system. Matte blue, Duo-Tone or Wonder finish. Imported 1992 to 2004.
9mm, .40 S&W . . . . **NiB $453 Ex $359 Gd $273**
.38 Super, 10mm, .45 ACP . . . . **NiB $453 Ex $359 Gd $273**
w/Duo-Tone finish (disc.), add $40
w/Wonder finish, add $20

WITNESS LIMITED CLASS . . . . **NiB $909 Ex $734 Gd $559**
Single action. Semi-automatic. Calibers: .38 Super, 9mm Parabellum, .40 S&W, .45 ACP. 10-round magazine, 4.75-inch bbl., Weight: 37 oz. Checkered competition-style walnut grips. Long slide w/post front sight, fully adj. rear. Matte blue finish. Imported 1994 to 1998.

WITNESS SUBCOMPACT DA AUTO PISTOL
Calibers: 9mm Para., .40 S&W, 41 AK, .45 ACP. 13-round magazine in 9mm, 9-round in .40 S&W, 3.66-inch bbl., 7.25 inches overall. Weight: 30 oz. Blade front sight, rear sight adj. for windage. Blued, satin chrome or blue/chrome finish. Imported from 1995 to 1997.
9mm blue . . . . **NiB $408 Ex $281 Gd $204**
9mm chrome or blue/chrome. . **NiB $453 Ex $306 Gd $225**
.40 S&W blue . . . . **NiB $453 Ex $306 Gd $225**
**.40 S&W chrome or
   blue/chrome** . . . . **NiB $497 Ex $366 Gd $229**
.41 AE blue . . . . **NiB $525 Ex $429 Gd $308**
**.41 AE chrome or
   blue/chrome** . . . . **NiB $577 Ex $448 Gd $319**
.45 ACP blued. . . . . **NiB $525 Ex $336 Gd $308**
**.45 ACP chrome
   or blue/chrome**. . . . . **NiB $500 Ex $439 Gd $321**

WITNESS TARGET PISTOLS
Similar to standard Witness model except fitted w/2- or 3-port compensator, competition frame and S/A target trigger. Calibers: 9mm Para., 9x21, .40 S&W, 10mm and .45 ACP, 5.25-inch match bbl., 10.5 inches overall. Weight: 38 oz. Square post front sight, fully adj. rear or drilled and tapped for scope. Blued or hard chrome finish. Low-profile competition grips. Imported 1992 to date.
**Silver Team (blued w/2-port
   compensator)** . . . . **NiB $895 Ex $785 Gd $561**
**Gold Team (chrome
   w/3-port compensator)** . . . **NiB $1810 Ex $1632 Gd $1331**

FAS — Malino, Italy
Currently imported by Nygord Precision Products.
Previously by Beeman Precision Arms and Osborne's, Cheboygan, MI.

OP601 SEMIAUTOMATIC MATCH TARGET PISTOL
Caliber: .22 Short. Five-round top-loading magazine, 5.6-inch ported and ventilated bbl., 11 inches overall. Weight:

Feather Guardian Angel Derringer

FEG Mark II AP-.22

41.5 oz. Removable, adj. trigger group. Blade front sight, open-notch fully adj. rear. Stippled walnut wraparound or adj. target grips.
Right-hand model . . . . NiB $1076 Ex $930 Gd $714
Left-hand model . . . . NiB $1153 Ex $985 Gd $755

602 SEMIAUTOMATIC MATCH TARGET PISTOL
Similar to Model FAS 601 except chambered for .22 LR. Weight: 37 oz.
Right-hand model . . . . NiB $960 Ex $705 Gd $581
Left-hand model . . . . NiB $1030 Ex $830 Gd $691

CF603 SEMIAUTOMATIC
MATCH TARGET PISTOL . . . . NiB $1030 Ex $816 Gd $647
Similar to Model FAS 601 except chambered for .32 S&W (wadcutter).

SP607 SEMIAUTOMATIC
MATCH TARGET PISTOL . . . . NiB $1030 Ex $804 Gd $658
Similar to Model FAS 601 except chambered for .22 LR, w/ removable bbl. weights. Imported 1995 to date.

FEATHER INDUSTRIES — Boulder, Colorado

GUARDIAN ANGEL DERRINGER
Double-action over/under derringer w/interchangeable drop-in loading blocks. Calibers: .22 LR, .22 WMR, 9mm, .38

Spec. Two-round capacity, 2-inch bbl., 5 inches overall. weight: 12 oz. Stainless steel. Checkered black grip. Made 1988 to 1995.
.22 LR, .22 WMR . . . . NiB 165 Ex $101 Gd $81
9mm, .38 Special (disc. 1989) . . . NiB $233 Ex $189 Gd $150

FEG (FEGYVERGYAN) — Budapest, Soroksariut, Hungary

Currently imported by KBI, Inc. and Century International Arms. Previously by Interarms.

MARK II AP-.22 DA
AUTOMATIC PISTOL . . . . NiB $271 Ex $219 Gd $179
Caliber: .22 LR. 8-round magazine, 3.4-inch bbl., Weight: 23 oz. Drift-adj. sights. Double action, all-steel pistol. Imported 1997 to 1998.

MARK II AP-.380 DA AUTOMATIC
PISTOL . . . . NiB $271 Ex $219 Gd $179
Caliber: .380. 7-round magazine, 3.9-inch bbl., weight 27 oz. Drift-adj. sights. Double action, all-steel pistol. Imported 1997 to 1998.

MARK II APK-.380 DA AUTOMATIC
PISTOL . . . . NiB $271 Ex $219 Gd $179
Caliber: .380. 7-round magazine, 3.4-inch bbl., weight: 25 oz. Drift-adj. sights. Double action, all-steel pistol. Imported 1997 to 1998.

MODEL GKK-9 (92C)
AUTO PISTOL . . . . NiB $321 Ex $240 Gd $204
Improved version of the double-action FEG Model MBK. Caliber: 9mm Para. 14-round magazine, 4-inch bbl., 7.4 inches overall. Weight: 34 oz. Blade front sight, rear sight adj. for windage. Checkered wood grips. Blued finish. Imported from 1992 to 1993.

MODEL GKK-.45 AUTO PISTOL
Improved version of the double-action FEG Model MBK. Caliber: .45 ACP. Eight-round magazine, 4.1-inch bbl., 7.75 inches overall. Weight: 36 oz. Blade front sight, adj. rear sight w/3-dot system. Checkered walnut grips. Blued or chrome finish. Imported 1993 to 1996.
Blued model (disc. 1994) . . . . . NiB $325 Ex $265 Gd $204
Chrome model . . . . NiB $362 Ex $281 Gd $220

MODEL MBK-9HP
AUTO PISTOL . . . . NiB $469 Ex $306 Gd $281
Similar to the double-action Browning Hi-Power. Caliber: 9mm Para. 14-round magazine, 4.6-inch bbl., 8 inches overall. Weight: 36 oz. Blade front sight, rear sight adj. for windage. Checkered wood grips. Blued finish. Imported 1992 to 1993.

Model PA-63 AUTO PISTOL . . . . Ex $175 Gd $95
Hungary's military pistol. Similar to the Walther PP. Caliber: 9x18mm Makarov. 7-round magazine, 3.95-inch bbl., 6.9 inches overall. Weight: 21 oz. Fixed sights. Two-tone finish; blued slide natutal aluminum frame. Checkered plasic grips. Military surplus.

MODEL PJK-9HP AUTO PISTOL
Similar to the single-action Browning Hi-Power. Caliber: 9mm Para. 13-round magazine, 4.75-inch bbl., 8 inches overall. Weight: 21 oz. Blade front sight, rear sight adj. for windage

FEG Model PJK-9HP

F.I.E. Model A27BW

F.I.E. Arminius

w/3-dot system. Checkered walnut or rubber grips. Blued or chrome finish. Imported 1992 to 2003.
Blued model . . . . NiB $469 Ex $388 Gd $265
Chrome model . . . . NiB $500 Ex $408 Gd $316

MODEL PSP-.25 AUTO PISTOL
Similar to the Browning .25. Caliber: .25 ACP. Six-round magazine, 2.1-inch bbl., 4.1 inches overall. Weight: 9.5 oz. Fixed sights. Checkered composition grips. Blued or chrome finish.
Blued model . . . . NiB $316 Ex $204 Gd $150
Chrome model . . . . NiB $316 Ex $204 Gd $150

MODEL SMC-.22 . . . . NiB $222 Ex $130 Gd $79
Same general specifications as FEG Model SMC-.380 except in .22 LR. Eight-round magazine, 3.5-inch bbl., 6.1 inches overall. Weight: 18.5 oz. Blade front sight, rear sight adj. for

windage. Checkered composition grips w/thumbrest. Blued finish.

MODEL SMC-.380 . . . . NiB $222 Ex $130 Gd $79
Similar to the Walther DA PPK w/alloy frame. Caliber: .380 ACP. Six-round magazine, 3.5-inch bbl., 6.1 inches overall. Weight: 18.5 oz. Blade front sight, rear sight adj. for windage. Checkered composition grips w/ thumbrest. Blued finish. Imported 1993 to 1997.

MODEL SMC-918 . . . . NiB $203 Ex $120 Gd $90
Same general specifications as FEG Model SMC-.380 except chambered in 9x18mm Makarov. Imported from 1994 to 1997.

FIALA OUTFITTERS, INC. — New York

REPEATING PISTOL . . . . NiB $689 Ex $479 Gd $365
Hand-operated, not semi-auto. Caliber: .22 LR. 10-round magazine, bbl. lengths: 3-, 7.5- and 20-inch. 11.25 inches overall (with 7.5-inch bbl.). Weight: 31 oz. (with 7.5-inch bbl.). Target sights. Blued finish. Plain wood grips. Shoulder stock was originally supplied for use w/20-inch bbl. Made from 1920 to 1923. Value shown is for pistol w/one bbl., no shoulder stock. Three bbl. cased sets start at $3,030.

F.I.E. CORPORATION — Hialeah, Florida
The F.I.E. Corporation became QFI (Quality Firearms Corp.) of Opa Locka, Fl., about 1990, when most of F.I.E.'s models were discontinued.

MODEL A27 "THE BEST"
SEMI-AUTO . . . . NiB $140 Ex $95 Gd $55
Caliber: .25 ACP. Six-round magazine, 2.5-inch bbl., 6.75 inches overall. Weight: 13 oz. Fixed sights. Checkered walnut grip. Discontinued in 1990.

ARMINIUS DA STANDARD REVOLVER
Calibers: .22 LR, .22 combo w/interchangeable cylinder, .32 S&W, .38 Special, .357 Magnum. Six, 7 or 8 rounds depending on caliber. Swing-out cylinder. bbl., lengths: 2-, 3-, 4, 6-inch. Vent rib on calibers other than .22, 11 inches overall (with 6-inch bbl.). Weight: 26 to 30 oz. Fixed or micro-adj. sights. Checkered plastic or walnut grips. Blued finish. Made in Germany. Disc.
.22 LR . . . . NiB $130 Ex $89 Gd $67
.22 Combo . . . . NiB $198 Ex $148 Gd $101
.32 S&W . . . . NiB $207 Ex $149 Gd $101
.38 Special . . . . NiB $161 Ex $95 Gd $70
.357 Magnum . . . . NiB $240 Ex $179 Gd $135

BUFFALO SCOUT SA REVOLVER
Calibers: .22 LR, .22 WRF, .22 combo w/interchangeable cylinder. 4.75-inch bbl., 10 inches overall. Weight: 32 oz. Adjustable sights. Blued or chrome finish. Smooth walnut or black checkered nylon grips. Made in Italy. Disc.
Blued standard . . . . NiB $84 Ex $62 Gd $40
Blued convertible . . . . NiB $91 Ex $62 Gd $40
Chrome standard . . . . NiB $91 Ex $62 Gd $40
Chrome convertible . . . . NiB $91 Ex $62 Gd $40

HOMBRE SA REVOLVER . . . . . . NiB $230 Ex $179 Gd $105
Calibers: .357 Magnum, .44 Magnum, .45 Colt. Six-round cylinder. bbl. lengths: 6 or 7.5 inches, 11 inches overall (with -inch bbl.). Weight: 45 oz. (6-inch bbl.). Fixed sights.

F.I.E. Titan Tiger

F.I.E. Titan II

F.I.E. Model TZ75

Firearms International Model D

Blued bbl., w/color-casehardened receiver. Smooth walnut grips. Made from 1979 to 1990.

SUPER TITAN II
Caliber: .32 ACP or .380 ACP, 3.25-inch bbl., weight: 28 oz. Blued or chrome finish. Disc. 1990.

.32 ACP blue;	NiB $138	Ex $95	Gd $70
.32 ACP chrome	NiB $138	Ex $95	Gd $70
.380 ACP blue;	NiB $138	Ex $95	Gd $70
.380 ACP chrome	NiB $138	Ex $95	Gd $70

TEXAS RANGER SINGLE-ACTION REVOLVER
Calibers: .22 LR, .22 WRF, .22 combo w/interchangeable cylinder. bbl., lengths: 4.75-, 6.5-, 9-inch. 10 inches overall (with 4.75-inch bbl.). Weight: 32 oz. (with 4.75-inch bbl.). Fixed sights. Blued finish. Smooth walnut grips. Made 1983 to 1990.

Standard	NiB $97	Ex $75	Gd $55
Convertible	NiB $97	Ex $75	Gd $55

LITTLE RANGER SA REVOLVER
Same as the TExas Ranger except w/3.25-inch bbl. and bird's-head grips. Made from 1986 to 1990.

Standard	NiB $97	Ex $75	Gd $55
Convertible	NiB $109	Ex $81	Gd $61

TITAN TIGER DA REVOLVER ..... NiB $78 Ex $47 Gd $35
Caliber: .38 Special. Six-round cylinder, 2- or 4-inch bbl., 8.25 inches overall (with 4-inch bbl.). Weight: 30 oz. (4-inch bbl.). Fixed sights. Blued finish. Checkered plastic or walnut grips. Made in the U.S. Disc. 1990.

TITAN II SEMIAUTOMATIC
Caiibers: .22 LR, .32 ACP, .380 ACP. 10-round magazine, integral tapered post front sight, windage-adjustable rear sight. European walnut grips. Blued or chrome finish. Disc. 1990.

.22 LR in blue	NiB $140	Ex $108	Gd $88
.32 ACP in blued	NiB $211	Ex $170	Gd $128
.32 ACP in chrome	NiB $221	Ex $176	Gd $141
.380 ACP in blue	NiB $221	Ex $176	Gd $141
.380 ACP in chrome	NiB $235	Ex $181	Gd $158

MODEL TZ75 DA SEMIAUTOMATIC
Double action. Caliber: 9mm. 15-round magazine, 4.5-inch bbl., 8.25 inches overall. Weight: 35 oz. Ramp front sight, windage-adjustable rear sight. European walnut or black rubber grips. Imported from 1988 to 1990.

Blued finish	NiB $387	Ex $302	Gd $214
Satin chrome	NiB $425	Ex $321	Gd $255

YELLOW ROSE SA REVOLVER
Same general specifications as the Buffalo Scout except in .22 combo w/interchangeable cylinder and plated in 24-karat gold. Limited Edition w/scrimshawed ivory polymer grips and American walnut presentation case. Made from 1987 to 1990.

Yellow Rose .22 combo	NiB $140	Ex $93	Gd $59
Yellow Rose Limited Edition	NiB $292	Ex $229	Gd $188

FIREARMS INTERNATIONAL CORP. — Washington, D.C.

MODEL D AUTOMATIC PISTOL NiB $219 Ex $179 Gd $95
Caliber: .380 Automatic. Six-round magazine, 3.3-inch bbl., 6.13 inches overall. Weight: 19.5 oz. Blade front sight, windage-adjustable rear sight. Blued, chromed, or military finish. Checkered walnut grips. Made from 1974 to 1977.

**Firearms
International Regent**

**FN Browning
6.35mm Pocket**

**FN Browning
1900 Pocket**

**FN Browning 1910
Pocket**

REGENT DA REVOLVER . . . . . . NiB $189 Ex $130 Gd $101
Calibers: .22 LR, .32 S&W Long. Eight-round cylinder (.22 LR), or 7-round (.32 S&W). Bbl. lengths: 3-, 4-, 6-inches (.22 LR) or 2.5-, 4-inches (.32 S&W). Weight: 28 oz.(with 4-inch bbl.). Fixed sights. Blued finish. Plastic grips. Made 1966-72.

FN BROWNING — Liege, Belgium. Mfd. by Fabrique Nationale Herstal

See also Browning handguns

6.35MM POCKET AUTO PISTOL
See FN Browning Baby Auto Pistol.

**MODEL 1900 POCKET
AUTO PISTOL** . . . . NiB $842 Ex $702 Gd $485
Caliber: .32 Automatic (7.65mm). Seven-round magazine, 4-inch bbl., 6.75 inches overall. Weight: 22 oz. Fixed sights. Blued finish. Hard rubber grips. Made from 1899 to 1910.

MODEL 1903 MILITARY AUTO PISTOL
Caliber: 9mm Browning Long. Seven-round magazine, 5-inch bbl., 8 inches overall. Weight: 32 oz. Fixed sights. Blued finish. Hard rubber grips. Note: Aside from size, this pistol is of the same basic design as the Colt Pocket .32 and .380 Automatic pistols. Made from 1903 to 1939.
Standard. . . . . NiB $1285 Ex $1152 Gd $880
w/slotted backstrap. . . . . NiB $1285 Ex $1152 Gd $880
**w/slotted backstrap, shoulder stock
   and extended magazine** . . NiB $2525 Ex $2270 Gd $1790

**MODEL 1910
POCKET AUTO PISTOL** . . . . . . NiB $577 Ex $431 Gd $286
Calibers: .32 Auto (7.65mm), .380 Auto (9mm). Seven-round magazine (.32 cal.), or 6-round (.380 cal.), 3.5-inch bbl., 6 inches overall. Weight: 20.5 oz. Fixed sights. Blued finish. Hard rubber grips. Made from 1910 to 1954.

MODEL 1922 (10/.22) POLICE/MILITARY AUTO
Calibers: .32 Auto (7.65mm), .380 Auto (9mm). Nine-round magazine (.32 cal.), or 8-round (.380 cal.), 4.5-inch bbl., 7 inches overall. Weight: 25 oz. Fixed sights. Blued finish. Hard rubber grips. Made from 1922 to 1959.
Model 1922 commercial. . . . . . NiB $459 Ex $326 Gd $265
Model 1922 Military contract . . NiB $414 Ex $301 Gd $204
Model 1922 (w/Nazi proofs) . . NiB $414 Ex $326 Gd $265

MODEL 1935 MILITARY HI-POWER PISTOL
Variation of the Browning-Colt .45 Auto design. Caliber: 9mm Para.13-round magazine, 4.63-inch bbl., 7.75 inches overall. Weight: About 35 oz. Adjustable rear sight and fixed front, or both fixed. Blued finish (Canadian manufacture Parkerized). Checkered walnut or plastic grips. Note: Above specifications in general apply to both the original FN production and the pistols made by John Inglis Company of Canada for the Chinese government. A smaller version, w/shorter bbl. and slide and 10-round magazine, was made by FN for the Belgian and Rumanian Governments about 1937 to 191940. Both types were made at the FN plant during the German occupation of Belgium.
**Pre-war commercial
   (w/fixed sights)** . . . . NiB $1152 Ex $918 Gd $729
**Pre-war commercial
   (w/tangent sight only)** . . . . NiB $2040 Ex $1347 Gd $712

**FN Browning 1922
Police/Military**

**FN Browning 1935
Military Hi-Power**

**FN Browning
Baby**

**Pre-war commercial
(w/tangent sight, slotted
backstrap)** . . . . NiB $3014 Ex $2652 Gd $1448
**Pre-war Belgian military
contract** . . . . NiB $1234 Ex $1020 Gd $704
**Pre-war Foreign military
contract** . . . . NiB $2212 Ex $1785 Gd $1225
**War production
(w/fixed sights)** . . . . NiB $861 Ex $674 Gd $485
**War production
(w/tangent sight only)** . . . . NiB $1405 Ex $1133 Gd $783
**War production (w/tangent sight and slotted
backstrap)** . . . . NiB $3488 Ex $2770 Gd $1913
**Post-war/pre-BAC
(w/fixed sights)** . . . . NiB $842 Ex $577 Gd $392
**Post-war/pre-BAC
(w/tangent sight only)** . . . . . . NiB $893 Ex $577 Gd $392
**Post-war/pre-BAC (w/tangent sight,
slotted backstrap)** . . . . NiB $663 Ex $784 Gd $756

**Inglis manufacture Canadian military
(w/fixed sights)** . . . . NiB $1015 Ex $743 Gd $571
**Canadian military
(w/fixed sight, slotted)** . . . . NiB $1871 Ex $1494 Gd $1021
**Canadian military
(w/tangent sight, slotted)** . . . NiB $1533 Ex $1235 Gd $884
**Canadian military
(marked w/Inglis logo)** . . . . NiB $2654 Ex $2149 Gd $1462
**Chinese military contract
(w/tangent sight, slotted)** . . NiB $3421 Ex $2754 Gd $1876
**Canadian military
(w/fixed sight, slotted backstrap)** . . . NiB $1879 Ex $1503
Gd $1029
**Canadian military (marked
w/Inglis logo)** . . . . NiB $2642 Ex $2147 Gd $1460
w/issue wooden holster, add. $408

BABY AUTO PISTOL . . . . NiB $638 Ex $530 Gd $377
Caliber: .25 Automatic (6.35mm). Six-round magazine, 2.13-
inch bbl., 4 inches overall. Weight: 10 oz. Fixed sights. Blued
finish. Hard rubber grips. Made from 1931 to 1983.

FOREHAND & WADSWORTH —
Worcester, Massachusetts

*See listings of comparable Harrington & Richardson and Iver
Johnson revolvers for values.*

FORT WORTH FIREARMS — Fort Worth, Texas

MATCH MASTER STANDARD . . . NiB $499 Ex $283 Gd $225
Semi-automatic. Caliber: .22LR. Equipped with 3 7/8-, 4 1/2-,
5 1/2-, 7 1/2- or 10-inch bull bbl., double Extractors, includes
upper push button and standard magazine release, angled grip,
low profile frame. Made from 1995 to 2000.

MATCH MASTER DOVETAIL . . . . NiB $500 Ex $408 Gd $321
Similar to Match Master except has 3 7/8-, 4 1/2-, or 5 1/2-inch
bbl. with dovetail rib.

MATCH MASTER DELUXE . . . . NiB $581 Ex $464 Gd $367
Similar to Match master Standard except has Weaver rib on bbl.
w/10-in. bbl., add. $128

SPORT KING. . . . . NiB $601 Ex $321 Gd $270
Semi-automatic. Caliber: .22 LR. Equipped with 4 1/2- or 5
1/2-inch bbl., blued finish, military grips, drift sights, 10 round
magazine. Made from 1995 to 2000.

CITATION . . . . NiB $439 Ex $319 Gd $265
Semi-automatic. Caliber: .22 LR. Equipped with 5 1/2-inch bull
bbl. or 7 1/2-inch fluted bbl., military grips, 10-round magazine.

TROPHY . . . . NiB $433 Ex $332 Gd $270
Semi-automatic. Caliber: .22 LR. Equipped with 5 1/2- or 7 1/2-
inch bull bbl. blued finish, military grips, 10-round magazine.
w/LH action (5 1/2-inch bbl. only), add $65

VICTOR . . . . NiB $499 Ex $398 Gd $301
Semi-automatic. Caliber: .22LR. Equipped with 3 7/8-, 4 1/2-
(VR or Weaver rib), 8- (Weaver rib) or 10-inch (Weaver rib)
bbls.; blued finish, military grips, 10-round magazine.

w/4 1/2- or 4 1/2-inch Weaver rib bbls, add $100
w/8- or 10-inch Weaver rib bbls, add $190

OLYMPIC . . . . NiB $668 Ex $525 Gd $410
Semi-automatic. Caliber: .22 LR or Short. Equipped with 6 1/2-inch fluted bbl., blued finish, military grips, 10-round magazine.

SHARPSHOOTER . . . . NiB $499 Ex $365 Gd $259
Semi-automatic. Caliber: .22 LR. Equipped with 5 1/2-inch bull bbl.,blued finish, military grips, 10-round magazine.

Freedom Arms
Model 83 Varmint

LE FRANCAIS — St. Etienne, France
Produced by Manufacture Francaise d'Armes et Cycles.

ARMY MODEL
AUTOMATIC PISTOL . . . . . . NiB $1749 Ex $1305 Gd $842
Similar in operation to the Le Francais .25 Automatics. Caliber: 9mm Browning Long. Eight-round magazine, 5-inch bbl., 7.75 inches overall. Weight: About 34 oz. Fixed sights. Blued finish. Checkered walnut grips. Made from 1928 to 1938.

POLICEMAN MODEL
AUTOMATIC PISTOL . . . . NiB $1020 Ex $917 Gd $416
DA. Hinged bbl., Caliber: .25 Automatic (6.35mm). Seven-round magazine, 3.5-inch bbl., 6 inches overall. Weight: About 12 oz. Fixed sights. Blued finish. Hard rubber grips. Introduced in 1914. disc.

STAFF OFFICER MODEL
AUTOMATIC PISTOL . . . . NiB $388 Ex $301 Gd $205
Caliber: .25 Automatic. Similar to the "Policeman" model except no cocking-piece head, barrel, is about an inch shorter and weight is an ounce less. Introduced in 1914. disc.

FREEDOM ARMS — Freedom, Wyoming

MODEL 97 PREMIER GRADE SA REVOLVER
Calibers: .17 HMR, .22 LR, .224-32 F.A., .327 Fed., .32 H&R Mag., .357 Mag., .41 Mag. or .45 LC. Five- or 6-round cylinder, 4.25, 5, 5.5, 6 or 7.5-inch bbl., removable front blade with adjustable or fixed rear sight. Hardwood or black Micarta grips. Satin stainless finish. Made from 1997 to date.
Premier grade 97 . . . . NiB $2178 Ex $1775 Gd $890
w/extra cylinder, add $225
w/fixed sights, deduct. $150

MODEL 83 FIELD GRADE
SA REVOLVER . . . . NiB $2283 Ex $1825 Gd $870
Calibers: .22LR, .357 Mag., .41 Mag., .44 Mag., .454 Casull, .475 Linebaugh , .50 AE or .500 Wyoming Express. Five-round cylinder, bbl. lengths: 4.75-, 6-, 7.5-, 9- or 10-in. Adj. sight or fixed. Impregnated hardwood grips. Brushed matte stainless steel finish. Made from 1988 to date.

MODEL 83 FIELD GRADE HUNTER PACK
SA REVOLVER . . . . NiB $1160 Ex $900 Gd $710
Similar to Model 83 Field Grade except calibers: .357 Mag., .44 Mag., or .454 Casull only. 7.5-in. bbl., sling studs. Made from 1990 to 1993.

MODEL 83 PREMIER GRADE
SA REVOLVER . . . . NiB $2686 Ex $2175 Gd $1000

Calibers: .357 Mag., .41 Mag., .44 Mag., .454 Casull, .475 Linebaugh, .50 AE or .500 Wyoming Express.Adjustable sight or fixed. Impregnated hardwood grips. Brushed bright stainless steel finish. Made from 1983 to date.

MODEL 83 PREMIER GRADE HUNTER PACK
SA REVOLVER . . . . NiB $1400 Ex $930 Gd $760
Similar to Model 83 Field Grade except calibers: .357 Mag., .44 Mag., or .454 Casull only. 7.5-in. bbl., sling studs. Made from 1990 to 1993.

MODEL 83 RIMFIRE GRADE
SA REVOLVER . . . . NiB $2484 Ex $1525 Gd $800
Calibers: .22 LR. Bbl. length: 10-in. Adjustable sights. Brushed matte stainless finish. Rosewood grips. Made from 1991 to date.

MODEL 83 SILHOUETTE GRADE (RIMFIRE)
SA REVOLVER . . . . NiB $2603 Ex $1875 Gd $830
Calibers: .22 LR. Bbl. lengths: 5.13 or 10 inches. Adjustable competition silhouette sights. Brushed or matte stainless finish. Black Micarta grips. Made from 1991 to date.

MODEL 83 SILHOUETTE GRADE (CENTERFIRE)
SA REVOLVER . . . . NiB $2318 Ex $1975 Gd $1000
Calibers: .357 Mag., .41 Mag., or .44 Mag. Bbl. lengths: 9- or 10-in. Removable blade front sight w/hood, adjustable rear. Brushed matte stainless finish. Wood grips.
.454 Casull . . . . NiB $1600 Ex $1080 Gd $850

MODEL U.S. DEPUTY MARSHAL
SA REVOLVER . . . . NiB $1330 Ex $780 Gd $540
Bbl. lengths: 3-in. Adj. or fixed sights. No ejector rod. Brushed matte stainless. Made from 1990 to 1993.

MODEL FA-L-22LR
MINI-REVOLVER . . . . NiB $204 Ex $159 Gd $103
Caliber: .22 LR, 1.75-inch contoured bbl., partial high-gloss stainless steel finish. Bird's-head-type grips. Disc. 1987.

MODEL FA-S-22LR
MINI-REVOLVER . . . . NiB $214 Ex $189 Gd $105
Caliber: .22 LR. One-inch contoured bbl., partial high-gloss stainless steel finish. Disc. 1988.
w/1.75-in. bbl . . . . NiB $204 Ex $159 Gd $103
w/3-in. bbl . . . . NiB $237 Ex $165 Gd $128

MODEL FA-S-22M
MINI-REVOLVER . . . . NiB $189 Ex $135 Gd $101
Same general specifications as Model FA-S-22LR except in caliber .22 WMR. Disc. 1988.

FRENCH MILITARY PISTOLS — Cholet, France
Manufactured originally by Société Alsacienne de Constructions Mécaniques (S.A.C.M.). Currently made by

Manufacture d'Armes Automatiques, Lotissement Industriel des Pontots, Bayonne.

MODEL 1935A
AUTOMATIC PISTOL . . . . NiB $377 Ex $274 Gd $143
Caliber: 7.65mm Long. Eight-round magazine, 4.3-inch bbl., 7.6 inches overall. Weight: 26 oz. Two-lug locking system similar to the Colt U.S. M1911A1. Fixed sights. Blued finish. Checkered grips. Made 1935-45. Note: This pistol was used by French troops during WW II and in Indo-China 1945 to 1954.

MODEL 1935S
AUTOMATIC PISTOL . . . . NiB $342 Ex $281 Gd $135
Similar to Model 1935A except 4.1-inch bbl., 7.4 inches overall and 28 oz. Single-step lug locking system.

MODEL 1950
AUTOMATIC PISTOL . . . . NiB $485 Ex $397 Gd $270
Caliber: 9mm Para. Nine-round magazine, 4.4-inch bbl., 7.6 inches overall. Weight: 30 oz. Fixed sights, tapered post front and U-notched rear. Similar in design and function to the U.S. .45 service automatic except no bbl. bushing.

MODEL MAB F1
AUTOMATIC PISTOL . . . . NiB $653 Ex $587 Gd $270
Similar to Model MAB P-15 except w/6-inch bbl. and 9.6 inches overall. Adjustable target-style sights. Parkerized finish.

MODEL MAB P-8
AUTOMATIC PISTOL . . . . NiB $576 Ex $464 Gd $342
Similar to Model MAB P-15 except w/8-round magazine,

MODEL MAB P-15
AUTOMATIC PISTOL . . . . NiB $632 Ex $474 Gd $385
Caliber: 9mm Para. 15-round magazine, 4.5-inch bbl., 7.9 inches overall. Weight: 38 oz. Fixed sights, tapered post front and U-notched rear.

FROMMER — Budapest, Hungary
Manufactured by Fémáru-Fegyver-és Gépgyár R.T.

LILIPUT POCKET
AUTOMATIC PISTOL . . . . NiB $437 Ex $362 Gd $240
Caliber: .25 Automatic (6.35mm). Six-round magazine, 2.14-inch bbl., 4.33 inches overall. Weight: 10.13 oz. Fixed sights. Blued finish. Hard rubber grips. Made during early 1920s. Note: Although similar in appearance to the Stop and Baby, this pistol is designed for blowback operation.

Frommer Stop

STOP POCKET
AUTOMATIC PISTOL . . . . NiB $414 Ex $321 Gd $165
Locked-breech action, outside hammer. Calibers: .32 Automatic (7.65mm), .380 Auto (9mm short). Seven-round (.32 cal.) or 6-round (.380 cal.) magazine, 3.88-inch bbl., 6.5 inches overall. Weight: About 21 oz. Fixed sights. Blued finish. Hard rubber grips. Made 1912 to 1920.

BABY POCKET
AUTOMATIC PISTOL . . . . NiB $321 Ex $262 Gd $143
Similar to Stop model except has 2-inch bbl., 4.75 inches overall. Weight 17.5 oz. Magazine capacity is one round less than Stop Model. Intro. shortly after WW I.

GALENA INDUSTRIES INC. — Sturgis, South Dakota
Galena Industries purchased the rights to use the AMT trademark in 1998. Many, but not all, original AMT designs were included in the transaction.

AMT BACKUP. . . . . NiB $474 Ex $291 Gd $219
Caliber: .380 (small frame, 2.5-inch bbl. only), .38 Super, .357 Sig, .40 S&W, .400 CorBon, .45 ACP, 9mm; magazine capacity: 5 or 6 rounds. Double action, 3-inch bbl., weight: 18 oz. (in .380), or 23 oz.
.38 Super, .357 Sig, .400 CorBon, add. $75

AUTOMAG II SEMI AUTO . . . . NiB $831 Ex $587 Gd $321
Caliber: .22 WMR, 9-round magazine (except 7-round in 3.38-inch bbl.); 3.38- 4.5- or 6-inch bbls.; weight: About 32 oz.

AUTOMAG III . . . . NiB $561 Ex $500 Gd $377
Similar to Automag II except chambered for the .30 Carbine cartridge, 6.38-inch bbl., stainless steel finish, weight: About 43 oz.

AUTOMAG IV. . . . . NiB $561 Ex $500 Gd $377
Caliber: .45 Winchester Magnum; 7-round magazine, 6.5-inch bbl., weight: 46 oz.

AUTOMAG .440 CORBON. . . . NiB $816 Ex $689 Gd $571
Semiautomatic, 7.5-inch bbl., 5-round magazine, checkered walnut grips, matte black finish, weight: 46 oz. Intro. in 2000.

COMMANDO. . . . . NiB $474 Ex $326 Gd $220
Similar to Hardballer model except caliber: .40 S&W, 4-inch bbl., 8-round magazine capacity, stainless steel finish, weight: About 38 ounces.

HARDBALLER II . . . . NiB $505 Ex $347 Gd $235
Based on the Colt Model 1911 frame. Caliber: .45 ACP, .40 S&W, .400 CorBon, 7-round magazine capacity, 5-inch bbl., weight: About 38 oz.

HARDBALLER II LONGSLIDE. . NiB $530 Ex $431 Gd $342
Similar to Hardballer model except caliber: .45 ACP, 7-inch bbl., 7-round magazine capacity, stainless steel finish, weight: About 46 ounces.

HARDBALLER ACCELERATOR . . NiB $587 Ex $437 Gd $332
Similar to Hardballer model except caliber: .400 CorBon, 7-inch bbl., 7-round magazine capacity, stainless steel finish, weight: About 46 ounces.

**Galesi
Model 6 Pocket**

**Glock Model 19
Gen 1**

**Glock
Model 30
Gen 3**

GALESI — Collebeato (Brescia), Italy

Manufactured by Industria Armi Galesi.

MODEL 6

POCKET AUTOMATIC PISTOL . NiB $227 Ex $179 Gd $128
Calibers: .22 Long, .25 Automatic (6.35mm). Six-round magazine, 2.25-inch bbl., 4.38 inches overall. Weight: About 11 oz. Fixed sights. Blued finish. Plastic grips. Made from 1930 disc.

MODEL 9 POCKET AUTOMATIC PISTOL

Calibers: .22 LR, .32 Auto (7.65mm), .380 Auto (9mm Short). Eight-round magazine, 3.25-inch bbl., 5.88 inches overall.

Weight: About 21 oz. Fixed sights. Blued finish. Plastic grips. Made from 1930 disc.

AUTOMATIC PISTOL

Note: Specifications vary, but those shown for .32 Automatic are common.

**.22 LR or
.380 Auto** . . . . NiB $273 Ex $191 Gd $135
.32 Auto . . . . NiB $265 Ex $180 Gd $110

GLISENTI — Carcina (Brescia), Italy

Mfd. by Societa Siderurgica Glisenti.

MODEL 1910 ITALIAN

SERVICE AUTOMATIC . . . . NiB $1397 Ex $1214 Gd $1015
Caliber: 9mm Glisenti. Seven-round magazine, 4-inch bbl., 8.5 inches overall. Weight: About 32 oz. Fixed sights. Blued finish. Hard rubber or plastic grips. Adopted 1910 and used through WWII.

BRIXIA MODEL . . . . NiB $1627 Ex $1122 Gd $943
Similar to Glisenti Model 1910 except mass produced using simplified mfg. techniques for the civilian market.

SOSSO MODEL . . . . **EXTREMELY RARE**
Experimental semi-auto. Cal.: 9 mm Para. Double action (marked "Sosso"), later single action. Mag.: 19 or 21 rounds. Made by FNA. Fewer than 10 made.

GLOCK, INC. — Austria

Manufactured in Austria and since 2005 in Smyrna, Georgia. NOTE: From 1986 to 1988 Generation 1 models were produced with a pepple texture grip; from 1988 to 1997 Generation 2 models were produced with a checkered grenade type grip texture with horizontal serrations on the front and back grips straps; from 1995 to 2014 Generation 3 models were first produced w/finger grooves in the front grip strap and thumbrests, they then transitioned into finger grooves with thumbrests and checkered finished frame with a front accessory rail. Generation 4 production began from 2010 to date and have interchangable backstraps. The "C" suffix added to model numbers indicated a compensated model. All use a striker-fired system and generally differ in barrel length, overal size, caliber and magazine capacity.

MODEL 17 . . . . NiB $505 Ex $385 Gd $301
Striker-fire action. Caliber: 9mm Parabellum. 10-, 17- or 19-round magazine, 4.5-inch bbl., 7.2 inches overall. Weight: 22 oz. w/o magazine, Polymer frame, steel bbl., slide and springs. Fixed or adj. rear sights. Matte, nonglare finish. Made of only 35 components, including three internal safety devices. Imported from 1985 to date.
Model 17C (compensated bbl.) . . NiB $672 Ex $562 Gd $398
w/adjustable sights, add $75
w/Meprolight sights, add $100
w/Trijicon sights, add $120
Gen4 variant, add $50

MODEL 17L . . . . NiB $714 Ex $577 Gd $396
Same general specifications as Model 17 except w/long slide and with 6-in. bbl., 8.85 inches overall., weight: 23.35 oz. Imported 1988 to 1999, Gen 3 1998 to date.
w/ported bbl., (early production), add $75
w/adjustable sights, add $50

MODEL 19 COMPACT....... NiB $499 Ex $395 Gd $255
Same general specifications as Model 17 except smaller compact version with 4-inch bbl., 6.85 inches overall and weight: 21 oz. Imported from 1988 to date.
Model 20C (compensated bbl.).. NiB $602 Ex $498 Gd $362
w/adjustable sights, add $75
w/Meprolight sights, add $95
w/Trijicon sights, add $120
Gen4 variant, add................................ $50

MODEL 20............... NiB $530 Ex $377 Gd $270
Caliber: 10mm. 15-round, hammerless, 4.6-inch bbl., 7.59 inches overall. Weight: 26.3 oz. Fixed sights. Matte, non-glare finish. Made from 1990 to date.
Model 19C (compensated bbl.).. NiB $632 Ex $485 Gd $377
w/adjustable sights, add $75
w/Meprolight sights, add $95
w/Trijicon sights, add $120
Gen4 variant, add................................ $50

MODEL 21............... NiB $530 Ex $377 Gd $270
Caliber: .45 ACP. 13-round magazine, 7.59 inches overall. Weight: 25.2 oz. Imported from 1990 to date.
Model 21C (compensated bbl.).. NiB $632 Ex $485 Gd $377
w/adjustable sights, add $75
w/Meprolight sights, add $95
w/Trijicon sights, add $120
Gen4 variant, add................................ $50

MODEL 22............... NiB $505 Ex $348 Gd $270
Similar to Model 17 except chambered for .40 S&W. 15-round magazine, 7.4 inches overall. Imported from 1990 to date.
Model 22C (compensated bbl.) NiB $612 Ex $362 Gd $281
w/adjustable sights, add $75
w/Meprolight sights, add $95
w/Trijicon sights, add $120
Gen4 variant, add................................ $50

MODEL 23 COMPACT....... NiB $505 Ex $348 Gd $270
Same general specifications as Model 19 except chambered for .40 S&W. 13-round magazine, 6.97 inches overall, fixed sights. Imported from 1990 to date.
Model 23C (compensated bbl.).... NiB $586 Ex $434 Gd $357
w/adjustable sights, add $50
w/Meprolight sights, add $80
w/Trijicon sights, add $105
Gen4 variant, add................................ $50

MODEL 24 COMPETITION... NiB $617 Ex $530 Gd $431
Caliber: .40 S&W, 10- and 15-round magazine, 6.02-in. bbl., 8.85 inches overall. Weight: 26.5 oz., fixed sights. Made from 1994-99.
Model 24C (compensated bbl.)... NiB $816 Ex $648 Gd $500
w/adjustable sights, add $75

MODEL 26 SUB-COMPACT... NiB $505 Ex $357 Gd $306
Caliber: 9mm, 10-round magazine, 3.47-inch bbl., 6.3 inches overall. Weight: 19.77 oz., fixed sights. Imported from 1995 to date.
w/adjustable sights, add $75
Gen4 variant, add................................ $50

MODEL 27 SUB-COMPACT.... NiB $505 Ex $389 Gd $290
Similar to the Model 22 except subcompact. Caliber: .40 S&W, 10-round magazine, 3.5-inch bbl., Weight: 21.7 oz. Polymer stocks, fixed sights. Imported from 1995 to date.
w/adjustable sights, add $75

w/Meprolight sights, add $95
w/Trijicon sights, add $120

MODEL 29 SUB-COMPACT... NiB $546 Ex $365 Gd $270
Similar to the Model 20 except subcompact. Caliber: 10mm. 10-round magazine, 3.8-inch bbl., weight: 27.1 oz. Polymer stocks, fixed sights. Imported from 1997 to date.
w/adjustable sights, add $75
w/Meprolight sights, add $95
w/Trijicon sights, add $120
Gen4 variant, add................................ $50

MODEL 30 SUB-COMPACT... NiB $546 Ex $365 Gd $270
Similar to the Model 21 except subcompact. Caliber: .45 ACP. 10-round magazine, 3.8-inch bbl., weight: 26.5 oz. Polymer stocks, fixed sights. Imported from 1997 to date.
w/adjustable sights, add $75
w/Meprolight sights, add $90
w/Trijicon sights, add $120
Gen4 variant, add................................ $50

MODEL 31............... NiB $546 Ex $357 Gd $270
Caliber: .357 Sig. 10- 15- or 17-round magazine, 4.49-inch bbl., weight: 23.28 oz., fixed sights. Imported from 1998 to date.
Model 31C (compensated bbl.). NiB $612 Ex $464 Gd $270
w/adjustable sights, add $75
w/Meprolight sights, add $95
w/Trijicon sights, add $120
Gen4 variant, add................................ $50

MODEL 32 COMPACT....... NiB $546 Ex $357 Gd $270
Caliber: .357 Sig., safe action system. 10- 13- or 15-round magazine, 4.02-inch bbl., weight: 21.52 oz. Imported from 1998 to date.Model 32C ..... NiB $648 Ex $485 Gd $395
w/adjustable sights, add $75
w/Meprolight sights, add $95
w/Trijicon Sights, add $120
Gen4 variant, add................................ $50

MODEL 33 SUB-COMPACT... NiB $530 Ex $357 Gd $286
Caliber: .357 Sig., safe action system. Nine- or 11-round magazine, 3.46-inch bbl. Weight: 19.75 oz. Imported from 1998 to date.
w/adjustable sights, add $75
w/Meprolight sights, add $95
w/Trijicon sights, add $120
Gen4 variant, add................................ $50

MODEL 34 COMPETITION.... NiB $577 Ex $485 Gd $377
Similar to Model 17 except w/longer slide and extended slide-stop lever and magazine release. 10-, 17- or 19-round magazine, 5.31-in. bbl. Weight: 22.9 oz., adj. sights. Imported from 1998 to date.
Gen4 variant, add................................ $50

MODEL 35 COMPETITION... NiB $581 Ex $469 Gd $362
Similar to Model 34 except .40 S&W. Imported from 1998 to date.
Gen4 variant, add................................ $50

MODEL 36 SUB-COMPACT.... NiB $536 Ex $444 Gd $342
Similar to Model 30 sub-compact except w/6-round single stackmagazine. Weight: 20.11 oz. Imported from 1999 to date.
w/adjustable sights, add $75
w/Meprolight sights, add $95
w/Trijicon sights, add $120

MODEL 37............... NiB $614 Ex $450 Gd $290
Similar to Model 21 except chambered in .45 G.A.P. Made from 2003 to date.
Gen4 variant, add...............................$50

MODEL 38 COMPACT....... NiB $614 Ex $450 Gd $290
Similar to Model 37 except more compact w/4-in. bbl. Made from 2005 to date.
Gen4 variant, add...............................$50

MODEL 39 SUB-COMPACT... NiB $614 Ex $450 Gd $290
Similar to Model 37 except more sub-compact w/3.4-in. bbl. Made from 2005 to date.
Gen4 variant, add...............................$50

MODEL 41................ NiB $599 Ex $395 Gd $340
Similar to Model 21 except w/long slide and 5.3-in. bbl. Made 2014 to date.

MODEL 42 SUB-COMPACT... NiB $599 Ex $395 Gd $340
Caliber: .380 ACP; 3.25-inch bbl. Weight: 13.7 ozs. Made 2014 to date.

**DESERT STORM
COMMEMORATIVE**...... NiB $1525 Ex $1375 Gd $1225
Same specifications as Model 17 except "Operation Desert Storm, January 16-February 27, 1991" engraved on side of slide w/list of coalition forces. Limited issue of 1,000 guns. Made in 1991.

GREAT WESTERN ARMS CO. — North Hollywood, California

NOTE: *Values shown are for improved late model revolvers early Great Westerns are variable in quality and should be evaluated accordingly. It should also be noted that, beginning about July 1956, these revolvers were offered in kit form. Values of guns assembled from these kits will, in general, be of less value than factory-completed weapons.*

DOUBLE BARREL DERRINGER.. NiB $884 Ex $780 Gd $536
Replica of Remington Double Derringer. Caliber: .38 S&W, .38 S&W Spl. . Double bbls. (superposed), 3-inch bbl. Overall length: 5 inches. Fixed sights. Blued finish. Checkered black plastic grips. Made 1953 to 1962 in various configurations.

SA FRONTIER REVOLVER..... NiB $793 Ex $530 Gd $388
Replica of the Colt Single Action Army Revolver. Calibers: .22 LR, .22 WMR, .357 Magnum, .38 Special, .44 Special, .44 Magnum .45 Colt. Six-round cylinder, bbl. lengths: 4.75-, 5.5 and 7.5-inches. Weight: 40 oz. in .22 cal. w/5.5-inch bbl. Overall length: 11.13 inches w/5.5-inch bbl. Fixed sights. Blued finish. Imitation stag grips. Made from 1951 to 1962.

SHERIFF'S MODEL........... NiB $791 Ex $638 Gd $500
Reportedly made from old Colt parts inventory. Cal.: .45 Long Colt. Blue, nickel, or case-colored finish. Plastic staghorn grips.

FAST DRAW MODEL........ NiB $714 Ex $601 Gd $439
Similar to Frontier model. Bbl.: 4.75 inches. Brass backstrap and trigger guard; blue finish; plastic staghorn grips. Longer, turned-up hammer spur.

TARGET MODEL.... .... NiB $740 Ex $616 Gd $474
Similar to Frontier model. Cal.: .22 LR. Adj. rear sights, Micro front blade. Blue or case colored frame. Bbl.: Various lengths.

Grendel Model P-12

DEPUTY MODEL............ NiB $831 Ex $709 Gd $500
Cal.: .22 LR, .38 Spl., .357 Mag. Bbl.: 4 inches. Deluxe blue finish, walnut grips. Adj. rear sight. Fewer than 100 made.

GRENDEL, INC. — Rockledge, Florida

MODEL P-10 AUTOMATIC PISTOL
Hammerless, blow-back action. DAO with no external safety. Caliber: .380 ACP. 10-round box magazine integrated in grip. Three-inch bbl., 5.3 inches overall. Weight: 15 oz. Matte blue, nickel or green Teflon finish. Made from 1988 to 1991.
Blued finish................NiB $219 Ex $160 Gd $105
Nickel finish ....NiB $227 Ex $179 Gd $120
Green finish ....NiB $227 Ex $179 Gd $105
w/compensated bbl., add $65

MODEL P-12 DA AUTOMATIC PISTOL
Caliber: .380 ACP. 11-round Zytel magazine, 3-inch bbl., 5.3 inches overall. Weight: 13 oz. Fixed sights. Polymer DuPont ST-800 grip. Made from 1991 to 1995.
Standard model............NiB $214 Ex $135 Gd $105
Electroless nickel...........NiB $219 Ex $135 Gd $105

MODEL P-30 AUTOMATIC PISTOL
Caliber: .22 WMR. 30-round magazine, 5-or 8-inch bbl., 8.5 inches overall w/5-inch bbl., weight: 21 oz. Blade front sight, fixed rear sight. Made from 1991 to 1995.
w/5-inch bbl.,..............NiB $337 Ex $255 Gd $214
w/8-inch bbl.,..............NiB $337 Ex $255 Gd $214

**MODEL P-31
AUTOMATIC PISTOL**........ NiB $474 Ex $352 Gd $281
Caliber: .22 WMR. 30-round Zytel magazine, 11-inch bbl., 17.3 inches overall. Weight: 48 oz. Adjustable blade front sight, fixed rear. Checkered black polymer DuPont ST-800 grip and forend. Made from 1991 to 1995.

GUNSITE — Paulden, Arizona

"ADVANCED TACTICAL" SA AUTO PISTOL
Manufactured w/Colt 1911 or Springfield 1911 parts. Caliber: .45 ACP. Eight-round magazine, 3.5-, 4.25-, 5-inch bbl. Weight: 32-38 oz. Checkered or laser-engraved walnut grips. Fixed or Novak Lo-mount sights.

**Hämmerli Model
33MP Free Pistol**

**Hämmerli Model
101**

**Hämmerli
Model 102 Deluxe**

**Hämmerli Model
105**

**Hämmerli
Model 106**

Stainless finish. . . . . NiB $1193 Ex $974 Gd $704
Blued finish. . . . . NiB $1030 Ex $836 Gd $621

"CUSTOM CARRY" SA AUTO PISTOL
Caliber: .45 ACP. Eight-round magazine, 3.5-, 4.25-, 5-inch bbl., Weight: 32-38 oz. Checkered or laser-engraved walnut grips. Fixed Novak Lo-mount sights. Single action, manufactured based on enhanced colt models.

Stainless finish. . . . . NiB $1219 Ex $990 Gd $740
Blued finish. . . . . NiB $1151 Ex $927 Gd $709

H&R 1871, INC. — Gardner, Massachusetts

NOTE: *In 1991, H&R 1871, Inc. was formed from the residual of the parent company, Harrington & Richardson, and then took over the New England Firearms facility. H&R 1871 produced firearms under both their logo and the NEF brand name until 1999, when the Marlin Firearms Company acquired the assets of H&R 1871. See listings under Harrington & Richardson, Inc.*

HÄMMERLI — Lenzburg, Switzerland.

Currently imported by Sigarms, Inc., Exeter, NH. Previously by Hammerli, USA; Beeman Precision Arms & Mandall Shooting Supplies.

MODEL 33MP FREE PISTOL . . . NiB $964 Ex $863 Gd $577

System Martini single-shot action, set trigger. Caliber: .22 LR. 11.5-inch octagon bbl., 16.5 inches overall. Weight: 46 oz. Micrometer rear sight, interchangeable front sights. Blued finish. Walnut grips, forearm. Imported from 1933 to 1949.

MODEL 100 FREE PISTOL
Same general specifications as Model 33MP. Improved action and sights, redesigned stock. Standard model has plain grips and forearm, deluxe model has carved grips and forearm. Imported 1950 to 1956.
Standard model. . . . . NiB $938 Ex $775 Gd $556
Deluxe model . . . . NiB $1020 Ex $893 Gd $612

MODEL 101 . . . . NiB $913 Ex $791 Gd $612
Similar to Model 100 except has heavy round bbl. w/matte finish, improved action and sights, adj. grips. Weight: About 49 oz. Imported from 1956 to 1960.

MODEL 102
Same as Model 101 except bbl., has highly polished blued finish. Deluxe model (illustrated) has carved grips and forearm. Made from 1956 to 1960.
Standard model. . . . . NiB $928 Ex $760 Gd $561
Deluxe model . . . . NiB $1035 Ex $791 Gd $602

MODEL 103 . . . . NiB $969 Ex $826 Gd $536
Same as Model 101 except has lighter octagon bbl. (as in Model 100) w/highly polished blued finish, grips and forearm of select French walnut. Weight: About 46 oz. Imported 1956 to 1960.

MODEL 104 . . . . NiB $804 Ex $673 Gd $439
Similar to Model 102 except has lighter round bbl., improved action redesigned grips and forearm. Weight: 46 oz. Imported 1961 to 1965.

MODEL 105 . . . . NiB $960 Ex $779 Gd $500
Similar to Model 103 except has improved action, redesigned grips and forearm. Imported from 1961 to 1965.

MODEL 106 . . . . NiB $933 Ex $796 Gd $464
Similar to Model 104 except has improved trigger and grips. Made from 1966 to 1971.

**Hämmerli
Model 107 Deluxe**

**Hämmerli
Model 120 Heavy Barrel**

**Hämmerli
Model 120-1**

**Hämmerli
Model 150**

**Hämmerli
Model 160**

MODEL 107
Similar to Model 105 except has improved trigger and stock. Deluxe model (illustrated) has engraved receiver and bbl., carved grips and forearm. Imported from 1966 to 1971.
Standard model . . . . NiB $1034 Ex $831 Gd $462
Deluxe model . . . . NiB $1025 Ex $826 Gd $474

Model 120 Heavy Barrel
Same as Models 120-1 and 120-2 except has 5.7-inch heavy bbl., weight: 41 oz. Avail. w/standard or adj. grips. 1,000 made. Imported from 1972.
w/standard grips . . . . NiB $627 Ex $459 Gd $388
w/adj. grips . . . . NiB $761 Ex $588 Gd $377

MODEL 120-1 SINGLE-
SHOT FREE PISTOL . . . . NiB $658 Ex $536 Gd $385
Side lever-operated bolt action. Adj. single-stage or two-stage trigger. Caliber: .22 LR, 9.9-inch bbl., 14.75 inches overall. Weight: 44 oz. Micrometer rear sight, front sight on high ramp. Blued finish bbl., and receiver, lever and grip frame anodized aluminum. Checkered walnut thumbrest grips. Imported from 1972 to date.

MODEL 120-2 . . . . NiB $734 Ex $648 Gd $377
Same as Model 120-1 except has hand-contoured grips w/adj. palm rest (available for right or left hand). Imported from 1972 to date.

MODELS 150/151 FREE PISTOLS
Improved Martini-type action w/lateral-action cocking lever. Set trigger adj. for weight, length and angle of pull. Caliber: .22 LR, 11.3-inch round free-floating bbl., 15.4 inches overall. Weight: 43 oz. (w/Extra weights, 49.5 oz.). Micrometer rear sight, front sight on high ramp. Blued finish. Select walnut forearm and grips w/adj. palm shelf. Imported 1972-93.
Model 150 (disc. 1989) . . . . NiB $1938 Ex $1709 Gd $1020
Model 151 (disc. 1993) . . . . NiB $1938 Ex $1709 Gd $1020

MODEL 152 ELECTRONIC PISTOL
Same general specifications as Model 150 except w/electronic trigger. Made from 1990 to 1992
Right hand . . . . NiB $1812 Ex $1700 Gd $1036
w/adj. grips, add $306

MODELS 160/162 FREE PISTOLS
Caliber: .22 LR. Single-shot. 11.31-inch bbl., 17.5 inches overall. Weight: 46.9 oz. Interchangeable front sight blades, fully adj. match rear. Match-style stippled walnut grips w/adj. palm shelf and poly-carbon fiber forend. Imported from 1993 to 2002.
**Model 160 w/mechanical
  set trigger (disc. 2000) . . . NiB $1812 Ex $1681 Gd $1005**
Model 162 w/electronic triggerNiB $1982 Ex $1622 Gd$1132

MODEL 208 STANDARD
AUTO PISTOL . . . . NiB $1802 Ex $1488 Gd $959
Caliber: .22 LR. Eight-round magazine, 5.9-inch bbl., 10 inches overall. Weight: 35 oz. (bbl. weight adds 3 oz.). Micrometer rear sight, ramp front. Blued finish. Checkered walnut grips w/adj. heel plate. Imported from 1966 to 1988.

MODEL 208S
TARGET PISTOL . . . . NiB $2540 Ex $2232 Gd $2066
Caliber: .22 LR. Eight-round magazine, 6-inch bbl., 10.2 inches overall. Weight: 37.3 oz. Micrometer rear sight, ramp front sight. Blued finish. Stippled walnut grips w/adj. heel plate. Imported from 1988 to 2000.

MODEL 211 . . . . NiB $1601 Ex $1458 Gd $847
Same as Model 208 except has standard. Thumbrest grips. Imported from 1966 to 1990.

**Hämmerli
Model 208**

**Hämmerli
Model 215**

**Hämmerli
International Model 206**

**Hämmerli
International Model 207**

**Hämmerli
Model 232 Rapid Fire**

MODEL 212
HUNTER'S PISTOL . . . . **NiB $2146 Ex $1816 Gd $1436**
Caliber: .22 LR, 4.88-inch bbl., 8.5 inches overall. Weight: 31 oz. Blade front sight, square-notched fully adj. rear. Blued finish. Checkered walnut grips. Imported 1984-93.

MODEL 215
. . . . **NiB $2368 Ex $2035 Gd $1734**
Similar to the Model 208 except w/heavier bbl. and fewer deluxe features. Imported from 1990 to 1993.

MODEL 230-1 RAPID FIRE
AUTO PISTOL. . . . . **NiB $755 Ex $576 Gd $478**
Caliber: .22 Short. Five-round magazine, 6.3-inch bbl., 11.6 inches overall. Weight: 44 oz. Micrometer rear sight, post front. Blued finish. Smooth walnut thumbrest grips. Imported from 1970 to 1983.

MODEL 230-2 RAPID FIRE
AUTO PISTOL. . . . . **NiB $785 Ex $601 Gd $444**
Same as Model 230-1 except has checkered walnut grips w/ adj. heel plate. Imported from 1970 to 1983.

MODEL 232 RAPID FIRE
AUTO PISTOL. . . . . **NiB $1454 Ex $1256 Gd $780**
Caliber: .22 Short. Six-round magazine, 5.1-inch ported bbl., 10.5 inches overall. Weight: 44 oz. Fully adj. target sights. Blued finish. Stippled walnut wraparound target grips. Imported 1984 to 1993.

INTERNATIONAL MODEL 206
AUTO PISTOL. . . . . **NiB $709 Ex $469 Gd $306**
Calibers: .22 Short, .22 LR. Six-round (.22 Short) or 8-round (.22 LR) magazine, 7.1-inch bbl. w/muzzle brake, 12.5 inches overall. Weight: 33 oz. (.22 Short), 39 oz. (.22 LR) (supplementary weights add 5 and 8 oz.). Micrometer rear sight, ramp front. Blued finish. Standard thumbrest grips. Imported from 1962 to 1969.

INTERNATIONAL MODEL 207
AUTO PISTOL. . . . . **NiB $760 Ex $621 Gd $469**
Same as Model 206 except has grips w/adj. heel plate, weight: 2 oz. more. Made from 1962 to 1969.

INTERNATIONAL MODEL 209
AUTO PISTOL. . . . . **NiB $825 Ex $672 Gd $562**
Caliber: .22 Short. Five-round mag., 4.75-inch bbl., w/muzzle brake and gas-escape holes, 11 inches overall. Weight: 39 oz. (interchangeable front weight adds 4 oz.). Micrometer rear sight, post front. Blued finish. Standard thumbrest grips of checkered walnut. Imported from 1966 to 1970.

INTERNATIONAL MODEL 210 . . **NiB $827 Ex $676 Gd $530**
Same as Model 209 except has grips w/adj. heel plate, is 0.8-inch longer and weighs 1 ounce more. Made from 1966 to 1970.Model 280 Target Pistol Carbon-reinforced synthetic frame and bbl., housing. Calibers: .22 LR, .32 S&W Long WC. Six-round (.22 LR) or 5-round (.32 S&W) magazine, 4.5-inch bbl. w/interchangeable metal or carbon fiber counterweights. 11.88 inches overall. Weight: 39 oz. Micro-adj. match sights w/interchangeable elements. Imported from 1988 to 2000.
.22 LR . . . . **NiB $1550 Ex $1295 Gd $627**
.32 S&W Long WC . . . . **NiB $1729 Ex $1550 Gd $842**
.22/.32 Conversion kit, add **$816**

**Hämmerli
International Model 210**

**Hämmerli-Walther
Olympia Model 203 1958-Type**

**Hämmerli-Walther
Olympia Model 205**

**SIG-Hämmerli
Model P240 Target**

5.5-inch bbl.). Weight: 40 oz. (with 5.5-inch bbl.). Fixed sights. Blued bbl. and cylinder, casehardened frame, chrome-plated grip frame and trigger guard. One-piece smooth walnut stock. Imported from 1973 to 1976 by Interarms, AlExandria, Va.

**WALTHER OLYMPIA MODEL 200 AUTOMATIC
PISTOL, 1952-TYPE . . . . NiB $704 Ex $598 Gd $479**
Similar to 1936 Walther Olympia Funfkampf model. Calibers: .22 Short, .22 LR. Six-round (.22 Short) or 10-round (.22 LR) magazine, 7.5-inch bbl., 10.7 inches overall. Weight: 27.7 oz. (.22 Short, light alloy breechblock), 30.3 oz. (.22 LR). Supplementary weights provided. Adj. target sights. Blued finish. Checkered walnut thumbrest grips. Imported 1952 to 1958.

**WALTHER OLYMPIA
MODEL 200,1958-TYPE . . . . . . NiB $780 Ex $632 Gd $530**
Same as Model 200 1952 type except has muzzle brake, 8-round magazine (.22 LR). 11.6 inches overall. Weight: 30 oz. (.22 Short), 33 oz. (.22 LR). Imported 1958 to 1963.

**WALTHER OLYMPIA
MODEL 201 . . . . NiB $704 Ex $546 Gd $437**
Same as Model 200,1952-Type except has 9.5-inch bbl. Imported from 1955 to 1957.

**WALTHER
OLYMPIA MODEL 202 . . . . NiB $780 Ex $632 Gd $530**
Same as Model 201 except has grips w/adjustable heel plate. Imported from 1955 to 1957.

WALTHER OLYMPIA MODEL 203
Same as corresponding Model 200 (1955 type lacks muzzle brake) except has grips w/adjustable heel plate. Imported 1955 to 1963.
1955 type . . . . NiB $794 Ex $638 Gd $479
1958 type . . . . NiB $842 Ex $709 Gd $475

WALTHER OLYMPIA MODEL 204
American model. Same as corresponding Model 200 (1956-Type lacks muzzle brake) except in .22 LR only, has slide stop and micrometer rear sight. Imported from 1956 to 1963.
1956-type . . . . NiB $760 Ex $606 Gd $464
1958-type . . . . NiB $816 Ex $680 Gd $556

WALTHER OLYMPIA MODEL 205
American model. Same as Model 204 except has grips w/ adjustable heel plate. Imported from 1956 to 1963.
1956-type . . . . NiB $842 Ex $714 Gd $610
1958-type . . . . NiB $893 Ex $727 Gd $556

MODEL P240 TARGET AUTO PISTOL
Calibers: .32 S&W Long (wadcutter), .38 Special (wadcutter). Five-round magazine, 5.9-inch bbl., 10 inches overall. Weight: 41 oz. Micrometer rear sight, post front. Blued finish/smooth walnut thumbrest grips. Accessory .22 LR conversion unit available. Imported from 1975 to 1986.
.32 S&W Long. . . . . NiB $1540 Ex $1329 Gd $755
.38 Special . . . . NiB $2545 Ex $2353 Gd $2025
.22 LR conversion unit, add $561

VIRGINIAN SA REVOLVER. . . NiB $780 Ex $602 Gd $ 440
Similar to Colt Single-Action Army except has base pin safety system (SWISSAFE). Calibers: .357 Magnum, .45 Colt. Six-round cylinder. 4.63-, 5.5- or 7.5-inch bbl., 11 inches overall (with

HARRINGTON & RICHARDSON, INC. —
Gardner, Massachusetts
Formerly Harrington & Richardson Arms Co. of Worcester, Mass. One of the oldest and most distinguished manufacturers of handguns, rifles and shotguns, H&R suspended operations

Harrington & Richardson SL .32

Harrington & Richardson USRA Model Single-Shot Target Pistol

Harrington & Richardson Model 4

Harrington & Richardson Model 5

Harrington & Richardson Model 6

on January 24, 1986. In 1987, New England Firearms was established as an independent company producing selected H&R models under the NEF logo. In 1991, H&R 1871, Inc., was formed from the residual of the parent company and then took over the New England Firearms facility. H&R 1871 produced firearms under both its logo and the NEF brand name until 1999, when the Marlin Firearms Company acquired the assets of H&R 1871.

NOTE: For ease in finding a particular firearm, H&R handguns are grouped into Automatic/Single-Shot Pistols, followed by Revolvers. For a complete listing, please refer to the index.

- AUTOMATIC/SINGLE-SHOT PISTOLS -

SL .25 PISTOL . . . . NiB $587 Ex $405 Gd $290
Modified Webley & Scott design. Caliber: .25 Auto. Six-round magazine, 2-inch bbl., 4.5 inches overall. Weight: 12 oz. Fixed sights. Blued finish. Black hard rubber grips. Made from 1912 to 1916.

SL .32 PISTOL . . . . NiB $562 Ex $321 Gd $205
Modified Webley & Scott design. Caliber: .32 Auto. Eight-round magazine, 3.5-inch bbl., 6.5 inches overall. Weight: About 20 oz. Fixed sights. Blued finish. Black hard rubber grips. Made from 1916 to 1924.

USRA MODEL SINGLE-SHOT
TARGET PISTOL . . . . NiB $548 Ex $500 Gd $288
Hinged frame. Caliber: .22 LR, bbl. lengths: 7-, 8- and 10-inch. Weight: 31 oz. w/10-inch bbl., Adj. target sights. Blued finish. Checkered walnut grips. Made from 1928 to 1941.

- REVOLVERS -

MODEL 4 (1904) DA . . . . NiB $255 Ex $180 Gd $90
Solid frame. Calibers: .32 S&W Long, .38 S&W. Six-round cylinder (.32 cal.), or 5-round (.38 cal.), bbl. Lengths: 2.5-, 4.5- and 6-inch. Weight: About 16 oz. (in .32 cal.) Fixed sights. Blued or nickel finish. Hard rubber grips. Disc. prior to 1942.

MODEL 5 (1905) DA . . . . NiB $237 Ex $159 Gd $77
Solid frame. Caliber: .32 S&W. Five-round cylinder, bbl., lengths: 2.5-,4.5- and 6-inch. Weight: About 11 oz. Fixed sights. Blued or nickel finish. Hard rubber grips. Disc. prior to 1942.

MODEL 6 (1906) DA . . . . NiB $198 Ex $115 Gd $75
Solid frame. Caliber: .22 LR. Seven-round cylinder, bbl. lengths: 2.5, 4.5- and 6-inches. Weight: About 10 oz. Fixed sights. Blued or nickel finish. Hard rubber grips. Disc. prior to 1942.

.22 SPECIAL DA . . . . NiB $351 Ex $197 Gd $101
Heavy hinged frame. Calibers: .22 LR, .22 Mag. Nine-round cylinder, 6-inch bbl., weight: 23 oz. Fixed sights, front gold-plated. Blued finish. Checkered walnut grips. Recessed safety cylinder on later models for high-speed ammunition. Disc. prior to 1942.

MODEL 199 SPORTSMAN
SA Revolver . . . . NiB $347 Ex $291 Gd $158
Hinged frame. Caliber: .22 LR. Nine-round cylinder, 6-inch bbl., 11 inches overall. Weight: 30 oz. Adj. target sights. Blued finish. Checkered walnut grips. Disc. 1951.

Harrington & Richardson
.22 Special

Harrington & Richardson
Model 199 Sportsman

Harrington & Richardson
Model 622

Harrington & Richardson
Model 632

Harrington & Richardson
Model 649

MODEL 504 DA . . . . **NiB $255 Ex $189 Gd $143**
Caliber: .32 H&R Magnum. Five-round cylinder, 4- or 6-inch
bbl., (square butt), 3- or 4-inch bbl., round butt. Made 1984
to 1986.

MODEL 532 DA . . . . **NiB $179 Ex $129 Gd $88**
Caliber: .32 H&R Magnum. Five-round cylinder, 2.5- or 4-inch
bbl., weight: Approx. 20 and 25 oz. respectively. Fixed sights.
American walnut grips. Lustre blued finish. Made 1984 to 1986.

MODEL 586 DA . . . . **NiB $290 Ex $188 Gd $130**
Caliber: .32 H&R Magnum. Five-round cylinder. bbl. lengths:
4.5, 5.5, 7.5, 10 inches. Weight: 30 oz. average. Adj. rear sight,
blade front. Walnut finished hardwood grips. Made from 1984
to 1986.

MODEL 603 TARGET . . . . **NiB $219 Ex $158 Gd $115**
Similar to Model 903 except in .22 WMR. Six-round capacity
w/unfluted cylinder. Made from 1980 to 1983.

MODEL 604 TARGET . . . . **NiB $219 Ex $158 Gd $115**
Similar to Model 603 except w/6-inch bull bbl., weight: 38 oz.
Made from 1980 to 1983.

MODEL 622/623 DA . . . . **NiB $170 Ex $128 Gd $79**
Solid frame. Caliber: .22 Short, Long, LR, 6-round cylinder.
bbl., lengths: 2.5-, 4-, 6-inches. Weight: 26 oz. (with 4-inch
bbl.). Fixed sights. Blued finish. Plastic grips. Made from 1957

to 1986. Note: Model 623 is same except chrome or nickel
finish.

MODEL 632/633
GUARDSMAN DA REVOLVER . . **NiB $171 Ex $128 Gd $79**
Solid Frame. Caliber: .32 S&W Long. Six-round cylinder, bbl.,
lengths: 2.5- or 4-inch. Weight: 19 oz. (with 2.5-inch bbl.).
Fixed sights. Blued or chrome finish. Checkered Tenite grips
(round butt on 2.5-inch, square butt on 4-inch). Made from
1953 to 1986. Note: Model 633 is the same except for chrome
or nickel finish.

MODEL 649/650 DA . . . . **NiB $265 Ex $158 Gd $95**
Solid frame. Side loading and ejection. Convertible model w/
two 6-round cylinders. Calibers: .22 LR, .22 WMR. 5.5-inch
bbl., Weight: 32 oz. Adj. rear sight, blade front. Blued finish.
One-piece, Western-style walnut grip. Made from 1976 to
1986. Note: Model 650 is same except nickel finish.

MODEL 666 DA . . . . **NiB $151 Ex $104 Gd $64**
Solid frame. Convertible model w/two 6-round cylinders.
Calibers: .22 LR, .22 WMR. Six-inch bbl., weight: 28 oz. Fixed
sights. Blued finish. Plastic grips. Made from 1976 to 1978.

MODEL 676 DA . . . . **NiB $283 Ex $200 Gd $104**
Solid frame. Side loading and ejection. Convertible model
w/two 6-round cylinders. Calibers: .22 LR, .22 WMR, bbl.
lengths: 4.5, 5.5, 7.5, 12-inches. Weight: 32 oz. (with 5.5-inch
bbl.). Adj. rear sight, blade front. Blued finish, color-casehardened frame. One-piece, Western-style walnut grip. Made from
1976 to 1980.

MODEL 686 DA . . . . **NiB $306 Ex $205 Gd $128**
Caliber: .22 LR and .22 WMR. Six-round magazine, 4.5, 5.5,
7.5, 10 or 12-inch bbl. Adj. rear sight, ramp and blade front.
Blued, color-casehardened frame. Weight: 31 oz. (with 4.5-
inch bbl.). Made from 1980 to 1986.

MODEL 732/733 DA . . . . **NiB $198 Ex $129 Gd $83**
Solid frame, swing-out 6-round cylinder. Calibers: .32 S&W,
.32 S&W Long. bbl., lengths: 2.5 and 4-inch. Weight: 26
oz. (with 4-inch bbl.). Fixed sights (windage adj. rear on

Harrington & Richardson
Model 666

Harrington & Richardson
Model 686

Harrington & Richardson
Model 830

Harrington & Richardson
Model 733

Harrington & Richardson
Model 900

4-inch bbl. model). Blued finish. Plastic grips. Made from 1958 to 1986. Note: Model 733 is the same except with nickel finish.

MODEL 826 DA . . . . NiB $200 Ex $135 Gd $88
Caliber: .22 WMR. Six-round magazine, 3-inch bull bbl., ramp and blade front sight, adj. rear. American walnut grips. Weight: 28 oz. Made from 1981 to 1983.

MODEL 829/830 DA
Same as Model 826 except in .22 LR caliber. Nine round capacity. Made from 1981 to 1983.
Model 829, blued . . . . NiB $189 Ex $143 Gd $94
Model 830, nickel. . . . . NiB $181 Ex $135 Gd $90

MODEL 832/833 DA
Same as Model 826 except in .32 SW Long. Blued or nickel finish. Made from 1981 to 1983.
Model 832, blued . . . . NiB $199 Ex $112 Gd $77
Model 833, nickel. . . . . NiB $199 Ex $112 Gd $77

MODEL 900/901 DA . . . . NiB $179 Ex $105 Gd $70
Solid frame, snap-out cylinder. Calibers: .22 Short, Long, LR. Nine-round cylinder, bbl. lengths: 2.5, 4, and 6-inches. Weight: 26 oz. (with 6-inch bbl.). Fixed sights. Blued finish. Cycolac grips. Made from 1962 to 1973. Note: Model 901 (disc. in 1963) is the same except has chrome finish and white Tenite grips.

MODEL 903 TARGET . . . . NiB $240 Ex $177 Gd $112
Caliber: .22 LR. Nine round capacity. SA/DA, 6-inch target-weight flat-side bbl., swing-out cylinder. Weight: 35 oz. Blade front sight, adj. rear. American walnut grips. Made from 1980 to 1983.

MODEL 904 TARGET . . . . NiB $265 Ex $177 Gd $116
Similar to Model 903 except 4 or 6-inch bull bbl. Weight: 32 oz. with 4-inch bbl. Made from 1980 to 1986. MODEL 905
TARGET . . . . NiB $270 Ex $183 Gd $137
Same as Model 904 except w/4-inch bbl. only. Nickel finish. Made from 1981 to 1983.

MODEL 922 DA REVOLVER
FIRST ISSUE . . . . NiB $232 Ex $189 Gd $148
Solid frame. Caliber: .22 LR. Nine-round cylinder, 10-inch octagon bbl., (early model) or 6-inches, round bbl. (later production). Weight: 26 oz. (with 6-inch bbl.). Fixed sights. Blued finish. Checkered walnut grips. Safety cylinder on later models. Disc. prior to 1942.

MODEL 922/923 DA REVOLVER,
SECOND ISSUE . . . . NiB $220 Ex $112 Gd $88
Solid frame. Caliber: .22 LR. Nine-round cylinder, bbl. lengths: 2.5, 4, and 6-inches. Weight: 24 oz. (with 4-inch bbl.). Fixed sights. Blued finish. Plastic grips. Made 1950 to 1986. Note: Second Issue Model 922 has a different frame from that

Harrington & Richardson
Model 903

Harrington & Richardson
Model 905

Harrington & Richardson
Model 925

Harrington & Richardson
Model 922, First Issue

Harrington & Richardson
Model 926

Harrington & Richardson
Model 922, Second Issue

of the First Issue. Model 923 is same as Model 922, Second Issue except for nickel finish.

MODEL 925
DEFENDER . . . . **NiB $255 Ex $148 Gd $110**
DA. Hinged frame. Caliber: .38 S&W. Five-round cylinder, 2.5-inch bbl., weight: 22 oz. Adj. rear sight, fixed front. Blued finish. One-piece wraparound grip. Made from 1964 to 1978.

MODEL 926 DA . . . . **NiB $255 Ex $158 Gd $110**
Hinged frame. Calibers: .22 LR, .38 S&W. Nine-round (.22 LR) or 5-round (.38) cylinder, 4-in. bbl., weight: 31 oz. Adj. rear sight, fixed front. Blued finish. Checkered walnut grips. Made 1968 to 1978.

MODEL 929/930
SIDEKICK DA REVOLVER . . . . . **NiB $219 Ex $130 Gd $95**
Caliber: .22 LR. Solid frame, swing-out 9-round cylinder, bbl. lengths: 2.5-, 4-, 6-inches. Weight: 24 oz. (with 4-inch bbl.). Fixed sights. Blued finish. Checkered plastic grips. Made from 1956 to 1986. Note: Model 930 is same except with nickel finish.

MODEL 939/940 ULTRA SIDEKICK
DA REVOLVER . . . . **NiB $290 Ex $187 Gd $112**
Solid frame, swing-out 9-round cylinder. Safety lock. Calibers: .22 Short, Long, LR. Flat-side 6-inch bbl. w/vent rib. Weight: 33 oz. Adj. rear sight, ramp front. Blued finish. Checkered walnut grips. Made 1958 to 1986, reintroduced by H&R 1871 in 1992. Note: Model 940 is same except has round bbl.

MODEL 949/950 FORTY-NINER
DA REVOLVER . . . . **NiB $270 Ex $190 Gd $110**
Solid frame. Side loading and ejection. Calibers: .22 Short, Long, LR. Nine-round cylinder, 5.5- or 7.5 inch bbl., weight: 31 to 38 oz. Adj. rear sight, blade front. Blued or nickel finish. One-piece, Western-style walnut grip. Made 1960 to 1986,

Harrington & Richardson
Model 939

Harrington & Richardson
Model 929

Harrington & Richardson
Model 950

Harrington & Richardson
Model 999, First Issue

Harrington & Richardson
Model 999, Second Issue

reintroduced by H&R 1871 in 1992 to 1999. Note: Model 950 is same except has nickel finish.

MODEL 976 DA . . . . NiB $310 Ex $197 Gd $109
Same as Model 949 except has color-casehardened frame, 7.5-inch bbl. Weight: 36 oz. Intro. 1977. Disc.

**MODEL 999 SPORTSMAN DA REVOLVER,
FIRST ISSUE** . . . . NiB $499 Ex $316 Gd $200

Hinged frame. Calibers: .22 LR, .22 Mag. Same specifications as Model 199 Sportsman Single Action. Disc. before 1942.

**MODEL 999 SPORTSMAN DA REVOLVER
SECOND ISSUE** . . . . NiB $464 Ex $309 Gd $197
Hinged frame. Caliber: .22 LR. Nine-round cylinder, 6-inch bbl. w/vent rib. Weight: 30 oz. Adj. sights. Blued finish. Checkered walnut grips. Made from 1950 to 1986.

**(NEW) MODEL 999 SPORTSMAN
DA REVOLVER** . . . . NiB $499 Ex $316 Gd $197
Hinged frame. Caliber: .22 Short, Long, LR. Nine-round cylinder. Six-inch bbl. w/vent rib. Weight: 30 oz. Blade front sight adj. for elevation, square-notched rear adj. for windage. Blued finish. Checkered hardwood grips. Reintroduced by H&R 1871 in 1992.

AMERICAN DA . . . . NiB $245 Ex $115 Gd $79
Solid frame. Calibers: .32 S&W Long, .38 S&W. Six-round (.32 cal.) or 5-round (.38 cal.) cylinder, bbl. lengths: 2.5-,4.5- and 6-inches. Weight: About 16 oz. Fixed sights. Blued or nickel finish. Hard rubber grips. Disc. prior to 1942.

**AUTOMATIC EJECTING
DA REVOLVER** . . . . NiB $231 Ex $174 Gd $120
Hinged frame. Calibers: .32 S&W Long, .38 S&W. Six-round (.32 cal.) or 5-round (.38 cal.) cylinder, bbl. lengths: 3.25-, 4-, 5- and 6-inches. Weight: 16 oz. (.32 cal.), 15 oz. (.38 cal.). Fixed sights. Blued or nickel finish. Black hard rubber grips. Disc. prior to 1942.

BOBBY DA . . . . NiB $316 Ex $219 Gd $160
Hinged frame. Calibers: .32 S&W, .38 S&W. Six-round cylinder (.32 cal.) or 5-round (.38 cal.). Four-inch bbl., 9 inches overall. Weight: 23 oz. Fixed sights. Blued finish. Checkered walnut grips. Disc. 1946. Note: Originally designed and produced for use by London's bobbies.

DEFENDER .38 DA . . . . NiB $346 Ex $219 Gd $110
Hinged frame. Based on the Sportsman design. Caliber: .38 S&W. Bbl. lengths: 4- and 6-inches, 9 inches overall (with 4-inch bbl.). Weight: 25 oz. with 4-inch bbl. Fixed sights. Blued finish. Black plastic grips. Disc. 1946. Note: This model was manufactured during WW II as an arm for plant guards, auxiliary police, etc.

EXPERT MODEL DA . . . . NiB $499 Ex $283 Gd $110
Same specifications as .22 Special except has 10-inch bbl., weight: 28 oz. Disc. prior to 1942.

**Harrington & Richardson
Automatic Ejecting**

**Harrington & Richardson
Premier**

Harrington & Richardson Bobby

**Harrington & Richardson
Defender .38**

**Harrington & Richardson
Hammerless, Small Frame**

**HAMMERLESS DA,
LARGE FRAME** . . . . .NiB $206 Ex $137 Gd $115
Hinged frame. Calibers: .32 S&W Long 38 S&W. Six-round (.32 cal.), or 5-round (.38 cal.) cylinder, bbl. lengths: 3.25, 4, and 6-inches. Weight: About 17 oz. Fixed sights. Blued or nickel finish. Hard rubber grips. Disc. prior to 1942.

**HAMMERLESS DA,
SMALL FRAME** . . . . .NiB $189 Ex $130 Gd $101
Hinged frame. Calibers: .22 LR, .32 S&W. Seven-round (.22 cal.) or 5-round (.32 cal.) cylinder, bbl. lengths: 2, 3, 4, 5 and 6-inches. Weight: About 13 oz. Fixed sights. Blued or nickel finish. Hard rubber grips. Disc. prior to 1942.

HUNTER MODEL DA . . . . .NiB $601 Ex $410 Gd $309
Solid frame. Caliber: .22 LR. Nine-round cylinder, 10-inch octagon bbl., weight: 26 oz. Fixed sights. Blued finish. Checkered walnut grips. Safety cylinder on later models. Note: An earlier Hunter Model was built on the smaller 7-round frame. Disc. prior to 1942.

NEW DEFENDER DA . . . . .NiB $346 Ex $244 Gd $189
Hinged frame. Caliber: .22 LR. Nine-round cylinder, 2-inch bbl., 6.25 inches overall. Weight: 23 oz. Adj. sights. Blued finish. Checkered walnut grips, round butt. Note: Basically, this is the Sportsman DA w/a short bbl., Disc. prior to 1942.

PREMIER DA . . . . .NiB $306 Ex $198 Gd $109
Small hinged frame. Calibers: .22 LR, .32 S&W. Seven-round (.22 LR) or 5-round (.32) cylinder. Bbl. Lengths: 2, 3, 4, 5, and 6-inches. Weight: 13 oz. (in .22 LR), 12 oz. (in .32 S&W). Fixed sights. Blued or nickel finish. Black hard rubber grips. Disc. prior to 1942.

**MODEL STR 022
BLANK REVOLVER** . . . . .NiB $143 Ex $90 Gd $70
Caliber: .22 RF blanks. Nine-round cylinder, 2.5-inch bbl. Weight: 19 oz. Satin blued finish.

**MODEL STR 032
BLANK REVOLVER** . . . . .NiB $148 Ex $95 Gd $75
Same general specifications as STR 022 except chambered for .32 S&W blank cartridges.

Harrington & Richardson Target

Harrington & Richardson Trapper

Harrington & Richardson Ultra Sportsmen

Harrington & Richardson Vest Pocket

Harrington & Richardson Young American

TARGET MODEL DA . . . . NiB $237 Ex $166 Gd $120
Small hinged frame. Calibers: .22 LR, .22 W.R.F. Seven-round cylinder, 6-inch bbl., weight: 16 oz. Fixed sights. Blued finish. Checkered walnut grips. Disc. prior to 1942.

TRAPPER MODEL DA . . . . NiB $388 Ex $219 Gd $130
Solid frame. Caliber: .22 LR. Seven-round cylinder, 6-inch octagon bbl., weight: 12.5 oz. Fixed sights. Blued finish. Checkered walnut grips. Safety cylinder on later models. Disc. prior to 1942.

ULTRA SPORTSMAN . . . . NiB $321 Ex $219 Gd $165
SA. Hinged frame. Caliber: .22 LR. Nine-round cylinder, 6-inch bbl., weight: 30 oz. Adj. target sights. Blued finish. Checkered walnut grips. This model has short action, wide hammer spur, cylinder is length of a .22 LR cartridge. Disc. prior to 1942.

VEST POCKET DA . . . . NiB $138 Ex $95 Gd $70
Solid frame. Spurless hammer. Calibers: .22 Rimfire, .32 S&W. Seven-round (.22 cal.) or 5-round (.32 cal.) cylinder, 1.13-inch bbl., weight: About 9 oz. Blued or nickel finish. Hard rubber grips. Disc. prior to 1942.

YOUNG AMERICA DA . . . . NiB $241 Ex $109 Gd $81
Solid frame. Calibers: .22 Long, .32 S&W. Seven-round (.22 cal.) or 5-round (.32 cal.) cylinder. Bbl. lengths: 2-, 4.5- and 6-inches. Weight: About 9 oz. Fixed sights. Blued or nickel finish. Hard rubber grips. Disc. prior to 1942.

HARTFORD ARMS & EQUIPMENT CO. — Hartford, Connecticut

Hartford pistols were the forebearer of the original High Standard line. High Standard Mfg. Corp. acquired Hartford Arms & Equipment Co. in 1932. The High Standard Model B is essentially the same as the Hartford Automatic.

AUTOMATIC
TARGET PISTOL . . . . NiB $648 Ex $534 Gd $431
Caliber. .22 LR. 10-round magazine, 6.75-inch bbl., 10.75 inches overall. Weight: 31 oz. Target sights. Blued finish. Black rubber grips. This gun closely resembles the early Colt Woodsman and High Standard pistols. Made 1929 to 1930.
REPEATING PISTOL . . . . NiB $785 Ex $576 Gd $342
Check for authenticity. This model is a hand-operated repeating pistol similar to the Fiala and Schall pistols Made from 1929 to 1930.

SINGLE-SHOT
TARGET PISTOL . . . . NiB $785 Ex $577 Gd $342
Similar in appearance to the Hartford Automatic. Caliber: .22 LR, 6.75-inch bbl., 10.75 inches overall. Weight: 38 oz. Target sights. Mottled frame and slide, blued bbl., Black rubber or walnut grips. Made from 1929 to 1930.

HASKELL MANUFACTURING — Lima, Ohio
See listings under Hi-Point.

HAWES FIREARMS — Van Nuys, California

DEPUTY MARSHAL SA REVOLVER
Calibers: .22 LR, also .22 WMR in two-cylinder combination. Six-round cylinder, 5.5-inch bbl., 11 inches overall. Weight: 34 oz. Adj. rear sight, blade front. Blued finish. Plastic or walnut grips. Imported 1973 to 1981.
.22 LR (plastic grips).........**NiB $219 Ex $120 Gd $88**
Combination, .22 LR/.22 WMR
   (plastic)...............**NiB $293 Ex $219 Gd $130**
Walnut grips, add..............................**$20**

Hawes
Deputy Marshal

DEPUTY DENVER MARSHAL
Same as Deputy Marshal SA except has brass frame. Imported 1973 to 1981.
.22 LR (plastic grips)........**NiB $265 Ex $212 Gd $110**
Combination, .22 LR/.22 WMR
   (plastic)................**NiB $293 Ex $219 Gd $130**
Walnut grips add............................. **$10**

DEPUTY MONTANA MARSHAL
Same as Deputy Marshal except has brass grip frame. Walnut grips only. Imported from 1973 to 1981.
.22 LR....................**NiB $283 Ex $198 Gd $118**
Combination, .22 LR/.22 WMR...**NiB $321 Ex $235 Gd $128**

Hawes
Deputy Montana Marshal

DEPUTY SILVER CITY MARSHAL
Same as Deputy Marshal except has chrome-plated frame, brass grip frame, blued cylinder and bbl., Imported from 1973 to 1981.
.22 LR (plastic grips).........**NiB $281 Ex $209 Gd $158**
Combination, .22 LR/.22 WMR
   (plastic)................**NiB $306 Ex $205 Gd $115**
Walnut grips, add.............................**$15**

Hawes
Deputy Silver City

DEPUTY TEXAS MARSHAL
Same as Deputy Marshal except has chrome finish. Imported 1973 to 1981.
.22 LR (plastic grips)........**NiB $293 Ex $205 Gd $110**
Combination, .22 LR/.22 WMR
   (plastic)................**NiB $306 Ex $190 Gd $110**
Walnut grips, add.............................**$15**

Hawes
Deputy Texas Marshal

FAVORITE SINGLE-SHOT
TARGET PISTOL............. **NiB $219 Ex $128 Gd $90**
Replica of Stevens No. 35. Tip-up action. Caliber: .22 LR. Eight-inch bbl., 12 inches overall. Weight: 24 oz. Target sights. Chrome-plated frame. Blued bbl., Plastic or rosewood grips (add $5). Imported 1972- to 1976.

SAUER CHIEF MARSHAL SA TARGET REVOLVER
Same as Western Marshal except has adjustable rear sight and front sight, oversized rosewood grips. Not made in .22 caliber. Imported from 1973 to 1981.
.357 Magnum or .45 Colt.....**NiB $326 Ex $254 Gd $189**
.44 Magnum...............**NiB $362 Ex $282 Gd $214**
Combination .357 Magnum and 9mm Para.
   .45 Colt and .45 Auto.......**NiB $362 Ex $282 Gd $214**
Combination
   .44 Magnum and .44-40.....**NiB $369 Ex $290 Gd $225**

Hawes Sauer Chief
Marshal

SAUER FEDERAL MARSHAL
Same as Western Marshal except has color-casehardened frame, brass grip frame, one-piece walnut grip. Not made in .22 caliber. Imported from 1973 to 1981.

Hawes Sauer
Federal Marshal

Hawes Sauer
Montana Marshal .22

Hawes Sauer
Silver City Marshal

Hawes Sauer
Texas Marshal

Hawes Sauer
Western Marshal

.357 Magnum or .45 Colt . . . . . NiB $321 Ex $235 Gd $198
.44 Magnum . . . . NiB $362 Ex $235 Gd $198
Combination .357 Magnum and 9mm Para.,
    .45 Colt and .45 Auto . . . . NiB $362 Ex $290 Gd $198
Combination .44 Magnum
    and .44-40 . . . . NiB $369 Ex $305 Gd $189

SAUER MONTANA MARSHAL
Same as Western Marshal except has brass grip frame.
Imported from 1973 to 1981.
.357 Magnum or .45 Colt . . . . . NiB $326 Ex $270 Gd $190
.44 Magnum . . . . NiB $357 Ex $281 Gd $214
Combination .357 Magnum and 9mm Para.,
    .45 Colt and .45 Auto . . . . NiB $377 Ex $301 Gd $219
Combination .44 Magnum
    and .44-40 . . . . NiB $385 Ex $309 Gd $220
.22 LR . . . . NiB $306 Ex $240 Gd $180
Combination .22 LR
    and .22 WMR . . . . NiB $332 Ex $281 Gd $190

SAUER SILVER CITY MARSHAL
Same as Western Marshal except has nickel plated frame, brass
grip frame, blued cylinder and barrel, pearlite grips. Imported
from 1973 to 1981.
.44 Magnum . . . . NiB $377 Ex $289 Gd $219
Combination .357 Magnum and 9mm Para.,
    .45 Colt and .45 Auto . . . . NiB $362 Ex $270 Gd $180
Combination .44 Magnum
    and .44-40 . . . . NiB $365 Ex $270 Gd $214

SAUER TEXAS MARSHAL
Same as Western Marshal except nickel plated, has pearlite
grips. Imported from 1973 to 1981.

.357 Magnum or .45 Colt . . . . . NiB $362 Ex $270 Gd $204
.44 Magnum . . . . NiB $365 Ex $303 Gd $214
Combination .357 Magnum and 9mm Para.,
    .45 Colt and .45 Auto . . . . NiB $388 Ex $321 Gd $225
Combination .44 Magnum
    and .44-40 . . . . NiB $395 Ex $332 Gd $239
.22 LR . . . . NiB $321 Ex $244 Gd $189
Combination .22 LR
    and .22 WMR . . . . NiB $336 Ex $265 Gd $189

SAUER WESTERN MARSHAL SA REVOLVER
Calibers: .22 LR (disc.), .357 Magnum, .44 Magnum,
.45 Auto. Also in two-cylinder combinations: .22 WMR
(disc.), 9mm Para., .44-40, .45 Auto. Six-round cylinder,
bbl. lengths: 5.5-inch (disc.), 6-inch, 11.75 inches overall
(with 6-inch bbl.). Weight: 46 oz. Fixed sights. Blued finish.
Originally furnished w/simulated stag plastic grips. Recent
production has smooth rosewood grips. Made from 1968
by J. P. Sauer & Sohn, Eckernforde, Germany. Imported from
1973 to 1981.
.357 Magnum or .45 LC . . . . . . NiB $357 Ex $265 Gd $200
.44 Magnum . . . . NiB $377 Ex $290 Gd $219
Combination .357 Magnum and 9mm Para.,
    .45 Colt and .45 Auto . . . . NiB $385 Ex $270 Gd $214
Combination .44 Magnum
    and .44-40 . . . . NiB $385 Ex $270 Gd $214
.22 LR . . . . NiB $281 Ex $198 Gd $160
Combination .22 LR
    and .22 WMR . . . . NiB $281 Ex $198 Gd $160

HECKLER & KOCH — Oberndorf am Neckar, Germany, and Chantilly, Virginia

MODEL HK4 DA AUTO PISTOL

Calibers: .380 Automatic (9mm Short), .22 LR, .25 Automatic (6.35mm), .32 Automatic (7.65mm) w/conversion kits. Seven-round magazine (.380 Auto), 8-round in other calibers, 3.4-inch bbl., 6.19 inches overall. Weight: 18 oz. Fixed sights. Blued finish. Plastic grip. Disc. 1984.

.22 LR or .380 units to kit. . . . . . NiB $536 Ex $388 Gd $265
.25 ACP or .32 ACP units to kit. . . . NiB $536 Ex $377 Gd $255
.380 units to kit w/.22
  conversion unit. . . . . NiB $530 Ex $357 Gd $225
.380 units to kit w/.22, .25, .32
  conversion units . . . . NiB $530 Ex $357 Gd $225

Heckler & Koch
Model HK4

MARK 23 DA

AUTO PISTOL . . . . NiB $2356 Ex $1831 Gd $1290
Short-recoil semiautomatic pistol w/polymer frame and steel slide. Caliber: .45 ACP. 10-round magazine, 5.87-inch bbl., 9.65 inches overall. Weight: 43 oz. Seven interchangeable rear sight adjustment units w/3-dot system. Developed primarily in response to specifications by the Special Operations Command (SOCOM) for a Special Operations Forces Offensive Handgun Weapon System. Imported from 1996 to date.

MODEL P7 K3 DA AUTO PISTOL

Caliber: .380 ACP. Eight-round magazine, 3.8 inch-bbl., 6.3 inches overall. Weight: About 26 oz. Adj. rear sight. Imported 1988 to 1994.

.380 Cal. . . . . NiB $954 Ex $785 Gd $546
.22 LR conversion kit . . . . NiB $713 Ex $611 Gd $434
.32 ACP conversion kit . . . . . . NiB $388 Ex $328 Gd $228

Heckler & Koch
Mark 23

MODEL P7 M8 . . . . NiB $1295 Ex $804 Gd $577

Squeeze-cock SA semiautomatic pistol. Caliber: 9mm Para. Eight-round magazine, 4.13-inch bbl., 6.73 inches overall. Weight: 29.9 oz. Matte black or nickel finish. Adjustable rear sight. Imported from 1985 to 2005.

MODEL P7 M10

Caliber: .40 S&W. Nine-round magazine, 4.2-inch bbl., 6.9 inches overall. Weight: 43 oz. Fixed front sight blade, adj. rear w/3-dot system. Imported from 1992 to 1994.

Blued finish . . . . NiB $1163 Ex $879 Gd $643
Nickel finish . . . . NiB $1163 Ex $879 Gd $643

Heckler & Koch
Model P7K3

MODEL P7 M13. . . . . NiB $2219 Ex $1848 Gd $1632

Caliber: 9mm. 13-round magazine, 4.13-inch bbl., 6.65 inches overall. Weight: 34.42 oz. Matte black finish. Adj. rear sight. Imported 1985 to 1994.

MODEL P7 (PSP). . . . . NiB $917 Ex $701 Gd $510

Caliber: 9mm Para. Eight-round magazine, 4.13-inch bbl., 6.54 inches overall. DA. Weight: About 33.5 oz. Blued finish. Imported 1983 to 1985 and 1990 with limited availability.

MODEL P9S DA AUTOMATIC PISTOL

Calibers: 9mm Para., .45 Automatic. Nine-round (9mm) or 7-round (.45 Auto) magazine. Four-inch bbl., 7.63 inches overall. Weight: 32 ounces. Fixed sights. Blued finish. Contoured plastic grips. This model disc. 1986.

Heckler & Koch
Model P7M13

**Heckler & Koch
Model P7 (PSP)**

**Heckler & Koch
Model USP9 Compact (Stainless)**

**Heckler & Koch
Model P9S DA**

Heckler & Koch USP45

9mm . . . . NiB $893 Ex $663 Gd $486
.45 Automatic . . . . NiB $918 Ex $713 Gd $500

MODEL P9S TARGET COMPETITION KIT
Same as Model P9S Target except comes w/Extra 5.5-inch bbl. and bbl. weights. Also available w/walnut competition grip.
w/standard grip . . . . NiB $1061 Ex $973 Gd $745
w/competition grip . . . . NiB $1199 Ex $1121 Gd $891

MODEL SP89 . . . . NiB $4023 Ex $3224 Gd $2227
Semiautomatic, recoil-operated, delayed roller-locked bolt system. Caliber: 9mm Para. 15-round magazine, 4.5-inch bbl., 13 inches overall. Weight: 68 oz. Hooded front sight, adj. rotary-aperture rear. Imported 1989 to 1993.

MODEL USP . . . . NiB $928 Ex $627 Gd $468
Polymer integral grip/frame design w/recoil reduction system. Calibers: 9mm Para., .40 S&W or .45 ACP. 15-round (9mm) or 13-round (.40 S&W and .45ACP) magazine, 4.13- or 4.25-inch bbl., 6.88 to 7.87 inches overall. Weight: 26.5-30.4 oz. Blade front sight, adj. rear w/3-dot system. Matte black finish. Stippled black polymer grip. Available in SA/DA or DAO. Imported 1993 to date.
Stainless finish. . . . . NiB $816 Ex $510 Gd 332
w/Tritium sights, add $100
w/ambidextrous decocking lever, add $30

MODEL USP9 COMPACT. . . NiB $1301 Ex $1193 Gd $1029
Caliber: 9mm. 10-round magazine, 4.25-inch bbl., 7.64 inches overall. Weight: 25.5 oz. Short recoil w/modified Browning action. 3-dot sighting system. Polymer frame w/integral grips, blued slide finish. Imported from 1993 to date.
Stainless slide finish . . . . . . NiB $1301 Ex $1193 Gd $1029
w/ambidextrous decocking lever, add $75

MODEL USP40 COMPACT
Caliber: .40 S&W. 10-round magazine, 3.58- inch bbl., 6.81 inches overall. Weight: 27 oz. Short recoil w/modified Browning action. 3-dot sighting system. Polymer frame w/ integral grips, blued slide finish. Imported from 1993 to date.

Heckler & Koch Model USP45 Compact 50th Anniversary

Heckler & Koch Model USP Expert

Heckler & Koch Model USP Tactical

Blued finish. . . . . NiB $857 Ex $615 Gd $437
Stainless finish. . . . . NiB $774 Ex $627 Gd $431
w/ambidextrous decocking lever, add $50

MODEL USP45 COMPACT . . . NiB $918 Ex $615 Gd $410
Caliber: .45 ACP. Eight-round magazine, 3.8- inch bbl., 7.09 inches overall. Weight: 28 oz. Short recoil w/modified Browning action. 3-dot sighting system. Polymer frame w/integral grips. Imported from 1998 to date.
Stainless slide finish . . . . NiB $816 Ex $639 Gd $431
w/ambidextrous decocking lever, add $50
50th Anniversary
   (1 of 1,000). . . . . NiB $1199 Ex $947 Gd $709

MODEL USP EXPERT . . . . . . NiB $1301 Ex $1142 Gd $842
Caliber: .45 ACP. 10-round magazine, 6.2- inch bbl., 9.65 inches overall. Weight: 30 oz. Adjustable 3-dot target sights. Short recoil modified Browning action w/recoil reduction system. Reinforced polymer frame w/integral grips and match-grade slide. Imported from 1999 to 2009.

MODEL USP TACTICAL . . . . . NiB $1178 Ex $933 Gd $638
SOCOM Enhanced version of the USP Standard Model, w/4.92-inch threaded bbl. Chambered for .45 ACP only. Imported from 1998 to date.

MODEL VP 70Z AUTO PISTOL NiB $791 Ex $536 Gd $377
Caliber: 9mm Para. 18-round magazine, 4.5-inch bbl., 8 inches overall. Weight: 32.5 oz. DA Fixed sights. Blued slide, polymer receiver and grip. Disc. 1986.

Heckler & Koch Model VP 7OZ

HELWAN
See listings under Interarms.

HERITAGE MANUFACTURING — Opa Locka, Florida

Acquired by Taurus Int'l. in 2012

Heritage Rough Rider shown w/
birds head grip

Heritage
Sentry

MODEL H-25 AUTO PISTOL
Caliber: .25 ACP. Six-round magazine, 2.5-inch bbl., 4.63
inches overall. Weight: 12 oz. Fixed sights. Blued or chrome
finish. Made 1995 to 1999.
Blued. . . . . NiB $136 Ex $95 Gd $75
Nickel, add $20

ROUGH RIDER SA REVOLVER
Calibers: .22 LR, .22 Mag. Six-round cylinder. bbl. lengths:
2.75, 3.75, 4.75, 6.5 or 9 inches. Weight: 31-38 oz. Blade front
sight, fixed rear. High-polished blued finish w/gold accents.
Smooth walnut grips. Made from 1993 to date.
.22 LR . . . . NiB $247 Ex $115 Gd $95
.22 LR/.22 Mag. combo . . . . . . NiB $291 Ex $179 Gd $110

SENTRY DA REVOLVER
Calibers: .22 LR, .22 Mag., .32 Mag., 9mm or .38 Special.
Six- or 8-round (rimfire) cylinder, 2- or 4-inch bbl., 6.25 inches
overall (2-inch bbl.). Ramp front sight, fixed rear. Blued or
nickel finish. Checkered polymer grips. Made from 1993 to
1997.
Blued. . . . . NiB $131 Ex $95 Gd $75
Nickel, add $15

STEALTH DA AUTO PISTOL . . . NiB $241 Ex $179 Gd $101
Calibers: 9mm, .40 S&W. 10-round magazine, 3.9-inch bbl.,
weight: 20.2 oz. Gas-delayed blowback, double action only.
AmbidExtrous trigger safety. Blade front sight, drift-adj. rear.
Black chrome or stainless slide. Black polymer grip frame.
Made from 1996 to 2000.

HI-POINT FIREARMS — Mansfield, Ohio

MODEL JS-9MM
AUTO PISTOL. . . . . NiB $158 Ex $101 Gd $75
Caliber: 9mm Para. Eight-round magazine, 4.5-inch bbl., 7.75
inches overall. Weight: 39 oz. Fixed low-profile sights w/3-dot
system. Matte blue, matte black or chrome finish. Checkered
synthetic grips. Made from 1990 to 2000.

MODEL JS-9MM COMPETITION
PISTOL (STALLARD) . . . . NiB $151 Ex $90 Gd $69
Similar to standard JS-9 except w/4-inch compensated bbl.
w/ shortened slide and adj. sights. 10-round magazine, 7.25
inches overall. Weight: 30 oz. Made from 1998 to 2006.

MODEL JS-9MM/C-9MM COMPACT PISTOL
(BEEMILLER) . . . . NiB $148 Ex $90 Gd $75
Similar to standard JS-9 except w/3.5-inch bbl. and shortened
slide w/alloy or polymer frame. 6.72 inches overall. Weight:
29 oz. or 32 oz. Three-dot-style sights. Made from 1993 to
date.

MODEL CF-.380
POLYMER . . . . NiB $158 Ex $88 Gd $61
Caliber: .380 ACP. Eight-round magazine, 3.5-inch bbl., 6.72
inches overall. Weight: 32 oz. Three-dot sights. Made from
1994 to date.

MODEL JS-.40/JC-.40 AUTO PISTOL
(IBERIA) . . . . NiB $171 Ex $110 Gd $75
Similar to Model JS-9mm except in caliber .40 S&W.

MODEL JS-.45/JH-.45 AUTO PISTOL
(HASKELL). . . . . NiB $150 Ex $101 Gd $70
Similar to Model JS-9mm except in caliber .45 ACP w/7-round
magazine and two-tone Polymer finish.

J. C. HIGGINS
See Sears, Roebuck & Company.

HIGH STANDARD SPORTING FIREARMS
— East Hartford, Connecticut
*Formerly High Standard Mfg. Co., Hamden, ConnecticutA
long-standing producer of sporting arms, High Standard disc.
its operations in 1984. See new High Standard models under
separate entry, HIGH STANDARD MFG. CO., INC.*

NOTE: *For ease in finding a particular firearm, High Standard
handguns are grouped into three sections: Automatic pistols,
derringers and revolvers. For a complete listing, please refer to
the Index.*

- AUTOMATIC PISTOLS -

MODEL A
HAMMERLESS. . . . . NiB $847 Ex $748 Gd $497
Caliber: .22 LR. 10-round magazine, bbl. lengths: 4.5-, 6.75-
inch. 11.5 inches overall (6.75-inch bbl.). Weight: 36 oz. (in
6.75-inch bbl.). Adj. target sights. Blued finish. Checkered
walnut grips. Made from 1938 to 1942.

MODEL B
AUTOMATIC PISTOL . . . . NiB $668 Ex $444 Gd $367
Original Standard pistol. Hammerless. Caliber: .22 LR.
10-round magazine, bbl. lengths: 4.5-, 6.75-inch, 10.75 inches

High Standard
Model A

High Standard
Model B

High Standard
Model D

overall (with 6.75-inch bbl.). Weight: 33 oz. (6.75-inch bbl.). Fixed sights. Blued finish. Hard rubber grips. Made from 1932 to 1942.

MODEL C
AUTOMATIC PISTOL . . . . NiB $979 Ex $826 Gd $549
Same as Model B except in .22 Short. Made 1935 to 1942.

MODEL D
AUTOMATIC PISTOL . . . . NiB $1020 Ex $774 Gd $544
Same general specifications as Model A but heavier bbl., weight: 40 oz. (6.75-inch bbl.). Made from 1937 to 1942.

DURA-MATIC . . . . NiB $362 Ex $301 Gd $204
Takedown. Caliber: .22 LR. 10-round magazine, 4.5 or 6.5 inch interchangeable bbl., 10.88 inches overall (6.5-inch bbl.). Weight: 35 oz. (in 6.5-inch bbl.). Fixed sights. Blued finish. Checkered grips. Made from 1952 to 1970.

MODEL E
AUTOMATIC PISTOL . . . . . . NiB $1275 Ex $1051 Gd $929
Same general specifications as Model A but w/Extra heavy bbl. and thumbrest grips. Weight: 42 oz. (6.75-inch bbl.). Made 1937 to 1942.

FIELD-KING AUTOMATIC PISTOL FIRST MODEL
Same general specifications as Sport-King but w/heavier bbl. and target sights. Late model 6.75-inch bbls. have recoil stabilizer and lever take-down feature. Weight: 43 oz. (6.75-inch bbl.). Made from 1951 to 1958.
w/one bbl. . . . . NiB $683 Ex $529 Gd $408
w/both bbls., add $204

FIELD-KING AUTOMATIC PISTOL SECOND MODEL
Same general specifications as First Model Field-King but w/ button take-down and marked FK 100 or FK 101.
w/one bbl. . . . . NiB $852 Ex $588 Gd $324
w/both bbls., add $204

FLITE-KING AUTOMATIC PISTOL — FIRST MODEL
Same general specifications as Sport-King except in .22. Short w/aluminum alloy frame and slide and marked FK 100 or FK 101. Weight: 26 oz. (6.5-inch bbl.). Made 1953-58.
w/one bbl. . . . . NiB $668 Ex $469 Gd $342
w/both bbls. . . . . NiB $872 Ex $660 Gd $546

High Standard Dura-Matic

High Standard
Model E

**High Standard
G-380**

**High Standard
Model G-B**

**High Standard
Model G-E**

**High Standard
Model H-A**

**High Standard
Model H-B**

FLITE-KING AUTOMATIC PISTOL — SECOND MODEL
Same as Flite-King—First Model except w/steel frame and marked in the 102 or 103 series. Made from 1958 to 1966.
Model 102 . . . . NiB $556 Ex $398 Gd $265
Model 103 . . . . NiB $536 Ex $388 Gd $219

MODEL G-380
AUTOMATIC PISTOL . . . . NiB $668 Ex $571 Gd $408
Lever takedown. Visible hammer. Thumb safety. Caliber: .380 Automatic. Six-round magazine, 5-inch bbl., weight: 40 oz. Fixed sights. Blued finish. Checkered plastic grips. Made 1943 to 1950.

MODEL G-B AUTOMATIC PISTOL
Lever takedown. Hammerless. Interchangeable bbls. Caliber: .22 LR. 10-round magazine, bbl. lengths: 4.5, 6.75 inches, 10.75 inches overall (with 6.75-inch bbl.). Weight: 36 oz. (with 6.75-inch bbl.). Fixed sights. Blued finish. Checkered plastic grips. Made 1948 to 1951.
w/one bbl. . . . . NiB $689 Ex $500 Gd $365
w/both bbls. . . . . NiB $893 Ex $704 Gd $576

MODEL G-D AUTOMATIC PISTOL
Lever takedown. Hammerless. Interchangeable bbls. Caliber: .22 LR. 10-round magazine, bbl. lengths: 4.5, 6.75 inches. 11.5 inches overall (with 6.75-inch bbl.). Weight: 41 oz. (6.75-inch bbl.). Target sights. Blued finish. Checkered walnut grips. Made 1948 to 1951.
w/one bbl. . . . . NiB $1076 Ex $917 Gd $709
w/both bbls. . . . . NiB $1275 Ex $1048 Gd $898

MODEL G-E AUTOMATIC PISTOL
Same general specifications as Model G-D but w/Extra heavy bbl. and thumbrest grips. Weight: 44 oz. (with 6.75-inch bbl.). Made from 1949 to 1951.
w/one bbl. . . . . NiB $1488 Ex $1266 Gd $1015
w/both bbls. . . . . NiB $1692 Ex $1470 Gd $1200

MODEL H-A
AUTOMATIC PISTOL . . . . . . NiB $2230 Ex $1355 Gd $859
Same as Model A but w/visible hammer, no thumb safety. Made from 1939 to 1942.

MODEL H-B
AUTOMATIC PISTOL . . . . NiB $816 Ex $590 Gd $433
Same as Model B but w/visible hammer, no thumb safety. Made from 1940 to 1942.

MODEL H-D
AUTOMATIC PISTOL . . . . . . NiB $1282 Ex $1122 Gd $806
Same as Model D but w/visible hammer, no thumb safety. Made from 1939 to 1942.

MODEL H-DM
AUTOMATIC PISTOL . . . . NiB $663 Ex $524 Gd $429
Also called H-D Military. Same as Model H-D but w/thumb safety. Made from 1941 to 1951.

**High Standard
Olympic Military**

**High Standard
Model H-E**

**High Standard Olympic
Automatic – First Model**

**High Standard Olympic
Automatic – Second Model**

**High Standard
Olympic I.S.U.**

**High Standard Olympic
I.S.U. Military**

MODEL H-E
AUTOMATIC PISTOL . . . . . NiB $2275 Ex $2142 Gd $1197
Same as Model E but w/visible hammer, no thumb safety. Made from 1939 to 1942.

OLYMPIC AUTOMATIC PISTOL FIRST MODEL (G-O)
Same general specifications as Model G-E but in .22 Short w/ light alloy slide. Made from 1950 to 1951.
w/one bbl. . . . . NiB $1785 Ex $1153 Gd $629
w/both bbls, add. $408

OLYMPIC AUTOMATIC SECOND MODEL
Same general specifications as Supermatic but in .22 Short w/light alloy slide. Weight: 39 oz. (6.75-inch bbl.). Made 1951 to 1958.
w/one bbl. . . . . NiB $1325 Ex $1076 Gd $730
w/both bbls, add. $306

OLYMPIC AUTOMATIC PISTOL,
THIRD MODEL. . . . . NiB $1213 Ex $984 Gd $734
Same as Supermatic Trophy w/bull bbl. except in .22 Short. Made from 1963 to 1966.

OLYMPIC COMMEMORATIVE
Limited edition of Supermatic Trophy Military issued to commemorate the only American-made rimfire target pistol ever to win an Olympic gold medal. Highly engraved w/Olympic rings inlaid in gold. Deluxe presentation case. Two versions issued: In 1972 (.22 LR) and 1980 (.22 Short).
1972 issue. . . . . NiB $6523 Ex $5416 Gd $3550
1980 issue. . . . . NiB $2243 Ex $1877 Gd $1215

OLYMPIC I.S.U . . . . NiB $1316 Ex $1020 Gd $798
Same as Supermatic Citation except caliber .22 Short, 6.75- or 8-inch tapered bbl. w/stabilizer, detachable weights. Made from 1958 to 1977. Eight-inch bbl. disc. in 1966.

OLYMPIC I.S.U. MILITARY . . . NiB $1120 Ex $940 Gd $702
Same as Olympic I.S.U. except has military grip and bracket rear sight. Intro. in 1965. Disc.

OLYMPIC MILITARY . . . . NiB $1142 Ex $932 Gd $755
Same as Olympic — Third Model except has military grip and bracket rear sight. Made in 1965.

SHARPSHOOTER
AUTOMATIC PISTOL . . . . NiB $385 Ex $267 Gd $197
Takedown. Hammerless. Caliber: .22 LR. 10-round magazine, 5.5-inch bull bbl., 9 inches overall. Weight: 42 oz. Micrometer rear sight, blade front sight. Blued finish. Plastic grips. Made from 1971 to 1983.

**High Standard Sport-King
Automatic — First Model**

**High Standard Sport-King
Automatic — Second Model**

**High Standard Sport-King
Automatic — Third Model**

High Standard Supermatic

**High Standard Mfg. Co.
10-X Supermatic Citation
(current mfg.)**

SPORT-KING AUTOMATIC PISTOL FIRST MODEL

Takedown. Hammerless. Interchangeable barrels. Caliber: .22 LR. 10-round magazine, barrel lengths: 4.5-, 6.75-inches. 11.5 inches overall (with 6.75-inch barrel). Weight: 39 oz. (with 6.75-inch barrel). Fixed sights. Blued finish. Checkered plastic thumbrest grips. Made from 1951 to 1958. Note: 1951 to 1954 production has lever takedown as in "G" series. Later version (illustrated at left) has push-button takedown.

w/one bbl. . . . . NiB $388 Ex $306 Gd $220
w/both bbls. . . . . NiB $590 Ex $500 Gd $408

SPORT-KING AUTOMATIC PISTOL

SECOND MODEL . . . . NiB $357 Ex $279 Gd $204
Caliber: .22 LR. 10-round magazine, 4.5- or 6.75 inch interchangeable bbl. 11.25 inches overall (with 6.75-inch barrel). Weight: 42 oz. (with 6.75-inch barrel). Fixed sights. Blued finish. Checkered grips. Made from 1958 to 1970.

SPORT-KING AUTOMATIC PISTOL

THIRD MODEL . . . . NiB $305 Ex $204 Gd $135
Similar to Sport-King — Second Model with same general specifications for weight and length. Blued or nickel finish. Introduced in 1974. Disc.

SPORT-KING LIGHTWEIGHT

Same as standard Sport-King except lightweight has forged aluminum alloy frame. Weight: 30 oz. with 6.75-inch barrel Made from 1954 to 1965.

w/one bbl. . . . . NiB $590 Ex $380 Gd $255
w/both bbls. . . . . NiB $791 Ex $602 Gd $453

SUPERMATIC AUTOMATIC PISTOL

Takedown. Hammerless. Interchangeable bbls. Caliber: .22 LR. 10-round magazine, barrel lengths: 4.5-, 6.75-inches. Late model 6.75-inch barrel have recoil stabilizer feature. Weight: 43 oz. (with 6.75-inch barrel) 11.5 inches overall (with 6.75-inch barrel). Target sights. Elevated serrated rib between sights. Adjustable barrel weights add 2 or 3 oz. Blued finish. Checkered plastic thumb-rest grips. Made from 1951 to 1958.

w/one bbl. . . . . NiB $872 Ex $683 Gd $509
w/both bbls. . . . . NiB $1070 Ex $893 Gd $714

SUPERMATIC CITATION

Same as Supermatic Tournament except 6.75-, 8- or 10-inch tapered bbl. with stabilizer and two removable weights. Also furnished with Tournament's 5.5-inch bull barrel, adjustable trigger pull, recoil-proof click-adjustable rear sight (barrel-mounted on 8- and 10-inch barrels), checkered walnut thumbrest grips on bull barrel model. Currently manufactured with only bull barrel. Made from 1958 to 1966.

**High Standard Victor
Solid Rib Barrel**

w/5.5-inch bull bbl. . . . . NiB $893 Ex $612 Gd $377
w/6.75-inch tapered bbl. . . . . NiB $893 Ex $612 Gd $377
w/8-inch tapered bbl. . . . . . . NiB $1066 Ex $760 Gd $536
w/10-inch tapered bbl. . . . . . NiB $1099 Ex $811 Gd $571

SUPERMATIC CITATION MILITARY
Same as Supermatic Citation except has military grip and bracket rear sight as in Supermatic Trophy. Made from 1965 to 1973.
w/bull bbl. . . . . NiB $897 Ex $581 Gd $499
w/fluted bbl. . . . . NiB $964 Ex $806 Gd $602

SUPERMATIC
TOURNAMENT . . . . NiB $734 Ex $587 Gd $362
Takedown. Caliber: .22 LR. 10-round magazine, interchangeable 5.5-inch bull or 6.75-inch heavy tapered bbl., notched and drilled for stabilizer and weights. 10 inches overall (with 5.5-inch bbl.). Weight: 44 oz. (5.5-inch bbl.). Click adj. rear sight, undercut ramp front. Blued finish. Checkered grips. Made from 1958 to 1966.

SUPERMATIC TOURNAMENT
MILITARY . . . . NiB $1305 Ex $997 Gd $836
Same as Supermatic Tournament except has military grip. Made from 1965 to 1971.

SUPERMATIC TROPHY
Same as Supermatic Citation except with 5.5-inch bull bbl., or 7.25-inch fluted bbl., w/detachable stabilizer and weights, Extra magazine, High-luster blued finish, checkered walnut thumbrest grips. Made from 1963 to 1966.
w/bull bbl. . . . . NiB $1305 Ex $1090 Gd $638
w/fluted bbl. . . . . NiB $1305 Ex $1090 Gd $638

SUPERMATIC TROPHY MILITARY
Same as Supermatic Trophy except has military grip and bracket rear sight. Made from 1965 to 1984.
w/bull bbl. . . . . NiB $1357 Ex $1060 Gd $760
w/fluted bbl. . . . . NiB $1408 Ex $1120 Gd $813

THE VICTOR AUTOMATIC . . . NiB $3299 Ex $2798 Gd $2550
Takedown. Caliber: .22 LR. 10-round magazine, 4.5-inch solid or vent rib and 5.5-inch vent rib, interchangeable bbl., 9.75 inches overall (with 5.5-inch bbl.). Weight: 52 oz. (with 5.5-inch bbl.). Rib mounted target sights. Blued finish. Checkered walnut thumbrest grips. Standard or military grip configuration. Made from 1972 to 1984 (standard-grip model made from 1974 to 1975).

**High Standard
Supermatic Citation Bull Barrel**

**High Standard
Supermatic Citation Military Fluted Barrel**

**High Standard
Supermatic Tournament Bull Barrel**

**High Standard
Supermatic Tournament Military Tapered Barrel**

**High Standard
Supermatic Trophy Bull Barrel**

High Standard Derringer

High Standard Double-Nine — Steel Frame

High Standard Durango

High Standard Sierra

- DERRINGERS -

DERRINGER
Hammerless, double action, two-round, double bbl. (over/under). Calibers: .22 Short, Long, LR or .22 Magnum Rimfire, 3.5-inch bbls., 5 inches overall. Weight: 11 oz. Standard model has blued or nickel finish w/plastic grips. Presentation model is goldplated in walnut case. Standard model made from 1963 (.22 S-L-LR) and 1964 (.22 MRF) to 1984. Gold model, made from 1965 to 1983.

Standard model (blue) . . . . NiB $332 Ex $225 Gd $204
Standard model (nickel) . . . . . . NiB $332 Ex $225 Gd $204
Standard model
(Electroless nickel). . . . . NiB $337 Ex $291 Gd $230
Gold Presentation
One Derringer. . . . . NiB $541 Ex $362 Gd $286
Silver Presentation
One Derringer. . . . . NiB $592 Ex $431 Gd $342
Presentation Set, Matched pair, consecutive
numbers (1965 only) . . . . NiB $1392 Ex $1180 Gd $836

- REVOLVERS -

CAMP GUN . . . . NiB $270 Ex $220 Gd $189
Same as Sentinel Mark I/Mark IV except has 6-inch bbl., adj. rear sight, target-style checkered walnut grips. Caliber: .22 LR or .22 WMR. Made from 1976 to 1983.

DOUBLE-NINE DA REVOLVER —ALUMINUM FRAME
Western-style version of Sentinel. Blued or nickel finish w/ simulated ivory, ebony or stag grips, 5.5-inch bbl., 11 inches overall. Weight: 27.25 oz. Made from 1959 to 1971.
Blue model . . . . NiB $255 Ex $190 Gd $150

DOUBLE-NINE—STEEL FRAME
Similar to Double-Nine—Aluminum Frame, w/same general specifications except w/steel frame and has Extra cylinder for .22 WMR, walnut grips. Intro. in 1971. Disc.
Blue model . . . . NiB $291 Ex $225 Gd $179
Nickel model. . . . . NiB $306 Ex $225 Gd $190

DOUBLE-NINE DELUXE. . . . . . NiB $326 Ex $240 Gd $198
Same as Double-Nine Steel Frame except has adj. target rear sight. Intro. in 1971. Disc.

DURANGO
Similar to Double-Nine—Steel Frame except .22 LR only, available w/4.5- or 5.5-inch bbl. Made from 1971 to 1973.
Blue model . . . . NiB $275 Ex $189 Gd $150
Nickel model. . . . . NiB $301 Ex $219 Gd $170

HIGH SIERRA DA REVOLVER
Similar to Double-Nine—Steel Frame except has 7-inch octagon bbl., w/gold-plated grip frame, fixed or adj. sights. Made 1973 to 1983.
w/fixed sights . . . . NiB $352 Ex $286 Gd $214
w/adj. sights . . . . NiB $362 Ex $306 Gd $230

HOMBRE
Similar to Double-Nine—Steel Frame except .22 LR only, lacks single-action type ejector rod and tube, has 4.5-inch bbl. Made from 1971 to 1973.
Blue model . . . . NiB $281 Ex $204 Gd $143
Nickel model. . . . . NiB $306 Ex $220 Gd $165

KIT GUN DA REVOLVER . . . . . NiB $275 Ex $214 Gd $150
Solid frame, swing-out cylinder. Caliber: .22 LR. Nine-round cylinder, 4-inch bbl., 9 inches overall. Weight: 19 oz. Adj. rear sight, ramp front. Blued finish. Checkered walnut grips. Made from 1970 to 1973.

LONGHORN ALUMINUM FRAME
Similar to Double-Nine—Aluminum Frame except has Longhorn hammer spur, 4.5-, 5.5- or 9.5-inch bbl., Walnut, simulated pearl or simulated stag grips. Blued finish. Made from 1960 to 1971.
w/4.5- or 5.5-inch bbl. . . . . NiB $357 Ex $254 Gd $190
w/9.5-inch bbl . . . . NiB $357 Ex $254 Gd $190

High Standard Longhorn
Steel Frame

High Standard
Kit Gun

High Standard
Sentinel

High Standard
Longhorn Aluminum Frame

High Standard
Natchez

High Standard
Posse

LONGHORN STEEL FRAME
Similar to Double-Nine — Steel Frame except has 9.5-inch bbl. w/fixed or adj. sights. Made from 1971 to1983
w/fixed sights . . . . NiB $362 Ex $270 Gd $204
w/adj. sights . . . . NiB $377 Ex $316 Gd $229

NATCHEZ . . . . NiB $418 Ex $270 Gd $209
Similar to Double-Nine — Aluminum Frame except 4.5-inch bbl., 10 inches overall, weight: 25.25 oz., blued finish, simulated ivory bird's-head grips. Made 1961-66.

POSSE . . . . NiB $281 Ex $180 Gd $148
Similar to Double-Nine — Aluminum Frame except 3.5-inch bbl., 9 inches overall, weight: 23.25 oz. Blued finish, brass-grip frame and trigger guard, walnut grips. Made from 1961 to 1966.

SENTINEL DA REVOLVER
Solid frame, swing-out cylinder. Caliber: .22 LR. Nine-round cylinder, 3- 4- or 6-inch bbl. Nine inches overall (with 4-inch-bbl.). Weight: 19 oz. (with 4-inch bbl.). Fixed sights. Aluminum frame. Blued or nickel finish. Checkered grips. Made from 1955 to 1956.
Blue model . . . . NiB $302 Ex $156 Gd $120
Blue/green model . . . . NiB $577 Ex $439 Gd $319
Gold model . . . . NiB $555 Ex $397 Gd $317
Nickel model . . . . NiB $270 Ex $214 Gd $158
Pink model . . . . NiB $536 Ex $306 Gd $180

SENTINEL DELUXE
Same as Sentinel except w/4- or 6-inch bbl., wide trigger, drift-adj. rear sight, two-piece square-butt grips. Made from 1957 to 1974. Note: Designated Sentinel after 1971.
Blue model . . . . NiB $270 Ex $170 Gd $128
Nickel model . . . . NiB $296 Ex $189 Gd $160

SENTINEL IMPERIAL
Same as Sentinel except has onyx-black or nickel finish, two-piece checkered walnut grips, ramp front sight. Made from 1962 to 1965.
Blue model . . . . NiB $270 Ex $179 Gd $130
Nickel model . . . . NiB $281 Ex $189 Gd $143

High Standard Sentinel I

High Standard Sentinel Mark II

High Standard Sentinel Mark III

High Standard Sentinel Snub

SENTINEL MARK 1 DA REVOLVER
Steel frame. Caliber: .22 LR. Nine-round cylinder, bbl. lengths: 2-, 3-, 4-inch, 6.88 inches overall (with 2-inch bbl.). Weight: 21.5 oz. (2-inch bbl.). Ramp front sight, fixed or adj. rear. Blued or nickel finish. Smooth walnut grips. Made from 1974 to 1983.
Blue model . . . . NiB $265 Ex $219 Gd $179
Nickel model. . . . . NiB $296 Ex $255 Gd $190
w/adj. sights . . . . NiB $337 Ex $270 Gd $225

SENTINEL MARK II
DA REVOLVER . . . . NiB $326 Ex $255 Gd $179
Caliber: .357 Magnum. Six-round cylinder, bbl. lengths: 2.5-, 4-, 6-inch, 9 inches overall w/4-inch bbl., weight: 38 oz. (with 4-inch bbl.). Fixed sights. Blued finish. Walnut service or combat-style grips. Made from 1974 to 1976.

SENTINEL MARK III . . . . NiB $326 Ex $255 Gd $175
Same as Sentinel Mark II except has ramp front and adj. rear sights. Weight: 40 oz. (with 4-inch bbl.). Blued finish. Made 1974 to 1976.

SENTINEL MARK IV
Same as Sentinel Mark I except in .22 WMR. Made 1974 to 1983.
Blue model . . . . NiB $301 Ex $230 Gd $175
Nickel model. . . . . NiB $326 Ex $265 Gd $198
w/adj. sights . . . . NiB $352 Ex $255 Gd $220

SENTINEL SNUB
Same as Sentinel Deluxe except w/2.75-inch bbl., (7.25 inches overall, weight: 15 oz.), checkered bird's head-type grips. Made 1957 to 1974.
Blued finish. . . . . NiB $255 Ex $190 Gd $148
Nickel finish . . . . NiB $274 Ex $160 Gd $109

HIGH STANDARD MFG. CO., INC. — Houston, Texas

In 1993, High Standard acquired original assets and moved to Houston, Texas. The first Texas-manufactured firearms began shipping in March 1994 to date.

VICTOR 10X AUTO PISTOL . . . NiB $1120 Ex $840 Gd $540
Caliber: .22 LR. 10-round magazine, 5.5-inch bbl., 9.5 inches overall. Weight: 45 oz. Checkered walnut grips. Blued finish. Made from 1994 to date.

OLYMPIC I.S.U. AUTOMATIC PISTOL
Same specifications as the 1958 I.S.U. issue. See listing under previous High Standard Section.
Olympic I.S.U. model . . . . NiB $592 Ex $345 Gd $270
Olympic I.S.U. military model . . . NiB $816 Ex $577 Gd $336

SPORT KING AUTO PISTOL . . . NiB $694 Ex $434 Gd $305
Caliber: .22 LR. 10-round magazine, 4.5- or 6.75-inch bbl., 8.5 or 10.75 inches overall. Weight: 44 oz. (with 4.5-inch bbl.), 46 oz. (with 6.75-inch bbl.). Fixed sights, slide mounted. Checkered walnut grips. Parkerized finish. Manufactured in limited quantities.

SUPERMATIC CITATION
AUTO PISTOL . . . . **NiB $536 Ex $399 Gd $254**
Caliber: .22 LR. 10-round magazine, 5.5- or 7.75-inch bbl., 9.5 or 11.75 inches overall. Weight: 44 oz. (with 5.5-inch bbl.), 46 oz. (with 7.75-inch bbl.). Frame-mounted, micro-adj. rear sight, undercut ramp front sight. Blued or Parkerized finish. Made from 1994 to 2003.
.22 Short conversion . . . . **NiB $408 Ex $337 Gd $255**

CITATION MS
AUTO PISTOL . . . . **NiB $821 Ex $638 Gd $474**
Similar to the Supermatic Citation except has 10-inch bbl., 14 inches overall. Weight: 49 oz. Made from 1994 to date.

SUPERMATIC TOURNAMENT . **NiB $745 Ex $377 Gd $274**
Caliber: .22 LR. 10-round magazine, bbl. lengths: 4.5, 5.5, or 6.75 inches, overall length: 8.5, 9.5 or 10.75 inches. Weight: 43, 44 or 45 oz. depending on bbl. length. Micro-adj. rear sight, undercut ramp front sight. Checkered walnut grips. Parkerized finish. Made from 1995 to 1997.

SUPERMATIC TROPHY . . . . **NiB $719 Ex $356 Gd $220**
Caliber: .22 LR. 10-round magazine, 5.5 or 7.25-inch bbl., 9.5 or 11.25 inches overall. Weight: 44 oz. (with 5.5-inch bbl.). Micro-adj. rear sight, undercut ramp front sight. Checkered walnut grips w/thumbrest. Blued or Parkerized finish. Made from 1994 to date.
.22 Short Conversion . . . . **NiB $1301 Ex $890 Gd $779**

VICTOR AUTOMATIC . . . . **NiB $723 Ex $475 Gd $270**
Caliber: .22 LR.10-round magazine, 4.5- or 5.5-inch ribbed bbl., 8.5 or 9.5 inches overall. Weight: 45 oz. (with 4.5-inch bbl.), 46 oz. (with 5.5-inch bbl.). Micro-adj. rear sight, post front. Checkered walnut grips. Blued or Parkerized finish. Made from 1994 to date.
.22 Short conversion . . . . **NiB $1193 Ex $925 Gd $780**

HOPKINS & ALLEN ARMS CO. — Norwich, Connecticut

See listings of comparable Harrington & Richardson and Iver Johnson models for values.

INGRAM — Powder Springs, GA

See listings under M.A.C. (Military Armament Corp.)

Note: *Military Armament Corp. ceased production of the select-fire automatic, M10 (9mm & .45 ACP) and M11 (.380 ACP) in 1977. Commercial production resumed on semiautomatic versions under the M.A.C. banner until 1982.*

INTERARMS — Alexandria, Virginia

Also see Bersa.

HELWAN BRIGADIER
AUTO PISTOL . . . . **NiB $265 Ex $203 Gd $143**
Caliber: 9mm Para. Eight-round magazine, 4.25-inch bbl., 8 inches overall. Weight: 32 oz. Blade front sight, dovetailed rear. Blued finish. Grooved plastic grips. Imported from 1987 to 1995.

VIRGINIAN DRAGOON SA REVOLVER
Calibers: .357 Magnum, .44 Magnum, .45 Colt. Six-round cylinder. Bbls.: 5- (not available in .44 Magnum), 6-, 7.5-,

Interarms/Helwan Brigadier

Interarms Virginian SA Revolver

8.38-inch (latter only in .44 Magnum w/adj. sights), 11.88 inches overall with (6-inch bbl.). Weight: 48 oz. (with 6-inch bbl.). Fixed sights or micrometer rear and ramp front sights. Blued finish w/color-casetreated frame. Smooth walnut grips. SWISSAFE base pin safety system. Mfg. by Interarms Industries Inc., Midland, VA. from 1977 to 1984.
Standard Dragoon . . . . **NiB $388 Ex $281 Gd $214**
Engraved Dragoon . . . . **NiB $785 Ex $530 Gd $362**
Deputy model . . . . **NiB $377 Ex $274 Gd $179**
Stainless . . . . **NiB $398 Ex $265 Gd $165**

VIRGINIAN REVOLVER
SILHOUETTE MODEL . . . . **NiB $385 Ex $274 Gd $244**
Same general specifications as regular model except designed in stainless steel w/untapered bull bbl., lengths of 7.5, 8.38 and 10.5 inches. Made from 1985 to 1986.

VIRGINIAN SA REVOLVER . . . . **NiB $388 Ex $270 Gd $265**
Similar to Colt Single Action Army except has base pin safety system. Imported from 1973-76. (See also listing under Hämmerli.)

INTRATEC U.S.A., INC. — Miami, Florida

CATEGORY 9 DAO
SEMIAUTOMATIC . . . . **NiB $270 Ex $177 Gd $120**
Blowback action w/polymer frame. Caliber: 9mm Par Eight-round magazine, 3-inch bbl., 7.7 inches overall. Weight: 18 oz. TExtured black polymer grips. Matte black finish. Made from 1993 to 2000.

CATEGORY 40
DAO SEMIAUTOMATIC . . . . . . **NiB $270 Ex $177 Gd $120**
Locking-breech action w/polymer frame. Caliber: .40 S&W. Seven-round magazine, 3.25-inch bbl., 8 inches overall. Weight: 21 oz. TExtured black polymer grips. Matte black fin-

**Japanese
Model 14 (1925)**

**Japanese
Model 26 DAO Revolver**

ish. Made from 1994 to 2000.
**CATEGORY 45
DAO SEMIAUTOMATIC** . . . . . . NiB $295 Ex $184 Gd $133
Locking-breech action w/polymer frame. Caliber: .45 ACP. Six-round magazine, 3.25-inch bbl., 8 inches overall. Weight: 21 oz. TExtured black polymer grips. Matte black finish. Made from 1994 to 2000.

MODEL PROTEC .25 ACP DA SEMIAUTOMATIC
Caliber: .25 ACP. 10-round magazine, 2.5-inch bbl., 5 inches overall. Weight: 14 oz. Wraparound composition grips. Black Teflon, satin grey or Tec-Kote finish. Disc. 2000..
ProTec .25 standard . . . . NiB $128 Ex $88 Gd $61
ProTec .25 w/satin or Tec-Kote . . . NiB $130 Ex $90 Gd $65

MODEL TEC-DC9 SEMIAUTOMATIC
Caliber: 9mm Para. 20- or 36-round magazine, 5-inch bbl., weight: 50-51 oz. Open fixed front sight, adj. rear. Military nonglare blued or stainless finish.
Tec-9 w/blued finish . . . . NiB $510 Ex $332 Gd $270
Tec-9 w/Tec Kote finish. . . . . . NiB $546 Ex $342 Gd $301
Tec 9S w/stainless finish . . . . . NiB $576 Ex $398 Gd $301

MODEL TEC-DC9M SEMIAUTOMATIC
Same specifications as Model Tec-9 except has 3-inch bbl. without shroud and 20-round magazine, blued or stainless finish.
Tec-9M w/blued finish . . . . . . NiB $546 Ex $337 Gd $281
Tec-9MS w/stainless finish . . . . NiB $622 Ex $398 Gd $255

MODEL TEC-22T SEMIAUTOMATIC
Caliber: .22 LR. 10/.22-type 30-round magazine, 4-inch bbl., 11.19 inches overall. Weight: 30 oz. Protected post front sight, adj. rear sight. Matte black or Tec-Kote finish. Made from 1991

to 1994.
Tec-22T standard . . . . NiB $434 Ex $220 Gd $189
Tec-22TK Tec-Kote, add. $50

TEC-38 DERRINGER . . . . NiB $183 Ex $129 Gd $101
Calibers: .22 Mag., .32 H&R Mag., .357 Mag., .38 Special. Two-round capacity, 3-inch blued bbl., 4.63 inches overall. Weight: 13 oz. Fixed sights. Synth. black frame. Double-action. Made from 1986 to 1988.

ISRAEL ARMS — Kfar Sabs, Israel
Imported by Israel Arms International, Houston, TX.

**BUL-M5 LOCKED BREECH (2000)
AUTO PISTOL**. . . . . NiB $398 Ex $235 Gd $148
Similar to the M1911 U.S. Government model. Caliber: .45 ACP. Seven-round magazine, 5-inch bbl., 8.5 inches overall. Weight: 38 oz. Blade front and fixed, low-profile rear sights.

KAREEN MK II (1500) AUTO PISTOL
Single-action only. Caliber: 9mm Para. 10-round magazine, 4.75-inch bbl., 8 inches overall. Weight: 33.6 oz. Blade front sight, rear adjustable for windage. TExtured black composition or rubberized grips. Blued, two-tone, matte black finish. Imported from 1997 to 1998.
Blued or matte black finish. . . . NiB $386 Ex $301 Gd $219
Two-tone finish . . . . NiB $556 Ex $386 Gd $304
Meprolite sights, add $50

**KAREEN MK II COMPACT
(1501) AUTO PISTOL** . . . . NiB $386 Ex $290 Gd $204
Similar to standard Kareen MKII except w/3.85-inch bbl., 7.1 inches overall. Weight: 32 oz. Imported 1999 to 2000.

GOLAN MODEL (2500) AUTO PISTOL
Single or double action. Caliber: 9mm Para., .40 S&W. 10-round magazine, 3.85-inch bbl., 7.1 inches overall. Weight: 34 oz. Steel slide and alloy frame w/ambidExtrous safety and decocking lever. Matte black finish. Imported 1999.
9mm Para.. . . . . NiB $954 Ex $755 Gd $536
.40 S&W . . . . NiB $954 Ex $755 Gd $536

**GAL MODEL
(5000) AUTO PISTOL** . . . . NiB $437 Ex $289 Gd $220
Caliber: .45 ACP. Eight-round magazine, 4.25-inch bbl., 7.25 inches overall. Weight: 42 oz. Low profile 3-dot sights. Combat-style black rubber grips. Imported from 1999 to 2001.

JAPANESE MILITARY PISTOLS — Tokyo, Japan
Manufactured by Government Plant.

**MODEL 14 (1925)
AUTOMATIC PISTOL** . . . . . . NiB $1423 Ex $1009 Gd $658
Modification of the Nambu Model 1914, changes chiefly intended to simplify mass production. Standard round trigger guard or oversized guard for use w/gloves. Caliber: 8mm Nambu. Eight-round magazine, 4.75-inch bbl., 9 inches overall. Weight: About 29 oz. Fixed sights. Blued finish. Grooved wood grips. Intro. 1925 and mfd. through WW II.

MODEL 26 DAO REVOLVER NiB $1586 Ex $1120 Gd $779
Top-break frame. Caliber: 9mm. Six-round cylinder w/ automatic Extractor/ejector, 4.7-inch bbl., adopted by the Japanese Army from 1893 to 1914, replaced by the Model 14

Automatic Pistol but remained in service through World War II.

MODEL 94 (1934)
AUTOMATIC PISTOL . . . . NiB $780 Ex $464 Gd $342
Poorly designed and constructed, this pistol is unsafe and can be fired merely by applying pressure on the sear, which is Exposed on the left side. Caliber: 8mm Nambu. Six-round magazine, 3.13-inch bbl., 7.13 inches overall. Weight: About 27 oz. Fixed sights. Blued finish. Hard rubber or wood grips. Intro. in 1934, principally for Export to Latin American countries, production continued thru WW II.

NAMBU MODEL
1914 AUTOMATIC PISTOL. . . NiB $1389 Ex $989 Gd $785
Original Japanese service pistol, resembles Luger in appearance and Glisenti in operation. Caliber: 8mm Nambu. Seven-round magazine, 4.5-inch bbl., 9 inches overall. Weight: About 30 oz. Fixed front sight, adj. rear sight. Blued finish. Checkered wood grips. Made from 1914 to 1925.

Japanese Model 94 (1934)

JENNINGS FIREARMS INC. — Irvine, CA

Currently Manufactured by Bryco Arms, Irvine, California. Previously by Calwestco, Inc. & B.L. Jennings. See additional listings under Bryco Arms.

MODEL J-22 AUTO PISTOL
Calibers: .22 LR, .25 ACP. Six-round magazine, 2.5-inch bbl., about 5 inches overall. Weight: 13 oz. Fixed sights. Chrome, satin nickel or black Teflon finish. Walnut, grooved black Cycolac or resin-impregnated wood grips. Made from 1981-85 under Jennings and Calwestco logos; disc. 1985 by Bryco Arms.
Model J-22 . . . . NiB $81 Ex $50 Gd $40
Model J-25 . . . . NiB $91 Ex $61 Gd $50

Jennings Model J Auto Pistol

IVER JOHNSON ARMS, INC. — Jacksonville, Arkansas

Operation of this company dates back to 1871, when Iver Johnson and Martin Bye partnered to manufacture metallic cartridge revolvers. Johnson became the sole owner and changed the name to Iver Johnson's Arms & Cycle Works, which it was known as for almost 100 years. Modern management shortened the name, and after several owner changes the firm was moved from Massachusetts, its original base, to Jacksonville, Arkansas. In 1987, the American Military Arms Corporation (AMAC) acquired the operation, which subsequently ceased in 1993.

NOTE: *For ease in finding a particular firearm, Iver Johnson handguns are divided into two sections: Automatic Pistols (below) and Revolvers, which follow. For the complete handgun listing, please refer to the Index.*

- AUTOMATIC PISTOLS -

9MM DA AUTOMATIC . . . . . . NiB $474 Ex $357 Gd $265
Caliber: 9mm. Six-round magazine, 3-inch bbl., 6.5 inches overall. Weight: 26 oz. Blade front sight, adj. rear. Smooth hardwood grip. Blued or matte blued finish. Intro. 1986.

COMPACT .25 ACP. . . . . NiB $273 Ex $190 Gd $148
Bernardelli V/P design. Caliber: .25 ACP. Five-round magazine, 2.13-inch bbl., 4.13 inches overall. Weight: 9.3 oz. Fixed sights. Checkered composition grips. Blued slide, matte blued frame and color-casehardened trigger. Made from 1991 to 1993.

Iver Johnson Enforcer

ENFORCER . . . . NiB $893 Ex $643 Gd $431
Caliber: .30 U.S. Carbine. Five-, 15-, or 30-round magazine, 9.5- inch bbl., weight: 5.5 lbs. Adj. sights. Walnut stock. Made 1986.

I.J. SUPER ENFORCER . . . . NiB $893 Ex $643 Gd $431
Caliber: .30 U.S. Carbine. Fifteen- or 30-round magazine, 9.5-inch bbl., 17 inches overall. Weight: 4 pounds. Adj. peep rear sight, blade front. American walnut stock. Made from 1978 to 1993.

PONY AUTOMATIC PISTOL
Caliber: .380 Auto. Six-round magazine, 3.1-inch bbl., 6.1 inches overall. Blue, matte blue, nickel finish or stainless. Weight: 20 oz. Wooden grips. Smallest of the locked breech automatics. Made from 1982-88. Reintro. 1989-91.
Blue or matte blue finish . . . . . NiB $434 Ex $342 Gd $270
Nickel finish . . . . NiB $464 Ex $345 Gd $290

Iver Johnson
Model TP

Iver Johnson
Model 57A Target

Iver Johnson
Model 55 Target

Iver Johnson
Model 55-S

Iver Johnson
Model 56 Blank Revolver

Deluxe finish. . . . . NiB $464 Ex $377 Gd $281

MODEL TP-22 DA
AUTOMATIC. . . . . NiB $316 Ex $219 Gd $160
Calibers: .22 LR, Seven-round magazine, 2.85-inch bbl., 5.39 inches overall. Blued finish. Weight: 14.46 oz. Made from 1982 to 1989.

MODEL TP25 DA
POCKET PISTOL . . . . NiB $271 Ex $190 Gd $143
Double-action automatic. Caliber: .25 ACP. Seven-round magazine, 3-inch bbl., 5.5 inches overall. Weight: 12 oz. Black plastic grips and blued finish. Made from 1981 to 1982.

TRAILSMAN AUTOMATIC PISTOL
Caliber: .22 LR. 10-round magazine, 4.5 or 6-inch bbl., 8.75 inches overall (with 4.5-inch bbl.). Weight: 46 oz. Fixed target-type sights. Checkered composition grips. Made 1985-91.
Standard model. . . . . NiB $306 Ex $220 Gd $160
Deluxe model . . . . NiB $321 Ex $230 Gd $170

- REVOLVERS -

MODEL 55
TARGET DA REVOLVER . . . . . . NiB $237 Ex $160 Gd $115
Solid frame. Caliber: .22 LR. Eight-round cylinder, bbl. lengths: 4.5-, 6-inches. 10.75 inches overall (with 6-inch bbl.). Weight: 30.5 oz. (with 6-inch bbl.). Fixed sights. Blued finish. Walnut grips. Note: Original model designation was 55; changed to 55A when loading gate was added in 1961. Made 1955-60.

MODEL 55-S REVOLVER. . . . . . NiB $265 Ex $165 Gd $110
Same general specifications as the Model 55 except for 2.5-inch bbl. and small, molded pocket-size grip.

MODEL 56
BLANK REVOLVER . . . . NiB $128 Ex $81 Gd $55
Solid frame. Caliber: .22 blanks only. Eight-round cylinder, 2.5-inch solid bbl., 6.75 inches overall. Weight: 10 oz.

MODEL 57A
TARGET DA REVOLVER . . . . . . NiB $255 Ex $143 Gd $101
Solid frame. Caliber: .22 LR. Eight-round cylinder, bbl. lengths: 4.5, and 6-inches. 10.75 inches overall. Weight: 30.5 oz. with 6-inch bbl. Adj. sights. Blued finish. Walnut grips. Note: Original model designation was 57, changed to 57A when loading gate was added in 1961. Made from 1961 to 1978.

TRAILSMAN
DA REVOLVER . . . . NiB $306 Ex $209 Gd $160
Hinged frame. Rebounding hammer. Caliber: .22 LR. Eight-round cylinder, 6-inch bbl., 11 inches overall. Weight: 34 oz. Adj. sights. Blued finish. Walnut grips. Made 1985-91.

MODEL 67
VIKING DA REVOLVER . . . . . . NiB $273 Ex $165 Gd $110
Hinged frame. Caliber: .22 LR. Eight-round cylinder, bbl. lengths: 4.5- and 6-inches, 11 inches overall (with 6-inch bbl.). Weight: 34 oz. (with 6-inch bbl.). Adj. sights. Walnut grips w/ thumbrest. Made 1964 to 1978.

MODEL 67S VIKING
SNUB REVOLVER . . . . NiB $286 Ex $189 Gd $179
DA. Hinged frame. Calibers: .22 LR, .32 S&W Short and Long, .38 S&W. Eight-round cylinder in .22, 5-round in .32 and .38 calibers; 2.75-inch bbl. Weight: 25 oz. Adj. sights. Tenite grips. Made from 1964 to 1978.

MODEL 1900 DA REVOLVER . . . . NiB $158 Ex $90 Gd $65
Solid frame. Calibers: .22 LR, .32 S&W, .32 S&W Long, .38 S&W. Seven-round cylinder in .22 cal. , 6-round (.32 S&W), 5-round (.32 S&W Long, .38 S&W); bbl. lengths: 2.5-, 4.5- and 6-inches. Weight: 12 oz. (in .32 S&W w/2.5-inch bbl.). Fixed sights. Blued or nickel finish. Hard rubber grips. Made from 1900 to 1941.

MODEL 1900
TARGET DA REVOLVER . . . . . . NiB $222 Ex $175 Gd $135
Solid frame. Caliber: .22 LR. Seven-round cylinder, bbl. lengths: 6- and 9.5-inches. Fixed sights. Blued finish. Checkered walnut grips. (This earlier model does not have counterbored chambers as in the Target Sealed 8. Made from 1925 to 1942.)

AMERICAN BULLDOG DA REVOLVER
Solid frame. Calibers: .22 LR, .22 WMR, .38 Special. Six-round cylinder in .22, 5-round in .38. Bbl. lengths: 2.5-, 4-inch. 9 inches overall (with 4-inch bbl.). Weight: 30 oz. (with 4-inch bbl.). Adj. sights. Blued or nickel finish. Plastic grips. Made from 1974 to 1976.
.38 Special . . . . NiB $464 Ex $286 Gd $204
Other calibers. . . . . NiB $464 Ex $286 Gd $204

ARMSWORTH MODEL 855 SA . . . NiB $464 Ex $290 Gd $198
Hinged frame. Caliber: .22 LR. Eight-round cylinder, 6-inch bbl., 10.75 inches overall. Weight: 30 oz. Adj. sights. Blued finish. Checkered walnut one-piece grip. Adj. finger rest. Made from 1955 to 1957.

CADET DA REVOLVER . . . . NiB $255 Ex $165 Gd $101
Solid frame. Calibers: .22 LR, .22 WMR, .32 S&W Long, .38 S&W, .38 Special. Six- or 8-round cylinder in .22, 5-round in other calibers, 2.5-inch bbl., 7 inches overall. Weight: 22 oz. Fixed sights. Blued finish or nickel finish. Plastic grips. Note: Loading gate added in 1961, .22 cylinder capacity changed from 8 to 6 rounds in 1975. Made 1955 to 1977.

CATTLEMAN SA REVOLVER . . . NiB $369 Ex $301 Gd $170
Patterned after the Colt Army SA revolver. Calibers: .357 Magnum, .44 Magnum, .45 Colt. Six-round cylinder. Bbl. lengths: 4.75-, 5.5- (not available in .44), 6- (.44 only), 7.25-inch. Weight: About 41 oz. Fixed sights. Blued bbl., and cylinder color-casehardened frame, brass grip frame. One-piece walnut grip. Made by Aldo Uberti, Brescia, Italy, from 1973 to 1978.
.44 Magnum, add $50

CATTLEMAN BUCKHORN SA REVOLVER
Same as standard Cattleman except has adj. rear and ramp front sights. Bbl. lengths: 4.75- (.44 only), 5.75- (not available

Iver Johnson
Model 66 Trailsman

Iver Johnson
Model 67 Viking

Iver Johnson
Model 67S Viking Snub

Iver Johnson
Model 1900 Target

Iver Johnson
Cadet

in .44), 6- (.44 only), 7.5- or 12-inches bbl., weight: About 44 oz. Made from 1973 to 1978.
.357 Magnum or .45
  Colt w/12-inch bbl. . . . . NiB $439 Ex $326 Gd $219
.357 Magnum or .45

Iver Johnson
Cattleman

Iver Johnson
Champion .22 Target

Iver Johnson
Protector Sealed 8

Iver Johnson
Rookie

Iver Johnson
Safety Hammer

Colt w/5.75- or 7.5-inch bbl. NiB $342 Ex $255 Gd $158
.44 Magnum, w/12-inch bbl. . . NiB $459 Ex $367 Gd $279
.44 Magnum, other bbls.. . . . . . NiB $439 Ex $326 Gd $219

CATTLEMAN BUNTLINE SA REVOLVER
Same as Cattleman Buckhorn except has 18-inch bbl., walnut
shoulder stock w/brass fittings. Weight: About 56 oz. Made
from 1973 to 1978.

.44 Magnum . . . . NiB $443 Ex $332 Gd $225
Other calibers. . . . . NiB $443 Ex $332 Gd $225

CATTLEMAN
TRAIL BLAZER . . . . NiB $377 Ex $274 Gd $189
Similar to Cattleman Buckhorn except .22 caliber has interchangeable .22 LR and .22 WMR cylinders, 5.5- or 6.5-inch
bbl., weight: About 40 oz. Made from 1973 to 1978.

CHAMPION 822
.22 TARGET SA . . . . NiB $499 Ex $326 Gd $175
Hinged frame. Caliber: .22 LR. Eight-round cylinder. Single
action. Counterbored chambers as in Sealed 8 model, 6-inch
bbl., 10.75 inches overall. Weight: 28 oz. Adj. target sights.
Blued finish. Checkered walnut grips, adj. finger rest. Made
from 1938 to 1948.

DELUXE TARGET. . . . . NiB $305 Ex $225 Gd $175
Same as Sportsman except has adj. sights. Made 1975-76.

PROTECTOR SEALED 8
DA REVOLVER . . . . NiB $453 Ex $337 Gd $204
Hinged frame. Caliber: .22 LR. Eight-round cylinder, 2.5-inch
bbl., 7.25 inches overall. Weight: 20 oz. Fixed sights. Blued
finish. Checkered walnut grips. Made from 1933 to 1949.

ROOKIE DA REVOLVER . . . . . . NiB $270 Ex $204 Gd $90
Solid frame. Caliber: .38 Special. Five-round cylinder, 4-inch
bbl., 9-inches overall. Weight: 30 oz. Fixed sights. Blued or
nickel finish. Plastic grips. Made from 1975 to 1977.

SAFETY HAMMER
DA REVOLVER . . . . NiB $342 Ex $170 Gd $105
Hinged frame. Calibers: .22 LR, .32 S&W, .32 S&W Long,
.38 S&W. Seven-round cylinder in .22 cal.,or 6-round (.32
S&W Long), 5-round (.32 S&W, .38 S&W). bbl. lengths: 2,
3, 3.25, 4, 5 or 6 inches. Weight w/4-inch bbl.: 15 oz. (.22,
.32 S&W), 19.5 oz. (.32 S&W Long) or 19 oz. (.38 S&W).
Fixed sights. Blued or nickel finish. Hard rubber, round butt
grips or square butt, rubber or walnut grips available. Note:
.32 S&W Long and .38 S&W models built on heavy frame.
Made 1892-1950.

SAFETY HAMMERLESS
DA REVOLVER . . . . NiB $337 Ex $219 Gd $129
Similar to the Safety Hammer Model except w/shrouded ham-
merless frame. Made from 1895 to 1950.

SIDEWINDER
DA REVOLVER. . . . . NiB $281 Ex $179 Gd $110
Solid frame. Caliber: .22 LR. Six- or 8-round cylinder, bbl.
lengths: 4.75, 6 inches; 11.25 inches overall (with 6-inch bbl.).
Weight: 31 oz. (with 6-inch bbl.). Fixed sights. Blued or nickel
finish w/plastic staghorn grips or color-casehardened frame
w/walnut grips. Note: Cylinder capacity changed from 8 to 6
rounds in 1975. Made from1961 to 1978

SIDEWINDER "S". . . . . NiB $281 Ex $179 Gd $110
Same as Sidewinder except has interchangeable cylinders
in .22 LR and .22 WMR, adj. sights. Intro. 1974. Disc.

SPORTSMAN
DA REVOLVER . . . . NiB $222 Ex $165 Gd $109
Solid frame. Caliber: .22 LR. Six-round cylinder. Bbl. lengths:
4.75-, 6-inches, 10.75 inches overall (with 6-inch bbl.).
Weight: 30.5 oz. (with 6-inch bbl.). Fixed sights. Blued finish.
Plastic grips. Made 1974 to 1976.

Iver Johnson
Sidewinder

Iver Johnson
Supershot Sealed 8

Iver Johnson Target Sealed 8

SUPERSHOT .22 DA
REVOLVER . . . . **NiB $273 Ex $175 Gd $119**
Hinged frame. Caliber: .22 LR. Seven-round cylinder, 6-inch bbl. Fixed sights. Blued finish. Checkered walnut grips. This earlier model does not have counterbored chambers as in the Supershot Sealed 8. Made from 1929 to 1949.

SUPERSHOT 9
DA REVOLVER . . . . **NiB $273 Ex $175 Gd $119**
Same as Supershot Sealed 8 except has nine non-counterbored chambers. Made from 1929 to 1949.

SUPERSHOT
MODEL 844 DA . . . . **NiB $336 Ex $204 Gd $129**
Hinged frame. Caliber: .22 LR. Eight-round cylinder, bbl. lengths: 4.5- or 6-inch, 9.25 inches overall (with 4.5-inch bbl.). Weight: 27 oz. (4.5-inch bbl.). Adj. sights. Blued finish. Checkered walnut one-piece grip. Made 1955-56.

SUPERSHOT SEALED
8 DA REVOLVER . . . . **NiB $316 Ex $180 Gd $140**
Hinged frame. Caliber: .22 LR. Eight-round cylinder, 6-inch bbl., 10.75 inches overall. Weight: 24 oz. Adj. target sights. Blued finish. Checkered walnut grips. Postwar model does not have adj. finger rest as earlier version. Made 1931-57.

SWING-OUT DA REVOLVER
Calibers: .22 LR, .22 WMR, .32 S&W Long, .38 Special. Six-round cylinder in .22, 5-round in .32 and .38. Two, 3-, 4-inch plain bbl., or 4- 6-inch vent rib bbl., 8.75 inches overall (with 4-inch bbl.). Fixed or adj. sights. Blue or nickel finish. Walnut grips. Made in 1977.
w/plain barrel, fixed sights . . . . **NiB $220 Ex $158 Gd $115**
w/vent rib, adj. sights . . . . **NiB $204 Ex $148 Gd $110**

TARGET 9 DA REVOLVER . . . . . **NiB $265 Ex $180 Gd $135**
Same as Target Sealed 8 except has nine non-counterbored chambers. Made from 1929 to 1946.

TARGET SEALED
8 DA REVOLVER . . . . **NiB $273 Ex $166 Gd $135**
Solid frame. Caliber: .22 LR. Eight-round cylinder, bbl. lengths: 6- and 10-inches. 10.75 inches overall (with 6-inch bbl.).

Weight: 24 oz. (with 6-inch bbl.). Fixed sights. Blued finish. Checkered walnut grips. Made from 1931 to 1957.

TRIGGER-COCKING
SA TARGET . . . . **NiB $321 Ex $239 Gd $187**
Hinged frame. First pull on trigger cocks hammer, second pull releases hammer. Caliber: .22 LR. Eight-round cylinder, counterbored chambers, 6-inch bbl., 10.75 inches overall. Weight: 24 oz. Adj. target sights. Blued finish. Checkered walnut grips. Made 1940 to 1947.

KAHR ARMS — Worcester, Massachusetts
Formerly Pearl River, New York.

MODEL K9 DAO AUTO PISTOL
Caliber: 9mm Para. Seven-round magazine, 3.5-inch bbl., 6 inches overall. Weight: 24 oz. Fixed sights. Matte black, electroless nickel, Birdsong Black-T or matte stainless finish. Wraparound textured polymer or hardwood grips. Made from 1994 to 2003.
Duo-Tone finish . . . . **NiB $587 Ex $464 Gd $321**
Electroless nickel finish. . . . . . . **NiB $657 Ex $577 Gd $395**
Black-T finish . . . . **NiB $740 Ex $602 Gd $464**
Matte stainless finish. . . . . **NiB $785 Ex $631 Gd $453**
Kahr Lady K9 model . . . . **NiB $530 Ex $345 Gd $270**
Elite model . . . . **NiB $836 Ex $610 Gd $399**
Tritium Night Sights, add $100

MODEL K40 DAO AUTO PISTOL
Similar to Model K9 except chambered .40 S&W w/5- or 6-round magazine, Weight: 26 oz. Made from 1997 to 2003.
Matte black finish . . . . **NiB $590 Ex $433 Gd $321**
Electroless nickel finish. . . . . . . **NiB $668 Ex $595 Gd $395**
Black-T finish . . . . **NiB $740 Ex $562 Gd $362**
Matte black stainless finish . . . . **NiB $653 Ex $485 Gd $345**
Covert model
(shorter grip-frame) . . . . **NiB $536 Ex $395 Gd $306**
Elite model . . . . **NiB $826 Ex $602 Gd $437**
Tritium Night Sights, add $100

MODEL K9 DAO AUTO PISTOL
Similar to Model K9 except w/Micro-Compact frame. Six- or 7- round magazine, 3- inch bbl., 5.5 inches overall. Weight: 22 oz. Stainless or Duo-Tone finish. Made from 1993 to 2003.
Duo-Tone finish . . . . **NiB $665 Ex $530 Gd $398**
Matte stainless
finish . . . . **NiB $437 Ex $347 Gd $301**
Elite model . . . . **NiB $830 Ex $544 Gd $429**
Tritium Night Sights, add $100

Kahr Model K9

Kel-Tec Model P-11

CW SERIES DAO AUTO PISTOL NiB $425 Ex $325 Gd $250
Caliber: 9mm Para., .40 S&W, .45 ACP. Seven-round magazine (9mm Para), 3.6-inch bbl., 6 inches overall. Weight: 15.8 oz. Fixed sights. Textured black polymer frame, matte stainless steel slide. Made from 2005 (9mm para), 2008 (.40 S&W, .45 ACP).

CM SERIES DAO AUTO PISTOL NiB $450 Ex $350 Gd $250
Caliber: 9mm Para., .40 S&W, .45 ACP. Six-round magazine (9mm Para), 3-inch bbl., 6 inches overall. Weight: 15.8 oz. Fixed sights. Textured black polymer frame, matte stainless steel slide. Made from 2011 (9mm para), 2012 (.40 S&W), 2013 (.45 ACP).

E9 DAO AUTO PISTOL . . . . NiB $425 Ex $340 Gd $250
Caliber: 9mm Para. Seven-round magazine, 3.5-inch bbl., 6 inches overall. Weight: 15.8 oz. Fixed sights. Textured black polymer frame. Made from 1997, reintro. 2003.

MK MICRO SERIES
DAO AUTO PISTOL . . . . NiB $450 Ex $350 Gd $250
Caliber: 9mm Para., .40 S&W. Six-round magazine (9mm para), 3-inch bbl., 5.5 inches overall. Weight: 15.8 oz. Fixed sights., Matte stainless steel slide and frame. Made from 1998-99 (9mm para), intro. 1999 (.40 S&W).

T SERIES DAO AUTO PISTOL . . NiB $600 Ex $450 Gd $290
Caliber: 9mm Para., .40 S&W. 8-round magazine (9mm para), 4-inch bbl., 6.5 inches overall. Weight: 26 oz. Fixed sights., Matte stainless steel slide and frame, wood grips. Made from 2002 (9mm para), 2004 (.40 S&W).

TP SERIES DAO AUTO PISTOL . . . NiB $500 Ex $430 Gd $285
Similar to T series except polymer frame and matte stainless steel slide. Made from 2004.

KBI, INC — Harrisburg, Pennsylvania

MODEL PSP-.25 AUTO PISTOL . . . NiB $308 Ex $244 Gd $157
Caliber: .25 ACP. Six-round magazine, 2.13-inch bbl., 4.13 inches overall. Weight: 9.5 oz. All-steel construction w/dual safety system. Made 1994.

KEL-TEC CNC INDUSTRIES, INC. — Cocoa, Florida

MODEL P-11 DAO PISTOL
Caliber: 9mm Parabellum or .40 S&W. 10-round magazine, 3.1- inch bbl., 5.6 inches overall. Weight: 14 oz. Blade front sight, drift adjustable rear. Aluminum frame w/steel slide. Checkered black, gray, or green polymer grips. Matte blue, nickel, stainless steel or Parkerized finish. Made from 1995 to date.
9mm . . . . NiB $305 Ex $214 Gd $156
.40 S&W . . . . NiB $590 Ex $399 Gd $243
Parkerized finish, add $75
Nickel finish (disc. 1995) add $75
Stainless finish, (1996 to date) add $75
Tritium Night Sights, add $90
.40 S&W conversion kit, add $204

P-32 . . . . NiB $291 Ex $170 Gd $90
Semi-auto, double-action. Cal.: .32 ACP. Internal block safety. 7-round mag. Bbl.: 2.68 inches; Parkerized, blue, or chrome finish. Choice of ivory or colored grips. Weight: 6.6 oz.

P-3AT . . . . NiB $301 Ex $180 Gd $95
Similar to P-32. Cal.: .380 ACP. Bbl.: 2.76 inches. 6-round mag. Black composite frame with Parkerized steel slide. Weight: 8.3 oz.

P-40 . . . . NiB $290 Ex $175 Gd $88
Semi-auto, double-action. 9- or 10-round mag. Composite frame with steel slide. Bbl.: 3.3 inches. Parkerized, blue, or chrome finish. Made from 1999 to 2001.
Parkerized finish, add $50
Hard chrome finish, add. $70

PLR-16 . . . . NiB $638 Ex $495 Gd $281
M-16-type gas operated. Cal.: .223 Rem., 10-round mag. Bbl.: 9.2 inches. Upper w/Picatinny accessory rail. Black composite frame. Weight: 3.2 lbs.

PLR-22 . . . . NiB $357 Ex $265 Gd $170
Similar to PLR-16 except in .22 LR; 26-round mag. Weight: 2.8 lbs.

PF-9 . . . . NiB $306 Ex $198 Gd $143
Similar to P-11, cal.: 9 mm Para. Bbl.: 3.1 inches. 7-round mag., lower accessory rail. Black finish. Weight: 12.7 oz. Limited production in 2006, reintro. 2008.
Parkerized finish, add $50
Hard chrome finish, add. $65

Kimber Model Classic .45

PMR-30. . . . . **NiB $408 Ex $301 Gd $189**
Cal.: .22 Mag. Bbl.: 4.3 inches. 30-round mag, blowback action, manual safety. Picatinny accessory rail. Steel slide and bbl., fiber optic sights. Weight: 19.5 oz. Made 2010 to date.

KIMBER MANUFACTURING, INC. — Yonkers, New York

Formerly Kimber of America, Inc.

MODEL CLASSIC .45
Similar to Government 1911 built on steel, polymer or alloy full-size or compact frame. Caliber: .45 ACP. Seven-, 8-, 10- or 14-round magazine, 4- or 5-inch bbl., 7.7 or 8.75 inches overall. Weight: 28 oz. (Compact LW), 34 oz. (Compact or Polymer) or .38 oz. (Custom FS). McCormick low-profile combat or Kimber adj. target sights. Blued, matte black oxide or stainless finish. Checkered custom wood or black synthetic grips. Made from 1994 to date.

Custom (matte black) . . . . NiB $882	Ex $599	Gd $431
Custom Royal (polished blue) . . . . NiB $774	Ex $612	Gd $443
Custom stainless (satin stainless) . . . NiB $737	Ex $577	Gd $439
Custom Target (matte black) . . . NiB $755	Ex $581	Gd $453
Target Gold Match (polished blue) . . . . NiB $1020	Ex $755	Gd $587
Target stainless Match (polished stainless) . . . . NiB $852	Ex $669	Gd $474
Polymer (matte black) . . . . NiB $852	Ex $669	Gd $474
Polymer Stainless (satin stainless slide) . . . . NiB $967	Ex $784	Gd $577
Polymer Target (matte black slide) . . . . NiB $918	Ex $744	Gd $536
Compact (matte black) . . . . NiB $644	Ex $541	Gd $377
Compact stainless (satin stainless) . . . . NiB $714	Ex $559	Gd $437
Compact LW (matte black w/alloy frame) . . . . NiB $733	Ex $577	Gd $408

SERIES II MODELS

Similar to Classic 1911 models except includes firing pin block safety and denoted with "II" following all model names. Size configurations vary per model and include from smallest to largest: Micro (2.75-in. bbl., micro frame), Ultra (3-in. bbl., short frame), Ultra+ (3-in. bbl., full size frame), Compact (4-in. bbl., short frame), Pro (4-in. bbl., full size frame), Custom (5-in. bbl., full size frame). Made from 2001 to date.

Aegis II (intro. 2006)	NiB $1200	Ex $1140	Gd $840
CDP II (intro. 2000)	NiB $1150	Ex $1095	Gd $805
Compact II	NiB $960	Ex $912	Gd $500
Covert II (intro. 2007)	NiB $1450	Ex $1100	Gd $650
Crimson Cary II (laser grip) . .	NiB $1050	Ex $900	Gd $735
Custom II	NiB $730	Ex $525	Gd $330
Custom II Stainless	NiB $855	Ex $655	Gd $365
Custom Royal II	NiB $1900	Ex $1000	Gd $580
Eclipse II (intro. 2002)	$1100	Ex $1045	Gd $570
Gold Match II	NiB $1300	Ex $1000	Gd $580
Master Carry II (intro. 2013)	NiB $1330	Ex $1265	Gd $931
Micro Carry (intro. 2013, .380 ACP)	NiB $580	Ex $475	Gd $375
Raptor II (intro. 2004)	NiB $1300	Ex $1235	Gd $910
Super Carry II (intro. 2010)	NiB $1350	Ex $1285	Gd $945
Tactical II (intro. 2003)	NiB $1130	Ex $1075	Gd $795
Ultra Carry II (intro. 1999)	NiB $800	Ex $760	Gd $560
Custom Royal II	NiB $1900	Ex $1000	Gd $580

KORTH — Lollar, Germany

Previously Ratzeburg, Germany. Currently imported by Korth USA (Earl's Repair Service, Tewkberry, MA). Previously by Keng's Firearms Specialty, Inc., Beeman Precision Arms; Osborn Beeman Precision Arms; Osborne's and Mandall Shooting Supply.

REVOLVERS COMBAT, SPORT, TARGET
Calibers: .357 Mag. and .22 LR w/interchangeable combination cylinders of .357 Mag./9mm Para. or .22 LR/.22 WMR also .22 Jet, .32 S&W and .32 H&R Mag. Bbls: 2.5-, 3-, 4-inch (combat) and 5.25- or 6-inch (target). Weight: 33 to 42 oz. Blued, stainless, matte silver or polished silver finish. Checkered walnut grips. Imported 1967 to date.

Standard rimfire model	NiB $4590	Ex $2735	Gd $1895
Standard centerfire model .	NiB $6899	Ex $5100	Gd $4029
ISU Match Target model . . .	NiB $7429	Ex $5433	Gd $3329
Custom stainless finish, add			$485
Matte silver finish, add			$689
Polished silver finish, add			$950

SEMI-AUTOMATIC PISTOL
Calibers: 30 Luger, 9mm Para., .357 SIG, .40 S&W, 9x21mm. 10- or 14-round magazine, 4- or 5-inch bbl., all-steel construction, recoil-operated. Ramp front sight, adj. rear. Blued, stainless, matte silver or polished silver finish. Checkered walnut grips. Limited import from 1988 .

Standard model	NiB $6495	Ex $5040	Gd $3934
Matte silver finish, add			$332
Polished silver finish, add			$791

LAHTI — Sweden & Finland

Mfd. by Husqvarna Vapenfabriks A. B. Huskvarna, Sweden, and Valtion Kivaar Tedhas ("VKT") Jyväskyla, Finland.

AUTOMATIC PISTOL
Caliber: 9mm Para. Eight-round magazine, 4.75-inch bbl., weight: About 46 oz. Fixed sights. Blued finish. Plastic grips. Specifications given are those of the Swedish Model 40 but also apply in general to the Finnish Model L-35, which differs only slightly. A considerable number of Swedish Lahti pistols were imported and sold in the U.S. The Finnish model, somewhat better made, is rare. Finnish Model L-35

Lahti Automatic Pistol

L.A.R. Mark I Grizzly

**Laseraim
Series I**

**Laseraim
Series II**

adopted 1935. Swedish Model 40 adopted 1940, mfd. through 1944.

Finnish L-35 model
(1st Variation) . . . . NiB $4120 Ex $3020 Gd $2455
Swedish 40 model . . . . NiB $648 Ex $449 Gd $332

L.A.R. MANUFACTURING, INC. — West Jordan, Utah

MARK I GRIZZLY WIN. MAG. AUTOMATIC PISTOL
Calibers: .357 Mag., .45 ACP, .45 Win. Mag. Seven-round magazine, 6.5-inch bbl., 10.5 inches overall. Weight: 48 oz. Fully adj. sights. Checkered rubber combat-style grips. Blued finish. Made from 1983 to date. 8- or 10-inch bbl., Made from 1987 to 1999.
.357 Mag. (6.5 inch barrel) . . . . NiB $918 Ex $643 Gd $434
.45 Win. Mag.(6.5 inch barrel) NiB $918 Ex $740 Gd $444
8-inch barrel . . . . NiB $1237 Ex $1040 Gd $943
10-inch barrel . . . . NiB $1320 Ex $1118 Gd $1029

MARK 4 GRIZZLY
AUTOMATIC PISTOL . . . . NiB $918 Ex $740 Gd $629
Same general specifications as the L.A.R. Mark I except chambered for .44 Magnum, has 5.5- or 6.5-inch bbl., beavertail grip safety, matte blued finish. Made from 1991 to 1999.

MARK 5 AUTO PISTOL . . . . . . NiB $918 Ex $734 Gd $631
Similar to the Mark I except chambered in 50 Action Express. Six-round magazine, 5.4- or 6.5-inch bbl., 10.6 inches overall (with 5.4-inch bbl.). Weight: 56 oz. Checkered walnut grips. Made 1993 to 1999.

LASERAIM TECHNOLOGIES, INC. — Little Rock, Arkansas

SERIES I SA AUTO PISTOL
Calibers: .40 S&W, .45 ACP, 10mm. Seven or 8- round magazine, 3.875- or 5.5-inch dual-port compensated bbl., 8.75 or 10.5 inches overall. Weight: 46 or 52 oz. Fixed sights w/ Laseraim or adjustable Millet sights. TExtured black composition grips. Extended slide release, ambidExtrous safety and beveled magazine well. Stainless or matte black Teflon finish. Made from 1993 to 1999.
Series I w/adjustable sights . . . . NiB $362 Ex $255 Gd $188
Series I w/fixed sights . . . . NiB $362 Ex $255 Gd $188
Series I w/fixed sights (HotDot) . . NiB $479 Ex $270 Gd $203
Series I Dream Team (RedDot) . . NiB $479 Ex $ 270 Gd $203
Series I Illusion (Laseraim) . . . . NiB $479 Ex $270 Gd $203

SERIES II SA AUTO PISTOL
Similar to Series I except w/stainless finish and no bbl., compensator. Made from 1993 to 1996.
Series II w/adjustable sights . . . NiB $530 Ex $365 Gd $265
Series II w/fixed sights . . . . NiB $530 Ex $365 Gd $265
Series II Dream Team . . . . NiB $602 Ex $437 Gd $279
Series II Illusion . . . . NiB $540 Ex $439 Gd $321

SERIES III SA AUTO PISTOL
Similar to Series II except w/serrated slide and 5-inch compensated bbl., only. Made 1994. Disc.
Series III w/adjustable sights . . NiB $632 Ex $536 Gd $398
Series III w/fixed sights . . . . . . NiB $632 Ex $599 Gd $362

VELOCITY SERIES SA AUTO PISTOL
Similar to Series I except chambered for .357 Sig. or .400 Cor-Bon, 3.875-inch unported bbl., (compact) or 5.5-inch dual-port compensated bbl. Made from 1993 to 1999. See illustration previous page.

Compact model (unported).... NiB $362 Ex $290 Gd $204
Government model (ported)... NiB $362 Ex $290 Gd $204
w/wireless laser (HotDot), add..................... $175

LIGNOSE — Suhl, Germany
Aktien-Gesellschaft "Lignose" Abteilung

The following Lignose pistols were manufactured from 1920 to the mid-1930s. They were also marketed under the Bergmann name.

EINHAND MODEL 2A
POCKET AUTO PISTOL ...... NiB $434 Ex $305 Gd $209
As the name implies, this pistol is designed for one-hand operation, pressure on a "trigger" at the front of the guard retracts the slide. Caliber: .25 Auto. (6.35 mm). Six-round magazine, 2-inch bbl., 4.75 inches overall. Weight: About 14 oz. Blued finish. Hard rubber grips.

MODEL 2 POCKET
AUTO PISTOL.............. NiB $362 Ex $237 Gd $175
Conventional Browning type. Same general specifications as Einhand Model 2A but lacks the one-hand operation.

EINHAND MODEL
3A POCKET AUTO PISTOL.... NiB $479 Ex $369 Gd $270
Same as the Model 2A except has longer grip, 9-round magazine, weight: About 16 oz.

LLAMA — Vitoria, Spain

Manufactured by Gabilondo y Cia, Vitoria, Spain, imported by S.G.S., Wanamassa, New Jersey.

NOTE: *For ease in finding a particular Llama handgun, the listings are divided into two groupings: Automatic Pistols (below) and Revolvers, which follow. For a complete listing of Llama handguns, please refer to the index.*

-AUTOMATIC PISTOLS -

MODEL IIIA
AUTOMATIC PISTOL .... NiB $337 Ex $170 Gd $109
Caliber: .380 Auto. Seven-round magazine, 3.69-inch bbl., 6.5 inches overall. Weight: 23 oz. Adj. target sights. Blued finish. Plastic grips. Intro. 1951. Disc.

MODELS IIIA, XA, XV DELUXE
Same as standard Model IIIA, XA and XV except engraved w/ blued or chrome finish and simulated pearl grips.
Chrome-engraved finish ...... NiB $365 Ex $306 Gd $219
Blue-engraved finish .... NiB $356 Ex $290 Gd $204

MODEL VIII
AUTOMATIC PISTOL .... NiB $377 Ex $306 Gd $255
Caliber: .38 Super. Nine-round magazine, 5-inch bbl., 8.5 inches overall. Weight: 40 oz. Fixed sights. Blued finish. Wood grips. Intro. in 1952. Disc.

MODELS VIII, IXA, XI DELUXE
Same as standard Models VIII, IXA and XI except finish (chrome engraved or blued engraved) and simulated pearl grips. Disc. 1984.
Chrome-engraved finish ...... NiB $377 Ex $290 Gd $190
Blue-engraved finish .... NiB $377 Ex $290 Gd $190

**Laseraim Series III
w/LA93 Illusion III scope**

**Llama Model IIIA
Deluxe Chrome Engraved First Issue**

**Llama Model IIIA
Deluxe Blue Engraved Second Issue**

Llama Model XA First Issue

Llama Model CE-IIIA

Llama Model Compact

Llama Model C-XI

MODEL XI
AUTOMATIC PISTOL . . . . NiB $377 Ex $290 Gd $190
Same as model VIII except 9mm Para.

MODEL XV
AUTOMATIC PISTOL . . . . NiB $321 Ex $255 Gd $170
Same as model XA except .22 LR.

MODELS BE-IIIA,
BE-XA, BE-XV . . . . NiB $530 Ex $332 Gd $235
Same as models IIIA, XA and XV except w/blued-engraved finish. Made from 1977-84.

MODELS BE-VIII,
BE-IXA, BE-XI DELUXE . . . . NiB $530 Ex $398 Gd $281
Same as models VIII, IXA and XI except w/blued-engraved finish. Made from 1977 to 1984.

MODELS C-IIIA, C-XA, C-XV . . NiB $408 Ex $365 Gd $259
Same as models IIIA, XA and XV except in satin chrome.

MODELS C-VIII, C-IXA, C-XI . . NiB $475 Ex $357 Gd $244
Same as models VIII, IXA and XI except in satin chrome.

MODELS CE-IIIA,
CE-XA, CE-XV . . . . NiB $398 Ex $347 Gd $230
Same as models IIIA, XA and XV except w/chrome engraved finish. Made from 1977 to 1984.

MODELS CE-VIII,
CE-IXA, CE-XI . . . . NiB $475 Ex $357 Gd $244
Same as models VIII, IXA and XI, w/except chrome engraved finish. Made from 1977 to 1984.

COMPACT FRAME
AUTO PISTOL . . . . NiB $345 Ex $270 Gd $204
Calibers: 9mm Para., .38 Super, .45 Auto. Seven-, 8- or 9-round magazine, 5-inch bbl., 7.88 inches overall. Weight: 34 oz. Blued, satin-chrome or Duo-Tone finishes. Made from 1986 to 1997. Duo-Tone disc. 1993.

DUO-TONE LARGE
FRAME AUTO PISTOL . . . . NiB $449 Ex $368 Gd $305
Caliber: .45 ACP. Seven-round magazine, 5-inch bbl., 8.5 inches overall. Weight: 36 oz. Adj. rear sight. Blued finished w/ satin chrome. Polymer black grips. Made from 1991 to 1993.

DUO-TONE SMALL
FRAME AUTO PISTOL . . . . NiB $306 Ex $209 Gd $150
Calibers: .22 LR, .32 and .380 Auto. Seven- or 8-round magazine, 3.69 inch bbl., 6.5 inches overall. Weight: 23 oz. Square-notch rear sight, Partridge-type front. Blued finish w/chrome. Made from 1990 to 1993.

MODEL IXA
AUTOMATIC PISTOL . . . . NiB $377 Ex $290 Gd $190
Same as model VIII except .45 Auto, 7-round magazine,

MODEL XA
AUTOMATIC PISTOL . . . . NiB $377 Ex $290 Gd $190
Same as model IIIA except .32 Auto, 8-round magazine,

**Llama M-82
DA Auto**

Llama MINI-MAX II

Llama MAX-I

**Llama
Comanche I**

MODEL G-IIIA DELUXE . . . NiB $2520 Ex $1944 Gd $1659
Same as Model IIIA except gold damascened w/simulated pearl grips. Disc. 1982.

LARGE-FRAME AUTOMATIC PISTOL (IXA)
Caliber: .45 Auto. 7-rnd. magazine, 5-in. bbl., weight: 2 lbs., 8 oz. Adj. rear sight, Partridge-type front. Walnut grips or teakwood on satin chrome model. Later models w/polymer grips.
Blued finish. . . . . NiB $369 Ex $258 Gd $198
Satin chrome finish. . . . . NiB $538 Ex $444 Gd $290

**M-82 DA
AUTOMATIC PISTOL . . . . NiB $587 Ex $398 Gd $270**
Caliber: 9mm Para. 15-round magazine, 4.25-inch bbl., 8 inches overall. Weight: 39 oz. Drift-adj. rear sight. Matte blued finish. Matte black polymer grips. Made from 1988 to 1993.

**M-87 COMPETITION
PISTOL . . . . NiB $1029 Ex $816 Gd $634**
Caliber: 9mm Para. 15-round magazine, 5.5-inch bbl., 9.5 inches overall. Weight: 40 oz. Low-profile combat sights. Satin nickel finish. Matte black grip panels. Built-in ported compensator to minimize recoil and muzzle rise. Made 1989-93.

MICRO-MAX SA AUTOMATIC PISTOL
Caliber: .380 ACP. Seven-round magazine, 3.125-inch bbl., weight: 23 oz. Blade front sight, drift adjustable rear w/3-dot system. Matte blue or satin chrome finish. Checkered polymer grips. Imported from 1997 to 2005.
Matte blue finish. . . . . NiB $281 Ex $204 Gd $165
Satin chrome finish. . . . . NiB $288 Ex $230 Gd $219

MINI-MAX SA AUTOMATIC PISTOL
Calibers: 9mm, .40 S&W or .45 ACP. Six- or 8-round magazine, 3.5-inch bbl., 8.3 inches overall. Weight: 35 oz. Blade front sight, drift adjustable rear w/3-dot system. Matte blue, Duo-Tone or satin chrome finish. Checkered polymer grips. Imported 1996 to 2005.
Duo-Tone finish . . . . NiB $290 Ex $204 Gd $158
Matte blue finish. . . . . NiB $306 Ex $220 Gd $170
Satin chrome finish. . . . . NiB $326 Ex $240 Gd $190
Stainless (disc.) . . . . NiB $359 Ex $301 Gd $235

MINI-MAX II SA AUTOMATIC PISTOL
Cal: .45 ACP only. 10-round mag., 3.625 inch bbl., 7.375 inch overall. Wt: 37 oz. Blade front sight, drift adj. rear w/3-dot system. Shortened barrel and grip. Matte and Satin Chrome finish. Imp. 2005.
Matte blue finish. . . . . NiB $290 Ex $225 Gd $170
Satin chrome finish. . . . . NiB $316 Ex $255 Gd $189

MAX-I SA AUTOMATIC PISTOL
Calibers: 9mm or .45 ACP. 7- or 9-round magazine, 4.25- to 5.125 inch bbl., weight: 34 or 36 oz. Blade front sight, drift adj. rear w/3-dot system. Matte blue, Duo-Tone or satin chrome finish. Checkered black rubber grips. Imported from 1995 to 1999.
Duo-Tone finish . . . . NiB $306 Ex $265 Gd $198
Matte blue finish. . . . . NiB $301 Ex $240 Gd $189
Satin chrome finish. . . . . NiB $316 Ex $270 Gd $219

**Llama
Comanche III Chrome**

**Llama
Martial Double-Action Revolver**

**Llama
Martial Deluxe Gold-Damascened**

**Llama
Super Comanche IV**

MAX-II SA AUTOMATIC PISTOL
Same as the MAX-I with 4.25 bbl. except w/10-round mag. Weight 40 oz., made 2005.
Matte blue finish. . . . . NiB $306 Ex $265 Gd $198
Satin chrome finish. . . . . NiB $332 Ex $270 Gd $219

OMNI 45 DOUBLE-ACTION
AUTOMATIC PISTOL . . . . NiB $437 Ex $291 Gd $220
Caliber: .45 Auto. Seven-round magazine, 4.25-inch bbl.,

7.75 inches overall. Weight: 40 oz. Adj. rear sight, ramp front. Highly polished deep blued finish. Made from 1984-86.

OMNI 9MM DOUBLE-ACTION
AUTOMATIC. . . . . NiB $469 Ex $347 Gd $290
Same general specifications as .45 Omni except chambered for 9mm w/13-round magazine. Made from 1983-86.

SINGLE-ACTION
AUTOMATIC PISTOL . . . . NiB $485 Ex $386 Gd $270
Calibers: .38 Super, 9mm, .45 Auto. Nine-round magazine (7-round for .45 Auto), 5-inch bbl., 8.5 inches overall. Weight: 2 lbs., 8 oz. Intro. in 1981.

SMALL-FRAME AUTOMATIC PISTOL
Calibers: .380 Auto (7-round magazine), .22 RF (8-round magazine), 3.69-inch bbl., weight: 23 oz. Partridge-blade front sight, adj. rear. Blued or satin-chrome finish. Disc. 1997.
Blued finish. . . . . NiB $255 Ex $204 Gd $165
Satin-chrome finish. . . . . NiB $270 Ex $220 Gd $175

- REVOLVERS -

MARTIAL DOUBLE-
ACTION REVOLVER . . . . NiB $255 Ex $170 Gd $120
Calibers: .22 LR, .38 Special. Six-round cylinder, bbl. lengths: 4-inch (.38 Special only) or 6-inch; 11.25 inches overall (w/6-inch bbl.). Weight: About 36 oz. w/6-inch bbl. Target sights. Blued finish. Checkered walnut grips. Made from 1969 to 1976.

MARTIAL DOUBLE-ACTION DELUXE
Same as standard Martial except w/satin chrome, chrome-engraved, blued engraved or gold damascened finish. Simulated pearl grips. Made from 1969 to 1976.
Satin-chrome finish. . . . . NiB $306 Ex $225 Gd $165
Chrome-engraved finish . . . . . . NiB $581 Ex $431 Gd $286
Blue-engraved finish . . . . NiB $638 Ex $453 Gd $332
Gold-damascened finish . . . NiB $2810 Ex $2647 Gd $2299

COMANCHE I . . . . NiB $270 Ex $204 Gd $160
Same general specifications as Martial .22. Made 1977 to 1982.

COMANCHE II . . . . NiB $265 Ex $189 Gd $150
Same general specifications as Martial .38. Made 1977-82.

COMANCHE III . . . . NiB $306 Ex $219 Gd $144
Caliber: .357 Magnum. Six-round cylinder, 4-inch bbl., 9.25 inches overall. Weight: 36 oz. Adj. rear sight, ramp front. Blued finish. Checkered walnut grips. Made from 1975 to 1995. Note: Prior to 1977, this model was designated "Comanche."

COMANCHE III CHROME . . . . NiB $362 Ex $270 Gd $204
Same gen. specifications as Comanche III except has satin chrome finish, 4- or 6-inch bbl. Made from 1975 to 1995.

SUPER COMANCHE IV . . . . . . NiB $388 Ex $301 Gd $204
Caliber: .44 Magnum. Six-round cylinder, 6-inch bbl., 11.75 inches overall. Weight: 50 oz. Adj. rear sight, ramp front. Polished deep blued finish. Checkered walnut grips. Disc. 1998.

SUPER COMANCHE V . . . . NiB $362 Ex $270 Gd $214
Caliber: .357 Mag. Six-round cylinder, 4-, 6- or 8.5-inch bbl., weight: 48 ozs. Ramped front blade sight, click-adj. Rear. Made from 1980 to 1988.

**Luger 1900
American Eagle**

LORCIN ENGINEERING CO., INC. — Mira Loma, California

MODEL L-22

SEMIAUTOMATIC PISTOL . . . . . . NiB $120 Ex $90 Gd $70
Caliber: 22 LR. Nine-round magazine, 2.5-inch bbl., 5.25 inches overall. Weight: 16 oz. Blade front sight, fixed notch rear w/3-dot system. Black Teflon or chrome finish. Black, pink or pearl composition grips. Made from 1990 to 1998.

MODEL L-25, LT-.25 SEMIAUTOMATIC PISTOL

Caliber: 25 ACP. Seven-round magazine, 2.4-inch bbl., 4.8 inches overall. Weight: 12 oz. (LT-25) or 14.5 oz. (L-25). Blade front sight, fixed rear. Black Teflon or chrome finish. Black, pink or pearl composition grips. Made from 1989-98.
Model L-25 . . . . NiB $89 Ex $61 Gd $40
Model LT-25 . . . . NiB $79 Ex $50 Gd $35
Model Lady Lorcin . . . . NiB $81 Ex $55 Gd $35

MODEL L-32

SEMIAUTOMATIC PISTOL . . . . NiB $90 Ex $65 Gd $50
Caliber: 32 ACP. Seven-round magazine, 3.5-inch bbl., 6.6 inches overall. Weight: 27 oz. Blade front sight, fixed notch rear. Black Teflon or chrome finish. Black composition grips. Made from 1992 to 1998.

MODEL L-380 SEMIAUTOMATIC PISTOL

Caliber: .380 ACP. Seven- or 10-round magazine, 3.5-inch bbl., 6.6 inches overall. Weight: 23 oz. Blade front sight, fixed notch rear. Matte Black finish. Grooved black composition grips. Made 1994 to 1998.
Model L-380 (10-round) . . . . NiB $158 Ex $95 Gd $65
Model L-380 (13-round) . . . . NiB $128 Ex $90 Gd $61

MODEL L9MM SEMIAUTOMATIC PISTOL

Caliber: 9mm Parabellum. 10- or 13-round magazine, 4.5-inch bbl., 7.5 inches overall. Weight: 31 oz. Blade front sight, fixed notch rear w/3-dot system. Black Teflon or chrome finish. Black composition grips. Made from 1992 to 1998.
Model L-9mm (7-round) . . . . NiB $158 Ex $95 Gd $65
Model L-9mm (10-round) . . . . NiB $158 Ex $95 Gd $65

O/U DERRINGER . . . . NiB $198 Ex $105 Gd $70

Caliber: .38 Special/.357 Mag., .45LC. Two-round derringer. 3.5-inch bbls. 6.5 inches overall. Weight: 12 oz. Blade front sight, fixed notch rear. Stainless finish. Black composition grips. Made from 1996-98.

LUGER — Manufactured by Deutsche Waffen und Munitionsfabriken (DWM), Berlin, Germany

1900 AMERICAN EAGLE . . NiB $6900 Ex $6555 Gd $4830
Caliber: 7.65 mm. Eight-round magazine; thin, 4.75-inch; tapered bbl.; 9.5 inches overall. Weight: 32 oz. Fixed rear sight, dovetailed front sight. Grip safety. Checkered walnut grips. Early-style toggle, narrow trigger, wide guard, no stock lug. American Eagle over chamber. Estimated 8,000 production.

1900 COMMERCIAL. . . . . . NiB $6910 Ex $6565 Gd $4837
Same specifications as Luger 1900 American Eagle except DWM on early-style toggle, no chamber markings. Estimated 8000 production.

1900 SWISS . . . . NiB $6700 Ex $6365 Gd $4700
Same specifications as Luger 1900 American Eagle except Swiss cross in sunburst over chamber. Estimated 9,000 production.

1902 AMERICAN EAGLE. . . NiB $16,650 Ex $14,000 Gd $12,990
Caliber: 9mm Para. Eight-round magazine, 4-inch heavy tapered bbl., 8.75 inches overall. Weight: 30 oz. Fixed rear sight, dovetailed front sight. Grip safety. Checkered walnut grips. American Eagle over chamber, DWM on early-style toggle, narrow trigger, wide guard, no stock lug. Estimated 700 production.

1902 CARBINE
Caliber: 7.65mm. Eight-round magazine, 11.75-inch tapered bbl., 16.5 inches overall. Weight: 46 oz. Adj. 4-position rear sight, long ramp front sight. Grip safety. Checkered walnut grips and forearm. DWM on early-style toggle, narrow trigger, wide guard, no chamber markings, stock lug. Estimated 3,200 production.
Model 1902 carbine
(gun only) . . . . NiB $12,245 Ex $11,353 Gd $7015
Model 1902 carbine
(gun only, American Eagle), add 45%
w/issued stock and matching numbers, add 20%
w/original stock and non-matching numbers, deduct. . . 20%

1902 CARTRIDGE
COUNTER. . . . . NiB $45,200 Ex $38,990 Gd $29,900
Caliber: 9mm Para. Eight-round magazine, Heavy, tapered 4-inch bbl., 8.75 inches overall. Weight: 30 oz. Fixed rear sight, dovetailed front sight. Grip safety. Checkered walnut grips. DWM on dished toggle w/lock, American Eagle over chamber when marked. No stock lug. Estimated production unknown.

1902 COMMERCIAL . . . NiB $13,600 Ex $10,895 Gd $5,500
Same basic specifications as Luger 1902 Cartridge Counter except DWM on early-style toggle, narrow trigger, wide guard, no chamber markings, no stock lug. Estimated 400 production.

1902 AMERICAN EAGLE . . . NiB $16,600 Ex $13,995 Gd $7,900
Same basic specifications as Luger 1902 Commercial except American Eagle over chamber, DWM on early-style toggle, narrow trigger, wide guard, no stock lug. Estimated 700 production.

1902 AMERICAN EAGLE CARTRIDGE
COUNTER. . . . . NiB $45,200 Ex $38,650 Gd $15,088
Same basic specifications as Luger 1902 Cartridge Counter except American Eagle over chamber, DWM on early-style toggle, narrow trigger, wide guard, no stock lug. Estimated 700 production.

1904 GL "BABY" . . NiB $197,500 Ex $166,000 Gd $110,000
Caliber: 9mm Para. Seven-round magazine, 3.25-inch bbl., 7.75 inches overall. Weight: Approx. 20 oz. Serial number 10077B. "GL" marked on rear of toggle. Georg Luger's personal sidearm. Only one made in 1904.

**1904 NAVAL
(REWORKED) . . . . NiB $14,000 Ex $11,000 Gd $8,250**
Caliber: 9mm Para. Eight-round magazine, bbl., length altered to 4 inches., 8.75 inches overall. Weight: 30 oz. Adj. two-position rear sight, dovetailed front sight. Thumb lever safety. Checkered walnut grips. Heavy tapered bbl., DWM on new-style toggle w/lock, 1902 over chamber. w/or without grip safety and stock lug. Estimated 800 production. Untouched original (rare) worth $50,000.

1906 (11.35MM). . . NiB $119,000 Ex $95,900 Gd $66,500
Caliber: .45 ACP. Six-round magazine, 5-inch bbl., 9.75 inches overall. Weight: 36 oz. Fixed rear sight, dovetailed front sight. Grip safety. Checkered walnut grips. GL monogram on rear toggle link, larger frame w/altered trigger guard and trigger, no proofs, no markings over chamber. No stock lug. Only two were known to be made. Note: This version of the Luger pistol is the most valuable nExt to the "GL" Baby Luger.

**1906 AMERICAN EAGLE
(7.65MM) . . . . NiB $4235 Ex $3300 Gd $2200**
Caliber: 7.65mm. Eight-round magazine, thin 4.75-inch tapered bbl., 9.5 inches overall. Weight: 32 oz. Fixed rear sight, dovetailed front sight. Grip safety. Checkered walnut grips. DWM on new-style toggle, American Eagle over chamber. No stock lug. Estimated 8,000 production.

1906 AMERICAN EAGLE (9MM). . . NiB $4600 Ex $4370 Gd $2000
Same basic specifications as the 7.65mm 1906 except in 9mm Para. w/4-inch barrel, 8.75 inches overall, weight: 30 oz. Estimated 3,500 production.

1906 BERN (7.65MM). . . . . NiB $4430 Ex $2520 Gd $1996
Same basic specifications as the 7.65mm 1906 American Eagle except checkered walnut grips w/.38-inch borders, Swiss Cross on new-style toggle, Swiss proofs, no markings over chamber, no stock lug. Estimated 17,874 production.

1906 BRAZILIAN (7.65MM) . . . . NiB $3550 Ex $3375 Gd $1910
Same general specifications as the 7.65mm 1906 American Eagle except w/Brazilian proofs, no markings over chamber, no stock lug. Estimated 4,500 produced.

1906 BRAZILIAN (9MM) . . NiB $1691 Ex $1390 Gd $1039
Same basic specifications as the 9mm 1906 American Eagle except w/Brazilian proofs, no markings over chamber, no stock lug. Production fewer than 4,000 estimated.

1906 COMMERCIAL. . . . . . NiB $4000 Ex $3400 Gd $1500
Calibers: 7.65mm or 9mm. Same specifications as the 1906 American Eagle versions (above) except no chamber markings and no stock lug. Estimated production: 6,000 (7.65mm) and 3,500 (9mm).

1906 DUTCH . . . . NiB $4200 Ex $3699 Gd $2809
Caliber: 9mm Para. Same specifications as the 9mm 1906 American Eagle except tapered bbl., w/proofs, no markings over chamber, no stock lug. Arsenal rework. Estimated 3,000 production.
Original finish, add 100%

**1906 LOEWE
AND COMPANY. . . . . NiB $4823 Ex $3899 Gd $2744**
Caliber: 7.65mm. Eight-round magazine, 6-inch tapered bbl., 10.75 inches overall. Weight: 35 oz. Adj. two-position rear sight, dovetailed front sight. Grip safety. Checkered walnut grips. Loewe & Company over chamber, Naval proofs, DWM on new-style toggle, no stock lug. Estimated production unknown.

1906 NAVY
Caliber: 9mm Para. Eight-round magazine, 6-inch tapered bbl., 10.75 inches overall. Weight: 35 oz. Adj. two-position rear sight, dovetailed front sight. Grip safety and thumb safety w/lower marking (1st issue), higher marking (2nd issue). Checkered walnut grips. No chamber markings, DWM on new-style toggle w/o lock, but w/stock lug. Est. production: 9,000 (lst issue); 2,000 (2nd issue).

First issue . . . . NiB $7020 Ex $5630 Gd $4490

1906 NAVY COMMERCIAL. . NiB $5600 Ex $5320 Gd $2350
Same as the 1906 Navy except lower marking on thumb safety, no chamber markings. DWM on new-style toggle, w/stock lug and commercial proofs. Estimated 3,000 production.

1906 PORTUGUESE ARMY . . NiB $3400 Ex $3230 Gd $1720
Same specifications as the 7.65mm 1906 American Eagle except w/Portuguese proofs, crown and crest over chamber. No stock lug. Estimated 3,500 production.

**1906 PORTUGUESE
NAVAL . . . . NiB $11,560 Ex $9260 Gd $7300**
Same as the 9mm 1906 American Eagle except w/Portuguese proofs, crown and anchor over chamber, no stock lug.

1906 RUSSIAN . . . . . NiB $18,650 Ex $15,767 Gd $12,890
Same general specifications as the 9mm 1906 American Eagle except thumb safety has markings concealed in up position, DWM on new-style toggle, DWM bbl., proofs, crossed rifles over chamber. Estimated production unknown.

1906 SWISS . . . . NiB $3900 Ex $2709 Gd $2100
Same general specifications as the 7.65mm 1906 American Eagle Luger except Swiss Cross in sunburst over chamber, no stock lug. Estimated 10,300 production.

1906 SWISS (REWORK) . . . NiB $3750 Ex $3250 Gd $2000
Same basic specifications as the 7.65mm 1906 Swiss except in bbl. lengths of 3.63, 4 and 4.75 inches, overall length 8.38 inches (with 4-inch bbl.). Weight 32 oz. (with 4-inch bbl.). DWM on new-style toggle, bbl., w/serial number and proof marks, Swiss Cross in sunburst or shield over chamber, no stock lug. Estimated production unknown.

1906 SWISS POLICE. . . . . . NiB $3189 Ex $2910 Gd $2397
Same general specifications as the 7.65mm 1906 Swiss except DWM on new-style toggle, Swiss Cross in matted field over chamber, no stock lug. Estimated 10,300 production.

1908 BULGARIAN . . . . NiB $3860 Ex $2450 Gd $2600
Caliber: 9mm Para. Eight-round magazine, 4-inch tapered bbl., 8.75 inches overall. Weight: 30 oz. Fixed rear sight dovetailed front sight. Thumb safety w/lower marking concealed. Checkered walnut grips. DWM chamber marking, no proofs, crown over shield on new-style toggle lanyard loop, no stock lug. Estimated production unknown.

1908 COMMERCIAL......NiB $2560 Ex $2010 Gd $1713
Same basic specifications as the 1908 Bulgarian except higher marking on thumb safety. No chamber markings, commercial proofs, DWM on new-style toggle, no stock lug. Estimated 4,000 production.

1908 ERFURT MILITARY...NiB $2555 Ex $2055 Gd $1824
Caliber: 9mm Para. Eight-round magazine, 4-inch tapered bbl., 8.75 inches overall. Weight: 30 oz. Fixed rear sight dovetailed front sight. Thumb safety w/higher marking concealed. Checkered walnut grips. Serial number and proof marks on barrel, crown and Erfurt on new-style toggle, dated chamber, but no stock lug. Estimated production unknown.

1908 MILITARY
Same general specifications as the 9mm 1908 Erfurt Military Luger except first and second issue have thumb safety w/higher marking concealed, serial number on bbl., no chamber markings, proofs on frame, DWM on new-style toggle but no stock lug. Estimated production: 10,000 (first issue) and 5000 (second issue). Third issue has serial number and proof marks on barrel, dates over chamber, DWM on new-style toggle but no stock lug. Estimated 3,000 production.
First issue ....NiB $2460 Ex $2160 Gd $1645
Second issue ....NiB $2010 Ex $1605 Gd $1320
Third issue..............NiB $2299 Ex $1897 Gd $1645

1908 NAVY...........NiB $8405 Ex $79849 Gd $3475
Same basic specifications as the 9mm 1908 military Lugers except w/6-inch bbl, adj. two-position rear sight, no chamber markings, DWM on new-style toggle, w/stock lug. Estimated 26,000 production.

1908 NAVY (COMMERCIAL) ...NiB $6600 Ex $6270 Gd $4620
Same specifications as the 1908 Naval Luger except no chamber markings or date. Commercial proofs, DWM on new-style toggle, w/stock lug. Estimated 1,900 produced.

1914 ERFURT ARTILLERY...NiB $4670 Ex $4435 Gd $3040
Caliber: 9mm Para. Eight-shot magazine, 8-inch tapered bbl., 12.75 inches overall. Weight: 40 oz. Artillery rear sight, Dovetailed front sight. Thumb safety w/higher marking concealed. Checkered walnut grips. Serial number and proof marks on barrel, crown and Erfurt on new-style toggle, dated chamber, w/stock lug. Estimated production unknown.

1914 ERFURT MILITARY...NiB $2170 Ex $2061 Gd $1190
Same specifications as the 1914 Erfurt Artillery except w/4-inch bbl., and corresponding length, weight, etc.; fixed rear sight. Estimated 3,000 production.

1914 NAVY.............NiB $6000 Ex $5700 Gd $3000
Same specifications as 9mm 1914 Lugers except has 6-inch bbl. w/corresponding length and weight, adj. two-position rear sight. Dated chamber, DWM on new-style toggle, w/stock lug. Estimated 40,000 produced.

1914–1918 DWM ARTILLERY ...NiB $3600 Ex $3090 Gd $1997
Caliber: 9mm Para. Eight-shot magazine, 8-inch tapered bbl., 12.75 inches overall. Weight: 40 oz. Artillery rear sight, dovetailed front sight. Thumb safety w/higher marking concealed. Checkered walnut grips. Serial number and proof marks on barrel, DWM on new-style toggle, dated chamber, w/stock lug. Estimated 3,000 production.

1914–1918 DWM MILITARY....NiB $2200 Ex $1899 Gd $1100
Same specifications as the 9mm 1914-1918 DWM Artillery

except w/4-inch tapered bbl., and corresponding length, weight, etc., and fixed rear sight. Production unknown.

1920 CARBINE
Caliber: 7.65mm. Eight-round magazine, 11.75-inch tapered bbl., 15.75 inches overall. Weight: 44 oz. Four-position rear sight, long ramp front sight. Grip (or thumb) safety. Checkered walnut grips and forearm. Serial numbers and proof marks on barrel, no chamber markings, various proofs, DWM on new-style toggle, w/stock lug. Estimated production unknown.
gun only ....NiB $7430 Ex $7058 Gd $3000
w/shoulder stock, add...........................35%

1920 NAVY CARBINE.....NiB $4800 Ex $4560 Gd $3360
Caliber: 7.65mm. Eight-round magazine, 11.75-inch tapered bbl., 15.75 inches overall. Two-position sliding rear sight. Naval military proofs and no forearm. Production unknown.

1920 COMMERCIAL......NiB $1450 Ex $1250 Gd $1018
Calibers: 7.65mm, 9mm Para. Eight-round magazine, 3.63-, 3.75-, 4-, 4.75-, 6-, 8-, 10-, 12-, 16-, 18- or 20-inch tapered bbl., overall length: 8.375 to 24.75 inches. Weight: 30 oz. (with 3.63-inch bbl.). Varying rear sight configurations, dovetailed front sight. Thumb safety. Checkered walnut grips. Serial numbers and proof marks on barrel, no chamber markings, various proofs, DWM or crown over Erfurt on new-style toggle, w/stock lug. Production not documented.

1920 POLICE ....NiB $1410 Ex $1200 Gd $931
Same specifications as 9mm 1920 DWM w/some dated chambers, various proofs, DWM or crown over Erfurt on new-style toggle, identifying marks on grip frame, w/stock lug. Estimated 3,000 production.

1923 COMMERICAL......NiB $1600 Ex $1520 Gd $1120
Calibers: 7.65mm and 9mm Para. Eight-round magazine, 3.63, 3.75, 4, 6, 8, 12 or 16-inch tapered bbl., overall length: 8.38 inches (with 3.63-inch bbl.). Weight: 30 oz. (with 3.63-inch bbl.). Various rear sight configurations, dovetailed front sight. Thumb lever safety. Checkered walnut grips. DWM on new-style toggle, serial number and proofs on barrel, no chamber markings, w/stock lug. Estimated 15,000 production.

1923 DUTCH COMMERICAL ...NiB $2320 Ex $2088 Gd $1872
Same basic specifications as 1923 Commercial Luger w/ same caliber offerings, but only 3.63 or 4-inch bbl. Fixed rear sight, thumb lever safety w/arrow markings. Production unknown.

1923 KRIEGHOFF COMMERCIAL ....NiB $2340 Ex $2223 Gd $1638
Same specifications as 1923 Commercial Luger, w/same caliber offerings but bbl., lengths of 3.63, 4, 6, and 8 inches. "K" marked on new-style toggle. Serial number, proofs and Germany on barrel. No chamber markings, but w/ stock lug. Production unknown.

1923 SAFE AND LOADED...NiB $2460 Ex $2337 Gd $1722
Same caliber offerings, bbl., lengths and specifications as the 1923 Commercial except thumb lever safety, "safe" and "loaded" markings, w/stock lug. Estimated 10,000 production.

Luger 1923 Stoeger

1923 STOEGER

Same general specifications as the 1923 Commercial Luger with the same caliber offerings and bbl., lengths of 3.75, 4, 6, 8 and up to 24 inches. Thumb lever safety. DWM on new-style toggle, serial number and/or proof marks on barrel. American Eagle over chamber but no stock lug. Estimated production less than 1000 (also see Stoeger listings). Note: Qualified appraisals should be obtained on all Stoeger Lugers with bbl. lengths over 8 inches to ensure accurate values.

3.75-, 4-, or 6-inch bbl. . . . NiB $5660 Ex $5377 Gd $2730
8-inch bbl.. . . . . NiB $6350 Ex $6035 Gd $2255

1926 "BABY"

PROTOTYPE . . . . . . NiB $112,750 Ex $90,295 Gd $62,355
Calibers: 7.65mm Browning and 9mm Browning (short). Five-round magazine, 2.31-inch bbl., about 6.25 inches overall. Small-sizedframe and toggle assembly. Prototype for a Luger "pocket pistol," but never manufactured commercially. Checkered walnut grips, slotted for safety. Only four known to exist, but as many as a dozen could have been made.

1929 SWISS . . . . NiB $2017 Ex $1486 Gd $989
Caliber: 7.65mm. Eight-round magazine, 4.75-inch tapered bbl., 9.5 inches overall. Weight: 32 oz. Fixed rear sight, dovetailed front sight. Long grip safety and thumb lever w/S markings. Stepped receiver and straight grip frame. Checkered plastic grips. Swiss Cross in shield on new-style toggle. Serial numbers and proofs on barrel, no markings over chamber and no stock lug. Estimated 1,900 production.

1934 KRIEGHOFF COMMERCIAL
(SIDE FRAME). . . . . NiB $ 7100 Ex $6350 Gd $2895
Caliber: 7.65mm or 9mm Para. Eight-round magazine, bbl. lengths: 4, 6, and 8 inches, overall length: 8.75 (with 4-inch bbl.). Weight: 30 oz. (with 4-inch bbl.). Various rear sight configurations w/dovetailed front sight. Thumb lever safety. Checkered brown plastic grips. Anchor w/H K Krieghoff Suhl on new-style toggle, but no chamber markings. Tapered bbl., w/serial number and proofs; w/stock lug. Estimated 1,700 production.

1934 KRIEGHOFF S CODE MODELS
Caliber: 9mm Para. Eight-round magazine, 4-inch tapered bbl., 8.75 inches overall. Weight: 30 oz. Fixed rear sight, dovetailed front sight. Thumb lever safety. Anchor w/H K Krieghoff Suhl on new-style toggle, S dated chamber, bbl., proofs and stock lug. Early model: Checkered walnut or plastic grips. Estimated 2,500 production. Late model: Checkered brown plastic grips. Estimated 1,200 production.

Early model. . . . . NiB $4660 Ex $4077 Gd $2976
Late model . . . . NiB $4460 Ex $3900 Gd $1464

1934 BYF . . . . NiB $2170 Ex $1950 Gd $1000
Caliber: 9mm Para. Eight-round magazine, 4-inch tapered bbl., 8.75 inches overall. Weight: 30 oz. Fixed rear sight, dovetailed front sight. Thumb lever safety. Checkered walnut or plastic grips. "byf" on new-style toggle, serial number and proofs on bbl., 41-42 dated chamber and w/stock lug. Estimated 3,000 productlon.

1934 MAUSER S/42 K. . . . . NiB $7950 Ex $6800 Gd $3500
Caliber: 9mm Para. Eight-round magazine, 4-inch tapered bbl., 8.75 inches overall. Weight: 30 oz. Fixed rear sight dovetailed front sight. Thumb lever safety. Checkered walnut or plastic grips. "42" on new-style toggle, serial number and proofs on barrel, 1939-40 dated chamber markings and w/stock lug. Estimated 10,000 production.

1934 MAUSER S/42
(DATED) . . . . NiB $2244 Ex $2117 Gd $1599
Same specifications as Luger 1934 Mauser 42 except 41 dated chamber markings and w/stock lug. Production unknown.

1934 MAUSER BANNER
(MILITARY) . . . . NiB $4190 Ex $3455 Gd $3097
Same specifications as Luger 1934 Mauser 42 except Mauser in banner on new-style toggle, tapered bbl., w/serial number and proofs usually, dated chamber markings and w/stock lug. Production unknown.

1934 MAUSER BANNER
COMMERCIAL . . . . NiB $4400 Ex $3760 Gd $3156
Same specifications as Luger 1934 Mauser 42 except checkered walnut grips. Mauser in banner on new-style toggle, tapered bbl., usually w/serial number and proofs, no chamber markings, but w/ stock lug. Production unknown.

1934 MAUSER
BANNER DUTCH . . . . NiB $3787 Ex $3375 Gd $3099
Same specifications as Luger 1934 Mauser 42 except checkered walnut grips. Mauser in banner on new-style toggle, tapered bbl., w/caliber, 1940 dated chamber markings and w/ stock lug. Production unknown.

1934 MAUSER LATVIAN. . . NiB $3260 Ex $2355 Gd $1989
Caliber: 7.65mm. Eight-round magazine, 4-inch tapered bbl., 8.75 inches overall. Weight: 30 oz. Fixed square-notched rear sight, dovetailed Partridge front sight. Thumb lever safety. Checkered walnut stocks. Mauser in banner on new-style toggle, 1937 dated chamber markings and w/stock lug. Production unknown.

1934 MAUSER
(OBERNDORF) . . . . NiB $3155 Ex $2535 Gd $1733
Same as 1934 Mauser 42 except checkered walnut grips. Oberndorf 1934 on new-style toggle, tapered bbl., w/proofs and caliber, Mauser banner over chamber and w/stock lug (also see Mauser).

1934 SIMSON-S TOGGLE . . . NiB $4459 Ex $4188 Gd $3799
Same as 1934 Mauser 42 except checkered walnut grips, "S" on new-style toggle, tapered bbl., w/proofs and S/N, no chamber markings; w/stock lug. Estimated 10,000 production.

Luger S42

42 MAUSER

BANNER (BYF) . . . . NiB $3877 Ex $3078 Gd $2689
Same specifications as Luger 1934 Mauser 42 except weight:
32 oz. Mauser in banner on new-style toggle, tapered bbl., w/
serial number and proofs usually, dated chamber markings and
w/stock lug. Estimated 3,500 production.

ABERCROMBIE AND

FITCH . . . . NiB $5465 Ex $4876 Gd $2879
Calibers: 7.65mm and 9mm Para. Eight-round magazine, 4.75-
inch tapered bbl., 9.5 inches overall. Weight: 32 oz. Fixed rear
sight, dovetailed front sight. Grip safety. Checkered walnut
grips. DWM on new-style toggle Abercrombie & Fitch markings on barrel, Swiss Cross in sunburst over chamber, no stock
lug. Est. 100 production.

DUTCH ROYAL

AIR FORCE . . . . NiB $3324 Ex $2190 Gd $998
Caliber: 9mm Para. Eight-round magazine, 4-inch tapered bbl.,
8.75 inches overall. Weight: 30 oz. Fixed rear sight dovetailed
front sight. Grip safety and thumb safety w/markings and arrow.
Checkered walnut grips. DWM on new-style toggle, bbl., dated
w/serial number and proofs, no markings over chamber, no
stock lug. Estimated 4,000 production.

DWM (G DATE) . . . . NiB $2189 Ex $1953 Gd $1645
Caliber: 9mm Para. Eight-round magazine, 4-inch tapered bbl.,
8.75 inches overall. Weight: 30 oz. Fixed rear sight, dovetailed front sight. Thumb lever safety. Checkered walnut grips.
DWM on new-style toggle, serial number and proofs on barrel, G (1935 date) over chamber and w/stock lug. Production
unknown.

DWM AND ERFURT . . . . NiB $1357 Ex $1134 Gd $876
Caliber: 9mm Para. Eight-round magazine, 4- or 6-inch tapered
bbl., overall length: 8.75 or 10.75 inches. Weight: 30 or 38
oz. Fixed rear sight, dovetailed front sight. Thumb safety.
Checkered walnut grips. Serial numbers and proof marks on
barrel, double dated chamber, various proofs, DWM or crown
over Erfurt on new-style toggle and w/stock lug. Production
unknown.

KRIEGHOFF 36 . . . . NiB $4550 Ex $3799 Gd $1899
Caliber: 9mm Para. Eight-round magazine, 4-inch tapered bbl.,
8.75 inches overall. Weight: 30 oz. Fixed rear sight, dovetailed
front sight. Thumb lever safety. Checkered brown plastic grips.
Anchor w/H K Krieghoff Suhl on new-style toggle, 36 dated

chamber, serial number and proofs on barrel and w/stock lug.
Estimated 700 production.

KRIEGHOFF DATED (1936 - 1945)
Same specifications as Luger Krieghoff 36 except 1936-45
dated chamber, bbl. proofs. Est. 8,600 production.
1936, 1937 and 1940 . . . . . NiB $5500 Ex $4779 Gd $2735
1938 and 1941 . . . . NiB $6500 Ex $5779 Gd $2735
1942 thru 1943, add 60%
1945, add 110%

KRIEGHOFF (GRIP SAFETY) . . . NiB $4977 Ex $3965 Gd $2790
Same specifications as Luger Krieghoff 36 except grip safety
and thumb lever safety. No chamber markings, tapered bbl.,
w/serial number, proofs and caliber, no stock lug. Production
unknown.

MAUSER BANNER

(GRIP SAFETY) . . . . NiB $2874 Ex $2050 Gd $1465
Caliber: 7.65mm. Eight-round magazine, 4.75-inch tapered
bbl., 9.5 inches overall. Weight: 30 oz. Fixed rear sight, dovetailed front sight. Grip safety and thumb lever safety. Checkered
walnut grips. Mauser in banner on new-style toggle, serial
number and proofs on barrel, 1939 dated chamber markings,
but no stock lug. Production unknown.

MAUSER BANNER 42

(DATED) . . . . NiB 2170 Ex $1196 Gd $100
Caliber: 9mm Para. Eight-round magazine, 4-inch tapered bbl.,
8.75 inches overall. Weight: 30 oz. Fixed rear sight, dovetailed
front sight. Thumb lever safety. Checkered walnut or plastic
grips. Mauser in banner on new-style toggle serial number and
proofs on bbl., (usually) 1942 dated chamber markings and
stock lug. Production unknown.

MAUSER BANNER

(SWISS PROOF) . . . . NiB $3460 Ex $2830 Gd $1540
Same specifications as Luger Mauser Banner 42 except checkered walnut grips and 1939 dated chamber.

MAUSER FREISE . . . . NiB $4960 Ex $4090 Gd $2866
Same specifications as Mauser Banner 42 except checkered
walnut grips, tapered bbl. w/proofs on sight block and Freise
above chamber. Production unknown.

S/42
Caliber: 9mm Para. Eight-round magazine, 4-inch tapered barrel. 8.75 inches overall. Weight: 30 oz. Fixed rear sight, dovetailed front sight. Thumb lever safety. Checkered walnut grips.
S/42 on new-style toggle, serial number and proofs on barrel
and w/stock lug. Dated Model: Has dated chamber; estimated
3000 production. G Date: Has G (1935 date) over chamber;
estimated 3000 production. K Date: Has K (1934 date) over
chamber; production unknown.
Dated model . . . . NiB $6780 Ex $5977 Gd $4538
G date model . . . . NiB $2669 Ex $2380 Gd $2010
K date model . . . . NiB $6876 Ex $5986 Gd $4610

RUSSIAN COMMERCIAL . . . NiB $3146 Ex $2548 Gd $1713
Caliber: 7.65mm. Eight-round magazine, 3.63-inch tapered
bbl., 8.38 inches overall. Weight: 30 oz. Fixed rear sight,
dovetailed front sight. Thumb lever safety. Checkered walnut grips. DWM on new-style toggle, Russian proofs on
barrel, no chamber markings but w/stock lug. Production
unknown.

**Luna Model 200
Free Pistol**

SIMSON AND COMPANY

Calibers: 7.65mm and 9mm Para. Eight-round magazine, Weight: 32 oz. Fixed rear sight, dovetailed front sight. Thumb lever safety. Checkered walnut grips. Simson & Company Suhl on new-style toggle, serial number and proofs on barrel, date over chamber and w/stock lug. Estimated 10,000 production.

Simson and Company
(9mm w/1925 date) . . . . . . NiB $6300 Ex $5300 Gd $300
Simson and Company
(undated) . . . . NiB $4300 Ex $3650 Gd $200
Simson and Company
(S code) . . . . NiB $5600 Ex $4800 Gd $2389

VICKERS-DUTCH . . . . NiB $4375 Ex $3968 Gd $3316
Caliber: 9mm Para. Eight-round magazine, 4-inch tapered bbl., 8.75 inches overall. Weight: 30 oz. Fixed rear sight, dovetailed front sight. Grip safety and thumb lever w/arrow markings. Checkered walnut grips (coarse). Vickers LTD on new-style toggle, no chamber markings, dated barrel but no stock lug. Estimated 10,000 production.

LUNA FREE PISTOL — Zella-Mehlis, Germany
Originally mfd. by Ernst Friedr. Buchel and later by Udo Anschutz.

MODEL 200 FREE PISTOL . . NiB $1198 Ex $1027 Gd $784
Single-shot. System Aydt action. Set trigger. Caliber: .22 LR. Eleven-inch bbl., weight: 40 oz. Target sights. Blued finish. Checkered and carved walnut grip and forearm; improved design w/adj. hand base on later models of Udo Anschutz manufacture. Made prior to WWII.

M.A.C. (Military Armament Corp.) — Ducktown, Tennessee

INGRAM MODEL 10 AUTO PISTOL
Select fire (NFA-Title II-Class III) SMG based on Ingram M10 blowback system using an open bolt design with or without telescoping stock. Calibers: 9mm or .45 ACP. Cyclic rate: 750 RPM (9mm) or 900 RPM (.45 ACP). 32- or 30-round magazine, 5.75-inch threaded bbl. (to accept muzzle brake) bbl. Extension or suppressor, 10.5 inches overall w/o stock or 10.6 (w/telescoped stock) and 21.5 (w/Extended stock). Weight: 6.25 pounds. Front protected post sight, fixed aperture rear sight.

9mm model . . . . NiB $1113 Ex $920 Gd $669
ACP model . . . . NiB $998 Ex $877 Gd $668
w/bbl. extension, add $255
w/suppressor, add $587

INGRAM MODEL 10A1S SEMIAUTOMATIC
Similar to the Model 10 except (Class I) semiautomatic w/ closed bolt design to implement an interchangable component system to easily convert to fire 9mm and .45 ACP.
9mm model . . . . NiB $408 Ex $332 Gd $225
.45 ACP model . . . . NiB $431 Ex $342 Gd $235
w/bbl. extension, add $204
w/fake suppressor, add $225

INGRAM MODEL 11 SEMIAUTOMATIC
Similar to the Model 10A1 except (Class I) semiautomatic chambered .380 ACP.
.380 ACP model . . . . NiB $862 Ex $714 Gd $536
w/bbl. extension, add $204
w/fake suppressor, add $225

MAGNUM RESEARCH, INC. (MRI) — Minneapolis, Minnesota
Originally mfd. by IMI (Isreal Military Industries). MRI purchased by Kahr Arms in 2010.

BABY EAGLE
SEMI-AUTOMATIC . . . . NiB $577 Ex $479 Gd $365
DA. Calibers: 9mm, .40 S&W, .41 AE. 15-shot magazine (9mm), 9-round magazine (.40 S&W), 10-round magazine (.41 AE), 4.75-inch bbl., 8.15 inches overall. Weight: 35.4 oz. Combat sights. Matte blued finish. Imported from 1991-96 and 1999 to 2007.

BABY EAGLE II
SEMI-AUTOMATIC . . . . NiB $656 Ex $430 Gd $335
Similar to Baby Eagle except w/accessory rail. Imported from 2008 to date.

BFR LONG CYLINDER
REVOVER . . . . NiB $1050 Ex $780 Gd $550
SA. Calibers: .30-30 Win., .444 Marlin, .45 LC/.410, .450 Marlin, .45-70 Gov't., .460 S&W Mag., and .50 S&W Mag. 5-round cylinder, bbl. lengths: 7.5- or 10-in. Stainless finish. Weight: 4-4.4 lbs. Rubber grips. Made from 1999 to date.

BFR SHORT
CYLINDER REVOVER . . . . NiB $1050 Ex $780 Gd $550
SA. Calibers: .44 Mag., .454 Casull, .475 Linebaugh, and .480 Ruger, 5-round cylinder, bbl. lengths: 5-, or 7.5-in. Stainless finish. Rubber grips. Weight: 3.2-4.4 lbs. Made 1999 to date.

DESERT EAGLE MK VII SEMIAUTOMATIC
Gas-operated. Calibers: .357 Mag., .41 Mag., .44 Mag., .50 Action Express (AE). Eight- or 9-round magazine, 6-inch w/ standard bbl., or 10- and 14-inch w/polygonal bbl., 10.6 inches overall (with 6-inch bbl.). Weight: 52 oz. (w/alum. alloy frame) to 67 oz. (w/steel frame). Fixed or adj. combat sights. Combat-type trigger guard. finish: Military black oxide, nickel, chrome, stainless or blued. Wraparound rubber grips. Made from 1983 to 1995 and 1998 to 2001.

.357 standard (steel)
or alloy (6-inch bbl.) . . . . NiB $903 Ex $658 Gd $562
.357 stainless steel (6-inch bbl.) . . . . NiB $940 Ex $704 Gd $536
.41 Mag. standard (steel) or alloy
(6-inch bbl.) . . . . NiB $1099 Ex $831 Gd $638
.41 Mag. stainless steel
(6-inch bbl.) . . . . NiB $1145 Ex $984 Gd $780
.44 Mag. standard (steel) or alloy
(6-inch bbl.) . . . . NiB $1015 Ex $798 Gd $567

Magnum Research Model Desert Eagle Mark XIX shown w/optional Leupold scope

Magnum Research Model One Pro .45

Magnum Research SSP-91 Lone Eagle Pistol shown w/Optional Leupold Scope

.44 Mag. stainless steel
   (6-inch bbl.) . . . . NiB $991   Ex $806   Gd $559
.50 AE Magnum standard . . . . NiB $1135   Ex $968   Gd $689
For 10-inch bbl., add . . . . NiB $204   Ex $148   Gd $110
For 14-inch bbl., add . . . . NiB $225   Ex $175   Gd $128

DESERT EAGLE MARK XIX SEMI-AUTOMATIC PISTOL

Interchangeable component system based on .50-caliber frame. Calibers: .357 Mag., .44 Mag., .50 AE. Nine-, 8-, 7-round magazine, 6- or 10-inch bbl. w/dovetail design and cross slots to accept scope rings. Weight: 70.5 oz. (6-inch bbl.) or 79 oz. 10.75 or 14.75 inches overall. Sights: Post front and adjustable rear. Blue, chrome or nickel finish; available brushed, matte or polished. Hogue soft rubber grips. Made from 1995 to 1998.

.357 Mag. and .44 Mag.
   (w/6-inch bbl.) . . . . NiB $1400   Ex $1150   Gd $900
.50 AE (w/6-inch bbl.) . . . . NiB $1435   Ex $1164   Gd $989

w/10-inch bbl., add $100
Two caliber conversion (bbl., bolt & mag.), add $444
XIX Platform System (three-caliber conversion kit
   w/six bbls.) . . . . NiB $4335   Ex $3799   Gd $3260
XIX6 System (two-caliber conversion kit
   w/two 6-inch bbls.) . . . . . NiB $2675   Ex $2254   Gd $1969
XIX10 System (two-caliber conversion
   kit w/two 10-inch bbls.) . . . NiB $2150   Ex $1720   Gd $1196
Custom shop finish, add $20%
24K gold finish, add $40%

MICRO DESERT EAGLE. . . . . . NiB $647   Ex $380   Gd $265
DAO. Calibers: .380 ACP. 6-shot magazine, 2-2-inch bbl. Weight: 14 oz. Imported from 2009 to 2013.

(ASAI) MODEL ONE PRO .45 PISTOL

Calibers: .45 ACP or .400 COR-BON, 3.75- inch bbl., 7.04 or 7.83 (IPSC Model) inches overall. Weight: 23.5 (alloy frame) or 31.1 oz. 10-round magazine. Short recoil action. SA or DA mode w/de-cocking lever. Steel or alloy grip-frame. Textured black polymer grips. Imported from 1998.
Model 1P45 . . . . NiB $740   Ex $567   Gd $399
Model 1C45/400 (compensator kit), add $204
Model 1C400NC (400 conversion kit), add $150

MOUNTAIN EAGLE SEMIAUTOMATIC

Caliber: .22 LR. 15-round polycarbonate resin magazine, 6.5-inch injection-molded polymer and steel bbl., 10.6 inches overall. Weight: 21 oz. Ramp blade front sight, adj. rear. Injection-molded, checkered and textured grip. Matte black finish. Made 1992 to 1996.
Standard, w/6-inch bb. . . . . NiB $214   Ex $160   Gd $143
Compact, w/4.5-inch bbl. . . . . . NiB $190   Ex $143   Gd $110
Target, w/8-inch bbl. . . . . NiB $240   Ex $150   Gd $120

SSP-91 LONE EAGLE PISTOL

Single-shot action w/interchangeable rotating breech bbl., assembly. Calibers: .22 LR, .22 Mag., .22 Hornet, .22-250, .223 Rem., .243 Win., 6mm BR, 7mm-08, 7mm BR, .30-06, .30-30, .308 Win., .35 Rem., .357 Mag., .44 Mag., .444 Marlin. 14-inch interchangeable bbl. assembly, 15 inches overall. Weight: 4.5 lbs. Black or chrome finish. Made from 1991 to 2001.
Black finish . . . . NiB $434   Ex $321   Gd $165
Chrome finish. . . . . NiB $464   Ex $342   Gd $186
Extra 14-inch bbl., black finish $150
Extra 14-inch bbl., chrome finish, ... $175
Ambidextrous stock assembly (only). $220
w/muzzle brake, add $408
w/open sights, add $45

MAUSER — Oberndorf, Germany, Waffenfabrik Mauser of Mauser-Werke A.G.

MODEL 80-SA AUTOMATIC. . . NiB $577   Ex $395   Gd $255
Caliber: 9mm Para. 13-round magazine, 4.66-inch bbl., 8 inches overall. Weight: 31.5 oz. Blued finish. Hardwood grips. Made 1992 to 1996.

MODEL 90 DA AUTOMATIC . . NiB $530   Ex $354   Gd $234
Caliber: 9mm Para. 14-round magazine, 4.66-inch bbl., 8 inches overall. Weight: 35 oz. Blued finish. Hardwood grips. Made 1992 to 1996.

**Mauser
Model 80-SA**

**Mauser
Model 90-DA**

**Mauser Model 1898
(1896) Military**

MODEL 90 DAC COMPACT . . . NiB $571 Ex $405 Gd $270
Caliber: 9mm Para. 14-round magazine, 4.13-inch bbl., 7.4 inches overall. Weight: 33.25 oz. Blued finish. Hardwood grips. Made 1992 to 1996.

MODEL 1898 (1896) "BROOMHANDLE" MILITARY AUTO PISTOL
Caliber: 7.63mm Mauser, but also chambered for 9mm Mauser and 9mm Para. w/the latter being identified by a large red "9"

in the grips. 10-round box magazine, 5.25-inch bbl., 12 inches overall. Weight: 45 oz. Adj. rear sight. Blued finish. Walnut grips. Made from 1897 to 1939. Note: Specialist collectors recognize a number of variations at significantly higher values. Price here is for more common commercial and military types with original finish.

Commercial model (pre-war). . . NiB $3520 Ex $2735 Gd $1096
Commercial model
(wartime) . . . . NiB $3015 Ex $2512 Gd $1040
Red 9 Commercial model
(fixed sight). . . . . NiB $3265 Ex $2979 Gd $1049
Red 9 WWI Contract
(tangent sight). . . . . NiB $3300 Ex $2670 Gd $1300
w/stock sssembly (matching S/N), add $1300

MODEL HSC DA AUTO PISTOL
Calibers: .32 Auto (7.65mm), .380 Auto (9mm Short). Eight-round (.32) or 7-round (.380) magazine, 3.4-inch bbl., 6.4 inches overall. Weight: 23.6 oz. Fixed sights. Blued or nickel finish. Checkered walnut grips. Made from 1938 to 1945 and from 1968 to 1996.

Military model
(low grip screw) . . . . NiB $6200 Ex $5110 Gd $2820
Commercial model (wartime) . . . NiB $536 Ex $398 Gd $249
Nazi military model (pre-war) . . . NiB $1148 Ex $974 Gd $632
Nazi military model (wartime) . . . .NiB $600 Ex $499 Gd $270
French production (postwar) . . . . NiB $474 Ex $398 Gd $239
Mauser production (postwar) . . . NiB $497 Ex $377 Gd $235
Recent importation
(Armes De Chasse) . . . . NiB $478 Ex $398 Gd $270
Recent importation
(Interarms) . . . . NiB $388 Ex $289 Gd $230
Recent importation
(European Amer. Arms). . . . . NiB $328 Ex $196 Gd $115
Recent importation
(Gamba, USA) . . . . NiB $431 Ex $316 Gd $194
American Eagle model
(1 of 5000) . . . . NiB $562 Ex $433 Gd $319

LUGER LANGE PISTOL 08
Caliber: 9mm Para. Eight-inch bbl., Checkered grips. Blued finish. Accessorized w/walnut shoulder stock, front sight tool, spare magazine, leather case. Currently in production. Commemorative version made in limited quantities w/ivory grips and 14-carat gold monogram plate.

Commemorative model
(100 produced). . . . . . . NiB $2855 Ex $2330 Gd $1875
Commemorative matched
pair. . . . . NiB $5423 Ex $4412 Gd $3099
Cartridge counter model. . . NiB $4010 Ex $2907 Gd $2017
Carbine model (w/matching
buttstock) . . . . NiB $8025 Ex $6309 Gd $3718

PARABELLUM LUGER AUTO PISTOL
Current commercial model. Swiss pattern with grip safety. Calibers: 7.65mm Luger, 9mm Para. Eight-round magazine, bbl. lengths: 4-, 6-inch, 8.75 inches overall (with 4-inch bbl.). Weight: 30 oz. (with 4-inch bbl.). Fixed sights. Blued finish. Checkered walnut grips. Made from 1970 to date. Note: Pistols of this model sold in the U.S. have the American Eagle stamped on the receiver.

Standard model (blue) . . . . . NiB $1603 Ex $1230 Gd $704

POCKET MODEL 1910 AUTO PISTOL
Caliber: .25 Auto (6.35mm). Nine-round magazine, 3.1-inch bbl., 5.4 inches overall. Weight: 15 oz. Fixed sights. Blued finish. Checkered walnut or hard rubber grips. Made 1910-34.

**Mauser Parabellum Luger
shown w/6-in. barrel**

Model 1910 (standard) . . . . **NiB $691 Ex $461 Gd $306**
Model 1910 (w/side latch) . . . . **NiB $546 Ex $431 Gd $309**

POCKET MODEL 1914 . . . . . . **NiB $691 Ex $485 Gd $314**
Similar to Pocket Model 1910. Caliber: .32 Auto (7.65mm). Eight-round magazine, 3.4-inch bbl., 6 inches overall. Weight: 21 oz. Fixed sights. Blued finish. Checkered walnut or hard rubber grips. Made 1914 to 1934

POCKET MODEL 1934 . . . . **NiB $816 Ex $595 Gd $410**
Similar to Pocket Models 1910 and 1914 in the respective calibers. Chief difference is in the more streamlined, one-piece grips. Made from 1934 to 1939.

WTP MODEL I AUTO PISTOL . **NiB $779 Ex $610 Gd $413**
"Westentaschen-Pistole" (Vest Pocket Pistol). Caliber: .25 Automatic (6.35mm). Six-round magazine, 2.5-inch bbl., 4 inches overall. Weight: 11.5 oz. Blued finish. Hard rubber grips. Made from 1922 to 1937.

**WTP MODEL II
AUTO PISTOL** . . . . **NiB $1398 Ex $1137 Gd $895**
Similar to Model I but smaller and lighter. Caliber: .25 Automatic (6.35mm). Six-round magazine, 2-inch bbl., 4 inches overall. Weight: 9.5 oz. Blued finish. Hard rubber grips. Made from 1938 to 1940.

MERWIN HULBERT & CO. — New York

**FIRST MODEL
FRONTIER ARMY** . . . . **NiB $9679 Ex $8023 Gd $6029**
Single action, .44 caliber, 7.5-inch bbl. Square butt, open top, scoop flutes on cylinder, two screws above trigger guard

**SECOND MODEL
FRONTIER ARMY** . . . . **NiB $8617 Ex $7608 Gd $6138**
Similar to First Model except has only one screw above trigger guard.

**SECOND MODEL
POCKET ARMY** . . . . **NiB $7740 Ex $ 6487 Gd $5009**
Similar to Second Model except has bird's-head butt instead of square butt, 3.5- or 7-inch (scarce) bbl. Some models may be marked "Pocket Army."

**THIRD MODEL
FRONTIER ARMY** . . . . **NiB $6995 Ex $3429 Gd $2152**
Caliber: .44, 7-inch round bbl. with no rib, single action.

Square butt, top strap, usually has conventional fluting on cylinder but some have scoop flutes.

**THIRD MODEL DA
FRONTIER ARMY** . . . . **NiB $6775 Ex $5254 Gd $4890**
Similar to Third Model Frontier Army SA except is double action.

**THIRD MODEL
POCKET ARMY** . . . . **NiB $7610 Ex $5366 Gd $4997**
Caliber: .44, 3.5- or 7.5-inch bbl. with no rib. Single action, bird's-head butt, top strap.

**THIRD MODEL
POCKET ARMY DA** . . . . **NiB $6648 Ex $5096 Gd $3930**
Similar to Third Model Pocket Army SA except is double action.

**FOURTH MODEL
FRONTIER ARMY** . . . . **NiB $9010 Ex $8188 Gd $4992**
Caliber: .44, 3.5- 5- or 7-inch unique ribbed bbl. Single action, square butt, top strap, conventional flutes on cylinder.

**FOURTH MODEL FRONTIER
ARMY DA** . . . . **NiB $8189 Ex $5883 Gd $5409**
Similar to Fourth Model Frontier Army SA except double action.

NOTE: *The following handguns are foreign copies of Merwin Hulbert Co. guns and may be marked as such, or as "Sistema Merwin Hulbert," but rarely with the original Hopkins & Allen markings. These guns will usually bring half or less of a comparable genuine Merwin Hulbert product.*

FIRST POCKET MODEL . . . **NiB $2270 Ex $1996 Gd $1416**
Caliber: .38 Special, 5-round cylinder (w/cylinder pin Exposed at front of frame), single action. Spur trigger; round loading hole in recoil shield, no loading gate.

SECOND POCKET MODEL . . . **NiB $1815 Ex $1595 Gd $1416**
Similar to First Pocket Model except has sliding loading gate.

THIRD POCKET MODEL. . . . **NiB $1633 Ex $1270 Gd $1111**
Similar to First Pocket Model except has enclosed cylinder pin.

**THIRD POCKET MODEL W/TRIGGER
GUARD.** . . . . **NiB $1517 Ex $1319 Gd $1133**
Similar to First Pocket Model except w/conventional trigger guard.

**SMALL FRAME
POCKET MODEL** . . . . **NiB $1360 Ex $1120 Gd $601**
Caliber: .38 Spec., 5-rnd. cylinder, DA, may have hammer spur.

**SMALL FRAME
POCKET MODEL 32** . . . . **NiB $1377 Ex $1190 Gd $979**
Similar to Medium Frame Pocket Model except .32 caliber, 7-round cylinder, double action.

TIP-UP MODEL 22 . . . . **NiB $1579 Ex $1367 Gd $1056**
Similar to S&W Model One except .22 caliber, 7-round cylinder, spur trigger. Scarce.

Mitchell Arms
Citation II

Mitchell Arms
Sharpshooter II

Mitchell Arms SA
Army Revolver

MITCHELL ARMS, INC. — Santa Ana, CA

MODEL 1911 GOLD SIGNATURE
Caliber: .45 ACP. Eight-round mag, 5-inch bbl., 8.75 inches overall. Weight: 39 oz. Interchangeable blade front sight, drift-adj. combat or fully adj. rear. Smooth or checkered walnut grips. Made 1994 to 1996.
Blued model w/fixed sights. . . . NiB $512 Ex $393 Gd $301
Blued model w/adj. sights. . . . . NiB $554 Ex $456 Gd $412
Stainless model w/fixed sights . . . NiB $709 Ex $549 Gd $464
Stainless model w/adj. sights . . . . NiB $755 Ex $601 Gd $530

ALPHA MODEL AUTO PISTOL
Dual action w/interchangeable trigger modules. Caliber: .45 ACP. Eight-round magazine, 5-inch bbl., 8.75 inches overall. Weight: 39 oz. Interchangeable blade front sight, drift-adj. rear. Smooth or checkered walnut grips. Blued or stainless finish. Made in 1994. Advertised in 1995 but not manufactured.

AMERICAN EAGLE
LUGER PISTOL . . . . NiB $900 Ex $678 Gd $369
Stainless-steel re-creation of the American Eagle Parabellum auto pistol. Caliber: 9mm Para. Seven-round magazine, 4-inch bbl., 9.6 inches overall. Weight: 26.6 oz. Blade front sight, fixed rear. Stainless finish. Checkered walnut grips. Made from 1993 to 1994.

CITATION II AUTO PISTOL . . . NiB $433 Ex $309 Gd $228
Re-creation of the High Standard Supermatic Citation Military. Caliber: .22 LR. 10-round magazine, 5.5-inch bull bbl. or 7.25 fluted bbl., 9.75 inches overall (5.5-inch bbl.). Weight: 44.5 oz. Ramp front sight, slide-mounted micro-adj. rear. Satin blued or stainless finish. Checkered walnut grips w/thumbrest. Made 1992 to 1996.

OLYMPIC I.S.U.
AUTO PISTOL . . . . NiB $659 Ex $556 Gd $434
Similar to the Citation II model except chambered in .22 Short, 6.75-inch round tapered bbl. w/stabilizer and removable counterweights. Made from 1992 to 1996.

SHARPSHOOTER I
AUTO PISTOL . . . . NiB $362 Ex $288 Gd $212
Re-creation of the High Standard Sharpshooter. Caliber: .22 LR. 10-round magazine, 5-inch bull bbl., 10.25 inches overall. Weight: 42 oz. Ramp front sight, slide-mounted micro-adj. rear. Satin blued or stainless finish. Checkered walnut grips w/thumbrest. Made 1992 to 1996.

MODEL SA SPORT KING II . . . NiB $304 Ex $226 Gd $170
Caliber: .22 LR. 10-round magazine, 4.5- or 6.75-inch bbl., 9 or 11.25 inches overall. Weight: 39 or 42 oz. Checkered walnut or black plastic grips. Blade front sight and drift adjustable rear. Made 1993 to 1994.

SA ARMY REVOLVER
Calibers: .357 Mag., .44 Mag., .45 Colt/.45 ACP. Six-round cylinder. bbl., lengths: 4.75, 5.5, 7.5 inches, weight: 40-43 oz. Blade front sight, grooved top strap or adj. rear. Blued or nickel finish w/color-casehardened frame. Brass or steel backstrap/trigger guard. Smooth one-piece walnut grips. Imported from 1987-94 and 1997. Disc.
Standard model w/blued finish . . NiB $431 Ex $319 Gd $235
Standard model w/nickel finish. . . .NiB $464 Ex $398 Gd $303
Standard model w/steel
    backstrap . . . . NiB $541 Ex $422 Gd $317
.45 Combo w/blued finish . . . . NiB $544 Ex $429 Gd $346
.45 Combo w/nickel finish . . . . NiB $601 Ex $562 Gd $433

TROPHY II
AUTO PISTOL . . . . NiB $464 Ex $337 Gd $270
Similar to the Citation II model except w/gold-plated trigger and gold-filled markings. Made from 1992 to 1996.

VICTOR II AUTO PISTOL . . . . . NiB $544 Ex $419 Gd $342
Re-creation of the High Standard Victor w/full-length vent rib. Caliber: .22 LR. 10-round magazine, 4.5- or 5.5-inch bbl., 9.75 inches overall (with 5.5-inch bbl.). Weight: 52 oz. (with

**Mitchell Arms
Victor II**

MKE Kirikkale

**MOA Maximum
Carbine Pistol**

**Mossberg Brownie
"Pepperbox" Pistol**

5.5-inch bbl.). Rib-mounted target sights. Satin blued or stainless finish. Checkered walnut grips w/thumbrest. Made from 1992 to 1996.

GUARDIAN ANGEL

DERRINGER . . . . **NiB $158 Ex $120 Gd $101**
Hammerless, double-action O/U derringer w/interchangeable drop-in breech block. Calibers: .22 LR, .22 WRM. Two-round capacity. Two-inch bbl., 5 inches overall. Weight: 12 oz. Blue, nickel or gold finish. Blade front and fixed rear sights. Checkered black grips. Made from 1996 to 1997.

GUARDIAN II . . . . **NiB $327 Ex $235 Gd $169**
Caliber: .38 Special, Six-round cylinder, 2-, 4- or 6-inch bbl., 8.5 inches overall (with 4-inch bbl.). Weight: 32 oz (with 4-inch bbl.). Blade ramp front and fixed rear sights. Checkered combat or target grips. Blued finish. Made in 1995.

GUARDIAN III . . . . **NiB $369 Ex $272 Gd $181**
Same specifications as Guardian II model except w/adjustable rear sights. Made in 1995.

TITAN II DA . . . . **NiB $295 Ex $259 Gd $175**
Caliber: .357 Mag. Six-round cylinder. 2-, 4- or 6-inch bbl., 7.75 inches overall (with 4-inch bbl.). Weight: 38 oz (with 4-inch bbl.). Blade front and fixed rear sights. Crane mounted cylinder release. Blued or stainless finish. Made in 1995.

TITAN III DA . . . . **NiB $345 Ex $204 Gd $119**
Same specification as the Titan II except w/adjustable rear sight. Made in 1995.

MKE — Ankara, Turkey

Manufactured by Makina ve Kimya Endüstrisi Kurumu.

KIRIKKALE DA

AUTOMATIC PISTOL . . . . **NiB $399 Ex $283 Gd $212**
Similar to Walther PP. Calibers: .32 Auto (7.65mm), .380 Auto (9mm Short). Seven-round magazine, 3.9-inch bbl., 6.7 inches overall. Weight: 24 oz. Fixed sights. Blued finish. Checkered plastic grips. Made from 1948 to 1988. Note: This is a Turkish Army standard service pistol.

MOA CORPORATION — Dayton, Ohio

MAXIMUM SINGLE-SHOT PISTOL
Calibers: .22 Hornet to .454 Casull Mag. Armoloy, Chromoloy or stainless falling block action fitted w/blued or stainless 8.75-, 10- or 14-inch Douglas bbl., weight: 60-68 oz. Smooth walnut grips. Made from 1986.
Chromoloy receiver
   (blued bbl.). . . . . **NiB $806 Ex $588 Gd $475**
Armoloy receiver (blued bbl.) . . . **NiB $933 Ex $836 Gd $497**
Stainless receiver (blued bbl.) . . **NiB $1028 Ex $916 Gd $689**
w/stainless bbl., add **$306**
w/Extra bbl., add **$388**

MAXIMUM CARBINE PISTOL
Similar to Maximum Pistol except w/18-inch bbl. Made intermittently from 1986-88 and from 1994 to date.
MOA Maximum (blued bbl.). . . **NiB $984 Ex $780 Gd $601**
**MOA Maximum
   (stainless bbl.)**. . . . . **NiB $1100 Ex $890 Gd $597**

Navy Arms
Model 1875 Schofield

Navy Arms
Model 1875 SA Revolver

Navy Arms
Frontier Standard

Navy Arms
Frontier Target Model

O.F. MOSSBERG & SONS, INC. — North Haven, Connecticut

BROWNIE "PEPPERBOX" PISTOL NiB $816 Ex $562 Gd $375
Hammerless, top-break, double-action, four bbls. w/revolving firing pin. Caliber: .22 LR, 2.5-inch bbls., weight: 14 oz. Blued finish. Serrated grips. Approximately 37,000 made from 1919-32.

MODEL 715P PISTOL........NiB $308 Ex $270 Gd $260
Semi-automatic. Uses a Model 702 Plinkster barreled action. Caliber: .22 LR, 10- or 20-rnd. magazine. 6-inch bbl. Weight: 48 oz. Blued finish. Polymer grips. Made from 2014 to present.
w/red dot optic, add............................$45
Duck Commander, add..........................$100

NAMBU

See Listings under Japanese Military Pistols.

NAVY ARMS COMPANY — Martinsburg, WV

MODEL 1873 SA REVOLVER
Calibers: .44-40, .45 Colt. Six-round cylinder, bbl. lengths: 3, 4.75, 5.5, 7.5 inches, 10.75 inches overall (with 5.5-inch bbl.). Weight: 36 oz. Blade front sight, grooved topstrap rear. Blued w/color-casehardened frame or nickel finish. Smooth walnut grips. Made from 1991 to 2009.
Blued finish w/brass
   backstrap .... NiB $468 Ex $357 Gd $235
U.S. Artillery model w/5-inch
   bbl.....................NiB $544 Ex $386 Gd $270
U.S. Cavalry model w/7-inch
   bbl ....NiB $544 Ex $386 Gd $270
Bisley model ....NiB $536 Ex $359 Gd $225
Sheriff's model (disc. 1998)....NiB $434 Ex $356 Gd $220

MODEL 1875 SCHOFIELD REVOLVER
Replica of S&W Model 3, top-break single-action w/auto ejector. Calibers: .44-40 or .45 LC. Six-round cylinder, 5- or 7-inch bbl., 10.75 or 12.75 inches overall. Weight: 39 oz. Blade front sight, square-notched rear. Polished blued finish. Smooth walnut grips. Made from 1999 to 2009.
Cavalry model (7-inch bbl.) ...NiB $668 Ex $544 Gd $336
Deluxe Cavalry model
   (engraved) ....NiB $1720 Ex $1398 Gd $1176
Wells Fargo model (5-inch bbl.).. NiB $840 Ex $636 Gd $447
Deluxe Wells Fargo
   model (engraved) ....NiB $1479 Ex $1266 Gd $1122
Hideout model
   (3.5-inch bbl.)...........NiB $748 Ex $590 Gd $398

1875 REMINGTON
SA REVOLVER..............NiB $398 Ex $283 Gd $194
Replica of Remington Model 1875. Calibers: .357 Magnum, .44-40, .45 Colt. Six-round cylinder, 7.5-inch bbl., 13.5 inches overall. Weight: About 48 oz. Fixed sights. Blued or nickel finish. Smooth walnut grips. Made in Italy c.1955-1980 and 1994 to 2000. Originally marketed in the U.S. as Replica Arms Model 1875 (that firm was acquired by Navy Arms Co).

FRONTIER SA REVOLVER.....NiB $397 Ex $290 Gd $224
Calibers: .22 LR, .22 WMR, .357 Mag., .45 Colt. Six-round cylinder, bbl. lengths: 4.5-, 5.5-, 7.5-inches, 10.25 inches overall (with 4.5-inch bbl.). Weight: About 36 oz. (with 4.5-inch bbl.). Fixed sights. Blued bbl., and cylinder, color-casehardened frame, brass grip frame. One-piece smooth walnut grip. Imported from 1975 to 1979.

FRONTIER TARGET MODEL...NiB $416 Ex $312 Gd $225
Same as standard Frontier except has adj. rear sight and ramp front sight. Imported from 1975 to 1979.

BUNTLINE FRONTIER ....NiB $569 Ex $467 Gd $342
Same as Target Frontier except has detachable shoulder stock and 16.5-inch bbl. Calibers: .357 Magnum and .45 Colt only. Made from 1975 to 1979.

LUGER AUTOMATIC . . . . **NiB $166 Ex $112 Gd $88**
Caliber: .22 LR, standard or high velocity. 10-round magazine, bbl. length: 4.5 inches, 8.9 inches overall. Weight: 1 lb., 13.5 oz. Square blade front sight w/square notch, stationary rear sight. Walnut checkered grips. Non-reflecting black finish. Made 1986 to 1988.

ROLLING BLOCK
SINGLE-SHOT PISTOL . . . . **NiB $418 Ex $345 Gd $231**
Calibers: .22 LR, .22 Hornet, .357 Magnum. Eight-inch bbl., 12 inches overall. Weight: About 40 oz. Adjustable sights. Blued bbl., color-casehardened frame, brass trigger guard. Smooth walnut grip and forearm. Imported from 1965 to 1980.

TT-OLYMPIA PISTOL. . . . . **NiB $283 Ex $214 Gd $170**
Reproduction of the Walther Olympia Target Pistol. Caliber: .22 LR. Eight inches overall 4.6-inch bbl., weight: 28 oz. Blade front sight, adj. rear. Blued finish. Checkered hardwood grips. Imported 1992 to 1994.

NEW ENGLAND FIREARMS — Gardner, Massachusetts

In 1987, New England Firearms was established as an independent company producing select H&R models under the NEF logo. In 1991, H&R 1871, Inc. was formed from the residual of the parent company and took over the New England Firearms facility. H&R 1871 produced firearms under both their logo and the NEF brand name until 1999, when the Marlin Firearms Company acquired the assets of H&R 1871. Purchased by Freedom Group in 2008.

MODEL R73 REVOLVER . . . . **NiB $158 Ex $98 Gd $67**
Caliber: .32 H&R Mag. Five-round cylinder, 2.5- or 4-inch bbl., 8.5 inches overall (with 4-inch bbl.). Weight: 26 oz. (with 4 inch bbl.). Fixed or adjustable sights. Blued or nickel finish. Walnut-finish hardwood grips. Made from 1988 to 1999.

MODEL R92 REVOLVER . . . . **NiB $137 Ex $90 Gd $64**
Same general specifications as Model R73 except chambered for .22 LR. Nine-round cylinder. Weight: 28 oz. w/4 inch bbl., Made 1988 to 1999.

MODEL 832 STARTER PISTOL . . **NiB $148 Ex $101 Gd $75**
Calibers: .22 Blank, .32 Blank. Nine- and 5-round cylinders, respectively. Push-pin swing-out cylinder. Solid wood grips w/ NEF medallion insert.

ULTRA REVOLVER . . . . **NiB $170 Ex $109 Gd $70**
Calibers: .22 LR, .22 Mag. Nine-round cylinder in .22 LR, 6-round cylinder in .22 Mag., 4- or 6-inch ribbed bull bbl., 10.75 inches overall (with 6-inch bbl.). Weight: 36 oz. (with 6-inch bbl.). Blade front sight, adj. square-notched rear. Blued or nickel finish. Walnut-finish hardwood grips. Made from 1989 to 1999.

LADY ULTRA REVOLVER . . . . . **NiB $169 Ex $144 Gd $106**
Same basic specifications as the Ultra except in .32 H&R Mag. w/5-round cylinder and 3-inch ribbed bull bbl., 7.5 inches overall. Weight: 31 oz. Made from 1992 to 1999.

NORTH AMERICAN ARMS — Provo, Utah

MODEL .22LR. . . . . **NiB $175 Ex $149 Gd $70**
Same as Model 22S except chambered for .22 LR., is

Navy Arms
Rolling Block Single-Shot

Navy Arms
TT-Olympia Pistol

New England Firearms
Model R73 Revolver

New England Firearms
Model 832 Starter Pistol

3.88-inches overall, weight: 4.5 oz. Made from 1975 to date.

MODEL 22S MINI REVOLVER . . **NiB $170 Ex $150 Gd $70**
Single-Action. Caliber: .22 Short. Five-round cylinder, 1.13-inch bbl., 3.5-inches overall. Weight: 4 oz. Fixed sights. Stainless steel. Plastic grips. Made from 1975 to date.

MODEL 450 MAGNUM EXPRESS
Single-Action. Calibers: .450 Magnum Express, .45 Win. Mag. Five-round cylinder, 7.5- or 10.5-inch bbl., matte or polished

Ortgies
Pocket Automatic Pistol

stainless steel finish. Walnut grips. Presentation case. Disc. 1984.

Matte stainless model . . . . . . NiB $1259 Ex $1066 Gd $808
Polished stainless model . . . . NiB $1528 Ex $1234 Gd $856
w/10-inch bbl., add $281
w/combo cylinder, add. $255

BLACK WIDOW REVOLVER
SA. Calibers: .22 LR., .22 WMR. Five-round cylinder, 2-inch heavy vent bbl., 5.88-inches overall. Weight: 8.8 oz. Fixed or adj. sights. Full-size black rubber grips. Stainless steel brush finish. Made from 1990 to date.

Adj. sight model . . . . NiB $257 Ex $188 Gd $135
Adj. sight combo model, add $45
Fixed sight model . . . . NiB $257 Ex $188 Gd $135
Fixed sight combo model, add $40

GUARDIAN DAO PISTOL . . . . NiB $377 Ex $286 Gd $198
Caliber: .25 ACP, .32 ACP or .380. Six-round magazine (.32 ACP), 2-inch bbl., 4.4 inches overall. Weight: 13.5 oz. Fixed sights. Black synthetic grips. Stainless steel. Made from 1997 to date.

MINI-MASTER TARGET REVOLVER
SA. Calibers: .22 LR., .22 WMR. Five-round cylinder, 4-inch heavy vent rib bbl., 7.75-inches overall. Weight: 10.75 oz. Fixed or adj. sights. Black rubber grips. Stainless steel brush finish. Made from 1990 to date.

Adj. sight model . . . . NiB $270 Ex $214 Gd $165
Adj. sight combo model, add $35
Fixed sight model . . . . NiB $270 Ex $214 Gd $165
Fixed sight combo model, add $35

NORWEGIAN MILITARY PISTOLS — Manufactured by Kongsberg Vaapenfabrikk, Government Arsenal at Kongsberg, Norway

MODEL 1912 . . . . NiB $2885 Ex $2289 Gd $1588
Same as the model 1914 except has conventional slide stop. Only 500 were made.

MODEL 1914
AUTOMATIC PISTOL . . . . NiB $511 Ex $378 Gd $283
Similar to Colt Model 1911 .45 Automatic w/same general specifications except has lengthened slide stop. Made 1919-46.

OLYMPIC ARMS, INC. — Olympia, WA

OA-93 AR SEMIAUTOMATIC PISTOL
AR-15 style receiver with no buffer tube or charging handle. Caliber: .223 Rem. or 7.62x39mm. Five-, 20- or 30-round detachable magazine, 6-, 9- or 14-inch stainless steel bbl., 15.75 inches overall w/6-inch bbl., weight: 4 lbs., 3 oz. Flattop upper with no open sights. VortEx flash suppressor. A2 stowaway pistol grip and forward pistol grip. Made 1993-94. Note: All post-ban versions of OA-93 style weapons are classified by BATF as "Any Other Weapon" and must be transferred by a Class III dealer. Values listed here are for limited-production, pre-ban guns.

(.223 Rem.) . . . . NiB $1134 Ex $871 Gd $687
(7.62x39mm) . . . . NiB $2234 Ex $1669 Gd $1378

OA-96 AR SEMI-AUTOMATIC
PISTOL . . . . NiB $904 Ex $804 Gd $637
Similar to Model OA-93 AR except w/6.5-inch bbl. only chambered for .223 Rem. Additional compliance modifications include a fixed (nonremovable) well-style magazine and no forward pistol grip. Made from 1996 to 2000.

WHITNEY WOLVERINE . . . . . . NiB $294 Ex $265 Gd $235
Similar to original Whitney Wolverine from 1950s except w/ polymer frame and ventalated rib. .22 LR, 10-rnd. magazine. Finish: black, pink, desert tan, coyote brown. Weight: 19.2 oz. Made from 2010 to date.

ORTGIES PISTOLS — Erfurt, Germany
Manufactured by Deutsche Werke A.G.

POCKET
AUTOMATIC PISTOL . . . . NiB $399 Ex $305 Gd $225
Calibers: .32 Auto (7.65mm), .380 Auto (9mm). Seven-round magazine (.380 cal.), 8-round (.32 cal.), 3.25-inch bbl., 6.5-inches overall. Weight: 22 oz. Fixed sights. Blued finish. Plain walnut grips. Made in 1920's.

VEST POCKET
AUTOMATIC PISTOL . . . . NiB $365 Ex $289 Gd $203
Caliber: .25 Auto (6.35mm). Six-round magazine, 2.75-inch bbl., 5.19 inches overall. Weight: 13.5 oz. Fixed sights. Blued finish. Plain walnut grips. Made in 1920's.

PARA USA, INC. — Pineville, NC
Purchased by Freedom Group in 2012.

LIMITED EDITION SERIES
Custom-tuned and fully accessorized "Limited Edition" versions of standard "P" Models. Enhanced-grip frame and serrated slide fitted w/match-grade bbl., and full-length recoil spring guide system. Beavertail grip safety and skeletonized hammer. Ambidextrous safety and trigger-stop adjustment. Fully adjustable or contoured low-mount sights. For pricing see individual models.

P-10 SA AUTO PISTOL
Super compact. Calibers: .40 S&W, .45 ACP. 10-round magazine, 3-inch bbl., weight: 24 oz. (alloy frame) or 31 oz. (steel frame). Ramp front sight and drift adjustable rear w/3-dot system. Steel or alloy frame. Matte black, Duo-Tone or stainless

Olympic Arms OA-93

Para-Ordnance
P-12 Compact

Para-Ordnance
P-14 Auto Pistol

finish. Made from 1997 to 2002.
Alloy model . . . . NiB $637 Ex $540 Gd $413
Duo-Tone model . . . . NiB $688 Ex $581 Gd $464
Stainless steel model . . . . NiB $693 Ex $577 Gd $447
Steel model . . . . NiB $648 Ex $536 Gd $410
Limited model (tuned & accessorized), add $150

P-12 COMPACT AUTO PISTOL
Calibers: .45 ACP. 11-round magazine, 3.5-inch bbl., 7-inches overall. Weight: 24 oz. (alloy frame). Blade front sight, adj. rear w/3-dot system. Textured composition grips. Matte black alloy or steel finish. Made from 1990 to 2003.
Model P1245 (alloy) . . . . NiB $779 Ex $606 Gd $530
Model P1245C (steel) . . . . NiB $857 Ex $686 Gd $541
Limited model (tuned & accessorized), add $150

P-13 AUTO PISTOL
Same general specifications as Model P-12 except w/12-round magazine, 4.5-inch bbl., 8-inches overall. Weight: 25 oz. (alloy frame). Blade front sight, adj. rear w/3-dot system. TExtured composition grips. Matte black alloy or steel finish. Made from 1993 to 2003.
Model P1345 (alloy) . . . . NiB $779 Ex $606 Gd $530
Model P1345C (steel) . . . . NiB $772 Ex $586 Gd $337
**Limited model
(tuned & accessorized), add** $150

P-14 AUTO PISTOL
Caliber: .45 ACP. 13-round magazine, 5-inch bbl., 8.5 inches overall. Weight: 28 oz. Alloy frame. Blade front sight, adj. rear w/3-dot system. TExtured composition grips. Matte black alloy or steel finish. Made from 1990 to 2003.
Model P1445 (alloy) . . . . NiB $685 Ex $474 Gd $332
Model P1445C (stainless) . . . . . NiB $755 Ex $546 Gd $395
Limited model (tuned & accessorized), add $128

P-15 AUTO PISTOL
Caliber: .40 S&W. 10-round magazine, 4.25-inch bbl., 7.75 inches overall. Weight: 28 to 36 oz. Steel, alloy or stainless receiver. Matte black, Duotone or stainless finish. Made 1996 to 1999.
Model P1540 (alloy) . . . . NiB $740 Ex $495 Gd $362
Model P1540C (steel) . . . . NiB $665 Ex $544 Gd $468
Duotone stainless model . . . . . . NiB $740 Ex $495 Gd $362
Stainless model . . . . NiB $700 Ex $602 Gd $536

P-16 SA AUTO PISTOL
Caliber: .40 S&W. 10- or 16-round magazine, 5-inch bbl., 8.5 inches overall. Weight: 40 oz. Ramp front sight and drift adjustable rear w/3-dot system. Carbon steel or stainless frame. Matte black, Duotone or stainless finish. Made from 1995 to 2002.
Blue steel model . . . . NiB $683 Ex $536 Gd $437
Duotone model . . . . NiB $709 Ex $572 Gd $362
Stainless model . . . . NiB $740 Ex $576 Gd $485
Limited model (tuned & accessorized), add $175

P-18 SA AUTO PISTOL
Caliber: 9mm Parabellum. 10- or 18-round magazine, 5-inch bbl., 8.5 inches overall. Weight: 40 oz. Dovetailed front sight and fully adjustable rear. Bright stainless finish. Made from 1998 to 2003.
Stainless model . . . . NiB $816 Ex $652 Gd $523
Limited model (tuned & accessorized), add $150

PXT SINGLE STACK SERIES AUTO PISTOL
Caliber: 9mm Para. , .38 Super or .45 ACP. Eight- or 9-round (9mm Para) magazine, 3-, 3.5-, 4.25-, 5- or 6-inch bbl., 8.5 inches overall (5-in. bbl.). Weight: 30 oz. (5-in. bbl.). Steel or stainless frame. Blade front sight, adj. rear w/3-dot system. Textured composition grips. Matte black alloy or steel finish. Made from 2004 to date.
1911 OPS (disc. 2008) . . . . NiB $980 Ex $931 Gd $450
1911 LTC (intro. 2009) . . . . NiB $780 Ex $741 Gd $330

Plainfield Model 71

Plainfield Model 72

Radom P-35

P18.9 (9mm Para, 18-rnd.
magazine). . . . . NiB $1030 Ex $840 Gd $470
Warthog (.45 ACP, 10-rnd.
magazine). . . . . NiB $900 Ex $700 Gd $400

PHOENIX ARMS — Ontario, California

MODEL HP22/HP25 SA
AUTO PISTOLS. . . . . NiB $170 Ex $95 Gd $66
Caliber: .22 LR, .25 ACP. 10-round magazine, 3-inch bbl., 5.5
inches overall. Weight: 20 oz. Checkered synthetic grips. Blade
front sight, adj. rear. Blue, chrome or nickel finish. Made from
1994 to date.

MODEL HP RANGE-MASTER TARGET SA
AUTO PISTOL. . . . . NiB $170 Ex $95 Gd $66
Similar to Model HP .22 except w/5.5-inch target bbl. and
Extended magazine, Ramp front sight, adj. notch rear on vent
rib. Checkered synthetic grips. Blue or satin nickel finish. Made
from 1998 to date.

MODEL HP RANGE-MASTER DELUXE TARGET
SA AUTO PISTOL. . . . . NiB $204 Ex $165 Gd $110
Similar to Model HP Rangemaster Target model except w/dual-
2000 laser sight and custom wood grips. Made from 1998 to date.

RAVEN SA AUTO PISTOL. . . . . NiB $88 Ex $61 Gd $45
Caliber: .25 ACP. Six-round magazine, 2.5 inch bbl., 4.75
inches overall. Weight: 15 oz. Ivory, pink pearl, or black slotted
stocks. Fixed sights. Blue, chrome or nickel finish. Made from
1993 to 1998.

PLAINFIELD MACHINE COMPANY — Dunellen, New Jersey

This firm disc. operation about 1982.

MODEL 71 AUTOMATIC PISTOL
Calibers: .22 LR, .25 Automatic w/conversion kit available.
10-round magazine (.22 LR) or 8-round (.25 Auto), 2.5-
inch bbl., 5.13 inches overall. Weight: 25 oz. Fixed sights.
Stainless steel frame/slide. Checkered walnut grips. Made
from 1970-82.
.22 LR or .25 Auto . . . . NiB $200 Ex $177 Gd $128
w/conversion kit. . . . . NiB $222 Ex $188 Gd $119

MODEL 72 AUTOMATIC PISTOL
Same as Model 71 except has aluminum slide, 3.5-inch bbl., 6
inches overall. Made from 1970 to 1982
.22 LR or .25 Auto only . . . . . . NiB $220 Ex $177 Gd $101
w/conversion kit. . . . . NiB $235 Ex $166 Gd $128

POLISH MILITARY PISTOLS — Radom, Poland

Manufactured at Lucznik Arms Factory.

MODEL P-64. . . . . NiB n/a Ex $250 Gd $125
SA/DA. Similar to Walther PPK. Caliber: 9x18mm Makarov.
3.3-in. bbl., 22 ozs. Military surplus. Made 1965 to date.

MODEL P-83 WANAD . . . . NiB n/a Ex $350 Gd $220
SA/DA. Caliber: 9x18mm Makarov. 8-round magazine. 3.5-in.
bbl., 26 ozs. Military surplus. Made 1983 to date.

1911 Wild Bunch (intro. 2011). . . NiB $660 Ex $550 Gd $340
GI Expert (intro. 2009). . . . . . . NiB $580 Ex $440 Gd $355
Slim Hawg (.45 ACP, 3-in. bbl.). . . NiB $860 Ex $670 Gd $400

PXT HIGH CAPACITY SERIES AUTO PISTOL
Similar to PXT Single Stack series except 10-, 14-, or 18-round
magazine. Made from 2004 to date.
P14.45 (.45 ACP, 14-rnd.
magazine). . . . . NiB $880 Ex $650 Gd $410

P-83 Wanad

PROFESSIONAL ORDNANCE, INC. —
Lake Havasu City, Arizona

MODEL CARBON-15 TYPE 20
SEMIAUTOMATIC PISTOL . . . . NiB $944 Ex $819 Gd $581
Similar to Carbon-15 Type 97 except w/unfluted barrel. Weight: 40 oz. Matte black finish. Made from 1999 to 2000.

MODEL CARBON-15 TYPE 97
SEMIAUTOMATIC PISTOL . . . NiB $1030 Ex $927 Gd $588
AR-15 operating system w/recoil reduction system. Caliber: .223 Rem. 10-round magazine, 7.25-inch fluted bbl., 20 inches overall. Weight: 46 oz. Ghost ring sights. Carbon-fiber upper and lower receivers w/Chromoly bolt carrier. Matte black finish. Checkered composition grip. Made from 1996 to 2003.

RADOM — Radom, Poland
Manufactured by the Polish Arsenal.

P-35 AUTOMATIC PISTOL
Variation of the Colt Government Model .45 Auto. Caliber: 9mm Para. Eight-round magazine, 4.75-inch bbl., 7.75 inches overall. Weight: 29 oz. Fixed sights. Blued finish. Plastic grips. Made from 1935 thru WWII.
Commercial model
(Polish Eagle) . . . . NiB $4599 Ex $4370 Gd $2555
Nazi military model
(w/slotted backstrap) . . . . . NiB $1629 Ex $1199 Gd $877
Nazi military model
(w/takedown lever) . . . . . . NiB $1300 Ex $1000 Gd $431
Nazi military model
(No takedown lever or slot) . . NiB $459 Ex $356 Gd $232
Nazi military model (Parkerized), add $357

RANDALL FIREARMS COMPANY —
Sun Valley, California

The short-lived Randall firearms Company (1982 to 1984) was a leader in the production of stainless steel semi-autimatic handguns, particularly in left-handed configurations. Prices shown are for production models. Add 50% for prototype

models (t-prefix on serial numbers) and $125 for guns with serial numbers below 2000. Scare models (C311, C332, etc., made in lots of four pieces or less) valued substantially higher to avid collectors.

MODEL A111 . . . . NiB $791 Ex $479 Gd $316
Caliber: .45 Auto. Barrel: 5 inches. Round-slide top; right-hand model. Sights: Fixed. Total production: 3,431 pieces.

MODEL A112 . . . . NiB $920 Ex $689 Gd $581
Calibers: 9mm. Barrel: 5 inches. Round-slide top; right-hand model. Sights: Fixed.

MODEL A121 . . . . NiB $734 Ex $643 Gd $377
Caliber: .45 Auto. Barrel: 5 inches. Flat-slide top; right-hand model. Sights: Fixed.

MODEL A211 . . . . NiB $785 Ex $571 Gd $479
Caliber: .45 Auto. Barrel: 4.25 inches. Round-slide top; right-hand model. Sights: Fixed.

MODEL A232 . . . . NiB $1560 Ex $1357 Gd $1100
Caliber: 9mm. Barrel: 4.25 inches. Flat-slide top; right-hand model. Sights: Fixed.

MODEL A331 . . . . NiB $1808 Ex $1566 Gd $1234
Caliber: .45 Auto. Barrel: 4.25 inches. Flat-slide top; right-hand model. Sights: Fixed.

MODEL B111 . . . . NiB $1270 Ex $1124 Gd $890
Caliber: .45 Auto. Barrel: 5 inches. Round-slide top; left-hand model. Sights: Fixed. Toatal production: 297 pieces

MODEL B131 . . . . NiB $1470 Ex $1326 Gd $1152
Caliber: .45 Auto. Barrel: 5 inches. Flat-slide top; left-hand model. Sights: Millet. Total production: 225 pieces.

MODEL B311 . . . . NiB $1632 Ex $1418 Gd $1206
Caliber: .45 Auto. Barrel: 4.25 inches. Round-slide top; left-hand model. Sights: Fixed. Total production: 52 pieces.

MODEL B312 LEMAY . . . . . NiB $5170 Ex $1669 Gd $3090
Caliber: 9mm. Barrel: 4.25 inches. Round-slide top; left-hand model. Sights: Fixed. Total production: 9 pieces.

MODEL B331 . . . . NiB $1800 Ex $1589 Gd $1356
Caliber: .45 Auto. Barrel: 4.25 inches. Flat-slide top; left-hand model. Sights: Millet. Total production: 45 pieces.

RECORD-MATCH PISTOLS — Zella-Mehlis, Germany. Manufactured by Udo Anschütz

MODEL 200 FREE PISTOL . . . NiB $1039 Ex $760 Gd $616
Basically the same as Model 210 except w/different stock design and conventional set trigger, spur trigger guard. Made prior to WW II.

MODEL 210 FREE PISTOL . . NiB $1355 Ex $1206 Gd $919
System Martini action, set trigger w/button release. Caliber: .22 LR. Single-shot, 11-inch bbl., weight: 46 oz. Target sights micrometer rear. Blued finish. Carved and checkered walnut forearm and stock w/adj. hand base. Also made w/ dual action (Model 210A); weight 35 oz. Made prior to WWII.

Remington
95 Double Derringer

Record-Match
Model 200 Free Pistol

REISING ARMS CO. — Hartford, Connecticut

TARGET AUTOMATIC PISTOL . . . NiB $1132 Ex $862 Gd $587
Hinged frame. Outside hammer. Caliber: .22 LR. 12-round magazine, 6.5-inch bbl., fixed sights. Blued finish. Hard rubber grips. Made 1921 to 1924.

REMINGTON ARMS COMPANY — Madison, NC
Manufacturing in Ilion, New York; Lonoke, AR; and Mayfield, KY. Owned by the Freedom Group.

MODEL 51 AUTOMATIC PISTOL
Calibers: .32 Auto, .380 Auto. Seven-round magazine, 3.5-inch bbl., 6.63 inches overall. Weight: 21 oz. Fixed sights. Blued finish. Hard rubber grips. Made from 1918 to 1926.
.32 ACP . . . . NiB $887 Ex $780 Gd $453
.380 ACP . . . . NiB $899 Ex $790 Gd $495

MODEL 95 DOUBLE DERRINGER
SA. Caliber: 41 Short Rimfire. Three-inch double bbls. (superposed), 4.88 inches overall. Early models have long hammer spur and two-armed Extractor, but later guns have short hammer spur and sliding Extractor (a few have no Extractor). Fixed blade front sight and grooved rear. finish: Blued, blued w/nickel-plated frame or fully nickel-plated; also w/factory engraving. Grips: Walnut, checkered hard rubber, pearl, ivory. Weight: 11 oz. Made 1866-1935. Approximately 150,000 were manufactured. Note: Duringthe 70 years of its production, serial numbering of

this model was repeated two or three times. Therefore, aside from hammer and Extractor differences between the earlier and later models, the best clue to the age of a Double Derringer is the stamping of the company's name on the top of the bbl., or side rib. Prior to 1888, derringers were stamped "E. Remington & Sons, Ilion, N.Y." on one side rib and "Elliot's Patent Dec. 12, 1865" on the other (Type I-early & mid-production) and on the top rib (Type I-late production). In 1888-1911, "Remington Arms Co., Ilion, N.Y." and patent date were stamped on the top rib (Type II) and from 1912-35 "Remington Arms - U.M.C. Co., Ilion, N.Y." and patent date were stamped on the top rib.

Model 95 (Early Type I,
  w/o Extractor) . . . . NiB $6600 Ex $5000 Gd $3800
Model 95 (Mid Type I,
  w/Extractor) . . . . NiB $11,000 Ex $8000 Gd $4000
Model 95 (Late Type I,
  w/Extractor) . . . . NiB $5000 Ex $4219 Gd $1000
M95 (TYPE II
  produced 1888-1911) . . . . NiB $3700 Ex $2588 Gd $909
Model 95 (Type III,
  produced 1912-35) . . . . . NiB $3600 Ex $3000 Gd $1099
Factory-engraved model w/ivory
  or pearl grips, add 40%

NEW MODEL SINGLE-SHOT TARGET PISTOL
Also called Model 1901 Target. Rolling-block action. Calibers: .22 Short & Long, .25 Stevens, .32 S&W, .44 S&W Russian. 10-inch half-octagon bbl., 14 inches overall. Weight: 45 oz. (.22 cal.). Target sights. Blued finish. Checkered walnut grips and forearm. Made from 1901 to 1909.
Model 1901 (.22 caliber) . . NiB $3750 Ex $2550 Gd $1203
Model 1901
  (.25 Stevens, .32 S&W) . . . NiB $3449 Ex $2988 Gd $1380
Model 1901 (.44 Russian) . . NiB $3969 Ex $2709 Gd $1190

MODEL XP-100
SINGLE-SHOT PISTOL . . . . . . NiB $984 Ex $622 Gd $464
Bolt action. Caliber: 221 Rem. Fireball. 10.5-inch vent rib bbl., 16.75 inches overall. Weight: 3.75 lbs. Adj. rear sight, blade front, receiver drilled and tapped for scope mounts. Blued finish. One-piece brown nylon stock. Made from 1963 to 1988.

MODEL XP-100
CUSTOM PISTOL . . . . NiB $1096 Ex $755 Gd $596
Bolt-action, single-shot, long-range pistol. Calibers: .223 Rem., 7mm-08 or .35 Rem. 14.5-inch bbl., standard contour or heavy. Weight: About 4.25 lbs. Currently in production.

MODEL XP-100 SILHOUETTE . NiB $984 Ex $622 Gd $464
Same general specifications as Model XP-100 except chambered for 7mm BR Rem. and 35 Rem. 14.75-inch bbl., weight: 4.13 lbs. Made from 1987 to 1992.

MODEL XP-100
VARMINT SPECIAL . . . . NiB $984 Ex $622 Gd $464
Bolt-action, single-shot, long-range pistol. Calibers: .223 Rem., 7mm BR. 14.5-inch bbl., 21.25 inches overall. Weight: About 4.25 lbs. One-piece Du Pont nylon stock w/universal grips. Made from 1986 to 1992.

MODEL XP-100R
CUSTOM REPEATER
Same general specifications as Model XP-100 Custom except 4- or 5- round repeater chambered for .22-250, .223 Rem., .250 Savage, 7mm-08 Rem., .308 Win., .35 Rem. and .350

Rem. Mag. Kevlar-reinforced synthetic or fiberglass stock w/ blind magazine and sling swivel studs. Made from 1992-94 and from 1998 to 1999.

Model XP-100R (fiberglass stock) . . . . **NiB $984 Ex $622 Gd $464**

Model XP-100R KS (kevlar stock) . . . . **NiB $984 Ex $622 Gd $464**

NOTE: *The following Remington derringers were produced from the mid-1860s through the mid-1930s. The Zig-Zag model is reputed to be the first cartridge handgun ever produced at the Remington plant. Few if any Remington derringers Exiswt in "new" or "in box" condition, therefore, guns in 90-percent condition command top price.*

ZIG-ZAG DERRINGER . . . . **NiB $6155 Ex $5875 Gd $4145**
Caliber: .22S, L, LR. Six shot, six-barrel (rotating) cluster. 3-inch bbl., blued, ring trigger. Two-piece rubber grips. Fewer than 1,000 pieces produced from 1861 to 1863.

ELIOT'S FIVE-SHOT DERRINGER . . . . **NiB $1897 Ex $1268 Gd $1091**
Caliber: .22S, L, LR. Five shot, five-barrel fixed cluster. 3-inch bbl., ring trigger, blue and/or nickel finish. Two-piece rubber, walnut, ivory or pearl grips.

ELIOT'S FOUR-SHOT DERRINGER . . . . **NiB $5000 Ex $4275 $3795**
Caliber: .32. Four shot, four-barrel fixed cluster. 3-3/8 inch bbl., ring trigger, blue and/or nickel finish. Two-piece rubber, walnut, ivory or pearl grips. Approx. 25,000 pieces (.22 and .32) produced.

VEST POCKET DERRINGER . . . . **NiB $3255 Ex $2920 Gd $2635**
Caliber: .22, .30, .32, .41 rimfire . Two shot, various bbl. lengths, blue or nickel finish. Two-piece walnut grips. Spur trigger. Made from 1865 to 1888.

OVER AND UNDER DERRINGER . . . . **NiB $6270 Ex $4720 Gd $3955**
Caliber: .41 rimfire. Two shot, 3-inch super imposed bbl., spur trigger, blue and/or nickel finish. Two-piece rubber, walnut, ivory or pearl grips. Oscillating firing pin. Produced 1866-1934. Also known as Double Derringer or Model 95. Type 1 and variatitons bear maker's name, patent data stamped between the barrels, with or without Extractor. Types Two and Three marked "Remington Arms Company, Ilion, NY. Type Four marked on top of barrel, "Remington Arms-U.M.C. Co. Ilion, NY."

MODEL 1866 ROLLING BLOCK PISTOL . . . **NiB $6210 Ex $4329 Gd $3144**
Caliber: .50 rimfire. Single-shot, 8-1/2 inch round, blue finish. Walnut grip and forearm. Spur trigger. Made from 1866-67. Mistakenly designated as Model 1865 Navy. Top values are for military-marked, pristine pieces. Very few of these guns remain in original condition.

MODEL 1870 NAVY ROLLING BLOCK PISTOL . . . **NiB $4225 Ex $3199 Gd $1905**
Caliber: .50 centerfire. Single shot, 7-inch round bbl. Standard trigger with trigger guard, walnut grip and forearm. Approx. 6,400 pieces made from 1870-75. Modified for the Navy from Model 1866. Higher values are for 8--inch commercial version without proof marks.

RIDER'S MAGAZINE PISTOL . . . . . . **NiB $3577 Ex $2885 Gd $2389**
Caliber: .32. Five shot, 3-inch octagon bbl. blued (add 50 percent for case-hardened receiver). Walnut, rosewood, ivory or pearl grips. Spur trigger. Made from 1871 to 1888.

ELIOT'S VEST POCKET SINGLE-SHOT DERRINGER . . . . **NiB $3387 Ex $1109 Gd $879**
Caliber: .41 rimfire. Single-shot, 2-1/2-inch round bbl., blue and/or nickel finish. Also known as "Mississippi Derringer." Two-piece walnut grips. Spur trigger. Approx. 10,000 made from 1867 to 1888.

MODEL 1890 SINGLE-ACTION REVOLVER . . . . **NiB $15,210 Ex $14,070 Gd $7680**
Caliber: .41 centerfire . Six shot, 5-3/4 or 7-1/2-inch round bbl., blue or nickel finish. Standard trigger with trigger guard. Two-piece ivory or pearl grips with Remington monogram. nickel finish valued about 15 percent less.

MODEL 1911 REMINGTON UMC . . . . . . **NiB $7000 Ex $5550 Gd $1650**
Caliber: .45 ACP. WWII military contract production. Blued finish. Made from 1918 to 1919, with serial numbers 1 to 21,676.

MODEL 1911A1 REMINGTON RAND . . . . . **NiB $2500 Ex $2079 Gd $1086**
Caliber: .45 ACP. Parkerized finish. Two-piece walnut grips. Made from 1943-45 by Remington Rand Co., not Remington Arms Co.

RG (Röhm Gesellschaft)—Germany

Imported by R.G. Industries, Miami, FL., then manufactured until 1986.

MODEL 23 . . . . **NiB $115 Ex $88 Gd $70**
SA/DA. 6-round magazine, swing-out cylinder. Caliber: .22 LR. 1.75- or 3.38-inch bbl., Overall length: 5.13 and 7.5 inches. Weight: 16-17 oz. Fixed sights. Blued or nickel finish. Disc. 986.

MODEL 385
SA/DA. Caliber: .38 Special. Six-round magazine, swing-out cylinder. Three- or 4-inch bbl., overall length: 8.25 and 9.25 inches. Weight: 32-34 oz. Windage-adj. rear sight. Blued finish. Disc. 1986.
w/plastic grips . . . . **NiB $177 Ex $140 Gd $101**
w/wood grips . . . . **NiB $212 Ex $130 Gd $95**

ROSSI — Sáo Leopoldo, Brazil

Manufactured by Amadeo Rossi S.A., imported by BrazTech, Int'l., in Miami, Florida; previously by Interarms, Alexandria, VA.

MODEL 31 DA REVOLVER . . . . . . **NiB $144 Ex $78 Gd $62**
Caliber: .38 Special. Five-round cylinder, 4-inch bbl., weight: 20 oz. Blued or nickel finish. Disc. 1985.

MODEL 51 DA REVOLVER . . . . . . **NiB $147 Ex $82 Gd $61**
Caliber: .22 LR. Six-round cylinder, 6-inch bbl., weight: 28 oz. Blued finish. Disc. 1985.

MODEL 68 . . . . **NiB $177 Ex $147 Gd $101**
Caliber: .38 Special. Five-round magazine, 2- or 3-inch bbl., overall length: 6.5 and 7.5 inches. Weight: 21-23 oz. Blued finish. Nickel finish available w/3-inch bbl. Disc. 1998.

MODEL 84 DA REVOLVER . . . . NiB $209 Ex $160 Gd $110
Caliber: .38 Special. 6-rnd. cylinder, 3-in. bbl., 8-in. overall. Weight: 27.5 oz. Stainless steel finish. Imported 1984 to 1986.

MODEL 85 DA REVOLVER . . . . NiB $209 Ex $160 Gd $110
Same as Model 84 except has vent rib. Imported 1985-86.

MODEL 88 DA REVOLVER
Caliber: .38 Special. Five-round cylinder, 2- or 3-inch bbl., weight: 21 oz. Stainless steel finish. Imported from 1988 to 98.
Model 88 (disc.) . . . . NiB $219 Ex $180 Gd $148
Model 88 Lady Rossi
  (round butt) . . . . NiB $225 Ex $189 Gd $152

MODEL 88/2 DA REVOLVER . . NiB $219 Ex $180 Gd $140
Caliber: .38 Special. Five-round cylinder, 2- or 3-inch bbl., 6.5 inches overall. Weight: 21 oz. Stainless steel finish. Imported 1985 to 1987.

MODEL 89 DA REVOLVER . . . . . NiB $184 Ex $110 Gd $75
Caliber: .32 S&W. Six-round cylinder, 3-inch bbl., 7.5 inches overall. Weight: 17 oz. Stainless steel finish. Imported 1989 to 1990.

MODEL 94 DA REVOLVER. . . . . NiB $175 Ex $109 Gd $88
Caliber: .38 Special. Six-round cylinder, 3-inch bbl., 8 inches overall. Weight: 29 oz. Imported from 1985 to 1988.

MODEL 95 (951) REVOLVER . . NiB $219 Ex $175 Gd $141
Caliber: .38 Special. 6-rnd. cylinder, 3-in. bbl., 8-in. overall. Weight: 27.5 oz. Vent rib. Blued finish. Imported 1985 to 1990.

MODEL 351/352 REVOLVERS
Caliber: .38 Special. Five-round cylinder, 2-inch bbl., 6.87 inches overall. Weight: 22 oz. Ramp front and rear adjustable sights. Stainless or matte blued finish. Imported 1999 to date.
Model 351 (matte blue finish) . NiB $362 Ex $255 Gd $186
Model 352 (stainless finish) . . . NiB $437 Ex $326 Gd $265

MODEL 461/462 REVOLVERS
Caliber: .357 Magnum. Six-round cylinder, 2-inch heavy bbl., 6.87 inches overall. Weight: 26 oz. Rubber grips w/ serrated ramp front sight. Stainless or matte blued finish. Imported 1999 to date.
Model 461 (matte blue finish) . NiB $365 Ex $265 Gd $188
Model 462 (stainless finish) . . . NiB $439 Ex $290 Gd $219

MODEL 511 DA REVOLVER . . . . NiB $195 Ex $170 Gd $75
Similar to the Model 51 except in stainless steel. Imported 1986 to 1990.

MODEL 515 DA REVOLVER . . . . NiB $214 Ex $105 Gd $70
Calibers: .22 LR, .22 Mag. Six-round cylinder, 4-inch bbl., 9 inches overall. Weight: 30 oz. Red ramp front sight, adj. square-notched rear. Stainless finish. Checkered hardwood grips. Imported from 1994 to 1998.

MODEL 518 DA REVOLVER . . . . NiB $214 Ex $105 Gd $70
Similar to the Model 515 except in caliber .22 LR. Imported from 1993 to 1998.

MODEL 677 DA REVOLVER . . . NiB $225 Ex $180 Gd $128
Caliber: .357 Mag. Six-round cylinder, 2-inch bbl., 6.87 inches overall. Weight: 26 oz. Serrated front ramp sight, chan-

nel rear. Matte blue finish. Contoured rubber grips. Imported 1997-98.

MODEL 720 DA REVOLVER . . . NiB $235 Ex $170 Gd $141
Caliber: .44 Special. Five-round cylinder, 3-inch bbl., 8 inches overall. Weight: 27.5 oz. Red ramp front sight, adj. square-notched rear. Stainless finish. Checkered Neoprene combat-style grips. Imported from 1992 to 1998.

MODEL 841 DA REVOLVER . . . NiB $319 Ex $225 Gd $160
Same general specifications as Model 84 except has 4-inch bbl., (9 inches overall), weight: 30 oz. Imported 1985-86.

MODEL 851 DA REVOLVER . . . NiB $336 Ex $259 Gd $158
Same general specifications as Model 85 except w/3-or 4-inch bbl., 8 inches overall (with 3-inch bbl.). Weight: 27.5 oz. (with 3-inch bbl.). Red ramp front sight, adj. square-notched rear. Stainless finish. Checkered hardwood grips. Imported from 2001 to 2009 to date.

MODEL 877 DA REVOLVER . . . NiB $230 Ex $160 Gd $110
Same general specifications as Model 677 except stainless steel. Made from 1996 to date.

MODEL 941 DA REVOLVER . . . . NiB $214 Ex $109 Gd $82
Caliber: .38 Special. Six-round cylinder, 4-inch bbl., 9 inches overall. Weight: 30 oz. Blued finish. Imported from 1985-86.

MODEL 951 DA REVOLVER . . . . NiB $214 Ex $109 Gd $82
Previous designation M95 w/same general specifications.

MODEL 971 DA REVOLVER
Caliber: .357 Magnum. Six-round cylinder, 2.5-, 4- or 6-inch bbl., 9 inches overall (with 4-inch bbl.). Weight: 36 oz. (with 4-inch bbl.). Blade front sight, adj. square-notched rear. Blued or stainless finish. Checkered hardwood grips. Imported from 1988 to 1998.
Blued finish. . . . . NiB $219 Ex $166 Gd $129
Stainless finish. . . . . NiB $240 Ex $175 Gd $101
w/compensated bbl., add $25

MODEL 971 VRC
DA REVOLVER . . . . NiB $321 Ex $270 Gd $175
Same general specifications as Model 971 stainless except w/ ventilated rib and compensated bbl. Made 1988 to 1998.

CYCLOPS DA REVOLVER . . . . . NiB $425 Ex $362 Gd $274
Caliber: .357 Mag. Six-round cylinder, 6- or 8-inch compensated slab-sided bbl., 11.75 or 13.75 inches overall. Weight: 44 oz. or 51 oz. Undercut blade front sight, fully adjustable rear. B-Square scope mount and rings. Stainless steel finish. Checkered rubber grips. Made from 1997 to 1998.

DA REVOLVER . . . . NiB $220 Ex $170 Gd $124
Calibers: .22 LR, .32 S&W Long, .38 Special. 5-rnd. (.38) or 6-rnd. cylinder (other calibers), bbl. lengths: 3-, 6-inches. Weight: 22 oz. (3-inch bbl.). Adj. Rear sight, ramp front. Blued or nickel finish. Wood or plastic grips. Imported from 1965-91.

SPORTSMAN'S .22 . . . . NiB $279 Ex $219 Gd $170
Caliber: .22 LR. Six-round magazine, 4-inch bbl., 9 inches overall. Weight: 30 oz. Stainless steel finish. Disc. 1991.

**Ruger Mark I Target w/5.5-inch
Untapered Bull Barrel**

Ruger Mark II

**Ruger Mark II
22/45**

RUGER — Southport, Connecticut

*Manufactured by Sturm, Ruger & Co. Rugers made in 1976
are designated "Liberty" in honor of the U.S. Bicentennial and
bring a premium of approximately 25% in value over regular
models.*

NOTE: *For ease in finding a particular Ruger handgun, the
listings are divided into two groups: Automatic/Single-Shot
Pistols (below) and Revolvers, which follow. For a complete
listing, please refer to the index.*

- AUTOMATIC/SINGLE-SHOT PISTOLS -

22 CHARGER AUTOMATIC... NiB $330 Ex $230 Gd $180
Uses Ruger 10/22 action. Caliber: .22 LR, 10-in. bbl., black/
grey laminated pistol grip and forend, bipod, matte black finish. Made from 2008 to 2012.

**HAWKEYE SINGLE-SHOT
PISTOL** . . . . NiB $2555 Ex $2427 Gd $1000
Built on a SA revolver frame w/cylinder replaced by a swing-out
breechblock and fitted w/a bbl., w/integral chamber. Caliber:
.256 Magnum. 8.5-inch bbl., 14.5 inches overall. Weight: 45
oz. Blued finish. Ramp front sight, click adj. rear. Smooth walnut grips. Made from 1963 to 1965 (3,300 produced).

MARK I TARGET MODEL AUTOMATIC PISTOL
Caliber: .22 LR. 10-round magazine, 5.25- and 6.88-inch heavy
tapered or 5.5-inch untapered bull bbl., 10.88 inches overall (with
6.88-inch bbl.). Weight: 42 oz. (in 5.5- or 6.88-inch bbl.). Undercut
target front sight, adj. rear. Blued finish. Hard rubber grips or checkered walnut thumbrest grips. Made from 1952 to 1982.
Standard model . . . . NiB $877 Ex $791 Gd $612
w/red medallion . . . . NiB $975 Ex $859 Gd $712
Walnut grips, add $434

MARK II AUTOMATIC PISTOL
Caliber: .22 LR, standard or high velocity 10-round magazine,
4.75- or 6-inch tapered bbl., 8.31 inches overall (with 4.75-
inch bbl.). Weight: 36 oz. Fixed front sight, square notch rear.
Blued or stainless finish. Made from 1982 to 2004.
Blued. . . . . NiB $265 Ex $305 Gd $158
Stainless . . . . NiB $321 Ex $265 Gd $204
**Bright stainless (ltd. prod.
5,000 in 1982)** . . . . NiB $590 Ex $479 Gd $346

MARK II 22/45 AUTOMATIC PISTOL
Same general specifications as Ruger Mark II .22 LR except
w/blued or stainless receiver and bbl., in four lengths: 4-inch
tapered w/adj. sights (P4), 4.75-inch tapered w/fixed sights
(KP4), 5.25-inch tapered w/adj. sights (KP 514) and 5.5-inch
bull (KP 512). Fitted w/Zytel grip frame of the same design as
the Model 1911 45 ACP. Made from 1993 to 2004.
Model KP4 (4.75-inch bbl.). . . . NiB $255 Ex $177 Gd $140
**Model KP512, KP514
(w/5.5- or 5.25-inch bbl.).** . . . NiB $365 Ex $229 Gd $126
**Model P4, P512
(Blued w/4- or 5.5-inch bbl.)** NiB $270 Ex $216 Gd $160

MARK II BULL BARREL MODEL
Same as standard Mark II except for bull bbl. (5.5- or 10-inch).
Weight: About 2.75 lbs.
Blued finish. . . . . NiB $319 Ex $237 Gd $175
Stainless finish (intro. 1985) . . . NiB $430 Ex $379 Gd $128

RUBY — Manufactured by Gabilondo y Urresti, Eibar, Spain, and others

**7.65MM
AUTOMATIC PISTOL** . . . . NiB $342 Ex $255 Gd $129
Secondary standard service pistol of the French Army in world
wars I and II. Essentially the same as the Alkartasuna (see
separate listing). Other manufacturers: Armenia Elgoibarresa
y Cia., Eceolaza y Vicinai y Cia., Hijos de Angel Echeverria
y Cia., Bruno Salaverria y Cia., Zulaika y Cia., all of Eibar,
Spain-Gabilondo y Cia., Elgoibar Spain; Ruby Arms Company,
Guernica, Spain. Made from 1914 to 1922.

Ruger P-89 DAC/ DAO

Ruger P-90

MARK II GOVERNMENT MODEL AUTO PISTOL
Civilian version of the Mark II used by U.S. Armed Forces. Caliber: .22LR. 10-round magazine, 6.88-inch bull bbl., 11.13 inches overall. Weight: 44 oz. Blued or stainless finish. Made from 1986 to 1999.
Blued model (MK687G commercial) . . . . NiB $388 Ex $286 Gd $198
Stainless steel model (KMK678G commercial) . . . . NiB $444 Ex $337 Gd $270
w/U.S. markings (military model) . . . NiB $1148 Ex $910 Gd $629

MARK II TARGET MODEL
Caliber: .22 LR. 10-round magazine, 4-, 5.5- and 10-inch bull bbl. or 5.25- and 6.88-inch heavy tappered bbl., weight: 38 oz. to 52 oz. 11.13 inches overall (with 6.88-inch bbl.). Made 1982 to 2004.
Blued. . . . . NiB $375 Ex $303 Gd $128
Stainless steel . . . . NiB $444 Ex $377 Gd $290

MARK III AUTOMATIC PISTOL
Similar to Mark II pistol except w/magazine button on left side grip, tapered bolt ears, and improved ejection port. Made from 2005 to date.
Blued. . . . . NiB $389 Ex $190 Gd $120

MARK III TARGET AUTOMATIC PISTOL
Same as Mark III pistol except w/tapered barrel, adj. rear sight, laminated grips. Made from 2005 to date.
Blued. . . . . NiB $460 Ex $240 Gd $180

Stainless steel . . . . NiB $569 Ex $290 Gd $190
Government Competition . . . . . NiB $659 Ex $350 Gd $250

MARK III 22/45 AUTOMATIC PISTOL
Similar to Mark II 22/45 pistol except w/Mark III improvements. Made from 2005 to 2012.
Blued. . . . . NiB $265 Ex $180 Gd $140
Stainless steel . . . . NiB $335 Ex $200 Gd $150
Hunter (fluted bbl.). . . . . NiB $435 Ex $250 Gd $170
Lite (2012 to date) . . . . NiB $499 Ex $330 Gd $270
Target (4- or 5.5-in. bull bbl.) . . NiB $359 Ex $255 Gd $175
Threaded Barrel (2011 to date) NiB $449 Ex $230 Gd $175

MODEL LCP AUTOMATIC PISTOL NiB $379 Ex $230 Gd $150
DOA. Caliber: .380 ACP, 6- or 7-round magazine, 2.75 in. bbl. Weight: 9.4 oz. Fixed sights. Made from 2008 to date.
w/Crimsontrace sight, add $150
w/LaserMax sight, add $75
Stainless steel slide finish . . . . NiB $429 Ex $225 Gd $175

MODEL LC9 PISTOL . . . . NiB $379 Ex $230 Gd $150
DAO. Caliber: 9mm. 7- or 9-round magazine, 3.12 inch bbl. Weight: 17.1 oz. Fixed 3-dot sights. Blued finish. Made from 2011 to date.
w/Crimsontrace sight, add $150
w/LaserMax sight, add $75

MODEL LC380 PISTOL . . . . . . NiB $379 Ex $230 Gd $150
Similar to LC9 pistol except chambered in .380 ACP. Blued finish. Made from 2013 to date.
w/Crimsontrace sight, add $150
w/LaserMax sight, add $75

MODEL P-85 AUTOMATIC PISTOL
Caliber: 9mm. DA, recoil-operated. 15-round capacity, 4.5 inch bbl., 7.84 inches overall. Weight: 32 oz. Fixed rear sight, square-post front. Available w/decocking levers, ambidExtrous safety or in DA only. Blued or stainless finish. Made from 1987 to 1992.
Blued finish. . . . . NiB $332 Ex $214 Gd $110
Stainless steel finish . . . . NiB $439 Ex $365 Gd $291

MODEL P-89 AUTOMATIC PISTOL
Caliber: 9mm. DA w/slide-mounted safety levers. 15-round magazine, 4.5-inch bbl., 7.84 inches overall. Weight: 32 oz. Square-post front sight, adj. rear w/3-dot system. Blued or stainless steel finish. Grooved black Xenoy grips. Made from 1992 to 2007.
P-89 blued . . . . NiB $434 Ex $321 Gd $225
P-89 stainless . . . . NiB $546 Ex $453 Gd $388

MODEL P-89 DAC/DAO AUTO PISTOLS
Similar to the standard Model P-89 except the P-89 DAC has ambidExtrous decocking levers. The P-89 DAO operates in double-action-only mode. Made from 1991 to 2009.
P-89 DAC blued . . . . NiB $431 Ex $316 Gd $225
P-89 DAC/DAO stainless . . . . . NiB $530 Ex $431 Gd $316

MODEL P-90, KP90 DA AUTOMATIC PISTOL
Caliber: .45 ACP. Seven-round magazine, 4.5-inch bbl., 7.88 inches overall. Weight: 33.5 oz. Square-post front sight adj. square-notched rear w/3-dot system. Grooved black Xenoy composition grips. Blued or stainless finish. DAC model has ambidExtrous decocking levers. Made from 1991 to 2010.

Ruger P-93
Compact

MODEL P-97D AUTOMATIC PISTOL
Caliber: .45 ACP. Eight-round magazine, 4.5- inch bbl., 7.25 inches overall. Weight: 30.5 oz. Square-post front sight adj. square-notched rear w/3-dot system. Grooved black Xenoy composition grips. Blued or stainless finish. DAC model has ambidExtrous decocking levers. Made from 2002 to 2004.
Model KP-97 DAO stainless . . . NiB $444 Ex $289 Gd $225
Model P-97D DAC (decockers) . . NiB $377 Ex $306 Gd $219

MODEL P-345 AUTOMATIC PISTOL
SA/DA. Caliber: .45 ACP. 8-round magazine, 4.25-in. bbl. Black polymer frame w/rail, blued steel slide. Weight: 29 oz. Fixed sights. Ambidextrous safety or decocking levers. Made from 2005 to 2012.
P345 . . . . NiB $490 Ex $340 Gd $225
KP345 (decocker) . . . . NiB $520 Ex $350 Gd $230

MODEL P-944 . . . . NiB $450 Ex $300 Gd $220
Similar to Model P-94 except in .40 S&W, ambidextrous safety and blued finish. Many variations of safety type, decocker or DAO. Made from 1999 to 2010.
Stainless finish, add. $50

MODEL SR22 . . . . NiB $399 Ex $265 Gd $230
SA/DA. Caliber: .22 LR. 10-round magazine, 3.25-in. bbl. Polymer frame, steel slide w/front/rear serrations. Weight: 17.5 oz. 3-dot adj. sights. Blued finish. Two backstrap inserts. Made 2012 to date.
Threaded barrel, add. $50
Two-tone finish, add $30

MODEL SR9 . . . . NiB $399 Ex $265 Gd $230
Striker fired system. Caliber: 9mm. 10- or 17-round magazine, 4.1-in. bbl. Polymer frame w/reversible backstrap. Weight: 26.5 oz. 3-dot low profile sights. Black stainless, brushed stainless, or OD green finish. Made 2007 to date.
Black stainless finish . . . . NiB $529 Ex $400 Gd $280
Matte stainless finish. . . . . NiB $529 Ex $400 Gd $280
OD green finish (2009-10) . . . . NiB $529 Ex $400 Gd $280

MODEL SR9C . . . . NiB $529 Ex $360 Gd $280
Similar to SR9 except compcat version w/3.5-in. bbl. Made 2010 to date.

MODEL SR40 . . . . NiB $529 Ex $360 Gd $280
Similar to SR9 except chambered in .40 S&W. Made 2011 to date.

MODEL SR40C . . . . NiB $529 Ex $360 Gd $280
Similar to SR40 except compcat version w/3.5-in. bbl. Made 2011 to date.

MODEL SR45 . . . . NiB $529 Ex $360 Gd $280
Similar to SR9 except chambered in .45 ACP. Made 2013 to date.

MODEL SR1911 . . . . NiB $829 Ex $470 Gd $330
1911 platform. Caliber: .45 ACP. 5-in. bbl., 7- and 8-round magazine. Stainless steel, checkered cocobola grips. Navak 3-dot sights. Made 2011 to date.
Commander model (4.25-in. bbl.) . . . NiB $829 Ex $470 Gd $330

STANDARD MODEL AUTOMATIC PISTOL
Caliber: .22 LR. Nine-round magazine, 4.75- or 6-in. bbl., 8.75 inches overall (with 4.75-inch bbl.). Weight: 36 oz. (with 4.75 inch bbl.). Fixed sights. Blued finish. Hard rubber or checkered walnut grips. Made from 1949 to 1952. Known as the "Red

Model P-90 blued . . . . NiB $530 Ex $342 Gd $240
Model P-90 DAC (decocker) . . . NiB $530 Ex $342 Gd $240
Model KP-90 DAC stainless. . . . NiB $536 Ex $367 Gd $270
Model KP-90 DAC (decocker) . . NiB $536 Ex $367 Gd $270

MODEL P-91 DA AUTOMATIC PISTOL
Same general specifications as the Model P-90 except chambered for .40 S&W w/12-round double-column magazine, Made 1992 to 1994.
Model P-91 DAC (decockers) . . NiB $444 Ex $289 Gd $225
Model P-91 DAO (DA only) . . . NiB $444 Ex $289 Gd $225

MODEL P-93D AUTO PISTOL
Similar to the standard Model P-89 except w/3.9-inch bbl., (7.3 inches overall). Weight: 31 oz. Stainless steel finish. Made from 1993 to 2004.
Model P-93 DAC (decocker)
(disc. 1994). . . . . NiB $444 Ex $289 Gd $225
Model P-93 Stainless. . . . . NiB $485 Ex $357 Gd $283

MODEL P-94 AUTOMATIC PISTOL
Similar to the Model P-91 except w/4.25-inch bbl., Calibers: 9mm or .40 S&W. Blued or stainless steel finish. Made 1994 to 2004.
Model KP-94 DAC
(S/S decocker) . . . . NiB $444 Ex $289 Gd $225
Model KP-94 DAO
(S/S dble. action only) . . . . . NiB $444 Ex $289 Gd $225
Model P-94 DAC
(Blued decocker) . . . . NiB $444 Ex $289 Gd $225
Model P-94 DAO
(blued dble. action only) . . . NiB $395 Ex $290 Gd $198

MODEL P-95PR AUTO PISTOL
Caliber: 9mm Parabellum. 10-round magazine, 3.9-inch bbl., 7.3 inches overall. Weight: 27 oz. Square-post front sight, drift adjustable rear w/3-dot system. Molded polymer grip-frame fitted w/stainless or chrome-moly slide. AmbidExtrous decocking levers (P-95D) or double action only (DAO). Matte black or stainless finish. Made 1997 to date.
P-95 blued . . . . NiB $444 Ex $289 Gd $225
KP-95PR stainless . . . . NiB $398 Ex $270 Gd $190

Ruger P-97

**Ruger Bearcat SA
(Old Model)**

**Ruger Bisley
Colt .45 Long (New Model)**

**Ruger Bisley
Single-Six Small Frame**

Ruger Blackhawk

- REVOLVERS -

BEARCAT, SUPER
(OLD MODEL) . . . . NiB $602 Ex $365 Gd $291
Same general specifications as Bearcat except has steel frame. Weight: 25 oz. Made from 1971 to 1974.

NEW MODEL BEARCAT REVOLVER
Same general specifications as Super Bearcat except all steel frame and trigger guard. Interlocked mechanism and transfer bar. Calibers: .22 LR and .22WMR. Interchangeable 6-round cylinders (disc. 1996). Smooth walnut stocks w/Ruger medallion. Made from 1994 to date.
**Convertible model (disc.
1996 after factory recall)** . . . . . NiB $469 Ex $362 Gd $291
Standard model (.22 LR only) . . . NiB $485 Ex $326 Gd $225

BISLEY SA REVOLVER, LARGE FRAME
Calibers: .357 Mag., .41 Mag. .44 Mag., .45 Long Colt. 7.5-inch bbl., 13 inches overall. Weight: 48 oz. Non-fluted or fluted cylinder, no engraving. Ramp front sight, adj. rear. Satin blued or stainless. Made from 1986 to date.
Blued finish . . . . NiB $485 Ex $365 Gd $270
**Vaquero/Bisley (blued w/case
   colored fr.)** . . . . NiB $612 Ex $474 Gd $398
**Vaquero/Bisley (stainless
   steel)** . . . . NiB $587 Ex $434 Gd $357
w/ivory grips, add $50

BISLEY SINGLE-SIX REVOLVER, SMALL FRAME
Calibers: .22 LR and .32 Mag. Six-round cylinder, 6.5-inch bbl., 11.5 inches overall. Weight: 41 oz. Fixed rear sight, blade front. Blue finish. Goncalo Alves grips. Made 1986 to date.
.22 caliber . . . . NiB $485 Ex $365 Gd $270
.32 H&R Mag. . . . . NiB $693 Ex $601 Gd $479

BLACKHAWK SA CONVERTIBLE (OLD MODEL)
Same as Blackhawk except has Extra cylinder. Caliber combinations: .357 Magnum and 9mm Para., .45 Colt and .45 Automatic. Made 1967 to 1972.
**.357/9mm combo (early w/o
   prefix S/N)** . . . . .NiB $556 Ex $437 Gd $290
**.357/9mm combo (late
   w/prefix S/N)** . . . . NiB $556 Ex $437 Gd $290
**.45 LC/.45 ACP combo
(1967-85 & 1999 to date)** . . . . . NiB $556 Ex $437 Gd $290

BLACKHAWK SA REVOLVER (OLD MODEL)
Calibers: .30 Carbine, .357 Mag., .41 Mag., .45 Colt. Six-round cylinder, bbl. lengths: 4.63-inch (.357, .41, .45 caliber),

Eagle Automatic," this early type is now a collector's item. Note: After the death of Alexander Sturm in 1951, the color of the eagle on the grip medallion was changed from red to black as a memorial. Made from 1952 to 1981.
w/red eagle medallion . . . . NiB $689 Ex $536 Gd $431
w/black eagle medallion . . . . . . NiB $430 Ex $379 Gd $170
Walnut grips, add $40

Ruger Super Blackhawk

**Ruger GP-100
DA Revolver**

Ruger New Model Blackhawk Convertible

**Ruger Blackhawk High-Gloss Stainless
(New Model) .357 Magnum**

6.5-inch (.357, .41 caliber), 7.5-inch (.30, .45 caliber). 10.13 inches overall (.357 Mag. w/4.63-inch bbl.). Weight: 38 oz. (.357 w/4.63-inch bbl.). Ramp front sight, adj. rear. Blued finish. Checkered hard rubber or smooth walnut grips. Made from 1955 to 1962.

.30 Carbine, .357 Mag.	NiB $510	Ex $432	Gd $325
.41 Mag.	NiB $760	Ex $660	Gd $265
.45 Colt	NiB $875	Ex $532	Gd $255

BLACKHAWK SA "FLAT-TOP" REVOLVER (OLD MODEL)

Similar to standard Blackhawk except w/"Flat Top" cylinder strap. Calibers: .357 Mag. or .44 Mag. Six-round fluted cylinder, 4.625-, 6.5-, 7.5- or 10-inch bbl., adj. rear sight, ramp front. Blued finish. Black rubber or smooth walnut grips. Made from 1955 to 1962.

.357 Mag. (w/4.625-inch bbl.)	NiB $1235	Ex $1148	Gd $975
.357 Mag. (w/6.5-inch bbl.)	NiB $479	Ex $342	Gd $198
.357 Mag. (w/10-inch bbl.)	NiB $2540	Ex $1650	Gd $1030
.44 Mag. (w/fluted cylinder/4.625-inch bbl.)	NiB $1336	Ex $1270	Gd $1030
.44 Mag. (w/fluted cylinder/ 6.5-inch bbl.)	NiB $1020	Ex $666	Gd $408
.44 Mag. (w/fluted cylinder/ 10-inch bbl.)	NiB $2540	Ex $1945	Gd $1779

GP-100 DA REVOLVER

Caliber: .357 Magnum. Three- to 4-inch heavy bbl., or 6-inch standard or heavy bbl., Overall length: 9.38 or 11.38 inches. Cushioned grip panels. Made from 1986 to date.

Blued finish.	NiB $590	Ex $434	Gd $274
Stainless steel finish	NiB $570	Ex $410	Gd $290

GP-100 MATCH CHAMPION . . . NiB $899 Ex $580 Gd $430

Similar to GP-100 except yuned for competiotion w/slab side, half under lug 4.25-in. bbl. Matte stainless finish. Hogue stippled hardwood grip. Made from 2014 to date.

LCR DAO REVOLVER . . . . NiB $545 Ex $670 Gd $300

DAO. Caliber: .22 LR, .22 WMR, .38 Spl.+P, or .357 Mag. Hammless design, polymer fire control housing, monolithic aluminum frame, stainless cylinder, 1.87-in. bbl., fixed sights, Hogue rubber grip. Made from 2010 to date.

.357 Mag., add.	$80
Crimson Trace laser grips, add.	$280
LCRX model (external hammer), add.	$50
LCRX model (3-in. bbl.), add	$20

NEW MODEL BLACKHAWK SA REVOLVER

Safety transfer bar mechanism. SA. Calibers: .30 Carbine, .357 Magnum, .357 Maximum, .41 Magnum, .44 Magnum, .44 Special, .45 Colt. Six-round cylinder, bbl. lengths: 4.63-inch (.357, .41, .45 Colt); 5.5 inch (.44 Mag., .44 Spec.); 6.5-inch (.357, .41, .45 Long Colt); 7.5-inch (.30, .45, .44 Special, .44 Mag.); 10.5-inch in .44 Mag; 10.38 inches overall (.357 Mag. w/4.63-inch bbl.). Weight: 40 oz. (.357 w/4.63-inch bbl.). Adj. rear sight, ramp front. Blued finish or stainless steel; latter only in .357 or .45 LC. Smooth walnut grips. Made from 1973 to date.

Blued finish.	NiB $464	Ex $326	Gd $203
High-gloss stainless (.357 Mag., .45 LC)	NiB $459	Ex $316	Gd $190
Satin stainless (.357 Mag., .45 LC)	NiB $418	Ex $332	Gd $265
.357 Maximum SRM (1984-85)	NiB $452	Ex $357	Gd $226

NEW MODEL BLACKHAWK BISLEY

Similar to New Model Blackhawk except w/Bisley shaped grip and hammer, fluted or unfluted cylinder. Made 1986 to date.

Blued finish.	NiB $799	Ex $430	Gd $320
Unfluted cylinder, add			$120

**Ruger Single-Six SSM
(New Model)**

**Ruger Super Blackhawk
(New Model)**

**Ruger Super Single-Six
Convertible (New Model)**

**Ruger Police Service-Six
Stainless Steel**

NEW MODEL BLACKHAWK CONVERTIBLE
Same as New Model Blackhawk except has Extra cylinder. Blued finish only. Caliber combinations: .357 Magnum/9mm Para., .44 Magnum/.44-40, .45 Colt/.45 ACP. (Limited Edition Buckeye Special .32-20/.32 H&R Mag. or .38-40/10mm). Made from 1973 to 1985. Reintro. 1999.

.32-20/.32 H&R Mag. (1989-90)	NiB $556	Ex $386	Gd $259
.38-40/10mm (1990-91)	NiB $556	Ex $386	Gd $259
.357/9mm combo	NiB $556	Ex $386	Gd $259
.44/.44-40 combo (disc.1982)	NiB $834	Ex $579	Gd $389
.45 LC/.45 ACP combo (disc. 1985)	NiB $556	Ex $386	Gd $259

NEW MODEL SUPER SINGLE-SIX SSM
SA REVOLVER . . . . NiB $555 Ex $480 Gd $209
Same general specifications as standard Single-Six except

chambered for .32 H&R Magnum cartridge. Bbl. lengths: 4.63, 5.5, 6.5 or 9.5 inches.

NEW MODEL SUPER BLACKHAWK SA REVOLVER
Safety transfer bar mechanism. SA. Caliber: .44 Magnum. Six-round cylinder, 5.5-inch, 7.5-inch and 10.5-inch bull bbl. 13.38 inches overall. Weight: 48 oz. Adj. rear sight, ramp front. Blued and stainless steel finish. Smooth walnut grips. Made 1973 to date, 5.5-inch bbl. made from 1973 to date.

Blued finish	NiB $570	Ex $477	Gd $281
High-gloss stainless (1994-96)	NiB $580	Ex $486	Gd $290
Satin stainless steel	NiB $570	Ex $480	Gd $295
Stainless steel Hunter (intro. 2002)	NiB $780	Ex $490	Gd $295

NEW MODEL SUPER BLACKHAWK BISLEY
Similar to New Model Super Blackhawk except w/Bisley shaped grip and hammer, fluted or unfluted cylinder. Made from 1986 to date.

Blued finish	NiB $729	Ex $330	Gd $260
Stainless Hunter model	NiB $859	Ex $480	Gd $340

NEW MODEL SUPER SINGLE-SIX CONVERTIBLE REVOLVER
Safety transfer bar mechanism. SA. Calibers: .22 LR and .22 WMR. Interchangeable 6-round cylinders. Bbl. lengths: 4.63, 5.5, 6.5, 9.5 inches. 10.81 inches overall (with 4.63 inch bbl.). Weight: 33 oz. (with 4.63-inch bbl.). Adj. rear sight, ramp front. Blued finish or stainless steel; latter only w/5.5- or 6.5-inch bbl., smooth walnut grips. Made from 1994 to 2004.

Blued finish	NiB $500	Ex $306	Gd $190
Stainless steel	NiB $530	Ex $316	Gd $219
Stainless steel Hunter (intro. 2002)	NiB $660	Ex $560	Gd $295
Stainless steel Hunter 17 HMR/.17 Mach 2 (2005-06)	NiB $760	Ex $560	Gd $295

NEW MODEL VAQUERO . . . . . NiB $590 Ex $431 Gd $316
Similar to Vaquero except w/smaller pre-1962 XR-3 style grip frame, reverse indexing cylinder, recontoured hammer, beveled cylinder, cresent shaped ejector rod. Blued w/case-color or bright stainless finish. Checkered rubber or smooth rosewood grips. Made 2005 to date.

NEW MODEL VAQUERO BISLEY . . . NiB $810 Ex $440 Gd $315
Similar to New Model Vaquero except w/Bisley shaped grip and hammer, fluted cylinder. Made from 2009 to date.

POLICE SERVICE-SIX
Same general specifications as Speed-Six except has square butt. Stainless steel models and 9mm Para. caliber available w/ only 4-inch bbl., Made from 1971 to 1988.

.38 Special, blued finish	NiB $434	Ex $306	Gd $230
.38 Special, stainless steel	NiB $345	Ex $290	Gd $270
.357 Magnum or 9mm Para., blued finish	NiB $444	Ex $309	Gd $235
.357 Magnum, stainless steel	NiB $439	Ex $306	Gd $225

REDHAWK DA REVOLVER
Calibers: .357 Mag., .41 Mag., .45 LC, .44 Mag. Six-round cylinder, 5.5-and 7.5-inch bbl., 11 and 13 inches overall, respectively. Weight: About 52 oz. Adj. rear sight, interchangeable front sights. Stainless finish. Made from 1979 to 2009;

**Ruger Super Redhawk
Stainless shown w/optional
scope**

Ruger Redhawk

**Ruger
Super Redhawk Stainless**

**Ruger
Single-Six**

53 to 58 oz. Integral scope mounting system w/stainless rings. Adjustable rear sight. Cushioned grip panels. Made from 1987 to date.

**Model .44 Mag. 7.5- inch
bbl., stainless** . . . . NiB $795 Ex $546 Gd $434
**Model .44 Mag. 9.5- inch
bbl., stainless** . . . . NiB $830 Ex $577 Gd $444
**Model .454 Casull & .480 Ruger
Stainless/target gray stainless** . . NiB $862 Ex $590 Gd $474
Alaskan (intro. 2005) . . . . NiB $880 Ex $590 Gd $480

SECURITY-SIX DA REVOLVER
Caliber: .357 Magnum, handles .38 Special. Six-round cylinder, bbl. lengths: 2.25-, 4-, 6-inch, 9.25 inches overall (with 4-inch bbl.). Weight: 33.5 oz. (with 4-inch bbl.). Adj. rear sight, ramp front. Blued finish or stainless steel. Square butt. Checkered walnut grips. Made 1971 to 1985.
Blued finish . . . . NiB $410 Ex $280 Gd $214
Stainless steel . . . . NiB $420 Ex $300 Gd $265

SINGLE-SIX REVOLVER (OLD MODEL)
Calibers: .22 LR, .22 WMR. Six-round cylinder. bbl., lengths: 4.63, 5.5, 6.5, 9.5 inches, 10.88 inches overall (with 5.5-inch bbl.). Weight: About 35 oz. Fixed sights. Blued finish. Checkered hard rubber or smooth walnut grips. Made 1953-73. Note: Pre-1956 model w/flat loading gate is worth about twice as much as later version.
Standard . . . . NiB $879 Ex $602 Gd $439
**Convertible (w/two cylinders,
.22 LR/.22 WMR)** . . . . NiB $561 Ex $398 Gd $272

SINGLE-SIX - LIGHTWEIGHT NiB $1086 Ex $816 Gd $530
Same general specifications as Single-Six except has 4.75-inch bbl., lightweight alloy cylinder and frame, 10 inches overall length, weight: 23 oz. Made in 1956.

SINGLE-NINE . . . . NiB $639 Ex $380 Gd $280
Same general specifications as New Model Single-Six except chambered in .22 WMR, 9-round cylinder, 6.5-in. bbl. Stainless steel. Made in 2013 to date.

SINGLE-TEN . . . . NiB $639 Ex $370 Gd $270
Same general specifications as New Model Single-Six except w/10-round cylinder, 5.5-in. bbl. Stainless steel. Made in 2012 to date.

SP101 DA REVOLVER
Calibers: .22 LR, .32 Mag., 9mm, .38 Special+P, .357 Mag. Five- or 6-round cylinder, 2.25-, 3.06- or 4-inch bbl., weight: 25-34 oz. Stainless steel finish. Cushioned grips. Made from 1989 to date.
Standard model . . . . NiB $530 Ex $321 Gd $204
**DAO model (DA only, spurless
hammer)** . . . . NiB $530 Ex $321 Gd $204

SPEED-SIX DA REVOLVER
Calibers: .38 Special, .357 Magnum, 9mm Para. Six-round cylinder, 2.75-, 4-inch bbl., (9mm available only w/2.75-inch bbl.). 7.75 inches overall (2.75-inch bbl.). Weight: 31 oz. (with 2.75-inch bbl.). Fixed sights. Blued or stainless steel finish; latter available in .38 Special (with 2.75 inch bbl.), .357 Magnum and 9mm w/either bbl., Round butt. Checkered walnut grips. Made from 1973 to 1987.
blued finish . . . . NiB $439 Ex $272 Gd $190
stainless steel . . . . NiB $449 Ex $303 Gd $214

.357 Mag. disc. 1986. Alloy steel model w/blued finish intro. in 1986 in .41 Mag. and .44 Mag. calibers.
Blued finish . . . . NiB $620 Ex $450 Gd $270
Stainless steel . . . . NiB $789 Ex $499 Gd $300

SUPER REDHAWK DA REVOLVER
Calibers: .44 Mag., .454 Casull and .480 Ruger. Six-round cylinder, 7.5- to 9.5- inch bbl., 13 to 15 inches overall. Weight:

Ruger
Single-Six Lightweight

Ruger
Super Single-Six Convertible

Ruger Single-Six Fixed Sight

Ruger Vaquero Stainless Steel

Ruger Vaquero Blued

Ruger Speed-Six Stainless Steel

9mm Para., blued finish . . . . . . NiB $689 Ex $522 Gd $440
9mm Para., stainless steel . . . . . NiB $690 Ex $540 Gd $442

SUPER BLACKHAWK (OLD MODEL)
SA w/heavy frame and unfluted cylinder. Caliber: .44
Magnum. Six-round cylinder. 6.5- or 7.5-inch bbl., Adj. rear
sight, ramp front. Steel or brass grip frame w/square-back
trigger guard. Smooth walnut grips. Blued finish. Made from
1956 to 1973.
w/6.5-inch bbl., ... NiB $1316 Ex $1148 Gd $918
w/7.5-inch bbl., ... NiB $806 Ex $385 Gd $281
w/brass gripframe . . . . NiB $1599 Ex $1316 Gd $1153

VAQUERO . . . . NiB $590 Ex $431 Gd $316
SA. Calibers: .357 Mag., .44-40, .44 Magnum, .45 Colt.
Six-round cylinder. Bbl. lengths: 4.625, 5.5, 7.5 inches,
13.63 inches overall (with 7.5-inch bbl.). Weight: 41 oz.
(with 7.5-inch bbl.). Blade front sight, grooved topstrap rear.
Blued w/color casehardened frame or polished stainless finish. Smooth rosewood grips w/Ruger medallion. Made from
1993 to 2004.

VAQUERO BISLEY . . . . NiB $575 Ex $460 Gd $230
Similar to Vaquero except w/Bisley shaped grip and hammer,
fluted cylinder. Blued or bright stainless finish. Made from
1999 to 2004.

RUSSIAN SERVICE PISTOLS —
Manufactured by Government plants at Tula and elsewhere

Note: Tokarev-type pistols have also been made in Hungary,
Poland, Yugoslavia, People's Republic of China, N. Korea.

MODEL TT30 TOKAREV SERVICE AUTOMATIC
Modified Colt-Browning type. Caliber: 7.62mm Russian Auto
(also uses 7.63mm Mauser Auto cartridge). Eight-round maga-
zine, 4.5-inch bbl., 7.75 inches overall. Weight: About 29 oz.
Fixed sights. Made from 1930 to mid-1950s. Note: A slightly
modified version w/improved locking system and different dis-
connector was adopted in 1933.
Standard Service Model
  TT30 . . . . NiB $1239 Ex $1127 Gd $918
Standard Service Model
  TT33 . . . . NiB $2490 Ex $2285 Gd $1879
Recent imports (distinguished by importer
  marks) . . . . NiB $209 Ex $158 Gd $109

Tokarev TT30

Sako Model .22-.32 Olympic

Sauer 1930 Pocket

Recent non-Russian imports (distinguished
by importer marks) . . . . NiB $434 Ex $306 Gd $170

SAKO — Riihimaki, Finland

Manufactured by Oy Sako Ab.

.22-.32 OLYMPIC PISTOL (TRIACE)

Calibers: .22 LR, .22 Short, .32 S&W Long. Five-round magazine, 6- or 8.85- (.22 Short) inch bbl., weight: About 46 oz. (.22 LR); 44 oz. (.22 Short); 48 oz. (.32). Steel frame. ABS plastic, anatomically designed grip. Non-reflecting matte black upper surface and chromium-plated slide. Equipped w/carrying case and tool set. Limited importation from 1983 to 1989.

Sako .22 or .32
  Single pistol . . . . NiB $1355 Ex $1240 Gd $1090
Sako Triace, triple-barrel set
  w/wooden grip . . . . NiB $2647 Ex $2279 Gd $2045

SAUER — Germany

Manufactured through WW II by J. P. Sauer & Sohn, Suhl, Germany. Now manufactured by J. P. Sauer & Sohn, GmbH, Ecmernförde, West Germany. Also see listings under Sig Sauer for automatic pistols, Hawes for single action revolvers.

MODEL 1913 POCKET PISTOL . . NiB $342 Ex $240 Gd $179
Semi-automatic pistol. Caliber: .32 ACP (7.65mm). Seven-round magazine, 3-inch bbl., 5.88 inches overall. Weight: 22 oz. Fixed sights. Blued finish. Black hard rubber grips. Made from 1913 to 1930.

MODEL 1930 POCKET AUTOMATIC PISTOL

Authority Model (Behorden Model). Successor to Model 1913, has improved grip and safety. Caliber: .32 Auto (7.65mm). Seven-round magazine, 3-inch bbl., 5.75 inches overall. Weight: 22 oz. Fixed sights. Blued finish. Black hard rubber grips. Made from 1930-38. Note: Some pistols made w/indicator pin showing when cocked. Also mfd. w/dual slide and receiver; this type weight: about 7 oz. less than the standard model.
Steel model . . . . NiB $405 Ex $290 Gd $203
Dural (alloy) model . . . . NiB $1454 Ex $1367 Gd $1209

MODEL 38H DA AUTOMATIC PISTOL

Calibers: .25 Auto (6.35mm), .32 Auto (7.65mm), .380 Auto (9mm). Specifications shown are for .32 Auto model. Seven-round magazine, 3.25-inch bbl., 6.25 inches overall. Weight: 20 oz. Fixed sights. Blued finish. Black plastic grips. Also made in dual model weighing about 6 oz. less. Made 1938-1945. Note: This pistol, designated Model .38, was mfd. during WW II for military use. Wartime models are inferior in design to earlier production, as some lack safety lever.
.22 caliber . . . . NiB $5625 Ex $3410 Gd $2200
.32 ACP . . . . NiB $643 Ex $410 Gd $281
.32 ACP (w/Nazi proofs) . . . . . . NiB $709 Ex $453 Gd $326
.380 ACP . . . . NiB $4500 Ex $4255 Gd $3975

POCKET .25 (1913) . . . . NiB $398 Ex $286 Gd $214
Smaller version of Model 1913, issued about same time as .32 caliber model. Caliber: .25 Auto (6.35mm). Seven-round magazine, 2.5-inch bbl., 4.25 inches overall. Weight: 14.5 oz. Fixed sights. Blued finish. Black hard rubber grips. Made 1913 to 1930.

MODEL PM

MAKAROV PISTOL . . . . NiB $3000 Ex $2445 Gd $2000
Double-action, blowback design. Semi-automatic. Caliber: 9x18mm Makarov. Eight-round magazine, 3.8-inch bbl., 6.4 inches overall. Weight: 26 oz. Blade front sight, square-notched rear. Checkered composition grips. Numerous examples exist from former Eastern Bloc countries such as Bulgaria and East Germany as well as China.
Standard Service Model PM
(Pistole Makarov) . . . . NiB $3595 Ex $3125 Gd $2890

Savage Model 101

Sears/J.C. Higgins
Model 88 DA Revolver

SAVAGE ARMS — Utica, New York

MODEL 101 SA SINGLE-SHOT
PISTOL . . . . NiB $255 Ex $170 Gd $105
Barrel integral w/swing-out cylinder. Calibers: .22 Short, Long, LR. 5.5-inch bbl. Weight: 20 oz. Blade front sight, slotted rear, adj. for windage. Blued finish. Grips of compressed, impregnated wood. Made 1960 to 1968.

MODEL 501/502F "STRIKER" SERIES PISTOLS
Calibers: .22 LR., and .22 WMR. 5- or 10- round magazine, 10-inch bbl., 19 inches overall. Weight: 4 lbs. Drilled and tapped sights for scope mount (installed). AmbidExtrous rear grip. Made from 2000 to 2005.
Model 501F, .22 LR. . . . . NiB $359 Ex $206 Gd $165
Model 502F, .22 WMR . . . . NiB $301 Ex $190 Gd $158

MODEL 510/516 "STRIKER" SERIES PISTOLS
Calibers: .223 Rem., .22-250 Rem., .243 Win., 7mm-08 Rem., .260 Rem., and .308 Win. Three-round magazine, 14-inch bbl., 22.5 inches overall. Drilled and tapped for scope mounts. Left hand bolt with right hand ejection. Stainless steel finish. Made from 1998 to 2005.
Model 510F. . . . . NiB $495 Ex $395 Gd $235
Model 516FSAK . . . . NiB $546 Ex $474 Gd $230
Model 516FSS. . . . . NiB $546 Ex $474 Gd $230
Model 516FSAK . . . . NiB $704 Ex $468 Gd $408
Model 516BSS. . . . . NiB $755 Ex $500 Gd $437

MODEL 1907 AUTOMATIC PISTOL
Caliber: .32 ACP, 10-round magazine, 3.25-inch bbl., 6.5 inches overall. Weight: 19 oz. Checkered hard rubber or steel grips marked "Savage Quality," circling an Indian-head logo. Optional pearl grips. Blue, nickel, silver or gold finish. Made from 1910 to 1917.

Blued model (.32 ACP) . . . . . . NiB $610 Ex $430 Gd $175
Blued model (.380 ACP) . . . . . . NiB $709 Ex $495 Gd $326

MODEL 1907 AUTOMATIC PISTOL
Calibers: .32 Auto, .380 Auto. 10-round magazine (.32 cal.), 9-round (.380 cal.). 3.75-inch bbl., (.32 cal.), 4.25-inch (.380 cal.). 6.5 inches overall (.32 cal.), 7 inches (.380 cal.). Weight: About 23 oz. Fixed sights. Blued finish. Hard rubber grips. Made in hammerless type w/grip safety or w/Exposed hammer spur. Made from 1910 to 1917.
.32 ACP. . . . . NiB $601 Ex $457 Gd $270
.380 ACP. . . . . NiB $700 Ex $560 Gd $499

MODEL 1915 AUTOMATIC PISTOL
Same general specifications as the Savage Model 1907 except the Model 1915 is hammerless and has a grip safety. It is also chambered for both the .32 and .380 ACP. Made froim 1915 to 1917.
.32 ACP. . . . . NiB $930 Ex $729 Gd $500
.380 ACP. . . . . NiB $1400 Ex $857 Gd $643

U.S. ARMY TEST MODEL . . . . NiB $12,650 Ex $8990 Gd $653
Caliber: .45 ACP, Seven-round magazine w/Exposed hammer. An enlarged version of the Model 1910 manufactured for military trials between 1907 and 1911. Note: Most "Trial Pistols" were refurbished and resold as commercial models. Values are for original Government Test Issue models.

MODEL 1917 AUTOMATIC PISTOL
Same specifications as 1910 Model except has spur-type hammer and redesigned, heavier grip. Made from 1917 to 1928.
.32 ACP. . . . . NiB $564 Ex $445 Gd $279
.380 ACP. . . . . NiB $646 Ex $486 Gd $336

SEARS, ROEBUCK & COMPANY — Chicago, Illinois

J.C. HIGGINS MODEL 80
AUTO PISTOL. . . . . NiB $281 Ex $165 Gd $109
Caliber: .22 LR. 10-round magazine, 4.5- or 6.5-inch interchangeable bbl., 10.88 inches overall (with 6.5-inch bbl.). Weight: 41 oz. (with 6.5-inch bbl.). Fixed Partridge sights. Blued finish. Checkered grips w/thumbrest.

J.C. HIGGINS MODEL 88
DA REVOLVER . . . . NiB $209 Ex $105 Gd $75
Caliber: .22 LR. Nine-round cylinder, 4- or 6-inch bbl., 9.5 inches (with 4-inch bbl.). Weight: 23 oz. (with 4-inch bbl.). Fixed sights. Blued or nickel finish. Checkered plastic grips.

J.C. HIGGINS RANGER
DA REVOLVER . . . . NiB $219 Ex $137 Gd $88
Caliber: .22 LR. Nine-round cylinder, 5.5-inch bbl., 10.75 inches overall. Weight: 28 oz. Fixed sights. Blued or chrome finish. Checkered plastic grips.

SECURITY INDUSTRIES OF AMERICA — Little Ferry, New Jersey

MODEL PM 357
DA REVOLVER . . . . NiB $255 Ex $198 Gd $160
Caliber: .357 Magnum. Five-round cylinder, 2.5-inch bbl., 7.5 inches overall. Weight: 21 oz. Fixed sights. Stainless steel. Walnut grips. Made 1975. Disc..

**Security Industries of
America Model PM 357**

**Security Industries of
America Model PPM 357**

**Security Industries of
America Model PSS38**

**MODEL PPM357
DA REVOLVER** . . . . **NiB $255 Ex $198 Gd $160**
Caliber: .357 Magnum. Five-round cylinder, 2-inch bbl., 6.13 inches overall. Weight: 18 oz. Fixed sights. Stainless steel. Walnut grips. Made in 1975. Note: Spurless hammer (illustrated) was disc. in 1975; this model has the same conventional hammer as other Security revolvers.

MODEL PSS 38 DA REVOLVER . . . **NiB $197 Ex $112 Gd $90**
Caliber: .38 Special. Five-round cylinder, 2-inch bbl., 6.5 inches overall. Weight: 18 oz. Fixed sights. Stainless steel. Walnut grips. Intro. 1973. disc.

R. F. SEDGLEY. INC. — Philadelphia, PA

**BABY HAMMERLESS
EJECTOR REVOLVER** . . . . **NiB $704 Ex $556 Gd $290**
DA. Solid frame. Folding trigger. Caliber: .22 Long. Six-round cylinder, 4 inches overall. Weight: 6 oz. Fixed sights. Blued or nickel finish. Rubber grips. Made 1930 to 1939.

L. W. SEECAMP, INC. — Milford, CT

MODEL LWS .25 DAO PISTOL . . . **NiB $439 Ex $398 Gd $281**
Caliber: .25 ACP. Seven-round magazine, 2-inch bbl., 4.125 inches overall. Weight: 12 oz. Checkered black polycarbonate grips. Matte stainless finish. No sights. Made from 1981 to 1985.

MODEL LWS 32 DAO PISTOL
Caliber: .32 ACP. Six-round magazine, 2-inch bbl., 4.25 inches overall. Weight: 12.9 oz. Ribbed sighting plane with no sights. Checkered black LExon grips. Stainless steel. Made from 1985 to date. Limited production results in inflated resale values.
Matte stainless finish. . . . . **NiB $464 Ex $398 Gd $272**
Polished stainless finish, add. **$128**

**MODEL LWS-380
DAO PISTOL**. . . . . **NiB $795 Ex $650 Gd $470**
Similar to LWS 32 except chambered in .380 ACP. Made from 2000 to date.

SHERIDAN PRODUCTS, INC. — Racine, WI

**KNOCKABOUT
SINGLE-SHOT PISTOL** . . . . **NiB $305 Ex $189 Gd $108**
Tip-up type. Caliber: .22 LR, Long, Short; 5-inch bbl., 6.75 inches overall. Weight: 24 oz. Fixed sights. Checkered plastic grips. Blued finish. Made from 1953 to 1960.

SIG — Neuhausen am Rheinfall, Switzerland

See also listings under SIG-Sauer.

MODEL P210-1 PISTOL . . . **NiB $2878 Ex $2662 Gd $2288**
Semi-automatic. Calibers: .22 LR, 7.65mm Luger, 9mm Para. Eight-round magazine, 4.75-inch bbl., 8.5 inches overall. Weight: 33 oz. (.22 cal.) or 35 oz. (7.65mm, 9mm). Fixed sights. Polished blued finish. Checkered wood grips. Made from 1949 to 1986.

MODEL P210-2. . . . . **NiB $1835 Ex $1590 Gd $1409**
Same as Model P210-1 except has sandblasted finish, plastic grips. Not avail. in .22 LR. Disc. 2002.

**SIG
Model P210-1**

**SIG
Model P210-6 Target Pistol**

**SIG Sauer
P220**

**SIG Sauer
P225**

MODEL P210-5
TARGET PISTOL . . . . NiB $2330 Ex $2190 Gd $1902
Same as Model P210-2 except has 6-inch bbl., micrometer adj. rear sight, target front sight, adj. trigger stop, 9.7 inches overall. Weight: About 38.3 oz. Disc. 2007.

MODEL P210-6
TARGET PISTOL . . . . NiB $1910 Ex $1720 Gd $1525
Same as Model P210-2 except has micrometer adj. rear sight, target front sight, adj. trigger stop. Weight: About 37 oz. Disc. 1987.

P210 .22 CONVERSION UNIT, add $1525
Converts P210 pistol to .22 LR. Consists of bbl., w/recoil spring, slide and magazine,

SIG SAUER — Neuhausen, Switzerland and Exeter, New Hampshire
Manufactured by J. P. Sauer & Sohn of Germany, SIG of Switzerland, and other manufacturers.

MODEL P220 DA/DAO AUTOMATIC PISTOL
Calibers: 22LR, 7.65mm, 9mm Para., .38 Super, .45 ACP. Seven-round in .45 ACP, 9-round in other calibers, 4.4-inch bbl., 8 inches overall. Weight: 26.5 oz. (9mm). Fixed sights. Blue, electroless nickel, K-Kote, Duo/nickel or Ilaflon finish. Alloy frame. Checkered plastic grips. Imported from 1976 to date. Note: Also sold in U.S. as Browning BDA.
Blue finish. . . . . NiB $918 Ex $734 Gd $499
Duo/nickel finish . . . . NiB $1030 Ex $712 Gd $523
Nickel finish . . . . NiB $988 Ex $784 Gd $546
K-Kote finish . . . . NiB $974 Ex $693 Gd $474
Ilaflon finish . . . . NiB $969 Ex $689 Gd $507
.22 LR conversion kit, add $434
w/Siglite sights, add $100

MODEL P220 SPORT
AUTOMATIC. . . . . NiB $1415 Ex $1119 Gd $1016
Similar to Model P220 except .45 ACP only w/4.5-inch compensated bbl., 10-round magazine, adj. target sights. Weight: 46.1 oz. Stainless finish. Made from 1999 to date.

MODEL P225 DA AUTOMATIC
Caliber: 9mm Para. Eight-round magazine, 3.85-inch bbl., 7 inches overall. Weight: 26.1 oz. Blue, nickel, K-Kote, Duo/nickel or Ilaflon finish.
Blued finish. . . . . NiB $628 Ex $556 Gd $431
Duo/nickel finish . . . . NiB $669 Ex $588 Gd $500
Nickel finish . . . . NiB $700 Ex $612 Gd $478
K-Kote finish . . . . NiB $700 Ex $612 Gd $478
w/Siglite sights, add $128

MODEL P226 DA/DAO AUTOMATIC
Caliber: .357 SIG, 9mm Para., .40 S&W, 10- or 15-round magazine, 4.4-inch bbl., 7.75 inches overall. Weight: 29.5 oz. Alloy frame. Blue, electroless nickel, K-Kote, Duo/nickel or Nitron finish. Imported from 1983 to date.
Blued finish. . . . . NiB $882 Ex $724 Gd $444
Duo/nickel finish . . . . NiB $898 Ex $809 Gd $496
Nickel finish . . . . NiB $804 Ex $659 Gd $478
K-Kote finish . . . . NiB $804 Ex $639 Gd $485

SIG Sauer P230

Nitron finish
(blackened stainless). . . . . . . NiB $826 Ex $658 Gd $479
w/Siglite sights, add $100

MODEL P228 DA AUTOMATIC
Same general specifications as Model P226 except w/3.86-inch
bbl., 7.13 inches overall. 10- or 13-round magazine, Imported
1990 to 1997.
Blued finish. . . . . NiB $831 Ex $709 Gd $455
Duo/nickel finish . . . . NiB $860 Ex $755 Gd $499
Electroless nickel finish. . . . . . NiB $895 Ex $780 Gd $530
K-Kote finish . . . . NiB $882 Ex $743 Gd $541
w/Siglite night sights, add $130

MODEL P229 DA/DAO AUTOMATIC
Same general specifications as Model P228 except w/3.86-inch
bbl., 10- or 12-round magazine, weight: 32.5 oz. Nitron or
Satin Nickel finish. Imported from 1991 to date.
Nitron finish
(Blackened stainless). . . . . . . NiB $860 Ex $755 Gd $464
Satin nickel finish . . . . NiB $890 Ex $791 Gd $500
For Siglite nite sights, add. $128

MODEL P229
SPORT AUTOMATIC. . . . . . . NiB $1292 Ex $1035 Gd $871
Similar to Model P229 except .357 SIG only w/4.5-inch compensated bbl., adj. target sights. Weight: 43.6 oz. Stainless
finish. Made from 1998 to 2003. Reintroduced 2003 to 2005.

MODEL P230 DA AUTOMATIC PISTOL
Calibers: .22 LR, .32 Auto (7.65mm), .380 Auto (9mm Short),
9mm Ultra. 10-round magazine in .22, 8-round in .32, 7-round
in 9mm; 3.6-inch bbl., 6.6 inches overall. Weight: 18.2 oz. or
22.4 oz. (steel frame). Fixed sights. Blued or stainless finish.
Plastic grips. Imported 1976 to 1996.
Blued finish. . . . . NiB $530 Ex $408 Gd $308
Stainless finish (P230SL) . . . . . . NiB $602 Ex $500 Gd $367

MODEL P232 DA/DAO AUTOMATIC PISTOL
Caliber: .380 ACP. Seven-round magazine, 3.6-inch bbl., 6.6
inches overall. Weight: 16.2 oz. or 22.4 oz. (steel frame).
Double/single action or double action only. Blade front
and notch rear drift adjustable sights. Alloy or steel frame.
Automatic firing pin lock and heelmounted magazine release.
Blue, Duo or stainless finish. Stippled black composite stocks.
Imported 1997 to date.
Blued finish. . . . . NiB $576 Ex $467 Gd $316

Duo finish. . . . . NiB $601 Ex $498 Gd $321
Stainless finish. . . . . NiB $588 Ex $523 Gd $433
w/Siglite night sights, add. $65

MODEL P239 DA/DAO AUTOMATIC PISTOL
Caliber: .357 SIG, 9mm Parabellum or .40 S&W. Seven- or
8-round magazine, 3.6-inch bbl., 6.6 inches overall. Weight:
28.2 oz. Double/single action or double action only. Blade
front and notch rear adjustable sights. Alloy frame w/stainless
slide. AmbidExtrous frame- mounted magazine release. Matte
black or Duo finish. Stippled black composite stocks. Made
from 1996 to date.
Matte black finish. . . . . NiB $590 Ex $524 Gd $301
DAO finish . . . . NiB $638 Ex $530 Gd $365
w/Siglite night sights, add $128

SMITH & WESSON — Springfield, Massachusetts

NOTE: *For ease in locating a particular S&W handgun, the
listings are divided into two groupings: Automatic/Single-Shot
Pistols (below) and Revolvers (page 156). For a complete
handgun listing, please refer to the index.*

*In 1957 S&W started to use a number system for each
model. Models with a dash followed by a one, two or three
digit number indicate a model that has had a design and/or
production change, i.e.: Model 29-2 indicates this Model 29
was produced during the second design and/or production
change. To determine the model number of a revolver, swing
out the cylinder and where the yoke meets the frame the model
name is stamped.*

*Since 1990 S&W's Performance Center has been building or
modfiying existing guns. Many handguns have come out of
the shop and it is difficult to keep an accurate accounting of
all models and variants. Note that guns from the Performance
Center in the past decade are marked with the Performance
Center logo on the frame. Champion and Pros Series handguns
are designed in collaboration with professional competition
shooters. Since 2007, S&W began the Classics Series reissuing
revolvers with aestetics of classic revolver models.*

- AUTOMATIC/SINGLE-SHOT PISTOLS -

MODEL 35 (1913)
AUTOMATIC PISTOL . . . . NiB $979 Ex $780 Gd $469
Caliber: 35 S&W Auto. Seven-round magazine, 3.5-inch bbl.,
(hinged to frame). 6.5 inches overall. Weight: 25 oz. Fixed
sights. Blued or nickel finish. Plain walnut grips. Made from
1913 to 1921.

MODEL 32
AUTOMATIC PISTOL . . . . . NiB $3097 Ex $2315 Gd $1699
Caliber: .32 Automatic. Same general specifications as .35
caliber model, but barrel is fastened to the receiver instead of
hinged. Made from 1924 to 1937.

MODEL 22A SPORT SERIES
Caliber: .22 LR. 10-round magazine, 4-, 5.5- or 7-inch standard (A-series) or bull bbl., (S-series). Single action. Eight,
9.5 or 11 inches overall. Weight: 28 oz. to 33 oz. Partridge
front sight, fully adjustable rear. Alloy frame w/stainless slide.
Blued finish. Black polymer or Dymondwood grips. Made
1997-2014.
Model 22A (w/4-inch bbl.) . . . . NiB $255 Ex $190 Gd $105

Smith & Wesson
Model 22A Sport Series

Smith & Wesson
Model 41

Smith & Wesson
Model 22S Sport Series
w/Dymondwood Grips

Smith & Wesson
Model 41 .22 w/muzzle brake

Model 22A (w/5.5-inch bbl.) .... NiB $265 Ex $204 Gd $120
Model 22A (w/7-inch bbl.) .... NiB $265 Ex $204 Gd $120
Model 22S (w/5.5-inch bbl.)... NiB $362 Ex $290 Gd $214
Model 22S (w/7-inch bbl.) .... NiB $395 Ex $337 Gd $265
w/bull bbl., add $65
w/Dymondwood grips, add $100

MODEL 39 9MM DA AUTO PISTOL

Calibers: 9mm Para. Eight-round magazine, 4-inch barrel. Overall length: 7.44-inches. Steel or alloy frames. Weight: 26.5 oz. (w/alloy frame). Click adjustable rear sight, ramp front. Blued or nickel finish. Checkered walnut grips. Made 1954-82. Note: Between 1954 and 1966, 927 pistols were produced w/steel instead of alloy. In 1970, Model 39-1 w/alloy frame and steel slide. In 1971, Model 39-2 was introduced as an improved version of the original Model 39 w/modified Extractor. Model 39 (early production) 1954-70.

First series (S/N 1000-2600) ... NiB $1566 Ex $1418 Gd $1299
9mm blue (w/steel frame & slide,
produced 1966) .... NiB $1866 Ex $1618 Gd $1299
9mm blue (w/alloy frame) .... NiB $622 Ex $437 Gd $225
Nickel finish, add $45
Models 39-1, 39-2 (late production, 1970-82),
9mm blue (w/alloy frame) ... NiB $534 Ex $331 Gd $220
Nickel finish, add $50

MODEL 41 .22 AUTOMATIC PISTOL

Caliber: .22 LR, .22 Short (not interchangeably). 10-round magazine, bbl. lengths: 5-, 5.5-, 7.75-inches; latter has detachable muzzle brake, 12 inches overall (with 7.75-inch bbl.). Weight: 43.5 oz. (with 7.75-inch bbl.). Click adj. rear sight, undercut Partridge front. Blued finish. Checkered walnut grips w/thumbrest. 1957 to date.

.22 LR model. .... NiB $1200 Ex $870 Gd $529
.22 Short model (w/counter-
weights & muzzle brake) ...NiB $2700 Ex $1299 Gd $1120
w/Extended sight, add. $128
w/muzzle brake, add $50

MODEL 46 .22

AUTO PISTOL. .... NiB $1225 Ex $765 Gd $448
Caliber: .22 LR. 10-round magazine, bbl. lengths: 5-, 5.5-, 7-inches. 10.56 inches overall (with 7-inch bbl.). Weight: 42 oz. (with 7-inch bbl.). Click adj. rear sight, undercut Partridge front. Blued finish. Molded nylon grips w/thumbrest. Only 4,000 produced. Made from 1957 to 1966.

MODEL 52 .38 MASTER AUTO

Caliber: .38 Special (midrange wadcutter only). Five-round magazine, 5-inch bbl., overall length: 8.63 inches. Weight: 41 oz. Micrometer click rear sight, Partridge front on ramp base. Blued finish. Checkered walnut grips. Made from 1961 to 1963.

Model 52 (1961-63) .... NiB $1109 Ex $915 Gd $546
Model 52-1 (1963-71). ...... NiB $1029 Ex $915 Gd $546
Model 52-2 (1971-93). ...... NiB $1029 Ex $915 Gd $546
Model 52-A USA Marksman (fewer
than 100 mfg.) .... NiB $3820 Ex $3470 Gd $3139

**Smith & Wesson
Model 52**

**Smith & Wesson
Model 59**

**Smith & Wesson
Model 422**

**Smith & Wesson
Model 439**

MODEL 59 9MM DA AUTO

Similar specifications as Model 39 except has 14-round staggered column magazine, checkered nylon grips. Made 1971 to 1981.

Model 59, blue . . . . NiB $549 Ex $431 Gd $290
Model 59, nickel. . . . . NiB $600 Ex $444 Gd $326
Model 59 (early production
  w/smooth grip frame). . . . NiB $1647 Ex $1508 Gd $1015

MODEL 61 ESCORT POCKET AUTOMATIC PISTOL

Caliber: .22 LR. Five-round magazine, 2.13-inch bbl., 4.69 inches overall. Weight: 14 oz. Fixed sights. Blued or nickel finish. Checkered plastic grips. Made from 1970 to 1974.

Model 61, blue . . . . NiB $380 Ex $270 Gd $165
Model 61, nickel. . . . . NiB $431 Ex $316 Gd $220

MODEL 410 AUTO PISTOL . . . NiB $561 Ex $444 Gd $244

Caliber: .40 S&W. Double action. 10-round magazine, 4-inch bbl., 7.5 inches overall. Weight: 28.5 oz. Alloy frame w/steel slide. Post front sight, fixed rear w/3-dot system. Matte blue finish. Checkered synthetic grips w/straight backstrap. Made from 1996 to 2007.

MODEL 411 AUTO PISTOL . . . NiB $530 Ex $433 Gd $386

Similar to S&W Model 915 except in caliber .40 S&W. 11-round magazine, made from 1994 to 1996.

MODEL 422 SA AUTO PISTOL

Caliber: .22 LR. 10-round magazine, 4.5- or 6-inch bbl., 7.5 inches overall (with 4.5-inch bbl.). Weight: 22-23.5 oz. Fixed or adjustable sights. Checkered plastic or walnut grips. Blued finish. Made from 1987 to 1996.

Standard model. . . . . NiB $220 Ex $175 Gd $150
Target model. . . . . NiB $274 Ex $198 Gd $170

MODEL 439 9MM AUTOMATIC

DA. Caliber: 9mm Para. Two 8-round magazines, 4-inch bbl., 7.44 inches overall. Alloy frame. Weight: 30 oz. Serrated ramp square front sight, square notch rear. Checkered walnut grips. Blued or nickel finish. Made from 1979 to 1988.

Model 439, blue . . . . NiB $530 Ex $368 Gd $306
Model 439, nickel. . . . . NiB $529 Ex $386 Gd $316
w/adjustable sights, add $40

MODEL 457
COMPACT AUTO PISTOL. . . . . NiB $571 Ex $434 Gd $265

Caliber: .45 ACP. Double action. Seven-round magazine, 3.75-inch bbl., 7.25 inches overall. Weight: 29 oz. Alloy frame w/steel slide. Post front sight, fixed rear w/3-dot system. Bobbed hammer. Matte blue finish. Wraparound synthetic grip w/straight backstrap. Made from 1996 to 2006.

MODEL 459 DA AUTOMATIC

Caliber: 9mm Para. Two 14-round magazines, 4-inch bbl., 7.44 inches overall. Alloy frame. Weight: 28 oz. Blued or nickel finish. Made from 1979 to 1987.

Model 459, blue . . . . NiB $485 Ex $431 Gd $319
Model 459, nickel. . . . . NiB $527 Ex $475 Gd $377
FBI Model (brushed finish) . . . . NiB $733 Ex $599 Gd $437

MODEL 469
(MINI) AUTOMATIC. . . . . NiB $485 Ex $388 Gd $270

DA. Caliber: 9mm Para. Two 12-round magazines, 3.5-inch bbl., 6.88 inches overall. Weight: 26 oz. Yellow ramp front

Smith & Wesson
Model 459

Smith & Wesson
Model 645

Smith & Wesson
Model 469

Smith & Wesson
Model 639

sight, dovetail mounted square-notch rear. Sandblasted blued finish. Optional ambidExtrous safety. Made from 1982 to 1988.

MODEL 539 DA AUTOMATIC
Similar to Model 439 except w/steel frame. Caliber: 9mm Para. Two 8-round magazines, 4-inch bbl., 7.44 inches overall. Weight: 36 oz. Blued or nickel finish. Made 1980-83.
Model 539, blue . . . . NiB $590 Ex $486 Gd $368
Model 539, nickel. . . . . NiB $601 Ex $530 Gd $408
w/adjustable sights, add $50

MODEL 559 DA AUTOMATIC
Similar to Model 459 except w/steel frame. Caliber: 9mm Para. Two 14-round magazines, 4-inch bbl., 7.44 inches overall. Weight: 39.5 oz. Blued or nickel finish. (3750 produced) Made 1980 to 1983.
Model 559, blue . . . . NiB $612 Ex $536 Gd $408
Model 559, nickel. . . . . NiB $648 Ex $561 Gd $444
w/adjustable sights, add $50

MODEL 622 SA AUTO PISTOL
Same general specifications as Model 422 except w/stainless finish. Made from 1989 to 1996.
Standard model. . . . . NiB $265 Ex $197 Gd $120
Target model . . . . NiB $309 Ex $212 Gd $146

MODEL 639 AUTOMATIC . . . . NiB $530 Ex $377 Gd $304
Caliber: 9mm Para. Stainless. Two 12-round magazines, 3.5-inch bbl., 6.9 inches overall. Weight: 36 oz. Made 1986-88.

MODEL 645 DA AUTOMATIC
Caliber: .45 ACP. Eight-round. 5-inch bbl., overall length: 8.5 inches. Weight: Approx. 38 oz. Red ramp front, fixed rear sights. Stainless. Made from 1986-88.
Model 645 (w/fixed sights) . . . . NiB $601 Ex $433 Gd $346
Model 645 (w/adjustable sights)NiB $638 Ex $464 Gd $366

MODEL 659 9MM AUTOMATIC
DA. Similar to S&W Model 459 except weight: 39.5 oz. and finish is satin stainless steel finish. Made from 1983-88.
Model 659 (w/fixed sights) . . . . NiB $517 Ex $419 Gd $326
Model 659 (w/adjustable sights). . . NiB $528 Ex $444 Gd $356

MODEL 669 AUTOMATIC . . . . NiB $559 Ex $345 Gd $274
Caliber: 9mm. 12-round magazine, 3.5 inch bbl., 6.9 inches overall. Weight: 26 oz. Serrated ramp front sight w/red bar, fixed rear. Non-glare stainless steel finish. Made from 1986-88.

MODEL 745 AUTOMATIC PISTOL
Caliber: .45 ACP. Eight-round magazine, 5-inch bbl., 8.63 inches overall. Weight: 38.75 oz. Fixed sights. Blued slide,

Smith & Wesson
Model 659

Smith & Wesson
Model 745

Smith & Wesson
Model 1026

MODEL 1000 SERIES DA AUTO

Caliber: 10mm. Nine-round magazine, 4.25- or 5-inch bbl., 7.88 or 8.63 inches overall. Weight: About 38 oz. Post front sight, adj. or fixed square-notched rear w/3-dot system. One-piece Xenoy wraparound grips. Stainless slide and frame. Made from 1990-94.

Model 1006 (fixed sights,
5-inch bbl.) . . . . NiB $724   Ex $530   Gd $433
Model 1006 (adj. sights,
5-inch bbl.) . . . . NiB $740   Ex $544   Gd $479
Model 1026 (fixed sights, 5-inch
bbl., decocking lever) . . . . . . NiB $724   Ex $530   Gd $433
Model 1066 (fixed
sights, 4.25 inch bbl.) . . . . NiB $678   Ex $530   Gd $362
Model 1076 (fixed sights, 4.25 inch bbl., frame-mounted
decocking lever, ... NiB $730   Ex $536   Gd $439
Model 1076 (same as above
w/Tritium night sight) . . . . . . NiB $730   Ex $536   Gd $439
Model 1086 (same as model
1076 in DA only) . . . . NiB $760   Ex $544   Gd $429

MODEL 2206 SA AUTOMATIC PISTOL

Similar to Model 422 except w/stainless-steel slide and frame, weight: 35-39 oz. Partridge front sight on adj. sight model; post w/white dot on fixed sight model. Plastic grips. Made from 1990-96.

Standard model. . . . . NiB $342   Ex $227   Gd $130
Target model . . . . NiB $377   Ex $239   Gd $178

MODEL 2213

SPORTSMAN AUTO . . . . NiB $279   Ex $180   Gd $119
Caliber: .22 LR. Eight-round magazine, 3-inch bbl., 6.13 inches overall. Weight: 18 oz. Partridge front sight, fixed square-notched rear w/3-dot system. Black synthetic molded grips. Stainless steel slide w/alloy frame. Made from 1992-99.

MODEL 2214

SPORTSMAN AUTO . . . . NiB $362   Ex $190   Gd $126
Same general specifications as Model 2214 except w/blued slide and matte black alloy frame. Made from 1990-99.

MODEL 3904/3906 DA AUTO PISTOL

Caliber: 9mm. Eight-round magazine, 4-inch bbl., 7.5 inches overall. Weight: 25.5 oz. (Model 3904) or 34 oz. (Model 3906).

stainless frame. Checkered walnut grips. Similar to the model 645, but w/o DA capability. Made from 1987-90.

w/standard competition
features. . . . . NiB $760   Ex $549   Gd $433
IPSC Commemorative
(first 5,000). . . . . NiB $798   Ex $638   Gd $429

MODEL 908/910 AUTO PISTOLS

Caliber: 9mm Parabellum. Double action. Eight-round (Model 908), 9-round (Model 909) or 10-round (Model 910) magazine; 3.5- or 4-inch bbl.; 6.83 or 7.38 inches overall. Weight: 26 oz. to 28.5 oz. Post front sight, fixed rear w/3-dot system. Matte blue steel slide w/alloy frame. Delrin synthetic wrap-around grip w/straight backstrap. Made from 1994 to date.

Model 908 . . . . NiB $541   Ex $397   Gd $272
Model 909 (disc 1996) . . . . . . NiB $479   Ex $347   Gd $239
Model 910 . . . . NiB $497   Ex $348   Gd $255

MODEL 915 AUTO PISTOL . . . NiB $434   Ex $306   Gd $220
DA. Caliber: 9mm Para. 15-round magazine, 4-inch bbl., 7.5 inches overall. Weight: 28.5 oz. Post front sight, fixed square-notched rear w/3-dot system. Xenoy wraparound grip. Blued steel slide and alloy frame. Made from 1992-94.

Smith & Wesson
Model 3906

Smith & Wesson
Model 3953

Fixed or adj. sights. Delrin one-piece wraparound checkered grips. Alloy frame w/blued carbon steel slide (Model 3904) or satin stainless (Model 3906). Made from 1989 to 1991.

Model 3904 w/adj. sights . . . . . NiB $536 Ex $362 Gd $287
Model 3904 w/fixed sights . . . . NiB $497 Ex $328 Gd $249
Model 3904 w/Novak LC sight . . . NiB $536 Ex $362 Gd $287
Model 3906 w/adj. sights . . . . . NiB $576 Ex $497 Gd 431
Model 3906 w/Novak LC
    sight . . . . NiB $546 Ex $499 Gd $366

MODEL 3913/3914 DA AUTOMATIC

Caliber: 9mm Parabellum (Luger). Eight-round magazine, 3.5-inch bbl., 6.88 inches overall. Weight: 25 oz. Post front sight, fixed or adj. square-notched rear. One-piece Xenoy wraparound grips w/straight backstrap. Alloy frame w/stainless or blued slide. Made from 1990 to 1999.

Model 3913 stainless . . . . NiB $577 Ex $449 Gd $346
Model 3913LS Lady Smith stainless
    w/contoured trigger guard . . . NiB $755 Ex $588 Gd $479
Model 3913TSW (intro. 1998) . . . NiB $739 Ex $596 Gd $479
Model 3914 blued compact
    (disc 1995) . . . . NiB $559 Ex $467 Gd $386

MODEL 3953/3954 DA AUTO PISTOL

Same general specifications as Model 3913/3914 except double action only. Made from 1990 to 2002.

Model 3953 stainless,
    double action only . . . . NiB $590 Ex $444 Gd $396
Model 3954 blued, double
    action only (disc. 1992) . . . . . NiB $530 Ex $431 Gd $340

MODEL 4000 SERIES DA AUTO

Caliber: .40 S&W. 11-round magazine, 4-inch bbl., 7.88 inches overall. Weight: 28-30 oz. w/alloy frame or 36 oz. w/ stainless frame. Post front sight, adj. or fixed square-notched rear w/2 white dots. Straight backstrap. One-piece Xenoy wraparound grips. Blued or stainless finish. Made between 1991 to 1993.

Model 4003 stainless w/alloy
    frame . . . . NiB $658 Ex $498 Gd $388
Model 4003 TSW w/
S&W Tactical options . . . . NiB $870 Ex $779 Gd $608
Model 4004 blued w/alloy
    frame . . . . NiB $601 Ex $449 Gd $397
Model 4006 stainless
    frame, fixed sights. . . . . NiB $711 Ex $562 Gd $431
Model 4006 stainless
    frame, Adj. sights . . . . NiB $744 Ex $634 Gd $498
Model 4006 TSW w/
S&W Tactical options . . . . . . NiB $855 Ex $760 Gd $475
Model 4013 stainless frame,
    fixed sights . . . . NiB $622 Ex $419 Gd $377
Model 4013 TSW w/
S&W Tactical options . . . . . . NiB $855 Ex $760 Gd $475
Model 4014 blued, fixed sights
    (disc. 1993) . . . . NiB $581 Ex $419 Gd $398
Model 4026 w/decocking
    Lever (disc. 1994) . . . . NiB $659 Ex $562 Gd $449
Model 4043 DA only, stainless
    w/alloy frame . . . . NiB $693 Ex $580 Gd $497
Model 4044 DA only,
    blued w/alloy frame . . . . NiB $569 Ex $448 Gd $346
Model 4046 DA only, stainless
    frame, fixed sights. . . . . NiB $739 Ex $668 Gd $499
Model 4046 TSW w/
S&W Tactical options . . . . . . NiB $700 Ex $632 Gd $485
Model 4046 DA only, stainless
    frame, Tritium night sight . . . NiB $724 Ex $634 Gd $475

MODEL 4013/4014 DA AUTOMATIC

Caliber: .40 S&W. Eight-round capacity, 3.5-inch bbl., 7 inches overall. Weight: 26 oz. Post front sight, fixed Novak LC rear w/3-dot system. One-piece Xenoy wraparound grips. Stainless or blued slide w/alloy frame. Made from 1991 to 1996.

Model 4013 w/stainless slide
    (disc. 1996) . . . . NiB $643 Ex $536 Gd $327
Model 4013 Tactical w/stainless
    slide . . . . NiB $860 Ex $693 Gd $588
Model 4014 w/blued slide
    (disc. 1993) . . . . NiB $587 Ex $464 Gd $328

MODEL 4053/4054 DA AUTO PISTOL

Same general specifications as Model 4013/4014 except double action only. Alloy frame fitted w/blued steel slide. Made from 1991 to 1997.

Model 4053 DA only w/stainless
    slide . . . . NiB $668 Ex $530 Gd $458
Model 4053 TSW w/ S&W
    Tactical options. . . . . NiB $760 Ex $648 Gd $541
Model 4054 DA only w/blued slide
(disc. 1992) . . . . NiB $709 Ex $464 Gd $378

Smith & Wesson
Model 4013

Smith & Wesson
Model 4046

Smith & Wesson
Model 4053

Smith & Wesson
Model 4586

MODEL 4500 SERIES DA AUTOMATIC

Caliber: .45 ACP. Six-, 7- or 8-round magazine, bbl. lengths: 3.75, 4.25 or 5 inches; 7.13 to 8.63 inches overall. Weight: 34.5 to 38.5 oz. Post front sight, fixed Novak LC rear w/3-dot system or adj. One-piece Xenoy wraparound grips. Satin stainless finish. Made from 1991 to 1997.

Model 4505 w/fixed sights,
  5-inch bbl. . . . . NiB $693 Ex $597 Gd $386
Model 4505 w/Novak LC sight,
  5-inch bbl. . . . . NiB $653 Ex $578 Gd $431
Model 4506 w/fixed sights,
  5-inch bbl. . . . . NiB $744 Ex $581 Gd $523
Model 4506 w/Novak LC sight,
  5-inch bbl. . . . . NiB $755 Ex $590 Gd $500
Model 4513T (TSW) w/3.75-inch
  bbl.Tactical Combat . . . . NiB $781 Ex $633 Gd $499
Model 4516 w/3.75-inch bbl . . . NiB $724 Ex $622 Gd $479
Model 4526 w/5-inch bbl., alloy frame,
  decocking lever, fixed sights . . . NiB $734 Ex $590 Gd $500
Model 4536, decocking lever . . . NiB $734 Ex $590 Gd $500
Model 4546, w/3.75-inch bbl.,
  DA only . . . . NiB $734 Ex $590 Gd $500
Model 4553T (TSW) w/3.75-inch
  bbl. Tactical Combat. . . . . . . NiB $780 Ex $665 Gd $459
Model 4556, w/3.75-inch bbl.,
  DA only . . . . NiB $700 Ex $601 Gd $397
Model 4563 TSW w/4.25-inch bbl.
  Tactical Combat . . . . NiB $779 Ex $658 Gd $499
Model 4566 w/4.25-inch bbl., ambidextrous
  safety, fixed sights. . . . . NiB $693 Ex $536 Gd $453
Model 4566 TSW w/4.25-inch
  bbl. Tactical Combat. . . . . . . NiB $693 Ex $536 Gd $453
Model 4576 w/4.25-inch bbl.,
  decocking lever. . . . . NiB $691 Ex $607 Gd $449
Model 4583T TSW w/4.25-inch bbl.
  Tactical Combat . . . . NiB $780 Ex $665 Gd $459
Model 4586 w/4.25-inch bbl.,
  DA only . . . . NiB $780 Ex $610 Gd $500
Model 4586 TSW w/4.25-inch bbl.
  Tactical Combat . . . . NiB $734 Ex $590 Gd $500

MODEL 5900 SERIES DA AUTOMATIC

Caliber: 9mm. 15-round magazine, 4-inch bbl., 7.5 inches overall. Weight: 26-38 oz. Fixed or adj. sights. One-piece Xenoy wraparound grips. Alloy frame w/stainless-steel slide (Model 5903) or blued slide (Model 5904) stainless-steel frame and slide (Model 5906). Made from 1990 to 1997.

Model 5903 w/adjustable
  sights . . . . NiB $693 Ex $556 Gd $386
Model 5903 w/Novak LC rear
  sight . . . . NiB $780 Ex $691 Gd $386
Model 5903 TSW w/4-inch bbl.,
  Tactical Combat . . . . NiB $767 Ex $658 Gd $497
Model 5904 w/adjustable
  sights . . . . NiB $581 Ex $468 Gd $376
Model 5904 w/Novak LC rear
  sight . . . . NiB $599 Ex $474 Gd $398
Model 5905 L/C Adjustable
  Sights . . . . NiB $693 Ex $549 Gd $398
Model 5905 w/Novak LC rear
  sight . . . . NiB $733 Ex $634 Gd $464

Smith & Wesson Model 5904 w/ Adjustable Sights

Model 5906 w/adjustable
sights . . . . NiB $658 Ex $544 Gd $439
Model 5906 w/Novak LC rear
sight . . . . NiB $658 Ex $544 Gd $439
Model 5906 w/Tritium night
sight . . . . NiB $755 Ex $650 Gd $562
Model 5906 TSW w/4-inch bbl.,
Tactical Combat . . . . NiB $862 Ex $733 Gd $544
Model 5924 w/anodized frame,
blued slide . . . . NiB $659 Ex $508 Gd $337
Model 5926 w/stainless frame,
decocking lever. . . . . NiB $644 Ex $543 Gd $444
Model 5943 w/alloy frame/
stainless slide, DA only . . . . . NiB $601 Ex $444 Gd $351
Model 5943 TSW w/4-inch bbl.,
DA only . . . . NiB $650 Ex $546 Gd $429
Model 5944 w/alloy frame/
blued slide, DA only . . . . NiB $689 Ex $556 Gd $456
Model 5946 w/stainless frame/slide,
DA only . . . . NiB $658 Ex $534 Gd $376
Model 5946 TSW w/4-inch bbl.,
DA only . . . . NiB $774 Ex $632 Gd $337

MODEL 6900 COMPACT SERIES
Double action. Caliber: 9mm. 12-round magazine, 3.5-inch bbl., 6.88 inches overall. Weight: 26.5 oz. AmbidExtrous safety. Post front sight, fixed Novak LC rear w/3-dot system. Alloy frame w/blued carbon steel slide (Model 6904) or stainless steel slide (Model 6906). Made 1989 to 1997.
Model 6904 . . . . NiB $601 Ex $499 Gd $377
Model 6906 w/fixed sights . . . . NiB $621 Ex $546 Gd $499
Model 6906 w/Tritium night
sight . . . . NiB $843 Ex $621 Gd $500
Model 6926 w/decocking lever . . NiB $691 Ex $587 Gd $374
Model 6944 in DA only . . . . NiB $612 Ex $546 Gd $342
Model 6946
in DA only ,fixed sights. . . . . NiB $709 Ex $577 Gd $395
Model 6946 w/Tritium night
sight . . . . NiB $709 Ex $544 Gd $433

M&P9 AUTOMATIC PISTOL . . . NiB $569 Ex $320 Gd $270
Striker fired action. Caliber: 9mm. 10- or 17-round magazine, 4.25-in. bbl., polymer frame w/three interchangeable grip inserts and accessory rail, low profile fixed sights, w/ or w/o thumb safety. Weight: 24 oz. Black Melonite finish. Made from 2006 to date.
M&P9L (5-in. bbl.,
discont. 2010) . . . . NiB $575 Ex $400 Gd $330
M&P9 Compact (3.5-in. bbl.) . . NiB $569 Ex $320 Gd $270
M&P9 JG (Julie Goloski-Golob design collaboration,
discont. 2012). . . . . NiB $465 Ex $330 Gd $280
M&P9 VTAC (Viking Tactics design collaboration, 4.5-in. bbl.
w/full size frame, FDE finish) . . .NiB $799 Ex $430 Gd $330

M&P9 C.O.R.E.
AUTOMATIC PISTOL . . . . NiB $729 Ex $480 Gd $350
Similar to M&P9 or M&P40 except set up for competition w/ optic mount, fixed 3-dot sights. Made from 2013 to date.

M&P9 PRO SERIES
AUTOMATIC PISTOL . . . . NiB $699 Ex $410 Gd $310
Similar to M&P9 except w/5-in. bbl., fiber optic Novak sights, optic ready. Made from 2012 to date.

M&P40 AUTOMATIC PISTOL . . . NiB $569 Ex $320 Gd $270
Similar to M&P9 except in .40 S&W w/10- or 15-round magazine. Made from 2006 to date.
M&P40 Compact (3.5-in. bbl.) . . .NiB $569 Ex $320 Gd $270
M&P40 VTAC (Viking Tactics design collaboration, 4.5-in.
bbl. w/full size frame, FDE finish) . . NiB $799 Ex $430 Gd $330

M&P40 PRO SERIES
AUTOMATIC PISTOL . . . . NiB $699 Ex $410 Gd $310
Similar to M&P40 except w/5-in. bbl., fiber optic Novak sights, optic ready. Made from 2012 to date.

M&P45 AUTOMATIC PISTOL . . . NiB $599 Ex $330 Gd $270
Similar to M&P9 except in .45 ACP w/10-round magazine. Made from 2006 to date.
M&P45 Compact (4-in. bbl.) . . . NiB $599 Ex $330 Gd $270

M&P357 AUTOMATIC PISTOL . . . NiB $585 Ex $380 Gd $280
Similar to M&P9 except in .357 SIG w/10- or 15-round magazine. Made from 2006 to 2010.
M&P357 Compact (3.5-in. bbl.) . . . NiB $585 Ex $380 Gd $280

M&P BODYGUARD
AUTOMATIC PISTOL . . . . NiB $380 Ex $240 Gd $185
DAO. Caliber: .380 ACP. 6-nd. magazine, 2.75-in. bbl., polymer frame. Weight: 11.9 oz. Black Melonite finish. Made 2014 to date.

SIGMA SW380
AUTOMATIC PISTOL . . . . NiB $536 Ex $357 Gd $290
Caliber: .380 ACP. Double-action only. Six-round magazine, 3-inch bbl., weight: 14 oz. Black integral polymer gripframe w/checkered back and front straps. Fixed channel sights. Polymer frame w/hammerless steel slide. Made from 1994 to 1996.

SIGMA SW9 SERIES AUTOMATIC PISTOL
Caliber: 9mm Parabellum. Double action only. 10-round magazine, 3.25-, 4- or 4.5-inch bbl., weight: 17.9 oz. to 24.7 oz. Polymer frame w/hammerless steel slide. Post front sight and drift adjustable rear w/3-dot system. Gray or black integral polymer gripframe w/checkered back and front straps. Made from 1994 to 1996.
Model SW9C (compact w/3.25-inch
bbl.) . . . . NiB $500 Ex $425 Gd $326

**Smith & Wesson
Model 1**

**Model SW9F (blue slide w/4.5-inch
bbl.)** . . . . NiB $500 Ex $425 Gd $326
**Model SW9M (compact w/3.25-inch
bbl.)** . . . . NiB $342 Ex $255 Gd $165
**Model SW9V (stainless slide w/4-inch
bbl.)** . . . . NiB $408 Ex $304 Gd $229
Tritium night sight, add. $25

M&P SHIELD
AUTOMATIC PISTOL . . . . NiB $449 Ex $280 Gd $210
Similar to M&P9 and M&P40 except sub-compact variant w/3.1-in. bbl., 6-, 7- or 8-round magazine. Weight: 19 oz. Black Melonite finish. Made from 2012 to date.

SW40 SERIES AUTOMATIC PISTOL
Same general specifications as SW9 series except chambered for .40 S&W w/4- or 4.5-inch bbl., weight: 24.4 to 26 oz. Made 1994 to 1998.
**Model SW40C (compact w/4-inch
bbl.)** . . . . NiB $497 Ex $346 Gd $249
**Model SW40F (blue slide w/4.5-inch
bbl.)** . . . . NiB $497 Ex $346 Gd $249
**Model SW40V (stainless slide
w/4-inch bbl.)** . . . . NiB $497 Ex $346 Gd $249
w/Tritium night sight, add. $25

MODEL 1891 SINGLE-SHOT TARGET PISTOL, FIRST MODEL
Hinged frame. Calibers: .22 LR, .32 S&W, .38 S&W. Bbl. lengths: 6-, 8- and 10-inches, approx. 13.5 inches overall (with 10-inch bbl.). Weight: About 25 oz. Target sights, barrel catch rear adj. for windage and elevation. Blued finish. Square butt, hard rubber grips. Made 1893-1905. Note: This model was available also as a combination arm w/accessory .38 revolver bbl. and cylinder enabling conversion to a pocket revolver. It has the frame of the .38 SA revolver Model 1891 w/side flanges, hand and cylinder stop slots.
Single-shot pistol, .22 LR . . NiB $2890 Ex $2643 Gd $2425
**Single-shot pistol, .32 S&W
or .38 S&W** . . . . NiB $2320 Ex $1996 Gd $1748
**Combination set, revolver
and single-shot barrel** . . . . . NiB $3635 Ex $3145 Gd $2869

MODEL 1891 SINGLE-SHOT TARGET PISTOL,
SECOND MODEL . . . . NiB $2797 Ex $2466 Gd $1580
Similar to the First Model except side flanges, hand and stop slots eliminated, cannot be converted to revolver, redesigned rear sight. Caliber: .22 LR only, 10-inch bbl. only. Made from 1905 to 1909.

PERFECTED SINGLE-SHOT TARGET PISTOL
Similar to Second Model except has double-action lockwork. Caliber: .22 LR only, 10-inch bbl. Checkered walnut grips, Extended square-butt target type. Made 1909-23. Note: In 1920 and thereafter, this model was made w/barrels having bore diameter of .223 instead of .226 and tight, short chambering. The first group of these pistols was produced for the U.S. Olympic Team of 1920, thus the designation Olympic Model.
Pre-1920 type . . . . NiB $2314 Ex $1945 Gd $1566
Olympic model . . . . NiB $2665 Ex $2380 Gd $2235

STRAIGHT LINE SINGLE-SHOT
TARGET PISTOL . . . . NiB $3345 Ex $3267 Gd $3095
Frame shaped like that of an automatic pistol, barrel swings to the left on pivot for Extracting and loading, straight-line trigger and hammer movement. Caliber: .22 LR. 10-inch bbl., 11.25 inches overall. Weight: 34 oz. Target sights. Blued finish. Smooth walnut grips. Supplied in metal case w/screwdriver and cleaning rod. Made from 1925 to 1936.

- REVOLVERS -

MODEL 1 HAND EJECTOR
DA REVOLVER . . . . NiB $2670 Ex $2000 Gd $1289
First Model. Forerunner of the .32 Hand Ejector and Regulation Police models, this was the first S&W revolver of the solid-frame, swing-out cylinder type. Top strap of this model is longer than those of later models, and it lacks the usual S&W cylinder latch. Caliber: .22 Long. Bbl., lengths: 3.25-, 4.25-, and 6-inches. Fixed sights. Blued or nickel finish. Round butt, hard rubber stocks. Made from 1896 to 1903.

NO. 3 SA FRONTIER . . . . . NiB $5170 Ex $4350 Gd $3095
Caliber: .44-40 WCF. Bbl., lengths: 4-, 5- and 6.5-inch. Fixed or target sights. Blued or nickel finish. Round, hard rubber or checkered walnut grips. Made from 1885 to 1908.

NO. 3 SA (NEW MODEL) . . NiB $7245 Ex $6095 Gd $4270
Hinged frame. Six-round cylinder. Caliber: .44 S&W Russian. Bbl., lengths: 4-, 5-, 6-, 6.5-, 7.5- and 8-inches. Fixed or target sights. Blued or nickel finish. Round, hard rubber or checkered walnut grips. Made from 1878 to 1908. Note: Value shown is for standard model. Specialist collectors recognize numerous variations w/a range of higher values.
**Performance Center Schofield Model of 2000
(modern repro)** . . . . NiB $1800

NO. 3 SA TARGET. . . . . . . NiB $6996 Ex $3890 Gd $3175
Hinged frame. Six-round cylinder. Calibers: .32/.44 S&W, .38/.44 S&W Gallery & Target. 6.5-inch bbl. only. Fixed or target sights. Blued or nickel finish. Round, hard rubber or checkered walnut grips. Made from 1887 to 1910.

MODEL 10 .38 MILITARY & POLICE DA
Also called Hand Ejector Model of 1902, Hand Ejector Model of 1905, Model K. Manufactured substantially in its present form since 1902, this model has undergone numerous changes, most of them minor. Round- or square-butt models, the latter intro. in 1904. Caliber: .38 Special. Six-round cylinder, bbl. lengths: 2-(intro. 1933), 4-, 5-, 6- and 6.5-inch (latter disc. 1915) also 4-inch heavy bbl., (intro. 1957); 11.13 inches overall (square-butt model w/6-inch bbl.). Round-butt model is 1/4-inch shorter, weight: About 1/2 oz. less. Fixed sights. Blued or nickel

**Smith & Wesson
Model 10 (Two-inch Barrel)**

**Smith & Wesson
Model 12 (Two-inch Barrel)**

**Smith & Wesson Model 13
(Heavy Barrel)**

**Smith & Wesson
Model 14**

finish. Checkered walnut grips, hard rubber available in round-butt style. Current Model 10 has short action. Made 1902 to date. Note: S&W Victory Model, wartime version of the M & P .38, was produced for the U.S. Government from 1940 to the end of the war. A similar revolver, designated .38/200 British Service Revolver, was produced for the British Government during the same period. These arms have either brush-polish or sandblast blued finish, and most of them have plain, smooth walnut grips, lanyard swivels.

Model of 1902 (1902-05)	NiB $639	Ex $536	Gd $362
Model of 1905 (1905-40)	NiB $1165	Ex $910	Gd $602
.38/200 British Service			
(1940-45)	NiB $1165	Ex $910	Gd $602
Victory Model (1942-45)	NiB $643	Ex $529	Gd $425
Model of 1944 (1945-48)	NiB $785	Ex $431	Gd $319
Model 10 (1948-date)	NiB $530	Ex $437	Gd $319

MODEL 10 .38 MILITARY
& POLICE HEAVY BARREL .... NiB $632 Ex $499 Gd $337
Same as standard Model 10 except has heavy 4-inch bbl., weight: 34 oz. Made from 1957 to 1986.

MODEL 10 CLASSICS SERIES .. NiB $632 Ex $499 Gd $337
Recent manufacture of Model 10 except chambered in .38 Spl.+P and w/heavy 4-in. bbl., fixed sights, blued finish, checkered wood grips. Made from 2010 to date.

MODEL 12 .38 M&P
AIRWEIGHT .... NiB $544 Ex $388 Gd $290
Same as standard Military & Police except has light alloy frame, f8rnished w/2- or 4-inch bbl. only, weight: 18 oz. (w/2-inch bbl.). Made from 1952 to 1986.

MODEL 12/13 (AIR FORCE MODEL)
DA REVOLVER .... NiB $536 Ex $439 Gd $265
Special "Air Force" Model designed with alloy cylinder and frame to be used as a "Survival Weapon" for air crews. Athough this weapon was actually a first-series Model 12, the Air Force stamped "M13" on the top strap. Issued 1953 but recalled for function problems in 1954.

MODEL 13 .357
MILITARY/POLICE .... NiB $487 Ex $318 Gd $204
Same as Model 10 .38 Military & Police Heavy Barrel except chambered for .357 Magnum and .38 Special w/3- or 4-inch bbl. Round or square butt configuration. Made 1974-98.

MODELS 14 (K-38) AND 16 (K-32) MASTERPIECE REVOLVERS
Calibers: .22 LR, .22 Magnum Rimfire, .32 S&W Long, .38 Special. Six-round cylinder. DA/SA. Bbl. lengths: 4- (.22 WMR only), 6-, 8.38-inch (latter not available in K32), 11.13 inches overall (with 6-inch bbl.). Weight: 38.5 oz. (with 6-inch bbl.). Click adj. rear sight, Partridge front. Blued finish. Checkered walnut grips. Made from 1947 to date. (Model 16 disc. 1974; 3,630 produced; reissued 1990 to 1993.)

Model 14 (K-38 DA)	NiB $577	Ex $318	Gd $209
Model 14 (K-38 SA, 6-in. bbl.)	NiB $693	Ex $366	Gd $220
Model 14 (K-38 SA, 8.38-in. bbl.)	NiB $474	Ex $351	Gd $259
Model 16 (K-32 DA) 1st Issue	NiB $3500	Ex $3316	Gd $889
Model 16 (K-32 DA)	NiB $2579	Ex $1138	Gd $974

**Smith & Wesson
Model 15**

**Smith & Wesson
Model 17 K-22**

**Smith & Wesson
Model 18 (See Model 15 for description)**

**Smith & Wesson
Model 19 (Round Butt)**

MODEL 14 CLASSICS SERIES . . . . NiB $695 Ex $375 Gd $340
Recent manufacture of Model 14 except chambered in .38 Spl.+P and 6-in. bbl., adj. sights, blued or nickel finish, checkered wood grips. Made from 2009 to 2011.

MODELS 15 (.38) AND 18 (.22) COMBAT MASTERPIECE DA REVOLVERS
Same as K-22 and K-38 Masterpiece but w/2- (.38) or 4-inch bbl., and Baughman quick-draw front sight. 9.13 inches overall w/4-inch bbl., Weight: 34 oz. (.38 cal.). Made 1950-99.
Model 15 . . . . NiB $805 Ex $602 Gd $456
Model 18 (disc. 1985) . . . . NiB $691 Ex $523 Gd $487
w/target options TH & TT, add $50

MODEL 15 CLASSICS SERIES . . . . NiB $780 Ex $300 Gd $270
Recent manufacture of Model 15 except chambered in .38 Spl.+P and 4-in. bbl., adj. sights, blued finish, checkered wood grips. Made from 2010 to 2011.

MODEL 17 K-22 MASTERPIECE DA REVOLVER
Caliber: 22 LR. Six-round cylinder, Bbl lengths: 4, 6 or 8.38 inches. 11.13 inches overall (with 6-inch bbl.). Weight: 38 oz. (with 6-inch bbl.). Partridge-type front sight, S&W micrometer click rear. Checkered walnut Service grips with S&W momogram. S&W blued finish. Made from 1947-93 and from 1996-98.
Model 17 (4-inch bbl.) . . . . NiB $632 Ex $453 Gd $347
Model 17 (6-inch bbl.) . . . . NiB $632 Ex $453 Gd $347
Model 17 (8.38-inch bbl.) . . . . . NiB $823 Ex $546 Gd $479
w/target options TH & TT, add $50

MODEL 17 CLASSICS SERIES . . . . NiB $989 Ex $480 Gd $430
Recent manufacture of Model 17 except w/6-in. bbl., adj. sights, blued finish, checkered wood grips. Made from 2009 to date.

MODEL 18 . . . . NiB $750 Ex $480 Gd $420
Similar to Model 17 except w/4-in. bbl., adj. sights, blued finish, checkered wood grips. Made from 1949 to 1986.

MODEL 18 CLASSICS SERIES . . . . NiB $695 Ex $400 Gd $360
Recent manufacture of Model 18. Made from 2009 to 2011.

MODEL 19 .357 COMBAT MAGNUM DA REVOLVER
Caliber: .357 Magnum. Six-round cylinder, bbl. lengths: 2.5 (round butt), 4, or 6 inches, 9.5 inches overall (with 4-inch bbl.). Weight: 35 oz. (with 4-inch bbl.). Click adj. rear sight, ramp front. Blued or nickel finish. Target grips of checkered Goncalo Alves. Made from 1956 to date (2.5- and 6-inch bbls. were disc. in 1991).
Model 19 (2.5-inch bbl.) . . . . . . NiB $601 Ex $431 Gd $319
Model 19 (4-inch bbl.) . . . . NiB $601 Ex $431 Gd $319
Model 19 (6-inch bbl.) . . . . NiB $601 Ex $431 Gd $319
Model 19 (8.38-inch bbl.) . . . . . NiB $601 Ex $431 Gd $319
w/target options TH & TT, add $75

MODEL 20 .38/44 HEAVY DUTY DA
Caliber: .38 Special. Six-round cylinder, bbl. lengths: 4, 5 and 6.5 inches;10.38 inches overall (with 5-inch bbl.). Weight: 40 oz. (with 5-inch bbl.). Fixed sights. Blued or nickel finish. Checkered walnut grips. Short action after 1948. Made from 1930-56 and from 1957 to 67.
Pre-World War II . . . . NiB $1970 Ex $1770 Gd $525
Post-war . . . . NiB $2270 Ex $1620 Gd $910

Smith & Wesson
Model 22/32 Target Revolver

Smith & Wesson
Model 19 (Square Butt)

Smith & Wesson
Model 20

Smith & Wesson
Model 22

Smith & Wesson
Model 22/32 Kit Gun

MODEL 21 .44 MILITARY DA REVOLVER

Postwar version of the 1926 Model 44 Military. Caliber: .44 Special, 6-round cylinder. Bbl. lengths: 4-, 5- and 6.5-inches. 11.75 inches overall (w/6.5-inch bbl.) Weight: 39.5 oz. (w/6.5-inch bbl.). Fixed front sight w/square-notch rear sight; target model has micrometer click rear sight adj. for windage and elevation. Checkered walnut grips w/S&W monogram. Blued or nickel finish. Made 1950 to 1967.

Model 21 (4- or 5-inch bbl.) ...NiB $2979 Ex $2035 Gd $809
Model 21 (6.5-inch bbl.), add 50%

MODEL 22 1950 ARMY DA ...NiB $2025 Ex $1735 Gd $816
Postwar version of the 1917 Army w/same general specifications except redesigned hammer. Made from 1950 to 1967.

MODEL 22 CLASSICS SERIES ... NiB $850 Ex $470 Gd $420
Recent manufacture of Model 22 except in .45 ACP, 4- or 5.5-in. bbl., blued finish, Altamont wood grip. Made 2007-10.

MODEL 22 CLASSICS SERIES

MODEL OF 1917 ....NiB $999 Ex $470 Gd $420
Recent manufacture of Model 1917 except in .45 ACP, 5.5-in. bbl., N-Frame, lanyard loop, blued finish, Altamont wood grip. Made from 2008 to 2012.

.22/.32 TARGET DA REVOLVER

Also known as the "Bekeart Model." Design based upon ".32 Hand Ejector." Caliber: .22 LR (recessed head cylinder for high-speed cartridges intro. 1935). Six-round cylinder, 6-inch bbl., 10.5 inches overall. Weight: 23 oz. Adj. target sights. Blued finish. Checkered walnut grips. Made from 1911-53. Note: In 1911, San Francisco gun dealer Phil Bekeart, who suggested this model, received 292 pieces. These are the true "Bekeart Model" revolvers and are marked with separate identification numbers on the base of the wooden grip.

.22/.32 Standard Model ..... NiB $1160 Ex $760 Gd $498
.22/.32 (early prod. 1-3000), add 20%
.22/.32 Bekeart model ..... NiB $1565 Ex $1329 Gd $752

.22/.32 KIT GUN ....NiB $850 Ex $580 Gd $319
Same as .22/.32 Target except has 2- or 4-inch bbl., round grips, 6 or 8 inches overall, weight: 19-21oz. Made 1935-53.

Smith & Wesson
Model 23

Smith & Wesson
Model 24 Target

Smith & Wesson
Model 25 Target

Smith & Wesson
Model 27

MODEL 23 .38-44 OUTDOORSMAN DA REVOLVER

Target version of the .38/44 Heavy Duty. 6.5- or 8.75-inch bbl., weight: 41.75 oz. Target sights, micrometer-click rear on postwar models. Blued or nickel finish. 1950 transition model has ribbed barrel, redesigned hammer. Made from 1930 to 1967.

Pre-war model (plain bbl.)...NiB $2555 Ex $1958 Gd $1278
Post-war (ribbed bbl.)......NiB $1724 Ex $1398 Gd $780

MODEL 24 1950 .44 TARGET DA REVOLVER

Postwar version of the 1921 Model .44 Hand Ejector. .44 Special with 4-, 5- or 6.5-inch ribbed bbl., redesigned hammer, micrometer click rear sight. Matte or polished blue finish. Made from 1950-67. Model 24 reintroduced in 1983 only.

Model 24 (1950 w/6.5-inch
   bbl...................NiB $2770 Ex $1696 Gd $897
Model 24 (1950) w/4-inch bbl., add................20%
Model 24 (1950) w/5-inch bbl., add..............100%
Model 24 (1950) w/polished
   blue finish, add.............................25%
Model 24 (1950)
   w/nickel finish, add..........................65%
Model 24 .44 Target reintroduced (7,500 produced
   in 1983-84) (w/4-inch bbl.)....NiB $760 Ex $560 Gd $402
Model 24 (w/6.5-inch bbl.)....NiB $730 Ex $553 Gd $365
Model 24-3 .44
Lew Horton Special
w/3-inch bbl. (prod. in 1983)..NiB $860 Ex $654 Gd $380
Classics w/6.5-inch bbl.
   (2008-2012)............NiB $770 Ex $554 Gd $370
Classics w/ nickel finish, add.....................8%

MODEL 24-6

CLASSICS SERIES...........NiB $770 Ex $470 Gd $420
Recent manufacture of Model 24 except in .45 ACP, 3- or 6.5-in. bbl., blued or nickel finish, square butt wood grip. Made from 2006 to 2012.

MODEL 25 1955 .45 TARGET DA REVOLVER

Same as 1950 Model .44 Target, but chambered for .45 ACP, .45 Auto Rim or .45 LC w/4-, 6- or 6.5-inch bbl. Made from 1955 to 1991 in several variations. Note: In 1961, the .45 ACP was designated Model 25-2, and in 1978 the .45 LC was designated Model 25-5.

Model 25 1955 .45 Target
.45 ACP w/4- or 6-inch bbl....NiB $780 Ex $587 Gd $434
.45 ACP w/6.5-inch pinned bbl...NiB $767 Ex $660 Gd $449
.45 LC early production...NiB $4245 Ex $4040 Gd $3779
Model 25-2 .45 ACP
Lew Horton Special w/3-inch
   bbl....................NiB $541 Ex $453 Gd $346
Model 25-2 (w/4-inch bbl.)....NiB $601 Ex $485 Gd $402
Model 25-3 (w/6.5-inch bbl.)..NiB $734 Ex $544 Gd $429
Model 25-5 .45 LC w/4-inch
   bbl....................NiB $601 Ex $484 Gd $377
Model 25-3 (w/6.5-inch bbl.)..NiB $648 Ex $530 Gd $362
Model 25 Classics
   (reintro. 2008)...........NiB $980 Ex $530 Gd $362

MODEL 25 CLASSICS SERIES....NiB $1010 Ex $470 Gd $420

Recent manufacture of Model 25 except w/3- or 6.5-in. bbl., blued or nickel finish, square butt, wood grip. Made from 2007 to date.

MODEL 26 1950 .45 LIGHT TARGET DA REVOLVER

Similar to 1950 Model Target except w/lighter bbl. Note: Lighter profile was not well received. (Only 2,768 produced)

Model 26 (.45 ACP or .45 Auto Rim
   w/6.5-inch bbl.).......NiB $4590 Ex $4295 Gd $3988
Model 26 .45 LC, (200
   produced)............NiB $4590 Ex $4295 Gd $3988
w/4- or 5-inch bbl.,..............................$50

Smith & Wesson
Model 28

Smith & Wesson
Model 29

Smith & Wesson
Model 31

MODEL 27 .357 MAGNUM DA

Caliber: .357 Magnum. Six-round cylinder, bbl. lengths: 3.5-, 4-, 5-, 6-, 6.5-and 8.38-inches, 11.38 inches overall (with 6-inch bbl.). Weight: 44 oz. (with 6-inch bbl.). Adj. target sights, Baughman quick-draw ramp front sight on 3.5-inch bbl., Blued or nickel finish. Checkered walnut grips. Made from 1935-94. Note: Until 1938, the .357 Magnum was custom made in any barrel length from 3.5-inch to 8.75-inch. Each of these revolvers was accompanied by a registration certificate and has its registration number stamped on the inside of the yoke. Postwar magnums have a redesigned hammer w/short-ened fall and the new S&W micrometer click rear sight.

Pre-war model
(Reg number on yoke). . . . . NiB $893 Ex $730 Gd $615
Pre-war model w/out reg
number . . . . NiB $862 Ex $653 Gd $612
Early model w/pinned bbl.,
recessed cyl. . . . . NiB $895 Ex $755 Gd $624
Late model w/8. 38-inch bbl. . . NiB $895 Ex $755 Gd $624
Late model w/3.5 to 5-inch bbl . . NiB $895 Ex $755 Gd $624
Late model, other bbl. lengths . . NiB $915 Ex $785 Gd $612

MODEL 27 CLASSICS SERIES . . NiB $1020 Ex $470 Gd $420

Recent manufacture of Model 25 except w/4- or 6.5-in. bbl., blued or nickel finish, wood grip. Made from 2008 to date.

MODEL 28 HIGHWAY PATROLMAN

Caliber: .357 Magnum. Six-round cylinder, bbl. lengths: 4- or 6-inches, 11.25 inches overall (with 6-inch bbl.). Weight: 44 oz. (with 6-inch bbl.). Adj. rear sight, ramp front. Blued finish. Checkered walnut grips, Magna or target type. Made from 1954 to 1986.

Pre-war registered model
(reg number on yoke) . . . . NiB $893 Ex $780 Gd $610
Pre-war model without registration
number . . . . NiB $1190 Ex $975 Gd $700
Early model w/pinned bbl.,
recessed cylinder, 5-screws . NiB $895 Ex $734 Gd $632
Late model, all bbl. lengths. . . . NiB $536 Ex $362 Gd $255

MODEL 29 .44 MAGNUM DA REVOLVER

Caliber: .44 Magnum. Six-round cylinder. bbl., lengths: 4-, 5-, 6.5-, 8.38-inches. 11.88 inches overall (with 6.5-inch bbl.). Weight: 47 oz. (with 6.5-inch bbl.). Click adj. rear sight, ramp front. Blued or nickel finish. Checkered Goncalo Alves target grips. Made from 1956 to 1998. Early Production Standard Series (disc. 1983)

3-Screw model (1962-83) . . . . . NiB $970 Ex $843 Gd $686
4-Screw model (1957-61) . . . NiB $2200 Ex $1693 Gd $880
5-Screw model (1956-57) . . NiB $3497 Ex $2895 Gd $2630
w/5-inch bbl., 3- or 4-screw models, add 100%Late
Production standard series (disc. 1998)
Model 29 (w/4- or 6.5-inch
bbl.) . . . . .NiB $870 Ex $669 Gd $432
Model 29 (w/3-inch bbl.,
Lew Horton Special) . . . . .NiB $920 Ex $689 Gd $432
Model 29 (w/8.38-inch bbl.). . .NiB $895 Ex $679 Gd $432
Model 29 Classic (w/5- or 6.5-inch
bbl.) . . . . .NiB $610 Ex $539 Gd $332
Model 29 Classic (w/8.38-inch
bbl.) . . . . .NiB $630 Ex $540 Gd $345
Model 29 Classic DX (w/6.5-in. and
8.38-in. bbl.) . . . . .NiB $1260 Ex $648 Gd $556
Model 29 Classic DX (w/5-inch
bbl.) . . . . .NiB $1410 Ex $798 Gd $656
Model 29 Magna Classic (w/7.5-inch
ported bbl.). . . . . .NiB $1170 Ex $859 Gd $537
Model 29 Silhouette (w/10.63-inch
bbl.) . . . . .NiB $860 Ex $656 Gd $437

MODEL 29 CLASSICS SERIES . . NiB $999 Ex $480 Gd $420

Recent manufacture of Model 29 except w/3-, 4- or 6.5-in. bbl., blued or nickel finish, wood grip. Made from 2008 to date.

MODEL 30 .32 HAND EJECTOR

DA REVOLVER . . . . .NiB $554 Ex $469 Gd $356
Caliber: .32 S&W Long. Six-round cylinder, bbl. lengths: 2- (intro. 1949), 3-, 4- and 6-inches, 8 inches overall (with 4-inch bbl.). Weight: 18 oz. (with 4-inch bbl.). Fixed sights. Blued or nickel finish. Round, checkered walnut or hard rubber grips. Made from 1903-76.

MODELS 31 & 33 REGULATION POLICE DA REVOLVER

Same basic type as .32 Hand Ejector except has square butt-grips. Calibers: .32 S&W Long (Model 31) .38 S&W (Model 33). Six-round cylinder in .32 cal., 5-round in .38 caliber. Bbl., lengths: 2- (intro. 1949), 3-, 4- and 6-inches in .32 cal., 4-inch only in .38 cal., 8.5 inches overall (with 4-inch bbl.). Weight:

**Smith & Wesson
Model 32**

**Smith & Wesson
Model 34**

**Smith & Wesson
Model 36**

**Smith & Wesson
Model 37**

18 oz. (.38 cal. w/4-inch bbl.), 18.75 oz. (.32 cal. w/4-inch bbl.). Fixed sights. Blued or nickel finish. Checkered walnut grips. Made from 1917. Model 33 disc. in 1974; Model 31 disc. in 1992.

Model 31 . . . . NiB $546 Ex $306 Gd $255
Model 33 . . . . NiB $448 Ex $283 Gd $198

MODEL 32 DA REVOLVER . . . NiB $546 Ex $467 Gd $219
Hinged frame. Caliber: .32 S&W. Five-round cylinder, bbl. lengths: 3-, 3.5- and 6-inches. Fixed sights. Blued or nickel finish. Hard rubber grips. Made from 1880-1919. Note: Value shown applies generally to the several varieties. exception is the rare first issue of 1880 (identified by squared sideplate and serial no. 1 to 30) valued up to $2,500.

MODEL 32 TERRIER DA . . . . . . NiB $479 Ex $342 Gd $255
Caliber: .38 S&W. Five-round cylinder, 2-inch bbl., 6.25 inches overall. Weight: 17 oz. Fixed sights. Blued or nickel finish. Checkered walnut or hard rubber grips. Built on .32 Hand Ejector frame. Made from 1936-74.

**MODEL 33 .32-20 MILITARY & POLICE
DA REVOLVER** . . . . NiB $2845 Ex $2719 Gd $2530
Same as M&P 38 except chambered for .32-20 Winchester cartridge. First intro. in the 1899 model, M&P revolvers were produced in this caliber until about 1940. Values same as M&P .38 models.

MODEL 34 DA REVOLVER . . . . NiB $756 Ex $408 Gd $305
Caliber: .22 LR. Six-shot cylinder, 2-inch or 4-inch bbl. and round or square grips, blued or nickel finish. Made from 1936-91.

**MODEL 35 1953
.22/.32 TARGET** . . . . NiB $772 Ex $590 Gd $362
Same general specifications as previous model .22/.32 Target except has micrometer-click rear sight. Magna type target grips. Weight: 25 oz. Made from 1953-74.

MODEL 36 CHIEFS SPECIAL DA
Based on .32 Hand Ejector w/frame lengthened to permit longer cylinder for .38 Special cartridge. Caliber: .38 Special. Five-round cylinder, bbl. lengths: 2- or 3-inches, 6.5 inches overall (with 2-inch bbl.). Weight: 19 oz. Fixed sights. Blued or nickel finish. Checkered walnut grips, round or square butt. Made from 1952 to date.

Blued model . . . . NiB $638 Ex $425 Gd $255
Nickel model . . . . NiB $648 Ex $437 Gd $265
**Early model (5-screw, small trigger
    guard, S/N 1-2500)** . . . . NiB $668 Ex $541 Gd $386
**Model 36 Ladysmith
    (1990-2008)** . . . . NiB $480 Ex $290 Gd $186

**MODEL 37 AIRWEIGHT
CHIEFS SPECIAL** . . . . NiB $500 Ex $366 Gd $225
Same general specifications as standard Chiefs Special except has light alloy frame, weight: 12.5 oz. w/2-inch bbl., blued finish only. Made from 1954 to 1995

MODEL 38 BODYGUARD AIRWEIGHT DA REVOLVER
Shrouded hammer. Light alloy frame. Caliber: .38 Special. Five-round cylinder, 2- or 3-inch bbl., 6.38 inches overall (w/2-inch bbl.) Weight: 14.5 oz. Fixed sights. Blued or nickel finish. Checkered walnut grips. Made from 1955 to 1998.

**Smith & Wesson
Model 38 Bodyguard Airweight**

Blued model . . . . NiB $479 Ex $347 Gd $235
Nickel model. . . . . NiB $500 Ex $362 Gd $274
Early model (pinned bbl. &
   recessed cyl., pre-1981) . . . . NiB $485 Ex $342 Gd $243

MODEL .38 DA REVOLVER. . . . NiB $945 Ex $734 Gd $544
Hinged frame. Caliber: .38 S&W. Five-round cylinder, bbl. lengths: 4-, 4.25-, 5-, 6-, 8- and 10-inch. Fixed sights. Blued or nickel finish. Hard rubber grips. Made from 1880-1911. Note: Value shown applies generally to the several varieties. exceptions are the first issue of 1880 (identified by squared sideplate and serial no. 1 to 4,000) and the 8- and 10-inch bbl. models of the third issue (1884 to 1995).

MODEL .38 HAND EJECTOR DA
Military & Police — First Model. Resembles Colt New Navy in general appearance, lacks bbl., lug and locking bolt common to all later S&W hand ejector models. Caliber: .38 Long Colt. Six-round cylinder, bbl. lengths: 4-, 5-, 6- and 6.5-inch, 11.5 inches overall (with 6.5-inch bbl.). Fixed sights. Blued or nickel finish. Round, checkered walnut or hard rubber grips. Made from 1899 to 1902.
Standard model
(civilian issue) . . . . NiB $1870 Ex $1322 Gd $1132
Army Model (marked U.S.
Army Model, 1000 issued) . NiB $3725 Ex $3397 Gd $2935
Navy Model (marked USN,
   1000 issued) . . . . NiB $4495 Ex $3800 Gd $3412

.38 MILITARY & POLICE
TARGET DA. . . . . NiB $3725 Ex $3397 Gd $2740
Target version of the Military & Police w/standard features of that model. Caliber: .38 Special, six-inch bbl. Weight: 32.25 oz. Adj. target sights. Blued finish. Checkered walnut grips. Made from 1899 to1940. For values, add $175 for corresponding M&P 38 models.

MODEL .38
PERFECTED DA. . . . . NiB $1465 Ex $1336 Gd $1145
Hinged frame. Similar to earlier .38 DA Model but heavier frame, side latch as in solid-frame models, improved lockwork. Caliber: .38 S&W. Five-round cylinder, bbl. lengths: 3.25, 4, 5 and 6 inches. Fixed sights. Blued or nickel finish. Hard rubber grips. Made 1909 to 1920.

MODEL 40 CENTENNIAL DA HAMMERLESS REVOLVER
Similar to Chiefs Special but has Safety Hammerless-type mechanism w/grip safety. Two-inch bbl. Weight: 19 oz. Made from 1953 to 1974.
Blued model . . . . NiB $633 Ex $437 Gd $398
Nickel model. . . . . NiB $1319 Ex $1109 Gd $895

MODEL 42 CENTENNIAL AIRWEIGHT
Same as standard Centennial model except has light alloy frame, weight: 13 oz. Made from 1954 to 1974.
Blued model . . . . NiB $648 Ex $429 Gd $351
Nickel model. . . . . NiB $1250 Ex $1062 Gd $884

MODEL 42 CLASSICS SERIES . . NiB $999 Ex $480 Gd $420
Recent manufacture of Model 42 except in .38 Spl.+P w/1.87-in. bbl., aluminum frame, grip safety, blued finish, checkered wood grip. Made from 2009 to 2010.

MODEL 43 1955 .22/.32
KIT GUN AIRWEIGHT . . . . NiB $760 Ex $543 Gd $274
Same as Model 34 Kit Gun except has light alloy frame, square grip. Furnished w/3.5-inch bbl., weight: 14.25 oz. Made 1954 to 1974.

MODEL 44 1926 MILITARY DA REVOLVER
Same as the early New Century model with Extractor rod casing but lacking the "Triple Lock" feature. Caliber: .44 S&W Special. Six-round cylinder, bbl. lengths: 4, 5 and 6.5 inches, 11.75 inches overall (with 6.5-inch bbl.). Weight: 39.5 oz. (with 6.5-inch bbl.). Fixed sights. Blued or nickel finish. Checkered walnut grips. Made 1926 to 1941.
Standard model. . . . . NiB $3715 Ex $3409 Gd $3135
Target model w/6.5-inch bbl.,
   target sights, blued . . . . . NiB $3715 Ex $3409 Gd $3095

.38 AND .44 DA REVOLVERS
Also called Wesson Favorite (lightweight model), Frontier (caliber .44-40). Hinged frame. Six-round cylinder. Calibers: .44 S&W Russian, .38-40, .44-40. Bbl. lengths: 4-, 5-, 6- and 6.5-inch. Weight: 37.5 oz. (with 6.5-inch bbl.). Fixed sights. Blued or nickel finish. Hard rubber grips. Made from 1881 to 1913, Frontier disc. 1910.
Standard model, .44
   Russian . . . . NiB $10,930 Ex $9795 Gd $6579
Standard model, .38-40 . . . NiB $6030 Ex $5095 Gd $1479
Frontier model . . . . NiB $5089 Ex $3240 Gd $1939
Favorite model . . . . NiB $10,600 Ex $8499 Gd $2977

.44 HAND EJECTOR MODEL DA REVOLVER
First Model, New Century, also called "Triple Lock" because of its third cylinder lock at the crane. Six-round cylinder. Calibers: .44 S&W Special, .450 Eley, .455 Mark II. Bbl. lengths: 4-, 5-, 6.5- and 7.5-inch. Weight: 39 oz. (with 6.5-inch bbl.). Fixed sights. Blued or nickel finish. Checkered walnut grips. Made 1907 to 1966. Second Model is basically the same as New Century except crane lock ("Triple Lock" feature) and Extractor rod casing eliminated. Calibers: .44 S&W Special .44-40 Win. .45 Colt. Bbl. lengths: 4-, 5-, 6.5- and 7.5-inch; 11.75 inches overall (with 6.5-inch bbl.). Weight: 38 oz. (with 6.5-inch bbl.). Fixed sights. Blued or nickel finish. Checkered walnut grips. Made from 1915 to 1937.
First Model w/triple lock (1907-15)
Standard model,
   .44 S&W Special. . . . . NiB $4735 Ex $4380 Gd $4335
Standard model
   other calibers. . . . . NiB $2865 Ex $2555 Gd $2339
British .455
   Target model . . . . NiB $3520 Ex $3299 Gd $1135
Second Model
   w/o triple lock (1915-37) . . NiB $3520 Ex $3266 Gd $1117
.44 S&W Special. . . . . NiB $2420 Ex $2119 Gd $1972
Second model,
   other calibers . . . . NiB $5200 Ex $4190 Gd $3977

170

Smith & Wesson
Model 48

Smith & Wesson
Model 63

Smith & Wesson
Model 49 Bodyguard

Smith & Wesson
Model 64

Smith & Wesson
Model 57

Smith & Wesson
Model 60

.44 HAND EJECTOR, SECOND MODEL
DA REVOLVER . . . . NiB $2425 Ex $2174 Gd $1981
Basically the same as New Century except crane lock ("Triple Lock" feature) and Extractor rod casing eliminated. Calibers: .44 S&W Special .44-40 Win. .45 Colt. Bbl. lengths: 4-, 5-, 6.5- and 7.5-inches, 11.75 inches overall (with 6.5-inch bbl.). Weight: .38 oz. (with 6.5-inch bbl.). Fixed sights. Blued or nickel finish. Checkered walnut grips. Made from 1915 to 1937.

MODEL 48 (K-22) MASTERPIECE M.R.F. DA REVOLVER
Caliber: .22 Mag. and .22 LR. Six-round cylinder, bbl. lengths: 4, 6 and 8.38 inches, 11.13 inches overall (w/ 6-inch bbl.). Weight: 39 oz. Adj. rear sight, ramp front. Made from 1959 to 1986.
Model 48 (4- or 6-inch bbl.) . . . NiB $862 Ex $668 Gd $495
Model 48 (8.38-inch bbl.) . . . . . NiB $826 Ex $612 Gd $439
w/target options TH & TT, add $75

MODEL 48 CLASSICS SERIES . . NiB $999 Ex $480 Gd $420
Recent manufacture of Model 48 except w/4- or 6-in. bbl., blued finish, checkered wood grip. Made from 2010 to date.

MODEL 49 BODYGUARD
Same as Model 38 Bodyguard Airweight except has steel frame, weight: 20.5 oz. Made from 1959 to 1996.
Blued model . . . . NiB $478 Ex $337 Gd $244
Nickel model. . . . . NiB $530 Ex $377 Gd $270

MODEL 51 1960 .22/.32
KIT GUN. . . . . NiB $755 Ex $549 Gd $319
Same as Model 34 Kit Gun except chambered for .22 WMR 3.5-inch bbl., weight: 24 oz. Made from 1960 to 1974.

**Smith & Wesson
Model 66 Combat Magnum**

**Smith & Wesson
Model 67 Combat Masterpiece**

MODEL 53 .22 REM. JET DA
Caliber: .22 Rem. Jet C.F. Magnum. Six-round cylinder (inserts permit use of .22 Short, Long, or LR cartridges). Bbl. lengths: 4, 6, 8.38 inches, 11.25 inches overall (with 6-inch bbl.). Weight: 40 oz. (with 6-inch bbl.). Micrometer-click rear sight ramp front. Checkered walnut grips. Made from 1960 to 1974.
Model 53 (4- or 6-inch bbl.)...NiB $933 Ex $749 Gd $633
Model 53 (8.38-inch bbl.)....NiB $1040 Ex $844 Gd $704
w/target options TH & TT, add $75

MODEL 57 .41 MAGNUM DA REVOLVER
Caliber: 41 Magnum. Six-round cylinder, bbl. lengths: 4-, 6-, 8.38-inch. Weight: 40 oz. (with 6-inch bbl.). Micrometer click rear sight, ramp front. Target grips of checkered Goncalo Alves. Made from 1964 to 1993.
Model 57 (w/4- or 6-inch bbl.) NiB $812 Ex $627 Gd $429
Model 57 (w/8.63-inch bbl.)...NiB $852 Ex $677 Gd $449
Model 57 (w/pinned bbl., recessed cylinder), add 10%

MODEL 57 CLASSICS SERIES NiB $1010 Ex $470 Gd $420
Recent manufacture of Model 57 except w/4- or 6-in. bbl., blued finish, checkered wood grip. Made from 2009 to date.

MODEL 58 .41 MILITARY& POLICE
DA REVOLVER ....NiB $855 Ex $709 Gd $576
Caliber: 41 Magnum. Six-round cylinder, 4-inch bbl. 9.25 inches overall. Weight: 41 oz. Fixed sights. Checkered walnut grips. Made from 1964 to 1982.

MODEL 58 CLASSICS SERIES .. NiB $780 Ex $470 Gd $420
Recent manufacture of Model 58 except w/blued or nickel finish, checkered wood grip. Made from 2009 to 2011.

MODEL 60 STAINLESS DA
Caliber: .38 Special or .357 Magnum. Five-round cylinder, bbl. lengths: 2, 2.1 or 3 inches, 6.5 or 7.5 inches overall. Weight: 19 to 23 oz. Square-notch rear sight, ramp front. Satin finish stainless steel. Made from 1965-96 (.38 Special) and from 1996 to date (.357/.38).
.38 Special (disc. 1996) ......NiB $474 Ex $346 Gd $270
.357 Mag. ....NiB $498 Ex $366 Gd $283
Lady Smith (w/smaller grip) ...NiB $544 Ex $377 Gd $280

MODEL 63 (1977)
KIT GUN DA..............NiB $474 Ex $319 Gd $265
Caliber: .22 LR. Six-round cylinder, 2- or 4-inch bbl., 6.5 or 8.5 inches overall. Weight: 19 to 24.5 oz. Adj. rear sight, ramp front. Stainless steel. Checkered walnut or synthetic grips.

MODEL 64 .38 M&P
STAINLESS ....NiB $498 Ex $362 Gd $287
Same as standard Model 10 except satin-finished stainless steel, square butt w/4-inch heavy bbl., or round butt w/2-inch bbl. Made from 1970 to date.

MODEL 65 .357 MILITARY/
POLICE STAINLESS .... NiB $499 Ex $357 Gd $290
Same as Model 13 except satin-finished stainless steel. Made 1974 to 2004.
Lady Smith (w/smaller grip) ...NiB $540 Ex $377 Gd $302

MODEL 66 .357 COMBAT MAGNUM STAINLESS
Same as Model 19 except satin-finished stainless steel. Made from 1971 to date.
Model 66 (2.5-inch bbl.)......NiB $536 Ex $439 Gd $328
Model 66 (3-inch bbl.) ....NiB $536 Ex $431 Gd $303
Model 66 (4-inch bbl.) ....NiB $536 Ex $431 Gd $303
Model 66 (6-inch bbl.) ....NiB $562 Ex $456 Gd $346
w/target options TH & TT, add $65

MODEL 67 .38 COMBAT
MASTERPIECE STAINLESS.....NiB $597 Ex $440 Gd $337
Same as Model 15 except satin-finished stainless steel available only w/4-inch bbl. Made from 1972-1988 and from 1991-1998.

MODEL 68 .38 COMBAT
MASTERPIECE STAINLESS.....NiB $831 Ex $668 Gd $601
Same as Model 66 except w/4- or 6-inch bbl., chambered for .38 Special. Made to accommodate CA Highway Patrol because they were not authorized to carry .357 magnums. Made from 1976 yo 1983. (7,500 produced)

125th Anniversary Commemorative
Issued to celebrate the 125th anniversary of the 1852 partnership of Horace Smith and Daniel Baird Wesson. Standard Edition is a Model 25 revolver in .45 Colt w/6.5-inch bbl., bright blued finish, gold-filled bbl., roll mark "Smith & Wesson 125th Anniversary," sideplate marked w/gold-filled Anniversary seal, smooth Goncalo Alves grips, in presentation case w/ nickel silver Anniversary medallion and book, "125 Years w/ Smith & Wesson," by Roy Jinks. Deluxe Edition is same except revolver is Class A engraved w/gold-filled seal on sideplate, ivory grips, Anniversary medallion is sterling silver and book is leather bound. Limited to 50 units. Total issue is 10,000 units, of which 50 are Deluxe Edition and two are a Custom Deluxe Edition and not for sale. Made in 1977.
Standard edition ....NiB $648 Ex $377 Gd $305
Deluxe edition ....NiB $2579 Ex $2365 Gd $2094

MODEL 242 AIRLITE TI
CENTENNIAL............. **NiB $500 Ex $300 Gd $220**
DAO. Caliber: .38 Spl.+P. 7-round titanium cylinder, 2.5-in. bbl., alloy L-frame. Uncle Mike's boot grip. Made 1990 only.

MODEL 296 AIRLITE TI
CENTENNIAL............. **NiB $650 Ex $400 Gd $260**
DAO. Caliber: .44 Spl. 5-round titanium cylinder, 2.5-in. bbl., alloy L-frame. Uncle Mike's boot grip. Made 1990 only.

MODEL 310 NIGHTGUARD.. **NiB $895 Ex $540 Gd $360**
SA/DA. Caliber: .40 S&W or 10mm. 6-round stainless cylinder, 2.5-in. bbl., scandium alloy N-frame. Fixed sights. Pachmayr grip. Made 2009 to 2010.

MODEL 315 NIGHTGUARD ...**NiB $895 Ex $540 Gd $360**
SA/DA. Caliber: .40 S&W or 10mm. 6-round stainless cylinder, 2.5-in. bbl., scandium alloy N-frame. Fixed sights. Pachmayr grip. Made 2009 to 2010.

MODEL 317 AIRLITE DA REVOLVER
Caliber: .22 LR. Eight-round cylinder, 1.88- or 3-in. bbl., 6.3 or 7.2 inches overall. Weight: 9.9 oz. or 11 oz. Ramp front sight, notched frame rear. Aluminum, carbon fiber, stainless and titanium construction. Brushed aluminum finish. Synthetic or Dymondwood grips. Made from 1997 to date.
w/1.88-in. bbl..............**NiB $590 Ex $380 Gd $306**
w/3-in. bbl................**NiB $683 Ex $453 Gd $356**
w/Dymondwood grips, add **$100**

MODEL 325 NIGHTGUARD ...**NiB $830 Ex $430 Gd $350**
SA/DA. Caliber: .45 ACP. 6-round stainless cylinder, 2.5-in. bbl., alloy N-frame. Fixed sights. Weight: 26.5 oz. Pachmayr rubber grip. Made 2008 to 2012.

MODEL 325 PD-AIRLITE SC......**NiB $800 Ex $490 Gd $340**
SA/DA. Caliber: .45 ACP. 6-round titanium cylinder, 2.5- or 4-in. bbl., scandium alloy N-frame. Weight: 21.5-25 oz. Hogue rubber grip. Made 2004 to 2007.

MODEL 327 NIGHTGUARD ...**NiB $830 Ex $430 Gd $350**
SA/DA. Caliber: .357 Mag. 8-round stainless cylinder, 2.5-in. bbl., alloy N-frame. Fixed sights. Weight: 28 oz. Pachmayr rubber grip. Made 2008 to 2012.

MODEL 327 PD-AIRLITE SC....**NiB $960 Ex $460 Gd $320**
SA/DA. Caliber: .357 Mag. 8-round titanium cylinder, 4-in. bbl., scandium alloy N-frame. Fixed sights. Weight: 28 oz. Wood grip. Made 2008 to 2009.

MODEL 329
NIGHTGUARD .... **NiB $830 Ex $430 Gd $350**
SA/DA. Caliber: .44 Mag. 6-round stainless cylinder, 2.5-in. bbl., alloy N-frame. Fixed sights. Weight: 28 oz. Pachmayr rubber grip. Made 2008 to 2012.

MODEL 329
PD-AIRLITE SC............**NiB $1160 Ex $530 Gd $350**
SA/DA. Caliber: .44 Mag. 6-round titanium cylinder, 4-in. bbl., scandium alloy N-frame. Fixed sights. Weight: 28 oz. Wood grip. Made 2003 to date.

MODEL 331 AIRLITE TI
CHIEFS SPECIAL .... **NiB $675 Ex $465 Gd $310**
SA/DA. Caliber: .32 H&R Mag. 6-round titanium cylinder, 1.87-in. bbl., alloy J-frame. Fixed sights. Weight: 28 oz. Wood or Uncle Mike's grip. Made 1999 to 2003.

MODEL 332 AIRLITE TI
CENTENNIAL .... **NiB $575 Ex $455 Gd $310**
DAO. Caliber: .32 H&R Mag. 6-round titanium cylinder, 1.87-in. bbl., alloy J-frame. Fixed sights. Weight: 28 oz. Uncle Mike's grip. Made 1999 to 2003.

MODEL 337 AIRLITE TI
CHIEFS SPECIAL .... **NiB $675 Ex $465 Gd $310**
SA/DA. Caliber: .38 Spl.+P. 5-round titanium cylinder, 1.87-in. bbl., alloy J-frame. Fixed sights. Weight: 12 oz. Made 1999 to 2003.

MODEL 337 AIRLITE TI
KIT GUN .... **NiB $600 Ex $350 Gd $290**
SA/DA. Caliber: .38 Spl.+P. 5-round cylinder, 3.12-in. bbl., J-frame. Fixed sights. Weight: 12 oz. Made 2000 to 2003.

MODEL 337 PD AIRLITE TI ... **NiB $585 Ex $345 Gd $315**
SA/DA. Caliber: .38 Spl.+P. 5-round titanium cylinder, 1.87-in. bbl., alloy J-frame. Fixed sights. Weight: 10.7 oz. Made 2000 to 2003.

MODEL 340 AIRLITE SC
CENTENNIAL .... **NiB $775 Ex $410 Gd $350**
DAO. Caliber: .357 Mag. 5-round titanium cylinder, 1.87-in. bbl., alloy J-frame. Fixed sights. Weight: 10.7 oz. Made 2001 to 2008.

MODEL 340 PD-AIRLITE SC
CENTENNIAL .... **NiB $775 Ex $410 Gd $350**
DAO. Caliber: .357 Mag. 5-round titanium cylinder, 1.87-in. bbl., alloy J-frame. HiViz fixed sights. Weight: 10.7 oz. Made 2000 to date.

MODEL 340 M&P
CENTENNIAL .... **NiB $869 Ex $500 Gd $280**
DAO. Caliber: .357 Mag. 5-round stainless cylinder, 1.87-in. bbl., alloy J-frame. HiViz fixed sights. Weight: 10.7 oz. Made 2007 to date.

MODEL 342 AIRLITE TI
CENTINNIAL............. **NiB $575 Ex $355 Gd $310**
DAO. Caliber: .38 Spl.+P. 5-round titanium cylinder, 1.87-in. bbl., alloy J-frame. Fixed sights. Weight: 12 oz. Made 1999 to 2003.

MODEL 342 PD AIRLITE TI
CENTINNIAL............. **NiB $575 Ex $355 Gd $310**
DAO. Caliber: .38 Spl.+P. 5-round titanium cylinder, 1.87-in. bbl., alloy J-frame. Fixed sights. Weight: 10.8 oz. Made 1999 to 2003.

MODEL 351 PD AIRLITE SC
CHIEFS SPECIAL .... **NiB $759 Ex $400 Gd $310**
SA/DA. Caliber: .22 WMR. 7-round cylinder, 1.87-in. bbl., alloy J-frame. Fixed sights. Weight: 10.6 oz. Made 2004 to date.

MODEL 351 PD AIRLITE
CENTINNIAL............. **NiB $689 Ex $375 Gd $300**
DAO. Caliber: .22 WMR. 7-round cylinder, 1.87-in. bbl., alloy J-frame. Fixed sights. Weight: 11 oz. Made 2010 to date.

MODEL 357 PD............ **NiB $815 Ex $405 Gd $345**
SA/DA. Caliber: .41 Mag. 6-round titanium cylinder, 4-in. bbl., scandium alloy N-frame. HiViz front, adj. rear sights. Weight: 27.5 oz. Ahrends wood grip. Made 2005 to 2007.

Smith & Wesson Model 500

MODEL 357 NIGHTGUARD . . NiB $895 Ex $430 Gd $355
SA/DA. Caliber: .41 Mag. 6-round stainless cylinder, 2.5-in. bbl., alloy N-frame. Fixed sights. Weight: 29.7 oz. Rubber grip. Made 2010 only.

MODEL 360 AIRLITE SC
CHEIFS SPECIAL . . . . NiB $780 Ex $410 Gd $345
SA/DA. Caliber: .357 Mag. 5-round titanium cylinder, 1.87-in. bbl., alloy J-frame. Fixed sights. Weight: 12 oz. Hogue rubber grip. Made 2001 to 2007.
Kit Gun model (3.1-in. bbl.) . . . . NiB $775 Ex $440 Gd $330

MODEL 360 PD AIRLITE SC
CHEIFS SPECIAL . . . . NiB $1020 Ex $400 Gd $345
SA/DA. Caliber: .357 Mag. 5-round titanium cylinder, 1.87-in. bbl., alloy J-frame. Fixed sights. Weight: 12 oz. Hogue rubber grip. Matte grey finish. Made 2002 to date.

MODEL 360 M&P
CHEIFS SPECIAL . . . . NiB $1020 Ex $400 Gd $345
SA/DA. Caliber: .357 Mag. 5-round stainless cylinder, 1.87-in. bbl., scandium alloy J-frame. Fixed sights. Weight: 13.3 oz. Rubber grip. Matte black finish. Made 2007 to 2010.

MODEL 386 AIRLITE SC
MOUNTAIN LITE . . . . NiB $660 Ex $3700 Gd $325
SA/DA. Caliber: .357 Mag. 7-round titanium cylinder, 2.5- or 3.1-in. bbl., scandium alloy L-frame. HiViz front, adj. rear sights. Weight: 18.5 oz. Rubber grip. Matte black finish. Made 2001 to 2007.

MODEL 386 PD-AIRLITE SC . . . NiB $1020 Ex $400 Gd $345
SA/DA. Caliber: .357 Mag. 7-round titanium cylinder, 2.5-in. bbl., scandium alloy L-frame. Adj. sights. Weight: 17.5 oz. Hogue rubber grip. Matte grey finish. Made 2001 to 2005.

MODEL 386 SC/S . . . . NiB $780 Ex $390 Gd $340
SA/DA. Caliber: .357 Mag. 7-round stainless cylinder, 2.5-in. bbl., scandium alloy L-frame. Adj. sights. Weight: 21.2 oz. Made 2007 to 2008.

MODEL 386 NIGHTGUARD . . NiB $750 Ex $460 Gd $410
SA/DA. Caliber: .357 Mag. 7-round stainless cylinder, 2.5-in. bbl., alloy L-frame. Fixed sights. Weight: 24.5 oz. Made 2008 to 2012.

MODEL 386 XL HUNTER
AIRLITE SC. . . . . NiB $795 Ex $430 Gd $380
SA/DA. Caliber: .357 Mag. 7-round stainless cylinder, 6-in. bbl., alloy L-frame. Fixed sights. Weight: 30 oz. Matte black finish. Made 2010 to 2012.

MODEL 396 AIRLITE TI
MOUNTAIN LITE. . . . . NiB $625 Ex $360 Gd $320
SA/DA. Caliber: .44 Spl. 5-round titanium cylinder, 3.1-in. bbl., alloy L-frame. Adj. sights. Weight: 18 oz. Matte grey finish. Made 2001 to 2004.

MODEL 396 NIGHTGUARD. . . NiB $825 Ex $480 Gd $430
SA/DA. Caliber: .44 Spl. 5-round stainless cylinder, 2.5-in. bbl., alloy L-frame. Fixed sights. Weight: 24.2 oz. Made 2008 to 2009.

MODEL 431 AIRWEIGHT . . . . NiB $525 Ex $355 Gd $300
SA/DA. Caliber: .32 H&R Mag. 6-round cylinder, 2-in. bbl., J-frame. Fixed sights. Blued finish. Made 2004 to 2005.

MODEL 431 CENTENNIAL
AIRWEIGHT. . . . . NiB $5505 Ex $380 Gd $310
DAO. Caliber: .32 H&R Mag. 6-round cylinder, 2-in. bbl., J-frame. Fixed sights. Blued finish. Made 2004 to 2005.

MODEL 438 AIRWEIGHT . . . . NiB $525 Ex $355 Gd $300
SA/DA. Caliber: .38 Spl.+P. 5-round cylinder, 1.87-in. bbl., J-frame. Fixed sights. Weight: 15 oz. Matte black finish. Made 2004 to 2005.

MODEL 442 AIRWEIGHT
CENTINNIAL . . . . NiB $470 Ex $220 Gd $180
DAO. Caliber: .38 Spl.+P. 5-round cylinder, 1.87-in. bbl., J-frame. Fixed sights. Weight: 15 oz. Matte black, blued, or nickel finish. Made 1993 to date.
442 Pro Series (moon clips) . . . . NiB $499 Ex $230 Gd $190

MODEL 469 V/XVR . . . . NiB $1370 Ex $700 Gd $600
SA/DA. Caliber: .460 S&W Mag. 5-round cylinder, 5- or 8.5-in. bbl., X-frame. HiViz adj. sights. Matte stainless finish. Made 2005 to date.

MODEL 500
Caliber: .500 S&W Magnum. Uses S&W's largest revolver frame: X-frame. 5-round cylinder, bbl. lengths: 4, 6.5 and 8.38 inches, ported barrel, overall length: 15 inches (8.38-inch bbl.). Weight: 71.9 oz. (8.38-inch bbl.). Interchangeable front sight, micrometer-click adj. rear. Synthetic grip. Satin stainless finish. Made from 2003 to date.
w/6- or 8.38-inch bbl.. . . . . . . NiB $1299 Ex $740 Gd $459
w/4-inch bbl. , add $70
w/ factory HI-VIZ sights (8.38-in. bbl.), add $70

MODEL 520
DA REVOLVER . . . . NiB $556 Ex $410 Gd $321
Caliber: .357 Mag. Six-round cylinder. N-Frame w/4-inch bbl. Weight: 40 oz. Fixed sights. In 1980, 3000 pieces were made for the N.Y. State Police but that agency did not purchase those firearms, so they were sold commercially.

MODEL 547
DA REVOLVER . . . . NiB $816 Ex $709 Gd $499
Caliber: 9mm. Six-round cylinder, bbl. length: 3 or 4 inches, 7.31 inches overall. Weight: 32 oz. Square-notch rear sight, ramp front. Disc. 1986.

**Smith & Wesson
Model 586 Distinguished Combat Magnum**

**Smith & Wesson
Model 625**

**Smith & Wesson
Model 629 Classic**

**Smith & Wesson
Model 629**

MODEL 581 DISTINGUISHED
SERVICE MAGNUM . . . . **NiB $7ˇ50 Ex $520 Gd $420**
SA/DA. Caliber: .357 Mag. 6-round cylinder, 4-in. full lug bbl., L-frame, fixed sights, blued or nickel finish. Made from 1981 to 1992.
Nickel finish, add **$25**

MODEL 586 DISTINGUISHED COMBAT MAGNUM
Caliber: .357 Magnum. Six-round cylinder, bbl. lengths: 4, 6 and 8.38 inches, overall length: 9.75 inches (with 4-inch bbl.). Weight: 42, 46, 53 oz., respectively. Red ramp front sight, micrometer-click adj. rear. Checkered grip. Blued or nickel finish. Made 1980 to 1999.
Model 586 (w/4- or 6-inch bbl.)NiB $691 Ex $479 Gd $345
Model 586 (w/8.63-inch bbl.). . NiB $709 Ex $499 Gd $359
Model 586 (w/adjustable front sight), add **$50**
Model 586 (w/nickel finish), add **$65**

MODEL 610 DA REVOLVER . . . NiB $755 Ex $612 Gd $500
Similar to Model 625 except in caliber .40 S&W/10mm. Magna classic grips. Made from 1990 to 1991 and from 1998 to 2004.

MODEL 610 CLASSIC. . . . . . . NiB $860 Ex $580 Gd $480
SA/DA. Caliber: .40 S&W/10mm. 6-round fluted or unfluted cylinder. 4-, 5- or 6.5-in. full lug bbl. N-frame, Adj. sights, stainless finish. Made from 1990; 1998 to 2005; 2009.
10-round cylinder, add **$80**

MODEL 617 K-22
MASTERPIECE. . . . . **NiB $830 Ex $480 Gd $360**
SA/DA. Caliber: .22 LR. 6- or 10-round cylinder. 4-, 6- or 8.37-in. full lug bbl. K-frame, Adj. sights, matte stainless finish, Hogue rubber grips. Made from 1990 to date.
Semi-target model w/4- or 6-inch
bbl.. **NiB $648 Ex $530 Gd $362**
Target model w/6-inch bbl.. . . . **NiB $648 Ex $530 Gd $362**
Target model w/8.38-inch bbl. . **NiB $615 Ex $485 Gd $332**
w/10-round cylinder, add **$128**

MODEL 619. . . . . **NiB $450 Ex $230 Gd $190**
SA/DA. Caliber: .357 Mag. 7-round cylinder. 5-in. bbl. L-frame, fixed sights, matte stainless finish, rubber grips. Made from 2005 to 2006.

MODEL 620 . . . . NiB $450 Ex $230 Gd $190
SA/DA. Caliber: .357 Mag. 7-round cylinder. 4-in. bbl., L-frame, adj. sights, matte stainless finish, rubber grips. Made from 2005 to 2009.

MODEL 624 . . . . NiB $750 Ex $530 Gd $460
SA/DA. Caliber: .44 Spl. 6-round cylinder. 4- or 6.5-in. bbl., N-frame, adj. sights, matte stainless finish. Made from 1986 to 1987.

MODEL 625 DA REVOLVER . . . NiB $866 Ex $733 Gd $569
Same general specifications as Model 25 except 3-, 4- or 5-inch bbl., round-butt Pachmayr grips and satin stainless steel finish. Made 1989 to 2007.

MODEL 625 JM . . . . NiB $979 Ex $480 Gd $430
SA/DA. Caliber: .45 ACP. 6-round cylinder. 3-, 4- or 5-in. full lug bbl., N-frame, adj. sights, matte stainless finish, made in colaboration with competitive shooter Jerry Miculek. Made from 1988 to date.

**Smith & Wesson
Model 642 Centennial Airweight**

**Smith & Wesson
Model 640**

MODEL 627 DA REVOLVER ... NiB $730 Ex $427 Gd $337
SA/DA. Caliber: .357 Mag. unfluted cylinder, 5.5-in. full lug bbl., N-frame, adj. sights, satin stainless steel finish. Made from 1989 to 2008.

MODEL 627 .... NiB $730 Ex $427 Gd $337
SA/DA. Caliber: .357 Mag. 8-round cylinder. 4-in. bbl., N-frame, adj. sights, satin stainless steel finish. Made from 2008 to 2009.

MODEL 629 DA REVOLVER
Same as Model 29 in .44 Magnum except in stainless steel. Classic made from 1990 to date.
w/ 3-inch bbl.(Backpacker
  model) .... NiB $774 Ex $567 Gd $408
w/4- or 6-inch bbls. .... NiB $774 Ex $567 Gd $408
w/8.38-inch bbl............. NiB $774 Ex $567 Gd $408
Classic model (w/5- or 6.5-inch
  bbl.) .... NiB $829 Ex $581 Gd $444
Classic model (w/8.38-inch
  bbl.) .... NiB $685 Ex $576 Gd $469
Classix DX model (w/6.5-inch
  bbl.) .... NiB $685 Ex $576 Gd $469
Classic DX model (w/8.38-inch
  bbl.) .... NiB $685 Ex $576 Gd $469
Magna Classic model .... NiB $979 Ex $680 Gd $530

MODEL 631 DA REVOLVER
Similar to Model 31 except chambered for .32 H&R Mag. Goncalo Alves combat grips. Made in 1991 to 1992.
Fixed sights, 2-inch bbl. ...... NiB $800 Ex $659 Gd $246
Adjustable sights, 4-inch bbl., add 10%
Lady Smith, 2-inch bbl........ NiB $410 Ex $329 Gd $246
Lady Smith, 2-inch bbl.
  (black stainless). .... NiB $420 Ex $329 Gd $246

MODEL 632 CENTENNIAL DA REVOLVER
Same general specifications as Model 640 except chambered for .32 H&R Mag. 2- or 3-inch bbl., weight: 15.5 oz. Stainless slide w/alloy frame. Fixed sights. Santoprene combat grips. Made 1991 to 1992.
w/2-inch bbl. .... NiB $693 Ex $408 Gd $321
w/3-inch bbl. .... NiB $789 Ex $485 Gd $930

**MODEL 637 CHIEFS SPECIAL AIRWEIGHT
DA REVOLVER .... NiB $485 Ex $357 Gd $289**
Same general specifications as Model 37 except w/clear anodized fuse alloy frame and stainless cylinder. 560 made in 1991 and reintroduced in 1996.

**MODEL 638 BODYGUARD
AIRWEIGHT DA .... NiB $468 Ex $367 Gd $326**
Same general specifications as Model .38 except w/clear anodized fuse alloy frame and stainless cylinder. 1,200 made in 1990 and reintroduced in 1998.

MODEL 640 CENTENNIAL DA .. NiB $648 Ex $398 Gd $326
Caliber: .38 Special. Five-round cylinder, 2, 2.1 or 3-inch bbl., 6.31 inches overall. Weight: 20-22 oz. Fixed sights. Stainless finish. Smooth hardwood service grips. Made 1990 to date.

**MODEL 642 CENTENNIAL AIRWEIGHT
DA Revolver .... NiB $479 Ex $365 Gd $290**
Same general specifications as Model 640 except w/stainless steel/aluminum alloy frame and finish. Weight 15.8 oz. Santoprene combat grips. Made from 1990-93 and reintroduced 1996.
Lady Smith model
  (w/smaller grip) .... NiB $648 Ex $478 Gd $377
2.125-in. bbl. w/ PowerPort (2009-2010), add........ $150
Pro Series w/ full moon clips (intro. 2010), add........ $30

**MODEL 648
DA REVOLVER .... NiB $695 Ex $506 Gd $450**
Same general specifications as Models 17/617 except in stainless and chambered for .22 Mag. Made from 1990 to 1993.
Model 648-2 (2003-2005)..... NiB $660 Ex $500 Gd $390

**MODEL 649 BODYGUARD
DA REVOLVER .... NiB $644 Ex $369 Gd $290**
Caliber: .38 Special. Five-round cylinder, bbl. length: 2 inches, 6.25 inches overall. Weight: 20 oz. Square-notch rear sight ramp front. Stainless frame and finish. Made from 1986 to date.

MODEL 650 . . . . **NiB $856 Ex $680 Gd $525**
Caliber: .22 Mag. Six-round cylinder, 3-inch bbl., 7 inches overall. Weight: 23.5 oz. Serrated ramp front sight, fixed square-notch rear. Round butt, checkered walnut mono-grammed grips. Stainless steel finish. Made 1983 to 1986.

MODEL 651 STAINLESS DA
Caliber: .22 Mag. Rimfire. Six-round cylinder, bbl. length: 3 and 4 inches, 7 and 8.63 inches, respectively, overall. Weight: 24.5 oz. Adj. rear sight, ramp front. Made from 1983 to 1987 and from 1990 to 1998. Note: .22 LR cylinder available during early production.
w/3- or 4-inch bbl. . . . . NiB $561 Ex $366 Gd $345
w/extra cylinder . . . . NiB $862 Ex $386 Gd $365

MODEL 657 REVOLVER
Caliber: 41 Mag. Six-round cylinder. Bbl. lengths: 4, 6 or 8.4 inches; 9.6, 11.4, and 13.9 inches overall. Weight: 44.2, 48 and 52.5 oz. Serrated black ramp front sight on ramp base click rear, adj. for windage and elevation. Satin finished stainless steel. Made from 1986 to 2008.
w/4- or 6-inch bbl. . . . . NiB $601 Ex $433 Gd $398
w/8.4-inch bbl. . . . . NiB $882 Ex $464 Gd $377

MODEL 681 DSM . . . . NiB $464 Ex $329 Gd $255
Same as S&W Model 581 except in stainless finish only. Made 1991 to 1993.

MODEL 686
Same as S&W Model 586 Distinguished Combat Magnum except in stainless finish w/additional 2.5-inch bbl. Made from 1991 to date.
w/2.5-inch bbl. . . . . NiB $639 Ex $434 Gd $332
w/4- or 6-inch bbl. . . . . NiB $639 Ex $434 Gd $332
w/8.63-inch bbl. . . . . NiB $639 Ex $434 Gd $332
Model 686 (w/adjustable
  front sight), add $50

MODEL 686 PLUS
Same as standard Model 686 Magnum except w/7-round cylinder and 2.5-, 4- or 6-inch bbl. Made from 1996 to date.
w/2.5-inch bbl. . . . . NiB $689 Ex $617 Gd $499
w/4-inch bbl. . . . . NiB $704 Ex $595 Gd $408
w/6-inch bbl. . . . . NiB $700 Ex $631 Gd $429

MODEL 696 . . . . NiB $546 Ex $386 Gd $337
Caliber: .44 S&W Special. L-Frame w/five-round cylinder, 3-inch shrouded bbl., 8.38 inches overall. Weight: 48 oz. Red ramp front sight, micrometer-click adj. rear. Checkered synthetic grip. Satin stainless steel. Made from 1997 to 2002.

MODEL 940 CENTENNIAL DA . . **NiB $479 Ex $367 Gd $290**
Same general specifications as Model 640 except chambered for 9mm. Two- or 3-inch bbl., Weight: 23-25 oz. Santoprene combat grips. Made from 1991 to 1998.

MODEL 1891
SA REVOLVER . . . . **NiB $2779 Ex $2465 Gd $2190**
Hinged frame. Caliber: .38 S&W. Five-round cylinder, bbl. lengths: 3.25, 4, 5 and 6-inches. Fixed sights. Blued or nickel finish. Hard rubber grips. Made 1891-1911. Note: Until 1906, an accessory single-shot target bbl. (see Model 1891 Single-Shot Target Pistol) was available for this revolver.
w/extra .22 single-shot bbl. . . NiB $5300 Ex $4220 Gd $3690

Smith & Wesson
Model 696

Smith & Wesson
Model K-22 Outdoorsman

Smith & Wesson
Lady Smith First Model

Smith & Wesson
Lady Smith Second Model

**Smith & Wesson
Regulation Police Target**

**Smith & Wesson
Safety Hammerless**

MODEL 1917 ARMY DA REVOLVER

Caliber: .45 Automatic, using 3-cartridge half-moon clip or .45 Auto Rim, without clip. Six-round cylinder, 5.5-inch bbl., 10.75 inches overall. Weight: 36.25 oz. Fixed sights. Blued finish (blue-black finish on commercial model, brush polish on military). Checkered walnut grips (commercial model, smooth on military). Made under U.S. Government contract 1917-19 and produced commercially 1919-1941. Note: About 175,000 of these revolvers were produced during WW I. The DCM sold these to NRA members during the 1930s at $16.15 each.

Commercial model . . . . NiB $2500 Ex $2168 Gd $1870
Military model . . . . NiB $1860 Ex $1640 Gd $1389

K-22 MASTERPIECE DA . . . NiB $5100 Ex $4390 Gd $2724
Improved version of K-22 Outdoorsman w/same specifications but w/micrometer-click rear sight, short action and antibacklash trigger. Fewer than 1,100 manufactured in 1940.

K-22 OUTDOORSMAN DA NiB $2552 Ex $1906 Gd $1392
Design based on the .38 Military & Police Target. Caliber: .22 LR. Six-round cylinder, 11.13 inches overall. Weight: 35 oz. Adj. target sights. Blued finish. Checkered walnut grip. Made 1931 to 1940.

K-32 AND K-38 HEAVY MASTERPIECES

Same as K32 and K38 Masterpiece but w/heavy bbl. Weight: 38.5 oz. Made 1950-53. Note: All K32 and K38 revolvers made after September 1953 have heavy bbls. and the "Heavy Masterpiece" designation was disc. Values for Heavy Masterpiece models are the same as shown for Models 14 and 16. (See separate listing).

K-32 TARGET

DA REVOLVER . . . . NiB $18,600 Ex $15,400 Gd $9900
Same as .38 Military & Police Target except chambered for .32 S&W Long cartridge, slightly heavier bbl., weight: 34 oz. Only 98 produced. Made from 1938 to 1940.

LADY SMITH (MODEL M HAND EJECTOR) DA REVOLVER

Caliber: .22 LR. Seven-round cylinder, bbl. length: 2.25-, 3-, 3.5- and 6-inch (Third Model only), approximately 7 inches overall w/3.5-inch bbl., weight: About 9.5 oz. Fixed sights, adj. target sights available on Third Model. Blued or nickel finish. Round butt, hard rubber grips on First and Second models; checkered walnut or hard rubber square buttgrips on Third Model. First Model —1902-06: Cylinder locking bolt operated by button on left side of frame, no bbl., lug and front locking bolt. Second Model —1906-11: Rear cylinder latch eliminated, has bbl. lug, forward cylinder lock w/draw-bolt fastening. Third Model —1911-21: Same as Second Model except has square grips, target sights and 6-inch bbl. available. Note: Legend has it that a straight-laced D.B. Wesson ordered discontinuance of the Lady Smith when he learned of the little revolver's reputed popularity w/ladies of the evening. The story, which undoubtedly has enhanced the appeal of this model to collectors, is not true: The Lady Smith was disc. because of difficulty of manufacture and high frequency of repairs.

First model . . . . NiB $3140 Ex $2130 Gd $1696
Second model . . . . NiB $2315 Ex $1779 Gd $1015
Third model, w/fixed sights,
   2.25- or 3.5-inch bbl. . . NiB $2315 Ex $1779 Gd $1015
Third model, w/fixed sights,
   6-inch bbl. . . . . NiB $2315 Ex $1779 Gd $1015
Third model, w/adj. sights,
   6-inch bbl. . . . . NiB $2215 Ex $1888 Gd $934

REGULATION POLICE

DA (I Frame) . . . . NiB $811 Ex $602 Gd $434
Calibers: .32 S&W (6-round) or .38 S&W (5-round) built on .32 Hand Ejector frames. Two-, 3-, 3.25-, 4-, 4.25- or 6-inch bbl., weight: 20-24 oz. Fixed sights. Blue or nickel finish. Checkered walnut grips. Made 1917-57. Note: After 1957 "J" Frames replaced the older "I" Frames and designations changed to Model 31 and 33 respectively.

Regulation Police, .32 S&W . . NiB $1097 Ex $920 Gd $599
Regulation Police, .38 S&W . . NiB $1097 Ex $920 Gd $599

REGULATION POLICE TARGET DA

Target version of the Regulation Police w/standard features of that model. Calibers: .32 S&W Long or .38 S&W. 6-inch bbl., 10.25 inches overall. Weight: 20 oz. Adjustable target sights. Blue or nickel finish. Checkered walnut grips. Made from about 1917 to 1957.

Regulation Police Target,
  .32 S&W . . . . NiB $2600 Ex $2470 Gd $780
Regulation Police Target,
  .38 S&W (pre-war) . . . . . . NiB $3000 Ex $2855 Gd $900

SAFETY HAMMERLESS . . . . NiB $1396 Ex $1178 Gd $1024
Also called New Departure Double Action. Hinged frame. Calibers: .32 S&W, .38 S&W. Five-round cylinder, bbl. lengths: 2, 3- and 3.5-inch (.32 cal.) or 2-, 3.25-, 4-, 5- and 6-inch (.38 cal.); 6.75 inches overall (.32 cal. w/3-inch bbl.) or 7.5 inches (.38 cal. w/3.25-inch bbl.). Weight: 14.25 oz. (.32 cal. w/3-inch bbl.) or 18.25 oz. (.38 cal. 2.5-inch bbl.). Fixed sights. Blued or nickel finish. Hard rubber grips. Made from 1888 to 1937 (.32 cal.); 1887 to 1941 (.38 cal. w/various minor changes.)

TEXAS RANGER

COMMEMORATIVE . . . . NiB $658 Ex $359 Gd $270
Issued to honor the 150th anniversary of the TExas Rangers. Model 19 .357 Combat Magnum w/4-inch bbl., sideplate stamped w/TExas Ranger Commemorative Seal, smooth Goncalo Alves grips. Special Bowie knife in presentation case. 8,000 sets made in 1973. Top value is for set in new condition.

**Sphinx
Model AT2000S w/optional
scope**

SPHINX ENGINEERING S.A. — Matten b. Interlaken, Switzerland

MODEL AT-380 DA PISTOL
Caliber: .380 ACP. 10-round magazine, 3.27- inch bbl., 6.03 inches overall. Weight: 25 oz. Stainless steel frame w/blued slide or Palladium finish. Slide latch w/ambidExtrous magazine release. Imported from 1993 to 1996.
Two-tone (w/blued slide) . . . . . NiB $474 Ex $336 Gd $240
w/Palladium finish . . . . NiB $561 Ex $431 Gd $336

NOTE: *The AT-88 pistol series was previously manufactured by ITM in Switzerland and imported by Action Arms before Sphinx-Muller resumed production of these firearms, now designated as the AT-2000 series.*

MODEL 2000S DA AUTOMATIC PISTOL
Calibers: 9mm Parabellum, .40 S&W. 15- or 11-round magazine respectively, 4.53-inch bbl., (S-standard), 3.66-inch bbl., (P-compact), 3.34-inch bbl., (H-subcompact), 8.25 inches overall. Weight: 36.5 oz. Fixed sights w/3-dot system. Stainless frame w/blued slide or Palladium finish. AmbidExtrous safety. Checkered walnut or neoprene grips. Imported 1993 to 1996.
Standard model. . . . . NiB $990 Ex $903 Gd $581
Compact model . . . . NiB $890 Ex $755 Gd $536
Sub-compact model . . . . NiB $890 Ex $755 Gd $536
.40 S&W, add $50
Palladium finish, add. $100

MODEL AT2000C/2000CS COMPETITOR
Similar to the Model AT2000S except also chambered for 9x21mm. 10-round magazine, 5.31-inch compensated bbl., 9.84 inches overall. Weight: 40.56 oz. Fully adjustable BoMar or ProPoint sights. Made 1993 to 1996.
w/Bomar sight . . . . NiB $1844 Ex $1599 Gd $1418
w/ProPoint sight . . . . NiB $2254 Ex $1923 Gd $1690

MODEL AT2000GM/GMS GRAND MASTER
Similar to the AT2000C except single action only w/square trigger guard and Extended beavertail grip. Imported 1993-96.
w/BoMar sight . . . . NiB $1872 Ex $1624 Gd $1375
w/ProPoint sight . . . . NiB $2179 Ex $1919 Gd $1699

**Springfield Armory
1911-A1 Post '90 Series Trophy Model**

**Springfield Armory
1911-A1 PDP Series Defender**

**Springfield Armory
1911-A1 Champion**

**Springfield Armory
1911-A1 Compact**

SPRINGFIELD ARMORY — Geneseo, Illinois

Formerly U.S. Government run Springfield Armory in Springfield, Massachusetts. Springfield Armory name purchased in 1974 for commercial/civilian manufacturing.

MODEL M1911 SERIES AUTO PISTOL

Springfield builds the "PDP" (Personal Defense Pistol) Series based on the self-loading M 1911-A1 pistol (military specifications model) as adopted for a standard service weapon by the U.S. Army. With enhancements and modifications they produce a full line of firearms including Ultra-Compacts, Lightweights, Match Grade and Competition Models. For values see specific models.

MODEL 1911-A1 GOVERNMENT

Calibers: 9mm Para., .38 Super, .40 S&W, 10mm or .45 ACP., 7-, 8-, 9- or 10-round magazine, 4- or 5-inch bbl., 8.5 inches overall. Weight: 36 oz. Fixed combat sights. Blued, Parkerized or Duo-Tone finish. Checkered walnut grips. Note: This is an Exact duplicate of the Colt M1911-A1 that was used by the U.S. Armed Forces as a service weapon.

Blued finish . . . . NiB $453 Ex $347 Gd $265
Parkerized finish . . . . NiB $453 Ex $347 Gd $265

MODEL 1911-A1 (PRE '90 SERIES)

Calibers: 9mm Parabellum, .38 Super, 10mm, .45 ACP. Seven-, 8-, 9- or 10-round magazine, bbl. length: 3.63, 4, 4.25 or 5 inches, 8.5 inches overall. Weight: 36 oz. Fixed combat sights. Blued, Duo-Tone or Parkerized finish. Checkered walnut stocks. Made 1985 to 1990.

Government model (blued) . . . . NiB $453 Ex $347 Gd $265
Government model
  (Parkerized) . . . . NiB $621 Ex $436 Gd $362
Bullseye model (wadcutter) . . NiB $1474 Ex $1345 Gd $866
Combat Commander model
  (blued) . . . . NiB $474 Ex $386 Gd $321
Combat Commander model
  (Parkerized) . . . . NiB $650 Ex $475 Gd $353
Commander model (blued) . . . . NiB $479 Ex $306 Gd $219
Commander model (Duo-Tone) . . NiB $567 Ex $473 Gd $397
Commander model (Parkerized) . . NiB $650 Ex $536 Gd $386
Compact model (blued) . . . . . NiB $ 470 Ex $347 Gd $265
Compact model (Duo-Tone) . . . NiB $559 Ex $500 Gd $434
Compact model (Parkerized) . . NiB $668 Ex $500 Gd $342
Defender model (blued) . . . . . . NiB $546 Ex $434 Gd $290
Defender model (Parkerized) . . NiB $704 Ex $556 Gd $377
Defender model
  (Custom Carry) . . . . NiB $540 Ex $429 Gd $326
National Match model
  (Hardball) . . . . NiB $829 Ex $709 Gd $546
Trophy Master (Competition) . . NiB $1355 Ex $1265 Gd $918
Trophy Master
  (Distinguished) . . . . NiB $2152 Ex $2030 Gd $1234
Trophy Master (Expert) . . . . NiB $1723 Ex $1528 Gd $1322

MODEL 1911-A1 (CUSTOM LOADED SERIES)

1911 style operating system w/steel or alloy frame. Calibers: 9mm Parabellum, .38 Super, .40 S&W, 10mm, .45 ACP. Seven-, 8-, 9- or 10-round magazine, bbl. length: 3.63, 4, 4.25 or 5 inches; 8.5 inches overall. Weight: 28 oz. to 36 oz. Fixed combat sights. Blued, Duo-Tone, Parkerized or stainless finish. Checkered composition or walnut stocks. Made 1990 to 1998.

Mil-Spec model (blued) . . . . . . NiB $595 Ex $419 Gd $340
Mil-Spec model (Parkerized) . . . NiB $809 Ex $644 Gd $444

Standard model (blued) . . . . . . NiB $879 Ex $689 Gd $499
Standard model (Parkerized) . . NiB $1068 Ex $998 Gd $826
Standard model (stainless) . . . . NiB $806 Ex $699 Gd $497
Trophy model (blued) . . . . . . NiB $1440 Ex $1240 Gd $989
Trophy model (Hi-Tone) . . . NiB $1437 Ex $1245 Gd $1029
Trophy model (stainless) . . . . . . NiB $709 Ex $577 Gd $429

MODEL 1911-A1 PDP SERIES

PDP Series (Personal Defense Pistol). Calibers: .38 Super, .40 S&W, .45 ACP. Seven-, 8-, 9-, 10-, 13- or 17-round magazine, bbl. length: 4, 5, 5.5 or 5.63 inches, 9 to 11 inches overall w/ compensated bbl. Weight: 34.5 oz. to 42.8 oz. Post front sight, adjustable rear w/3-dot system. Blued, Duo-Tone, Parkerized or stainless finish. Checkered composition or walnut stocks. Made from 1991 to 1998.

Defender model (blued) . . . . . . NiB $910 Ex $780 Gd $586
Defender model (Duo-Tone) . . . NiB $910 Ex $780 Gd $586
Defender model (Parkerized) . . NiB $910 Ex $780 Gd $586
.45 ACP Champion Comp
  (blued) . . . . NiB $780 Ex $562 Gd $431
.45 ACP Compact Comp HC
  (blued) . . . . NiB $602 Ex $453 Gd $398
.380 Sup Factory Comp (blued) . . NiB $740 Ex $546 Gd $431
.45 ACP Factory Comp (blued) NiB $866 Ex $780 Gd $544
.380 Sup Factory Comp HC
  (blued) . . . . NiB $740 Ex $546 Gd $398
.45 ACP Factory Comp HC
  (blued) . . . . NiB $733 Ex $789 Gd $556

MODEL M1911-A1 CHAMPION

Calibers: .380 ACP, 9mm Para., .45 ACP. Six- or 7-round magazine, 4-inch bbl. Weight: 26.5 to 33.4 oz. Low profile post front sight and drift adjustable rear w/3-dot sighting system. Commander-style hammer and slide. Checkered walnut grips. Blue, Bi-Tone, Parkerized or stainless finish. Made from 1992 to 2002.

.380 ACP standard
  (disc. 1995) . . . . NiB $850 Ex $807 Gd $479
.45 ACP (parkerized or blued) . . NiB $700 Ex $665 Gd $480
.45 ACP (Bi-Tone) (B/H Model) . . NiB $912 Ex $790 Gd $386
.45 ACP (stainless) . . . . NiB $742 Ex $707 Gd $522
.45 ACP Super Tuned (1997-1999) . . NiB $850 Ex $807 Gd $479

MODEL M1911-A1 COMPACT

Similar to the standard M1911 w/champion length slide on a steel or alloy frame w/a shortened grip. Caliber: .45 ACP. Six- or 7-round magazine (10+ law enforcement only), 4-inch bbl. weight: 26.5 to 32 oz. Low profile sights w/3-dot system. Checkered walnut grips. Matte blue, Duo-Tone or Parkerized finish. Made 1991 to 1996.

Compact (Parkerized) . . . . NiB $464 Ex $380 Gd $290
Compact (blued) . . . . NiB $464 Ex $380 Gd $290
Compact (Duo-Tone) . . . . NiB $577 Ex $500 Gd $434
Compact (stainless) . . . . NiB $556 Ex $376 Gd $270
Compact Comp (ported) . . . . . . NiB $882 Ex $792 Gd $587
High capacity (blued) . . . . NiB $595 Ex $369 Gd $321
High capacity (stainless) . . . . . . NiB $831 Ex $638 Gd $499

MODEL M1911-A1 ULTRA COMPACT

Similar to M1911 Compact except chambered for .380 ACP or .45 ACP. 6- or 7-round magazine, 3.5-inch bbl., weight: 22 oz. to 30 oz. Matte Blue, Bi-Tone, Parkerized (military specs) or stainless finish. Made from 1995 to 2003.

.380 ACP Ultra (disc. 1996) . . . NiB $740 Ex $585 Gd $388
.45 ACP Ultra (Parkerized
  or blued) . . . . NiB $740 Ex $585 Gd $388

**Springfield Armory
M1911-A1 Ultra
Compact Parkerized**

**Springfield Armory
M1911-A1 Ultra Compact Bi-Tone**

**Springfield Armory
P9 Combat**

**Springfield Armory
M1911-A1 Ultra Compact Stainless**

Springfield Armory Panther

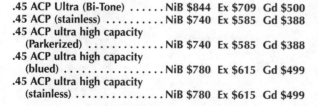

.45 ACP Ultra (Bi-Tone) . . . . . . NiB $844 Ex $709 Gd $500
.45 ACP (stainless) . . . . NiB $740 Ex $585 Gd $388
.45 ACP ultra high capacity
(Parkerized) . . . . NiB $740 Ex $585 Gd $388
.45 ACP ultra high capacity
(blued) . . . . NiB $780 Ex $615 Gd $499
.45 ACP ultra high capacity
(stainless) . . . . NiB $780 Ex $615 Gd $499

.45 ACP V10 ultra comp
(Parkerized) . . . . NiB $979 Ex $806 Gd $495
.45 ACP V10 ultra comp
(blued) . . . . NiB $979 Ex $806 Gd $495
.45 ACP V10 ultra comp
(stainless) . . . . NiB $979 Ex $806 Gd $495
.45 ACP V10 ultra (super
tuned) . . . . NiB $1090 Ex $974 Gd $577

**MODEL 1911-A1 TRP (TACITCAL RESPONSE PISTOL)
OPERATOR**
SA AUTO PISTOL . . . . NiB $1620 Ex $1460 Gd $780
1911 style operating system w/steel frame. Caliber: .45 ACP.
Seven-round magazine, bbl. length: 5 inches; 8.5 inches over-
all. Weight: 36 oz. Fixed combat sights. Black Armory Kote
or stainless finish. Checkered front strap, composition stocks.
Made from 2008 to date.

MODEL 1911-A1 LONG SLIDE CUSTOM LOADED
SA AUTO PISTOL . . . . NiB $1100 Ex $960 Gd $480
1911 style operating system w/steel frame. Caliber: .45 ACP
or .45 Super. Seven-round magazine, bbl. length: 6 inches;

8.5 inches overall. Weight: 36 oz. Fixed combat sights. Black Armory Kote or stainless finish. Checkered wood stocks. Made from 2001 to 2012.

FIRECAT AUTOMATIC PISTOL
Calibers: 9mm, .40 S&W. Eight-round magazine (9mm) or 7-round magazine (.40 S&W), 3.5-inch bbl., 6.5 inches overall. Weight: 25.75 oz. Fixed sights w/3-dot system. Checkered walnut grip. Matte blued finish. Made from 1991 to 1993.

9mm . . . . .NiB $556 Ex $408 Gd $289
.40 S&W . . . . .NiB $556 Ex $408 Gd $289

PANTHER AUTO PISTOL . . . . .NiB $606 Ex $453 Gd $346
Calibers: 9mm, .40 S&W. 15-round magazine (9mm) or 11-round magazine (.40 S&W), 3.8-inch bbl., 7.5 inches overall. Weight: 28.95 oz. Blade front sight, rear adj. for windage w/3-dot system. Checkered walnut grip. Matte blued finish. Made from 1991 to 1993.

MODEL P9 DA COMBAT SERIES
Calibers: 9mm, .40 S&W, .45 ACP. Magazine capacity: 15-round (9mm), 11-round (.40 S&W) or 10-round (.45 ACP), 3.66-inch bbl., (Compact and Sub-Compact), or 4.75-inch bbl., (Standard), 7.25 or 8.1 inches overall. Weight: 32 to 35 oz. Fixed sights w/3-dot system. Checkered walnut grip. Matte blued, Parkerized, stainless or Duo-Tone finish. Made from 1990 to 1994.

Compact model (9mm,
   Parkerized) . . . . .NiB $464 Ex $342 Gd $279
Sub-Compact model (9mm,
   Parkerized) . . . . .NiB $433 Ex $309 Gd $235
Standard model (9mm,
   Parkerized) . . . . .NiB $498 Ex $377 Gd $304
w/blued finish, add $50
w/Duo-Tone finish, add $100
w/stainless finish, add $128
.40 S&W, add $35
.45 ACP add $50

MODEL P9 COMPETITION SERIES
Same general specifications as Model P9 except in target configuration w/5-inch bbl., (LSP Ultra) or 5.25-inch bbl. Factory Comp model w/dual port compensator system, Extended safety and magazine release.

Factory Comp model
   (9mm Bi-Tone) . . . . .NiB $648 Ex $444 Gd $337
Factory Comp model
   (9mm stainless) . . . . .NiB $733 Ex $431 Gd $281
IPSC Ultra model
   (9mm Bi-Tone) . . . . .NiB $689 Ex $431 Gd $270
LSP Ultra model
   (9mm stainless) . . . . .NiB $785 Ex $580 Gd $425
.40 S&W, .45 ACP: add $128

XD SERIES
Based on HS 2000 pistol manufactured in Croatia. Striker fired. Calibers: 9mm, .357 SIG, .40 S&W, .45 ACP or .45 G.A.P. Polymer frame. 9-, 10-, 12- or 15-rnd. magazine depending on caliber. Matte black or bi-tone finish. Imported 2002 to date.

5-in. bbl. NiB $599 Ex $400 Gd $270
4-in. bbl. NiB $580 Ex $370 Gd $240
3-in. bbl. NiB $550 Ex $370 Gd $240

XD(M) Series. . . . . .NiB $697 Ex $470 Gd $320
Similar to XD series except w/modular backstraps, diagonal slide serrations. Striker fired. Calibers: 9mm, .40 S&W, or .45

ACP. Bbl. lengths: 3.8- or 4.5-in. Made 2008 to date.
Compact . . . . .NiB $700 Ex $470 Gd $320
Competition . . . . .NiB $780 Ex $550 Gd $350

STALLARD ARMS — Mansfield, Ohio
See listings under Hi-Point.

STAR — Eibar, Spain
Manufactured by Star, Bonifacio Echeverria, S.A.

MODEL 30M DA AUTO PISTOL NiB $431 Ex $288 Gd $189
Caliber: 9mm Para. 15-round magazine, 4.38-inch bbl., 8 inches overall. Weight: 40 oz. Steel frame w/combat features. Adj. sights. Checkered composition grips. Blued finish. Made from 1984 to 1991.

MODEL 30PK DA AUTO PISTOL NiB $431 Ex $288 Gd $189
Same gen. specifications as Star Model 30M except 3.8-inch bbl., weight: 30 oz. Alloy frame. Made from 1984 to 1989.

MODEL 31P DA AUTO PISTOL
Same general specifications as Model 30M except removable backstrap houses complete firing mechanism. Weight: 39.4 oz. Made from 1990 to 1994.
Blued finish. . . . . .NiB $431 Ex $288 Gd $189
Starvel finish, add $50

MODEL 31 PK DA AUTO PISTOL . . . NiB $431 Ex $288 Gd $189
Same general specifications as Model 31P except w/alloy frame. Weight: 30 oz. Made from 1990 to 1997.

Star Model 30M

Star Model 30PK

Star Model AS

Star Model BKS

Star Model F

**Star Model F
Olympic Rapid-Fire**

MODEL A AUTOMATIC PISTOL . . **NiB $365 Ex $259 Gd $169**
Modification of the Colt Government Model .45 Auto, which it closely resembles, but lacks grip safety. Caliber: .38 Super. Eight-round magazine, 5-inch bbl., 8 inches overall. Weight: 35 oz. Fixed sights. Blued finish. Checkered grips. Made from 1934-97. (No longer imported.)

MODELS AS, BS, PS . . . . **NiB $500 Ex $380 Gd $279**
Same as Models A, B and P except have magazine safety. Made in 1975.

MODEL B . . . . **NiB $498 Ex $365 Gd $259**
Same as Model A except in 9mm Para. Made 1934 to 1975.

MODEL BKM . . . . **NiB $398 Ex $306 Gd $225**
Similar to Model BM except has aluminum frame weight: 25.6 oz. Made from 1976 to 1992.

**MODEL BKS STARLIGHT
AUTOMATIC PISTOL** . . . . **NiB $431 Ex $279 Gd $209**
Light alloy frame. Caliber: 9mm Para. Eight-round magazine, 4.25-inch bbl., 7 inches overall. Weight: 25 oz. Fixed sights. Blued or chrome finish. Plastic grips. Made from 1970 to 1981.

MODEL BM AUTOMATIC PISTOL
Caliber: 9mm. Eight-round magazine, 3.9-inch bbl., 6.95 inches overall. Weight: 34.5 oz. Fixed sights. Checkered walnut grips. Blued or Starvel finish. Made from 1976 to 1992.
Blued finish. . . . . **NiB $367 Ex $279 Gd $220**
Starvel finish. . . . . **NiB $380 Ex $304 Gd $240**

**MODEL CO POCKET
AUTOMATIC PISTOL** . . . . **NiB $316 Ex $217 Gd $126**
Caliber: .25 Automatic (6.35mm), 2.75-inch bbl., 4.5 inches overall. Weight: 13 oz. Fixed sights. Blued finish. Plastic grips. Made from 1941 to 197.

**MODEL CU STARLET
POCKET PISTOL** . . . . **NiB $291 Ex $198 Gd $124**
Light alloy frame. Caliber: .25 Auto (6.35mm). Eight-round magazine, 2.38-inch bbl., 4.75 inches overall. Weight: 10.5 oz. Fixed sights. Blued or chrome-plated slide w/frame anodized in black, blue, green, gray or gold. Plastic grips. Made from 1957 to 1997. (U.S. importation disc. 1968.)

**MODEL F
AUTOMATIC PISTOL** . . . . **NiB $362 Ex $268 Gd $130**
Caliber: .22 LR. 10-round magazine, 4.5-inch bbl., 7.5 inches overall. Weight: 25 oz. Fixed sights. Blued finish. Plastic grips. Made from 1942 to 1967.

**MODEL F
OLYMPIC RAPID-FIRE** . . . . **NiB $556 Ex $408 Gd $230**
Caliber: .22 Short. Nine-round magazine, 7-inch bbl., 11.06 inches overall. Weight: 52 oz. w/weights. Adj. target sight. Adj. 3-piece bbl. weight. Aluminum alloy slide. Muzzle brake. Plastic grips. Made from 1942 to 1967.

MODEL FM. . . . . **NiB $362 Ex $279 Gd $171**
Similar to Model FR except has heavier frame w/web in front of trigger guard, 4.25-inch heavy bbl., Weight: 32 oz. Made from 1972 to 1991.

MODEL FR . . . . **NiB $362 Ex $279 Gd $171**
Similar to Model F w/same general specifications but restyled, has slide stop and adj. rear sight. Made from 1967 to 1972.

Star Model FS

**Star
Model M Military**

**Star
Model PD**

MODEL FR SPORT . . . . NiB $398 Ex $306 Gd $229
Same as Model FR except has 6-inch bbl., weight: 28 oz. Also avail. in chrome finish. Made from 1967 to 1991.

MODEL FS . . . . NiB $362 Ex $309 Gd $165
Same as regular Model F but w/6-inch bbl. and adj. sights. Weight: 27 oz. Made from 1942 to 1967.

**MODEL HK LANCER
AUTOMATIC PISTOL**. . . . . NiB $319 Ex $225 Gd $249
Similar to Starfire w/same general specifications except .22 LR. Made from 1955 to 1968.

**MODEL HN
AUTOMATIC PISTOL** . . . . NiB $431 Ex $279 Gd $220
Caliber: .380 Auto (9mm Short). Six-round magazine, 2.75-inch bbl., 5.56 inches overall. Weight: 20 oz. Fixed sights. Blued finish. Plastic grips. Made from 1934 to 1941.

MODEL H . . . . NiB $357 Ex $281 Gd $165
Same as Model HN except .32 Auto (7.65mm), 7-round magazine, weight: 20 oz. Made from 1934 to 1941.

**MODEL I
AUTOMATIC PISTOL** . . . . NiB $398 Ex $302 Gd $177
Caliber: .32 Auto (7.65mm). Nine-round magazine, 4.81-inch bbl., 7.5 inches overall. Weight: 24 oz. Fixed sights. Blued finish. Plastic grips. Made from 1934 to 1936.

MODEL IN. . . . . NiB $434 Ex $290 Gd $175
Same as Model I except caliber .380 Auto (9mm Short), 8-round magazine, weight: 24.5 oz. Made from 1934-36.

**MODEL M MILITARY
AUTOMATIC PISTOL** . . . . NiB $398 Ex $337 Gd $219
Modification of the Model M without grip safety. Calibers: 9mm Bergmann (Largo), .45 ACP, 9mm Para. Eight-round magazine except 7-shot in .45 caliber, 5-inch bbl., 8.5 inches overall. Weight: 36 oz. Fixed sights. Blued finish. Checkered grips. Made from 1934 to 1939.

MODELS M40, M43, M45 FIRESTAR AUTO PISTOLS
Calibers: 9mm, .40 S&W, .45 ACP. Seven-round magazine (9mm) or 6-round (other calibers). 3.4-inch bbl., 6.5 inches overall. Weight: 30.35 oz. Blade front sight, adj. rear w/3-dot system. Checkered rubber grips. Blued or Starvel finish. Made 1990 to 1997.
M40 blued (.40 S&W) . . . . NiB $367 Ex $289 Gd $232
M40 Starvel (.40 S&W) . . . . . . NiB $398 Ex $304 Gd $239
M43 blued (9mm) . . . . NiB $365 Ex $294 Gd $237
M43 Starvel (9mm) . . . . NiB $398 Ex $304 Gd $239
M45 blued (.45 ACP) . . . . NiB $357 Ex $270 Gd $120
M45 Starvel (.45 ACP) . . . . . . NiB $377 Ex $290 Gd $143

MEGASTAR AUTOMATIC PISTOL
Calibers: 10mm, .45 ACP. 12-round magazine, 4.6-inch bbl., 8.44 inches overall. Weight: 47.6 oz. Blade front sight, adj. rear. Checkered composition grip. finishes: Blued or Starvel. Made from 1992 to 1997.
Blued finish, 10mm or .45 ACP . . . NiB $500 Ex $397 Gd $274
Starvel finish, 10mm or .45 ACP . . . NiB $544 Ex $416 Gd $305

MODEL P . . . . NiB $464 Ex $345 Gd $283
Same as Model A except caliber .45 Auto, has 7-round magazine. Made from 1934 to 1975.

MODEL PD AUTOMATIC PISTOL
Caliber: .45 Auto. Six-round magazine, 3.75-inch bbl., 7 inches overall. Weight: 25 oz. Adj. rear sight, ramp front. Blued or Starvel finish. Checkered walnut grips. Made from 1975 to 1992.
Blued finish. . . . . NiB $398 Ex $304 Gd $224
Starvel finish . . . . NiB $422 Ex $342 Gd $270

MODEL S . . . . NiB $319 Ex $220 Gd $159
Same as Model SI except caliber .380 Auto (9mm), 7-round magazine, weight: 19 oz. Made from 1941 to 1965.

MODEL SI

AUTOMATIC PISTOL . . . . **NiB $316 Ex $225 Gd $130**
Reduced-size modification of the Colt Government Model .45 Auto, lacks grip safety. Caliber: .32 Auto (7.65mm). Eight-round magazine, 4-inch bbl., 6.5 inches overall. Weight: 20 oz. Fixed sights. Blued finish. Plastic grips. Made from 1941 to 1965.

STARFIRE DK

AUTOMATIC PISTOL . . . . **NiB $453 Ex $337 Gd $255**
Light alloy frame. Caliber: .380 Automatic (9mm Short). Seven-round magazine, 3.13-inch bbl.. 5.5 inches overall. Weight: 14.5 oz. Fixed sights. Blued or chrome-plated slide w/frame anodized in black, blue, green, gray or gold. Plastic grips. Made 1957-97. U.S. importation disc. 1968.

MODEL SUPER A

AUTOMATIC PISTOL . . . . **NiB $499 Ex $431 Gd $220**
Caliber: .38 Super. Improved version of Model A but has disarming bolt permitting easier takedown, cartridge indicator, magazine safety, take-down magazine, improved sights w/luminous spots for aiming in darkness. This is the standard service pistol of the Spanish Armed Forces, adopted 1946.

MODEL SUPER B AUTOMATIC PISTOL

Caliber: 9mm Para. Similar to Model B except w/improvements described under Model Super A. Made 1946 to 1990.
Super blued finish . . . . **NiB $453 Ex $342 Gd $225**
Starvel finish . . . . **NiB $456 Ex $366 Gd $249**

MODELS SUPER M, SUPER P . . **NiB $852 Ex $685 Gd $478**
Calibers: .45 ACP, 9mm Parabellum or 9mm Largo, (Super M) and 9mm Parabellum (Super P). Improved versions of the Models M & P w/same general specifications, but has disarming bolt permitting easier takedown, cartridge indicator, magazine safety, take-down magazine, improved sights w/luminous spots for aiming in darkness.

MODELS SUPER SI, SUPER S . . **NiB $332 Ex $239 Gd $274**
Same general specifications as the regular Model SI and S except w/improvements described under Super Star. Made 1946 to 1972.

MODEL SUPER SM . . . . **NiB $398 Ex $386 Gd $204**
Similar to Model Super S except has adj. rear sight, wood grips. Made from 1973 to 1981.

SUPER TARGET MODEL . . . **NiB $1595 Ex $1396 Gd $1309**
Same as Super Star model except w/adj. target sight. (Disc.)

ULTRASTAR DA

AUTOMATIC PISTOL . . . . **NiB $365 Ex $290 Gd $200**
Calibers: 9mm Parabellum or .40 S&W. Nine-round magazine, 3.57-inch bbl., 7 inches overall. Weight: 26 oz. Blade front, adjustable rear w/3-dot system. Polymer frame. Blue metal finish. Checkered black polymer grips. Imported from 1994 to 1997.

STENDA-WERKE — Suhl, Germany

POCKET AUTOMATIC PISTOL . **NiB $337 Ex $279 Gd $160**
Essentially the same as the Beholla (see listing of that pistol for specifications). Made circa 1920-.25. Note: This pistol may be marked "Beholla" along w/the Stenda name and address.

**Sterling
Model 283 Target 300**

**Sterling
Model 284 Target 300L**

**Sterling
Model 285 Husky**

**Sterling
Model 286 Trapper**

**Sterling
Model 300**

**Sterling Model
400**

MODEL 287 PPL-.380
AUTOMATIC PISTOL . . . .**NiB $179 Ex $115 Gd $90**
Caliber: .380 Auto. Six-round magazine, 1-inch bbl., 5.38 inches overall. Weight: 22.5 oz. Fixed sights. Blued finish. Plastic grips. Made from 1971 to 1972.

MODEL 300
AUTOMATIC PISTOL . . . .**NiB $150 Ex $90 Gd $75**
Caliber: .25 Auto. Six-round magazine, 2.33-inch bbl., 4.5 inches overall. Weight: 13 oz. Fixed sights. Blued or nickel finish. Plastic grips. Made from 1972 to 1983.

MODEL 300S . . . .**NiB $179 Ex $115 Gd $90**
Same as Model 300 except in stainless steel. Made 1976-83.

MODEL 302 . . . .**NiB $179 Ex $115 Gd $90**
Same as Model 300 except in .22 LR. Made 1973 to 1983.

MODEL 302S . . . .**NiB $179 Ex $115 Gd $90**
Same as Model 302 except in stainless steel. Made 1976-83.

MODEL 400 DA
AUTOMATIC PISTOL . . . .**NiB $309 Ex $214 Gd $129**
Caliber: .380 Auto. Seven-round magazine, 3.5-inch bbl., 6.5 inches overall. Weight: 24 oz. Adj. rear sight. Blued or nickel finish. Checkered walnut grips. Made from 1975 to 1983.

MODEL 400S . . . .**NiB $309 Ex $214 Gd $129**
Same as Model 400 except stainless steel. Made1977-83.

MODEL 450 DA AUTO PISTOL . .**NiB $309 Ex $214 Gd $129**
Caliber: .45 Auto. Eight-round magazine, 4-inch bbl., 7.5 inches overall. Weight: 36 oz. Adj. rear sight. Blued finish. Smooth walnut grips. Made from 1977 to 1983.

MODEL PPL-22
AUTOMATIC PISTOL . . . .**NiB $309 Ex $214 Gd $129**
Caliber: .22 LR. 10-round magazine, 1-inch bbl., 5.5 inches overall. Weight: About 24 oz. Fixed sights. Blued finish. Wood grips. Only 382 made in 1970 to 1971.

STERLING ARMS CORPORATION —
Gasport, New York

MODEL 283 TARGET 300
AUTO PISTOL. . . . .**NiB $189 Ex $109 Gd $90**
Caliber: .22 LR. 10-round magazine, bbl. lengths: 4.5-, 6- 8-inch. 9 inches overall w/4.5-inch bbl., Weight: 36 oz. w/4.52-inch bbl. Adj. sights. Blued finish. Plastic grips. Made from 1970 to 1971.

MODEL 284 TARGET 300L . . . . .**NiB $179 Ex $115 Gd $90**
Same as Model 283 except has 4.5- or 6-inch Luger-type bbl. Made from 1970 to 1971.

MODEL 285 HUSKY. . . . .**NiB $179 Ex $115 Gd $90**
Same as Model 283 except has fixed sights, 4.5-inch bbl only. Made from 1970 to 1971.

MODEL 286 TRAPPER . . . .**NiB $129 Ex $115 Gd $90**
Same as Model 284 except w/fixed sights. Made 1970-71.

J. STEVENS ARMS & TOOL CO. —
Chicopee Falls, Massachusetts

This firm was established in Civil War era by Joshua Stevens, for whom the company was named. In 1999 Savage Arms began manufacture of Stevens designs.

NO. 10 SINGLE-SHOT
TARGET PISTOL . . . .**NiB $249 Ex $207 Gd $160**
Caliber: .22 LR. 8-inch bbl., 11.5 inches overall. Weight: 37 oz. Target sights. Blued finish. Hard rubber grips. In External appearance this arm resembles an automatic pistol but it has a tip-up action. Made from 1919 to 1939.

NO. 35 OFFHAND MODEL SINGLE-SHOT
TARGET PISTOL . . . .**NiB $377 Ex $301 Gd $255**
Tip-up action. Caliber: .22 LR. Bbl. lengths: 6, 8, 10, 12.25 inches. Weight: 24 oz. w/6-inch bbl. Target sights. Blued finish. Walnut grips. Note: This pistol is similar to the earlier "Gould" model. Made from 1907 to 1939.

Stevens No. 10

Stevens No. 35

Stevens No. 38

OFFHAND NO. 35 SINGLE-SHOT
PISTOL/SHOTGUN . . . . NiB $377 Ex $301 Gd $255
Same general specifications as the standard No. 35 pistol except chambered for the .410 shotshell. Six-, 8-, 10-, or 12-inch half-ocatagonal bbl., iron frame either blued, nickel plated, or casehardened. BATF Class 3 license required to purchase. Made from 1923 to 1942.

NO. 36 SINGLE-SHOT PISTOL . . NiB $842 Ex $577 Gd $439
Tip-up action. Calibers: .22 Short and LR, .22 WRF, .25 Stevens, .32 Short Colt, .38 Long Colt, .44 Russian. 10- or 12-inch half-octagonal bbl., iron or brass frame w/nickel plated finish. Blued bbl. Checkered walnut grips. Made from 1880 to 1911.

NO. 37 SINGLE-SHOT PISTOL. . .NiB $1020 Ex $836 Gd $544
Similar specifications to the No. 38 except the finger spur on the trigger guard has been omitted. Made from 1889 to 1919.

NO. 38 SINGLE-SHOT PISTOL NiB $536 Ex $437 Gd $247
Tip-up action. Calibers: .22 Short and LR, .22 WRF, .25 Stevens, .32 Stevens, .32 Short Colt. Iron or brass frame. Checkered grips. Made from 1884 to 1903.

NO. 41 TIP-UP
SINGLE-SHOT PISTOL . . . . NiB $342 Ex $281 Gd $204
Tip-up action. Caliber: .22 Short, 3.5-inch half-octagonal bbl. Blued metal parts w/optional nickel frame. Made from 1896 to1915.

STEYR — Steyr, Austria

GB SEMIAUTOMATIC PISTOL
Caliber: 9mm Para. 18-round magazine, 5.4-inch bbl., 8.9 inches overall. Weight: 2.9 lbs. Post front sight, fixed, notched rear. Double, gas-delayed, blow-back action. Made from 1981 to 1988.
Commercial model . . . . NiB $680 Ex $530 Gd $337
Military model
(Less than 1000 imported) . . NiB $800 Ex $652 Gd $377

STEYR-HAHN (M12) AUTOMATIC PISTOL
Caliber: 9mm Steyr. Eight-round fixed magazine, charger loaded; 5.1-inch bbl., 8.5 inches overall. Weight: 35 oz. Fixed sights. Blued finish. Checkered wood grips. Made from 1911-19. Adopted by the Austro-Hungarian Army in 1912. Note: Confiscated by the Germans in 1938, an estimated 250,000 of these pistols were converted to 9mm Para. and stamped w/an identifying "08" on the left side of the slide. Mfd. by Osterreichische Waffenfabrik-Gesellschaft.
Commercial model (9mm Steyr) . .NiB $544 Ex $468 Gd $377
Military model (9mm Steyr-Austro
-Hungarian Army) . . . . .NiB $568 Ex $479 Gd $229
Military model (9mm Parabellum
Conversion marked "08") . .NiB $1033 Ex $879 Gd $498

STOEGER LUGERS — South Hackensack, NJ
Formerly manufactured by Stoeger Industries, So. Hackensack, New Jersey; later by Classic Arms, Union City, New Jersey.

AMERICAN EAGLE LUGER
Caliber: 9mm Para. 7-rnd. magazine, 4- or 6-in. bbl., 8.25 inches overall (with 4-inch bbl.). or 10.25 inches (with 6-inch bbl.). Weight: 30 or 32 oz. Checkered walnut grips. Stainless steel w/brushed or matte black finish. Intro. 1994. Disc.
Model P-08 stainless (4-inch
bbl.) . . . . NiB $774 Ex $499 Gd $366
Navy model (6-inch bbl.) . . . . .NiB $854 Ex $811 Gd $400
w/matte black finish, add $85

STANDARD LUGER . . . . .NiB $299 Ex $137 Gd $101
Caliber: .22 LR. 10-round magazine, 4.5- or 5.5-inch bbl., 8.88 inches overall (with 4.5-inch bbl.). Weight: 29.5 oz. (with 4.5-inch bbl.). Fixed sights. Black finish. Smooth wood grips. Made 1969 to 1986.

STEEL FRAME LUGER . . . . .NiB $290 Ex $133 Gd $95
Caliber: .22 LR. 10-round magazine, 4.5-inch bbl., 8.88 inches overall. Blued finish. Checkered wood grips. Features one piece forged and machined steel frame. Made 1980 to 1986.

TARGET LUGER
.22 AUTO PISTOL . . . . .NiB $227 Ex $160 Gd $110
Same as Standard Luger .22 except has target sights 9.38 inches overall w/4.5-inch bbl., Checkered wood grips. Made from 1975 to 1986.

**Stoeger
American Eagle Luger P08 Stainless**

**Stoeger
American Eagle Luger Navy Model**

**Stoeger
Standard Luger .22**

**Targa
Model GT380XE**

TARGA PISTOLS — Italy
Manufactured by Armi Tanfoglio Guiseppe.

**MODEL GT26S
AUTO PISTOL**. . . . . NiB $166 Ex $98 Gd $79
Caliber: .25 ACP. Six-round magazine, 2.5-inch bbl., 4.63 inches overall. Weight: 15 oz. fixed sights. Checkered composition grips. Blued or chrome finish. Disc. 1990.

MODEL GT32 AUTO PISTOL
Caliber: .32 ACP. Six-round magazine, 4.88-inch bbl., 7.38 inches overall. Weight: 26 oz. fixed sights. Checkered composition or walnut grips. Blued or chrome finish.
Blued finished. . . . . NiB $166 Ex $109 Gd $88
Chrome finish. . . . . NiB $179 Ex $118 Gd $89

MODEL GT380 AUTOMATIC PISTOL
Same as the Targa GT32 except chambered for .380 ACP.
Blued finish. . . . . NiB $179 Ex $118 Gd $89
Chrome finish. . . . . NiB $197 Ex $137 Gd $101

**MODEL GT380XE
AUTOMATIC PISTOL**. . . . . NiB $220 Ex $165 Gd $101
Caliber: .380 ACP. 11-round magazine, 3.75-inch bbl., 7.38 inches overall. Weight: 28 oz. Fixed sights. Blued or satin nickel finish. Smooth wooden grips. Made from 1980 to 1990.

TAURUS INT'L. MFG. — Porto Alegre, Brazil
Manufactured by FORJAS TAURUS S.A. Porto Alegre, Brazil; imported Miami, FL.

NOTE: *For ease in locating a particular Taurus handgun, the listings are divided into two groupings: Automatic Pistols (page 192) and Revolvers (below). For a complete handgun listing, please refer to the index.*

- REVOLVERS -

MODEL GAUCHO. . . . . NiB $425 Ex $285 Gd $245
SA. Colt SAA reproduction. Caliber: .357 Mag., .44-40, or .45 LC. Six-round cylinder, 4.75-, 5.5-, 7.5- or 12-in. bbl. Blued, case color, matte or bright stainless finish. Made from 2005 to 2007.

MODEL 17C. . . . . NiB $300 Ex $190 Gd $170
SA/DA. Caliber: .17 HMR or .17 Mach 2. 8-round cylinder, 2-, 4-, 5-in. bbl. Adj. sights, rubber grips. Blued finish. Made from 2003 to 2007.
Ultra-Lite (2-in. bbl.). . . . . NiB $340 Ex $200 Gd $180
Polished stainless finish. . . . . . NiB $330 Ex $195 Gd $175

MODEL 17IB. . . . . NiB $295 Ex $185 Gd $170
SA/DA. Caliber: .17 HMR or .17 Mach 2. 8- or 9-round cylinder, 1.75-in. bbl. Adj. sights, rubber grips. Blued finish. Made from 2005 to 2007.
Matte stainless finish. . . . . NiB $330 Ex $195 Gd $175

Taurus Model .44

Taurus Model 66

**Taurus
Model 74 Target Grade**

Taurus Model 80

Taurus Model 82

MODEL 17 TRACKER . . . . **NiB $481 Ex $265 Gd $225**
SA/DA. Caliber: .17 HMR. 7-round cylinder, 4-, 6.5-, 8.6-in. vent rib bbl. Adj. sights, rubber grips. Made from 2003 to date.
Matte stainless, add **$50**
Two-tone finish, add **$50**
Silhoutte model (12-in. bbl., optic mount,
    discont. 2004). . . . .**NiB $320 Ex $205 Gd $185**

MODEL 21T TRACKER . . . . . . **NiB $330 Ex $205 Gd $185**
SA/DA. Caliber: .218 Bee. 7-round cylinder, 6.5-in. vent rib bbl. Adj. sights, rubber grips. Made from 2003 to 2005.

**MODEL 22H
RAGING HORNET** . . . . **NiB $800 Ex $530 Gd $455**
SA/DA. Caliber: .22 Hornet. 8-round cylinder, 10-in. vent rib bbl. Adj. sights, optic mount, rubber grips. Made from 1999 to 2004.

**MODEL 30C RAGING THIRTY
HUNTER** . . . . **NiB $800 Ex $530 Gd $455**
SA/DA. Caliber: .30 Carbine. 8-round cylinder, 12-in. vent rib full lug bbl. Adj. sights, optic mount, adj. trigger, rubber grips. Made from 2003 to 2004.
Silhoutte model (12-in. half lug bbl., optic mount,
    discont. 2004). . . . .**NiB $795 Ex $525 Gd $450**

MODEL 44 DA REVOLVER
Caliber: .44 Mag. Six-round cylinder, 4-, 6.5-, or 8.38-inch bbl. Weight: 44.75 oz., 52.5 or 57.25 oz. Brazilian hardwood grips. Blued or stainless steel finish. Made from 1994 to 2004.
Blued finish. . . . .**NiB $433 Ex $327 Gd $220**
Model 44SS Stainless finish
    (intro. 1994) . . . .**NiB $600 Ex $487 Gd $274**

MODEL 44C TRACKER . . . . . . **NiB $646 Ex $430 Gd $380**
SA/DA. Caliber: .44 Mag. 5-round cylinder, 4-in. ported bbl. Blued or matte stainless finish. Made from 2005 to date.

MODEL 45-410 "THE JUDGE" . . . .**NiB $610 Ex $355 Gd $300**
SA/DA. Caliber: .45 LC/.410 3-in. chamber. 5-round cylinder, 2.5-, 3-, 6.5-in. bbl. Blued or matte stainless finish. Made from 2006 to date.
Ultra-Lite . . . .**NiB $580 Ex $400 Gd $355**

**MODEL 45-410 "THE JUDGE"
PUBLIC DEFENDER** . . . . **NiB $610 Ex $355 Gd $300**
SA/DA. Caliber: .45 LC/.410 2.5-in. chamber. 5-round stainless or titanium cylinder, 2-in. bbl. smaller hammer. Blued or matte stainless finish. Made from 2009 to date.
Ultra-Lite . . . .**NiB $580 Ex $400 Gd $355**
Polymer frame. . . . .**NiB $550 Ex $400 Gd $355**

MODEL 65 DA REVOLVER
Caliber: .357 Magnum. 6-round cylinder, 3- or 4-inch bbl., weight: 32 oz. Front ramp sight, square notch rear. Checkered walnut target grip. Royal blued or satin nickel finish. Imported 1992 to 1997 and from 1999 to date.
Blue finish. . . . .**NiB $398 Ex $289 Gd $171**
Stainless finish. . . . .**NiB $427 Ex $351 Gd $212**

MODEL 66 DA REVOLVER
Calibers: .357 Magnum, .38 Special. Six-round cylinder, 3-, 4- and 6-inch bbl., weight: 35 oz. Serrated ramp front sight, rear click adj. Checkered walnut grips. Royal blued or nickel finish. Imported 1992-1997 and from 1999 to date.
Blue finish. . . . .**NiB $500 Ex $351 Gd $212**
Model 66SS Stainless finish. . . . .**NiB $550 Ex $398 Gd $229**

Taurus Model 83

Taurus Model 84

Taurus Model 85 Concealed Hammer

Taurus Model 86

Taurus Model 85 w/Spur Hammer

MODEL 73 DA REVOLVER . . . . NiB $211 Ex $121 Gd $101
Caliber: .32 Long. Six-round cylinder, 3-inch heavy bbl., weight: 20 oz. Checkered grips. Blued or satin nickel finish. Disc. 1993.

MODEL 76 TARGET . . . . NiB $244 Ex $279 Gd $118
Caliber: .32 S&W Long. Six-round cylinder, 3-inch bbl., 8.25 inches overall. Weight: 20 oz. Adj. rear sight, ramp front. Blued or nickel finish. Checkered walnut grips. Made from 1971 to 1990.

MODEL 80 DA REVOLVER
Caliber: .38 Special. Six-round cylinder, bbl. lengths: 3, 4 inches, 9.25 inches overall (with 4-inch bbl.). Weight: 30 oz. (with 4-inch bbl.) Fixed sights. Blued or nickel finish. Checkered walnut grips. Made 1996 to 1997.
Blued finish. . . . . NiB $214 Ex $140 Gd $98
Model 80SS Stainless finish. . . . NiB $431 Ex $337 Gd $258

MODEL 82 HEAVY BARREL
Same as Model 80 except has heavy bbl., weight: 33 oz. w/4-inch bbl., Made from 1971 to date.
Blued finish. . . . . NiB $366 Ex $290 Gd $212
Model 82SS Stainless finish
** (intro. 1993) . . . . NiB $437 Ex $327 Gd $259**

MODEL 83 HEAVY BARREL TARGET GRADE
Same as Model 84 except has heavy bbl., weight: 34.5 oz. Made from 1977 to date.
Blued finish. . . . . NiB $255 Ex $160 Gd $105
Model 83SS Stainless finish. . . . NiB $281 Ex $198 Gd $128

MODEL 84 TARGET
GRADE REVOLVER . . . . NiB $312 Ex $235 Gd $170
Caliber: .38 Special. Six-round cylinder, 4-inch bbl., 9.25 inches overall. Weight: 31 oz. Adj. rear sight, ramp front. Blued or nickel finish. Checkered walnut grips. from 1971 to 1989.

MODEL 85 DA REVOLVER
Caliber: .38 Special. Five-round cylinder, 2- or 3-inch. bbl., weight: 21 oz. Fixed sights. Checkered walnut grips. Blued, satin nickel or stainless-steel finish. Model 85CH is the same as the standard version except for concealed hammer. Made from 1997 to 2012.
Blued or satin nickel finish . . . . NiB $377 Ex $302 Gd $143
Stainless steel finish . . . . NiB $437 Ex $362 Gd $189
Titanium Ultra-Lightweight. . . . NiB $540 Ex $370 Gd $320

MODEL 85PLYB2
"PROTECTOR PLY" . . . . NiB $355 Ex $230 Gd $210
SA/DA. Caliber: .38 Spl.+P. Five-round blued or matte stainless cylinder, 1.25- or 1.75-in. vent rib bbl., polymer frame. Weight: 16.5 oz. Fixed fiber optic sights. Made from 2011 to 2012.

MODEL 86 CUSTOM TARGET
DA REVOLVER . . . . NiB $301 Ex $208 Gd $110
Caliber: .38 Special. Six-round cylinder, 6-inch bbl., 11.25 inches overall. Weight: 34 oz. Adj. rear sight, Partridge-type front. Blued finish. Checkered walnut grips. Made 1971-94.

MODEL 94 DA REVOLVER
Same as Model 74 except .22 LR. w/9-round cylinder, 3- or 4-inch bbl., weight: 25 oz. Blued or stainless finish. Made from 1971 to date.
Blued finish. . . . . NiB $362 Ex $306 Gd $219
Model 94SS Stainless finish. . . . NiB $386 Ex $348 Gd $255

MODEL 96 TARGET SCOUT...NiB $301 Ex $209 Gd $112
Same as Model 86 except in .22 LR. Made from 1971 to 1998.

MODEL 431 DA REVOLVER
Caliber: .44 Spec. Five-round cylinder, 3- or 4-inch solid-rib bbl. w/ejector shroud. Weight: 35 oz. w/4-inch bbl., Serrated ramp front sight, notched topstrap rear. Blued or stainless finish. Made 1992 to 1997.
Blued finish................NiB $239 Ex $198 Gd $144
Stainless finish..............NiB $434 Ex $306 Gd $265

MODEL 441 DA REVOLVER
Similar to the Model 431 except w/6-inch bbl. and fully adj. target sights. Weight: 40 oz. Made from 1991 to 1997.
Blued finish................NiB $306 Ex $237 Gd $144
Stainless finish..............NiB $434 Ex $306 Gd $225

MODEL 445 DA REVOLVER
Caliber: .44 Special. Five-round cylinder, 2-inch bbl., 6.75 inches overall. Weight: 28.25 oz. Serrated ramp front sight, notched frame rear. Standard or concealed hammer. Santoprene I grips. Blue or stainless finish. Imported from 1997 to 2003.
Blued finish................NiB $306 Ex $239 Gd $190
Stainless finish..............NiB $342 Ex $265 Gd $204

MODEL 454 DA RAGING BULL REVOLVER
Caliber: .454 Casull. Five-round cylinder, ported 6.5- or 8.4-inch vent rib bbl., 12 inches overall (w/6.5-inch bbl.). Weight: 53 or 63 oz. Partridge front sight, micrometer adj. rear. Santoprene I or walnut grips. Blue or stainless finish. Imported 1997 to date.
Blued finish................NiB $862 Ex $730 Gd $587
Stainless finish..............NiB $877 Ex $791 Gd $648

MODEL 669/669VR DA REVOLVER
Caliber: .357 Mag. Six-round cylinder, 4- or 6-inch solid-rib bbl. w/ejector shroud Model 669VR has vent rib bbl., weight: 37 oz. w/4-inch bbl., Serrated ramp front sight, micro-adj. rear. Royal blued or stainless finish. Checkered Brazilian hardwood grips. Made from 1989 to 1998.
Blued finish................NiB $283 Ex $214 Gd $165
Stainless finish..............NiB $362 Ex $286 Gd $240
Model 669VR, blued finish....NiB $301 Ex $225 Gd $175
Model 669VR, stainless finish..NiB $362 Ex $286 Gd $255

MODEL 741/761 DA REVOLVER
Caliber: .32 H&R Mag. Six-round cylinder, 3- or 4-inch solid-rib bbl. w/ejector shroud. Weight: 20 oz. w/3-inch bbl., Serrated ramp front sight, micro-adj. rear. Blued or stainless finish. Checkered Brazilian hardwood grips. Made 1991-97.
Blued finish................NiB $225 Ex $129 Gd $90
Stainless finish ....NiB $291 Ex $204 Gd $150
MODEL 761(6-inch bbl.),
** 34 oz., blued finish).......NiB $281 Ex $204 Gd $143**

MODEL 941 TARGET REVOLVER
Caliber: .22 Magnum. Eight-round cylinder. Solid-rib bbl. w/ejector shroud. Micro-adj. rear sight. Brazilian hardwood grips. Blued or stainless finish.
Blued finish...............NiB $357 Ex $306 Gd $204
Stainless finish..............NiB $408 Ex $365 Gd $274

**Taurus
Model 669**

**Taurus
Model PT-22**

**Taurus
Model PT-58**

**Taurus
Model PT-92AF**

**Taurus
Model PT-99AF**

**Taurus
Model PT-908**

- AUTOMATIC PISTOLS -

MODEL 22 PLY . . . . NiB $285 Ex $177 Gd $101
DAO. Caliber: .22 LR. 8-round magazine, tip-up 2.3-in. bbl., polymer frame. Weight: 10.8 oz. Fixed sights. Made from 2012 to date.

MODEL 25 PLY . . . . NiB $285 Ex $177 Gd $101
Similar to Model 22 PLY model except chambered in .25 ACP. Made from 2012 to date.

MODEL PT-22 . . . . NiB $285 Ex $177 Gd $101
SA/DA. Caliber: .22 LR. Nine-round magazine, 2.75-inch bbl., weight: 12.3 oz. Fixed open sights. Brazilian hardwood grips. Blued finish. Made from 1991 to date.

MODEL PT-24/7 . . . . NiB $455 Ex $300 Gd $260
DAO. Caliber: 9mm, .40 S&W or .45 ACP. 10-, 12-, 15, or 17-round magazine, 4-in. bbl. Polymer frame w/blued or stainless slide. 3-dot sights. Acessory rail. Made from 2004 to 2005.

**MODEL PT-24/7
PRO FULL SIZE** . . . . NiB $420 Ex $290 Gd $240
SA with DA second strike trigger. Caliber: 9mm, .40 S&W or .45 ACP. 10-, 12-, 15, or17-round magazine, 4-in. bbl. Polymer frame w/blued or stainless slide. 3-dot sights. Acessory rail. Made from 2006 to 2010.
Pro Compact (3.1-in. bbl.) . . . . NiB $420 Ex $280 Gd $250
Pro Long Slide (5.2-in. bbl.) . . . NiB $450 Ex $295 Gd $255

MODEL PT-24/7 G2 . . . . NiB $530 Ex $300 Gd $260
SA with DA second strike trigger. Caliber: 9mm, .40 S&W or .45 ACP. 10-, 12-, 15, or17-round magazine, 4-in. bbl. Polymer frame w/interchangeable backstraps, ambidextrous controls, blued or stainless slide. 3-dot sights. Acessory rail. Made from 2011 to date.

Compact (3.1-in. bbl.) . . . . NiB $530 Ex $300 Gd $260

MODEL PT-24/7 OSS . . . . NiB $480 Ex $330 Gd $290
Similar to PT-24/7 Pro Full Size except w/5.25-in. bbl. and tan or black polymer frame. Made from 2007 to 2010.

MODEL PT-25 . . . . NiB $285 Ex $170 Gd $92
Same general specifications as Model PT 22 except in .25 ACP w/eight-round magazine. Made from 1992 to date.

MODEL PT-58 . . . . NiB $408 Ex $332 Gd $240
Caliber: .380 ACP. Twelve-round magazine, 4-inch bbl., 7.2 inches overall. Weight: 30 oz. Blade front sight, rear adj. for windage w/3-dot sighting system. Blued, satin nickel or stainless finish. Made from 1988 to 1996.

MODEL PT-92AF
SA/DA. Similar to Beretta M92 SB-F. Caliber: 9mm Para. 15-round magazine, 5-inch bbl., 8.5 inches overall. Weight: 24 oz. Blade front sight, notched bar rear. Smooth Brazilian walnut grips. Blued, satin nickel or stainless finish. Made from 1991 to date.
Blued finish . . . . NiB $670 Ex $377 Gd $286
Satin nickel finish . . . . NiB $720 Ex $418 Gd $319
Stainless finish . . . . NiB $679 Ex $398 Gd $306
Deluxe (blue/gold or
    stainless/gold) . . . . NiB $520 Ex $390 Gd $300

MODEL PT-92AFC COMPACT PISTOL
Same general specs as Model PT-92AF except w/13-round magazine, 4.25-inch bbl., 7.5 inches overall. Weight: 31 oz. Made 1991 to 1996
Blued finish . . . . NiB $362 Ex $283 Gd $214
Satin nickel finish . . . . NiB $408 Ex $328 Gd $266
Stainless finish . . . . NiB $434 Ex $346 Gd $220

MODEL PT-99AF
SEMI-AUTOMATIC PISTOL . . . . NiB $530 Ex $437 Gd $301
Same general specifications as Model PT-92AF except rear sight is adj. for elevation and windage, and finish is blued or satin nickel.

MODEL PT-100 DA AUTOMATIC PISTOL
Caliber: .40 S&W. Eleven-round magazine, 5-inch bbl., weight: 34 oz. Fixed front sight, adj. rear w/3-dot system. Smooth hardwood grip. Blued, satin nickel or stainless finish. Made from 1991 to 1997.
Blued finish . . . . NiB $500 Ex $444 Gd $362
Satin finish . . . . NiB $546 Ex $469 Gd $377
Stainless finish . . . . NiB $536 Ex $444 Gd $367

MODEL PT-101 DA AUTOMATIC PISTOL
Same general specifications as Model 100 except w/micrometer click adj. sights. Made from 1992 to 1996.
Blued finish . . . . NiB $536 Ex $444 Gd $367
Satin nickel finish . . . . NiB $576 Ex $453 Gd $367
Stainless finish . . . . NiB $536 Ex $444 Gd $367

MODEL PT-111 MILLENNIUM DAO PISTOL
Caliber: 9mm Parabellum. 10-round magazine, 3.12-inch bbl., 6 inches overall. Weight: 19.1 oz. Fixed low-profile sights w/3-dot system. Black polymer grip/frame. Blue or stainless slide. Imported from 1998 to 2004.
Blue finish . . . . NiB $362 Ex $265 Gd $130
Stainless finish . . . . NiB $380 Ex $286 Gd $185

MODEL PT-908 SEMIAUTOMATIC PISTOL
Caliber: 9mm Para. Eight-round magazine, 3.8-inch bbl., 7 inches overall. Weight: 30 oz. Post front sight, drift-adj. com-

bat rear w/3-dot system. Blued, satin nickel or stainless finish. Made 1993 to 1997.

Blued finish. . . . . NiB $357 Ex $286 Gd $204
Satin nickel finish . . . . NiB $388 Ex $316 Gd $205
Stainless finish. . . . . NiB $431 Ex $321 Gd $265

MODEL PT-911 COMPACT SEMIAUTOMATIC PISTOL
Caliber: 9mm Parabellum. 10-round magazine, 3.75-inch bbl., 7.05 inches overall. Weight: 28.2 oz. Fixed low-profile sights w/3-dot system. Santoprene II grips. Blue or stainless finish. Imported from 1997 to date.

Blued finish. . . . . NiB $546 Ex $408 Gd $270
Stainless finish. . . . . NiB $546 Ex $408 Gd $270

MODEL PT-938 COMPACT SEMIAUTOMATIC PISTOL
Caliber: 380 ACP. 10-round magazine, 3.72-inch bbl., 6.75 inches overall. Weight: 27 oz. Fixed low-profile sights w/3-dot system. Santoprene II grips. Blue or stainless finish. Imported 1997 to 2005.

Blue finish. . . . . NiB $499 Ex $357 Gd $265
Stainless finish. . . . . NiB $469 Ex $377 Gd $286

MODEL PT-940 COMPACT SEMIAUTOMATIC PISTOL
Caliber: .40 S&W. 10-round magazine, 3.75-inch bbl., 7.05 inches overall. Weight: 28.2 oz. Fixed low-profile sights w/3-dot system. Santoprene II grips. Blue or stainless finish. Imported from 1997 to date.

Blue finish. . . . . NiB $546 Ex $437 Gd $290
Stainless finish. . . . . NiB $571 Ex $499 Gd $316

MODEL PT-945 COMPACT SEMIAUTOMATIC PISTOL
Caliber: .45 ACP. Eight-round magazine, 4.25-inch bbl., 7.48 inches overall. Weight: 29.5 oz. Fixed low-profile sights w/3-dot system. Santoprene II grips. Blue or stainless finish. Imported from 1995 to date.

Blue finish. . . . . NiB $601 Ex $530 Gd $377
Stainless finish. . . . . NiB $587 Ex $437 Gd $316

TEXAS ARMS — Waco, Texas

DEFENDER DERRINGER. . . . . . NiB $306 Ex $218 Gd $120
Calibers: 9mm, .357 Mag., .44 Mag., .45 ACP, .45 Colt/.410. Three-inch bbl., 5 inches overall. Weight: 21 oz. Blade front sight, fixed rear. Matte gun-metal gray finish. Smooth grips. Made from 1993 to 1999.

TEXAS LONGHORN ARMS — Richmond, TX

"THE JEZEBEL" PISTOL. . . . . . . NiB $337 Ex $265 Gd $200
Top-break, single-shot. Caliber: .22 Short, Long or LR. Six-inch half-round bbl., 8 inches overall. Weight: 15 oz. Bead front sight, adj. rear. One-piece walnut grip. Stainless finish. Intro. in 1987.

SA REVOLVER CASED SET
Set contains one each of the Texas Longhorn Single Actions. Each chambered in the same caliber and w/the same serial number. Intro. in 1984.

Standard set . . . . NiB $1620 Ex $1400 Gd $1000
Engraved set . . . . NiB $1820 Ex $1615 Gd $1219

SOUTH TEXAS ARMY LIMITED
EDITION SA REVOLVER. . . NiB $1840 Ex $1418 Gd $1120
Calibers: All popular centerfire pistol calibers. Six-round cylin-

Thompson/Center
Vent Rib Barrel

TThompson/Center
Contender Bull Barrel

der, 4.75-inch bbl.,10.25 inches overall. Weight: 40 oz. Fixed sights. Color casehardened frame. One-piece deluxe walnut grips. Blued bbl., Intro. in 1984.

SESQUICENTENNIAL
SA REVOLVER. . . . . NiB $2613 Ex $2114 Gd $1489
Same as South Texas Army Limited Edition except engraved and nickel-plated w/one-piece ivory grip. Intro. in 1986.

TEXAS BORDER SPECIAL
SA REVOLVER. . . . . NiB $1744 Ex $1316 Gd $954
Same as South Texas Army Limited Edition except w/3.5-inch bbl. and bird's-head grips. Intro. in 1984.

WEST TEXAS FLAT TOP
TARGET SA REVOLVER. . . . . NiB $1633 Ex $1316 Gd $896
Same as South TExas Army Limited Edition except w/choice of bbl. lengths from 7 .5 to 15 inches. Same special features w/ flat-top style frame and adj. rear sight. Intro. in 1984.

THOMPSON — West Hurley, New York

Manufactured by Auto-Ordnance Corporation; owned by Kahr Arms. Also see Auto-Ordnance handgun section.

MODEL 1927A-5 . . . . NiB $1071 Ex $855 Gd $668
Similar to Thompson Model 1928A submachine gun except has no provision for automatic firing, does not have detachable buttstock. Caliber: .45 Auto, 20-round detachable box magazine (5-, 15- and 30-round box magazines, 39-round drum also available), 13-inch finned bbl., overall length: 26 inches. Weight: About 6.75 lbs. Adj. rear sight, blade front. Blued finish. Walnut grips. Intro. in 1977.

THOMPSON/CENTER ARMS — Rochester, New Hampshire
Acquired by Smith & Wesson in 2006.

CONTENDER SINGLE-SHOT PISTOL

Break frame, underlever action. Calibers: (rimfire) .22 LR. .22 WMR, 5mm RRM; (standard centerfire), .218 Bee, .22 Hornet, .22 Rem. Jet, .221 Fireball, .222 Rem., .25-35, .256 Win. Mag., .30 M1 Carbine, .30-30, .38 Auto, .38 Special .357 Mag./ Hot Shot, 9mm Para., .45 Auto, .45 Colt, .44 Magnum/Hot Shot; (wildcat centerfire) .17 Ackley Bee, .17 Bumblebee, .17 Hornet, .17 K Hornet, .17 Mach IV, .17-.222, .17-.223, .22 K Hornet, .30 Herrett, .357 Herrett, .357-4 B&D. Interchangeable bbls.: 8.75- or 10-inch standard octagon (.357 Mag., .44 Mag. and .45 Colt available w/detachable choke for use w/Hot Shot cartridges); 10-inch w/vent rib and detachable internal choke tube for Hot Shots, .357 and .44 Magnum only; 10-inch bull bbl., .30 or .357 Herrett only. 13.5 inches overall w/10-inch bbl., Weight: 43 oz. (w/standard 10-inch bbl.). Adj. rear sight, ramp front; vent rib model has folding rear sight, adj. front; bull bbl., available w/or w/o sights. Lobo 1.5/ scope and mount (add $40 to value). Blued finish. Receiver photoengraved. Checkered walnut thumbrest grip and forearm (pre-1972 model has different grip w/silver grip cap). Made from 1967 to date, w/the following revisions and variations.

Standard model. . . . . NiB $419 Ex $321 Gd $204
Vent rib model . . . . NiB $439 Ex $342 Gd $230
Bull bbl. model, w/sights . . . . . NiB $434 Ex $326 Gd $214
Bull bbl. model, without sights . . NiB $431 Ex $316 Gd $204
Extra standard bbl, add. $255
Extra vent rib or bull bbl, add. $306

CONTENDER BULL BARREL. . . NiB $408 Ex $321 Gd $204

Caliber offerings of the bull bbl. version Expanded in 1973 and 1978, making it the Contender model w/the widest range of caliber options: .22 LR, .22 Win. Mag., .22 Hornet, .223 Rem., 7mm T.C.U., 7x30 Waters, .30 M1 Carbine, .30-30 Win., .32 H&R Mag., .32-20 Win., .357 Rem. Max., .357 Mag., 10mm Auto, .44 Magnum, .445 Super Magnum. 10-inch heavy bbl., Partridge-style iron sights. Contoured Competitor grip. Blued finish.

CONTENDER INTERNAL

CHOKE MODEL . . . . NiB $434 Ex $347 Gd $225
Originally made in 1968-69 w/octagonal bbl., this Internal Choke version in .45 Colt/.410 caliber only was reintroduced in 1986 w/10-inch bull bbl. Vent rib also available. Fixed iron rear sight, bead front. Detachable choke screws into muzzle. Blued finish. Contoured American black walnut Competitor grip, also since 1986, has nonslip rubber insert permanently bonded to back of grip.

w/bull bbl, add $50
w/vent rib, add $61

CONTENDER OCTAGON

BARREL. . . . . NiB $388 Ex $290 Gd $204
The original Contender design, this octagonal bbl., version began to see the discontinuance of caliber offerings in 1980. Now it is available in .22 LR only, 10-inch octagonal bbl., Partridge-style iron sights. Contoured Competitor grip. Blued finish.

**Uberti
Rolling Block Target**

CONTENDER STAINLESS

Similar to the standard Contender models except stainless steel w/blued sights. Black Rynite forearm and ambidExtrous finger-groove grip. Made from 2006 to date.

Standard SS model (10-inch bbl.) . . NiB $469 Ex $386 Gd $306
SS Super 14. . . . . NiB $377 Ex $291 Gd $143
SS Super 16. . . . . NiB $377 Ex $291 Gd $143

CONTENDER SUPER (14 IN./16 IN.)

Calibers: .22 LR, .222 Rem., .223 Rem., 6mm T.C.U., 6.5mm T.C.U., 7mm T.C.U., 7x30 Waters, .30 Herrett, .30-30 Win., .357 Herrett, .357 Rem. Max., .35 Rem., 10mm Auto, .44 Mag., .445 Super Mag. 14- or 16.25-inch bull bbl., 18 or 20.25 inches overall. Weight: 43-65 oz. Partridge-style ramp front sight, adj. target rear. Blued finish. Made from 1978 to 1997.

Super 14 . . . . NiB $380 Ex $306 Gd $204
Super 16 . . . . NiB $380 Ex $306 Gd $204

CONTENDER TC ALLOY II

Calibers: .22 LR, .223 Rem., .357 Magnum, .357 Rem. Max., .44 Magnum, 7mm T.C.U., .30-30 Win., .45 Colt/.410 (w/internal choke), .35 Rem. and 7-30 Waters (14-inch bbl.). 10- or 14-inch bull bbl. or 10-inch vent rib bbl. (w/internal choke). All metal parts permanently electroplated w/T/C Alloy II, which is harder than stainless steel, ensuring smoother action, 30 percent longer bbl. life. Other design specifications the same as late model Contenders. Made from 1986 to 1989.

w/10-inch bull bbl. . . . . NiB $377 Ex $306 Gd $214
w/vent rib bbl. and choke. . . . . NiB $464 Ex $377 Gd $286
Super 14 . . . . NiB $388 Ex $306 Gd $219

ENCORE SINGLE-SHOT PISTOL

Similar to the standard Contender models except w/10-, 12- or 15-inch bbl., Calibers: .22-250 Rem., .223 Rem., .243 Win., .260 Rem., .270 Win., 7mm BR Rem., 7mm-08 Rem., 7.62x39mm, .308 Win., .30-06 Spfd., .44 Rem. Mag., .444 Marlin, .45-70 Govt., .45 LC/410. Blue or stainless finish. Walnut or composition, ambidExtrous finger-groove grip. Hunter Model w/2.5-7x pistol scope. Note: Encore bbls. are not interchangeable with Contenter models. Made from 1998 to date.

w/10-inch bbl. (blue, disc.). . . . NiB $561 Ex $499 Gd $270
w/12-inch bbl., blued . . . . NiB $561 Ex $499 Gd $270
w/15-inch bbl., blued . . . . NiB $576 Ex $464 Gd $286
Hunter model w/2,5-7x scope . . NiB $755 Ex $546 Gd $365
Encore model (stainless finish), add $25

G2 CONTENDER SINGLE-SHOT PISTOL

Similar to the Contender model except w/12- or 14-in. bbl., various rimfire and centerfire calibers. Walnut grip. Note: older Contender bbls. are compatiable with G2 Contenter models. Made from 2002 to 2012.

Blued finish. . . . . NiB $650 Ex $400 Gd $350
Stainless finish. . . . . NiB $695 Ex $425 Gd $370

PRO-HUNTER SINGLE-SHOT

PISTOL. . . . . NiB $655 Ex $430 Gd $360
Similar to the Contender model except w/15-in. fluted stainless steel bbl., various calibers. Walnut or composite grip. Made from 2006 to 2012.

UBERTI — Ponte Zanano, Italy

Manufactured by Aldo Uberti, imported by Uberti USA, Inc. Manufactures many reproduction revolvers for a variety of companies including EMF, Taylor's & Co., and Cimarron Firearms.

**Uberti
Model 1873 Cattleman**

**Uberti
Cattleman Buntline Target**

MODEL 1871 ROLLING BLOCK
TARGET PISTOL . . . . NiB $418 Ex $321 Gd $230
Single shot. Calibers: .22 LR, .22 Magnum, .22 Hornet and .357 Magnum; 9.5-inch bbl., 14 inches overall. Weight: 44 oz. Ramp front sight, fully adjustable rear. Smooth walnut grip and forearm. Color casehardened frame w/brass trigger guard. Blued half-octagon or full round barrel. Made 2002 to 2006.

MODEL 1873 CATTLEMAN SA REVOLVER
Calibers: .357 Magnum, .38-40, .44-40, .44 Special, .45 Long Colt, .45 ACP. Six-round cylinder, Bbl length: 3.5, 4.5, 4.75, 5.5, 7.5 or 18 inches; 10.75 inches overall (5.5-inch bbl.). Weight: 38 oz. (5.5-inch bbl.). Color casehardened steel frame w/steel or brass back strap and trigger guard. Nickel-plated or blued barrel and cylinder. First issue imported from 1997 to 2004; new models from 2002 to date.
First issue . . . . NiB $459 Ex $386 Gd $235
Bisley . . . . NiB $459 Ex $386 Gd $235
Bisley (flattop) . . . . NiB $459 Ex $386 Gd $235
Buntline (reintroduced 1992) . NiB $500 Ex $395 Gd $244
Quick Draw . . . . NiB $459 Ex $386 Gd $235
Sabre (bird head) . . . . NiB $459 Ex $386 Gd $235
Sheriff's model . . . . NiB $459 Ex $386 Gd $235
Convertible cylinder, add $75
Stainless steel, add $150
Steel backstrap and trigger guard, add $75
Target sights, add $75

MODEL 1875 REMINGTON OUTLAW
Replica of Model 1875 Remington. Calibers: .357 Mag., .44-40, .45 ACP, .45 Long Colt. Six-round cylinder, 5.5- to 7.5-inch bbl., 11.75 to13.75 inches overall. Weight: 44 oz. (with 7.5 inch bbl). Color casehardened steel frame w/steel or brass back strap and trigger guard. Blue or nickel finish.
Blue finish. . . . . NiB $479 Ex $366 Gd $219
Nickel finish (disc. 1995) . . . . . NiB $541 Ex $473 Gd $321
**Convertible cylinder
(.45 LC/.45 ACP), add** $50

MODEL 1890 REMINGTON POLICE
Similar to Model 1875 Remington except without the web under the ejector housing.

Blue Model . . . . NiB $464 Ex $346 Gd $198
Nickel finish (disc. 1995) . . . . NiB $862 Ex $704 Gd $345
Convertible Cylinder (.45 LC/.45 ACP), add $50

ULTRA LIGHT ARMS, INC — Granville, West Virginia

MODEL 20 SERIES PISTOLS
Calibers: .22-250 thru .308 Win. Five-round magazine, 14-inch bbl., weight: 4 lbs. Composite Kevlar, graphite reinforced stock. Benchrest grade action available in right- or left-hand models. Timney adjustable trigger w/three function safety. Bright or matte finish. Made 1987 to 1999.
**Model 20 Hunter's Pistol
(disc. 1989).** . . . . NiB $1295 Ex $1057 Gd $974
**Model 20 Reb Pistol
(disc. 1999).** . . . . NiB $1508 Ex $1345 Gd $1199

UNIQUE — Hendaye, France
Manufactured by Manufacture d'Armes des Pyrénées. Currently imported by Nygord Precision Products, previously by Beeman Precision Arms.

MODEL B/CF
AUTOMATIC PISTOL . . . . NiB $220 Ex $115 Gd $70
Calibers: .32 ACP, .380 ACP. 9-rnd. (.32) or 8-rnd. (.38) magazine, 4-inch bbl., 6.6 inches overall. Weight: 24.3 oz. Blued finish. Plain or thumbrest plastic grips. Intro. in 1954. Disc.

MODEL D2
MODEL D2. . . . . NiB $326 Ex $219 Gd $177
Same as Model D6 except has 4.5-inch bbl., 7.5 inches overall, weight: 24.5 oz. Made from 1954. Disc.

MODEL D6
AUTOMATIC PISTOL . . . . NiB $332 Ex $239 Gd $118
Caliber: .22 LR. 10-round magazine, 6-inch bbl., 9.25 inches overall. Weight: About 26 oz. Adj. sights. Blued finish. Plain or thumbrest plastic grips. Intro. in 1954. Disc.

MODEL DES/32U RAPID FIRE PISTOL
Caliber: .32 S&W Long (wadcutter). Five- or 6-round magazine, 5.9-inch bbl., weight: .40.2 oz. Blade front sight, micro-adj. rear. Trigger adj. for weight and position. Blued finish. Stippled handrest grips. Imported from 1990 to date.
Right-hand model . . . . NiB $1418 Ex $1316 Gd $1155
Left-hand model . . . . NiB $1486 Ex $1366 Gd $1220

MODEL DES/69-U STANDARD MATCH PISTOL
Caliber: .22 LR. Five-round magazine, 5.9-inch bbl., w/250 gm counterweight. 10.6 inches overall. Trigger adjusts for position and pull. Weight: 35.3 oz. Blade front sight, micro-adj. rear. Checkered walnut thumbrest grips w/adj. handrest. Blued finish. Imported from 1969 to 1999.
Right-hand model . . . . NiB $1234 Ex $1138 Gd $909
Left-hand model . . . . NiB $1240 Ex $1144 Gd $941

MODEL DES 823U RAPID FIRE
MATCH AUTOMATIC PISTOL NiB $1122 Ex $950 Gd $836
Caliber: .22 Short. Five-round magazine, 5.9-inch bbl., 10.4 inches overall. Weight: 43 oz. Click adj. rear sight blade front. Checkered walnut thumbrest grips w/adj. handrest. Trigger adj. for length of pull. Made from 1974 to 1998.

Unique D6

**Unique
DES/69 Standard Match**

**Unique
Model DES/VO Rapid Fire Match**

**Unique
Mikros Pocket**

U.S. Arms Abilene

KRIEGSMODELL L
AUTOMATIC PISTOL . . . . **NiB $362 Ex $255 Gd $180**
Caliber: .32 Auto (7.65mm). Nine-round magazine, 3.2-inch bbl., 5.8 inches overall. Weight: 26.5 oz. Fixed sights. Blued finish. Plastic grips. Mfd. during German occupation of France 1940 to 194545. Note: Bears the German military acceptance marks and may have grips marked "7.65m/m 9 SCHUSS."

MODEL L
AUTOMATIC PISTOL . . . . **NiB $283 Ex $204 Gd $149**

Calibers: .22 LR, .32 Auto (7.65mm), .380 Auto (9mm Short). 10-round magazine in .22, 7 in .32, 6 in .380; 3.3-inch bbl.; 5.8 inches overall. Weight: 16.5 oz. (.380 Auto w/light alloy frame), 23 oz. (w/steel frame). Fixed sights. Blued finish. Plastic grips. Intro. in 1955. Disc.

MODEL MIKROS POCKET
Automatic Pistol . . . . **NiB $225 Ex $150 Gd $97**
Calibers: .22 Short, .25 Auto (6.35mm). Six-round magazine, 2.25-inch bbl., 4.44 inches overall. Weight: 9.5 oz. (light alloy frame), 12.5 oz. (steel frame.). Fixed sights. Blued finish. Plastic grips. Intro. in 1957. Disc.

MODEL RR
AUTOMATIC PISTOL . . . . **NiB $218 Ex $109 Gd $68**
Postwar commercial version of WWII Kriegsmodell w/same general specifications. Intro. in 1951. Disc.

MODEL 2000-U MATCH PISTOL
Caliber: .22 Short. Designed for U.I.T. rapid fire competition. Five-round top-inserted magazine, 5.5-inch bbl., w/five vents for recoil reduction. 11.4 inches overall. Weight: 43.4 oz. Special light alloy frame, solid steel slide and shock absorber. Stippled French walnut w/adj. handrest. Imported from 1990 to 1996.
Right-hand model . . . . **NiB $1367 Ex $1199 Gd $1122**
Left-hand model . . . . **NiB $1398 Ex $1250 Gd $1196**

UNITED STATES ARMS CORPORATION — Riverhead, New York

ABILENE SA REVOLVER
Safety Bar action. Calibers: .357 Mag., .41 Mag., .44 Mag., .45 Colt and .357/9mm convertible model w/two cylinders. Six-round cylinder, bbl. lengths: 4.63-, 5.5-, 6.5-inch, 7.5- and 8.5-inches in .44 Mag. only. Weight: About 48 oz. Adj. rear sight, ramp front. Blued finish or stainless steel. Smooth walnut grips. Made 1976 to 1983.
.44 Magnum, blued finish . . . . . **NiB $365 Ex $306 Gd $225**
Magnum, stainless steel . . . . . . **NiB $437 Ex $336 Gd $265**
Other calibers, blued finish . . . **NiB $327 Ex $209 Gd $200**
.357 Magnum, stainless steel . . **NiB $433 Ex $342 Gd $266**
Convertible, .357 Mag./9mm
   Para., blued finish. . . . . **NiB $362 Ex $224 Gd $207**

UNITED STATES FIRE ARMS MFG CO., INC. — Hartford, CT

Manufacturer of high quality reproduction Colt SAA revolver and Colt 1911 pistols from 1995 to 2012. The facility was once located in the old Colt factory building.

1910 COMMERCIAL MODEL
AUTOMATIC PISTOL . . . . . . **NiB $1650 Ex $1300 Gd $800**
Full size 1911-style pistol. Caliber: .45 ACP, 7-round magazine, 5-inch bbl., 8.3 inches overall. High polish Armory Blue finish, checkered walnut grips. Made from 2006 to 2009.
1911 Military Model (similar
   Colt 1911 rollmarks). . . . **NiB $1650 Ex $1300 Gd $800**
1911 Super 38 (.38 Super) . **NiB $1650 Ex $1300 Gd $800**

SINGLE ACTION ARMY REVOLVER
PREMIUM GRADE . . . . **NIB $910 EX $660 GD $400**
Calibers: .22 LR, .22 WMR, .32-20, .357 Mag., .38 Special,

Universal Enforcer (3000)

**Uzi
Semi-automatic Pistol**

.38-40, .41 Colt, .44-40, .44 Special, .45 Long Colt, .45 ACP. Six-round cylinder, Bbl length: 3, 4, 4.75, 5.5, 7.5 or 10 inches. Dome Blue, Old Armory, Bone Case or nickel finish.

Flat Top (adj. sights)	NiB $1509	Ex $1186	Gd $710
U.S. Pre-War.	NiB $1400	Ex $1000	Gd $610
New Buntline Special (16-in. bbl., skeleton stock)	NiB $1900	Ex $1550	Gd $990
Bisley	NiB $1560	Ex $1210	Gd $710
Sheriff's Model	NiB $1060	Ex $900	Gd $500
Rodeo (matte finish)	NiB $700	Ex $500	Gd $350
Cowboy (Dome Blue finish, brown rubber grips)	NiB $775	Ex $600	Gd $400
Omni-Potent (Bisley grip) . . .	NiB $1500	Ex $1060	Gd $675

UNIVERSAL FIREARMS CORPORATION — Hialeah, Florida

This company was purchased by Iver Johnson Arms in the mid-1980s, when the Enforcer listed below was disc. An improved version was issued under the Iver Johnson name (see separate listing).

ENFORCER (3000)
SEMIAUTOMATIC PISTOL . . . . NiB $479 Ex $337 Gd $265
M-1 Carbine-type action. Caliber: 30 Carbine. Five-, 15- or 30-round clip magazine, 10.25-inch bbl., 17.75 inches overall. Weight: 4.5 lbs. (with 30-round magazine). Adj. rear sight, blade front. Blued finish. Walnut stock w/pistol grip and handguard. Made from 1964 to 1983.

UZI — Israel
Manufactured by Israel Military Industries, Israel currently imported by UZI America.

SEMIAUTOMATIC PISTOL . . . NiB $1044 Ex $855 Gd $658
Caliber: 9mm Para. 20-round magazine, 4.5-inch bbl., about 9.5 inches overall. Weight: 3.8 lbs. Front post-type sight, rear open-type, both adj. Disc. in 1993.

"EAGLE" SERIES SEMIAUTOMATIC DA PISTOL
Caliber: 9mm Parabellum, .40 S&W, .45 ACP (Short Slide). 10-round magazine, 3.5-, 3.7- and 4.4-inch bbl., weight: 32 oz. to 35 oz. Blade front sight, drift adjustable tritium rear. Matte blue finish. Black synthetic grips. Imported from 1997 to 1998.

Compact model (DA or DAO) . . .	NiB $540	Ex $406	Gd $317
Polymer compact model	NiB $540	Ex $496	Gd $317
Full-size model	NiB $540	Ex $496	Gd $317
Short slide model	NiB $540	Ex $496	Gd $317

WALTHER — Manufactured by German, French, Swiss and U.S. firms
The following Walther pistols were made before and during World War II by Waffenfabrik Walther, Zella-Mehlis (Thür.), Germany.

MODEL 1
AUTOMATIC PISTOL . . . . NiB $900 Ex $581 Gd $316
Caliber: .25 Auto (6.35mm). Six-round. 2.1-inch bbl., 4.4 inches overall. Weight: 12.8 oz. Fixed sights. Blued finish. Checkered hard rubber grips. Intro. in 1908.

MODEL 2 AUTOMATIC PISTOL
Caliber: .25 Auto (6.35mm). Six-round magazine, 2.1-inch bbl., 4.2 inches overall. Weight: 9.8 oz. Fixed sights. Blued finish. Checkered hard rubber grips. Intro. in 1909.

Standard model.	NiB $663	Ex $468	Gd $227
Pop-up sight model	NiB $1950	Ex $1345	Gd $1188

MODEL 3
AUTOMATIC PISTOL . . . . NiB $4010 Ex $3286 Gd $1005
Caliber: .32 Auto (7.65mm). Six-round magazine, 2.6-inch bbl., 5 inches overall. Weight: 16.6 oz. Fixed sights. Blued finish. Checkered hard rubber grips. Intro. in 1910.

MODEL 4
AUTOMATIC PISTOL . . . . NiB $556 Ex $425 Gd $235
Caliber: .32 Auto (7.65mm). Eight-round magazine, 3.5-inch bbl., 5.9 inches overall. Weight: 18.6 oz. Fixed sights. Blued finish. Checkered hard rubber grips. Made from 1910 to 1918.

MODEL 5
AUTOMATIC PISTOL . . . . NiB $660 Ex $541 Gd $204
Improved version of Model 2 w/same general specifications, distinguished chiefly by better workmanship and appearance. Intro. in 1913.

MODEL 6
AUTOMATIC PISTOL . . . . . NiB $9570 Ex $7933 Gd $5420
Caliber: 9mm Para. Eight-round magazine, 4.75-inch bbl., 8.25 inches overall. Weight: 34 oz. Fixed sights. Blued finish. Checkered hard rubber grips. Made from 1915-17. Note: The 9mm Para. cartridge is too powerful for the simple blow-back system of this pistol, so firing is not recommended.

MODEL 7
AUTOMATIC PISTOL . . . . NiB $759 Ex $553 Gd $301
Caliber: .25 Auto. (6.35mm). Eight-round magazine, 3-inch bbl., 5.3 inches overall. Weight: 11.8 oz. Fixed sights. Blued finish. Checkered hard rubber grips. Made from 1917 to 1918.

MODEL 8
AUTOMATIC PISTOL . . . . NiB $770 Ex $639 Gd $240
Caliber: .25 Auto. (6.35mm). Eight-round magazine, 2.88-inch bbl., 5.13 inches overall. Weight: 12.38 oz. Fixed sights. Blued finish. Checkered plastic grips. Made from 1920 to 1945.

MODEL 8 LIGHTWEIGHT
AUTOMATIC PISTOL . . . . NiB $733 Ex $530 Gd $422
Same as standard Model Eight except about 25 percent lighter due to use of aluminum alloys.

MODEL 9 VEST POCKET
AUTOMATIC PISTOL . . . . NiB $779 Ex $577 Gd $396
Caliber: .25 Auto (6.35mm). Six-round magazine, 2-inch bbl., 3.94 inches overall. Weight: 9 oz. Fixed sights. Blued finish. Checkered plastic grips. Made from 1921 to 1945.

Walther Model 5

Walther Model 8

Walther Model 9

MODEL HP DOUBLE-ACTION AUTOMATIC
Prewar commercial version of the P38 marked with an "N" proof over an "Eagle" or "Crown." The "HP" is an abbreviation of "Heeres Pistole" (Army Pistol). Caliber: 9mm Para. 8-round magazine, 5-inch bbl., 8.38 inches overall. Weight: About 34.5 oz. Fixed sights. Blued finish. Checkered wood or plastic grips. The Model HP is distinguished by its notably fine material and workmanship. Made from 1937 to 1944. (S/N range 1000-25900)

First production (Swedish Trials
model H1000-H2000)..... NiB $3595 Ex $2765 Gd $2064
Standard commercial production
(2000-24,000)......... NiB $2152 Ex $1825 Gd $1743
War production - marked "P38"
(24,000-26,000)....... NiB $1722 Ex $1550 Gd $1289
w/Nazi proof "Eagle/359," add $270

OLYMPIA FUNFKAMPF
MODEL AUTOMATIC..... NiB $3266 Ex $2430 Gd $2220
Caliber: .22 LR. 10-round magazine, 9.6-inch bbl., 13 inches overall. Weight: 33 oz., less weight. Set of 4 detachable weights. Adj. target sights. Blued finish. Checkered grips. Intro. in 1936.

OLYMPIA HUNTING
MODEL AUTOMATIC..... NiB $2762 Ex $2430 Gd $2220
Same general specifications as Olympia Sport Model but w/4-inch bbl., Weight: 28.5 oz.

OLYMPIA RAPID
FIRE AUTO............. NiB $2550 Ex $1620 Gd $1244
Caliber: .22 Short. Six-round magazine, 7.4-inch bbl., 10.7 inches overall. Weight: (without 12.38 oz. detachable muzzle weight,) 27.5 oz. Adj. target sights. Blued finish. Checkered grips. Made 1936 to 1940.

OLYMPIA SPORT
MODEL AUTOMATIC..... NiB $2090 Ex $1398 Gd $1269
Caliber: .22 LR. 10-round magazine, 7.4-inch bbl., 10.7 inches overall. Weight: 30.5 oz., less weight. Adj. target sights. Blued finish. Checkered grips. Set of four detachable weights was supplied at Extra cost. Made about 1936 to 1940.

P38 MILITARY DA AUTOMATIC
Modification of the Model HP adopted as an official German Service arm in 1938 and produced throughout WW II by Walther (code "ac"), Mauser (code "byf") and a few other manufacturers. General specifications and appearance same as Model HP, but w/a vast difference in quality, the P38 being a mass-produced military pistol. Some of the late wartime models were very roughly finished and tolerances were quite loose.
War Production w/Walther banner (1940)
Zero S/N 1st issue
    (S/N01-01,000)........ NiB $8130 Ex $6160 Gd $2445
Zero S/N. 2nd issue
    (S/N 01,000-03,500).... NiB $6515 Ex $5125 Gd $2309
Zero S/N. 3rd issue
    (S/N 03,500-013,000)... NiB $3130 Ex $2112 Gd $1021

WALTHER CONTRACT PISTOLS (LATE 1940-44)
"480" code Series
    (S/N 1-7,600)......... NiB $5745 Ex $3937 Gd $1590
"ac" code Ser. w/no date
    (S/N 7,350-9,700)...... NiB $6079 Ex $4390 Gd $2244
"ac" code Ser. w/.40 below
    code (S/N 9,700-9,900A) NiB $4435 Ex $3866 Gd $1879
"ac40" code inline Ser.
    (S/N 1-9,900B)......... NiB $2360 Ex $1966 Gd $909
"ac" code Ser. w/41 below code
    (S/N 1-4,5001)......... NiB $1897 Ex $1633 Gd $974
"ac" code Ser. w/42 below code
    (S/N 4,500I-9,300K)..... NiB $1610 Ex $1364 Gd $869
"ac" code Ser. w/43 date
    (inline or below).......... NiB $831 Ex $633 Gd $478
"ac" code Ser. w/45
    (inline or below).......... NiB $780 Ex $599 Gd $439

MAUSER CONTRACT PISTOLS (LATE 1942-44)
"byf" code Ser. w/42 date
    (19,000 prod.) .... NiB $1418 Ex $1023 Gd $816
"bcf" code Ser. w/43, 44 or 45 date
    (inline or below) .... NiB $984 Ex $744 Gd $612
"svw" code Ser. (French prod. w/Nazi
    proofs) .... NiB $1316 Ex $1066 Gd $693
"svw" code Ser. (French prod.
    w/star proof) .... NiB $576 Ex $500 Gd $376

SPREEWERKE CONTRACT PISTOLS (LATE 1942-45)
"cyq" code 1st Ser. w/Eagle over
    359 (500 prod.) .... NiB $1866 Ex $1598 Gd $1135
"cyq" code Standard Ser.
    (300,000 prod.) .... NiB $989 Ex $590 Gd $478
"cyq" code "0" Ser.
    (5,000 prod.) .... NiB $1132 Ex $741 Gd $562

Walther PP
(Prewar)

MODEL PP DA AUTOMATIC PISTOL

Polizeipistole (Police Pistol). Calibers: .22 LR (5.6mm), .25 Auto (6.35mm), .32 Auto (7.65mm), .380 Auto (9mm). Eight-round magazine, (7-round in .380), 3.88-inch bbl., 6.94 inches overall. Weight: 23 oz. Fixed sights. Blued finish. Checkered plastic grips. 1929-45. Post-War production and importation 1963 to 2000.

NOTE: *Wartime models are inferior in quality to prewar commercial pistols.*

COMMERICAL MODEL WITH CROWN "N" PROOF

.22 cal.	NiB $1599	Ex $1033	Gd $713
.25 cal.	NiB $8554	Ex $3390	Gd $1729
.32 cal.	NiB $890	Ex $568	Gd $376
.32 cal. (w/Dural alloy frame)	NiB $1025	Ex $979	Gd $377
.32 cal. (w/Verchromt Fin., pre-war)	NiB $3560	Ex $2533	Gd $907
.32 cal. (A.F.Stoeger Contract, pre-war)	NiB $2550	Ex $1656	Gd $691
.32 cal. (Allemagne French contract, pre-war)	NiB $1489	Ex $1189	Gd $712
.380 cal. (w/Comm. Crown "N" proof)	NiB $1578	Ex $1266	Gd $831
.380 cal. (w/Verchromt Fin., pre-war)	NiB $2779	Ex $2465	Gd $1109

WARTIME MODEL WITH EAGLE "N" PROOF

.32 cal. (w/Waffenampt proofs)	NiB $980	Ex $544	Gd $475
.32 cal. (w/Eagle "C" Nazi Police markings)	NiB $1056	Ex $744	Gd $496
.32 cal. (w/Eagle "F" Nazi Police markings)	NiB $1060	Ex $748	Gd $500
.32 cal. (w/NSKK markings)	NiB $3277	Ex $3417	Gd $1100
.32 cal. (w/NSDAP Gruppe markings)	NiB $2660	Ex $2245	Gd $1033
.380 cal. (w/Waffenampt proofs)	NiB $1440	Ex $1187	Gd $899

COMMERCIAL MODEL (POST-WAR)

.22 cal. (German manufacture)	NiB $1203	Ex $1032	Gd $601
.32 cal. (German manufacture)	NiB $1044	Ex $806	Gd $577
.380 cal. (German manufacture)	NiB $1181	Ex $1099	Gd $444
.22 cal. (French manufacture)	NiB $601	Ex $498	Gd $290
.32 cal. (French manufacture)	NiB $601	Ex $498	Gd $290
.380 cal. (French manufacture)	NiB $610	Ex $567	Gd $289
.22, .32 or .380 Cal. (other foreign manuf.)	NiB $449	Ex $346	Gd $240

MODEL PP SPORT DA AUTOMATIC PISTOL

Target version of the Model PP. Caliber: .22 LR. Eight-round magazine, 5.75- to 7.75 inch bbl. w/adjustable sights. Blue or nickel finish. Checkered plastic grips w/thumbrest. Made from 1953 to 1970.

Walther manufacture	NiB $1233	Ex $730	Gd $464
Manurhin manufacture	NiB $990	Ex $834	Gd $561
C Model (comp./SA)	NiB $1294	Ex $920	Gd $668
w/nickel finish, add			$204
w/matched bbl., weights, add			$100

MODEL PP DELUXE ENGRAVED

These elaborately engraved models are available in blued finish, silver- or gold-plated.

Blued finish	NiB $ 1667	Ex $1462	Gd $1230
Silver-plated	NiB $1922	Ex $1530	Gd $1306
Gold-plated	NiB $2130	Ex $1830	Gd $1488
w/ivory grips, add			$281
w/presentation case, add			$4750
.22 caliber, add			$75
.380 caliber, add			100%

MODEL PP LIGHTWEIGHT

Same as standard Model PP except about 25 percent lighter due to use of aluminum alloys (Dural). Values 40 percent higher. (See individual listings).

MODEL PP SUPER

DA PISTOL . . . . NiB $1066 Ex $831 Gd $623
Caliber: 9x18mm. Seven-round magazine, 3.6-inch bbl., 6.9 inches overall. Weight: 30 oz. Fixed sights. Blued finish. Checkered plastic grips. Made from 1973 to 1979.

MODEL PP 7.65MM

PRESENTATION . . . . NiB $2100 Ex $1596 Gd $1214
Made of soft aluminum alloy in green-gold color, these pistols were not intended to be fired.

MODEL PPK DOUBLE-ACTION AUTOMATIC PISTOL

Polizeipistole Kriminal (Detective Pistol). Calibers: .22 LR (5.6mm), .25 Auto (6.35mm), .32 Auto (7.65mm), .380 Auto (9mm). Seven-round magazine, (6-round in .380), 3.25-inch bbl., 5.88 inches overall. Weight: 19 oz. Fixed sights. Blued finish. Checkered plastic grips.

Note: *Wartime models are inferior in workmanship to prewar commercial pistols. Made 1931 to 1945.*

NOTE: *After both World Wars, the Walther manufacturing facility was required to cease the production of "restricted" firearms as part of the armistice agreements. Following WW II, Walther moved its manufacturing facility from the original location in Zella/Mehilis, Germany to Ulm/Donau. In 1950, the firm Manufacture de Machines du Haut Rhine at Mulhouse, France was licensed by Walther and started production of PP and PPK models at the Manurhin facility in 1952. The MK II Walthers as produced at Manurhin were imported into the U.S. until 1968 when CGA importation requirements restricted the PPK firearm configuration from further importation. As a result, Walther developed the PPK/S to conform to the new regulations and licensed Interarms to produce the firearm in the U.S. from 1986-99. From 1984-86, Manurhin imported PP and PPK/S type firearms under the Manurhin logo. Additional manufacturing facilities (both licensed & unlicensed) that produced PP and PPK type firearms were established after WW II in various locations and other countries including: China, France, Hungary, Korea, Romania and Turkey. In 1996, Walther was sold to UmarEx Sportwaffen GmbH and manufacturing facili-*

ties were relocated in Arnsberg, Germany. In 1999, Walther formed a partnership with Smith and Wesson and selected Walther firearms were licensed for production in the U.S.

COMMERCIAL MODEL W/EAGLE PROOF (PREWAR)
.22 cal. . . . . NiB $2560 Ex $1735 Gd $1509
.25 cal. . . . . NiB $10,620 Ex $6387 Gd $4960
.32 cal. . . . . NiB $1533 Ex $831 Gd $567
.380 cal. . . . . NiB $4530 Ex $3789 Gd $3320

WARTIME MODEL W/EAGLE "N" PROOF
.22 cal. . . . . NiB $2522 Ex $1733 Gd $1458
.22 cal. (w/Dural frame). . . NiB $1920 Ex $1779 Gd $1357
.32 cal. . . . . NiB $1599 Ex $1022 Gd $879
.32 cal. (w/Dural frame). . . NiB $1199 Ex $ 1022 Gd $879
.32 cal. (w/Verchromt Fin.,
   Pre-War). . . . . NiB $1199 Ex $1022 Gd $879
.380 cal. . . . . NiB $3885 Ex $2345 Gd $2097
.380 cal. (w/Dural frame). . NiB $3885 Ex $2345 Gd $2097
.380 cal. (w/Verchromt Fin.,
   Pre-War). . . . . NiB $3885 Ex $2345 Gd $2097
.32 cal. (w/Waffenampt
   proofs) . . . . NiB $2132 Ex $882 Gd $453
.32 cal. (w/Eagle "C" Nazi
   Police markings) . . . . NiB $2132 Ex $882 Gd $453
.32 cal. (w/Eagle "F" Nazi
   Police markings) . . . . NiB $2566 Ex $1145 Gd $650
.32 cal. (w/NSKK markings). . NiB $2366 Ex $1918 Gd $1333
.32 cal. (w/NSDAP
   Gruppe markings). . . . . . NiB $8560 Ex $5788 Gd $1225
.380 cal. (w/Waffenampt
   proofs) . . . . NiB $1474 Ex $1198 Gd $1029

COMMERCIAL MODEL (POST-WAR)
.22 cal. (German manufacture) . . . NiB $1076 Ex $945 Gd $411
.32 cal. (German manufacture) . . . NiB $850 Ex $601 Gd $383
.380 cal. (German manufacture). . NiB $1091 Ex $591 Gd $498
.22 cal. (French manufacture) . . NiB $2212 Ex $924 Gd $538

Walther PPK (WW II)

Walther PPK Silver-Plated

.32 cal. (French manufacture) . . NiB $857 Ex $651 Gd $437
.380 cal. (French manufacture). . NiB $1173 Ex $839 Gd $452
.22, .32 or .380 cal. (other foreign
   manuf.). . . . . NiB $332 Ex $281 Gd $201

COMMERCIAL MODEL (U.S. PRODUCTION 1986-2001)
.380 cal. (w/blue finish) . . . . . . NiB $658 Ex $499 Gd $403
.380 cal. (w/nickel finish). . . . . NiB $658 Ex $499 Gd $403
.32 or .380 Cal. (stainless steel). . NiB $658 Ex $499 Gd $403

MODEL PPK DELUXE ENGRAVED
These elaborately engraved models are available in blued finish, chrome-, silver- or gold-plated.
Blued finish . . . . NiB $1932 Ex $1543 Gd $1199
Chrome-plated . . . . NiB $3087 Ex $2156 Gd $1779
Silver-plated . . . . NiB $2234 Ex $1789 Gd $1418
Gold-plated. . . . . NiB $2567 Ex $1979 Gd $1598
w/ivory grips, add. $306
w/Presentation case, add $791
.22 cal, add. $75
.25 cal, add. $128
.380 cal, add. $110

MODEL PPK LIGHTWEIGHT
Same as standard Model PPK except about 25 percent lighter due to aluminum alloys. Values 50 percent higher.

MODEL PPK 7.65MM
PRESENTATION . . . . NiB $1856 Ex $1418 Gd $966
Made of soft aluminum alloy in green-gold color, these pistols were not intended to be fired.

MODEL PPK/S DA AUTOMATIC PISTOL
Designed to meet the requirements of the U.S. Gun Control Act of 1968, this model has the frame of the PP and the shorter slide and bbl., of the PPK. Overall length: 6.1 inches. Weight: 23 oz. Other specifications are the same as those of standard PPK except steel frame only. German, French and U.S. production 1971 to date. U.S. version made by Interarms 1978-1999, Smith & Wesson production from 2002-2009.
.22 cal. (German manufacture). . NiB $1336 Ex $1016 Gd $660
.32 cal. (German manufacture). . NiB $997 Ex $789 Gd $497
.380 cal. (German
   manufacture) . . . . NiB $1321 Ex $997 Gd $577
.22 cal. (French manufacture). . NiB $968 Ex $760 Gd $561
.32 cal. (French manufacture). . NiB $973 Ex $781 Gd $577
.380 cal. (French
   manufacture) . . . . NiB $944 Ex $632 Gd $500
.22, .32 or .380 cal., blue
   (U.S. manufacture) . . . . NiB $638 Ex $508 Gd $398
.22, .32 or .380 cal.,
   stainless (U.S. manufacture) NiB $638 Ex $508 Gd $398

NOTE: *Interarms (Interarmco) acquired a license from Walther in 1978 to manufacturer PP and PPK models at the Ranger Manufacturing Co., Inc. in Gadsden, Alabama. In 1988 the Ranger facility was licensed as EMCO and continued to produce Walther firearms for Interarms until 1996. From 1996-99, Black Creek in Gadsden, Alabama, produced Walther pistols for Interarms. In 1999, Smith & Wesson acquired manufacturing rights for Walther firearms at the Black Creek facility.*

MODELS PPK/S DELUXE ENGRAVED
These elaborately engraved models are available in blued finish, chrome-, silver- or gold-plated.
Blued finish. . . . . NiB $1634 Ex $1216 Gd $1094
Chrome-plated . . . . NiB $1552 Ex $1268 Gd $976
Silver-plated . . . . NiB $1755 Ex $1296 Gd $966

Walther Free Pistol

Walther GSP

Walther P5

Gold-plated. . . . . NiB $1889 Ex $1566 Gd $1034

NOTE: *The following Walther pistols are now manufactured by Carl Walther, Waffenfabrik, Ulm/Donau, Germany.*

SELF-LOADING
SPORT PISTOL . . . . NiB $866 Ex $856 Gd $546
Caliber: .22 LR. 10-rnd. magazine, bbl. lengths: 6- and 9-in. 9.88 inches overall w/6-inch bbl. Target sights. Blued finish. One-piece, wood or plastic grips, checkered. Intro. in 1932.

MODEL FREE PISTOL . . . . . NiB $1533 Ex $1367 Gd $1159
Single-Shot. Caliber: .22 LR. 11.7-inch heavy bbl., Weight: 48 oz. Adj. grips and target sights w/electronic trigger. Importation disc. 1991.

MODEL GSP TARGET AUTOMATIC PISTOL
Calibers: .22 LR, .32 S&W Long Wadcutter. Five-round magazine, 4.5-inch bbl., 11.8 inches overall. Weights: 44.8 oz. (.22 cal.) or 49.4 oz. (.32 cal.). Adj. target sights. Black finish. Walnut thumbrest grips w/adj. handrest. Made 1969 to 1994.

.22 LR . . . . NiB $1598 Ex $1432 Gd $889
.32 S&W Long Wadcutter. . NiB $2773 Ex $2513 Gd $2122
Conversion unit. .22 Short or .22 LR, add $1071

MODEL OSP RAPID
FIRE TARGET PISTOL . . . . . NiB $1744 Ex $1509 Gd $1345
Caliber: .22 Short. Five-round magazine, 4.5-inch bbl., 11.8 inches overall. Weight: 42.3 oz. Adj. target sights. Black finish. Walnut thumbrest grips w/ adj. handrest. .22 LR conversion unit available (add $281.) Made from 1968 to 1994.

MODEL P4 (P38-LV)
DA PISTOL. . . . . NiB $844 Ex $712 Gd $448
Similar to P38 except has an uncocking device instead of a manual safety. Caliber: 9mm Para. 4.3-inch bbl., 7.9 inches overall. Other general specifications same as for current model P38. Made from 1974 to 1982.

MODEL P5 DA PISTOL
. . . . . . NiB $1654 Ex $804 Gd $543
Alloy frame w/frame-mounted decocking levers. Caliber: 9mm Para. Eight-round magazine, 3.5-inch bbl., 7 inches overall. Weight: 28 oz. blued finish. Checkered walnut or synthetic grips. Made from 1997 to date.

MODEL P5 COMPACT
DA PISTOL . . . . NiB $1693 Ex $988 Gd $497
Similar to model P5 except w/3.1-inch bbl. and weight: 26 oz. Imported from 1987.

MODEL P1 DA AUTOMATIC
Postwar commercial version of the P38, has light alloy frame. Calibers: .22 LR, 7.65mm Luger, 9mm Para. Eight-round magazine, bbl., lengths: 5.1-inch in .22 caliber, 4.9- inch in 7.65mm and 9mm, 8.5 inches overall. Weight: 28.2 oz. Fixed sights. Nonreflective black finish. Checkered plastic grips. Made from 1957 to 1989. Note: The "P1" was W. German Armed Forces official pistol.
.22 LR . . . . NiB $805 Ex $644 Gd $433
Other calibers. . . . . NiB $806 Ex $610 Gd $398

MODEL P38 DELUXE ENGRAVED PISTOL
Elaborately engraved, available in blued or chrome-, silver- or gold-plated finish.
Blued finish. . . . . NiB $2077 Ex $1566 Gd $1028
Chrome-plated . . . . NiB $1776 Ex $1432 Gd $998
Silver-plated . . . . NiB $1712 Ex $1429 Gd $1043
Gold-plated. . . . . NiB $1987 Ex $1603 Gd $1163

MODEL P38K
. . . . NiB $886 Ex $781 Gd $468
Short-barreled version of current P38, the "K" standing for "kurz" (meaning short). Same general specifications as standard model except 2.8-inch bbl., 6.3 inches overall, weight: 27.2 oz. Front sight is slide mounted. Caliber: 9mm Para. Made from 1974 to 1980.

MODEL P88 DA AUTOMATIC
PISTOL . . . . NiB $1132 Ex $988 Gd $774
Caliber: 9mm Para. 15-round magazine, 4-inch bbl., 7.38 inches overall. Weight: 31.5 oz. Blade front sight, adj. rear. Checkered black synthetic grips. External hammer w/ambidExtrous decocking levers. Alloy frame w/matte blued steel slide. Made 1987 to 1993.

MODEL P88 DA COMPACT
Similar to the standard P88 Model except w/10- or 13-round magazine, 3.8-inch bbl., 7.1 inches overall. Weight: 29 oz. Imported from 1993 to 2003.

Walther P38

Walther P38K

Walther P88

Walther TPH

Model P88
(early importation) . . . . NiB $1088 Ex $975 Gd $648
Model P88
(post 1994 importation) . . . . NiB $1088 Ex $975 Gd $648

MODEL P99 DA
AUTOMATIC PISTOL . . . . NiB $756 Ex $576 Gd $486
Calibers: 9mm Para., .40 S&W or 9x21mm. 10-round magazine, 4-inch bbl., 7.2 inches overall. Weight: 22-25 oz. AmbidExtrous magazine release, decocking lever and 3-function safety. Interchangeable front post sight, micro-adj. rear. Polymer gripframe w/blued slide. Imported from 1995 to date.

MODEL TPH DA POCKET PISTOL
Light alloy frame. Calibers: .22 LR, .25 ACP (6.35mm). Six-round magazine, 2.25-inch bbl., 5.38 inches overall. Weight: 14 oz. Fixed sights. Blued finish. Checkered plastic grips. Made 1968 to date. Note: Few Walther-made models reached the U.S. because of import restrictions. A U.S.-made version was mfd. by Interarms from 1986 to 1999.
German model . . . . NiB $1100 Ex $756 Gd $602
U.S. model . . . . NiB $900 Ex $743 Gd $436

NOTE: *The Walther Olympia Model pistols were manufactured 1952-1963 by Hämmerli AG Jagd-und Sportwaffenfabrik, Lenzburg, Switzerland, and marketed as "Hämmerli-Walther." See Hämmerli listings for specific data.*

OLYMPIA MODEL 200 AUTO PISTOL,
1952 TYPE. . . . . NiB $729 Ex $612 Gd $453
Similar to 1936 Walther Olympia Funfkampf Model.
Note: For Hammerli-Walther Models—200, 201, 202, 203, 204, and 205—see listings under Hammerli Section.

WARNER — Norwich, Connecticut
Warner Arms Corp. or Davis-Warner Arms Co.

INFALLIBLE POCKET
AUTOMATIC PISTOL . . . . NiB $507 Ex $356 Gd $253
Caliber: .32 Auto. Seven-round magazine, 3-inch bbl., 6.5 inches overall. Weight: About 24 oz. Fixed sights. Blued finish. Hard rubber grips. Made from 1917 to 1919.

WEBLEY & SCOTT LTD. — London and Birmingham, England

MODEL 1909 9MM MILITARY
& POLICE AUTOMATIC . . . NiB $2090 Ex $1465 Gd $1288
Caliber: 9mm Browning Long. Eight-round magazine, 8 inches overall. Weight: 32 oz. Fixed sights. Blued finish. Checkered Vulcanite grips. Made from 1909 to 1930.

Walther P99

**Webley 9MM
Military Police Automatic**

**Webley Mark III
38 Military & Police Revolver**

MODEL 1907 HAMMER
AUTOMATIC . . . . NiB $1006 Ex $866 Gd $207
Caliber: .25 Automatic. Six-round magazine, overall length: 4.75 inches. Weight: 11.75 oz. No sights. Blued finish. Checkered Vulcanite grips. Made from 1906 to 1940.

MODEL 1912 HAMMERLESS
AUTOMATIC. . . . . NiB $1500 Ex $1306 Gd $1233
Caliber: .25 Automatic. Six-round magazine, overall length: 4.25 inches, weight: 9.75 oz. Fixed sights. Blued finish. Checkered Vulcanite grips. Made from 1909 to 1940.

MARK I 455
AUTOMATIC PISTOL . . . . . NiB $2505 Ex $1988 Gd $1600
Caliber: .455 Webley Auto. Seven-round magazine, 5-inch bbl., 8.5 inches overall. Weight: About 39 oz. Fixed sights. Blued finish. Checkered Vulcanite grips. Made 1913-31. Reissued during WWII. Total production about 9,300. Note: Mark I No. 2 is same pistol w/adj. rear sight and modified manual safety.

MARK III 38 MILITARY & POLICE
DA REVOLVER . . . . NiB $974 Ex $789 Gd $633
Hinged frame. DA. Caliber: .38 S&W. Six-round cylinder, bbl. lengths: 3- and 4-inches. 9.5 inches overall (with 4-inch bbl.). Weight: 21 oz. (with 4-inch bbl.). Fixed sights. Blued finish. Checkered walnut or Vulcanite grips. Made from 1897 to 1945.

MARK IV 22 CALIBER
TARGET REVOLVER . . . . NiB $806 Ex $691 Gd $386
Same frame and general appearance as Mark IV .38. Caliber: .22 LR. Six-round cylinder, 6-inch bbl., 10.13 inches overall. Weight: 34 oz. Target sights. Blued finish. Checkered grips. Disc. in 1945.

MARK IV 38 MILITARY & POLICE
DA REVOLVER . . . . NiB $806 Ex $691 Gd $386
Identical in appearance to the double-action Mark IV .22 w/ hinged frame except chambered for .38 S&W. Six-round cylinder, bbl. length: 3-, 4- and 5-inches; 9.13 inches overall (with 5-inch bbl.). Weight: 27 oz. (with 5-inch bbl.). Fixed sights. Blued finish. Checkered grips. Made from 1929 to 1957.

MARK VI NO. 1 BRITISH SERVICE
DA REVOLVER . . . . NiB $691 Ex $567 Gd $478
Hinged frame. Caliber: 455 Webley. Six-round cylinder, bbl. lengths: 4-, 6- and 7.5-inches; 11.25 inches overall (with 6-inch bbl.). Weight: 38 oz. (with 6-inch bbl.). Fixed sights. Blued finish. Checkered walnut or Vulcanite grips. Made from 1915 to 1947.

MARK VI 22
TARGET REVOLVER . . . . NiB $1266 Ex $1096 Gd $909
Same frame and general appearance as the Mark VI 455. Caliber: .22 LR. Six-round cylinder, 6-inch bbl., 11.25 inches overall. Weight: 40 oz. Target sights. Blued finish. Checkered walnut or Vulcanite grips. Disc. in 1945.

METROPOLITAN POLICE
AUTOMATIC PISTOL . . . . . NiB $1629 Ex $1528 Gd $1266
Calibers: .32 Auto, .380 Auto. Eight-round (.32) or 7-round (.380) magazine, 3.5-inch bbl., 6.25 inches overall. weight: 20 oz. Fixed sights. Blued finish. Checkered Vulcanite grips. Made from 1906-40 (.32) and 1908 to 1920 (.380).

R.I.C. MODELS DA REVOLVER NiB $950 Ex $700 Gd $500
Royal Irish Constabulary or Bulldog Model. Solid frame. Caliber: .455 Webley. Five-round cylinder, 2.25-inch bbl., weight: 21 oz. Fixed sights. Blued finish. Checkered walnut or vulcanite grips. Made from 1897-1939.

SEMIAUTOMATIC
SINGLE-SHOT PISTOL . . . . . NiB $1090 Ex $ 916 Gd $617
Similar in appearance to the Webley Metropolitan Police Automatic, this pistol is "semiautomatic" in the sense that the fired case is Extracted and ejected and the hammer cocked as in a blow-back automatic pistol; it is loaded singly and the slide manually operated in loading. Caliber: .22 Long, 4.5- or 9-inch bbl., 10.75 inches overall (with 9-inch bbl.). Weight: 24 oz. (with 9-inch bbl.). Adj. sights. Blued finish. Checkered Vulcanite grips. Made from 1911 to 1927.

SINGLE-SHOT
TARGET PISTOL . . . . NiB $1588 Ex $1469 Gd $1190
Hinge frame. Caliber: .22 LR. 10-inch bbl., 15 inches overall. Weight: 37 oz. Fixed sights on earlier models, current production has adj. rear sight. Blued finish. Checkered walnut or Vulcanite grips. Made from 1909.

WEBLEY-FOSBERY AUTOMATIC REVOLVER
Hinged frame. Recoil action revolves cylinder and cocks hammer. Caliber: 455 Webley. Six-round cylinder, 6-inch bbl., 12 inches overall. Weight: 42 oz. Fixed or adjustable sights. Blued finish. Checkered walnut grips. Made 1901-1939. Note: A few were produced in caliber .38 Colt Auto w/an 8-shot cylinder (very rare).
1901 model. . . . . NiB $12,600 Ex $8600 Gd $5500
1902 model .38 Colt (8-round), add, add. 300%
1903 model. . . . . NiB $10,000 Ex $7600 Gd $4600
Target model w/adjustable sights, add 20%

**Webley-Fosbery Automatic
Revolver**

**Dan Wesson
Model 14-2 Service**

**Dan Wesson
Model 15-2H Interchangeable Heavy Barrels**

WESSON FIREARMS CO., INC. — Palmer, MA

Renamed Dan Wesson Firearms, Inc. Acquired by CZ-USA in 2005 and renamed Dan Wesson. Also see Dan Wesson for current production.

Note: *Models with a three digit model number that begins with a "7" are starinless steel models.*

MODEL 8 SERVICE
Same general specifications as Model 14 except caliber .38 Special. Made from 1971 to 1975. Values same as for Model 14.

MODEL 8-2 SERVICE
Similar as Model 14-2 except caliber .38 Special. Made from 1975 to date. Values same as for Model 14-2.

MODEL 9 TARGET
Same as Model 15 except caliber .38 Special. Made from 1971 to 1975. Values same as for Model 15.

MODEL 9-2 TARGET
Same as Model 15-2 except caliber .38 Special. Made from 1975 to date. Values same as for Model 15-2.

MODEL 9-2H HEAVY BARREL
Same general specifications as Model 15-2H except caliber .38 Special. Made from 1975 to date. Values same as for Model 15-2H. Disc. 1983.

MODEL 9-2HV VENT RIB HEAVY BARREL
Same as Model 15-2HV except caliber .38 Special. Made from 1975 to date. Values same as for Model 15-2HV.

MODEL 9-2V VENT RIB
Same as Model 15-2V except caliber .38 Special. Made from 1975 to date. Values same as for Model 15-2H.

MODEL 11 SERVICE DA REVOLVER
Caliber: .357 Magnum. Six-round cylinder. bbl. lengths: 2.5-, 4-, 6-inches interchangeable bbl. assemblies, 9 inches overall (with 4-inch bbl.). Weight: 38 oz. (with 4-inch bbl.). Fixed

sights. Blued finish. Interchangeable grips. Made from 1970-71. Note: The Model 11 has an External bbl. nut.
w/one bbl. assembly and grip . . NiB $274 Ex $180 Gd $101
Extra bbl. assembly, add $75
Extra grip, add $50

MODEL 12 TARGET
Same general specifications as Model 11 except has adj. sights. Made from 1970-71.
w/one-bbl. assembly and grip . . NiB $290 Ex $204 Gd $135
Extra bbl. assembly, add $75
Extra grip, add $50

MODEL 14 SERVICE DA REVOLVER
Caliber: .357 Magnum. Six-round cylinder, bbl. length: 2.25-, 3.75, 5.75-inches; interchangeable bbl. assemblies, 9 inches overall (with 3.75-inch bbl.). Weight: 36 oz. (with 3.75-inch bbl.). Fixed sights. Blued or nickel finish. Interchangeable grips. Made 1971-75. Note: Model 14 has recessed bbl. nut.
w/one-bbl. assembly and grip . . NiB $225 Ex $158 Gd $101
Extra bbl. assembly, add $61
Extra grip, add $25

MODEL 14-2 SERVICE DA REVOLVER
Caliber: .357 Magnum. Six-round cylinder, bbl. lengths: 2.5-, 4-, 6-, 8-inch; interchangeable bbl. assemblies, 9.25 inches overall (with 4-inch bbl.) Weight: 34 oz. (with 4-inch bbl.). Fixed sights. Blued finish. Interchangeable grips. Made from 1975 to 1995. Note: Model 14-2 has recessed bbl. nut.
**w/one bbl. assembly
    (8 inch) and grip . . . . NiB $270 Ex $204 Gd $158**
**w/one bbl. assembly
    (other lengths) and grip . . . . NiB $270 Ex $204 Gd $158**
Extra bbl. assembly, 8 inch, add $75
**Extra bbl. assembly,
    other lengths, add. $75**
Extra grip, add $50

MODEL 15 TARGET
Same general specifications as Model 14 except has adj. sights. Made from 1971 to 1975.
w/one bbl. assembly and grip . . NiB $306 Ex $230 Gd $190
Extra bbl. assembly, add $75
Extra grip, add $50

MODEL 15-2 TARGET
Same general specifications as Model 14-2 except has adj. rear sight and interchangeable blade front; also avail. w/10-, 12- or 15-inch bbl., Made from 1975 to 1995.
w/one bbl. assembly (8 inch) and grip . . NiB $362 Ex $289 Gd $187
**w/one bbl. assembly (10 inch)
    and grip . . . . NiB $362 Ex $289 Gd $187**
**w/one bbl. assembly
    (12 inch)/grip. Disc. . . . . NiB $362 Ex $289 Gd $187**
**w/one bbl. assembly
    (15 inch)/grip. Disc. . . . . NiB $362 Ex $289 Gd $187**
**w/one-bbl. assembly
    (other lengths)/grip. . . . . NiB $244 Ex $159 Gd $133**
Extra bbl. assembly, add $75
Extra grip, add $50

MODEL 15-2H HEAVY BARREL
Same as Model 15-2 except has heavy bbl., assembly weight: with 4-inch bbl., 38 oz. Made from 1975 to 1983.
w/one bbl. assembly . . . . NiB $500 Ex $345 Gd $235
Extra bbl. assembly, add $75
Extra grip, add $50

MODEL 15-2HV VENT RIB HEAVY BARREL

Same as Model 15-2 except has vent rib heavy bbl. assembly; weight: (w/4-inch bbl.) 37 oz. Made from 1975 to 1995.

w/one bbl. assembly
(8 inch) and grip . . . . NiB $303 Ex $240 Gd $162
w/one bbl. assembly
(10 inch) and grip . . . . NiB $303 Ex $240 Gd $162
w/one bbl. assembly
(12 inch) and grip . . . . NiB $303 Ex $240 Gd $162
w/one bbl. assembly
(15 inch) and grip . . . . NiB $321 Ex $273 Gd $192
w/one bbl. assembly
(other lengths) and grip . . . . NiB $198 Ex $241 Gd $163
Extra bbl. assembly (8 inch), add $75
Extra bbl. assembly (10 inch), add $75
Extra bbl. assembly (12 inch), add $75
Extra bbl. assembly (15 inch), add $75
Extra bbl. assembly (other lengths), add $75
Extra grip, add $50

MODEL 15-2V VENT RIB

Same as Model 15-2 except has vent rib bbl. assembly, weight: 35 oz. (with 4-inch bbl.). Made from 1975 to date. Values same as for 15-2H.

HUNTER PACS

Dan Wesson Hunter Pacs are offered in all Magnum calibers and include heavy vent rib 8-inch shrouded bbl., Burris scope mounts, bbl. changing tool in a case.

HP22M-V . . . . NiB $893 Ex $660 Gd $473
HP22M-2 . . . . NiB $733 Ex $612 Gd $447
HP722M-V . . . . NiB $843 Ex $632 Gd $439
HP722M-2 . . . . NiB $806 Ex $612 Gd $408
HP32-V . . . . NiB $785 Ex $571 Gd $395
HP32-2 . . . . NiB $691 Ex $530 Gd $425
HP732-V . . . . NiB $816 Ex $597 Gd $434
HP732-2 . . . . NiB $755 Ex $608 Gd $449
HP15-V . . . . NiB $755 Ex $608 Gd $449
HP15-2 . . . . NiB $780 Ex $601 Gd $437
HP715-V . . . . NiB $831 Ex $654 Gd $479
HP715-2 . . . . NiB $755 Ex $657 Gd $478
HP41-V . . . . NiB $688 Ex $556 Gd $425
HP741-V . . . . NiB $841 Ex $689 Gd $495
HP741-2 . . . . NiB $739 Ex $607 Gd $439
HP44-V . . . . NiB $884 Ex $700 Gd $536
HP44-2 . . . . NiB $739 Ex $607 Gd $439
HP744-V . . . . NiB $933 Ex $781 Gd $576
HP744-2 . . . . NiB $897 Ex $738 Gd $546
HP40-V . . . . NiB $616 Ex $497 Gd $366
HP40-2 . . . . NiB $827 Ex $691 Gd $496
HP740-V . . . . NiB $988 Ex $816 Gd $590
HP740-2 . . . . NiB $918 Ex $729 Gd $526
HP375-V . . . . NiB $595 Ex $500 Gd $356
HP375-2 . . . . NiB $944 Ex $786 Gd $590
HP45-V . . . . NiB $734 Ex $626 Gd $439

WHITNEY FIREARMS COMPANY —
Hartford, Connecticut

NOTE: *Since 2004 the Whitney Wolverine design is currently manufactured by Olympic Arms, Olympia, WA. Also see Olympic Arms.*

WOLVERINE AUTOMATIC PISTOL

Dural frame/shell contains all operating components. Caliber: .22 LR. 10-round magazine, 4.63-inch bbl., 9 inches overall.

Whitney Firearms Company Wolverine w/ nickel finish

Weight: 23 oz. Partridge-type sights. Blued or nickel finish. Plastic grips. Made from 1955 to 1962.
Blue finish . . . . NiB $680 Ex $575 Gd $383
Nickel finish . . . . NiB $1330 Ex $1080 Gd $610

WICHITA ARMS — Wichita, Kansas

CLASSIC PISTOL

Caliber: Chambered to order. Bolt-action, single-shot. 11.25-inch octagonal bbl., 18 inches overall. Weight: 78 oz. Open micro sights. Custom-grade checkered walnut stock. Blued finish. Made from 1980 to 1997.
Standard . . . . NiB $3310 Ex $2546 Gd $2245
Presentation grade
(engraved) . . . . NiB $5379 Ex $3916 Gd $2166

HUNTER PISTOL . . . . NiB $1433 Ex $1096 Gd $872
Bolt-action, single-shot. Calibers: .22 LR, .22 WRF, 7mm Super Mag., 7-30 Waters, .30-30 Win., .32 H&R Mag., .357 Mag., .357 Super Mag. 10.5-inch bbl., 16.5 inches overall, weight: 60 oz. No sights (scope mount only). Stainless steel finish. Walnut stock. Made from 1983 to 1994.

INTERNATIONAL PISTOL . . . . . NiB $733 Ex $567 Gd $453
Top-break, single-shot. SA. Calibers: 7-30 Waters, 7mm Super Mag., 7R (.30-30 Win. necked to 7mm), .30-30 Win. .357 Mag., .357 Super Mag., .32 H&R Mag., .22 Mag., .22 LR. 10- and 14-inch bbl. (10.5 inch for centerfire calibers). Weight: 50-71 oz. Partridge front sight, adj. rear. Walnut forend and grips.

MK-40 SILHOUETTE . . . . . . NiB $1613 Ex $1407 Gd $1206
Calibers: .22-250, 7mm IHMSA, .308 Win. Bolt-action, single-shot. 13-inch bbl., 19.5 inches overall. Weight: 72 oz. Wichita Multi-Range sight system. Aluminum receiver w/blued bbl., gray Fiberthane glass stock. Made from 1981 to 1994.

SILHOUETTE PISTOL . . . NiB $1587 Ex. . $1453 Gd $1356
Calibers: .22-250, 7mm IHMSA 308 Win. Bolt-action, single-shot. 14.94-inch bbl., 21.38 inches overall. Weight: 72 oz. Wichita Multi-Range sight system. Blued finish. Walnut or gray Fiberthane glass stock. Walnut center or rear grip. Made from 1979 to 1994.

WILKINSON ARMS — Parma, Idaho

LINDA . . . . NiB $680 Ex $557 Gd $360
Semi-automatic. Caliber: 9mm Para. 31-rnd. magazine, 8.25-in. bbl., 12.25 inches overall. Weight: 77 oz. Rear peep sight w/blade front. Blued finish. Checkered composition grips. Made from 2000 to 2005.

SHERRY . . . . NiB $274 Ex $188 Gd $126
Semi-automatic. Caliber: .22 LR. 8-rnd. magazine, 2.13-in. bbl., 4.38 inches overall. Weight: 9.25 oz. Crossbolt safety.

Wilkinson Arms Linda

Zastava M88A

Zastava CZ999

Zastava M57

Zastava M70

Fixed sights. Blued or blue-gold finish. Checkered composition grips. Made from 2000 to 2005.

DIANE. . . . . **NiB $160 Ex $97 Gd $55**
Semi-automatic. Caliber: .25 ACP, 6-rnd. magazine, 2.125-in. bbl. Weight: 77 oz. Rear peep sight w/blade front. Blued finish. Checkered composition grips. Made from 2000 to 2005.

ZASTAVA ARMS — Serbia

NOTE: *Established in 1853, Zastava firearms have been imported into the U.S. by Century Arms International, EAA, Remington and others.*

CZ999 . . . . **NiB $475 Ex $420 Gd $265**
Semi-automatic. DA/SA. Caliber: 9mm, 10- or 15-rnd. magazine, 4.25-in. bbl., 7.8 inches overall. Weight: 33.5 oz. Fixed sight. Finish: matte black. Checkered polymer grips. Made from 2013 to date.

CZ999 Compact (3.5-in. bbl.) . . **NiB $475 Ex $420 Gd $265**

M57 . . . . **NiB $310 Ex $300 Gd $180**
Similar to Soviet TT. Semi-automatic. SA. Caliber: 7.62x25mm Tokarev, 9-rnd. magazine, 4.5-in. bbl., 7.9 inches overall. Weight: 31 oz. Fixed sight. Finish: blued. Polymer grips. Manual safety. Made from 2013 to date.

M70A . . . . **NiB $310 Ex $300 Gd $180**
Similar to Soviet TT. Semi-automatic. SA. Caliber: 9mm, 9-rnd. magazine, 4.5-in. bbl., 7.9 inches overall. Weight: 31 oz. Fixed sight. Finish: blued. Polymer grips. Manual safety. Made from 2013 to date.

M88 . . . . **NiB $310 Ex $300 Gd $180**
Semi-automatic. SA. Caliber: 9mm, 9-rnd. magazine, 3.8-in. bbl., 6.9 inches overall. Weight: 29.9 oz. Fixed sight. Finish: blued. Polymer grips. Manual safety. Made from 2013 to date.

Rifles

A.A. ARMS — Monroe, North Carolina

AR-9 SEMIAUTOMATIC
CARBINE . . . .**NiB $805 Ex $641 Gd $439**
Semiautomatic recoil-operated rifle w/side-folding metal stock design. Fires from a closed bolt. Caliber: 9mm Parabellum. 20-round magazine. 16.25-inch bbl., 33 inches overall. Weight: 6.5 lbs. Fixed blade, protected postfront sight adjustable for elevation, winged square notched rear. Matte phosphate/blue or nickel finish. Checkered polymer grip/frame. Made 1991 to 1994 (banned).

ACCURACY INTERNATIONAL LTD. (AI) — Hampshire, England

Currently U.S. office Fredericksburg, VA; formerly Orchard Park, NY.

AE MODEL . . . .**NiB $3600 Ex $3330 Gd $2780**
Similar to AWP Model. Caliber: .243 Win., .260 Rem., or 6.5 Creedmoor, 5-rnd. magazine. 20- or 24-inch bbl. Weight: 8.5 lbs. Imported 2002 to present.

AW MODEL . . . .**NiB $6050 Ex $5600 Gd $4700**
Bolt-action. Caliber: .243 Win., .260 Rem., 6.5 Creedmoor, .300 Win. Mag., or .338 Lapua Mag. 10-rnd. magazine. 20-, 24-, 26- or 27-inch bbl. Weight: 14 lbs. Imported 1995 to present.

AWP MODEL . . . .**NiB $4300 Ex $3700 Gd $3200**
Similar to AW model except 20- or 24-in. bbl. w/o muzzle device. Weight: 15 lbs. Imported 1995 to 2007.

AW50 MODEL . . . .**NiB $12,500 Ex $10,600 Gd $9000**
Bolt-action. Caliber: .50 BMG. 5-rnd. magazine. 27-in. bbl. w/ muzzle brake. Weight: 30 lbs. Imported 1998 to 2012.

AWM MODEL . . . .**NiB $12,500 Ex $10,600 Gd $9000**
Bolt-action. Caliber: .300 Win. Mag. or .338 Lapua Mag. 5-rnd. magazine. 20-, 24-, 26- or 27-in. bbl. w/ or w/o muzzle brake. Weight: 15.5 lbs. Imported 1995 to 2009.

AX MODEL . . . .**NiB $6500 Ex $6000 Gd $5500**
Bolt-action. Caliber: .243 Win., .260 Rem., 6.5 Creedmoor, .308 Win., or .338 Lapua Mag. 10-rnd. magazine. 20-, 24-, 26- or 27-inch bbl. Folding chassis. Finish: black, green or dark earth.

AXMC MODEL . . . .**NiB $6500 Ex $6000 Gd $5500**
Bolt-action, multi-caliber system. Caliber: .308 Win., .300 Win. Mag. or .338 Lapua Mag. 10-rnd. magazine. 20-, 24-, 26- or 27-inch bbl. Weight: 14.6 lbs. Folding chassis. Finish: black, green or pale brown. Imported 2014 to present.

ACTION ARMS — Philadelphia, Pennsylvania

MODEL B SPORTER
SEMI-AUTOMATIC CARBINE . . . . .**NiB $650 Ex $572 Gd $380**
Similar to Uzi Carbine (see separate listing) except w/thumbhole stock. Caliber: 9mm Parabellum, 10-round magazine. 16-inch bbl. Weight: 8.75 lbs. Post front sight; adj. rear. Imported 1994.

TIMBER WOLF REPEATING RIFLE
Calibers: .357 Mag./.38 Special and .44 Mag. slide-action. Tubular magazine holds 10 and 8 rounds, respectively. 18.5-inch bbl. 36.5 inches overall. Weight: 5.5 lbs. Fixed blade front sight; adj. rear. Receiver w/integral scope mounts. Checkered walnut stock. Imported from 1989 to 1993, later by I.M.I. Israel.
Blued model . . . .**NiB $338 Ex $271 Gd $190**
Chrome model, add **$75**
.44 Mag., add **$126**

ALPHA ARMS, INC. — Dallas, Texas

CUSTOM BOLT-ACTION RIFLE . **NiB $1707 Ex $1335 Gd $876**
Calibers: .17 Rem. thru .338 Win. Mag. Right or left-hand action in three action lengths w/three-lug locking system and 60-degree bolt rotation. 20- to 24-inch round or octagonal bbl. Weight: 6 to 7 lbs. No sights. Presentation-grade California Claro walnut stock w/hand-rubbed oil finish, custom inletted sling swivels and ebony forend tip. Made from 1984 to 1987.

ALASKAN BOLT-ACTION RIFLE . . **NiB $1706 Ex $1337 Gd $869**
Similar to Custom model but w/stainless-steel bbl. and receiver w/ all other parts coated w/Nitex. Weight: 6.75 to 7.25 lbs. Open sights w/bbl-band sling swivel. Classic-style Alpha wood stock w/Niedner-style steel grip cap and solid recoil pad. Made from 1985 to 1987.

GRAND SLAM
BOLT-ACTION RIFLE. . . . .**NiB $1322 Ex $1065 Gd $795**
Same as Custom model but has Alphawood (fiberglass and wood) classic-style stock featuring Niedner-style grip cap. Wt: 6.5 lbs. Left-hand models same value. Made 1985 to 1987.custom Bolt-Action Rifle Same as Custom Rifle except designed on Mauser-style action w/claw extractor drilled and tapped for scope. Originally designated Alpha Model 1. Calibers: .243, 7mm-08, .308 original chambering (1984 to 1985) up to .338 Win. Mag. in standard model; .338 thru .458 Win. Mag. in Big Five model (1987). Teflon-coated trigger guard/floorplate assembly. Made from1984 to 1987.

Action Arms Timber Wolf

Alpha Arms Custom

Alpha Arms Alaskan

Alpha Arms Jaguar

Jaguar Grade I . . . . NiB $1035 Ex $855 Gd $624
Jaguar Grade II. . . . . NiB $1268 Ex $684 Gd $707
Jaguar Grade III . . . . NiB $1319 Ex $1046 Gd $756
Jaguar Grade IV . . . . NiB $1424 Ex $1056 Gd $755
Big Five model . . . . NiB $1717 Ex $1198 Gd $977

AMERICAN ARMS — N. Kansas City, Missouri

1860 HENRY. . . . . NiB $926 Ex $698 Gd $530
Replica of 1860 Henry rifle. Calibers: .44-40 or .45 LC. 24.25-inch half-octagonal bbl. 43.75 inches overall. Weight: 9.25 lbs. Brass frame and appointments. Straight-grip walnut buttstock.

1866 WINCHESTER
Replica of 1866 Winchester. Calibers: .44-40 or .45 LC. 19-inch round tapered bbl. (carbine) or 24.25-inch tapered octagonal bbl. (rifle). 38 to 43.25 inches overall. Weight: 7.75 or 8.15 lbs. Brass frame, elevator and buttplate. Walnut buttstock and forend.
Carbine. . . . . NiB $743 Ex $625 Gd $409
Rifle . . . . NiB $743 Ex $625 Gd $409

1873 WINCHESTER
Replica of 1873 Winchester rifle. Calibers: .44-40 or .45 LC. 24.25-inch tapered octagonal bbl. w/tubular magazine. Color casehardened steel frame w/brass elevator and ejection port cover. Walnut buttstock w/steel buttplate.
Standard model. . . . . NiB $876 Ex $710 Gd $419
Deluxe model . . . . NiB $1141 Ex $924 Gd $640

AMERICAN SPIRIT ARMS CORP. — Scottsdale, Arizona

A2 CAR CARBINE. . . . . NiB $1041 Ex $703 Gd $544
Caliber: 9mm Parabellum. Forged receiver, non-collapsible stock. Bbl.: 16-inch Wilson w/o muzzle brake, bird cage flash hider (pre-ban) or muzzle brake (post-ban).

ASA 24-INCH MATCH RIFLE NiB $1806 Ex $1106 Gd $789
Caliber: .308 Win. Bbl.: 24-in. stainless steel match w/ or w/o fluting/porting. Side-charging handle; pistol grip. Introduced 2002.

ASA A2 RIFLE . . . . NiB $926 Ex $633 Gd $509
Caliber: .223 Rem. A2 receiver; 20-inch National Match barrel. Intro. 1999.

ASA BULL BARREL A2 RIFLE . . NiB $989 Ex $733 Gd $535
Similar to Flattop Rifle except has A2 upper receiver with carrying handle and sights. Introduced 1999.

ASA BULL BARREL FLATTOP NiB $1043 Ex $709 Gd $533
Semi-automatic. Caliber: .223 Rem. Patterned after AR-15. Forged steel lower receiver, aluminum flattop upper receiver, 24-in. stainless bull barrel, free-floating aluminum hand guard, includes Harris bipod.

ASA CARBINE. . . . . NiB $1077 Ex $707 Gd $589
Caliber: .223 Rem. or Short. Side-charging, flattop receiver; M4 hand guard; 16-inch National Match bbl. w/slotted muzzle brake.

ASA M4 RIFLE. . . . . NiB $944 Ex $679 Gd $482
Caliber: .223 Rem. Non-collapsible stock, M4 hand guard, 16-inch bbl. w/muzzle brake; aluminum flattop upper receiver.

Anschutz Model 54.18MS-REP

ASA TACTICAL RIFLE . . . . . . NiB $1788 Ex $1096 Gd $780
Caliber: .308 Win. Bbl.: 16-inch stainless steel regular or match; side-charging handle; pistol grip.
Match (w/fluted bbl. match trigger, chrome finish) Add $525

BULL BARREL A2 INVADER . . NiB $1032 Ex $710 Gd $544
Caliber: .223 Rem. Similar to ASA 24-inch bull bbl. rifle except has 16-inch stainless steel bbl.. Introduced 1999.

DCM SERVICE RIFLE . . . . NiB $1412 Ex $915 Gd $618
Caliber: .223 Rem. Bbl.: 20-inch stainless steel match type with free-floating shroud. National Match front and rear sights; match trigger; pistol grip.

FLATTOP CAR RIFLE . . . . NiB $1041 Ex $703 Gd $544
Caliber: 9mm Parabellum. Similar to A2 CAR Rifle except flattop design w/o sights. Introduced 2002.

LIMITED MATCH RIFLE . . . . . NiB $1411 Ex $909 Gd $579
Caliber: .223 Rem. Bbl.: 16-inch fluted stainless steel match with round shroud. National Match front and rear sights; match trigger.

OPEN MATCH RIFLE . . . . . . NiB $1471 Ex $1097 Gd $745
Caliber: .223 Rem. Bbl.: 16-inch fluted and ported stainless steel match with round shroud. Flattop without sights, forged upper and lower receiver, match trigger. Introduced 2001.

POST-BAN CARBINE . . . . NiB $909 Ex $690 Gd $482
Caliber: .223 Rem. Wilson 16-inch National Match bbl.; non-collapsible stock. Introduced 1999.

AMT (ARCADIA MACHINE & TOOL) — Irwindale, California (1998)

BOLT-ACTION REPEATING RIFLE
Winchester-type push-feed or Mauser-type controlled-feed short-, medium- or long-action. Calibers: .223 Remi., .22-250 Rem., .243 A, .243 Win., 6mm PPC, .25-06 Rem., 6.5x08, .270 Win., 7x57 Mauser, 7mm-08 Rem., 7mm Rem. Mag., 7.62x39mm, .308 Win., .30-06, .300 Win. Mag., .338 Win. Mag., .375 H&H, .416 Rem., .416 Rigby, .458 Win. Mag. 22- to 28-inch number 3 contour bbl. Weight: 7.75 to 8.5 lbs. Sights: None furnished; drilled and tapped for scope mounts. Classic composite or Kevlar stock. Made from 1996 to 1997.
Standard model . . . . NiB $899 Ex $720 Gd $531
Deluxe model . . . . NiB $1087 Ex $830 Gd $529

BOLT-ACTION SINGLE-SHOT RIFLE
Winchester-type cone breech push-feed or Mauser-type controlled-feed action. Calibers: .22 Hornet, .22 PPC, .222 Rem., .223 Rem., .22-250 Rem., .243 A, .243 Win., 6mm

PPC, 6.5x08, .270 Win., 7mm-08 Rem., .308 Win. 22- to 28-inch #3 contour bbl. Weight: 7.75 to 8.5 lbs. Sights: None furnished; drilled and tapped for scope mounts. Classic composite or Kevlar stock. Made from1996.
Standard model . . . . NiB $865 Ex $733 Gd $520
Deluxe model . . . . NiB $1077 Ex $744 Gd $500

CHALLENGER AUTOLOADING TARGET RIFLE SERIES I, II & III
Similar to Small Game Hunter except w/McMillan target fiberglass stock. Caliber: .22 LR. 10-round magazine. 16.5-, 18-, 20- or 22-inch bull bbl. Drilled and tapped for scope mount; no sights. Stainless steel finish. Made from 1994 to 1998.bull bbl. Drilled and tapped for scope mount; no sights. Stainless steel finish. Made from 1994 to 1998.
Challenger I Standard . . . . NiB $822 Ex $577 Gd $409
Challenger II w/muzzle brake . . NiB $926 Ex $755 Gd $554
Challenger III w/bbl extension NiB $976 Ex $588 Gd $452
w/jeweled trigger, add $227

LIGHTNING 25/22
AUTOLOADING RIFLE . . . . NiB $316 Ex $237 Gd $170
Caliber: .22 LR. 25-round magazine. 18-inch tapered or bull bbl. Weight: 6 lbs. 37 inches overall. Sights: Adj. rear; ramp front. Folding stainless-steel stock w/matte finish. Made 1986 to 1993.

MAGNUM HUNTER RIFLE . . . NiB $495 Ex $455 Gd $240
Similar to Lightning Small Game Hunter II model except chambered in .22 WRF w/22-inch match-grade bbl. Made from 1995 to 1998.

SMALL GAME HUNTER SERIES
Similar to AMT 25/22 except w/conventional matte black fiberglass/nylon stock. 10-round rotary magazine. 22-inch bbl. 40.5 inches overall. Weight: 6 lbs. Grooved for scope; no sights. Made from 1986 to 1994 (Series I), and 1993 (Series II).
Hunter I . . . . NiB $333 Ex $218 Gd $155
Hunter II (w/22-inch
heavy target bbl.) . . . . NiB $269 Ex $223 Gd $159

ANSCHUTZ — Ulm, Germany

Currently imported by Merkel USA. Anschutz models 1407 ISU, 1408-ED, 1411, 1413, 1418, 1432, 1433, 1518 and 1533 were marketed in the U.S. by Savage Arms. Further, Anschutz models 1403, 1416, 1422D, 1441, 1516 and 1522D were sold as Savage/Anschutz with Savage model designations (see also listings under Savage Arms).

MODEL 54.18MS . . . . NiB $1300 Ex $899 Gd $469
Bolt-action, single-shot, Caliber: .22 LR. 22-inch bbl. European hardwood stock w/cheekpiece. Stipple-checkered forend and Wundhammer swell pistol-grip. Receiver grooved, drilled and tapped for scope blocks. Weight: 8.4 lbs. Imported 1982 to 1997.

Anschutz Model 1416D

Anschutz Model 1418

MODEL 54.18MS-REP REPEATING RIFLE
Same as model 54.18MS except w/repeating action and 5-round magazine. 22- to 30-inch bbl. 41-49 inches overall. Avg. weight: 7 lbs., 12 oz. Hardwood or synthetic gray thumbhole stock. Imported from 1989 to 1997.
Standard MS-REP model . . . . NiB $2050 Ex $1569 Gd $880
Left-hand model . . . . NiB $2070 Ex $1579 Gd $790

MODEL 64S BOLT-ACTION SINGLE-SHOT RIFLE
Bolt-action, single-shot. Caliber: .22 LR. 26-inch bbl. Checkered European hardwood stock w/Wundhammer swell pistol-grip and adj. buttplate. Single-stage trigger. Aperture sights. Weight: 8.25 lbs. Imported from 1963 to 1981.
Standard . . . . NiB $480 Ex $370 Gd $250
Left-hand model . . . . NiB $480 Ex $370 Gd $250

MODEL 64MS BOLT-ACTION SINGLE-SHOT RIFLE
Bolt-action, single-shot. Caliber: .22 LR. 21.25-inch bbl. European hardwood silhouette-style stock w/cheekpiece. Forend base and Wundhammer swell pistol-grip, stipple-checkered. Adj. two-stage trigger. Receiver grooved, drilled and tapped for scope blocks. Weight: 8 lbs. Imported from 1982 to 1996.
Standard or Featherweight
(disc. 1988) . . . . NiB $1133 Ex $780 Gd $620
Left-hand model . . . . NiB $1133 Ex $780 Gd $620

MODEL 64MSR BOLT-ACTION REPEATER
Similar to Anschutz Model 64MS except repeater w/5-round magazine. Imported from 1996.
Standard model . . . . NiB $1045 Ex $789 Gd $603
Left-hand model . . . . NiB $1045 Ex $789 Gd $603

MODEL 520/61 SEMIAUTOMATIC . . NiB $331 Ex $270 Gd $167
Caliber: .22 LR. 10-round magazine. 24-inch bbl. Sights: Folding leaf rear, hooded ramp front. Receiver grooved for scope mounting. Rotary-style safety. Monte Carlo stock and beavertail forend, checkered. Weight: 6.5 lbs. Imported from 1982 to 1983.

MODEL 525 AUTOLOADER
Caliber: .22 LR. 10-round magazine. 20- or 24-inch bbl. 39 to 43 inches overall. Weight: 6.1 to 6.5 lbs. Adj. folding rear sight; hooded ramp front. Checkered European hardwood Monte Carlo style buttstock and beavertail forend. Sling swivel studs. Imported 1984 to 1995.
Carbine model (disc. 1986) . . . NiB $430 Ex $324 Gd $227
Rifle model (24-inch bbl.) . . . . . NiB $500 Ex $443 Gd $319

MODEL 1403B . . . . NiB $904 Ex $745 Gd $440
A lighter-weight model designed for Biathlon competition. Caliber: .22 LR. 21.5-inch bbl. Adj. two-stage trigger. Adj.

grooved wood buttplate, stipple-checkered deep thumbrest flute and straight pistol-grip. Weight: 9 lbs. w/sights. Imported from 1990 to 1992.

MODEL 1403D MATCH SINGLE-SHOT TARGET RIFLE
Caliber: .22 LR. 25-inch bbl. 43 inches overall. Weight: 8.6 lbs. No sights, receiver grooved for Anschutz target sights. Walnut-finished hardwood target stock w/adj. buttplate. Importation disc. 1992.
Standard model . . . . NiB $707 Ex $567 Gd $417
w/match sights . . . . NiB $988 Ex $779 Gd $555

MODEL 1407 I.S.U. MATCH 54 RIFLE
Bolt-action, single-shot, caliber: .22 LR. 26.88-inch bbl. Scope bases. Receiver grooved for Anschutz sights. Single-stage adj. trigger. Select walnut target stock w/deep forearm for position shooting, adj. buttplate, hand stop and swivel. Weight: 10 lbs. Imported 1970 to 1981.
Standard model . . . . NiB $653 Ex $535 Gd $291
Left-hand model . . . . NiB $653 Ex $535 Gd $291
w/international sights, add $75

MODEL 1408 . . . . NiB $466 Ex $408 Gd $370
Bolt-action, single-shot, caliber: .22 LR. 23.5-inch bbl. w/sliding weights. No metallic sights. Receiver drilled and tapped for scope-sight bases. Single-stage adj. trigger. Oversize bolt knob. Select walnut stock w/thumbhole, adj. comb and buttplate. Weight: 9.5 lbs. Intro. 1976. Disc. Add $175 for ED model.

MODEL 1411 MATCH 54 RIFLE
Bolt-action, single-shot. Caliber: .22 LR. 27.5-inch extra heavy bbl. w/mounted scope bases. Receiver grooved for Anschutz sights. Single-stage adj. trigger. Select walnut target stock w/ cheekpiece (adj. in 1973 and later production), full pistol-grip, beavertail forearm, adj. buttplate, hand stop and swivel. Model 1411-L has left-hand stock. Weight: 11 lbs. Disc.
w/Non-adj. cheekpiece . . . . NiB $678 Ex $423 Gd $269
w/adj. cheekpiece . . . . NiB $703 Ex $532 Gd $402
w/Anschutz International Sight set, add $300

MODEL 1413 SUPER MATCH 54 RIFLE
Freestyle international target rifle w/specifications similar to those of Model 1411, except w/special stock w/thumbhole, adj. pistol grip, adj. cheekpiece in 1973 and later production, adj. hook buttplate, adj. palmrest. Model 1413-L has left-hand stock. Weight: 15.5 lbs. Disc.
w/non-adj. cheekpiece . . . . NiB $830 Ex $733 Gd $400
w/adj. cheekpiece . . . . NiB $704 Ex $572 Gd $399
w/Anschutz International sight set, add $300

MODEL 1416D . . . . NiB $790 Ex $577 Gd $368
Bolt-action sporter. Caliber: .22 LR. 22.5-inch bbl. Sights: Folding leaf rear; hooded ramp front. Receiver grooved for

Anschutz Model 1422D

Anschutz Model 1427B

Anschutz Model 1432

Anschutz Model 1432D

scope mounting. Select European stock w/cheekpiece, skip-checkered pistol grip and forearm. Weight: 6 lbs. Imported 1982 to 2007.

MODEL 1416D CLASSIC/CUSTOM SPORTERS
Same as Model 1416D except w/American classic-style stock (Classic) or modified European-style stock w/Monte Carlo roll-over cheekpiece and Schnabel forend (Custom). Weight: 5.5 lbs. (Classic); 6 lbs. (Custom). Imported 1986 to 2007.
Model 1416D Classic . . . . NiB $995 Ex $549 Gd $380
Model 1416D Classic,
  "True" left-hand . . . . NiB $1095 Ex $577 Gd $419
Model 1416D Custom. . . . . . . NiB $980 Ex $750 Gd $380
Model 1416D fiberglass (1991-92)NiB $760 Ex $623 Gd $445

MODEL 1418 BOLT-ACTION
SPORTER. . . . . NiB $452 Ex $352 Gd $200
Caliber: .22 LR. 5- or 10-rnd. magazine. 19.75-in. bbl. Sights: Folding leaf rear; hooded ramp front. Receiver grooved for scope mounting. Select walnut stock, Mannlicher type w/cheekpiece, pistol-grip and forearm skip checkered. Weight: 5.5 lbs. Intro. 1976. Disc.

MODEL 1418D BOLT-ACTION
SPORTER. . . . . NiB $1008 Ex $886 Gd $533
Caliber: .22 LR. 5- or 10-round magazine. 19.75-inch bbl. European walnut Monte Carlo stock, Mannlicher type w/cheekpiece, pistolgrip and forend skip-line checkered, buffalo horn Schnabel tip. Weight: 5.5 lbs. Imported from 1982 to 1995 and 1998 to 2003.

MODEL 1422D CLASSIC/CUSTOM RIFLE
Bolt-action sporter. Caliber: .22 LR. Five-round removable straight-feed clip magazine. 24-inch bbl. Sights: Folding leaf rear; hooded ramp front. Select European walnut stock, classic type (Classic); Monte Carlo w/hand-carved rollover cheek-

piece (Custom). Weight: 7.25 lbs. (Classic) 6.5 lbs. (Custom). Imported 1982 to 1989.
Model 1422D Classic . . . . NiB $833 Ex $670 Gd $432
Model 1422D Custom. . . . . . . NiB $896 Ex $833 Gd $479

Model 1427B Biathlon Rifle . NiB $1943 Ex $1377 Gd $937
Bolt-action clip repeater. Caliber: .22 LR. 21.5-inch bbl. Two-stage trigger w/wing-type safety. Hardwood stock w/deep fluting, pistol grip and deep forestock with adj. hand stop rail. Target sights w/adjustable weights. Advertised in 1981 but imported from 1982 to date as Model 1827B.

MODEL 1430D MATCH . . . . . . NiB $976 Ex $650 Gd $429
Improved version of Model 64S. Bolt-action, single-shot. Caliber: .22 LR. 26-inch medium-heavy bbl. Walnut Monte Carlo stock w/cheekpiece, adj. buttplate, deep midstock tapered to forend. Pistol-grip and contoured thumb groove w/stipple checkering. Single-stage adj. trigger. Target sights. Weight: 8.38 lbs. Imported 1982 to 1990.

MODEL 1432 BOLT-ACTION SPORTER
Caliber: .22 Hornet. 5-round box magazine. 24-inch bbl. Sights: Folding leaf rear, hooded ramp front. Receiver grooved for scope mounting. Select walnut stock w/Monte Carlo comb and cheekpiece, pistol-grip and forearm skip-checkered. Weight: 6.75 lbs. Imported from 1974 to 1987. (Reintroduced as 1707/1730 series)
Early model (1974-85) . . . . . . NiB $1347 Ex $988 Gd $721
Late model (1985-87) . . . . NiB $1145 Ex $933 Gd $631

MODEL 1432D CLASSIC/CUSTOM RIFLE
Bolt-action sporter similar to Model 1422D except chambered for Caliber: .22 Hornet. 4-round magazine. 23.5-inch bbl. Weight: 7.75 lbs. (Classic); 6.5 lbs. (Custom). Classic stock on Classic model; fancy-grade Monte Carlo w/hand-carved rollover cheekpiece (Custom). Imported from 1982 to 1987. (Reintroduced as 1707/1730 series)
Model 1432D Classic . . . . NiB $1347 Ex $982 Gd $733
Model 1432D Custom. . . . . . . NiB $1175 Ex $923 Gd $634

Anschutz Model 1707

Model 1518 . . . . NiB $766 Ex $650 Gd $423
Model 1518D . . . . NiB $974 Ex $788 Gd $544
w/set trigger, add $150

MODEL 1433 BOLT-ACTION SPORTER . . . NiB $1131 Ex $916 Gd $650
Caliber: .22 Hornet. 5-round box magazine. 19.75-inch bbl.
Sights: Folding leaf rear, hooded ramp front. Receiver grooved
for scope mounting. Single-stage or double-set trigger. Select
walnut Mannlicher stock; cheekpiece, pistol-grip and forearm
skip-checkered. Weight: 6.5 lbs. Imported from 1976 to 1986.

MODEL 1448D . . . . NiB $421 Ex $324 Gd $236
Similar to Model 1449 except chambered for Caliber: .22 LR.
w/22.5-inch smooth bore bbl. and no sights. Walnut-finished
hardwood stock. Imported from 1999 to 2001.

MODEL 1449D YOUTH SPORTER NiB $300 Ex $233 Gd $177
Bolt-action sporter version of Model 2000. Caliber: .22 LR.
5-round box magazine. 16.25-inch bbl. Weight: 3.5 lbs.
Hooded ramp front sight, addition. Walnut-finished hardwood
stock. Imported from 1990 to 1991.

MODEL 1450B TARGET RIFLE . NiB $703 Ex $533 Gd $397
Biathlon rifle developed on 2000 Series action. 19.5-inch bbl.
Weight: 5.5 lbs. Adj. buttplate. Target sights. Imported 1993 to 1994.

MODEL 1451 E/R SPORTER/TARGET
Bolt-action, single-shot (1451E) or repeater (1451R). Caliber:
.22 LR. 22- or 22.75-inch bbl. w/o sights. Select hardwood
stock w/stippled pistolgrip and vented forearm. beavertail
forend, adj. cheekpiece, and deep thumb flute. Weight: 6.5 lbs.
Imported from 1996 to 2001.
Model 1451E (disc. 1997) . . . . NiB $487 Ex $370 Gd $254
Model 1451R . . . . NiB $479 Ex $455 Gd $310

MODEL 1451D CLASSIC/CUSTOM RIFLE
Same as Model 1451R except w/walnut-finished hardwood
stock (Classic) or modified European-style walnut stock
w/Monte Carlo rollover cheekpiece and Schnabel forend
(Custom). Weight: 5 lbs. Imported from 1998 to 2001.
Model 1451D Classic (Super) . . NiB $367 Ex $288 Gd $199
Model 1451D Custom. . . . . NiB $488 Ex $455 Gd $321
MODEL 1451 ST- R RIFLE . . . . . NiB $499 Ex $454 Gd $342
Same as Model 1451R except w/two-stage trigger and walnut-
finished hardwood uncheckered stock. Imported 1996 to 2001.

MODEL 1516D CLASSIC/CUSTOM RIFLE
Same as Model 1416D except chambered for Caliber: .22
Magnum RF, with American classic-style stock (Classic) or
modified European-style stock w/Monte Carlo rollover cheek-
piece and Schnabel forend (Custom). Weight: 5.5 lbs. (Classic),
6 lbs. (Custom). Imported from1986 to 2003.
Model 1516D Classic . . . . NiB $704 Ex $572 Gd $379
Model 1516D Custom. . . . . NiB $639 Ex $600 Gd $423

MODELS 1516D/1518D LUXUS RIFLES
The alpha designation for these models was changed from Custom
to Luxus in 1996 to 1998. (See Custom listings for Luxus values.)

MODELS 1518/1518D SPORTING RIFLES
Same as Model 1418 except chambered for .22 Magnum RF,
4-round box magazine. Model 1518 intro. 1976. Disc. Model
1518D has full Mannlicher-type stock. Imported from 1982 to 2001.

MODEL 1522D CLASSIC/CUSTOM RIFLE
Same as Model 1422D except chambered for .22 Magnum
RF, 4-round magazine. Weight: 6.5 lbs. (Custom). Fancy-
grade Classic or Monte Carlo stock w/hand-carved roll-
over cheekpiece. Imported 1982 to 1989. (Reintroduced as
1707D/1730D series)
Model 1522D Classic . . . . NiB $1197 Ex $869 Gd $633
Model 1522D Custom. . . . . . . NiB $1197 Ex $869 Gd $633

MODEL 1532D CLASSIC/CUSTOM RIFLE
Same as Model 1432D except chambered for .222 Rem.
Three-round mag. Weight: 6.5 lbs. (Custom). Classic stock on
Classic Model; fancy-grade Monte Carlo stock w/handcarved
rollover cheekpiece (Custom). Imported from 1982 to 1989.
(Reintroduced as 1707D/174 D0 series)
Model 1532D Classic . . . . NiB $1019 Ex $795 Gd $448
Model 1532D Custom. . . . . . . NiB $1297 Ex $996 Gd $698

MODEL 1533 . . . . NiB $1090 Ex $844 Gd $589
Same as Model 1433 except chambered for .222 Rem. Three-
shot box magazine. Imported from 1976 to 1994.

MODEL 1707 SERIES BOLT-ACTION REPEATER
Match 54 Sporter. Calibers: .22 LR., .22 Mag., .22 Hornet,
.222 Rem. Five-shot removable magazine 24-inch bbl. 43
inches overall. Weight: 7.5 lbs. Folding leaf rear sight, hooded
ramp front. Select European walnut stock w/cheekpiece and
Schnabel forend tip. Imported from 1989 to 2001.
Standard Model 1707
Bavarian — rimfire cal. . . . . . . NiB $1018 Ex $933 Gd $580
Standard Model 1707
Bavarian — centerfire cal. . . NiB $1342 Ex $1056 Gd $697
Model 1707D Classic (Classic stock, 6.75 lbs.)
rimfire cal. . . . . NiB $1179 Ex $994 Gd $698
Model 1707D
Classic — centerfire cal.. . NiB $1279 Ex $1044 Gd $748
Model 1707D
Custom — rimfire cal. . . . . NiB $1094 Ex $893 Gd $633
Model 1707D
Custom — centerfire cal. NiB $1332 Ex $1088 Gd $775
Model 1707D Graphite Cust. (McMillan graphite reinforced
stock, 22-inch bbl., intro. 1991) . . . NiB $1156 Ex $985 Gd $641
Select walnut and gold trigger, add $200
Model 1707 FWT (featherweight, 6.5 lbs.) –
rimfire cal. . . . . NiB $1122 Ex $909 Gd $641
Model 1707 FWT — centerfire
cal. . . . . NiB $1289 Ex $1136 Gd $703

MODEL 1733D MANNLICHER NiB $1370 Ex $1168 Gd $860
Same as Model 1707D except w/19-inch bbl. and Mannlicher-
style stock. 39 inches overall. Weight: 6.25 lbs. Imported from
1993 to 1995 (Reintroduced in 1998, disc. 2001).

MODEL 1740 MONTE CARLO SPORTER
Caliber: .22 Hornet or .222 Rem. Three and 5-round magazines
respectively. 24-inch bbl. 43.25 inches overall. Weight: 6.5 lbs.
Hooded ramp front, folding leaf rear. Drilled and tapped for
scope mounts. Select European walnut stock w/roll-over cheekpiece, checkered grip and forend. Imported from 1998 to 2006.

Anschutz Model 1803D

Anschutz Model 1907

Model 1740 Classic
  (Meistergrade) . . . . **NiB $1504 Ex $1237 Gd $866**
Model 1740 Custom . . . . **NiB $1370 Ex $1089 Gd $733**

MODEL 1743 MONTE CARLO
SPORTER. . . . . **NiB $1370 Ex $1132 Gd $769**
Similar to Model 1740 except w/Mannlicher full stock.
Imported from 1997 to 2001.

MODEL 1903D MATCH SINGLE-SHOT TARGET RIFLE
Caliber: .22 LR. 25.5-inch bbl. 43.75 inches overall. Weight:
8.5 lbs. No sights; receiver grooved, drilled and tapped for
scope mounts. Blonde or walnut-finished hardwood stock w/
adj. cheekpiece, stippled grip and forend. Left-hand version.
Imported 1987 to 1993.
Right-hand model
  (Reintroduced as 1903D) . . . **NiB $1006 Ex $844 Gd $544**
Left-hand model . . . . **NiB $1108 Ex $866 Gd $633**

MODEL 1807 ISU
STANDARD MATCH . . . . **NiB $1359 Ex $1094 Gd $708**
Bolt-action single-shot. Caliber: 22 LR. 26-inch bbl. Improved
Super Match 54 action. Two-stage match trigger. Removable
cheekpiece, adj. buttplate, thumbpiece and forestock w/
stipple-checkered. Weight: 10 lbs. Imported 1982 to 1988.
(Reintroduced as 1907 ISU)

MODEL 1808ED SUPER RUNNING TARGET
Bolt-action single-shot. Caliber: .22 LR. 23.5-inch bbl. w/slid-
ing weights. Improved Super Match 54 action. Heavy beavertail forend w/adj.cheekpiece and buttplate. Adj. single-stage
trigger. Weight: 9.5 lbs. Imported from 1982 to 1998.
Right-hand model . . . . **NiB $1677 Ex $1328 Gd $869**
Left-hand model . . . . **NiB $1688 Ex $1377 Gd $973**

MODEL 1808MS-R
METALLIC SILHOUETTE . . . . **NiB $2021 Ex $1565 Gd $932**
Bolt-action repeater. Caliber: .22 LR. 19.2-inch bbl. w/o sights.
Thumbhole Monte Carlo stock w/grooved forearm enhanced
w/ "Anschutz" logo. Weight: 8.2 lbs. Imported from 1998 to
date.

MODEL 1810 SUPER MATCH II NiB $1979 Ex $1440 Gd $937
A less detailed version of the Super Match 1813 model.
Tapered forend w/deep receiver area. Select European hardwood stock. Weight: 13.5 lbs. Imported from 1982 to 1988
(reintroduced as 1910 series).

MODEL 1811 PRONE MATCH NiB $1843 Ex $1623 Gd $877
Bolt-action single-shot. Caliber: .22 LR. 27.5-inch bbl.
Improved Super Match 54 action. Select European hardwood
stock w/beavertail forend, adj. cheekpiece, and deep thumb
flute. Thumb groove and pistol grip w/stipple checkering.
Adj. buttplate. Weight: 11.5 lbs. Imported 1982 to 1988.
(Reintroduced as 1911 Prone Match)

MODEL 1813 SUPER MATCH NiB $2281 Ex $1951 Gd $869
Bolt-action single-shot. Caliber: .22 LR. 27.5-inch bbl. Improved
Super Match 54 action w/light firing pin, one-point adj. trigger.
European walnut thumbhole stock, adj. palm rest, forend and
pistol grip stipple checkered. Adj. cheekpiece and hook buttplate. Weight: 15.5 lbs. Imported 1979 to 1988. Reintroduced
as 1913 Super Match.

MODEL 1827B BIATHLON RIFLE
Bolt-action clip repeater. Caliber: .22 LR. 21.5-inch bbl. 42.5
inches overall. Weight: 8.5 to 9 lbs. Slide safety. Adj. target
sight set w/snow caps. European walnut stock w/cheekpiece,
stippled pistol grip and forearm w/adj. weights. Fortner straight
pull bolt option offered in 1986. Imported from 1982 to date.
Model 1827B w/Sup. Mat. 54
  action . . . . **NiB $2359 Ex $2153 Gd $1020**
Model 1827B, left-hand . . . **NiB $2101 Ex $1716 Gd $1224**
Model 1827BT w/Fortner
  Option, right-hand . . . . . **NiB $2467 Ex $2261 Gd $1032**
Model 1827BT, left-hand . . **NiB $2604 Ex $2127 Gd $1513**
Model 1827BT w/laminated stock, add **$175**
w/stainless steel bbl., add **$205**

MODEL 1907 ISU INTERNATIONAL MATCH RIFLE
Updated version of Model 1807 w/same general specifications
as Model 1913 except w/26-inch bbl. 44.5 inches overall.
Weight: 11 lbs. Designed for ISU 3-position competition. Fitted
w/vented beechwood or walnut, blonde or color-laminated
stock. Imported from 1989 to date.
Right-hand model . . . . **NiB $1544 Ex $1353 Gd $838**
Left-hand model . . . . **NiB $1730 Ex $1415 Gd $1012**
w/laminated stock, add **$135**
w/walnut stock, add **$100**
w/stainless steel bbl., add **$130**

MODEL 1910 INTERNATIONAL SUPER MATCH RIFLE
Updated version of Model 1810 w/same general specifications
Model 1913 except w/less-detailed hardwood stock w/tapered
forend. Weight: 13.5 lbs. Imported from 1989 to 1998.
Right-hand model . . . . **NiB $2566 Ex $2077 Gd $1103**
Left-hand model . . . . **NiB $2560 Ex $2097 Gd $1506**

Anschutz Model 2013

Anschutz Achiever

MODEL 1911 PRONE MATCH RIFLE
Updated version of Model 1811 w/same general specifications Model 1913 except w/specialized prone match hardwood stock w/beavertail forend. Weight: 11.5 lbs. Imported from 1989 to date.
Right-hand model . . . . NiB $1854 Ex $1764 Gd $849

MODEL 1912
LADIES' SPORT RIFLE. . . . . NiB $1837 Ex $1932 Gd $865
Similar to the Model 1907 designed for ISU 3-position competition w/same general U.I.T. specifications except w/shorter dimensions to accomodate smaller competitors. Weight: 11.4 lbs. Imported from 1999 to date.

MODEL 1913
STANDARD RIFLE . . . . NiB $1611 Ex $1235 Gd $909
Similar to 1913 Super Match w/economized appointments. Imported from 1997 to date.

MODEL 1913 SUPER MATCH RIFLE
Bolt-action single-shot Super Match (updated version of Model 1813). Caliber: .22 LR. 27.5-inch bbl. Weight: 14.2 lbs. Adj. two-stage trigger. Vented International thumbhole stock w/adj. cheek-piece, hand and palm rest, fitted w/10-way butthook. Imported from 1989 to date.
Right-hand model . . . . NiB $3310 Ex $1989 Gd $879
Left-hand model . . . . NiB $2370 Ex $1909 Gd $1343
W/laminated stock, add $150
W/stainless steel bbl., add $175

MODEL 2007 ISU STANDARD RIFLE
Bolt-action single-shot. Caliber: .22 LR. 19.75-inch bbl. 43.5 to 44.5 inches overall. Weight: 10.8 lbs. Two-stage trigger. Standard ISU stock w/adj. cheekpiece. Imported from 1992 to date.
Right-hand model . . . . NiB $1997 Ex $1529 Gd $909
Left-hand model . . . . NiB $2040 Ex $1719 Gd $1244
W/stainless steel bbl., add $175

MODEL 2013
LADIES' SPORT RIFLE. . . . . NiB $2197 Ex $2021 Gd $933
Similar to the Model 2007 designed for ISU 3-position competition w/same general U.I.T. specifications except w/shorter dimensions to accomodate smaller competitors. Weight: 11.4 lbs. Imported from 1999 to date.

MODEL 2013
BENCHREST RIFLE (BR-50). . NiB $1889 Ex $1624 Gd $877
Bolt-action single-shot. Caliber: .22 LR. 19.6-inch bbl. 43 inches overall. Weight: 10.3 lbs. Adjustable trigger for single or two-stage function. Benchrest-configuration stock. Imported 1999 to date.

MODEL 2013
SILHOUETTE RIFLE. . . . . . . NiB $2187 Ex $1675 Gd $944
Bolt-action single-shot. Caliber: .22 LR. 20-inch bbl. 45.5 inches overall. Weight: 11.5 lbs. Two-stage trigger. Thumbhole black synthetic or laminated stock w/adj. cheekpiece, hand and palm rest. Imported from 1994 to date.

MODEL 2013 SUPER MATCH RIFLE
Bolt-action single-shot. Caliber: .22 LR. 19.75- or 27.1-inch bbl. 43 to 50.1 inches overall. Weight: 15.5 lbs. Two-stage trigger. International thumbhole, black synthetic or laminated stock w/adj. cheekpiece, hand and palm rest; fitted w/10-way butthook. Imported from 1992 to date.
Right-hand model . . . . NiB $3566 Ex $2317 Gd $1149
Left-hand model . . . . NiB $2588 Ex $1290 Gd $1482
W/laminated stock, add $200

ACHIEVER BOLT-ACTION RIFLE . . NiB $422 Ex $337 Gd $219
Caliber: .22 LR. 5-round magazine. Mark 2000-type repeating action. 19.5-inch bbl. 36.5 inches overall. Weight: 5 lbs. Adj. open rear sight; hooded ramp front. Plain European hardwood target-style stock w/vented forend and adj. buttplate. Imported 1987 to 1995.

ACHIEVER ST-SUPER TARGET. . NiB $559 Ex $431 Gd $269
Same as Achiever except single-shot w/22-inch bbl. and adj. stock. 38.75 inches overall. Weight: 6.5 lbs. Target sights. Imported since 1994 to 1995.

BR-50 BENCH REST RIFLE . NiB $2123 Ex $1707 Gd $1026
Single-shot. Caliber: .22 LR. 19.75-inch bbl. (23 inches w/ muzzle weight). 37.75-42.5 inches overall. Weight: 11 lbs. Grooved receiver, no sights. Walnut-finished hardwood or synthetic benchrest stock w/adj. cheekpiece. Imported from 1994 to 1997. (Reintroduced as Model 2013 BR-50)

KADETT BOLT-ACTION
REPEATING RIFLE. . . . . NiB $370 Ex $241 Gd $198
Caliber: .22 LR. 5-round detachable box magazine. 22-inch bbl. 40 inches overall. Weight: 5.5 lbs. Adj. folding leaf rear sight; hooded ramp front. Checkered European hardwood stock w/walnut-finish. Imported 1987.

Armalite AR-10

Armalite AR-10 (T) Target Carbine

MARK 2000 MATCH . . . . NiB $448 Ex $355 Gd $221
Takedown, bolt-action single-shot. Caliber: .22 LR. 26-inch heavy bbl. Walnut stock w/deep-fluted thumb-groove, Wundhammer swell pistol grip, beavertail forend. Adj. butt-plate, single-stage adj. trigger. Weight: 8 lbs. Imported from 1982 to 1988.

ARMALITE, INC. — Geneseo, Illinois

Formerly Costa Mesa, California. Armalite was in Costa Mesa, California from 1959-73. Following the acquisition by Eagle Arms in 1995, production resumed under the Armalite, Inc. Logo in Geneseo, Illinois.

Production by ARMALITE

AR-7 EXPLORER SURVIVAL RIFLE NiB $469 Ex $345 Gd $290
Takedown. Semiautomatic. Caliber: .22 LR. Eight-round box magazine. 16-inch cast aluminum bbl. w/steel liner. Sights: Peep rear; blade front. Brown plastic stock, recessed to stow barrel, action, and magazine. Weight: 2.75 lbs. Will float stowed or assembled. Made from 1959-1973 by Armalite; from 1974-90 by Charter Arms; from 1990-97 by Survival Arms, Cocoa, FL.; from 1997 to date by Henry Repeating Arms Co., Brooklyn, NY.

AR-7 EXPLORER CUSTOM RIFLE . NiB $325 Ex $270 Gd $199
Same as AR-7 Survival Rifle except w/deluxe walnut stock w/cheekpiece and pistol grip. Weight: 3.5 lbs. Made from 1964 to 1970.

AR-180 SEMIAUTOMATIC RIFLE
Commercial version of full automatic AR-18 Combat Rifle. Gas-operated semiautomatic. Caliber: .223 Rem. (5.56mm). 5-, 20-, 30-round magazines. 18.25-inch bbl. w/flash hider/muzzle brake. Sights: Flip-up "L" type rear, adj. for windage; post front, adj. for elevation. Accessory: 3x scope and mount (add $60 to value). Folding buttstock of black nylon, rubber buttplate and pistol grip, heat dissipating fiberglass forend (hand guard), swivels, sling. 38 inches overall, 28.75 inches folded. Weight: 6.5 lbs. Note: Made by Armalite Inc. 1969 to 1972, manufactured for Armalite by Howa Machinery Ltd., Nagoya, Japan, from 1972 to 1973; by Sterling Armament Co. Ltd., Dagenham, Essex, England, from 1976 to 1994. Importation disc.
Armalite AR-180 (Mfg. by
  Armalite-Costa Mesa) . . . . NiB $2189 Ex $1543 Gd $1043
Armalite AR-180 (Mfg. by Howa) NiB $2109 Ex $1535 Gd $990
Armalite AR-180 (Mfg. by Sterling) NiB $1809 Ex $1404 Gd $933
w/3x scope and mount, add $250

AR-10 SEMIAUTOMATIC SERIES
Gas-operated semiautomatic action. Calibers: .243 Win. or .308 Win. (7.62 x 51mm). 10-round magazine. 16- or 20-inch bbl. 35.5 or 39.5 inches overall. Weight: 9 to 9.75 lbs. Post front sight, adj. aperature rear. Black or green composition stock. Made from 1995 to date.
AR-10 A2 (Std. carbine) . . . . NiB $1190 Ex $1088 Gd $707
AR-10 A2 (Std. rifle) . . . . NiB $1190 Ex $1088 Gd $707
AR-10 A4 (S.P. carbine) . . . . . NiB $1080 Ex $905 Gd $600
AR-10 A4 (S.P. rifle) . . . . NiB $1080 Ex $905 Gd $600
w/stainless steel bbl., add $150

AR-10 T (TARGET)
Similar to AR-10A except in National Match configuration w/three-slot short Picatinny rail system and case deflector. Additional calibers: .260 Rem., .300 RUM, 7mm-08 Rem., .338 Fed. 16- or 24-inch bbl. Weight: 8.25 to 10.4 lbs. Composite stock and handguard. No sights. Optional National Match carry handle and detachable front sight. Made from 1995 to date.
AR-10 T (Rifle) . . . . NiB $1579 Ex $1289 Gd $1043
AR-10 T (Carbine) . . . . NiB $1479 Ex $1289 Gd $1043

MODEL AR-50 SS
BOLT-ACTION RIFLE. . . . . . NiB $3198 Ex $2645 Gd $1370
Caliber: .50 BMG. 31-inch bbl. w/muzzle brake. 59 inches overall. Weight: 41 lbs. Modified octagonal-form receiver, drilled and slotted for scope rail. Single-stage trigger. Triple front-locking bolt lug w/spring-loaded plunger for automatic ejection. Magnesium phosphate steel, hard-anodized aluminum finish. Made from 1999 to date.

M15 SERIES
Gas-operated semiautomatic w/A2-style forward-assist mechanism and push-type pivot pin for easy takedown. Caliber: .223 Rem., 5.56 NATO or 6.8 SPC. 7-round magazine. 16-, 20- or 24-inch bbl. Weight: 7-9.2 lbs. Composite or retractable stock. Fully adj. sights. Black anodized finish. Made from 1995 to date.
M-15A2 (Carbine) . . . . NiB $927 Ex $800 Gd $647
M-15A2 (Service Rifle) . . . . NiB $989 Ex $845 Gd $655
M-15A2 (National Match) . . . NiB $1350 Ex $1123 Gd $770
M-15A2 (Golden Eagle
  heavy bbl.) . . . . NiB $1332 Ex $1086 Gd $730
M-15A2 M4C (retractable stock,
  disc. 1997) . . . . NiB $1299 Ex $1021 Gd $698
M-15A4 (Action Master,
  disc. 1997) . . . . NiB $1139 Ex $934 Gd $670
M-15A4 (Predator) . . . . NiB $977 Ex $855 Gd $654

Armalite M-15A2 National Match

Armalite M-15A2 HBAR

**M-15A4 S.P. R. (Special Purpose
Rifle)**.................NiB $956 Ex $799 Gd $535
M-15A4 (S.P. Carbine) ....NiB $875 Ex $720 Gd $463
M-15A4T (Eagle Eye Carbine)...NiB $1326 Ex $1090 Gd $775
M-15A4T (Eagle Eye Rifle) ..NiB $1377 Ex $1030 Gd $755

ARMI JAGER — Turin, Italy

AP-74 COMMANDO ....NiB $322 Ex $248 Gd $166
Similar to standard AP-74 but styled to resemble original version of Uzi 9mm submachine gun w/wood buttstock. Lacks carrying handle and flash suppressor. Has different type front sight mount and guards, wood stock, pistol grip and forearm. Intro. 1976. Disc.

AP-74 SEMIAUTOMATIC RIFLE
Styled after U.S. M16 military rifle. Caliber: .22 LR, .32 Auto (pistol cartridge). Detachable clip magazine; capacity: 14 rounds caliber .22 LR, 9 rounds .32 ACP. 20-inch bbl. w/flash suppressor. Weight: 6.5 lbs. M16 type sights. Stock, pistol-grip and forearm of black plastic, swivels and sling. Intro. 1974. Disc.
.22 LR. ....NiB $359 Ex $290 Gd $200
.32 Auto ....NiB $379 Ex $322 Gd $209

AP-74 WOOD STOCK MODEL
Same as standard AP-74 except w/wood stock, pistol-grip and forearm weight: 7 lbs. Disc.
.22 LR ....NiB $448 Ex $380 Gd $250
.32 Auto ....NiB $448 Ex $380 Gd $250

ARMSCOR (Arms Corp.) — Manila, Philippines *Imported by Armscor Precision Int'l.*

MODEL 20 AUTO RIFLE
Caliber: .22 LR. 15-round magazine. 21-inch bbl. 39.75 inches overall. Weight: 6.5 lbs. Sights: Hooded front; adj. rear. Checkered or plain walnut finished mahogany stock. Blued finish. Imported 1990 to 1991. (Reinstated by Ruko in the M series.)
Model 20 (checkered stock) ....NiB $167 Ex $130 Gd $97
Model 20C (carbine-style stock) NiB $144 Ex $122 Gd $98
Model 20P (plain stock) ....NiB $126 Ex $100 Gd $78

MODEL 1600 AUTO RIFLE
Caliber: .22 LR. 15-round magazine. 19.5-inch bbl. 38 inches overall. Weight: 6 lbs. Sights: Post front; aperture rear. Plain mahogany stock. Matte black finish. Imported 1987 to 1991. (Reinstated by Ruko in the M series.)
Standard model.............NiB $180 Ex $155 Gd $100
Retractable stock model ......NiB $190 Ex $167 Gd $110

MODEL AK22 AUTO RIFLE
Caliber: .22 LR. 15- or 30-round magazine. 18.5-inch bbl. 36 inches overall. Weight: 7 lbs. Sights: Post front; adj. rear. Plain mahogany stock. Matte black finish. Imported 1987 to 1991.
Standard model.............NiB $179 Ex $150 Gd $110
Folding stock model ....NiB $269 Ex $220 Gd $166

MODEL M14 SERIES BOLT-ACTION RIFLE
Caliber: .22 LR. 10-round magazine. 23-inch bbl. Weight: 6.25 lbs. Open sights. Walnut or mahogany stock. Imported 1991 to 1997.
M14P Standard model ....NiB $129 Ex $98 Gd $70
**M14D Deluxe model
(checkered stock, disc. 1995)** ...NiB $149 Ex $110 Gd $90

MODEL M20 SERIES SEMIAUTOMATIC RIFLE
Caliber: .22 LR. 10- or 15-round magazine. 18.25- or 20.75-inch bbl. Weight:5.5 to 6.5 lbs. 38 to 40.5 inches overall. Hooded front sight w/windage adj. rear. Walnut finished mahogany stock. Imported 1990 to 1997.
M20C (carbine model) ....NiB $144 Ex $109 Gd $80
M20P (standard model) ....NiB $128 Ex $100 Gd $78
**M20S Sporter Deluxe (w/checkered
mahogany stock)**...........NiB $167 Ex $150 Gd $97
**M20SC Super Classic (w/checkered
walnut stock)** ....NiB $281 Ex $227 Gd $108

MODEL M1400 BOLT-ACTION RIFLE
Similar to Model 14P except w/checkered stock w/Schnabel forend. Weight: 6 lbs. Imported from 1990 to 1997.
M1400LW (Lightweight, disc. 1992)...NiB $239 Ex $199 Gd $137
M1400S (Sporter) ....NiB $177 Ex $150 Gd $100
M1400SC (Super Classic) .....NiB $300 Ex $255 Gd $179

Armi Jager AP-74 Wood Stock

MODEL M1500 BOLT-ACTION RIFLE
Caliber: .22 Mag. 5-round magazine. 21.5-inch bbl. Weight: 6.5 lbs. Open sights. Checkered mahogany stock. Imported 1991 to 1997.
M1500 (standard) . . . . NiB $198 Ex $137 Gd $105
M1500LW (Euro-style walnut
   stock, disc. 1992) . . . . NiB $219 Ex $188 Gd $135
M1500SC (Monte Carlo stock) . . . NiB $224 Ex $190 Gd $140

MODEL M1600 AUTO RIFLE
Rimfire replica of Armalite Model AR 180 (M16) except chambered for Caliber .22 LR. 15-round magazine. 18-inch bbl. Weight: 5.25 lbs. Composite or retractable buttstock w/ composite handguard and pistol grip. Carrying handle w/adj. aperture rear sight and protected post front. Black anodized finish. Imported from 1991 to 1997.
M-1600 (standard w/fixed stock). . . NiB $190 Ex $149 Gd $110
M-1600R (retractable stock). . . NiB $200 Ex $161 Gd $120

MODEL M1800 BOLT-ACTION RIFLE
Caliber: .22 Hornet. 5-round magazine. 22-inch bbl. Weight: 6.6 lbs. Checkered hardwood or walnut stock. Sights: Post front; adj. rear. Imported from 1996 to 1997.
M-1800 (standard) . . . . NiB $310 Ex $233 Gd $175
M-1800SC (checkered walnut stock) . . . NiB $400 Ex $327 Gd $255

MODEL M2000 BOLT-ACTION RIFLE
Similar to Model 20P except w/checkered mahogany stock and adj. sights. Imported from 1991 to 1997.
M2000S (standard) . . . . NiB $177 Ex $139 Gd $100
M2000SC (w/checkered
   walnut stock) . . . . NiB $279 Ex $220 Gd $167

ARNOLD ARMS — Arlington, Washington

AFRICAN SAFARI
Calibers: .243 to .458 Win. Mag. and proprietary cartridges. 22- to 26-inch bbl. Weight: 7-9 lbs. Scope mount standard or w/optional M70 Express sights. Chrome-moly in four finishes. "A" and "AA" Fancy Grade English walnut stock with number 5 standard wraparound checkering pattern. Ebony forend tip. Made from 1994 to 2001.
w/ "A" Grade English
   walnut stock, blue finish NiB $4732 Ex $3841 Gd $2690
Std. polish. . . . . NiB $4969 Ex $4000 Gd $2821
Hi-Luster. . . . . NiB $5189 Ex $4290 Gd $2950
Stainless steel matte . . . . . . NiB $4733 Ex $3847 Gd $2993
w/ "AA" Grade English walnut stock,
   C-M matte blue finish. . . NiB $4707 Ex $3810 Gd $2688
Std. polish. . . . . NiB $4988 Ex $4037 Gd $2835
Hi-Luster. . . . . NiB $5188 Ex $4200 Gd $2969
Stainless steel matte finish. . . . NiB $4707 Ex $3875 Gd $2710

ALASKAN TROPHY
Calibers: .300 Magnum to .458 Win. Magnum. 24- to 26-inch bbl. Weight: 7-9 lbs. Scope mount w/Express sights standard.

Stainless steel or chrome-moly Apollo action w/fibergrain or black synthetic stock. Barrel band on 357 H&H and larger magnums. Made from 1996 to 2000.
Matte finish. . . . . NiB $3330 Ex $2689 Gd $1900
Std. polish. . . . . NiB $3559 Ex $2900 Gd $2044
Stainless steel . . . . NiB $3386 Ex $2744 Gd $1935

A-SQUARE COMPANY INC. — Glenrock, Wyoming

CAESAR BOLT-ACTION RIFLE
Custom rifle built on Remington's 707 receiver. Calibers: Same as Hannibal, Groups I, II and III. 20- to 26-inch bbl. Weight: 8.5 to 11 lbs. Express 3-leaf rear sight, ramp front. Synthetic or classic Claro oil-finished walnut stock w/flush detachable swivels and Coil-Chek recoil system. Three-way adj. target trigger; 3-position safety. Right- or left-hand. Made from 1986 to 2012.
Synthetic stock model . . . . NiB $3512 Ex $2790 Gd $1947
Walnut stock model. . . . . . NiB $4044 Ex $2379 Gd $1756

GENGHIS KHAN BOLT-ACTION RIFLE
Custom varmint rifle developed on Winchester's M70 receiver; fitted w/heavy tapered bbl. and Coil-Chek stock. Calibers: .22-250 Rem., .243 Win., .25-06 Rem., 6mm Rem. Weight: 8-8.5 lbs. Made from 1995 to 2012.
Synthetic stock model. . . . . NiB $3566 Ex $2312 Gd $2044
Walnut stock model . . . . . . NiB $3482 Ex $2854 Gd $2023

HAMILCAR BOLT-ACTION RIFLE
Similar to Hannibal Model except lighter. Calibers: .25-06, .257 Wby., 6.5x55 Swedish, .270 Wby., 7x57, 7mm Rem., 7mm STW, 7mm Wby., .280 Rem., .30-06, .300 Win., .300 Wby., .338-06, 9.3x62. Weight: 8-8.5 lbs. Made from 1994 to 2012.
Synthetic stock model. . . . . NiB $3554 Ex $2909 Gd $2011
Walnut stock model . . . . . . NiB $3508 Ex $2866 Gd $2009

HANNIBAL BOLT-ACTION RIFLE
Custom rifle built on reinforced P-17 Enfield receiver. Calibers: Group I: 30-06; Group II: 7mm Rem. Mag., .300 Win. Mag., .416 Taylor, .425 Express, .458 Win. Mag.; Group III: .300 H&H, .300 Wby. Mag., 8mm Rem. Mag., .340 Wby. Mag., .375 H&H, .375 Wby. Mag., .404 Jeffery, .416 Hoffman, .416 Rem Mag., .450 Ackley, .458 Lott; Group IV: .338 A-Square Mag., .375 A-Square Mag., .378 Wby. Mag., .416 Rigby, .416 Wby. Mag., .460 Short Square Mag., .500 A-Square Mag. 20- to 26-inch bbl. Weight: 9 to 11.75 lbs. Express 3-leaf rear sight, ramp front. Classic Claro oil-finished walnut stock or synthetic stock w/flush detachable swivels and Coil-Chek recoil system. Adj. trigger w/2-position safety. Made from 1986 to 2012.
Synthetic stock model. . . . . NiB $3614 Ex $2870 Gd $1921
Walnut stock model . . . . . . NiB $3707 Ex $2795 Gd $2021

RIFLES

A-Square Hannibal

Auto-Ordnance
Thompson Model 27A-1
Deluxe

Auto-Ordnance
Thompson Model 27A-1
Standard Carbine

Auto-Ordnance
Thompson M1 Carbine

AUSTRIAN MILITARY RIFLES — Steyr, Austria *Manufactured at Steyr Armory.*

MODEL 90
STEYR-MANNLICHER . . . . **NiB $337 Ex $189 Gd $139**
Straight-pull bolt action. Caliber: 8mm. 5-round magazine. Open sights. 10-inch bayonet. Cartridge clip forms part of the magazine mechanism. Some of these rifles were provided with a laced canvas hand guard, others were of wood.

MODEL 90 STEYR-MANNLICHER
CARBINE. . . . . **NiB $339 Ex $228 Gd $139**
Same general specifications as Model 90 rifle except w/19.5-inch bbl., weight 7 lbs. No bayonet stud or supplemental forend grip.

MODEL 95 STEYR-MANNLICHER
CARBINE. . . . . **NiB $329 Ex $250 Gd $141**
Same general specifications as Model 95 rifle except w/19.5-inch bbl., weight 7 lbs. Post front sight; adj. rear carbine sight.

MODEL 95 STEYR-MANNLICHER
SERVICE RIFLE . . . . **NiB $299 Ex $190 Gd $137**
Straight-pull bolt action. Caliber: 8x50R Mannlicher (many of these rifles were altered during World War II to use the 7.9mm German service ammunition). 5-round Mannlicher-type box magazine. 30-inch bbl. Weight: 8.5 lbs. Sights: Blade front; rear adj. for elevation. Military-type full stock.

AUTO-ORDNANCE CORPORATION — Worcester, Massachusetts

A division of Kahr Arms.

THOMPSON 22-27A-3 . . . . . . **NiB $997 Ex $754 Gd $498**
Similar as Deluxe Model 27A-1 except 22 LR w/lightweight alloy receiver, weight 6.5 lbs. Magazines include 5-, 20-, 30- and 50-round box types, 80-round drum. Made from 1977 to 1994.

THOMPSON 27A-1 DELUXE. NiB $1100 Ex $879 Gd $530
Same as Standard Model 27A-1 except w/finned bbl. w/compensator, adj. rear sight, pistol-grip forestock. Caliber: .22 LR, l0mm (1991 to 1993) or 45 ACP. Weight: 11.5 lbs. Made from 1976 to 1999.
.22 LR (Limited production) . . . **NiB $1190 Ex $1000 Gd $770**
10-round stick magazine, add **$70**
20- or 30-round stick magazine, add **$80**
10-round drum magazine, add **$200**
50-round drum magazine, add **$300**

100-round drum magazine, add $600
Violin carrying case, add $227
Hard carrying case, add $200
Detacable stock/horizontal grip (2007), add $440

THOMPSON 27A-1 STANDARD
SEMIAUTO CARBINE . . . . **NiB $689 Ex $641 Gd $440**
Similar to Thompson submachine gun ("Tommy Gun") except has no provision for automatic firing. Caliber: .45 ACP. 20-round detachable box magazine (5-,15- and 30-round box magazines, 39-round drum also available). 16-inch plain bbl. Weight: 14 lbs. Sights: Aperture rear; blade front. Walnut buttstock, pistol grip and grooved forearm, sling swivels. Made from 1976-86.

THOMPSON
27A-1C LIGHTWEIGHT . . . . . **NiB $1090 Ex $900 Gd $707**
Similar to Model 27A-1 except w/lightweight alloy receiver. Weight: 9.25 lbs. Made 1984 to date.

THOMPSON M1 . . . . **NiB $1070 Ex $660 Gd $479**
Similar to Model 27A-1 except in M-1 configuration w/side cocking lever and horizontal forearm. Weight: 11.5 lbs. Made from 1986 to date.
M1-C (lightweight) . . . . **NiB $1080 Ex $860 Gd $570**

THOMPSON
27A-1 COMMANDO . . . . **NiB $1098 Ex $860 Gd $579**
Similar to Model 27A-1 except parkerized finish and black stock. 13 lbs. Made from 1997 to date.

BAIKAL — Izhevsk, Russia
Imported by RWC, Tullytown, PA. Formerly imported by EAA, Corp., Rockledge, Florida.

IZH-18MN Single Shot . . . . **NiB $250 Ex $190 Gd $110**
Boxlock, break action. Caliber: .222 Rem., .223 Rem., .243 Win., .270 Win., 7.62x39mm, .308 Win., .30-06, or .45-70. 23.5-inch bbl., 40 inches overall. Matte blue finish, checkered walnut stock. Imported from 2003 to 2009.

MP161K Semi Automatic . . . . . **NiB $330 Ex $250 Gd $170**
Caliber: .17 HMR, .22 LR or .22 WMR. 10-round magazine. 19.5-inch bbl., 39 inches overall. Matte blue finish, polymer thumbhole stock. Imported from 2009 to date.
.17 HMR or .22 WMR, add 20%

MP221 Side By Side . . . . **NiB $910 Ex $700 Gd $300**
Double barrel, boxlock, break action. Caliber: .223 Rem., .270 Win., .30-06, .308 Win., or .45-70. 23.5-inch bbl., 40 inches overall. Matte blue finish, checkered walnut stock. Imported from 2003 to 2009, reintro. 2011 to date.

BALLARD ARMS, INC. — Onsted, MI
Formerly Ballard Rifle LLC, Cody, WY. Firearms manufactured since 1996.

1-1/2 HUNTER'S RIFLE . . . . **NiB $3200 Ex $2440 Gd $1833**
Calibers: Seven calibers from .22 LR to .50-70. Single trigger, S-style lever action; uncheckered stock. Weight: 10.5 lbs.

1-3/4 FAR WEST RIFLE . . . . **NiB $2902 Ex $2045 Gd $1471**
Calibers: Eight calibers from .32-40 WCF to .50-90 SS. Patterned after original Ballard Far West model. 30 or 32-inch bbl., standard or heavyweight octagon; double set triggers; ring-style lever. Weight: 9.75 to 10.5 lbs.

NO. 5 PACIFIC . . . . **NiB $3208 Ex $2460 Gd $1996**
Calibers: Nine calibers between .32-40 WCF and .50-90 SS. Similar to No. 1-3/4 Far West model but with under-barrel wiping rod.

NO. 4-1/2 MID-RANGE
RIFLE . . . . **NiB $2900 Ex $2080 Gd $1765**
Calibers: Five calibers between .32-40 WCF and .45-110. Designed for black powder silhouette shooting. 30 or 32-inch bbl., half-octagonal heavyweight; single or double set triggers; pistol grip stock; full loop lever; hard rubber Ballard buttplate; Vernier tang sight. Weight: 10.75 to 11.5 lbs.

NO. 7 LONG-RANGE
RIFLE . . . . **NiB $3369 Ex $2390 Gd $1479**
Caliber: Five calibers between .40-65 Win. and .45-110. Similar to No. 4-1/2 Mid-Range Rifle; designed for long-range shooting. 32 or 34-inch half-octagon standard or heavyweight bbl.

MODEL 1885
HIGH WALL RIFLE . . . . **NiB $3190 Ex $2444 Gd $1954**
Calibers: Various. Exact replica of Winchester Model 1885 (parts are interchangeable). 30 or 32-inch bbl., octagon; case-colored receiver, uncheckered straight-grip stock and forearm. Weight: Approx. 9 lbs. Introduced 2001.
Deluxe model, add $1717
Sporting model, add $250
Shuetzen model, add $400

BANSNER'S ULTIMATE RIFLES, LLC — Adamstown, Pennsylvania
Established in 1981 in Adamstown, Pennsylvania, as Basner's Gunsmithing Specialties. Company name changed in 2000.

HIGH TECH SERIES . . . . **NiB $1032 Ex $790 Gd $641**
Calibers: Various. Steel or stainless steel action with factory bbl. Bansner's synthetic stock and Pachmayer decelerator pad.
Stainless steel model, add $300

SAFARI HUNTER . . . . **NiB $6200 Ex $4396 Gd $2398**
Calibers: Various dangerous game calibers. Based on Model 70 Classic action; muzzle brake; Lilja Precision stainless steel barrel; synthetic stock; matte black Teflon metal finish. Introduced 2003.

ULTIMATE ONE . . . . **NiB $5540 Ex $3766 Gd $3060**
Calibers: Various. Bolt-action, modeled on Winchester M70 and Remington 707 actions. Various metal finishes; muzzle brake; custom trigger; custom stock; Pachmayer decelerator pad; custom scope mounts and bases.
Three-position safety, add $250

WORLD SLAM LIMITED EDITION
RIFLE . . . . **NiB $5345 Ex $3850 Gd $2300**
Calibers: Various. Customized Model 707 action; fluted bold body. jeweled trigger. three-position safety; synthetic stock. Only 25-50 of limited edition models were made beginning in 2003.

BARRETT FIREARMS MFG., INC. — Murfreesboro, Tennessee

MODEL 82A1
SEMI-AUTOMATIC RIFLE . . NiB $8900 Ex $7760 Gd $5100
Caliber: .50 BMG. 10-round detachable box magazine. 29-inch recoiling bbl. w/muzzle brake. 57 inches overall. Weight: 28.5 lbs. Open iron sights and 10x scope. Composit stock w/ Sorbothance recoil pad and self-leveling bipod. Blued finish. Made in various configurations from 1985 to date.

MODEL 90 BOLT-ACTION
RIFLE . . . . NiB $3530 Ex $3099 Gd $2020
Caliber: .50 BMG. Five round magazine. 29-inch match bbl. 45 inches overall. Weight: 22 lbs. Composite stock w/retractable bipod. Made from 1990 to 1995.

MODEL 95 BOLT-ACTION . . NiB $6635 Ex $4890 Gd $3530
Similar to Model 90 bullpup except w/improved muzzle brake and extendable bipod. Made from 1995 to date.

MODEL 98B BOLT-ACTION . . . NiB $4699 Ex $4400 Gd $2530
Caliber: .338 Lapua Mag. 20-, 26-, or 27-in. bbl. Weight: 13.5 lbs. 10-rnd. magazine. Muzzle brake, adj. stock. Made from 2009 to date.

MODEL M4468
SEMI-AUTOMATIC . . . . NiB $2100 Ex $1707 Gd $1000
AR-style rifle. Caliber: 6.8 SPC. 16-inch bbl. Weight: 8 lbs. 5-, 10-, 30-round magazine. Made from 2005 to 2008.

BEEMAN PRECISION ARMS INC. — Santa Rosa, California

Since 1993 all European firearms imported by Beeman have been distributed by Beeman Outdoor Sports, Div., Roberts Precision Arms, Inc., Santa Rosa, CA.

WEIHRAUCH HW MODELS 60J AND 60J-ST BOLT-ACTION RIFLES
Calibers: .22 LR (60J-ST), .222 Rem. (60J). 22.8-inch bbl. 41.7 inches overall. Weight: 6.5 lbs. Sights: Hooded blade front; open adj. rear. Blued finish. Checkered walnut stock w/cheekpiece. Made from 1988 to 1994.
Model 60J . . . . NiB $835 Ex $746 Gd $615
Model 60J-ST . . . . NiB $655 Ex $539 Gd $398

WEIHRAUCH HW MODEL 60M
Small Bore Rifle . . . . NiB $690 Ex $579 Gd $389
Caliber: .22 LR. Single-shot. 26.8-inch bbl. 45.7 inches overall. Weight: 10.8 lbs. Adj. trigger w/push-button safety. Sights: Hooded blade front on ramp, precision aperture rear. Target-style stock w/stippled forearm and pistol grip. Blued finish. Made from 1988 to 1994.

WEIHRAUCH HW MODEL 660
MATCH RIFLE . . . . NiB $1023 Ex $855 Gd $445
Caliber: .22 LR. 26-inch bbl. 45.3 inches overall. Weight: 10.7 lbs. Adj. match trigger. Sights: globe front, precision aperture rear. Match-style walnut stock w/adj. cheekpiece and buttplate. Made from 1988 to 1994.

FEINWERKBAU MODEL 2600 SERIES TARGET RIFLE
Caliber: .22 LR. Single-shot. 26.3-inch bbl. 43.7 inches overall. Weight: 10.6 lbs. Match trigger w/fingertip weight adjustment dial. Sights: Globe front; micrometer match aperture rear. Laminated hardwood stock w/adj. cheekpiece. Made from 1988 to 1994.

Standard Model 2600 (left-hand) NiB $1733 Ex $1360 Gd $944
**Standard Model 2600
(right-hand) . . . . NiB $1560 Ex $1239 Gd $816**
**Free Rifle Model 2602
(left-hand) . . . . NiB $2196 Ex $1755 Gd $1024**
**Free Rifle Model 2602
(right-hand) . . . . NiB $2196 Ex $1755 Gd $1024**

BELGIAN MILITARY RIFLES — Belgium

Mfd. by Fabrique Nationale D'Armes de Guerre, Herstal, Belgium; Fabrique D'Armes de L'Etat, Lunich, Belgium. Hopkins & Allen Arms Co. of Norwich, Conn., as well as contractors in Birmingham, England, also produced these guns during World War I.

MODEL 1889 MAUSER
MILITARY RIFLE . . . . NiB $279 Ex $230 Gd $156
Caliber: 7.65mm Belgian Service (7.65mm Mauser). 5-round projecting box magazine. 30.75-inch bbl. w/jacket. Weight: 8.5 lbs. Adj. rear sight, blade front. Straight-grip military stock. This, and the carbine version, was the principal weapon of the Belgian Army at the start of WWII. Made from 1889 to c.1935.

MODEL 1916 MAUSER CARBINE . . . NiB $300 Ex $240 Gd $190
Same as Model 1889 Rifle except w/20.75-inch bbl. Weighs 8 lbs. and has minor differences in the rear sight graduations, lower band closer to the muzzle and swivel plate on side of buttstock.

MODEL 1935 MAUSER
MILITARY RIFLE . . . . NiB $370 Ex $292 Gd $169
Same general specifications as F.N. Model 1924; minor differences. Caliber: 7.65mm Belgian Service. Mfd. by Fabrique Nationale D'Armes de Guerre.

MODEL 1936 MAUSER
MILITARY RIFLE . . . . NiB $378 Ex $290 Gd $166
An adaptation of Model 1889 w/German M/98-type bolt, Belgian M/89 protruding box magazine. Caliber: 7.65mm Belgian Service. Mfd. by Fabrique Nationale D'Armes de Guerre.

BENELLI — Urbino, Itay

Imported by Benelli USA, Accokeek, MD.

R1 Semi-Automatic . . . . NiB $910 Ex $700 Gd $500
Caliber: .270 WSM, .308 Win., .30-06, .300 WSM, .300 Win. Mag. or .338 Win. Mag. 20-, 22- or 24-inch bbl. Matte black finish, checkered walnut or polymer stock. Designated Argo in Europe. Imported from 2002 to date.
ComforTech stock, add $125

BENTON & BROWN FIREARMS, INC. — Fort Worth, Texas

MODEL 93 BOLT-ACTION RIFLE
Similar to Blaser Model R84 (the B&B rifle is built on the Blaser action, see separate listing) with an interchangeable bbl. system. Calibers: .243 Win., 6mm Rem., .25-06, .257 Wby., .264 Win., .270 Win., .280 Rem., 7mm Rem Mag., .30-06, .308, .300 Wby., .300 Win. Mag., .338 Win., .375 H&H. 22- or 24-inch bbl. 41 or 43 inches overall. Bbl.-mounted scope rings and one-piece base; no sights. Two-piece walnut or fiberglass stock. Made 1993–1996.
Walnut stock model . . . . . . NiB $1896 Ex $1744 Gd $1012
Fiberglass stock model add $227
Extra bbl. assembly, add $525
Extra bolt assembly, add $450

Beretta 501
Bolt-Action Sporter

Beretta AR-70

BERETTA U.S.A. CORP. — Accokeek, Maryland *Manufactured by Fabbrica D'Armi Pietro Beretta, S.P.A., Gardone Val Trompia (Brescia), Italy.*

455 SIDE BY SIDE EXPRESS DOUBLE RIFLE
Sidelock action w/removable sideplates. Calibers: .375 H&H, .458 Win. Mag., .470 NE, .500 NE (3 inches), .416 Rigby. Bbls.: 23.5 or 25.5-inch. Weight: 11 lbs. Double triggers. Sights: Blade front; V-notch folding leaf rear. Checkered European walnut forearm and buttstock w/recoil pad. Color casehardened receiver w/blued bbls. Various grades of engraving. Custom built. Made from 1990 to date.
Model 455 . . . . NiB $100,000
Model 455EELL . . . . NiB $150,000

500 BOLT-ACTION SPORTER
Centerfire bolt-action rifle w/Sako A I short action. Calibers: .222 Rem., .223 Rem. Five round magazine. 23.63-inch bbl. Weight: 6.5 lbs. Available w/ or w/o iron sights. Tapered dovetailed receiver. European walnut stock. Disc. 1998.
Standard . . . . NiB $707 Ex $590 Gd $475
DL Model . . . . NiB $1590 Ex $1288 Gd $909
500 EELLEngraved . . . . NiB $1670 Ex $1465 Gd $990
w/iron sights, add 10%

501 BOLT-ACTION SPORTER
Same as Model 500 except w/Sako A II medium action. Calibers: .243 Win., .308 Win. Weight: 7.5 lbs. Disc. 1986.
Standard . . . . NiB $625 Ex $466 Gd $420
Standard w/iron sights . . . . NiB $707 Ex $650 Gd $430
DL model . . . . NiB $1386 Ex $1097 Gd $944
501 EELL (engraved) . . . . NiB $1607 Ex $1329 Gd $989
w/iron sights, add 10%

502 BOLT-ACTION SPORTER
Same as Model 500 except w/Sako A III long action. Calibers: .270 Win., 7mm Rem. Mag., .30/06, 375 H&H. Weight: 8.5 lbs. Disc. 1986.
Standard model . . . . NiB $675 Ex $534 Gd $460
DL model . . . . NiB $1565 Ex $1299 Gd $980
502 EELL (engraved) . . . . . . NiB $1607 Ex $1347 Gd $1088
w/iron sights, add 10%

AR-70 SEMIAUTOMATIC
RIFLE . . . . NiB $2020 Ex $1788 Gd $1077
Caliber: .223 Rem. (5.56mm). 30-round magazine. 17.75-inch bbl. Weight: 8.25 lbs. Sights: Rear peep adj. for windage and elevation; blade front. High-impact synthetic buttstock. Imported 1984-89.

EXPRESS S686/S689 SILVER SABLE O/U RIFLE
Calibers: .30-06 Spfld., 9.3x74R, and .444 Marlin. 24-inch bbl. Weight: 7.7 lbs. Drilled and tapped for scope mount. European-style cheek rest and ventilated rubber recoil pad. Imported 1995.
Model S686/S689 Silver
Sable II . . . . NiB $4720 Ex $3800 Gd $2244
Model S689 Gold Sable . . . NiB $6347 Ex $5329 Gd $3144
Model S686/S689 EELL
Diamond Sable . . . . . . NiB $13,325 Ex $9765 Gd $6479
w/extra bbl. set, add $350
w/detachable claw mounts, add $645

EXPRESS SSO O/U EXPRESS DOUBLE RIFLE
Sidelock. Calibers: .375 H&H Mag., .458 Win. Mag., 9.3 x 74R. 23-24- or 25.5-inch blued bbls. Weight: 11 lbs. Double triggers. Express sights w/blade front and V-notch folding leaf rear. Optional Zeiss scope w/claw mounts. Color casehardened receiver w/scroll engraving, game scenes and gold inlays on higher grades. Checkered European walnut forearm and buttstock w/cheekpiece and recoil pad. Imported 1985 to 1989.
Model SS0 (disc. 1989) NiB $15,800 Ex $10,600 Gd $6545
Model SS05 (disc. 1990) NiB $18600 Ex $14,300 Gd $7600
Model SS06 Custom . . . . NiB $75,000
Model SS06 EELL Gold Custom . . . . NiB $125,000
Extra bbl. assembly, add $7070
Claw mounts, add $800

MATO . . . . NiB $1015 Ex $733 Gd $533
Calibers: .270 Win., .280 Rem., 7mm Rem. Mag, .300 Win. Mag., .338 Win. Mag., .375 H&H. 23.6-inch bbl. Weight: 8 lbs. Adjustable trigger. Drop-out box magazine. Drilled and tapped for scope w/ or w/o adj. sights. Walnut or synthetic stock. Manufactured based on Mauser 98 action. Made from 1997 to 2002.
Deluxe model . . . . NiB $2015 Ex $1723 Gd $976
.375 H&H w/iron sights, add $350

SMALL BORE SPORTING CARBINE/TARGET RIFLE
Semiautomatic w/bolt handle in raised or conventional single-shot bolt-action w/handle in lowered position. Caliber: .22 LR. Four, 5-, 8-, 10- or 20-round magazines. 20.5-inch standard or heavy bbl. Sights: 3-leaf folding rear, partridge front. Target or sporting stock w/checkered pistol grip and forend and sling swivels. Weight: 5.5 to 6 lbs.
Sporter model (Super Sport X) . NiB $460 Ex $355 Gd $256
Target model (Olympia X) . . . . . NiB $340 Ex $520 Gd $345

Blaser Model R84

VINCENZO BERNARDELLI — Brescia, Italy

Currently headquartered in Brescia, Italy, Bernardelli arms were manufactured from 1721 to 1997 in Gardone, Italy. Imported and distributed by Armsport, Inc., Miami, Florida. Also handled by Magnum Research, Inc., Quality Arms, Inc., Armes De Chasse, Stoeger and Action Arms.

CARBINA .22 . . . . NiB $580 Ex $300 Gd $170
Semi-auto. Caliber: .22 rimfire. Blow-back action. Imported from 1990 to 1997.

EXPRESS VB . . . . NiB $5768 Ex $4755 Gd $3690
Double barrel. Calibers: Various. Side-by-side sidelock action. Ejectors, double triggers. Imported from 1990 to1997.
Deluxe model (w/double triggers), add $1125

EXPRESS 2000 . . . . NiB $2707 Ex $2025 Gd $1580
Calibers: .30-06, 7x65R, 8x57JRS, 9.3x74R. Over/under box-lock design. Single or double triggers, extractors. Checkered walnut stock and forearm. Imported from 1994 to 1997.
Single trigger, add $200

MINERVA EXPRESS . . . . . . NiB $5200 Ex $3890 Gd $4098
Caliber: Various. Exposed hammers. Extractors, double triggers. Moderate engraving. Imported from 1995 to 1997.

MODEL 120 . . . . NiB $2120 Ex $1587 Gd $1100
Combination gun; over-under boxlock; 12 gauge over .22 Hornet, .222 Rem., 5.6x50R Mag., .243 Win., 6.5x57R, .270 Win., 7x57R, .308 Win., .30-06, 6.5x55, 7x65R, 8x57JRS, 9.3x74R. Iron sights. Checkered walnut stock and forearm. Double triggers, automatic ejectors or extractors. Ventilated recoil pad. Engraved action. Made in Italy. Discontinued.

MODEL 190 . . . . NiB $1489 Ex $1129 Gd $1069
Combination gun; over-under boxlock. Calibers: 12, 16 or 20 ga. Over .222 Rem., .243 Win., .30-06, .308 Win., 5.6x50R Mag., .5.6x57R, 6.5x55, 6.5x57R, 7x57R, 7x65R, 8x57JRS, 9.3x74R. Iron sights. Checkered walnut stock. Double triggers; extractors. Made in Italy. Introduced in 1969, discontinued 1989.

MODEL 2000 . . . . NiB $2713 Ex $1866 Gd $1390
Combination gun; over-under boxlock action. Calibers: 12, 16 or 20 ga. Over .222 Rem., .22 Hornet, 5.6x50R Mag., .243 Win., 6.5x55, 6.5x57R, .270 Win., 7x57R, .308 Win., .30-06, 8x57JRS, 9.3x74R. Bbl: 23 inches. Sights: Blade front, open rear. Hand checkered, oil-finished select European walnut stock, double-set triggers, auto ejectors. Silvered, engraved action. Made in Italy. Introduced in 1990, disconti nued 1991.
Extra bbl. assembly, add $595

BLASER U.S.A., INC. — Fort Worth, Texas

Manufactured by Blaser Jagdwaffen GmbH, Germany, imported by Sigarms, Exeter, NH; Autumn Sales, Inc., Fort Worth, Texas.

MODEL R-84 BOLT-ACTION RIFLE
Calibers: .22-250, .243, 6mm Rem., .25-06, .270, .280 Rem., .30-06- .257 Wby. Mag., .264 Win. Mag., 7mm Rem Mag., .300 Win. Mag., .300 Wby. Mag., .338 Win. Mag., .375 H&H. Interchangeable bbls. w/standard or Magnum bolt assemblies. Bbl. length: 23 inches (standard); 24 inches (Magnum). 41 to 42 inches overall. Weight: 7 to 7.25 lbs. No sights. Bbl.-mounted scope system. Two-piece Turkish walnut stock w/solid black recoil pad. Imported from 1989 to 1994.
Model R84 Standard . . . . . NiB $2245 Ex $1725 Gd $1190
Model R84 Deluxe
(engraved game scene) . . NiB $2400 Ex $2021 Gd $1200
Model R84 Super Deluxe
(Gold and silver inlays) . . . . NiB $2449 Ex $1990 Gd $1590
Left-hand model, add $150
Extra bbl. assembly, add $600

MODEL R-93 SAFARI SERIES BOLT-ACTION REPEATER
Similar to Model R-84 except restyled action w/straight-pull bolt, unique safety and searless trigger mechanism. Additional chamberings: 6.5x55, 7x57, .308, .416 Rem. Optional open sights. Imported 1994 to 1998.
Model R93 Safari . . . . NiB $3598 Ex $2277 Gd $1844
Model R93 Safari Deluxe . . NiB $3943 Ex $4134 Gd $3297
Model R84 Safari Super Deluxe . . . NiB $4854 Ex $4326 Gd $3458
Extra bbl. assembly, add $600

MODEL R-93 CLASSIC SERIES BOLT-ACTION REPEATER
Similar to Model R-93 Safari except w/expanded model variations. Imported from 1998 to 2002.
Model R93 Attache (Premium wood,
fluted bbl.) . . . . NiB $3566 Ex $3887 Gd $3110
Model R93 Classic
(.22-250 to .375 H&H) . . NiB $3525 Ex $2889 Gd $2009
Model R93 Classic Safari
(.416 Rem.) . . . . NiB $3535 Ex $3279 Gd $2270
Model R93 LX (.22-250
to .416 Rem.) . . . . NiB $1799 Ex $1445 Gd $996
Model R93 Synthetic (.22-250
to .375 H&H) . . . . NiB $1908 Ex $1235 Gd $855
Extra bbl. assembly, add $600

BRITISH MILITARY RIFLES — England

Manufactured at Royal Small Arms Factory, Enfield Lock, Middlesex, England, private contractors.

RIFLE NO. 1 MARK III . . . . NiB $338 Ex $209 Gd $144
Short magazine Lee-Enfield (S.M.L.E.). Bolt action. Caliber: .303 British. 10-round box magazine. 25.25-inch bbl. Weight: 8.75 lbs. Sights: Adj. rear; blade front w/guards. Two-piece, full-length military stock. Note: The earlier Mark III (approved 1907) is virtually the same as Mark III (adopted 1918) except for sights and different magazine cut-off that was eliminated on the latter.

RIFLE NO. 3 MARK I
(PATTERN 14) . . . . NiB $347 Ex $255 Gd $160
Modified Mauser-type bolt action. Except for caliber .303 British and long-range sight, this rifle is the same as U.S. Model 1917 Enfield. See listing of the latter for general specifications.

RIFLE NO. 4 MARK I . . . . NiB $278 Ex $230 Gd $155
Post-World War I modification of the S.M.L.E. intended to simplify mass production. General specifications same as Rifle No. 1 Mark III except w/aperture rear sight and minor differences in construction and weighs 9.25 lbs.

Brno Model II

Brno Model 21H
Bolt-Action Sporting Rifle

LIGHT RIFLE NO. 4 MARK I...NiB $227 Ex $170 Gd $133
Modification of the S.M.L.E. Caliber: .303 British. 10-round box magazine. 23-inch bbl. Weight: 6.75 lbs. Sights: Micrometer click rear peep; blade front. One-piece military-type stock w/recoil pad. Made during WWII.

RIFLE NO. 5 MARK I . . . . NiB $369 Ex $244 Gd $175
Jungle Carbine. Modification of the S.M.L.E. similar to Light Rifle No. 4 Mark I except w/20.5-inch bbl. w/flash hider, carbine-type stock. Made during WWII, originally designed for use in the Pacific Theater.

BRNO SPORTING RIFLES — Brno, Czech Republic

Manufactured by Ceska Zbrojovka; Imported by Euro-Imports, El Cajon, California, previously by Bohemia Arms & Magnum Research. See also CZ rifles.

MODEL I BOLT-ACTION
SPORTING RIFLE . . . . NiB $689 Ex $615 Gd $437
Caliber: .22 LR. Five round detachable magazine. 22.75-inch bbl. Weight: 6 lbs. Sights: three-leaf open rear; hooded ramp front. Sporting stock w/checkered pistol grip, swivels. Made 1946 to 1973.

MODEL II BOLT-ACTION
SPORTING RIFLE . . . . NiB $641 Ex $543 Gd $444
Same as Model I except w/deluxe grade stock. Made 1949 to 1957.

MODEL III BOLT-ACTION
TARGET RIFLE. . . . . NiB $707 Ex $567 Gd $495
Same as Model I except w/heavy bbl. and target stock. Made from 1948-56.

MODEL IV BOLT-ACTION
TARGET RIFLE. . . . . NiB $755 Ex $587 Gd $488
Same as Model III except w/improved target trigger mechanism. Made 1956 to 1962.

MODEL V BOLT-ACTION
SPORTING RIFLE . . . . NiB $789 Ex $633 Gd $456
Same as Model I except w/improved trigger mechanism. Made from 1956 to 1973.

MODEL 21H BOLT-ACTION
SPORTING RIFLE . . . . NiB $1590 Ex $1325 Gd $1009
Mauser-type action. Calibers: 6.5x57mm, 7x57mm 8x57mm. Five round box magazine. 20.5-inch bbl. Double set trigger. Weight: 6.75 lbs. Sights: Two-leaf open rear-hooded ramp front. Half-length sporting stock w/cheekpiece, checkered pistol-grip and forearm, swivels. Made from 1946 to 1955.

MODEL 22F . . . . NiB $1408 Ex $1010 Gd $679
Same as Model 21H except w/full-length Mannlicher-type stock, weight: 6 lbs., 14 oz. Disc.

MODEL 98 STANDARD
Calibers: .243 Win., .270 Win., .30-06, .308 Win., .300 Win. Mag., 7x57mm, 7x64mm, or 9.3x62mm. 23.8-inch bbl. Overall 34.5 inches. Weight: 7.25 lbs. Checkered walnut stock w/Bavarian cheekpiece. Imported from 1998. Disc.
Standard calibers . . . . NiB $560 Ex $439 Gd $300
Calibers .300 Win., Mag.,
9.3x62mm . . . . NiB $580 Ex $469 Gd $386
w/single set trigger, add $150

MODEL 98 MANNLICHER
Similar to Model 98 Standard except full length stock and set triggers. Imported from 1998. Disc.
Standard calibers . . . . NiB $724 Ex $545 Gd $390
Calibers .300 Win. Mag., 9.3x62mm . . . NiB $755 Ex $600 Gd $445

ZKB-110 SINGLE-SHOT
Calibers: .22 Hornet, .222 Rem., 5.6x52R, 5.6x50 Mag., 6.5x57R, 7x57R, and 8x57JRS. 23.8-inch bbl. Weight: 6.1 lbs. Walnut checkered buttstock and forearm w/Bavarian cheekpiece. Imported from 1998 to 2003.
Standard model. . . . . NiB $279 Ex $218 Gd $177
Lux model . . . . NiB $448 Ex $333 Gd $266
Calibers 7x57R and 8x57 JRS, add $50
w/interchangeable 12 ga. shotgun bbl., add $150

HORNET BOLT-ACTION
SPORTING RIFLE . . . . NiB $1278 Ex $1043 Gd $689
Miniature Mauser action. Caliber: .22 Hornet. Five-round detachable box magazine. 23-inch bbl. Double set trigger. Weight: 6.25 lbs. Sights: Three-leaf open rear hooded ramp front. Sporting stock w/checkered pistol grip and forearm, swivels. Made 1949-74. Note: This rifle was also marketed in U.S. as "Z-B Mauser Varmint Rifle." (Reintroduced as Model ZKB 689)

MODEL ZKB 689
BOLT-ACTION RIFLE. . . . . NiB $482 Ex $345 Gd $296
Calibers .22 Hornet, .222 Rem. Five-round detachable box magazine. 23.5-inch bbl. Weight: 5.75 lbs. Double-set triggers. Adj. open rear sight, hooded ramp front. Walnut stock. Imported 1985–92.

MODEL ZKM 611 SEMIAUTOMATIC RIFLE
Caliber: .22 WMR. Six-round magazine. 20-inch bbl. 37 inches overall. Weight: 6.2 lbs. Hooded front sight; mid-mounted rear sight. Checkered walnut or beechwood stock. Single thumbscrew takedown. Grooved receiver for scope mounting. Imported from 2006 to date.
Standard beechwood model . . . NiB $508 Ex $412 Gd $389
Deluxe walnut model . . . . NiB $600 Ex $482 Gd $328

Brno Model 22F

Brno Model-ZKM 611

Brown Precision High Country Youth Rifle

Standard Pro-Hunter......NiB $4597 Ex $3150 Gd $2370
Pro-Hunter Elite (1993 to date) ...NiB $6066 Ex $3886 Gd $2125
Pro-Hunter w/Rem 40X action add $650

PRO-VARMINTER BOLT-ACTION RIFLE
Custom varminter built on a Remington 707 or 40X action fitted w/Shilen stainless steel benchrest bbl. Varmint or benchrest-style stock. Made from 1993 to date.
Standard Pro-Varminter ....NiB $3735 Ex $2966 Gd $969

SELECTIVE TARGET MODEL..NiB $1044 Ex $835 Gd $590
Tactical law-enforcement rifle built on a Remington 707V action. Caliber: .308 Win. 20-, 22- or 24-inch bbl. Synthetic stock. Made from 1989 to 1992.

TACTICAL ELITE RIFLE ....NiB $4566 Ex $3290 Gd $1977
Similar to Selective Target Model except fitted w/select match-grade Shilen benchrest heavy stainless bbl. Calibers: .223, .308, .300 Win. Mag. Black or camo Kevlar/graphite composite fiberglass stock w/adj. buttplate. Non-reflective black Teflon metal finish. Made from 1997 to date.

BROWN PRECISION COMPANY — Los Molinos, California

MODEL 7 SUPER LIGHT
SPORTER ....NiB $1128 Ex $1086 Gd $775
Lightweight sporter built on a Remington Model 7 barreled action w/18-inch factory bbl. Weight: 5.25 lbs. Kevlar stock. Made from 1984 to 1992.

HIGH COUNTRY BOLT-ACTION SPORTER
Custom sporting rifles built on Blaser, Remington 707, Ruger 77 and Winchester 70 actions. Calibers: .243 Win., .25-06, .270 Win., 7mm Rem. Mag., .308 Win., .30-06. Five-round magazine (4-round in 7mm Mag.). 22- or 24-inch bbl. Weight: 6.5 lbs. Fiberglass stock w/recoil pad, sling swivels. No sights. Made from 1975 to 1992.
Standard High Country.....NiB $1624 Ex $1043 Gd $855
Custom High Country.....NiB $4490 Ex $3124 Gd $1876
Left-hand action, add $250
Stainless bbl., add..............................$250
70, 77 or Blaser actions, add $150
70 SG action, add.............................$400

HIGH COUNTRY
YOUTH RIFLE............ NiB $1336 Ex $1023 Gd $688
Similar to standard Model 7 Super Light except w/Kevlar or graphite stock, scaled-down to youth dimensions. Calibers: .223, .243, 6mm, 7mm-08, .308. Made from 1993 to 2000.

PRO-HUNTER BOLT-ACTION RIFLE
Custom sporting rifle built on Remington 707 or Winchester 70 SG action fitted w/match-grade Shilen bbl. chambered in customer's choice of caliber. Matte blued, nickel or Teflon finish. Express-style rear sight hooded ramp front. Synthetic stock. Made 1989 to date

BROWNING — Morgan, Utah
Manufactured for Browning by Fabrique Nationale d'Armes de Guerre (now Fabrique Nationale Herstal), Herstal, Belgium; Miroku Firearms Mfg. Co., Tokyo, Japan; A.T.I., Salt Lake City, UT; Oy Sako Ab, Riihimaki, Finland.

.22 AUTOMATIC RIFLE, GRADE I
Similar to discontinued Remington Model 241A. Autoloading. Take-down. Calibers: .22 LR. .22 Short (not interchangeably). Tubular magazine in buttstock holds 11 LR. 16 Short. Bbl. lengths: 19.25 inches (.22 LR), 22.25 inches (.22 Short). Weight: 4.75 lbs. (.22 LR); 5 lbs. (.22 Short). Receiver scroll engraved. Open rear sight, bead front. Checkered pistol-grip buttstock, semibeavertail forearm. Made from 1956 to 1972 by FN; from 1972 to date by Miroku. Note: Illustrations are of rifles manufactured by FN.
FN manufacture ....NiB $899 Ex $500 Gd $265
Miroku manufacture.........NiB $650 Ex $398 Gd $327

Brown Precision Pro-Hunter

Brown Precision Tactical Elite

.22 AUTOMATIC RIFLE, GRADE II

Same as Grade I except satin chrome-plated receiver engraved w/small game animal scenes, gold-plated trigger select walnut stock and forearm. .22 LR only. Made from 1972 to 1984.
FN manufacture . . . . **NiB $1200 Ex $909 Gd $369**
Miroku manufacture . . . . **NiB $554 Ex $439 Gd $300**

.22 AUTOMATIC RIFLE, GRADE III

Same as Grade I except satin chrome-plated receiver elaborately hand-carved and engraved w/dog and game-bird scenes, scrolls and leaf clusters: gold-plated trigger, extra-fancy walnut stock and forearm, skip-checkered. .22 LR only. Made from 1972 to 1984.
FN manufacture . . . . **NiB $1500 Ex $1125 Gd $880**
Miroku manufacture . . . . **NiB $822 Ex $590 Gd $480**

.22 AUTOMATIC, GRADE VI . . . NiB $1190 Ex $798 Gd $600

Same general specifications as standard .22 Automatic except for engraving, high-grade stock w/checkering and glossy finish. Made by Miroku from 1986 to date.

MODEL 52 BOLT-ACTION RIFLE . . . NiB $800 Ex $655 Gd $443

Limited edition of Winchester Model 52C Sporter. Caliber: .22 LR. Five-round magazine. 24-inch bbl. Weight: 7 lbs. Micro-Motion trigger. No sights. Checkered select walnut stock w/rosewood forend and metal grip cap. Blued finish. 5000 made from 1991 to 1992.

MODEL 53 LEVER-ACTION RIFLE . . . NiB $833 Ex $724 Gd $480

Limited edition of Winchester Model 53. Caliber: .32-20. Seven-round tubular half-magazine. 22-inch bbl. Weight: 6.5 lbs. Adj. rear sight, bead front. Select walnut checkered pistol-grip stock w/high-gloss finish. Classic-style forearm. Blued finish. 5000 made in 1990.

MODEL 65 GRADE I LEVER-ACTION

RIFLE . . . . **NiB $730 Ex $445 Gd $370**
Caliber: .218 Bee. 7-round tubular half-magazine. 24-inch bbl. Weight: 6.75 lbs. Sights: Adj. buckhorn-style rear, hooded bead front. Select walnut pistol-grip stock w/high-gloss finish. Semibeavertail forearm. Limited edition of 3500 made in 1989.

MODEL 65 HIGH GRADE RIFLE . . . NiB $1009 Ex $733 Gd $528

Same general specifications as Model 65 Grade I except w/ engraving and gold-plated animals on grayed receiver. Cut checkering on pistol grip and forearm. Limited edition of 1500 made in 1989.

MODEL 71 GRADE I CARBINE . . . NiB $880 Ex $640 Gd $455

Same general specifications as Model 71 Grade I Rifle except carbine w/20-inch round bbl. and weighs 8 lbs. Limited edition of 4000 made in 1986 to 1987.

MODEL 71 GRADE I LEVER-ACTION

RIFLE . . . . **NiB $916 Ex $710 Gd $497**
Caliber: .348 Win. 4-round magazine. 24-inch round bbl. Weight: 8 lbs., 2 oz. Open buckhorn sights. Select walnut straight grip stock w/satin finish. Classic-style forearm, flat metal buttplate. Limited edition of 3000 made in 1986 to 1987.

MODEL 71 HIGH-GRADE

CARBINE . . . . **NiB $1332 Ex $1123 Gd $765**
Similar to Model 71 High Grade Rifle, except carbine w/20-inch round bbl. Limited edition of 3000 made 1986 to 1988.

MODEL 71 HIGH-GRADE

RIFLE . . . . **NiB $3866 Ex $3121 Gd $2140**
Caliber: .348 Win. Four round magazine. 24-inch round bbl. Weight: 8 lbs., 2 oz. Engraved receiver. Open buckhorn sights. Select walnut checkered pistol-grip stock w/high-gloss finish. Classic-style forearm, flat metal buttplate. Limited edition of 3000 made in 1987.

M-78 BICENTENNIAL SET . . . NiB $3866 Ex $3121 Gd $2140

Special Model 78 .45-70 w/same specifications as standard type, except sides of receiver engraved w/bison and eagle, scroll engraving on top of receiver, lever, both ends of bbl. and buttplate; high-grade walnut stock and forearm. Accompanied by an engraved hunting knife and stainless steel commemorative medallion, all in an alder wood presentation case. Each item in set has matching serial number beginning with "1776" and ending with numbers 1 to 1,000. Edition limited to 1,000 sets. Made in 1976.

MODEL 78 SINGLE-SHOT RIFLE

Falling-block lever-action similar to Winchester 1885 High Wall single-shot rifle. Calibers: .22-250, 6mm Rem., .243 Win., .25-06, 7mm Rem. Mag., .30-06, .45-70 Govt. 26-inch octagon or heavy round bbl.; 24-inch octagon bull bbl. on .45-70 model. Weight: 7.75 lbs. w/octagon bbl.; w/round bbl., 8.5 lbs.; .45-70, 8.75 lbs. Furnished w/o sights except .45-70 model w/open rear sight, blade front. Checkered fancy walnut stock and forearm. .45-70 model w/straight-grip stock and curved buttplate; others have Monte Carlo comb and cheekpiece, pistol-grip w/cap, recoil pad. Made from 1973 to 1983 by Miroku. Reintroduced in 1985 as Model 1885.
All calibers except .45-70 . . **NiB $1500 Ex $1274 Gd $1010**
.45-70 . . . . **NiB $970 Ex $766 Gd $523**

MODEL 1885 SINGLE-SHOT RIFLE

Calibers: .22 Hornet, .223, .243, (Low Wall); .357 Mag., .44 Mag., .45 LC (L/W Traditional Hunter); .22-250, .223 Rem.,

Browning Model 53
Lever-Action Limited Edition

Browning Model 71
Grade I Lever-Action

Browning Model 71
High-Grade Carbine

Browning Model 71
High-Grade

Browning Model 78
Single-Shot .45-70

Browning Model 1885
High-Wall Single-Shot

Browning Model 1885
High-Wall Traditional Hunter

Browning Model 1885
Low-Wall Single-Shot

Browning Model 1885
BPCR Single-Shot

Browning Model 1886
Grade I

Browning Model 1886
High-Grade

Browning Model 1895
Grade I

Browning
A-Bolt Eclipse

.270 Win., 7mm Rem. Mag., .30-06, .454 Casull Mag., .45.70 (High Wall); .30.30 Win., .38-55 WCF, .45 Govt. (H/W Traditional Hunter); .40-65, .45 Govt. and .45.90 (BPCR). 24-, 28-, 30 or 34-inch round, octagonal or octagonal and round bbl. 39.5, 43.5, 44.25 or 46.125 inches overall. Weight: 6.25, 8.75, 9, 11, or 11.75 lbs. respectively. Blued or color casehardened receiver. Gold-colored adj. trigger. Drilled and tapped for scope mounts w/no sights or vernier tang rear sight w/globe front and open sights on .45-70 Govt. Walnut straight-grip stock and Schnabel forearm w/cut checkering and high-gloss or oil finish. Made from 1985 to 2001.

Low Wall model w/o sights
   (Intro. 1995). . . . . **NiB $1400 Ex $976 Gd $540**
Traditional Hunter model
   (Intro. 1998). . . . . **NiB $1450 Ex $990 Gd $575**
High Wall model w/o sights
   (Intro. 1985) . . . . **NiB $1390 Ex $1020 Gd $770**
Traditional Hunter model
   (Intro. 1997). . . . . **NiB $1390 Ex $1020 Gd $770**
BPCR model w/o
   ejector (Intro. 1996). . . . **NiB $1933 Ex $1442 Gd $1041**
BPCR Creedmoor Model .45-90
   (Intro. 1998). . . . . **NiB $1933 Ex $1442 Gd $1041**

MODEL 1886 MONTANA
CENTENNIAL RIFLE . . . . . . **NiB $2120 Ex $1670 Gd $1097**
Same general specifications as Model 1886 High Grade lever-action except w/specially engraved receiver designating Montana Centennial; also different stock design. Made in 1986 in limited issue by Miroku.

MODEL 1886 GRADE I LEVER-ACTION
RIFLE. . . . . **NiB $1255 Ex $712 Gd $495**
Caliber: .45-70 Govt., 8-round magazine. 26-inch octagonal bbl. 45 inches overall. Weight: 9 lbs., 5 oz. Deep blued finish on receiver. Open buckhorn sights. Straight-grip walnut stock. Classic-style forearm. Metal buttplate. Satin finish. Made in 1986 in limited issue 7070 by Miroku.

MODEL 1886 HIGH-GRADE
LA RIFLE . . . . **NiB $2055 Ex $1359 Gd $933**
Same general specifications as the Model 1886 Grade I except receiver is grayed, steel embellished w/scroll; elk and American bison engraving. High-gloss stock. Made in 1986 in limited issue of 3000 by Miroku.

MODEL 1895 GRADE I
LA RIFLE . . . . **NiB $979 Ex $911 Gd $765**
Caliber: .30-06, .30-40 Krag. Four round magazine. 24-inch round bbl. 42 inches overall. Weight: 8 lbs. French walnut stock and Schnabel forend. Sights: Rear buckhorn; gold bead on elevated ramp front. Made in 1984 in limited issue of 8,000 (2,000 chambered for .30-40 Krag and 6,000 chambered for .30-06). Mfd. by Miroku.

MODEL 1895 HIGH-GRADE
LA RIFLE . . . . **NiB $1630 Ex $1379 Gd $996**
Similar to Model 1895 Grade I except engraved receiver and Grade III French walnut stock and forend w/fine checkering. Made in 1985 in limited issue of 1000 in each caliber by Miroku.

MODEL AB3 . . . . **NiB $600 Ex $500 Gd $475**
Bolt-action. Calibers: .270 Win., .30-06 or .300 Win. Mag. 5-rnd. detachable magazine. 22- or 26-in. bbl. Weight: 7 lbs. Finish: matte blue. Made from 2014 to date.

MODEL ACERA. . . . . **NiB $896 Ex $800 Gd $660**
Straight pull action. Calibers: .30-06 or .300 Win. Mag. Detachable magazine. 22- or 24-in. bbl. Weight: 7 lbs. Finish: gloss blue. Stock: checkered walnut. Made from 1999 to 2000.

MODEL A-BOLT .22 RIFLE
Calibers: .22 LR, .22 Magnum. Five- and 15-round magazines. 22-inch round bbl. 40.25 inches overall. Weight: 5 lbs., 9 oz. Gold-colored adj. trigger. Laminated walnut stock w/checkering. Rosewood forend grip cap; pistol grip. With or w/o sights. Ramp front and adj. folding leaf rear on open sight model. 22 LR made 1985 to 1996; 22 Magnum, 1990 to 1996.

GRADING: **NiB** = New in Box   **Ex** = Excellent or NRA 95%   **Gd** = Good or NRA 68%

Browning A-Bolt .22

Browning A-Bolt Euro-Bolt

Browning A-Bolt Hunter

Browning A-Bolt Hunter with BOSS

Browning A-Bolt Medallion Custom Trophy

Grade I .22 LR . . . . NiB $575 Ex $340 Gd $255
Grade I .22 Magnum. . . . . NiB $600 Ex $423 Gd $269
Deluxe Grade Gold Medallion. . . NiB $620 Ex $479 Gd $354

MODEL A-BOLT ECLIPSE BOLT RIFLE
Similar as Hunter Grade except fitted w/gray and black laminated thumbhole stock. Available in both short and long action w/two bbl. configurations w/BOSS. Mfd. by Miroku 1996 to 2006.
Eclipse w/standard bbl.. . . . . . . NiB $955 Ex $821 Gd $677
Eclipse Varmint w/heavy bbl. . NiB $1123 Ex $978 Gd $720
Eclipse M-1000
   Target (.300 Win. Mag.) . . NiB $1304 Ex $1038 Gd $796

MODEL A-BOLT EURO-BOLT RIFLE
Same general specifications as Hunter Grade except w/checkered satin-finished walnut stock. W/continental-style cheekpiece, palm-swell grip and Schnabel forend. Mannlicher-style spoon bolt handle and contoured bolt shroud. 22- or 26-inch bbl. w/satin blued finish. Weight: 6.8 to 7.4 lbs. Calibers: .22-250 Rem., .243 Win., .270 Win., .30.06, .308 Win., 7mm Rem. Mag. Mfd. by Miroku 1993 to 1994; 1994 to 1996 (Euro-Bolt II).
Euro-Bolt. . . . . NiB $679 Ex $536 Gd $369
Euro-Bolt II. . . . . NiB $755 Ex $640 Gd $470
BOSS option, add $100

MODEL A-BOLT HUNTER GRADE RIFLE
Calibers: .22 Hornet, .223 Rem., .22-250 Rem., .243 Win., .257 Roberts, 7mm-08 Rem., .308 Win., (short action) .25-06 Rem., .270 Win., .280 Rem., .284 Win., .30-06, 7mm Rem. Mag., .300 Win. Mag., .338 Win. Mag. Four-round magazine (standard), 3-round (magnum). 22-inch bbl. (standard), 24-inch (magnum). Weight: 7.5 lbs. (standard), 8.5 lbs. (magnum). With or w/o sights. Classic-style walnut stock. Produced in two action lengths w/nine locking lugs, fluted bolt w/60 degree rotation. Mfd. by Miroku from 1985 to 1993; from 1994 to 2007 (Hunter II).
Hunter . . . . NiB $489 Ex $333 Gd $269
Hunter II. . . . . NiB $590 Ex $389 Gd $310
Hunter Micro . . . . NiB $596 Ex $395 Gd $317
BOSS option, add $100
Open sights, add. $75

MODEL A-BOLT MEDALLION GRADE RIFLE
Same as Hunter Grade except w/high-gloss deluxe stock rosewood grip cap and forend; high-luster blued finish. Also in .375 H&H w/open sights. Left-hand models available in long action only. Mfd. by Miroku from 1988 to 1993; from 1994 to 2009 (Medallion II). Bighorn Sheep Ltd. Ed.
.270 Win. (600 made 1986) . NiB $1412 Ex $1096 Gd $790
Gold Medallion Deluxe Grade . . . NiB $679 Ex $500 Gd $346
Gold Medallion II Deluxe
   Grade . . . . NiB $670 Ex $525 Gd $380
Medallion, Standard Grade . . . NiB $633 Ex $488 Gd $354
Medallion II, Standard Grade . . NiB $655 Ex $500 Gd $397
Medallion, .375 H&H . . . . NiB $999 Ex $770 Gd $488
Medallion II, .375 H&H . . . . . NiB $1012 Ex $790 Gd $497
Micro Medallion . . . . NiB $690 Ex $557 Gd $367
Micro Medallion II . . . . NiB $707 Ex $569 Gd $415
Pronghorn Antelope Ltd. Ed. 243 Win.
   (500 made 1987) . . . . NiB $1266 Ex $1139 Gd $923
w/BOSS option, add $100
w/Open sights, add. $75

MODEL A-BOLT STALKER RIFLE
Same general specifications as Model A-Bolt Hunter Rifle except w/checkered graphite-fiberglass composite stock and

Browning A-Bolt
Medallion White Gold

Browning A-Bolt
Medallion

Browning A-Bolt
Medallion (Left-Handed)

Browning A-Bolt
Composite Stalker

Browning A-Bolt Stainless
Stalker

Browning BAR, Grade IV

Browning BAR, Grade V

GRADING: **NiB** = New in Box   **Ex** = Excellent or NRA 95%   **Gd** = Good or NRA 68%   **229**

Browning BAR Mark II Safari

Browning BAR Mark II Safari

matte blued or stainless metal. Non-glare matte finish of all exposed metal surfaces. 3 models: Camo Stalker orig. w/multi-colored laminated wood stock, matte blued metal; Composite Stalker w/graphite-fiberglass stock, matte blued metal; w/ composite stock, stainless metal. Made by Miroku from 1987 to 1993; 1994 to date. (Stalker II).

Camo Stalker (orig. laminated stock)	NiB $960	Ex $709	Gd $350
Composite Stalker	NiB $990	Ex $656	Gd $433
Composite Stalker II	NiB $990	Ex $656	Gd $433
Stainless Stalker	NiB $1045	Ex $745	Gd $500
Stainless Stalker II	NiB $876	Ex $655	Gd $571
Stainless Stalker, .375 H&H	NiB $909	Ex $808	Gd $667
W/BOSS option, add			$100
Left-hand model, add			$100

MODEL A-BOLT
VARMINT II RIFLE . . . . NiB $805 Ex $723 Gd $577
Same general specifications as Stalker model except w/22-inch heavy bbl. w/BOSS system and varmint-style black laminated wood stock. Calibers: .22-250, .223 or .308. No sights. Bright blue or satin finish. Made by Miroku from 2002 to 2008.

MODEL B-92 LEVER-ACTION
RIFLE . . . . NiB $534 Ex $467 Gd $288
Calibers: .357 Mag. and .44 Rem. Mag. 11-round magazine. 20-inch round bbl. 37.5 inches overall. Weight: 5.5 to 6.4 lbs. Seasoned French walnut stock w/high gloss finish. Cloverleaf rear sight; steel post front. Made from 1979 to 1989 by Miroku.

BAR AUTOMATIC RIFLE, GRADE I,
STANDARD CALIBERS . . . . . . NiB $805 Ex $623 Gd $455
Gas-operated semiautomatic. Calibers: .243 Win., .270 Win., .280 Rem., .308 Win., .30-06. Four-round box magazine. 22-inch bbl. Weight: 7.5 lbs. Folding leaf rear sight, hooded ramp front. French walnut stock and forearm checkered, QD swivels. Made from 1967 to 1992 by FN.

BAR, GRADE I, MAGNUM
CALIBERS . . . . NiB $809 Ex $733 Gd $590
Same as BAR in standard calibers, except w/24-inch bbl. 7mm Rem. Mag. or .300 Win. Mag. .338 Win. Mag. w/3-round box magazine and recoil pad. Weight: 8.5 lbs. Made 1969 to 1992 by FN.

BAR, GRADE II
Same as Grade I except receiver engraved w/big-game heads (deer and antelope on standard-caliber rifles, ram and grizzly on Magnum-caliber) and scrollwork, higher grade wood. Made 1967 to 1974 by FN.
Standard calibers . . . . NiB $1229 Ex $976 Gd $657
Magnum calibers . . . . NiB $1338 Ex $875 Gd $617

BAR, GRADE III
Same as Grade I except receiver of grayed steel engraved w/big-game heads (deer and antelope on standard-caliber rifles, moose and elk on Magnum-caliber) framed in fine-line scrollwork, gold-plated trigger, stock and forearm of highly figured French walnut, hand-checkered and carved. Made from 1971 to 1974 by FN.
Standard calibers . . . . NiB $1554 Ex $993 Gd $591
Magnum calibers . . . . NiB $1617 Ex $1230 Gd $725

BAR, GRADE IV
Same as Grade I except receiver of grayed steel engraved w/full detailed rendition of running deer and antelope on standard-caliber rifles, moose and elk on Magnum-caliber gold-plated trigger, stock and forearm of highly figured French walnut, hand checkered and carved. Made frm 1971 to 1986 by FN.
Standard calibers . . . . NiB $2490 Ex $1546 Gd $1110
Magnum calibers . . . . NiB $2669 Ex $1721 Gd $1300

BAR, GRADE V
Same as Grade I except receiver w/complete big-game scenes executed by a master engraver and inlaid w/18K gold (deer and antelope on standard-caliber rifles, moose and elk on Magnum caliber), gold-plated trigger, stock and forearm of finest French walnut, intricately hand-checkered and carved. Made from 1971 to 1974 by FN.
Standard calibers . . . . NiB $6457 Ex $4707 Gd $2897
Magnum calibers . . . . NiB $6844 Ex $5110 Gd $3194

BAR MARK II SAFARI AUTOMATIC RIFLE
Same general specifications as standard BAR semiautomatic rifle, except w/redesigned gas and buffer systems, new bolt release lever, and engraved receiver. Made from 1993 to date.
Standard calibers . . . . NiB $1019 Ex $707 Gd $505
Magnum calibers . . . . NiB $1040 Ex $808 Gd $617
Lightweight (alloy receiver
   w/20-inch bbl.) . . . . NiB $765 Ex $588 Gd $380
BAR Mk II Grade III
   (intro. 1996) . . . . NiB $3520 Ex $2377 Gd $1290
BAR Mk II Grade IV
   (intro. 1996) . . . . NiB $3609 Ex $2303 Gd $1829
W/BOSS option, add $75
W/open sights, add $25

BAR LONGTRAC . . . . NiB $1230 Ex $990 Gd $880
Similar to BAR Shorttrac except in .270 Win., .30-06, .300 Win. Mag., or 7mm Rem. Made in Belgium from 2005 to date.
WSM calibers, add $120
Stalker (matte black finish,
   composite stock) . . . . NiB $1260 Ex $1050 Gd $880
Camo, add $100

BAR SHORTTRAC . . . . NiB $1230 Ex $990 Gd $880
Semi-automatc. Gas operated. Calibers: .243 Win., .270 WSM, .300 WSM, .308 Win., 7mm-08, 7mm WSM or .325 WSM. 3- or 4-rnd. detacable magazine. 22- or 23-in. bbl. Weight: 6.6-7.25 lbs. Stock: satin or oil finish walnut. Finish: black or stain nickel. Made in Belgium from 2005 to date.
WSM calibers, add $120
Stalker (matte black finish,
   composite stock) . . . . NiB $1260 Ex $1050 Gd $880
Camo, add $100

Browning BBR Lightning

Browning BL-22, Grade I

Browning BPR
Pump Rifle

Browning
BL-22 II

Browning
BLR Model '81

Browning High-Power
Bolt-Action Rifle, Medallion Grade

Browning High-Power
Safari Grade Medium Action, Heavy Barrel

RIFLES

BAR 22 AUTOMATIC RIFLE
Semiautomatic. Caliber: .22 LR. Tubular magazine holds 15 rounds. 20.25-inch bbl. Weight: 6.25 lbs. Sights: Folding-leaf rear, gold bead front on ramp. Receiver grooved for scope mounting. French walnut pistol-grip stock and forearm checkered. Made from 1977 to 1985.

Grade I . . . . NiB $641 Ex $369 Gd $322
Grade II . . . . NiB $1011 Ex $555 Gd $375

BBR LIGHTNING BOLT-ACTION
RIFLE. . . . . NiB $606 Ex $495 Gd $400
Bolt-action rifle w/short bolt throw of 60 degrees. Calibers: .25-06 Rem., .270 Win., .30-06, 7mm Rem. Mag., .300 Win. Mag. 24-inch bbl. Weight: 8 lbs. Made from 1979 to 1984.

BL-17 GRADE I . . . . NiB $480 Ex $380 Gd $290
Similar to BL-22 except .17 Mach 2. Made from 2005 to date.

Grade II, add $50
Grade II Field Octagon, add $330

BL-22 LEVER-ACTION REPEATING RIFLE
Short-throw lever-action. Caliber: .22 LR, Long, Short. Tubular magazine holds 15 LR, 17 Long 22 Short rounds. 20-inch bbl. Weight: 5 lbs. Sights: Folding leaf rear; bead front. Receiver grooved for scope mounting. Walnut straight-grip stock and forearm, bbl. band. Made from 1970 to date by Miroku.

Grade I . . . . NiB $445 Ex $379 Gd $290
Grade II (w/scroll engraving) . . NiB $498 Ex $390 Gd $300

BLR LEVER-ACTION REPEATING RIFLE
Calibers: (short action only) .243 Win., .308 Win., .358 Win. Four round detachable box magazine. 20-inch bbl. Weight: 7 lbs. Sights: Windage and elevation adj. open rear; hooded ramp front. Walnut straight-grip stock and forearm, checkered, bbl. band, recoil pad. Made in 1966 by BAC/USA; from 1969 to 1973 by FN; from 1974 to 1980 by Miroku. Note: USA manufacture of this model was limited to prototypes and pre-production guns only and may be identified by the "MADE IN USA" roll stamp on the bbl.

FN model . . . . NiB $1000 Ex $699 Gd $554
Miroku model . . . . NiB $690 Ex $500 Gd $398
USA model . . . . NiB $1245 Ex $1097 Gd $686

BLR LIGHTNING MODEL
Lightweight version of the Browning BLR '81 w/forged alloy receiver and redesigned trigger group. Calibers: Short Action—.22-250 Rem., .223 Rem., .243 Win., 7mm-08 Rem., .308 Win.; Long Action— .270 Win., 7mm Rem. Mag., .30-06, .300 Win. Mag. Three or 4-round detachable box magazine. 20-, 22- or 24-inch bbl. Weight: 6.5 to 7.75 lbs. Pistol-grip style walnut stock and forearm, cut checkering and recoil pad. Made by Miroku from 1995 to 2002.

Short action model . . . . NiB $690 Ex $586 Gd $390
Long action model . . . . NiB $707 Ex $596 Gd $400

BLR MODEL '81
Redesigned version of the Browning BLR. Calibers: .222-50 Rem., .243 Win., .308 Win., .358 Win; Long Action— .270 Win., 7mm Rem. Mag., .30-06. Fourround detachable box magazine. 20-inch bbl. Weight: 7 lbs. Walnut straight-grip stock and forearm, cut checkering, recoil pad. Made by Miroku from 1981 to 1995; Long Action intro. 1991.

Short action model . . . . NiB $780 Ex $592 Gd $396
Long action model . . . . NiB $850 Ex $505 Gd $390

BPR-22 PUMP RIFLE
Hammerless slide-action repeater. Specifications same as for BAR-.22, except also available chambered for .22 Magnum RF; magazine capacity, 11 rounds. Made from 1977 to 1982 by Miroku.

Model I . . . . NiB $355 Ex $274 Gd $200
Model II . . . . NiB $425 Ex $437 Gd $262

BPR PUMP RIFLE
Slide-action repeater based on proven BAR designs w/forged alloy receiver and slide that cams down to clear bbl. and receiver. Calibers: .243 Win., .308 Win., .270 Win., .30-06, 7mm Rem. Mag. .300 Win. Mag. Three or 4-round detachable box magazine. 22- or 24-inch bbl. w/ramped front sight and open adj. rear. Weight: 7.2 to 7.4 lbs. Made from 1997 to 2001 by Miroku.

BPR Model standard calibers . . NiB $743 Ex $533 Gd $390
BPR Model magnum calibers add $75

EXPRESS RIFLE . . . . NiB $6010 Ex $5600 Gd $4800
Custom shop. Superposed Superlight action. Calibers: .270, .30-06 or 9.3x74R. O/U barrels 24-in. Stock: straight grip. Single trigger. Weight: 6.8 lbs. Cased. Made in Belgium. Discontinued 1986.

Grade I . . . . NiB $7600 Ex $6600 Gd $5600

HIGH-POWER BOLT-ACTION RIFLE, MEDALLION GRADE . . . . NiB $3877 Ex $3488 Gd $1967
Same as Safari Grade except receiver and bbl. scroll engraved, ram's head engraved on floorplate; select walnut stock w/rosewood forearm tip, grip cap. Made from 1961 to 1974.

HIGH-POWER BOLT-ACTION RIFLE, OLYMPIAN GRADE . . . . . NiB $3831 Ex $3435 Gd $1925
Same as Safari Grade except bbl. engraved; receiver, trigger guard and floorplate satin chrome-plated and engraved w/game scenes appropriate to caliber; finest figured walnut stock w/ rosewood forearm tip and grip cap, latter w/18K-gold medallion. Made from 1961 to 1974.

HIGH-POWER BOLT-ACTION RIFLE SAFARI GRADE, MEDIUM ACTION. . NiB $1443 Ex $988 Gd $733
Same as Standard except medium action. Calibers: .22-250, .243 Win., .264 Win. Mag., .284 Win. Mag., .308 Win. Bbl.: 22-inch lightweight bbl.; .22-250 and .243 also available w/24-inch heavy bbl. Weight: 6 lbs., 12 oz. w/lightweight bbl.; 7 lbs. 13 oz. w/heavy bbl. Made 1963 to 1974 by Sako.

HIGH-POWER BOLT-ACTION RIFLE, SAFARI GRADE, SHORT ACTION . . . . NiB $1722 Ex $933 Gd $747
Same as Standard except short action. Calibers: .222 Rem., .222 Rem. Mag. 22-inch lightweight or 24-inch heavy bbl. No sights. Weight: 6 lbs., 2 oz. w/lightweight bbl.; 7.5 lbs. w/heavy bbl. Made from 1963 to 1974 by Sako.

HIGH-POWER BOLT-ACTION RIFLE, SAFARI GRADE, STANDARD ACTION . . . . . . NiB $1523 Ex $1133 Gd $944
Mauser-type action. Calibers: .270 Win., .30-06, 7mm Rem. Mag., .300 H&H Mag., .300 Win. Mag., .308 Norma Mag. .338 Win. Mag., .375 H&H Mag., .458 Win. Mag. Cartridge capacity: 6 rounds in .270, .30-06; 4 in Magnum calibers. Bbl. length: 22 in., in .270, .30-06; 24 in., in Magnum calibers. Weight: 7 lbs., 2 oz., in .270, .30-06; 8.25 lbs. in Mag. calibers. Folding leaf rear sight, hooded ramp front. Checkered stock w/ pistol grip, Monte Carlo cheekpiece, QD swivels; recoil pad on Magnum models. Made from 1959 to 1974 by FN.

T-BOLT T-1 .22 REPEATING RIFLE
Straight-pull bolt action. Caliber: .22 LR. Five round clip magazine. 24-inch bbl. Peep rear sight w/ramped blade front. Plain

Browning High-Power
Safari Grade Short Action, Heavy Barrel

Browning High-Power
Safari Grade Standard Action

BSA
Model 12/15 Martini

BSA
Model 15 Martini

walnut stock w/pistol grip and laquered finish. Weight: 6 lbs. Also left-hand model. Made from 1965 to 1974 by FN.
Right-hand model . . . . NiB $650 Ex $469 Gd $300
Left-hand model . . . . NiB $675 Ex $512 Gd $409

T-BOLT T-2
Same as T-1 Model except w/checkered fancy figured walnut stock. Made from 1966-74 by FN. (Reintroduced briefly during the late 1980's with oil-finished stock)
Original model . . . . NiB $909 Ex $579 Gd $289
Reintroduced model . . . . NiB $589 Ex $433 Gd $266

F.N. BROWNING FAL SEMIAUTOMATIC RIFLE
Same as F.N. FAL Semiautomatic Rifle. See F.N. listing for specifications. Sold by Browning for a brief period c. 1960.
F.N. FAL standard
  model (G-series) . . . . NiB $4977 Ex $3677 Gd $2928
F.N. FAL lightweight
  model (G-series) . . . . NiB $5310 Ex $4400 Gd $3090
F.N. FAL heavy bbl.
  model (G-series) . . . . NiB $7175 Ex $6230 Gd $4956
BAC FAL model . . . . NiB $5320 Ex $4952 Gd $4915

X-BOLT HUNTER . . . . NiB $910 Ex $800 Gd $750
Bolt-action, short and long actions. Similar calibers as A-Bolt series except w/adj. 22- or 26-in. free float bbl. Feather trigger. 3- or 4-rnd. detachable magazine. Stock: Satin walnut. Finish: low luster blue. Weight: 6.5-7 lbs. Optic ready. Made 2008 to date.
Eclipse Hunter (laminated thumbhole stock,
  matte blue finish) . . . . NiB $1020 Ex $860 Gd $770
Micro Hunter (youth stock) . . NiB $1020 Ex $860 Gd $770
RMEF Special Hunter, add $150

X-BOLT MEDALLION . . . . NiB $1040 Ex $900 Gd $850
Similar to X-Bolt Hunter except w/high gloss walnut stock and rosewod pistol cap and forend cap. Made 2008 to date.
Gold Medallion (stainless finish w/scroll
  engraving) . . . . NiB $1420 Ex $1130 Gd $950

X-BOLT COMPOSITE STALKER NiB $860 Ex $730 Gd $600
Similar to X-Bolt Hunter except w/matte black finish, composite stock w/DuraTouch. Weight: 6.2-6.7 lbs. Made 2009 to date.
Stainless Stalker (matte stainless
  finish) . . . . NiB $1020 Ex $860 Gd $770
Varmint Stalker (heavy bbl.) . . NiB $1070 Ex $930 Gd $730

BSA GUNS LTD. — Birmingham, England
Previously imported by Samco Global Arms, BSA Guns Ltd and Precision Sports.

MODEL 12 MARTINI SINGLE-SHOT
TARGET RIFLE. . . . . NiB $766 Ex $567 Gd $433
Caliber .22 LR. 29-inch bbl. Weight: 8.75 lbs. Parker-Hale Model 7 rear sight and Model 2 front sight. Straight-grip stock, checkered forearm. Note: This model was also available w/open sights or w/BSA No. 20 and 30 sights. Made before WWII.

MODEL 12/15
MARTINI HEAVY . . . . NiB $765 Ex $544 Gd $379
Same as Standard Model 12/15 except w/extra heavy bbl., weighs 11 lbs.

MODEL 12/15 MARTINI SINGLE-SHOT
TARGET RIFLE. . . . . NiB $650 Ex $479 Gd $355
Caliber: .22 LR. 29-inch bbl. Weight: 9 lbs. Parker-Hale No. PH-7A rear sight and No. FS-22 front sight. Target stock w/high comb and cheekpiece, beavertail forearm. Note: This is a post-WWII model; however, a similar rifle, the BSA-Parker Model 12/15, was produced c. 1938.

MODEL 13 MARTINI SINGLE-SHOT
TARGET RIFLE. . . . . NiB $756 Ex $579 Gd $443
Caliber: .22 LR. Lighter version of the No.12 w/same general specifications except w/25-inch bbl., weighs 6.5lbs. Made before WWII.

BSA CFT Target

BSA
Martini-International ISU Match

MODEL 13 SPORTING RIFLE

Same as No. 13 Target except fitted w/Parker-Hale "Sportarget" rear sight and bead front sight. Also available in .22 Hornet. Made before WWII.

.22 Long Rifle . . . . NiB $756 Ex $579 Gd $443
.22 Hornet . . . . NiB $976 Ex $800 Gd $579

MODEL 15 MARTINI SINGLE-SHOT

TARGET RIFLE. . . . . NiB $765 Ex $577 Gd $338
Caliber: .22 LR. 29-inch bbl. Weight: 9.5 lbs. BSA No. 30 rear sight and No. 20 front sight. Target stock w/cheekpiece and pistol-grip, long, semi-beavertail forearm. Made before WWII.

CENTURION MODEL MATCH

RIFLE. . . . . NiB $522 Ex $423 Gd $320
Same general specifications as Model 15 except w/Centurion match bbl. Made before WWII.

CF-2 BOLT-ACTION HUNTING

RIFLE . . . . NiB $543 Ex $399 Gd $265
Mauser-type action. Calibers: 7mm Rem. Mag., .300 Win. Mag. Three-round magazine. 23.6-inch bbl. Weight: 8 lbs. Sights: Adj. rear; hooded ramp front. Checkered walnut stock w/Monte Carlo comb, rollover cheekpiece, rosewood forend tip, recoil pad, sling swivels. Made 1975 to 1987.

CF-2 STUTZEN RIFLE . . . . NiB $577 Ex $437 Gd $333

Calibers: .222 Rem., .22-250, .243 Win., .270 Win., .308 Win. .30-06. Four round capacity (5 in 222 Rem.). 20.6-inch bbl. 41.5 inches (approx.) overall length. Weight: 7.5 to 8 lbs. Williams front and rear sights. Hand-finished European walnut stock. Monte Carlo cheekpiece and Wundhammer palm swell. Double-set triggers. Importation disc. 1987.

CFT TARGET RIFLE . . . . NiB $926 Ex $735 Gd $533

Single-shot bolt action. Caliber: 7.62mm. 26.5-inch bbl. About 47.5 inches overall. Weight: 11 lbs., incl. accessories. Bbl. and action weight: 6 lbs., 12 oz. Importation disc. 1987.

MAJESTIC DELUXE FEATHERWEIGHT
BOLT-ACTION HUNTING RIFLE

Mauser-type action. Calibers: .243 Win., .270 Win., .308 Win., .30-06, .458 Win. Mag. Four round magazine. 22-inch bbl. w/ BESA recoil reducer. Weight: 6.25 lbs.; 8.75 lbs. in 458. Folding leaf rear sight, hooded ramp front. Checkered European-style walnut stock w/cheekpiece, pistol-grip, Schnabel forend, swivels, recoil pad. Made from 1959 to 1965.

.458 Win. Mag. caliber . . . . . . NiB $650 Ex $508 Gd $380
Other calibers. . . . . NiB $506 Ex $433 Gd $298

BSA MAJESTIC DELUXE STANDARD

WEIGHT . . . . NiB $508 Ex $332 Gd $255
Same as Featherweight model except heavier bbl. w/o recoil reducer. Calibers: .22 Hornet, .222 Rem., .243 Win., 7x57mm, .308 Win., .30-06. Weight: 7.25 to 7.75 lbs. Disc.

MARTINI-INTERNATIONAL ISU

MATCH RIFLE . . . . NiB $944 Ex $708 Gd $577
Similar to MK III, but modified to meet International Shooting Union "Standard Rifle" specifications. 28-inch standard weight bbl. Weight: 10.75 lbs. Redesigned stock and forearm, latter attached to bbl. w/"V" section alloy strut. Intro. 1968. Disc.

MARTINI-INTERNATIONAL

MARK V MATCH RIFLE . . . . . . NiB $1077 Ex $897 Gd $623
Same as ISU model except w/heavier bbl. Weight: 12.25 lbs. Intro. 1976. Disc.

MARTINI-INTERNATIONAL MATCH RIFLE SINGLE-SHOT

HEAVY PATTERN . . . . NiB $866 Ex $630 Gd $443
Caliber: .22 LR. 29-inch heavy bbl. Weight: 14 lbs. Parker-Hale "International" front and rear sights. Target stock w/full cheekpiece and pistol-grip, broad beavertail forearm, handstop, swivels. Right- or left-hand models. Made from 1950 to 1953.

MARTINI-INTERNATIONAL MATCH

RIFLE — LIGHT PATTERN. . . . . NiB $775 Ex $584 Gd $455
Same general specifications as Heavy Pattern except w/26-inch lighter weight bbl. Weight: 11 lbs. Disc.

MARTINI-INTERNATIONAL MK II

MATCH RIFLE . . . . NiB $1043 Ex $720 Gd $630
Same general specifications as original model. Heavy and Light Pattern. Improved trigger mechanism and ejection system. Redesigned stock and forearm. Made from 1953 to 1959.

MARTINI-INTERNATIONAL MK III

MATCH RIFLE . . . . NiB $1044 Ex $812 Gd $613
Same general specifications as MK II Heavy Pattern. Longer action frame w/I-section alloy strut to which forearm is attached; bbl. is fully floating. Redesigned stock and forearm. Made 1959 to 1967.

MONARCH DELUXE BOLT-ACTION

HUNTING RIFLE . . . . NiB $714 Ex $349 Gd $260
Same as Majestic Deluxe Standard Weight model except w/redesigned stock of U.S. style w/contrasting hardwood forend tip and grip cap. Calibers: .222 Rem., .243 Win., .270 Win., 7mm Rem. Mag., .308 Win., .30-06. 22-inch bbl. Weight: 7 to 7.25 lbs. Made 1965 to 1974.

BSA
Martini-International Mark V Match

BSA
Martini-International MK III Match

BSA
Monarch Deluxe Varmint

MONARCH DELUXE VARMINT
RIFLE . . . . NiB $710 Ex $420 Gd $290
Same as Monarch Deluxe except w/24-inch heavy bbl. and weighs 9 lbs. Calibers: .222 Rem., .243 Win.

BUSHMASTER FIREARMS — Ilion, NY
Quality Parts Company. Currently Ilion, NY, formerly Windham, Maine. Purchased by Freedom Group Inc. 2011.

M17S BULLPUP . . . . NiB $735 Ex $600 Gd $466
Caliber: .223. 21.5-inch bbl. Weight: 8.2 lbs. Polymer stocks. Handle w/fixed open sights w/Weaver-type rail for any optics. Semi-auto, self-compensating short stroke gas piston. Forward trigger/grip w/rear chamber. Bullpup style. Alloy receiver. Synthetic lower receiver is hinged to upper w/hinged takedown system. Accepts M-16 type magazines. Made from 1992 to 2005.

MODEL XM15 E2S SERIES
Caliber: .223. 16-, 20-, 24- or 26-inch bbl. Weight: 7 to 8.6 lbs. Polymer stocks. Adjustable sights w/dual flip-up aperture; optional flattop rail accepts scope. Direct gas-operated w/rotating bolt. Forged alloy receiver. All steel-coated w/manganese phosphate. Accepts M-16 type magazines. Made from 1989 to date.
XM15 E2S Carbine . . . . NiB $1210 Ex $989 Gd $750
XM15 E2S Target Rifle . . . . . NiB $1244 Ex $1018 Gd $707

CABELA'S, INC. — Sidney, Nebraska
Cabela's is a sporting goods dealer and catalog company headquartered in Sidney, Nebraska. Cabela's imports black powder cartridge Sharps replicas, revolvers and other reproductions and replicas manufactured in Italy by A. Uberti, Pedersoli, Pietta and others.

1858 HENRY REPLICA . . . . NiB $707 Ex $599 Gd $524
Lever-action. Modeled after the original Henry rifle. Caliber: .44-40. Thirteen-round magazine; Bbl: 24 inches. Overall length: 43 inches. Weight: 9 pounds. European walnut stock. Sights: Bead front, open adjustable rear. Brass receiver and buttplate. Introduced 1994.

1866 WINCHESTER REPLICA . . NiB $599 Ex $425 Gd $347
Lever-action modeled after the original Model 1866 rifle. Caliber: .44-40. Thirteen-round magazine. Bbl: 24 inches, octagonal; overall length: 43 inches. Weight: 9 pounds. European walnut stock, brass receiver, butt plate and forend cap. Sights: Bead front, open adjustable rear.

1873 WINCHESTER REPLICA . . NiB $525 Ex $455 Gd $390
Lever-action modeled after the original Model 1873 rifle. Caliber: .44-40, .45 Colt. Thirteen-round magazine. Bbl: 30 inches. Overall length: 43 inches. Weight: 8 pounds. European walnut stock. Sights: Bead front, open adjustable rear or globe front and tang rear. Color case-hardened steel receiver. Introduced 1994.
w/tang rear sight, globe front, add $175

1873 SPORTING MODEL
REPLICA . . . . NiB $655 Ex $577 Gd $500
Same as 1873 Winchester except with 30-inch bbl.
w/half-round, half-octagonal bbl., half magazine, add . . $126

CATTLEMAN CARBINE . . . . NiB $355 Ex $290 Gd $227
Revolver with shoulder stock. Caliber: .44-40; six-round cylinder. Bbl: 18 inches. Overall length: 34 inches. Weight: 4 pounds. European walnut stock. Sights: Blade front, notch rear. Color case-hardened frame, remainder blued. Introduced 1994.

SHARPS SPORTING RIFLE . . . . NiB $879 Ex $779 Gd $576
Single-shot. Caliber: .45-70. Bbl: Tapered octagon, 32 inches. Overall length: 47 inches. Weight: 9 pounds. Checkered walnut stock. Sights: Blade front, open adjustable rear. Color case-hardened receiver and hammer; remainder blued. Introduced 1995.

CALICO LIGHT WEAPONS SYSTEMS — Cornelius, OR
Formerly Bakersville, California.

LIBERTY 50/100 SEMIAUTOMATIC RIFLE
Retarded blowback action. Caliber: 9mm. 50- or 100-round helical-feed magazine. 16.1-inch bbl. 34.5 inches overall. Weight: 7 lbs. Adjustable post front sight and aperture rear. Ambidextrous rotating safety. Glass-filled polymer or thumbhole-style wood stock. Made 1995 to 2001; reintro. 2007.

Model Liberty 50 . . . . NiB $800 Ex $668 Gd $410
Model Liberty 100 . . . . NiB $909 Ex $869 Gd $495

MODEL M-100 SEMIAUTOMATIC SERIES
Similar to the Liberty 100 Model except chambered for .22 LR. Weight: 5 lbs. 34.5 inches overall. Folding or glass-filled polymer stock and forearm. Made from 1986 to 1994; reintro. 2007.
Model M-100 w/folding
  stock (disc. 1994) . . . . NiB $600 Ex $355 Gd $300
Model M-100 FS w/fixed
  stock disc. 1996 . . . . NiB $400 Ex $379 Gd $320

MODEL M-105 SEMI-AUTOMATIC
SPORTER. . . . . NiB $688 Ex $492 Gd $333
Similar to the Liberty 100 Model except fitted w/walnut butt-stock and forearm. Made from 1989 to 1994.

MODEL M-900 SEMIAUTOMATIC CARBINE
Caliber: 9mm Parabellum. 50- or 100-round magazine. 16.1-inch bbl. 28.5 inches overall. Weight: 3.7 lbs. Post front sight adj. for windage and elevation, fixed notch rear. Collapsible steel buttstock and glass-filled polymer grip. Matte black finish. Made from 1989 to 1990, 1992 to 1993 and 2007.
Model M-100 w/folding
  stock (disc. 1994) . . . . NiB $808 Ex $497 Gd $338
Model M-100 FS w/fixed
  stock (intro. 1996) . . . . NiB $677 Ex $533 Gd $390

MODEL M-951 TACTICAL CARBINE
Similar to Model 900 except w/long compensator and adj. forward grip. Made from 1990 to 1994.
Model 951 . . . . NiB $725 Ex $533 Gd $445
Model 951-S . . . . NiB $725 Ex $533 Gd $445

CANADIAN MILITARY RIFLES — Quebec, Canada

Manufactured by Ross Rifle Co.

MODEL 1907 MARK II ROSS
MILITARY RIFLE . . . . NiB $409 Ex $299 Gd $277
Straight-pull bolt action. Caliber: .303 British. Five-round box magazine. 28-inch bbl. Weight: 8.5 lbs. Sights: adj. rear; blade front. Military-type full stock. Note: The Ross was originally issued as a Canadian service rifle in 1907. There were several variations; it was the official weapon at the start of WWI, but has been obsolete for many years. For Ross sporting rifle, see listing under Ross Rifle company.

CENTURY INTERNATIONAL ARMS, INC. — Delray Beach, Florida

Importer of military surplus and sporting firearms as well as manufacturer of firearms.

CENTURION M38/M96 BOLT-ACTION SPORTER
Sporterized Swedish M38/96 Mauser action. Caliber: 6.5x55mm. Five-round magazine. 24-inch bbl. 44 inches overall. Adj. rear sight. Blade front. Black synthetic or checkered European hardwood Monte Carlo stock. Holden Ironsighter see-through scope mount. Imported from 1987 to date.
w/hardwood stock . . . . NiB $277 Ex $190 Gd $133
w/synthetic stock . . . . NiB $280 Ex $198 Gd $144

Century International Arms GP WASR-10

Century International Arms Tantal Sporter

Century International Arms VZ 2008 Sporter

Century International Arms GP 1975

Century International Arms Degtyarev DP28

Century International Arms Sterling SA

CENTURION M98 BOLT-ACTION SPORTER
Sporterized VZ24 or 98 Mauser action. Calibers: .270 Win., 7.62x39mm, .308 Win., .30-06. Five round magazine. 22-inch bbl. 44 inches overall. Weight: 7.5 lbs. W/Millet or Weaver scope base(s), rings and no iron sights. Classic or Monte Carlo laminated hardwood, black synthetic or checkered European hardwood stock. Imported from 1992 to date.
M98 Action W/black
  synthetic stock (w/o rings) . . NiB $300 Ex $220 Gd $167
M98 Action W/hardwood Stock
  (w/o rings) . . . . NiB $290 Ex $190 Gd $126
VZ24 action w/laminated
  hardwood stock (Elite) . . . . . NiB $355 Ex $289 Gd $188
VZ24 action w/black synthetic stock NiB $338 Ex $269 Gd $175
w/Millet base and rings, add. $45

Churchill "One of One Thousand"

Churchill Regent

CENTURION P-14 SPORTER
Sporterized P-14 action. Caliber: 7mm Rem. Mag., .300 Win. Mag. Five-round magazine. 24-inch bbl. 43.4 inches overall. Weight: 8.25 lbs. Weaver-type scope base. Walnut stained hardwood or fiberglass stock. Imported from 1987 to date.
w/hardwood stock . . . . NiB $269 Ex $211 Gd $157
w/fiberglass stock . . . . NiB $299 Ex $223 Gd $167

CETME SPORTER . . . . NiB $754 Ex $577 Gd $387
Cal.: .308 Win. Bbl.: 19.5 inches. 20-round mag. Blue or Mossy Oak Break-Up camo finish, wood or synthetic stock w/ pistol grip. Vented forearm. Weight: 9.7 lbs.

DEGTYAREV DP28 . . . . NiB $4125 Ex $3155 Gd $2390
Semi-auto, top-mounted magazine. Cal.: 7.62x54R. Gas operated. Full stock. 47- to 50-round mag. Weight: 10 lbs. Disc.
DPM 28 (pistol grip) . . . . . . NiB $3970 Ex $3289 Gd $2410
DPX Tank Model . . . . NiB $3970 Ex $3289 Gd $2410

ENFIELD SPORTER 4 BOLT-ACTION RIFLE
Sporterized Lee-Enfield action. Caliber: .303 British. 10-rnd. magazine. 25.25-inch bbl. 44.5 inches overall. Blade front sight, adj. aperture rear. Sporterized beechwood military stock or checkered walnut Monte Carlo stock. Blued finish. Imported from 1987. Disc.
w/sporterized military stock . . . . NiB $169 Ex $128 Gd $90
w/checkered walnut stock . . . . NiB $223 Ex $190 Gd $135

GAMESTALKER . . . . NiB $1399 Ex $1088 Gd $946
Cal.: .243 WSSM, .25 WSSM, .300 WSSM. Bbl.: 22 inches, stainless steel, flattop upper, free-floating aluminum hand guard. ACE skeleton stock with ERGO Sure Grip. 100% camo. Weight: 7 lbs.

G-3 SPORTER . . . . NiB $866 Ex $633 Gd $425
Semi-auto. Cal.: .308 Win. Made from G3 parts, American-made receiver with integrated scope rail. Bbl.: 19 inches. 20-round mag. Pistol grip stock, matte black finish. Weight: 9.3 pounds. Imported 1999 to 2006.

GP 1975 . . . . NiB $650 Ex $440 Gd $300
Cal.: 7.62x39mm. Bbl.: 16.25 inches. Black synthetic furniture, U.S.-made receiver and bbl. Weight: 7.4 lbs.

GP WASR-10 . . . . NiB $555 Ex $370 Gd $244
AK-47 type by Romarm. Cal.: 7.62x39mm. Bbl.: 16.25 inches. Wood stock and forearm, 5- and 10-round mag. Weight: 7.5 lbs.
High-Cap series . . . . NiB $529 Ex $345 Gd $221

GOLANI SPORTER . . . . NiB $835 Ex $650 Gd $456
Made in Israel. Cal.: .223 Rem. Bbl.: 21 inches. Folding stock, opt. bayonet lug., 35-round mag. Weight: 8 lbs. Disc.

L1A1 FAL SPORTER . . . . NiB $944 Ex $749 Gd $588
Sporterized L1A1 FAL semiautomatic. Caliber: .308 Win. 20.75-inch bbl. 41 inches overall. Weight: 9.75 lbs. Protected front post sight, adj. aperture rear. Matte blued finish. Black or camo Bell & Carlson thumbhole sporter stock w/rubber buttpad. Imported from 1988-98.

L1A1/R1A1 SPORTER . . . . . . NiB $1044 Ex $835 Gd $229
Modeled after British L1A1. Cal.: .308 Win. Bbl.: 22.5 inches. Carrying handle, synthetic furn. 20-round mag. Folding rear sight. Weight: 9.5 lbs.

M-14 SPORTER . . . . NiB $460 Ex $338 Gd $255
Sporterized M-14 gas operated semiautomatic action. Caliber: .308 Win. 10-round magazine. 22-inch bbl. 41 inches overall. Weight: 8.25 lbs. Blade front sight, adj. aperture rear sight. Parkerized finish. Walnut stock w/rubber recoil pad. Forged receiver. Imported from 1991 Disc.

M-76 SNIPER . . . . NiB $1956 Ex $1538 Gd $967
Semi-auto version of Yugoslav M76. Cal.: 8mm Mauser. Bbl.: 21.5 inches. U.S.-made receiver. Includes scope, mount and 10-round mag. Weight: 11.3 lbs. Disc.

MODEL B-82 . . . . NiB $835 Ex $600 Gd $380
Limited production Italian police model; serial no. with "D" suffix. Cal.: .30 Luger, .32 ACP, 9 mm Ultra.

PAR 1 . . . . NiB $439 Ex $300 Gd $218
AK-47 receiver, made by PAR. Cal.: 7.62x39mm; 10-round mag. Bbl.: 20.9 inches. Weight: 7.6 lbs. Imported 2002 to 2009.
PAR 3 (.223 Rem.) . . . . NiB $439 Ex $300 Gd $218

S.A.R. 1 . . . . NiB $835 Ex $600 Gd $380
AK-47-type by Romarm. Cal.: 7.62x39mm. Bbl.: 16 inches. Wood stock and forearm. Includes one 10 and one 30-round double-stack magazine. Disc. 2003.
S.A.R. 2 (5.45x39mm) . . . . NiB $835 Ex $600 Gd $380
S.A.R. 3 (.223 Rem.) . . . . NiB $835 Ex $600 Gd $380

STERLING SA . . . . NiB $745 Ex $560 Gd $380
Semi-auto version of Sterling sub-machine gun. Cal.: 9mm Para., 34-round mag. Bbl.: 16 inches. U.S.-made receiver and bbl., crinkle finish; folding stock. Disc.

TANTAL SPORTER . . . . NiB $735 Ex $555 Gd $455
Cal.: 5.45x39mm. Bbl.: 18 inches, flash hider. Folding wire stock. Parkerized finish. Includes extra mag. Weight: 8 lbs.

TIGER DRAGUNOV . . . . NiB $1023 Ex $790 Gd $545
Russian SVD semiautomatic sniper rifle. Caliber: 7.62x54R. Five-round magazine. 21-inch bbl. 43 inches overall. Weight: 8.5 lbs. Blade front sight, open rear adj. for elevation. Blued

finish. European laminated hardwood thumbhole stock. 4x range-finding scope w/lighted reticle and sunshade. Quick detachable scope mount. Imported from 1994 to 1995.

VZ 2008 SPORTER . . . . **NiB $865 Ex $645 Gd $465**
Copy of the Czech V258. Cal.: 7.62x39mm. Bbl.: 16.25 inches; steel receiver w/matte finish; wood or plastic stock. Weight: 7 lbs. Disc.

CHARTER ARMS CORPORATION — Shelton, CT

AR-7 EXPLORER SURVIVAL RIFLE . . . **NiB $139 Ex $120 Gd $99**
Same as Armalite AR-7, except w/black, instead of brown, "wood grain" plastic stock. See listing of that rifle for specifications. Made from 1973 to 1990.

CHIPMUNK RIFLES — Milltown, PA

Formerly Prospect, Oregon. Manufactured by Rogue Rifle Company, formerly Oregon Arms Company and Chipmunk Manufacturing, Inc.

BOLT-ACTION SINGLE-SHOT RIFLE
Calibers: .22 LR. or .22 WMR. 16.13-inch standard or 18.13-inch bull bbl. Weight: 2.5 lbs. (standard) or 4 lbs. (Bull bbl.) Peep sight rear; ramp front. Plain or checkered American walnut, laminated or black hardwood stock. Made from 1982 to 2007.
Standard model w/plain walnut
   stock. . . . . .NiB $235 Ex $156 Gd $103
Standard model
   w/black hardwood stock. . . . . NiB $195 Ex $155 Gd $99
Standard model
   w/camouflage stock . . . . NiB $227 Ex $170 Gd $130
Standard model
   w/laminated stock . . . . NiB $200 Ex $160 Gd $126
Deluxe grade
   w/checkered walnut stock . . NiB $289 Ex $227 Gd $144
.22 WMR, add $40

E.J. CHURCHILL — England

Manufactured in High Wycombe, England, imported by Elliot Brothers, Chapin, SC.

HIGHLANDER BOLT-ACTION RIFLE . . **NiB $439 Ex $367 Gd $298**
Calibers: .243 Win., .25-06 Rem., .270 Win., .308 Win., .30-06, 7mm Rem. Mag., .300 Win. Mag. Four round magazine (standard); 3-round (magnum). Bbl. length: 22-inch (standard); 24-inch (magnum). 42.5 to 44.5 inches overall. Weight: 7.5 lbs. Adj. rear sight, blade front. Checkered European walnut pistol-grip stock. Imported from 1986 to 1991.

"ONE OF ONE
THOUSAND" . . . . **NiB $4220 Ex $2535 Gd $1966**
Made for Interarms to commemorate that firm's 20th anniversary. Mauser-type action. Calibers: .270, 7mm Rem. Mag., .308, .30-06, .300 Win. Mag., .375 H&H Mag., .458 Win. Mag. Five round magazine (3-round in Magnum calibers). 24-inch bbl. Weight: 8 lbs. Classic-style French walnut stock w/cheekpiece, black forend tip, checkered pistol grip and forearm, swivel-mounted recoil pad w/cartridge trap, pistol-grip cap w/trap for extra front sight, barrel-mounted sling swivel. Limited issue of 1,000 rifles made in 1973. See illustration next page.

REGENT BOLT-ACTION RIFLE . . . **NiB $577 Ex $423 Gd $290**
Calibers: .243 Win., .25-06 Rem., .270 Win., .308 Win., .30-06, 7mm Rem. Mag., .300 Win. Mag. Four round magazine. 22-inch round bbl. 42.5 inches overall. Weight: 7.5 lbs. Ramp front sight w/gold bead; adj. rear. Hand-checkered Monte Carlo-style stock of select European walnut; recoil pad. Made from 1986 to 1988.

CIMARRON ARMS — Fredericksburg, Texas

Importer of reproductions and replicas manufactured in Italy by A. Uberti, Pedersoli, Pietta and others.

1860 HENRY LEVER-ACTION REPLICA
Replica of 1860 Henry w/original Henry loading system. Calibers: .44-40, .44 Special, .45 Colt. 13-round magazine. 22-inch bbl. (carbine) or 24.25-inch bbl. (rifle). 43 inches overall (rifle). Weight: 9.5 lbs. (rifle). Bead front sight, open adj. rear. Brass receiver and buttplate. Smooth European walnut buttstock. Imported from 1991.
Carbine model . . . . NiB $1460 Ex $1096 Gd $735
Rifle model . . . . NiB $1390 Ex $1087 Gd $675
Civil War model (U.S. issue
   martially marked) . . . . NiB $1466 Ex $1100 Gd $709
w/ standard engraving add $2550
w/standard engraving, deluxe wood, add $3150
w/Lincoln hand engraving (disc. 2009), add $4500
w/Lincoln hand engraving,
   deluxe wood (disc. 2009), add $5000

1866 YELLOWBOY LEVER-ACTION
Replica of 1866 Winchester. Calibers: .22 LR, 22WMR, .38 Special, .44-40, .45 Colt. 16-inch round bbl. (Trapper), 19-inch round bbl. (Carbine) or 24.25-inch ocatgonal bbl. (rifle). 43 inches overall (rifle). Weight: 9 lbs. (rifle). Bead front sight, open adj. rear. Brass receiver, buttplate and forend cap. Smooth European walnut stock. Imported 1991 to date.
Carbine . . . . NiB $1075 Ex $787 Gd $581
Rifle . . . . NiB $1050 Ex $612 Gd $406
Indian model (disc.) . . . . NiB $895 Ex $585 Gd $379
Trapper Model (.44-40 WCF only, disc.) NiB $995 Ex $756 Gd $502
w/A-engraving, add. $2025
w/B-engraving, add. $2500
w/C-engraving, add. $3000

1873 LEVER-ACTION
Replica of 1873 Winchester. Calibers: .22 LR. .22WMR, .357 Magnum, .44-40 or .45 Colt. 16-inch round bbl. (Trapper), 19-inch round bbl. (SRC), 20-inch octagonal bbl. (short rifle), 24.25-inch octagonal bbl. (sporting rifle) and 30-inch octagonal bbl. (express rifle). 43 inches overall (sporting rifle). Weight: 8 lbs. Fixed blade front sight, adj. semi-buckhorn rear or tang peep sight. Walnut stock and forend. Color case-hardened receiver. Imported from 1989 to date.
Express Rifle . . . . NiB $1235 Ex $960 Gd $677
Short Rifle (disc.) . . . . NiB $1235 Ex $960 Gd $677
Sporting Rifle . . . . NiB $1235 Ex $960 Gd $677
SRC Carbine . . . . NiB $1235 Ex $960 Gd $677
Trapper (disc.). . . . . NiB $1268 Ex $980 Gd $697
One of 1000 engraved model NiB $2409 Ex $2033 Gd $1354

1874 FALLING BLOCK SPORTING RIFLE
Replica of 1874 Sharps Sporting Rifle. Calibers: .45-65, .45-70, .45-90 or .45-120. 32- or 34-inch round or octagonal bbl. Weight: 9.5 to 10 lbs. Blade or globe front sight w/adj. open rear or sporting tang peep sight. Single or double set triggers.

Cimarron 1883 Burgess Rifle

Cimarron Adobe Walls Falling Block Rifle

Cimarron Sharps Rocky Mountain II Model 74

Cimarron Civil War Henry Rifle

Cimarron 1876 Centennial Sporting Rifle

Cimarron 1892 Carbine

Checkered walnut stock and forend w/nose cap. Color case-hardened receiver. Imported from 1997 to date.

1874 Sporting Rifle - Billy Dixon
Model . . . . NiB $1754 Ex $1289 Gd $1100
1874 Sporting Rifle - Quigley
Model . . . . NiB $1556 Ex $1178 Gd $909
Sharps Sporting No. 1 Silhoette
Rifle . . . . NiB $1577 Ex $1133 Gd $926

1883 BURGESS RIFLE . . . . . NiB $1489 Ex $1077 Gd $744
Caliber: .45 Long Colt. Bbl.: 20 or 25 ½ inches. Reproduction. Importation began in 2010.

LIGHTNING RIFLE . . . . . . NiB $1488 Ex $1088 Gd $755
Reproduction of Colt Lightning Rifle. Cal.: .357 Mag., .44-40 WCF or .45 Long Colt. Bbl.: round; 20 or 24 inches; octagon: 20, 24, or 26 inches. Blue or case-colored frame.
W/octagon bbl., add. $150
Color case-hardened frame, add. $300

MODEL 1871 ROLLING BLOCK
BABY CARBINE . . . . NiB $379 Ex $290 Gd $195
Remington repro. Caliber: .22 LR, .22 Hornet, .22 Mag. Or .357 Mag. Bbl: 22 inches. Walnut stock and forearm. Brass trigger guard and buttplate. Disc. 1990.
Deluxe model . . . . NiB $785 Ex $580 Gd $338

LONG RANGE CREEDMOOR . . NiB $1279 Ex $899 Gd $655
Cal.: .45-70 Gov't. Barrel: 30-inch octagon. Deluxe checkered walnut stock.

ADOBE WALLS FALLING
BLOCK RIFLE . . . . NiB $1754 Ex $1310 Gd $976
Cal.: .45-70 Gov't. Bbl.: 30 inches, octagon. Case hardened receiver, hand checkered walnut stock, German silver nose cap. Optional Creedmoor sights.

SHARPS NO. 1 RIFLE. . . . . . . NiB $1087 Ex $755 Gd $544
Sharps reproduction. Cal.: .40-65 Win. or .45-70 Gov't. Bbl.: 32 inches, octagon; pistol grip stock. Imported 2000 to 2002.
No. 1 Silhouette . . . . NiB $1588 Ex $1011 Gd $744

MODEL 1874 SPORTING RIFLE . NiB $1377 Ex $986 Gd $650
Armi-Sport Billy Dixon model. Cal.: .38-55 WCF, .45-70 Gov't., .45-90 Win., .45-110, .50-90. Bbl.: 32 inches. Checkered deluxe walnut stock. Double set triggers.
Pedersoli model . . . . NiB $1809 Ex $1335 Gd $1088
Quigley II model . . . . NiB $1569 Ex $1104 Gd $854
Pedersoli Quigley. . . . . NiB $2188 Ex $1598 Gd $1077
Big 50 model . . . . NiB $2769 Ex $1988 Gd $1369
Sharps Pride model . . . . . . NiB $2240 Ex $1674 Gd $1290
Pride II model . . . . NiB $1544 Ex $1068 Gd $909
Professional Hunter. . . . . . . NiB $1357 Ex $1068 Gd $909
Texas Ranger . . . . NiB $1271 Ex $933 Gd $730

SHARPS ROCKY MOUNTAIN II
MODEL 74 . . . . NiB $1498 Ex $1043 Gd $677
Repro. Cal.: .45-70 Gov't. Bbl.: 30 inches, octagon. Silver receiver, checkered walnut stock. Optional 6x Malcolm rifle scope.
w/scope, add $650

MODEL 1860 SPENCER RIFLE . . . NiB $1560 Ex $1154 Gd $933
By Armi Sport. Cal.: 56-50. Bbl.: 30 inches. Plain walnut stock and forearm. Case hardened receiver, trigger guard and hammer. Three barrel bands.

MODEL 1865 SPENCER
REPEATING RIFLE. . . . . NiB $1490 Ex $1167 Gd $770
By Armi Sport. Cal.: .44-40 WCF, .45 Schofield, .45 Long Colt, .56-50. Bbl.: 20 or 30 inches (in 56-50 only, disc. 2009). Blue finish, color case hardened frame. Straight grip walnut stock.
w/30-inch bbl., add $227

CIVIL WAR HENRY RIFLE. . . NiB $1344 Ex $1269 Gd $976
By Uberti. Cal.: .44-40 WCF or .45 Long Colt. Bbl.: 24 inches. Includes military inspector's marks and cartouche; military-type sling swivels.

1866 YELLOWBOY CARBINE . . . NiB $1192 Ex $1054 Gd $593
By Uberti. Cal.: .32-20 WCF, .38 SP, .38-55 WCF, .44 SP, .44-40 WCF, .45 Long Colt. Similar to Model 1866 Sporting Rifle except w/19-inch round bbl., two barrel bands, saddle ring, smooth walnut stock, and forearm.
Trapper model. . . . . NiB $1167 Ex $866 Gd $546
Indian Carbine model. . . . . . NiB $1056 Ex $679 Gd $496
Red Cloud model . . . . NiB $1056 Ex $679 Gd $496

1873 SADDLE RING CARBINE . . . NiB $1355 Ex $1089 Gd $733
Cal.: .22 LR, .22 Mag., .32-20 WCF, .357 Mag./.38 SP, .38-40 WCF, .44 SP., .44-40 WCF, .45 Long Colt. Bbl.: 19 inches, round. Blued receiver, saddle ring.
Trapper Carbine . . . . NiB $1490 Ex $1100 Gd $977

1876 CENTENNIAL
SPORTING RIFLE. . . . . NiB $1525 Ex $1260 Gd $995
Cal.: .40-60 WCF, .45-60 WCF, .45-70 WCF,.50-95 WCF; bbl.: 22 or 28 inches, octagon. Blue finish, case hardened frame. Full-length magazine, iron sights, walnut stock, and forearm.

1876 CARBINE . . . . NiB $1788 Ex $1388 Gd $1100
By Uberti. Cal.: .45-60 WCF, .45-75. Bbl.: 22 inches, round. Full length fore end and barrel band. Canadian NWMP model has blued frame and saddle ring.

1885 HI-WALL RIFLE . . . . . . NiB $1169 Ex $977 Gd $749
Cal.: .30-40 Krag, .348 Win., .38-55 Win., .405 Win., .40-65 WCF, .45-70 Gov't., .45-90 WCF, .45-120 WCF. Bbl.: 28 or 30 inches, octagon. Case hardened finish frame. Iron sights standard or optional aperture rear and globe front offered.
Pedersoli mode . . . . NiB $2378 Ex $1956 Gd $1100

1885 LOW-WALL RIFLE. . . . . NiB $1077 Ex $800 Gd $654
Cal.: .22 LR, .22 Hornet, .22 Mag., .30-30 Win., .32-20 WCF, .357 Mag., .38-40 WCF, .44 Mag., .38-55, .44-40 WCF, .45-70 Gov't., .45 Long Colt. Bbl.: 30 inches. Hand checkered walnut stock, single- or double-set trigger.
Deluxe model, add $200
Standard custom engraving, add. $1750
Double set triggers, add $400

1892 RIFLE. . . . . NiB $1288 Ex $800 Gd $643
Cal.: .357 Mag., .44 Mag., .44-40 WCF, .45 Long Colt. Bbl.: 20 or 24 inches. Solid or take-down frame, smooth walnut stock and forearm, case colored receiver.
w/take-down frame, add $200
.44-40 WCF, .44 Mag., add. $50

1892 CARBINE . . . . NiB $1235 Ex $866 Gd $650
Cal.: .357 Mag., .44 Mag., .44-40 WCF, .45 Long Colt. Bbl.: 16 (Trapper model) or 20 inches. Solid frame, choice of big loop lever (El Dorado) or standard with 20-inch bbl. Saddle ring with 20-inch bbl. only.

CLERKE RECREATION PRODUCTS — Santa Monica, California

DELUXE HI-WALL. . . . . NiB $337 Ex $290 Gd $219
Same as standard model, except w/adj. trigger, half-octagon bbl., select wood, stock w/cheekpiece and recoil pad. Made 1972-74.

HI-WALL SINGLE-SHOT RIFLE. . . . NiB $310 Ex $234 Gd $177
Falling-block lever-action similar to Winchester 1885 High Wall S.S. Color casehardened investment-cast receiver. Calibers: .222 Rem., .22-250, .243 Rem., 6mm Rem., .25-06, .270 Win., 7mm Rem. Mag., .30-06, .45-70 Govt. 26-inch medium-weight bbl. Weight: 8 lbs. Furnished w/o sights. Checkered walnut pistol-grip stock and Schnabel forearm. Made 1972-74.

CLIFTON ARMS — Medina, Texas

SCOUT BOLT-ACTION RIFLE
Custom rifle built on the Dakota 76, Ruger 77 or Winchester 70 action. Shilen match-grade barrel cut and chambered to customer's specification. Clifton composite stock fitted and finished to customer's preference. Made from 1992 to 1997.
African Scout . . . . NiB $3175 Ex $2690 Gd $2310
Pseudo Scout . . . . NiB $3160 Ex $2211 Gd $1589
Standard Scout . . . . NiB $3122 Ex $2520 Gd $1443
Super Scout. . . . . NiB $3145 Ex $2175 Gd $1590

COLT'S MFG. CO., INC. — West Hartford, Connecticut

NOTE: *Add $200 to pre-ban models made prior to 10/13/94.*

AR-15 A2 DELTA MATCH H-BAR
RIFLE. . . . . NiB $2300 Ex $1977 Gd $1492
Similar to AR-15A2 Government Model except w/standard stock and heavy refined bbl. Furnished w/3-9x rubber armored scope and removeable cheekpiece. Made from 1986 to 1991.

AR-15 A2 GOVERNMENT MODEL
CARBINE. . . . . NiB $1945 Ex $1044 Gd $813
Caliber: .223 Rem., Five-round magazine. 16-inch bbl. w/flash suppressor. 35 inches overall. Weight: 5.8 lbs. Telescoping aluminum buttstock; sling swivels. Made from 1985 to 1991.

AR-15 A2 SPORTER II. . . . . NiB $1937 Ex $1347 Gd $1136
Same general specifications as standard AR-15 Sporter except heavier bbl., improved pistol-grip. Weight 7.5 lbs.; optional 3x or 4x scope. Made from 1985 to 1989.

AR-15 COMPACT 9MM
CARBINE. . . . . NiB $2255 Ex $1990 Gd $1176
Semiautomatic. Caliber: 9mm NATO. 20-round detachable magazine. Bbl.: 16-inch round. Weight: 6.3 lbs. Adj. rear and front sights. Adj. buttstock. Ribbed round handguard. Made from 1985 to 1986.

AR-15 SEMIAUTOMATIC SPORTER
Commercial version of U.S. M16 rifle. Gas-operated. Takedown. Caliber: .223 Rem. (5.56mm). 20-round magazine w/spacer to reduce capacity to 5 rounds. 20-inch bbl. w/flash suppressor. Sights: Rear peep w/windage adjustment in carrying handle; front adj. for windage. 3x scope and mount optional. Black molded buttstock of high-impact synthetic material, rubber buttplate. Barrel surrounded by handguard of black fiberglass w/heat-reflecting inner shield. Swivels, black web sling strap. Weight: w/o accessories, 6.3 lbs. Made from 1964 to 1994.
Standard Sporter . . . . NiB $1951 Ex $1447 Gd $1133
w/adj. stock, redesigned forearm (disc. 1988), add $227
w/3x scope and mount, add $126

AR-15 SPORTER COMPETITION
H-BAR RIFLE . . . . NiB $1997 Ex $1126 Gd $766
Similar to AR-15 Sporter Target model except w/integral Weaver-type mounting system on a flat-top receiver. 20-inch bbl. w/counter-bored muzzle and 1:9 rifling twist. Made from 1991 to date.

AR-15 SPORTER
COMPETITION H-BAR (RS) . NiB $2009 Ex $1143 Gd $931
Similar to AR-15 Sporter Competition H-BAR Model except "Range Selected" for accuracy w/3x9 rubber-clad scope w/ mount. Carrying handle w/iron sights. Made from 1992 to 1994.

AR-15 SPORTER MATCH TARGET LIGHTWEIGHT
Calibers: .223 Rem., 7.62x39mm, 9mm. Five-round magazine. 16-inch bbl. (non-threaded after 1994). 34.5-35.5 inches overall. Weight: 7.1 lbs. Redesigned stock and shorter handguard. Made from 1991 to 2002.
Standard LW Sporter (except 9mm)NiB $976 Ex $755 Gd $612
Standard LW Sporter, 9mm . . NiB $1077 Ex $776 Gd $556
.22 LR conversion (disc. 1994), add $200

AR-15 SPORTER TARGET RIFLE
Caliber: .223 Rem. Five-round magazine. 20-inch bbl. w/flash suppressor (non-threaded after 1994). 39 inches overall. Weight:

Colt AR-15 A2

Colt AR-15 A2 Delta Match H-BAR

Colt AR-15 A2 Government Model

Colt AR-15 Sporter Competition H-BAR

Colt Stagecoach

Colteer 1-.22

Colteer .22 Autoloader

GRADING: **NiB** = New in Box   **Ex** = Excellent or NRA 95%   **Gd** = Good or NRA 68%

7.5 lbs. Black composition stock, grip and handguard. Sights: post front; adj. aperture rear. Matte black finish. Made from 1993 to date.

Sporter Target Rifle . . . . NiB $1244 Ex $1087 Gd $722
.22 LR conversion (disc. 1994), add $227

LIGHTNING MAGAZINE RIFLE - LARGE FRAME
Similar to Medium Frame model except w/large frame to accommodate larger calibers: .38-56, .44-60, .45-60, .45-65, .45-85, or .50-95 Express. Standard 22-inch (carbine & baby carbine) or 28-inch round or octagonal bbl. (rifle). Note: Additional bbl. lengths optional. Weight: 8 to 10.5 lbs. Sights: Open rear; bead or blade front. Walnut stock and checkered forearm. Made 1887 to 1994. (6,496 produced)

Rifle . . . . NiB $11,765 Ex $7390 Gd $3469
Carbine . . . . NiB $10,576 Ex $7798 Gd $4479
Baby Carbine . . . . NiB $14,475 Ex $9077 Gd $5796
.50-95 Express, add. 40%

LIGHTNING MAGAZINE RIFLE - MEDIUM FRAME
Slide-action w/12-round tubular magazine Carbine & Baby Carbine) or 15-round tubular magazine (rifle). Calibers: .32-20, .38-40, .44-40. Standard 20-inch (Carbine & Baby Carbine) or 26-inch round or octagonal bbl.(rifle). Note: Additional bbl. lengths optional. Weight: 5.5 lbs. (Baby Carbine), 6.25 lbs. (carbine) or 7 to 9 lbs. (rifle). Sights: Open rear; bead or blade front. Walnut stock and checkered forearm. Blue finish w/color case-hardened hammer. Made from 1884 to 1902. (89,777 produced)

Rifle . . . . NiB $6096 Ex $3822 Gd $2274
Carbine . . . . NiB $7778 Ex $4966 Gd $2988
Baby Carbine . . . . NiB $9380 Ex $5246 Gd $4012
Military model w/bayonet
   lug & sling swivels . . . . . NiB $5250 Ex $3844 Gd $2691

LIGHTNING MAGAZINE RIFLE - SMALL FRAME
Similar to Medium Frame model except w/smaller frame and chambered for .22 caliber only. Standard 24-inch round or octagonal bbl. w/half magazine. Note: Additional bbl. lengths optional. Weight: 6 lbs. Sights: Open rear; bead or blade front. Walnut stock and checkered forearm. Made from 1884 to 1902. (89,912 produced)

Standard Rifle model . . . . . NiB $5599 Ex $4125 Gd $2889
W/Deluxe or optional features, add 25%

STAGECOACH .22
AUTOLOADER . . . . NiB $395 Ex $298 Gd $200
Same as Colteer .22 Autoloader except w/engraved receiver, saddle ring, 16.5-inch bbl. Weight: 4 lbs., 10 oz. Made from 1965 to 1975.

COLTEER 1-.22 SINGLE-SHOT
BOLT-ACTION RIFLE. . . . . NiB $403 Ex $397 Gd $159
Caliber: .22 LR. Long, Short. 20- or 22-inch bbl. Sights: Open rear; ramp front. Pistol-grip stock w/Monte Carlo comb. Weight: 5 lbs. Made from 1957 to 1967.

.22 AUTOLOADER
.22 AUTOLOADER . . . . NiB $390 Ex $288 Gd $227
Caliber: .22 LR. 15-round tubular magazine. 19.38-inch bbl. Sights: Open rear; hooded ramp front. Straight-grip stock, Western carbine-style forearm w/bbl. band. Weight: 4.75 lbs. Made 1964 to 1975.

CUSTOM BOLT-ACTION SPORTING
RIFLE. . . . . NiB $600 Ex $498 Gd $338
FN Mauser action, side safety, engraved floorplate. Calibers: .30-06, .300 H&H Mag. Five round box magazine. 24-inch bbl., rampfront sight. Fancy walnut stock. Monte Carlo comb, cheekpiece, pistol-grip, checkered, QD swivels. Weight: 7.25 lbs. Made 1957 to 1961.

DELUXE RIFLE . . . . NiB $977 Ex $798 Gd $569
FN Mauser action. Same as Custom model, except plain floor-

plate, plainer wood and checkering. Made from 1957-61. Value shown is for rifle as furnished by manufacturer w/o rear sight.

1957 SERIES RIFLES
Sako medium action. Calibers: .243, .308. Weight: 6.75 lbs. Other specifications similar to those of models w/FN actions. Made from 1957 to 1961.

Standard . . . . NiB $755 Ex $486 Gd $417
Custom . . . . NiB $944 Ex $697 Gd $488
Deluxe . . . . NiB $944 Ex $697 Gd $488

1961 MODEL CUSTOM RIFLE NiB $733 Ex $568 Gd $422
Sako action. Calibers: .222, .222 Mag., .223, .243, .264, .270, .308, .30-06, .300 H&H. 23-, 24-inch bbl. Sights: Folding leaf rear; hooded ramp front. Fancy French walnut stock w/Monte Carlo comb, rosewood forend tip and grip cap skip checkering, recoil pad, sling swivels. Weight: 6.5 - 7.5 lbs. Made from 1963 to 1965.

1961 MODEL, STANDARD RIFLE. . . NiB $744 Ex $578 Gd $432
Same as Custom model except plainer, American walnut stock. Made from 1963 to 1965.

STANDARD RIFLE. . . . . NiB $689 Ex $533 Gd $390
FN Mauser action. Same as Deluxe model except in .243, .30-06, .308, .300 Mag. and stock w/o cheekpiece, bbl. length 22 inches. Made from 1957 to 1961. Value shown is for rifle as furnished by manufacturer w/o rear sight.

COLT-SAUER DRILLINGS *See Colt shotgun listings.*

GRAND AFRICAN . . . . NiB $2656 Ex $1966 Gd $1049
Same specifications as standard model except .458 Win. Mag., weight: 9.5 lbs. Sights: Adj. leaf rear; hooded ramp front. Magnum-style stock of Bubinga. Made from 1973 to 1985.

GRAND ALASKAN . . . . NiB $2606 Ex $1989 Gd $1008
Same specifications as standard model except .375 H&H, weight: 8.5 lbs. Sights: Adj. leaf rear; hooded ramp front. Magnum-style stock of walnut.

MAGNUM. . . . . NiB $2506 Ex $1923 Gd $778
Same specifications as standard model except calibers 7mm Rem. Mag., .300 Win. Mag., .300 Weatherby. Weight: 8.5 lbs. Made from 1973 to 1985.

SHORT ACTION . . . . NiB $2390 Ex $1613 Gd $766
Same specifications as standard model except shorter action chambered for the following calibers: .22-250, .243 Win., .308 Win. and similar length cartridges. Weight: 7.5 lbs.; 8.25 lbs. (.22-250). Drilled and tapped for scope mount. No front or rear open sights. Made from 1973 to 1988.

SPORTING RIFLE, STANDARD
MODEL. . . . . NiB $2077 Ex $1405 Gd $766
Sauer 80 non-rotating bolt action. Calibers: .25-06, .270 Win., .30-06. Three-round detachable box magazine. 24-inch bbl. Weight: 7.75 lbs., 8.5 lbs. (.25-06). Furnished w/o sights. American walnut stock w/Monte Carlo cheekpiece, checkered pistol grip and forearm, rosewood forend tip and pistol-grip cap, recoil pad. Made from 1973 to 1988.

COMMANDO ARMS — Knoxville, Tennessee

Formerly Volunteer Enterprises, Inc.

MARK III SEMIAUTOMATIC CARBINE
Blow-back action, fires from closed bolt. Caliber: .45 ACP. 15- or 30-round magazine. 16.5-inch bbl. w/cooling sleeve

Coltsman 1961 Custom

Coltsman 1961 Standard

Colt-Sauer Grand African

Colt-Sauer Short Action

Cooper Arms Model 22 Pro Varmint

and muzzle brake. Weight: 8 lbs. Sights: peep rear; blade front. "Tommy Gun" style stock and forearm or grip. Made from 1969 to 1976.

w/horizontal forearm . . . . NiB $510 Ex $399 Gd $277

MARK 9
Same specifications as Mark III and Mark 45 except caliber 9mm Luger. Made from 1976 to 1981.

w/horizontal forearm . . . . NiB $545 Ex $439 Gd $333
w/vertical foregrip . . . . NiB $650 Ex $565 Gd $389

MARK 45
Same specifications as Mark III. Has redesigned trigger housing and magazines. Made from 1976 to 1988.

w/horizontal forearm . . . . NiB $499 Ex $438 Gd $293
w/vertical foregrip . . . . NiB $596 Ex $484 Gd $341

CONTINENTAL ARMS CORP. — New York, NY
Manufactured in Belgium for Continental Arms Corp., New York, New York.

DOUBLE RIFLE
Calibers: .270, .303 Sav., .30-40, .348 Win., .30-06, .375 H&H, .400 Jeffrey, .465, .470, .475 No. 2, .500, .600. Side-by-side. Anson-Deeley reinforced boxlock action w/triple bolting lever work. Two triggers. Non-automatic safety. 24- or 26-inch bbls. Sights: Express rear; bead front. Checkered cheekpiece stock and forend. Weight: From 7 lbs., depending on caliber. Imported from 1956 to 1975.

.270 to .348 Win. . . . . NiB $5077 Ex $3966 Gd $3095
.375 H&H & larger calibers, add 60%

COOPER FIREARMS OF MONTANA, INC. — Stevensville, Montana (Previously COOPER ARMS)

MODEL 21
Similar to Model 36C except in calibers .17 Rem., .17 Mach IV, .221 Fireball, .222, .223, 6x45, 6x47. 24-inch stainless or chrome-moly bbl. 43.5 inches overall. Weight: 8.75 lbs. Made from 1994 to date.

21 Benchrest . . . . NiB $1513 Ex $1207 Gd $943
21 Classic . . . . NiB $2223 Ex $1766 Gd $1007
21 Custom Classic . . . . NiB $2178 Ex $1859 Gd $1032
21 Western Classic . . . . NiB $3030 Ex $1956 Gd $1043
21 Varminter . . . . NiB $1408 Ex $976 Gd $800
21 Varmint Extreme . . . . NiB $1944 Ex $1244 Gd $976

CZ Model ZKK 600

CA Model ZKM 452 LUX Model

CZ 511

CZ Model ZKM 527

CZ 550 LUX Model

MODEL 22

Bolt-action, single-shot. Calibers: .22 BR. .22-250 Rem., .220 Swift, .243 Win., 6mm PPC, 6.5x55mm, 25-06 Rem., 7.62x39mm 26-inch bbl, 45.63 inches overall. Weight: 8 lbs., 12 oz. Single-stage trigger. AAA Claro walnut stock. Made from 1999 to date.

22 Benchrest	NiB $1533	Ex $1377	Gd $1079
22 Classic	NiB $2176	Ex $1312	Gd $755
22 Custom Classic	NiB $1370	Ex $1244	Gd $879
22 Western Classic	NiB $2244	Ex $1359	Gd $954
22 Varminter	NiB $1468	Ex $934	Gd $650
22 Pro-Varmint Extreme	NiB $2011	Ex $1143	Gd $836
22 Black Jack	NiB $1895	Ex $1154	Gd $846

MODEL 36 RF/BR 50 . . . . . . NiB $1608 Ex $1266 Gd $880
Caliber: .22 LR. Bolt-action. Single-shot. 22-inch bbl. 40.5 inches overall. Weight: 6.8 lbs. No sights. Fully-adj. match-grade trigger. Stainless barrel. McMillan benchrest stock. Three mid-bolt locking lugs. Made from 1993 to 1999.

MODEL 36 CF BOLT-ACTION RIFLE

Calibers: .17 CCM, .22 CCM, .22 Hornet. Four-round mag. 23.75 inch bbl. 42.5 inch overall. Weight: 7 lbs. Walnut or synthetic stock. Made from 1992 to 1994.

Marksman	NiB $1635	Ex $880	Gd $654
Sportsman	NiB $730	Ex $544	Gd $343
Classic Grade	NiB $1863	Ex $1154	Gd $866
Custom Grade	NiB $1744	Ex $937	Gd $665
Custom Classic Grade	NiB $1706	Ex $1266	Gd $876

MODEL 36 RF BOLT-ACTION RIFLE

Similar to Model 36CF except in caliber .22 LR. Five round magazine. Weight: 6.5-7 lbs. Made from 1992 to 1994.

BR-50 (22-inch stainless bbl.)	NiB $1755	Ex $1139	Gd $768
Custom Grade	NiB $1756	Ex $906	Gd $675
Custom Classic Grade	NiB $1670	Ex $951	Gd $688
Featherweight	NiB $1617	Ex $988	Gd $709

MODEL 36 TRP-1 SERIES

Similar to Model 36RF except in target configuration w/ ISU or silhouette-style stock. Made from 1992 to 1993.

TRP-1 (ISU single-shot)	NiB $944	Ex $778	Gd $533
TRP-1S (Silhouette)	NiB $944	Ex $778	Gd $533

MODEL 38 SINGLE SHOT

Similar to Model 36CF except in calibers .17 or .22 CCM w/3-round magazine. Weight: 8 lbs. Walnut or synthetic stock. Made 1992 to 1993.

Standard Sporter	NiB $1544	Ex $1023	Gd $688
Classic Grade	NiB $2239	Ex $1836	Gd $989
Custom Grade	NiB $3035	Ex $1997	Gd $977
Custom Classic Grade	NiB $1570	Ex $1267	Gd $855

MODEL 40 CLASSIC BOLT-ACTION RIFLE

Calibers: .17 CCM, .17 Ackley Hornet, .22 Hornet, .22K Hornet, .22 CCM, 4- or 5-round magazine. 23.75-inch bbl. Checkered oil-finished AAA Claro walnut stock. Made from 1995 to 1996.

Classic	NiB $1644	Ex $1233	Gd $886
Custom Classic	NiB $1844	Ex $1450	Gd $1139
Classic Varminter	NiB $1844	Ex $1450	Gd $1139

CUMBERLAND MOUNTAIN ARMS — Winchester, Tennessee

PLATEAU RIFLE
Falling block action w/underlever. Calibers: .40-65, and .45-70. 32-inch round bbl. 48 inches overall. Weight: 10.5 lbs. American walnut stock. Bead front sight, adj. buckhorn rear. Blued finish. Lacquer finish walnut stock w/crescent buttplate. Made from 1993 to 1999.
Standard model............ NiB $1133 Ex $829 Gd $631
Deluxe model, add $375

CZ (CESKA ZBROJOVKA), INC. — Uherský Brod, Moravia, Czech Republic
Formerly Strankonice, Czechoslovakia, currently CZ-USA Kansas City, Kansas, formerly Czechpoint, Inc. See also listings under Brno Sporting Rifles and Springfield, Inc.

ZKK 600 BOLT-ACTION RIFLE
Calibers: .270 Win., 7x57, 7x64, .30-06. Five round magazine. 23.5- inch bbl. Weight: 7.5 lbs. Adj. folding-leaf rear sight, hooded ramp front. Pistol-grip walnut stock. Imported from 1990 to 1995.
Standard model............. NiB $613 Ex $479 Gd $350
Deluxe model .... NiB $688 Ex $554 Gd $400

ZKK 601 BOLT-ACTION RIFLE
Similar to Model ZKK 600 except w/short action in calibers .223 Rem., .243 Win., .308 Win. 43 inches overall. Weight: 6 lbs., 13 oz. Checkered walnut pistol-grip stock w/Monte Carlo cheekpiece. Imported from 1990 to 1995.
Standard model............. NiB $570 Ex $495 Gd $443
Deluxe model .... NiB $641 Ex $567 Gd $423

ZKK 602 BOLT-ACTION RIFLE
Similar to Model ZKK 600 except w/Magnum action in calibers .300 Win. Mag., 8x68S, .375 H&H, .458 Win. Mag. 25-inch bbl. 45.5 inches overall. Weight: 9.25 lbs. Imported from 1990 to 1997.
Standard model............. NiB $727 Ex $650 Gd $468
Deluxe model .... NiB $896 Ex $744 Gd $505

452 BOLT-ACTION REPEATING RIFLE
Calibers: .22 LR. or .22 WMR. Five, 6- or 10-round magazine. 25-inch bbl. 43.5 inches overall. Weight: 6 lbs. Adj. rear sight, hooded bead front. Oil-finished beechwood or checkered walnut stock w/Schnabel forend. Imported 1995 and 2007.
Standard model (22 LR) ...... NiB $455 Ex $338 Gd $200
Deluxe model (22 LR)....... NiB $455 Ex $338 Gd $200
Varmint model (22 LR)....... NiB $458 Ex $370 Gd $215
.22 WMR, add................................ $50

527 BOLT-ACTION RIFLE
Calibers: .22 Hornet, .222 Rem., .223 Rem., 7.62x39mm. Five round magazine. 23.5-inch bbl. 42.5 inches overall. Weight: 6.75 lbs. Adj. rear sight, hooded ramp front. Grooved receiver. Adj. double-set triggers. Oil-finished beechwood or checkered walnut stock . Imported 1995.
Standard model............. NiB $650 Ex $465 Gd $340
Classic model .... NiB $655 Ex $470 Gd $338
Carbine model
   (shorter configuration) ..... NiB $600 Ex $466 Gd $345
Deluxe model .... NiB $657 Ex $572 Gd $373

537 SPORTER BOLT-ACTION RIFLE
Calibers: .243 Win., .270 Win., 7x57mm, .308 Win., .30-06. Four or 5-round magazine. 19- or 23.5-inch bbl. 40.25 or 44.75 inches overall. Weight: 7 to 7.5 lbs. Adj. folding leaf rear sight, hooded ramp front. Shrouded bolt. Standard or Mannlicher-style checkered walnut stock. Imported 1995.
Standard model............. NiB $529 Ex $460 Gd $345
Mountain Carbine model ..... NiB $555 Ex $439 Gd $326

511 SEMI-AUTO RIFLE .... NiB $355 Ex $252 Gd $155
Mannlicher model, ... add $126
Caliber: .22 LR. 8-round magazine. 22- inch bbl., 38.6 inches overall. Weight: 5.39 lbs. Receiver top fitted for telescopic sight mounts. Walnut wood-lacquered checkering stock. Imported 1996, 1998 to 2001, 2005 to 2006.

550 BOLT-ACTION SERIES
Calibers: .243 Win., 6.5x55mm, .270 Win., 7mm Mag., 7x57, 7x64, .30-06, .300 Win Mag., .375 H&H, .416 Rem., .416 Rigby, .458 Win. Mag., 9.3x62. Four or 5-round detachable magazine. 20.5- or 23.6-inch bbl. Weight: 7.25 to 8 lbs. No sights or Express sights on magnum models. Receiver drilled and tapped for scope mount. Standard or Mannlicher-style checkered walnut stock w/buttpad. Imported 1995 to 2000.
Standard .... NiB $510 Ex $423 Gd $326
Magnum .... NiB $855 Ex $633 Gd $465
Lux .... NiB $530 Ex $456 Gd $355
Battue Lux (1998)......... NiB $500 Ex $426 Gd $325
Mannlicher .... NiB $817 Ex $579 Gd $370
Calibers .416 Rem., .416 Rigby, .458 Win. Mag., add... $100

CZECHOSLOVAKIAN MILITARY RIFLES — Brno, Czechoslovakia *Manufactured by Ceska Zbrojovka.*

MODEL 1924 (VZ24) MAUSER
MILITARY RIFLE .... NiB $331 Ex $243 Gd $176
Similar to German Kar., 98k and F.N. (Belgian Model 1924.) Caliber: 7.9mm Mauser. Five round box magazine. 23.25-inch bbl. Weight: 8.5 lbs. Sights: Adj. rear; blade front w/ guards of Belgian-type military stock, full handguard. Made from 1924 thru WWII. Many of these rifles were made for export. As produced during the German occupation, this model was known as Gewehr 24t.

MODEL 1933 (VZ33) MAUSER
MILITARY CARBINE .... NiB $380 Ex $300 Gd $227
Modification of German M/98 action w/smaller receiver ring. Caliber: 7.9mm Mauser. 19.25-inch bbl. Weight: 7.5 lbs. Sights: Adj. rear; blade front w/guards. Military-type full stock. Mfd. 1933 thru WWII. A similar model, produced during the German occupation, was designated Gew. 33/40.

DAEWOO PRECISION INDUSTRIES — Korea
Manufactured in Korea, previously imported by Kimber of America; Daewoo Precision Industries; Nationwide Sports and KBI, Inc.

DR200 SA SEMIAUTOMATIC SPORTER
Caliber: .223 Rem. (5.56mm). Six or 10-round magazine. 18.4-inch bbl. 39.25 inches overall. Weight: 9 lbs. Protected post front sight, fully-adj. aperture rear. Forged aluminum receiver w/rotating locking bolt assembly. Synthetic sporterized thumb-hole stock. Imported from 1994 to 1996.
Sporter model............. NiB $679 Ex $545 Gd $459
Varmint model .... NiB $650 Ex $579 Gd $356

RIFLES

Daisy V/L Collector's Kit

Daisy V/L Standard

DR300 SA SEMIAUTOMATIC

SPORTER. . . . . **NiB $670 Ex $602 Gd $421**
Similar to Model Daewoo DR200 except chambered for 7.62x39mm. Imported from 1994 to 1996.

DAISY — Rogers, Arkansas

Daisy V/L rifles carry the first and only commercial caseless cartridge system. These rifles are expected to appreciate considerably in future years. The cartridge, no longer made, is also a collector's item. Production was discontinued following BATF ruling the V/L model to be a firearm.

COLLECTOR'S KIT . . . . **NiB $590 Ex $427 Gd $304**
Presentation-grade rifle w/gold plate inscribed w/owner's name and gun serial number mounted on the stock. Also includes a special gun case, pair of brass gun cradles for wall-hanging, 300 rounds of 22 V/L ammunition and a certificate signed by Daisy president Cass S. Hough. Approx. 1,000 manufactured from 1968 to 1969.

PRESENTATION GRADE . . . . . . **NiB $347 Ex $296 Gd $245**
Same specifications as standard model except w/walnut stock. Approx. 4,000 manufactured from 1968 to 1969.

STANDARD RIFLE . . . . **NiB $269 Ex $224 Gd $175**
Single-shot under-lever action. Caliber: .22 V/L (caseless cartridge, propellant ignited by jet of hot air). 18-inch bbl. Weight: 5 lbs. Sights: Adj. open rear, ramp w/blade front. Wood-grained Lustran stock (foam-filled). About 19,000 manufactured 1968 to 1969.

DAKOTA ARMS, INC. — Sturgis, SD
Currently owned by Freedom Arms Inc.

MODEL 10 SINGLE-SHOT RIFLE
Chambered for most commercially-loaded calibers. 23-inch bbl. 39.5 inches overall. Weight: 5.5 lbs. Top tang safety. No sights. Checkered pistol-grip buttstock and semi-beavertail forearm, QD swivels, rubber recoil pad. Made from 1992 to date.
Standard calibers . . . . **NiB $4679 Ex $3066 Gd $1977**
Deluxe model, add **$1,375**

MODEL 22 BOLT-ACTION
SPORTER RIFLE. . . . . **NiB $2735 Ex $1217 Gd $823**
Calibers: .22 LR. .22 Hornet. Five round magazine. 22-inch bbl. Weight: 6.5 lbs. Adj. trigger. Checkered classic-style Claro or English walnut stock w/black recoil pad. Made from 2003 to 2004.

MODEL 76 AFRICAN
BOLT-ACTION RIFLE. . . . . . **NiB $7998 Ex $4056 Gd $2597**
Same general specifications as Model 76 Safari. Calibers: .404 Jeffery, .416 Rigby, .416 Dakota, .450 Dakota. 24-inch bbl. Weight: 8 lbs. Checkered select walnut stock w/two cross bolts. "R" prefix on ser. nos. Intro. 1989.

MODEL 76 ALPINE BOLT-ACTION
RIFLE. . . . . **NiB $5634 Ex $2789 Gd $2009**
Same general specifications as Model 76 Classic except short action w/blind magazine. Calibers: .22-250, .243, 6mm Rem., .250-3000, 7mm-08, .308. 21-inch bbl. Weight: 7.5 lbs. Made 1989 to 1992.

MODEL 76 CLASSIC BOLT-ACTION
RIFLE. . . . . **NiB $5629 Ex $3467 Gd $2240**
Calibers: .257 Roberts, .270 Win., .280 Rem., .30-06, 7mm Rem. Mag., .300 Win. Mag., .338 Win. Mag., .375 H&H Mag., .458 Win. Mag. 21- or 23-inch bbl. Weight: 7.5 lbs. Receiver drilled and tapped for sights. Adj. trigger. Classic-style checkered walnut stock w/steel grip cap and solid recoil pad. Right- and left-hand models. Made from 1987 to date.

MODEL 76 LONGBOW TACTICAL
BOLT-ACTION RIFLE. . . . . . **NiB $4466 Ex $3459 Gd $2390**
Calibers: .300 Dakota Mag., .330 Dakota Mag., .338 Lapua Mag. Blind magazine. Ported 28-inch bbl. 50 to 51 inches overall. Weight: 13.7 lbs. Black or oliver green fiberglass stock w/adj. cheekpiece and buttplate. Receiver drilled and tapped w/one-piece rail mount and no sights. Made from 1997 to 2009.

Dakota Model 10 Single-Shot Rifle

Dakota Arms Model 76 African Grade

Dakota Arms Model 76 Classic Grade

Dakota Arms Model 97 Hunter

MODEL 76 SAFARI BOLT-ACTION
RIFLE . . . . NiB $7533 Ex $5416 Gd $2307
Calibers: .300 Win. Mag., .338 Win. Mag., .375 H&H Mag.
.458 Win. Mag. 23-inch bbl. w/bbl. band swivel. Weight: 8.5
lbs. Ramp front sight, standing leaf rear. Checkered fancy walnut stock w/ebony forend tip and solid recoil pad. Made from
1987 to date.

MODEL 76 TRAVELER SERIES RIFLES
Threadless take-down action w/interchangeable bbl. capability
based on the Dakota 76 design. Calibers: .257 through .458
Win (Standard-Classic & Safari) and .416 Dakota, .404 Jeffery,
.416 Rigby, .338 Lapua and .450 Dakota Mag. (E/F Family-
African Grade). 23- to 24- inch bbl. Weight: 7.5 to 9.5 lbs.
Right or left-hand action. X grade (Classic) or XXX grade (Safari
or African) oil finish English Bastogne or Claro walnut stock.
Made from 1999 to date.
Classic Grade . . . . NiB $6644 Ex $5428 Gd $2380
Safari Grade . . . . NiB $8577 Ex $6502 Gd $2866
African Grade . . . . NiB $9233 Ex $7544 Gd $3209
Interchangeable bbl. assemblies
   Standard calibers, add $2500
   Safari calibers, add $2700
   African calibers, add $2970

MODEL 76 VARMINT BOLT-ACTION
RIFLE . . . . NiB $2710 Ex $1988 Gd $1165
Similar to Model 76 Classic except single-shot action w/ heavy
bbl. chambered for .17 Rem. to 6mm PPC. Weight: 13.7 lbs.
Checkered walnut or synthetic stock. Receiver drilled and tapped
for scope mounts and no sights. Made from 1994 to 1998.

MODEL 97 HUNTER BOLT-ACTION SERIES
Calibers: .22-250 Rem. to .330 Dakota Mag.(Lightweight), .25-
06 to .375 Dakota Mag. (Long Range). 22-, 24- or 26-inch bbl.
43 to 46 inches overall. Weight: 6.16 lbs. to 7.7 lbs.
Black composite fiberglass stock w/recoil pad. Fully adj. match
trigger. Made from 1997 to 2004.

Lightweight . . . . NiB $2744 Ex $1675 Gd $944
Long Range . . . . NiB $3440 Ex $2475 Gd $1755

MODEL 97 VARMINT HUNTER
BOLT-ACTION RIFLE . . . . . . NiB $3734 Ex $2566 Gd $1896
Similar to Model 97 Hunter except single-shot action w/ heavy bbl.
chambered .22-250 Rem. to .308 Win. Checkered walnut stock.
Receiver drilled and tapped for scope mounts and no sights. Made
from 1998 to 2004.

CHARLES DALY — Harrisburg,
Pennsylvania *Imported by K.B.I., Inc., Harrisburg, PA;
previously by Outdoor Sports Headquarters, Inc.*

EMPIRE GRADE BOLT-ACTION RIFLE (RF)
Similar to Superior Grade except w/checkered California wal-
nut stock w/rosewood grip cap and forearm cap. High polished
blued finish and damascened bolt. Made from 1998. Disc.
Empire Grade (.22 LR) . . . . NiB $370 Ex $324 Gd $223
Empire Grade (.22WMR) . . . . . NiB $406 Ex $322 Gd $235
Empire Grade (.22 Hornet) . . . . NiB $556 Ex $444 Gd $320

FIELD GRADE BOLT-ACTION RIFLE (RF)
Caliber: .22 LR. 16.25-, 17.5- or 22.63-inch bbl. 32 to 41
inches overall. Single-shot (True Youth) and 6- or 10-round
magazine. Plain walnut-finished hardwood or checkered polymer stock. Blue or stainless finish. Imported from 1998. Disc.
Field Grade (Standard w/22.63-inch
   bbl.) . . . . NiB $157 Ex $128 Gd $95
Field Grade (Youth w/17.5-inch bbl.) . . . NiB $170 Ex $139 Gd $99
Field Grade (True Youth
   w/16.25-inch bbl.) . . . . NiB $188 Ex $155 Gd $131
Field Grade (Polymer w/stainless
   action) . . . . NiB $158 Ex $130 Gd $100

FIELD GRADE HUNTER BOLT-ACTION RIFLE
Calibers: .22 Hornet, .223 Rem., .243 Win., .270 Win., 7mm
Rem. Mag. .308 Win., .30-06, .300 Win. Mag., .300 Rem. Ultra
Mag., .338 Win. Mag. Three, 4-, or 5-round magazine. 22- or

24-inch bbl. w/o sights. Weight: 7.2 to 7.4 lbs. Checkered walnut or black polymer stock. Receiver drilled and tapped. Blue or stainless finish. Imported from 1998. Disc.

Field Grade Hunter (walnut stock) .... **NiB $572 Ex $457 Gd $339**
Field Grade Hunter (polymer stock) ... **NiB $589 Ex $478 Gd $339**
w/Left-hand model, add **$35**

HAMMERLESS DRILLING
See listing under Charles Daly shotguns.

HORNET RIFLE .... **NiB $1299 Ex $1088 Gd $759**
Same as Herold Rifle. See listing of that rifle for specifications. Imported during the 1930s. Disc.

MAUSER 98
Calibers: .243 Win., .270 Win., 7mm Rem. Mag. .308 Win., .30-06, .300 Win. Mag., .375 H&H, or .458 Win. Mag. Three, 4-, or 5-round magazine. 23-inch bbl. 44.5 inches overall. Weight: 7.5 lbs. Checkered European walnut (Superior) or fiberglass/graphic (Field) stock w/recoil pad. Ramped front sight, adj. rear. Receiver drilled and tapped w/side saftey. Imported from 1998. Disc.

Field Grade (standard calibers)
   Disc..................... **NiB $466 Ex $423 Gd $155**
Field Grade (375 H&H
   and 458 Win. Mag.) .... **NiB $669 Ex $572 Gd $354**
Superior Grade (standard calibers)
   Disc.................... **NiB $669 Ex $572 Gd $454**
Superior Grade (magnum calibers)
   Disc.................... **NiB $903 Ex $766 Gd $641**

MINI-MAUSER 98
Similar to Mauser 98 except w/19.25-inch bbl. chambered for .22 Hornet, .22-250 Rem., .223 Rem., or 7.62x39mm. Five round magazine. Imported from 1998. Disc.

Field Grade .... **NiB $409 Ex $358 Gd $233**
Superior Grade .... **NiB $533 Ex $447 Gd $259**

SUPERIOR GRADE BOLT-ACTION RIFLE
Calibers: .22 LR. .22 WMR, .22 Hornet. 20.25- to 22.63-inch bbl. 40.5 to 41.25 inches overall. Five, 6-, or 10-round magazine. Ramped front sight, adj. rear w/grooved receiver. Checkered walnut stock. Made from 1998. Disc.

Superior Grade (.22 LR) ...... **NiB $179 Ex $150 Gd $100**
Superior Grade (.22WMR) .... **NiB $244 Ex $190 Gd $145**
Superior Grade (.22 Hornet).. **NiB $399 Ex $345 Gd $239**

SEMIAUTOMATIC RIFLE
Caliber: .22 LR. 20.75-inch bbl. 40.5 inches overall. 10-round magazine. Ramped front sight, adj. rear w/grooved receiver. Plain walnut-finished hardwood stock (Field), checkered walnut (Superior), checkered polymer stock or checkered California walnut stock w/rosewood grip cap and forearm cap (Empire). Blue or stainless finish. Imported from 1998. Disc.

Field Grade .... **NiB $145 Ex $126 Gd $85**
Field Grade (Polymer
   w/stainless action) .... **NiB $161 Ex $136 Gd $92**
Superior Grade .... **NiB $215 Ex $188 Gd $132**
Empire Grade .... **NiB $355 Ex $290 Gd $200**

BOLT ACTION RIFLE
.... **NiB $922 Ex $659 Gd $560**
Calibers: .22 Hornet. Bbl.: 24 inches. Five round box magazine, hinged floorplate. Sights: Ramp front, leaf rear. Walnut stock, checkered grip and forearm. Early version rifle, introduced 1931 by Franz Jaeger Co. Discontinued 1939. Imported by Charles Daly but same model was imported by A. F. Stoeger as Herold Rifle.

SUPERIOR
COMBINATION GUN .... **NiB $1354 Ex $1149 Gd $1013**
Calibers: 12-guage shotgun over .22 Hornet, .223 Remington, .22-250, .243 Win., .270 Win., or .30-06. Barrels: 23 1/2 inches. Shotgun choked Imp. Cyl. Weight: About 7.5 pounds. Checkered walnut, pistol grip, semi-beavertail forend. Silvered, engraved receiver. Chrome-moly steel barrels, double triggers, extractors. Gold bead front sight. Introduced 1997, imported by K.B.I.

EMPIRE COMBINATION GUN...**NiB $1743 Ex $1540 Gd $1179**
Similar to Superior Combination Gun but with fancy grade wood, European style comb and cheekpiece, slimmer forend. Introduced 1997, imported by K.B.I.

FIELD GRADE AUTO RIFLE .... **NiB $167 Ex $109 Gd $94**
Calibers: .22 LR. Semiautomatic, 10-round magazine, shell deflector. Bbl.: 20 3/4 inches. Weight: 6.5 pounds. Overall length: 40.5 inches. Stock: Hardwood, walnut-finished, Monte Carlo style. Sights: Hooded front, adjustable open rear. Grooved for scope mounting. Blued finish. Introduced 1998. Imported by K. B. I.

EMPIRE GRADE AUTO RIFLE .. **NiB $210 Ex $166 Gd $135**
Similar to Field Grade Auto Rifle but with select California walnut stock, hand checkering. Contrasting forend and grip caps. Damascened bolt, high-polish blued finish. Introduced 1998; discontinued.

TRUE YOUTH BOLT-ACTION RIFLE... **NiB $156 Ex $100 Gd $75**
Caliber: .22 LR. Single-shot., bolt-action. Bbl.: 16.25 inches. Weight: 3 pounds. Overall length: 32 inches. Walnut-finished hardwood stock. Sights: Blade front, adjustable rear. Blued finish. Introduced 1998. Imported by K. B. I.

DPMS FIREARMS — St. Cloud, MN *Previously in Becker, MN; previously called DPMS, Inc. (Defense Procurement Manufacturing Facilities); currently owned by The Freedom Group.*

PANTHER CARBINE .... **NiB $830 Ex $450 Gd $410**
Semi-automatic AR15 platform. Caliber: .223 Rem. 30-round magazine. 16-in. heavy bbl. w/A2 flash hider, A3 flat top upper, A2 pistol grip, Pardus collapsible buttstock. Weight: 7.1 lbs. Made 1993 to date.

6.8mm Carbine (2006-2011) .. **NiB $880 Ex $600 Gd $520**
6.8mm SPCII Hunter
   (2011-2012) .... **NiB $1050 Ex $730 Gd $630**
7.62x39mm Carbine (2000-2011)... **NiB $730 Ex $480 Gd $430**
A2 "The Agency" (16-in. bbl., Surefire flashlight, EOTech
   sight, 2007-2012) .... **NiB $1730 Ex $650 Gd $580**
A2 Tactical (16-in. heavy bbl., A2 handguard,
   2004-2013) .... **NiB $740 Ex $480 Gd $430**
AP4 (16-in. M4 contour bbl., fixed M4 buttstock
   2004-2012)............. **NiB $630 Ex $480 Gd $380**
DCM (20-in. heavy stainless bbl.,
   1998-2003; 2006-2012) .... **NiB $970 Ex $600 Gd $520**
Lo-Pro Classic (16-in. heavy bbl., A2 buttstock,
   flat top upper, 2002-2012) .. **NiB $650 Ex $450 Gd $400**
Pardus (16-in. heavy stainless bbl., aluminum free
   float handguard, adj. stock,
   2006-2008)............. **NiB $1350 Ex $800 Gd $680**
Race Gun (24-in. stainless bbl., Hot Rod handguard, IronStone
   stock, 2001-2008)........ **NiB $1450 Ex $950 Gd $840**
SDM-R (20-in. heavy bbl., aluminum free float handguard,
   Harris bipod, 2007-2008) .. **NiB $1180 Ex $830 Gd $730**
Tuber (16-in. heavy bbl., aluminum free float handguard,
   flat top upper, 2002-2008) .. **NiB $650 Ex $450 Gd $400**

PANTHER .22............ **NiB $780 Ex $550 Gd $480**
Similar to Panther model except chambered in .22 LR w/16-in. heavy bbl. Weight: 7.85 lbs. Made 2003 to 2008.
AP4 (16-in. M4 contour bbl.,
  2004-2008)............. **NiB $750 Ex $500 Gd $470**
DCM (20-in. fluted bbl.,
  2004-2008)............. **NiB $850 Ex $550 Gd $480**

PANTHER LR-.308........ **NiB $1200 Ex $650 Gd $580**
Similar to Panther model except chambered in .308 Win. w/24-in. free float heavy bbl. Weight: 11.25 lbs. Made 2003 to date.
LR-.308B (18-in. bbl., 2003-12)... **NiB $995 Ex $650 Gd $580**
LR-.308T (24-in. bbl., 7.62x51mm NATO,
  2004-2012)............. **NiB $995 Ex $650 Gd $580**
LR-.308 AP4 (20-in. bbl., 7.62x51mm NATO,
  2003-2012)............. **NiB $1100 Ex $730 Gd $600**
LR-.308C (20-in. bbl., 7.62x51mm NATO, A3 flat top w/
  handle 2003-2012)....... **NiB $1050 Ex $730 Gd $600**

PANTHER LR-30S......... **NiB $1050 Ex $730 Gd $600**
Similar to Panther LR-.308 model except chambered in .300 RSUM w/20-in. free float heavy bbl. Made 2004 to 2008.

PANTHER LR-243........ **NiB $1280 Ex $730 Gd $600**
Similar to Panther LR-.308 model except chambered in .243 Win. w/20-in. free float heavy bbl. Made 2006 to 2013.

PANTHER CSAT TACTICAL.. **NiB $1500 Ex $830 Gd $730**
Similar to Panther model except chambered in 5.56x45mm NATO. w/16-in. bbl., Magpul buttstock and psitol grip. Weight: 7.8 lbs. Made 2010 to 2012.

PANTHER RAPTR.......... **NiB $1400 Ex $850 Gd $730**
Similar to Panther model except chambered in 5.56x45mm NATO. w/16-in. bbl., Crimson Trace laser, Ergo Z-Rail, AP4 buttstock Weight: 8.2 lbs. Made 2010 to 2011.

PANTHER REPR......... **NiB $2590 Ex $1400 Gd $1200**
Similar to Panther LR-.308 model except w/18- or 20-in. free float fluted heavy bbl., Magpul stock, Hogue rubber pistol grip, Gem Tech flash hider. Made 2009 to date.

PRAIRIE PANTHER........ **NiB $1240 Ex $750 Gd $580**
Similar to Panther model except w/20-in. heavy fluted free floated bbl. Weight: 8.75 lbs. Made 1993 to 1999; 2010 to date.

EAGLE ARMS INC. — Geneseo, Illinois

Previously Coal Valley, Illinois. In 1995, Eagle Arms Inc., became a division of ArmaLite and reintroduced that logo. For current ArmaLite production see models under that listing.

MODEL EA-15 CARBINE
Caliber: .223 Rem. (5.56mm). 30-round magazine. 16-inch bbl. and collapsible buttstock. Weight: 5.75 lbs. (E1); 6.25 lbs. (E2 w/heavy bbl. & National Match sights). Made 1990 to 1995; reintro. 2002 to 2005.
E1 Carbine............... **NiB $976 Ex $739 Gd $510**
E2 Carbine............... **NiB $976 Ex $739 Gd $510**

MODEL EA-15 GOLDEN
EAGLE MATCH RIFLE....... **NiB $1244 Ex $977 Gd $657**
Same general specifications as EA-15 Standard, except w/E2-style National Match sights. 20-inch Douglas Heavy Match bbl. NM trigger and bolt-carrier group. Weight: 12.75 lbs. Made 1991 to 1995, reintro. 2002.

MODEL EA-15............ **NiB $1221 Ex $722 Gd $504**
Same as EA-15 Carbine except 20-inch bbl., 39 inches overall and weighs 7 lbs. Made from 1990 to 1993; reintro. 2002 to 2005.

EMF COMPANY, INC. — Santa Ana, California

MODEL AP-74 SEMI-AUTOMATIC
CARBINE.................. **NiB $397 Ex $300 Gd $221**
Calibers: .22 LR or .32 ACP, 15-round magazine. 20-inch bbl. w/flash reducer. 38 inches overall. Weight: 6.75 lbs. Protected pin front sight; protected rear peep sight. Lightweight plastic buttstock; ventilated snap-out forend. Importation disc. 1989.

MODEL AP74-W SPORTER
CARBINE.................. **NiB $419 Ex $321 Gd $213**
Sporterized version of AP-74 w/wood buttstock and forend. Importation disc. 1989.

MODEL AP74 PARATROOPER ...**NiB $433 Ex $260 Gd $242**
Same general specifications as Model AP74-W except w/folding tubular buttstock. Made in .22 LR. only. Importation disc. 1987.

MODEL 1860 HENRY RIFLE
Calibers: .44-40 and .45 LC. 24.25-inch bbl.; upper-half octagonal w/magazine tube in one-piece steel. 43.75-inches overall. Weight: 9.25 lbs. Varnished American walnut wood stock. Polished brass frame and brass buttplate. Original rifle was patented by B. Tyler Henry and produced by the New Haven Arms Company, when Oliver Winchester was president. Imported 1987 to 2008.
Deluxe model............. **NiB $968 Ex $688 Gd $347**
Engraved model........... **NiB $1123 Ex $832 Gd $560**

MODEL 1866 YELLOW BOY RIFLE...**NiB $754 Ex $558 Gd $359**
Calibers: .44-40, .45 LC and .38 Special. Lever-action. Bbl: 24 inches, 43 inches overall. Bead front sight. Offered w/blued finish, walnut stock and brass frame 2005 to 2008.

MODEL 1866 YELLOW BOY CARBINE
Same features as 1866 Yellow Boy Rifle except carbine.
Standard carbine........... **NiB $933 Ex $465 Gd $333**
Engraved carbine........... **NiB $933 Ex $465 Gd $333**

MODEL 1873 SPORTING RIFLE
Calibers: .22 LR. .22 WMR, .357 Mag., .44-40 and .45 LC. 24.25-inch octagonal bbl. 43.25 inches overall. Weight: 8.16 lbs. Color casehardened frame w/blued steel magazine tube. Walnut stock and forend.
Standard Rifle.............. **NiB $922 Ex $707 Gd $459**
Engraved Rifle............. **NiB $1007 Ex $657 Gd $482**
Boy's Rifle (Youth Model, .22 LR)... **NiB $674 Ex $558 Gd $369**

MODEL 1873 SPORTING RIFLE CARBINE
Same features as 1873 sporting rifle except w/19-inch bbl. Overall length: 38.25 inches. Weight: 7.38 lbs. Color casehardened or blued frame. Made 1988 to 1989.
Standard carbine........... **NiB $904 Ex $689 Gd $466**

ERMA-WERKE — Dachau, Germany

Previously imported by Precision Sales International; Nygord Precision Products; Mandall's Shooting Supplies.

MODEL EG72 PUMP-ACTION
REPEATER.................. **NiB $158 Ex $110 Gd $98**
Visible hammer. Caliber: .22 LR. 15-round magazine. 18.5-inch bbl. Weight: 5.25 lbs. Sights: open rear; hooded ramp

RIFLES

Erma EG712

Erma EGM1

Erma EM1 22

front. Receiver grooved for scope mounting. Straight-grip stock, grooved slide handle. Imported from 1970 to 1976.

MODEL EG73 . . . . NiB $288 Ex $223 Gd $172
Same as Model EG712 except chambered for .22 WMR w/12-round tubular magazine, 19.3-inch bbl. Imported from 1973 to 1997.

MODEL EG712 LEVER-ACTION
REPEATING CARBINE . . . . NiB $297 Ex $229 Gd $167
Styled after Winchester Model 94. Caliber: .22 LR. Long, Short. Tubul33 magazine holds 15 LR, 17 Long, 21 Short. 18.5-inch bbl. Weight: 5.5 lbs. Sights: Open rear; hooded ramp front. Receiver grooved for scope mounting. Western carbine-style stock and forearm w/bbl. band. Imported 1976 to 1997. Note: A similar carbine by Erma was marketed in U.S. as Ithaca Model 72 Saddle Gun.

MODEL EGM1 . . . . NiB $290 Ex $247 Gd $180
Same as Model EM1 except w/unslotted buttstock, ramp front sight, 5-round magazine standard. Imported from 1970 to 1995.

MODEL EM1 .22 SEMIAUTOMATIC
CARBINE . . . . NiB $387 Ex $320 Gd $222
Styled after U.S. Carbine cal. 30 M1. Caliber: .22 LR. 10- or 15-round magazine. 18-inch bbl. Weight: 5.5 lbs. Carbine-type sights. Receiver grooved for scope mounting. Military stock/handguard. Imported 1966 to 1997.

EUROPEAN AMERICAN ARMORY —
Sharpes, Florida

MODEL HW 660 BOLT-ACTION
SINGLE-SHOT RIFLE . . . . NiB $909 Ex $745 Gd $495
Caliber: .22 LR. 26.8-inch bbl., 45.7 inches overall. Weight: 10.8 lbs. Match-type aperture rear sight; Hooded ramp front. Stippled walnut stock. Imported from 1992 to 1996.

MODEL HW BOLT-ACTION SINGLE-SHOT
TARGET RIFLE . . . . NiB $895 Ex $740 Gd $485
Same general specification as Model HW 660 except equipped w/ target stock. Imported from 1995 to 1996.

MODEL SABITTI SP1822
Caliber: .22 LR. 10-round detachable magazine. 18.5 inch bbl. 37.5 inches overall. Weight: 5.25 to 7.15 lbs. No sights. Hammer-forged heavy non-tapered bbl. Scope-mounted rail. Flush-mounted magazine release. Alloy receiver w/non-glare finish. Manual bolt lock. Wide claw extractor. Blowback action. Cross-trigger safety. Imported 1994 to 1996.
Traditional Sporter model . . . . . NiB $259 Ex $206 Gd $149
Thumbhole Sporter
  model (synthetic stock) . . . . . NiB $379 Ex $312 Gd $221

FABRIQUE NATIONALE HERSTAL —
Herstal & Liege, Belgium
Formerly Fabrique Nationale d'Armes de Guerre.

MODELS 1924, 1934/30 AND 1930
MAUSER MILITARY RIFLES . . . NiB $445 Ex $337 Gd $241
Similar to German Kar. 98k w/straight bolt handle. Calibers: 7mm, 7.65mm and 7.9mm Mauser. Five round box magazine. 23.5-inch bbl. Weight: 8.5 lbs. Sights: Adj. rear; blade front. Military stock of M/98 pattern w/slight modification. Model differences are minor. Also produced in a short carbine model w/17.25-inch bbl. Note: These rifles were manufactured under contract for Abyssinia, Argentina, Belgium, Bolivia, Brazil, Chile, China, Colombia, Ecuador, Iran, Luxembourg, Mexico, Peru, Turkey, Uruguay and Yugoslavia. Such arms usually bear the coat of arms of the country for which they were made together with the contractor's name and date of manufacture. Also sold commercially and exported to all parts of the world.

MODEL 1949 SEMIAUTOMATIC
MILITARY RIFLE . . . . NiB $799 Ex $647 Gd $328
Gas-operated. Calibers: 7mm, 7.65mm, 7.92mm, .30-06. 10-round box magazine, clip fed or loaded singly. 23.2-inch bbl. Weight: 9.5 lbs. Sights: Tangent rear-shielded post front. Pistol-grip stock, handguard. Note: Adopted by Belgium in 1949; also by Belgian Congo, Brazil, Colombia, Luxembourg, Netherlands, East Indies, and Venezuela. Approx. 160,000 were made.

MODEL 1950 MAUSER
MILITARY RIFLE . . . . NiB $533 Ex $360 Gd $287

F.N. Model 1949

F.N. Model 1950 Mauser

F.N. Deluxe Mauser

Same as previous F.N. models of Kar. 98k type except chambered for .30-06.

DELUXE MAUSER BOLT-ACTION
SPORTING RIFLE . . . . **NiB $799 Ex $689 Gd $443**
American calibers: .220 Swift, .243 Win., .244 Rem.,
.250/3000, .257 Roberts, .270 Win., 7mm, .300 Sav., .308
Win. .30-06. European calibers: 7x57, 8x57JS, 8x60S, 9.3x62,
9.5x57, 10.75x68mm. Five round box magazine. 24-inch bbl.
Weight: 7.5-8.25 lbs. American model is standard w/hooded
ramp front sight and Tri-Range rear; Continental model w/two-
leaf rear. Checkered stock w/cheekpiece, pistol-grip, swivels.
Made from 1947 to 1963.

DELUXE MAUSER — PRESENTATION
GRADE . . . . **NiB $1337 Ex $1096 Gd $752**
Same as regular model except w/select grade stock; engraving
on receiver, trigger guard, floorplate and bbl. breech. Disc.
1963.

FAL/FNC/LAR SEMIAUTOMATIC
Same as standard FAL military rifle except w/o provision for
automatic firing. Gas-operated. Calibers: 7.62mm NATO (.308
Win.) or 5.56mm (.223 Rem.). 10- or 20-round box magazine.
25.5-inch bbl. (including flash hider). Weight: 9 lbs. Sights:
Post front; aperture rear. Fixed wood or folding buttstock,
pistol-grip, forearm/handguard w/carrying handle and sling
swivels. Disc. 1988.
F.N. FAL/LAR model (Light
 Automatic Rifle) . . . . **NiB $2594 Ex $2216 Gd $1402**
F.N. FAL/HB model (h. bbl.). **NiB $2955 Ex $2343 Gd $1644**
F.N. FAL/PARA (Paratrpr) . . **NiB $3566 Ex $2886 Gd $1854**
F.N. FNC Carbine
 model (.223 cal.) . . . . . . **NiB $2715 Ex $1954 Gd $1294**
F.N. FNC Carbine model w/flash
 suppresser (.223 cal.) . . . **NiB $2790 Ex $2033 Gd $1387**

SUPREME MAUSER BOLT-ACTION
SPORTING RIFLE . . . . **NiB $808 Ex $865 Gd $443**
Calibers: .243, .270, 7mm, .308, .30-06. Four round magazine
in .243 and .308; 5-round in other calibers. 22-inch bbl. in
.308; 24-inch in other calibers. Sights: Hooded ramp front,
Tri-Range peep rear. Checkered stock w/ Monte Carlo cheekpiece, pistol-grip, swivels. Weight: 7.75 lbs. Made from 1957
to 1975.

SUPREME MAGNUM MAUSER NiB $865 Ex $689 Gd $474
Calibers: .264 Mag., 7mm Mag., .300 Win. Mag. Similar as
standard caliber model except 3-round magazine capacity.

FEATHER INDUSTRIES, INC. — Boulder, Colorado

See MITCHELL ARMS for current production.

MODEL AT-9 SEMIAUTOMATIC RIFLE
Caliber: 9mm Parabellum. 10-, 25-, 32-, or 100-round magazine. 17-inch bbl. 35 inches overall (extended). Hooded post
front sight, adj. aperture rear. Weight: 5 lbs. Telescoping wire
stock w/composition pistol-grip and barrel-shroud handguard.
Matte black finish. Made from 1988 to 1995.
Model AT-9 . . . . **NiB $898 Ex $714 Gd $479**
w/32-round magazine, add. **$100**
w/100-round drum magazine, add **$300**

MODEL AT-22 . . . . **NiB $355 Ex $232 Gd $171**
Caliber: .22 LR. 20-round magazine. 17-inch bbl. 35 inches
overall (extended). Hooded post front sight; adj. aperture rear.
Weight: 3.25 lbs. Telescoping wire stock w/composition pistol-
grip and barrel shroud handguard. Matte black finish.

MODEL F2 SA CARBINE. . . . . . . **NiB $331 Ex $258 Gd $149**
Similar to AT-22, except w/fixed Polymer stock and pistol-grip.
Made from 1992 to 1995.

MODEL F9 SA CARBINE. . . . . . . **NiB $758 Ex $599 Gd $400**
Similar to AT-9, except w/fixed Polymer stock and pistol-grip.
Made from 1992 to 1995.

FINNISH LION — Jyväkylylä, Finland
Manufactured by Valmet Oy, Tourula Works.

CHAMPION FREE RIFLE. . . . . . . **NiB $688 Ex $545 Gd $390**
Bolt-action single-shot target rifle. Double-set trigger. Caliber:
.22 LR. 28.75-inch heavy bbl. Weight: 16 lbs. Sights: Extension
rear peep; aperture front. Walnut free-rifle stock w/full pistol-
grip, thumbhole, beavertail forend, hook buttplate, palm rest,
hand stop, swivel. Made from 1965 to 1972.

STANDARD ISU TARGET RIFLE . . **NiB $421 Ex $337 Gd $213**
Bolt-action, single-shot. Caliber: .22 LR. 27.5-inch bbl. Weight:
10.5 lbs. Sights: extension rear peep; aperture front. Walnut target stock w/full pistol-grip, checkered beavertail forearm, adj.
buttplate, sling swivel. Made from 1966 to 1977.

F.N. Supreme Mauser

F.N. FAL Semiautomatic

MATCH RIFLE.............**NiB $569 Ex $510 Gd $343**
Bolt-action, single-shot. Caliber: .22 LR. 28.75-inch heavy bbl.
Weight: 14.5 lbs. Sights: Extension rear peep; aperture front.
Walnut free-rifle stock w/full pistol-grip, thumbhole, beavertail
forearm, hook buttplate, palm rest, hand stop, swivel. Made
1937 to 1972.

STANDARD TARGET RIFLE
Bolt-action, single-shot. Caliber: .22 LR. 27.5-inch bbl. 44.5
inches overall. Weight: 10.5 lbs. No sights; micrometer rear
and globe front International-style sights available. Select wal-
nut stock in target configuration. Made 1966 to 1997..
Standard model.............**NiB $808 Ex $679 Gd $448**
Thumbhole stock model......**NiB $893 Ex $733 Gd $533**
Deluxe model..............**NiB $439 Ex $350 Gd $259**

LUIGI FRANCHI, S.P.A. — Brescia, Italy

CENTENNIAL AUTOMATIC RIFLE
Commemorates Franchi's 100th anniversary (1868-1968).
Centennial seal engraved on receiver. Semiautomatic. Takedown. Caliber: .22 LR. 11-round magazine in buttstock. 21-inch
bbl. Weight: 5.13 lbs. Sights: Open rear; gold bead front on
ramp. Checkered walnut stock and forend. Deluxe model w/
fully engraved receiver, premium grade wood. Made in 1968.
Standard model.............**NiB $433 Ex $321 Gd $224**
Engraved model ....**NiB $478 Ex $379 Gd $270**

FRANCOTTE — Leige, Belgium
*Imported by Armes de Chasse, Hertford, NC; previously by
Abercrombie & Fitch.*

BOLT-ACTION RIFLE
Custom rifle built on Mauser style bolt action. Available in three
action lengths. Calibers: .17 Bee to .505 Gibbs. Barrel length: 21-
to 24.5-inches. Weight: 8 to 12 lbs. Stock dimensions, wood type
and style to customer's specifications. Engraving, appointments
and finish to customer's preference. Note: Deduct 25% for models
w/o engraving.
Short action ....**NiB $9770 Ex $7725 Gd $4690**
Standard action.........**NiB $7859 Ex $6233 Gd $3834**
Magnum Francotte action ..**NiB $14,000 Ex $11,770 Gd $7690**

BOXLOCK MOUNTAIN RIFLE
Custom single-shot rifle built on Anson & Deeley style boxlock
or Holland & Holland style sidelock action. 23- to 26-inch barrels chambered to customer's specification. Stock dimensions,
wood type and style to customer's specifications. Engraving,
appointments and finish to customer's preference. Note:
Deduct 30% for models w/o engraving.
Boxlock.............**NiB $14,299 Ex $12,200 Gd $7800**
Sidelock ....**NiB $22,438 Ex $17,950 Gd $12,206**

DOUBLE RIFLE
Custom side-by-side rifle. Built on Francotte system boxlock
or back-action sidelock. 23.5- to 26-inch barrels chambered
to customer's specification. Stock dimensions, wood type and
style to customer's specifications. Engraving, appointments and
finish to customer's preference. Note: Deduct 30% for models
w/o engraving.
Boxlock...........**NiB $26,750 Ex $16,875 Gd $10,270**
Sidelock ....**NiB $31,760 Ex $26,900 Gd $16,975**

FRENCH MILITARY RIFLE — Saint Etienne, France

MODEL 1936 MAS MILITARY RIFLE ..NiB $209 Ex $170 Gd $103
Bolt-action. Caliber: 7.5mm MAS. Five-round box magazine.
22.5-inch bbl. Weight: 8.25 lbs. Sights: Adj. rear; blade front.
Two-piece military-type stock. Bayonet carried in forend tube.
Made from 1936 to 1940 by Manufacture Francaise d'Armes et
de Cycles de St. Etienne (MAS).

GALIL — Israel
*Manufactured by Israel Military Industries, Israel. Not current-
ly imported, previously imported by UZI America Inc., North
Haven, CT; previously by Action Arms, Springfield Armory
and Magnum Research, Inc.*

AR SEMIAUTOMATIC RIFLE
Calibers: .308 Win. (7.62 NATO), .223 Rem. (5.56mm). 25-round
(.308) or 35-round (.223) magazine. 16-inch (.223) or 18.5-inch
(.308) bbl. w/flash suppressor. Weight: 9.5 lbs. Folding aperture
rear sight, post front. Folding metal stock w/carrying handle.
Imported 1982 to 1994. Currently select fire models available to
law enforcement only.
Model .223 AR ....**NiB $3233 Ex $1998 Gd $1200**
Model .308 AR ....**NiB $3233 Ex $1998 Gd $1200**
Model .223 ARM.........**NiB $3227 Ex $2290 Gd $1669**
Model .308 ARM.........**NiB $3227 Ex $2290 Gd $1669**

SPORTER SEMIAUTOMATIC
RIFLE...................**NiB $1723 Ex $1009 Gd $707**
Same general specifications as AR Model except w/hardwood
thumbhole stock and 5-round magazine. Weight: 8.5 lbs.
Imported 1991 to 1994.

GARCIA CORPORATION — Teaneck, New Jersey

BRONCO 22 SINGLE-SHOT RIFLE .. NiB $151 Ex $112 Gd $88
Swing-out action. Takedown. Caliber: .22 LR, Long, Short.
16.5-inch bbl. Weight: 3 lbs. Sights: Open rear-blade front.

Finnish Lion Champion

Finnish Lion Match

Franchi Deluxe Centennial

Francotte Sidelock Double Rifle

Francotte Boxlock Mountain Rifle w/
claw mounts and scope

Galil .223 AR Semiautomatic Rifle

Carl Gustaf Model 2000

One-piece stock and receiver, crackle finish. Intro. 1967. Discontinued.

GERMAN MILITARY RIFLES — Germany

Manufactured by Ludwig Loewe & Co., Berlin, other contractors and by German arsenals and various plants under German government control.

MODEL 24T (GEW. 24T)
MAUSER RIFLE . . . . NiB $598 Ex $443 Gd $300
Same general specifications as Czech Model 24 (VZ24) Mauser Rifle w/minor modification and laminated wood stock. Weight: 9.25 lbs. Made in Czechoslovakia during German occupation; adopted 1940.

MODEL 29/40 (GEW. 29/40)
MAUSER RIFLE . . . . NiB $433 Ex $329 Gd $244
Same general specifications as Kar. 98K w/minor differences. Made in Poland during German occupation; adopted 1940.

MODEL 33/40 (GEW. 33/40)
MAUSER RIFLE . . . . NiB $1030 Ex $799 Gd $515
Same general specifications as Czech Model 33 (VZ33) Mauser Carbine w/minor modifications and laminated wood stock as found in war-time Model 98K carbines. Made in Czechoslovakia during German occupation; adopted 1940.

MODELS 41 AND 41-W (GEW. 41, GEW. 41-W)
SEMIAUTOMATIC MILITARY RIFLES
Gas-operated, muzzle cone system. Caliber: 7.9mm Mauser. Ten-round box magazine. 22.5-inch bbl. Weight: 10.25 lbs. Sights: Adj. leaf rear; blade front. Military-type stock w/semi-pistol grip, plastic handguard. Note: Model 41 lacks bolt release found on Model 41-W; otherwise, the models are the same. These early models were mfd. in Walther's Zella-Mehlis plant. Made c.1941 to 1943.
Model 41 . . . . NiB $4460 Ex $3588 Gd $2510
Model 41-W . . . . NiB $3488 Ex $2789 Gd $1809

MODEL 43 (GEW. 43, KAR. 43)
SEMIAUTO MILITARY RIFLES NiB $1399 Ex $1125 Gd $848
Gas-operated, bbl. vented as in Russian Tokarev. Caliber: 7.9mm Mauser. 10-round detachable box magazine. 22- or 24-inch bbl. Weight: 9 lbs. Sights: Adj. rear; hooded front. Military-type stock w/semi-pistol-grip, wooden handguard. Note: These rifles are alike except for minor details, have characteristic late WWII mfg. short cuts: cast receiver and bolt cover, stamped steel parts, etc. Gew. 43 may have either 22- or 24-inch bbl. The former length was standardized in late 1944, when weapon designation was changed to "Kar. 43." Made from 1943 to 1945.

MODEL 1888 (GEW. 88) MAUSER- MANNLICHER
SERVICE RIFLE . . . . NiB $433 Ex $265 Gd $221
Bolt-action w/straight bolt handle. Caliber: 7.9mm Mauser (8x57mm). Five round Mannlicher box magazine. 29-inch bbl. w/jacket. Weight: 8.5 lbs. Fixed front sight, adj. rear. Military-type full stock. Mfd. by Ludwig Loewe & Co., Haenel, Schilling and other contractors.

MODEL 1888 (KAR. 88) MAUSER- MANNLICHER
CARBINE. . . . . NiB $337 Ex $249 Gd $245
Same general specifications as Gew. 88 except w/18-inch bbl., w/o jacket, flat turned-down bolt handle, weight: 6.75 lbs. Mfd. by Ludwig Loewe & Co., Haenel, Schilling and other contractors.

MODEL 1898 (GEW. 98) MAUSER MILITARY
RIFLE. . . . . NiB $572 Ex $434 Gd $270
Bolt action with straight bolt handle. Caliber: 7.9mm Mauser (8x57mm). Five round box magazine. 29-inch stepped bbl. Weight: 9 lbs. Sights: Blade front; adj. rear. Military-type full stock w/rounded bottom pistol grip. Adopted 1898.

MODEL 1898A (KAR. 98A)
MAUSER CARBINE . . . . NiB $521 Ex $433 Gd $329
Same general specifications as Model 1898 (Gew.98) Rifle except has turned-down bolt handle, smaller receiver ring, light 23.5-inchstraight taper bbl., front sight guards, sling is attached to left side of stock, weight: 8 lbs. Note: Some of these carbines are marked "Kar. 98;" the true Kar. 98 is the earlier original M/98 carbine w/17-inch bbl. and is rarely encountered.

MODEL 1898B (KAR. 98B)
MAUSER CARBINE . . . . NiB $475 Ex $397 Gd $294
Same general specifications as Model 1898 (Gew.98) Rifle except has turned-down bolt handle and sling attached to left side of stock. This is post-WWI model.

MODEL 1898K (KAR. 98K)
MAUSER CARBINE . . . . NiB $515 Ex $423 Gd $320
Same general specifications as Model 1898 (Gew.98) Rifle except has turned-down bolt handle, 23.5-inch bbl., may have hooded front sight, sling attached to left side of stock, weighs about 8.5 lbs. Adopted in 1935, this was the standard German service rifle of WWII. Note: Late-war models had stamped sheet steel trigger guards and many of the Model 98K carbines made during WWII had laminated wood stocks These weigh .5 to .75 pound more than the previous Model 98K. Value shown is for earlier type.

MODEL VK 98 PEOPLE'S RIFLE
("VOLKSGEWEHR") . . . . NiB $290 Ex $233 Gd $166
Kar. 98K-type action. Caliber: 7.9mm. Single-shot or repeater (latter w/rough hole-in-the-stock 5-round "magazine" or fitted w/10-round clip of German Model 43 semiauto rifle). 20.9-inch bbl. Weight: 7 lbs. Fixed V-notch rear sight dovetailed into

Carl Gustaf Deluxe

Carl Gustaf Grand Prix

Carl Gustaf Sporter

front receiver ring; front blade welded to bbl. Crude, unfinished, half-length stock w/o buttplate. Last ditch weapon made in 1945 for issue to German civilians. Note: Of value only as a military arms collector's item, this hastily-made rifle should be regarded as unsafe to shoot.

GÉVARM — Saint Etienne, France
Manufactured by Gevelot.

E-1 AUTOLOADING RIFLE . . . . NiB $234 Ex $190 Gd $150
Caliber: .22 LR. 8-rnd. clip magazine. 19.5-in. bbl. Sights: Open rear; post front. Pistol-grip stock and forearm of French walnut.

GOLDEN EAGLE — Houston, Texas
Manufactured by Nikko Firearms Ltd., Tochigi, Japan.

MODEL 7000 GRADE I
AFRICAN . . . . NiB $743 Ex $578 Gd $468
Same as Grade I Big Game except: Caliber: .375 H&H Mag. and .458 Win. Mag. Two-round magazine in .458, weight: 8.75 lbs. in .375 and 10.5 lbs. in .458, furnished w/sights. Imported 1976–81.

MODEL 7000 BIG GAME SERIES
Bolt action. Calibers: .22-250, .243 Win., .25-06, .270 Win., Weatherby Mag., 7mm Rem. Mag., .30-06, .300 Weatherby Mag., .300 Win. Mag., .338 Win. Mag. Magazine capacity: 4 rounds in .22-250, 3 rounds in other calibers. 24- or 26-inch bbl. (26-inch only in 338). Weight: 7 lbs., .22-250; 8.75, lbs., other calibers. Furnished w/o sights. Fancy American walnut stock, skip checkered, contrasting wood forend tip and grip cap w/gold eagle head, recoil pad. Imported 1976 to 1981.
Grade I . . . . NiB $722 Ex $630 Gd $455
Grade II . . . . NiB $755 Ex $689 Gd $479

GREIFELT & CO. — Suhl, Germany

SPORT MODEL 22 HORNET BOLT-ACTION
RIFLE. . . . . NiB $2388 Ex $1907 Gd $1412

Caliber: .22 Hornet. Five round box magazine. 22-inch Krupp steel bbl. Weight: 6 lbs. Sights: Two-leaf rear; ramp front. Walnut stock, checkered pistol-grip and forearm. Made before WWII.

CARL GUSTAF — Eskilstuna, Sweden
Manufactured by Carl Gustaf Stads Gevärsfaktori.

MODEL 2000 BOLT-ACTION RIFLE
Calibers: .243, 6.5x55, 7x64, .270, .308 Win., .30-06, 7mm Rem. Mag., .300 Win. Mag. Three round magazine. 24-inch bbl. 44 inches overall. Weight: 7.5 lbs. Receiver drilled and tapped. Hooded ramp front sight, open rear. Adj. trigger. Checkered European walnut stock w/Monte Carlo cheekpiece and Wundhammer palmswell grip. Imported 1991 to 1995
w/o sights . . . . NiB $1443 Ex $1235 Gd $879
w/sights. . . . . NiB $1790 Ex $1390 Gd $1009
LUXE. . . . . NiB $1744 Ex $1689 Gd $1035

DELUXE . . . . NiB $707 Ex $579 Gd $522
Same specifications as Monte Carlo Standard. Calibers: 6.5x55, 308 Win., .30-06, 9.3x62. Four round magazine in 9.3x62. Jeweled bolt. Engraved floorplate and trigger guard. Deluxe French walnut stock w/rosewood forend tip. Imported 1970 to 1977.

GRAND PRIX SINGLE-SHOT
TARGET RIFLE . . . . NiB $577 Ex $459 Gd $202
Special bolt action with "world's shortest lock time." Single-stage trigger adjusts down to 18 oz. Caliber: .22 LR. 26.75-inch heavy bbl. w/adj. trim weight. Weight: 9.75 lbs. Furnished w/o sights. Target-type Monte Carlo stock of French walnut, adj. cork buttplate. Imported from 1970 to 1977.

MONTE CARLO STANDARD BOLT-ACTION
SPORTING RIFLE . . . . NiB $507 Ex $422 Gd $370
Carl Gustaf 1900 action. Calibers: 6.5x55, 7x64, .270 Win., 7mm Rem. Mag., .308 Win., .30-06, 9.3x62. Five round magazine, except 4-round in 9.3x62 and 3-round in 7mm Rem. Mag. 23.5-inch bbl. Weight: 7 lbs. Sights: Folding leaf rear; hooded ramp front. French walnut Monte Carlo stock w/ cheekpiece, checkered forearm and pistol grip, sling swivels. Also available in left-hand model. Imported from 1970 to 1977.

Hammerli Model 45

Hammerli-Tanner 300M

Harrington & Richardson
Model 60 Reising

SPECIAL . . . . NiB $575 Ex $401 Gd $376
Also designated "Grade II" in U.S. and "Model 9000" in
Canada. Same specifications as Monte Carlo Standard.
Calibers: .22-250, .243 Win., .25-06, .270 Win., 7mm Rem.
Mag., .308 Win., .30-06, .300 Win. Mag. Three round maga-
zine in magnum calibers. Select wood stock w/rosewood
forend tip. Left-hand model avail. Imported from 1970 to 1977.

SPORTER. . . . . NiB $512 Ex $355 Gd $291
Also designated "Varmint-Target" in U.S. Fast bolt action w/
large Bakelite bolt knob. Trigger pull adjusts down to 18 oz.
Calibers: .222 Rem., .22-250, .243 Win., 6.5x55. Five round
magazine except 6-round in .222 Rem. 26.75-inch heavy bbl.
Weight: 9.5 lbs. Furnished w/o sights. Target-type Monte Carlo
stock of French walnut. Imported from 1970 to 1977.

STANDARD. . . . . NiB $512 Ex $355 Gd $291
Same specifications as Monte Carlo Standard. Calibers: 6.5x55,
7x64, .270 Win., .308 Win., .30-06, 9.3x62. Classic-style stock
w/o Monte Carlo. Imported from 1970 to 1977.

TROFÉ. . . . . NiB $588 Ex $479 Gd $382
Also designated "Grade III" in U.S. and "Model 8000"
in Canada. Same specifications as Monte Carlo Standard.
Calibers: .22-250, .25-06, 6.5x55, .270 Win., 7mm Rem. Mag.,
.308 Win., .30-06, .300 Win. Mag. Three round magazine in
magnum calibers. Furnished w/o sights. Fancy wood stock w/
rosewood forend tip, high-gloss lacquer finish. Imported from
1970 to 1977.

C.G. HAENEL — Suhl, Germany

'88 MAUSER SPORTER . . . . NiB $813 Ex $508 Gd $380
Same general specifications as Haenel Mauser-Mannlicher
except w/Mauser 5-round box magazine.

**MAUSER-MANNLICHER BOLT-ACTION
SPORTING RIFLE** . . . . NiB $821 Ex $572 Gd $400
Mauser M/88-type action. Calibers: 7x57, 8x57, 9x57mm.
Mannlicher clip-loading box magazine, 5-round. 22- or 24-inch

half or full octagon bbl. w/raised matted rib. Double-set trigger.
Weight: 7.5 lbs. Sights: Leaf-type open rear; ramp front. Sporting
stock w/cheekpiece, checkered pistol-grip, raised side-panels,
Schnabel tip, swivels.

HÄMMERLI AG JAGD-UND-SPORTWAFFENFABRIK — Lenzburg, Switzerland
*Imported by Sigarms, Exeter, NH; previ-
ously by Hammerli USA; Mandall Shooting Supplies, Inc. &
Beeman Precision Arms.*

**MODEL 45 SMALLBORE BOLT-ACTION SINGLE-SHOT
MATCH RIFLE** . . . . NiB $765 Ex $654 Gd $453
Calibers: .22 LR. 22 Extra Long. 27.5-inch heavy bbl. Weight:
15.5 lbs. Sights: Micrometer peep rear; globe front. Free-rifle
stock w/cheekpiece, full pistol-grip, thumbhole, beavertail
forearm, palmrest, Swiss-type buttplate, swivels. Made from
1945 to 1957.

**MODEL 54 SMALLBORE
MATCH RIFLE** . . . . NiB $709 Ex $544 Gd $423
Bolt-action, single-shot. Caliber: .22 LR. 27.5-inch heavy bbl.
Weight: 15 lbs. Sights: Micrometer peep rear; globe front. Free-
rifle stock w/cheekpiece, thumbhole, adj. hook buttplate, palm
rest, swivel. Made from 1954 to 1957.

MODEL 508 FREE RIFLE . . . . . . NiB $707 Ex $546 Gd $413
Bolt-action, single-shot. Caliber: .22 LR. 27.5-inch heavy bbl.
Weight: 15 lbs. Sights: Micrometer peep rear; globe front. Free-
rifle stock w/cheekpiece, thumbhole, adj. hook buttplate, palm
rest, swivel. Made from 1957 to 1962.

**MODEL 506 SMALLBORE
MATCH RIFLE** . . . . NiB $769 Ex $650 Gd $439
Bolt-action, single-shot. Caliber: .22 LR. 26.75-inch heavy bbl.
Weight: 16.5 lbs. Sights: Micrometer peep rear; globe front.
Free-rifle stock w/cheekpiece, thumbhole adj. hook buttplate,
palmrest, swivel. Made from 1963 to 1966.

Harrington & Richardson
Model 65 Military

Harrington & Richardson
Model 150 Leatherneck

Harrington & Richardson
Model 155

Harrington & Richardson
Model 157

Harrington & Richardson
Model 158 Topper Jet

Harrington & Richardson
Model 158C w/extra shotgun barrel

Harrington & Richardson
Model 171

Harrington & Richardson
Model 171 Deluxe

Harrington & Richardson
Model 172

Harrington & Richardson
Model 173

MODEL OLYMPIC 300 METER BOLT-ACTION SINGLE-SHOT FREE RIFLE . . . . NiB $905 Ex $755 Gd $556
Calibers: .30-06, .300 H&H Magnum for U.S.A.; ordinarily produced in 7.5mm, other calibers available on special order. 29.5-inch heavy bbl. Double-pull or double-set trigger. Sights: Micrometer peep rear, globe front. Free-rifle stock w/cheekpiece, full pistol grip, thumbhole, beavertail forend, palmrest, Swiss-type buttplate, swivels. Made 1945 to 1959.

TANNER 300 METER FREE RIFLE . . . NiB $937 Ex $740 Gd $534
Bolt-action, single-shot. Caliber: 7.5mm standard, available in most popular centerfire calibers. 29.5-inch heavy bbl. Weight: 16.75 lbs. Sights: Micrometer peep rear; globe front. Free-rifle stock w/cheekpiece, thumbhole, adj. hook buttplate, palmrest, swivel. Intro. 1962. Disc. See Illustration previous page.

HARRINGTON & RICHARDSON, INC. — Gardner, Massachusetts

Currently H&R 1872, formerly Harrington & Richardson Arms Co. of Worcester, Mass. One of the oldest and most distinguished manufacturers of handguns, rifles and shotguns, H&R suspended operations on January 24, 1986. In 1987, New England Firearms was established as an independent company producing selected H&R models under the NEF logo. In 1991, H&R 1871, Inc. was formed from the residual of the parent company and that took over the New England Firearms facility. H&R 1871 produced firearms under both its logo and the NEF brand name until 1999, when the Marlin Firearms Company acquired the assets of H&R 1871. Marlin was purchased by the Freedom Group Inc. in 2008.

MODEL 60 REISING SEMI-AUTOMATIC
RIFLE. . . . . NiB $1266 Ex $899 Gd $598
Caliber: .45 Automatic. 12- and 20-round detachable box magazines. 18.25-inch bbl. Weight: 7.5 lbs. Sights: Open rear; blade front. Plain pistol-grip stock. Made from 1944 to 1946.

MODEL 65 MILITARY
AUTOLOADING RIFLE . . . . . . NiB $496 Ex $322 Gd $208

Also called "General." Caliber: .22 LR. 10-round detachable box magazine. 23-inch heavy bbl. Weight: 9 lbs. Sights: Redfield 70 rear peep, blade front w/protecting "ears." Plain pistol-grip stock, "Garand" dimensions. Made from 1944 to 1946. Note: This model was used as a training rifle by the U.S. Marine Corps.

MODEL 150 LEATHERNECK
AUTOLOADER . . . . NiB $338 Ex $234 Gd $110
Caliber: .22 LR. only. Five round detachable box magazine. 22-inch bbl. Weight: 7.25 lbs. Sights: Open rear; blade front, on ramp. Plain pistol-grip stock. Made from 1949 to 1953.

MODEL 151 . . . . NiB $338 Ex $234 Gd $110
Same as Model 150 except w/Redfield 70 rear peep sight.

MODEL 155 SINGLE-SHOT
RIFLE. NiB $279 Ex $178 Gd $126
Model 158 action. Calibers: .44 Rem. Mag., .45-70 Govt. 24- or 28-inch bbl. (latter in .44 only). Weight: 7 or 7.5 lbs. Sights: Folding leaf rear; blade front. Straight-grip stock, forearm w/ bbl. band, brass cleaning rod. Made from 1972 to 1982.

MODEL 157 SINGLE-SHOT
RIFLE. NiB $333 Ex $154 Gd $121
Model 158 action. Calibers: .22 WMR, .22 Hornet, .30-30. 22-inch bbl. Weight: 6.25 lbs. Sights: Folding leaf rear; blade front. Pistol-grip stock, full-length forearm, swivels. Made from 1976 to 1986.

MODEL 158 TOPPER JET SINGLE-SHOT COMBINATION RIFLE
Shotgun-type action w/visible hammer, side lever, auto ejector. Caliber: .22 Rem. Jet. 22-inch bbl. (interchanges with .30-30, .410 ga., 20 ga. bbls.). Weight: 5 lbs. Sights: Lyman folding adj. open rear; ramp front. Plain pistol-grip stock and forearm, recoil pad. Made from 1963 to 1967.
Rifle only. . . . . NiB $250 Ex $171 Gd $126
Interchangeable bbl. .30-30, shotgun, add $75

MODEL 158C . . . . NiB $250 Ex $171 Gd $126
Same as Model 158 Topper Jet except calibers .22 Hornet, .30-30, .357 Mag., .357 Mag., .44 Mag. Straight-grip stock. Made 1963 to 1986.

Harrington & Richardson
Model 174 Little Big Horn Commemorative

Harrington & Richardson
Model 178

Harrington & Richardson
Model 300

Harrington & Richardson
Model 301 Carbine

Harrington & Richardson
Model 317P

Harrington & Richardson
Model 330

Harrington & Richardson
Model 360 Ultra

Harrington & Richardson
Model 370 Ultra Medalist

GRADING: **NiB** = New in Box   **Ex** = Excellent or NRA 95%   **Gd** = Good or NRA 68%   **259**

MODEL 163 MUSTANG
SINGLE-SHOT RIFLE . . . . NiB $250 Ex $168 Gd $124
Same as Model 158 Topper except w/gold-plated hammer and trigger, straight-grip stock and contoured forearm. Made 1964 to 1967.

MODEL 165 LEATHERNECK
AUTOLOADER . . . . NiB $250 Ex $170 Gd $126
Caliber: .22 LR. 10-round detachable box magazine. 23-inch bbl. Weight: 7.5 lbs. Sights: Redfield 70 rear peep; blade front, on ramp. Plain pistol-grip stock, swivels, web sling. Made from 1945 to 1961.

MODEL 171 . . . . NiB $633 Ex $466 Gd $257
Model 1873 Springfield Cavalry Carbine replica. Caliber: .45-70. 22-inch bbl. Weight: 7 lbs. Sights: Leaf rear; blade front. Plain walnut stock. Made from 1972 to 1981.

MODEL 171 DELUXE . . . . NiB $776 Ex $523 Gd $309
Same as Model 171 except engraved action and different sights. Made from 1972-86. See illustration next page.

MODEL 172 . . . . NiB $759 Ex $588 Gd $454
Same as Model 171 Deluxe except silver-plated, w/fancy walnut stock, checkered, w/grip adapter; tang-mounted aperture sight. Made from 1972 to 1986.

MODEL 173 . . . . NiB $1663 Ex $963 Gd $538
Model 1873 Springfield Officer's Model replica, same as 100th Anniversary Commemorative except w/o plaque on stock. Made from 1972 to 1986.

MODEL 174 . . . . NiB $1266 Ex $1009 Gd $633
Little Big Horn Commemorative Carbine. Same as Model 171 Deluxe except w/tang-mounted aperture sight, grip adapter. Made from 1972 to 1984.

MODEL 178 . . . . NiB $735 Ex $422 Gd $328
Model 1873 Springfield Infantry Rifle replica. Caliber: .45-70. 32-inch bbl. Weight: 8 lbs. 10 oz. Sights: Leaf rear; blade front. Full-length stock w/bbl. bands, swivels, ramrod. Made 1973 to 1986.

MODEL 250 SPORTSTER BOLT-ACTION
REPEATING RIFLE . . . . NiB $220 Ex $111 Gd $80
Caliber: .22 LR. Five-round detachable box magazine. 23-inch bbl. Weight: 6.5 lbs. Sights: Open rear; blade front, on ramp. Plain pistol-grip stock. Made from 1948 to 1961.

MODEL 251 . . . . NiB $255 Ex $128 Gd $90
Same as Model 250 except w/Lyman No. 55H rear sight.

MODEL 265 "REG'LAR" BOLT- ACTION
REPEATING RIFLE . . . . NiB $337 Ex $140 Gd $98
Caliber: .22 LR. 10-round detachable box magazine. 22-inch bbl. Weight: 6.5 lbs. Sights: Lyman No. 55 rear peep; blade front, on ramp. Plain pistol-grip stock. Made from 1946 to 1949.

MODEL 300 ULTRA . . . . NiB $572 Ex $521 Gd $302
Mauser-type action. Calibers: .22-250, .243 Win., .270 Win., .30-06, .308 Win., 7mm Rem. Mag., .300 Win. Mag. Three round magazine in 7mm and .300 Mag. calibers, 5-round in others. 22- or 24-inch bbl. Sights: Open rear; ramp front. Checkered stock w/rollover cheekpiece and full pistol grip, contrasting wood forearm tip and pistol grip, rubber buttplate, sling swivels. Weight: 7.25 lbs. Made 1965 to 1982.

MODEL 301 CARBINE . . . . NiB $523 Ex $412 Gd $287
Same as Model 300 except w/18-inch bbl., Mannlicher-style stock, weighs 7.25 lbs.; not available in caliber .22-250. Made 1967–82.

MODEL 308 AUTOMATIC RIFLE . . . NiB $531 Ex $390 Gd $277
Original designation of the Model 360 Ultra. Made 1965 to 1967.

MODEL 317 ULTRA WILDCAT
BOLT-ACTION RIFLE . . . . NiB $650 Ex $495 Gd $380
Sako short action. Calibers: .17 Rem. 17/.223 (handload), .222 Rem., .223 Rem. Six round magazine. 20-inch bbl. No sights, receiver dovetailed for scope mounts. Checkered stock w/ cheekpiece and full pistol grip, contrasting wood forearm tip and pistol-grip cap, rubber buttplate. Weight: 5.25 lbs. Made from 1968 to 1976.

MODEL 317P PRESENTATION
GRADE . . . . NiB $710 Ex $546 Gd $488
Same as Model 317 except w/select grade fancy walnut stock w/basket weave carving on forearm and pistol-grip. Made from 1968 to 1976.

MODEL 330 HUNTER'S RIFLE . . . NiB $439 Ex $326 Gd $244
Similar to Model 300, but w/plainer stock. Calibers: .243 Win., .270 Win., .30-06, .308 Win., 7mm Rem. Mag., .300 Win. Mag. Weight: 7.13 lbs. Made from 1967 to 1972.

MODEL 333 . . . . NiB $439 Ex $326 Gd $244
Plainer version of Model 300 w/uncheckered walnut-finished hardwood stock. Calibers: 7mm Rem. Mag. and .30-06. 22-inch bbl. Weight: 7.25 lbs. No sights. Made in 1974.

MODEL 340 . . . . NiB $450 Ex $341 Gd $259
Mauser-type action. Calibers: .243 Win., .308 Win., .270 Win., .30-06, 7x57. 22-inch bbl. Weight: 7.25 lbs. Hand-checkered American walnut stock. Made from 1982 to 1984.

MODEL 360 ULTRA . . . . NiB $534 Ex $380 Gd $300
Gas-operated semiautomatic. Calibers: .243 Win., .308 Win. Three round detachable box magazine. 22-inch bbl. Sights: Open rear; ramp front. Checkered stock w/rollover cheekpiece, full pistol grip, contrasting wood forearm tip and pistol-grip cap, rubber buttplate, sling swivels. Weight: 7.25 lbs. Made from 1967 to 1978.

MODEL 361 . . . . NiB $556 Ex $439 Gd $333
Same as Model 360 except w/full rollover cheekpiece for right- or left-hand shooters. Made from 1970 to 1973.

MODEL 369 ACE BOLT-ACTION
SINGLE-SHOT RIFLE . . . . NiB $178 Ex $140 Gd $96
Caliber: .22 LR. 22-inch bbl. Weight: 6.5 lbs. Sights: Lyman No. 55 rear peep, blade front, on ramp. Plain pistol-grip stock. Made 1946 to 1947.

MODEL 370 ULTRA MEDALIST NiB $555 Ex $423 Gd $320
Varmint and target rifle based on Model 300. Calibers: .22-250, .243 Win., 6mm Rem. Three round magazine. 24-inch varmint weight bbl. No sights. Target-style stock w/semibeavertail forearm. Weight: 9.5 lbs. Made from 1968 to 1973.

MODEL 422 SLIDE-ACTION
REPEATER . . . . NiB $375 Ex $234 Gd $141
Caliber: .22 LR. Long, Short. Tubular magazine holds 21 Short, 17 Long, 15 LR. 24-inch bbl. Weight: 6 lbs. Sights: Open rear; ramp front. Plain pistol-grip stock grooved slide handle. Made 1956–58.

Harrington & Richardson
Model 700 Deluxe

Harrington & Richardson
Model 750 Pioneer

Harrington & Richardson
"New" Model 750

Harrington & Richardson
Model 755

Harrington & Richardson
Model 760

Harrington & Richardson
Model 866

Harrington & Richardson
Model 1873 — 100th Anniversary

GRADING: **NiB** = New in Box   **Ex** = Excellent or NRA 95%   **Gd** = Good or NRA 68%

**Harrington & Richardson
Ultra Varmint**

MODEL 450 . . . . NiB $403 Ex $221 Gd $130
Same as Model 451 except w/o front and rear sights.

**MODEL 451 MEDALIST BOLT-ACTION
TARGET RIFLE.** . . . . NiB $433 Ex $222 Gd $130
Caliber: .22 LR. Five round detachable box magazine. 26-inch bbl. Weight: 10.5 lbs. Sights: Lyman No. 524F extension rear; Lyman No. 77 front, scope bases. Target stock w/full pistol-grip and forearm, swivels and sling. Made from 1948 to 1961.

**MODEL 465 TARGETEER SPECIAL
BOLT-ACTION REPEATER** . . . . . NiB $423 Ex $233 Gd $144
Caliber: .22 LR. 10-round detachable box magazine. 25-inch bbl. Weight: 9 lbs. Sights: Lyman No. 57 rear peep; blade front, on ramp. Plain pistol-grip stock, swivels, web sling strap. Made from 1946 to 1947.

MODEL 707 AUTOLOADER . . . NiB $456 Ex $321 Gd $188
Caliber: .22 WMR. Five-round magazine. 22-inch bbl. Weight: 6.5 lbs. Sights: Folding leaf rear; blade front, on ramp. Monte Carlo-style stock of American walnut. Made from 1977 to 1986.

MODEL 707 DELUXE . . . . NiB $508 Ex $381 Gd $285
Same as Model 707 Standard except w/select custom polished and blued finish, select walnut stock, hand checkering, and no iron sights. Fitted w/H&R Model 432 4x scope. Made from 1980 to 1986.

**MODEL 750 PIONEER BOLT-ACTION
SINGLE-SHOT RIFLE.** . . . . NiB $145 Ex $104 Gd $80
Caliber: .22 LR, Long, Short. 22- or 24-inch bbl. Weight: 5 lbs. Sights: Open rear; bead front. Plain pistol-grip stock. Made from 1954 to 1981; redesigned 1982; disc. 1985.

MODEL 751 SINGLE-SHOT RIFLE . . NiB $170 Ex $95 Gd $77
Same as Model 750 except w/Mannlicher-style stock. Made in 1971.

**MODEL 755 SAHARA SINGLE-SHOT
RIFLE.** . . . . NiB $166 Ex $90 Gd $67
Blow-back action, automatic ejection. Caliber: .22 LR, Long, Short. 18-inch bbl. Weight: 4 lbs. Sights: Open rear; military-type front. Mannlicher-style stock. Made from 1963 to 1971.

MODEL 760 SINGLE-SHOT . . . . NiB $188 Ex $100 Gd $80
Same as Model 755 except w/conventional sporter stock. Made from 1965 to 1970.

**MODEL 765 PIONEER BOLT-ACTION
SINGLE-SHOT RIFLE** . . . . NiB $188 Ex $97 Gd $66
Caliber: .22 LR, Long, Short. 24-inch bbl. Weight: 5 lbs. Sights: Open rear; hooded bead front. Plain pistol-grip stock. Made 1948 to 1954.

**MODEL 800 LYNX AUTOLOADING
RIFLE.** . . . . NiB $407 Ex $224 Gd $119
Caliber: .22 LR. Five or 10-round clip magazine. 22-inch bbl. Open sights. Weight: 6 lbs. Plain pistol-grip stock. Made 1958 to 1960.

**MODEL 852 FIELDSMAN BOLT-ACTION
REPEATER** . . . . NiB $198 Ex $101 Gd $89
Caliber: .22 LR, Long, Short. Tubular magazine holds 21 Short, 17 Long, 15 LR. 24-inch bbl. Weight: 5.5 lbs. Sights: Open rear; bead front. Plain pistol-grip stock. Made from 1952 to 1953.

**MODEL 865 PLAINSMAN BOLT-ACTION
REPEATER** . . . . NiB $167 Ex $115 Gd $80
Caliber .22 LR, Long, Short. Five round detachable box magazine. 22- or 24-inch bbl. Weight: 5.25 lbs. Sights: Open rear, bead front. Plain pistol-grip stock. Made from 1949 to 1986.

**MODEL 866
BOLT-ACTION REPEATER** . . . . . . NiB $197 Ex $115 Gd $80
Same as Model 865, except w/Mannlicher-style stock. Made 1971.

**MODEL 1873 100TH ANNIVERSARY (1871-1971)
COMMEMORATIVE OFFICER'S SPRINGFIELD
REPLICA** . . . . NiB $866 Ex $659 Gd $475
Model 1873 "trap door" single-shot action. Engraved breech block, receiver, hammer, lock, band and buttplate. Caliber: .45-70. 26-inch bbl. Sights: Peep rear; blade front. Checkered walnut stock w/anniversary plaque. Ramrod. Weight: 8 lbs. 10,000 made in 1971.

MODEL 5200 SPORTER . . . . . . NiB $677 Ex $376 Gd $277
Turn-bolt repeater. Caliber: .22 LR. 24-inch bbl. Classic-style American walnut stock. Adj. trigger. Sights: Peep receiver; hooded ramp front. Weight: 6.5 lbs. Disc. 1983.

MODEL 5200 MATCH RIFLE . . NiB $590 Ex $495 Gd $368
Same action as 5200 Sporter. Caliber: .22 LR. 28-inch target weight bbl. Target stock of American walnut. Weight: 11 lbs. Made 1982 to 1986.

CUSTER MEMORIAL ISSUE
Limited Edition Model 1873 Springfield Carbine replica, richly engraved and inlaid w/gold, fancy walnut stock, in mahogany display case. Made in 1973.
Officers' Model
     Limited to 25 pieces . . . NiB $4125 Ex $2990 Gd $12423
Enlisted Men's model,
     limited to 243 pieces . . . . NiB $2033 Ex $1021 Gd $690

**TARGETEER JR. BOLT-ACTION
RIFLE** . . . . NiB $227 Ex $177 Gd $145
Caliber: .22 LR. Five-round detachable box magazine. 20-inch bbl. Weight: 7 lbs. Sights: Redfield 70 rear peep; Lyman No. 17A front. Target stock, junior-size w/pistol grip, swivels and sling. Made 1948 to 1951.

ULTRA SINGLE-SHOT RIFLE
Side-lever single-shot. Calibers: .22-250 Rem., .223 Rem., .25-06 Rem., .308 Win. 22- to 26-inch bbl. Weight: 7-8 lbs. Curly maple or laminated stock. Barrel-mounted scope mount, no sights. Made from 1993 to date.
Ultra Hunter (.25-06, .308) . . . NiB $257 Ex $166 Gd $167
Ultra Varmint . . . . NiB $288 Ex $230 Gd $188

Heckler & Koch
Model HK91 A-2

Heckler & Koch
Model HK91 A-3

Heckler & Koch
Model HK93 A-2

Heckler & Koch
Model HK940 Carbine

Heckler & Koch
Model HK PSG-1

Heckler & Koch
Model SL-8

GRADING: **NiB** = New in Box   **Ex** = Excellent or NRA 95%   **Gd** = Good or NRA 68%

HARRIS GUNWORKS — Phoenix, Arizona

Formerly McMillan Gun Works. Sporting line of firearms discontinued, now specializes in sniper and tactical arms.

SIGNATURE ALASKAN BOLT-ACTION

RIFLE . . . . NiB $3510 Ex $3108 Gd $2110
Same general specifications as Classic Sporter except w/match-grade bbl. Rings and mounts. Sights: Single-leaf rear, bbl. band front. Checkered Monte Carlo stock w/palmswell and solid recoil pad. Nickel finish. Calibers: LA (long): .270 Win., .280 Rem., .30-06, MA (Magnum): 7mm Rem. Mag., .300 Win. Mag., .300 Wby. Mag., .340 Wby. Mag., .358 Win., .375 H&H Mag. Made from 1990. Disc.

SIGNATURE CLASSIC SPORTER

The prototype for Harris' Signature Series, this bolt-action rifle is available in three lengths: SA (standard/ short) — from .22-250 to .350 Rem Mag.; LA (long) — .25-06 to .30-06; MA (Magnum) — 7mm STW to .416 Rem. Mag. Four-round or 3-round (Magnum) magazine. Bbl. lengths: 22, 24 or 26 inches. Weight: 7 lbs. (short action). No sights; rings and bases provided. Harris fiberglass stock, Fibergrain or wood stock optional. Stainless, matte black or black chrome sulfide finish. Available in right- and left-hand models. Made from 1987. Disc. Has pre-64 Model 70-style action for dangerous game.
Classic Sporter, standard . . . NiB $2565 Ex $2347 Gd $1424
Classic Sporter, stainless . . . NiB $2565 Ex $2347 Gd $1424
Talon Sporter . . . . NiB $2613 Ex $2092 Gd $1474

SIGNATURE MOUNTAIN

RIFLE . . . . NiB $3037 Ex $2977 Gd $1609
Same general specifications as Harris (McMillan) Classic Sporter except w/titanium action and graphite-reinforced fiberglass stock. Weight: 5.5 lbs. Calibers: .270 Win., .280 Rem., .30-06, 7mm Mag., .300 Win. Mag. Other calibers on special order. Made from 1995. Disc.

SIGNATURE SUPER

VARMINTER . . . . NiB $2512 Ex $2233 Gd $1429
Same general specifications as Harris (McMillan) Classic Sporter except w/heavy, contoured bbl., adj. trigger, fiberglass stock and field bipod. Calibers: .223, .22-250, .220 Swift, .244 Win., 6mm Rem., .25-06, 7mm-08, .308 Win., .350 Win. Mag. Made from 1995. Disc.

TALON SAFARI RIFLE

Same general specifications as Harris (McMillan) Classic Sporter except w/Harris Safari-grade action, match-grade bbl. and "Safari" fiberglass stock. Calibers: Magnum — .300 H&H Mag., .300 Win Mag., .300 Wby. Mag., .338 Win. Mag., .340 Wby. Mag., .375 H&H Mag., .404 Jeffrey, .416 Rem. Mag., .458 Win., Super Mag. — .300 Phoenix, .338 Lapua, .378 Wby. Mag., .416 Rigby, .416 Wby. Mag., .460 Wby. Mag. Matte black finish. Other calibers available on special order, and at a premium, but the "used gun" value remains the same. Imported 1989. Disc.
Safari Magnum . . . . NiB $3809 Ex $3166 Gd $2179
Safari Super Magnum . . . . . NiB $4322 Ex $3561 Gd $2574

HECKLER & KOCH, GMBH — Oberndorf am Neckar, Germany.

Imported by Heckler & Koch, Inc., Sterling, VA.

MODEL 911 SEMIAUTO

RIFLE . . . . NiB $1970 Ex $1723 Gd $1019
Caliber: .308 (7.62mm). Five-round magazine. 19.7-inch bull bbl. 42.4 inches overall. Sights: Hooded post front; adj. aperture rear. Weight: 11 lbs. Kevlar-reinforced fiberglass thumbhole-stock. Imported 1989 to 1993.

MODEL HK91 A-2

SEMIAUTO . . . . NiB $2634 Ex $2133 Gd $1388
Delayed roller-locked blow-back action. Caliber: 7.62mmx51 NATO (308 Win.) 5- or 20-round box magazine. 19-inch bbl. Weight: W/o magazine, 9.37 lbs. Sights L "V" and aperture rear, post front. Plastic buttstock and forearm. Disc. 1991.

MODEL HK91 A-3 . . . . NiB $2721 Ex $2490 Gd $1665
Same as Model HK91 A-2 except w/retractable metal buttstock, weighs 10.56 lbs. Disc. 1991.

MODEL HK93 SEMIAUTOMATIC

Delayed roller-locked blow-back action. Caliber: 5.56mmx45 (.223 Rem.). 5- or 20-round magazine. 16.13-inch bbl. Weight: W/o magazine, 7.6 lbs. Sights: "V" and aperture rear; post front. Plastic buttstock and forearm. Disc. 1991.
HK93 A-2 . . . . NiB $2835 Ex $2177 Gd $1198
HK93 A-3 w/retractable stock NiB $3590 Ex $2816 Gd $2021

MODEL HK94 SEMIAUTOMATIC CARBINE

Caliber: 9mm Para. 15-round magazine. 16-inch bbl. Weight: 6.75 lbs. Aperture rear sight, front post. Plastic buttstock and forend or retractable metal stock. Imported from 1983 to 1991.
HK94-A2 w/standard stock NiB $4054 Ex $3209 Gd $2775
HK94-A3 w/retractable stock, add 20%

MODEL HK300

SEMIAUTOMATIC . . . . NiB $1423 Ex $955 Gd $600
Caliber: .22 WMR. Five- or 15-round box magazine. 19.7-inch bbl. w/polygonal rifling. Weight: 5.75 lbs. Sights: V-notch rear; ramp front. High-luster polishing and bluing. European walnut stock w/ cheekpiece, checkered forearm and pistol-grip. Disc. 1989.

MODEL HK630

SEMIAUTOMATIC . . . . NiB $1733 Ex $1277 Gd $1009
Caliber: .223 Rem. Four- or 10-round magazine. 24-inch bbl. Overall length: 42 inches. Weight: 7 lbs. Sights: Open rear; ramp front. European walnut stock w/Monte Carlo cheekpiece. Imported from 1983 to 1990.

MODEL HK770

SEMIAUTOMATIC . . . . NiB $2244 Ex $1703 Gd $1099
Caliber: .308 Win. Three- or 10-round magazine. Overall length: 44.5 inches. Weight: 7.92 lbs. Sights: Open rear; ramp front. European walnut stock w/Monte Carlo cheekpiece. Imported from 1983 to 1986.

MODEL HK940

SEMIAUTOMATIC . . . . NiB $2055 Ex $1833 Gd $1079
Caliber: .30-06 Springfield. Three- or 10-round magazine. Overall length: 47 inches. Weight: 8.8 lbs. Sights: Open rear; ramp front. European walnut stock w/Monte Carlo cheekpiece. Imported from 1983 to 1986.

MODEL HK PSG-1

MARKSMAN'S RIFLE . . . NiB $12,790 Ex $10,879 Gd $8966
Caliber: .308 (7.62mm). Five- and 20-round magazine. 25.6-inch bbl. 47.5 inches overall. Hensoldt 6x42 telescopic sight. Weight: 17.8 lbs. Matte black composite stock w/pistol-grip. Imported from 1988 to 1998.

MODEL SL8-1 RIFLE . . . . NiB $2006 Ex $1409 Gd $987
Caliber: .223 Win. Ten-round magazine. 20.80- inch bbl. 38.58 inches overall. Weight: 8.6 lbs. Gas-operated, short-stroke piston w/rotary locking bolt. Rear adjustable sight w/ambidextrous

Heckler & Koch
Model USC Carbine

Heym
Model SR-20 Standard

Heym
Model SR-20L Mannlicher

safety selector lever. Polymer receiver w/adjustable buttstock. Introduced in 1999.

MODEL SR-9 SEMIAUTO
RIFLE . . . . NiB $2130 Ex $1850 Gd $1044
Caliber: .308 (7.62mm). Five round magazine. 19.7-inch bull bbl. 42.4 inches overall. Hooded post front sight; adj. aperture rear. Weight: 11 lbs. Kevlar-reinforced fiberglass thumbhole-stock w/wood grain finish. Imported from 1989 to 1993.

MODEL SR-9 TARGET RIFLE. . NiB $2844 Ex $2166 Gd $1482
Same general specifications as standard SR-9 except w/ PSG-1 trigger group and adj. buttstock. Imported from 1992 to 1994.

MODEL USC CARBINE RIFLE. . . NiB $1675 Ex $1133 Gd $790
Caliber: 45 ACP. 10-round magazine. 16- inch bbl., 35.43 inches overall. Weight: 6 lbs. Blow-back operating system. Polymer receiver w/integral grips. Rear adjustable sight w/ ambidextrous safety selector lever. Introduced in 1999.

HENRY REPEATING ARMS — Bayonne, NJ

MINI BOLT . . . . NiB $260 Ex $215 Gd $90
Caliber: .22 Short, LR. Single shot. 16.25-inch bbl. Stainless steel receiver, synthetic stock. Made 2002 to date.

ACU-BOLT . . . . NiB $335 Ex $225 Gd $120
Caliber: .17 HMR, .22 LR or .22 WMR. Single shot. 20-inch bbl. Stainless steel receiver, synthetic stock. Made 2004 to date.

LEVER ACTION . . . . NiB $335 Ex $225 Gd $120
Caliber: .17 HMR, .22 Short, Long, LR or .22 WMR. Lever action, 15-round (.22 LR) tube magazine. 16.12-, 18.25-, 19.25-, or 20-inch round or octagon bbl. Blued receiver, American walnut stock. Made 1997 to date.
Carbine Large Loop. . . . . NiB $290 Ex $186 Gd $130
Golden Boy (brass receiver) . . . NiB $430 Ex $275 Gd $160

"BIG BOY" LEVER ACTION . . . NiB $335 Ex $225 Gd $120
Caliber: .38 Special/.357 Mag., 17 HMR, .44 Special/.44 Mag. or .45 LC. Lever action, 10-round tube magazine. 20-inch

octagon bbl. Brass receiver, American walnut stock. Made 2003 to date.
Deluxe II (hand engraved) . . NiB $1725 Ex $1230 Gd $710

.30-30 LEVER ACTION . . . . . . NiB $335 Ex $225 Gd $120
Caliber: .30-30 Win. Lever action, 6-round tube magazine. 20-inch round or octagon bbl. Blued receiver, American walnut stock. Made 2008 to date.
Brass receiver/octagon bbl., add. $220

PUMP ACTION . . . . NiB $335 Ex $225 Gd $120
Caliber: .22 Short, Long, LR or .22 WMR. Pump action, 16-round (.22 LR) tube magazine. 18.25- or 20.5-inch round bbl. Blued receiver, American walnut stock. Made 1999 to date.

U.S. SURVIVAL .22
SEMI-AUTOMATIC . . . . NiB $225 Ex $170 Gd $115
Similar to Armalite AR-7 takedown rifle. Caliber: .22 LR. Semi-auto action, 8-round magazine. Made 1997 to date.

HEROLD — Suhl, Germany
Made by Franz Jaeger & Company.

BOLT-ACTION REPEATING
SPORTING RIFLE . . . . NiB $1044 Ex $800 Gd $634
"Herold-Repetierbüchse." Miniature Mauser-type action w/ unique 5-round box magazine on hinged floorplate. Double-set triggers. Caliber: .22 Hornet. 24-inch bbl. Sights: Leaf rear; ramp front. Weight: 7.75 lbs. Fancy checkered stock. Made before WWII. Note: These rifles were imported by Charles Daly and A.F. Stoeger Inc. of New York City and sold under their names.

HEYM RIFLES AMERICA, INC. — Germany
Manufactured by Heym, GmbH & Co JAGWAFFEN KD., Gleichamberg, Germany (previously imported by Heym America, Inc.; Heckler & Koch; JagerSport, Ltd.)

MODEL 55B DOUBLE RIFLE
Kersten boxlock action w/double cross bolt and cocking indicators. Calibers: .308 Win., .30-06, .375 H&H, .458 Win. Mag., .470 N.E. 25-inch bbl. 42 inches overall. Weight: 8.25 lbs. Sights: fixed V-type rear; front ramp w/silver bead.

**High Standard
Flite-King Pump**

Engraved receiver w/optional sidelocks, interchangeable bbls. and claw mounts. Checkered European walnut stock. Imported from Germany.

Model 55 (boxlock). . . . . . . NiB $6677 Ex $6488 Gd $5745
Model 55 (sidelock). . . . . . NiB $9544 Ex $7890 Gd $6791
w/extra rifle bbls., add $6000
w/extra shotgun bbls., add $3000

MODEL 88B DOUBLE RIFLE
Modified Anson & Deeley boxlock action w/standing gears, double underlocking lugs and Greener extension w/crossbolt. Calibers: 8x57 JRS, 9.3x74R, .30-06, .375 H&H, .458 Win. Mag., .470 Nitro Express, .500 Nitro Express. Other calibers available on special order. Weight: 8 to 10 lbs. Top tang safety and cocking indicators. Double triggers w/front set. Fixed or 3-leaf express rear sight, front ramp w/silver bead. Engraved receiver w/optional sidelocks. Checkered French walnut stock. Imported from Germany.

Model 88B Boxlock. . . . . NiB $11,669 Ex $8875 Gd $6067
Model 88B/SS Sidelock . . .NiB $15,538 Ex $10,850 Gd $7410
Model 88B Safari (Magnum). . .NiB $15,038 Ex $12,050 Gd $8226

EXPRESS BOLT-ACTION RIFLE
Same general specifications as Model SR-20 Safari except w/modified magnum Mauser action. Checkered AAA-grade European walnut stock w/cheekpiece, solid rubber recoil pad, rosewood forend tip and grip cap. Calibers: .338 Lapua Magnum, .375 H&H, .378 Wby. Mag., .416 Rigby .450 Ackley, .460 Wby. Mag., .500 A-Square, .500 Nitro Express, .600 Nitro Express. Other calibers available on special order, but no change in used gun value. Imported from Germany 1989 to 1995.

Standard Express Magnum . NiB $5644 Ex $4490 Gd $3230
600 Nitro Express . . . . NiB $5895 Ex $5133 Gd $3190
Left-hand models, add $750

SR-20 BOLT-ACTION RIFLE
Calibers: .243 Win., .270 Win., .308 Win., .30-06, 7mm Rem. Mag., .300 Win. Mag., .375 H&H. Five round (standard) or 3-round (Magnum) magazine. Bbl. length: 20.5-inch (SR-20L); 24-inch (SR-20N); 26-inch (SR-20G). Weight: 7.75 lbs. Adj. rear sight, blade front. Checkered French walnut stock in Monte Carlo style (N&G Series) or full Mannlicher (L Series). Imported from Germany. Disc. 1992.

SR-20L. . . . . NiB $2316 Ex $1832 Gd $1209
SR-20N . . . . NiB $2279 Ex $1856 Gd $1200
SR-20G . . . . NiB $2865 Ex $2379 Gd $1600

SR-20 CLASSIC BOLT-ACTION RIFLES
Same as SR-20 except w/.22-250 and .338 Win. Mag. plus metric calibers on request. 24-inch (standard) or 25-inch (Magnum) bbl. Checkered French walnut stock. Left-hand models. Imported from Germany since 1985; Sporter version 1989 to 1993.

Classic (Standard) . . . . NiB $1860 Ex $1875 Gd $1423
Classic (Magnum) . . . . NiB $2355 Ex $2216 Gd $1466
**Classic Sporter (Std.
    w/22-inch bbl.)**. . . . . NiB $2556 Ex $2203 Gd $1499
**Classic Sporter (Mag.
    w/24-inch bbl.)**. . . . . NiB $1899 Ex $2288 Gd $1633
Left-hand models, add $350

SR-20 ALPINE, SAFARI AND TROPHY SERIES
Same general specifications as Model SR-20 Classic Sporter except Alpine Series w/20-inch bbl., Mannlicher stock, chambered in standard calibers only; Safari Series w/24-inch bbl., 3-leaf express sights and magnum action in calibers .375 H & H, .404 Jeffrey, .425 Express, .458 Win. Mag.; Trophy Series w/Krupp-Special tapered octagon bbl. w/quarter rib and open sights, standard and Magnum calibers. Imported from Germany from 1989 to 1993.

Alpine Series. . . . . NiB $1969 Ex $1812 Gd $1492
Safari Series . . . . NiB $2308 Ex $2177 Gd $1545
Trophy Series (Stand. calibers) . . NiB $2589 Ex $2115 Gd $1904
**Trophy Series
    (Magnum calibers)**. . . . . . NiB $2733 Ex $2118 Gd $1944

J.C. HIGGINS RIFLES
See Sears, Roebuck & Company.

HI-POINT FIREARMS — Dayton, Ohio

MODEL 995 CARBINE
Semiautomatic recoil-operated carbine. Calibers: 9mm Parabellum or 40 S&W. 10-round magazine. 16.5-inch bbl. 31.5 inches overall. Protected post front sight, aperture rear w/integral scope mount. Matte blue, chrome or Parkerized finish. Checkered polymer grip/frame. Made from 1996 to date.

**Model 995, 9mm
    (blue or Parkerized)** . . . . NiB $233 Ex $179 Gd $130
**Model 995, .41 S&W
    (blue or Parkerized)** . . . . NiB $248 Ex $211 Gd $146
w/laser sights, add $50
w/chrome finish, add $25

HIGH STANDARD SPORTING FIREARMS — East Hartford, Connecticut
Formerly High Standard Mfg. Co., Hamden, CT. A long-standing producer of sporting arms, High Standard discontinued its operations in 1984.

SPORT-KING PUMP RIFLE . . . . . NiB $207 Ex $144 Gd $98
Hammerless slide-action. Caliber: .22 LR, .22 Long, .22 Short. Tubular mag. holds 17 LR, 19 Long, or 24 Short. 24-inch bbl. Weight: 5.5 lbs. Sights: Partridge rear; bead front. Monte Carlo stock w/pistol grip, serrated semibeavertail forearm. Made from 1963 to 1976.

HI-POWER DELUXE RIFLE . . . . NiB $475 Ex $315 Gd $221
Mauser-type bolt action, sliding safety. Calibers: .270, .30-06. Four round magazine. 22-inch bbl. Weight: 7 lbs. Sights: Folding open rear; ramp front. Walnut stock w/checkered pistol-grip and forearm, Monte Carlo comb, QD swivels. Made from 1962 to 1965.

**HI-POWER FIELD BOLT-ACTION
RIFLE**. . . . . NiB $255 Ex $179 Gd $126
Same as Hi-Power Deluxe except w/plain field style stock. Made from 1962 to 1966.

High Standard
Hi-Power Deluxe

Holland & Holland
Best Quality Magazine

Holland & Holland
Royal Deluxe Double

Howa
Model 1500 Hunter

Howa
Model 1500 Lightning

RIFLES

**SPORT-KING AUTO- LOADING
CARBINE.** . . . . NiB $379 Ex $318 Gd $200
Same as Sport-King Field Autoloader except w/18.25-inch bbl.,
Western-style straight-grip stock w/bbl. band, sling and swivels.
Made from 1964 to 1973.

**SPORT-KING DELUXE
AUTOLOADER** . . . . NiB $280 Ex $213 Gd $100
Same as Sport-King Special Autoloader except w/checkered
stock. Made from 1966 to 1975.

**SPORT-KING FIELD
AUTOLOADER** . . . . NiB $229 Ex $130 Gd $90
Calibers: .22 LR, .22 Long, .22 Short (high speed). Tubular
magazine holds 15 LR, 17 Long, or 21 Short. 22.25-inch bbl.
Weight: 5.5 lbs. Sights: Open rear; beaded post front. Plain
pistol-grip stock. Made from 1960 to 1966.

**SPORT-KING SPECIAL
AUTOLOADER** . . . . NiB $210 Ex $166 Gd $106
Same as Sport-King Field except stock w/Monte Carlo comb
and semibeavertail forearm. Made from 1960 to 1966.

HOLLAND & HOLLAND, LTD. — London, England

Imported by Holland & Holland, New York, NY.

**NO. 2 MODEL HAMMERLESS EJECTOR
DOUBLE RIFLE** . . . . . NiB $15,650 Ex $12,800 Gd $10,770
Same general specifications as Royal Model except plainer
finish. Disc. 1960.

**BEST QUALITY MAGAZINE
RIFLE.** . . . . NiB $15,300 Ex $12,000 Gd $9890
Mauser or Enfield action. Calibers: .240 Apex, .300 H&H Mag.,
.375 H&H Magnum. Four round box magazine. 24-inch bbl.
Weight: 7.25 lbs., 240 Apex; 8.25 lbs., .300 Mag. and .375 Mag.
Sights: Folding leaf rear; hooded ramp front. Detachable French
walnut stock w/cheekpiece, checkered pistol-grip and forearm,
swivels. Currently mfd. Specifications given apply to most models.

**DE LUXE MAGAZINE
RIFLE.** . . . . NiB $16,780 Ex $13,966 Gd $9566
Same specifications as Best Quality except w/exhibition-grade
stock and special engraving. Currently mfd.

GRADING: **NiB** = New in Box   **Ex** = Excellent or NRA 95%   **Gd** = Good or NRA 68%

ROYAL HAMMERLESS
EJECTOR RIFLE . . . . . NiB $43,000 Ex $33,900 Gd $24,775
Sidelock. Calibers: .240 Apex, 7mm H&H Mag., .300 H&H Mag., .300 Win. Mag., .30-06, .375 H&H Mag., .458 Win. Mag., .465 H&H Mag. 24- to 28-inch bbls. Weight: From 7.5 lbs. Sights: Folding leaf rear, ramp front. Cheekpiece stock of select French walnut, checkered pistol-grip and forearm. Currently mfd. Same general specifications apply to prewar model.

ROYAL DELUXE DOUBLE
RIFLE . . . . NiB $57,956 Ex $47,888 Gd $32,600
Formerly designated "Modele Deluxe." Same specifications as Royal Model except w/exhibition-grade stock and special engraving. Currently mfd.

HOWA — Tokyo, Japan
Imported by Legacy Sports Int., Reno, NV. See also Mossberg (1500) Smith & Wesson (1500 & 1707) and Weatherby (Vanguard).

MODEL 1500 HUNTER
Similar to Trophy Model except w/standard walnut stock. No Monte Carlo cheekpiece or grip cap. Imported from 1988 to 1989.
Standard calibers . . . . NiB $508 Ex $455 Gd $337
Magnum calibers . . . . NiB $520 Ex $466 Gd $350
Stainless steel, add $100

MODEL 1500 LIGHTNING BOLT-ACTION RIFLE
Similar to Hunter Model except fitted w/black Bell & Carlson Carbelite stock w/checkered grip and forend. Weight: 7.5 lbs. Imported 1988.
Standard calibers . . . . NiB $479 Ex $336 Gd $269
Magnum calibers . . . . NiB $482 Ex $410 Gd $312

MODEL 1500 PCS BOLT-ACTION RIFLE
Similar to Hunter Model except in Police Counter Sniper configuration and chambered for .308 Win. only. Walnut or synthetic stock w/checkered grip and forend. Receiver drilled and tapped but w/o sights. Weight: 8.5 to 9.3 lbs. Imported from 1999 to 2000.
PCS Model w/walnut stock . . . NiB $433 Ex $337 Gd $249
PCS Model w/synthetic stock . NiB $479 Ex $388 Gd $307
Stainless steel, add $100

MODEL 1500 REALTREE
CAMO RIFLE . . . . NiB $546 Ex $489 Gd $333
Similar to Trophy Model except fitted w/Camo Bell & Carlson Carbelite stock w/checkered grip and forend. Weight: 8 lbs. Stock, action and barrel finished in Realtree camo. Available in standard calibers only. Imported 1993 to 1994.

MODEL 1500 TROPHY/VARMINT BOLT-ACTION RIFLE
Calibers: .22-250, .223, .243 Win., .270 Win., .308 Win., .30-06, 7mm Mag., .300 Win. Mag., .338 Win. Mag. 22-inch bbl. (standard); 24-inch bbl. (Magnum). 42.5 inches overall (standard). Weight: 7.5 lbs. Adj. rear sight hooded ramp front. Checkered walnut stock w/Monte Carlo cheekpiece. Varmint Model w/24-inch heavy bbl., weight of 9.5 lbs. in calibers .22-250, .223 and .308 only. Imported 1988 to 1992 and 2001 to 2008.
Trophy Standard . . . . NiB $575 Ex $499 Gd $370
Trophy Magnum . . . . NiB $590 Ex $508 Gd $379
Varmint (Parkerized finish) . . . . NiB $602 Ex $488 Gd $380
Stainless steel, add $100

MODEL 1500 WOODGRAIN LIGHTNING RIFLE
Calibers: .243, .270, 7mm Rem. Mag., .30-06. Mag. Five round magazine 22-inch. 42 inches overall. Weight: 7.5 lbs. Receiver drilled and tapped for scope mount, no sights. Checkered woodgrain synthetic polymer stock. Imported from 1993 to 1994.
Standard calibers . . . . NiB $488 Ex $419 Gd $374
Magnum calibers . . . . NiB $500 Ex $443 Gd $399

H-S PRECISION — Rapid City, South Dakota

PRO-SERIES
Custom rifle built on Remington 707 bolt action. Calibers: .22 to .416, 24- or 26-inch bbl. w/fluted option. Aluminum bedding block system w/take-down option. Kevlar/carbon fiber stock to customer's specifications. Appointments and options to customer's preference. Made from 1990 to date.
Sporter model . . . . NiB $2180 Ex $1830 Gd $1100
Pro-Hunter model (PHR) . . NiB $2866 Ex $2033 Gd $1108
Long-Range Model . . . . NiB $4597 Ex $3766 Gd $2080
Long-Range takedown
model . . . . NiB $2355 Ex $1944 Gd $1390
Marksman model . . . . NiB $2966 Ex $1830 Gd $1106
Marksman takedown model NiB $2977 Ex $2133 Gd $1490
Varmint takedown model
(VTD) . . . . NiB $4369 Ex $2835 Gd $2000
Left-hand models, add $227

HUNGARIAN MILITARY RIFLES — Budapest, Hungary
Manufactured at government arsenal.

MODEL 1935M MANNLICHER
MILITARY RIFLE . . . . NiB $370 Ex $287 Gd $186
Caliber: 8x52mm Hungarian. Bolt action, straight handle. Five round projecting box magazine. 24-inch bbl. Weight: 9 lbs. Adj. leaf rear sight, hooded front blade. Two-piece military-type stock. Made from 1935 to 1940.

MODEL 1943M (GERMAN GEW 98/40) MANNLICHER
MILITARY RIFLE . . . . NiB $388 Ex $322 Gd $200
Modification, during German occupation, of Model 1935M. Caliber: 7.9mm Mauser. Turned-down bolt handle and Mauser M/98-type box magazine; other differences are minor. Made from 1940 to end of war in Europe.

HUSQVARNA VAPENFABRIK A.B. — Husqvarna, Sweden

MODEL 456 LIGHTWEIGHT
FULL-STOCK SPORTER . . . . NiB $713 Ex $466 Gd $339
Same as Series 4000/4100 except w/sporting style full stock w/slope-away cheekrest. Weight: 6.5 lbs. Made from 1959 to 1970.

SERIES 1000 SUPER GRADE . . . NiB $572 Ex $479 Gd $339
Same as 1951 Hi-Power except w/European walnut sporter stock w/Monte Carlo comb and cheekpiece. Made from 1952 to 1956.

SERIES 1100 DELUXE MODEL HI-POWER BOLT-ACTION
SPORTING RIFLE . . . . NiB $557 Ex $468 Gd $339
Same as 1951 Hi-Power, except w/jeweled bolt, European walnut stock. Made from 1952 to 1956.

Husqvarna
Series 1100 Deluxe

Husqvarna 1951
Hi-Power

Husqvarna 3000
Crown Grade

Husqvarna 4100
Lightweight

Husqvarna 6000
Imperial Custom

Interarms Mark X
Lightweight Sporter

Interarms Mini-Mark X

RIFLES

1950 HI-POWER SPORTING RIFLE...NiB $554 Ex $415 Gd $300
Mauser-type bolt action. Calibers: .220 Swift, .270 Win. .30-06 (see note below), 5-round box magazine. 23.75-inch bbl. Weight: 7.75 lbs. Sights: Open rear; hooded ramp front. Sporting stock of Arctic beech, checkered pistol grip and forearm, swivels. Note: Husqvarna sporters were first intro. in U.S. about 1948; earlier models were also available in calibers 6.5x55, 8x57 and 9.3x57. Made from 1946 to 1951.

1951 HI-POWER RIFLE......NiB $554 Ex $415 Gd $300
Same as 1950 Hi-Power except w/high-comb stock, low safety.

SERIES 3000 CROWN GRADE . NiB $643 Ex $455 Gd $300
Same as Series 3100, except w/Monte Carlo comb stock.

SERIES 3100 CROWN GRADE . NiB $643 Ex $455 Gd $300
HVA improved Mauser action. Calibers: .243, .270, 7mm, .30-06, .308 Win. Five round box magazine. 23.75-inch bbl. Weight: 7.75 lbs. Sights: Open rear; hooded ramp front. European walnut stock, checkered, cheekpiece, pistol-grip cap, black forend tip, swivels. Made from 1954 to 1972.

SERIES 4000 LIGHTWEIGHT RIFLE...NiB $699 Ex $433 Gd $297
Same as Series 4100 except w/Monte Carlo comb stock and no rear sight.

SERIES 4100 LIGHTWEIGHT RIFLE .. NiB $616 Ex $423 Gd $260
HVA improved Mauser action. Calibers: .243, .270, 7mm, .30-06, .308 Win. Five round box magazine. 20.5-inch bbl. Weight: 6.25 lbs. Sights: Open rear; hooded ramp front. Lightweight walnut stock w/cheekpiece, pistol grip, Schnabel forend tip, checkered, swivels. Made from 1954 to 1972.

SERIES 6000 IMPERIAL CUSTOM GRADE ....NiB $877 Ex $633 Gd $409
Same as Series 3100 except fancy-grade stock, 3-leaf folding rear sight, adj. trigger. Calibers: .243, .270, 7mm Rem. Mag. .308, .30-06. Made from 1968 to 1970.

SERIES 7070 IMPERIAL MONTE CARLO LIGHTWEIGHT ......NiB $920 Ex $577 Gd $400
Same as Series 4000 Lightweight except fancy-grade stock, 3-leaf folding rear sight, adj. trigger. Calibers: .243, .270, .308, .30-06. Made from 1968 to 1970.

SERIES 8000 IMPERIAL GRADE .... NiB $831 Ex $569 Gd $389
Same as Model 9000 except w/jeweled bolt, engraved floorplate, deluxe French walnut checkered stock, no sights. Made 1971 to 1972.

SERIES 9000 CROWN GRADE .... NiB $633 Ex $459 Gd $348
New design Husqvarna bolt action. Adj. trigger. Calibers: .270, 7mm Rem. Mag., .30-06, .300 Win. Mag. Five round box magazine, hinged floorplate. 23.75-inch bbl. Sights: Folding leaf rear; hooded ramp front. Checkered walnut stock w/Monte Carlo cheekpiece, rosewood forend tip and pistol-grip cap. Weight: 7 lbs. 3 oz. Made from 1971 to 1972.

SERIES P-3000 PRESENTATION... NiB $1179 Ex $889 Gd $627
Same as Crown Grade Series 3000 except w/selected stock, engraved action, adj. trigger. Calibers: .243, .270, 7mm Rem. Mag., .30-06. Made from 1968 to 1970.

INTERARMS — Alexandria, Virginia
The following Mark X rifles are manufactured by Zavodi Crvena Zastava, Belgrade, Yugoslavia.

MARK X ALASKAN ....NiB $708 Ex $447 Gd $321
Same specs as Mark X Sporter, except chambered for .375 H&H Mag. and .458 Win. Mag. w/3-round magazine. Stock w/recoil-absorbing cross bolt and heavy duty recoil pad. Weighs 8.25 lbs. Made from 1976 to 1984.

MARK X BOLT-ACTION SPORTER SERIES
Mauser-type action. Calibers: .22-250, .243, .25-06, .270, 7x57, 7mm Rem. Mag., .308, .30-06, .300 Win. Mag. Five round magazine (3-round in magnum calibers). 24-inch bbl. Weight: 7.5 lbs. Sights: Adj. leaf rear; ramp front, w/hood. Classic-style stock of European walnut w/Monte Carlo comb and cheekpiece, checkered pistol grip and forearm, black forend tip, QD swivels. Made from 1972 to 1997.

Mark X Standard ....NiB $479 Ex $355 Gd $260
Mark X Camo (Realtree)......NiB $499 Ex $440 Gd $327
American Field, std.
  (rubber recoil pad) ....NiB $570 Ex $460 Gd $368
American Field, Magnum
  (rubber recoil pad) ....NiB $689 Ex $572 Gd $408

MARK X CAVALIER..........NiB $460 Ex $355 Gd $260
Same specifications as Mark X Sporter except w/contemporary-style stock w/rollover cheekpiece, rosewood forend tip/grip cap, recoil pad. Intro. 1974; Disc.

MARK X CONTINENTAL MANNLICHER STYLE CARBINE ....NiB $643 Ex $412 Gd $277
Same specifications as Mark X Sporter except straight European-style comb stock w/sculptured cheekpiece. Precise double-set triggers and classic "butterknife" bolt handle. French checkering. Weight: 7.25 lbs. Disc.

MARK X LIGHTWEIGHT SPORTER ... NiB $445 Ex $355 Gd $260
Calibers: .22-250 Rem., .270 Win., 7mm Rem. Mag., .30-06 or 7mm Mag. Four- or 5-round magazine. 20-inch bbl. Synthenic Carbolite stock. Weight: 7 lbs. Imported from 1988-90. Reintro. 1994-97.

MARK X MARQUIS MANNLICHER-STYLE CARBINE ....NiB $575 Ex $408 Gd $290
Same specifications as Mark X Sporter except w/20-inch bbl., full-length Mannlicher-type stock w/metal forend/muzzle cap. Calibers: .270, 7x57, .308, .30-06. Imported 1976 to 1984.

MINI-MARK X BOLT-ACTION RIFLE... NiB $448 Ex $359 Gd $260
Miniature M98 Mauser action. Caliber: .223 Rem. Five round magazine. 20-inch bbl. 39.75 inches overall. Weight: 6.25 lbs. Adj. rear sight, hooded ramp front. Checkered hardwood stock. Imported from 1987 to 1994.

MARK X VISCOUNT........NiB $440 Ex $368 Gd $258
Same specifications as Mark X Sporter except w/plainer field grade stock. Imported from 1974 to 1987.

AFRICAN SERIES..........NiB $1035 Ex $603 Gd $422
Mauser-type bolt-action. Calibers: .375 H&H Mag., .458 Win. Mag. Three round magazine. 24-inch bbl. Weight: 8 lbs. Sights: 3-leaf express open rear, ramp front w/hood. English-style stock of European walnut, w/cheekpiece, black forend tip, checkered pistol grip and forearm, recoil pad, QD swivels. Imported from 1974 to 1996 by Whitworth Rifle Co., England.

ITALIAN MILITARY RIFLES — Italy
Manufactured by government plants at Brescia, Gardone, Terni, and Turin, Italy.

Italian Model 38 Military Rifle

Ithaca Model 49

Ithaca Model 49
Presentation

Ithaca Model 49R
Sporter

Ithaca Model 72
Saddlegun

Ithaca Model 72
Saddlegun Deluxe

Ithaca
Model LSA-65 Standard

RIFLES

**Ithaca
Model X5-T**

MODEL 38 MILITARY RIFLE. . . . NiB $167 Ex $120 Gd $85
Modification of Italian Model 1891 Mannlicher-Carcano Military Rifle w/turned-down bolt handle, detachable folding bayonet. Caliber: 7.35mm Italian Service (many arms of this model were later converted to the old 6.5mm caliber). Six round box magazine. 21.25-inch bbl. Weight: 7.5 lbs. Sights: Adj. rear-blade front. Military straight-grip stock. Adopted 1938.

ITHACA GUN COMPANY, INC. — King Ferry, New York

Formerly Ithaca, New York.

**MODEL 49 SADDLEGUN LEVER ACTION
SINGLE-SHOT RIFLE. . . . . NiB $166 Ex $135 Gd $96**
Martini-type action. Hand-operated rebounding hammer. Caliber: .22 LR, Long, Short. 18-inch bbl. Open sights. Western carbine-style stock. Weight: 5.5 lbs. Made from 1961 to 1978.

**MODEL 49 SADDLEGUN—
DELUXE . . . . NiB $220 Ex $167 Gd $121**
Same as standard Model 49 except w/gold-plated hammer and trigger, figured walnut stock, sling swivels. Made from 1962 to 1975.

**MODEL 49 SADDLEGUN—
MAGNUM. . . . . NiB $205 Ex $188 Gd $130**
Same as standard Model 49 except chambered for .22 WMR cartridge. Made from 1962 to 1978.

**MODEL 49 SADDLEGUN—
PRESENTATION . . . . NiB $333 Ex $239 Gd $166**
Same as standard Model 49 Saddlegun except w/gold-plated hammer and trigger, engraved receiver, full fancy-figured walnut stock w/gold nameplate. Available in .22 LR or .22 WMR. Made from 1962 to 1974.

**MODEL 49 SADDLEGUN—
ST. LOUIS BICENTENNIAL. . . . NiB $370 Ex $333 Gd $169**
Same as Model 49 Deluxe except w/commemorative inscription. 200 made in 1964. Top value is for rifle in new, unfired condition.

**MODEL 49R SADDLEGUN
REPEATING RIFLE. . . . . NiB $298 Ex $243 Gd $154**
Similar in appearance to Model 49 Single-Shot. Caliber: .22 LR, Long, Short. Tubular magazine holds 15 LR, 17 Long, 21 Short. 20-inch bbl. Weight: 5.5 lbs. Sights: Open rear-bead front. Western-style stock, checkered grip. Made from 1968 to 1971.

MODEL 49 YOUTH SADDLEGUN . . NiB $177 Ex $138 Gd $105
Same as standard Model 49 except shorter stock for young shooters. Made from 1961 to 1978.

REPEATING CARBINE. . . . . NiB $379 Ex $300 Gd $208
Caliber: .22 LR, Long, Short. Tubular magazine holds 15 LR, 17 Long, 21 Short. 18.5-inch bbl. Weight: 5.5 lbs. Sights: Open rear; hooded ramp front. Receiver grooved for scope mounting.

Western carbine stock and forearm of American walnut. Made 1973 to 1978.

**MODEL 72 SADDLEGUN—
DELUXE . . . . NiB $443 Ex $370 Gd $250**
Same as standard Model 72 except w/silver-finished and engraved receiver, octagon bbl., higher grade walnut stock and forearm. Made from 1974 to 1976.

**MODEL LSA-65 BOLT ACTION
STANDARD GRADE . . . . NiB $479 Ex $443 Gd $337**
Same as Model LSA-55 Standard Grade except calibers .25-06, .270, .30-06; 4-round magazine, 23-inch bbl., weight: 7 lbs. Made from 1969 to 1977.

MODEL LSA-65 DELUXE . . . . . NiB $590 Ex $531 Gd $355
Same as Model LSA-65 Standard Grade except w/special features of Model LSA-55 Deluxe. Made from 1969 to 1977.

**MODEL X5-C LIGHTNING
AUTOLOADER . . . . NiB $222 Ex $177 Gd $123**
Takedown. Caliber: .22 LR. Seven round clip magazine. 22-inch bbl. Weight: 6 lbs. Sights: Open rear; Ray-bar front. Pistol-grip stock, grooved forearm. Made from 1958 to 1964.

**MODEL X5-T LIGHTNING AUTOLOADER
TUBULAR REPEATING RIFLE . . NiB $222 Ex $177 Gd $123**
Same as Model X5-C except w/16-round tubular magazine, stock w/plain forearm.

**MODEL X-15 LIGHTNING
AUTOLOADER . . . . NiB $222 Ex $177 Gd $123**
Same general specifications as Model X5-C except forend is not grooved. Made from 1964 to 1967.

**BSA CF-2 BOLT-ACTION REPEATING
RIFLE. . . . . NiB $510 Ex $370 Gd $277**
Mauser-type action. Calibers: 7mm Rem. Mag., .300 Win. Mag. Three round magazine. 23.6-inch bbl. Weight: 8 lbs. Sights: Adj. rear; hooded ramp front. Checkered walnut stock w/Monte Carlo comb, rollover cheekpiece, rosewood forend tip, recoil pad, sling swivels. Imported from 1976 to 1977. Mfd. by BSA Guns Ltd., Birmingham, England.

JAPANESE MILITARY RIFLES — Tokyo, Japan
Manufactured by government plant.

MODEL 38 ARISAKA SERVICE RIFLE. . . NiB $656 Ex $390 Gd $220
Mauser-type bolt action. Caliber: 6.5mm Japanese. Five round box magazine. Bbl. lengths: 25.38 and 31.25 inches. Weight: 9.25 lbs. w/long bbl. Sights: fixed front, adj. rear. Military-type full stock. Adopted in 1905, the 38th year of the Meiji reign hence, the designation "Model 38."

MODEL 38 ARISAKA CARBINE . . . NiB $656 Ex $390 Gd $220
Same general specifications as Model 38 Rifle except w/19-inch bbl., heavy folding bayonet, weight 7.25 lbs.

MODEL 44 CAVALRY CARBINE . . . NiB $1190 Ex $690 Gd $355
Same general specifications as Model 38 Rifle except w/19-inch bbl., heavy folding bayonet, weight 8.5 lbs. Adopted in 1911, the 44th year of the Meiji reign, hence the designation, "Model 44."

Ithaca
Model X-15

Ithaca
BSA CF-2

Johnson Model 1941

Johnson Sporting Rifle

Iver Johnson Model M-1

Iver Johnson Model SC30FS

Iver Johnson Survival
Semiautomatic Carbine

Iver Johnson Trailblazer

MODEL 99 SERVICE RIFLE . . . . NiB $577 Ex $255 Gd $200
Modified Model 38. Caliber: 7.7mm Japanese. Five round box magazine. 25.75-inch bbl. Weight: 8.75 lbs. Sights: Fixed front; adj. aperture rear; anti-aircraft sighting bars on some early models; fixed rear sight on some late WWII rifles. Military-type full stock, may have bipod. Takedown paratroop model was also made during WWII. Adopted in 1939, (Japanese year 2599) from which the designation "Model 99" is taken. Note: The last Model 99 rifles made were of poor quality; some with cast steel receivers. Value shown is for earlier type.
Sniper Rifle (with 4x scope) NiB $3900 Ex $3431 Gd $1817

JARRETT CUSTOM RIFLES — Jackson, SC

**MODEL NO. 2 WALK ABOUT
BOLT-ACTION RIFLE. . . . . . NiB $4788 Ex $3077 Gd $2043**
Custom lightweight rifle built on Remington M707 action. Jarrett match- grade barrel cut and chambered to customer's specification in short action calibers only. McMillan fiberglass stock pillar-bedded to action. Made 1995 to 2003.

**MODEL NO. 3 CUSTOM
BOLT-ACTION RIFLE. . . . . . NiB $4800 Ex $3147 Gd $2090**
Custom rifle built on Remington M707 action. Jarrett match grade barrel cut and chambered to customer's specification. McMillan classic fiberglass stock pillar-bedded to action and finished to customer's preference. Made from 1989 to date.

**MODEL NO. 4 PROFESSIONAL HUNTER
BOLT-ACTION RIFLE. . . . . . NiB $6988 Ex $5876 Gd $4490**
Custom magnum rifle built on Winchester M70 "controlled feed" action. Jarrett match grade barrel cut and chambered to customer's specification in magnum calibers only. Quarter rib w/iron sights and two Leupold scopes w/Q-D rings and mounts. McMillan classic fiberglass stock fitted and finished to customer's preference.

JOHNSON AUTOMATICS, INC. — Providence, Rhode Island

**MODEL 1941 SEMIAUTO MILITARY
RIFLE. . . . . NiB $7433 Ex $5740 Gd $3328**
Short-recoil operated. Removable, air-cooled, 22-inch bbl. Caliber: .30-06, 7mm Mauser. 10-round rotary magazine. Two-piece wood stock, pistol grip, perforated metal radiator sleeve over rear half of bbl. Sights: Receiver peep; protected post front. Weight: 9.5 lbs. Note: The Johnson M/1941 was adopted by the Netherlands government in 1940-41 and the major portion of the production of this rifle, 1941-43, was on Dutch orders. A quantity was also bought by the U.S. government for use by Marine Corps parachute troops (1943) and for Lend Lease. All these rifles were caliber .30-06; the 7mm Johnson rifles were made for the South American government.

**SPORTING RIFLE
PROTOTYPE . . . . NiB $14,000 Ex $11,500 Gd $7595**
Same general specifications as military rifle except fitted w/ sporting stock, checkered grip and forend. Blade front sight; receiver peep sight. Less than a dozen made prior to World War II.

IVER JOHNSON ARMS, INC. — Jacksonville, Arkansas
(formerly of Fitchburg, Massachusetts, and Middlesex, New Jersey)

**LI'L CHAMP BOLT-ACTION
RIFLE . . . . .NiB $227 Ex $146 Gd $90**
Caliber: .22 Short, Long, LR. Single-shot. 16.25-inch bbl. 32.5 inches overall. Weight: 3.25 lbs. Adj. rear sight, blade front. Synthetic composition stock. Made from 1986 to 1988.

MODEL M-1 SEMIAUTOMATIC CARBINE
Similar to U.S. M-1 Carbine. Calibers: 9mm Parabellum 30 U.S. Carbine. 15- or 30-round magazine. 18-inch bbl. 35.5 inches overall. Weight: 6.5 lbs. Sights: blade front, w/guards; adj. peep rear. Walnut, hardwood or collapsible wire stock. Parkerized finish.
(30 cal. w/hardwood) . . . . NiB $460 Ex $340 Gd $220
(30 cal. w/walnut) . . . . NiB $506 Ex $374 Gd $242
(30 cal. w/wire) . . . . NiB $469 Ex $388 Gd $222
5.7mm or 9mm, add. 30%

**MODEL PM.30 SEMIAUTOMATIC
CARBINE. . . . . NiB $413 Ex $320 Gd $190**
Similar to U.S. Carbine, Cal. 30 M1. 18-inch bbl. Weight: 5.5 lbs. 15- or 30-round detachable magazine. Both hardwood and walnut stock.

**MODEL SC30FS SEMIAUTOMATIC
CARBINE. . . . . NiB $466 Ex $390 Gd $233**
Similar to Survival Carbine except w/folding stock. Made from 1983 to 1989.

**SURVIVAL SEMIAUTOMATIC
CARBINE . . . . NiB $433 Ex $399 Gd $230**
Similar to Model PM.30 except in stainless steel. Made from 1983 to 1989. W/folding high-impact plastic stock add $35.

**TRAILBLAZER SEMIAUTO
RIFLE. . . . . NiB $277 Ex $160 Gd $126**
Caliber: .22 LR. 18-inch bbl. Weight: 5.5 lbs. Sights: Open rear, blade front. Hardwood stock. Made from 1983 to 1985.

MODEL X BOLT-ACTION RIFLE . . . NiB $270 Ex $189 Gd $115
Takedown, Single-shot. Caliber: .22 Short, Long and LR. 22-inch bbl. Weight: 4 lbs. Sights: Open rear; blade front. Pistol-grip stock w/knob forend tip. Made from 1928 to 1932.

MODEL XX (2X) . . . . NiB $323 Ex $170 Gd $100
Improved version of Model X w/heavier 24-inch bbl. larger stock (w/o knob tip), weight: 4.5 lbs. Made from 1932 to 1955.

K.B.I., INC. — Harrisburg, Pennsylvania

See listing under Armscor; Charles Daly; FEG; Liberty and I.M.I.

SUPER CLASSIC
Calibers: .22 LR, .22 Mag., RF, .22 Hornet. Five- or 10-round capacity. Bolt and semiauto action. 22.6- or 20.75-inch bbl. 41.25 or 40.5 inches overall. Weight: 6.4 to 6.7 lbs. Blue finish. Oil-finished American walnut stock w/hardwood grip cap and forend tip. Checkered Monte Carlo comb and cheekpiece. High polish blued barreled action w/damascened bolt. Dovetailed receiver and iron sights. Recoil pad. QD swivel posts.
M-1500 SC, .22 LR . . . . NiB $482 Ex $223 Gd $170
M-1500SC, .22 WMR . . . . NiB $289 Ex $233 Gd $177
M-1800-S, .22 Hornet. . . . . NiB $455 Ex $380 Gd $256
M-2000 SC, semiauto, .22 LR . . NiB $290 Ex $244 Gd $179

Iver Johnson Model XX (2X) Bolt-Action Rifle

Kel-Tec
Sub-Series Semiautomatic Rifles
shown expanded and folded

K.D.F. INC. — Sequin, Texas

MODEL K15 BOLT-ACTION RIFLE
Calibers: (Standard) .22-250, .243 Win., 6mm Rem., .25-06, .270 Win., .280 Rem., 7mm Mag., .30-60; (Magnum) .300 Wby., .300 Win., .338 Win., .340 Wby., .375 H&H, .411 KDF, .416 Rem., .458 Win. Four round magazine (standard), 3-shot (magnum). 22-inch (standard) or 24-inch (magnum) bbl. 44.5 to 46.5 inches overall. Weight: 8 lbs. Sights optional. Kevlar composite or checkered walnut stock in Classic, European or thumbhole-style. Note: U.S. Manufacture limited to 25 prototypes and pre-production variations.
Standard model. . . . . NiB $1796 Ex $1721 Gd $977
Magnum model. . . . . NiB $1834 Ex $1597 Gd $1106

KEL-TEC CNC INDUSTRIES, INC. — Cocoa, FL

SUB-SERIES SEMIAUTOMATIC RIFLES
Semiautomatic blow-back action w/pivoting bbl., takedown. 9mm Parabellum or 40 S&W. Interchangeable grip assembly accepts most double column, high capacity handgun magazines. 16.1-inch bbl. 31.5 inches overall. Weight: 4.6 lbs. Hooded post front sight, flip-up rear. Matte black finish. Tubular buttstock w/grooved polymer buttplate and vented handguard. Made from 1997 to 2000.
Sub-9 model (9mm) . . . . NiB $395 Ex $333 Gd $265
Sub-40 model (.40 S&W) . . . . . NiB $395 Ex $333 Gd $265

SUB-2000 . . . . NiB $380 Ex $300 Gd $200
Similar to Sub-9 and Sub-40. Accepts Glock, Beretta, S&W or SIG pistol magazines. Made 2001 to date.

SU-16A . . . . NiB $640 Ex $500 Gd $360
Semi-automatic w/pivoting bbl. Caliber: 5.56 NATO. Compatibale with AR-style magazines. 16- or 18.5-inch bbl. Weight: 4.7 lbs. Matte black, OD green or tan finish. Polymer stock. Made from 2003 to date.

KIMBER MANUFACTURING, INC. — Elmsford, NY

Manufactured by Kimber Manufacturing, Inc., Yonkers, NY, formerly Kimber of America, Inc.; Kimber of Oregon, Inc.

Note: *From 1980-91, Kimber of Oregon produced Kimber firearms. A redesigned action designated by serialization with a "B" suffix was introduced 1986. Pre-1986 production is recognized as the "A" series but is not so marked. These early models in rare configurations and limited-run calibers command premium prices from collectors. Kimber of America, in Clackamas, Oregon, acquired the Kimber trademark and resumed manufactured of Kimber rifles. During this transition, Nationwide Sports Distributors, Inc. in Pennsylvania and Nevada became exclusive distributors of Kimber products. In 1997, Kimber Manufacturing acquired the trademark with manufacturing rights and expanded production to include a 1911-A1-style semiautomatic pistol, the Kimber Classic 45. Rifle production resumed in late 1998 with the announcement of an all-new Kimber .22 rifle and a refined Model 84 in both single-shot and repeater configurations.*

MODEL 82 BOLT-ACTION RIFLE
Small action based on Kimber's "A" Model 82 rimfire receiver w/ twin rear locking lugs. Calibers: .22 LR, .22 WRF, .22 Hornet, .218 Bee, .25-20. 5- or 10-round magazine (.22 LR); 5-round magazine (22WRF); 3-round magazine (.22 Hornet). .218 Bee and .25-20 are single-shot. 18- to 25-inch bbl. 37.63 to 42.5 inches overall. Weight: 6 lbs. (Light Sporter), 6.5 lbs. (Sporter), 7.5 lbs. (Varmint); 10.75 lbs. (Target). Right- and left-hand actions are available in distinctive stock styles.
Cascade (disc. 1987). . . . . NiB $890 Ex $674 Gd $388
Classic (disc. 1988). . . . . NiB $885 Ex $674 Gd $388
Continental . . . . NiB $1482 Ex $1197 Gd $823
Custom Classic (disc. 1988) . . NiB $1041 Ex $833 Gd $579
Mini Classic . . . . NiB $679 Ex $555 Gd $389
Super America . . . . NiB $1307 Ex $1165 Gd $909

Kimber Model 82 Rimfire Classic

Kimber Model 82C Rimfire Classic

Kimber Model 84 Classic

Super Continental.........NiB $2220 Ex $1390 Gd $925
All-American Match.......NiB $1978 Ex $1165 Gd $789
Deluxe Grade (disc. 1990)..NiB $1388 Ex $1097 Gd $898
Hunter (w/laminated stock) ...NiB $912 Ex $833 Gd $523
Government Target.........NiB $660 Ex $550 Gd $330

MODEL 82C CLASSIC BOLT-ACTION RIFLE
Caliber: .22 LR. Four- or 10-round magazine. 21-inch air-gauged bbl. 40.5 inches overall. Weight: 6.5 lbs. Receiver drilled and tapped for Warne scope mounts; no sights. Single-set trigger. Checkered Claro walnut stock w/red buttpad and polished steel grip cap. Reintroduced 1993.
Classic model..............NiB $833 Ex $688 Gd $495
Left-hand model, add.........................$100

MODEL 84 BOLT-ACTION RIFLE
Classic (disc. 1988) Compact-medium action based on a scaled-down Mauser-type receiver, designed to accept small base centerfire cartridges. Calibers: .17 Rem., .221 Fireball, .222 Rem., .223 Rem. Five round magazine. Same general barrel and stock specifications as Model 82.
Classic (disc. 1988)........NiB $1100 Ex $821 Gd $577
Continental ....NiB $1400 Ex $1098 Gd $769
Custom Classic (disc. 1988) ..NiB $1410 Ex $978 Gd $713
Super America (disc. 1988)..NiB $1925 Ex $1078 Gd $757
Super Continental I
(disc. 1988)...........NiB $2100 Ex $1170 Gd $844
1990 Classifications
Deluxe Grade (disc. 1990).. NiB $1310 Ex $1044 Gd $733
Hunter/Sporter (laminated stock)...NiB $1010 Ex $943 Gd $665
Super America (disc. 1991)..NiB $1988 Ex $1146 Gd $825
Super Varmint (disc. 1991) ..NiB $1137 Ex $1187 Gd $825
Ultra Varmint (disc. 1991) ..NiB $1189 Ex $1123 Gd $779

MODEL 89 BGR (BIG GAME RIFLE)
Large action combining the best features of the pre-64 Model 70 Winchester and the Mauser 98. Three action lengths are offered in three stock styles. Calibers: .257 Roberts, .25-06, 7x57, .270 Win., .280 Win., .30-06, 7mm Rem. Mag., .300 Win. Mag., .300 H&H, .338 Win., 35 Whelen, .375 H&H, .404 Jeffrey, .416 Rigby, .460 Wby., .505 Gibbs (.308 cartridge family to follow). Five round magazine (standard calibers); 3-round magazine (Magnum calibers). 22- to 24-inch bbl. 42 to 44 inches overall. Weight: 7.5 to 10.5 lbs. Model 89 African features express sights on contoured quarter rib, banded front sight. Barrel-mounted recoil lug w/integral receiver lug and twin recoil crosspins in stock.
BGR Long Action Classic
(disc. 1988)...............NiB $944 Ex $844 Gd $588
Custom Classic (disc. 1988)...NiB $1288 Ex $1044 Gd $745
Super America ....NiB $1548 Ex $1270 Gd $926
1990 Classifications Deluxe Grade:
Featherweight ....NiB $1995 Ex $1490 Gd $1044
Medium................NiB $1866 Ex $1566 Gd $1135
.375 H&H..............NiB $1956 Ex $1577 Gd $1145
Hunter Grade (laminated stock)
.270 and .30-06........NiB $1370 Ex $1105 Gd $800
.375 H&H...............NiB $1676 Ex $1356 Gd $944
Super America: Featherweight ...NiB $2088 Ex $1703 Gd $1213
Medium.................NiB $2189 Ex $1760 Gd $1217
.375 H&H..............NiB $2788 Ex $2274 Gd $1590
African — All calibers.....NiB $5635 Ex $3955 Gd $2766

KNIGHT'S ARMAMENT COMPANY — Titusville, FL,

Formerly, Vero Beach, FL.

SR-15 SEMIAUTOMATIC MATCH
RIFLE.................NiB $1733 Ex $1544 Gd $1103
AR-15 configuration. Caliber: .223 Rem. (5.56mm). Five- or 10-round magazine. 20-inch w/free-floating, match-grade bbl., 38 inches overall. Weight: 7.9 lbs. Integral Weaver-style rail. Two-stage target trigger. Matte black oxide finish. Black synthetic AR-15A2-style stock and forearm. Made from 1997 to 2008.

SR-15 M-4 SEMIAUTOMATIC CARBINE
Similar to SR-15 rifle except w/16-inch bbl. Sights and mounts optional. Fixed synthetic or collapsible buttstock. Made from 1997 to 2008.
Model SR-15 Carbine
(w/collapsible stock)....NiB $1520 Ex $1388 Gd $1077

Kimber Model 89 Big Game 375 Caliber

Kimber Model 89 Big Game 375 H&H Caliber

SR-15 M-5
SEMIAUTOMATIC RIFLE. . . NiB $1765 Ex $1488 Gd $1165
Caliber: .223 Rem. (5.56mm). Five- or 10-round magazine. 20-inch bbl. 38 inches overall. Weight: 7.6 lbs. Integral Weaver-style rail. Two-stage target trigger. Matte black oxide finish. Black synthetic AR-15A2-style stock and forearm. Made from 1997 to 2008.

SR-25 MATCH RIFLE
Similar to SR-25 Sporter except w/free floating 20- or 24-inch match bbl. 39.5-43.5 inches overall. Weight: 9.25 and 10.75 lbs., respectively. Integral Weaver-style rail. Sights and mounts optional. 1 MOA guaranteed. Made from 1993 to 2008.
Model SR-25 LW Match
  (w/20-inch bbl.) . . . . NiB $5744 Ex $3289 Gd $2665
W/RAS (Rail Adapter System), add $350

SR-25 SEMIAUTOMATIC CARBINE
Similar to SR-25 Sporter except w/free floating 16-inch bbl. 35.75 inches overall. Weight: 7.75 lbs. Integral Weaver-style rail. Sights and mounts optional. Made from 1995 to 2008.
Model SR-25 Carbine (w/o sights) . . . NiB $6000 Ex $3927 Gd $1949
w/RAS (Rail Adapter System), add $300

SR-25 SEMIAUTOMATIC SPORTER
RIFLE. . . . . NiB $2784 Ex $2409 Gd $1709
AR-15 configuration. Caliber: .308 Win. (7.62 NATO). Five, 10- or 20-round magazine. 20-inch bbl. 39.5 inches overall. Weight: 8.75 lbs. Integral Weaver-style rail. Protected post front sight adjustable for elevation, detachable rear adjustable for windage. Two-stage target trigger. Matte black oxide finish. Black synthetic AR-15A2-style stock and forearm. Made from 1993 to 1997.

SR-50 SEMIAUTOMATIC LONG RANGE
PRECISION RIFLE . . . . NiB $6833 Ex $6096 Gd $3597
Gas-operated semiautomatic action. Caliber: .50 BMG. 10-round magazine. 35.5-inch bbl. 58.5 inches overall. Weight: 31.75 lbs. Integral Weaver-style rail. Two-stage target trigger. Matte black oxide finish. Tubular-style stock. Limited production from 1996 to 2008.

KONGSBERG — Kongsberg, Norway
Imported by Kongsberg America L.L.C., Fairfield, CT.

MODEL 393 CLASSIC SPORTER
Calibers: .22-250 Rem., .243 Win., 6.5x55, .270 Win., 7mm Rem. Mag., .30-06, .308 Win. .300 Win. Mag., .338 Win. Mag. Three-

or 4-round rotary magazine. 23-inch bbl. (Standard) or 26-inch bbl. (magnum). Weight: 7.5 to 8 lbs. 44 to 47 inches overall. No sights w/ dovetailed receiver or optional hooded blade front sight, adjustable rear. Blue finish. Checkered European walnut stock w/ rubber buttplate. Imported from 1994 to 1998.
Standard calibers . . . . NiB $957 Ex $779 Gd $597
Magnum calibers . . . . NiB $1289 Ex $1100 Gd $800
Left-hand model, add $150
w/optional sights, add. $75

MODEL 393 DELUXE SPORTER
Similar to Classic Model except w/deluxe European walnut stock. Imported from 1994 to 1998.
Standard calibers . . . . NiB $1017 Ex $909 Gd $599
Magnum calibers . . . . NiB $1347 Ex $1117 Gd $809
Left-hand model, add $150
w/optional sights, add. $75

MODEL 393 THUMBHOLE SPORTER
Calibers: 22-250 Rem. or 308 Win. Four round rotary magazine. 23-inch heavy bbl. Weight: 8.5 lbs. 44 inches overall. No sights, dovetailed receiver. Blue finish. Stippled American walnut thumbhole stock w/adjustable cheekpiece. Imported from 1993 to 1998.
Right-hand model . . . . NiB $1453 Ex $1347 Gd $650
Left-hand model . . . . NiB $1533 Ex $1377 Gd $800

KRICO — Stuttgart-Hedelfingen, Germany
Manufactured by Sportwaffenfabrik, Kriegeskorte GmbH; imported by Northeast Arms, LLC, Ft. Fairfield, Maine; previously by Beeman Precision Arms, Inc. and Mandell Shooting Supplies.

MODEL 260
SEMIAUTOMATIC RIFLE. . . . . . NiB $744 Ex $656 Gd $459
Caliber: .22 LR. 10-round magazine. 20-inch bbl. 38.9 inches overall. Weight: 6.6 lbs. Hooded blade front sight; adj. rear. Grooved receiver. Beech stock. Blued finish. Introduced 1989. Disc.

MODEL 300 BOLT-ACTION RIFLE
Calibers: .22 LR. .22 WMR, .22 Hornet. 19.6-inch bbl. (22 LR), 23.6-inch (22 Hornet). 38.5 inches overall. Weight: 6.3 lbs. Double-set triggers. Sights: Ramped blade front, adj. open rear. Checkered walnut-finished hardwood stock. Blued finish. Introduced 1989. Disc.
Model 300 Standard . . . . NiB $735 Ex $568 Gd $445
Model 300 Deluxe . . . . NiB $779 Ex $589 Gd $455
Model 300 SA (Monte Carlo walnut
  stock) . . . . NiB $897 Ex $744 Gd $553
Model 300 Stutzen (full-length walnut
  stock) . . . . NiB $1023 Ex $864 Gd $654

Krico Model 400

MODEL 311 SMALL-BORE RIFLE
Bolt action. Caliber: .22 LR. 5- or 10-rnd. clip magazine. 22-in. bbl. Weight: 6 lbs. Single- or double-set trigger. Sights: Open rear; hooded ramp front; available w/factory-fitted Kaps 2.5x scope. Checkered stock w/cheekpiece, pistol-grip and swivels. Disc. 1962.
w/scope sight . . . . NiB $376 Ex $347 Gd $233
w/iron sights only . . . . NiB $355 Ex $333 Gd $270

MODEL 320 BOLT-ACTION
SPORTER. . . . . NiB $920 Ex $622 Gd $423
Caliber: .22 LR. Five round detachable box magazine. 19.5-inch bbl. 38.5 inches overall. Weight: 6 lbs. Adj. rear sight, blade ramp front. Checkered European walnut Mannlicher-style stock w/low comb and cheekpiece. Single or double-set triggers. Imported from 1986 to 1988.

MODEL 340 METALLIC SILHOUETTE
BOLT-ACTION RIFLE. . . . . NiB $788 Ex $658 Gd $466
Caliber: .22 LR. Five round magazine. 21-inch heavy, bull bbl. 39.5 inches overall. Weight: 7.5 lbs. No sights. Grooved receiver for scope mounts. European walnut stock in off-hand, match-style configuration. Match or double-set triggers. Imported from 1983 to 1988. Disc.

MODEL 360S BIATHLON
RIFLE . . . . NiB $1455 Ex $1188 Gd $687
Caliber: .22 LR. Five 5-round magazines. 21.25-inch bbl. w/snow cap. 40.5 inches overall. Weight: 9.25 lbs. Straight-pull action. Match trigger w/17-oz. pull. Sights: Globe front, adj. match peep rear. Biathlon-style walnut stock w/high comb and adj. butt-plate. Imported from 1991. Disc.

MODEL 360 S2 BIATHLON
RIFLE. NiB $1423 Ex $1189 Gd $655
Similar to Model 360S except w/pistol-grip activated action. Biathlon-style walnut stock w/black epoxy finish. Imported from 1991. Disc.

MODEL 400 BOLT-ACTION
RIFLE. NiB $889 Ex $766 Gd $544
Caliber: .22 Hornet. Five round detachable box magazine. 23.5-inch bbl. Weight: 6.75 lbs. Adj. open rear sight, ramp front. European walnut stock. Disc. 1990.

MODEL 420 BOLT-ACTION
RIFLE. NiB $1043 Ex $833 Gd $568
Same as Model 400 except w/full-length Mannlicher-style stock and double-set triggers. Scope optional, extra. Disc. 1989.

MODEL 440 S BOLT-ACTION
RIFLE . . . . NiB $889 Ex $745 Gd $540
Caliber: .22 Hornet. Detachable box magazine. 20-inch bbl. 36.5 inches overall. Weight: 7.5 lbs. No sights. French walnut stock w/ventilated forend. Disc. 1988.

MODEL 500 MATCH RIFLE NiB $3633 Ex $2988 Gd $1077
Caliber: .22 LR. Single-shot. 23.6-inch bbl. 42 inches overall. Weight: 9.4 lbs. Kricotronic electronic ignition system. Sights: Globe front; match micrometer aperture rear. Match-style European walnut stock w/adj. butt.

MODEL 600 BOLT-ACTION
RIFLE. . . . . NiB $1177 Ex $1055 Gd $733
Same general specifications as Model 707 except w/short action. Calibers: .17 Rem., .222, .223, .22-250, .243, 5.6x50 Mag. and 308. Introduced 1983. Disc.

MODEL 620 BOLT-ACTION
RIFLE. . . . . NiB $1206 Ex $1119 Gd $726
Same as Model 600 except w/short-action-chambered for .308 Win. only and full-length Mannlicher-style stock w/Schnabel forend tip. 20.75-inch bbl. Weight: 6.5 lbs. No longer imported.

MODEL 640 SUPER SNIPER BOLT-ACTION
REPEATING RIFLE. . . . . NiB $1863 Ex $1277 Gd $905
Calibers: .223 Rem., .308 Win. Three round magazine. 26-inch bbl. 44.25 inches overall. Weight: 9.5 lbs. No sights drilled and tapped for scope mounts. Single or double-set triggers. Select walnut stock w/adj. cheekpiece and recoil pad. Disc. 1989.

MODEL 640 VARMINT RIFLE . . NiB $997 Ex $844 Gd $638
Caliber: .222 Rem. Four round magazine. 23.75-inch bbl. Weight: 9.5 lbs. No sights. European walnut stock. No longer imported.

MODEL 707 BOLT-ACTION RIFLE
Calibers: .17 Rem., .222, .222 Rem. Mag., .223, .22-250, 5.6x50 Mag., .243, 5.6x57 RSW, 6x62, 6.5x55, 6.5x57, 6.5x68 .270 Win., 7x64, 7.5 Swiss, 7mm Mag., .30-06, .300 Win., 8x68S, 9.3x64. 24-inch (standard) or 26-inch (magnum) bbl. 44 inches overall (standard). Weight: 7.5 lbs. Adj. rear sight; hooded ramp front. Checkered European-style walnut stock w/Bavarian cheekpiece and rosewood Schnabel forend tip. Imported from 1983 to date.
Hunter . . . . NiB $1146 Ex $896 Gd $790
Deluxe . . . . NiB $1244 Ex $1043 Gd $733
Deluxe R. . . . . NiB $1096 Ex $790 Gd $695
Deluxe Stutzen . . . . NiB $1290 Ex $770 Gd $655

MODEL 720 BOLT-ACTION RIFLE
Same general specifications as Model 707 except in calibers .270 Win. and .30-06 w/full-length Mannlicher-style stock and Schnabel forend tip. 20.75-inch bbl. Weight: 6.75 lbs. Disc. importing 1990.
Sporter Model . . . . NiB $1144 Ex $1043 Gd $728
Ltd. Edition . . . . NiB $2419 Ex $2179 Gd $1188

BOLT-ACTION SPORTING
RIFLE . . . . NiB $733 Ex $634 Gd $438
Miniature Mauser action. Single- or double-set trigger. Calibers: .22 Hornet, .222 Rem. Four round clip magazine. 22-24- or 26-inch bbl. Weight: 6.25 lbs. Sights: Open rear; hooded ramp front. Checkered stock w/cheekpiece, pistol-grip, black forend tip, sling swivels. Imported from 1956 to 1962. Disc.

CARBINE . . . . NiB $743 Ex $637 Gd $440
Same as Krico Sporting Rifle except w/20- or 22-inch bbl., full-length Mannlicher-type stock. Disc. 1962.

SPECIAL VARMINT RIFLE . . . . . NiB $743 Ex $637 Gd $440
Same as Krico Rifle except w/heavy bbl., no sights, weight: 7.25 lbs. Caliber: .222 Rem. only. Disc. 1962.

Krico Model 420

Krico 640 Varmint

Krieghoff Teck Boxlock Over/Under

Krieghoff Teck Sidelock Over/Under

Lakefield Model 64B

Lakefield Model 92S Target

RIFLES

KRIEGHOFF — Ulm (Donau), Germany

Manufactured by H. Krieghoff Jagd und Sportwaffenfabrik. See also Combination Guns under Krieghoff shotgun listings.

TECK OVER/UNDER RIFLE
Kersten action, double crossbolt, double underlugs. Boxlock. Calibers: 7x57r5, 7x64, 7x65r5, .30-30, .308 Win. .30-06, .300 Win. Mag., 9.3x74r5, .375 H&H Mag. .458 Win. Mag. 25-inch bbls. Weight: 8 to 9.5 lbs. Sights: Express rear; ramp front. Checkered walnut stock and forearm. Made from 1967. Disc.
Standard calibers . . . . NiB $8843 Ex $6953 Gd $5442
.375 H&H Mag. (Disc. 1988) and
  .458 Win. Mag . . . . NiB $10650 Ex $7566 Gd $6831

ULM OVER/ UNDER
RIFLE. . . . . NiB $14,790 Ex $11,110 Gd $6990
Same general specifications as Teck model except w/sidelocks w/leaf Arabesque engraving. Made from 1963. Disc.

ULM-PRIMUS OVER/UNDER
RIFLE. . . . . NiB $20,244 Ex $16,277 Gd $10,550
Delux version of Ulm model, w/detachable sidelocks, higher grade engraving and stock wood. Made from 1963. Disc.

LAKEFIELD ARMS LTD. — Ontario, Canada

See also listing under Savage for production since 1994.

MODEL 64B SEMIAUTOMATIC
RIFLE. . . . . NiB $150 Ex $110 Gd $85
Caliber: .22 LR. 10-round magazine. 20-inch bbl. Weight: 5.5 lbs. 40 inches overall. Bead front sight, adj. rear. Grooved receiver for scope mounts. Stamped checkering on walnut-finished hardwood stock w/Monte Carlo cheekpiece. Imported from 1990 to 1994.

MODEL 90B BOLT-ACTION
TARGET RIFLE. . . . . NiB $476 Ex $359 Gd $232
Caliber: .22 LR. Five round magazine. 21-inch bbl. w/snow cap. 39.63 inches overall. Weight: 8.25 lbs. Adj. receiver peep sight; globe front w/colored inserts. Receiver drilled and tapped for scope mounts. Biathlon-style natural finished hardwood stock w/shooting rails, hand stop and butthook. Made from 1991 to 1994.

MODEL 91T/91TR BOLT-ACTION TARGET RIFLE
Calibers: .22 Short, Long, LR. 25-inch bbl. 43.63 inches overall. Weight: 8 lbs. Adj. rear peep sight; globe front w/inserts. Receiver drilled and tapped for scope mounts. Walnut-finished hardwood stock w/shooting rails and hand stop. Model 91TR is a 5-round clip-fed repeater. Made from 1991 to 1994.
Model 91T single-shot. . . . . NiB $378 Ex $299 Gd $148
Model 91TR repeater (.22 LR only)NiB $416 Ex $266 Gd $171

MODEL 92S TARGET RIFLE . . . NiB $300 Ex $257 Gd $184
Same general specifications as Model 90B except w/conventional target-style stock. 8 lbs. No sights, but drilled and tapped for scope mounts. Made from 1993 to 1995.

MODEL 93M BOLT ACTION . . NiB $188 Ex $157 Gd $110
Caliber: .22 WMR. 5-rnd. magazine. 20.75-inch bbl. 39.5 inches overall. Weight: 5.75 lbs. Bead front sight, adj. open rear. Receiver grooved for scope mount. Thumb-operated rotary safety. Checkered walnut-finished hardwood stock. Blued finish. Made in 1995.

MARK I BOLT-ACTION RIFLE. . . . NiB $133 Ex $98 Gd $77
Calibers: .22 Short, Long, LR. Single-shot. 20.5-inch bbl. (19-inch Youth Model); available in smoothbore. Weight: 5.5 lbs. 39.5 inches overall. Bead front sight; adj. rear. Grooved receiver for scope mounts. Checkered walnut-finished hardwood stock w/Monte Carlo and pistol-grip. Blued finish. Made from 1990 to 1994.

MARK II BOLT-ACTION RIFLE
Same general specifications as Mark I except has repeating action w/10-round detachable box magazine. .22 LR. only. Made 1992 to 1994.
Mark II standard model . . . . NiB $137 Ex $120 Gd $80
Mark II Youth model
  (w/19-inch bbl.) . . . . NiB $132 Ex $111 Gd $83
Mark II left-hand model . . . . . . NiB $169 Ex $137 Gd $100

L.A.R. MANUFACTURING, INC. — West Jordan, Utah

BIG BOAR COMPETITOR BOLT-ACTION
RIFLE. . . . . NiB $2230 Ex $1966 Gd $1429
Single-shot, bull-pup action. Caliber: .50 BMG. 36-inch bbl. 45.5 inches overall. Weight: 28.4 lbs. Made from 1994 to date.

LAURONA — Eibar, Spain

Manufactured in Eibar, Spain; imported by Galaxy Imports, Victoria, TX.

MODEL 2000X O/U EXPRESS RIFLE
Calibers: .30-06, 8x57 JRS, 8x75 JR, .375 H&H, 9.3x74R Five round magazine. 24-inch separated bbls. Weight: 8.5 lbs. Quarter rib drilled and tapped for scope mount. Open sights. Matte black chrome finish. Monte Carlo-style checkered walnut buttstock; tulip forearm. Custom orders only. Imported from 1993 to date.
Standard calibers . . . . NiB $3166 Ex $2480 Gd $1723
Magnum calibers . . . . NiB $3790 Ex $3044 Gd 2133

LUNA — Mehlis, Germany

Manufactured by Ernst Friedr. Büchel.

SINGLE-SHOT TARGET RIFLE NiB $1043 Ex $788 Gd $558
Falling block action. Calibers: .22 LR. .22 Hornet. 29-inch bbl. Weight: 8.25 lbs. Sights: Micrometer peep rear tang; open rear; ramp front. Cheekpiece stock w/full pistol-grip, semibeavertail forearm, checkered, swivels. Made before WWII.

MAGNUM RESEARCH, INC. — Minneapolis, Minnesota

MOUNTAIN EAGLE BOLT-ACTION RIFLE SERIES
Calibers: .222 Rem., .223 Rem., .270 Win., .280 Rem., 7mm Rem. Mag., 7mm STW, .30-06, .300 Win. Mag., .338 Win. Mag., .340 Wby. Mag., .375 H&H, .416 Rem. Mag. Five round (std.) or 4-round (Mag.). 24- or 26-inch bbl. 44 to 46 inches overall. Weight: 7.75 to 9.75 lbs. Receiver drilled and tapped for scope mount; no sights. Blued finish. Fiberglass composite stock. Made from 1994 to 2000.
Standard model. . . . . NiB $1379 Ex $1209 Gd $744
Magnum model. . . . . NiB $1997 Ex $1202 Gd $931
Varmint model (Intro. 1996) NiB $1498 Ex $1216 Gd $938
Calibers .375 H&H, .416 Rem. Mag., add $325
Left-hand model, add $110

Magnum Research Mountain Eagle Bolt-Action Rifle

Mannlicher Model L Rifle

Mannlicher Model M Carbine

Mannlicher Model M Professional

MAGTECH — Las Vegas, Nevada

Manufactured by CBC, Brazil.

**MODEL MT 122.2/S BOLT-ACTION
RIFLE**..................... **NiB $135 Ex $121 Gd $75**
Calibers: .22 Short, Long, Long Rifle. Six- or 10-round clip.
Bolt action.   25-inch free-floating bbl. 43 inches overall.
Weight: 6.5 lbs. Double locking bolt. Red cocking indicator.
Safety lever. Brazilian hardwood finish. Double extractors.
Beavertail forearm. Sling swivels. Imported from 1994. Disc.

MODEL MT 122.2/R.......... **NiB $140 Ex $116 Gd $88**
Same as Model MT 122.2/S except adj. rear sight and post front
sight. Introduced 1994. Disc.

MODEL MT 122.2/T.......... **NiB $151 Ex $122 Gd $93**
Same as Model MT 122.2/S except w/adj. micrometer-type rear
sight and ramp front sight. Introduced 1994. Disc.

MANNLICHER SPORTING RIFLES —
Austria *Manufactured by Steyr-Daimler-Puch, A.-G.*

NOTE: *Certain Mannlicher-Schoenauer models were produced
before WWII. Manufacture of sporting rifles and carbines was*
*resumed at the Steyr-Daimler-Puch plant in Austria in 1950 during
which time the Model 1950 rifles and carbines were introduced.*

*In 1967, Steyr-Daimler-Puch introduced a series of sporting
rifles with a bolt action that is a departure from the Mannlicher-
Schoenauer system of earlier models. In the latter, the action is
locked by lugs symmetrically arranged behind the bolt head as well
as by placing the bolt handle ahead of the right flank of the receiver, the rear section of which is open on top for backward movement of the bolt handle. The current action, made in four lengths
to accommodate different ranges of cartridges, has a closed-top
receiver; the bolt locking lugs are located toward the rear of the
bolt (behind the magazine). The Mannlicher-Schoenauer rotary
magazine has been redesigned as a detachable box type made of
Makrolon. Imported by Gun South, Inc. Trussville, AL.*

MODEL L CARBINE .... **NiB $1666 Ex $1189 Gd $835**
Same general specifications as Model SL Carbine except w/
type "L" action, weight: 6.2 lbs. Calibers same as for Model L
Rifle. Imported 1968 to 1996.

MODEL L RIFLE .... **NiB $2177 Ex $1508 Gd $1009**
Same general specifications as Model SL Rifle except w/type "L"
action, weighs 6.3 lbs. Calibers: .22-250, 5.6x57 (disc. 1991),
..243 Win., 6mm Rem. .308 Win. Imported 1968 to 1996.

MODEL L VARMINT RIFLE . . **NiB $2107 Ex $1600 Gd $977**
Same general specs as Model SL Varmint Rifle except w/type
"L" action. Calibers: .22-250, .243 Win., .308 Win. Imported
1969–96.

Mannlicher Model
M Rifle

Mannlicher Model SL Rifle
w/Single-Set Trigger

Mannlicher-Schoenauer
Model 1950 Sporting Rifle

Mannlicher-Schoenauer
Model 1950 Carbine

Mannlicher-Schoenauer
Model 1950 Carbine

Mannlicher-Schoenauer Model
1950 Sporting Rifle

Mannlicher-Schoenauer Model
1950 Improved Carbine

MODEL LUXUS BOLT-ACTION RIFLE

Same general specifications as Models L and M except w/3-round detachable box magazine and single-set trigger. Full or half-stock w/low-luster oil or high-gloss lacquer finish. Disc. 1996.

Full stock. . . . . **NiB $2133 Ex $1790 Gd $1305**
Half stock . . . . **NiB $2733 Ex $1966 Gd $928**

MODEL M CARBINE

Same general specifications as Model SL Carbine except w/ type "M" action, stock w/recoil pad, weighs 6.8 lbs. Left-hand version w/additional 6.5x55 and 9.3x62 calibers intro. 1977. Imported 1969 to 1996.

Right-hand carbine . . . . **NiB $1688 Ex $1570 Gd $909**
Left-hand carbine . . . . **NiB $2088 Ex $1964 Gd $1507**

MODEL M PROFESSIONAL RIFLE . . **NiB $1079 Ex $800 Gd $633**

Same as standard Model M Rifle except w/synthetic (Cycolac) stock, weighs 7.5 lbs. Calibers: 6.5x55, 6.5x57, .270 Win., 7x57, 7x64, 7.5 Swiss, .30-06, 8x57JS, 9.3x62. Imported 1977 to 1993.

MODEL M RIFLE

Same general specifications as Model SL Rifle except w/type "M" action, stock w/forend tip and recoil pad; weighs 6.9 lbs. Calibers: 6.5x57, .270 Win., 7x57, 7x64, .30-06, 8x57JS, 9.3x62. Made 1969 to date. Left-hand version also in calibers 6.5x55 and 7.5 Swiss. Imported 1977 to 1996.

Right-hand rifle . . . . **NiB $1667 Ex $1188 Gd $832**
Left-hand rifle . . . . **NiB $2317 Ex $1951 Gd $1489**

MODEL S RIFLE . . . . **NiB $1674 Ex $1203 Gd $855**

Same general specs as Model SL Rifle except w/type "S" action, 4-round magazine, 25.63-inch bbl., stock w/forend tip and recoil pad, weighs 8.4 lbs. Calibers: 6.5x68, .257 Weatherby Mag., .264 Win. Mag., 7mm Rem. Mag., .300 Win. Mag., .300 H&H Mag., .308 Norma Mag., 8x68S, .338 Win. Mag., 9.3x64, .375 H&H Mag. Imported 1970 to 1996.

MODEL SL CARBINE . . . . . . **NiB $1664 Ex $1176 Gd $815**

Same general specifications as Model SL Rifle except w/20-inch bbl. and full-length stock, weight: 6 lbs. Imported 1968 to 1996.

MODEL SL RIFLE . . . . **NiB $1744 Ex $1278 Gd $823**

Steyr-Mannlicher SL bolt action. Calibers: .222 Rem., .222 Rem., .222 Rem. Mag., .223 Rem. Five round rotary magazine, detachable. 23.63-inch bbl. Weight: 6 lbs. Single- or double-set trigger (mechanisms interchangeable). Sights: Open rear; hooded ramp front. Half stock of European walnut w/Monte Carlo comb and cheekpiece, skip-checkered forearm and pistol grip, rubber buttpad, QD swivels. Imported 1967 to 1996.

MODEL SL VARMINT RIFLE . . . **NiB $1233 Ex $1198 Gd $854**

Same general specifications as Model SL Rifle except caliber .222 Rem. only, w/25.63-inch heavy bbl., no sights, weighs 7.92 lbs. Imported 1969 to 1996.

MODEL SSG MATCH TARGET RIFLE

Type "L" action. Caliber: .308 Win. (7.62x51 NATO). Five- or 10-round magazine, single-shot plug. 25.5-inch heavy bbl. Weight: 10.25 lbs. Single trigger. Sights: Micrometer peep rear; globe front. Target stock, European walnut or synthetic, w/full pistol-grip, wide forearm w/swivel rail, adj. rubber buttplate. Imported 1969 to date.

w/walnut stock . . . . **NiB $2388 Ex $1956 Gd $1267**
w/synthetic stock . . . . **NiB $1488 Ex $1131 Gd $709**

MODEL S/T RIFLE. . . . . **NiB $1278 Ex $1564 Gd $931**

Same as Model S Rifle except w/heavy 25.63-inch bbl., weight: 9 lbs. Calibers: 9.3x64, .375 H&H Mag., .458 Win. Mag.

Option of 23.63-inch bbl. in latter caliber. Imported 1975 to 1996.

MODEL 1903 BOLT-ACTION SPORTING

CARBINE. . . . . **NiB $2790 Ex $2133 Gd $1500**
Caliber: 6.5x53mm (referred to in some European gun catalogs as 6.7x53mm, following the Austrian practice of designating calibers by bullet diameter). Five round rotary magazine. 450mm (17.7-inch) bbl. Weight: 6.5 lbs. Double-set trigger. Sights: Two-leaf rear; ramp front. Full-length sporting stock w/ cheekpiece, pistol-grip, trap buttplate, swivels. Pre-WWII.

MODEL 1905 CARBINE . . . . . **NiB $1966 Ex $904 Gd $633**
Same as Model 1903 except w/19.7-inch bbl.chambered 9x56mm and weight: 6.75 lbs. Pre-WWII.

MODEL 1908 CARBINE . . . . . **NiB $1910 Ex $909 Gd $640**
Same as Model 1905 except calibers 7x57mm and 8x56mm Pre-WWII.

MODEL 1910 CARBINE . . . . **NiB $1823 Ex $1535 Gd $870**
Same as Model 1905 except in 9.5x57mm. Pre-WWII.

MODEL 1924 CARBINE . . . **NiB $1767 Ex $1543 Gd $1067**
Same as Model 1905 except caliber .30-06 (7.62x63mm). Pre-WWII.

MODEL 1950 BOLT-ACTION

SPORTING RIFLE . . . . **NiB $1947 Ex $1466 Gd $590**
Calibers: .257 Roberts, .270 Win., .30-06. Five round rotary magazine. 24-inch bbl. Weight: 7.25 lbs. Single trigger or double-set trigger. Redesigned low bolt handle, shotgun-type safety. Sights: Folding leaf open rear; hooded ramp front. Improved half-length stock w/cheekpiece, pistol grip, checkered, ebony forend tip, swivels. Made from 1950 to 1952.

MODEL 1950 CARBINE . . . . **NiB $2065 Ex $1567 Gd $997**
Same general specifications as Model 1950 Rifle except w/20-inch bbl., full-length stock, weighs 7 lbs. Made from 1950 to 1952.

MODEL 1950 6.5 CARBINE **NiB $2060 Ex $1550 Gd $990**
Same as other Model 1950 Carbines except caliber 6.5x53mm, w/18.25-inch bbl., weighs 6.75 lbs. Made from 1950 to 1952.

MODEL 1952 IMPROVED

CARBINE. . . . . **NiB $1866 Ex $1444 Gd $905**
Same as Model 1950 Carbine except w/swept-back bolt handle, redesigned stock. Calibers: .257, .270, 7mm, .30-06. Made 1952 to 1956.

MODEL 1952 IMPROVED

6.5 CARBINE. . . . . **NiB $2088 Ex $1091 Gd $623**
Same as Model 1952 Carbine except caliber 6.5x53mm, w/18.25-inch bbl. Made from 1952 to 1956.

MODEL 1952 IMPROVED

SPORTING RIFLE . . . . **NiB $1847 Ex $1350 Gd $896**
Same as Model 1950 except w/swept-back bolt handle, redesigned stock. Calibers: .257, .270, .30-06, 9.3x62mm. Made from 1952 to 1956 and imported exclusively by Stoeger Arms Corp.

MODEL 1956 CUSTOM

CARBINE . . . . **NiB $2055 Ex $831 Gd $567**
Same general specifications as Models 1950 and 1952 Carbines except w/redesigned stock w/high comb. Drilled and tapped for scope mounts. Calibers: .243, 6.5mm, .257, .270, 7mm, .30-06, .308. Made 1956 to 1960.

RIFLES

**Mannlicher Schoenauer
High Velocity Bolt-Action Sporting Rifle**

Marlin Model 9 9mm Carbine

Marlin Model 9N Nickel-Teflon

CARBINE, MODEL 1961-MCA . . . NiB $1867 Ex $1278 Gd $990
Same as Model 1956 Carbine except w/universal Monte Carlo design stock. Calibers: .243 Win., 6.5mm, .270, .308, .30-06. Made from 1961 to 1971.

RIFLE, MODEL 1961-MCA . . NiB $2159 Ex $1389 Gd $997
Same as Model 1956 Rifle except w/universal Monte Carlo design stock. Calibers: .243, .270, .30-06. Made from 1961 to 1971.

**HIGH VELOCITY BOLT-ACTION
SPORTING RIFLE . . . . NiB $2650 Ex $1630 Gd $1190**
Calibers: 7x64 Brenneke, .30-06 (7.62x63), 8x60 Magnum, 9.3x62, 10.75x68mm. 23.6-inch bbl. Weight: 7.5 lbs. Sights: British-style 3-leaf open rear; ramp front. Half-length sporting stock w/cheek-piece, pistol grip, checkered, trap buttplate, swivels. Also produced in a takedown model. Pre-WWII. See illustration next page.
10.75x68mm, add 105%

M72 MODEL L/M CARBINE . . NiB $1043 Ex $762 Gd $513
Similar to M72 Model L/M Rifle except w/20-inch bbl. and full-length stock, weight: 7.2 lbs. Imported from 1972 to date.

M72 MODEL L/M RIFLE . . . . . . NiB $906 Ex $821 Gd $600
M72 bolt-action, type L/M receiver front-locking bolt internal rotary magazine (5-round). Calibers: .22-250, 5.6x57, 6mm Rem., .243 Win., 6.5x57, .270 Win., 7x57, 7x64, .308 Win., .30-06. 23.63-inch bbl. Weight: 7.3 lbs. Single- or double-set trigger (mechanisms interchangeable). Sights: Open rear; hooded ramp front. Half stock of European walnut, checkered forearm and pistol-grip, Monte Carlo cheekpiece, rosewood forend tip, recoil pad QD swivels. Imported 1972 to 1981.

M72 MODEL S RIFLE . . . . NiB $876 Ex $756 Gd $544
Same general specifications as M72 Model L/M Rifle except w/ magnum action, 4-round magazine, 25.63-inch bbl., weighs 8.6 lbs. Calibers: 6.5x68, 7mm Rem. Mag., 8x68S, 9.3x64, .375 H&H Mag. Imported from 1972 to 1981.

M72 MODEL S/T RIFLE . . . . NiB $1755 Ex $1461 Gd $999
Same as M72 Model S Rifle except w/heavy 25.63-inch bbl., weighs 9.3 lbs. Calibers: .300 Win. Mag. 9.3x64, .375 H&H Mag., .458 Win. Mag. Option of 23.63-inch bbl. in latter caliber. Imported from 1975 to 1981.

MODEL SBS FORESTER RIFLE
Calibers: .243 Win., .25-06 Rem., .270 Win., .6.5x55mm, 6.5x57mm, 7x64mm, 7mm-08 Rem., .30-06, .308 Win. 9.3x64mm. Four round detachable magazine. 23.6-inch bbl. 44.5 inches overall. Weight: 7.5 lbs. No sights w/drilled and tapped for Browning A-Bolt configuration. Checkered American walnut stock w/Monte Carlo cheekpiece and Pachmayr swivels. Polished or matte blue finish. Imported from 1997 to date.
Standard calibers . . . . NiB $955 Ex $823 Gd $595
Mountain Rifle (w/20-inch bbl.) . . NiB $975 Ex $805 Gd $555
For magnum calibers, add $50
For metric calibers, add $126

MODEL SBS PRO-HUNTER RIFLE
Similar to the Forester Model, except w/ASB black synthetic stock. Matte blue finish. Imported from 1997 to date.
Standard calibers . . . . NiB $1000 Ex $879 Gd $467
Mountain Rifle (w/20-inch bbl.) NiB $897 Ex $689 Gd $523
.376 Steyr . . . . NiB $887 Ex $679 Gd $513
Youth/Ladies rifle . . . . NiB $720 Ex $689 Gd $523
For magnum calibers, add $50
For metric calibers, add $150
w/walnut stock . . . . NiB $2307 Ex $1896 Gd $1371
w/synthetic stock, add $150

MARLIN FIREARMS CO. — Ilion, NY

Formerly manufactured in North Haven, Connecticut, acquired by Freedom Group Inc. in 2007 and manufactured in Ilion, New York. In 2000 Marlin acquired H&R 1871 including Harrington & Richardson (H&R) New England Firearms, and Wesson & Harrington. See Shotgun section for L.C. Smith listings.

To facilitate locating Marlin rifles, models are grouped into categories: Centerfire Bolt-action Rifles, Centerfire Lever-Action Rifles, Centerfire Semi-automatic Rifles, Rimfire Bolt-action Rifles, Rimfire Lever-action Rifles, Rimfire Semi-

Marlin Model 455 Sporter

Marlin-Glenfield Model 30A

automatic Rifles, Slide-action (pump) Rifles. For a complete listing, please refer to the index.

- CENTERFIRE BOLT-ACTION RIFLES -

MODEL 322 BOLT-ACTION
VARMINT RIFLE . . . . **NiB $597 Ex $390 Gd $278**
Sako short Mauser action. Caliber: .222 Rem. Three round clip magazine. 24-inch medium weight bbl. Checkered stock. Sights: Two-position peep rear; hooded ramp front. Weight: 7.5 lbs. Made from 1954-57.

MODEL 455 BOLT-ACTION SPORTER
FN Mauser action w/Sako trigger. Calibers: .30-06 or .308. Five round box magazine. 24-inch medium weight stainless-steel bbl. Monte Carlo stock w/cheekpiece, checkered pistol grip and forearm. Lyman No. 48 receiver sight; hooded ramp front. Weight: 8.5 lbs. Made from 1957 to 1959.
.30-06 Spfd., 1079 produced . . **NiB $707 Ex $535 Gd $325**
.308 Win., 59 produced . . . . . . **NiB $800 Ex $610 Gd $475**

MODEL MR-7 . . . . **NiB $555 Ex $380 Gd $277**
Bolt action. Calibers: .25-06 Rem., .270 Win., .280 Rem., .308 Win. or .30-06. Four round magazine. 22-inch bbl. w/ or w/o sights. 43.31 inches overall. Weight: 7.5 lbs. Checkered American walnut or birch stock w/recoil pad and sling-swivel studs. Jeweled bolt w/cocking indicator and 3-position safety. Made from 1996 to 1999.
w/birch stock, intro. 1998 . . . . **NiB $460 Ex $379 Gd $255**
w/open sights, add **$50**

MODEL X-7 . . . . **NiB $403 Ex $355 Gd $305**
Bolt action, short or long action. Calibers: .223 Rem., .243 Win., .25-06 Rem., .270 Win., 7mm-08, .308 Win. or .30-06. Four round internal magazine. 22-inch bbl. w/o sights. 43.31 inches overall. Weight: 6.5 lbs. Black synthetic stock. Two-position safety. Scope bases. Blued finish. Made from 2008 to 2015.
X7C (camo stock), add **$20**
X7W (wood stock), add **$110**

- CENTERFIRE LEVER-ACTION RIFLES -

MODEL 30/30A AND 30AS LEVER-ACTION
Caliber: .30/30 Win. Six-round tubular magazine. 20-inch bbl. w/Micro-Groove rifling. 38.25 inches overall. Weight: 7 lbs. Brass bead front sight, adj. rear. Solid top receiver, offset hammer spur for scope use. Walnut-finished hardwood stock w/ pistol-grip. Mar-Shield finish. Made from 1964 to 2000.
Model 30/30A . . . . **NiB $290 Ex $198 Gd $160**
Model 30AS . . . . **NiB $290 Ex $198 Gd $160**
Model 30AS w/4x scope, add **$25**

MODEL 30 . . . . **NiB $280 Ex $133 Gd $100**
Lever action. Same as Marlin Model 336C except chambered for .30-30 only, w/4-round magazine, plainer stock and forearm of walnut-finished hardwood. Made 1966 to 1968.

MODEL 30A . . . . **NiB $279 Ex $190 Gd $139**
Lever action. Same as Model 336C but chambered for .30-30 only, w/checkered walnut-finished hardwood stock. Made 1969 to 1983.

MODEL 36G . . . . **NiB $879 Ex $633 Gd $260**
Same as Marlin Model 336C except chambered for .30-30 only, w/5-round magazine, plainer stock. Made 1960 to 1965.

MODEL 36 LEVER-ACTION REPEATING CARBINE
Calibers: .30-30, .32 Special. Seven-round tubular magazine. 20-inch bbl. Weight: 6.5 lbs. Sights: Open rear; bead front. Pistol-grip stock, semibeavertail forearm w/carbine bbl. band. Early production w/receiver, lever and hammer color casehardened and the remaining metal blued. Late production w/blued receiver. Made 1936 to 1948. Note: In 1936, this was designated "Model 1936" and was so marked on the upper tang. In 1937, the model designation was shortened to "36". An "RC" serial number suffix identifies a "Regular/Carbine".
Model 1936 CC receiver
  (w/long tang, no SN prefix) . **NiB $909 Ex $744 Gd $500**
Model 1936 CC receiver
  (w/short tang, no SN prefix) **NiB $645 Ex $531 Gd $390**
Model 1936 CC receiver
  (w/SN prefix) . . . . **NiB $534 Ex $488 Gd $345**
Model 36, CC receiver
  (w/SN prefix) . . . . **NiB $508 Ex $433 Gd $300**
Model 36, blued receiver
  (w/SN prefix) . . . . **NiB $482 Ex $390 Gd $289**

MODEL 36 SPORTING CARBINE
Same as M36 carbine except w/6-round, (2/3 magazine) and weighs 6.25 lbs.
Model 1936, CC receiver
  (w/long tang, no SN prefix) . **NiB $860 Ex $707 Gd $499**
Model 1936, CC receiver
  (w/short tang, no SN prefix) **NiB $656 Ex $567 Gd $380**
Model 1936, CC receiver
  (w/SN prefix) . . . . **NiB $588 Ex $497 Gd $355**

RIFLES

Marlin Model 62

Marlin Model 93 Musket

Marlin Model 93 Lever Action

Marlin Model 94 Sporting Carbine

Model 36, CC receiver
(w/SN prefix).............NiB $555 Ex $457 Gd $339
Model 36, blued receiver
(w/SN prefix) .... NiB $480 Ex $413 Gd $303

MODEL 36A/36A-DL LEVER-ACTION REPEATING RIFLE
Same as Model 36 Carbine except has 24-inch bbl. w/hooded front sight and 2/3 magazine holding 6 cartridges. Weight: 6.75 lbs. Note: An "A" serial number suffix identifies a Rifle while an "A-DL" suffix designates a Deluxe Model w/checkered stock, semibeavertail forearm, swivels and sling. Made from 1936 to 1948.
Model 1936, CC receiver (w/long tang,
no SN prefix) ....NiB $1180 Ex $1077 Gd $790
Model 1936, CC receiver
(w/short, tang, no SN prefix) NiB $795 Ex $556 Gd $378
Model 1936, CC receiver
(w/SN prefix) ....NiB $845 Ex $589 Gd $465
MODEL 36, CC receiver,
(w/SN prefix) ....NiB $775 Ex $451 Gd $348
Model 36, blued receiver
(w/SN prefix) ....NiB $744 Ex $440 Gd $332
ADL model, add $25%

MODEL 62 LEVERMATIC RIFLE NiB $555 Ex $440 Gd $190
Lever-action. Calibers: .256 Magnum, .30 Carbine. Four round clip magazine. 23-inch bbl. Weight: 7 lbs. Sights: Open rear; hooded ramp front. Monte Carlo-style stock w/pistol-grip, swivels and sling. Made in .256 Magnum 1963 to 1966; in .30 Carbine 1963 to 1969.

MODEL 92 LEVER-ACTION REPEATING RIFLE
Calibers: .22 Short, Long, LR. .32 Short, Long (rimfire or centerfire by changing firing pin). Tubular magazines holding 25 Short, 20 Long, 18 LR (.22); or 17 Short, 14 Long (.32); 16-inch bbl. model w/shorter magazine holding 15 Short, 12 Long, 10 LR. Bbl. lengths: 16 (.22 cal. only) 24, 26, 28 inches. Weight: 5.5 lbs. w/24-inch bbl. Sights: open rear; blade front. Plain

straight-grip stock and forearm. Made 1892 to 1916. Note: Originally designated "Model 1892."
Model 92 (.22 caliber) .....NiB $1598 Ex $1400 Gd $883
Model 92 (.32 caliber) .....NiB $1554 Ex $1268 Gd $956

MODEL 93/93SC CARBINE
Same as Standard Model 93 Rifle except in calibers .30-30 and .32 Special only. Model 93 w/7-round magazine. 20-inch round bbl., carbine sights, weight: 6.75 lbs. Model 93SC magazine capacity 5 rounds, weight 6.5 lbs.
Model 93 Carbine
(w/saddle ring) ....NiB $1689 Ex $1423 Gd $1108
Model 93 Carbine "Bull's-Eye"
(w/o saddle ring) ....NiB $1449 Ex $1188 Gd $976
Model 93SC Sporting
Carbine...............NiB $1377 Ex $1087 Gd $915

MODEL 93 LEVER-ACTION
REPEATING RIFLE........NiB $2833 Ex $2022 Gd $1370
Solid frame or takedown. Calibers: .25-36 Marlin, .30-30, .32 Special, .32-40, .38-55. Tubular magazine holds 10 cartridges. 26-inch round or octagon bbl. standard; also made w/28-, 30- and 32-inch bbls. Weight: 7.25 lbs. Sights: Open rear; bead front. Plain straight-grip stock and forearm. Made from 1893 to 1936. Note: Before 1915 designated "Model 1893."

MODEL 93 MUSKET..... NiB $5610 Ex $ 3766 Gd $2833
Same as Standard Model 93 except w/30-inch bbl., angular bayonet, ramrod under bbl., musket stock, full-length military-style forearm. Weight: 8 lbs. Made from 1893 to 1915.

MODEL 94 ....NiB $2655 Ex $1840 Gd $989
Lever action. Solid frame or takedown. Calibers: .25-20, .32-20, .38-40, .44-40. 10-round tubular magazine. 24-inch round or octagon bbl. Weight: 7 lbs. Sights open rear; bead front. Plain straight-grip stock and forearm (also available w/ pistol-grip stock). Made from 1894 to 1934. Note: Before 1906 designated "Model 1894."

Marlin Model 336A

Marlin Model 336A-DL

Marlin Model 336 Cowboy

MODEL 94 LEVER-ACTION COWBOY SERIES

Calibers: .357 Mag., .44-40, .44 Mag., .45 LC. 10-round magazine. 24-inch tapered octagon bbl. Weight: 7.5 lbs. 41.5 inches overall. Marble carbine front sight, adjustable semi-buckhorn rear. Blue finish. Checkered, straight-grip American black walnut stock w/hard rubber buttplate. Made from 1996 to date. Cowboy II introduced in 1997.

Cowboy model (.45 LC) . . . . . NiB $833 Ex $650 Gd $466
Cowboy II model (.357 Mag., .44-40,
   .44 Mag.) . . . . NiB $854 Ex $659 Gd $572

MODEL 308MX . . . . NiB $686 Ex $2022 Gd $1370
Lever action. Calibers: .308 Marlin Express. 5-rnd. tube magazine. 22-inch bbl. Weight: 7.25 lbs. Blue finish. Checkered, pistol-grip American black walnut stock w/rubber butt pad. Made from 2007 to date.
308MXLR (stainless, 24-in. bbl.), add $200

MODEL 336A . . . . NiB $570 Ex $400 Gd $338
Lever action. Improved version of Model 36A Rifle w/same general specifications except w/improved action w/round breech bolt. Calibers: .30-30, .32 Special (disc. 1963), .35 Rem. (intro. 1952). Made from 1948-63; reintroduced 1973, disc. 1980.

MODEL 336A-DL . . . . NiB $665 Ex $544 Gd $351
Same as Model 336A Rifle except w/deluxe checkered stock and forearm, swivels and sling. Made from 1948-63.

MODEL 336AS . . . . NiB $475 Ex $291 Gd $139
Lever action. Similar to Model 30AS. Caliber: .30-30 Win., Six round tubular magazine. 20- inch Micro-Groove bbl. 38.25 inches overall. Weight: 7 lbs. Maine birch pistol grip stock w/ swivel studs and hard rubber butt plate. Tapped for scope mount and receiver sight. Screw-adjustable open rear and ramp front sight. Checkered walnut finish. Made from 1999 to date.

MODEL 336C . . . . NiB $559 Ex $398 Gd $290
Improved version of Model 36 Carbine w/same general specifications except w/improved action w/round breech bolt.

Original calibers: .30-30 and .32 Win. Spec. Made from 1948-83. Note: Caliber .35 Rem. intro. 1953. Caliber .32 Winchester Special disc. 1963.

MODEL 336 COWBOY
LEVER-ACTION RIFLE . . . . NiB $600 Ex $445 Gd $380
Calibers: .30-30 Win., or .38-55 Win., 6- round tubular magazine. 24- inch tapered octagon bbl. 42.5 inches overall. Weight: 7.5 lbs. American black walnut checkering stock. Marble carbine front sight w/solid top receiver drilled and tapped for scope mount. Mar-Shield finish. Made from 1998 to date.

MODEL 336CS W/SCOPE . . . . . NiB $479 Ex $338 Gd $266
Lever-action w/hammer block safety. Caliber: .30/30 Win. or .35 Rem. Six round tubular magazine. 20-inch round bbl. w/ Micro-Groove rifling. 38.5 inches overall. Weight: 7 lbs. Ramp front sight w/hood, adj. semi-buckhorn folding rear. Solid top receiver drilled and tapped for scope mount or receiver sight; offset hammer spur for scope use. American black walnut stock w/pistol-grip, fluted comb. Mar-Shield finish. Made 1984 to date.

MODEL 336DT DELUXE TEXAN . . NiB $500 Ex $466 Gd $359
Same as Model 336T except w/select walnut stock and forearm, hand-carved longhorn steer and map of Texas on buttstock. Made 1962 to 1964.

MODEL 336M LEVER-ACTION
RIFLE . . . . NiB $590 Ex $495 Gd $359
Calibers: .30-30 Win., 6- round tubular magazine. 20- inch stainless steel Micro Groove bbl., 38.5 inches overall. Weight: 7 lbs. American black walnut w/checkered pistol-grip stock. Adjustable folding semi-buckhorn rear and ramp front sight w/brass bead and removable Wide-Scan hood. Tapped for receiver sight and scope mount. Mar-Shield finish. Made from 1999 to date.

MODEL 336 MARAUDER . . . . . NiB $600 Ex $485 Gd $300
Same as Model 336 Texan Carbine except w/16.25-inch bbl., weight: 6.25 lbs. Made from 1963 to 1964.

MODEL 336-MICRO
GROOVE ZIPPER . . . . NiB $845 Ex $633 Gd $390
General specifications same as Model 336 Sporting Carbine except caliber .219 Zipper. Made from 1955 to 1961.

Marlin Model 336M

Marlin Model 336DT Deluxe Texan

Marlin Model 336T Texan

Marlin Model 336 Marauder

MODEL 336 OCTAGON......**NiB $570 Ex $498 Gd $300**
Same as Model 336T except chambered for .30-30 only w/22-inch octagon bbl. Made in 1973.

**MODEL 336 SPORTING
CARBINE.**...................**NiB $845 Ex $589 Gd $445**
Same as Model 336A rifle except w/20-inch bbl., weight: 6.25 lbs. Made from 1948 to 1963.

MODEL 336T TEXAN CARBINE...**NiB $369 Ex $277 Gd $228**
Same as Model 336 Carbine except w/straight-grip stock and is not available in caliber .32 Special. Made 1953-83. Caliber .44 Magnum made 1963 to 1967.

MODEL 336TS.............. **NiB $400 Ex $333 Gd $190**
Lever-action w/hammer-block safety. Caliber: .30-30 Win. Six round tubular magazine. 18.5-inch Micro-Groove bbl. 37 inches overall. Weight: 6.5 lbs. Ramp front sight, adj. semi-buckhorn folding rear. Straight-grip American black walnut stock. Made 1983–87.

**MODEL 336 ZANE GREY
CENTURY.**....................**NiB $488 Ex $439 Gd $300**
Similar to Model 336A except w/22-inch octagonal bbl., caliber .30-30, Zane Grey Centennial 1872-1972 medallion inlaid in receiver; select walnut stock w/classic pistol-grip and forearm; brass buttplate, forend cap. Weight: 7 lbs. 10,000 produced (numbered ZG1 through ZG10,000). Made in 1972.

MODEL 338MX............ **NiB $685 Ex $545 Gd $380**
Simialr to the 308MX except chambered in .338 Marlin Express. Made from 2014 to date.
338MXLR (stainless, 24-in. bbl.), add...............**$200**

MODEL 375..............**NiB $845 Ex $589 Gd $445**
Same as Model 336CS except chambered in .375 Win. Made from 1980 to 1983.

MODEL 444 LEVER-ACTION..**NiB $482 Ex $390 Gd $235**
Action similar to Model 336. Caliber: .444 Marlin. Four round tubular magazine. 24-inch bbl. Weigh: 7.5 lbs. Sights: Open rear; hooded ramp front. Monte Carlo stock w/straight grip, recoil pad. Carbine-style forearm w/bbl. band. Swivels, sling. Made from 1965 to 1971.

MARLIN MODEL 444 SPORTER..**NiB $576 Ex $445 Gd $235**
Same as Model 444 Rifle except w/22-inch bbl., pistol-grip stock and forearm as on Model 336A, recoil pad, QD swivels and sling. Made from 1972 to 1983.

MODEL 444P (OUTFITTER)...**NiB $559 Ex $447 Gd $255**
Lever action. Caliber: .444 Marlin. Five round tubular magazine. 18.5-inch ported bbl., 37 inches overall. Weight: 6.75 lbs. Ramp front and adjustable folding rear sights, Black walnut straight grip stock w/cut checkering and Mar-Shield finish. Made from 1999 to 2002.

MODEL 444SS.............**NiB $570 Ex $449 Gd $240**
Same general specifications as Model 444 except w/hammer safety. Made from 1984-2002. (Changed to M444 in 2001.)

MODEL 1894 LEVER-ACTION RIFLE
See Marlin Model 94 listed previously under this section.

MODEL 1894 CARBINE......**NiB $415 Ex $300 Gd $245**
Replica of original Model 94. Caliber: .44 Rem. 10-round magazine. 20-inch round bbl. Weight: 6 lbs. Sight: Open rear; ramp front. Straight-grip stock. Made from 1969 to 1984.
Octagon bbl. (made 1973)....**NiB $525 Ex $390 Gd $239**
Sporter model (w/22-inch bbl.
made 1973).............**NiB $585 Ex $369 Gd $345**

Marlin Model 336 Zane Grey Century

Marlin Model 444SS

Marlin Model 1894 Carbine

Marlin Model 1894CL

RIFLES

MODEL 1894CL CLASSIC.....NiB $743 Ex $545 Gd $355
Calibers: .218 Bee, .25-20 Win., .32-20 Win. Six round tubular magazine. 22-inch bbl. 38.75 inches overall. Weight: 6.25 lbs. Adj. semibuckhorn folding rear sight, brass bead front. Receiver tapped for scope mounts. Straight-grip American black walnut stock w/Mar-Shield finish. Made from 1988 to 1994.

MODEL 1894CS LEVER-ACTION...NiB $779 Ex $545 Gd $369
Caliber: .357 Magnum, .38 Special. Nine round tubular magazine. 18.5-inch bbl. 36 inches overall. Weight: 6 lbs. Side ejection. Hammer block safety. Square finger lever. Bead front sight, adj. semi-buckhorn folding rear. Offset hammer spur for scope use. Two-piece straight grip American black walnut stock w/white buttplate spacer. Mar-Shield finish. Made from 1984 to 2002.

MODEL 1894S LEVER-ACTION NiB $522 Ex $347 Gd $245
Calibers: .41 Mag., .44 Rem. Mag., .44 S&W Special, .45 Colt.10-shot tubular magazine. 20-inch bbl.37.5 inches overall. Weight: 6 lbs. Sights and stock same as Model 1894M. Made 1984 to 2002.

MODEL 1895 .45-70 REPEATER .. NiB $445 Ex $390 Gd $235
Model 336-type action. Caliber: .45-70 Government. Four round magazine. 22-inch bbl. Weight: 7 lbs. Sights: Open rear; bead front. Straight-grip stock, forearm w/metal end cap, QD swivels, leather sling. Made 1972 to 1979.

MODEL 1895 ....NiB $447 Ex $393 Gd $236
Lever-action repeater. Solid frame or takedown. Calibers: .33 WCF, .38-56, .40-65, .40-70, .40-82, .45-70. Nine round tubular magazine. 24-inch round or octagongon bbl. standard (other lengths available). Weight: 8 lbs. Sights: Open rear; bead front. Plain stock and forearm (also available w/pistol-grip stock). Made 1895 to 1915.

MODEL 1895G (GUIDE GUN) ...NiB $590 Ex $389 Gd $280
Lever action. Caliber: .45-70 Govt., 4- round magazine. 18.5-inch ported bbl., 37 inches overall. Weight: 6.75 lbs. Ramp front and adjustable folding rear sights. Black walnut straight grip stock w/cut checkering and Mar-Shield finish. 2,500 made starting in 1998.

MODEL 1895M. ....NiB $448 Ex $290 Gd $144
Lever action. Caliber: .450 Marlin. Four round tubular magazine., 18.5- inch ported bbl. w/Ballard-type rifling. 37 inches overall. Weight: 6.75 lbs. Genuine American black walnut straight-grip stock w/checkering. Ventilated recoil pad. Adjustable folding semi-buckhorn rear and ramp front sights. Mar-Shield finish. Made 2000 to date.
Model 1895GBL (big loop).....NiB $595 Ex $340 Gd $165

MODEL 1895SS ....NiB $609 Ex $448 Gd $356
Lever action. Caliber: .45-70 Govt. Four round tubular magazine. 22-inch bbl. w/Micro-Groove rifling. 40.5 inches overall. Weight: 7.5 lbs. Ramp front sight w/brass bead and Wide-Scan hood; adj. semi-buckhorn folding rear. Solid top receiver tapped for scope mount or receiver sight. Off-set hammer spur for scope use. Two-piece American black walnut stock w/fluted comb, pistol-grip, sling swivels. Made 1984 to date. (Changed to M1895 in 2001.)

MODEL 1936 LEVER-ACTION CARBINE
See Marlin Model 36 listed previously under this section.

- CENTERFIRE SEMI-AUTOMATIC RIFLES -

MODEL 9 SEMIAUTOMATIC CARBINE
Calibers: 9mm Parabellum. 12-round magazine. 16.5-inch bbl. 35.5 inches overall. Weight: 6.75 lbs. Manual bolt hold-open.

Marlin Model 1894CS

Marlin Model 1894S

Marlin Model 1895
.45-70 (New Model)

Marlin Model 1895G

Sights: Hooded post front; adj. open rear. Walnut-finished hardwood stock w/rubber buttpad. Blued or nickel-Teflon finish. Made 1985 to 1999.

Model 9 . . . . NiB $525 Ex $387 Gd $213
Model 9N, nickel-Teflon (disc. 1994) . . NiB $475 Ex $390 Gd $146

MODEL 45 . . . . NiB $390 Ex $290 Gd $198
Semiautomatic action. Caliber: .45 Auto. Seven round clip.16.5-inch bbl. 35.5 inches overall. Weight: 6.75 lbs. Manual bolt hold-open. Sights: Ramp front sight w/brass bead, adj. folding rear. Receiver drilled and tapped for scope mount. Walnut-finished hardwood stock. Made from 1986 to 1999.

- RIMFIRE BOLT-ACTION RIFLES -

MODEL 10 . . . . NiB $140 Ex $110 Gd $85
Bolt-action. Same as Marlin Model 101 except w/walnut-finished hardwood stock. Made 1966-79. Note: Later production featuring hot-ironstamped wood pistol grip to simulate checkering/carving; plain forend.

MODEL 15Y/15YN

Bolt-action, single-shot "Little Buckaroo" rifle. Caliber: .22 Short, Long or LR. 16.25-inch bbl. Weight: 4.25 lbs. Thumb safety. Ramp front sight; adj. open rear. One-piece walnut Monte Carlo stock w/full pistol-grip. Made 1984 to 1988. Reintroduced in 1989 as Model 15YN.

Model 15Y . . . . NiB $200 Ex $130 Gd $98
Model 15YN . . . . .NiB $215 Ex $140 Gd $110

MODEL 20 . . . . NiB $779 Ex $439 Gd $310
Bolt-action. Same as Marlin Model 80/780 except w/bead front sight, walnut-finished hardwood stock. Made 1966 to 1982. Note: Recent production has stamped pistol grip; plain forend.

MODEL 25MB BOLT-ACTION

RIFLE . . . . NiB $179 Ex $110 Gd $95
Caliber: .22 Short, Long or LR; 7-round clip. 22-inch bbl. Weight: 5.5 lbs. Ramp front sight, adj. open rear. One-piece walnut Monte Carlo stock w/full pistol-grip Mar-Shield finish. Made 1984 to 1988.

MODEL 25M BOLT ACTION

W/SCOPE . . . . NiB $167 Ex $119 Gd $95
Caliber: .22 WMR. 7-round clip. 22-inch bbl. Weight: 6 lbs. Ramp front sight w/brass bead, adj. open rear. Walnut-finished stock w/Monte Carlo styling and full pistol-grip. Sling swivels. Made 1986 to 1988.

Marlin Model 1895M

Marlin Model 1895SS

Marlin Model 9 9mm Carbine

Marlin-Glenfield Model 10

MODEL 25MB MIDGET
MAGNUM. . . . . **NiB $190 Ex $126 Gd $99**
Bolt action. Caliber: .22 WMR. Seven round capacity.16.25-inch bbl. Weight: 4.75 lbs. Walnut-finished Monte Carlo-style stock w/full pistol grip and abbreviated forend. Sights: Ramp front w/brass bead, adj. open rear. Thumb safety. Made from 1986 to 1988.

MODEL 25MG/25MN/25N/25NC BOLT-ACTION RIFLE
Caliber: .22 WMR (Model 25MN) or .22 LR. (Model 25N). Seven round clip magazine. 22-inch bbl. 41 inches overall. Weight: 5.5 to 6 lbs. Adj. open rear sight, ramp front; receiver grooved for scope mounts. One piece walnut-finished hardwood Monte Carlo stock w/pistol grip. Made from 1989 to 2003.
Model 25MG (Garden Gun) . . . NiB $218 Ex $179 Gd $126
Model 25MN . . . . NiB $200 Ex $167 Gd $110
Model 25N . . . . NiB $177 Ex $155 Gd $109
Model 25 NC (camo stock), add. $50

MODEL 65 BOLT-ACTION SINGLE-SHOT
RIFLE. . . . . **NiB $139 Ex $93 Gd $70**
Takedown. Caliber: .22 LR, Long, Short. 24-inch bbl. Weight: 5 lbs. Sights: Open rear; bead front. Plain pistol-grip stock w/ grooved forearm. Made 1932-38. Model 65E is same as Model 65 except w/rear peep sight and hooded front sight.

MODEL 70 . . . . NiB $188 Ex $95 Gd $65
Bolt-action. Same as Marlin Model 989M2 except w/walnut-finished hardwood stock; no handguard. Made 1966 to 1969.

MODEL 80 BOLT-ACTION REPEATING RIFLE
Takedown. Caliber: .22 LR, Long, Short. Eight round detach-able box magazine. 24-inch bbl. Weight: 6 lbs. Sights: Open rear; bead front. Plain pistol-grip stock. Made from 1934 to 1939. Model 80E, w/peep rear sight; hooded front, made from 1934 to 1940.
Model 80 Standard . . . . NiB $190 Ex $135 Gd $95
Model 80E. . . . . NiB $175 Ex $110 Gd $85

MODEL 80C/80DL BOLT-ACTION REPEATER
Improved version of Model 80. Model 80C w/bead from sight, semibeavertail forearm; made 1940-70. Model 80DL w/peep rear sight; hooded blade front sight on ramp, swivels; made 1940 to 1965.
Model 80C . . . . NiB $200 Ex $155 Gd $100
Model 80DL . . . . NiB $167 Ex $110 Gd $90

MODEL 80G. . . . . NiB $100 Ex $65 Gd $45
Bolt action. Same as Marlin Model 80C except w/plain stock, bead front sight. Made 1960 to 1965.

MODEL 81/81E BOLT-ACTION REPEATER
Takedown. .22 LR, Long, Short. Tubular magazine holds 24 Short, 20 Long, 18 LR. 24-inch bbl. Weight: 6.25 lbs. Sights: Open rear, bead front. Plain pistol-grip stock. Made from 1937 to 1940. Model 81E w/peep rear sight; hooded front w/ramp.
Model 81 . . . . NiB $220 Ex $176 Gd $110
Model 81E. . . . . NiB $245 Ex $195 Gd $139

MODEL 81C/81DL BOLT-ACTION REPEATER
Improved version of Model 81 w/same general specifications. Model 81C w/bead front sight, semibeavertail forearm; made 1940 to 1970. Model 81 DL w/peep rear sight, hooded front, swivels; disc. 1965.
Model 81C . . . . NiB $239 Ex $188 Gd $100
Model 81DL . . . . NiB $220 Ex $199 Gd $110

Marlin Model 15Y "Little Buckaroo"

Marlin Model 15YN

Marlin Model 20

Marlin Model 25M Bolt-Action Rifle

Marlin Model 25MB
Midget Magnum

MODEL 81G . . . . **NiB $110 Ex $78 Gd $66**
Bolt action. Same as Marlin Model 81C except w/plain stock, bead front sight. Made from 1960 to 1965.

MODEL 100 BOLT-ACTION
SINGLE-SHOT RIFLE . . . . **NiB $200 Ex $123 Gd $90**
Takedown. Caliber: .22 LR, Long, Short. 24-inch bbl. Weight: 4.5 lbs. Sights: Open rear; bead front. Plain pistol-grip stock. Made 1936 to 1960.

MODEL 100SB . . . . **NiB $120 Ex $90 Gd $65**
Same as Model 100 except smoothbore for use w/22 shot cartridges, shotgun sight. Made from 1936 to 1941.

MODEL 100 TOM MIX
SPECIAL . . . . **NiB $315 Ex $200 Gd $146**
Same as Model 100 except w/peep rear sight; hooded front; sling. Made from 1936 to 1946.

MODEL 101 . . . . **NiB $100 Ex $75 Gd $55**
Improved version of Model 100 w/same general specifications, except w/stock w/beavertail forearm, weighs 5 lbs. Intro. 1951. Disc.

MODEL 101 DL . . . . **NiB $119 Ex $85 Gd $70**
Same as Model 101 except has peep rear sight; hooded front, swivels. Disc.

MODEL 101G . . . . **NiB $110 Ex $79 Gd $55**
Bolt action. Same as Marlin Model 101 except w/plain stock. Made 1960 to 1965.

MODEL 122 SINGLE-SHOT JUNIOR
TARGET RIFLE. . . . . **NiB $135 Ex $95 Gd $75**
Bolt action. Caliber: .22 LR, .22 Long, .22 Short. 22-inch bbl. Weight: 5 lbs. Sights: Open rear; hooded ramp front. Monte Carlo stock w/pistol-grip, swivels, sling. Made from 1961 to 1965.

MODEL 780/781/782/783 BOLT-ACTION REPEATER SERIES
Bolt action. Caliber: .22 LR, Long, Short. Seven round clip magazine. 22-inch bbl. Weight: 5.5 to 6 lbs. Sights: Open rear; hooded ramp front. Receiver grooved for scope mounting. Monte Carlo stock w/checkered pistol-grip and forearm. Made from 1971 to 1988.
Standard model. . . . . NiB $145 Ex $100 Gd $85
w/17-round tubular mag. . . . . . . NiB $145 Ex $100 Gd $85
.22 WMR w/swivels, sling. . . . . . NiB $145 Ex $100 Gd $85
w/12-round tubular mag. . . . . . . NiB $145 Ex $100 Gd $85

Marlin-Glenfield Model 70

Marlin-Glenfield Model 80G

Marlin Model 80C

Marlin Model 80DL

Marlin Model 81DL

Marlin Model 780

RIFLES

Marlin Model 781

Marlin Model 783

Marlin Model 882L

Marlin Model 883N

Marlin Model 980

Marlin Model 2000

MODEL 880/881/882/883 BOLT-ACTION REPEATER SERIES
Caliber: .22 rimfire. Seven round magazine. 22-inch bbl. 41 inches overall. Weight: 5.5 to 6 lbs. Hooded ramp front sight; adj. folding rear. Grooved receiver for scope mounts. Checkered Monte Carlo-style walnut stock w/QD studs and rubber recoil pad. Made from 1989 to 1997.

.22 LR . . . . NiB $220 Ex $177 Gd $115
Stainless .22 LR . . . . NiB $269 Ex $200 Gd $150
Squirrel .22 LR . . . . NiB $269 Ex $223 Gd $160

Model 881 w/7-rd. tub. mag.   NiB $244 Ex $175 Gd $110
Model 882 (.22 WMR) . . . . NiB $235 Ex $189 Gd $115
w/laminated hardwood stock . . NiB $277 Ex $189 Gd $120
Stainless w/Fire sights . . . . NiB $290 Ex $222 Gd $167
Stainless .22 LR . . . . NiB $195 Ex $227 Gd $170
Model 883 (.22 WMR w/12-round
   tubular mag.) . . . . NiB $235 Ex $179 Gd $120
w/nickel-Teflon finish . . . . NiB $279 Ex $226 Gd $180
Stainless w/laminated stock . . . NiB $297 Ex $200 Gd $177

Marlin Model 39
Carbine

Marlin Model 39
Century Ltd.

Marlin Model 39 Carbine
90th Anniversary

Marlin Model 39 Rifle
Original First Issue

Marlin Model 39A
90th Anniversary Rifle

Marlin Model 39 — ADL

Marlin Model 39AS

GRADING: **NiB** = New in Box   **Ex** = Excellent or NRA 95%   **Gd** = Good or NRA 68%

Marlin Model 56

Marlin Model 57

MODEL 980 .22 MAGNUM . . .NiB $290 Ex $167 Gd $135
Bolt action. Caliber: .22 WMR. Eight round clip magazine. 24-inch bbl. Weight: 6 lbs. Sights: Open rear; hooded ramp front. Monte Carlo stock, swivels, sling. Made from 1962 to 1970.

MODEL 2000 TARGET RIFLE . .NiB $590 Ex $479 Gd $338
Bolt-action single-shot. Caliber: .22 LR. Optional 5-round adapter kit available. 22-inch bbl. 41 inches overall. Weight: 8 lbs. Globe front sight, adj. peep or aperture rear. two-stage target trigger. Textured composite Kevlar or black/gray laminated stock. Made from 1991 to 1995.
w/adj. comb (made 1994 only) NiB $643 Ex $522 Gd $355
w/laminated stock (intro. 1996)NiB $654 Ex $535 Gd $429

- RIMFIRE LEVER-ACTION RIFLES -

MODEL 39 CARBINE . . . . .NiB $556 Ex $355 Gd $298
Same as 39M except w/lightweight bbl., 3/4 magazine (capacity: 18 Short, 14 Long, 12 LR), slimmer forearm. Weight: 5.25 lbs. Made 1963 to 1967.

MODEL 39 90TH ANNIVERSARY
CARBINE. . . . . .NiB $1244 Ex $976 Gd $835
Carbine version of 90th Anniversary Model 39A. 500 made in 1960. Top value is for carbine in new, unfired condition.

MODEL 39 CENTURY LTD. . . .NiB $670 Ex $370 Gd $259
Commemorative version of Model 39A. Receiver inlaid w/ brass medallion, "Marlin Centennial 1870-1970." Square lever. 20-inch octagon bbl. Fancy walnut straight-grip stock and forearm; brass forend cap, buttplate, nameplate in buttstock. 35,388 made in 1970.

MODEL 39 LEVER-ACTION
REPEATER . . . . .NiB $3145 Ex $1189 Gd $1018
Takedown. Casehardened receiver. Caliber: .22 LR, Long, Short. Tubular magazine holds 25 Short, 20 Long, 18 LR. 24-inch octagon bbl. Weight: 5.75 lbs. Sights: Open rear; bead front. Plain pistol-grip stock and forearm. Made from 1922 to 1938.

MODEL 39A
General specifications same as Model 39 except w/blued receiver, round bbl., heavier stock w/semibeavertail forearm, weight 6.5 lbs. Made from 1939 to 1960.
Early model (no prefix) . . . . .NiB $1500 Ex $1178 Gd $800
Late model ("B" prefix). . . . . .NiB $1166 Ex $895 Gd $650

MODEL 39A 90TH
ANNIVERSARY RIFLE . . . . . .NiB $1268 Ex $1140 Gd $835
Commemorates Marlin's 90th anniversary. Same general specifications as Golden 39A except w/chrome-plated bbl. and action, stock and forearm of select walnut-finely checkered,

carved figure of a squirrel on right side of buttstock. 500 made in 1960. Top value is for rifle in new, unfired condition.

MODEL 39A ARTICLE II RIFLE NiB $489 Ex $420 Gd $338
Commemorates National Rifle Association Centennial 1871-1971. "The Right to Bear Arms" medallion inlaid in receiver. Similar to Model 39A. Magazine capacity: 26 Short, 21 Long, 19 LR. 24-inch octagon bbl. Fancy walnut pistol-grip stock and forearm; brass forend cap, buttplate. 6,244 made in 1971. Golden 39A/39AS Rifle Same as Model 39A except w/gold-plated trigger, hooded ramp front sight, sling swivels. Made from 1960-87 (39A); Model 39AS from 1988 to date.
Golden 39A . . . . .NiB $479 Ex $300 Gd $190
Golden 39AS (W/hammer
**   block safety) . . . . .NiB $479 Ex $300 Gd $190**

MODEL 39A "MOUNTIE" LEVER- ACTION
REPEATING RIFLE. . . . . .NiB $479 Ex $300 Gd $190
Same as Model 39A except w/lighter, straight-grip stock, slimmer forearm. Weight: 6.25 lbs. Made from 1953 to 1960.
Carbine . . . . NiB $495 Ex $300 Gd $190

MODEL 39A OCTAGON . . . . .NiB $645 Ex $579 Gd $390
Same as Golden 39A except w/oct. bbl., plain bead front sight, slimmer stock and forearm, no pistol-grip cap or swivels. Made in 1973. (2551 produced).

MODEL 39D. . . . . .NiB $440 Ex $280 Gd $200
Same as Model 39M except w/pistol-grip stock, forearm w/bbl. band. Made from 1970 to 1974.

39M ARTICLE II CARBINE . . . .NiB $488 Ex $469 Gd $300
Same as 39A Article II Rifle except w/straight-grip buttstock, square lever, 20-inch octagon bbl., reduced magazine capacity. 3,824 units, made in 1971.

GOLDEN 39M
Calibers: .22 Short, Long and LR. Tubular magazine holds 21 Short, 16 Long or 15 LR cartridges. 20-inch bbl. 36 inches overall. Weight: 6 lbs. Gold-plated trigger. Hooded ramp front sight, adj. folding semi-buckhorn rear. Two-piece, straight-grip American black walnut stock. Sling swivels. Mar-Shield finish. Made from 1960 to 1987.
Golden 39M . . . . .NiB $445 Ex $338 Gd $266
octagonal bbl. (1973 only) . . . NiB $495 Ex $469 Gd $390

MODEL 39M "MOUNTIE" CARBINE
Same as Model 39A "Mountie" Rifle except w/20-inch bbl. Weight: 6 lbs. 500 made in 1960. (For values See Marlin 39 90th Anniversary Carbine)

MODEL 39TDS CARBINE . . . . .NiB $545 Ex $369 Gd $290
Same general specifications as Model 39M except takedown style w/16.5-inch bbl. and reduced magazine capacity. 32.63 inches overall. Weight: 5.25 lbs. Made from 1988 to 1995.

Marlin Model 1894M

Marlin Model 1897
Cowboy

Marlin Model 60C

MODEL 56 LEVERMATIC RIFLE . . .NiB $345 Ex $250 Gd $149
Same as Model 57 except clip-loading. Magazine holds eight rounds. Weight: 5.75 lbs. Made from 1955 to 1964.

MODEL 57 LEVERMATIC RIFLE . . .NiB $375 Ex $227 Gd $132
Lever-action. Cal: .22 LR, 22 Long, 22 Short. Tubular mag. holds 19 LR, 21 Long, 27 Short. 22 inch bbl. Wt: 6.25 lbs. Sights: Open rear, adj. for windage and elevation; hooded ramp front. Monte Carlo-style stock w/pistol-grip. Made from 1959 to 1965.

MODEL 57M LEVERMATIC. . . . NiB $415 Ex $255 Gd $148
Same as Model 57 except chambered for 22 WMR cartridge, w/24-inch bbl., 15-round magazine. Made from 1960 to 1969.

MODEL 97 . . . . NiB $2590 Ex $2066 Gd $1269
Lever action. Takedown. Caliber: .22 LR, Long, Short. Tubular magazine; full length holds 25 Short, 20 Long, 18 LR; half length holds 16 Short, 12 Long and 10 LR. Bbl. lengths: 16, 24, 26, 28 inches. Weight: 6 lbs. Sights: Open rear; bead front. Plain, straight-grip stock and forearm (also avail. w/pistol-grip stock). Made from 1897 to 1922. Note: Before 1905 designated "Model 1897."

MODEL 1870-1970 CENTENNIAL MATCHED PAIR,
MODELS 336 AND 39 . . . . NiB $2230 Ex $1766 Gd $1180
Presentation-grade rifles in luggage-style case. Matching serial numbers. Fancy walnut straight-grip buttstock and forearm brass buttplate and forend cap. Engraved receiver w/inlaid medallion; square lever. 20-inch octagon bbl. Model 336: .30-30, 7-round capacity; weight: 7 lbs. Model 39: .22 Short, Long, LR, tubular magazine holds 21 Short, 16 Long, 15 LR. 1,000 sets produced. Made in 1970. Top value is for rifles in new, unfired condition. See image on page 291.

MODEL 1894M. . . . . NiB $495 Ex $443 Gd $233
Lever action. Caliber: .22 WMR.11-round tubular magazine. 20-inch bbl. Weight: 6.25 lbs. Sights: Ramp front w/brass bead and Wide-Scan hood; adj. semi-buckhorn folding rear. Offset hammer spur for scope use. Straight-grip American black walnut stock w/white buttplate spacer. Squared finger lever. Made from 1986 to 1988.

MODEL 1897 COWBOY . . . . . NiB $643 Ex $489 Gd $369
Lever action. Caliber: .22 LR., capacity: 19 LR, 21 L, or 26 S, tubular magazine. 24-inch tapered octagon bbl., 40 inches overall. Weight: 6.5 lbs. Marble front and adjustable rear sight, tapped for scope mount. Black walnut straight grip stock w/cut checkering and Mar-Shield finish. Made from 1999 to 2001.

- RIMFIRE SEMI-AUTOMATIC RIFLES -

MODEL 49/49DL AUTOLOADING RIFLE
Same as Model 99C except w/two-piece stock, checkered after 1970. Made 1968-71. Model 49DL w/scrollwork on sides of receiver, checkered stock and forearm; made from 1971 to 1978.
Model 49 . . . . NiB $200 Ex $190 Gd $145
Model 49DL . . . . NiB $227 Ex $179 Gd $144

MODEL 50/50E AUTOLOADING RIFLE
Takedown. Cal: .22 LR. Six round detachable box mag. 22 inch bbl. Wt: 6 lbs. Sights: Open rear; bead front; Mdl. 50E w/ peep rear sight, hooded front. Plain pistol-grip stock, forearm w/finger grooves. Made from 1931 to 1934.
Model 50 . . . . NiB $227 Ex $190 Gd $124
Model 50E. . . . . NiB $235 Ex $200 Gd $130

MODEL 60 SEMI-AUTOMATIC
RIFLE . . . . .NiB $227 Ex $145 Gd $90
Caliber: .22 LR. 14-round tubular magazine. 22-inch bbl. 40.5 inches overall. Weight: 5.5 lbs. Grooved receiver. Ramp front sight w/removable hood; adj. open rear. Anodized receiver w/ blued bbl. Monte Carlo-style walnut-finished hardwood stock w/Mar-Shield finish. Made 1981 to date. Note: Marketed 1960 to 1980 under Glenfield promotion logo and w/slightly different stock configuration.

MODEL 60C SELF-LOADING
RIFLE . . . . .NiB $198 Ex $130 Gd $107
Caliber: .22 LR. 14- round tubular mag. 22 inch Micro-Groove bbl., 40.5 inch overall. Wt: 5.5 lbs. Screw-adjustable open rear and ramp front sights. Aluminum receiver, grooved for scope mount. Hardwood Monte Carlo stock w/Mossy Oak "Break-Up" camouflage pattern. Made from 2000 to date.

MODEL 60SS SEMI-AUTOMATIC RIFLE
Same general specifications as Model 60 except w/stainless bbl. and magazine tube. Synthetic, uncheckered birch or laminated black/ gray birch stock w/nickel-plated swivel studs. Made 1993 to date.

Marlin Model 60SS

Marlin Model 70HC w/7-Shot Clip

Marlin Model 70P

w/uncheckered birch stock.... NiB $278 Ex $200 Gd $135
w/laminated birch stock...... NiB $270 Ex $197 Gd $126
w/fiberglass stock .... NiB $260 Ex $188 Gd $126

MODEL 70HC SEMI-AUTOMATIC
Caliber: .22 LR. Seven and 15-round magazine. 18-inch bbl. Weight: 5.5 lbs. 36.75 inches overall. Ramp front sight; adj. open rear. Grooved receiver for scope mounts. Walnut-finished hardwood stock w/Monte Carlo and pistol-grip. Made from 1988 to 1996.
Marlin model .... NiB $200 Ex $155 Gd $124
Glenfield model .... NiB $155 Ex $126 Gd $100

MODEL 70P SEMIAUTOMATIC...NiB $290 Ex $189 Gd $100
"Papoose" takedown. Caliber: .22 LR. Seven round clip. 16.25-inch bbl. 35.25 inches overall. Weight: 3.75 lbs. Sights: Ramp front, adj. open rear. Side ejection, manual bolt hold-open. Cross-bolt safety. Walnut-finished hard-wood stock w/abbreviated forend, pistol-grip. Made 1984 to 1994.

MODEL 70PSS .... NiB $338 Ex $200 Gd $175
Semi-automatic "Papoose" takedown carbine. Caliber: .22 LR. Seven round clip. 16.25- inch bbl., 35.25 inches overall. Weight: 3.25 lbs. Ramp front and adjustable open rear sights. Automatic last-shot hold open (1996). Black fiberglass synthetic stock. Made from 1995 to date.

MODEL 75C
SEMI-AUTOMATIC .... NiB $233 Ex $158 Gd $109
Caliber: .22 LR. 13-round tubular magazine.18-inch bbl. 36.5 inches overall. Weight: 5 lbs. Side ejection. Cross-bolt safety. Sights: Ramp-mounted blade front; adj. open rear. Monte Carlo-style walnut-finished hardwood stock w/pistol-grip. Made 1975 to 1992.

MODEL 88-C/88-DL TAKEDOWN RIFLE
Takedown. Caliber: .22 LR. Tubular magazine in buttstock holds 14 cartridges. 24-inch bbl. Weight: 6.75 lbs. Sights: Open rear; hooded front. Plain pistol-grip stock. Made from 1947-56. Model 88-DL w/received peep sight, checkered stock and sling swivels, made 1953 to 1956.
Model 88-C................ NiB $200 Ex $145 Gd $100
Model 88-DL.............. NiB $200 Ex $145 Gd $100

MODEL 89C/89DL AUTOLOADING RIFLE
Clip magazine version of Model 88-C. Seven round clip (12-round in later models); other specifications same. Made from 1950 to 1961. Model 89-DL w/receiver peep sight, sling swivels.
Model 89-C................ NiB $200 Ex $145 Gd $100
Model 89-DL.............. NiB $210 Ex $150 Gd $105

MODEL 98 AUTOLOADING
RIFLE..................... NiB $255 Ex $138 Gd $100
Solid frame. Caliber: .22 LR. Tubular magazine holds 15 cartridges. 22-inch bbl. Weight: 6.75 lbs. Sights: Open rear; hooded ramp front. Monte Carlo stock w/cheekpiece. Made from 1950 to 1961.

MODEL 99 AUTOLOADING
RIFLE..................... NiB $255 Ex $138 Gd $100
Caliber: .22 LR. Tubular magazine holds 18 cartridges. 22-inch bbl. Weight: 5.5 lbs. Sights: Open rear; hooded ramp front. Plain pistol-grip stock. Made from 1959 to 1961.

MODEL 99C .... NiB $209 Ex $177 Gd $119
Same as Model 99 except w/gold-plated trigger, receiver grooved for tip-off scope mounts, Monte Carlo stock (checkered in later production). Made from 1962 to 1978.

MODEL 99DL.............. NiB $266 Ex $255 Gd $144
Same as Model 99 except w/gold-plated trigger, jeweled breech bolt, Monte Carlo stock w/pistol-grip, swivels and sling. Made 1960 to 1965.

MODEL 99M1 CARBINE........ NiB $200 Ex $99 Gd $80
Same as Model 99C except styled after U.S. .30 M1 Carbine; 9-round tubular magazine, 18-inch bbl. Sights: Open rear; military-style ramp front; carbine stock w/handguard and bbl. band, sling swivels. Weight: 4.5 lbs. Made 1966 to 1979.

MODEL 795 SELF-LOADING
RIFLE .... NiB $167 Ex $130 Gd $115
Caliber: .22 LR. 10- round clip. 18- inch Micro-Groove bbl., 37 inches overall. Weight: 5 lbs. Screw-adjustable open rear and ramp front sight. Monte Carlo synthetic stock with checkering swivel studs. Made from 1999 to date.

MODEL 922 MAGNUM SELF-LOADING
RIFLE..................... NiB $390 Ex $244 Gd $160
Similar to Model 9 except chambered for .22 WMR. Seven round magazine. 20.5-inch bbl. 39.5 inches overall. Weight: 6.5 lbs. American black walnut stock w/Monte Carlo. Blued finish. Made 1993 to 2001.

Marlin Model 989

Marlin Model 989M2

Marlin Model 990

Marlin Model 990L

Marlin Model 995

Marlin Model A-1 Autoloader

RIFLES

MODEL 989 AUTOLOADING
RIFLE . . . . **NiB $210 Ex $144 Gd $110**
Caliber: .22 LR. Seven round clip magazine. 22-inch bbl. Weight: 5.5 lbs. Sights: Open rear; hooded ramp front. Monte Carlo walnut stock w/pistol grip. Made from 1962 to 1966.

MODEL 989M2 CARBINE . . . . . **NiB $250 Ex $145 Gd $100**
Semi-automatic. Same as Model 99M1 except clip-loading, 7-round magazine. Made from 1966 to 199.

MODEL 990 SEMI-AUTOMATIC
Caliber: .22 LR. 17-round tubular magazine. 22-inch bbl. 40.75 inches overall. Weight: 5.5 lbs. Side ejection. Cross-bolt safety. Ramp front sight w/brass bead; adj. semi-buckhorn folding rear. Receiver grooved for scope mount. Monte Carlo-style American black walnut stock w/checkered pistol grip and forend. Made from 1979 to 1987.
Model 990 Semiautomatic . . . . . **NiB $135 Ex $100 Gd $85**
w/14-round mag, laminated hardwood stock,
  QD swivels, blackrecoil pad. Made 1992
  to date) . . . . **NiB $208 Ex $155 Gd $110**

MODEL 995
SEMI-AUTOMATIC . . . . **NiB $233 Ex $167 Gd $110**
Caliber: .22 LR. Seven round clip magazine.18-inch bbl. 36.75 inches overall. Weight: 5 lbs. Cross-bolt safety. Sights: Ramp front w/brass bead; adj. folding semi-buckhorn rear. Monte Carlo-style American black walnut stock w/checkered pistol grip and forend. Made from 1979 to 1994.

MODEL 7000 . . . . **NiB $255 Ex $190 Gd $146**
Semi-automatic. Caliber: .22 LR. 10-round magazine. 18-inch bbl. Weight: 5.5 lbs. Synthetic stocks. No sights; receiver grooved for scope. Semi-auto. Side ejection. Manual bolt hold-open. Cross-bolt safety. Matte finish. Made from 1997 to 2001.
Model 7000T . . . . **NiB $390 Ex $290 Gd $220**

MODEL A-1 . . . . **NiB $185 Ex $110 Gd $90**
Semi-automatic. Takedown. Caliber: .22 LR. Six round detachable box magazine. 24-inch bbl. Weight: 6 lbs. Open rear sight. Plain pistol-grip stock. Made from 1935 to 1946.

MODEL A-1C . . . . **NiB $185 Ex $110 Gd $90**
Improved version of Model A-1 w/same general specifications, stock w/semibeavertail forend. Made from 1940 to 1946.

MODEL A-1DL . . . . **NiB $185 Ex $110 Gd $90**
Same as Model A-1C above, except w/peep rear sight; hooded front, swivels.

MODEL A-1E . . . . **NiB $190 Ex $126 Gd $95**
Same as Model A-1 except w/peep rear sight; hooded front.

MODEL 99G . . . .**NiB $170 Ex $75 Gd $65**
Semi-automatic. Same as Marlin Model 99C except w/plain stock, bead front sight. Made from 1960 to 1965.

MODEL 989G . . . .**NiB $179 Ex $110 Gd $79**
Semi-automatic. Same as Marlin Model 989 except w/plain stock, bead front sight. Made from 1962 to 1964.

- SLIDE-ACTION RIFLES (CENTERFIRE AND RIMFIRE)-

MODEL 18 BABY . . . .**NiB $1405 Ex $1105 Gd $610**
Slide-action repeater. Exposed hammer. Solid frame. Caliber: .22 Short, Long, LR. Tubular magazine holds 14 Short cartridges. 20-inch bbl., round or octagon. Weight: 3.75 lbs. Sights: Open rear; bead front. Plain straight-grip stock and slide handle. Made from 1906 to 1909.

MODEL 20 SLIDE-ACTION . . .**NiB $1405 Ex $1105 Gd $605**
Exposed hammer. Takedown. Caliber: .22 LR, Long, Short. Tubular magazine: Half-length holds 15 Short, 12 Long, 10 LR; full-length holds 25 Short, 20 Long, 18 LR. 24-inch octagon bbl. Weight: 5 lbs. Sights: Open rear; bead front. Plain straight-grip stock, grooved slide handle. Made from 1907 to 1922. Note: After 1920 was designated "Model 20-S."

MODEL 25 SLIDE-ACTION
REPEATER . . . .**NiB $879 Ex $540 Gd $431**
Exposed hammer. Takedown. Caliber: .22 Short (also handles 22 CB caps). Tubular magazine holds 15 Short. 23-inch bbl. Weight: 4 lbs. Sights: Open rear; beaded front. Plain straight-grip stock and slide handle. Made from 1909 to 1910.

MODEL 27 . . . .**NiB $1159 Ex $909 Gd $650**
Slide-action repeater. Exposed hammer. Takedown. Calibers: .25-20, .32-20. Magazine (tubular) holds 7 rounds. 24-inch octagon bbl. Weight: 5.75 lbs. Sights: Open rear; bead front. Plain, straight-grip stock, grooved slide handle. Made from 1910 to 1916.

MODEL 27S . . . .**NiB $909 Ex $579 Gd $388**
Same as Model 27 except w/round bbl., also chambered for .25 Stevens rimfire Made from 1920 to 1932.

MODEL 29 SLIDE-ACTION
REPEATER . . . .**NiB $660 Ex $388 Gd $290**
Similar to Model 20 w/23-inch round bbl., half magazine only, weight 5.75 lbs. Made from 1913 to 1916.

MODEL 32 SLIDE-ACTION
REPEATER . . . .**NiB $1154 Ex $690 Gd $533**
Hammerless. Takedown. Caliber: .22 LR, Long, Short. Tubular magazine holds 15 Short, 12 Long, 10 LR; full magazine, 25 Short, 20 Long, 18 LR. 24-inch octagon bbl. Weight: 5.5 lbs. Sights: Open rear; bead front. Plain pistol-grip stock, grooved slide handle. Made from 1914 to 1915.

MODEL 37 . . . .**NiB $650 Ex $442 Gd $237**
Slide action. Similar to Model 29 except w/24-inch bbl. and full magazine. Weight: 5.25 lbs. Made from 1913 to 1916.

MODEL 38 . . . .**NiB $744 Ex $418 Gd $339**
Slide action. Hammerless. Takedown. Caliber: .22 LR, Long, Short. 2/3 magazine (tubular) holds 15 Short, 12 Long, 10 LR. 24-inch octagon or round bbls. Weight: 5.5 lbs. Sights: Open rear; bead front. Plain shotgun-type pistol-grip buttstock w/hard rubber buttplate, grooved slide handle. Ivory bead front sight; adj. rear. About 20,000 Model 38 rifles were made 1920 to 1930.

MAUSER SPORTING RIFLES — Oberndorf am Neckar, Germany

Manufactured by Mauser-Werke GmbH. Imported by Blaser USA in San Antoinio; previously by Brolin Arms, Pomona, CA; Gun South, Inc.; Gibbs Rifle Co.; Precision Imports, Inc. and KDF, Inc.

Before the end of WWI the name of the Mauser firm was "Waffenfabrik Mauser A.-G." Shortly after WWI it was changed to "Mauser-Werke A.-G." This information may be used to determine the age of genuine original Mauser sporting rifles made before WWII because all bear either of these firm names as well as the Mauser banner trademark. The first four rifles listed were manufactured before WWI. Those that follow were produced between World Wars I and II. The early Mauser models can generally be identified by the pistol grip, which is rounded instead of capped, and the M/98 military-type magazine floorplate and catch. The later models have hinged magazine floorplates with lever or button release.

NOTE: *The "B" series of Mauser .22 rifles (Model ES340B, MS350B, etc.) were improved versions of their corresponding models and were introduced about 1935.*

- PRE-WORLD WAR I MODELS -

BOLT-ACTION SPORTING CARBINE
Calibers: 6.5x54, 6.5x58, 7x57, 8x57, 957mm. 19.75-inch bbl. Weight: 7 lbs. Full-stocked to muzzle. Other specifications same as for standard rifle.
W/20-inch bbl. (Type M) . .**NiB $2489 Ex $2066 Gd $1445**
W/20- or 24-inch bbl. (Type S)NiB $2566 Ex $2155 Gd $1486

BOLT-ACTION SPORTING RIFLE
Calibers: 6.5x55, 6.5x58, 7x57, 8x57, 9x57, 9.3x62 10.75x68. Five-round box magazine, 23.5-inch bbl. Weight: 7 to 7.5 lbs. Pear-shaped bolt handle. Double-set or single trigger. Sights: Tangent curve rear; ramp front. Pistol-grip stock, forearm w/ Schnabel tip and swivels.
Type A, English export . . . .**NiB $2669 Ex $2276 Gd $1559**
Type B . . . .**NiB $1790 Ex $1466 Gd $1080**

BOLT-ACTION SPORTING RIFLE,
MILITARY MODEL TYPE C .**NiB $3854 Ex $3165 Gd $2189**
So called because of stepped M/98-type bbl., military front sight and double-pull trigger. Calibers: 7x57, 8x57, 9x57mm. Other specifications same as for standard rifle.

BOLT-ACTION SPORTING RIFLE
SHORT MODEL TYPE K . . .**NiB $3856 Ex $3169 Gd $2190**
Calibers: 6.5x54, 8x51mm. 19.75-inch bbl. Weight: 6.25 lbs. Other specifications same as for standard rifle.

- PRE-WORLD WAR II MODELS -

MODEL DSM34 BOLT-ACTION SINGLE-SHOT
SPORTING RIFLE . . . .**NiB $670 Ex $445 Gd $338**
Also called "Sport-model." Caliber: .22 LR. 26-inch bbl. Weight: 7.75 lbs. Sights: Tangent curve open rear; Barleycorn front. M/98 military-type stock, swivels. Intro. c. 1935.

MODEL EL320 BOLT-ACTION SINGLE-SHOT
SPORTING RIFLE . . . .**NiB $556 Ex $449 Gd $339**
Caliber: .22 LR. 23.5-inch bbl. Weight: 4.25 lbs. Sights: Adj. open rear; bead front. Sporting stock w/checkered pistol grip, swivels.

Mauser Model ES350

Mauser Type "A" Pattern No. 1 shown
with floorplate opened.

Mauser Type "B" Pattern No. 60

Mauser Type "M" Pattern No. 270

RIFLES

**MODEL EN310 BOLT-ACTION SINGLE-SHOT
SPORTING RIFLE** . . . . NiB $499 Ex $420 Gd $298
Caliber: .22 LR. ("22 Lang fur Buchsen.") 19.75-inch bbl.
Weight: 4 lbs. Sights: Fixed open rear, blade front. Plain pistol-
grip stock.

**MODEL ES340 BOLT-ACTION SINGLE-SHOT
TARGET RIFLE** . . . . NiB $765 Ex $455 Gd $338
Caliber: .22 LR. 25.5-inch bbl. Weight: 6.5 lbs. Sights: Tangent
curve rear; ramp front. Sporting stock w/checkered pistol-grip
and grooved forearm, swivels.

**MODEL ES340B BOLT-ACTION SINGLE-SHOT
TARGET RIFLE** . . . . NiB $765 Ex $445 Gd $356
Caliber: .22 LR. 26.75-inch bbl. Weight: 8 lbs. Sights: Tangent
curve open rear; ramp front. Plain pistol-grip stock, swivels.

**MODEL ES350 BOLT-ACTION SINGLE-SHOT
TARGET RIFLE** . . . . NiB $977 Ex $775 Gd $558
"Meistershaftsbuchse" (Championship Rifle). Caliber: .22 LR.
27.5-inch bbl. Weight: 7.75 lbs. Sights: Open micrometer rear;
ramp front. Target stock w/checkered pistol-grip and forearm,
grip cap, swivels.

**MODEL ES350B BOLT-ACTION SINGLE-SHOT
TARGET RIFLE** . . . . NiB $970 Ex $668 Gd $495
Same general specifications as Model MS350B except single-
shot, weight: 8.25 lbs.

**MODEL KKW BOLT-ACTION SINGLE-SHOT
TARGET RIFLE** . . . . NiB $944 Ex $667 Gd $544

Caliber: .22 LR. 26-inch bbl. Weight: 8.75 lbs. Sights: Tangent
curve open rear; Barleycorn front. M/98 military-type stock,
swivels. Note: This rifle has an improved design Mauser 22
action w/separate nonrotating bolt head. In addition to being
produced for commercial sale, this model was used as a training rifle by the German armed forces; it was also made by
Walther and Gustoff. Intro. just before WWII.

**MODEL MM410 BOLT-ACTION REPEATING
SPORTING RIFLE** . . . . NiB $2166 Ex $1590 Gd $955
Caliber: .22 LR. Five round detachable box magazine. 23.5-
inch bbl. Weight: 5 lbs. Sights: Tangent curve open rear; ramp
front. Sporting stock w/checkered pistol-grip, swivels.

**MODEL MM410B BOLT-ACTION REPEATING
SPORTING RIFLE** . . . . NiB $2166 Ex $1590 Gd $955
Caliber: .22 LR. Five round detachable box magazine. 23.5-inch
bbl. Weight: 6.25 lbs. Sights: Tangent curve open rear; ramp front.
Lightweight sporting stock w/checkered pistol-grip, swivels.

**MODEL MS350B BOLT-ACTION REPEATING
TARGET RIFLE** . . . . NiB $1268 Ex $800 Gd $556
Caliber: .22 LR. Five round detachable box magazine. Receiver and
bbl. grooved for detachable rear sight or scope. 26.75-inch bbl.
Weight: 8.5 lbs. Sights: Micrometer open rear; ramp front. Target
stock w/checkered pistol grip and forearm, grip cap, sling swivels.

**MODEL MS420 BOLT-ACTION REPEATING
SPORTING RIFLE** . . . . NiB $1145 Ex $879 Gd $606
Caliber: .22 LR. Five round detachable box magazine. 25.5-
inch bbl. Weight: 6.5 lbs. Sights: Tangent curve open rear; ramp
front. Sporting stock w/checkered pistol grip, grooved forearm
swivels.

MODEL MS420B BOLT-ACTION REPEATING
TARGET RIFLE . . . . NiB $1156 Ex $922 Gd $633
Caliber: .22 LR. Five round detachable box magazine. 26.75-inch bbl. Weight: 8 lbs. Sights: Tangent curve open rear; ramp front. Target stock w/checkered pistol grip, grooved forearm, swivels.

STANDARD MODEL RIFLE . . . . NiB $339 Ex $210 Gd $159
Refined version of German Service Kar. 98k. Straight bolt handle. Calibers: 7mm Mauser (7x57mm), 7.9mm Mauser (8x57mm). Five round box magazine. 23.5-inch bbl. Weight: 8.5 lbs. Sights: Blade front; adj. rear. Walnut stock of M/98 military-type. Note: These rifles were made for commercial sale and are of the high quality found in the Oberndorf Mauser sporters. They bear the Mauser trademark on the receiver ring.

TYPE "A" BOLT-ACTION SPORTING
RIFLE . . . . NiB $7000 Ex $6200 Gd $3005
Special British Model. 7x57, 30-06 (7.62x63), 8x60, 9x57, 9.3x62mm. Five round box mag. 23.5-inch round bbl. Weight: 7.25 lbs. Mil.-type single trigger. Sights: Express rear; hooded ramp front. Circassian walnut sporting stock w/checkered pistol-grip and forearm, w/ or w/o cheekpiece, buffalo horn forend tip and grip cap, detachable swivels. Variations: Octagon bbl., double-set trigger, shotgun-type safety, folding peep rear sight, tangent curve rear sight, three-leaf rear sight.

TYPE "A" BOLT-ACTION SPORTING RIFLE,
MAGNUM MODEL . . . . NiB $5598 Ex $3473 Gd $2745
Same general specifications as standard Type "A" except w/ Magnum action, weighs 7.5 to 8.5 lbs. Calibers: .280 Ross, .318 Westley Richards Express, 10.75x68mm, .404 Nitro Express.

TYPE "A" BOLT-ACTION SPORTING RIFLE,
SHORT MODEL . . . . NiB $6149 Ex $4144 Gd $2448
Same as standard Type "A" except w/short action, 21.5-inch round bbl., weight 6 lbs. Calibers: .250-3000, 6.5x54, 8x51mm.

TYPE "B" BOLT-ACTION SPORTING
RIFLE . . . . NiB $5005 Ex $4885 Gd $2544
Normal Model. Calibers: 7x57, .30-06 (7.62x63), 8x57, 8x60, 9x57, 9.3x62, 10.7568mm. Five round box magazine. 23.5-inch round bbl. Weight: 7.25 lbs. Double-set trigger. Sights: Three-leaf rear, ramp front. Fine walnut stock w/checkered pistol-grip, Schnabel forend tip, cheekpiece, grip cap, swivels. Variations: Octagon or half-octagon bbl., military-type single trigger, shotgun-type safety, folding peep rear sight, tangent curve rear sight, telescopic sight.

TYPE "K" BOLT-ACTION SPORTING
RIFLE . . . . NiB $8177 Ex $6805 Gd $4285
Light Short Model. Same specifications as Normal Type "B" model except w/short action, 21.5-inch round bbl., weight: 6 lbs. Calibers: .250-3000, 6.5x54, 8x51mm.

TYPE "M" BOLT-ACTION
SPORTING CARBINE . . . . . NiB $6000 Ex $5133 Gd $3200
Calibers: 6.5x54, 7x57, .30-06 (7.62x63), 8x51, 8x60, 9x57mm. Five round box magazine. 19.75-inch round bbl. Weight: 6 to 6.75 lbs. Double-set trigger, flat bolt handle. Sights: Three-leaf rear; ramp front. Stocked to muzzle, cheekpiece, checkered pistol-grip and forearm, grip cap, steel forend cap, swivels. Variations: Military-type single trigger, shotgun-type trigger, shotgun-type safety, tangent curve rear sight, telescopic sight.

TYPE "S" BOLT-ACTION SPORTING
CARBINE . . . . NiB $6000 Ex $5009 Gd $3005
Calibers: 6.5x54 7x57, 8x51, 8x60, 9x57mm. Five-round box magazine. 19.75-inch round bbl. Weight: 6 to 6.75 lbs. Double-set trigger. Sights: Three-leaf rear; ramp front. Stocked to muzzle, Schnabel forend tip, cheekpiece, checkered pistol-grip w/cap, swivels. Variations: Same as listed for Normal Model Type "B."

- POST-WORLD WAR II MODELS -

NOTE: *Production of original Mauser sporting rifles (66 series) resumed at the Oberndorf plant in 1965 by Mauser-Jagdwaffen GmbH, now Mauser-Werke Oberndorf GmbH. The Series 2000-3000-4000 rifles, however, were made for Mauser by Friedrich Wilhelm Heym Gewehrfabrik, Muennerstadt, West Germany.*

MODEL 66S BOLT-ACTION STANDARD SPORTING RIFLE
Telescopic short action. Bbls. interchangeable within cal. group. Single- or double-set trigger (interchangeable). Cal: .243 Win., 6.5x57, .270 Win., 7x64, .308 Win., .30-06. Three round mag. 23.6 inch bbl. (25.6inch in 7x64). Wt: 7.3 lbs. (7.5 lbs. in 7x64). Sights: Adj. open rear, hooded ramp front. Select Eur. walnut stock, Monte Carlo w/cheekpiece, rosewood forend tip and pistol-grip cap, skip checkering, recoil pad, sling swivels. Made from 1974 to 1995, export to U.S. disc. 1974. Note: U.S. designation, 1971 to 1973, was "Model 660."
Model 66S . . . . NiB $4739 Ex $3054 Gd $2044
w/extra bbl. assembly, add $600

MODEL 66S DELUXE SPORTER
Limited production special order. Model 66S rifles and carbines are available with elaborate engraving, gold and silver inlays and carved select walnut stocks. Added value is upward of $4500.

MODEL 66S ULTRA
Same general specifications as Model 66S Standard except with 20.9-inch bbl., weight: 6.8 lbs.
Model 66S Ultra . . . . NiB $1754 Ex $1644 Gd $1097
w/extra bbl. assembly, add $600

MODEL 66SG BIG GAME . . NiB $3077 Ex $2100 Gd $1388
Same general specifications as Model 66S Standard except w/25.6-inch bbl., weight 9.3 lbs. Calibers: .375 H&H Mag., .458 Win. Mag. Note: U.S. designation, 1971-73, was "Model 660 Safari."
w/ extra bbl. assembly, add $600

MODEL 66SH HIGH
PERFORMANCE . . . . NiB $1706 Ex $1530 Gd $1109
Same general specifications as Model 66S Standard except w/25.6-inch bbl., weighs 7.5 lbs. (9.3 lbs. in 9.3x64). Calibers: 6.5x68, 7mm Rem. Mag., 7mm S.E.v. Hoffe, .300 Win. Mag., 8x68S, 9.3x64.

MODEL 66SP SUPER MATCH BOLT-ACTION
TARGET RIFLE . . . . NiB $4198 Ex $3707 Gd $2033
Telescopic short action. Adj. single-stage trigger. Caliber: .308 Win. (chambering for other cartridges available on special order). Three round magazine. 27.6-inch heavy bbl. w/muzzle brake, dovetail rib for special scope mount. Weight: 12 lbs. Target stock w/wide and deep forearm, full pistol-grip, thumbhole adj. cheekpiece, adj. rubber buttplate.

MODEL 66ST CARBINE . . . . NiB $2635 Ex $1710 Gd $1277
Same general specifications as Model 66S Standard except w/20.9-inch bbl., full-length stock, weight: 7 lbs.

Mauser Model 66S Deluxe

Mauser Model 66SP
Super Match Target Rifle

Mauser Model 66ST Carbine

w/extra bbl. assembly, add $600

MODEL 83 . . . . **NiB $2215 Ex $2188 Gd $1360**
Centerfire single-shot, bolt-action rifle for 300-meter competition. Caliber: .308 Win. 25.5-inch fluted bbl. Weight: 10.5 lbs. Adj. micrometer rear sight globe front. Fully adj. competition stock. Disc. 1988.

MODEL 96 . . . . **NiB $677 Ex $633 Gd $455**
Calibers: .25-06, .270 Win., 7x64, .308 Win., .30-06, 7mm Rem. Mag., .300 Win. Mag. 22-inch bbl. Weight: 6.25 lbs. No sights; drilled and tapped for scope. Walnut stock. Five-round top-loading magazine. 3-position safety.

MODEL 99 CLASSIC BOLT-ACTION RIFLE
Calibers: .243 Win., .25-06, .270 Win., .30-06, .308 Win., .257 Wby., .270 Wby., 7mm Rem. Mag., .300 Win., .300 Wby. .375 H&H. Four round magazine (standard), 3-round (Magnum). Bbl.: 24-inch (standard) or 26-inch (Magnum). 44 inches overall (standard). Weight: 8 lbs. No sights. Checkered European walnut stock w/rosewood grip cap available in Classic and Monte Carlo styles w/High-Luster or oil finish. Disc. importing 1994.
Standard Classic or
   Monte Carlo (oil finish) . . **NiB $1156 Ex $1077 Gd $710**
Magnum Classic or
   Monte Carlo (oil finish) . . **NiB $1266 Ex $1109 Gd $800**
Standard Classic or
   Monte Carlo (H-L finish) . **NiB $1188 Ex $1098 Gd $775**
Magnum Classic or
   Monte Carlo (H-L finish) . **NiB $1347 Ex $1109 Gd $790**

MODEL 107 BOLT-ACTION
RIFLE. . . . . **NiB $369 Ex $277 Gd $210**

Caliber: .22 LR. Mag. Five round magazine. 21.5-inch bbl. 40 inches overall. Weight: 5 lbs. Receiver drilled and tapped for rail scope mounts. Hooded front sight, adj. rear. Disc. importing 1994.

MODEL 201/201 LUXUS BOLT-ACTION RIFLE
Calibers: .22 LR. .22 Win. Mag. Five round magazine. 21-inch bbl. 40 inches overall. Weight: 6.5 lbs. Receiver drilled and tapped for scope mounts. Sights optional. Checkered walnut-stained beech stock w/Monte Carlo. Model 201 Luxus w/checkered European walnut stock QD swivels, rosewood forend and rubber recoil pad. Made from 1989 to 1997.
Standard model. . . . . **NiB $670 Ex $555 Gd $400**
Magnum . . . . **NiB $722 Ex $569 Gd $440**
Luxus Standard model. . . . . **NiB $756 Ex $544 Gd $468**
Luxus Magnum model. . . . . **NiB $844 Ex $633 Gd $560**

MODEL 2000 BOLT-ACTION
SPORTING RIFLE . . . . **NiB $539 Ex $355 Gd $290**
Modified Mauser-type action. Calibers: .270 Win., .308 Win., .30-06. Five-round magazine. 24-inch bbl. Weight: 7.5 lbs. Sights: Folding leaf rear; hooded ramp front. Checkered walnut stock w/Monte Carlo comb and cheekpiece, forend tip, sling swivels. Made from 1969 to 1971. Note: Model 2000 is similar in appearance to Model 3000.

MODEL 2000 CLASSIC BOLT-ACTION SPORTING RIFLE
Calibers: .22-250 Rem., .234 Win., .270 Win., 7mm Mag., .308 Win., .30-06, .300 Win. Mag. Three or 5-round magazine. 24-inch bbl. Weight: 7.5 lbs. Sights: Folding leaf rear; hooded ramp front. Checkered walnut stock w/Monte Carlo comb and cheekpiece, forend tip, sling swivels. Imported 1998. Note: The Model 2000 Classic is designed to interchange bbl. assemblies within a given caliber group.
Classic model . . . . **NiB $1696 Ex $ 1377 Gd $1044**
Professional model . . . . **NiB $3228 Ex $2709 Gd $1995**
w/recoil compensator . . . . . **NiB $3245 Ex $2730 Gd $1100**
Sniper model. . . . . **NiB $2010 Ex $1544 Gd $1120**
Varmint model . . . . **NiB $1996 Ex $1528 Gd $965**
Extra bbl. assembly, add $950

RIFLES

Mauser Model 99

Mauser Model 201

Mauser Model 3000

Mauser Model 4000

Midland Model 2707 Bolt-Action Rifle

Merkel Model 220

MODEL 3000 BOLT-ACTION
SPORTING RIFLE . . . . NiB $570 Ex $440 Gd $400
Modified Mauser-type action. Calibers: .243 Win., .270 Win., .308 Win., .30-06. Five round magazine. 22-inch bbl. Weight: 7 lbs. No sights. Select European walnut stock, Monte Carlo style w/cheekpiece, rosewood forend tip and pistol-grip cap, skip checkering, recoil pad, sling swivels. Made from 1971 to 1974.

MODEL 3000 MAGNUM . . . . . NiB $641 Ex $486 Gd $379
Same general specifications as standard Model 3000, except w/3-round magazine, 26-inch bbl., weight: 8 lbs. Calibers: 7mm Rem. Mag., .300 Win. Mag., .375 H&H Mag.

MODEL 4000 VARMINT RIFLE NiB $466 Ex $380 Gd $269
Same general specifications as standard Model 3000, except w/smaller action, folding leaf rear sight; hooded ramp front, rubber buttplate instead of recoil pad, weight 6.75 lbs. Calibers: .222 Rem., .223 Rem. 22-inch bbl. Select European walnut stock w/rosewood forend tip and pistol-grip cap. French checkering and sling swivels.

McMILLAN GUN WORKS — Phoenix, Arizona *See Harris Gunworks.*

GEBRÜDER MERKEL — Suhl, Germany
For Merkel combination guns and drillings, see listings under Merkel shotguns.

OVER/UNDER RIFLES ("BOCK-DOPPELBÜCHSEN")
Calibers: 5.6x35 Vierling, 6.5x58r5, 7x57r5, 8x57JR, 8x60R Magnum, 9.3x53r5, 9.3x72r5, 9.3x74r5, 10.3x60R as well as most of the British calibers for African and Indian big game. Various bbl. lengths, weights. In general, specifications correspond to those of Merkel over/under shotguns. Values of

Mossberg Model 25

these over/under rifles (in calibers for which ammunition is obtainable) are about the same as those of comparable shotgun models currently manufactured. For more specific data, see Merkel shotgun models indicated below.

Model 210 . . . . NiB $5766 Ex $4470 Gd $3210
Model 210E. . . . . NiB $6630 Ex $4950 Gd $3765
Model 213 . . . . NiB $13,760 Ex $10,550 Gd $7330
Model 240E1. . . . . NiB $7113 Ex $4966 Gd $3412
Model 313E. . . . . . . NiB $19,670 Ex $16,750 Gd $10,355
Model 320E. . . . . NiB $15,770 Ex $12,559 Gd $9220
Model 321 . . . . NiB $17,210 Ex $13,880 Gd $9155
Model 321E. . . . . NiB $17,998 Ex $14,760 Gd $9970
Model 322 . . . . NiB $12,550 Ex $14,770 Gd $10,049
Model 323E. . . . . . . NiB $23,760 Ex $19,210 Gd $12,960
Model 324 . . . . NiB $27,650 Ex $21,880 Gd $15,330

MEXICAN MILITARY RIFLE — Mexico

Manufactured by Government Arsenal, Mexico, D.F.

MODEL 1936 MAUSER
MILITARY RIFLE . . . . NiB $221 Ex $169 Gd $95
Same as German Kar.98k w/minor variations and U.S. M/1903 Springfield-type knurled cocking piece.

MIDLAND RIFLES — Martinsburg, West Virginia

Manufactured by Gibbs Rifle Company, Inc., Martinsburg, West Virginia.

MODEL 2100 BOLT-ACTION
RIFLE . . . . NiB $413 Ex $338 Gd $228
Calibers: .22-250, .243 Win., 6mm Rem., .270 Win., 6.5x55, 7x57, 7x64, .308 Win., and .30-06. Springfield 1903 action. Four-round magazine. 22-inch bbl. 43 inches overall. Weight: 7 lbs. Flip-up rear sight; hooded ramp front. Finely finished and checkered walnut stock w/pistol-grip cap and sling swivels. Steel recoil bar. Action drilled and tapped for scope mounts. Production disc.1997.

MODEL 2600 BOLT-ACTION
RIFLE . . . . NiB $445 Ex $370 Gd $220
Same general specifications as Model 2100 except no pistol-grip cap, and stock is walnut-finished hardwood. Made 1992 to 1997.

MODEL 2707 BOLT-ACTION
RIFLE . . . . NiB $443 Ex $284 Gd $220
Same general specifications as Model 2100 except the weight of this rifle as been reduced by utilizing a tapered bbl., anodized aluminum trigger housing and lightened stock. Weight: 6.5 lbs. Disc.

MODEL 2800 LIGHTWEIGHT
RIFLE . . . . NiB $466 Ex $355 Gd $269
Same general specifications as Model 2100 except w/laminated birch stock. Made from 1992 to 1994 and from 1996 to 1997.

MITCHELL ARMS, INC. — Fountain Valley, CA

Formerly Santa Ana, California.

MODEL 15/22 SEMIAUTOMATIC
High Standard-style action. Caliber: .22 LR. 15-round magazine (10-round after 10/13/94). 20.5-inch bbl. 37.5 inches overall. Weight: 6.25 lbs. Ramp front sight; adj. open rear. Blued finish. Mahogany stock; Monte Carlo-style American walnut stock on Deluxe model. Made from 1994 to 1996.
NiB $300 Ex $233 Gd $179 . . NiB $300 Ex $233 Gd $179
Carbine . . . . NiB $300 Ex $233 Gd $179
Deluxe . . . . NiB $259 Ex $166 Gd $126

MODEL 9300 SERIES BOLT-ACTION RIFLE
Calibers: .22 LR. .22 Mag. Five or 10-round magazine. 22.5-inch bbl. 40.75 inches overall. Weight: 6.5 lbs. Beaded ramp front sight; adj. open rear. Blued finish. American walnut stock. Made 1994 to 1995.
**Model 9302 (.22 LR w/checkered
  stock, rosewood caps)** . . . . . NiB $319 Ex $239 Gd $177
**Model 9302 (.22 Mag., checkered
  stock, rosewood caps)** . . . . . NiB $317 Ex $237 Gd $175
Model 9303 (.22 LR, plain stock) . . NiB $317 Ex $237 Gd $175
**Model 9304 (.22 Mag.,
  checkered stock)** . . . . NiB $266 Ex $201 Gd $177
**Model 9305 (.22 LR,
  special stock)** . . . . NiB $221 Ex $179 Gd $235

AK-22 SEMIAUTOMATIC RIFLE . . . NiB $359 Ex $248 Gd $189
Replica of AK-47 rifle. .22 LR. .22 WMR., 20-round magazine (.22 LR), 10-round (.22 WMR). 18-inch bbl. 36 inches overall. Weight: 6.5 lbs. Sights: Post front; open adj. rear. European walnut stock and forend. Matte black finish. Made from 1985 to 1994.

CAR-15 . . . . NiB $525 Ex $355 Gd $283
Replica of AR-15 CAR rifle. Caliber: .22 LR. 15-round magazine.16.25-inch bbl. 32 inches overall. Sights: Adj. post front; adj. aperture rear. Telescoping buttstock and ventilated forend. Matte black finish. Made 1990 to 1994.

GALIL 22 SEMIAUTOMATIC RIFLE . . . . NiB $439 Ex $289 Gd $198
Replica of Israeli Galil rifle. Calibers: .22 LR. .22 WMR., 20-round magazine (.22 LR), 10-round (.22 WMR). 18-inch bbl. 36 inches overall. Weight: 6.5 lbs. Sights: Adj. post front; rear adj. for windage. Folding metal stock w/European walnut grip and forend. Matte black finish. Made 1987 to 1993.

M-16A 22 SEMIAUTOMATIC RIFLE . . . NiB $479 Ex $266 Gd $179
Replica of AR-15 rifle. Caliber: .22 LR. 15-round magazine. 20.5-inch bbl. 38.5 inches overall. Weight: 7 lbs. Sights: Adj. post front, adj. aperture rear. Black composite stock and forend. Matte black finish. Made 1990 to 1994.

MAS 22 SEMIAUTOMATIC RIFLE . NiB $439 Ex $290 Gd $221
Replica of French MAS bullpup rifle. Caliber: .22 LR. 20-round magazine. 18-inch bbl. 28 inches overall. Weight: 7.5 lbs.

GRADING: **NiB** = New in Box **Ex** = Excellent or NRA 95% **Gd** = Good or NRA 68%

RIFLES

Mossberg Model 35A

Mossberg Model 40

Mossberg Model L42A

Sights: Adj. post front, folding aperture rear. European walnut buttstock and forend. Matte black finish. Made from 1987 to 1993.

PPS SEMIAUTOMATIC RIFLE
Caliber: .22 LR. 20-round magazine, 50-round drum. 16.5-inch bbl. 33.5 inches overall. Weight: 5.5 lbs. Sights: Blade front; adj. rear. European walnut stock w/ventilated bbl. shroud. Matte black finish. Made 1989 to 1994.
Model PPS (20-round magazine) NiB $370 Ex $259 Gd $188
Model PPS/50 (50-round drum) NiB $522 Ex $402 Gd $300

O.F. MOSSBERG & SONS, INC. — North Haven, Connecticut
Formerly New Haven, CT.

4X4 CENTERFIRE RIFLE . . . . . . NiB $485 Ex $410 Gd $380
Bolt-action. Calibers: .22-250, .25-06, .243, .270, .30-06, .270 WSM, 7mm-08, 7mm Rem., .300 Win. Mag., .300 WSM, or .338 Win. Mag. 4- or 5-rnd detacable magazine. Bbl: 22- or 24-in. (fluted). Weight: 6.7-7.8 lbs. Finish: blue or Marinecote. Stock: wood or polymer w/vent forearm. Sights: open sights (.30-06, .300 Win. Mag., or 338 Win. Mag. only), Weaver base. Sling swivel studs. Made from 2007 to 2015.

MODEL 10 BOLT-ACTION SINGLE-SHOT RIFLE . . . . NiB $338 Ex $190 Gd $120
Takedown. Caliber: .22 LR, Long, Short. 22-inch bbl. Weight: 4 lbs. Sights: Open rear; bead front. Plain pistol-grip stock w/ swivels, sling. Made 1933 to 1935.

MODEL 14 BOLT-ACTION SINGLE-SHOT RIFLE . . . . NiB $338 Ex $190 Gd $120
Takedown. Caliber: .22 LR, Long, Short. 24-inch bbl. Weight: 5.25 lbs. Sights: Peep rear; hooded ramp front. Plain pistol-grip stock w/semi-beavertail forearm, 1.25-inch swivels. Made 1934 to 1935.

MODEL 20 BOLT-ACTION SINGLE-SHOT RIFLE . . . . NiB $338 Ex $190 Gd $120
Takedown. Caliber: .22 LR, Long, Short. 24-inch bbl. Weight: 4.5 lbs. Sights: Open rear; bead front. Plain pistol-grip stock and forearm w/finger grooves, sling and swivels. Made from 1933 to 1935.

MODEL 25/25A BOLT-ACTION SINGLE-SHOT RIFLE
Takedown. Caliber: .22 LR, Long, Short. 24-inch bbl. Weight: 5 lbs. Sights: Peep rear; hooded ramp front. Plain pistol-grip stock w/semibeavertail forearm. 1.25-inch swivels. Made from 1935 to 1936.
Model 25 . . . . NiB $338 Ex $190 Gd $120
Model 25A (Improved Model 25, 1936-38) . . . . NiB $325 Ex $190 Gd $120

MODEL 26B/26C BOLT-ACTION SINGLE-SHOT
Takedown. Caliber: .22 LR. Long, Short. 26-inch bbl. Weight: 5.5 lbs. Sights; Rear, micrometer click peep or open; hooded ramp front. Plain pistol-grip stock swivels. Made from 1938 to 1941.
Model 26B . . . . NiB $338 Ex $190 Gd $120
Model 26C (No rear sights or sling swivels) . . . . . . NiB $250 Ex $132 Gd $91

MODEL 30 BOLT-ACTION SINGLE-SHOT RIFLE . . . . NiB $338 Ex $190 Gd $120
Takedown. Caliber: .22 LR. Long, Short. 24-inch bbl. Weight: 4.5 lbs. Sights: Peep rear; bead front, on hooded ramp. Plain pistol-grip stock, forearm w/finger grooves. Made from 1933 to 1935.

MODEL 34 BOLT-ACTION SINGLE-SHOT RIFLE . . . . NiB $338 Ex $190 Gd $120
Takedown. Caliber: .22 LR. Long, Short. 24-inch bbl. Weight: 5.5 lbs. Sights: Peep rear; hooded ramp front. Plain pistol-grip

Mossberg Model 42C

Mossberg Model L-43

Mossberg Model 43B

Mossberg Model 44US

Mossberg Model L45A
Left-Hand Model

stock w/semibeavertail forearm, 1.25-inch swivels. Made 1934 to 1935.

MODEL 35 TARGET GRADE BOLT-ACTION
SINGLE-SHOT RIFLE. . . . . **NiB $440 Ex $300 Gd $166**
Caliber: .22 LR. 26-inch heavy bbl. Weight: 8.25 lbs. Sights: Micrometer click rear peep; hooded ramp front. Large target stock w/full pistol grip, cheekpiece, full beavertail forearm, 1.25-inch swivels. Made from 1935 to 1937.

MODEL 35A BOLT-ACTION SINGLE-SHOT
RIFLE. . . . . **NiB $440 Ex $300 Gd $166**
Caliber: .22 LR. 26-inch heavy bbl. Weight: 8.25 lbs. Sights: Micrometer click peep rear; hooded front. Target stock w/ cheekpiece full pistol grip and forearm, 1.25-inch sling swivels. Made from 1937 to 1938.

MODEL 35A-LS. . . . . **NiB $440 Ex $300 Gd $166**
Caliber .22 LR. Same as Model 35A but w/Lyman No. 57 rear sight, 17A front. Target stock w/checkpiece, full pistol-grip and forearm.

MODEL 35B. . . . . **NiB $440 Ex $300 Gd $166**
Same specifications as Model 44B except single-shot. Made from 1938 to 1940.

MODEL 40 BOLT-ACTION
REPEATER . . . . **NiB $222 Ex $140 Gd $100**
Takedown. Caliber: .22 LR. Long, Short, 16-round tubular magazine. 24-inch bbl. Weight: 5 lbs. Sights: Peep rear; bead front, on hooded ramp. Plain pistol-grip stock, forearm w/finger grooves. Made 1933 to 1935.

MODEL 42 BOLT-ACTION
REPEATER . . . . **NiB $278 Ex $155 Gd $110**

Takedown. Caliber: .22 LR. Long, Short. Seven-round detachable box magazine. 24-inch bbl. Weight: 5 lbs. Sights: Receiver peep, open rear; hooded ramp front. Pistol-grip stock. 1.25-inch swivels. Made 1935 to 1937.

MODEL 42A/L42A BOLT-ACTION REPEATERS
Takedown. Caliber: .22 LR. Long, Short. Seven-round detachable box magazine. 24-inch bbl. Weight: 5 lbs. Sights: Receiver peep, open rear; ramp front. Plain pistol-grip stock. Made from 1937-38. Model L42A (left-hand action) made from 1937 to 1941.
Model 42A . . . . **NiB $279 Ex $169 Gd $120**
Model L42A . . . . **NiB $288 Ex $179 Gd $130**

MODEL 42B/42C BOLT-ACTION REPEATERS
Takedown. Caliber: .22 LR. Long, Short. Five-round detachable box magazine. 24-inch bbl. Weight: 6 lbs. Sights: Micrometer click receiver peep, open rear hooded ramp front. Plain pistol-grip stock, swivels. Made from 1938 to 1941.
Model 42B . . . . **NiB $289 Ex $190 Gd $100**
Model 42C (No rear peep sight). . .**NiB $235 Ex $155 Gd $110**

MODEL 42M BOLT-ACTION
REPEATER . . . . **NiB $345 Ex $233 Gd $135**
Caliber: .22 LR, Long, Short. Seven-round detachable box magazine. 23-inch bbl. Weight: 6.75 lbs. Sights: Microclick receiver peep, open rear; hooded ramp front. Two-piece Mannlicher-type stock w/cheekpiece and pistol-grip, swivels. Made from 1940 to 1950.

MODEL 43/L43 BOLT-ACTION
REPEATERS . . . . **NiB $376 Ex $256 Gd $198**
Speedlock, adj. trigger pull. Caliber: .22 LR. Seven-round detachable box (magazine. 26-inch heavy bbl. Weight: 8.25 lbs. Sights: Lyman No. 57 rear; selective aperture front. Target stock w/cheekpiece, full pistol-grip, beavertail forearm, adj. front swivel. Made from 1937-38. Model L43 is same as Model 43 except w/left-hand action.

Mossberg Model 45B

Mossberg Model L46A-LS

Mossberg Model 46B

Mossberg Model 46M

Mossberg Model 50

Mossberg Model 51

Mossberg Model 51M

Mossberg Model 140B

Mossberg Model 140K

MODEL 43B . . . . NiB $390 Ex $300 Gd $170
Same as Model 44B except w/Lyman No. 57 receiver sight and No. 17A front sight. Made from 1938 to 1939.

MODEL 44 BOLT-ACTION
REPEATER . . . . NiB $397 Ex $276 Gd $160
Takedown. Caliber: .22 LR, Long, Short. Tubular magazine holds 16 LR. 24-inch bbl. Weight: 6 lbs. Sights: Peep rear; hooded ramp front. Plain pistol-grip stock w/semi-beavertail forearm, 1.25-inch swivels. Made from 1934 to 1935. Note: Do not confuse this rifle w/later Models 44B and 44US, which are clip repeaters.

MODEL 44B BOLT-ACTION
TARGET RIFLE. . . . . NiB $389 Ex $266 Gd $160
Caliber: .22 LR. Seven-round detachable box magazine. Made from 1938 to 1941.

MODEL 44US BOLT-ACTION REPEATER
Caliber: .22 LR. Seven round detachable box magazine. 26-inch heavy bbl. Weight: 8.5 lbs. Sights: Micrometer click receiver peep, hooded front. Target stock, swivels. Made from 1943-48. Note: This model was used as a training rifle by the U.S. Armed Forces during WWII.
Model 44US . . . . NiB $395 Ex $279 Gd $145
Model 44US (marked U.S. Property) NiB $395 Ex $279 Gd $145

MODEL 45 BOLT-ACTION
REPEATER . . . . NiB $254 Ex $178 Gd $117
Takedown. Caliber: .22 LR, Long, Short. Tubular magazine holds 15 LR, 18 Long, 22 Short. 24-inch bbl. Weight: 6.75 lbs. Sights: Rear peep; hooded ramp front. Plain pistol-grip stock, 1.25-inch swivels. Made 1935 to 1937.

MODEL 45A, L45A, 45AC BOLT-ACTION REPEATERS
Takedown. Caliber: .22 LR, Long, Short. Tubular magazine holds 15 LR, 18 Long, 22 Short. 24-inch bbl. Weight: 6.75 lbs. Sights: Receiver peep, open rear; hooded blade front sight mounted on ramp. Plain pistol-grip stock, 1.25-inch sling swivels. Made 1937 to 1938.
Model 45A . . . . NiB $300 Ex $190 Gd $145
Model L45A (Left-hand action) NiB $655 Ex $355 Gd $279
Model 45AC
   (No receiver peep sight) . . . . NiB $249 Ex $177 Gd $123

MODEL 45B/45C BOLT-ACTION REPEATERS
Takedown. Caliber: .22 LR, Long, Short. Tubular magazine holds 15 LR, 18 Long, 22 Short. 24-inch bbl. Weight: 6.25 lbs. Open rear sight; hooded blade front sight mounted on ramp. Plain pistol-grip stock w/sling swivels. Made from 1938 to 1940.
Model 45B . . . . NiB $338 Ex $233 Gd $138
Model 45C (No sights, made 1935
   to 1937) . . . . NiB $338 Ex $233 Gd $138

MODEL 46 BOLT-ACTION
REPEATER . . . . NiB $338 Ex $233 Gd $138
Takedown. Caliber: .22 LR, Long, Short. Tubular magazine holds 15 LR, 18 Long, 22 Short. 26-inch bbl. Weight: 7.5 lbs. Sights: Micrometer click rear peep; hooded ramp front. Pistol-grip stock w/cheekpiece, full beavertail forearm, 1.25-inch swivels. Made from 1935 to 1937.

MODEL 46A, 46A-LS, L46A-LS BOLT-ACTION REPEATERS
Takedown. Caliber: .22 LR, Long, Short. Tubular magazine holds 15 LR, 18 Long, 22 Short. 26-inch bbl. Weight: 7.25 lbs. Sights: Micrometer click receiver peep, open rear; hooded ramp front. Pistol-grip stock w/cheekpiece and beavertail forearm, quick-detachable swivels. Made from 1937 to 1938.
Model 46A . . . . NiB $338 Ex $233 Gd $138
Mdl. 46A-LS (w/Lyman No. 57
   receiver sight) . . . . NiB $386 Ex $276 Gd $189
Model L46A-LS
   (Left-hand action) . . . . NiB $650 Ex $355 Gd $269

MODEL 46B BOLT-ACTION
REPEATER . . . . NiB $290 Ex $167 Gd $133
Takedown. Caliber: .22 LR, Long, Short. Tubular magazine holds 15 LR, 18 Long, 22 Short. 26-inch bbl. Weight: 7 lbs. Sights: Micrometer click receiver peep, open rear, hooded front. Plain pistol-grip stock w/cheekpiece, swivels. Note: Postwar version of this model has full magazine holding 20 LR, 23 Long, 30 Short. Made 1938 to 1950.

MODEL 46BT . . . . NiB $347 Ex $229 Gd $176
Same as Model 46B except w/heavier bbl. and stock. Weight: 7.75 lbs. Made from 1938 to 1939.

MODEL 46C . . . . NiB $347 Ex $229 Gd $176
Same as Model 46 except w/a heavier bbl. and stock than that model. Weight: 8.5 lbs. Made from 1936 to 1937.

MODEL 46M BOLT-ACTION
REPEATER . . . . NiB $347 Ex $229 Gd $176
Caliber: .22 LR, Long, Short. Tubular magazine holds 22 Short, 18 Long, 15 LR. 23-inch bbl. Weight: 7 lbs. Sights: Microclick receiver peep, open rear; hooded ramp front. Two-piece Mannlicher-type stock w/cheekpiece and pistol-grip, swivels. Made 1940 to 1952.

MODEL 50 AUTOLOADING RIFLE. . NiB $298 Ex $213 Gd $139
Same as Model 51 except w/plain stock w/o beavertail cheekpiece, swivels or receiver peep sight. Made from 1939 to 1942.

MODEL 51 AUTOLOADING RIFLE. . NiB $298 Ex $213 Gd $139
Takedown. Caliber: .22 LR. Fifteen-round tubular magazine in buttstock. 24-inch bbl. Weight: 7.25 lbs. Sights: Micrometer

Mossberg Model 144LS

Mossberg Model 146B

Mossberg Model 151M

Mossberg Model 152

click receiver peep, open rear; hooded ramp front. Cheekpiece stock w/full pistol grip and beavertail forearm, swivels. Made in 1939 only.

MODEL 51M AUTOLOADING
RIFLE. . . . . **NiB $278 Ex $154 Gd $123**
Caliber: .22 LR. Fifteen-round tubular magazine. 20-inch bbl. Weight: 7 lbs. Sights: Microclick receiver peep, open rear; hooded ramp front. Two-piece Mannlicher-type stock w/pistol-grip and cheekpiece, hard-rubber buttplate and sling swivels. Made from 1939 to 1946.

MODEL 140B SPORTER-TARGET
RIFLE. . . . . **NiB $254 Ex $186 Gd $134**
Same as Model 140K except w/peep rear sight, hooded ramp front sight. Made from 1957 to 1958.

MODEL 140K BOLT-ACTION
REPEATER . . . . **NiB $248 Ex $197 Gd $123**
Caliber: .22 LR, .22 Long, .22 Short. Seven-round clip magazine. 24.5-inch bbl. Weight: 5.75 lbs. Sights: Open rear; bead front. Monte Carlo stock w/cheekpiece and pistol-grip, sling swivels. Made 1955 to 1958.

MODEL 142-A BOLT-ACTION
REPEATING CARBINE. . . . . **NiB $277 Ex $233 Gd $166**
Caliber: .22 Short Long, LR. Seven-round detachable box magazine. 18-inch bbl. Weight: 6 lbs. Sights: Peep rear, military-

type front. Monte Carlo stock w/pistol-grip, hinged forearm pulls down to form hand grip; sling swivels mounted on left side of stock. Made from 1949 to 1957.

MODEL 142K . . . . **NiB $244 Ex $152 Gd $109**
Same as Model 142 except w/open rear sight. Made 1953 to 1957.

MODEL 144 BOLT-ACTION
TARGET RIFLE . . . . **NiB $390 Ex $288 Gd $215**
Caliber: .22 LR. Seven-round detachable box magazine. 26-inch heavy bbl. Weight: 8 lbs. Sights: Microclick receiver peep; hooded front. Pistol-grip target stock w/beavertail forearm, adj. hand stop, swivels. Made from 1949 to 1954. Note: This model designation was resumed c.1973 to replace Model 144LS, and then disc. again in 1985.

MODEL 144LS . . . . **NiB $385 Ex $277 Gd $205**
Same as Model 144 except w/Lyman No. 57MS or Mossberg S331 receiver sight and Lyman 17A front sight. Made from 1954 to date. Note: Since 1973, this model has been marketed as Model 144.

MODEL 146B BOLT-ACTION
REPEATER . . . . **NiB $347 Ex $190 Gd $139**
Takedown. Caliber: .22 LR, Long, Short. Tubular magazine holds 30 Short, 23 Long, 20 LR. 26-inch bbl. Weight: 7 lbs. Sights: Micrometer click rear peep, open rear; hooded front. Plain stock w/pistol-grip, Monte Carlo comb and cheekpiece, knob forend tip, swivels. Made from 1949 to 1954.

310

Mossberg Model 320B

Mossberg Model 320K

Mossberg Model 333

Mossberg Model 340K

RIFLES

MODEL 151K . . . . **NiB $290 Ex $193 Gd $130**
Same as Model 151M except w/24-inch bbl., weight: 6 lbs., w/o peep sight, plain stock w/Monte Carlo comb and cheek-piece, pistol-grip knob, forend tip, w/o swivels. Made from 1950 to 1951.

**MODEL 151M AUTOLOADING
RIFLE.** . . . . **NiB $370 Ex $199 Gd $138**
Improved version of Model 51M w/same general specifications, complete action is instantly removable w/o use of tools. Made 1946 to 1958.

**MODEL 152 AUTOLOADING
CARBINE.** . . . . **NiB $276 Ex $197 Gd $135**
Caliber: .22 LR. Seven-round detachable box magazine. 18-inch bbl. Weight: 5 lbs. Sights: Peep rear; military-type front. Monte Carlo stock w/pistol-grip, hinged forearm pulls down to form hand grip, sling mounted on swivels on left side of stock. Made 11948–57.

MODEL 152K. . . . . **NiB $233 Ex $176 Gd $121**
Same as Model 152 except w/open instead of peep rear sight. Made from 1950 to 1957.

**MODEL 320B BOY SCOUT TARGET
RIFLE.** . . . . **NiB $233 Ex $176 Gd $121**
Same as Model 340K except single-shot w/auto. safety. Made 1960 to 1971.

**MODEL 320K HAMMERLESS
BOLT-ACTION SINGLE-SHOT** . . **NiB $200 Ex $123 Gd $90**
Same as Model 346K except single-shot, w/drop-in loading plat-form, automatic safety. Weight: 5.75 lbs. Made from 1958 to 1960.

MODEL 321B . . . . **NiB $347 Ex $190 Gd $139**
Same as Model 321K except w/receiver peep sight. Made 1972-75.

**MODEL 321K BOLT-ACTION
SINGLE-SHOT.** . . . . **NiB $347 Ex $190 Gd $139**
Same as Model 341 except single-shot. Made from 1972 to 1980.

**MODEL 333 AUTOLOADING
CARBINE.** . . . . **NiB $266 Ex $180 Gd $145**
Caliber: .22 LR. 15-round tubular magazine. 20-inch bbl. Weight: 6.25 lbs. Sights: Open rear; ramp front. Monte Carlo stock w/checkered pistol grip and forearm, bbl. band, swivels. Made 1972 to 1973.

**MODEL 340B TARGET
SPORTER.** . . . . **NiB $231 Ex $188 Gd $133**
Same as Model 340K except w/peep rear sight, hooded ramp front sight. Made from 1958 to 1981.

**MODEL 340K HAMMERLESS BOLT-ACTION
REPEATER** . . . . **NiB $231 Ex $188 Gd $133**
Same as Model 346K except clip type, 7-round magazine. Made from 1958 to 1971.

MODEL 340M. . . . . **NiB $650 Ex $390 Gd $238**
Same as Model 340K except w/18.5-inch bbl., Mannlicher-style stock w/swivels and sling. Weight: 5.25 lbs. Made 1970 to 1971.

**MODEL 341 BOLT-ACTION
REPEATER** . . . . **NiB $290 Ex $144 Gd $110**
Caliber: .22 Short. Long, LR. Seven-round clip magazine. 24-inch bbl. Weight: 6.5 lbs. Sights: Open rear, ramp front. Monte Carlo stock w/checkered pistol-grip and forearm, sling swivels. Made 1972 to 1985.

**MODEL 342K HAMMERLESS BOLT-ACTION
CARBINE.** . . . . **NiB $240 Ex $150 Gd $113**

GRADING: NiB = New in Box   **Ex** = Excellent or NRA 95%   **Gd** = Good or NRA 68%

Mossberg Model 341

Mossberg Model 342K

Mossberg Model 346B

Mossberg Model 346K

Same as Model 340K except w/18-inch bbl., stock w/no cheekpiece, extension forend is hinged, pulls down to form hand grip; sling swivels and web strap on left side of stock. Weight: 5 lbs. Made 1958 to 1974.

MODEL 346B . . . . **NiB $240 Ex $180 Gd $113**
Same as Model 346K except w/peep rear sight, hooded ramp front sight. Made from 1958 to 1967.

MODEL 346K HAMMERLESS BOLT-ACTION
REPEATER . . . . **NiB $240 Ex $150 Gd $113**
Caliber: .22 Short. Long, LR. Tubular magazine holds 25 Short, 20 Long, 18 LR. 24-inch bbl. Weight: 6.5 lbs. Sights: Open rear; bead front. Walnut stock w/Monte Carlo comb, cheekpiece, pistol-grip, sling swivels. Made from 1958 to 1971.

MODEL 350K AUTOLOADING
RIFLE — CLIP TYPE . . . . **NiB $240 Ex $150 Gd $113**
Caliber: .22 Short (High Speed), Long, LR. Seven-round clip magazine. 23.5-inch bbl. Weight: 6 lbs. Sights: Open rear; bead front. Monte Carlo stock w/pistol-grip. Made from 1958 to 1971.

MODEL 351C AUTOLOADING
CARBINE. . . . . **NiB $240 Ex $150 Gd $113**
Same as Model 351K except w/18.5-inch bbl., Western carbine-style stock w/barrel band and sling swivels. Weight: 5.5 lbs. Made from 1965 to 1971.

MODEL 351K AUTOLOADING
SPORTER. . . . . **NiB $240 Ex $150 Gd $113**
Caliber: .22 LR. Fifteen-round tubular magazine in buttstock. 24-inch bbl. Weight: 6 lbs. Sights: Open rear; bead front. Monte Carlo stock w/pistol-grip. Made from 1960 to 1971.

MODEL 352K AUTOLOADING
CARBINE. . . . . **NiB $240 Ex $150 Gd $113**
Caliber: .22 Short, Long, LR. Seven-round clip magazine. 18-inch bbl. Weight: 5 lbs. Sights: Open rear; bead front. Monte Carlo stock w/pistol grip; extension forend of Tenite is hinged, pulls down to form hand grip; sling swivels, web strap. Made from 1958 to 1971.

MODEL 353 AUTOLOADING
CARBINE. . . . . **NiB $240 Ex $150 Gd $113**
Caliber: .22 LR. Seven round clip magazine. 18-inch bbl. Weight: 5 lbs. Sights: Open rear; ramp front. Monte Carlo stock w/checkered pistol-grip and forearm; black Tenite extension forend pulls down to form hand grip. Made 1972 to 1985.

MODEL 377 PLINKSTER
AUTOLOADER . . . . **NiB $278 Ex $200 Gd $155**
Caliber: .22 LR. Fifteen-round tubular magazine. 20-inch bbl. Weight: 6.25 lbs. 4x scope sight. Thumbhole stock w/rollover cheekpiece, Monte Carlo comb, checkered forearm; molded of modified polystyrene foam in walnut-finish; sling swivel studs. Made 1977 to 1979.

MODEL 380 SEMIAUTOMATIC
RIFLE. . . . . **NiB $278 Ex $200 Gd $155**
Caliber: .22 LR. Fifteen-round buttstock magazine. 20-inch bbl. Weight: 5.5 lbs. Sights: Open rear; bead front. Made 1980 to 1985.

MODEL 400 PALOMINO
LEVER-ACTION. . . . . **NiB $390 Ex $242 Gd $161**
Hammerless. Caliber: .22 Short, Long, LR. Tubular magazine holds 20 Short, 17 Long, 15 LR. 24-inch bbl. Weight: 5.5 lbs. Sights: Open rear; bead front. Monte Carlo stock w/checkered pistol-grip; beavertail forearm. Made 1959 to 1964.

MODEL 402 PALOMINO CARBINE. . . **NiB $390 Ex $242 Gd $161**
Same as Model 400 except w/18.5-inch (1961-64) or 20-inch bbl. (1964-71), forearm w/bbl. band, swivels; magazine holds two fewer rounds. Weight: 4.75 lbs. Made from 1961 to 1971.

MODEL 430 AUTOLOADING RIFLE. . . **NiB $340 Ex $180 Gd $135**
Caliber: .22 LR. Eighteen-round tubular magazine. 24-inch bbl. Weight: 6.25 lbs. Sights: Open rear; bead front. Monte Carlo stock w/checkered pistol grip; checkered forearm. Made 1970 to 1971.

MODEL 432 WESTERN-STYLE
AUTO . . . . **NiB $340 Ex $180 Gd $135**
Same as Model 430 except w/plain straight-grip carbine-type stock and forearm, bbl. band, sling swivels. Magazine capacity: 15 cartridges. Weight: 6 lbs. Made from 1970 to 1971.

Mossberg Model 350K
Autoloading — Clip Type

Mossberg Model 351K
Automatic Sporter

Mossberg Model 352K
Carbine

Mossberg Model 353
Carbine

Mossberg Model 377 Plinkster

Mossberg Model 400

Mossberg Model 402

MODEL 464 . . . . **NiB $530 Ex $440 Gd $385**
Lever-action. Caliber: .22 LR or .30-30, 7- or 14-rnd. magazine. 18- or 20-in. bbl. Stock: hardwood straight- or pistol-grip stock, smooth or checkered. Sights: adj. open, drilled and tapped. Top tang safety. Weight: 6.75 lbs. Caliber: .30-30. Made from 2008 to present.
.22 LR, subtract. **$35**
w/pistol-grip stock, add **$45**
SPX (polymer adj. stock), add. **$30**
ZMB (polymer adj. stock, flash hider), add. **$10**

MODEL 472 BRUSH GUN . . . . **NiB $340 Ex $180 Gd $135**
Same as Model 472 Carbine w/straight-grip stock except w/18-inch bbl., weight: 6.5 lbs. Caliber: .30-30. Magazine capacity: 5 rounds. Made from 1974 to 1976.

**MODEL 472 LEVER-ACTION
CARBINE.** . . . . **NiB $340 Ex $180 Gd $135**
Calibers: .30-30, .35 Rem. Six round tubular magazine. 20-inch bbl. Weight: 6.75 to 7 lbs. Sights: Open rear; ramp front. Pistol-grip or straight-grip stock, forearm w/bbl. band; sling swivels on pistol-grip model saddle ring on straight-grip model. Made from 1972 to 1979.

Mossberg Model 472
Brush Gun

Mossberg Model 472
Carbine (Pistol Grip)

Mossberg Model 472
Carbine (Straight Grip)

Mossberg Model
472 "One in Five
Thousand"

MODEL 472 ONE IN
FIVE THOUSAND.......... NiB $665 Ex $423 Gd $240
Same as Model 472 Brush Gun except w/Indian scenes etched on receiver; brass buttplate, saddle ring and bbl. bands, gold-plated trigger, bright blued finish, select walnut stock and forearm. Limited edition of 5,000; serial numbered 1 to 5,000. Made in 1974.

MODEL 472 RIFLE .... NiB $340 Ex $180 Gd $135
Same as Model 472 Carbine w/pistol-grip stock except w/24-inch bbl., 5-round magazine, weight: 7 lbs. Made from 1974 to 1976.

MODEL 479
Caliber: .30-30. Six-round tubular magazine. 20-inch bbl. Weight: 6.75 to 7 lbs. Sights: Open rear; ramp front. Made 1983 to 1985.
Model 479 Rifle .... NiB $340 Ex $180 Gd $135
Model 479PCA
 (carbine w/20-inch bbl.).... NiB $340 Ex $180 Gd $135
Model 479RR (Roy Rogers model,
 5000 Ltd. Ed.)............ NiB $665 Ex $423 Gd $240

MODEL 620K HAMMERLESS SINGLE-SHOT
BOLT-ACTION RIFLE........ NiB $290 Ex $179 Gd $133
Single shot. Caliber: .22 WMR. 24-inch bbl. Weight: 6 lbs. Sights: Open rear; bead front. Monte Carlo stock w/cheekpiece, pistol-grip, sling swivels. Made from 1959 to 1960.

MODEL 620K-A .... NiB $290 Ex $179 Gd $133
Same as Model 640K except w/sight modification. Made 1960–68.

MODEL 640K CHUCKSTER HAMMERLESS
BOLT-ACTION RIFLE........ NiB $338 Ex $228 Gd $136
Caliber: .22 WMR. Five-round detachable clip magazine. 24-inch bbl. Weight: 6 lbs. Sights: Open rear; bead front. Monte Carlo stock w/cheekpiece, pistol grip, sling swivels. Made from 1959 to 1984.

MODEL 640KS .... NiB $338 Ex $ 228 Gd $136
Deluxe version of Model 640K w/select walnut stock hand checkering; gold-plated front sight, rear sight elevator, and trigger. Made 1960 to 1964.

MODEL 640M............. NiB $665 Ex $423 Gd $240
Similar to Model 640K except w/heavy receiver and jeweled bolt. 20-inch bbl., full length Mannlicher-style stock w/Monte Carlo comb and cheekpiece, swivels and leather sling. 40.75 inches overall. Weight: 6 lbs. Made from 1971 to 1973.

MODEL 642K CARBINE ...... NiB $396 Ex $277 Gd $194
Caliber: .22 WMR. Five-round detachable clip magazine. 18-inch bbl. Weight: 5 lbs. 38.25 inches overall. Sights: Open rear; bead front. Monte Carlo walnut stock w/black Tenite forearm extension that pulls down to form hand grip. Made from 1961 to 1968.

MODEL 702 PLINKSTER....... NiB $187 Ex $100 Gd $85
Semi-automatic. Caliber: .22 LR, 10- or 20-rnd. magazine. 18- or 21-in. bbl. Weight: 4 lbs. Sights: Leaf rear; ramp front. Stock: wood, polymer sporter (black, camo, pink) or thumbhole (black). Made from 2006 to present.
Bantam, subtract................................ $10
Duck Commander, add.......................... $50

MODEL 715T .... NiB $375 Ex $330 Gd $300
Semi-automatic, AR-style. Caliber: .22 LR, 10- or 25-rnd. magazine. 16.25-in. bbl. Weight: 5-5.5 lbs. Sights: open/rail or rail onlt. Stock: polymer (black, camo, pink). Made from 2012 to present.
Duck Commander, add.......................... $100
Tatctcal Carry (18-in. bbl.), subtract................. $60

MODEL 800 BOLT-ACTION
CENTERFIRE RIFLE......... NiB $455 Ex $307 Gd $200
.222 Rem., .22-250, .243 Win., .308 Win. Four-round mag., 3-round in .222. 22-inch bbl. Weight: 7.5 lbs. Sights:

RIFLES

Mossberg Model 640KS

Mossberg Model 640M

Mossberg Model 642K shown w/forearm extension pulled down

Mossberg Model 800

Folding leaf rear; ramp front. Monte Carlo stock w/cheek-piece, checkered pistol-grip and forearm, sling swivels. Made from 1967 to 1979.

MODEL 800D SUPER GRADE . NiB $455 Ex $307 Gd $200
Deluxe version of Model 800 except w/stock w/rollover comb and cheekpiece, rosewood forend tip and pistol-grip cap. Weight: 6.75 lbs. Chambered for all calibers listed for the Model 800 except for .222 Rem. Sling swivels. Made from 1970 to 1973.

MODEL 800M. . . . . NiB $650 Ex $315 Gd $209
Same as Model 800 except w/flat bolt handle, 20-inch bbl., Mannlicher-style stock. Weight: 6.5 lbs. Calibers: .22-250, .243 Win., .308 Win. Made from 1969 to 1972.

MODEL 800VT
VARMINT/TARGET . . . . NiB $455 Ex $307 Gd $200
Similar to Model 800 except w/24-inch heavy bbl., no sights. Weight: 9.5 lbs. Calibers: .222 Rem., .22-250, .243 Win. Made 1968 to 1979.

MODEL 801 HALF-PINT
PLINKSTER . . . . NiB $230 Ex $200 Gd $175
Bolt-action, single shot. Caliber: .22 LR. 16-in. bbl. Weight: 4 lbs. Sights: Leaf rear; ramp front. Stock: hardwood (12.25 LOP). Made from 2008 to present.

MODEL 802 PLINKSTER. . . . . . NiB $230 Ex $200 Gd $175
Bolt-action. Caliber: .22 LR. 18- or 20-in. bbl. 10-rnd. maga-zine. Weight: 4 lbs. Sights: Leaf rear; ramp front. Stock: hard-wood, or polymer thumbhole (black or pink). Finish: blued or chrome. Made from 2006 to present.
Bantam (18-in. bbl., wood stock). . . NiB $230 Ex $200 Gd $175
Varmint (21-in. bull bbl.) . . . . . NiB $230 Ex $200 Gd $175

MODEL 810 BOLT-ACTION CENTERFIRE RIFLE
Calibers: .270 Win., .30-06, 7mm Rem. Mag., .338 Win. Mag. Detachable box magazine (1970-75) or internal magazine w/ hinged floorplate (1972 to date). Capacity: Four-round in .270 and .30-06, 3-round in Magnums. 22-inch bbl. in .270 and .30-06, 24-inch in Magnums. Weight: 7.5 to 8 lbs. Sights: Leaf rear; ramp front. Stock w/Monte Carlo comb and cheekpiece, checkered pistol-grip and forearm, grip cap, sling swivels. Made from 1970 to 1979.
Standard calibers . . . . NiB $390 Ex $333 Gd $232
Magnum calibers . . . . NiB $370 Ex $316 Gd $226

MODEL 817 . . . . NiB $219 Ex $190 Gd $155
Bolt-action. Caliber: .17 HMR. 21-in. bbl. 6-rnd. magazine. Weight: 4 lbs. Sights: Leaf rear; ramp front. Stock: Polymer thumbhole (black). Finish: blued or brushed chrome. Made from 2007 to present.
Varmint (21-in. bull bbl.) . . . . . NiB $261 Ex $220 Gd $185

GRADING: **NiB** = New in Box   **Ex** = Excellent or NRA 95%   **Gd** = Good or NRA 68%

Mossberg Model 800D

Mossberg Model 800M

Mossberg Model 810

Mossberg Model L

Mossberg Model R

MODEL 1500 MOUNTAINEER GRADE I
CENTERFIRE RIFLE . . . . **NiB $441 Ex $338 Gd $288**
Calibers: .223, .243, .270, .30-06, 7mm Mag. 22-inch or 24-inch (7mm Mag.) bbl. Weight: 7 lbs. 10 oz. Hardwood walnut-finished checkered stock. Sights: Hooded ramp front w/ gold bead; fully adj. rear. Drilled and tapped for scope mounts. Sling swivel studs. Imported from 1986 to 1987.Model 1500 Varmint Bolt-Action Rifle Same as Model 1500 Grade I except w/22-inch heavy bbl. Chambered in .222, .22-250, .223 only. High-luster blued finish or Parkerized satin finished stock. Imported from Japan 1986 to 1987.
High-luster blue . . . . **NiB $440 Ex $328 Gd $288**
Parkerized satin finish . . . . **NiB $455 Ex $338 Gd $298**

MODEL 1707LS CLASSIC HUNTER
BOLT-ACTION RIFLE. . . . . **NiB $479 Ex $369 Gd $266**
Same as Model 1500 Grade I except w/checkered classic-style stock and Schnabel forend. Chambered in 243, 270, 30-06 only. Imported from Japan 1986 to 1987.

MODEL ATR. . . . . **NiB $375 Ex $310 Gd $270**
Bolt-action. Calibers: .243, .270, 7mm-08, .308 or .30-06. 3-rnd interbal magazine. Bbl: 22-in. fluted or non-fluted. Weight: 7 lbs. Finish: blue or Marinecote. Stock: walnut, Durawood or polymer. Sights: open sights or Weaver base. Sling swivel studs. LBA adj. trigger standard in 2009. Made from 2005 to 2015.
w/camo stock, add **$50**
Bantam . . . . **NiB $375 Ex $310 Gd $270**
Deer Thug (scoped combo) . . . . **NiB $485 Ex $380 Gd $330**
Night Train Special (.308, w/scope) NiB $620 Ex $520 Gd $460

MODEL B BOLT-ACTION RIFLE. . . **NiB $340 Ex $205 Gd $113**
Takedown. Caliber: .22 LR, Long, Short. Single-shot. 22-inch bbl. Sights: Open rear; bead front. Plain pistol-grip stock. Made from 1930 to 1932.

MODEL BLAZE . . . . **NiB $187 Ex $160 Gd $100**
Semi-automatic. Caliber: .22 LR, 10- or 25-rnd. magazine. 16.5-in. bbl. Weight: 3.5 lbs. Stock: polymer. Length: 35.75 in. Sights: open sights. Finish: blued. Made from 2014 to present.
Camo finish, add **$90**
Combo (w/Dead Ringer green dot sight), add **$65**

MODEL BLAZE-47 . . . . **NiB $375 Ex $340 Gd $300**
Similar to Blaze except styled like an AK-47 w/wood stock and furniture. Adj. fiber optic sights. Finish: blued. Made from 2014 to present.
Polymer stock and furniture, subtract **$46**

MODEL K SLIDE-ACTION
REPEATER . . . . **NiB $545 Ex $390 Gd $233**
Hammerless. Takedown. Caliber: .22 LR, Long, Short. Tubular magazine holds 20 Short, 16 Long, 14 LR. 22-inch bbl. Weight: 5 lbs. Sights: Open rear; bead front. Plain, straight-grip stock. Grooved slide handle. Made from 1922 to 1931.

MODELS L42A, L43, L45A, L46A-LS
See Models 42A, 43, 45A and 46A-LS respectively; "L" refers to a left-hand version of those rifles.

MODEL L SINGLE-SHOT RIFLE . . . **NiB $850 Ex $535 Gd $429**
Martini-type falling-block lever-action. Takedown. Caliber: .22 LR, Long, Short. 24-inch bbl. Weight: 5 lbs. Sights: Open rear; bead front. Plain pistol-grip stock and forearm. Made from 1929 to 1932.

MODEL M SLIDE-ACTION

REPEATER . . . . **NiB $550 Ex $340 Gd $227**
Specifications same as for Model K except w/24-inch octagon bbl., pistol-grip stock, weighs 5.5 lbs. Made from 1928 to 1931.

MODEL MMR HUNTER

MODEL MMR HUNTER . . . . . **NiB $1028 Ex $980 Gd $800**
Semi-automatic, AR15 style. Calibers: 5.56mm NATO, 5-rnd. magazine, compatiable with AR15 magazines. 20-in.free floated bbl. Weight: 7 lbs. Stock: A2 style polymer. Length: 39 in. Sights: none, rail. Finish: Matte black, Mossy Oak Treestand or Mossy Oak Brush. Made from 2011 to present.
Camo finish, add **$100**

MODEL MMR TACTICAL . . . . **NiB $1028 Ex $980 Gd $800**
Simialr to MMR Hunter model except w/matte balck finish only, 10- or 30-rnd. magazine, adj. stock, Sights: adj/rail or rail only. Made from 2011 to present.
w/rail only, subtract **$40**

MODEL MVP FLEX . . . . **NiB $996 Ex $900 Gd $875**
Simialr to MVP Predator except FLEX system 6-position stock. Made from 2013 to present.
Scoped combo . . . . **NiB $1177 Ex $995 Gd $875**

MODEL MVP-LC . . . . **NiB $1438 Ex $1200 Gd $1000**
Bolt-action. Calibers: 5.56mm NATO or 7.62mm NATO, 10-rnd. magazine, compatiable with AR15 magazines. 16.25- or 18.5-in. (7.62mm NATO) fluted bbl. w/threaded muzzle. Weight: 8-10 lbs. Stock: light weight aluminum chassis. Length: 35.5-37.75 in. Sights: none, rail. Bipod. LBA adj. trigger. Made from 2015 to present.
Combo (Voretx scope) . . . . **NiB $2102 Ex $2000 Gd $1988**

MODEL MVP-LR . . . . **NiB $996 Ex $900 Gd $875**
Similar to MVP-LC except long range variant w/20-in. medium bull bbl., threaded muzzle. Weight: 7-8 lbs. Stock: Green textured w/adj comb, benchrest style. Length: 39-39.5 in. Sights: rail. Made from 2015 to present.
LR-T Tactical (16.25-in. bbl., sights) . . . **NiB $996 Ex $900 Gd $875**

MODEL MVP PATROL . . . . **NiB $748 Ex $700 Gd $685**
Simialr to MVP Predator except available also in .300 ACC BLK, 16.25-in. medium bull, fluted bbl. w/flash suppressor. Weight: 9.25-10 lbs. Stock: textured (tan or black). Length: 35.25-37.5 in. Sights: iron and rail. Made from 2013 to present.
Scoped combo, add **$100**
Thunder Ranch (green stock) . . **NiB $771 Ex $710 Gd $695**

MODEL MVP PREDATOR . . . . . **NiB $732 Ex $600 Gd $520**
Bolt-action. Calibers: 5.56mm NATO or 7.62mm NATO, 10-rnd. magazine, compatiable with AR15 magazines. 18.5- or 20-in.medium bull, fluted bbl. w/threaded muzzle. Weight: 8-8.5 lbs. Stock: laminated wood sporter style. Length: 37.5-40 in. Sights: none, rail. LBA adj. trigger. Made from 2011 to present.
Scoped combo, add **$50**

MODEL MVP SCOUT . . . . **NiB $777 Ex $700 Gd $685**
Simialr to MVP Predator except available only in 7.62mm NATO, 16.25-in. medium bull, bbl. w/flash suppressor. Weight: 6.75 lbs. Stock: synthetic (black). Length: 37.5 in. Sights: rail. Made from 2015 to present.
Scoped combo, add **$170**

MODEL MVP VARMINT . . . . . . **NiB $732 Ex $600 Gd $520**
Simialr to MVP Predator except available also in .204 Ruger, 24-in.medium bull, fluted bbl. w/threaded muzzle. Weight:

9.25-10 lbs. Stock: laminated wood bench rest style. Length: 43-44 in. Sights: none, rail. Made from 2011 to present.
Scoped combo w/bipod, add **$170**

MODEL PATRIOT . . . . **NiB $438 Ex $400 Gd $370**
Bolt-action. Calibers: .22-250, .243, .25-06, .270, 7mm-08, .308 or .30-06, 7mm Rem. Mag., .300 Win. Mag., .338 Win. Mag., or .375 Ruger. 4- or 5-rnd magazine. Bbl: 22-in. fluted or sporter style. Weight: 6.5-7.25 lbs. Finish: blue or Marinecote. Stock: walnut or sythetic. Sights: open sights or Weaver base. LBA adj. trigger. Sling swivel studs. Made from 2015 to present.
w/synthetic stock, subtract **$50**
Night Train (scope, bipod) . . . . **NiB $811 Ex $795 Gd $700**
Youth . . . . **NiB $438 Ex $400 Gd $370**

MODEL R BOLT-ACTION

REPEATER . . . . **NiB $379 Ex $265 Gd $190**
Takedown. Caliber: .22 LR, Long, Short. Tubular magazine. 24-inch bbl. Sights: Open rear; bead front. Plain pistol-grip stock. Made from 1930 to 1932.

MODEL SSI . . . . **NiB $480 Ex $400 Gd $370**
Lever-action, single shot. Calibers: .22-250, .223, .243, .270, .308, .30-06 or 12 gauge. Interchangable bbls., 24-in. Weight: 8-10 lbs. Finish: blued or camo. Stock: checkered walnut. Sights: drilled and tapped. Made from 2001 to 2004.

MUSGRAVE MFRS. & DIST. (PTY) LTD. — Bloemfontein, South Africa

PREMIER NR5 BOLT- ACTION

HUNTING RIFLE . . . . **NiB $460 Ex $375 Gd $288**
Calibers: .243 Win., .270 Win., .30-06, .308 Win., 7mm Rem. Mag. Five-round magazine. 25.5-inch bbl. Weight: 8.25 lbs. Furnished w/o sights, but drilled and tapped for scope mount. Select walnut Monte Carlo stock w/cheekpiece, checkered pistol-grip and forearm, contrasting pistol-grip cap and forend tip, recoil pad, swivel studs. Musgrave or Mauser action. Made from 1971 to 1976.

RSA NR1 BOLT-ACTION SINGLE-SHOT

TARGET RIFLE . . . . **NiB $449 Ex $420 Gd $300**
Caliber: .308 Win. (7.62mm NATO). 26.4-inch heavy bbl. Weight: 10 lbs. Sights: Aperture receiver; tunnel front. Walnut target stock w/beavertail forearm, handguard, bbl. band, rubber buttplate, sling swivels. Made from 1971 to 1976.

VALIANT NR6 HUNTING

RIFLE . . . . **NiB $415 Ex $369 Gd $255**
Similar to Premier except w/24-inch bbl.; stock w/straight comb, skip French-style checkering, no grip cap or forend tip. Sights: Leaf rear; hooded ramp front bead sight. Weight: 7.7 lbs. Made from 1971 to 1976.

MUSKETEER RIFLES — Washington, D.C.

Manufactured by Firearms International Corp.

MAUSER SPORTER

FN Mauser bolt action. .243, .25-06, .270, .264 Mag., .308, .30-06, 7mm Mag., .300 Win. Mag. Magazine holds 5 standard, 3 Magnum cartridges. 24-inch bbl. Weight: 7.25 lbs. No sights. Monte Carlo stock w/checkered pistol-grip and forearm, swivels. Made 1963 to 1972.
Standard Sporter . . . . **NiB $415 Ex $295 Gd $255**
Deluxe Sporter . . . . **NiB $459 Ex $380 Gd $276**
Standard Carbine . . . . **NiB $415 Ex $295 Gd $255**

RIFLES

Musgrave RSA NR1

Musgrave Valiant NR6

Musketeer Mauser Sporter

NAVY ARMS — Martinsburg, WV

Importer of reproduction firearms. A division of Forgett Trading LLC which also owns Gibbs Rifle Company. Previously Union City, NJ and Ridgefield, NJ.

.45-70 MAUSER CARBINE .... NiB $333 Ex $227 Gd $160
Same as .45-70 Mauser Rifle except w/18-inch bbl., straight-grip stock w/low comb, weight: 7.5 lbs. Disc.

.45-70 MAUSER RIFLE .... NiB $260 Ex $221 Gd $155
Siamese Mauser bolt action. Caliber: .45-70 Govt. Three-round magazine. 24- or 26-inch bbl. Weight: 8.5 lbs. w/26-inch bbl. Sights: Open rear; ramp front: Checkered stock w/Monte Carlo comb. Intoduced 1973. Disc.

MODEL 1873 WINCHESTER
BORDER RIFLE .... NiB $1077 Ex $869 Gd $378
Replica of Winchester Model 1873 Short Rifle. Calibers: .357 Mag., .44-40, and .45 Colt. 20- inch bbl., 39.25 inches overall. Weight: 7.6 lbs. Blued full octagonal barrel, color casehardened receiver w/walnut stocks. Made from 1999 to 2009.

MODEL 1873 CARBINE ..... NiB $1043 Ex $756 Gd $399
Similar to Model 1873 Rifle except w/blued receiver, 10-round magazine, 19-inch round bbl. carbine-style forearm w/bbl. band, weighs 6.75 lbs. Disc. Reissued in 1991 in .44-40 or .45 Colt.

MODEL 1873 LEVER-ACTION
RIFLE.................... NiB $1043 Ex $756 Gd $399
Replica of Winchester Model 1873. Casehardened receiver. Calibers: .22 LR, .357 Magnum, .44-40. 15-round magazine. 24-inch octagon bbl. Weight: 8 lbs. Sights: Open rear; blade front. Straight-grip stock, forearm w/end cap. Disc. Reissued in 1991 in .44-40 or .45 Colt w/12-round magazine. Disc. 1994.

MODEL 1873 TRAPPER ...... NiB $744 Ex $560 Gd $425
Same as Model 1873 Carbine, except w/16.5-inch bbl., 8-round magazine, weighs 6.25 lbs. Disc.

MODEL 1873 SPORTING CARBINE/RIFLE
Replica of Winchester Model 1873 Sporting Rifle. Calibers: .357 Mag. (24.25- inch bbl. only), .44-40 and .45 Colt. 24.25-inch bbl. (Carbine) or 30-inch bbl. (Rifle). 48.75 to 53 inches overall. Weight: 8.14 to 9.3 lbs. Octagonal barrel, casehardened receiver and checkered walnut pistol-grip. Made from 1999 to 2003.
Carbine model .... NiB $970 Ex $844 Gd $630
Rifle model .... NiB $1035 Ex $928 Gd $670

MODEL 1874 SHARPS CAVALRY
CARBINE................. NiB $1010 Ex $733 Gd $580
Replica of Sharps 1874 Cavalry Carbine. Similar to Sniper Model, except w/22-inch bbl. and carbine stock. Caliber: .45-70. Imported from 1997 to 2009.

MODEL 1874 SHARPS SNIPER RIFLE
Replica of Sharps 1874 Sharpshooter's Rifle. Caliber: .45-70. Falling breech, single-shot. 30-inch bbl. 46.75 inches overall. Weight: 8.5 lbs. Double-set triggers. Color casehardened receiver. Blade front sight; rear sight w/elevation leaf. Polished blued bbl. Military three-band stock w/patch box. Imported from 1994 to 2000.
Infantry model (single trigger) . NiB $933 Ex $790 Gd $630
Sniper model (double set trigger) .. NiB $2013 Ex $1118 Gd $956

ENGRAVED MODELS
Yellowboy and Model 1873 rifles are available in deluxe models w/select walnut stocks and forearms and engraving in three grades. Grade "A" has delicate scrollwork in limited areas. Grade "B" is more elaborate with 40 percent coverage. Grade "C" has highest grade engraving. Add to value:
Grade "A" .... NiB $1023 Ex $779 Gd $615
Grade "B" .... NiB $1126 Ex $986 Gd $813
Grade "C" .... NiB $1568 Ex $995 Gd $723

HENRY LEVER-ACTION RIFLE
Replica of the Winchester Model 1860 Henry Rifle. Caliber: .44-40. Twelve round magazine. 16.5-, 22- or 24.25-inch octagon bbl. Weight: 7.5 to 9 lbs. 35.4 to 43.25 inches overall.

Navy Arms 1873 Carbine

Navy Arms Model 1874
Sharps Carbine

Navy Arms 1874
Sharps Sniper Rifle

Sights: Blade front, adjustable ladder rear. European walnut straight grip buttstock w/bbl. and side stock swivels. Imported from 1985 to date. Brass or steel receiver. Blued or color case-hardened metal.

Carbine w/22-inch bbl.
(introduced 1992)........NiB $735 Ex $479 Gd $376
Military rifle model
(w/brass frame)..........NiB $989 Ex $688 Gd $482
Trapper model (w/brass frame)....NiB $735 Ex $479 Gd $376
Trapper model (w/iron frame) ...NiB $1055 Ex $800 Gd $479
w/"A" engraving, add $325
w/"B" engraving, add $550
w/"C" engraving, add $950

MARTINI TARGET RIFLE......NiB $556 Ex $379 Gd $333
Martini single-shot action. Calibers: .444 Marlin, .45-70. 26- or 30-inch half-octagon or full-octagon bbl. Weight: 9 lbs. w/26-inch bbl. Sights: Creedmoor tang peep, open middle, blade front. Stock w/cheekpiece and pistol-grip, forearm w/Schnabel tip, both checkered. Intro. 1972. Disc.

REVOLVING CARBINE ....NiB $641 Ex $540 Gd $400
Action resembles that of Remington Model 1875 Revolver. Casehardened frame. Calibers: .357 Magnum, .44-40, .45 Colt. Six round cylinder. 20-inch bbl. Weight: 5 lbs. Sights: Open rear; blade front. Straight-grip stock brass trigger guard and buttplate. Intro. 1968. Disc.

ROLLING BLOCK BABY
CARBINE..................NiB $255 Ex $190 Gd $155
Replica of small Remington Rolling Block single-shot action. Casehardened frame, brass trigger guard. Calibers: .22 LR, .22 Hornet, .357 Magnum, .44-40. 20-inch octagon or 22-inch round bbl. Weight: 5 lbs. Sights: Open rear; blade front. Straight-grip stock, plain forearm, brass buttplate. Imported from 1968 to 1981.

ROLLING BLOCK BUFFALO
CARBINE..................NiB $439 Ex $333 Gd $227
Same as Buffalo Rifle except w/18-inch bbl., weight: 10 lbs

ROLLING BLOCK BUFFALO
RIFLE......................NiB $720 Ex $572 Gd $338
Replica Remington Rolling Block single-shot action. Casehardened frame, brass trigger guard. Calibers: .444 Marlin, .45-70, .50-70. 26- or 30-inch heavy half-octagon or full-octagon bbl. Weight: 11 to 12 lbs. Sights: Open rear; blade front. Straight-grip stock w/brass buttplate, forearm w/brass bbl. band. Made from 1971 to 2003.

ROLLING BLOCK CREEDMOOR RIFLE
Same as Buffalo Rifle except calibers .45-70 and .50-70 only, 28- or 30-inch heavy half-octagon or full-octagon bbl., Creedmoor tang peep sight.
Target model.............NiB $1530 Ex $1109 Gd $775
Deluxe target model (disc. 1998) NiB$1677 Ex$1330 Gd$190

YELLOWBOY CARBINE ......NiB $865 Ex $590 Gd $443
Similar to Yellowboy Rifle except w/19-inch bbl., 10-round magazine (14-round in 22 Long Rifle), carbine-style forearm. Weight: 6.75 lbs. Disc. Reissued 1991 in .44-40 only.

YELLOWBOY LEVER-ACTION
REPEATER ....NiB $1035 Ex $567 Gd $359
Replica of Winchester Model 1866. Calibers: .38 Special, .44-40. 15-round magazine. 24-inch octagon bbl. Weight: 8 lbs. Sights: Folding leaf rear; blade front. Straight-grip stock, forearm w/end cap. Intro. 1966. Disc. Reissued 1991 in .44-40 only w/12-round magazine and adj. ladder-style rear sight.

YELLOWBOY TRAPPER'S ......NiB $723 Ex $500 Gd $379
Same as Yellowboy Carbine except w/16.5-inch bbl., 8-round magazine, weighs 6.25 lbs. Disc.

NEW ENGLAND FIREARMS — Gardner, Massachusetts

In 1987, New England Firearms was established as an independent company producing selected H&R models under the NEF logo. In 1991, H&R 1871, Inc. was formed from the residual of the

Navy Arms Martini
Target Rifle

Navy Arms
Yellowboy Carbine
.22 LR

Navy Arms
Revolving Carbine

Navy Arms
Rolling Block Baby Carbine

Navy Arms
Rolling Block Buffalo Rifle

Noble Model 10

Youth model . . . . NiB $300 Ex $233 Gd $144
10th Anniversary model . . . . . NiB $822 Ex $555 Gd $375
Trapper's Edition . . . . NiB $337 Ex $265 Gd $190

SUPER LIGHT HANDI-RIFLE . . NiB $378 Ex $229 Gd $145
Cal.: .22 Hornet, .223 Rem., .243 Win. Same as Handi Rifle
but with black synthetic stock and forearm, recoil pad. Bbl.:
20-inch special contour w/rebated muzzle. .223 Rem. model
includes scope base and hammer extension. Weight: 5.5 lbs.
Made 1997 to 2008.

*parent company and that took over the New England Firearms
facility. H&R 1871 produced firearms under both its logo and the
NEF brand name until 1999, when the Marlin Firearms Company
acquired the assets of H&R 1871.*

HANDI-RIFLE . . . . NiB $245 Ex $190 Gd $137
Single-shot, break-open action w/side-lever release. Calibers:
.22 Hornet, .22-250, .223, .243, .270, .30-30, .30-06, .45-
70. 22-inch bbl. Weight: 7 lbs. Sights: Ramp front; folding
rear. Drilled and tapped for scope mounts. Walnut-finished
hardwood or synthetic stock. Blued finish. Made from 1989
to 2008.
Synthetic . . . . NiB $290 Ex $200 Gd $128
Synthetic/Stainless . . . . NiB $325 Ex $266 Gd $159

SPORTSTER . . . . NiB $218 Ex $144 Gd $90
Cal.: .17 HMR, .17 Mach 2, .22 LR, .22 Mag. Bbl.: 20 or 22 inches,
Weaver-style rail, no sights. Adult or youth (.22 LR only) dimen-
sions. Stock and forearm: Black polymer. Made 1999 to 2008.

SURVIVOR . . . . NiB $297 Ex $195 Gd $115
Cal.: .223 Rem., .308 Win., .357 Mag., .410/.45 Long Colt.
Similar to Survivor series shotgun but with removable forearm

Noble Model 33

Noble Model 222

Noble Model 236

Noble Model 275

and thumbhole stock (both with ammo compartments). Bbl.: 20 or 22 inches, blue or nickel finish. Weight: 6 lbs. Made 1996 to 2008.

NEWTON SPORTING RIFLES — Buffalo, NY
Manufactured by Newton Arms Co., Charles Newton Rifles Corp. and Buffalo Newton Rifle Co.

BUFFALO SPORTING RIFLE NiB $2590 Ex $1800 Gd $970
Same general specifications as Standard Model, Second Type. Made c. 1922 to 1932 by Buffalo Newton Rifle Co.

MAUSER SPORTING RIFLE NiB $2125 Ex $1633 Gd $1110
Mauser (Oberndorf) action. Caliber: .256 Newton. Five round box magazine, hinged floorplate. Double-set triggers. 24-inch bbl. Open rear sight, ramp front sight. Sporting stock w/checkered pistol-grip. Weight: 7 lbs. Made c. 1914 by Newton Arms Co.

**STANDARD MODEL SPORTING RIFLE,
FIRST TYPE . . . . NiB $3597 Ex $2044 Gd $1035**
Newton bolt action, interrupted screw-type breech-locking mechanism, double-set triggers. Calibers: .22, .256, .280, .30, ,33, ,35 Newton; ,30-06. 24-inch bbl. Sights: Open rear or cocking-piece peep; ramp front. Checkered pistol-grip stock. Weight: 7 to 8 lbs.,depending on caliber. Made c. 1916 to 1918 by Newton Arms Co. Second type was prototype only; never manufactured.

NEWTON SPRINGFIELD . . . NiB $1568 Ex $1105 Gd $890
Kit including a Marlin-built sporting stock with .256 Newton barrel. Springfield 1903 action and sights provided by customer. Original has square-cut barrels marked "Newton Arms Co. Buffalo, NY." Mfg. 1914 to 1917.

NIKKO FIREARMS, LTD. — Tochiga, Japan
See listings under Golden Eagle Rifles.

NOBLE MFG. CO. — Haydenville, MA

**MODEL 10 BOLT-ACTION
SINGLE-SHOT RIFLE. . . . . NiB $121 Ex $89 Gd $73**
Caliber: .22 LR, Long, Short. 24-inch bbl. Plain pistol-grip stock. Sights: Open rear, bead front. Weight: 4 lbs. Made 1955 to 1958.

**MODEL 20 BOLT-ACTION
SINGLE-SHOT RIFLE. . . . . NiB $126 Ex $92 Gd $75**
Manually cocked. Caliber: .22 LR, Long, Short. 22-inch bbl. Weight: 5 lbs. Sights: Open rear; bead front. Walnut stock w/ pistol grip. Made from 1958 to 1963.

**MODEL 33 SLIDE-ACTION
REPEATER . . . . NiB $230 Ex $110 Gd $80**
Hammerless. Caliber: .22 LR, Long, Short. Tubular magazine holds 21 Short, 17 Long, 15 LR. 24-inch bbl. Weight: 6 lbs. Sights: Open rear; bead front. Tenite stock and slide handle. Made 1949 to 1953.

MODEL 33A . . . . NiB $115 Ex $89 Gd $69
Same general specifications as Model 33 except w/wood stock and slide handle. Made from 1953 to 1955.

**MODEL 222 BOLT-ACTION
SINGLE-SHOT RIFLE. . . . . NiB $240 Ex $120 Gd $80**
Manually cocked. Caliber: .22 LR, Long, Short. Barrel integral w/receiver. Overall length: 38 inches. Weight: 5 lbs. Sights: Interchangeable V-notch and peep rear; ramp front. Scope mounting base. Pistol-grip stock. Made from 1958 to 1971.

**MODEL 236 SLIDE-ACTION
REPEATING RIFLE. . . . . NiB $159 Ex $140 Gd $97**
Hammerless. Caliber: .22 Short, Long, LR. Tubular magazine holds 21 Short, 17 Long, 15 LR. 24-inch bbl. Weight: 5.5 lbs. Sights: Open rear; ramp front. Pistol-grip stock, grooved slide handle. Made from 1951 to 1971.

GRADING: **NiB** = New in Box   **Ex** = Excellent or NRA 95%   **Gd** = Good or NRA 68%

Olympic Arms LTF Tactical Rifle

Olympic Arms K4B

MODEL 278 LEVER-ACTION RIFLE... NiB $227 Ex $139 Gd $110
Hammerless. Caliber: .22 Short, Long, LR. Tubular magazine holds 21 Short, 17 Long, 15 LR. 24-inch bbl. Weight: 5.5 lbs. Sights: Open rear; ramp front. Stock w/semipistol-grip. Made from 1958 to 1971.

NORINCO — Beijing, China

Manufactured by Northern China Industries Corp., Beijing, China. Imported by Century International Arms; Interarms; KBI and others.

Model 81S/AK Semiautomatic Rifle
Semiautomatic Kalashnikov style AK-47 action. Caliber: 7.62x39mm. Five, 30- or 40-round magazine. 17.5-inch bbl. 36.75 inches overall. Weight: 8.5 lbs. Hooded post front sight, 500 meters leaf rear sight. Oil-finished hardwood (military style) buttstock, pistol grip, forearm and handguard or folding metal stock. Black oxide finish. Imported 1988 to 1989.
NIdek 81S (w/wood stock) . . . NiB $1244 Ex $965 Gd $733
Model 81S (w/folding
     metal stock) . . . . NiB $1266 Ex $1002 Gd $753
Model 81S-5/56S-2
     (w/folding metal stock) . . . NiB $1339 Ex $1027 Gd $755

MODEL 84S/AK SEMIAUTOMATIC RIFLE
Semiautomatic Kalashnikov style AK-47 action. Caliber: .223 (5.56mm). 30-round magazine. 16.25-inch bbl. 35.5 inches overall. Weight: 8.75 lbs. Hooded post front sight, 800 meters leaf rear sight. Oil-finished hardwood (military style) buttstock, pistol grip, forearm and handguard; sporterized composite fiberglass stock or folding metal stock. Black oxide finish. Imported from 1988 to 1989.
Model 84S (w/wood stock) . . NiB $1479 Ex $1032 Gd $678
Model 84S-3 (w/folding
     metal stock) . . . . NiB $1688 Ex $954 Gd $669
Model 84S-3 (w/composite
     stock) . . . . NiB $1337 Ex $1043 Gd $645
Model 84S-5 (w/folding metal
     stock) . . . . NiB $1613 Ex $981 Gd $687

MODEL AK-47 THUMBHOLE SPORTER
Semiautomatic AK-47 sporterized variant. Calibers: .223 (5.56mm) or 7.62x39mm. Five round magazine. 16.25-inch or 23.25-inch bbl. 35.5 or 42.5 inches overall. Weight: 8.5 to 10.3 lbs. Adj. post front sight, open adj. rear. Forged receiver w/ black oxide finish. Walnut-finished thumbhole stock w/recoil pad. Imported from 1991 to 1993.
5.56mm. . . . . NiB $775 Ex $466 Gd $337
7.62x39mm. . . . . NiB $564 Ex $466 Gd $339

MODEL MAK 90/01 SPORT . . . NiB $733 Ex $455 Gd $337
Similar to Model AK-47 Thumbhole Sporter except w/minor modifications implemented to meet importation requirements. Imported from 1994 to 1995.

OLYMPIC ARMS — Olympia, Washington

PCR SERIES Gas-operated semi-auto action. Calibers: .17 Rem., .223, 7.62x39, 6x45, 6PPC or 9mm, .40 S&W, 4.5ACP (in carbine version only). Ten-round magazine. 16-, 20- or 24-inch bbl. Weight: 7 to 10.2 lbs. Black composite stocks. Post front, rear adj. sights; scope ready flattop. Barrel fluting. William set trigger. Made from 1994 to date.
PCR-1 Ultra Match . . . . NiB $981 Ex $760 Gd $583
PCR-2 Mult-iMatch ML-1 . . . . NiB $1032 Ex $915 Gd $633
PCR-3 Multi-Match ML-2 . . . . NiB $1070 Ex $959 Gd $654
PCR-4 AR-15 Match . . . . NiB $877 Ex $808 Gd $521
MCR-5 CAR-15 (.223 Rem.) . . . NiB $977 Ex $803 Gd $522
PCR5 CAR-15
     (9mm, 40 S&W, .45 ACP) . . . NiB $903 Ex $794 Gd $538
PCR-5 CAR (.223 Rem.) . . . . . . NiB $955 Ex $731 Gd $510
PCR-6/A-2 (7.62x39mm) . . . . . NiB $895 Ex $692 Gd $486

BOLT-ACTION SAKO . . . . NiB $755 Ex $575 Gd $456
Cal.: Various from .17 Rem. to .416 Rem. Mag. Bbl.: Fluted; various stock options. Value is for base model without custom options.

ULTRA CSR TACTICAL . . . . NiB $1877 Ex $1355 Gd $1043
Cal.: .308 Win. Sako action. Bbl.: Heavy, 26 inches, broach cut. Stock: Bell & Carlson black or synthetic with aluminum bedding. Harris bipod included. Made from 1996 to 2000.

COUNTER SNIPER RIFLE. . NiB $1490 Ex $1266 Gd $1079
Bolt action. Cal.: .308 Win. Bbl.: Heavy, 26-inches. Stock: Camo fiberglass. Weight: 10.5 lbs. Disc. 1987.

SURVIVOR 1 . . . . NiB $455 Ex $276 Gd $264
Converts M1911 into bolt-action carbine. Cal.: .223 Rem., .45 ACP. Bbl.: 16.25 inches. Collapsible stock. Available for S&W and Browning Hi-Power. Weight: 5 lbs.

CAR 97. . . . . NiB $909 Ex $693 Gd $633
Cal.: .223 Rem., 9mm Para., 10mm, .40 S&W, .45 ACP. Similar to PCR-5 but w/ 16-inch button-rifled barrel. A2 sights, fixed CAR stock, post-ban muzzle brake. Weight: 7 lbs. Made from 1997 to 2004.
M-4 version (disc. 2004), add $75

FAR-15 . . . . NiB $1035 Ex $780 Gd $669
Featherweight model. Cal.: .223 Rem. Bbl.: 16 inches, lightweight, button-rifled, collapsible stock. Weight: 9.2 lbs. Made from 2001 to 2004.

GI-16 . . . . NiB $989 Ex $760 Gd $590
Cal.: .223 Rem. Forged aluminum receiver, matte finish. Bbl.: Match grade, 16 inches, button rifled. Collapsible stock. Weight: 7 lbs. Made 2004 and 2006.

GI-20 . . . . NiB $877 Ex $698 Gd $549
Cal. .223 Rem. Similar to GI-16 except w/20-inch heavy bbl., A-2 lower. Weight: 8.4 lbs. Made 2004.

Olympic Arms K7 Eliminator

Parker-Hale Model 81 Classic

Parker-Hale Model 87

Parker-Hale Model 1100 Lightweight

Parker-Hale Model 1200 Super Clip

OA-93 Carbine. . . . . **NiB $1390 Ex $1133 Gd $976**
Based on OA-93 pistol. Cal.: .223 Rem. Bbl.: 16 inches. Flattop receiver. Aluminum side folding stock, round aluminum hand-guard, Vortex flash supp. Weight: 7.5 lbs. Made 1998 and from 2004 to 2007.

OA-93PT . . . . **NiB $1077 Ex $976 Gd $692**
Similar to OA-93 carbine but with aluminum receiver, black matte anodized finish. Bbl.: 16 inches, match grade chromemo-ly steel with removable muzzle brake, push-button removable stock. Weight: 7 lbs. Made from 2006 to 2007.

LTF TACTICAL RIFLE . . . . . . **NiB $1338 Ex $1056 Gd $777**
Cal. .223 Rem. Bbl.: 16 inches, fluted or non-fluted w/flash supp. Black matte anodized receiver. Firsh-type forearm, Picatinny rails, Parkerized steel parts. Tube-style stock. Weight: 6.4 lbs.
Fluted bbl., add **10%**

K3B CARBINE . . . . **NiB $1189 Ex $873 Gd $689**
Cal. .223 Rem. Bbl.: 16 inches, match grade chromemoly steel w/flash supp. A2 rear sight and buttstock; adj. front post sight.
A3 Flattop receiver, add **$75**
FAR carbine, add **$75**
M4 carbine, add. **$75**
A3-TC carbine, add **$250**

K4B/K4B68 . . . . **NiB $1087 Ex $764 Gd $590**
Cal.: .223 Rem., 6.8 SPC. Bbl.: 20 inches, match grade, chromemoly steel, button rifled; flash supp. Adj. A2 rear sight and front post; A2 buttstock, upper receiver and hand guard. Weight: 8.5 lbs.
Flattop receiver, add **$150**

K4B-A4. . . . . **NiB $1034 Ex $766 Gd $588**
Cal.: .223 Rem. Bbl.: 20 inches w/A2 flash supp.; bayonet lug. Flattop receiver. Adj. post front sight. Firsh handguard, Picatinny rails. Made from 2006 to 2008.

K7 ELIMINATOR . . . . **NiB $1087 Ex $800 Gd $633**
Cal.: .223 Rem. Bbl.: 16 inches, stainless steel w/flash supp.; adj. A2 rear sight and front post; A2 buttstock. Weight: 7.8 lbs.

K8 TARGET MATCH . . . . **NiB $1087 Ex $723 Gd $572**
Cal.: .223 Rem. Bbl.: 20-inch bull bbl., stainless, button rifling; Picatinny flattop upper, A2 buttstock. Weight: 8.5 lbs.

K8-MAG . . . . **NiB $1423 Ex $1150 Gd $976**
Similar to Target Match model. Cal.: .223 WSSM, .243 WSSM, .25 WSSM, .300 WSM. 24-inch bbl. Weight: 9.4 lbs.

K9/K10/K40/K45 . . . . **NiB $1132 Ex $955 Gd $780**
Cal.: 9mm Para., 10mm Norma, .40 S&W, .45 ACP. Blow-back action. Bbl.: 16 inches w/flash suppressor and bayonet lug. Adj. A2 rear sight. Collapsible stock. Weight: 6.7 lbs.

K9GL/K40GL . . . . **NiB $1188 Ex $992 Gd $694**
Similar to K9 series. Cal.: 9mm Para., .40 S&W. Lower designed to accept Glock magazines. Bbl.: 16 inches; flash suppressor. Collapsible stock. No magazine furnished.
A3 upper, add $126

K16 . . . . **NiB $962 Ex $710 Gd $577**
Cal.: .223 Rem. Bbl.: 16 inches, free-floating, button rifled. Picatinny flattop upper; A2 buttstock. Weight: 7.5 lbs.
K30R . . . . **NiB $1077 Ex $879 Gd $683**
w/A3 upper, add $126

K-30 (.30 carbine) . . . . **NiB $978 Ex $668 Gd $533**
Cal.: 7.62x39mm. Bbl.: 16-inch stainless steel, adj. rear sight. Parkerized steel parts. Six-point collapsible stock.

K68 . . . . **NiB $1198 Ex $978 Gd $645**
Cal.: 6.8 Rem. SPC. Bbl.: 16-in. stainless steel, A2 upper with adj. rear sight and flash suppressor. Matte black anodized receiver, Parkerized steel parts. Six-position collapsible A2 stock w/pistol grip.
w/A3 upper, add $126

K74 . . . . **NiB $1027 Ex $903 Gd $645**
Cal.: 5.45x39mm. Bbl.: 16-in. button rifling; flash suppressor and adj. front sight. Six-position collapsible stock. Weight: 6.75 lbs.

PARKER-HALE LIMITED — Birmingham, England

MODEL 81 AFRICAN . . . . **NiB $909 Ex $789 Gd $533**
Same general specifications as Model 81 Classic except in caliber .375 H&H only. Sights: African Express rear; hooded blade front. Barrel-band swivel. All-steel trigger guard. Checkered European walnut stock w/pistol grip and recoil pad. Engraved receiver. Imported from 1986 to 1991.

MODEL 81 CLASSIC BOLT-ACTION
RIFLE . . . . **NiB $745 Ex $627 Gd $439**
Calibers: .22-250, .243 Win., .270 Win., 6mm Rem., 6.5x55, 7x57, 7x64, .308 Win., .30-06, .300 Win. Mag., 7mm Rem. Mag. Four round magazine. 24-inch bbl. Weight: 7.75 lbs. Sights: Adj. open rear, hooded ramp front. Checkered pistol-grip stock of European walnut. Imported from 1984 to 1991.

MODEL 85 SNIPER RIFLE . **NiB $2730 Ex $2161 Gd $1578**
Caliber: .308 Win. Ten or 20-round M-14-type magazine. 24.25-inch bbl. 45 inches overall. Weight: 12.5 lbs. Blade front sight, folding aperture rear. McMillan fiberglass stock w/ detachable bipod. Imported from 1989 to 1991.

MODEL 87 BOLT-ACTION REPEATING
TARGET RIFLE . . . . **NiB $1425 Ex $1233 Gd $757**
Calibers: .243 Win., 6.5x55, .308 Win., .30-06 Springfield, .300 Win. Mag. Five-round detachable box magazine.

26-inch bbl. 45 inches overall. Weight: 10 lbs. No sights; grooved for target-style scope mounts. Stippled walnut stock w/adj. buttplate. Sling swivel studs. Parkerized finish. Folding bipod. Imported 1988–91.

MODEL 1000 STANDARD RIFLE . . . **NiB $460 Ex $359 Gd $248**
Calibers: .22-250, .243 Win., .270 Win., 6mm Rem., .308 Win., .30-06. Four-round magazine. Bolt action. 22-inch or 24-inch (22-250) bbl. 43 inches overall. 7.25 lbs. Checkered walnut Monte Carlo-style stock w/satin finish. Imported from 1984 to 1988.

MODEL 1100 LIGHTWEIGHT BOLT-ACTION
RIFLE . . . . **NiB $535 Ex $443 Gd $337**
Same general specifications as Model 1000 Standard except w/22-inch lightweight profile bbl., hollow bolt handle, alloy trigger guard and floorplate, 6.5 lbs., Schnabel forend. Imported 1984 to 1991.

MODEL 1100M AFRICAN MAGNUM
RIFLE . . . . **NiB $858 Ex $745 Gd $500**
Same as Model 1000 Standard except w/24-inch bbl. in calibers .404 Jeffery, .458 Win. Mag. Weight: 9.5 lbs. Sights: Adj. rear; hooded post front. Imported from 1984 to 1991.

MODEL 1200 SUPER CLIP BOLT-ACTION
RIFLE . . . . **NiB $763 Ex $555 Gd $423**
Same as Model 1200 Super except w/detachable box magazine in calibers .243 Win., 6mm Rem., .270 Win. .30-06 and .308 Win., .300 Win. Mag., 7mm Rem. Mag. Imported from 1984 to 1991.

MODEL 1200 SUPER BOLT-ACTION
SPORTING RIFLE . . . . **NiB $586 Ex $480 Gd $355**
Mauser-type bolt action. Calibers: .22-250, .243 Win., 6mm Rem., .25-06, .270 Win., .30-06, .308 Win. Four round magazine. 24-inch bbl. Weight: 7.25 lbs. Sights: Folding open rear, hooded ramp front. European walnut stock w/rollover Monte Carlo cheekpiece, rosewood forend tip and pistol-grip cap, skip checkering, recoil pad, sling swivels. Imported from 1968 to 1991.

MODEL 1200 SUPER MAGNUM . . . **NiB $556 Ex $550 Gd $369**
Same general specifications as 1200 Super except calibers 7mm Rem. Mag. and .300 Win. Mag., 3-round magazine. Imported 1988 to 1991.

MODEL 1200P PRESENTATION NiB $580 Ex $459 Gd $347
Same general specifications as 1200 Super except w/scroll-engraved action, trigger guard and floorplate, no sights. QD swivels. Calibers: .243 Win. and .30-06. Imported from 1969 to 1975.

MODEL 1200V VARMINT . . . . . **NiB $557 Ex $498 Gd $425**
Same general specifications as 1200 Super, except w/24-inch heavy bbl., no sights, weight: 9.5 lbs. Calibers: .22-250, 6mm Rem., .25-06, .243 Win. Imported from 1969-89.

MODEL 1300C SCOUT . . . . . . **NiB $733 Ex $689 Gd $550**
Calibers: .243, .308 Win. 10-round magazine. 20-inch bbl. w/ muzzle brake. 41 inches overall. Weight: 8.5 lbs. No sights, drilled and tapped for scope. Checkered laminated birch stock w/QD swivels. Imported in 1991.

MODEL 2100 MIDLAND BOLT-ACTION
RIFLE . . . . **NiB $380 Ex $321 Gd $244**
Calibers: .22-250, .243 Win., 6mm Rem., .270 Win., 6.5x55, 7x57, 7x64, .308 Win, .30-06. Four-round box magazine.

Pedersen Model 3000
Grade III

Plainfield M-1 Carbine

Polish Model 1929 Mauser

Purdey Double Rifle

Purdey Bolt-Action Rifle

RIFLES

22-inch or 24-inch (22-250) bbl. 43-inches overall. Weight: 7 lbs. Sights: Adj. folding rear; hooded ramp front. Checkered European walnut Monte Carlo stock w/pistol-grip. Imported from 1984 to 1991.

MODEL 2707 LIGHTWEIGHT . NiB $370 Ex $329 Gd $237
Same general specifications as Model 2100 Midland except w/ tapered lightweight bbl. and aluminum trigger guard. Weight: 6.5 lbs. Imported in 1991.

MODEL 2800 MIDLAND . . . . . NiB $375 Ex $319 Gd $245
Same general specifications as model 2100 except w/laminated birch stock. Imported in 1991.

PEDERSEN CUSTOM GUNS — North Haven, Connecticut *Division of O.F. Mossberg & Sons, Inc.*

MODEL 3000 GRADE I BOLT-ACTION
RIFLE. . . . . NiB $1034 Ex $809 Gd $544
Richly engraved w/silver inlays, full-fancy American black walnut stock. Mossberg Model 810 action. Calibers: .270 Win., .30-06, 7mm Rem. Mag., .338 Win. Mag. Three-round magazine, hinged floorplate. 22-inch bbl. in .270 and .30-06, 24-inch in Magnums. Weight: 7 to 8 lbs. Sights: Open rear; hooded ramp front. Monte Carlo stock w/roll-over cheekpiece, wraparound hand checkering on pistol grip and forearm, rosewood pistol-grip cap and forend tip, recoil pad or steel buttplate w/trap, detachable swivels. Imported 1973 to 1975.

MODEL 3000 GRADE II . . . . . . NiB $733 Ex $480 Gd $380
Same as Model 3000 Grade I except less elaborate engraving, no inlays, fancy grade walnut stock w/recoil pad. Imported 1973 to 1975.

MODEL 3000 GRADE III. . . . . NiB $579 Ex $380 Gd $299
Same as Model 3000 Grade I except no engraving or inlays, select grade walnut stock w/recoil pad. Imported from 1973 to 1974.

MODEL 4700 CUSTOM DELUXE
LEVER-ACTION RIFLE. . . . . . . NiB $279 Ex $238 Gd $175
On Mossberg Model .472 action. Calibers: .30-30, 35 Rem. Five-round tubular magazine. 24-inch bbl. Weight: 7.5 lbs. Sights: Open rear, hooded ramp front. Hand-finished black walnut stock and beavertail forearm, barrel band swivels. Imported in 1975.

J.C. PENNEY CO., INC. — Dallas, Texas
Firearms sold under the J.C. Penney label were mfd. by Marlin, High Standard, Stevens, Savage and Springfield.

MODEL 2025 BOLT-ACTION
REPEATER . . . . NiB $100 Ex $65 Gd $55
Takedown. Caliber: .22 RF. Eight round detachable box magazine. 24-inch bbl. Weight: 6 lbs. Sights: Open rear; bead front. Plain pistol-grip stock. Manufactured by Marlin.

MODEL 2035 BOLT-ACTION
REPEATER . . . . NiB $100 Ex $65 Gd $55
Takedown. Caliber: .22 RF. Eight round detachable box magazine. 24-inch bbl. Weight: 6 lbs. Sights: Open rear; bead front. Plain pistol-grip stock. Manufactured by Marlin.

MODEL 2935 LEVER-ACTION
RIFLE. NiB $210 Ex $170 Gd $121
Same general specifications as Marlin Model 336.

GRADING: NiB = New in Box   **Ex** = Excellent or NRA 95%   **Gd** = Good or NRA 68%

MODEL 6400 BOLT-ACTION
CENTERFIRE RIFLE . . . . NiB $210 Ex $170 Gd $110
Same general specifications as Savage Model 340.

MODEL 6660 AUTOLOADING RIFLE. . . NiB $115 Ex $90 Gd $75
Caliber: .22 RF. Tubular magazine. 22-inch bbl. Weight: 5.5
lbs. Sights: Open rear; hooded ramp front. Plain pistol-grip
stock. Manufactured by Marlin.

PLAINFIELD MACHINE COMPANY —
Dunellen, New Jersey

M-1 CARBINE . . . . NiB $227 Ex $166 Gd $135
Same as U.S. Carbine, Cal. .30, M-1 except also available in
caliber 5.7mm (.22 caliber w/necked-down .30 Carbine cartridge case). Current production w/ventilated metal handguard
and barrel band w/o bayonet lug; earlier models have standard
military-type fittings. Made from 1960 to 1977.

M-1 CARBINE, COMMANDO
MODEL. . . . . NiB $232 Ex $171 Gd $145
Same as M-1 Carbine except w/paratrooper-type stock w/tele-
scoping wire shoulderpiece. Made from 1960 to 1977.

M-1 CARBINE, MILITARY SPORTER. . . NiB $227 Ex $166 Gd $135
Same as M-1 Carbine except w/unslotted buttstock and wood
handguard. Made from 1960 to 1977.

M-1 DELUXE SPORTER. . . . . . . NiB $232 Ex $171 Gd $145
Same as M-1 Carbine except w/Monte Carlo sporting stock
Made from 1960 to 1973.

POLISH MILITARY RIFLES — Poland
Manufactured by Government Arsenals at Radom and Warsaw, Poland.

MODEL 1898 (KARABIN 98, K98) MAUSER
MILITARY CARBINE . . . . NiB $331 Ex $210 Gd $166
Same as German Kar. 98A except for minor details. First manu-
factured during early 1920s.

MODEL 1898 (KARABIN 98, WZ98A) MAUSER
MILITARY RIFLE . . . . NiB $289 Ex $180 Gd $145
Same as German Kar. 98 used in WWI except for minor details.
Manufacture began c. 1921.

MODEL 1929 (KARABIN 29, WZ29) MAUSER
MILITARY RIFLE . . . . NiB $331 Ex $210 Gd $166
Same as Czech Model 24, mfd. 1929 thru WWII except for
minor details. A similar model produced during German occupation was designated Gew. 29/40.

WILLIAM POWELL & SON LTD. —
Birmingham, England

DOUBLE-BARREL RIFLE NiB $32,278 Ex $26,900 Gd $18,900
Boxlock. Made to order in any caliber during the time that rifle
was manufactured. Bbls.: Made to order in any legal length,
but 26 inches recommended. Highest grade French walnut
buttstock and forearm w/fine checkering. Metal is elaborately
engraved. Imported by Stoeger from 1938 to 1951.

BOLT-ACTION RIFLE. . . . . NiB $2888 Ex $2367 Gd $1699
Mauser-type bolt action. Calibers: 6x54 through .375 H&H
Magnum. Three and 4-shot magazine, depending upon chambering. 24-inch bbl. Weight: 7.5 to 8.75 lbs. Sights: Folding
leaf rear; hooded ramp front. Cheekpiece stock, checkered
forearm and pistol grip, swivels. Imported by Stoeger from
1938 to 1951.

PTR 91, INC. — Aynor, SC
Previously Bristol, CT and Farmington, CT.

MODEL PTR-91F
SEMI-AUTOMATIC . . . . NiB $1150 Ex $900 Gd $600
Delayed roller-locked blow-back action similar to H&K G3.
Caliber: .308 Win. 20-round magazine. 18-inch bbl. H&K
Navy type polymer trigger group. Sights: H&K style front post
and rear adj. diopter. Plastic buttstock. Matte black finish. and
forearm. Made from 2005 to date.
PTR-91 AI (match grade barrel,
**   2005-2008)**. . . . . NiB $1170 Ex $730 Gd $570
PTR-91 Classic (black or wood
**   stock, 2012)** . . . . NiB $880 Ex $650 Gd $460
PTR-91 KC (16-in. bbl.). . . . . NiB $1160 Ex $910 Gd $600
PTR-91T (green furniture). . . . NiB $900 Ex $850 Gd $550
PTR-MSG 91 Sniper (18-in. fluted
**   target bbl.)** . . . . NiB $1980 Ex $1600 Gd $900

PUMA — Brescia, Italy
*Manufactured by Armisport Chiappa in Brescia, Italy, and
imported by Legacy Sports Int'l., Reno, NV.*

Model 1886 Lever Action . . . . NiB $1260 Ex $880 Gd $625
Reproduction of Winchester 1886 lever action. Caliber: .45-70. 7-
or 8-round tube magazine. 22- or 26-inch round or octagon bbl.
Case colored receiver, Italian walnut stock. Made 2009 to date.

Model 92 Lever Action . . . . . . NiB $925 Ex $710 Gd $460
Caliber: .38 Special/.357 Mag., .44 Special/.44 Mag., .45 LC,
.454 Casull or .480 Ruger. Lever action, 9- or 10-round tube
magazine. 20-inch round or octagon bbl. Blue, brass or case
colored receiver, walnut stock. Made 2001 to date.

PPS/22 . . . . NiB $480 Ex $330 Gd $280
Caliber: .22 LR. Semi-auto action, 16-inch bbl., 10- or
50-round (drum) magazine. Made 2009 to 2010.

JAMES PURDEY & SONS LTD. — London, England

BOLT-ACTION RIFLE. NiB $22,800 Ex $19,970 Gd $12,770
Mauser-type bolt action. Calibers: 7x57, .300 H&H Magnum,
.375 H&H Magnum, 10.75x73. Three round magazine. 24-inch
bbl. Weight: 7.5 to 8.75 lbs. Sights: Folding leaf rear; hooded
ramp front. Cheekpiece stock, checkered forearm and pistol-
grip, swivels. Currently manufactured; same general specifications apply to pre-WWII model.

DOUBLE RIFLE
Sidelock action, hammerless, ejectors. Almost any caliber is
available but the following are the most popular: .375 Flanged
Magnum Nitro Express, .500/465 Nitro Express .470 Nitro Express,
.577 Nitro Express. 25.5-inch bbls. (25-inch in .375). Weight: 9.5
to 12.75 lbs. Sights: Folding leaf rear; ramp front. Cheekpiece
stock, checkered forearm and pistol-grip, recoil pad, swivels.
Currently manufactured to individual measurements and specifications; same general specifications apply to pre-WWII model.
H&H calibers . . . . . . NiB $72,665 Ex $57,550 Gd $38,750
NE calibers . . . . NiB $85,000 Ex $56,000 Gd $39,000

Remington No. 7
Target and Sporting Rifle

Remington
Model 40X Standard Rimfire

Remington
Model 40-XB Centerfire

RAPTOR ARMS COMPANY, INC. — Newport, New Hampshire

BOLT-ACTION RIFLE
Calibers: .243 Win., .270 Win., .30-06 or .308 Win. Four round magazine. 22-inch sporter or heavy bbl. Weight: 7.3 to 8 lbs. 42.5 inches overall. No sights w/drilled and tapped receiver or optional blade front, adjustable rear. Blue, stainless or "Taloncote" rust-resistant finish. Checkered black synthetic stock w/Monte Carlo cheepiece and vented recoil pad. Imported from 1997 to 1999.

Raptor Sporter model . . . . NiB $255 Ex $190 Gd $155
Raptor Deluxe Peregrine
  model (disc. 1998) . . . . NiB $258 Ex $195 Gd $159
Raptor heavy bbl. model . . . . . NiB $277 Ex $222 Gd $195
Raptor stainless bbl. model . . . . NiB $299 Ex $257 Gd $213
w/optional sights, add $40

REMINGTON ARMS COMPANY — Madison, NC
Manufacturing locations in Ilion, New York, Lonoke, AR, and Mayfield, Kentucky. Acquired by Freedom Group Inc. in 2007.

To facilitate locating Remington firearms, models are grouped into four categories: Single-shot rifles, bolt-action repeating rifles, slide-action (pump) rifles, and semiautomatic rifles. For a complete listing, please refer to the index.

- SINGLE-SHOT RIFLES -

NO. 1 SPORTING RIFLE . . . NiB $6223 Ex $3856 Gd $2210
Single-Shot, rolling-block action. Calibers: .40-50, .40-70, .44-77, .50-45, .50-70 Gov't. centerfire and .44 Long, .44 Extra Long, .45-70, .46 Long, .46 Extra Long, .50-70 rimfire. Bbl. lengths: 28- or 30-inch part octagon. Weight: 5 to 7.5 lbs. Sights: Folding leaf rear sight; sporting front, dovetail bases. Plain walnut straight stock; flanged-top, semicarbine buttplate. Plain walnut forend with thin, rounded front end. Made from 1868 to 1902.

NO. 1 1/2 SPORTING RIFLE . . . NiB $4190 Ex $1200 Gd $1888
Single-Shot, rolling-block action. Calibers: .22 Short, Long, or Extra Long. 25 Stevens, .32, and .38 rimfire cartridges. .32-20, .38-40 and .44-40 centerfire. Bbl. lengths: 24-, 26-, 28- or 30-inch part octagon. Remaining features similar to Remington No. 1. Made from 1869 to 1902.

NO. 2 SPORTING RIFLE
Single-shot, rolling-block action. Calibers: .22, .25, .32, .38, .44 rimfire or centerfire. Bbl. lengths: 24, 26, 28 or 30 inches. Weight: 5 to 6 lbs. Sights: Open rear; bead front. Straight-grip sporting stock and knobtip forearm of walnut. Made from 1873 to 1909.
Calibers: .22, .25, .32 . . . . . . NiB $3575 Ex $2040 Gd $989
Calibers: .38, .44 . . . . NiB $9650 Ex $8129 Gd $5450

NO. 3 CREEDMOOR AND SCHUETZEN
RIFLES . . . . NiB $16,187 Ex $12,750 Gd $10,510
Produced in a variety of styles and calibers, these are collector's items and bring far higher prices than the sporting types. The Schuetzen Special, which has an under-lever action, is especially rare — perhaps fewer than 100 have been made.

NO. 3 HIGH POWER RIFLE
Single-shot, Hepburn falling-block action w/side lever. Calibers: .30-30, .30-40, .32 Special, .32-40, .38-55, .38-72 (high-power cartridges). Bbl. lengths: 26-, 28-, 30-inch. Weight: About 8 lbs. Open sporting sights. Checkered pistol-grip stock and forearm. Made from 1893 to 1907.
Calibers: .30-30, .30-40,
  .32 Special, .32-40 . . . . . NiB $9775 Ex $7956 Gd $5110
Calibers: .38-55, .38-72 . . . NiB $9688 Ex $8154 Gd $6422

NO. 3 SPORTING RIFLE . . . NiB $9775 Ex $7279 Gd $6788
Single-shot, Hepburn falling-block action w/side lever. Calibers: .22 WCF, .22 Extra Long, .25-20 Stevens, .25-21 Stevens, .25-25 Stevens, .32 WCF, .32-40 Ballard & Marlin, .32-40 Rem., .38 WCF, .38-40 Rem., 38-.38-50 Rem., .38-55 Ballard & Marlin, .40-60 Ballard & Marlin, .40-60 WCF, .40-65 Rem. Straight, .40-82 WCF, .45-70 Gov., .45-90 WCF, also was supplied on special order in bottle-necked .40-50, .40-70, .40-90, .44-77, .44-90, .44-105, .50-70 Gov., .50-90 Sharps Straight.

Remington
Model 40-XB Varmint Special

Bbl. lengths: 26-inch (22, 25, 32 cal. only), 28-inch, 30-inch; half-octagon or full-octagon. Weight: 8 to 10 lbs. Sights: Open rear; blade front. Checkered pistol-grip stock and forearm. Made from 1880 to c. 1911.

NO. 4 SINGLE-SHOT RIFLE . . NiB $1630 EX $944 Gd $755
Rolling-block action. Solid frame or takedown. Calibers: .22 Short and Long, .22 LR, .25 Stevens R.F., .32 Short and Long R.F. 22.5-inch octagon bbl., 24-inch available in .32 caliber only. Weight: About 4.5 lbs. Sights: Open rear; blade front. Plain walnut stock and forearm. Made from 1890-1933.

NO. 4S MILITARY MODEL 22 SINGLE-SHOT
RIFLE. . . . . NiB $2650 Ex $2033 Gd $997
Rolling-block action. Calibers: .22 Short, Long LR. 28-inch bbl. Weight: About 5 lbs. Sights: Military-type rear; blade front. Military-type stock w/handguard, stacking swivel, sling. Has a bayonet stud on the barrel; bayonet and scabbard were regularly supplied. Note: At one time the Military Model was the official rifle of the Boy Scouts of America and was called the Boy Scout Rifle. Made from 1913 to 1933.

NO. 5 SPECIAL SINGLE-SHOT RIFLE
Single-shot, rolling-block action. Calibers: 7mm Mauser, .30-30, .30-40 Krag, .303 British, .32-40, .32 Special, .38-55 (high-power cartridges). Bbl. lengths: 24, 26 and 28 inches. Weight: About 7 lbs. Open sporting sights. Plain straight-grip stock and forearm. Made 1902 to 1918. Note: Models 1897 and 1902 Military Rifles, intended for the export market, are almost identical with the No. 5, except for 30-inch bbl. full military stock and weight (about 8.5 lbs.); a carbine was also supplied. The military rifles were produced in caliber 8mm Lebel for France, 7.62mm Russian for Russia and 7mm Mauser for the Central and South American government trade. Also offered to retail buyers.
Sporting model . . . . NiB $934 Ex $733 Gd $530
Military model . . . . NiB $731 Ex $554 Gd $400

NO. 6 TAKEDOWN RIFLE. . . . . NiB $675 Ex $535 Gd $459
Single-shot, rolling-block action. Calibers: .22 Short, Long, LR; .32 Short, Long RF. 20-inch bbl. Weight: Avg. 4 lbs. Sights: Open front and rear; tang peep. Plain straight-grip stock, forearm. Made from 1901 to 1933.

NO. 7 TARGET AND SPORTING
RIFLE. . . . . .NiB $9707 Ex $7235 Gd $6755
Single-shot. Rolling-block Army Pistol frame. Calibers: .22 Short, .22 LR. 25-10 Stevens R.F. (other calibers available on special order). Half-octagon bbls.: 24-, 26-, 28-inch. Weight: About 6 lbs. Sights: Lyman combination rear; Beach combination front. Fancy walnut stock, Swiss buttplate available. Made from 1903 to 1911.

MODEL 33 BOLT-ACTION
SINGLE-SHOT RIFLE. . . . . . . .NiB $278 EX $190 Gd $239
Takedown. Caliber: .22 Short, Long, LR. 24-inch bbl. Weight: About 4.5 lbs. Sights: Open rear, bead front. Plain, pistol-grip stock, forearm with grasping grooves. Made from 1931 to 1936.

MODEL 33 NRA JUNIOR
TARGET RIFLE. . . . . NiB $544 Ex $408 Gd $240

Same as Model 33 Standard except has Lyman peep rear sight, Partridge-type front sight, 0.88-inch sling and swivels, weighs about 5 lbs.

MODEL 40X CENTERFIRE
RIFLE . . . . .NiB $2690 Ex $2044 Gd $1107
Specifications same as for Model 40X Rimfire (heavy weight). Calibers: .222 Rem., .222 Rem. Mag., 7.62mm NATO, .30-06 (others were available on special order). Made from 1961 to 1964. Value shown is for rifle w/o sights.

MODEL 40X HEAVYWEIGHT BOLT-ACTION
TARGET RIFLE (RIMFIRE)
Caliber: .22 LR. Single shot. Action similar to Model 722. Click adj. trigger. 28-inch heavy bbl. Redfield Olympic sights. Scope bases. High-comb target stock bedding device, adj. swivel, rubber buttplate. Weight: 12.75 lbs. Made from 1955 to 1964.
w/ sights . . . . NiB $3370 Ex $2133 Gd $1320
w/o sights . . . . NiB $2390 Ex $1096 Gd $675

MODEL 40-X SPORTER . . . . NiB $3000 Ex $1947 Gd $944
Same general specifications as Model 707 C Custom (see that listing in this section) except in caliber .22 LR. Made from 1972 to 1977.

MODEL 40X STANDARD BARREL
Same as Model 40X Heavyweight except has lighter barrel. Weight: 10.75 lbs.
w/ sights . . . . NiB $579 Ex $416 Gd $322
w/o sights . . . . NiB $495 Ex $338 Gd $256

MODEL 40-XB CENTERFIRE
MATCH RIFLE. . . . . NiB $590 Ex $466 Gd $380
Bolt-action, single-shot. Calibers: .222 Rem., .222 Rem. Mag., .223 Rem., .22-250, 6x47mm, 6mm Rem., .243 Win., .25-06, 7mm Rem. Mag., .30-06, .308 Win. (7.62mm NATO), .30-338, (7.62mm NATO), .30-338, .300 Win. Mag. 27 25-inch standard or heavy bbl. Target stock w/adj. front swivel block on guide rail, rubber buttplate. Weight w/o sights: Standard bbl., 9.25 lbs.; heavy bbl., 11.25 lbs. Value shown is for rifle without sights. Made from 1964 to date.

MODEL 40-XB RANGEMASTER CENTERFIRE RIFLE
Single-shot target rifle with same basic specifications as Model 40-XB Centerfire Match. Additional calibers in .220 Swift, 6mm BR Rem. and 7mm BR Rem., and stainless bbl. only. American walnut or Kevlar (weighs 1 lb. less) target stock with forend stop. Discontinued 1994.
right-hand model . . . . NiB $835 Ex $600 Gd $444
left-hand model. . . . . NiB $835 Ex $600 Gd $444
Kevlar stock, right-hand model . . . NiB $2200 Ex $2011 Gd $1077
Kevlar stock, left-hand model . . . . NiB $2200 Ex $2011 Gd $1077
w/2 oz. trigger, add $126
Repeater model, add. $126

MODEL 40-XB RANGEMASTER RIMFIRE
MATCH RIFLE. . . . . NiB $877 Ex $792 Gd $440
Bolt-action, single-shot. Caliber: .22 LR. 28-inch standard or heavy bbl. Target stock with adj. front swivel block on guide rail, rubber buttplate. Weight w/o sights: Standard bbl., 10 lbs.; heavy bbl., 11.25 lbs. Value shown is for rifle without sights. Made 1964-74.

Remington
Model 40-XBR

Remington
Model 40-XC

Remington
Model 40-XR Custom Sporter Grade II

Remington
Model 40-XR Rimfire Position Rifle

**MODEL 40-XB VARMINT SPECIAL
RIFLE** . . . . **NiB $1367 Ex $899 Gd $466**
Same general specifications as Model 40-XB Repeater except
has synthetic stock (Kevlar). Made from 1987-94.

MODEL 40-XBBR BENCH REST RIFLE
Bolt action, single shot. Calibers: .222 Rem., .222 Rem.
Mag., .223 Rem., 6x47mm, .308 Win. (7.62mm NATO). 20-
or 26-inch unblued stainless-steel bbl. Supplied w/o sights.
Weight: With 20-inch bbl., 9.25 lbs., with 26-inch bbl.,12 lbs.
(Heavy Varmint class; 7.25 lbs. w/Kevlar stock (Light Varmint
class). Made from 1974 to 2004; reintroduced 2007.
Model 40-XBBR (disc.) . . . . **NiB $3550 Ex $2896 Gd $1600**
Model 40-XBBR KS
  (Kevlar stock) . . . . **NiB $3504 Ex $2973 Gd $1679**

MODEL 40-XC NATIONAL MATCH COURSE RIFLE
Bolt-action repeater. Caliber: .308 Win. (7.62mm NATO). Five
round magazine, clip slot in receiver. 24-inch bbl. Supplied
w/o sights. Weight: 11 lbs. Thumb groove stock w/adj. hand
stop and sling swivel, adj. buttplate. Disc 2004, reintroduced
2006.
W/wood stock, disc.) . . . . . **NiB $3170 Ex $2834 Gd $1566**
W/Kevlar stock, disc. 1994) NiB $3159 Ex $2833 Gd $1633

MODEL 40-XR CUSTOM SPORTER RIFLE
Caliber: .22 RF. 24-inch contoured bbl. Supplied w/o sights.
Made in four grades of checkering, engraving and other custom
features. Made from 1987 to date. High grade model discontinued 1991.

Grade I . . . . **NiB $1233 Ex $1099 Gd $820**
Grade II . . . . **NiB $2270 Ex $1833 Gd $1166**
Grade III . . . . **NiB $3077 Ex $2100 Gd $1310**
Grade IV . . . . **NiB $5055 Ex $4110 Gd $2966**

**MODEL 40-XR RIMFIRE POSITION
RIFLE** . . . . **NiB $1266 Ex $1087 Gd $677**
Bolt action, single shot. Caliber: .22 LR. 24-inch heavy bbl.
Supplied w/o sights. Weight: 10 lbs. Position-style stock w/
thumb groove, adj. hand stop and sling swivel on guide rail,
adj. buttplate. Made from 1974. Discontinued 2004.
KS model (w/Kevlar stock) . . **NiB $1387 Ex $1100 Gd $707**

**MODEL 41A TARGETMASTER BOLT-ACTION
SINGLE-SHOT RIFLE** . . . . **NiB $296 Ex $190 Gd $137**
Takedown. Caliber: .22 Short, Long, LR. 27-inch bbl. Weight:
About 5.5 lbs. Sights: Open rear; bead front. Plain pistol-grip
stock. Made 1936 to 1940.

MODEL 41AS . . . . **NiB $398 Ex $224 Gd $135**
Same as Model 41A except chambered for .22 Remington
Special (.22 W.R.F.).

MODEL 41P . . . . **NiB $323 Ex $200 Gd $135**
Same as Model 41A except has peep rear sight, hooded
front sight.

MODEL 41SB . . . . **NiB $439 Ex $167 Gd $154**
Same as Model 41A except smoothbore for use with shot
cartridges.

**Remington
Model 580**

MODEL 510A TARGETMASTER BOLT-ACTION
SINGLE-SHOT RIFLE.........NiB $255 Ex $170 Gd $130
Takedown. Caliber: 22 Short, Long, LR. 25-inch bbl. Weight:
About 5.5 lbs. Sights: Open rear; bead front. Plain pistol-grip
stock. Made from 1939 to 1962.

MODEL 510P ....NiB $277 Ex $175 Gd $131
Same as Model 510A except has peep rear sight, Patridge front
on ramp.

MODEL 510-X SB ....NiB $390 Ex $248 Gd $190
Same as Model 510A except smoothbore for use with shot
cartridges, shotgun bead front sight, no rear sight.

MODEL 510X BOLT-ACTION SINGLE-SHOT
RIFLE....................NiB $233 Ex $190 Gd $126
Same as Model 510A except improved sights. Made
from1964-66.

MODEL 514 BOLT-ACTION
SINGLE-SHOT..............NiB $180 Ex $157 Gd $126
Takedown. Caliber: .22 Short, Long, LR. 24-inch bbl. Weight:
4.75 lbs. Sights: Open rear; bead front. Plain pistol-grip stock.
Made from1948 to 1971.

MODEL 514BC BOY'S
CARBINE.................NiB $227 Ex $166 Gd $129
Same as Model 514 except has 21-inch bbl., 1-inch shorter
stock. Made from1961 to 1971.

MODEL 514P ....NiB $227 Ex $166 Gd $129
Same as Model 514 except has receiver peep sight.

MODEL 540-X RIMFIRE
TARGET RIFLE.............NiB $455 Ex $300 Gd $141
Bolt-action, single-shot. Caliber: .22 R. 26-inch heavy bbl.
Supplied w/o sights. Weight: About 8 lbs. Target stock w/Monte
Carlo cheekpiece and thumb groove, guide rail for hand stop
and swivel, adj. buttplate. Made from 1969 to 1974.

MODEL 540-XR POSITION
RIFLE.....................NiB $455 Ex $300 Gd $141
Bolt-action, single-shot. Caliber: .22 LR. 26-inch medium-
weight bbl. Supplied w/o sights. Weight: 8 lbs., 13 oz. Position-
style stock w/thumb groove, guide rail for hand stop and
swivel, adj. buttplate. Made from 1974 to 1984.

MODEL 540-XRJR..........NiB $415 Ex $338 Gd $200
Same as Model 540-XR except 1.75-inch shorter stock. Made
from 1974 to 1984.

MODEL 580 BOLT-ACTION
SINGLE-SHOT..............NiB $200 Ex $155 Gd $120
Caliber: .22 Short, Long, LR. 24-inch bbl. Weight: 4.75 lbs.
Sights: Bead front; U-notch rear. Monte Carlo stock. Made
1967 to 1978.

MODEL 580BR BOY'S RIFLE...NiB $200 EX $155 Gd $120
Same as Model 580 except w/1-inch shorter stock. Made 1971
to 1978.

MODEL 580SB SMOOTH BORE.. NiB $290 Ex $215 Gd $149
Same as Model 580 except smooth bore for .22 Long Rifle shot
cartridges. Made from 1967 to 1978.

INTERNATIONAL FREE RIFLE...NiB $1100 Ex $824 Gd $482
Same as Model 40-XB rimfire and centerfire except has free
rifle- type stock with adj. buttplate and hook, adj. palm rest,
movable front sling swivel, 2-oz. trigger. Weight: About 15 lbs.
Made from 1964 to 1974. Value shown is for rifle with profes-
sionally finished stock, no sights.

INTERNATIONAL MATCH FREE
RIFLE..................NiB $1133 Ex $1055 Gd $677
Calibers: .22 LR, .222 Rem., .222 Rem. Mag., 7.62mm
NATO, .30-06 (others were available on special order). Model
40X-type bolt- action, single-shot. 2-oz. adj. trigger. 28-inch
heavy bbl. Weight: About 15.5 lbs. Free rifle-style stock with
thumbhole (furnished semifinished by mfr.); interchangeable
and adj. rubber buttplate and hook buttplate, adj. palm rest,
sling swivel. Made 1961 to 1964. Value shown is for rifle with
professionally-finished stock, no sights.

NYLON 10 BOLT-ACTION SINGLE-SHOT
RIFLE....................NiB $580 Ex $475 Gd $280
Caliber: .22 Short, Long, LR. 19.13-inch bbl. Weight: 4.25
lbs. Open rear sight; ramped blade front. Receiver grooved for
scope mount. Brown nylon stock. Made from 1962 to 1966.

- BOLT-ACTION REPEATING RIFLES -

MODEL SEVEN CF BOLT-ACTION RIFLE
Calibers: .17 Rem., .222 Rem., .223 Rem., .243 Win., 6mm
Rem., 7mm-08 and .308 Win. Magazine capacity: 5-round
in .17 Rem., .222 Rem., .223 Rem., 4-round in other calibers.
18.5-inch bbl. Weight: 6.5 lbs. Walnut stock checkering, and
recoil pad. Made from 1983 to 1999. .223 Rem. added in
1984.
Standard calibers............NiB $525 Ex $459 Gd $325
.17 Rem & .222 Rem...........NiB $577 Ex $485 Gd $350

MODEL SEVEN FS RIFLE......NiB $559 Ex $495 Gd $356
Calibers: .243, 7mm-08 Rem., .308 Win. 18.5-inch bbl. 37.5
inches overall. Weight: 5.25 lbs. Hand layup fiberglass stock,
reinforced with DuPont Kevlar at points of bedding and stress.
Made 1987 to 1989.

MODEL SEVEN KS RIFLE ...NiB $2269 Ex $1090 Gd $789
Calibers: .223 Rem., 7mm-08, .308, .35 Rem. and .350 Rem.
Mag. 20-inch bbl. Custom-made in Remington's Custom Shop
with Kevlar stock. Made from 1987 to date.

MODEL SEVEN LS RIFLE......NiB $654 Ex $495 Gd $338
Calibers: .223 Rem., .243 Win., .260 Rem., 7mm-08 and
308 Win. 20-inch matte bbl. Laminated hardwood stock
w/matte brown finish. Weight: 6.5 lbs. Made from 2000 to
2005.

Remington
International Match

Remington
Nylon 10

Remington Model Seven

Remington Model Seven FS

Remington Model Seven
KS Custom Rifle

MODEL SEVEN LSS RIFLE . . . . . NiB $645 Ex $510 Gd $355
Similar to Model Seven LS except stainless bbl. w/o sights.
Calibers: .22-250 Rem., .243 Win. or 7mm-08. Made from
2000 to 2003.

**MODEL SEVEN MS CUSTOM
RIFLE. . . . . NiB $2655 Ex $2025 Gd $1043**
Similar to the standard Model Seven except fitted with a laminated full Mannlicher-style stock. Weight: 6.75 lbs. Calibers:
.222 Rem., .22-250, .243, 6mm Rem.,7mm-08, .308, .350
Rem. Additional calibers available on special order. Made from
1993 to 1999.

MODEL SEVEN SS RIFLE . . . . . . NiB $650 Ex $445 Gd $316
Same as Model Seven except 20-inch stainless bbl., receiver
and bolt; black synthetic stock. Calibers: .243, 7mm-08 or
.308. Made 1994 to 2006.

MODEL SEVEN YOUTH RIFLE . NiB $575 Ex $370 Gd $279
Similar to the standard Model Seven except fitted with hardwood stock with a 12.19-inch pull. Calibers: .243, 6mm, 7mm-
08 only. Made 1993 to 2007.

**MODEL 30A BOLT-ACTION
EXPRESS RIFLE . . . . NiB $650 Ex $522 Gd $361**
Standard Grade. Modified M/1917 Enfield Action. Calibers:
.25, .30, .32 and .35 Rem., 7mm Mauser, .30-06. Five round
box magazine. 22-inch bbl. Weight: About 7.25 lbs. Sights:
Open rear; bead front. Walnut stock w/checkered pistol grip
and forearm. Made 1921 to 1940. Note: Early Model 30s had
a slender forend with Schnabel tip, military-type double-pull
trigger.

MODEL 30R CARBINE . . . . NiB $655 Ex $540 Gd $433
Same as Model 30A except has 20-inch bbl., plain stock
weight about 7 lbs.

GRADING: **NiB** = New in Box **Ex** = Excellent or NRA 95% **Gd** = Good or NRA 68%

Remington Model 30A

Remington Model 30R

Remington Model 30S

Remington Model 34

MODEL 30S SPORTING RIFLE NiB $790 Ex $650 Gd $455
Special Grade. Same action as Model 30A. Calibers: .257 Roberts, 7mm Mauser, .30-06. Five round box magazine. 24-inch bbl. Weight: About 8 lbs. Lyman No. 48 Receiver sight, bead front sight. Special high comb stock with long, full forearm, checkered. Made 1930 to 1940.

**MODEL 34 BOLT-ACTION
REPEATER . . . . NiB $210 Ex $166 Gd $137**
Takedown. Caliber: .22 Short, Long, LR. Tubular magazine holds 22 Short, 17 Long or 15 LR. 24-inch bbl. Weight: 5.25 lbs. Sights: Open rear; bead front. Plain, pistol-grip stock, forearm w/grasping grooves. Made from 1932 to 1936.

MODEL 34 NRA TARGET RIFLE NiB $553 Ex $390 Gd $256
Same as Model 34 Standard except has Lyman peep rear sight, Partridge-type front sight, .88-inch sling and swivels, weight: About 5.75 lbs.

MODEL 37 RANGEMASTER BOLT-ACTION TARGET RIFLE (I)
Model of 1937. Caliber: .22 LR. Five round box magazine, single shot adapter also supplied as standard equipment. 28-inch heavy bbl. Weight: About 12 lbs. Remington front and rear sights, scope bases. Target stock, swivels, sling. Note: Original 1937 model had a stock with outside bbl. band similar in appearance to that of the old-style Winchester Model 52, forearm design was modified and bbl. band eliminated in 1938. Made from 1937 to 1940.
w/factory sights . . . . NiB $1190 Ex $715 Gd $380
w/out sights . . . . NiB $1010 Ex $599 Gd $338

MODEL 37 RANGEMASTER BOLT-ACTION TARGET RIFLE (II)
Model of 1940. Same as Model of 1937 except has "Miracle" trigger mechanism and Randle-design stock with high comb, full pistol-grip and wide beavertail forend. Made from 1940 to 1954.
w/factory sights . . . . NiB $1179 Ex $687 Gd $491
w/out sights . . . . NiB $977 Ex $569 Gd $338

**MODEL 40-XB CENTERFIRE
REPEATER . . . . NiB $2210 Ex $1088 Gd $779**
Same as Model 40-XB Centerfire except 5-round repeater. Calibers: .222 Rem., .222 Rem. Mag., .223 Rem., .22-250, 6x47mm, 6mm Rem., .243 Win., .308 Win. (7.62mm NATO). Heavy bbl. only. Discontinued.

**MODEL 788 SPORTSMAN
BOLT-ACTION RIFLE. . . . . NiB $496 Ex $390 Gd $322**
Similar to Model 707 ADL except with straight-comb walnut-finished hardwood stock in calibers .223 Rem., .243 Win., .270 Win., .30-06 Springfield and .308 Win. 22-inch bbl. Weight: 7 lbs. Adj. sights. Made from 1967 to 1983.

**MODEL 341A SPORTSMASTER
BOLT-ACTION REPEATER . . . . . NiB $295 Ex $167 Gd $135**
Takedown. Caliber: .22 Short, Long, LR. Tubular magazine holds 22 Short, 17 Long, 15 LR. 27-inch bbl. Weight: About 6 lbs. Sights: Open rear; bead front. Plain pistol-grip stock. Made 1936 to 1940.

MODEL 341P . . . . NiB $465 Ex $220 Gd $150
Same as Model 341A except has peep rear sight, hooded front sight.

MODEL 341SB . . . . NiB $533 Ex $280 Gd $198
Same as Model 341A previously listed except smoothbore for use with shot cartridges.

Remington Model 37 (1937)

Remington Model 37 (1940)

Remington Model 511X

Remington Model 512A

Remington Model 513S

Remington Model 513TR

MODEL 511A SCOREMASTER BOLT-ACTION
BOX MAGAZINE REPEATER . . . NiB $266 Ex $188 Gd $145
Takedown. Caliber: 22 Short, Long, LR. Six round detachable box magazine. 25-inch bbl. Weight: About 5.5 lbs. Sights: Open rear; bead front. Plain pistol-grip stock. Made 1939 to 1962.

MODEL 511P . . . . NiB $190 Ex $201 Gd $150
Same as Model 511A except has peep rear sight, Partridge-type blade front on ramp.

MODEL 511X BOLT-ACTION
REPEATER . . . . NiB $259 Ex $210 Gd $155
Clip type. Same as Model 511A except improved sights. Made from 1964 to 1966.

MODEL 512A SPORTSMASTER
BOLT-ACTION REPEATER . . . . . NiB $269 EX $179 Gd $139
Takedown. Caliber: .22 Short, Long, LR. Tubular magazine holds 22 Short, 17 Long, 15 LR. 25-inch bbl. Weight: About 5.75 lbs. Sights: Open rear; bead front. Plain pistol-grip stock w/semibeavertail forend. Made from 1940 to 1962.

MODEL 512P . . . . NiB $288 Ex $227 Gd $170
Same as Model 512A except has peep rear sight, blade front, on ramp.

MODEL 512X BOLT- ACTION
REPEATER . . . . NiB $277 Ex $228 Gd $180
Tubular magazine type. Same as Model 512A except has improved sights. Made from 1964 to 1966.

MODEL 513S BOLT-ACTION
RIFLE . . . . NiB $854 Ex $492 Gd $312
Caliber: .22 LR. Six round detachable box magazine. 27-inch bbl. Weight: About 6.75 lbs. Marble open rear sight, Partridge-type front. Checkered sporter stock. Made from 1941 to 1956.

MODEL 513TR MATCHMASTER BOLT-ACTION
TARGET RIFLE. . . . . NiB $450 Ex $299 Gd $211
Caliber: .22 LR. Six round detachable box magazine. 27-inch bbl. Weight: About 9 lbs. Sights: Redfield No. 75 rear; globe front. Target stock. Sling and swivels. Made from 1941 to 1969.

GRADING: **NiB** = New in Box   **Ex** = Excellent or NRA 95%   **Gd** = Good or NRA 68%

Remington Model 521TL

Remington Model 541-S

Remington Model 581-S

Remington Model 581

MODEL 521TL JUNIOR TARGET BOLT-ACTION
REPEATER . . . . NiB $398 Ex $269 Gd $191
Takedown. Caliber: .22 LR. Six round detachable box magazine. 25-inch bbl. Weight: About 7 lbs. Sights: Lyman No. 57RS rear; dovetailed blade front. Target stock. Sling and swivels. Made from 1947 to 1969.

MODEL 522 VIPER . . . . NiB $129 Ex $128 Gd $102
Calibers: .22 LR. 10-round magazine. 20-inch bbl. 40 inches overall. Weight: 4.63 lbs. Checkered black PET resin stock with beavertail forend. Dupont high-tech synthetic lightweight receiver. Matte black finish on all exposed metal. Made from 1993 to date.

MODEL 541-S CUSTOM
SPORTER . . . . NiB $750 Ex $599 Gd $418
Bolt-action repeater. Scroll engraving on receiver and trigger guard. Caliber: .22 Short, Long, LR. Five round clip magazine. 24-inch bbl. Weight: 5.5 lbs. Supplied w/o sights. Checkered walnut stock w/ rosewood-finished forend tip, pistol-grip cap and buttplate. Made from 1972 to 1984.

MODEL 541-T BOLT-ACTION RIFLE
Caliber: .22 RF. Clip-fed, Five round. 24-inch bbl. Weight: 5.88 lbs. Checkered walnut stock. Made from 1986 to date; heavy bbl. model intro. 1993.
Model 541-T Standard . . . . NiB $500 Ex $311 Gd $193
Model 541-T-HB heavy bbl. . . . NiB $466 Ex $337 Gd $249

MODEL 581 CLIP REPEATER . NiB $ 259 Ex $144 Gd $120
Same general specifications as Model 580 except has 5-round clip magazine. Made from 1967 to 1984.
Model 581 (left-hand, made 1969-84)NiB $257 Ex $142 Gd $118

MODEL 581-S BOLT-ACTION
RIFLE . . . . NiB $190 Ex $157 Gd $133
Caliber: .22 RF. Clip-fed, 5-round. 24-inch bbl. Weight: 4.75 lbs. Plain walnut-colored stock. Made from 1987 to 1992.

MODEL 582 TUBULAR
REPEATER . . . . NiB $256 Ex $179 Gd $127
Same general specifications as Model 580 except has tubular magazine holding 20 Short,15 Long,14 LR. Weight: About 5 lbs. Made from 1967 to 1984.

MODEL 591 BOLT-ACTION CLIP
REPEATER . . . . NiB $319 Ex $210 Gd $171
Caliber: 5mm Rimfire Magnum. Four round clip magazine. 24-inch bbl. Weight: 5 lbs. Sights: Bead front; U-notch rear. Monte Carlo stock. Made from 1970 to 1973.

MODEL 592 TUBULAR
REPEATER . . . . NiB $278 Ex $175 Gd $128
Same as Model 591 except has tubular magazine holding 10 rounds, weight: 5.5 lbs. Made from 1970 to 1973.

MODEL 600 BOLT-ACTION CARBINE
Calibers: .222 Rem., .223 Rem., .243 Win., 6mm Rem., .308 Win., 35 Rem., 5-round magazine (6-round in .222 Rem.) 18.5-inch bbl. with ventilated rib. Weight: 6 lbs. Sights: Open rear; blade ramp front. Monte Carlo stock w/pistol-grip. Made from 1964 to 1967.
.222 Rem. . . . . NiB $550 Ex $445 Gd $333
.223 Rem . . . . NiB $1109 Ex $923 Gd $715
.35 Rem. . . . . NiB $641 Ex $540 Gd $499
Standard calibers . . . . NiB $510 Ex $390 Gd $338

MODEL 600 MAGNUM . . . . . NiB $1044 Ex $800 Gd $645
Same as Model 600 except calibers 6.5mm Mag. and .350 Rem. Mag., 4-round magazine, special Magnum-type bbl. with bracket for scope back-up, laminated walnut and beech stock w/recoil pad. QD swivels and sling; weight: About 6.5 lbs. Made 1965 to 1967.

MODEL 600 MONTANA
TERRITORIAL CENTENNIAL . . . NiB $990 Ex $755 Gd $559
Same as Model 600 except has commemorative medallion embedded in buttstock. Made in 1964. Value is for rifle in new, unfired condition.

MODEL 660 STP
Calibers: .222 Rem., 6mm Rem., .243 Win., .308 Win., 5-round magazine. (6-round in .222 Rem.) 20-inch bbl. Weight: 6.5 lbs. Sights: Open rear; bead front on ramp. Monte Carlo stock, checkered, black pistol-grip cap and forend tip. Made from 1968 to 1971.
.222 Rem . . . . NiB $465 Ex $355 Gd $290
Other calibers. . . . . NiB $560 Ex $443 Gd $355

MODEL 660 MAGNUM . . . . . . NiB $970 Ex $766 Gd $641
Same as Model 660 except calibers 6.5mm Rem. Mag. and .350 Rem. Mag., 4-round magazine, laminated walnut-and-beech stock with recoil pad. QD swivels and sling. Made from 1968 to 1971.

Remington Model 591

Remington Model 592

Remington Model 600

Remington Model 600
Montana Territorial
Centennial

Remington Model 660

Remington Model 700 ADL

MODEL 700 ADL CENTERFIRE
RIFLE. . . . . **NiB $535 Ex $369 Gd $266**
Calibers: .22-250, .222 Rem., .25-06, 6mm Rem., .243 Win., .270 Win., .30-06, .308 Win., 7mm Rem. Mag. Magazine capacity: 6-round in .222 Rem.; 4-round in 7mm Rem. Mag. Five round in other calibers. Bbl. lengths: 24-inch in .22-250, .222 Rem., .25-06, 7mm Rem. Mag.; 22-inch in other calibers. Weight: 7 lbs. standard; 7.5 lbs. in 7mm Rem. Mag. Sights: Ramp front; sliding ramp open rear. Monte Carlo stock w/cheekpiece, skip checkering, recoil pad on Magnum. Laminated stock also avail. Made from 1962 to 2005.

MODEL 700 APR BOLT-ACTION
RIFLE. . . . . **NiB $2900 Ex $2290 Gd $1998**
Acronym for African Plains Rifle. Calibers: 7mm Rem. Mag., 7mm STW, 300 Win. Mag., 300 Wby. Mag., 300 Rem. Ultra Mag., 338 Win. Mag., 375 H&H. Three round magazine. 26-inch bbl. on a magnum action. 46.5 inches overall. Weight: 7.75 lbs. Matte blue finish. Checkered classic-style laminated wood stock w/black magnum recoil pad. Made 1994 to 2004.

MODEL 700 AS BOLT-ACTION RIFLE
Similar to the Model 700 BDL except with non-reflective matte black metal finish, including the bolt body. Weight: 6.5 lbs. Straight comb synthetic stock made of Arylon, a fiberglass-reinforced thermoplastic resin with non-reflective matte finish. Made from 1988 to 1992.
Standard caliber . . . . **NiB $555 Ex $440 Gd $339**
Magnum caliber . . . . **NiB $579 Ex $466 Gd $340**

MODEL 700 AWR BOLT-ACTION
RIFLE. . . . . **NiB $1566 Ex $1264 Gd $1090**
Acronym for Alaskan Wilderness Rifle, similar to Model 700 APR except w/24-inch stainless bbl. and black chromed action. Matte gray or black Kevlar stock w/straight comb and raised cheekpiece fitted w/black magnum recoil pad. Made from 1994 to 2004.

MODEL 700 BDL CENTERFIRE RIFLE
Same as Model 700 ADL except has hinged floorplate hooded ramp front sight, stock w/black forend tip and pistol-grip cap, cut checkering, QD swivels and sling. Additional calibers: .17 Rem., .223 Rem., .264 Win. Mag., 7mm-08, .280, .300 Sav., .300 Win. Mag., 8mm Rem. Mag., .338 Win. Mag., .35 Whelen. All have 24-inch bbls. Magnums have 4-round magazine, recoil pad, weighs 7.5 lbs; .17 Rem. has 6-round magazine, weighs 7 lbs. Made 1962 to date.
Standard calibers. . . . . **NiB $810 Ex $466 Gd $333**
Magnum calibers and .17
Rem. . . . . **NiB $855 Ex $555 Gd $380**
Left-hand, .270 Win. A
nd .30-06 . . . . **NiB $855 Ex $469 Gd $343**

GRADING: **NiB** = New in Box   **Ex** = Excellent or NRA 95%   **Gd** = Good or NRA 68%

**Remington Model 700
ADL w/Laminated Stock**

**Remington
Model 700 ADL Left Hand**

Remington Model 700 APR

Left hand, 7mm Rem. Mag. & .222
  Rem. . . . . .NiB $788 Ex $559 Gd $495

MODEL 700 BDL EUROPEAN RIFLE
Same general specifications as Model 700 BDL, except has
oil-finished walnut stock. Calibers: .243, .270, 7mm-08, 7mm
Mag., .280 Rem., .30-06. Made from 1993 to 1995.
Standard calibers . . . . .NiB $495 Ex $422 Gd $370
Magnum calibers . . . . .NiB $579 Ex $466 Gd $357

MODEL 700 BDL SS BOLT-ACTION RIFLE
Same as Model 700 BDL except w/24-inch stainless bbl.,
receiver and bolt plus black synthetic stock. Calibers: .223
Rem., .243 Win., 6mm Rem., .25-06 Rem., .270 Win. .280
Rem., 7mm-08, 7mm Rem. Mag., 7mm Wby. Mag., .30-06,
.300 Win., .308 Win., .338 Win. Mag. .375 H&H. Made from
1992 to 2004.
Standard calibers . . . . .NiB $625 Ex $509 Gd $347
Magnum calibers, add. $100
DM (detachable magazine), add. $50
DM-B (w/muzzle brake), add $126

MODEL 700 BDL VARMINT
SPECIAL. . . . . NiB $695 Ex $449 Gd $315
Same as Model 700 BDL except has 24-inch heavy bbl., no
sights, weighs 9 lbs. (8.75 lbs. in 308 Win.). Calibers: .22-250,
.222 Rem., .223 Rem., .25-06, 6mm Rem., .243 Win., .308
Win. Made 1967 to 1994.

MODEL 700 CS BOLT-ACTION RIFLE
Similar to Model 700 BDL except with nonreflective matte
black metal finish, including the bolt body. Straight comb syn-
thetic stock camouflaged in Mossy Oak Bottomland pattern.
Made 1992–94.
Standard calibers . . . . .NiB $590 Ex $495 Gd $369
Magnum calibers . . . . .NiB $641 Ex $500 Gd $370

MODEL 700 CLASSIC
Same general specifications as Model 700 BDL except has
"Classic" stock of high-quality walnut with full-pattern cut-check-

ering, special satin wood finish; Schnabel forend. Brown rubber
buttpad. Hinged floorplate. No sights. Weight: 7 lbs. Also cham-
bered for "Classic" cartridges such as .257 Roberts and .250-3000.
Introduced in 1981.
Standard calibers . . . . .NiB $916 Ex $588 Gd $369
Magnum calibers . . . . .NiB $977 Ex $588 Gd $369

MODEL 700 CUSTOM BOLT-ACTION RIFLE
Same general specifications as Model 700 BDL except custom-
built; available in choice of grades, each with higher qual-
ity wood, different checkering patterns, engraving, high-gloss
blued finish. Introduced in 1965.
C Grade I. . . . . NiB $1965 Ex $1110 Gd $800
C Grade II. . . . . .NiB $2490 Ex $1854 Gd $1354
C Grade III . . . . .NiB $2988 Ex $2360 Gd $1635
C Grade IV . . . . .NiB $4955 Ex $3290 Gd $2990
D Peerless Grade . . . . .NiB $2855 Ex $1590 Gd $1122
F Premier Grade . . . . .NiB $3634 Ex $2989 Gd $2190

MODEL 700 FS BOLT-ACTION RIFLE
Similar to Model 700 ADL except with straight comb fiberglass
stock reinforced with DuPont Kevlar, finished in gray or gray camo
with Old English-style recoil pad. Made from 1987 to 1989.
Standard calibers . . . . .NiB $600 Ex $479 Gd $259
Magnum calibers . . . . .NiB $720 Ex $590 Gd $433

MODEL 700 KS CUSTOM MOUNTAIN RIFLE
Similar to standard Model 700 MTN Rifle, except with custom
Kevlar reinforced resin synthetic stock with standard or wood-
grain finish. Calibers: .270 Win., .280 Rem., 7mm Rem Mag.,
.30-06, .300 Win. Mag., .300 Wby. Mag., 8mm Rem. Mag.,
.338 Win. Mag., .35 Whelen, .375 H&H. Four round maga-
zine. 24-inch bbl. Weight: 6.75 lbs. Made from 1986 to 2008.
Standard KS stock (disc. 1993)NiB $1899 Ex $1380 Gd $1079
Wood-grain KS stock. . . . . . . .NiB $1139 Ex $899 Gd $655
Stainless synthetic (1995-97) . . NiB $2090 Ex $1421 Gd $1008
Left-hand model, add $100

MODEL 700 LS BOLT-ACTION RIFLE
Similar to Model 700 ADL except with checkered Monte Carlo-
style laminated wood stock with alternating grain and wood

Remington Model 700 BDL

Remington Model 700 BDL Magnum

Remington Model 700 Classic

Remington Model 700 Custom Grade I

Remington Model 700 Custom Grade II

Remington Model 700 Custom Grade III

Remington Model 700 Custom Grade IV

Remington Model 700 FS

color, impregnated with phenolic resin and finished with a low satin luster. Made from 1988 to 1993.

Standard calibers . . . . NiB $690 Ex $550 Gd $395
Magnum calibers . . . . NiB $779 Ex $598 Gd $443

MODEL 700 LSS BOLT-ACTION RIFLE

Similar to Model 700 BDL except with stainless steel barrel and action. Checkered Monte Carlo-style laminated wood stock with alternating grain and gray tinted color impregnated with phenolic resin and finished with a low satin luster. Made from 1996 to 2004.

Standard calibers . . . . NiB $510 Ex $440 Gd $290
Magnum calibers . . . . NiB $588 Ex $479 Gd $466

MODEL 700 MOUNTAIN RIFLE

Lightweight version of Model 700. Calibers: .243 Win., .25-06, .257 Roberts, .270 Win., 7x57, 7mm-08 Rem., .280 Rem., .30-06 and .308 Win. Four round magazine. 22-inch bbl. Weight: 6.75 lbs. Satin blue or stainless finish. Checkered walnut stock and redesigned pistol grip, straight comb, contoured cheekpiece, Old English-style recoil pad and satin oil finish

Remington Model 700 KS
Custom Mountain Rifle

Remington Model 700
Mountain Rifle Deluxe

Remington Model 700 RS

Remington Model 700 Sendero

Remington Model 700 Safari

Remington Model 721A Deluxe

Remington Model 722A

or black synthetic stock with pressed checkering and blind magazine. Made from 1986 to 1994.

DM model (intro. 1995)	NiB $755	Ex $488	Gd $367
SS model (stainless synthetic, disc. 1993)	NiB $500	Ex $443	Gd $309
DM Model (New 1995)	NiB $685	Ex $443	Gd $339
SS Model stainless synthetic (disc. 1993)	NiB $450	Ex $390	Gd $287

MODEL 700 RS BOLT-ACTION RIFLE
Similar to the Model 700 BDL except with straight comb DuPont Rynite stock finished in gray or gray camo with Old English style recoil pad. Made from 1987 to 1990.

Standard calibers	NiB $600	Ex $433	Gd $380
Magnum calibers	NiB $677	Ex $535	Gd $390
.280 Rem. (Limited prod.)	NiB $739	Ex $596	Gd $415

MODEL 700 SAFARI GRADE
Big game heavy magnum version of the Model 700 BDL. 8mm Rem. Mag., .375 H&H Mag., .416 Rem. Mag. and .458 Win. Mag. 24-inch heavy bbl. Weight: 9 lbs. Blued or stainless finish. Checkered walnut stock in synthetic/Kevlar stock with standard matte or wood-grain finish with old English style recoil pad. Made from 1962 to 2000.

Safari Classic/Monte Carlo	NiB $1498	Ex $1044	Gd $610
Safari KS (Kevlar stock, intro. 1989)	NiB $1335	Ex $1155	Gd $927
Safari KS (wood-grain stock, intro. 1992)	NiB $1296	Ex $1133	Gd $909

Remington Nylon 11

Remington Nylon 12

Safari KS SS (stainless,
   intro. 1993) . . . . NiB $1577 Ex $1326 Gd $1055
Safari model, left-hand, add $126

MODEL 700 SENDERO BOLT-ACTION RIFLE
Same as Model 700 VS except chambered in long action and
magnum .25-06 Rem., .270 Win., .280 Rem., 7mm Rem. Mag.,
.300 Win. Made from 1994 to 2002.
Standard calibers . . . . NiB $707 Ex $589 Gd $390
Magnum calibers, add. $50
SF model (stainless, fluted bbl.), add $150

MODEL 700 VLS (VARMINT LAMINATED STOCK)
BOLT-ACTION RIFLE. . . . . NiB $899 Ex $555 Gd $390
Same as Model 700 BDL Varmint Special except with 26-inch
polished blue barrel. Laminated wood stock with alternating
grain and wood color impregnated with phenolic resin and
finished with a satin luster. Calibers: .222 Rem., .223 Rem., .22-
250 Rem., .243 Win., 7mm-08 Rem., .308 Win. Weight: 9.4 lbs.
Made from 1995 to date.

MODEL 700 VS BOLT-ACTION RIFLE
Same as Model 700 BDL Varmint Special except w/26-inch
matte blue or fluted stainless barrel. Textured black or gray synthetic stock reinforced with Kevlar, fiberglass and graphite with
full length aluminum bedding block. Calibers: .22-250 Rem.,
.220 Swift, .223 Rem., .308 Win. Made from 1992 to date.
Model 700 VS . . . . NiB $888 Ex $559 Gd $444
Model SF (fluted bbl.) . . . . NiB $790 Ex $677 Gd $535
Model 700 VS SF/SF-P
   (fluted & ported bbl.) . . . . . NiB $1043 Ex $866 Gd $657

MODEL 720A BOLT-ACTION
HIGH . . . . NiB $1379 Ex $1266 Gd $1108
Modified M/1917 Enfield action. .257 Roberts, .270 Win., .30-
06. Five round box magazine. 22-inch bbl. Weight: About 8
lbs. Sights: Open rear; bead front, on ramp. Pistol-grip stock,
checkered. Model 720R has 20-inch bbl.; Model 720S has
24-inch bbl. Made in 1941.

MODEL 721 STANDARD GRADE BOLT-ACTION
HIGH-POWER RIFLE . . . . NiB $495 Ex $433 Gd $356
Calibers: .270 Win., .30-06. Four round box magazine. 24-inch
bbl. Weight: About 7.25 lbs. Sights: Open rear; bead front, on
ramp. Plain sporting stock. Made from 1948 to 1962.

MODEL 721A MAGNUM STANDARD
GRADE . . . . NiB $655 Ex $499 Gd $439
Caliber: .264 Win. Mag. or .300 H&H Mag. Same as standard model
except has 26-inch bbl. Three round magazine and recoil pad. Weight:
8.25 lbs.

MODEL 721ADL/BDL DELUXE
Same as Model 721A Standard or Magnum except has deluxe
checkered stock and/or select wood.

Deluxe Grade . . . . NiB $744 Ex $548 Gd $433
.300 Win. Mag. Deluxe. . . . . . . NiB $790 Ex $775 Gd $600
Deluxe Special Grade . . . . NiB $844 Ex $645 Gd $500
.300 Mag. Deluxe . . . . NiB $833 Ex $689 Gd $567

MODEL 722A STANDARD GRADE SPORTER
Same as Model 721A bolt-action except shorter action. .222
Rem. mag., .243 Win., .257 Roberts, .308 Win., .300 Savage.
Four or 5-round magazine. Weight: 7-8 lbs. .222 Rem. introduced 1950; .244 Rem. introduced 1955. Made from 1948 to
1962.
.222 Rem. . . . . NiB $517 Ex $466 Gd $360
.244 Rem. . . . . NiB $500 Ex $380 Gd $278
.222 Rem. Mag. & .243 Win. . . NiB $465 Ex $390 Gd $288
Other calibers. . . . . NiB $466 Ex $398 Gd $270

MODEL 722ADL DELUXE GRADE
Same as Model 722A except has deluxe checkered stock.
Standard calibers . . . . NiB $590 Ex $513 Gd $398
.222 Rem. Deluxe Grade . . . . . NiB $690 Ex $579 Gd $455
.244 Rem. Deluxe Grade . . . . . NiB $835 Ex $733 Gd $495

MODEL 722BDL DELUXE SPECIAL GRADE
Same as Model 722ADL except select wood.
Standard calibers . . . . NiB $866 Ex $590 Gd $498
.222 Rem. Deluxe Special Grade NiB $866 Ex $590 Gd $498
.244 Rem. Deluxe Special Grade NiB $799 Ex $733 Gd $475

MODEL 725 KODIAK MAGNUM
RIFLE. . . . . NiB $4200 Ex $3543 Gd $2300
Similar to Model 725ADL. Calibers: .375 H&H Mag., .458
Win. Mag. Three round magazine. 26-inch bbl. with recoil
reducer built into muzzle. Weight: About 9 lbs. Deluxe, reinforced Monte Carlo stock with recoil pad, black forend tip
swivels, sling. Fewer than 100 made in 1961.

MODEL 725ADL BOLT-ACTION REPEATING RIFLE
Calibers: .222, .243, .244, .270, .280, .30-06. Four round box
mag. (5-round in 222). 22-inch bbl. (24-inch in .222). Weight:
About 7 lbs. Sights: Open rear, hooded ramp front. Monte
Carlo comb stock w/pistol-grip, checkered, swivels. Made from
1958 to 1961.
.222 Rem., .243 Win., .244 Rem NiB $855 Ex $690 Gd $505
.270 Win. . . . . NiB $767 Ex $659 Gd $467
.280 Win. . . . . NiB $977 Ex $800 Gd $509
.30-06 . . . . NiB $707 Ex $580 Gd $439

MODEL 788 CENTERFIRE BOLT-ACTION
Calibers: .222 Rem., .22-250, .223 Rem., 6mm Rem., .243
Win., 7mm-08 Rem., .308 Win., .30-30, .44 Rem. Mag. Three
round clip magazine (4-round in .222 and .223 Rem.). 24-inch
bbl. in .22s, 22-inch in other calibers. Weight: 7.5 lbs. with
24-inch bbl.; 7.25 lbs. with 22-inch bbl. Sights: Blade front
on ramp; U-notch rear. Plain Monte Carlo stock. Made 1967
to 1984.

RIFLES

Remington Model 121A

Remington Model 141A
Gamemaster

Remington Model 572A

Remington Model 572 BDL

.22-250, .223 Rem., 6mm Rem.,
.243 Win., .308 Win. . . . . NiB $522 Ex $339 Gd $243
.30-30 Win.. . . . . NiB $555 Ex $434 Gd $319
7mm-08 Rem.. . . . . NiB $733 Ex $423 Gd $333
.44 Mag.. . . . . NiB $650 Ex $449 Gd $339

NYLON 11 BOLT-ACTION
REPEATER . . . . NiB $495 Ex $322 Gd $209
Clip type. Caliber: .22 Short, Long, LR. Six- or 10-round clip mag. 19.63-inch bbl. Weight: 4.5 lbs. Sights: Open rear; blade front. Nylon stock. Made from 1962 to 1966.

NYLON 12 BOLT-ACTION
REPEATER . . . . NiB $545 Ex $433 Gd $245
Same as Nylon 11 except has tubular magazine holding 22 Short, 17 Long, 15 LR. Made from 1962 to 1966.

- SLIDE- AND LEVER-ACTION RIFLES -

MODEL SIX (6) SLIDE-ACTION
REPEATER . . . . NiB $698 Ex $390 Gd $288
Hammerless. Calibers: 6mm Rem., .243 Win., .270 Win. 7mm Express Rem., .30-06, .308 Win. 22-inch bbl. Weight: 7.5 lbs. Checkered Monte Carlo stock and forearm. Made 1981 to 1988.

MODEL SIX (6) SLIDE-ACTION REPEATER,
PEERLESS GRADE . . . . NiB $1864 Ex $1607 Gd $989
Same as Model Six Standard except has engraved receiver. Three versions made from 1981 to 1988.

MODEL SIX (6) SLIDE-ACTION REPEATER, PREMIUM GRADES
Same as Model Six Standard except has engraved receiver with gold inlay. Made from 1981 to 1988.
Peerless D Grade . . . . NiB $1977 Ex $1670 Gd $1120
Premier F Grade . . . . NiB $4509 Ex $3533 Gd $2410
Premier Gold F Grade. . . . . NiB $6212 Ex $4944 Gd $3490

MODEL 12A, 12B, 12C, 12CS SLIDE-ACTION REPEATERS
Standard Grade. Hammerless. Takedown. Caliber: .22 Short, Long or LR. Tubular magazine holds 15 Short, 12 Long or 10 LR cartridges. 22- or 24-inch round or octagonal bbl. Open rear sight, bead front. Plain, half-pistol-grip stock and grooved slide handle of walnut. Made from 1909 to 1936.
Model 12A . . . . NiB $600 Ex $399 Gd $278
Model 12B (22 Short only
  w/octagon bbl.) . . . . NiB $733 Ex $549 Gd $370
Model 12C
  (w/24-inch octagon bbl.) . . . NiB $623 Ex $544 Gd $355
Model 12CS (22 WRF w/24-inch
  octagon bbl.) . . . . NiB $570 Ex $445 Gd $315

MODEL 14A HIGH POWER SLIDE-ACTION
REPEATING RIFLE. . . . . NiB $1077 Ex $798 Gd $643
Standard grade. Hammerless. Takedown. Calibers: .25, .30, .32 and .35 Rem. Five round tubular magazine. 22-inch bbl. Weight: About 6.75 lbs. Sights: Open rear; bead front. Plain half-pistol-grip stock and grooved slide handle of walnut. Made from 1912 to 1935.

MODEL 14R CARBINE . . . . . NiB $1286 Ex $1044 Gd $590
Same as Model 14R except has 18.5-inch bbl., straight-grip stock, weight: About 6 lbs.

MODEL 14 1/2 CARBINE . . . NiB $1286 Ex $1044 Gd $590
Same as Model 14A Rifle previously listed, except has 9-round magazine, 18.5-inch bbl.

Remington Model 760
Bicentennial Commemorative

Remington Model 760
Gamemaster

Remington Model 7600 Carbine

MODEL 14 1/2 RIFLE......NiB $1688 Ex $1044 Gd $622
Similar to Model 14A except calibers: .38-40 and .44-40, 11-round full magazine, 22.5-inch bbl. Made from 1912 to early 1920's.

**MODEL 25A SLIDE-ACTION
REPEATER ....NiB $1094 Ex $744 Gd $500**
Standard Grade. Hammerless. Takedown. Calibers: .25-20, .32-20. 10-round tubular magazine. 24-inch bbl. Weight: About 5.5 lbs. Sights: Open rear; bead front. Plain, pistol-grip stock, grooved slide handle. Made from 1923 to 1936.

MODEL 25R CARBINE ......NiB $1190 Ex $745 Gd $533
Same as Model 25A except has 18-inch bbl. Six round magazine, straight-grip stock, weight: About 4.5 lbs.

**MODEL 121A FIELDMASTER SLIDE-ACTION
REPEATER ....NiB $677 Ex $500 Gd $355**
Standard Grade. Hammerless. Takedown. Caliber: .22 Short, Long, LR. Tubular magazine holds 20 Short, 15 Long or 14 LR cartridges. 24-inch round bbl. Weight: 6 lbs. Plain, pistol-grip stock and grooved semi-beavertail slide handle. Made from 1936 to 1954.

MODEL 121S ....NiB $599 Ex $500 Gd $443
Same as Model 121A except chambered for .22 Remington Special (.22 W.R.F.). Magazine holds 12 rounds. Disc.

MODEL 121SB ....NiB $707 Ex $553 Gd $439
Same as Model 121A except smoothbore. Disc.

**MODEL 141A GAMEMASTER SLIDE-ACTION
REPEATER ....NiB $543 Ex $359 Gd $269**
Standard Grade. Hammerless. Takedown. Calibers: .30, .32 and .35 Rem. Five round tubular magazine. 24-inch bbl. Weight: About 7.75 lbs. Sights: Open rear; bead front, on ramp. Plain, pistol-grip stock, semibeavertail forend (slide-handle). Made from 1936 to 1950.

**MODEL 572A FIELDMASTER SLIDE-ACTION
REPEATER ....NiB $290 Ex $179 Gd $130**
Hammerless. Caliber: .22 Short, Long, LR. Tubular magazine holds 20 Short, 17 Long, 15 LR. 23-inch bbl. Weight: About 5.5 lbs. Sights: Open rear; ramp front. Pistol-grip stock, grooved forearm. Made 1955 to 1988.

MODEL 572BDL DELUXE.....NiB $533 Ex $444 Gd $149
Same as Model 572A except has blade ramp front sight, sliding ramp rear; checkered stock and forearm. Made from 1966 to date.

MODEL 572SB SMOOTH BORE.. NiB $549 Ex $400 Gd $300
Same as Model 572A except smoothbore for .22 LR shot cartridges. Made from 1961 to date.

**MODEL 760 BICENTENNIAL
COMMEMORATIVE ....NiB $556 Ex $398 Gd $265**
Same as Model 760 except has commemorative inscription on receiver. Made in 1976.

MODEL 760 CARBINE ....NiB $480 Ex $390 Gd $245
Same as Model 760 Rifle except made in calibers .270 Win., .280 Rem., .30-06 and .308 Win. only, has 18.5-inch bbl., weight: 7.25 lbs. Made 1961 to 1980.

**MODEL 760 GAMEMASTER STANDARD GRADE
SLIDE-ACTION REPEATING RIFLE**
Hammerless. Calibers: .223 Rem., 6mm Rem., .243 Win., .257 Roberts, .270 Win. .280 Rem., .30-06, .300 Sav., .308 Win., .35 Rem. 22-inch bbl. Weight: About 7.5 lbs. Sights: Open rear; bead front, on ramp. Plain pistol-grip stock, grooved slide handle on early models; current production has checkered stock and slide handle. Made from 1952 to 1980.
.222 Rem................NiB $1195 Ex $1021 Gd $744
.223 Rem................NiB $1409 Ex $1135 Gd $739
.257 Roberts..............NiB $933 Ex $779 Gd $489
Other calibers..............NiB $460 Ex $407 Gd $375

MODEL 760ADL DELUXE GRADE... NiB $500 Ex $398 Gd $347
Same as Model 760 except has deluxe checkered stock, standard or high comb, grip cap, sling swivels. Made from 1953 to 1963.

MODEL 760BDL CUSTOM DELUXE .. NiB $655 Ex $449 Gd $325
Same as Model 760 Rifle except made in calibers .270, .30-06 and .308 only, has Monte Carlo cheekpiece stock forearm with black tip, basket-weave checkering. Available also in left-hand model. Made from 1953 to 1980.

MODEL 760D PEERLESS GRADE.... NiB $2589 Ex $1176 Gd $925
Same as Model 760 except scroll engraved, fancy wood. Made from 1953 to 1980.

MODEL 760F PREMIER GRADE
Same as Model 760 except extensively engraved with game scenes and scroll, finest grade wood. Also available with receiver inlaid with gold; adds 50 percent to value. Made from 1953 to 1980.

RIFLES

Remington Model 7600 Rifle

Remington Nylon 76 Lever-Action

Remington Sportsman 76

Premier F Grade . . . . NiB $5200 Ex $3288 Gd $2579
Premier Gold F Grade . . . . . NiB $7179 Ex $6088 Gd $4439

MODEL 7600 SLIDE-ACTION
CARBINE. . . . . NiB $698 Ex $449 Gd $370
Same general specifications as Model 7600 Rifle except has
18.5-inch bbl. and weighs 7.25 lbs. Made from 1987 to date.

MODEL 7600 SLIDE-ACTION
RIFLE . . . . NiB $707 Ex $451 Gd $370
Similar to Model Six except has lower grade finishes. Made
from 1981 to date.

MODEL 7600 SPECIAL
PURPOSE . . . . NiB $470 Ex $444 Gd $289
Same general specification as the Model 7600, except chambered only in .270 or .30-06. Special Purpose matte black
finish on all exposed metal. American walnut stock with SP
non-glare finish.

NYLON 76 LEVER-ACTION
REPEATER . . . . NiB $899 Ex $677 Gd $468
Short-throw lever action. Caliber: .22 LR. 14-round buttstock
tubular magazine. Weight: 4 lbs. Black (add $707) or brown
nylon stock and forend. Made 1962-64. Remington's only
lever-action rifle.

SPORTSMAN 76 SLIDE-ACTION
RIFLE. . . . . NiB $375 Ex $300 Gd $200
Caliber: .30-06, 4-round magazine. 22-inch bbl. Weight:
7.5 lbs. Open rear sight; front blade mounted on ramp.
Uncheckered hardwood stock and forend. Made from 1985
to 1987.

- SEMIAUTOMATIC RIFLES -

MODEL FOUR (4) AUTOLOADING RIFLE
Hammerless. Calibers: 6mm Rem., .243 Win., .270 Win. 7mm
Express Rem., .30-06, .308 Win. 22-inch bbl. Weight: 7.5 lbs.
Sights: Open rear; bead front, on ramp. Monte Carlo checkered
stock and forearm. Made from 1981 to 1988.

Standard model . . . . NiB $722 Ex $465 Gd $369
Peerless Grade (engraved
    receiver) . . . . NiB $2219 Ex $1266 Gd $909
Premier Grade (engraved
    receiver) . . . . NiB $4155 Ex $3265 Gd $2200
Premier Grade, (engraved
    receiver, gold inlay) . . . . NiB $6544 Ex $5233 Gd $3588

MODEL FOUR DIAMOND ANNIVERSARY
LTD. EDITION. . . . . NiB $1377 EX $1088 Gd $976
Same as Model Four Standard except has engraved receiver
w/inscription, checkered high-grade walnut stock and forend.
Only 1,500 produced. Made in 1981 only. (Value for new
condition.)

MODEL 8A AUTOLOADING
RIFLE. . . . . NiB $766 Ex $645 Gd $473
Standard Grade. Takedown. Calibers: .25, .30, .32 and .35 Rem.
Five-round, clip-loaded magazine. 22-inch bbl. Weight: 7.75 lbs.
Sights: Adj. and dovetailed open rear; dovetailed bead front. Half-
moon metal buttplate on plain straight-grip walnut stock; plain
walnut forearm with thin curved end. Made from 1906 to 1936.

MODEL 16 AUTOLOADING
RIFLE. . . . . NiB $755 Ex $523 Gd $390
Takedown. Closely resembles the Winchester Model 03 semi-
automatic rifle. Calibers: .22 Short, .22 LR, 22 Rem. Auto.
15-round tubular magazine in buttstock. 22-inch bbl. Weight:
5.75 lbs. Sights: Open rear; dovetailed bead front. Plain
straight-grip stock and forearm. Made from 1914 to 1928.
Note: In 1918 this model was discontinued in all calibers
except .22 Rem. Auto; specifications are for that model.

MODEL 24A AUTOLOADING
RIFLE . . . . NiB $498 Ex $343 Gd $244
Standard Grade. Takedown. Calibers: .22 Short only, .22 LR.
only. Tubular magazine in buttstock, holds 15 Short or 10 LR.
21-inch bbl. Weight: About 5 lbs. Sights: Dovetailed adj. open
rear; dovetailed bead front. Plain walnut straight-grip buttstock;
plain walnut forearm. Made 1922 to 1935.

MODEL 81A WOODSMASTER
AUTOLOADER . . . . NiB $590 Ex $498 Gd $300
Standard Grade. Takedown. Calibers: .30, .32 and .35 Rem.,
.300 Sav. Five round box magazine (not detachable). 22-inch

Remington Model 7400

bbl. Weight: 8.25 lbs. Sights: Open rear; bead front. Plain walnut pistol-grip stock, forearm. Made from 1936 to 1950.

MODEL 141A SPEEDMASTER
AUTOLOADER . . . . NiB $500 Ex $326 Gd $249
Standard Grade. Takedown. Calibers: .22 Short only, .22 LR. only. Tubular magazine in buttstock, holds 15 Short or 10 LR. 24-inch bbl. Weight: About 6 lbs. Sights: Open rear, bead front. Plain walnut stock and forearm. Made from 1935 to 1951.

MODEL 550A AUTOLOADER. . NiB $370 Ex $222 Gd $129
Has "Power Piston" or floating chamber, which permits interchangeable use of 22 Short, Long or LR cartridges. Tubular magazine holds 22 Short, 17 Long, 15 LR. 24-inch bbl. Weight: About 6.25 lbs. Sights: Open rear; bead front. Plain, one-piece pistol-grip stock. Made from 1941 to 1971.

MODEL 550P . . . . NiB $369 Ex $221 Gd $156
Same as Model 550A except has peep rear sight, blade front, on ramp.

MODEL 550-2G . . . . NiB $388 Ex $279 Gd $200
"Gallery Special." Same as Model 550A except has 22-inch bbl., screw eye for counter chain and fired shell deflector.

MODEL 552A SPEEDMASTER
AUTOLOADER . . . . NiB $339 Ex $229 Gd $133
Caliber: .22 Short, Long, LR. Tubular magazine holds 20 Short, 17 Long, 15 LR. 25-inch bbl. Weight: About 5.5 lbs. Sights: Open rear; bead front. Pistol-grip stock, semi-beavertail forearm. Made from 1957 to 1988.

MODEL 552BDL DELUXE. . . . . NiB $533 Ex $367 Gd $290
Same as Model 552A except has checkered walnut stock and forearm. Made from 1966 to date.

MODEL 552C CARBINE . . . . . . NiB $333 Ex $209 Gd $148
Same as Model 552A except has 21-inch bbl. Made 1961 to 1977.

MODEL 552GS GALLERY
SPECIAL . . . . NiB $387 Ex $265 Gd $190
Same as Model 552A except chambered for .22 Short only. Made from 1957 to 1977.

MODEL 740A WOODSMASTER AUTOLOADER
Standard Grade. Gas-operated. Calibers: .30-06 or .308. Four round detachable box magazine. 22-inch bbl. Weight: About 7.5 lbs. Plain pistol-grip stock, semibeavertail forend with finger grooves. Sights: Open rear; ramp front. Made from 1955 to 1959.
Rifle model . . . . NiB $369 Ex $278 Gd $199
Carbine model . . . . NiB $467 Ex $443 Gd $290

MODEL 740ADL/BDL DELUXE
Same as Model 740A except has deluxe checkered stock, standard or high comb, grip cap, sling swivels. Model 740 BDL also has select wood. Made from 1955 to 1960.

Model 740 ADL Deluxe Grade . . . NiB $480 Ex $572 Gd $410
Model 740 BDL Deluxe Special
 Grade . . . . NiB $480 Ex $572 Gd $410

MODEL 742 BICENTENNIAL
COMMEMORATIVE . . . . NiB $588 Ex $380 Gd $355
Same as Model 742 Woodsmaster rifle except has commemorative inscription on receiver. Made in 1976. (Value for new condition.)

MODEL 742 CARBINE . . . . . . NiB $522 Ex $355 Gd $260
Same as Model 742 Woodsmaster Rifle except made in calibers .30-06 and .308 only, has 18.5-inch bbl., weight 6.75 lbs. Made from 1961 to 1980.

MODEL 742 WOODSMASTER AUTOMATIC
BIG GAME RIFLE . . . . NiB $707 Ex $533 Gd $290
Gas-operated semiautomatic. Calibers: 6mm Rem., .243 Win., .280 Rem., .30-06, .308 Win. Four round clip magazine. 22-inch bbl. Weight: 7.5 lbs. Sights: Open rear; bead front, on ramp. Checkered pistol-grip stock and forearm. Made from 1960 to 1980.

MODEL 742BDL CUSTOM
DELUXE . . . . NiB $523 Ex $433 Gd $300
Same as Model 742 Rifle except made in calibers .30-06 and .308 only, Monte Carlo cheekpiece stock, forearm with black tip, basket-weave checkering. Available in left-hand model. Made from 1966 to 1980.

MODEL 742D PEERLESS
GRADE. . . . . NiB $2590 Ex $2020 Gd $1100
Same as Model 742 except scroll engraved, fancy wood. Made from 1961 to 1980.

MODEL 742F PREMIER GRADE
Same as Model 742 except extensively engraved with game scenes and scroll, finest grade wood. Also available with receiver inlaid with gold; adds 50 percent to value. Made from 1961 to 1980.
Premier F Grade . . . . NiB $5233 Ex $3288 Gd $2270
Premier Gold F Grade. . . . . NiB $7350 Ex $5093 Gd $3466

MODEL 7400 AUTOLOADER
Similar to Model Four w/lower grade finishes. Made from 1981 to date.
Model 7400 Standard . . . . NiB $559 Ex $433 Gd $310
Model 7400 HG (High gloss
 finish) . . . . NiB $559 Ex $433 Gd $310

MODEL 7400 CARBINE . . . . . . NiB $559 Ex $433 Gd $310
Caliber: .30-06 only. Similar to the Model 7400 rifle except has 18.5-inch bbl. and weight 7.25 lbs. Made from 1988 to date.

MODEL 7400 SPECIAL
PURPOSE . . . . NiB $476 Ex $434 Gd $289
Same general specification as the Model 7400 except chambered only in .270 or .30-06. Special Purpose matte black finish on metal. American walnut stock with SP nonglare finish. Made 1993 to 1995.

GRADING: **NiB** = New in Box   **Ex** = Excellent or NRA 95%   **Gd** = Good or NRA 68%

Remington Model 7400 Carbine

Remington Nylon 66 Mohawk

Remington Sportsman 74

NYLON 66 APACHE BLACK . . .NiB $279 Ex $169 Gd $130
Same as Nylon 66 Mohawk Brown listed below except bbl. and receiver cover chrome-plated, black stock. Made 1962 to 1984.

NYLON 66 BICENTENNIAL
COMMEMORATIVE . . . . .NiB $597 Ex $433 Gd $259
Same as Nylon 66 Mohawk Brown listed below except has commemorative inscription on receiver. Made 1976 only.

NYLON 66MB AUTOLOADING
RIFLE. .NiB $500 Ex $325 Gd $244
Similar to the early production Nylon 66 Black Apache except with blued bbl. and receiver cover. Made from 1978 to 1987.

NYLON 66 MOHAWK BROWN
AUTOLOADER . . . . .NiB $450 Ex $278 Gd $230
Caliber: .22 LR. Tubular magazine in buttstock holds 14 rounds. 19.5-inch bbl. Weight: About 4 lbs. Sights: Open rear; blade front. Brown nylon stock and forearm. Made from 1959 to 1987.

NYLON 77 CLIP REPEATER . . .NiB $400 Ex $295 Gd $220
Same as Nylon 66 except w/5-round clip magazine. Made 1970 to 1971.

SPORTSMAN 74 AUTOLOADING
RIFLE. .NiB $379 Ex $294 Gd $200
Caliber: .30-06, 4-round magazine. 22-inch bbl. Uncheckered buttstock and forend. Open rear sight; ramped blade front sight. Made 1985 to 1988.

JOHN RIGBY & CO. — Paso Robles, California

MODEL 278 MAGAZINE SPORTING
RIFLE. . . . . .NiB $6475 Ex $5144 Gd $3576
Mauser action. Caliber: .278 High Velocity or 7x57mm; 5-round box magazine. 25-inch bbl. Weight: about 7.5 lbs. Sights: Folding leaf rear; bead front. Sporting stock w/half-pistol-grip, checkered. Specifications given are those of current model; however, in general, they apply also to prewar model.

MODEL 278 LIGHTWEIGHT MAGAZINE
RIFLE. . . . . .NiB $5110 Ex $4122 Gd $2833
Same as standard .278 rifle except has 21-inch bbl. Weight: 6.75 lbs.

MODEL 350 MAGNUM MAGAZINE
SPORTING RIFLE . . . . .NiB $4332 Ex $3633 Gd $2490
Mauser action. Caliber: .350 Magnum. Five round box magazine. 24-inch bbl. Weight: About 7.75 lbs. Sights: Folding leaf rear; bead front. Sporting stock with full pistol-grip, checkered. Currently mfd.

MODEL 416 BIG GAME MAGAZINE
SPORTING RIFLE . . . . .NiB $7688 Ex $6133 Gd $4286
Mauser action. Caliber: .416 Big Game. Four round box magazine. 24-inch bbl. Weight: 9 to 9.25 lbs. Sights: Folding leaf rear; bead front. Sporting stock with full pistol-grip, checkered. Currently mfd.

BEST QUALITY HAMMERLESS EJECTOR
DOUBLE RIFLE . . . . . NiB $73,675 Ex $62,000 Gd $38,550
Sidelocks. Calibers: .278 Magnum, .350 Magnum, .470 Nitro Express. 24- to 28-inch bbls. Weight: 7.5 to 10.5 lbs. Sights: Folding leaf rear; bead front. Checkered pistol-grip stock and forearm.

SECOND QUALITY HAMMERLESS EJECTOR
DOUBLE RIFLE. . . . . NiB $13,600 Ex $11,290 Gd $10,375
Same general specifications as Best Quality double rifle except boxlock.

THIRD QUALITY HAMMERLESS EJECTOR
DOUBLE RIFLE. . . . . . NiB $11,689 Ex $10,450 Gd $7,800
Same as Second Quality double rifle except plainer finish and not of as high quality.

ROSS RIFLE CO. — Quebec, Canada

MODEL 1910 BOLT-ACTION SPORTING RIFLE
Straight-pull bolt-action with interrupted screw-type lugs. Calibers: .280 Ross, .303 British. Four round or 5-round magazine. Bbl. lengths: 22, 24, 26 inches. Sights: Two-leaf open rear; bead front. Checkered sporting stock. Weight: About 7 lbs. Made c. 1910 to end of World War I. Note: Most firearm authorities agree that this and other Ross models with interrupted screw-type lugs are unsafe to fire.
Military model . . . . NiB $2175 Ex $1370 Gd $989
Military Match Target
** model . . . . NiB $10,300 Ex $7227 Gd $3590**

ROSSI — Sao Leopoldo, Brazil
Currently imported exclusively by BrazTech Int'l. in Miami, FL since 1998; previously by Interarms in Alexandria. VA.

Rossi Model 62 Stainless Rifle

Rossi Model 62 Stainless Carbine

Rossi Model 62 WMR Rifle

Rossi Model 62 SAC Carbine

Rossi Model 62 Gallery Rifle

To facilitate locating Ruger firearms, models are grouped into three categories: Single-shot/Lever-action Rifles (below), Semi-automatic Rifles and Bolt-action Rifles. For a complete listing, please refer to the index.

MODEL 62 GALLERY SAC CARBINE
Same as standard Gallery Model except in .22 LR only with 16.25-inch bbl.; weight 5.5 lbs. Imported 1975 to 1998.
Blued finish. . . . . .NiB $215 Ex $159 Gd $126
Nickel finish . . . . .NiB $220 Ex $163 Gd $130
Stainless . . . . .NiB $220 Ex $163 Gd $130

MODEL 62 GALLERY
MAGNUM. . . . . .NiB $235 Ex $200 Gd $135
Same as standard Gallery Model except chambered for .22 WMR, 10-shot magazine. Imported from 1975 to 1998.

62 GALLERY MODEL SLIDE-ACTION REPEATER
Similar to Winchester Model 62. Calibers: .22 LR, Long, Short or .22 WMR. Tubular magazine holds 13 LR, 16 Long, 20 Short. 23-inch bbl. 39.25 inches overall. Weight: 5.75 lbs. Sights: Open rear; bead front. Straight-grip stock, grooved slide handle. Blued, nickel or stainless finish. Imported 1970 to 1998. Values same as SAC Model.

MODEL 65/92 LEVER-ACTION CARBINE
Similar to Winchester Model 92. Caliber: .38 Special/.357 Mag., .44 Mag., .44-40, .45 LC. 8- or 10-round magazine. 16-, 20- or 24-inch round or half-octagonal bbl. Weight: 5.5 to 6 lbs. 33.5- to 41.5-inches overall. Satin blue, chrome or stainless finish. Brazilian hardwood buttstock and forearm. Made from 1978 to 1998.
.45 LC. . . . . .NiB $338 Ex $250 Gd $190
.38/.357, .44 Mag. . . . . .NiB $338 Ex $250 Gd $190
W/octagon bbl.. . . . . .NiB $400 Ex $329 Gd $278
LL Lever model . . . . .NiB $510 Ex $396 Gd $280
Engraved, add $100
Chrome, add. $50
Stainless, add $50

RUGER — Southport, CT

Manufacturing facilities in Newport, NH, and Prescott, AZ; previously manufactured in Southport, CT.

- SINGLE-SHOT RIFLES / LEVER-ACTION RIFLES -

NO.1 LIGHT SPORTER. . . . . .NiB $1010 Ex $615 Gd $445
Same as No.1 Standard except has 22-inch bbl., folding leaf rear sight on quarter-rib and ramp front sight, Henry pattern forearm. Made from 1966 to date.

NO.1 MEDIUM SPORTER. . . .NiB $1010 Ex $615 Gd $445
Same as No. 1 Light Sporter except has 26-inch bbl. 22-inch in 45-70); weight: 8 lbs (7.25 lbs. in .45-70). Calibers: 7mm Rem. Mag., .300 Win. Mag., .45-70. Made from 1966 to date.
Stainless model (matte stainless finish, grey laminated
  stock, made 2001 to 2010) . . NiB $980 Ex $480 Gd $400

NO.1 "NORTH AMERICANS" PRESENTATION
RIFLE. . . . . NiB $53,950 Ex $43,550 Gd $38,770
Same general specifications as the Ruger No. 1 Standard except highly customized with elaborate engravings, carvings, fine-line checkering and gold inlays. This was a series of 21 rifles depicting a North American big-game animal, chambered in the caliber appropriate to the game. Stock is of Northern California English walnut. Comes in trunk-style Huey case with Leupold scope and other accessories.

NO.1 RSI INTERNATIONAL . .NiB $1010 Ex $615 Gd $445
Similar to the No. 1 Light Sporter except with lightweight 20-inch bbl. and full Mannlicher-style forend, in calibers .243 Win., .270 Win., 7x57mm, .30-06. Weight: 7.25 lbs.

NO.1 SPECIAL VARMINTER . .NiB $1010 Ex $615 Gd $445
Same as No. 1 Standard except has heavy 24-inch bbl. with target scope bases, no quarter-rib. Weight: 9 lbs. Calibers: .22-250, .25-06, 7mm Rem. Mag., .300 Win. Mag. Made from 1966 to date.
Stainless model (matte stainless finish, grey laminated stock,
  made 2001 to 2009). . . . . . . .NiB $930 Ex $430 Gd $360

NO.1 STANDARD RIFLE. . . . .NiB $1010 Ex $615 Gd $445

RIFLES

Ruger No. 1 Light Sporter

Ruger No. 1 Medium Sporter

Ruger No. 1 "North Americans"

Ruger Number One "North Americans" Presentation Set

Falling-block single-shot action with Farquharson-type lever. Calibers: .22-250, .243 Win., 6mm Rem., .25-06, .270 Win., .30-06, 7mm Rem. Mag., .300 Win. Mag. 26-inch bbl. Weight: 8 lbs. No sights, has quarter-rib for scope mounting. Checkered pistol-grip buttstock and semibeavertail forearm, QD swivels, rubber buttplate. Made from 1966 to date.
Stainless model (matte stainless finish, grey laminated stock, made 2001 to 2010).. NiB $980 Ex $480 Gd $400

NO.1 TROPICAL RIFLE . . . . . . NiB $1010 Ex $615 Gd $445
Same as No. 1 Light Sporter except has heavy 24-inch bbl.; calibers are .375 H&H .404 Jeffery, .416 Rigby, and .458 Win. Mag. Weight: 8.25 to 9 lbs. Made from 1966 to date.

Stainless model (matte stainless finish, grey laminated stock, made 2001 to 2009) . . . . NiB $930 Ex $430 Gd $360

NO.3 CARBINE . . . . NiB $800 Ex $495 Gd $355
Falling-block action with American-style lever. Calibers: .22 Hornet .223 Rem., .30-40 Krag, .357 Win., .44 Mag., .45-70. 22-inch bbl. Weight: 6 lbs. Sights: Folding leaf rear; gold bead front. Carbine-style stock w/curved buttplate, forearm with bbl. band. Made 1972 to 1987.

MODEL 96
Caliber: .22 LR, .22 Mag., .44 Mag. Detachable 10-, 9- or 4-round magazine. 18.5-inch bbl. Weight: 5.25 lbs. Front gold

Ruger No. 1
International

Ruger No. 1
Special Varminter

Ruger No. 1
Standard Rifle

Ruger No. 1 Tropical Rifle

bead sights. Drilled and tapped for scope. American hardwood stock. Made from 1996 to 2008.

96/22 (.22 LR). . . . . NiB $379 Ex $255 Gd $180
96/22M (.22 WMR) . . . . NiB $390 Ex $278 Gd $195
96/44 (.44 Mag.). . . . . NiB $390 Ex $278 Gd $195

- SEMI-AUTOMATIC RIFLES -

MODEL 10/22 CARBINE
Caliber: .22 LR. Detachable 10-round rotary magazine. 18.5-inch bbl. Weight: 5 lbs. Sights: Folding leaf rear; bead front. Carbine-style stock with bbl. band and curved buttplate (walnut stock discontinued 1980). Blued finish. Made from 1964 to date. International and Sporter versions discontinued 1971.

Standard (hardwood stock). . . . NiB $279 Ex $120 Gd $100
Standard (synthetic stock). . . . . NiB $279 Ex $120 Gd $100
Standard (synthetic stock, LaserMax sight), add $100
Standard (stainless finish) . . . . . NiB $310 Ex $130 Gd $110
Standard Sporter (checkered
  wood stock). . . . . NiB $379 Ex $215 Gd $180
Fingergroove Sporter (monte carlo wood stock,
  1966-1971). . . . . NiB $679 Ex $455 Gd $380
Fingergroove Sporter (checkered stock), add 30%
International (Mannlicher-style
  stock, 1966-69). . . . . NiB $680 Ex $460 Gd $375
K-10/22 RB (birch stock, stainless
  finish) . . . . NiB $260 Ex $178 Gd $144
Magnum (.22 WMR, 1999-06) . NiB $260 Ex $178 Gd $144
RB (birch stock, blued finish) . . NiB $260 Ex $178 Gd $144
RBI International (blued, Mannlicher-style
  stock, 1994-2003). . . . . NiB $260 Ex $120 Gd $110
RBI International (stainless, Mannlicher-style
  stock, 1994-2003). . . . . NiB $330 Ex $130 Gd $120

Rifle (20-in. bbl, 2004-06) . . . . NiB $220 Ex $110 Gd $100
SP Deluxe Sporter (intro. 1966) . . . NiB $260 Ex $178 Gd $144
Tactical (synthetic stock, flash
  hider 2010-date). . . . . NiB $339 Ex $150 Gd $120
Tactical Target (16.1-in. heavy bbl. w/spiral design, Hogue
  stock 2010-date). . . . . NiB $599 Ex $280 Gd $240
Takedown (synthetic stock, backpack
  2010-date) . . . . NiB $409 Ex $250 Gd $230
Takedown (w/threaded barrel,
  2013-date) . . . . NiB $429 Ex $250 Gd $230
Target (20-in. heavy bbl. w/spiral design, blued finish, brown
  laminated stock, 1996-date) NiB $550 Ex $210 Gd $180
Target (20-in. heavy bbl. w/spiral design, stainless finish, black
  laminated stock, 1996-date). . . . NiB $589 Ex $230 Gd $190
Target (thumbhole stock, 2001-02), add $100

MODEL 44
Gas-operated. Caliber: .44 Magnum. Four round tubular magazine (with magazine release button since 1967). 18.5-inch bbl. Weight: 5.75 lbs. Sights: Folding leaf rear; gold bead front. Carbine-style stock w/bbl. band and curved buttplate. Made from 1961 to 1986. International and Sporter versions discontinued 1971.

Standard . . . . NiB $588 Ex $434 Gd $338
International (Mannlicher-style
  stock). . . . . NiB $944 Ex $597 Gd $488
Sporter (MC stock w/finger
  groove) . . . . NiB $707 Ex $569 Gd $495
RS (peep rear sight, disc. 1978). . . NiB $695 Ex $487 Gd $388

MODEL 99/44 DEERFIELD . . . NiB $650 Ex $600 Gd $340
Similar to Model 44 except w/four-round rotary detachable box magazine, rotating bolt w/dual front locking lugs, integral scope mount. Made from 2000 to 2006.

Ruger No 3 Single-Shot Carbine

Ruger Model 10/22
Standard Rifle

Ruger Model 10/22
Deluxe Rifle

Ruger Model 44
Autoloading Carbine

Ruger Model 77 Round Top Receiver

Ruger Model 77
Ultra-Light Carbine

Blued finish. . . . . NiB $939 Ex $630 Gd $550
Blued finish (polymer stock), add $15
Stainless finish. . . . . NiB $979 Ex $680 Gd $580
Stainless finish (folding stock), add $350
Stainless finish (polymer stock) NiB $979 Ex $680 Gd $580
Stainless finish (6.8SPC,
    2007-11) . . . . NiB $979 Ex $680 Gd $580

MINI-14 TARGET . . . . NiB $1199 Ex $780 Gd $650
Similar to Mini-14 Ranch Rifle except w/22-in. stainless heavy
bbl. w/harmonic stabilizer, thumbhole stock. Made from 2007
to date.
w/Hogue synthetic stock . . . . NiB $1199 Ex $780 Gd $650

MINI-14 TACTICAL . . . . NiB $1019 Ex $680 Gd $550
Similar to Mini-14 Ranch Rifle except w/16.1-in. bbl. w/flash
hider, synthetic stock. Weight: 6.75 lbs. Made from 2009 to
date.
w/folding stock . . . . NiB $1019 Ex $680 Gd $550

MINI-14
Gas-operated. Caliber: .223 Rem. 5-, 10- or 20-round box
magazine. 18.5-inch bbl. Weight: About 6.5 lbs. Sights: Peep
rear; blade front mounted on removable barrel band. Pistol-
grip stock w/curved buttplate, handguard. Made from 1974
to 2004.
Blued finish. . . . . NiB $725 Ex $579 Gd $375
K-Mini-14/S stainless steel . . . . NiB $815 Ex $580 Gd $444
Mini-14/5F w/blued finish,
    folding stock. . . . . NiB $1144 Ex $995 Gd $790
K-Mini-14/SF w/stainless finish,
    folding stock. . . . . NiB $855 Ex $690 Gd $545

MINI-14 RANCH RIFLE
Similar to Mini-14 except w/receiver machined for scope
mounts. Recent manufacture chambered in 5.56mm NATO.
Weight: 7 lbs. Made from 1982 to date.

MINI-THIRTY
Similar to Mini-14 except chambered in 7.62 x 39mm. 5-round
detachable magazine. 18.5-inch bbl. 37.25 inches overall.

Ruger Model 77
International Carbine

Ruger Model 77
Varmint Rifle

Ruger Model 77 Mark II
All-Weather Rifle

Ruger Model 77 Mark II

Ruger Model 77/.22 Rimfire

Ruger Model 77/.22
All Weather

Ruger Model 77/.44
All Weather

**Stainless finish (polymer stock,
1990 to date)** . . . . NiB $979 Ex $730 Gd $580

PC SERIES SEMIAUTOMATIC CARBINES
Calibers: 9mm Parabellum or .40 S&W. 10-round magazine.
15.25-inch bbl. Weight: 6.25 lbs. Integral Ruger scope mounts
with or without sights. Optional blade front sight, adjustable
open rear. Matte black oxide finish. Matte black Zytel stock w/
checkered pistol-grip and forearm. Made from 1997 to date.

Weight: 7 lbs. 3 oz. Designed for use with telescopic sights.
Walnut stained stock. Sights: Peep rear; blade front mounted
on bbl. band. Blued or stainless finish. Made from 1987 to
2004.
Blued finish . . . . NiB $625 Ex $439 Gd $300
Stainless finish . . . . NiB $815 Ex $545 Gd $360

GRADING: **NiB** = New in Box   **Ex** = Excellent or NRA 95%   **Gd** = Good or NRA 68%   **349**

Model PC9 (no sights). . . . . NiB $510 Ex $440 Gd $300
Model PC4 (no sights). . . . . NiB $545 Ex $467 Gd $333
w/adjust. sights, add. $50

SR-556/SR-556 CARBINE. . . . NiB $2049 Ex $900 Gd $800
Semi-automatic AR15 platform w/gas piston system. Caliber: 5.56mm NATO. 10-, 25- or 30-round magazine. 16.1-in. bbl., adj. gas block, Troy folding sights, fixed or collapsible buttstock. Weight: 7.9 lbs. Made 2009 to date.
6.8mm SPC (2010-2011). . . . . NiB $2049 Ex $900 Gd $800
SR-556VT (20-in. bbl., A2 buttstock, Mappul
    grip 2013-date). . . . . NiB $2049 Ex $900 Gd $800

SR-762 CARBINE . . . . NiB $2269 Ex $1280 Gd $1050
Semi-automatic AR15 platform w/gas piston system. Caliber: 7.62mm NATO. 20-round magazine. 16.1-in. bbl., adj. gas block, adj. folding sights, collapsible buttstock. Weight: 8.6 lbs. Made 2013 to date.

- BOLT-ACTION RIFLES -

MODEL 77 BOLT-ACTION RIFLE
Receiver with integral scope mount base or with round top. Short stroke or magnum length action (depending on caliber) in the former type receiver, magnum only in the latter. .22-250, .220 Swift, 6mm Rem., .243 Win., .250-3000, .25-06, .257 Roberts, 6.5 Rem. Mag., .270 Win., 7x57mm, 7mm-08 7mm Rem. Mag., .280 Rem., .284 Win., .308 Win., .30-06, .300 Win. Mag. .338 Win. Mag., .350 Rem. Mag., .458 Win. Mag. Five round magazine standard, 4-round in .220 Swift, 3-round in magnum calibers. 22 24- or 26-inch bbl. (depending on caliber). Weight: About 7 lbs.; .458 Mag. model, 8.75 lbs. Round-top model furnished w/folding leaf rear sight and ramp front; integral base model furnished w/scope rings,with or w/o open sights. Stock w/checkered pistol grip and forearm, pistol-grip cap, rubber recoil pad, QD swivel studs. Made from 1968 to 1992.
Model 77 w/integral base, no sights . . NiB $500 Ex $408 Gd $321
6.5 Rem. Mag., add. $100
.284 Win., add $50
.338 Win. Mag., add. $75
.350 Rem. Mag., add. $75
Model 77RL Ultra Light, w/no
    sights . . . . NiB $545 Ex $438 Gd $290
Model 77RL Ultra Light, w/open
    sights. NiB $569 Ex $454 Gd $331
Model 77RS w/integral base,
    open sights . . . . NiB $569 Ex $454 Gd $331
.338 Win. Mag, .458 Win. Mag.,
    standard stock, add. $100
Model 77RSC, .458 Win. Mag.,
    w/walnut stock, add. $126
w/fancy grade Circassian walnut stock, add. $707
Model 77RSI International w/Mannlicher stock,
    short action, 18.5-inch bbl . . NiB $675 Ex $466 Gd $339
Model 77ST w/round top, open
    sights. NiB $575 Ex $439 Gd $369
.338 Win. Mag., add. $75
Model 77V Varmint
    w/integral base, no sights. . . NiB $588 Ex $466 Gd $300
Model 77 NV Varmint w/integral base, no sights, stainless steel
    bbl., laminated wood stock. . NiB $593 Ex $468 Gd $379

MODEL 77 MARK II ALL-WEATHER
RIFLE . . . . NiB $535 Ex $430 Gd $315
Revised Model 77 action. Same general specifications as Model M-77 Mark II except with stainless bbl. and action. Zytel injection-molded stock. Calibers: .223, .243, .270, .308,
.30-06, 7mm Mag., .300 Win. Mag., .338 Win. Mag. Made from 1999 to 2008.

MODEL 77 MARK II BOLT-ACTION RIFLE
Revised Model 77 action. Same general specifications as Model M-77 except with new 3-position safety and fixed blade ejector system. Calibers .22 PPC, .223 Rem., 6mm PPC, 6.5x55 Swedish, .375 H&H, .404 Jeffery and .416 Rigby also available. Weight: 6 to 10.25 lbs. Made from 1989 to 2012.
MKIIR w/integral base, no sights . . NiB $545 Ex $423 Gd $314
Left-hand model, add $50
MKII RL Ultralight, no sights . . NiB $545 Ex $423 Gd $314
MKII RLS w/open sights . . . . . . NiB $545 Ex $423 Gd $314
MKII RS w/integral base, open
    sights . . . . NiB $545 Ex $423 Gd $314
MKII RS Express w/fancy grade French walnut stock, integral
    base, open sights. . . . . NiB $1347 Ex $1116 Gd $835
MKII RSI International Mannlicher. . . NiB $799 Ex $479 Gd $368
MKII RSM Magnum w/fancy grade Circassian walnut stock,
    integral base, open sights NiB $1465 Ex $1143 Gd $870
77VT (VBZ or VTM) MKII Varmint/Target w/stainless steel
    action, laminated wood stock . . NiB $480 Ex $403 Gd $288

MODEL 77 GUNSITE SCOUT NiB $1075 Ex $480 Gd $400
Similar to Model 77 Mark II except w/16.5-in. bbl. w/flash hider, 10-shot detacable box magazine, .308 Win. only, forward scope mount, blued finish, laminated stock w/spacers. Weight: 7 lbs. Made from 2011 to date.
Blued finish (composite stock) NiB $1075 Ex $480 Gd $400
Stainless finish. . . . . NiB $1139 Ex $640 Gd $520
Stainless finish (composite stock). . . NiB $1139 Ex $640 Gd $520

MODEL 77/22 HORNET . . . . . NiB $556 EX $445 Gd $339
Mini-Sporter built on the 77/.22 action in caliber .22 Hornet. Six round rotary magazine. 20- inch bbl. 40 inches overall. Weight: 6 lbs. Receiver machined for Ruger rings (included). Beaded front sight and open adj. rear, or no sights. Blued or stainless finish. Checkered American walnut stock. Made from 1994 to date.
Model 77/22RH (rings, no sights) . . . NiB $625 Ex $470 Gd $369
Model 77/22RSH (rings & sights). . . NiB $625 Ex $470 Gd $369
Model 77/22VHZ (stainless finish,
    laminated wood stock) . . . . NiB $735 Ex $544 Gd $390

MODEL 77/22 RIMFIRE BOLT-ACTION RIFLE
Calibers: .22 LR or .22 WMR. 10-shot (.22 LR) or 9-shot (.22 WMR) rotary magazine. 20-inch bbl. 39.75 inches overall. Weight: 5.75 lbs. Integral scope bases; with or w/o sights. Checkered American walnut or Zytel injection-molded stock. Stainless or blued finish. Made 1983 to date. (Blued); stainless. Introduced 1989.
77/22R w/scope rings, no sights, walnut
    stock . . . . NiB $625 Ex $544 Gd $390
77/22RS w/scope rings, sights, walnut
    stock. . . . . NiB $625 Ex $544 Gd $390
77/22RP w/scope rings, no sights, synthetic
    stock . . . . NiB $625 Ex $544 Gd $390
77/22RSP w/scope rings, sights, synthetic
    stock . . . . NiB $625 Ex $544 Gd $390
K77/22RP w/stainless scope rings, no sights,
    synthetic stock . . . . NiB $625 Ex $544 Gd $390
K77/22RSP w/stainless scope rings, sights,
    synthetic stock . . . . NiB $625 Ex $544 Gd $390
77/22RM (.22 WMR) w/scope rings,no sights,
    walnut stock . . . . NiB $625 Ex $544 Gd $390
K77/22RSMP (.22 WMR) w/stainless scope rings,
    sights, synthetic stock. . . . . . NiB $735 Ex $579 Gd $437
K77/22RMP (.22 WMR) w/stainless scope rings, sights,
    synthetic stock . . . . NiB $625 Ex $544 Gd $390

Ruger Model 96/22 Lever-Action

Ruger Model 96/44 Lever-Action

Ruger Mini-14 Semiautomatic

Ruger Mini-14 with Folding Stock

Ruger Mini-Thirty Autoloader

Ruger Model PC9 w/Ghost Ring Sights

Sako Model 73

Sako Model 74 Carbine

GRADING: **NiB** = New in Box   **Ex** = Excellent or NRA 95%   **Gd** = Good or NRA 68%

**K77/22 VBZ (.22 WMR) w/no sights, laminated stock
(intro. 1993)** . . . . **NiB $735 Ex $579 Gd $437**

MODEL 77/44

Short-action, carbine-style M77 similar to the 77/22RH. Chambered .44 Rem. Mag. Four round rotary magazine. 18.5-inch bbl. 38.25 inches overall. Weight: 6 lbs. Gold bead front sight, folding adjustable rear w/integral scope base and Ruger rings. Blue or stainless finish. Synthetic or checkered American walnut stock w/rubber buttpad and swivels. Made from 1997 to 2004.

Blued finish . . . . **NiB $625 Ex $544 Gd $390**
Stainless finish . . . . **NiB $555 Ex $350 Gd $245**

AMERICAN RIFLE

Three-lug push-feed bolt w/70-degree bolt lift, short or long action, integral scope mount, adj. trigger, black polymer stock, flush-fit rotary magzine, no sights. Calibers: .223 Rem., .22-250, .243 Win., .270 Win., 7mm-08, .308 Win., or .30-06. 22-inch bbl. (depending on caliber). Weight: 6.1 to 6.4 lbs. Made 2012 to date.

Standard (blued finish) . . . . **NiB $459 Ex $280 Gd $250**
**All-Weather (22-in. bbl., stainless
 finish)** . . . . **NiB $595 Ex $320 Gd $280**
**All-Weather Compact (18-in. bbl.,
 stainless finish)** . . . . **NiB $595 Ex $320 Gd $280**
Compact (18-in. bbl., blued finish) . . . **NiB $459 Ex $280 Gd $250**

AMERICAN RIFLE RIMFIRE

Push-feed bolt w/60-degree bolt lift, integral scope mount, adj. trigger, black modular polymer stock w/adj. LOP, 22-in. bbl., 9- or 10-round flush-fit rotary magzine, no sights, blued finish. Calibers: .17 HMR, .22 LR, .22 Mag. Weight: 5.5 to 6 lbs. Made 2013 to date.

Standard . . . . **NiB $339 Ex $190 Gd $150**
Compact (18-in. bbl.) . . . . **NiB $339 Ex $190 Gd $150**
w/threaded barrel, add $30

GUIDE GUN

Similar to Model HM77 Hawkeye except w/20-in. stainless bbl. w/muzzle brake, adj. sights, laminated stock, matte stainless finish. Weight: 8.15 lbs. Made from 2013 to date.

Standard (blued finish) . . . . **NiB $939 Ex $320 Gd $270**

MODEL HM77 HAWKEYE

Revised Model 77 Mark II action w/same general specifications except w/Mauser style controlled feed, LC6 trigger, one-piece stainless bolt, integral scope base. no sights. Weight: 7 to 8.25 lbs. Made from 2007 to date.

Standard (blued finish) . . . . **NiB $939 Ex $320 Gd $270**
**African (adj. sights, wood stock w/ebony tip, blued finish,
 2007-12)** . . . . **NiB $939 Ex $400 Gd $370**
**African (muzzle brake, adj. sights, wood stock w/ebony tip
 blued finish, 2013-date)** . . . . **NiB $939 Ex $400 Gd $370**
**Alaskan (adj. sights, Hogue overmold stock stainless finish,
 2007-12)** . . . . **NiB $939 Ex $400 Gd $370**
**All-Weather (synthetic stock stainless
 finish)** . . . . **NiB $939 Ex $320 Gd $270**
**All-Weather Ultra Light (6.5 lbs., synthetic stock stainless
 finish, 2009 only)** . . . . **NiB $580 Ex $330 Gd $280**
**Compact (walnut stock, 16.5-in. bbl., blue finish,
 2009-date)** . . . . **NiB $939 Ex $320 Gd $270**
**Compact Laminate (laminate stock, 16.5-in. bbl., stainless
 finish, 2009-date)** . . . . **NiB $999 Ex $420 Gd $270**
**International (adj. sights, Mannlicher checkered stock matet
 blue finish, 2009-10)** . . . . . . **NiB $755 Ex $430 Gd $350**
**Laminated (laminated stock, stainless finish,
 2008-10)** . . . . **NiB $939 Ex $400 Gd $370**
**Magnum Hunter (Hogue green overmold stock, stainless
 finish, 24-in. bbl. w/muzzle brake, .300 Win. Mag. only,**

2013-date) . . . . **NiB $1139 Ex $530 Gd $455**
**Predator (22- or 24-in. heavy bbl., laminated stock, stainless
 finish,2009-date)** . . . . **NiB $1069 Ex $430 Gd $370**
**Sporter (22- or 24-in. bbl., brown or black laminate stock matte
 stainless finish, 2009-13)** . . . **NiB $765 Ex $320 Gd $270**
**Tactical (22-in. heavy bbl., Hogue black overmold stock, Harris
 bipod,matte blue finish, 2009-13)** . . **NiB $1050 Ex $650 Gd $580**
**Ultra Light (6.5 lbs., 20-in. bbl., no sights, walnut stock blue
 finish, 2009-10)** . . . . **NiB $695 Ex $410 Gd $360**

RUSSIAN MILITARY RIFLES — Tula, Russia
Principal U.S.S.R. Arms Plant, Tula.

MODEL 1891 MOSIN MILITARY

RIFLE. . . . . **NiB $485 Ex $269 Gd $187**
Nagant system bolt action. Caliber: 7.62mm Russian. Five round box magazine. 31.5-inch bbl. Weight: About 9 lbs. Sights: Open rear; blade front. Full stock w/straight grip. Specifications given are for WWII version; earlier types differ slightly. Note: In 1916, Remington Arms Co. and New England Westinghouse Co. produced 250,000 of these rifles on a contract from the Imperial Russian Government. Few were delivered to Russia and the balance bought by the U.S. Government for training in 1918. Eventually, many of these rifles were sold to N.R.A. members for about $3 each by the Director of Civilian Marksmanship.

TOKAREV MODEL 40 SEMIAUTOMATIC

MILITARY RIFLE . . . . **NiB $844 Ex $438 Gd $270**
Gas-operated. Caliber: 7.62mm Russian. 10-round detachable box magazine. 24.5-inch bbl. Muzzle brake. Weight: About 9 lbs. Sights: Leaf rear, hooded post front. Full stock w/pistol grip. Differences among Models 1938,1940 and 1941 are minor.

SAKO — Riihimaki, Finland
Manufactured by Sako L.T.D. Formerly imported by Stoeger Industries, Wayne NJ (formerly by Garcia Corp.) until 2000. Imported by Beretta USA 2001 to date.

MODEL 72 . . . . **NiB $1090 Ex $865 Gd $660**
Single model designation replacing Vixen Sporter, Vixen Carbine, Vixen Heavy Barrel, Forester Sporter, Forester Carbine, Forester Heavy Barrel, Finnbear Sporter, and Finnbear Carbine, with same specifications, except all but heavy barrel models fitted with open rear sight. Values same as for corresponding earlier models. Imported from 1972 to 1974.

MODEL 73 LEVER-ACTION RIFLE . . . **NiB $1670 Ex $988 Gd $690**
Same as Finnwolf except has 3-round clip magazine, flush floorplate; stock has no cheekpiece. Imported from 1973 to 1975.

MODEL 74 CARBINE . . . . **NiB $1141 Ex $735 Gd $600**
Long Mauser-type bolt action. Caliber: .30-06. Five round magazine. 20-inch bbl. Weight: 7.5 lbs. No sights. Checkered Mannlicher-type full stock of European walnut, Monte Carlo cheekpiece. Imported from 1974 to 1978.

MODEL 74 HEAVY BARREL RIFLE,

LONG ACTION . . . . **NiB $1165 Ex $755 Gd $634**
Same specifications as short action except w/24-inch heavy bbl., weighs 8.75 lbs.; magnum w/4-round magazine. Calibers: .25-06, 7mm Rem. Mag. Imported from 1974 to 1978.

MODEL 74 HEAVY BARREL RIFLE,

MEDIUM ACTION . . . . **NiB $1165 Ex $755 Gd $634**

Sako Model 74 Super Sporter

Sako Model 74 Super Rimfire

Sako Model 75 Hunter

Sako 75 Stainless Synthetic

Sako Model 75 Varmint Rifle

Sako Classic

Sako Fiberglass

Sako Finnfire

GRADING: **NiB =** New in Box   **Ex =** Excellent or NRA 95%   **Gd =** Good or NRA 68%

Same specifications as short action except w/23-inch heavy bbl., weighs 8.5 lbs. Calibers: .220 Swift, .22-250, .243 Win., .308 Win. Imported from 1974 to 1978.

MODEL 74 HEAVY BARREL RIFLE,
SHORT ACTION . . . . **NiB $1195 Ex $909 Gd $650**
Mauser-type bolt action. Calibers: .222 Rem., .223 Rem. Five round magazine. 23.5-inch heavy bbl. Weight: 8.25 lbs. No sights. Target-style checkered European walnut stock w/beavertail forearm. Imported from 1974 to 1978.

MODEL 74 SUPER SPORTER,
LONG ACTION . . . . **NiB $1165 Ex $755 Gd $634**
Same specifications as short action except w/24-inch bbl., weight: 8 lbs.; magnums have 4-round magazine, recoil pad. Calibers: .25-06, .270 Win. 7mm Rem. Mag., .30-06, .300 Win. Mag., .338 Win. Mag., .375 H&H Mag. Imported from 1974-78.

MODEL 74 SUPER SPORTER,
MEDIUM ACTION . . . . **NiB $1175 Ex $910 Gd $659**
Same specifications as short action except weight: 7.25 lbs. Calibers: .220 Swift, .22-250, .243 Win. Imported from 1974-78.

MODEL 74 SUPER SPORTER,
SHORT ACTION . . . . **NiB $1175 Ex $910 Gd $659**
Mauser-type bolt action. Calibers: .222 Rem., .223 Rem. Five round magazine. 23.5-inch bbl. Weight: 6.5 lbs. No sights. Checkered European walnut stock w/Monte Carlo cheekpiece, QD swivel studs. Imported 1974. Disc.

MODEL 75 DELUXE . . . . NiB $1190 Ex $944 Gd $690
Same specifications as Sako 75 Hunter Model except w/hinged floor plate, deluxe high gloss checkered walnut stock w/rosewood forend cap and grip cap w/silver inlay. Imported from 1998-2006. Disc.

MODEL 75 HUNTER . . . . NiB $1260 Ex $833 Gd $665
New bolt action design available in four action lengths fitted with a new bolt featuring three front locking lugs with an external extractor positioned under the bolt. Calibers: .17 Rem., .222 Rem., .223 Rem., (I); .22-250 Rem., .243 Win., 7mm-08 Rem., .308 Win., (III); .25-06 Rem., .270 Win., .280 Rem., .30-06, (IV); 7mm Rem Mag., .300 Win. Mag., .300 Wby. Mag., .338 Win. Mag. 7mm STW, .300 Wby. Mag., .340 Wby. Mag., .375 H&H Mag. and .416 Rem. Mag.,(V). 4-, 5- or 6-round magazine w/detachable magazine. 22-, 24-, and 26-inch bbls. 41.75 to 45.6 inches over all. Weight: 6.3 to 9 lbs. Sako dovetail scope base integral with receiver with no sights. Checkered high-grade walnut stock w/recoil pad and sling swivels. Made from 1997 to 2006.

MODEL 75 STAINLESS
SYNTHETIC . . . . .NiB $1279 Ex $877 Gd $685
Similar to Model 75 Hunter except chambered for .22-250 Rem., .243 Win., .25-06 Rem., .270 Win., 7mm-08 Rem., 7mm STW, .30-06, .308 Win., 7mm Rem Mag., .300 Win. Mag., .338 Win. Mag. or .375 H&H Mag. 22-, 24-, and 26-inch bbls. Black composite stock w/soft rubber grips inserts. Matte stainless steel finish. Made from 1997 to 2006.

MODEL 75 VARMINT
RIFLE .NiB $1471 Ex $835 Gd $656
Similar to Model 75 Hunter except chambered .17 Rem., .222 Rem., .223 Rem. and .22-250 Rem. 24-inch bbl. Matte lacquered walnut stock w/beavertail forearm. Made from 1998 to 2006.

MODEL 78 SUPER HORNET
SPORTER . . . . .NiB $654 Ex $535 Gd $338
Same specifications as Model 78 Rimfire except chambered for .22 Hornet, 4-round magazine. Imported from 1977 to 1987.

MODEL 78 SUPER RIMFIRE
SPORTER . . . . .NiB $587 Ex $466 Gd $338
Bolt action. Caliber: .22 LR. Five round magazine. 22.5-inch bbl. Weight, 6.75 lbs. No sights. Checkered European walnut stock, Monte Carlo cheekpiece. Imported from 1977 to 1986.

MODEL 85 CLASSIC BOLT-ACTION RIFLE
Calibers: .25-06 Rem., .270 Win., .30-06, .308 Win., .300 Win. Mga., .338 Win. Mag., .370 Sako Mag., .375 H&H Mag.., .270 WSM., .300 WSM., 7mm Mag. detachable mag., single stage trigger, pistol grip, checkered walnut stock. Weight: 7 lbs. New 2009.
Standard calibers . . . . **NiB $1937 Ex $1216 Gd $1019**
Magnum caliber, add **$126**

DELUXE GRADE AI. . . . . NiB $1266 Ex $870 Gd $633
Same specifications as Standard Grade except w/22 lines to the inch French checkering, rosewood grip cap and forend tip, semibeavertail forend. Disc.

DELUXE GRADE AII . . . . NiB $1145 Ex $790 Gd $556
Same specifications as Standard Grade except w/22 lines per inch French checkering, rosewood grip cap and forend tip, semi beavertail forend. Disc.

DELUXE GRADE AIII . . . . . . NiB $1482 Ex $1188 Gd $766
Same specifications as w/standard except w/French checkering, rosewood grip cap and forend tip, semibeavertail forend. Disc.

DELUXE LIGHTWEIGHT BOLT-ACTION
RIFLE . . . . .NiB $1190 Ex $1021 Gd $699
Same general specifications as Hunter Lightweight except w/beautifully grained French walnut stock; superb high-gloss finish, fine hand-cut checkering, rosewood forend tip and grip cap. Imported from 1985-97.

FIBERCLASS BOLT-ACTION
RIFLE . . . . .NiB $1137 Ex $1077 Gd $650
All-weather fiberglass stock version of Sako barreled long action. Calibers: .25-06, .270, .30-06, 7mm Rem. Mag., .300 Win. Mag., .338 Win. Mag., .375 H&H Mag. Bbl. length: 22.5 inches. Overall length: 44.25 inches. Weight: 7.25 lbs. Imported 1984 to 1996.

FINNBEAR CARBINE . . . . . . .NiB $1190 Ex $926 Gd $572
Same as Finnbear Sporter except w/20-inch bbl., Mannlicher-type full stock. Imported 1971. Disc.

FINNBEAR SPORTER . . . . . . .NiB $1190 Ex $926 Gd $572
Long Mauser-type bolt action. Calibers: .25-06, .264 Mag. .270, .30-06, .300 Win. Mag., .338 Mag., 7mm Mag., .375 H&H Mag. Magazine holds 5 standard or 4 magnum cartridges. 24-inch bbl. Weight: 7 lbs. Hooded ramp front sight. Sporter stock w/Monte Carlo cheekpiece, checkered pistol-grip and forearm, recoil pad, swivels. Imported from 1961 to 1971.

FINNFIRE BOLT-ACTION RIFLE
Mini-Sporter built for rimfires on a scaled-down Sako design. Caliber: .22 LR. 5- or 10-round magazine. 22-inch bbl. 39.5 inches overall. Weight: 5.25 lbs. Receiver machined for 11mm dovetail scope rings. Beaded blade front sight, open

Sako Finnfire Heavy Barrel

Sako Forester Sporter

Sako Golden Anniversary

Sako Hunter Lightweight

adj. rear. Blued finish. Checkered European walnut stock. Imported from 1994 to 2005.

Hunter model	NiB $926	Ex $694	Gd $533
Varmint model	NiB $988	Ex $696	Gd $580
Sporter model	NiB $1027	Ex $866	Gd $613

FINNWOLF LEVER-ACTION
RIFLE. . . . . NiB $975 Ex $733 Gd $621
Hammerless. Calibers: .243 Win., .308 Win. Four round clip magazine. 23-inch bbl. Weight: 6.75 lbs. Hooded ramp front sight. Sporter stock w/Monte Carlo cheekpiece, checkered pistol-grip and forearm, swivels (available w/right- or left-hand stock). Imported 1963 to 1972.

FINNSPORT 2707 . . . . NiB $808 Ex $597 Gd $466
Bolt-action centerfire rifle. Calibers: .270, .30-06, 7mm Rem. Mag., .300 Win. Mag. Bbl. length: 24 inches. Weight: 8 lbs. Imported 1984 to 1986.

FORESTER CARBINE . . . . NiB $1116 Ex $924 Gd $550
Same as Forester Sporter except w/20-inch bbl., Mannlicher-type full stock. Imported from 1958 to 1971.

FORESTER HEAVY BARREL . . . NiB $1423 Ex $988 Gd $713
Same as Forester Sporter except w/24-inch heavy bbl. Weight 7.5 lbs. Imported from 1958 to 1971.

FORESTER SPORTER . . . . NiB $1141 Ex $1015 Gd $559
Medium-length Mauser-type bolt action. Calibers: .22-250, .243 Win., .308 Win. Five round magazine. 23-inch bbl. Weight: 6.5 lbs. Hooded ramp front sight. Sporter stock w/ Monte Carlo cheekpiece, checkered pistol grip and forearm, swivels. Imported 1957 to 1971.

GOLDEN ANNIVERSARY
MODEL . . . . NiB $2866 Ex $2210 Gd $1570
Special presentation-grade rifle issued in 1973 to commemorate Sako's 50th anniversary. 1,000 (numbered 1 to 1,000) made. Same specifications as Deluxe Sporter: Long action, 7mm Rem. Mag. receiver, trigger guard and floorplate decorated w/gold oak leaf and acorn motif. Stock of select European walnut, checkering bordered w/hand-carved oak leaf pattern.

HIGH-POWER MAUSER
SPORTING RIFLE . . . . NiB $1154 Ex $1043 Gd $831
FN Mauser action. Calibers: .270, .30-06. Five round magazine. 24-inch bbl. Sights: Open rear leaf; Partridge front; hooded ramp. Checkered stock w/Monte Carlo comb and cheekpiece. Weight: 7.5 lbs. Imported from 1950 to 1957.

HUNTER LIGHTWEIGHT BOLT-ACTION RIFLE
5- or 6-round magazine. Bbl. length: 21.5 inches, AI; 22 inches, AII; 22.5 inches, AIII. Overall length: 42.25-44.5 inches. Weight: 5.75 lbs., AI; 6.75 lbs. AII; 7.25 lbs., AIII. Monte Carlo-style European walnut stock, oil finished. Hand-checkered pistol-grip and forend. Imported from 1985-97. Left-hand version intro. 1987.

AI (Short Action) .17 Rem.	NiB $1466	Ex $1224	Gd $1018
.222 Rem., .223 Rem.	NiB $1088	Ex $831	Gd $589
AII (Medium Action) .22-250 Rem.,			
.243 Win., .308 Win.	NiB $976	Ex $798	Gd $543
AII (Long Action) .25-06 Rem.			
.270 Win., .30-06	NiB $978	Ex $792	Gd $553
.338 Win. Mag.	NiB $1154	Ex $976	Gd $735
.375 H&H Mag.	NiB $1266	Ex $1044	Gd $766
Left-hand model (std cal.)	NiB $1294	Ex $1088	Gd $773
Magnum calibers	NiB $1590	Ex $1277	Gd $945

LAMINATED STOCK BOLT-ACTION RIFLES
Similar in style and specifications to Hunter Grade except w/ stock of resin-bonded hardwood veneers. Available 18 calibers

Sako Mannlicher-Style Carbine

Sako Sporter Deluxe

**Sako TRG-21
Target Rifle**

in AI (Short), AII (Medium) or AV action, left-hand version in 10 calibers, AV only. Imported from 1987 to 1995.
Short or medium action . . . . . **NiB $1043 Ex $899 Gd $577**
Long action/Magnum . . . . **NiB $1108 Ex $902 Gd $645**

MAGNUM MAUSER . . . . **NiB $1588 Ex $1244 Gd $909**
Similar specifications as Standard Model except w/recoil pad and redesigned longer AIII action to handle longer magnum cartridges. Calibers: .300 H&H Magnum, .375 H&H Magnum, standard at time of introduction. Disc.

MANNLICHER-STYLE CARBINE
Similar to Hunter Model except w/full Mannlicher-style stock and 18.5-inch bbl. Weighs 7.5 lbs. Chambered in .243, .25-06, .270, .308, .30-06, 7mm Rem. Mag., .300 Win. Mag., .338 Win. Mag., .375 H&H. Intro. in 1977. Disc.
Standard calibers . . . . **NiB $1287 Ex $1021 Gd $734**
Magnum calibers (except .375) . . . **NiB $1338 Ex $1055 Gd $733**
.375 H&H . . . . **NiB $1370 Ex $1094 Gd $790**

SAFARI GRADE . . . . **NiB $2576 Ex $1988 Gd $1166**
Classic bolt-action. Calibers: .300 Win. Mag., .338 Win. Mag., .375 H&H. Oil-finished European walnut stock w/hand-checkering. Barrel band swivel, express-type sight rib; satin or matte blue finish. Imported from 1980 to 1996.

SPORTER DELUXE . . . . **NiB $1290 Ex $1045 Gd $687**
Same as Vixen, Forester, Finnbear and Model 74 except w/ fancy French walnut stock w/skip checkering, rosewood forend tip and pistol-grip cap, recoil pad, inlaid trigger guard and floorplate. Disc.

STANDARD GRADE AI . . . . . . **NiB $1077 Ex $823 Gd $440**
Short bolt-action. Calibers: .17 Rem., .222 Rem., .223 Rem. Five round magazine. 23.5-inch bbl. Weight: 6.5 lbs. No sights. Checkered European walnut stock w/Monte Carlo cheekpiece, QD swivel studs. Imported 1978 to 1985.

STANDARD GRADE AII . . . . . **NiB $1090 Ex $840 Gd $456**
Medium bolt-action. Calibers: .22-250 Rem., .243 Win., .308 Win. 23.5-inch bbl. in .22-250; 23-inch bbl. in other calibers. Five round magazine. Weight: 7.25 lbs. Checkered European walnut stock w/Monte Carlo cheekpiece, QD swivel studs. Imported from 1978 to 1985.

STANDARD GRADE AIII . . . . . **NiB $1178 Ex $843 Gd $545**
Long bolt action. Calibers: .25-06 Rem., .270 Win., .30-06, 7mm Rem. Mag., .300 Win. Mag., .338 Win. Mag., .375 H&H. 24-inch bbl. 4-round magazine. Weight: 8 lbs. Imported from 1978 to 1984.

SUPER DELUXE RIFLE . . . . . **NiB $2544 Ex $2210 Gd $1347**
Available in AI, AII, AIII calibers. Select European walnut stock, hand-checkered, deep oak leaf hand-engraved design. Disc.

TRG BOLT-ACTION TARGET RIFLE
Caliber: .308 Win., .330 Win. or .338 Lapua Mag. Detachable 10-round magazine. 25.75- or 27.2-inch bbl. Weight: 10.5 to 11 lbs. Blued action w/stainless barrel. Adjustable two-stage trigger. modular reinforced polyurethane target stock w/adj. cheekpiece and buttplate. Options: Muzzle break; detachable bipod; QD sling swivels and scope mounts w/1-inch or 30mm rings. Imported from 1993 to 2004.
TRG 21 .308 Win . . . . **NiB $2376 Ex $2099 Gd $1545**
TRG 22 .308 Win. . . . . **NiB $2459 Ex $2288 Gd $1590**
TRG 41 .338 Lapua . . . . . . **NiB $2788 Ex $2690 Gd $1877**
**TRG-42 (.300 Win Mag. or .338
Lapua)** . . . . **NiB $3154 Ex $2651 Gd $1835**

TRG-S BOLT-ACTION RIFLE
Calibers: .243, 7mm-08, .270, .30-06, 7mm Rem. Mag., .300 Win. Mag., .338 Win. Mag. Five shot magazine (standard calibers), 4-shot (magnum), 22- or 24-inch bbl. 45.5 inches overall. Weight: 7.75 lbs. No sights. Reinforced polyurethane stock w/Monte Carlo. Introduced in 1993.
Standard calibers . . . . **NiB $823 Ex $707 Gd $466**
Magnum calibers . . . . **NiB $880 Ex $844 Gd $545**

VIXEN CARBINE . . . . **NiB $1096 Ex $954 Gd $868**
Same as Vixen Sporter except w/20-inch bbl., Mannlicher-type full stock. Imported from 1947 to 1971.

VIXEN HEAVY BARREL . . . . . . **NiB $1110 Ex $933 Gd $545**
Same as Vixen Sporter except calibers .222 Rem., .222 Rem. Mag., .223 Rem., heavy bbl., target-style stock w/beavertail forearm. Weight: 7.5 lbs. Imported from 1947-71.

VIXEN SPORTER . . . . **NiB $1100 Ex $969 Gd $546**
Short Mauser-type bolt-action. Cals.: .218 Bee, .22 Hornet, .222 Rem., .222 Rem. Mag., .223 Rem. Five round magazine.

Sako TRG-S Bolt-Action Rifle

Sako Vixen Heavy Barrel

Sako Vixen Sporter

23.5-inch bbl. Weight: 6.5 lbs. Hooded ramp front sight. Sporter stock w/Monte Carlo cheekpiece, checkered pistol-grip and forearm, swivels. Imported from 1946 to 1971.

J. P. SAUER & SOHN — Eckernforde, Germany

Formerly Suhl, Germany. Imported by Sigarms Exeter, NH, previously by Paul Company Inc. and G.U. Inc.

MAUSER BOLT-ACTION SPORTING
RIFLE. . . . . NiB $1457 Ex $1089 Gd $777
Calibers: 7x57 and 8x57mm most common, but these rifles were produced in a variety of calibers including most of the popular Continental calibers as well as our .30-06. Five round box magazine. 22- or 24-inch Krupp steel bbl., half-octagon w/raised matted rib. Double-set trigger. Weight: 7.5 lbs. Sights: Three-leaf open rear; ramp front. Sporting stock w/cheekpiece, checkered pistol grip, raised side-panels, Schnabel tip, swivels. Also made w/20-inch bbl. and full-length stock. Mfd. before WWII.

MODEL S-90 BOLT-ACTION RIFLES
Calibers: .243 Win., .308 Win. (Short action); .25-06, .270 Win., .30-06 (Medium action); 7mm Rem. Mag., .300 Win. Mag., .300 Wby., .338 Win., .375 H&H (Magnum action). Four round (standard) or 3-round magazine (magnum). Bbl. length: 20-inch (Stutzen), 24-inch. Weight: 7.6 to 10.75 lbs. Adjustable (Supreme) checkered Monte Carlo style stock. contrasting forend and pistol grip cap w/high-gloss finish or European (Lux) checkered Classic-style European walnut stock w/satin oil finish. Imported from 1983 to 1989.
S-90 Standard . . . . NiB $1154 Ex $990 Gd $587
S-90 Lux . . . . NiB $1389 Ex $1100 Gd $654
S-90 Safari. . . . . NiB $1411 Ex $1127 Gd $665
S-90 Stutzen . . . . NiB $1144 Ex $994 Gd $482
S-90 Supreme . . . . NiB $1490 Ex $1167 Gd $800
Grade I engraving, add $650
Grade II engraving, add $850
Grade III engraving add $1200
Grade IV engraving, add. $1717

MODEL 200 BOLT-ACTION RIFLES
Calibers: .243 Win., .25-06, .270 Win., 7mm Rem Mag., .30-06, .308 Win., .300 Win. Mag., Detachable box magazine.

24-inch (American) or 26-inch (European) interchangeable bbl. Standard (steel) or lightweight (alloy) action. Weight: 6.6 to 7.75 lbs. 44 inches overall. Stock options: American Model w/checkered Monte Carlo style 2-piece stock contrasting forend and pistol grip cap w/high gloss finish and no sights. European walnut stock w/Schnabel forend, satin oil finish and iron sights. Contemporary Model w/synthetic carbon fiber stock. Imported from 1986 to 1993.
Standard model. . . . . NiB $1266 Ex $1093 Gd $707
Lightweight model . . . . NiB $1278 Ex $1043 Gd $580
Contemporary model . . . . . . NiB $1260 Ex $1017 Gd $565
American model . . . . NiB $1260 Ex $1017 Gd $565
European model . . . . NiB $1395 Ex $1070 Gd $532
Left-hand model, add $200
Magnum calibers, add $130
Interchangeable barrel assembly, add. $325

MODEL 202 BOLT-ACTION RIFLES
Calibers: .243 Win., 6.5x55, 6.5x57, 6.6x68, .25-06, .270 Win., .280 7x64, .308, .30-06, Springfield, 7mm Rem. Mag., .300 Win. Mag., .300 Wby. Mag., 8x68S, .338 Win. Mag., .375 H&H Mag. Removable 3-round box magazine. 23.6- and 26-inch interchangable bbl. 44.3 and 46 inches overall. Modular receiver drilled and tapped for scope bases. Adjustable two-stage trigger w/dual release safety. Weight: 7.7 to 8.4 lbs. Stock options: Checkered Monte Carlo-style select American walnut two-piece stock; Euro-classic French walnut two-piece stock w/semi Schnabel forend and satin oil finish; Super Grade Claro walnut two-piece stock fitted w/rosewood forend and grip cap w/high-gloss epoxy finish. Imported from 1994 to 2004.
Standard model. . . . . NiB $2660 Ex $1848 Gd $983
Euro-Classic model . . . . NiB $1369 Ex $897 Gd $633
Super Grade model. . . . . NiB $1119 Ex $888 Gd $603
Left-hand model, add $150

Magnum calibers, add. $126
Interchangeable barrel assembly, add. $295

SAVAGE ARMS — Westfield, MA

Formerly Chicopee Falls, MA, and Utica, NY. Acquired by ATK in 2013.

NOTE: *Since J. Stevens Arms (see also separate listing) is a division of Savage Industries, certain Savage models carry the "Stevens" name.*

Savage Model 3

Savage Model 4

Savage Model 5

To facilitate locating Savage rifles, discontinued and current models are grouped into five categories: Bolt-action Rifles (below), Break-action Rifles, Lever-action Rifles, Semi-automatic Rifles, and Slide-Action Rifles. For complete model listings, please refer to the index.

- BOLT-ACTION RIFLES -

MODEL 1904 . . . . NiB $228 Ex $140 Gd $90
Bolt-action, single-shot. Takedown. .22 Short, Long, LR. 18-inch bbl. Weight: About 3 lbs. Sights: Open rear; bead front. Plain, straight-grip, one-piece stock. Made from 1904 to 1917.

MODEL 1905 . . . . NiB $220 Ex $138 Gd $85
Bolt-action, single-shot. Takedown. .22 Short, Long, LR. 22-inch bbl. Weight: About 5 lbs. Sights: Open rear; bead front. Plain, straight-grip one-piece stock. Made from 1905 to 1919.

**MODEL 3 BOLT-ACTION SINGLE-SHOT
RIFLE**. NiB $100 Ex $61 Gd $59
Takedown. Caliber: .22 Short, Long, LR. 26-inch bbl. on prewar rifles, postwar production w/24-inch bbl. Weight: 5 lbs. Sights: Open rear; bead front. Plain pistol-grip stock. Made 1933 to 1952.

MODEL 3S . . . . NiB $116 Ex $89 Gd $59
Same as Model 3 except w/peep rear sight, hooded front. Made 1933 to 1942.

MODEL 3ST . . . . NiB $120 Ex $85 Gd $50
Same as Model 3S except fitted w/swivels and sling. Made from 1933 to 1942.

**MODEL 4 BOLT-ACTION
REPEATER** . . . . NiB $149 Ex $90 Gd $59
Takedown. Caliber: .22 Short, Long, LR. Five round detachable box magazine. 24-inch bbl. Weight: 5.5 lbs. Sights: Open rear; bead front. Checkered pistol-grip stock on prewar models, early production had grooved forearm; postwar rifles have plain stocks. Made from 1933 to 1965.

MODEL 4M. . . . . NiB $121 Ex $87 Gd $64
Same as Model 4 except chambered for .22 Rimfire Magnum. Made from 1961 to 1965.

MODEL 4S . . . . NiB $130 Ex $78 Gd $47
Same as Model 4 except w/peep rear sight, hooded front. Made from 1933 to 1942.

MODEL 5 . . . . NiB $126 Ex $78 Gd $57
Same as Model 4 except w/tubular magazine (holds 21 Short, 17 Long, 15 LR), weight: 6 lbs. Made from 1936 to 1961.

MODEL 5S . . . . NiB $135 Ex $77 Gd $50
Same as Model 5 except w/peep rear sight, hooded front. Made 1936 to 1942.

MODEL 6 AUTOLOADING RIFLE . . . NiB $169 Ex $94 Gd $57
Takedown. Caliber: .22 Short, Long, LR. Tubular magazine holds 21 Short, 17 Long, 15 LR. 24-inch bbl. Weight: 6 lbs. Sights: Open rear; bead front. Checkered pistol-grip stock on prewar models, postwar rifles have plain stocks. Made from 1938 to 1968.

MODEL 6S . . . . NiB $170 Ex $95 Gd $48
Same as Model 6 except w/peep rear sight, bead front. Made 1938 to 1942.

MODEL 7 . . . . NiB $167 Ex $105 Gd $59
Same general specifications as Model 6 except w/5-round detachable box magazine. Made from 1939 to 1951.

MODEL 7S . . . . NiB $167 Ex $105 Gd $62
Same as Model 7 except w/peep rear sight, hooded front. Made from 1938 to 1942.

**MODEL 19 BOLT-ACTION
TARGET RIFLE**. . . . . NiB $325 Ex $270 Gd $209
Model of 1933. Speed lock. Caliber: .22 LR. Five round detachable box magazine. 25-inch bbl. Weight: 8 lbs. Adj. rear peep sight, blade front on early models, later production equipped w/extension rear sight, hooded front. Target stock w/full pistol-grip and beavertail forearm. Made 1933 to 1946.

**MODEL 19 NRA BOLT-ACTION
MATCH RIFLE**. . . . . NiB $300 Ex $205 Gd $126
Model of 1919. Caliber: .22 LR. Five round detachable box magazine. 25-inch bbl. Weight: 7 lbs. Sights: Adj. rear peep; blade front. Full military stock w/pistol-grip. Made from 1919 to 1933.

MODEL 19H. . . . . NiB $575 Ex $340 Gd $265
Same as standard Model 19 (1933) except chambered for .22 Hornet, w/Model 23D-type bolt mechanism, loading port and magazine. Made from 1933 to 1942.

MODEL 19L . . . . NiB $348 Ex $290 Gd $185
Same as standard Model 19 (1933) except equipped w/Lyman No. 48Y receiver sight, 17A front sight. Made from 1933 to 1942.

Savage Model 6

Savage Model 19 NRA (1933)

Savage Model 20

Savage Model 23AA

Savage Model 29

Savage Model 40

Savage Model 45

MODEL 19M . . . . NiB $356 Ex $465 Gd $227
Same as standard Model 19 (1933) except w/heavy 28-inch
bbl. w/scope bases, weight: 9.25 lbs. Made from 1933 to 1942.

MODEL 20-1926 HI-POWER . . NiB $944 Ex $725 Gd $420
Same as Model 1920, listed on page 354, except w/24-inch
medium weight bbl., improved stock, Lyman 54 rear peep
sight, weight: 7 lbs. Made from 1926 to 1929.

MODEL 23A . . . . NiB $270 Ex $208 Gd $177
Bolt-action. Caliber: 22 LR. Five round detachable box magazine. 23-inch bbl. Weight: 6 lbs. Sights: Open rear, blade
or bead front. Plain pistol-grip stock w/slender forearm and
Schnabel tip. Made 1923 to 1933.

MODEL 23AA . . . . NiB $370 Ex $278 Gd $200
Model of 1933. Improved version of Model 23A w/same
general specifications except w/speed lock, improved stock,
weighs 6.5 lbs. Made from 1933-42.

MODEL 23B . . . . NiB $333 Ex $235 Gd $179
Same as Model 23A except caliber .25-20, 25-inch bbl. Model of
1933 w/improved stock w/full forearm instead of slender forearm
w/Schnabel found on earlier production. Weight: 6.5 lbs. Made
from 1923 to 1942.

MODEL 23C . . . . NiB $389 Ex $290 Gd $175
Same as Model 23B except caliber .32-20. Made 1923 to
1942.

MODEL 23D . . . . NiB $415 Ex $300 Gd $220
Same as Model 23B except caliber .22 Hornet. Made 1933 to
1947.

MODEL 25
LIGHTWEIGHT VARMINTER . . NiB $772 Ex $640 Gd $580
Lightweight Varminter Series. Calibers: .17 Hornet, .22
Hornet, .204 Ruger or .223 Rem., 4-rnd detachable maga-
zine. 22- or 24-in. bbl. No sights, optic ready. Stock: laminate

GRADING: **NiB** = New in Box   **Ex** = Excellent or NRA 95%   **Gd** = Good or NRA 68%

Savage Model 60

wood. Finish: matte blue. Wieght: 8.25 lbs. Length: 43.75 in. Accutrigger. Made 2008 to date.
Varminter-T (thumbhole stock) NiB $824 Ex $690 Gd $580

MODEL 25
WALKING VARMINTER . . . . . . NiB $772 Ex $640 Gd $580
Lightweight Varminter Series. Similar to Lightweight Varminter except w/black synthetic stock. Made 2011 to date.
Camo stock (RealTree Extra or Realtree Max 1), add . . . $50

MODEL 35 . . . . NiB $90 Ex $80 Gd $70
Bolt-action. Caliber: .22 LR, 5-rnd. magazine. 22-inch bbl. Discontinued 1985.

MODEL 36 . . . . NiB $90 Ex $80 Gd $70
Simialr to Model 35 except single-shot. 22-inch bbl. Made 1983 to 1984.

MODEL 40 . . . . NiB $379 Ex $280 Gd $227
Bolt-action. Standard Grade. Calibers: .250-3000, .300 Sav., .30-30, .30-06. Four round detachable box magazine. 22-inch bbl. in calibers .250-3000 and .30-30; 24-inch in .300 Sav. and .30-06. Weight: 7.5 lbs. Sights: Open rear; bead front, on ramp. Plain pistol-grip stock w/tapered forearm and Schnabel tip. Made 1928 to 1940.

MODEL 45 SUPER SPORTER . . NiB $423 Ex $265 Gd $220
Special Grade. Same as Model 40 except w/checkered pistol-grip and forearm, Lyman No. 40 receiver sight. Made 1928 to 1940.

MODEL 46 . . . . NiB $90 Ex $80 Gd $70
Simialr to Model 35 except w/tubular magazine. Made 1969 to 1973.

MODEL 63K KEY LOCK BOLT-ACTION
SINGLE-SHOT RIFLE. . . . . NiB $120 Ex $90 Gd $60
Trigger locked w/key. Caliber: .22 Short, Long, LR. 18-inch bbl. Weight: 4 lbs. Sights: Open rear; hooded ramp front. Full-length stock w/pistol grip, swivels. Made from 1970 to 1972.

MODEL 63KM . . . . NiB $126 Ex $98 Gd $63
Same as Model 63K except chambered for .22 WMR. Made 1970 to 1972.

MODEL 93G BOLT-ACTION
RIFLE. NiB $227 Ex $166 Gd $126
Caliber: .22 Win Mag. 5-round magazine. 20.75-inch bbl. 39.5 inches overall. Weight: 5.75 lbs. Sights: Adj. open rear; bead front. Grooved receiver for scope mounts. Stamped checkering on walnut-finished hardwood stock w/Monte Carlo cheekpiece. Made from 1996 to date.

MODEL 93F BOLT-ACTION
RIFLE. NiB $277 Ex $124 Gd $110
Same general specifications as Model 93G except w/black graphite/polymer stock. Weight: 5.2 lbs. Made from 1997 to date.

MODEL 1920 HI-POWER BOLT-ACTION RIFLE
Short Mauser-type action. Calibers: .250/3000, .300 Sav. Five round box magazine. 22-inch bbl. in .250 cal.; 24-inch in .300 cal. Weight: About 6 lbs. Sights: Open rear; bead front. Checkered pistol-grip stock w/slender forearm and Schnabel tip. Made from 1920 to 1926.
.250-3000 Savage . . . . NiB $1029 Ex $833 Gd $690
.300 Savage. . . . . NiB $969 Ex $755 Gd $588

NOTE: *Anschutz In 1965, Savage began the importation of rifles manufactured by J. G. Anschutz GmbH, Ulm, West Germany. Models designated "Savage/Anschutz" are listed in this section, those marketed in the U.S. under the "Anschutz" name are included in that firm's listings. Anschutz rifles are now distributed in the U.S. by Precision Sales Int'l., Westfield, Mass. See "Anschutz" for detailed specifications.*

MARK 10 BOLT-ACTION
TARGET RIFLE. . . . . NiB $534 Ex $359 Gd $265
Single shot. Caliber: .22 LR. 26-inch bbl. Weight: 8.5 lbs. Sights: Anschutz micrometer rear; globe front. Target stock w/full pistol-grip and cheekpiece, adj. hand stop and swivel. Made 1967 to 1972.

MARK 10D. . . . . NiB $544 Ex $369 Gd $259
Same as Mark 10 except has redesigned stock with Monte Carlo comb, different rear sight. Weight: 7.75 lbs. Made in 1972.

MODEL 54 CUSTOM SPORTER NiB $766 Ex $639 Gd $400
Same as Anschutz Model 1422D.

MODEL 54M. . . . . NiB $945 Ex $670 Gd $439
Same as Anschutz Model 1522D.

MODEL 64 BOLT-ACTION
TARGET. . . . . NiB $655 Ex $512 Gd $338
Same as Anschutz Model 1403.

MODEL 153 BOLT-ACTION
SPORTER. . . . . NiB $697 Ex $488 Gd $349
Caliber: .222 Rem. Three round clip magazine. 24-inch bbl. Sights: Folding leaf open rear; hooded ramp front. Weight: 6.75 lbs. French walnut stock w/cheekpiece, skip checkering, rosewood forend tip and grip cap, swivels. Made from 1964 to 1967.

MODEL 153S . . . . NiB $770 Ex $556 Gd $390
Same as Model 153 except has double-set trigger. Made 1965 to 1967.

MODEL 164 CUST. SPORTER. NiB $775 Ex $561 Gd $195
Same as Anschutz Model 1416.

MODEL 164M. . . . . NiB $660 Ex $454 Gd $300
Same as Anschutz Model 1516.

MODEL 184 SPORTER . . . . NiB $638 Ex $484 Gd $288
Same as Anschutz Model 1441.

Savage Model 71 "Stevens Favorite"

Savage Model 90

Savage Model 99A 1971 Issue

Savage Model 99C

Savage Model 99CD

Savage Model 99DE

front. Monte Carlo stock w/checkered pistol grip and forearm. Made from 1982 to 1985.

MODEL 35M . . . . **NiB $219 Ex $140 Gd $100**
Same as Model 35 except chambered for .22 WMR. Made 1982 to 1985.

MODEL 46 . . . . **NiB $190 Ex $136 Gd $100**
Bolt-action. Caliber: .22 Short, Long, LR. Tubular magazine holds 22 Short, 17 Long, 15 LR. 20-inch bbl. Weight: 5 lbs. Plain pistol-grip stock on early production; later models have Monte Carlo stock w/checkering. Made from 1969 to 1073.

MODEL 65 . . . . **NiB $219 Ex $138 Gd $99**
Bolt-action. Caliber: .22 Short, Long, LR. Five round clip magazine. 20-inch bbl. Weight: 5 lbs. Sights: Open rear; ramp front. Monte Carlo stock w/checkered pistol grip and forearm. Made from 1969 to 1973.

**MODEL 34 BOLT-ACTION
REPEATER** . . . . **NiB $190 Ex $126 Gd $88**
Caliber: .22 Short, Long, LR. 20-inch bbl. Weight: 4.75 lbs. Sights: Open rear; bead front. Plain pistol-grip stock. Made 1965 to 1980.

MODEL 34M. . . . . **NiB $190 Ex $146 Gd $98**
Same as Model 34 except chambered for 22 WMR. Made 1969 to 1973.

MODEL 35 . . . . **NiB $190 Ex $146 Gd $98**
Bolt-action repeater. Caliber: 22 LR. Six round clip magazine. 22-inch bbl. Weight: About 5 lbs. Sights: Open rear; ramp

MODEL 65M. . . . . NiB $200 Ex $134 Gd $90
Same as Model 65 except chambered for .22 WMR, has 22-inch bbl., weighs 5.25 lbs. Made from 1969 to 1981.

**MODEL 73 BOLT-ACTION
SINGLE-SHOT.** . . . . NiB $159 Ex $138 Gd $89
Caliber: .22 Short, Long, LR. 20-inch bbl. Weight: 4.75 lbs. Sights: Open rear; bead front. Plain pistol-grip stock. Made 1965 to 1980.

MODEL 73Y YOUTH MODEL. . . NiB $150 Ex $110 Gd $90
Same as Model 73 except has 18-inch bbl., 1.5-inch shorter buttstock, weight: 4.5 lbs. Made from 1965 to 1980.

MODEL 74 LITTLE FAVORITE. . . NiB $167 Ex $115 Gd $98
Same as Model 72 Crackshot except has black-finished frame, 22-inch round bbl., walnut-finished hardwood stock. Weight: 4.75 lbs. Made from 1972 to 1974.

MODEL 93 BRJ . . . . NiB $542 Ex $520 Gd $485
Similar to Model 93 F series except w/21-in. spiral fluted bbl. Weight: 7 lbs. Stock: laminated wood. Blued finish. Made from 2010 to date.
**93 BSEV (stainless, laminate
    thumbhole stock)** . . . . NiB $646 Ex $620 Gd $590
**93 BTVSS (stainless, laminate
    thumbhole stock)** . . . . NiB $525 Ex $500 Gd $485

MODEL 93 CLASSIC MAGNUM . . NiB $590 Ex $430 Gd $370
Similar to Model 93 F series except w/24-in. bbl., w/ aperature or w/o sights. High luster blued finish. Made from 2008 to 2010.

MODEL 93 F . . . . NiB $259 Ex $230 Gd $185
Bolt-action. Caliber: .22 WMR, 5-rnd. magazine. 21-in. bbl. Weight: 5 lbs. Sights: optic ready. Stock: black synthetic. AccuTrigger added 2006. Made from 1996 to date.
Camo (synthetic stock, new 2002), add $100
93 FSS (stainless, new 1997). . . NiB $346 Ex $320 Gd $190
93 FV (heavy varmint bbl.), add $70
**93 FV-SR (16.5-in. heavy bbl., suppressor ready, optic
    ready, no sights, new 2014)** NiB $368 Ex $340 Gd $310
**93 FV-SR Landry (gator camo stock,
    new 2015)** . . . . NiB $424 Ex $400 Gd $385
93 FVSS (heavy varmint bbl., stainless), add. $100

MODEL 93R17 F. . . . . NiB $268 Ex $240 Gd $195
Similar to Model 93 F except in .17 HMR. Made from 2003 to date.
93R17 FSS (stainless) . . . . NiB $334 Ex $310 Gd $300
93R17 FV (heavy varmint bbl.), add $40
**93R17 FV-SR (16.5-in. heavy bbl., suppressor ready, optic
    ready, no sights).** . . . . NiB $368 Ex $340 Gd $310
93R17 FVSS (heavy varmint bbl., stainless), add. $100

MODEL 93R17 GV . . . . NiB $299 Ex $240 Gd $200
Similar to Model 93R17 F except w/high luster wood stock. Made from 2003 to date.
93R17 GLV (left hand), add $10

MODEL 93R17 TR. . . . . NiB $558 Ex $540 Gd $500
Simialr to Model 93R17 F except 22-in. fluted bbl. Stock: wood tactical style. Weight: 7.5 lbs. Made 2010 to date.
93R17 TRR-SR (additional Picatinny rails), add $100

NOTE: *The Model 110 series was first produced in 1958 and continues production to date with a variety of engineering and cosmetic changes along the way. The series uses a push-feed bolt-action. Recent changes include Savage logo etched on bolt (1994),*

pillar bedded stocks (1996), AccuTrigger (2003), left-hand ejection port with target actions (2007), Accustock (2009), dual port action (2009), stainless steel only target actions (2010). Model 10 rifles are short action rifles, Model 110 are long actions rifles. The Model 10/110 action is used with Model 11/111, 12/112, 14/114 and 16/116 models with differences as noted. Numerous Package models are fitted with factory mounted scopes.

MODEL 10 PRECISION CARBINE . . NiB $960 Ex $820 Gd $680
Calibers: .223, .308 or .300 AAC BLK., 4-rnd. detachable magazine. 20-in. bbl. w/ or w/o threaded muzzle. Weight: 7 lbs. Optic ready. Stock: camo Accustock. Oversized bolt handle. Made 2009 to 2015.

MODEL 10 PREDATOR HUNTER. . . NiB $999 Ex $850 Gd $700
Calibers: .204 Ruger, .22-250 Rem., .223 Rem., .243 Win., .260 Rem., 6.5 Creedmoor, or 6.5x285 Norma, detachable magazine. 22- or 24-in. bbl. Weight: 7.25 lbs. Optic ready. Stock: laminate or Accustock. Finish: Mossy Oak Brush, Snow or RealTree Max 1. Made 2007 to date.

MODEL 10BA . . . . NiB $2446 Ex $2100 Gd $1500
Law Enforcement Series. Calibers: .308 only, 10-rnd. detachable magazine. 24-in. bbl. w/muzzle brake. Weight: 13.4 lbs. Sights: optic ready. Stock: aluminum chassis w/Magpul PRS-G3 stock. Made 2009 to date.
**10BAT/S-K (adj. tactical stock, made 2009
    to 2013)** . . . . NiB $1750 Ex $1500 Gd $1200

**MODEL 10/110FCP
H-S PRECISION** . . . . NiB $1315 Ex $1100 Gd $930
Law Enforcement Series. Model 10 Calibers: .308 Win.; Model 110 Calibers: .300 Win. Mag. or .338 Lapua Mag. 4-rnd detachable magazine. 24- or 26-in. bbl. w/muzzle brake. 44.5-49.5 in. overall. Weight: 9-10.7 lbs. Stock: H-S Precision fiberglass. Matte black finish. Made from 2007 to date.

MODEL 10FCP MCMILLAN . . . . NiB $1591 Ex $1350 Gd $1030
SImilar to Model 10/110FCP H-S Precision except .308 Win. only and McMillian fiberglass stock. Made from 2007 to date.

MODEL 10FCP-K . . . . NiB $850 Ex $730 Gd $600
SImilar to Model 10/110FCP H-S Precision except .223 Rem. or .308 Win. only. Stock: Accustock. Made from 2009 to 2013.
10FLP-K (left hand) . . . . NiB $850 Ex $730 Gd $600

MODEL 10FCP-SR . . . . NiB $761 Ex $700 Gd $670
SImilar to Model 10/110FCP except .308 Win. only, 10-rnd detachable magazine. Suppressor ready. Stock: Accustock. Oversized bolt handle. Made from 2015 to date.
10FLCP-SR (left hand) . . . . NiB $761 Ex $700 Gd $670

MODEL 10FCM SCOUT . . . . . . NiB $730 Ex $580 Gd $460
Calibers: 7.62x39mm, .308 or 7mm-08, 4-rnd. detachable magazine. 20-in.bbl. Weight: 6.1 lbs. Sights: ghost ring/optic ready. Stock: black synthetic. Matte blue finish. Accustock standard in 2009. Made 1999 to 2003, reintro. 2007 to 2013.

MODEL 10FCM . . . . NiB $376 Ex $336 Gd $244
Calibers: .243 Win., .270 WSM, .300 WSM, .308 Win. or 7mm-08; Detachable magazine. 20-inch bbl. 41.5 inches overall. Weight: 6.25 lbs. No sights, drilled and tapped. Black graphite/fiberglass composition stock. Non-glare matte blue finish. Made 2005 to 2006.

MODEL 10FP POLICE RIFLE. . . NiB $630 Ex $510 Gd $430
Law Enforcement Series. Calibers: .223 or .308 Win., 4-rnd. interna box magazine. 20 or 24-in. heavy, free float bbl.

Savage Model 99E 1969 Issue

Savage Model 99EG (Post WWII)

Savage Model 99F

Savage Model 99G

Savage Model 99PE Early Issue

Savage Model 99PE Late Issue

Weight: 6.25 lbs. Stock: McMillian synthetic sporter style. No sights, optic read. Oversized bolt handle. Matte blue finish. Made from 1998 to 2010.

10FP Duty (open sights,
2002 only) . . . . **NiB $440 Ex $360 Gd $570**
10FP-SR (supressor ready,
2011-2013) . . . . **NiB $630 Ex $510 Gd $430**
10FLP (left hand) . . . . **NiB $630 Ex $510 Gd $430**
10FPCPXP (Burris or Leupold scope,
Harris bipod, 2002-2009) NiB $2300 Ex $1900 Gd $1600

MODEL 10GY . . . . **NiB $540 Ex $460 Gd $350**
Ladies/Youth series. Calibers: .223 Rem., .243 Win. or .308 Win., 22-in. bbl. Open sights. Discontinued 2007.
10GYXP3 Package (scope, bipod), add $70

MODEL 10GXP3 PACKAGE . . . **NiB $720 Ex $530 Gd $420**
Package series. Various short action calibers. 22- or 24-in. bbl. Stock: checkered wood. Factory mounted scope. Discontinued 2011.

MODEL 10/110 TROPHY
HUNTER XP PACKAGE . . . . **NiB $620 Ex $780 Gd $690**
Calibers: .22-250 Rem., .223 Rem., .243 Win., .270 Win., .308 Win., .30-06, .300 Win. Mag. or 7mm Rem. Mag., detachable magazine. 22- or 24-in. bbl. Weight: 8.3-9.3 lbs. Weaver 3-9x40 scope. Stock: satin wood. Finish: matte black. Current manufacture.

MODEL 110 . . . . **NiB $420 Ex $333 Gd $155**
Bolt-action. Calibers: .243, .270, .308, .30-06. 4-rnd. box magazine. 22-inch bbl. Weight: About 6.75 lbs. Sights: Open rear; ramp front. Standard sporter stock with checkered pistol-grip. Made 1958 to 1963.

MODEL 110B
Same as Model 110E except with checkered select walnut Monte Carlo-style stock (early models) or brown laminated stock (late models). Calibers: .243 Win., .270 Win. .30-06, 7mm Rem. Mag., .338 Win. Mag. Made from 1976 to 1991.
Early model . . . . **NiB $423 Ex $303 Gd $227**
Laminated stock model . . . . **NiB $367 Ex $299 Gd $211**

MODEL 110BA . . . . **NiB $2638 Ex $2200 Gd $1900**
Law Enforcement Series. Simialr to 10BA except in .300 Win. Mag. or .338 Lapua Mag. calibers. 26-in.bbl. w/muzzle brake. Weight: 15.75 lbs. Made 2009 to date.

Savage Model 99R (Pre-WWII)

Savage Model 99R (Post-WWII)

Savage Model 99RS (Pre-WWII)

Savage Model 99T

Savage Model 110B

MODEL 110BL . . . .**NiB $439 Ex $369 Gd $269**
Same as Model 110B except has left-hand action.

MODEL 110C
Calibers: .22-250, .243, .25-06, .270, .308, .30-06, 7mm Rem. Mag., .300 Win. Mag. Four round detachable clip magazine (3-round in Magnum calibers). 22-inch bbl. (24-inch in .22-250 Magnum calibers). Weight: 6.75 lbs., Magnum, 7.75 to 8 lbs. Sights: Open rear; ramp front. Checkered Monte Carlo-style walnut stock (Magnum has recoil pad). Made from 1966 to 1988.
Standard calibers . . . . .NiB $468 Ex $413 Gd $239
Magnum calibers . . . . .NiB $639 Ex $455 Gd $279

MODEL 110CL
Same as Model 110C except has left-hand action. (Available only in .243 Win., .30-06, .270 Win. and 7mm Mag.) Made 1963 to 1966.
Standard calibers . . . . .NiB $488 Ex $369 Gd $262
Magnum calibers . . . . .NiB $459 Ex $350 Gd $255

MODEL 110CY YOUTH/LADIES
RIFLE. . . . . .NiB $466 Ex $379 Gd $228

Same as Model 110G except w/walnut-finished hardwood stock and 12.5-inch LOP. Calibers: .243 Win. and .300 Savage. Made 1991 - 2009.

MODEL 110D
Similar to Model 110C except has internal magazine with hinged floorplate. Calibers: .243 Win., .270 Win., .30-06, 7mm Rem. Mag., .300 Win. Mag. Made from 1972 to 1988.
Standard calibers . . . . .NiB $390 Ex $310 Gd $240
Magnum calibers . . . . .NiB $453 Ex $390 Gd $259

MODEL 110DL
Same as Model 110D except has left-hand action. Discontinued.
Standard calibers . . . . .NiB $500 Ex $413 Gd $297
Magnum calibers . . . . .NiB $535 Ex $430 Gd $319

MODEL 110E . . . . .NiB $379 Ex $255 Gd $198
Calibers: .22-250, .223 Rem., .243 Win., .270 Win., .308, 7mm Rem. Mag., .30-06. Four round box magazine (3-round in Magnum). 20- or 22-inch bbl. (24-inch stainless steel in Magnum). Weight: 6.75 lbs.; Magnum, 7.75 lbs. Sights: Open rear; ramp front. Plain Monte Carlo stock on early production; current models have checkered stocks of walnut-finished hardwood (Magnum has recoil pad). Made 1963 to 1989.

MODEL 110EL . . . . NiB $370 Ex $248 Gd $185
Same as Model 110E except has left-hand action made in .30-06 and 7mm Rem. Mag. only. Made from 1969 to 1973.

MODEL 110F/110K BOLT-ACTION RIFLE
Same as Model 110E except Model 110F has black Rynite synthetic stock, swivel studs; made 1988 to 1993. Model 110K has laminated camouflage stock; made from 1986 to 1988.
adj. sights . . . . NiB $770 Ex $470 Gd $359
w/out sights . . . . NiB $735 Ex $355 Gd $277
Standard calibers . . . . NiB $355 Ex $320 Gd $256
Magnum calibers . . . . NiB $520 Ex $399 Gd $287

**MODEL 10/110FM SIERRA ULTRA
LIGHT** . . . . NiB $376 Ex $336 Gd $244
Calibers: .243 Win., .270 Win., .30-06, .308 Win. Five round magazine. 20-inch bbl. 41.5 inches overall. Weight: 6.25 lbs. No sights w/drilled and tapped receiver. Black graphite/fiberglass composition stock. Non-glare matte blue finish. Made 1996 to 2004.

**MODEL 10/110FP POLICE
RIFLE** . . . . NiB $610 Ex $355 Gd $265
Law Enforcement Series. Model 10 Calibers: .223 or .308 Win.; Model 110 Calibers: .26-06, .30-06, .300 Win. Mag. or 7mm Rem. Mag. Four round magazine. 24-inch bbl. 45.5 inches overall. Weight: 9 lbs. Black Rynite composite stock. Matte blue finish. Made from 1990 to date.

MODEL 10/110FCM . . . . NiB $376 Ex $336 Gd $244
Model 10 Calibers: .243 Win., .270 WSM, .300 WSM, .308 Win. or 7mm-08; Model 110 Calibers: .270 Win., .30-06, .308 Win. Five round magazine. 20-inch bbl. 41.5 inches overall. Weight: 6.25 lbs. No sights w/drilled and tapped receiver. Black graphite/fiberglass composition stock. Non-glare matte blue finish. Made 1996 to 2004.

MODEL 110G BOLT-ACTION RIFLE
Calibers: .223, .22-250, .243 Win., .270, 7mm Rem. Mag., .308 Win., .30-06, .300 Win. Mag. Five round (standard) or 4-round magazine (magnum). 22- or 24-inch bbl. 42.38 overall (standard). Weight: 6.75 to 7.5 lbs. Ramp front sight, adj. rear. Checkered walnut-finished hardwood stock with rubber recoil pad. Made from 1989 to 1993.
Standard calibers . . . . NiB $408 Ex $309 Gd $220
Magnum calibers . . . . NiB $455 Ex $338 Gd $259
Left-hand, no sights. . . . . NiB $355 Ex $369 Gd $271

**MODEL 110GV VARMINT
RIFLE.** . . . . NiB $369 Ex $338 Gd $268
Similar to the Model 110G except fitted with medium-weight varmint bbl. with no sights. Receiver drilled and tapped for scope mounts. Calibers .22-250 and .223 only. Made 1989-93.

MAGNUM 110M MAGNUM . . NiB $445 Ex $345 Gd $269
Same as Model 110MC except calibers: 7mm Rem. Mag. .264, .300 and .338 Win. 24-inch bbl. Stock with recoil pad. Weight: 7.75 to 8 lbs. Made from 1963 to 1969.

MODEL 110MC . . . . NiB $444 Ex $229 Gd $149
Same as Model 110 except has Monte Carlo-style stock. Calibers: .22-250, .243 Win., .270, .308, .30-06. 24-inch bbl. in .22-250. Made from 1959 to 1969.
Model 110MCL . . . . NiB $400 Ex $215 Gd $135

MODEL 110P PREMIER GRADE
Calibers: .243 Win., 7mm Rem. Mag., .30-06. Four round magazine (3-round in Magnum). 22-inch bbl. (24-inch stainless

steel in Magnum). Weight: 7 lbs.; Magnum, 7.75 lbs. Sights: Open rear folding leaf; ramp front. French walnut stock w/ Monte Carlo comb and cheekpiece, rosewood forend tip and pistol-grip cap, skip checkering, sling swivels (Magnum has recoil pad). Made 1964 to 1970.
Calibers .243 Win. and .30-06 . NiB $798 Ex $645 Gd $459
Caliber 7mm Rem. Mag . . . . . . NiB $945 Ex $765 Gd $545

MODEL 110PE PRESENTATION GRADE
Same as Model 110P except has engraved receiver, floorplate and trigger guard, stock of choice grade French walnut. Made 1968 to 1970.
Calibers .243 Win. and .30-06 . NiB $555 Ex $441 Gd $290
Caliber 7mm Rem. Mag . . . . . . NiB $600 Ex $455 Gd $347

MODEL 110PEL PRESENTATION GRADE
Same as Model 110PE except has left-hand action.
Calibers .243 Win. and .30-06 . NiB $807 Ex $654 Gd $458
Caliber 7mm Rem. Mag . . . . . . NiB $879 Ex $710 Gd $496

MODEL 110PL PREMIER GRADE
Same as Model 110P except has left-hand action.
Calibers .243 Win. and .30-06 . NiB $528 Ex $401 Gd $271
Caliber 7mm Rem. Mag . . . . . . NiB $549 Ex $401 Gd $293

MODEL 110S/110V
Same as Model 110E except Model 110S in .308 Win. only; discontinued 1985. Model 110V in .22-250 and .223 Rem. w/heavy 2-inch barrel, 47 inches overall, weight: 9 lbs. Discontinued 1989.
Model 110S. . . . . NiB $397 Ex $315 Gd $240
Model 110V . . . . NiB $416 Ex $322 Gd $248

MODEL 11/111 HOG HUNTER . . NiB $578 Ex $480 Gd $350
Specialty Series. Calibers: .223 Rem., .308 Win., or .338 Fed.; 4-rnd. internal magazine. 20-in. threaded bbl. Weight: 6 lbs. Sights: no sights, optic ready. Stock: matte wood. Matte black finish. Accutrigger. Made from 2012 to date.

MODEL 11/111 LADY HUNTER . . NiB $899 Ex $480 Gd $350
Specialty Series. Calibers: .223 Rem., .243 Win., 6.5 Creedmoor, .308 Win., 7mm-08 or .30-06; 4-rnd. detachable magazine. 20-in. mediun contour threaded bbl. Weight: 7.25 lbs. Sights: open sights, optic ready. Stock: green synthetic sporter. Matte black finish. Accutrigger. Made from 2012 to date.

**MODEL 11/111 LIGHTWEIGHT
HUNTER** . . . . NiB $991 Ex $830 Gd $690
Specialty Series. Calibers: .223 Rem., .243 Win., .260 Rem., 6.5 Creedmoor, .308 Win., 7mm-08 or .30-06; 4-rnd. detachable magazine. 20-in. bbl. Weight: 5.5 lbs. Sights: no sights, optic ready. Stock: wood sporter. Matte black finish. Accutrigger. Spiral fluted bolt, lightening cuts in receiver and stock. Made from 2011 to date.

**MODEL 11/111 LONG RANGE
HUNTER** . . . . NiB $1136 Ex $960 Gd $780
Specialty Series. Calibers: .260 Rem., 6.5 Creedmoor, 6.5x284 Norma, .308 Win., .300 WSM. .300 Win. Mag., 7mm Rem. Mag., .338 Fed. or .338 Lapua Mag. Internal or detachable magazine. 26-in. bbl. w/ muzzle brake. Weight: 8.4-9.25 lbs. Sights: no sights, optic ready. Stock: Accustock w/ adj. cheek riser. Matte black finish. Accutrigger. Made from 2011 to date.
.338 Lapua Mag., add $240

**MODEL 11F/111F
(11FNS/111FNS)** . . . . NiB $610 Ex $480 Gd $350
Model 11F Calibers: .22-250 Rem., .223 Rem., .243 Win., .260 Rem., .270 WSM, .308 Win., .300 RSUM, .300 WSM,

Savage Model 110BL

Savage Model 110C

Savage Model 110E

Savage Model 110 MCL

Savage Model 110P

Savage Model 110PE

7mm RSUM, 7mm WSM, 7mm-08; Model 111F Calibers: .270 Win., 7x57mm, 7mm Rem. Mag. .30-06. 3- or 4-rnd. internal or detacable magazine. 22-, 24, or 26-in. bbl. (26-in. in 111F). Weight: 6.5-6.75 lbs. Sights: optic ready. Stock: synthetic. Blued finish. Made from 1998 to 2011.

MODEL 11FCNS/111FCNS ... NiB $610 Ex $480 Gd $350
Similar to models 11F/111F except w/Accustock or pillar bedded synthetic stock, Accutrigger. Made from 1999 to 2001; reintro. 2003 to 2015.

MODEL 11G/111G
(11GNS/111GNS) .... NiB $700 Ex $510 Gd $420
Similar to models 11F/111F except wood stock w/pressed checkering. Blued finish. Made from 1998 to 2011.

MODEL 111 CHIEFTAIN BOLT-ACTION RIFLE
Calibers: .243 Win., .270 Win., 7x57mm, 7mm Rem. Mag. .30-06. 4-round clip magazine (3-round in Magnum). 22-inch

bbl. (24-inch in Magnum). Weight: 7.5 lbs., 8.25 lbs. Magnum. Sights: Leaf rear; hooded ramp front. Select walnut stock w/ Monte Carlo comb and cheekpiece, checkered, pistol-grip cap, QD swivels and sling. Made from 1974 to 1979.

Standard calibers .... NiB $444 Ex $389 Gd $259
Magnum calibers .... NiB $445 Ex $398 Gd $279

MODEL 111F, 111FC, 111FNS CLASSIC HUNTER RIFLE
Similar to the Model 111G except with graphite/fiberglass composite stock. Weight: 6.25 lbs. Made from 1994 to date.

Model 111F (right- or left-hand
w/box mag.) .... NiB $498 Ex $411 Gd $238
Model 111FC
(w/detachable mag.) ...... NiB $448 Ex $338 Gd $206
Model 111FNS (right- or left-hand
w/detachable mag.) .... NiB $469 Ex $355 Gd $228

MODEL 111G, 111GC, 111GNS CLASSIC HUNTER RIFLE
Calibers: .22-250 Rem., .223 Rem., .243 Win., .25-06 Rem. .250 Sav., .270 Win., 7mm-08 Rem., 7mm Rem. Mag., .30-06, .300 Sav., .300 Win. Mag., .308 Win., .338 Win. 22- or 24-inch bbl. Weight: 7 lbs. Ramp front sight, adj. open rear.

Savage Model 111 Chieftain

Savage Model 111F

Savage Model 112V

Savage Model 116FCSAK

Walnut-finished hardwood stock. Blued finish. Made from 1994 to date.

Model 111G (right- or left-hand
w/box mag.) . . . . **NiB $369 Ex $298 Gd $210**
Model 111GC (right- or left-hand
w/ detachable mag.) . . . . **NiB $465 Ex $358 Gd $227**
Model 111GNS (w box mag.,
no sights) . . . . **NiB $370 Ex $300 Gd $198**

MODEL 12 BENCHREST . . . **NiB $1678 Ex $1480 Gd $1260**
Target Series. Calibers: 6 Norma BR, 6.5x284 Norma or .308 Win., single shot. 29-in. heavy bbl. Wood laminate stock. Matte stainless finish. No sights, optic ready. Accutrigger. Weight: 12.75 lbs. Length: 49 in. Made from 2009 to date.

MODEL 12 F CLASS . . . . . . **NiB $1648 Ex $1450 Gd $1230**
Target Series. Similar to Model 12 Benchrest except in 6 Norma BR or 6.5x284 Norma only. 30-in. heavy bbl. Weight: 13.3 lbs. Length: 50 in. Left load port, right eject action. Made from 2009 to date.

MODEL 12 F/TR . . . . **NiB $1648 Ex $1450 Gd $1230**
Target Series. Similar to Model 12 Benchrest except in .223 Rem. or .308 Win. only. 30-in. heavy bbl. Weight: 12.65 lbs. Length: 50 in. Made from 2007 to date.

MODEL 12 LONG RANGE
PRECISION . . . . **NiB $1252 Ex $1050 Gd $890**
Target Series. Calibers: .243 Win., .260 Rem. or 6.5 Creedmoor, 4-rnd. detachable magazine. 26-in. heavy, fluted bbl. H-S Precision fiberglass stock. Blued. No sights, optic ready. Accutrigger. Weight: 11 lbs. Length: 46.25 in. Made from 2011 to date.

MODEL 12 PALMA . . . . . . **NiB $2147 Ex $1850 Gd $1630**
Target Series. Similar to Model 12 Benchrest except in .308 Win. only. 30-in. heavy bbl. Weight: 12.65 lbs. Length: 49.75

in. Stock: laminated wood, veted forend, adj. comb and LOP. Made from 2009 to date.

MODEL 12 VARMINT LOW
PROFILE . . . . **NiB $1146 Ex $960 Gd $770**
Varmint Series. Similar to Model 12BVSS/112BVSS except w/ smaller left-side ejection port. Made from 2004 to date.

MODEL 112BV, 12BVSS/112BVSS, 12BVSS-S/112BVSS-S
Varmint Series. Right bolt, left port ejection. Model 12 calibers: .204 Ruger, .22-250 Rem., .223 Rem., .243 Win., .300 WSM or .308 Win., 4-rnd. internal magazine. Model 112 calibers: .22-250 Rem., .223 Rem., .2506, .30-06, .308 Win., .300 Win. Mag. or 7mm Rem. Mag. 26-inch heavy fluted bbl. Laminated wood stock. Weight: 10 lbs. Length: 46.25 in. Accutrigger standard 2003. Made 1993 to date.

Model 112BV (Made 1993-94) NiB $520 Ex $378 Gd $266
Model 112BVSS (w/fluted stainless
bbl., intro. 1994) . . . . **NiB $556 Ex $422 Gd $315**
Model 12BVSS-S (stainless finish,
single-shot, 2002-2005) . . . . **NiB $721 Ex $610 Gd $495**
Model 112BVSS-S (stainless finish,
single-shot, 1994-2001) . . . . **NiB $595 Ex $520 Gd $430**
Model 112BT Cometition Grade (black stainless finish, .223
or .308, five-shot, 1994-2001) . . **NiB $595 Ex $520 Gd $430**
Model 12BTCSS (stainless finish, .204 Ruger,
.22-250 or .223, thumb hole stock,
2008-present) . . . . **NiB $595 Ex $520 Gd $430**
Model 112BT-S Cometition Grade (black stainless
finish, .300 Win. Mag., five-shot,
1995-2001) . . . . **NiB $595 Ex $520 Gd $430**

MODEL 12FV/112FV, 12FVSS/112FVSS, 12FVSS-S/112FVSS-S
Varmint Series. Similar to models 12BVSS/112BVSS except w/ blued finish, black synthetic stock, 9 lbs. Made from 1993 to date.
Model 12FV . . . . **NiB $732 Ex $620 Gd $480**
Model 12FVY (youth) . . . . **NiB $732 Ex $620 Gd $480**

Savage Model 219

Savage Model 219L

Model 12FVSS (stainless finish,
1998-2012).............**NiB $895   Ex $700   Gd $610**
Model 12FVSS-S (stainless finish,
single-shot, 1998-2001) .... **NiB $550   Ex $490   Gd $398**
Model 112FV (1991-1998) .... **NiB $410   Ex $380   Gd $360**
Model 112FV-S (single-shot,
1992-1993).............**NiB $410   Ex $380   Gd $360**
Model 112FVSS (stainless finish,
1993-2002).............**NiB $569   Ex $500   Gd $430**
Model 112FVSS-S (stainless finish,
single-shot, 1994-2001) .... **NiB $550   Ex $490   Gd $398**

MODEL 12FCV ....**NiB $781   Ex $590   Gd $300**
Varmint Series. Caliber: .204 Ruger, .223 Rem. or .22-250,
4-rnd. detachable box. 26-in. heavy bbl. Drlled and tapped.
Weight: 9 lbs. Stock: synthetic. Accutrigger. Made from 2015
to date.

MODEL 112V VARMINT RIFLE ...**NiB $389   Ex $289   Gd $200**
Bolt action, single shot. Caliber: .220 Swift, .222 Rem., .223
Rem., .22-250, .243 Win., .25-06. 26-inch heavy bbl. with
scope bases. Supplied w/o sights. Weight: 9.25 lbs. Select wal-
nut stock in varmint style w/checkered pistol-grip, high comb,
QD sling swivels. Made from 1975 to 1979.

MODEL 14/114 AMERICAN
CLASSIC/CLASSIC .... **NiB $949   Ex $800   Gd $680**
Classic Series. Various short- and long-action calibers. 22- or
24-in. bbl. Weight: 7 lbs. Detachable 3- or 4-round magazine. No
sights, drilled and tapped. Accutrigger. Right- or left-hand actions.
Stock: checkered walnut w/black forend tip. Finish: high luster
blue. Made 2005 to date.

MODEL 14/114 EURO
CLASSIC................. **NiB $949   Ex $800   Gd $680**
Classic Series. Similar to 14/114 American Classic/Classic
except in .22-250, .243 or .308 and checkered walnut w/black
forend tip and cheek rest. Made 2006 to 2010.

MODEL 114C, 114CE, 114CU BOLT-ACTION RIFLES
Calibers: .270 Win., 7mm Rem. Mag., .30-06, .300 Win. Mag.
22- or 24-inch bbl. Weight: 7 lbs. Detachable 3- or 4-round
magazine. Ramp front sight; adjustable, open rear; (114CU has
no sights). Checkered select walnut stock w/oil finish, red butt
pad. Schnabel forend and skip-line checkering (114CE). High-
luster blued finish. Made 1991 to date.
Model 114C (Classic) ....**NiB $745   Ex $588   Gd $338**
Model 114CE (Classic European) NiB $533   Ex $390   Gd $300

Model 114CU (Classic Ultra) .. **NiB $540   Ex $400   Gd $310**

MODEL 116 ALASKA BRUSH
HUNTER .... **NiB $761   Ex $630   Gd $520**
Specialty Series. Calibers: .338 Win. Mag. or .375 Ruger,
internal magazine. 20-in. bbl. w/open sights. Synthetic stock,
Accutrigger. Weight: 7.6 lbs. Length: 41.5 in. Made 2012 to
date.

MODEL 16/116 BEAR
HUNTER .... **NiB $1066   Ex $930   Gd $620**
Specialty Series. Calibers: .300 WSM, .325 WSM, .300 Win.
Mag., .338 Win. Mag. or .375 Ruger, internal magazine.
23-in. bbl. w/muzzle brake. Synthetic Accustock, Accutrigger.
Weight: 7.5-7.75 lbs. Made 2011 to date.

MODEL 16/116 TROPHY HUNTER XP
PACKAGE................. **NiB $1066   Ex $930   Gd $620**
Package Series. Various calibers. 22- or 24-in. bbl. Black syn-
thetic stock, Accutrigger. Finish: stainless. Weight: 7.25 lbs.
Factory mounted Nikon 3-9x40mm scope. Made 2012 to date.

MODELS 16/116BSS WEATHER WARRIOR BOLT-ACTION
RIFLES
Similar to the Model 16/116FSS except w/brown laminated
checkered wood stock. Weight: 7.75 lbs.
Model 16BSS (2002-2003).... **NiB $668   Ex $570   Gd $470**
Model 116BSS (2001-2002) ...**NiB $644   Ex $580   Gd $490**

MODELS 16/116FCSAK, 116FSAK BOLT-ACTION RIFLES
Similar to the Model 116FSK except in calibers .270 Win., .30-
06, 7mm Mag., .300 Win. Mag., .338 Win. Mag. Fluted 22-inch
stainless bbl. w/adj. muzzle brake. Weight: 6.5 lbs. Made from
1994 to date.
Model 16/116FCSAK
(detachable mag.) ....**NiB $661   Ex $570   Gd $500**
Model 116FSAK ....**NiB $590   Ex $443   Gd $338**

MODELS 16/116FCSS, 16/116FSS BOLT-ACTION RIFLES
Improved Model 110 with satin stainless action and bbl.
Calibers: .223, .243, .270, .30-06, 7mm Rem. Mag., .300 Win.
Mag., .338 Win. Mag. 22- or 24-inch bbl. Four or 5-round
capacity. Weight: About 7.5 lbs. Black Rynite stock w/recoil
pad and swivel studs. Receiver drilled and tapped for scope
mounts, no sights. Made from 1991 to date.
Model 16/116FSS ....**NiB $720   Ex $580   Gd $480**
Model 16/116FSC
(detachable magazine) .....**NiB $885   Ex $750   Gd $630**

MODEL 116FSK KODIAK RIFLE .. **NiB $535   Ex $380   Gd $278**
Similar to the Model 116FSS except with 22-inch bbl. chambered for 338 Win. Mag. only. "Shock Suppressor" recoil
reducer. Made from 1994 to 2000.

Savage Model 340

Savage Model 340C Carbine

Savage Model 1895 Replica

Savage/Anschutz Mark 10D

Savage-Stevens Model 34

MODEL 16/116FXP3 PACKAGE...NiB $782 Ex $630 Gd $500
Similar to the Model 16/116 Trophy Hunter XP Package except w/factory mounted nickel finish scope. Made from 2002 to 2011.

MODEL 116-SE, 116-US RIFLES
Calibers: .270 Win., 7mm Rem Mag., .30-06, .300 Win. Mag. (116US); .300 Win. Mag., .338 Win. mag., .425 Express, .458 Win. Mag. (116SE). 24-inch stainless barrel (with muzzle brake 116SE only). 45.5 inches overall. Weight: 7.2 to 8.5 lbs. Three round magazine. 3-leaf Express sights 116SE only. Checkered Classic style select walnut stock with ebony forend tip. Stainless finish. Made from 1994 to 2004.
Model 116SE (Safari Express) . . NiB $947 Ex $788 Gd $556
Model 116US (Ultra Stainless) . NiB $660 Ex $498 Gd $400

MODEL 340 BOLT-ACTION REPEATER
Calibers: .22 Hornet, .222 Rem., .223 Rem., .227 Win., .30-30. Clip magazine; 4-round capacity (3-round in 30-30). Bbl. lengths: Originally 20-inch in .30-30, 22-inch in .22 Hornet; later 22-inch in .30-30, 24-inch in other calibers. Weight: 6.5 to 7.5 lbs. depending on caliber and vintage. Sights: Open rear (folding leaf on recent production); ramp front. Early models had plain pistol-grip stock, checkered since 1965. Made from

1950-85. (Note: Those rifles produced between 1947-1950 were .22 Hornet Stevens Model .322 and .30-30 Model .325. The Savage model, however, was designated Model .340 for all calibers.)
Pre-1965 with plain stock.....NiB $266 Ex $190 Gd $105
Savage Model 340C Carbine...NiB $278 Ex $228 Gd $140

MODEL 340S DELUXE ....NiB $345 Ex $298 Gd $218
Same as Model 340 except has checkered stock, screw eyes for sling, peep rear sight, hooded front. Made from 1955 to 1960.

MODEL 342 ....NiB $345 Ex $298 Gd $218
Designation, 1950 to 1955, of Model 340 .22 Hornet.

MODEL 342S DELUXE ....NiB $355 Ex $325 Gd $227
Designation, 1950 to 1955, of Model 340S .22 Hornet.

MODEL AXIS ....NiB $362 Ex $340 Gd $290
WHeavy Barrel, add $20
SR (suppressor ready), add $25
XP (scope combo), add............................$40
XP Camo (scope combo), add.....................$110
XP Stainless (scope combo), add..................$160

MODEL AXIS II XP ....NiB $475 Ex $430 Gd $370
Similar to Axis XP except w/Accutrigger. Made from 2014 to date.
XP Youth (Muddy Girl), add $100

MODEL B.MAG. . . . . NiB $372 Ex $360 Gd $310
Bolt-action. Caliber: .17 WSM, 8-rnd. rotary magazine. 22-in. bbl. Weight: 4.5 lbs. Sights: optic ready. Stock: black synthetic. AccuTrigger. Made from 2013 to date.
Target (stainless, new 2015) . . . NiB $566 Ex $540 Gd $510
Stainless Heavy Barrel . . . . NiB $425 Ex $400 Gd $390

MODEL CUB . . . . NiB $227 Ex $180 Gd $160
Bolt-action, single-shot. Calibers: .17 Mach 2 or .22 LR. 16-in. bbl. Weight: 4.5 lbs. Sights: Open rear; ramp front. Stock: hardwood or polymer (pink). AccuTrigger added 2006. Made from 2003 to 2011.
Target (thumbhole stock), add $100

MODEL EDGE. . . . . NiB $330 Ex $340 Gd $300
Bolt-action. Caliber: .223., .22-250, .243, .25-06, .270, .308, .30-06 or 7mm-08, 4-rnd. detachable magazine. 22-in. bbl. Weight: 6.5 lbs. Drilled and tapped. Stock: black synthetic. Blued finish. Made from 2010 to 2011.
XP (scope combo), add $50

MODEL MARK I G . . . . NiB $272 Ex $240 Gd $190
Bolt-action, single-shot. Calibers: .22 Short, Long, LR. 18- or 20.75-in. bbl. Weight: 5 lbs. Sights: Open rear; ramp front. Stock: hardwood. AccuTrigger added 2006. Made from 1996 to date.
Mark I FVT (synthetic stock, new 2005), add $10
Mark I GY (youth model), subtract $40

MODEL MARK II BRJ . . . . NiB $519 Ex $500 Gd $490
Similar to Mark II F series except in .22 LR only, 5-rnd. magazine. 21-in. spiral fluted bbl. Weight: 7 lbs. Sights: optic ready. Stock: laminated wood. Blued finish. Made from 2010 to date.
Camo (synthetic stock, new 2002), add $30
Mark II BSEV (stainless, laminate
    thumbhole stock) . . . . NiB $620 Ex $600 Gd $580
Mark II BTV (laminate
    thumbhole stock) . . . . NiB $461 Ex $440 Gd $420
Mark II BTVLSS (left hand, stainless, laminate
    thumbhole stock) . . . . NiB $516 Ex $500 Gd $480
Mark II BTVSS (stainless, laminate
    thumbhole stock) . . . . NiB $516 Ex $500 Gd $480
Mark II BV (heavy bbl. laminate
    stock) . . . . NiB $400 Ex $390 Gd $340

MODEL MARK II F . . . . NiB $308 Ex $290 Gd $230
Bolt-action. Calibers: .17 Mach 2 or .22 LR, 10-rnd. magazine. 21-in. bbl. Weight: 5 lbs. Sights: Open rear; ramp front. Stock: black polymer. Blued finish. AccuTrigger added 2006. Made from 1998 to date.
Camo (synthetic stock, new 2002), subtract $30
Mark II FSS (stainless) . . . . NiB $336 Ex $300 Gd $265
Mark II FV (heavy varmint bbl.) . . NiB $344 Ex $310 Gd $280
Mark II FVT (heavy varmint bbl., target
    sights) . . . . NiB $471 Ex $440 Gd $400
Mark II FV-SR (.22 LR only, 16.5-in. heavy bbl.,
    suppressor ready, optic ready, no sights,
    new 2011) . . . . NiB $471 Ex $440 Gd $400
Mark II FV-SR Landry (gator camo stock,
    new 2015) . . . . NiB $461 Ex $430 Gd $390
Mark II FXP (.22 LR only, satin blue finish,
    optic ready, no sights, OD gren stock,
    new 2014) . . . . NiB $461 Ex $430 Gd $390

MODEL MARK II G . . . . NiB $242 Ex $210 Gd $185
Simialr to Model Mark II F except w/wood stock. Made 1996 to date.
Mark II GL (left hand) . . . . NiB $242 Ex $210 Gd $185

Mark II GLY (left hand youth) . . NiB $242 Ex $210 Gd $185
Mark II GY (youth) . . . . NiB $242 Ex $210 Gd $185

MODEL MARK II TR . . . . NiB $533 Ex $460 Gd $405
Simialr to Model Mark II F except .22 LR only, 22-in. fluted bbl. Stock: wood tactical style. Weight: 7.5 lbs. Made 2010 to date.
Mark II TRR-SR (additional Picatinny rails), add $100

MODEL RASCAL . . . . NiB $186 Ex $160 Gd $140
Bolt-action, single-shot. Caliber: .22 LR. 16-in. bbl. Weight: 4.5 lbs. Sights: Open rear; ramp front. Stock: hardwood or polymer (various colors). Weight: 2.6 lbs. AccuTrigger. Made from 2102 to date.

- BREAK-ACTION RIFLES -

MODEL 219 SINGLE-SHOT RIFLE NiB $227 Ex $119 Gd $67
Hammerless. Takedown. Shotgun-type action with top lever. Calibers: .22 Hornet, .25-20, .32-20, .30-30. 26-inch bbl. Weight: about 6 lbs. Sights: Open rear; bead front. Plain pistol-grip stock and forearm. Made from 1938 to 1965.
Model 219L (w/side lever,
    made 1965-67) . . . . NiB $155 Ex $100 Gd $70

MODEL 221-229 UTILITY GUNS
Same as Model 219 except in various calibers, supplied in combination with an interchangeable shotgun bbl. All versions discontinued.
Model 221 (.30-30,12-ga.
    30-inch bbl.) . . . . NiB $155 Ex $80 Gd $55
Model 222 (.30-30,16-ga.
    28-inch bbl.) . . . . NiB $155 Ex $80 Gd $55
Model 223 (.30-30, 20-ga.
    28-inch bbl.) . . . . NiB $155 Ex $80 Gd $55
Model 227 (.22 Hornet, 12-ga.
    30-inch bbl.) . . . . NiB $155 Ex $80 Gd $55
Model 228 (.22 Hornet, 16-ga.
    28-inch bbl.) . . . . NiB $155 Ex $80 Gd $55
Model 229 (.22 Hornet, 20-ga.
    28-inch bbl.) . . . . NiB $155 Ex $80 Gd $55

- LEVER-ACTION RIFLES -

MODEL 71 "STEVENS FAVORITE" SINGLE-SHOT
LEVER-ACTION RIFLE. . . . . NiB $229 Ex $114 Gd $98
Replica of original Stevens Favorite issued as a tribute to Joshua Stevens, "Father of .22 Hunting." Caliber: .22 LR. 22-inch full-octagon bbl. Brass-plated hammer and lever. Sights: Open rear; brass blade front. Weight: 4.5 lbs. Plain straight-grip buttstock and Schnabel forend; brass commemorative medallion inlaid in buttstock, brass crescent-shaped buttplate. 10,000 produced. Made in 1971 only. Top value is for new, unfired gun.

NOTE: *The Model 72 is a "Favorite"-type single-shot unlike the smaller, original "Crackshot" made by Stevens from 1913 to 1939. See "Stevens" for additional models.*

MODEL 72 CRACKSHOT SINGLE-SHOT
LEVER-ACTION RIFLE. . . . . NiB $190 Ex $109 Gd $79
Falling-block action. Casehardened frame. Caliber: .22 Short, Long, LR. 22-inch octagon bbl. Weight: 4.5lbs. Sights: Open rear; bead front. Plain straight-grip stock and forend of walnut. Made 1972–89.

MODEL 88 . . . . NiB $90 Ex $80 Gd $70
Similar to Model 60 except w/walnut stock. Made from 1969–72.

Savage-Stevens Model 46

Savage-Stevens Model 65

Savage-Stevens Model 72 — Crackshot

Savage-Stevens Model 73

Savage-Stevens Model 80

**MODEL 89 SINGLE-SHOT LEVER-ACTION
CARBINE.** . . . . **NiB $121 Ex $90 Gd $66**
Martini-type action. Caliber: .22 Short, Long, LR. 18.5-inch
bbl. Weight: 5 lbs. Sights: Open rear; bead front. Western-style
carbine stock w/straight grip, forearm with bbl. band. Made
1976 to 1989.

NOTE: *Introduced in 1899, the Model 99 has been produced in a variety of styles and calibers. Original designation
"Model 1899" was changed to "Model 99" c.1920. Earlier
rifles and carbines—similar to Models 99A, 99B and 99H—
were available in calibers .25-35, .30-30, .303 Sav., .32-40
and .38-55. Post-WWII Models 99A, 99C, 99CD, 99DE,
99DL, 99F and 99PE have top tang safety other 99s have
slide safety on right side of trigger guard. Models 99C and
99CD have detachable box magazine instead of traditional
rotary magazine.*

MODEL 99A (I). . . . . **NiB $1015 Ex $768 Gd $545**
Hammerless. Solid frame. Calibers: .30-30, .300 Sav., .303
Sav. Five-round rotary magazine. 24-inch bbl. Weight: 7.25
lbs. Sights: Open rear; bead front, on ramp. Plain straight-grip
stock, tapered forearm. Made from 1920 to 1936.

MODEL 99A (II) . . . . **NiB $915 Ex $668 Gd $445**
Current model. Similar to original Model 99A except w/top
tang safety, 22-inch bbl., folding leaf rear sight, no crescent
buttplate. Calibers: .243 Win., .250 Sav., .300 Sav., .308 Win.
Made from 1971 to 1982.

MODEL 99B . . . . **NiB $1245 Ex $938 Gd $577**
Takedown. Otherwise same as Model 99A except weight: 7.5
lbs. Made from 1920 to 1936.

MODEL 99C . . . . **NiB $560 Ex $488 Gd $399**
Current model. Same as Model 99F except w/clip magazine
instead of rotary. Calibers: .243 Win., .284 Win., .308 Win.
Four round detachable magazine holds one round less in .284.
Weight: 6.75 lbs. Made from 1965-98.

MODEL 99CD. . . . . **NiB $698 Ex $599 Gd $389**
Deluxe version of Model 99C. Calibers: .243 Win., .250 Sav.,
.308 Win. Hooded ramp front sight. Weight: 8.25 lbs. Stock
w/Monte Carlo comb and cheekpiece, checkered pistol-grip,
grooved forearm, swivels and sling. Made from 1975 to 81.

**MODEL 99DE CITATION
GRADE** . . . . **NiB $955 Ex $679 Gd $495**
Same as Model 99PE except w/less elaborate engraving. Made
from 1968-70.

GRADING: NiB = New in Box   **Ex** = Excellent or NRA 95%   **Gd** = Good or NRA 68%

Savage-Stevens Model 89

Savage-Stevens Model 987-T

walnut forearm w/bbl. band. Weight: 6.5 lbs. Open rear sights; ramped blade front sight. Other specifications same as Model 99A. Made 1931 to 1942.

MODEL 99DL DELUXE . . . . . . **NiB $745 Ex $576 Gd $359**
Postwar model. Calibers: .243 Win., .308 Win. Same as Model 99F, except w/high comb Monte Carlo stock, sling swivels. Weight: 6.75 lbs. Made from 1960-73.

MODEL 99E CARBINE (I) . . . . . **NiB $656 Ex $500 Gd $439**
Pre-WWII type. Solid frame. Calibers: .22 Hi-Power, .250/3000, .30/30, .300 Sav., .303 Sav. w/22-inch bbl.; .300 Sav. 24-inch. Weight: 7 lbs. Other specifications same as Model 99A. Made from 1920-36.

MODEL 99E CARBINE (II) . . . . **NiB $709 Ex $505 Gd $457**
Current model. Solid frame. Calibers: .250 Sav., .243 Win., .300 Sav., .308 Win. 20- or 22-inch bbl. Checkered pistol-grip stock and forearm. Made from 1960-89.

MODEL 99EG (I) . . . . **NiB $877 Ex $687 Gd $476**
Pre-WWII type. Solid frame. Plain pistol-grip stock and forearm. Otherwise same as Model G. Made from 1936 to 1941.

MODEL 99EG (II) . . . . **NiB $1023 Ex $799 Gd $600**
Post-WWII type. Same as prewar model except w/checkered stock and forearm. Calibers: .250 Sav., .300 Sav., .308 Win. (intro. 1955), .243 Win., and .358 Win. Made from 1946 to 1960.

MODEL 99F
FEATHERWEIGHT (I) . . . . **NiB $813 Ex $707 Gd $514**
Pre-WWII type. Takedown. Specifications same as Model 99E, except weight: 6.5 lbs. Made 1920 to 1942. Some marked 99M.

MODEL 99F
FEATHERWEIGHT (II) . . . . **NiB $945 Ex $735 Gd $567**
Postwar model. Solid frame. Calibers: .243 Win., .300 Sav., .308 Win. 22-inch bbl. Checkered pistol-grip stock and forearm. Weight: 6.5 lbs. Made from 195 to 1973.

MODEL 99G . . . . **NiB $1290 Ex $933 Gd $707**
Takedown. Checkered pistol-grip stock and forearm. Weight: 7.25 lbs. Other specifications same as Model 99E. Made 1920 to 1942.

MODEL 99H CARBINE . . . . . . **NiB $926 Ex $577 Gd $4455**
Solid frame. Calibers: .250/3000, .30/30, .303 Sav. 20-inch special weight bbl. Walnut carbine stock w/metal buttplate;

MODEL 99K . . . . **NiB $3854 Ex $2650 Gd $2128**
Deluxe version of Model G w/similar specifications except w/ fancy stock and engraving on receiver and bbl. Lyman peep rear sight and folding middle. Made from 1931 to 1942.

MODEL 99PE PRESENTATION
GRADE . . . . **NiB $2055 Ex $1717 Gd $854**
Same as Model 99DL except w/engraved receiver (game scenes on sides), tang and lever, fancy walnut Monte Carlo stock and forearm w/hand checkering, QD swivels. Calibers: .243, .284, .308. Made 1968 to 1970.

MODEL 99R (I) . . . . **NiB $735 Ex $588 Gd $499**
Pre-WWII type. Solid frame. Calibers: .250-3000 (22-inch bbl.), .300 Sav. (24-inch bbl.). Weight: 7.5 lbs. Special large pistol-grip stock and forearm, checkered. General specifications same as other Model 99 rifles. Made from 1936 to 1942.

MODEL 99R (II) . . . . **NiB $689 Ex $498 Gd $356**
Post-WWII type. Same as prewar mod except w/24-inch bbl. only, w/screw eyes for sling swivels. Calibers: .250 Sav., .300 Sav., .308 Win., .243 Win. and .358 Win. Made from 1946 to 1960.

MODEL 99RS (I) . . . . **NiB $944 Ex $650 Gd $489**
Pre-WWII type. Same as prewar Model 99R except equipped w/Lyman rear peep sight and folding middle sight, quick detachable swivels and sling. Made from 1932 to 1942.

MODEL 99RS (II) . . . . **NiB $756 Ex $600 Gd $467**
Post-WWII type. Same as postwar Model 99RS except equipped w/Redfield 70LH receiver sight, blank in middle sight slot. Made from 1946 to 1960.

MODEL 99T . . . . **NiB $1707 Ex $1032 Gd $744**
Featherweight. Solid frame. Calibers: .22 Hi-Power, .30/30, .303 Sav. w/20-inch bbl.; .300 Sav. w/22-inch bbl. Checkered pistol-grip stock and beavertail forearm. Weight: 7 lbs. General specifications same as other Model 99 rifles. Made from 1936 to 1942.

MODEL 99-358 . . . . **NiB $1156 Ex $903 Gd $657**
Similar to current Model 99A except caliber .358 Win. has grooved forearm, recoil pad, swivel studs. Made from 1977 to 1980.

ANNIVERSARY MODEL 1895
LEVER-ACTION. . . . . **NiB $6235 Ex $4589 Gd $2240**
Replica of Savage Model 1895 Hammerless Lever-Action Rifle issued to commemorate the 75th anniversary (1895-1970) of Savage Arms. Caliber: .308 Win. Five round rotary magazine. 24-inch full-octagon bbl. Engraved receiver. Brass-plated lever. Sights: Open rear; brass blade front. Plain straight-grip buttstock, Schnabel-type forend; brass medallion inlaid in buttstock, brass crescent-shaped buttplate. 9,999 produced. Made in 1970 only. Top value is for new, unfired specimen.

- SEMI-AUTOMATIC RIFLES -

MODEL 1912 AUTOLOADING
RIFLE. . . . . **NiB $800 Ex $533 Gd $337**
Takedown. Caliber: 22 LR. only. Seven round detachable box magazine. 20-inch bbl., plain stock and forearm. Made 1912 to 1916.

MODEL 60 AUTOLOADING
RIFLE. . . . . **NiB $115 Ex $80 Gd $48**
Caliber: .22 LR. 15-round tubular magazine. 20-inch bbl. Weight: 6 lbs. Sights: Open rear, ramp front. Monte Carlo stock of walnut w/checkered pistol-grip and forearm. Made from 1969 to 1972.

MODEL 64 G . . . . NiB $228 Ex $200 Gd $110
Semi-automatic. Caliber: .22 LR, 10-rnd magazine. 20.25-in. bbl. Weight: 5.5 lbs. Sights: Open rear; ramp front. Stock: wood. Made from 1996 to date.
Model 64 F (synthetic stock), subtract **$53**
Model 64 F Camo (camo synthetic stock), add. **$13**
Mark 64 FSS (stainless, synthetic
   stock) . . . . **NiB $264 Ex $240 Gd $200**
Mark 64 FV-SR (synthetic stock, blued, optic-ready, 16.5-in.
   bbl. suppressor ready) . . . . . **NiB $238 Ex $210 Gd $185**

MODEL 80 . . . . NiB $215 Ex $170 Gd $126
Semi-automatic. Caliber: 22 LR. 15-round tubular magazine. 20-inch bbl. Weight: 6 lbs. Sights: Open rear, bead front. Monte Carlo stock of walnut w/checkered pistol-grip and forearm. Made from 1976 to date. (Note: This rifle is essentially the same as the Model 60 of 1969 to 1972 except for a different style of checkering, side instead of top safety and plain bead instead of ramp front sight.)

MODEL 88 . . . . NiB $190 Ex $110 Gd $88
Similar to Model 80 except has walnut-finished hardwood stock, plain bead front sight. Weight: 5.75 lbs. Made from 1969 to 1972.

MODEL 90 . . . . NiB $194 Ex $161 Gd $126
Similar to Model 60 except w/16.5-inch bbl. w/folding leaf rear sight, bead front. 10-round tubular magazine. Uncheckered, carbine style walnut stock w/bbl. Band and sling swivels. Weight: 5.75 lbs. Made from 1969 to 1972.

MODEL 987-T. . . . . NiB $217 Ex $166 Gd $129
Semi-automatic. Caliber: .22 LR. 15-round tubular magazine. 20-inch bbl. Weight: 6 lbs. Sights: Open rear; ramp front. Monte Carlo stock w/checkered pistol grip and forearm. Made from 1981 to 1989.

MODEL A17. . . . . NiB $465 Ex $460 Gd $400
Semi-automatic. Caliber: .17 HMR, 10-rnd rotary magazine. 22-in. bbl. Weight: 5.4 lbs. Sights: optic ready. Stock: black sythetic. Made from 2015 to date.

- SLIDE-ACTION RIFLES -

MODEL 1903 SLIDE-ACTION
REPEATER . . . . **NiB $733 Ex $549 Gd $370**
Hammerless. Takedown. Caliber: .22 Short, Long, LR. Detachable box magazine. 24-inch octagon bbl. Weight: About 5 lbs. Sights: Open rear; bead front. Pistol-grip stock, grooved slide handle. Made 1903 to 1921.

MODEL 1909 SLIDE-ACTION
REPEATER . . . . **NiB $800 Ex $533 Gd $337**
Hammerless. Takedown. Similar to Model 1903 except has 20-inch round bbl., plain stock and forearm, weight: Approximately 4.75 lbs. Made from 1909 to 1915.

MODEL 1914 SLIDE-ACTION
REPEATER . . . . **NiB $520 Ex $347 Gd $239**
Hammerless. Takedown. Caliber: .22 Short, Long, LR, Tubular magazine holds 20 Short, 17 Long, 15 LR. 24-inch octagon bbl. Weight: About 5.75 lbs. Sights: Open rear; bead front. Plain pistol-grip stock, grooved slide handle. Made from 1914 to 1924.

MODEL 25 SLIDE-ACTION
REPEATER . . . . **NiB $346 Ex $391 Gd $237**
Takedown. Hammerless. Caliber: .22 Short, Long, LR. Tubular magazine holds 20 Short, 17 Long, 15 LR. 24-inch octagon bbl. Weight: 5.75 lbs. Sights: Open rear; blade front. Plain pistol-grip stock, grooved slide handle. Made from 1925 to 1929.

MODEL 29 SLIDE-ACTION
REPEATER . . . . **NiB $500 Ex $380 Gd $265**
Takedown. Hammerless. Caliber: .22 Short, Long, LR. Tubular magazine holds 20 Short, 17 Long, 15 LR. 24-inch bbl., octagon on prewar, round on postwar production. Weight: 5.5 lbs. Sights: Open rear; bead front. Stock w/checkered pistol grip and slide handle on prewar, plain stock and grooved forearm on postwar production. Made from 1929 to 1967.

MODEL 170 PUMP-ACTION . . NiB $249 Ex $190 Gd $106
Calibers: .30-30, .35 Rem. Three round tubular magazine. 22-inch bbl. Weight: 6.75 lbs. Sights: Folding leaf rear; ramp front. Select walnut stock w/checkered pistol-grip Monte Carlo comb, grooved slide handle. Made from 1970 to 1981.

MODEL 170C CARBINE . . . . . . NiB $280 Ex $322 Gd $166
Same as Model 170 Rifle except has 18.5-inch bbl., straight comb stock, weight: 6 lbs.; caliber .30-30 only. Made from 1974 to 1981.

V.C. SCHILLING — Suhl, Germany

MAUSER-MANNLICHER BOLT ACTION
SPORTING RIFLE . . . . **NiB $938 Ex $744 Gd $539**
Same general specifications as given for the Haenel Mauser-Mannlicher Sporter. See separate listing.

'88 MAUSER SPORTER . . . . NiB $909 Ex $722 Gd $515
Same general specifications as Haenel '88 Mauser Sporter. See separate listing.

SCHULTZ & LARSEN GEVAERFABRIK — Otterup, Denmark

MATCH RIFLE NO. 47 . . . . NiB $690 Ex $555 Gd $360
Caliber: .22 LR. Bolt-action, single-shot, set trigger. 28.5-inch heavy bbl. Weight: 14 lbs. Sights: Micrometer receiver,

RIFLES

Sedgley Springfield Sporter

Sedgley Springfield — Left Hand

Sedgley Springfield Mannlicher

globe front. Free-rifle stock w/cheekpiece, thumbhole, adj. Schuetzen-type buttplate, swivels, palmrest.

FREE RIFLE MODEL 54 . . . . . . NiB $866 Ex $780 Gd $598
Calibers: 6.5x55mm or any standard American centerfire caliber. Schultz & Larsen M54 bolt-action, single-shot, set trigger. 27.5-inch heavy bbl. Weight: 15.5 lbs. Sights: Micrometer receiver; globe front. Free-rifle stock w/cheekpiece, thumbhole, adj. Schuetzen-type buttplate, swivels, palm rest.

MODEL 54J
SPORTING RIFLE . . . . NiB $684 Ex $528 Gd $430
Calibers: .270 Win., .30-06, 7x61 Sharpe & Hart. Schultz & Larsen bolt action. Three-round magazine. 24-inch bbl. in .270 and .30-06, 26-inch in 7x61 S&H. Checkered stock w/Monte Carlo comb and cheekpiece. Value shown is for rifle less sights.

SEARS, ROEBUCK & COMPANY — Chicago, Illinois

The most encountered brands or model designations used by Sears are J. C. Higgins and Ted Williams. Firearms sold under these designations have been mfd. by various firms including Winchester, Marlin, Savage, Mossberg, etc.

MODEL 2C BOLT-ACTION
RIFLE. . . . . NiB $159 Ex $119 Gd $95
Caliber: .22RF. Seven round clip mag. 21-inch bbl. Weight: 5 lbs. Sights: Open rear; ramp front. Plain Monte Carlo stock. Mfd. by Win.

MODEL 42 BOLT-ACTION
REPEATER. . . . . NiB $159 Ex $119 Gd $95
Takedown. Caliber: .22RF. Eight round detachable box magazine. 24-inch bbl. Weight: 6 lbs. Sights: Open rear; bead front. Plain pistol-grip stock. Mfd. by Marlin.

MODEL 42DL
BOLT-ACTION REPEATER . . . . . . NiB $159 Ex $119 Gd $95
Same general specifications as Model 42 except fancier grade w/peep sight, hooded front sight and swivels.

MODEL 44DL LEVER-ACTION
RIFLE . . . . NiB $239 Ex $179 Gd $130
Caliber: .22RF. Tubular magazine holds 19 LR cartridges. 22-inch bbl. Weight: 6.25 lbs. Sights: Open rear; hooded ramp front. Monte Carlo-style stock w/pistol grip. Mfd. by Marlin.

MODEL 53 BOLT-ACTION
RIFLE. . . . . NiB $289 Ex $198 Gd $155
Calibers: .243, .270, .308, .30-06. Four-round magazine. 22-inch bbl. Weight: 6.75 lbs. Sights: Open rear; ramp front. Standard sporter stock w/pistol-grip, checkered. Mfd. by Savage.

MODEL 54 LEVER-ACTION
RIFLE. . . . . NiB $222 Ex $188 Gd $135
Similar general specifications as Winchester Model 94 carbine. Made in .30-30 caliber only. Mfd. by Winchester.

MODEL 103 SERIES BOLT-ACTION
REPEATER . . . . NiB $229 EX $121 Gd $98
Same general specifications as Model 103.2 w/minor changes. Mfd. by Marlin.

MODEL 103.2 BOLT-ACTION
REPEATER . . . . NiB $145 Ex $100 Gd $90
Takedown. Caliber: .22RF. Eight-round detachable box magazine. 24-inch bbl. Weight: 6 lbs. Sights: Open rear; bead front. Plain pistol-grip stock. Mfd. by Marlin.

R. F. SEDGLEY, INC. — Philadelphia, Pennsylvania

SPRINGFIELD SPORTER . . . . NiB $1290 Ex $1189 Gd $633
Springfield '03 bolt action. Calibers: .220 Swift, .218 Bee, .22-3000, R, .22-4000, .22 Hornet, .25-35, .250-3000, .257 Roberts, .270 Win., 7mm, .30-06. 24-inch bbl. Weight: 7.5 lbs. Sights: Lyman No. 48 receiver; bead front on matted ramp. Checkered walnut stock, grip cap, sling swivels. Disc. 1941.

SPRINGFIELD LEFT-HAND
SPORTER. . . . . NiB $1674 Ex $1412 Gd $954
Bolt-action reversed for left-handed shooter; otherwise the same as standard Sedgley Springfield Sporter. Disc. 1941.

SPRINGFIELD MANNLICHER-TYPE
SPORTER. . . . . NiB $1515 Ex $1479 Gd $1088

Shilen DGA Benchrest Rifle

Shilen DGA Sporter

Shilen DGA Varminter

Same as standard Sedgley Springfield Sporter except w/20-inch bbl., Mannlicher-type full stock w/cheekpiece, weight: 7.75 lbs. Disc. 1941.

SHILEN RIFLES, INC. — Enis, Texas

DGA BENCHREST RIFLE. . . . NiB $1529 Ex $1244 Gd $977
DGA single-shot bolt-action. Calibers as listed for Sporter. 26-inch medium-heavy or heavy bbl. Weight: From 10.5 lbs. No sights. Fiberglass or walnut stock, classic or thumbhole pattern. Currently manufactured.

DGA SPORTER . . . . NiB $1567 Ex $1189 Gd $843
DGA bolt action. Calibers: .17 Rem., .222 Rem., .223 Rem. .22-250, .220 Swift, 6mm Rem., .243 Win., .250 Sav., .257 Roberts, .284 Win., .308 Win., .358 Win. Three round blind magazine. 24-inch bbl. Average weight: 7.5 lbs. No sights. Select Claro walnut stock w/cheekpiece, pistol grip, sling swivel studs. Currently manufactured.

DGA VARMINTER . . . . NiB $1455 Ex $1209 Gd $1155
Same as Sporter except w/25-in. medium-heavy bbl. Weight: 9 lbs.

SHILOH RIFLE MFG. CO. — Big Timber, MT

SHARPS MODEL 1874
BUSINESS RIFLE . . . . NiB $1149 Ex $1072 Gd $698
Replica of 1874 Sharps similar to No. 3 Sporting Rifle. .32-40, .38-55, .40-50 BN, .40-70 BN, .40-90 BN, .45-70 ST, .45-90 ST, .50-70 ST, .50-100 ST. 28-inch round heavy bbl.

Blade front sight, buckhorn rear. Double-set triggers. Straight-grip walnut stock w/steel crescent buttplate. Made from 1986 to date.

SHARPS MODEL 1874 LONG RANGE
EXPRESS RIFLE . . . . NiB $1798 Ex $1703 Gd $1166
Replica of 1874 Sharps w/single-shot falling breech action. .32-40, .38-55, .40-50 BN, .40-70 BN, .40-90 BN, .45-70 ST, .45-90 ST, .45-110 ST, .50-70 ST, .50-90 ST, .50-110 ST. 34-inch tapered octagon bbl. 51 inches overall. Weight: 10.75 lbs. Globe front sight, sporting tang peep rear. Walnut buttstock w/pistol-grip and Schnabel-style forend. Color casehardened action w/double-set triggers Made from 1986 to date.

SHARPS MODEL 1874 SADDLE
RIFLE. . . . . NiB $1267 Ex $1133 Gd $723
Similar to 1874 Express Rifle except w/30-inch bbl., blade front sight and buckhorn rear. Made from 1986 to date.

SHARPS MODEL 1874 SPORTING
RIFLE NO. 1 . . . . NiB $1355 Ex $1187 Gd $745
Similar to 1874 Express Rifle except w/30-inch bbl., blade front sight and buckhorn rear. Made from 1986 to date.

SHARPS MODEL 1874 SPORTING
RIFLE NO. 3 . . . . NiB $1150 Ex $1007 Gd $688
Similar to 1874 Sporting Rifle No. 1 except w/straight-grip stock w/steel crescent buttplate. Made from 1986 to date.

SHARPS MODEL 1874 MONTANA ROUGHRIDER
Similar to 1874 Sporting Rifle No. 1 except w/24- to 34-inch half-octagon or full-octagon bbl. Standard or deluxe walnut stock w/pistol-grip or military-style buttstock. Made from 1989 to date.
Standard model. . . . . NiB $1154 Ex $715 Gd $646
Deluxe model . . . . NiB $1300 Ex $990 Gd $615

SIG SSG 3000 Patrol

SIG Tactical 2

Smith & Wesson
Model 1500DL

SIG SWISS INDUSTRIAL COMPANY — Neuhausen-Rhine Falls, Switzerland

AMT SEMIAUTOMATIC . . . NiB $4798 Ex $3270 Gd $2775
.308 Win.(7.62 NATO). Five, 10, or 20-round magazine. 18.5-inch bbl. w/flash suppressor. Weight: 9.5 lbs. Sights: Adj. aperture rear, post front. Walnut buttstock and forend w/synthetic pistol grip. Imported 1980 to 1988.

AMT SPORTING RIFLE . . . . NiB $4876 Ex $3129 Gd $2210
Semi-automatic version of SG510-4 automatic assault rifle based on Swiss Army SIGW57. Roller-delayed blowback action. Caliber: 7.62x51mm NATO (.308 Win.). Five, 10- and 20-round magazines. 19-inch bbl. Weight: 10 lbs. Sights, aperture rear, post front. Wood buttstock and forearm, folding bipod. Imported from 1960 to 1988.

**PE-57 SEMI-AUTOMATIC
RIFLE. . . . . NiB $6596 Ex $4348 Gd $3100**
Caliber: 7.5 Swiss. 24-round magazine. 23.75-inch bbl. Weight: 12.5 lbs. Sights: Adj. aperture rear; post front. High-impact synthetic stock. Imported from Switzerland during the 1980s.

SIG SAUER — Neuhausen, Switzerland
Manufactured and imported by SIG Sauer USA in Exeter, NH.

To facilitate locating SIG Sauer rifles, models are grouped into two categories: bolt-action rifles (below) and semi-automatic rifles. For a complete listing, please refer to the index.

- BOLT-ACTION RIFLES -

TACTICAL 2 . . . . NiB $4171 Ex $2400 Gd $1900
Push-feed, straight pull action. Calibers: .223 Rem., .308 Win., .300 Win. Mag. or .338 Lapua. 4- or 5-round detachable box magazine. 24.7-, 25.6-, or 27-in. fluted bbl. w/muzzle brake.

Aluminum chassis, adj. trigger, ambidextrous Blaser stock w/ adj. LOP and cheekpiece. Made from 2007 to 2015.

SIG50 . . . . NiB $9825 Ex $5100 Gd $4900
Push-feed action. .50 BMG only. 5-round detachable box magazine. 29-in. fluted bbl. w/muzzle brake. McMillan stock. Made 2011-12; 2014-15.

SSG 3000 . . . . NiB $2400 Ex $1500 Gd $1250
Push-feed action, .308 Win. only, 5-round detachable box magazine, 23.4-in. heavy bbl. w/muzzle brake, adj. McMillan stock. Made from 2000 to 2012.
Patrol (18-in. bbl.) . . . . NiB $1499 Ex $830 Gd $700

- SEMI-AUTOMATIC RIFLES -

SIG M400 . . . . NiB $1313 Ex $874 Gd $750
Semi-automatic AR15 platform w/gas impingment system. Caliber: 5.56mm NATO. 30-round magazine. 16-in. bbl., removable adj. sights. Weight: 6.5 lbs. Overall: 39.5 in. Made 2012 to date.
Hunting (20-in. bbl., 2012 only) . . . NiB $975 Ex $680 Gd $600
Varminter (22-in. bbl., 2013-15) . . NiB $1395 Ex $820 Gd $650

SIG551-A1 . . . . NiB $1599 Ex $930 Gd $800
Semi-automatic w/gas piston system. Caliber: 5.56mm NATO. 20- or 30-round Swiss 550-style clear magazine. 16-in. bbl., adj. sights, folding polymer stock. Weight: 7 lbs. Overall: 34.6 in. Made 2012 to 2015.

SIG556 CLASSIC . . . . NiB $1299 Ex $850 Gd $700
Similar to gas piston system SG550 military rifle except semi-automatic. Caliber: 5.56mm NATO. 30-round AR51-style magazine. 16-in. bbl., adj. sights, folding polymer stock. Weight: 8.2 lbs. Overall: 35.8 in. Made 2007 to 2013.
**DMR (Magpul PRS stock,18-in. heavy bbl., optic ready
2008-13) . . . . NiB $1732 Ex $930 Gd $800**
**Holo (M4-style stock, red dot
holographic sight) . . . . NiB $1832 Ex $1030 Gd $900**

Smith & Wesson
Model 1707 LS Classic Hunter

Springfield Armory
BM-59

Patrol (polymer handguard,
2010-13) . . . . NiB $1266 Ex $850 Gd $700
Patrol SWAT (aluminum handguard,
2010-13) . . . . NiB $1266 Ex $850 Gd $700
SWAT (quad-rail handguard), add $140

SIG556R . . . . NiB $1332 Ex $900 Gd $760
Similar to SG556 except chambered in 7.62x39mm. 30-round
AK-style magazine, red dot optic. Weight: 7 lbs. Made 2011
to 2013.

SMITH & WESSON — Springfield, MA

*Manufactured by Husqvarna, Vapenfabrik A.B., Huskvarna,
Sweden, & Howa Machinery LTD., Shinkawa-Chonear, Nagota
452, Japan.*

MODEL 1500 . . . . NiB $410 Ex $339 Gd $269
Bolt-action. .243 Win., .270 Win., .30-06, 7mm Rem. Mag.
22-inch bbl. (24-inch in 7mm Rem. Mag.). Weight: 7.5 lbs.
American walnut stock w/Monte Carlo comb and cheekpiece,
cut checkering. Sights: Open rear, hooded ramp, gold bead-
front. This model was also imported by Mossberg (see separate
listings); Imported from 1979 to 1984.

MODEL 1500DL DELUXE . . . . NiB $410 Ex $339 Gd $269
Same as standard model, except w/o sights; w/engine-turned
bolt, decorative scroll on floorplate, French checkering.
Imported from 1983 to 1984.

MODEL 1707 LS "CLASSIC
HUNTER" . . . . NiB $460 Ex $388 Gd $318
Bolt action. Calibers: .243 Win., .270 Win., .30-06, 5-round
magazine. 22-inch bbl. Weight: 7.5 lbs. Solid recoil pad, no
sights, Schnabel forend, checkered walnut stock. Imported
1983 to 1984.

MODEL A BOLT-ACTION RIFLE NiB $443 Ex $329 Gd $290
Similar to Husqvarna Model 9000 Crown Grade. Mauser-type
bolt action. Calibers: .22-250, .243 Win., .270 Win., .308
Win., .30-06, 7mm Rem. Mag., .300 Win. Mag. Five round
magazine except 3-round capacity in latter two calibers.

23.75-inch bbl. Weight: 7 lbs. Sights: Folding leaf rear; hooded
ramp front. Checkered walnut stock w/Monte Carlo cheekpiece, rosewood forend tip and pistol-grip cap, swivels. Made
from 1969 to 1972.

MODEL B . . . . NiB $460 Ex $367 Gd $238
Same as Model A except w/20.25-inch extra-light bbl., Monte
Carlo cheekpiece w/Schnabel-style forearm, weight: 6 lbs., 10
oz. Calibers: .243 Win., .30-06.

MODEL C . . . . NiB $460 Ex $367 Gd $238
Same as Model B except w/cheekpiece stock w/straight comb.

MODEL D . . . . NiB $588 Ex $469 Gd $240
Same as Model C except w/full-length Mannlicher-style forearm.

MODEL E . . . . NiB $588 Ex $469 Gd $240
Same as Model B except w/full-length Mannlicher-style forearm.

SPRINGFIELD ARMORY INC. — Colona,

Illinois *Formerly of Geneseo, IL. This is a private firm not
to be confused with the former U.S. Government facility in
Springfield, Mass.*

BM-59 SEMIAUTOMATIC RIFLE
Gas-operated. Caliber: .308 Win. (7.62mm NATO). 20-round
detachable box magazine. 19.3-inch bbl. w/flash suppressor.
About 43 inches overall. Weight: 9.25 lbs. Adj. military aperture rear sight, square post front; direct and indirect grenade
launcher sights. European walnut stock w/handguard or folding
buttstock (Alpine Paratrooper). Made from 1981 to 1990.
Standard model. . . . . NiB $1844 Ex $1329 Gd $911
Paratrooper model . . . . NiB $2136 Ex $1779 Gd $1533

M-1 GARAND SEMIAUTOMATIC RIFLE
Gas-operated. Calibers: .308 Win. (7.62 NATO), .30-06. Eight
round stripper clip. 24-inch bbl. 43.5 inches overall. Weight:
9.5 lbs. Adj. aperture rear sight, military square blade front.
Standard "Issue-grade" walnut stock or folding buttstock. Made
from 1979 to 1990.

GRADING: **NiB** = New in Box   **Ex** = Excellent or NRA 95%   **Gd** = Good or NRA 68%

**Springfield Armory
SAR-8 Sporter Rifle**

Standard model. . . . . NiB $779 Ex $588 Gd $353
National Match model . . . . NiB $909 Ex $799 Gd $489
Ultra Match model . . . . NiB $1000 Ex $808 Gd $589
Sniper model. . . . . NiB $1264 Ex $876 Gd $665
Tanker model . . . . NiB $954 Ex $677 Gd $498

MATCH M1A

Same as Standard M1A except w/National Match-grade bbl. w/modified flash suppressor, National Match sights, turned trigger pull, gas system assembly in one unit, modified mainspring guide glass-bedded walnut stock. Super Match M1A w/ premium-grade heavy bbl. (weight: 10 lbs).
Match M1A . . . . **NiB $1277 Ex $1879 Gd $1271**
Super Match M1A. . . . . . . **NiB $2695 Ex $1899 Gd $1721**

STANDARD M1A SEMIAUTOMATIC

Gas-operated. Similar to U.S. M14 service rifle except w/o provision for automatic firing. Caliber: 7.65mm NATO (.308 Win.). Five, 10- or 20-round detachable box magazine. 25.13-inch bbl w/flash suppressor. Weight: 9 lbs. Sights: Adj. aperture rear; blade front. Fiberglass, birch or walnut stock, fiberglass handguard, sling swivels. Made from 1996 to 2000.
w/fiberglass or birch stock. . . **NiB $1198 Ex $694 Gd $645**
w/walnut stock . . . . **NiB $1412 Ex $1100 Gd $833**

M-6 SCOUT RIFLE/SHOTGUN COMBO

Similar to (14-inch) short-barrel Survival Gun provided as backup weapon to U.S. combat pilots. Calibers: .22 LR/.410 and .22 Hornet/.410. 18.5-inch bbl. 32 inches overall. Weight: 4 lbs. Parkerized or stainless steel finish. Folding detachable stock w/storage for fifteen .22 LR cartridges and four .410 shells. Drilled and tapped for scope mounts. Intro. 1982 and imported from Czech Republic 1995 to 2004.
First Issue (no trigger guard) . . . . . NiB $1709 Ex $1443 Gd $1067
Second Issue (w/trigger guard) . . . NiB $1797 Ex $1449 Gd $1088

SAR-8 SPORTER RIFLE

Similar to H&K 911 semiautomatic rifle. Calibers: .308 Win., (7.62x51) NATO. Detachable 5- 10- or 20-round magazine. 18- or 20-inch bbl. 38.25 or 45.3 inches overall. Weight: 8.7 to 9.5 lbs. Protected front post and rotary adj. rear sight. Delayed roller-locked blow-back action w/fluted chamber. Kevlar-reinforced fiberglass thumb-hole style wood stock. Imported from 1990 to 1998.
w/wood stock (disc. 1994) . . . NiB $1077 Ex $877 Gd $658
w/thumb-hole stock . . . . NiB $1127 Ex $976 Gd $679

SAR-48, SAR-4800

Similar to Browning FN FAL/LAR semiautomatic rifle. Calibers: .233 Rem. (5.56x45) and 3.08 Win. (7.62x51) NATO. Detachable 5- 10- or 20-round magazine. 18- or 21-inch chrome-lined bbl. 38.25 or 45.3 inches overall. Weight: 9.5 to 13.25 lbs. Protected post front and adj. rear sight. Forged receiver and bolt w/adj. gas system. Pistol-grip or thumb-hole style; synthetic or wood stock. Imported 1985; reintroduced 1995.

w/pistol-grip stock, disc. 1989NiB $1788 Ex $1289 Gd $990
w/wood stock, disc. 1989. . NiB $2577 Ex $2066 Gd $1500
w/folding stock, disc. 1989 NiB $2854 Ex $2310 Gd $1669
w/thumb-hole stock . . . . NiB $1329 Ex $1100 Gd $796

SQUIRES BINGHAM CO., INC. — Makati, Rizal, Philippines

MODEL 14D DELUXE BOLT-ACTION
REPEATING RIFLE . . . . NiB $159 Ex $123 Gd $88
Caliber: .22 LR. Five round box magazine. 24-inch bbl. Sights: V-notch rear; hooded ramp front. Receiver grooved for scope mounting. Pulong Dalaga stock w/contrasting forend tip and grip cap, checkered forearm and pistol-grip. Weight: 6 lbs. Disc.

MODEL 15 . . . . NiB $189 Ex $127 Gd $115
Same as Model 14D except chambered for .22 WMR. Importation. Disc.

MODEL M16 SEMIAUTOMATIC
RIFLE. . . . . NiB $190 Ex $166 Gd $126
Styled after U.S. M16 military rifle. Caliber: .22 LR. 15-round box magazine. 19.5-inch bbl. w/muzzle brake/flash hider. Rear sight in carrying handle, post front on high ramp. Black-painted mahogany buttstock and forearm. Weight: 6.5 lbs. Importation disc.

MODEL M20D DELUXE . . . . . . NiB $277 Ex $227 Gd $131
Caliber: .22 LR. 15-round box magazine. 19.5-inch bbl. w/ muzzle brake/flash hider. Sights: V-notch rear; blade front. Receiver grooved for scope mounting. Pulong Dalaga stock w/ contrasting forend tip and grip cap, checkered forearm/pistol-grip. Weight: 6 lbs. Importation disc.

STAG ARMS, LLC — New Britain, CT

MODEL 1 . . . . NiB $949 Ex $600 Gd $500
Semi-automatic AR15 platform w/gas impingment system. Caliber: 5.56mm NATO. 30-round magazine. 16-in. bbl., milspec collapsible buttstock, A2 flashhider, sights and pistol grip. Removeable carry handle. Weight: 7 lbs. Made 2003 to date.
Model 1L (left-hand variant), add $40

MODEL 2 . . . . NiB $940 Ex $590 Gd $490
Similar to Model 1 except w/folding rear sight. Weight: 6.5 lbs. Made 2003 to date.
Model 2L (left-hand variant), add $40
Model 2T (quad rail handguard), add $190
Model 2TL (left-hand variant), add $215

MODEL 3 . . . . NiB $895 Ex $550 Gd $480
Similar to Model 1 except optic ready, Diamondhead VRS handguard. Weight: 6.1 lbs. Made 2011 to date.

**Star
Rolling Block Carbine**

Stevens No. 14 Little Scout

Stevens No. 14.5 Little Scout

Stevens No. 44 Ideal

Stevens Ideal Schuetzen Rifle

Stevens Model 87

Model 3L (left-hand variant), add $25
Model 3G (18-in. bbl. w/3G compensator, Magpul stock and
  pistols grip, Samson Evolution handguard, 6.1 lbs.,
  2011-date) . . . . NiB $1459 Ex $900 Gd $780
Model 3GL (left-hand variant), add $20
Model 3T (Diamondhead folding sights and handguard,
  7.4 lbs., 2014-date). . . . . NiB $999 Ex $600 Gd $530
Model 3TL (left-hand variant), add $20
Model 3T-M (Diamondhead folding sights and
  handguard, Magpul stock and pistol grip, 7.4 lbs.,
  2014-date) . . . . NiB $1160 Ex $700 Gd $580
Model 3TL-M (left-hand variant), add. $20

MODEL 4. . . . . NiB $1015 Ex $630 Gd $560
Similar to Model 1 except w/20-in. bbl., A2 buttstock, 5-round
magazine. Weight: 8.5 lbs. Made 2003 to date.
Model 4L (left-hand variant), add $50

MODEL 5. . . . . NiB $895 Ex $550 Gd $480
Similar to Model 1 except w/o rear sight, chambered in 6.8SPC
II. Weight: 6.4 lbs. Made 2011 to date.
Model 5L (left-hand variant), add $50

MODEL 6. . . . . NiB $1055 Ex $650 Gd $530
Similar to Model 1 except w/o sights, 24.1-in. heavy bbl., Hogue
aluminum handguard. Weight: 10 lbs. Made 2011 to date.
Model 6L (left-hand variant), add $40

MODEL 7. . . . . NiB $1055 Ex $650 Gd $530
Similar to Model 6 except w/20.8-in. heavy bbl., chambered in
6.8SPC II. Weight: 10 lbs. Made 2003 to date.
Model 7L (left-hand variant), add $40

GRADING: **NiB** = New in Box   **Ex** = Excellent or NRA 95%   **Gd** = Good or NRA 68%

MODEL 8 . . . . **NiB $1055 Ex $650 Gd $530**
Similar to Model 1 except w/gas piston system, Diamondhead flip-up sights. Weight: 6.9 lbs. Made 2011 to date.
Model 8L (left-hand variant), add $30
Model 8T (Diamondhead folding sights and handguard,
  7.2 lbs., 2013-date) . . . . **NiB $1275 Ex $730 Gd 600**
Model 8TL (left-hand variant), add $20

MODEL 9 . . . . **NiB $990 Ex $580 Gd $500**
Semi-automatic AR15 platform w/blowback system. Caliber: 9mm. 32-round magazine. 16-in. bbl., mil-spec collapsible buttstock, A2 flashhider and pistol grip, optic ready. Weight: 6.8 lbs. Made 2015 to date.
Model 9L (left-hand variant), add $35
Model 9T (Diamondhead folding sights and free float
  handguard, 7.9 lbs., 2015-date) . . . **NiB $1275 Ex $730 Gd 600**
Model 9TL (left-hand variant), add $20

STANDARD ARMS COMPANY —
Wilmington, Delaware

MODEL G AUTOMATIC RIFLE NiB $815 Ex $569 Gd $355
Gas-operated. Autoloading. Hammerless. Takedown. .25-35, .30-30, .25 Rem., .30 Rem., .35 Rem. Magazine capacity: 4 rounds in .35 Rem., 5 rounds in other calibers. 22.38-inch bbl. Weight: 7.75 lbs. Sights: Open sporting rear; ivory bead front. Shotgun-type stock. Made c. 1910. Note: This was the first gas-operated rifle manufactured in the U.S. While essentially an autoloader, the gas port can be closed and the rifle may be operated as a slide-action repeater.

MODEL M HAND-OPERATED
RIFLE . . . . **NiB $737 Ex $543 Gd $431**
Slide-action repeater w/same general specifications as Model G except lacks autoloading feature. Weight: 7 lbs.

STAR — Eibar, Spain
Manufactured by Bonifacio Echeverria, S.A.

ROLLING BLOCK CARBINE . . . **NiB $500 Ex $337 Gd $178**
Single-shot, similar to Remington Rolling Block. .30-30, .357 Mag., .44 Mag. 20-inch bbl. Weight: 6 lbs. Sights: Folding leaf rear; ramp front. Walnut straight-grip stock w/crescent buttplate, forearm w/bbl. band. Imported 1934 to 1975.

STERLING ARMAMENT, LTD. — Essex, England
Imported by Lanchester U.S.A., Inc., Dallas, Texas.

MARK 6 SEMIAUTOMATIC
CARBINE . . . . **NiB $1822 Ex $1177 Gd $987**
Caliber: 9mm Para 34-round magazine. Bbl.: 16.1 inches. Weight: 7.5 lbs. Flip-type rear peep sight, ramp front. Folding metal skeleton stock. Made from 1983 to 1994.

J. STEVENS ARMS CO. — Chicopee Falls, MA
A division of Savage Industries, Westfield, Massachusetts, owned by ATK since 2013. J. Stevens Arms eventually became a division of Savage Industries. Consequently, the "Stevens" brand name is used for some rifles by Savage; see separate Savage-Stevens listings under Savage.

NO. 12 MARKSMAN SINGLE-SHOT
RIFLE . . . . **NiB $456 Ex $324 Gd $189**

Lever-action, tip-up. Takedown. Calibers: .22 LR, .25 R.F., .32 R.F. 22-inch bbl. Plain straight-grip stock, small tapered forearm.

NO. 14 LITTLE SCOUT SINGLE-SHOT
RIFLE . . . . **NiB $455 Ex $310 Gd $180**
Caliber: .22 RF. 18-inch bbl. One-piece slab stock readily distinguishes it from the No. 14X that follows. Made from 1906 to 1910.

NO. 14 1/2 LITTLE SCOUT SINGLE-SHOT
RIFLE . . . . **NiB $455 Ex $309 Gd $200**
Rolling block. Takedown. Caliber: .22 LR. 18- or 20-inch bbl. Weight: 2.75 lbs. Sights: open rear; blade front. Plain straight-grip stock, small tapered forearm.

MODEL 15 . . . . **NiB $227 Ex $150 Gd $144**
Same as Stevens-Springfield Model 15 except w/24-inch bbl., weight: 5 lbs., w/redesigned stock. Made from 1948 to 1965.

MODEL 15Y YOUTH'S RIFLE . . **NiB $221 Ex $155 Gd $127**
Same as Model 15 except w/21-inch bbl., short buttstock, weight: 4.75 lbs. Made from 1958 to 1965.

NO. 44 IDEAL SINGLE-SHOT
RIFLE . . . . **NiB $689 Ex $466 Gd $380**
Rolling block. Lever-action. Takedown. Calibers: .22 LR, .25 R.F., .32 R.F., .25-20 S.S., .32-20, .32-40, .38-40, .38-55, .44-40. Bbl. lengths: 24-inch, 26-inch (round, half-octagon, full-octagon). Weight: 7 lbs w/26-inch round bbl. Sights: Open rear; Rocky Mountain front. Plain straight-grip stock and forearm. Made from 1894 to 1932.

NO. 44 1/2 IDEAL SINGLE-SHOT
RIFLE . . . . **NiB $990 Ex $848 Gd $578**
Falling-block. Lever-action rifle. Aside from the new design action intro. 1903, specifications of this model are the same as those of Model 44. Model 44X disc. 1916.

NOS. 45-54 IDEAL SINGLE-SHOT RIFLES
These are higher-grade models, differing from the standard No. 44 and 44.5 chiefly in finish, engraving, set triggers, levers, bbls., stock, etc. The Schuetzen types (including the Stevens-Pope models) are in this series. Model Nos. 45 to 54 were intro. 1896 and originally had the No. 44-type rolling-block action, which was superseded in 1903 by the No. 44.5-type falling-block action. These models were all disc. about 1916. Generally speaking, the 45-54 series rifles, particularly the Stevens Pope and higher grade Schuetzen models are collector's items, bringing much higher prices than the ordinary No. 44 and 44.5.

MODEL 66 BOLT-ACTION REPEATING
RIFLE . . . . **NiB $255 Ex $140 Gd $121**
Takedown. Caliber: .22 Short, Long, LR. Tubular magazine holds 13 LR, 15 Long, 19 Short. 24-inch bbl. Weight: 5 lbs. Sights: Open rear, bead front. Plain pistol-grip stock w/grooved forearm. Made from 1931 to 1935.

NO. 70 VISIBLE LOADING
SLIDE-ACTION . . . . **NiB $579 Ex $398 Gd $255**
Exposed hammer. Caliber: .22 LR, Long, Short. Tubular magazine holds 11 LR, 13 Long, 15 Short. 22-inch bbl. Weight: 4.5 lbs. Sights: Open rear; bead front. Plain straight-grip stock, grooved slide handle. Made 1907-34. Note: Nos. 702, 71, 712, 72, 722 essentially the same as No. 70, differing chiefly in bbl. length or sight tooling.

Stevens No. 414 Armory

Stevens Model 416

Stevens Buckhorn Model 53

Stevens Buckhorn Model 055

Stevens Buckhorn Model 56

Stevens Buckhorn Model 066

Stevens Buckhorn Model 66

Stevens Buckhorn Model 76

RIFLES

Stevens Crackshot No. 26

MODEL 87 AUTOLOADING
RIFLE. . . . . **NiB $167 Ex $121 Gd $90**
Takedown. Caliber: .22 LR. 15-round tubular magazine. 24-inch bbl. (20-inch on current model). Weight: 6 lbs. Sights: Open rear, bead front. Pistol-grip stock. Made 1938 to date. Note: This model originally bore the "Springfield" brand name, disc. in 1948.

MODEL 200 . . . . NiB $420 Ex $370 Gd $330
Bolt action. Calibers: .22-250 Rem., .223 Rem., .243 Win., .25-06, .270 Win., 7mm-08, .308 Win., .30-06 or .300 Win. Mag. 3- or 4-rnd. internal magazine. 22- or 24-in. bbl. Weight: 6.5 lbs. No sights. Stock: synthetic. Made from 2005 to 2013.

MODEL 300 . . . . NiB $205 Ex $180 Gd $160
Bolt action. Caliber: .22 LR, 10-rnd. magazine. 20.75-in. bbl. Weight: 5 lbs. Adj. sights. Stock: synthetic. Made from 2006 to 2013.

MODEL 305 . . . . NiB $205 Ex $180 Gd $160
Similar to Model 300 except in .22 WMR. Made 2006 to 2013.

MODEL 322 HI-POWER BOLT-ACTION
CARBINE. . . . . **NiB $487 Ex $333 Gd $202**
Caliber: .22 Hornet. 4-round detachable magazine. 21-inch bbl. Weight: 6.75 lbs. Sights: Open rear; ramp front. Pistol-grip stock. Made 1947 to 1950 (See Savage models 340, 342.)

MODEL 322-S . . . . NiB $479 Ex $338 Gd $200
Same as Model 325 except w/peep rear sight. (See Savage models 340S, 342S.)

MODEL 325 HI-POWER BOLT-ACTION
CARBINE. . . . . **NiB $479 Ex $338 Gd $200**
Caliber: .30-30. Three round detachable box magazine. 21-inch bbl. Weight: 6.75 lbs. Sights: Open rear; bead front. Plain pistol-grip stock. Made from 1947 to 1950. (See Savage Model 340.)

MODEL 325-S . . . . NiB $479 Ex $338 Gd $200
Same as Model 325 except w/peep rear sight. (See Savage Model 340S.)

NO. 414 ARMORY MODEL SINGLE-SHOT
RIFLE. . . . . **NiB $488 Ex $398 Gd $316**
No. 44-type lever-action. Calibers: .22 LR only, .22 Short only. 26-inch bbl. Weight: 8 lbs. Sights: Lyman receiver peep; blade front. Plain straight-grip stock, military-type forearm, swivels. Made from 1912 to 1932.

MODEL 416 BOLT-ACTION TARGET
RIFLE. . . . . **NiB $159 Ex $100 Gd $77**
Caliber: .22 LR. Five round detachable box magazine. 26-inch heavy bbl. Weight: 9.5 lbs. Sights: Receiver peep; hooded front. Target stock, swivels, sling. Made from 1937 to 1949.

NO. 419 JUNIOR TARGET MODEL BOLT-ACTION
SINGLE-SHOT RIFLE. . . . . **NiB $433 Ex $325 Gd $255**
Takedown. Caliber: .22 LR. 26-inch bbl. Weight: 5.5 lbs. Sights: Lyman No. 55 rear peep; blade front. Plain junior target stock w/pistol grip and grooved forearm, swivels, sling. Made 1932 to 1936.

BUCKHORN MODEL 053 BOLT-ACTION
SINGLE-SHOT RIFLE. . . . . **NiB $200 Ex $148 Gd $110**
Takedown. Calibers: .22 Short, Long, LR., .22 WRF. .25 Stevens R.F. 24-inch bbl. Weight: 5.5 lbs. Sights: Receiver peep; open middle; hooded front. Sporting stock w/pistol-grip and black forend tip. Made 1935 to 1948.

BUCKHORN MODEL 53 . . . . . NiB $220 Ex $179 Gd $122
Same as Buckhorn Model 053 except w/open rear sight and plain bead front sight.

BUCKHORN 055 . . . . NiB $233 Ex $188 Gd $126
Takedown. Same as Model 056 except in single-shot configuration. Weight: 5.5 lbs. Caliber: .22 LR, Long, Short. 24-inch bbl. Weight: 6 lbs. Sights: Receiver peep, open middle, hooded front. Made from 1935 to 1948.

BUCKHORN MODEL 056 . . . . NiB $230 Ex $190 Gd $131
Takedown. Bolt action. Caliber: .22 LR, Long, Short. Five round detachable box magazine. 24-inch bbl. Weight: 6 lbs. Sights: Receiver peep, open middle, hooded front. Sporting stock w/ pistol grip and black forend tip. Made from 1935 to 1948.

BUCKHORN MODEL 56 . . . . . NiB $230 Ex $190 Gd $131
Same as Buckhorn Model 056 except w/open rear sight and plain bead front sight.

BUCKHORN NO. 057 . . . . NiB $233 Ex $155 Gd $120
Same as Buckhorn Model 076 except w/5-round detachable box magazine. Made from 1939 to 1948.

BUCKHORN NO. 57 . . . . NiB $230 Ex $155 Gd $120
Same as Buckhorn Model 76 except w/5-round detachable box magazine. Made from 1939 to 1948.

BUCKHORN MODEL 066 . . . NiB $290 Ex $227 Gd $130
Takedown. Bolt action. Caliber: .22 LR, Long, Short. Tubular magazine holds 21 Short, 17 Long, 15 LR. 24-inch bbl. Weight: 6 lbs. Sights: Receiver peep; open middle; hooded front. Sporting stock w/pistol grip and black forend tip. Made from 1935 to 1948.

BUCKHORN MODEL 66 . . . . . NiB $219 Ex $133 Gd $210
Same as Buckhorn Model 066 except w/open rear sight, plain bead front sight.

BUCKHORN NO. 076 AUTOLOADING
RIFLE. . . . . **NiB $227 Ex $188 Gd $135**
Takedown. Caliber: .22 LR. 15-round tubular magazine. 24-inch bbl. Weight: 6 lbs. Sights: Receiver peep; open middle; hooded front. Sporting stock w/pistol grip, black forend tip. Made 1938 to 1948.

BUCKHORN NO. 76 . . . . NiB $227 Ex $188 Gd $135
Same as Buckhorn No. 076 except w/open rear sight, plain bead front sight.

Stevens Walnut Hill
No. 417-1

Stevens Walnut Hill
No. 417.5

Stevens Walnut Hill
No. 418

**CRACKSHOT NO. 26 SINGLE-SHOT
RIFLE**. . . . . .NiB $338 Ex $229 Gd $170
Lever-action. Takedown. Calibers: .22 LR, .32 R.F. 18-inch or
22-inch bbl. Weight: 3.25 lbs. Sights: Open rear; blade front.
Plain straight-grip stock, small tapered forearm. Made from
1913 to 1939.

CRACKSHOT NO. 26.5 . . . . . . NiB $325 Ex $220 Gd $195
Same as Crackshot No. 26 on previous page except w/smooth-
bore bbl. for shot cartridges.

"STEVENS FAVORITE"
Also see Savage Model 71.

**FAVORITE NO. 17 SINGLE-SHOT
RIFLE**. . . . . .NiB $333 Ex $227 Gd $200
Lever-action. Takedown. Calibers: .22 LR, .25 R.F., .32 R.F.
24-inch round bbl; other lengths were available. Weight: 4.5
lbs. Sights: Open rear; Rocky Mountain front. Plain straight-grip
stock, small tapered forearm. Made from 1894 to 1935.

FAVORITE NO. 18 . . . . .NiB $422 Ex $300 Gd $179
Same as Favorite No. 17 except w/Vernier peep rear sight, leaf
middle sight, Beach combination front sight.

FAVORITE NO. 19 . . . . .NiB $439 Ex $333 Gd $220
Same as Favorite No. 17 except w/Lyman combination rear
sight, leaf middle sight, Lyman front sight.

FAVORITE NO. 20 . . . . .NiB $420 Ex $325 Gd $215
Same as Favorite No. 17 except w/smoothbore barrel.

FAVORITE NO. 27 . . . . .NiB $439 Ex $333 Gd $220
Same as Favorite No. 17 except w/octagon bbl.

FAVORITE NO. 28 . . . . .NiB $439 Ex $333 Gd $220
Same as Favorite No. 18 except w/octagon bbl.

FAVORITE NO. 29 . . . . .NiB $439 Ex $333 Gd $220
Same as Favorite No. 19 except w/octagon bbl.

**WALNUT HILL NO. 417-0 SINGLE-SHOT
TARGET RIFLE**. . . . . .NiB $909 Ex $777 Gd $530
Lever-action. Calibers: .22 LR only, .22 Short only, .22
Hornet. 28-inch heavy bbl. (extra heavy 29-inch bbl. also
available). Weight: 10.5 lbs. Sights: Lyman No. 52L extension rear; 17A front, scope bases mounted on bbl. Target
stock w/full pistol-grip, beavertail forearm, bbl. band, swivels, sling. Made from 1932 to 1947.

WALNUT HILL NO. 417-1 . . . . NiB $909 Ex $750 Gd $521
Same as No. 417-0 except w/Lyman No. 48L receiver sight.

WALNUT HILL NO. 417-2 . . . . NiB $909 Ex $750 Gd $521
Same as No. 417-0 except w/Lyman No. 144 tang sight.

WALNUT HILL NO. 417-3 . . . . NiB $909 Ex $750 Gd $521
Same as No. 417-0 except w/o sights.

**WALNUT HILL NO. 417.5
SINGLE-SHOT RIFLE**. . . . . NiB $909 Ex $750 Gd $521
Lever-action. Calibers: .22 LR, .22 WMR, .25 R.F., .22 Hornet.
28-inch bbl. Weight: 8.5 lbs. Sights: Lyman No. 144 tang peep,
folding middle; bead front. Sporting stock w/pistol-grip, semi-
beavertail forearm, swivels, sling. Made from 1932 to 1940.

**WALNUT HILL NO. 418 SINGLE-SHOT
RIFLE**. . . . . .NiB $988 Ex $768 Gd $589
Lever-action. Takedown. Calibers: .22 LR only, .22 Short only.
26-inch bbl. Weight: 6.5 lbs. Sights: Lyman No. 144 tang peep;
blade front. Pistol-grip stock, semi-beavertail forearm, swivels,
sling. Made from 1932 to 1940.

WALNUT HILL NO. 418-5 . . . . NiB $988 Ex $768 Gd $589
Same as No. 418 except also available in calibers .22 WRF
and .25 Stevens R.F., w/Lyman No. 2A tang peep sight, bead
front sight.

Stevens-Springfield
Model 15

Stevens-Springfield
Model 82

Stevens-Springfield
Model 83

Stevens-Springfield
Model 84

Stevens-Springfield
Model 85

Stevens-Springfield
Model 86-S

STEVENS-SPRINGFIELD

**MODEL 82 BOLT-ACTION SINGLE-SHOT
RIFLE** . . . . **NiB $178 Ex $144 Gd $115**
Takedown. Caliber: .22 LR, Long, Short. 22-inch bbl. Weight: 4 lbs. Sights: Open rear; gold bead front. Plain pistol-grip stock w/grooved forearm. Made from 1935 to 1939.

**MODEL 83 BOLT-ACTION SINGLE-SHOT
RIFLE** . . . . **NiB $200 Ex $155 Gd $110**
Takedown. Calibers: .22 LR, Long, Short; .22 WRF, .25 Stevens R.F. 24-inch bbl. Weight: 4.5 lbs. Sights: Peep rear; open middle; hooded front. Plain pistol-grip stock w/grooved forearm. Made 1935 to 1939.

MODEL 84 . . . . **NiB $220 Ex $190 Gd $128**
Same as Model 86 except w/5-round detachable box magazine. Pre-1948 rifles of this model were designated Springfield Model 84, later known as Stevens Model 84. Made from 1940 to 1965.

MODEL 84-S (084) . . . . **NiB $220 Ex $190 Gd $128**
Same as Model 84 except w/peep rear sight and hooded front sight. Pre-1948 rifles of this model were designated Springfield Model 084, later known as Stevens Model 84-S. Disc.

MODEL 85 . . . . **NiB $244 Ex $199 Gd $139**
Same as Stevens Model 87 except w/5-round detachable box magazine. Made 1939 to date. Pre-1948 rifles of this model were designated Springfield Model 85, currently known as Stevens Model 85. Earlier models command slight premiums.

MODEL 85-S (085) . . . . **NiB $224 Ex $167 Gd $126**
Same as Model 85 except w/peep rear sight and hooded front sight. Pre-1948 models were designated Springfield Model 085; also known as Stevens Model 85-S.

MODEL 86 BOLT-ACTION . . . . **NiB $224 Ex $167 Gd $126**
Takedown. Caliber: .22 LR, Long, Short. Tubular magazine holds 15 LR, 17 Long, 21 Short. 24-inch bbl. Weight: 6 lbs. Sights: Open rear, gold bead front. Pistol-grip stock, black forend tip on later production. Made 1935 to 1965. Note: The Springfield brand name was disc. in 1948.

MODEL 86-S (086) . . . . **NiB $230 Ex $172 Gd $128**
Same as Model 86 except w/peep rear sight and hooded front sight. Pre-1948 rifles of this model were designated as Springfield Model 086, later known as Stevens Model 86-S. Disc.

MODEL 87-S (087) . . . . **NiB $233 Ex $215 Gd $156**
Same as Stevens Model 87 except w/peep rear sight and hooded front sight. Pre-1948 rifles of this model were designated as Springfield Model 087, later known as Stevens Model 87-S. Disc.

Thompson/Center
Contender Carbine

Thompson/Center TCR
'83 Aristocrat

Thompson/Center TCR '87
Hunter

STEYR DAIMLER PUCH A.G. — Steyr, Austria

See also listings under Mannlicher.

AUG-SA SEMIAUTOMATIC
RIFLE . . . . **NiB $4220 Ex $3370 Gd $2340**
Gas-operated. Caliber: .223 Rem. (5.56mm). Thirty or 40-round magazine. 20-inch bbl. standard; optional 16-inch or 24-inch heavy bbl. w/folding bipod. 31 inches overall. Weight: 8.5 lbs. Sights: Integral 1.5x scope and mount. Green high-impact synthetic stock w/folding vertical grip.

SMALL BORE CARBINE . . . . . . **NiB $440 Ex $300 Gd $166**
Bolt-action repeater. Caliber: .22 LR. Five round detachable box magazine. 19.5-inch bbl. Sights: Leaf rear; hooded bead front. Mannlicher-type stock, checkered, swivels. Made 1953 to 1967.

STOEGER — New York, NY

Manufactured by Franz Jaeger & Co., Suhl, Germany; dist. in the U.S. by A. F. Stoeger, Inc., New York, NY.

HORNET RIFLE . . . . **NiB $1388 Ex $1008 Gd $659**
Same specifications as Herold Rifle, designed and built on a Miniature Mauser-type action. See listing under Herold Bolt-Action Repeating Sporting Rifle for additional specifications. Imported during the 1930s.

SURVIVAL ARMS — Orange, Connecticut

AR-7 EXPLORER . . . . **NiB $180 Ex $155 Gd $98**
Caliber: .22 LR. Eight round magazine. Weight: 3 lbs. Polymer stocks. Drift adj. sights. Disassembles into five separate elements, allowing barrel, action and magazine to fit into butt-stock; assembles quickly w/o tools. Choice of camo, silvertone or black matte finishes. Made from 1992 to 1995.

THOMPSON/CENTER ARMS — Springfield, MA
Acquired by Smith & Wesson in 2007; formerly in Rochester, NH.

To facilitate locating Thompson/Center rifles, models are grouped into three categories: single-shot rifles (below), semi-automatic and bolt-action rifles. For a complete listing, please refer to the index.

- SINGLE-SHOT RIFLES -

CONTENDER CARBINE
Calibers: .22 LR, .22 Hornet, .222 Rem., .223 Rem., 7mm T.C.U., 7x30 Waters, .30-30 Win., .35 Rem., .44 Mag., .357 Rem. Max. and .410 bore. 21-inch interchangeable bbls. 35 inches overall. Adj. iron sights. Checkered American walnut or Rynite stock and forend. Made from 1986 to 2000.
Standard model (rifle calibers) NiB $466 Ex $287 Gd $198
Standard model (.410 bore) . . . NiB $459 Ex $280 Gd $210
Rynite stock model (rifle
   calibers) . . . . **NiB $390 Ex $290 Gd $245**
Rynite stock model (.410 bore) NiB $390 Ex $300 Gd $244
Youth model (all calibers) . . . . . NiB $495 Ex $320 Gd $235
Extra bbl. (rifle calibers), add **$25**
Extra bbl. (.410 bore), add **$35**

CONTENDER CARBINE
SURVIVAL SYSTEM . . . . **NiB $655 Ex $488 Gd $370**
Similar to standard Contender Carbine w/Rynite stock and forend. Comes w/two 16.25-inch bbls. chambered in .223 and .45/.410 bore. Camo Cordura case.

STAINLESS CONTENDER CARBINE
Same as standard Contender Carbine Model, except stainless steel w/blued sights. Calibers: .22 LR, .22 Hornet, .223 Rem., 7-30 Waters, .30-30 Win., .410. Walnut or Rynite stock and forend. Made from 1993 to 2000.
Walnut stock model . . . . **NiB $445 Ex $390 Gd $325**
Rynite stock model . . . . **NiB $495 Ex $425 Gd $300**
Youth stock model . . . . **NiB $467 Ex $388 Gd $287**
Extra bbls. (rifle calibers), add **$25**

Thompson/Center Icon Warlord

Thompson/Center Model R-55 Classic

Thompson/Center Dimension RH Scoped

Thompson/Center Encore Katahdin

ENCORE RIFLE . . . . **NiB $788 Ex $521 Gd $379**
Single-shot, break-action. Cal.: Rimfire and centerfire from .17 Mach 2 to .45-70 Gov't. Bbl.: 24 to 16 inches, interchangeable. Hammer block safety, trigger guard opening lever. Stock: Synthetic black, Realtree camo or American walnut; smooth forearm, Monte Carlo stock w/pistol grip.; adj. rear sight.
w/extra blued bbls., add **$245**
Camo models, add **$150**
w/thumbhole stock, add **$227**
.17 Mach 2, add **$75**
w/stainless bbl., add **$400**
Hunter pkg. (scope, bases, case), add **$300**

ENCORE KATAHDIN . . . . **NiB $633 Ex $467 Gd $379**
Same as Encore but with 18-inch blued bbl. Cal.: .444 Marlin, .450 Marlin or .45-70 Gov't. Stock: Black composite. Fiber optic sights, drilled and tapped for scope. Weight: 6.6 lbs. Made from 2002 to 2005.

PRO HUNTER RIFLE . . . . **NiB $944 Ex $670 Gd $433**
Cal.: Various. Bbl.: 28 inches, stainless steel. Recoil reducing Flex-Tech stock (thumbhole option) in black or camo.
w/camo stock, add **$100**
w/ extra bbl., add **$400**

HOTSHOT (CAMO STOCK) . . **NiB $395 Ex $299 Gd $214**
Youth model. Cal.: 22 LR. Bbl.: 19 inches. Stock: Black synthetic, Realtree AP camo or AP pink camo. Auto safety; drilled and tapped for scope. Weight: 3 lbs.
w/pink camo stock, add **$25**

TCR '83/ARISTOCRAT MODEL . . .**NiB $497 Ex $445 Gd $277**
Break frame, overlever action. Calibers: .223 Rem., .22/250 Rem., .243 Win., 7mm Rem. Mag., .30-06 Springfield. Interchangeable bbls.: 23 inches in length. Weight: 6 lbs., 14 oz. American walnut stock and forearm, checkered, black rubber recoil pad, cheekpiece. Made from 1983 to 1987.
Aristocrat model . . . . **NiB $569 Ex $439 Gd $280**
Extra bbl. (rifle calibers), add **$278**

TCR '87 HUNTER RIFLE . . . . . . **NiB $544 Ex $345 Gd $200**
Similar to TCR '83 except in calibers .22 Hornet, ..222 Rem., 223 Rem., .22-250 Rem., .243 Win., .270 Win., 7mm-08, .308 Win., .30-06, .32-40 Win. Also 12-ga. slug and 10- and 12-ga. field bbls. 23-inch standard or 25.88-inch heavy bbl. interchangeable. 39.5 to 43.38 inches overall. Weight: 6 lbs., 14 oz. to 7.5 lbs. Iron sights optional. Checkered American black walnut buttstock w/fluted end. Disc. 1992.
Extra bbl. (rifle calibers, 10- & 12-ga. field), add **$250**
Extra bbl. (12-ga. slug), add **$300**

- BOLT-ACTION RIFLES -

DIMENSION . . . . **NiB $689 Ex $380 Gd $300**
Push-feed, short or long action, interchangeable barrels. Calibers.: .204 Ruger, .22-250 Rem., .223 Rem., .243 Win., .270 Win., .308 Win., .30-06, .300 Win. Mag., 7mm-08, 7mm Rem. Mag. Bbl.: 22 or 24 in., 3-round detachable box magazine, black synthetic stock w/adj. LOP, Weaver style mounts. Made 2012 to date.

ICON . . . . **NiB $1167 Ex $855 Gd $766**
Bolt action. Cal.: .22-250 Rem., .270 Win., .30-06, .300 Win. Mag., .308 Win., .30 TC, 6.5 Creedmoor, 7mm Mag. Bbl.: 24 inches. Medium or long action, hinged floor plate (on long action). Stock: Black synthetic or RealTree camo, checkered American walnut, classic walnut or Ultra Wood; pistol grip and forearm. Adj. trigger, cocking indicator, three-shot magazine (on medium action). Jeweled bolt handle. Weaver-style bases. Weight: 7.5 pounds. Made 2007-12.
Walnut stock models, add **$75**

ICON PRECISION HUNTER . . . .**NiB $1355 Ex $988 Gd $778**
Bolt action. Cal.: .204 Ruger, .223 Rem., .22-250 Rem., .243 Win., 6.5 Creedmoor, .308 Win. Bbl.: 22 inches, fluted; 5R button rifling. Tactical-style bolt handle. Stock: Brown synthetic with cheekpiece and beavertail fore end. Detachable 3-round magazine with single-shot adapter. Picatinny rail, adj. trigger, sling studs. Made 2009-12.

ICON WARLORD . . . . **NiB $1370 Ex $1127 Gd $888**
Bolt action. Cal.: .308 Win. or .338 Lapua; 5- or 10-round magazine. Bbl.: Fluted, stainless steel, hand lapped. Stock: Carbon fiber tactical style with adj. cheek piece available in OD, flat black or desert sand. Adj. trigger, Picatinny rail. Weight: 12.75 to 13.75 lbs. Made 2010-11.

VENTURE . . . . **NiB $632 Ex $495 Gd $375**
Bolt action. Cal.: 270 Win., .30-06, 7 mm Rem. Mag., .300 Win. Mag. Bbl.: 24 inches, tapered match grade with 5R button rifling. Stock: Black synthetic, sporter design, textured grip. Adj. trigger, two-position safety. Made 2009 to date.

VENTURE PREDATOR . . . . **NiB $690 Ex $559 Gd $433**
Bolt action. Cal.: .204 Ruger, .223 Rem., .22-250 Rem. or .308 Win. Bbl.: 22 inches, fluted, 3-round magazine. Stock: Composite with 100% Realtree Max-1 camo coating; Hogue panels, Weather Shield bolt handle. Weight: 6.75 lbs. Made 2010 to date.

- SEMI-AUTOMATIC RIFLES -

SILVER LYNX . . . . **NiB $488 Ex $390 Gd $300**
Semi-auto. Cal.: .22 LR. Bbl.: 20 inches, match grade; 5-round magazine, stainless steel action and bbl. Stock: Black composite with Monte Carlo cheek piece. Weight: 5.5 lbs. Made 2004-05.

Tikka Model 412S
Double Rifle

Tikka Model LSA55
Deluxe

Tikka Model LSA65
Deluxe

Tikka
Model M65 Sporter

Tikka
Model M65 Wild Boar

RIFLES

MODEL R-55 CLASSIC. . . . . . . **NiB $629 Ex $428 Gd $326**
Semi-auto. Cal.: .17 Mach 2, .22 LR. Bbl.: 22 inches, match
grade; adj. rear sight; blue finish. Blow-back action. Smooth
Monte Carlo walnut stock. Weight: 5.5 lbs. Made 2000-09.
R-55 Target. . . . . **NiB $677 Ex $466 Gd $389**
R-55 Sporter . . . . **NiB $519 Ex $405 Gd $310**

TIKKA — Riihimaki, Finland
*Manufactured by Sako, Ltd. of Riihimaki, Finland and Armi
Marocchi in Italy. Acquired by Beretta Holdings in 2000.*

NOTE: *Tikka New Generation, Battue and Continental series
bolt action rifles are being manufactured by Sako, Ltd., in
Finland. Tikka O/U rifles (previously Valmet) are being manufactured in Italy by Armi Marocchi. For earlier importation see
additional listings under Ithaca LSA and Valmet 412S models.*

T3 HUNTER . . . . **NiB $655 Ex $535 Gd $390**
Calibers:..223, .22-250, .243Win., .308 Win., .25-06, .270
Win., 6.5x55, 270 WSM, 7mm Rem. Mag., .30-06, 300 WSM,
.300 Win. Mag., .338 Win. Mag., Bbl: 22 7/16 inches (24.37
in magnum calibers. Weight: 6.75 pounds. No sights. Walnut
stock with rubber butt pad. Introduced 2003.

T3 LAMINATED STAINLESS . . . **NiB $765 Ex $689 Gd $590**
Same as T3 Hunter but with stainless barrel and action; laminated
stock.

T3 LITE . . . . **NiB $555 Ex $489 Gd $410**
Similar to T3 Hunter but with synthetic stock; weight: 6
pounds, 3 ounces. Introduced 2003.

T3 LITE STAINLESS . . . . **NiB $589 Ex $469 Gd $370**
Same as T3 Lite but with stainless barrel and action.

T3 TACTICAL. . . . . **NiB $1469 Ex $1210 Gd $1077**
Calibers: .223, .308 Win. Similar to T3 Hunter but designed
for law enforcement. Bbl.: 20 inches. Black phosphate finish,
synthetic stock with adjustable comb. Five round detachable
magazine. Picatinny rail on action, fitted for muzzle brake and
bipod use.

T3 VARMINT. . . . . **NiB $844 Ex $707 Gd $567**
Calibers: .223, .22-250, .308 Win. Similar to T3 Hunter but
with heavy bull barrel, synthetic stock, adjustable trigger. Five
round detachable magazine.

T3 VARMINT STAINLESS. . . . . . NiB $844 Ex $707 Gd $567
Similar to T3 Varmint but with stainless barrel and action.

MODEL 412S DOUBLE RIFLE
Calibers: .308 Win., .30-06, 9.3x74R. 24-inch bbl. w/ quarter rib machined for scope mounts; automatic ejectors (9.3x74R only). 40 inches overall. Weight: 8.5 lbs. Ramp front and folding adj. rear sight. Barrel selector on trigger. European walnut buttstock and forearm. Model 412S was replaced by the 512S version in 1994. Imported from 1989 to 1993.
Model 412S (disc. 1993). . . . . NiB $1135 Ex $944 Gd $725
Extra bbl. assembly (O/U shotgun), add $707
Extra bbl. assembly (O/U Combo), add $800
Extra bbl. assembly (OU/rifle), add $1050

MODEL 512S DOUBLE RIFLE
Formerly Valmet 412S. In 1994, following the joint venture of 1989, the model designation was changed to 512S. Imported from 1994 to 1997.
Model 512S. . . . . NiB $1559 Ex $1440 Gd $1100
w/extra bbl. assembly (O/U rifle), add. $800

LSA55 DELUXE. . . . . NiB $590 Ex $534 Gd $450
Same as LSA55 Standard except w/rollover cheekpiece, rosewood grip cap and forend tip, skip checkering, high-luster blue. Imported from 1965 to 1988.

LSA55 SPORTER . . . . NiB $580 Ex $482 Gd $369
Same as LSA55 except has 22.8-inch heavy bbl. w/o sights, special stock w/beavertail forearm, not available in 6mm Rem. Weighs 9 lbs. Imported from 1965 to 1988.

LSA55 STANDARD BOLT-ACTION
REPEATER . . . . NiB $555 Ex $389 Gd $244
Mauser-type action. Calibers: .222 Rem., .22-250, 6mm Rem. Mag., .243 Win., .308 Win. Three round clip magazine. 22.8-inch bbl. Weight: 6.8 lbs. Sights: Folding leaf rear; hooded ramp front. Checkered walnut stock w/Monte Carlo cheekpiece, swivels. Made from 1965-88.

LSA65 DELUXE. . . . . NiB $598 Ex $522 Gd $369
Same as LSA65 Standard except w/special features of LSA55 Deluxe. Imported from 1970 to 1988.

LSA65 STANDARD . . . . NiB $495 Ex $398 Gd $277
Same as LSA55 Standard except calibers: .25-06, 6.5x55 .270 Win., .30-06. Five round magazine, 22-inch bbl., weight: 7.5 lbs. Imported 1970 to 1988.

MODEL M55
Bolt action. Calibers: .222 Rem., .22-250 Rem., .223 Rem. .243 Win., (6mm Rem. and 17 Rem. available in Standard and Deluxe models only). 23.2-inch bbl. (24.8-inch in Sporter and Heavy Barrel models). 42.8 inches overall (44 inches in Sporter and Heavy Barrel models). Weight: 7.25 to 9 lbs. Monte Carlo-style stock w/pistol-grip. Sling swivels. Imported 1965 to 1988.
Continental. . . . . NiB $745 Ex $560 Gd $420
Deluxe model . . . . NiB $808 Ex $579 Gd $443
Sporter . . . . NiB $733 Ex $577 Gd $400
Sporter w/sights . . . . NiB $755 Ex $572 Gd $390
Standard . . . . NiB $669 Ex $544 Gd $367
Super Sporter . . . . NiB $833 Ex $466 Gd $398
Super Sporter w/sights . . . . NiB $909 Ex $478 Gd $514
Trapper . . . . NiB $755 Ex $556 Gd $443

MODEL M65
Bolt action. Calibers: .25-06, .270 Win., .308 Win., .30-06, 7mm Rem. Mag., .300 Win. Mag. (Sporter and Heavy Bbl. models in .270 Win., .308 Win. and .30-06 only). 22.4-inch bbl. (24.8-inch in Sporter and Heavy Bbl. models). 43.2 inches overall (44 inches in Sporter, 44.8 in Heavy Bbl.). Weight: 7.5 to 9.9 lbs. Monte Carlo-style stock w/pistol-grip. Disc. 1989.
Continental. . . . . NiB $755 Ex $572 Gd $439
Deluxe Magnum . . . . NiB $800 Ex $677 Gd $495
Deluxe model . . . . NiB $770 Ex $587 Gd $467
Magnum . . . . NiB $709 Ex $540 Gd $440
Sporter . . . . NiB $579 Ex $555 Gd $398
Sporter w/sights . . . . NiB $789 Ex $645 Gd $445
Standard . . . . NiB $670 Ex $690 Gd $479
Super Sporter . . . . NiB $898 Ex $690 Gd $489
Super Sporter w/sights . . . . NiB $909 Ex $695 Gd $494
Super Sporter Master . . . . NiB $1143 Ex $944 Gd $643

MODEL M65 WILD BOAR . . . . NiB $790 Ex $650 Gd $469
Same general specifications as Model M 65 except 20.8-inch bbl., overall length of 41.6 inches, weight: of 7.5 lbs. Disc. 1989.

NEW GENERATION RIFLES
Short-throw bolt available in three action lengths. Calibers: .22-250 Rem., .223 Rem., .243 Win., .308 Win., (medium action) .25-06 Rem., .270 Win., .30.06, (Long Action) 7mm Rem. Mag., .300 Win. Mag., .338 Win. Mag., (Magnum Action). 22- to 26-inch bbl. 42.25 to 46 inches overall. Weight: 7.2 to 8.5 lbs. Available w/o sights or w/hooded front and open rear sight on quarter rib. Quick-release 3- or 5-round detachable magazine w/recessed side release. Barrel selector on trigger and cocking indicators in tang. European walnut buttstock and forearm matte lacquer finish. Imported 1989 to 1994.
Standard calibers . . . . NiB $769 Ex $688 Gd $487
Magnum calibers, add.. . . . . $50

PREMIUM GRADE RIFLE
Similar to New Generation rifles except w/hand-checkered deluxe wood stock w/roll-over check-piece and rosewood grip cap and forend tip. High polished blued finish. Imported from 1989 to 1994.
Standard calibers . . . . NiB $923 Ex $755 Gd $488
Magnum calibers, add.. . . . . $50

WHITETAIL BOLT-ACTION RIFLE SERIES
New Generation design in multiple model configurations and three action lengths chambered .22-250 to .338 Win. Mag.

BATTUE MODEL
Similar to Hunter Model except designed for snapshooting w/ hooded front and open rear sights on quarter rib. Blued finish. Checkered select walnut stock w/matt lacquered finish. Imported 1991 to 1997.
Battue model (standard w/sights) NiB $568 Ex $466 Gd $388
Magnum calibers, add.. . . . . $50

CONTINENTAL MODEL
Similar to Hunter Model except w/prone-style stock w/wider forearm and 26-inch heavy bbl. chambered for 17 Rem., .22-250 Rem., .223 Rem., .308 Win. (Varmint); .25-06 Rem., .270 Win., 7mm Rem. Mag., .300 Win. Mag. (Long Range). Weight: 8.6 lbs. Imported from 1991 to 2003.
Continental Long-Range model NiB $690 Ex $558 Gd $390
Continental Varmint model. . . . NiB $640 Ex $500 Gd $355
Magnum calibers, add.. . . . . 40%

Tikka Continental/
Varmint

Tikka
Premium Grade

Tikka Whitetail/
Battue

Tikka
Whitetail Hunter Deluxe

Tikka
Whitetail Hunter Synthetic

Tikka
Whitetail Hunter Stainless Synthetic

SPORTER MODEL. . . . . NiB $909 Ex $779 Gd $633
Similar to Hunter Model except 23.5-inch bbl. Five round
detachable mazigine. Chambered .22-250 Rem., .223 Rem.,
.308 Win. Weight: 8.6 lbs. Adjustable buttplate and cheekpiece
w/stippled pistol grip and forend. Imported from 1998 to 2003.

WHITETAIL HUNTER MODEL
Calibers: .22-250 Rem., .223 Rem., .243 Win., .25-06 Rem.,
.270 Win., 7mm Rem. Mag., .308 Win .30.06, .300 Win. Mag.,
.338 Win. Mag. Three or 5-round detachable box magazine.
20.5- to 24.5-inch bbl. with no sights. 42 to 44.5 inches overall. Weight: 7 to 7.5 lbs. Adj. single-stage or single-set trigger.
Blued or stainless finish. All-Weather synthetic or checkered
select walnut stock w/matt lacquered finish. Imported from
1991 to 2002.

Standard model. . . . . NiB $633 Ex $523 Gd $389
Deluxe model . . . . NiB $689 Ex $534 Gd $445
Synthetic model . . . . NiB $689 Ex $534 Gd $445
Stainless model . . . . NiB $689 Ex $534 Gd $445
Magnum calibers, add. $50
Left-hand model, add $100

UBERTI — Accokeek, Maryland

*Formerly in Lakeville, Connecticut. Manufactured By Aldo
Uberti, Ponte Zanano, Italy. Imported by Stoeger Industries,
Accokeek, MD. Division of Beretta Holdings.*

MODEL 1866 SPORTING RIFLE
Replica of Winchester Model 1866 lever-action repeater.
Calibers: .22 LR, .22 WMR, .38 Spec., .44-40, .45 LC. 24.25-
inch octagonal bbl. 43.25 inches overall. Weight: 8.25 lbs.
Blade front sight, rear elevation leaf. Brass frame and buttplate.
Bbl., magazine tube, other metal parts blued. Walnut buttstock
and forearm.
Rifle . . . . NiB $976 Ex $667 Gd $390
Carbine (19-inch round bbl.) . . NiB $944 Ex $600 Gd $409
Trapper (16-inch bbl., Disc. 1989NiB $1145 Ex $855 Gd $600
Rimfire (Indian Rifle) . . . . NiB $744 Ex $523 Gd $379
Rimfire (Indian Carbine). . . . . . NiB $744 Ex $523 Gd $379

MODEL 1873 SPORTING RIFLE
Replica of Winchester Model 1873 lever-action repeater.
Calibers: .22 LR, .22 WMR, .38 Spl., .357 Mag., .44-40, .45 LC.
24.25- or 30-inch octagonal bbl. 43.25 inches overall. Weight:

**Uberti Model
1873 Carbine**

8 lbs. Blade front sight; adj. open rear. Color case-hardened frame. Bbl., magazine tube, hammer, lever and buttplate blued. Walnut buttstock and forearm.

Rifle .NiB $1095 Ex $809 Gd $572
Carbine (19-inch round bbl.) . .NiB $790 Ex $666 Gd $445
Trapper (16-inch bbl.,
    disc. 1990) . . . . .NiB $1095 Ex $809 Gd $572

HENRY RIFLE
Replica of Henry lever-action repeating rifle. Calibers: .44-40, .45 LC. 24.5-inch half-octagon bbl. 43.75 inches overall. Weight: 9.25 lbs. Blade front sight; rear sight adj. for elevation. Brass frame, buttplate and magazine follower. Bbl., magazine tube and remaining parts blued. Walnut buttstock.

Rifle .NiB $1177 Ex $808 Gd $590
Carbine (22.5-inch bbl.) . . . . .NiB $1177 Ex $808 Gd $590
Trapper (16- or 18-inch bbl.) . NiB $1177 Ex $808 Gd $590
Steel frame, add $100

MODEL 1875 ARMY TARGET . . NiB $455 Ex $360 Gd $300
Calibers: .357 Mag., .44-40 Colt. Six-round cylinder. Bbl.: 18 inches. Overall length: 37 inches. Weight: 4 1/2 pounds. Carbine version of Model 1875 single-action revolver. Sights: Adjustable rear, ramp front. Plain walnut stock, polished brass butt plate and trigger guard. Case-hardened frame. Blued or nickel-plated cylinder and barrel. Made in Italy. Introduced in 1987, discontinued 1989.
Nickel finish, add $50

ROLLING BLOCK BABY
CARBINE . . . . .NiB $450 Ex $380 Gd $319
Calibers: .22 LR, .22WMR, .22 Hornet, .357 Mag. Bbl.: 22 inches. Overall length: 35 1/2 inches. Weight: 4 3/4 pounds. Copy of Remington New Model No. 4 carbine featuring brass butt plate and trigger guard; blued barrel; color case-hardened frame. Introduced in 1986.

ULTRA-HI PRODUCTS COMPANY — Hawthorne, New Jersey

MODEL 2200 SINGLE-SHOT BOLT-ACTION
RIFLE .NiB $235 Ex $166 Gd $120
Caliber: .22 LR, Long, Short. .23-inch bbl. Weight: 5 lbs. Sights: Open rear; blade front. Monte Carlo stock w/pistol grip. Made in Japan. Intro. 1977; Disc.

ULTRA LIGHT ARMS COMPANY — Granville, West Virginia

MODEL 20 BOLT-ACTION RIFLE
Calibers: .22-250 Rem., .243 Win., 6mm Rem., .250-3000 Savage, .257 Roberts, .257 Ack., 7mm Mauser, 7mm Ack., 7mm-08 Rem., .284 Win., .300 Savage, .308 Win., .358 Win. Box magazine. 22-inch ultra light bbl. Weight: 4.75 lbs. No sights. Synthetic stock of Kevlar or graphite finished, seven different colors. Nonglare matte or bright metal finish.

Medium-length action available L.H. models. Made from 1985 to 1999.
Standard model. . . . . .NiB $2270 Ex $2056 Gd $1190
Left-hand model, add $150

MODEL 20S BOLT-ACTION RIFLE
Same general specifications as Model 20 except w/short action in calibers 17 Rem., .222 Rem., .223 Rem., .22 Hornet only.
Standard model . . . . .NiB $2467 Ex $2144 Gd $1180
Left-hand model, add $126

MODEL 24 BOLT-ACTION RIFLE
Same general specifications as Model 20 except w/long action in calibers .25-06, .270 Win., .30-06 and 7mm Express only.
Standard model. . . . . .NiB $2350 Ex $2123 Gd $1179
Left-hand model, add $126

MODEL 28 BOLT-ACTION
RIFLE . . . . .NiB $2709 Ex $2033 Gd $1190
Same as Model 20 except w/long magnum action in calibers .264 Win. Mag., 7mm Rem. Mag., .300 Win. Mag., .338 Win. Mag. only. Offered w/recoil arrester. Left-hand model available.

MODEL 40 BOLT-ACTION RIFLE
Similar to Model 28 except in calibers .300 Wby. and .416 Rigby. Weight: 5.5 lbs. Made from 1994 to 1999.
Standard model. . . . . .NiB $2770 Ex $2055 Gd $1290
Left-hand, model, add $126

UNIQUE — Hendaye, France

Manufactured by Manufacture d'Armes des Pyrénées Francaises.

T66 MATCH RIFLE . . . . .NiB $469 Ex $388 Gd $289
Single-shot bolt-action rifle. Caliber: .22 LR. 25.5-inch bbl. Weight: 10.5 lbs. Sights: Micrometer aperture rear; globe front. French walnut target stock w/Monte Carlo comb, bull pistol-grip, wide and deep forearm, stippled grip surfaces, adj. swivel on accessory track, adj. rubber buttplate. Made in 1966. Disc.

U.S. MILITARY RIFLES — Springfield, Massachusetts

Manufactured by Springfield Armory, Remington Arms Co., Winchester Repeating Arms Co., Inland Mfg. Div. of G.M.C., and other contractors. Unless otherwise indicated, the following U.S. military rifles were mfg. at Springfield Armory, Springfield, Mass.

MODEL 1898 KRAG-JORGENSEN
CARBINE . . . . .NiB $2100 Ex $1879 Gd $1100
Same general specifications as Model 1898 Rifle except w/22-inch bbl., weight: 8 lbs., carbine-type stock. Note: The foregoing specifications apply, in general, to Carbine models 1896

U.S. Model 1903-A1
Springfield

U.S. Model 1903-A3
Springfield

U.S. Model 1917
Enfield

U.S. Rifle Caliber .30, M1
(Garand)

U.S. Carbine
Caliber .30, M1

RIFLES

and 1899, which differed from Model 1898 only in minor details.

MODEL 1898 KRAG-JORGENSEN

MILITARY RIFLE . . . . NiB $2100 Ex $1879 Gd $1100
Bolt action. Caliber: .30-40 Krag. Five round hinged box magazine. 30-inch bbl. Weight: 9 lbs. Sights: Adj. rear; blade front. Military-type stock, straight grip. Note: The foregoing specifications apply, in general, to Rifle models 1892 and 1896, which differed from Model 1898.

MODEL 1903 MARK I

SPRINGFIELD . . . . NiB $2144 Ex $1844 Gd $945
Same as Standard Model 1903 except altered to permit use of the Pedersen Device. This device, officially designated "U.S. Automatic Pistol Model 1918," converted the M/1903 to a semiautomatic weapon firing a .30 caliber cartridge similar to .32 automatic pistol ammunition. Mark I rifles have a slot milled in the left side of the receiver to serve as an ejection port when the Pedersen Device was in use; these rifles were also fitted w/a special sear and cut-off. Some 65,000 of these devices were manufactured and, presumably, a like number of M/1903 rifles were converted to handle them. During the early 1930s, all Pedersen Devices were ordered destroyed and the Mark I rifles were reconverted by replacement of the special sear and cut-off w/standard components. Some 20-odd specimens are known to have escaped destruction and are in government museums and private collections. Probably more are extant. Rarely is a Pedersen Device offered for sale, so a current value

cannot be assigned. However, many of the altered rifles were bought by members of the National Rifle Association through the Director of Civilian Marksmanship. Value shown is for the Mark I rifle w/o the Pedersen Device.

MODEL 1903 NATIONAL MATCH

SPRINGFIELD . . . . NiB $1755 Ex $1577 Gd $1109
Same general specifications as Standard Model 1903 except specially selected w/star-gauged bbl., Type C pistol-grip U.S. Model 1903 National Match Springfield (Con't) stock, polished bolt assembly; early types have headless firing pin assembly and reversed safety lock. Produced especially for target shooting.

MODEL 1903 SPRINGFIELD MILITARY RIFLE

Modified Mauser-type bolt action. Caliber: .30-06. Five round box magazine. 23.79-inch bbl. Weight: 8.75 lbs. Sights: Adj. rear; blade front. Military-type stock straight grip. Note: M/1903 rifles of Springfield manufacture w/serial numbers under 800,000 (1903 to 1918) have casehardened receivers; those between 800,000 and 1,278,767 (1918 to 1927) were double heat-treated; rifles numbered over 1,278,767 have nickle steel bolts and receivers. Rock Island production from No. 1 to 285,507 have case-hardened receivers. Improved heat treatment was adopted in May 1918 with No. 285,207; about three months later, with No. 319,921, the use of nickel steel was begun, but the production of some double-heat-treated carbon-steel receivers and bolts continued. Made 1903 to 1930 at Springfield Armory during WWI, M/1903 rifles were also made at Rock Island Arsenal, Rock Island, Ill.
w/case-hardened receiver. . NiB $5566 Ex $4769 Gd $2270
w/double heat-treated receiverNiB $4410 Ex $3636 Gd $1645
w/nickel steel receiver . . . . . NiB $1707 Ex $1530 Gd $977

MODEL 1903 SPRINGFIELD
SPORTER..............NiB $1449 Ex $1978 Gd $899
Same general specifications as National Match except w/sporting design stock, Lyman No. 48 receiver sight.

MODEL 1903 STYLE T SPRINGFIELD
MATCH RIFLE............NiB $1633 Ex $1290 Gd $934
Similar to Springfield Sporter except w/heavy bbl. (26-, 28- or 30-inch), scope bases, globe front sight, weight: 12.5 lbs. w/26-inch bbl.

MODEL 1903 TYPE A SPRINGFIELD
FREE RIFLE ....NiB $1900 Ex $1544 Gd $1150
Same as Style T except made w/28-inch bbl. only, w/Swiss buttplate, weight: 13.25 lbs.

MODEL 1903 TYPE B SPRINGFIELD
FREE RIFLE ....NiB $3510 Ex $2065 Gd $1400
Same as Type A, except w/cheekpiece stock, palm rest, Woodie double-set triggers, Garand fast firing pin, weight: 14.75 lbs.

MODEL 1903-A1 SPRINGFIELD
Same general specifications as Model 1903 except may have Type C pistol-grip stock adopted in 1930. The last Springfields produced at the Springfield Armory were of this type; final serial number was 1,532,878, made in 1939. Note: Late in 1941, Remington Arms Co., Ilion, N.Y., began production, under government contract, of Springfield rifles of this type w/a few minor modifications. These rifles are numbered 3,000,001-3,348,085 and were manufactured before the adoption of Model 1903-A3.
Springfield manufacture ....NiB $1444 Ex $1266 Gd $845
Remington manufacture ......NiB $955 Ex $855 Gd $577

MODEL 1903-A3
SPRINGFIELD............NiB $1698 Ex $1492 Gd $978
Same general specifications as Model 1903-A1, except modified to permit increased production and lower cost; may have either straight-grip or pistol-grip stock, bolt is not interchangeable w/earlier types, w/receiver peep sight, many parts are stamped sheet steel, including the trigger guard and magazine assembly. Quality of these rifles, lower than that of other 1903 Springfields, reflects the emergency conditions under which they were produced. Mfd. during WWII by Remington Arms Co. and L. C. Smith Corona Typewriters, Inc.

MODEL 1922-M1 22 SPRINGFIELD
TARGET RIFLE............NiB $1277 Ex $1068 Gd $788
Modified Model 1903. Caliber: .22 LR. Five round detachable box magazine. 24.5-inch bbl. Weight: 9 lbs. Sights: Lyman No. 48C receiver, blade front. Sporting-type stock similar to that of Model 1903 Springfield Sporter. Issued 1927. Note: The earlier Model 1922, which is seldom encountered, differs from the foregoing chiefly in the bolt mechanism and magazine.

M2 22 SPRINGFIELD TARGET
RIFLE..................NiB $1370 Ex $1123 Gd $580
Same general specifications as Model 1922-M1 except w/ speedlock, improved bolt assembly adj. for headspace. Note: These improvements were later incorporated in many rifles of the preceding models (M1922, M1922MI) and arms so converted were marked "M1922M2" or "M1922MII."

NOTE: *The WWII-vintage .30-caliber U.S. Carbine was mfd. by Inland Mfg. Div. of G.M.C., Dayton, OH; Winchester Repeating Arms Co., New Haven, CT, and other contractors: International Business Machines Corp., Poughkeepsie, NY; National Postal Meter Co., Rochester, NY; Quality Hardware &* Machine Co., and Rock-Ola Co., Chicago, IL; Saginaw Steering Gear Div. of G.M.C., Saginaw, M1; Standard Products Co., Port Clinton, OH; Underwood-Elliott-Fisher Co., Hartford, CT.

CALIBER .30, M1 (GARAND) MIL.
RIFLE..................NiB $1441 Ex $1206 Gd $1166
Clip-fed, gas-operated, air-cooled semiautomatic. Uses a clip containing 8 rounds. 24-inch bbl. Weight: W/o bayonet, 9.5 lbs. Sights: Adj. peep rear; blade front w/guards. Pistol-grip stock, handguards. Made 1937-57. Note: Garand rifles have also been produced by Winchester Repeating Arms Co., Harrington & Richardson Arms Co. and International Harvester Co. Deduct 25% for arsenal-assembled mismatches.

CALIBER .30, M1, NATIONAL
MATCH..................NiB $2389 Ex $1775 Gd $730
Accurized target version of the Garand. Glass-bedded stock; match grade bbl., sights, gas cylinder. "NM" stamped on bbl. forward of handguard.

MODEL 1917 ENFIELD MILITARY
RIFLE..................NiB $977 Ex $800 Gd $370
Modified Mauser-type bolt action. Caliber: .30-06. Five round box magazine. 26-inch bbl. Weight: 9.25 lbs. Sights: Adj. rear; blade front w/guards. Military-type stock w/semi-pistol-grip. This design originated in Great Britain as the, "Pattern 14" and was mfd. in caliber .303 for the British Government in three U.S. plants. In 1917, the U.S. Government contracted w/these firms to produce the same rifle in caliber .30-06; over two million of these Model 1917 Enfields were mfd. While no more were produced after WWI, the U.S. supplied over a million of them to Great Britain during WWII.

NOTE: *The U.S. Model 1917 Enfield was mfd. 1917 to 1918 by Remington Arms Co. of Delaware (later Midvale Steel & Ordnance Co., Eddystone, PA); Remington Arms Co., Ilion, NY; Winchester Repeating Arms Co., New Haven, CT.*

CARBINE, CALIBER .30, M1 ...NiB $844 Ex $677 Gd $497
Gas-operated (short-stroke piston), semiautomatic. 15- or 30-round detachable box magazine. 18-inch bbl. Weight: 5.5 lbs. Sights: adj. rear; blade front sight w/guards. Pistol-grip stock w/handguard, side-mounted web sling. Made 1942 to 1945. In 1963, 150,000 surplus M1 Carbines were sold at $20 each to members of the National Rifle Assn. by the Dept. of the Army. Note: For Winchester and Rock-Ola, add 30%; for Irwin Pedersen, add 80%. Quality Hardware did not complete its production run. Guns produced by other manufacturers were marked "Unquality" & command premium prices.

U.S. REPEATING ARMS CO.

See Winchester rifle listings.

UNIVERSAL FIREARMS, INC. — Miami, Florida

DELUXE CARBINE ....NiB $466 Ex $348 Gd $210
Same as standard model except also available in caliber .256, w/ deluxe walnut Monte Carlo stock and handguard. Made fro 1965 to 1987.

STANDARD M-1 CARBINE ... NiB $375 Ex $246 Gd $175
Same as U.S. Carbine, Cal. .30, M1 except may have either wood or metal handguard, bbl. band w/ or w/o bayonet lug; 5-round magazine standard. Made from 1964 to 1987.

Uzi Semiautomatic
Model B Carbine

Valmet M-62S

Valmet Hunter

Vickers Jubilee
Single-Shot Target Rifle

UZI — Ramat HaSharon, Israel
Manufactured by Israel Military Industries.

SEMIAUTOMATIC MODEL B CARBINE
Calibers: 9mm Parabellum, .41 Action Express, .45 ACP. 20- to 50-round magazine. 16.1-inch bbl. Weight: 8.4 lbs. Metal folding stock. Front post-type sight, open rear, both adj. Imported by Action Arms 1983 to 1989. NFA (Selective Fire) models imported by UZI America, INC., 1983 to 1994.

Model B Carbine (9mm or .45 ACP)... NiB $1500 Ex $1149 Gd $963
Model B Carbine (.41 AE)...NiB $1500 Ex $1149 Gd $963
Centerfire conversion unit, add $215
Rimfire conversion unit, add......................$150

SEMIAUTOMATIC MINI
CARBINE. ....NiB $2375 Ex $2153 Gd $1535
Similar to Uzi Model B except with 19.75-inch bbl.and chambered 9mm Parabellum only. 20-round magazine. Weight: 7.2 lbs. Imported in 1989.

VALMET — Jyväskylä, Finland
M-62S SEMIAUTOMATIC
RIFLE. ....NiB $2590 Ex $2088 Gd $1675
Semiautomatic version of Finnish M-62 automatic assault rifle based on Russian AK-47. Gas-operated rotating bolt action. Caliber: 7.62mmX39 Russian. 15- and 30-round magazines. 16.63-inch bbl. Weight: 8 lbs. w/metal stock. Sights: Tangent

aperture rear; hooded blade front w/luminous flip-up post for low-light use. Tubular steel or wood stock. Intro. 1962. Disc.

M-71S . . . . .NiB $1988 Ex $1766 Gd $1064
Same specifications as M-62S except caliber 5.56mmx45 (.223 Rem.), w/open rear sight, reinforced resin or wood stock, weight: 7.75 lbs. w/former. Made from 1971 to 1989.

M-76 SEMIAUTOMATIC RIFLE
Semiautomatic assault rifle. Gas-operated, rotating bolt action. Caliber: 223 Rem. 15- and 30-round magazines. Made 1984 to 1989.
Wood stock. . . . . .NiB $1788 Ex $1373 Gd $1055
Folding stock. . . . . .NiB $1947 Ex $1522 Gd $1140

M-78 SEMIAUTOMATIC
RIFLE. . . . . .NiB $1865 Ex $1492 Gd $1170
Caliber: 7.62x51 (NATO). 24.13-inch bbl. Overall length: 43.25 inches. Weight: 10.5 lbs.

M-82 SEMIAUTOMATIC
CARBINE. . . . . .NiB $1748 Ex $1399 Gd $1180
Caliber: .223 Rem. 15- or 30-round magazine. 17-inch bbl. 27 inches overall. Weight: 7.75 lbs.

MODEL 412 S DOUBLE
RIFLE. . . . . .NiB $1095 Ex $1077 Gd $933
Boxlock. Manual or automatic extraction. Calibers: .243, .308, .30-06, .375 Win., 9.3x74R. Bbls.: 24-inch over/under. Weight: 8.63 lbs. American walnut checkered stock and forend.

Valmet M-62S

Valmet Hunter

**Vickers Jubilee
Single-Shot Target Rifle**

**HUNTER SEMIAUTOMATIC
RIFLE**....................**NiB $955 Ex $755 Gd $639**
Similar to M-78 except in calibers .223 Rem. (5.56mm), .243 Win., .308 Win. (7.62 NATO) and .30-06. Five , 9- or 15-round magazine. 20.5-inch plain bbl. 42 inches overall. Weight: 8 lbs. Sights: Adj. combination scope mount/rear; blade front, mounted on gas tube. Checkered European walnut buttstock and extended checkered forend and handguard. Imported from 1986 to 1989.

VICKERS LTD. — Crayford, Kent, England

**JUBILEE MODEL SINGLE-SHOT-
TARGET RIFLE**.............**NiB $545 Ex $390 Gd $265**
Round-receiver Martini-type action. Caliber: .22 LR. 28-inch heavy bbl. Weight: 9.5 lbs. Sights: Parker-Hale No. 2 front; Perfection rear peep. One-piece target stock w/full forearm and pistol-grip. Made before WWII.

EMPIRE MODEL............**NiB $569 Ex $439 Gd $287**
Similar to Jubilee Model except w/27- or 30-inch bbl., straight-grip stock, weight: 9.25 lbs. w/30-inch bbl. Made before WWII.

VOERE — Vohrenvach, Germany

**VEC-91 LIGHTNING BOLT-ACTION
RIFLE**..................**NiB $2765 Ex $2165 Gd $1540**
Features unique electronic ignition system to activate or fire caseless ammunition. Calibers: 5.56 UCC (.222 Cal.), 6mm UCC caseless. Five round magazine. 20-inch bbl. 39 inches overall. Weight: 6 lbs. Open adj. rear sight. Drilled and tapped for scope mounts. European walnut stock w/cheekpiece. Twin forward locking lugs. Imported from 1992 to date.

VOERE, VOELTER & COMPANY — Vaehrenbach, Germany
Mauser-Werke acquired Voere in 1987 and all models are now marketed under new designations.

**MODEL 1007 BIATHLON
REPEATER**.................**NiB $466 Ex $350 Gd $254**
Caliber: 22 LR. Five round magazine. 19.5-inch bbl. 39 inches overall. Weight: 5.5 lb. Sights: Adj. rear, blade front. Plain beechwood stock. Imported from 1984 to 1986.

**MODEL 1013 BOLT-ACTION
REPEATER**.................**NiB $766 Ex $544 Gd $389**
Same as Model 1007 except w/military-style stock in 22 WMR caliber. Double-set triggers optional. Imported 1984 to 1986 by KDF, Inc.

MODEL 2107 BOLT-ACTION REPEATER
Caliber: 22 LR. Five or 8-round magazine. 19.5-inch bbl. 41 inches overall. Weight: 6 lbs. Sights: Adj. rear sight, hooded front. European hardwood Monte Carlo-style stock. Imported 1986 by KDF, Inc.
Standard model............**NiB $439 Ex $278 Gd $255**
Deluxe model..............**NiB $469 Ex $347 Gd $266**

WALTHER — Ulm and Arnsberg, Germany
Manufactured by the German firms of Waffenfabrik Walther and Carl Walther Sportwaffenfabrik.

The following Walther rifles were mfd. before WWII by Waffenfabrik Walther, Zella-Mehlis (Thür.), Germany.

**MODEL 1 AUTOLOADING RIFLE
(LIGHT)**...................**NiB $976 Ex $723 Gd $500**
Similar to Standard Model 2 but w/20-inch bbl., lighter stock, weight: 4.5 lbs.

**MODEL 2 AUTOLOADING
RIFLE**....................**NiB $1045 Ex $690 Gd $533**
Bolt-action, may be used as autoloader, manually operated repeater or single-shot. Caliber: .22 LR. Five or 9-round detachable box magazine. 24.5-inch bbl. Weight: 7 lbs. Sights: Tangent-curve rear; ramp front. Sporting stock w/checkered pistol grip, grooved forearm, swivels. Disc.

**OLYMPIC BOLT-ACTION
MATCH RIFLE**............**NiB $1354 Ex $1095 Gd $800**
Single-shot. Caliber: .22 LR. 26-inch heavy bbl. Weight: 13 lbs. Sights: Micrometer extension rear; interchangeable front. Target

Walther Model 1

Walther Model 2

Walther Model GX-1

Walther Model KKM-S

Walther Model U.I.T.
Super Match

stock w/checkered pistol-grip, thumbhole, full beavertail forearm, covered w/corrugated rubber, palm rest, adj. Swiss-type buttplate, swivels. Disc.

MODEL V BOLT-ACTION
SINGLE-SHOT RIFLE . . . . **NiB $645 Ex $544 Gd $368**
Caliber: .22 LR. 26-inch bbl. Weight: 7 lbs. Sights: Open rear; ramp front. Plain pistol-grip stock w/grooved forearm. Disc.

MODEL V MEISTERBÜCHSE
(CHAMPION) . . . . **NiB $675 Ex $494 Gd $338**
Same as standard Model V except w/micrometer open rear sight and checkered pistol-grip. Disc.

POST WWII MODELS
The Walther rifles listed below have been manufactured since WWII by Carl Walther Sportwaffenfabrik, Ulm (Donau), Germany.

MODEL GX-1 FREE RIFLE . . . **NiB $1985 Ex $1544 Gd $933**
Bolt-action, single-shot. Caliber: .22 LR. 25.5-inch heavy bbl. Weight: 15.9 lbs. Sights: Micrometer aperture rear; globe front. Thumbhole stock w/adj. cheekpiece and buttplate w/removable hook, accessory rail. Left-hand stock available. Accessories furnished include hand stop and sling swivel, palm rest, counterweight assembly.

MODEL KKJ SPORTER . . . . . **NiB $1355 Ex $1108 Gd $650**
Bolt action. Caliber: .22 LR. Five round box magazine. 22.5-inch bbl. Weight: 5.5 lbs. Sights: Open rear; hooded ramp

front. Stock w/cheekpiece, checkered pistol-grip and forearm, sling swivels. Disc.

MODEL KKJ-HO . . . . **NiB $1543 Ex $1337 Gd $1110**
Same as Model KKJ except chambered for .22 Hornet. Disc.

MODEL KKJ-MA . . . . **NiB $1321 Ex $1231 Gd $650**
Same as Model KKJ except chambered for .22 WMR. Disc.

MODEL KKM INTERNATIONAL
MATCH RIFLE . . . . **NiB $944 Ex $669 Gd $609**
Bolt-action, single-shot. Caliber: .22 LR. 28-inch heavy bbl. Weight: 15.5 lbs. Sights: Micrometer aperture rear; globe front. Thumbhole stock w/high comb, adj. hook buttplate, accessory rail. Left-hand stock available. Disc.

MODEL KKM-S . . . . **NiB $1000 Ex $877 Gd $641**
Same specifications as Model KKM, except w/adj. cheekpiece. Disc.

MOVING TARGET MATCH
RIFLE . . . . **NiB $1067 Ex $833 Gd $554**
Bolt-action, single-shot. Caliber: .22 LR. 23.6-inch bbl. w/ weight. Weight: 8.6 lbs. Supplied w/o sights. Thumbhole stock w/adj. cheekpiece and buttplate. Left-hand stock available.

PRONE 400 TARGET RIFLE . . . . **NiB $833 Ex $715 Gd $500**
Bolt-action, single-shot. Caliber: .22 LR. 25.5-inch heavy bbl. Weight: 10.25 lbs. Supplied w/o sights. Prone stock w/adj. cheekpiece and buttplate, accessory rail. Left-hand stock available. Disc.

MODEL SSV VARMINT RIFLE . . NiB $770 Ex $697 Gd $488
Bolt-action, single-shot. Calibers: .22 LR, .22 Hornet. 25.5-inch bbl. Weight: 6.75 lbs. Supplied w/o sights. Monte Carlo stock w/high cheekpiece, full pistol grip and forearm. Disc.

MODEL U.I.T. SPECIAL MATCH
RIFLE. . . . . NiB $1187 Ex $1070 Gd $833
Bolt-action, single-shot. Caliber: .22 LR. 25.5-inch bbl. Weight: 10.2 lbs. Sights: Micrometer aperture rear; globe front. Target stock w/high comb, adj. buttplate, accessory rail. Left-hand stock avail. Disc. 1993.

MODEL U.I.T. SUPER MATCH
RIFLE. . . . . NiB $1169 Ex $1966 Gd $788
Bolt-action, single-shot. Caliber: .22 LR. 25.5-inch heavy bbl. Weight: 10.2 lbs. Micrometer aperture rear; globe front. Target stock w/support for off-hand shooting, high comb, adj. buttplate and swivel. Left-hand stock available. Disc. 1993.

MONTGOMERY WARD — Chicago, Illinois
Firearms under the "private label" names of Western Field and Hercules are manufactured by such firms as Mossberg, Stevens, Marlin, and Savage for distribution and sale by Montgomery Ward.

MODEL 14M-497B WESTERN FIELD
BOLT-ACTION RIFLE. . . . . NiB $160 Ex $121 Gd $90
Caliber: .22 RF. Seven round detachable box magazine. 24-inch bbl. Weight: 5 lbs. Sights: Receiver peep; open rear; hooded ramp front. Pistol-grip stock. Mfg. by Mossberg.

MODEL M771 WESTERN FIELD
LEVER-ACTION RIFLE. . . . . NiB $221 Ex $177 Gd $135
Calibers: .30-30, .35 Rem. Six round tubular magazine. 20-inch bbl. Weight: 6.75 lbs. Sights: Open rear; ramp front. Pistol-grip or straight stock, forearm w/barrel band. Mfg. by Mossberg.

MODEL M772 WESTERN FIELD
LEVER-ACTION RIFLE. . . . . NiB $235 Ex $190 Gd $131
Calibers: .30-30, .35 Rem. Six round tubular magazine. 20-inch bbl. Weight: 6.75 lbs. Sights: Open rear; ramp front. Pistol-grip or straight stock, forearm w/bbl. band. Mfg. by Mossberg.

MODEL M775
BOLT-ACTION RIFLE . . . . NiB $158 Ex $139 Gd $99
Calibers: .222 Rem., .22-250, .243 Win., .308 Win. Four round magazine. Weight: 7.5 lbs. Sights: Folding leaf rear; ramp front. Monte Carlo stock w/cheekpiece, pistol-grip. Mfg by Mossberg.

MODEL M776 BOLT-ACTION
RIFLE. . . . . NiB $260 Ex $227 Gd $159
Calibers: .222 Rem., .22-250, .243 Win., .308 Win. Four round magazine. Weight: 7.5 lbs. Sights: Folding leaf rear; ramp front. Monte Carlo stock w/cheekpiece, pistol-grip. Mfg. by Mossberg.

MODEL M778 LEVER-ACTION NiB $255 Ex $188 Gd $138
Calibers: .30-30, .35 Rem. Six round tubular magazine. 20-inch bbl. Weight: 6.75 lbs. Sights: Open rear; ramp front. Pistol-grip or straight stock, forearm w/bbl. band. Mfg. by Mossberg.

MODEL M780 BOLT-ACTION
RIFLE. . . . . NiB $265 Ex $237 Gd $168
Calibers: .222 Rem., .22-250, .243 Win., .308 Win. Four round magazine. Weight: 7.5 lbs. Sights: Folding leaf rear; ramp front. Monte Carlo stock w/cheekpiece, pistol grip. Mfg. by Mossberg.

MODEL M782 BOLT-ACTION
RIFLE. NiB $259 Ex $233 Gd $177
Same general specifications as Model M780.

MODEL M808. . . . . NiB $155 Ex $133 Gd $90
Takedown. Caliber: .22RF. Fifteen round tubular magazine. Bbls.: 20- and 24-inch. Weight: 6 lbs. Sights: Open rear; bead front. Pistol-grip stock. Mfg. by Stevens.

MODEL M832 BOLT-ACTION RIFLE NiB $166 Ex $144 Gd $90
Caliber: .22 RF. Seven round clip magazine. 24-inch bbl. Weight: 6.5 lbs. Sights: Open rear; ramp front. Mfg. by Mossberg.

MODEL M836. . . . . NiB $169 Ex $122 Gd $95
Takedown. Caliber: .22RF. Fifteen round tubular magazine. Bbls.: 20- and 24-inch. Weight: 6 lbs. Sights: Open rear; bead front. Pistol-grip stock. Mfg. by Stevens.

MODEL M865 LEVER-ACTION
CARBINE. . . . . NiB $188 Ex $146 Gd $144
Hammerless. Caliber: .22RF. Tubular magazine. Made w/both 18.5-inch and 20-inch bbls., forearm w/bbl. band, swivels. Weight: 5 lbs. Mfg. by Mossberg.

MODEL M894 AUTO-LOADING
CARBINE. . . . . NiB $198 Ex $137 Gd $105
Caliber: .22 RF. Fifteen round tubular magazine. 20-inch bbl. Weight: 6 lbs. Sights: Open rear; ramp front. Monte Carlo stock w/pistol-grip. Mfg. by Mossberg.

MODEL M-SD57. . . . . NiB $178 Ex $133 Gd $95
Takedown. Caliber: .22RF. 15-round tubular magazine. Bbls.: 20- and 24-inch. Weight: 6 lbs. Sights: Open rear; bead front. Pistol-grip stock. Mfg. by Stevens.

WEATHERBY, INC. — Atascadero, California
Formerly South Gate, CA.

CROWN CUSTOM RIFLE . . NiB $8656 Ex $6298 Gd $4470
Calibers: .240, .30-06, .257, .270, 7mm, .300, and .340. Bbl.: Made to order. Super fancy walnut stock. Also available w/engraved barreled action including gold animal overlay.

DELUXE .378 MAGNUM
RIFLE. . . . . NiB $2233 Ex $2148 Gd $1490
Same general specifications as Deluxe Magnum in other calibers except caliber .378 W. M. Schultz & Larsen action; 26-inch bbl. Disc. 1958.

DELUXE MAGNUM RIFLE . NiB $1844 Ex $1623 Gd $1189
Calibers: .220 Rocket, .257 Weatherby Mag., .270 Wby. Mag, 7mm Wby. Mag., .300 Wby. Mag., .375 Wby. Mag. Specially processed FN Mauser action. 24-inch bbl. (26-inch in .375 cal.). Monte Carlo-style stock w/cheekpiece, black forend tip, grip cap, checkered pistol-grip and forearm, quick-detachable sling swivels. Value shown is for rifle w/o sights. Disc. 1958.

DELUXE RIFLE . . . . NiB $1844 Ex $1623 Gd $1189
Same general specifications as Deluxe Magnum except chambered for standard calibers such as .270, .30-06, etc. Disc. 1958.

FIBERGUARD RIFLE . . . . NiB $810 Ex $679 Gd $485
Same general specifications as Vanguard except for fiberglass stock and matte metal finish. Disc, 1988.

Weatherby Mark V Classicmark I

Weatherby Crown Custom

Weatherby Fiberguard

Weatherby Fibermark

Caliber .378 Wby. . . . . NiB $1177   Ex $944   Gd $577
Caliber .416 Wby. . . . . NiB $1150   Ex $922   Gd $535
Caliber .460 Wby. . . . . NiB $1313   Ex $1044   Gd $590

FIBERMARK RIFLE . . . . **NiB $1377   Ex $1043   Gd $707**
Same general specifications as Mark V except w/molded fiberglass stock, finished in a nonglare black wrinkle finish. The metal is finished in a non-glare matte finish. Disc. 1993.

MARK V ACCUMARK BOLT-ACTION REPEATING RIFLE
Weatherby Mark V magnum action. Calibers: .257 Wby., .270 Wby., 7mm Rem. Mag., 7mm Wby., 7mm STW, .300 Win. Mag., .300 Wby. Mag., .30-338 Wby., .30-378 Wby. and .340 Wby. 26- or 28-inch stainless bbl. w/black oxide flutes. 46.5 or 48.5 inches overall. Weight: 8 to 8.5 lbs. No sights, drilled and tapped for scope. Stainless finish w/blued receiver. H-S Precision black synthetic stock w/aluminum bedding plate, recoil pad and sling swivels. Imported from 1996 to date.
.30-338 & .30-378 Wby. Mag . . . NiB $1674   Ex $1198   Gd $865
All other calibers . . . . NiB $1589   Ex $1020   Gd $722
Left-hand model, add $100

MARK V ACCUMARK LIGHT
WEIGHT RIFLE . . . . NiB $1357   Ex $1154   Gd $744
Similar to the Mark V Accumark except w/LightWeight Mark V action designed for standard calibers w/sixlocking lugs rather than nine. 24-inch stainless bbl. Weight: 5.75 lbs. Gray or black Monte Carlo-style composite Kevlar/fiberglass stock w/ Pachmayr "Decelerator" pad. No sights. Imported from 1997 to 2004.

MARK V CLASSICMARK I RIFLE
Same general specifications as Mark V except w/checkered select American Claro walnut stock w/oil finish and presentation recoil pad. Satin metal finish. Imported from 1992 to 1993.
Calibers .240 to .300 Wby. . . . NiB $1135   Ex $884   Gd $572
Caliber .340 Wby. . . . . NiB $1135   Ex $884   Gd $572

MARK V CLASSICMARK LL RIFLE
Same general specifications as Classicmark I except w/checkered select American walnut stock w/oil finish steel grip cap and Old English recoil pad. Satin metal finish. Right-hand only. Imported from 1992 to 1993.
.240 to .340 Wby. (26-inch bbl.) . . NiB $1589   Ex $1043   Gd $844
.378 Wby. . . . . NiB $1188   Ex $1044   Gd $909
.426 Wby. . . . . NiB $1207   Ex $1044   Gd $1032
.460 Wby. . . . . NiB $1290   Ex $1170   Gd $1056

MARK V DELUXE RIFLE . . . **NiB $2633   Ex $1845   Gd $1579**
Similar to Mark V Sporter except w/Lightweight Mark V action designed for standard calibers w/sixlocking lugs rather than nine, 4- or 5-round magazine. 24-inch bbl. 44 inches overall. Weight: 6.75 lbs. Checkered Monte Carlo American walnut stock w/rosewood forend and pistol grip and diamond inlay. Imported from 1957 to date.

MARK V DELUXE BOLT-ACTION SPORTING RIFLE
Mark V action, right or left hand. Calibers: .22-250, .30-06- .224 Weatherby Varmintmaster; .240, .257, .270, 7mm, .300, .340, .375, .378, .416, .460 Weatherby Magnums. Box magazine holds 2 to 5 cartridges depending on caliber. 24- or 26-inch bbl. Weight: 6.5 to 10.5 lbs. Monte Carlo-style stock w/cheekpiece, skip checkering, forend tip, pistol-grip cap, recoil pad, QD swivels. Values shown are for rifles w/o sights. Made in Germany 1958 to 1969; in Japan 1970 to 1994. Values shown for Japanese production.
.22-250, .224 Wby. . . . . NiB $1790   Ex $1408   Gd $956
.375 H&H Magnum . . . . NiB $1835   Ex $1079   Gd $766
.378 Wby. Mag. . . . . NiB $2239   Ex $1177   Gd $897
.416 Wby. Mag. . . . . NiB $2210   Ex $1443   Gd $833
.460 Wby. Mag. . . . . NiB $2633   Ex $1399   Gd $1069

GRADING: **NiB** = New in Box   **Ex** = Excellent or NRA 95%   **Gd** = Good or NRA 68%

Weatherby Mark V Deluxe

Weatherby Mark V Euromark

Weatherby Mark V Lazermark

MARK V EUROMARK BOLT-ACTION RIFLE
Same general specifications as other Mark V rifles except w/ hand-rubbed, satin oil finish Claro walnut stock and nonglare special process blue matte barreled action. Left-hand models available. Imported from 1986 to 1993. Reintroduced in 1995.

.378 Wby. Mag.	NiB $1855	Ex $1190	Gd $943
.416 Wby. Mag.	NiB $1855	Ex $1190	Gd $943
.460 Wby. Mag.	NiB $1896	Ex $1497	Gd $1108
Other calibers	NiB $1590	Ex $800	Gd $555

MARK V LAZERMARK RIFLE
Same general specifications as Mark V except w/laser-carved stock.

.378 Wby. Mag.	NiB $2022	Ex $1598	Gd $938
.416 Wby. Mag.	NiB $2022	Ex $1598	Gd $938
.460 Wby. Mag.	NiB $1489	Ex $1134	Gd $822
Other calibers	NiB $1489	Ex $1134	Gd $822

MARK V SAFARI GRADE
RIFLE. . . . . NiB $2300 Ex $1841 Gd $1283
Same general specifications as Mark V except extra capacity magazine, bbl. sling swivel, and express rear sight typical "Safari" style.

MARK V SPORTER RIFLE
Sporter version of Mark V Magnum w/low-luster metal finish. Checkered Carlo walnut stock w/o grip cap or forend tip. No sights. Imported from 1993 to date.

Calibers .257 to .300 Wby	NiB $1488	Ex $920	Gd $723
.340 Wby. Mag.	NiB $1644	Ex $923	Gd $555
.375 H&H	NiB $1588	Ex $923	Gd $555

MARK V LIGHTWEIGHT SPORTER
RIFLE. . . . . NiB $1041 Ex $843 Gd $498
Similar to Mark V Sporter except w/Lightweight Mark V action designed for standard calibers w/six locking lugs rather than nine. Imported from 1998 to date.Mark V Stainless Rifle
Similar to the Mark V Magnum except in 400-series stainless steel w/bead-blasted matte finish. Weight: 8 lbs. Monte Carlo synthetic stock w/aluminum bedding block. Imported from 1997 to 2002.

.30-378 Wby Mag.	NiB $1488	Ex $967	Gd $641
.375 H&H	NiB $1455	Ex $975	Gd $643
All other calibers	NiB $1135	Ex $800	Gd $600
w/fluted bbl., add			$150

MARK V (LW) STAINLESS
RIFLE. . . . . NiB $1146 Ex $833 Gd $500

Similar to the Mark V (standard calibers) except in 400-series stainless steel w/bead-blasted matte finish. Five round magazine. 24-inch bbl. 44 inches overall. Weight: 6.5 lbs. Monte Carlo synthetic stock w/aluminum bedding block. Imported from 1997 to 2002.

MARK V SLS RIFLE
Acronym for Stainless Laminated Sporter. Similar to the Mark V Magnum Sporter, except w/stainless 400-series action and 24- or 26-inch stainless bbl. Laminated wood stock. Weight: 8.5 lbs. Black oxide bead-blasted matte blue finish. Imported from 1997 to date.

.340 Wby. Mag.	NiB $1267	Ex $1088	Gd $777
All other calibers	NiB $1200	Ex $955	Gd $724

MARK V SYNTHETIC RIFLE
Similar to the Mark V Magnum except w/Monte Carlo synthetic stock w/aluminum bedding block. 24- or 26-inch standard tapper or fluted bbl. Weight: 7.75 to 8 lbs. Matte blue finish. Imported from 1995 to date.

.340 Wby. Mag.	NiB $1096	Ex $790	Gd $533
.30-378 Wby. Mag.	NiB $1135	Ex $823	Gd $567
All other calibers	NiB $835	Ex $633	Gd $450
W/fluted bbl., add			$126

MARK V ULTRA LIGHT WEIGHT RIFLE
Similar to the Mark V Magnum except w/skeletonized bolt handle. 24- or 26-inch fluted stainless bbl. chambered .257 Wby., .270 Wby., 7mm Rem. Mag., 7mm Wby., .300 Win. Mag., .300 Wby. Monte Carlo synthetic stock w/aluminum bedding block. Weight: 6.75 lbs. Imported from 1998 to date.

Standard calibers	NiB $1648	Ex $1396	Gd $879
Weatherby calibers	NiB $1866	Ex $1545	Gd $1077
Left-hand action, add			$200

MARK XXII DELUXE .22 AUTOMATIC
SPORTER, CLIP-FED MODEL . . NiB $846 Ex $547 Gd $397
Semiautomatic w/single-shot selector. Caliber: .22 LR. Five and 10-round clip magazines. 24-inch bbl. Weight: 6 lbs. Sights: Folding leaf open rear; ramp front. Monte Carlo-type stock w/ cheekpiece, pistol-grip, forend tip, grip cap, skip checkering, QD swivels. Intro. 1964. Made in Italy from 1964 to 1969; in Japan, from 1970 to 191981; in the U.S., from 1982 to 1990.

MARK XXII, TUBULAR MAGAZINE
MODEL. . . . . NiB $844 Ex $546 Gd $397
Same as Mark XXII, clip-fed model except w/15-round tubular magazine. Made in Japan from 1973-81; in the U.S., from 1982-90.

VANGUARD (I) BOLT-ACTION SPORTING RIFLE
Mauser-type action. Calibers: .243 Win., .25-06, .270 Win., 7mm Rem. Mag., .30-06, .300 Win. Mag. Five round magazine; (3-round in Magnum calibers). 24-inch bbl. Weight: 7

Weatherby Mark V Safari Grade

Weatherby Mark XXII Deluxe .22 Automatic Sporter

Weatherby Vanguard (I) VGL Bolt-Action Sporting Rifle

Weatherby Varmintmaster

lbs. 14 oz. No sights. Monte Carlo-type stock w/cheekpiece, rosewood forend tip and pistol-grip cap, checkering, rubber buttpad, QD swivels. Imported from 1970 to 1984.

Standard model . . . . NiB $495 Ex $439 Gd $298
VGL model (w/20-inch bbl., plain checkered
  stock, matte finish) . . . . NiB $650 Ex $533 Gd $400
VGS model (w/24-inch bbl.) . . . NiB $440 Ex $388 Gd $338
VGX model (w/higher grade finish) NiB $655 Ex $493 Gd $339

VANGUARD CLASSIC I RIFLE . NiB $555 Ex $439 Gd $321
Same general specifications as Vanguard VGX Deluxe except w/hand-checkered classic-style stock, black buttpad and satin finish. Calibers .223 Rem., .243 Win. .270 Win., 7mm-08, 7mm Rem. Mag., .30-06 and .308 Win. Imported 1989 to 1994.

VANGUARD CLASSIC II RIFLE . . . NiB $720 Ex $587 Gd $444
Same general specifications as Vanguard VGX Deluxe except custom checkered classic-style American walnut stock w/black forend tip, grip cap and solid black recoil pad, satin finish. Imported 1989 to 1994.

VANGUARD VGX DELUXE . . . . NiB $650 Ex $456 Gd $398
Calibers: .22-250 Rem., .243 Rem., .270 Wby. Mag., .270 Win., 7mm Rem. Mag., .30-06, .300 Win. Mag., .300 Wby. Mag., .338 Win. Mag. Three or 5-round capacity. 24-inch bbl. About 44 inches overall. Weight: 7 to 8.5 lbs. Custom checkered American walnut stock w/Monte Carlo and recoil pad. Rosewood forend tip and pistol-grip cap. High-luster finish. Disc. 1994.

VARMINT SPECIAL BOLT-ACTION
RIFLE . . . . NiB $654 Ex $447 Gd $368
Calibers: .224 Wby., .22-250, 4-round magazine. 26-inch bbl. 45 inches overall. Weight: 7.75 lbs. Checkered walnut stock. No sights. Disc.

WEATHERMARK RIFLE
Same gen. specs. as Classicmark except w/checkered blk. Weathermark composite stock. Mark V bolt act. Cal: .240, .257, .270, .300, .340, .378, .416 and .460 Weatherby Mag.; plus .270 Win., 7mm Rem. Mag., .30-06 and .375 H&H Mag. Wt: 8 to 10 lbs. Right-hand only. Imp. 1992 to 1994.

Calibers .257 to .300 Wby. Mag . . . NiB $798 Ex $616 Gd $452
.340 Wby. Mag. . . . . NiB $835 Ex $647 Gd $445
.375 H&H . . . . NiB $1079 Ex $835 Gd $450
Non-Wby. calibers . . . . NiB $800 Ex $577 Gd $465

WEATHERMARK ALASKAN
RIFLE . . . . NiB $707 Ex $544 Gd $433
Same general specifications as Weathermark except w/nonglare electroless nickel finish. Right-hand only. Imported from 1992 to 1994.

WEIHRAUCH — Melrichstadt, Germany
Imported by European American Armory, Sharpes, FL.

MODEL HW 60 TARGET RIFLE NiB $677 Ex $559 Gd $445
Single-shot. Caliber: .22 LR. 26.75-inch bbl. Walnut stock. Adj. buttplate and trigger. Hooded ramp front sight. Push button safety. Imported 1995 to 1997.

MODEL HW 66 BOLT-ACTION
RIFLE . . . . NiB $645 Ex $482 Gd $338
Caliber: .22 Hornet. 22.75-inch bbl. 41.75 inches overall. Weight: 6.5 lbs. Walnut stock w/cheekpiece. Hooded blade ramp front sight. Checkered pistol grip and forend. Imported from 1989 to 1990.

MODEL HW 660 MATCH BOLT-ACTION
RIFLE . . . . NiB $942 Ex $745 Gd $500
Caliber: .22 LR. 26-inch bbl. 45.33 inches overall. Weight: 10.75 lbs. Walnut or laminated stock w/adj. cheekpiece and buttplate. Checkered pistol grip and forend. Adj. trigger. Imported 1991 to 2005.

RIFLES

WESTERN FIELD RIFLES

See listings under "W" for Montgomery Ward.

WESTLEY RICHARDS & CO., LTD. — London, England

BEST QUALITY DOUBLE
RIFLE . . . . **NiB $35,000 Ex $28,900 Gd $19,670**
Boxlock, hammerless, ejector. Hand-detachable locks. Calibers: .30-06, .318 Accelerated Express, .375 Mag., .425 Mag. Express, .465 Nitro Express, .470 Nitro Express. 25-inch bbls. Weight: 8.5 to 11 lbs. Sights: leaf rear; hooded front. French walnut stock w/cheekpiece, checkered pistol grip and forend.

BEST QUALITY MAGAZINE RIFLE
Mauser or Magnum Mauser action. Calibers: 7mm High Velocity, .30-06, .318 Accelerated Express, .375 Mag., .404 Nitro Express, .425 Mag. Bbl. lengths: 24-inch; 7mm, 22-inch; .425 caliber, 25-inch. Weight 7.25 to 9.25 lbs. Sights: Leaf rear; hooded front.
Standard action . . . . **NiB $11,970 Ex $7295 Gd $5790**
Magnum action . . . . . . **NiB $13,888 Ex $11,679 Gd $8957**

WICHITA ARMS — Wichita, Kansas

MODEL WCR CLASSIC BOLT-ACTION RIFLE
Single-shot. Calibers: .17 Rem through .308 Win. 21-inch octagon bbl. Hand-checkered walnut stock. Drilled and tapped for scope w/no sights. Right or left-hand action w/Canjar trigger. Non-glare blued finish. Made from 1978 to date.
Right-hand model . . . . **NiB $2578 Ex $2044 Gd $1760**
Left-hand model . . . . **NiB $3544 Ex $2967 Gd $2178**

MODEL WMR STAINLESS MAGNUM
BOLT-ACTION RIFLE . . . . . **NiB $2275 Ex $1938 Gd $1179**
Single-shot or w/blind magazine action chambered .270 Win. through .458 Win. Mag. Drilled and tapped for scope with no sights. Fully adj. trigger. 22- or 24-inch bbl. Hand-checkered select walnut stock. Made from 1980 to 1984.

MODEL WSR SILHOUETTE BOLT-ACTION RIFLE
Single-shot, bolt action, chambered in most standard calibers. Right or left-hand action w/fluted bolt. Drilled and tapped for scope mount with no sights. 24-inch bbl. Canjar trigger. Metallic gray Fiberthane stock w/vented rubber recoil pad. Made 1983 to 1995.
Right-hand model . . . . **NiB $2588 Ex $2066 Gd $1449**
Left-hand model . . . . **NiB $2744 Ex $2190 Gd $1633**

MODEL WVR VARMINT RIFLE
Calibers: .17 Rem through .308 Win. Three round magazine. Right or left-hand action w/jeweled bolt. 21-inch bbl. w/o sights. Drilled and tapped for scope. Hand-checkered American walnut pistol-grip stock. Made from 1978 to 1997.
Right-hand model . . . . **NiB $2577 Ex $2038 Gd $1289**
Left-hand model . . . . **NiB $2798 Ex $2260 Gd $1678**

WICKLIFFE RIFLES — Wickliffe, Ohio
Manufactured by Triple S Development Co., Inc.

'76 COMMEMORATIVE
MODEL . . . . **NiB $1169 Ex $1044 Gd $939**

Limited edition of 100. Same as Deluxe Model except w/filled etching on receiver sidewalls, U.S. silver dollar inlaid in stock, 26-inch bbl. only, comes in presentation case. Made in 1976 only.

'76 DELUXE MODEL . . . . **NiB $522 Ex $415 Gd $331**
Same as Standard Model except w/22-inch bbl. in .30-06 only; high-luster blued finish, fancy-grade figured American walnut stock w/nickel silver grip cap.

'76 STANDARD MODEL SINGLE-SHOT
RIFLE . . . . **NiB $443 Ex $300 Gd $217**
Falling-block action. Calibers: .22 Hornet, .223 Rem., .22-250, .243 Win., .25-06, .308 Win., .30-06, .45-70. 22-inch lightweight bbl. (.243 and .308 only) or 26-inch heavy sporter bbl. Weight: 6.75 or 8.5 lbs., depending on bbl. No sights. Select American walnut Monte Carlo stock w/right or left cheekpiece and pistol-grip, semi-beavertail forearm. Intro. 1976. Disc.

STINGER MODEL . . . . **NiB $433 Ex $300 Gd $217**
Falling block, single-shot. Calibers: .22 Hornet and .223 Rem. .22-inch bbl. w/no sights. American walnut Monte Carlo stock w/continental-type forend. Made from 1979-80.

TRADITIONALIST MODEL . . . . **NiB $441 Ex $339 Gd $200**
Falling block single-shot. Calibers: .30-06, .45-70. 24-inch bbl. w/open sights. Hand-checkered. American walnut classic-style buttstock and forearm. Made from 1979 to 1980.

WILKINSON ARMS CO. — Covina, California

TERRY CARBINE . . . . **NiB $551 Ex $408 Gd $354**
Caliber: 9mm Para. Semiautomatic. Thirty round magazine. 16-inch bbl. 30 inches overall. Weight: 6 lbs. Dovetailed receiver for scope mounting. Bolt-type safety. Ejection port w/automatic trap door. Blowback action. Fires from closed bolt. Made from 1975. Disc.

TED WILLIAMS RIFLES

See Sears, Roebuck and Company.

WINCHESTER — Columbia, SC
Formerly New Haven, Connecticut. In 1987 Fabrique Nationale d'Armes de Guerre (FN) acquired U.S. Repeating Arms Company, including the license to manufacture Winchester-brand firearms. Winchester has gone through numerous restructuring and slight name changes since 1866 when it first started production. Formerly known as Winchester Repeating Arms Co., and then mfd. by Winchester-Western Div., Olin Corp., later by U.S. Repeating Arms Company. In 1999, production rights were acquired by Browning Arms Company. FN acquired Browning in 1977.

EARLY MODELS 1873 (MFG. 1873 – 1918)
NOTE: *Most Winchester rifles manufactured prior to 1918 used the date of approximate manufacture as the model number. For example, the Model 1894 repeating rifle was manufactured from 1894 to 1937. When Winchester started using two-digit model numbers after 1918, the "18" was dropped and the rifle was then called the Model 94. The Model 1892 was called the Model 92, etc. Serial numbers for the Model*

Wickliffe '76 Standard
Single-Shot Rifle

Winchester Model 1873
Lever-Action Rifle

**Close-up barrel engraving on Winchester
Model 1873 One of One Thousand.**

*1973s manufactured from 1873-1918 include 1 to 700734.
There are numerous reproductions of the following models:
Model 1873, Model 1885, Model 1886, Model 1892, Model
1895, Model 53 and Model 71*

MODEL 1873 LEVER-ACTION
CARBINE . . . . **NiB $4820 Ex $3933 Gd $2577**
Same as Standard Model 1873 Rifle except w/20-inch bbl.,
12-round magazine, weight: 7.25 lbs.

MODEL 1873 LEVER-ACTION
RIFLE . . . . **NiB $5088 Ex $3482 Gd $2100**
Calibers: .32-20, .38-40, .44-40; a few were chambered for
.22 rimfire. Fifteen round magazine, also made w/6-round
half magazine. 24-inch bbl. (round, half-octagon, octagon).
Weight: 8.5 lbs. Sights: Open rear; bead or blade front. Plain
straight-grip stock and forearm. Made 1873 to 1924. 720,610
rifles of this model were mfd.

MODEL 1873 — ONE OF
ONE THOUSAND NiB **$196,000+ Ex $150,000 Gd $90,000**
During the late 1870s, Winchester offered Model 1873 rifles
of superior accuracy and extra finish, designated "One of
One Thousand" grade, at $100. These rifles are marked "1 of
1000" or "One of One Thousand." Only 136 of this model
are known to have been manufactured. This is one of the
rarest of rifles and, because so few have been sold in recent
years, it is extremely difficult to assign a value, however, an
"excellent" specimen would probably bring a price upward
of $200,000.

MODEL 1873 SPECIAL SPORTING
RIFLE . . . . **NiB $11,375 Ex $10,450 Gd $7,707**
Same as Standard Model 1873 Rifle except this type has
receiver casehardened in colors, pistol-grip stock of select
walnut, octagon bbl. only.

MODEL 1873 SHORT RIFLE (RECENT MFG.)
Similar to Standard Model 1873 Rifle except .357 Mag/.38
Spl. or .44-40. 20-in. round bbl. Straight grip. Blued.
Reintroduced 2013 to present.
Standard . . . . **NiB $1300 Ex $1150 Gd $995**
Case Hardened finish . . . . . **NiB $1580 Ex $1179 Gd $1100**
Sporter Octagon (straight grip; 24-in. bbl.; .357 Mag/.38
Spl., .44-40, .45 Long Colt; case hardened
finish . . . . **NiB $1740 Ex $1279 Gd $1200**
Sporter Octagon (pistol grip; 24-in. bbl.; .357 Mag/.38 Spl.,
.44-40, .45 Long Colt; case hardened
finish . . . . **NiB $1740 Ex $1279 Gd $1200**
Sporter Octagon (pistol grip; 24-in. bbl.;
.357 Mag/.38 Spl., .44-40, .45 Long Colt;
blued finish . . . . **NiB $1740 Ex $1279 Gd $1200**

MODEL 1885 SINGLE-SHOT RIFLE
Designed by John M. Browning, this falling-block, lever-action
rifle was manufactured from 1885 to 1920 in a variety of models
and chambered for most of the popular cartridges of the period
— both rimfire and centerfire from .22 to .50 caliber. There are
two basic styles of frames, low-wall and high-wall. The low-wall
was chambered only for the lower-powered cartridges, while the
high-wall was supplied in all calibers and made in three basic
types. The standard model for No. 3 and heavier barrels is the
type commonly encountered; the thin-walled version was supplied with No. 1 and No. 2 light barrels and the thick-walled
action in the heavier calibers. Made in both solid frame and
takedown versions. Barrels were available in five weights ranging
from the lightweight No. 1 to the extra-heavy No. 5 in round,
half-octagon and full-octagon styles. Many other variations were
also offered.

MODEL 1885 HIGH-WALL SINGLE-SHOT
SPORTING RIFLE . . . . **NiB $5335 Ex $3100 Gd $2066**
Solid frame or takedown. No. 3, 30-inch bbl., standard.
Weight: 9.5 lbs. Standard trigger and lever. Open rear sights;
blade front sight. Plain stock and forend.

MODEL 1885 LOW-WALL SINGLE-SHOT
SPORTING RIFLE . . . . **NiB $1550 Ex $1466 Gd $1000**
Solid frame. No. 1, 28-inch round or octagon bbl. Weight: 7
lbs. Open rear sight; blade front sight. Plain stock and forend.

MODEL 1885 SINGLE-SHOT SCHUETZEN
RIFLE . . . . **NiB $10,000 Ex $7860 Gd $5779**
Solid frame or takedown. High-wall action. Schuetzen double-
set trigger. Spur finger lever. No. 3, 30-inch octagon bbl.

Winchester Model 1886 Rifle w/ Case-colored Receiver

Winchester Model 1886 Rifle w/ Blued Receiver

Winchester Model 1886 Saddle-Ring Carbine

Winchester Model 1890

Winchester Model 1892

Weight: 12 lbs. Vernier rear peep sight; wind-gauge front sight. Fancy walnut Schuetzen stock with checkered pistol-grip and forend. Schuetzen buttplate; adj. palm rest.

MODEL 1885 SINGLE-SHOT SPECIAL
SPORTING RIFLE . . . . NiB $7335 Ex $5550 Gd $5090
Same general specifications as the standard high-wall model except with checkered fancy walnut stock and forend.

MODEL 1885
SINGLE-SHOT MUSKET . . . . NiB $1590 Ex $1171 Gd $878
Solid frame. Low-wall. .22 Short and Long Rifle. 28-inch round bbl. Weight: 8.6 lbs. Lyman rear peep sight; blade front sight. Military-type stock and forend. Note: The U.S. Government purchased a large quantity of these muskets during World War I for training purposes.

MODEL 1885 SINGLE-SHOT "WINDER"
MUSKET . . . . NiB $1488 Ex $1203 Gd $1037
Solid frame or takedown. High-wall. Plain trigger. 28-inch round bbl. Weight: 8.5 lbs. Musket rear sight; blade front sight. Military-type stock and forend w/bbl. band and sling stud/rings.

MODEL 1885 HIGH-WALL SINGLE-SHOT (RECENT MFG.)
Solid frame. 28-in., oct. bbl.; Calibers: .223 Rem., .22-250 Rem., .270 WSM, .300 WSM, or 7mm WSM. Weight: 8.5 lbs. No sights. Checkered stock. Adj. trigger. Blued finish. Made 2005 to 2006.
Standard model. . . . . NiB $1090 Ex $1000 Gd $800

BPCR (.45-70; 30-in. half-rnd., half-oct. bbl.; 10 lbs.; case hardened) . . . . . . NiB $10,270 Ex $7668 Gd $5790
Cenntenial Hunter (.30-06) NiB $1620 Ex $1530 Gd $1300

MODEL 1885 LOW-WALL SINGLE-SHOT (RECENT MFG.)
Solid frame. 24- or 24.5-in. half-rnd., half-oct. or oct. bbl.; Calibers: .17HMR, .22 LR, .22 Hornet, .223 Rem., .22-250 Rem., or .243 Win. Weight: 8 lbs. Smooth or checkered stock. Blued finish.
Grade I .22 LR (1999-2001) . . . NiB $828 Ex $740 Gd $630
High Grade .22 LR (1999-2001)NiB $1180 Ex $1060 Gd $880
Low Wall 1885 (2003-2006) . . NiB $1070 Ex $880 Gd $720
Hunter Rimfire (2014-present)NiB $1470 Ex $1330 Gd $1100

MODEL 1886 LEVER-ACTION RIFLE
Solid frame or takedown. .33 Win., .38-56, .38-70, .40-65, .40-70, .40-82, .45-70, .45-90, .50-100, .50-110. The .33 Win. and .45-70 were the last calibers in which this model was supplied. Eight round tubular magaine; also 4-round half-magazine. 26-inch bbl. (round, half-octagon, octagon). Weight: 7.5 lbs. Sights: Open rear; bead or blade front. Plain straight-grip stock and forend or standard models. Made 1886 to 1935.
Standard model. . . . . NiB $8288 Ex $6399 Gd $5100
Takedown model. . . . . NiB $10,270 Ex $7668 Gd $5790
Deluxe model (checkered pistol grip and high-quality walnut stock) . . . . NiB $17,689 Ex $13,790 Gd $10,777
Lightweight model (.45-70, .33 WCF; tapered round bbl.; half magazine; shotgun butt) . . . NiB $7689 Ex $5790 Gd $4999
Lightweight Deluxe model (checkered pistol grip and high-quality walnut stock) . . .NiB 19,600 Ex $17,000 Gd $13,300

MODEL 1886 SADDLE-RING
CARBINE. . . . . NiB $19,690 Ex $16,660 Gd $13,750
Same as standard rifle except with 22-in. bbl., carbine buttstock and forend. Saddle ring on left side of receiver. Made 1886 to 1935.

Winchester Model 1894

Winchester Model 1894
Fancy-Grade Takedown

Winchester Model 1894 Saddle-
Ring Carbine

MODEL 1886 GRADE I LEVER-ACTION RIFLE (RECENT MFG.)
Newr mfg., simialr to 1886 rifle except .45-70 only. 26-in. octagon bbl.; Weight: 7.5 lbs. Sights: Open rear; blade front. Straight-grip stock and forend. Blued finish. Made 1997 to 1998.
High Grade (gold inlays,
  checkered wood) . . . . . . NiB $1625 Ex $1325 Gd $1060
Takedown model. . . . . NiB $1200 Ex $1060 Gd $900
Extra Light Grade I (22-in. rnd. tapered bbl.; weight:
  7.25 lbs.; made 2000- 2001 and
  2010-2012) . . . . NiB $1270 Ex $1180 Gd $950
Extra Light High Grade (gold inlays, checkered wood; made
  2000-2001) . . . . NiB $1270 Ex $1180 Gd $950
Short Rifle (24-in. rnd. bbl.; weight: 8.37 lbs.; plain wood;
  made 2011-present) . . . . . NiB $1270 Ex $1180 Gd $950
Deluxe Case Hardened (24-in. octagon bbl.;
  weight: 9.75 lbs.; checkered wood; made
  2015-present) . . . . NiB $1740 Ex $1180 Gd $950

MODEL 1890 SLIDE-ACTION RIFLE
Visible hammer. Calibers: .22 Short, Long, LR; .22 WRF (not interchangeable). Tubular magazine holds 15 Short, 12 Long, 11 LR; 12 WRF. 24-inch octagon bbl. Weight: 5.75 lbs. Sights: Open rear; bead front. Plain straight-grip stock, grooved slide handle. Originally solid frame; after No. 15,499, all rifles of this model were takedown-type. Fancy checkered pistol-grip stock, nickel-steel bbl. supplied at extra cost, which can also increase the value by 100% or more. Made from 1890 to 1932.
.22 WRF, blued model. . . . . NiB $2079 Ex $1754 Gd $1166
.22 LR, blued model . . . . . . NiB $2148 Ex $2066 Gd $1180
Color casehardened receiver NiB $6689 Ex $5349 Gd $3730

MODEL 1892 LEVER-ACTION
RIFLE. . . . . NiB $3482 Ex $2210 Gd $1588
Solid frame or takedown. Calibers: .25-20, .32-20, .38-40, .44-40. Thirteen round tubular magazine; also 7-round half-magazine. 24-inch bbl. (round, octagon, half-octagon). Weight: from 6.75 lbs. up. Sights: Open rear; bead front. Plain straight-grip stock and forend. Made from 1892 to 1941.
Deluxe (pistol-grip stock) NiB $15,300 Ex $13,600 Gd $11,700
Musket (full length stock) NiB $21,800 Ex $18,200 Gd $14,600

MODEL 1892 SADDLE-RING
CARBINE. . . . . NiB $5321 Ex $2549 Gd $1266
Same general specifications as the Model 1892 rifle except carbine buttstock, forend and sights. 20-inch bbl. Saddle ring on left side of receiver.

Trapper (12-, 14-, 15-, 16-, or 18-in. bbl.; most common
  15-in.,) . . . . NiB $21,800 Ex $18,200 Gd $14,600

MODEL 1892 GRADE 1 LEVER-ACTION RIFLE (RECENT MFG.)
Similar to the original Model 1892. Calibers: .357 Mag., .44-40, .44 Mag., .45 LC. Ten round magazine. 24-inch round bbl. Weight: 6.25 lbs. 41.25 inches overall. Bead front sight, adjustable buckhorn rear. Etched receiver and gold trigger. Blue finish. Smooth straight-grip walnut stock and forewarn w/ metal grip cap. Made from 1997 to 1999.
Standard Rifle . . . . NiB $677 Ex $558 Gd $425
Short Rifle (20-inch bbl.,
  .44 Mag. only) . . . . NiB $669 Ex $500 Gd $488
Trapper (16-inch bbl., 2011-2012) . . . NiB $1070 Ex $799 Gd $730
Trapper Takedown (16-inch bbl.,
  2011-2012) . . . . NiB $1550 Ex $1100 Gd $960
Case Hardened
  (24-inch bbl., 2011-2012). . NiB $1270 Ex $899 Gd $820

MODEL 1892 CARBINE . . . . . NiB $1160 Ex $900 Gd $750
Similar to Model 1892 Grade 1 except 20-in. round bbl. Made 2011-2013.
Large Loop (2011-2012,
  reintro. 2014-current) . . . . NiB $1260 Ex $930 Gd $810
Short Rifle (2014-current). . . . NiB $1070 Ex $860 Gd $760

NOTE: *Winchester Model 1894 and Model 94 rifles are divided by dates of manufacture as pre-'64 and post-'64 models. Early Model 1894 rifles were manufactured from 1894 to 1898 (serial number range: 1-147684), those made from 1898 to 1929 (serial numbers continues to 1077097). Starting in 1929 only carbines were manufactured. Model 94 Saddle Ring models made from 1929 to late 1930s.*

MODEL 1894 LEVER-ACTION
RIFLE. . . . . NiB $6530 Ex $4739 Gd $3220
Solid frame or takedown. .25-35, .30-30, .32-40, .32 Special, .38-55. Seven round tubular magazine or 4-round half-magazine. 26-inch bbl. (round, octagon, half-octagon). Weight: about 7.35 lbs. Sights: Open rear; bead front. Plain straight-grip stock and forearm on standard model; crescent-shaped or shotgun-style buttplate. Made from 1894-1937. See also Winchester Model 94 for later variations of this model.

MODEL 1894 DELUXE . NiB $12,890 Ex $10,669 Gd $8777
Same general specifications as the standard rifle except checkered pistol-grip buttstock and forend using high-grade walnut. Engraved versions are considerably higher in value.

Winchester Model 1895
Carbine

Winchester Model 1895
Rifle

Winchester Model 1897
Lee Sporting Rifle

Winchester Model 1902

Winchester Model 1903

Winchester Model 1904

Winchester Model 1905

Winchester Model 1906

Winchester Model 1907

Winchester Model 1910

MODEL 1894 SADDLE-RING
CARBINE. . . . . **NiB $2866 Ex $1806 Gd $1100**
Same general specifications as the Model 1894 standard rifle except 20-inch bbl., carbine buttstock, forend, and sights. Saddle ring on left side of receiver. Weight: about 6.5 lbs. Made

MODEL 1894 STANDARD
CARBINE. . . . . **NiB $6798 Ex $4890 Gd $3855**
Same general specifications as Saddle-Ringle Carbine except shotgun type buttstock and plate, no saddle ring, standard open rear sight. Sometimes called "Eastern Carbine." See also Winchester Model 94 carbine.

1895 LEVER-ACTION
CARBINE. . . . . **NiB $4297 Ex $3037 Gd $1971**
Same as Model 95 Standard Rifle except has 22-inch bbl., carbine-style buttstock and forend, weight: About 8 lbs., calibers .30-40 Krag, .30-03, .30-06 and .303, solid frame only.

MODEL1895 LEVER- ACTION
RIFLE. . . . . **NiB $3364 Ex $2130 Gd $1266**
Calibers: .30-40 Krag, .30-03, .30-60, .303 British, 7.62mm Russian, .35 Win., .38-72, .40-72, .405 Win. Four round box magazine except .30-40 and .303, which have 5-round magazines. Bbl. lengths: 24-, 26-, 28-inches (round, half-octagon, octagon). Weight: About 8.5 lbs. Sights: Open rear; bead or blade front. Plain straight-grip stock and forend (standard). Both solid frame and takedown models were made from1897 to 1931.

MODEL 1895 GRADE 1 LEVER-ACTION RIFLE (RECENT MFG.)
Similar to the original Model 1895. Calibers: .270 Win., .30-06, .30-40 Krag, or .405 Win. 4-rnd. magazine. 24-inch round bbl. Weight: 8 lbs. Bead front sight, adjustable buckhorn rear. Top tang safety. Blue finish. Smooth straight-grip walnut stock and forewarm. Made from 1997 to 2004.
Standard model. . . . . **NiB $1180 Ex $1060 Gd $900**
Limited Edition (.30-06 only,
  1995-1997). . . . . **NiB $980 Ex $700 Gd $580**
Limited Edition High Grdae
  (.30-06, 1995-2002). . . . . **NiB $1760 Ex $1300 Gd $1000**

MODEL 1895 THEODORE ROOSEVELT SERIES (RECENT MFG.)
Similar to Model 1895 Grade 1 except .405 Win. only, high polish blue, gold inlays, engraved receiver.
150th Anniversary Custom Grade
  (2008). . . . . **NiB $2760 Ex $2360 Gd $1900**
150th Anniversary High Grade
  (2008). . . . . **NiB $1500 Ex $1300 Gd $1060**
Safari High Grade (2009) . . **NiB $1580 Ex $1360 Gd $1100**
Safari Custom Grade
  (2 gun set, 2009) . . . . . . **NiB $3360 Ex $2960 Gd $2500**

MODEL (1897) LEE BOLT-ACTION RIFLE
Straight-pull bolt-action. .236 U.S. Navy, 5-round box magazine, clip loaded. 24- and 28-inch bbl. Weight: 7.5 to 8.5 lbs.

Sights: Folding leaf rear sight on musket; open sporting sight on sporting rifle.
Musket model . . . . **NiB $1939 Ex $1777 Gd $1129**
Sporting rifle. . . . . **NiB $2000 Ex $1808 Gd $1110**

MODEL 1900 BOLT-ACTION SINGLE-SHOT
RIFLE. . . . . **NiB $628 Ex $499 Gd $356**
Takedown. Caliber: .22 Short and Long. 18-inch bbl. Weight: 2.75 lbs. Open rear sight; blade front sight. One-piece, straight-grip stock. Made from 1899 to 1902.

MODEL 1902 BOLT-ACTION SINGLE-SHOT
RIFLE. . . . . **NiB $495 Ex $369 Gd $269**
Takedown. Basically the same as Model 1900 with minor improvements. Calibers: .22 Short and Long, .22 Extra Long, .22 LR. Weight: 3 lbs. Made from 1902 to 1931.

MODEL 1903 SELF-LOADING
RIFLE. . . . . **NiB $1133 Ex $909 Gd $577**
Takedown. Caliber: .22 Win. Auto. Ten round tubular magazine in buttstock. 20-inch bbl. Weight: 5.75 lbs. Sights: Open rear; bead front. Plain straight-grip stock and forearm (fancy grade illustrated). Made from 1903 to 1936.

MODEL (1904) 99 THUMB-TRIGGER BOLT-ACTION
SINGLE-SHOT RIFLE. . . . . **NiB $833 Ex $707 Gd $510**
Takedown. Same as Model 1902 except fired by pressing a button behind the cocking piece. Made from 1904 to 1923.

MODEL 1904 BOLT-ACTION SINGLE-SHOT
RIFLE. . . . . **NiB $469 Ex $388 Gd $269**
Similar to Model 1902. Takedown. Caliber: 22 Short, Long Extra Long, LR. 21-inch bbl. Weight: 4 lbs. Made from 1904 to 1931.

MODEL 1905
SELF-LOADING RIFLE. . . . . **NiB $768 Ex $580 Gd $500**
Takedown. Calibers: .32 Win. SL or .35 Win. SL. Five or 10-round detachable box magazine. 22-inch bbl. Weight: 7.5 lbs. Sights: Open rear; bead front. Plain pistol-grip stock and forearm. Made from 1905 to 1920.

MODEL 1906
SLIDE-ACTION REPEATER . . **NiB $1590 Ex $1077 Gd $733**
Takedown. Visible hammer. Caliber: .22 Short, Long, LR. Tubular magazine holds 20 Short, 16 Long or 14 LR. 20-inch bbl. Weight: 5 lbs. Sights: Open rear; bead front. Straight-grip stock and grooved forearm. Made from 1906 to 1932.

MODEL 1907 SELF-LOADING
RIFLE . . . .**NiB $733 Ex $589 Gd $421**
Takedown. Caliber: .351 Win. SL. Five or 10-round detachable box magazine. 20-inch bbl. Weight: 7.75 lbs. Sights: Open rear; bead front. Plain pistol-grip stock and forearm. Made 1907 to 1957.

MODEL 1910 SELF-LOADING
RIFLE . . . .**NiB $910 Ex $707 Gd $533**
Takedown. Caliber: .401 Win. SL. Four round detachable box magazine. 20-inch bbl. Weight: 8.5 lbs. Sights: Open rear;

Winchester Model 47

Winchester Model 52
Standard Barrel

Winchester Model 52
International Match

Winchester Model 52
International Prone Target

Winchester Model 52-B
Standard Barrel

Winchester Model 52-B
Sporter

bead front. Plain pistol-grip stock and forearm. Made from 1910 to 1936.

MODEL 43 BOLT-ACTION
SPORTING RIFLE . . . . NiB $855 Ex $679 Gd $480
Standard Grade. Calibers: .218 Bee, .22 Hornet, .25-20, .32-20 (latter two discontinued 1950). Three round detachable box magazine. 24-inch bbl. Weight: 6 lbs. Sights: Open rear, bead front on hooded ramp. Plain pistol-grip stock with swivels. Made from 1949 to 1957.

MODEL 43 SPECIAL GRADE . . NiB $855 Ex $679 Gd $480
Same as Standard Model 43 except has checkered pistol-grip and forearm, grip cap.

MODEL 47 BOLT-ACTION SINGLE-SHOT
RIFLE. . . . . NiB $466 Ex $370 Gd $245
Caliber: .22 Short, Long, LR. 25-inch bbl. Weight: 5.5 lbs. Sights: Peep or open rear; bead front. Plain pistol-grip stock. Made from 1949 to 1954.

MODEL 52 BOLT-ACTION TARGET RIFLE
Standard bbl. First type. .22 LR. Five round box magazine. 28-inch bbl. Weight: 8.75 lbs. Sights: Folding leaf peep rear; blade front sight; standard sights various other combinations available. Scope bases. Semi-military-type target stock w/pistol grip; original model has grasping grooves in forearm; higher comb and semi-beavertail forearm on later models. Numerous changes were made in this model; the most important was the adoption of the speed lock in 1929. Model 52 rifles produced before this change are generally referred to as "slow lock" models. Last arms of this type bore serial numbers followed by the letter "A." Made 1919 to 1937.

**Winchester Model 52-C
Heavy Barrel**

Slow Lock model. . . . . .NiB $909 Ex $622 Gd $370
Speed Lock model. . . . . .NiB $733 Ex $466 Gd $379

MODEL 52 HEAVY BARREL . . .NiB $1379 Ex $1008 Gd $798
First type speed lock. Same general specifications as Standard Model 52 of this type except has heavier bbl., Lyman No. 17G front sight, weight: 10 lbs.

MODEL 52 INTERNATIONAL MATCH RIFLE
Similar to Model 52-D Heavy Barrel except has special lead-lapped bbl., laminated "free rifle"-style stock with high comb, thumbhole, hook buttplate, accessory rail, handstop/swivel assembly, palm rest. Weight: 13.5 lbs. Made from 1969 to 1978.
With standard trigger . . . . . .NiB $1577 Ex $1103 Gd $922
With Kenyon or I.S.U. trigger, add $350

MODEL 52 INTERNATIONAL
PRONE . . . . .NiB $1470 Ex $1133 Gd $909
Similar to Model 52-D Heavy Barrel except has special lead-lapped bbl., prone stock with full pistol-grip, rollover cheekpiece removable for bore-cleaning. Weight 11.5 lbs. Made from 1975 to 1980.

MODEL 52 SPORTING RIFLE
First type. Same as Standard Model 52 of this type except has lightweight 24-inch bbl., Lyman No. 48 receiver sight and gold bead front sight on hooded ramp, deluxe checkered sporting stock with cheekpiece, black forend tip, etc. Weight: 7.75 lbs. Made 1934 to 1958. Reintroduced 1993.
Model 52 Sporter . . . . .NiB $4677 Ex $3200 Gd $1590
Model 52A Sporter . . . . . . .NiB $3290 Ex $2733 Gd $1266
Model 52B Sporter . . . . . . .NiB $4633 Ex $2479 Gd $1790
Model 52C Sporter . . . . . . .NiB $5125 Ex $4120 Gd $2798
Model 52 C Sporter
   (1993 BAC re-issue) . . . . .NiB $650 Ex $500 Gd $433

MODEL 52-B BOLT-ACTION RIFLE
Standard bbl. Extensively redesigned action. Supplied with choice of "Target" stock, an improved version of the previous Model 52 stock, or "Marksman" stock with high comb, full pistol grip and beavertail forearm. Weight: 9 lbs. Offered with a wide choice of target sight combinations (Lyman, Marble-Goss, Redfield, Vaver, Winchester), value shown is for rifle less sight equipment. Other specifications as shown for first type. Made from 1935 to 1947. Reintroduced 1997.
Target model. . . . . .NiB $1270 Ex $968 Gd $755
BAC model (1997 BAC re-issue) . .NiB $1270 Ex $968 Gd $755
USRAC Sporting model. . . . . . .NiB $768 Ex $600 Gd $455

MODEL 52-B BULL GUN HEAVY
BARREL. . . . . .NiB $1880 Ex $1144 Gd $600
Same specifications as Standard Model 52-B except Bull Gun has extra heavy bbl., Marksman stock only, weight: 12 lbs. Heavy Bbl. model weight: 11 lbs. Made 1940 to 1947.

MODEL 52-C BOLT-ACTION RIFLE
Improved action with "Micro-Motion" trigger mechanism and new-type "Marksman" stock. General specifications same as shown for previous models. Made from 1947 to 1961, Bull Gun from 1952. Value shown is for rifle less sights.
Bull Gun (w/extra heavy bbl.,

wt. 12 lbs.) . . . . .NiB $1877 Ex $976 Gd $694
w/standard bbl. (wt. 9.75 lbs.) NiB $1466 Ex $800 Gd $659
Target model (w/heavy bbl.) . .NiB $1455 Ex $909 Gd $689

NOTE: *Following WWI, Winchester had financial difficulties and, like many other firearm firms of the day, failed. However, Winchester continued to operate in the hands of receivers. Then, in 1931, The Western Cartridge Co.—under the leadership of John Olin—purchased all assets of the firm. After that, Winchester leaped ahead of all other firms of the day in firearm and ammunition development.The first sporting firearm to come out of the Winchester plant after WWI was the Model 20 shotgun, but this was quickly followed by the famous Model 52 bolt-action rifle. This was also a time when Winchester dropped the four-digit model numbers and began using two-digit numbers instead. This model-numbering procedure, with one exception (Model 677), continued for the next several years.*

MODEL 52-D BOLT-ACTION
TARGET RIFLE. . . . . .NiB $1377 Ex $976 Gd $488
Redesigned Model 52 action, Single-Shot. Caliber: .22 LR. 28-inch standard or heavy bbl., free-floating, with blocks for standard target scopes. Weight: With standard bbl., 9.75 lbs., with heavy barrel, 11 lbs. Restyled Marksman stock with accessory channel and forend stop, rubber buttplate. Made 1961 to 1978. Value shown is for rifle without sights.

MODEL 53 LEVER-ACTION
REPEATER . . . . .NiB $2343 Ex $1869 Gd $1333
Modification of Model 92. Solid frame or takedown. Calibers: .25-20, .32-20, .44-40. Six round tubular half-magazine in solid frame model. Seven round in takedown. 22-inch nickel steel bbl. Weight: 5.5 to 6.5 lbs. Sights: Open rear; bead front. Redesigned straight-grip stock and forearm. Made from 1924 to 1932.

MODEL 54 BOLT-ACTION HIGH POWER
SPORTING RIFLE (I) . . . . .NiB $1570 Ex $933 Gd $667
First type. Calibers: .270 Win., 7x57mm, .30-30, .30-06, 7.65x53mm, 9x57mm. Five round box magazine. 24-inch bbl. Weight: 7.75 lbs. Sights: Open rear; bead front. Checkered stock w/pistol grip, tapered forearm w/Schnabel tip. This type has two-piece firing pin. Made from 1925 to 1930.

MODEL 54 BOLT-ACTION HIGH POWER
SPORTING RIFLE (II) . . . . . . .NiB $1180 Ex $922 Gd $744
Standard Grade. Improved type with speed lock and one-piece firing pin. Calibers: .22 Hornet, .220 Swift, .250/3000, .257 Roberts, .270 Win., 7x57mm, .30-06. Five round box magazine. 24-inch bbl., 26-inch in cal. .220 Swift. Weight: About 8 lbs. Sights: Open rear, bead front on ramp. NRA-type stock w/ checkered pistol-grip and forearm. Made 1930 to 1936. Add $200 for .22 Hornet caliber.

MODEL 54 CARBINE (I) . . . . .NiB $1495 Ex $884 Gd $601
First type. Same as Model 54 rifle except has 20-inch bbl., plain lightweight stock with grasping grooves in forearm. Weight: 7.25 lbs.

GRADING: **NiB** = New in Box   **Ex** = Excellent or NRA 95%   **Gd** = Good or NRA 68%

Winchester Model 53

Winchester Model 54
Super Grade

Winchester Model 55
"Automatic" Single-Shot

Winchester Model 55
Lever-Action

Winchester Model 56

Winchester Model 57
Target

MODEL 54 CARBINE (II) . . . . NiB $1566 Ex $912 Gd $648
Improved type. Same as Model 54 Standard Grade Sporting Rifle of this type except has 20-inch bbl. Weight: About 7.5 lbs. This model may have either NRA-type stock or the lightweight stock found on the first-type Model 54 Carbine.

**MODEL 54 NATIONAL MATCH
RIFLE. . . . . NiB $1722 Ex $967 Gd $679**
Same as Standard Model 54 except has Lyman sights, scope bases, Marksman-type target stock, weighs 9.5 lbs. Same calibers as Standard Model.

**MODEL 54 SNIPER'S MATCH
RIFLE. . . . . NiB $2489 Ex $1388 Gd $633**
Similar to the earlier Model 54 Sniper's Rifle except has Marksman-type target stock, scope bases, weight: 12.5 lbs. Available in same calibers as Model 54 Standard Grade.

MODEL 54 SNIPER'S RIFLE. . . NiB $2566 Ex $ 1534 Gd $770
Same as Standard Model 54 except has heavy 26-inch bbl., Lyman No. 48 rear peep sight and blade front sight semi-military stock, weight: 11.75 pounds, cal. .30-06 only.

MODEL 54 SUPER GRADE. . . NiB $3144 Ex $2057 Gd $1166
Same as Standard Model 54 Sporter except has deluxe stock with cheekpiece, black forend tip, pistol-grip cap, quick detachable swivels, 1-inch sling strap.

MODEL 54 TARGET RIFLE . . . . NiB $888 Ex $572 Gd $390
Same as Standard Model 54 except has 24-inch medium-weight bbl. (26-inch in cal. .220 Swift), Lyman sights, scope bases, Marksman-type target stock, weight: 10.5 lbs., same calibers as Standard Model.

**MODEL 55 "AUTOMATIC"
SINGLE-SHOT. . . . . NiB $379 Ex $290 Gd $210**
Caliber: .22 Short, Long, LR. 22-inch bbl. Sights: Open rear, bead front. One-piece walnut stock. Weight: About 5.5 lbs. Made from 1958 to 1960.

MODEL 55 LEVER-ACTION REPEATER
Modification of Model 94. Solid frame or takedown. Calibers: .25-35, .30-30, .32 Win. Special. Three round tubular half magazine. 24-inch nickel steel bbl. Weight: About 7 lbs. Sights: Open rear; bead front. Made from 1924 to 1932.
Standard model (straight grip)NiB $2133 Ex $1670 Gd $1006
Deluxe model (pistol grip) . NiB $2287 Ex $1744 Gd $1140

Winchester Model 58

Winchester Model 59

Winchester Model 60A

Winchester Model 61

MODEL 56 BOLT-ACTION SPORTING

RIFLE.................NiB $1179 Ex $1143 Gd $707
Solid frame. Caliber: .22 LR., .22 Short. Five or 10-round detachable box magazine. 22-inch bbl. Weight: 4.75 lbs. Sights: Open rear; bead front. Plain pistol-grip with Schnabel forend. Made 1926 to 1929.

MODEL 57 BOLT-ACTION RIFLE
Solid frame. Same as Model 56 except available (until 1929) in .22 Short as well as LR with 5- or 10-round magazine. Has semi-military style target stock, bbl. band on forend, swivels and web sling, Lyman peep rear sight, weight: 5 lbs. Made from 1926 to 1936.
Sporter model..............NiB $888 Ex $654 Gd $500
Target model..............NiB $733 Ex $679 Gd $500

MODEL 58 BOLT-ACTION

SINGLE-SHOT............NiB $1056 Ex $800 Gd $598
Similar to Model 52. Takedown. Caliber. .22 Short, Long LR. 18-inch bbl. Weight: 3 lbs. Sights, Open rear; blade front. Plain, flat, straight-grip hardwood stock. Not serial numbered. Made 1928 to 1931.

MODEL 59 BOLT-ACTION

SINGLE-SHOT............NiB $1268 Ex $1009 Gd $756
Improved version of Model 58, has 23-inch bbl., redesigned stock w/pistol grip, weight: 4.5 lbs. Made in 1930.

MODEL 60, 60A BOLT-ACTION SINGLE-SHOT
Redesign of Model 59. Caliber: .22 Short, Long, LR. 23-inch bbl. (27-inch after 1933). Weight: 4.25 lbs. Sights: Open rear, blade front. Plain pistol-grip stock. Made 1930 to 1934 (60), 1932 to 1939 (60A).
Model 60 ....NiB $445 Ex $276 Gd $200
Model 60A ....NiB $556 Ex $380 Gd $338

MODEL 60A TARGET RIFLE ...NiB $670 Ex $448 Gd $338
Essentially the same as Model 60 except has Lyman peep rear sight and square top front sight, semi-military target stock and web sling, weight: 5.5 lbs. Made 1932 to 1939.

MODEL 61 HAMMERLESS SLIDE-ACTION REPEATER
Takedown. Caliber: .22 Short, Long, LR. Tubular magazine holds 20 Short, 16 Long, 14 LR. 24-inch round bbl. Weight: 5.5 lbs. Sights: Open rear; bead front. Plain pistol-grip stock, grooved semi-beavertail slide handle. Also available with 24-inch full-octagon bbl. and only calibers .22 Short, .22 LR or .22 WRF. Note: Octagon barrel model discontinued 1943 to 1944; assembled 1948.
w/round bbl..............NiB $1330 Ex $987 Gd $478
w/grooved receiver........NiB $1268 Ex $1160 Gd $800
w/octagon bbl. ....NiB $1766 Ex $1447 Gd $1006

MODEL 61 MAGNUM ....NiB $2650 Ex $1854 Gd $1000
Same as Standard Model 61 except chambered for .22 WMR; magazine holds 12 rounds. Made from 1960 to 1963.

MODEL 62 VISIBLE

HAMMER ....NiB $1560 Ex $1288 Gd $1043
Modernized version of Model 1890. Caliber: .22 Short, Long, LR. 23-inch bbl. Weight: 5.5 lbs. Plain straight-grip stock, grooved semibeavertail slide handle. Also available in Gallery Model chambered for .22 Short only. Made from 1932 to 1959. Note: Pre-WWII model (small forearm) commands 25% higher price.

MODEL 63 SELF-LOADING RIFLE
Takedown. Caliber: .22 LR High Speed only. Ten round tubular magazine in buttstock. 23-inch bbl. Weight: 5.5 lbs. Sights: Open rear, bead front. Plain pistol-grip stock and forearm. Originally available with 20-inch bbl. as well as 23-inch. Made from 1933 to 1959. Reintroduced in 1997.
w/23-inch bbl. ....NiB $1144 Ex $996 Gd $573
w/20-inch bbl. ....NiB $2690 Ex $1877 Gd $1133
w/grooved receiver........NiB $2711 Ex $1912 Gd $995
Grade I (1997 BAC re-issue)...NiB $707 Ex $576 Gd $488
High Grade (1997 BAC re-issue)NiB $705 Ex $579 Gd $495

MODEL 67 BOLT-ACTION

SINGLE-SHOT RIFLE .... NiB $345 Ex $259 Gd $200
Takedown. Calibers: .22 Short, Long, LR, .22 LR round (smoothbore), .22 WRF. 27-inch bbl. Weight: 5 lbs. Sights: Open rear, bead front. Plain pistol-grip stock (original model had grasping grooves in forearm). Made from 1934 to 1963.

Winchester Model 62

Winchester Model 63

Winchester Model 64
Deer Rifle

Winchester Model 64
Standard

Winchester Model 64
1972-74 Type

Winchester Model 65

Winchester Model 67

Winchester Model 68

Winchester Model 69

MODEL 67 BOY'S RIFLE......NiB $345 Ex $259 Gd $200
Same as Standard Model 67 except has shorter stock, 20-inch bbl., weighs 4.25 lbs.

**MODEL 68 BOLT-ACTION
SINGLE-SHOT**..............NiB $345 Ex $259 Gd $200
Same as Model 67 except has rear peep sight. Made 1934 to 1946.

**MODEL 69 BOLT- ACTION
RIFLE'S** ....NiB $450 Ex $370 Gd $200
Takedown. Caliber: .22 Short, Long, LR. Five or 10-round box magazine. 25-inch bbl. Weight: 5.5 lbs. Peep or open rear sight. Plain pistol-grip stock. Rifle cocks on closing motion of the bolt. Made from 1935 to 1937.

MODEL 69A BOLT-ACTION RIFLE
Same as the Model 69 except cocking mechanism was changed to cock the rifle by the opening motion of the bolt. Made from 1937 to 1963. Note: Models with grooved receivers command 20% higher prices.
Model 69A standard ....NiB $489 Ex $397 Gd $290
Match model w/Lyman No. 57E
  receiver sight ....NiB $546 Ex $444 Gd $314
Target model w/Winchester
  peep rear sight, swivels, sling NiB $690 Ex $567 Gd $389

MODEL 70
Introduced in 1937, the Model 70 Bolt-Action Repeating Rifle was offered in several styles and calibers. Only minor design changes were made over a period of 27 years and more than 500,000 of these rifles were sold. The original model was dubbed "The Rifleman's Rifle." In 1964, the original Model 70 was superseded by a revised version with redesigned action, improved bolt, swaged (free-floating) barrel, restyled stock. This model again underwent major changes in 1972. Most visible: New stock with contrasting forend tip and grip cap, cut checkering (instead of impressed as in predecessor) knurled bolt handle. The action was machined from a solid block of steel with barrels made from chrome molybdenum steel. Other changes in the design and style of the Model 70 continued. The XTR models were added in 1978 along with the Model 70A, the latter omitting the white liners, forend caps and floor plates. In 1981, an XTR Featherweight Model was added to the line, beginning with serial number G1,440,000. This version featured lighter barrels, fancy-checkered stocks with Schnabel forend. After U.S. Repeating Arms took over the Winchester plant, the Model 70 went through even more changes as described under that section of Winchester rifles.

PRE-1964 MODEL 70

MODEL 70 AFRICAN RIFLE NiB $8000 Ex $5600 Gd $3809
Same general specifications as Super Grade Model 70 except w/25-inch bbl., 3-round magazine, Monte Carlo stock w/recoil pad. Weight: 9.5 lbs. Caliber: .458 Winchester Magnum. Made from 1956 to 1963.

MODEL 70 ALASKAN
Same as Standard Model 70 except calibers .338 Win. Mag., .375 H&H Mag.; 3-round magazine in .338, 4-round in .375 caliber; 25-inch bbl.; stock w/recoil pad. Weight: 8 lbs. in .338; 8.75 lbs. in .375 caliber. Made from 1960 to 1963.
.338 Win. Mag...........NiB $4135 Ex $2170 Gd $1166
.375 H&H Mag. ....NiB $4395 Ex $2100 Gd $1189

MODEL 70 BULL GUN.... NiB $4467 Ex $3889 Gd $2356
Same as Standard Model 70 except w/heavy 28-inch bbl., scope bases, Marksman stock, weighs 13.25 lbs., caliber .300 H&H Magnum and .30-06 only. Disc. in 1963.

MODEL 70 FEATHERWEIGHT SPORTER
Same as Standard Model 70 except w/redesigned stock and 22-inch bbl., aluminum trigger guard, floorplate and buttplate. Calibers: .243 Win., .264 Win. Mag., .270 Win., .308 Win., .30-06, .358 Win. Weight: 6.5 lbs. Made from 1952 to 1963.
.243 Win. ....NiB $1790 Ex $1019 Gd $707
.264 Win. Mag ....NiB $2164 Ex $1443 Gd $998
.270 Win. ....NiB $1869 Ex $1233 Gd $854
.30-06 Springfield ....NiB $1043 Ex $888 Gd $596
.308 Win. ....NiB $1278 Ex $866 Gd $658
.358 Win. ....NiB $4566 Ex $3000 Gd $2043

**MODEL 70 NATIONAL MATCH
RIFLE**....................NiB $3376 Ex $1943 Gd $1723
Same as Standard Model 70 except w/scope bases, Marksman-type target stock, weight: 9.5 lbs. caliber .30-06 only. Disc. 1960.

MODEL 70 STANDARD GRADE
Calibers: .22 Hornet, .220 Swift, .243 Win., .250-3000, .257 Roberts, .270 Win., 7x57mm, .30-06, .308 Win., .300 H&H Mag., .375 H&H Mag. Five round box magazine (4-round in Magnum calibers). 24-inch bbl. standard; 26-inch in .220 Swift and .300 Mag.; 25-inch in .375 Mag.; at one time a 20-inch bbl. was available. Sights: Open rear; hooded ramp front. Checkered walnut stock; Monte Carlo comb standard on later production. Weight: From 7.75 lbs. depending on caliber and bbl. length. Made from 1937 to 1963.
.22 Hornet (1937-58) .....NiB $3466 Ex $2033 Gd $1266
.220 Swift (1937-63).......NiB $1497 Ex $1266 Gd $879
.243 Win. (1955-63).......NiB $2145 Ex $1077 Gd $910
.250-3000 Sav. (1937-49) .NiB $5433 Ex $3810 Gd $2244
.257 Roberts (1937-59)....NiB $3809 Ex $2088 Gd $1110
.264 Win. Mag. (1959-63,
  ltd pr) ....NiB $1988 Ex $1154 Gd $877
.270 Win. (1937-63) ....NiB $2588 Ex $2000 Gd $1165
7x57mm Mauser (1937-49) .. NiB $6970 Ex $4650 Gd $4077
7.65 Argentine (1937, limited prod.) Very Rare
.30-06 Springfield
  (1937-63) ....NiB $3466 Ex $1880 Gd $1299
.308 Win. (1952-63, special order) Very Rare
  .300 H&H (1937-63) ...NiB $3598 Ex $2079 Gd $1599
.300 Sav. (1944-50, limited prod.) Rare
.300 Win. Mag. (1962-63) .NiB $2244 Ex $1867 Gd $1265
.338 Win. Mag. (1959-63, special
  order only) ....NiB $2144 Ex $1675 Gd $1197
.35 Rem. (1941-47, limited prod.) Very Rare
.358 Win. (1955-58) Very Rare
.375 H&H (1937-63) .....NiB $4676 Ex $4054 Gd $2354

RIFLES

Winchester Model 70
Basic Post-WWII Model

Winchester Model 70
Standard

Winchester Model 70
African (1964)

Winchester Model 70
Deluxe (1964)]

.458 Win. Mag. (1956-63) Super Grade
only. . . . . NiB $4000 Ex $2978 Gd $2369
9x57 Mauser (1937 only, limited prod.) Very Rare

MODEL 70 SUPER GRADE
Same as Standard Grade Model 70 except w/deluxe stock w/ cheekpiece, black forend tip, pistol-grip cap, quick detachable swivels, sling. Disc. 1960. Prices for Super Grade models also reflect rarity in both production and caliber. Values are generally twice that of standard models of similar configuration.

MODEL 70 SUPER GRADE FEATHERWEIGHT
Same as Standard Grade Featherweight except w/deluxe stock w/cheekpiece, black forend tip, pistol-grip cap, quick detachable swivels, sling. Disc. 1960. Note: SG-FWs are very rare, but unless properly documented will not command premium prices. Prices for authenticated Super Grades Featherweight models are generally 4 to 5 times that of a standard production Featherweight model w/similar chambering.

MODEL 70 TARGET RIFLE
Same as Standard Model 70 except w/24-inch medium-weight bbl., scope bases, Marksman stock, weight 10.5 lbs. Originally offered in all of the Model 70 calibers, this rifle was available later in calibers .243 Win. and .30-06. Disc. 1963. Values are generally twice that of standard models of similar configuration.

MODEL 70 TARGET HEAVY
WEIGHT . . . . NiB $3160 Ex $2244 Gd $1590
Same general specifications as Standard Model 70 except w/ either 24- or 26-inch heavy weight bbl. weight: 10.5 lbs. No checkering. .243 and .30-06 calibers.

MODEL 70 TARGET BULL
BARREL. . . . . NiB $4466 Ex $2587 Gd $1964
Same general specifications as Standard Model 70 except 28-inch heavy weight bbl. and chambered for either .30-06 or .300 H&H Mag. Drilled and tapped for front sight base. Receiver slotted for clip loading. Weight: 13.25 lbs.MODEL 70

VARMINT RIFLE . . . . NiB $2388 Ex $1454 Gd $1145
Same general specifications as Standard Model 70 except w/26-inch heavy bbl., scope bases, special varminter stock. Calibers: .220 Swift, .243 Win. Made from 1956 to 1963.

MODEL 70 WESTERNER. . . . . NiB $707 Ex $569 Gd $355
Same as Standard Model 70 except calibers .264 Win. Mag., .300 Win. Mag.; 3-round magazine; 26-inch bbl. in former caliber, 24-inch in latter. Weight: 8.25 lbs. Made from 1960 to 1963.

1964-TYPE MODEL 70

MODEL 70 AFRICAN . . . . NiB $595 Ex $397 Gd $338
Caliber: .458 Win. Mag. Three round magazine. 22-inch bbl. Weight: 8.5 lbs. Special "African" sights. Monte Carlo stock w/ebony forend tip, hand-checkering, twin stock-reinforcing bolts, recoil pad, QD swivels. Made from 1964 to 1971.

MODEL 70 DELUXE . . . . NiB $790 Ex $588 Gd $445
Calibers: .243, .270 Win., .30-06, .300 Win. Mag. Five round box magazine (3-round in Magnum). 22-inch bbl. (24-inch in Magnum). Weight: 7.5 lbs. Sights: Open rear; hooded ramp front. Monte Carlo stock w/ebony forend tip, hand-checkering, QD swivels, recoil pad on Magnum. Made from 1964 to 1971.

MODEL 70 INTERNATIONAL ARMY
MATCH RIFLE. . . . . NiB $1198 Ex $955 Gd $744
Caliber: .308 Win. (7.62 NATO). Five round box magazine. 24-inch heavy barrel. Externally adj. trigger. Weight: 11 lbs. ISU stock w/military oil finish, forearm rail for standard accessories, vertically adj. buttplate. Made in 1971. Value shown is for rifle w/o sights.

MODEL 70 MAGNUM
Calibers: 7mm Rem. Mag.; .264, .300, .338 Win. Mag.; .375 H&H Mag. Three round magazine. 24-inch bbl. Weight: 7.75 to 8.5 lbs. Sights: Open rear; hooded ramp front. Monte Carlo stock w/cheekpiece, checkering, twin stock-reinforcing bolts, recoil pad, swivels. Made from 1964 to 1971.
375 H&H Mag. . . . . NiB $1043 Ex $787 Gd $678
Other calibers. . . . . NiB $800 Ex $687 Gd $473

Winchester Model 70
Standard Weight Target Rifle

Winchester Model 70
Heavy Weight Target Rifle

vvinchester Model 70
Bull Gun

Winchester Model 70
(Pre-1964) Standard Model

MODEL 70 MANNLICHER . . NiB $1266 Ex $1090 Gd $789
Calibers: .243, .270, .308 Win., .30-06. Five round box magazine. 19-inch bbl. Sights: open rear; hooded ramp front. Weight: 7.5 lbs. Mannlicher-style stock w/Monte Carlo comb and cheekpiece, checkering, steel forend cap, QD sling swivels. Made from 1969 to 1971.

MODEL 70 STANDARD . . . . . . NiB $788 Ex $577 Gd $400
Calibers: .22-250, .222 Rem., .227, .243, .270, .308 Win., .30-06. Five round box magazine. 22-inch bbl. Weight: 7.5 lbs. Sights: Open rear; hooded ramp front. Monte Carlo stock w/cheekpiece, checkering, swivels. Made from 1964 to 1971.

MODEL 70 TARGET . . . . . . NiB $4200 Ex $2765 Gd $1489
Calibers: .308 Win. (7.62 NATO) and .30-06. Five round box magazine. 24-inch heavy bbl. Blocks for target scope. No factory sights installed, but drilled and tapped for front and rear sights. Weight: 10.25 lbs. High-comb Marksman-style stock, aluminum hand stop, swivels. Straight-grain, one-piece stock w/sling swivels, but no checkering. Made from 1964 to 1971.

MODEL 70 VARMINT . . . . . NiB $2160 Ex $1576 Gd $1009
Same as Model 70 Standard except w/24-inch target weight bbl., blocks for target scope. No factory sights installed, but drilled and tapped for front and rear sights. Available in calibers .22-250, .222 Rem., and .243 Win. only. Weight: 9.75 lbs. Made 1964 to 1971.

1972-TYPE MODEL 70

MODEL 70 AFRICAN . . . . NiB $909 Ex $733 Gd $523
Similar to Model 70 Magnum except w/22-inch bbl. caliber .458 Win. Mag. w/special African open rear sight, reinforced stock w/ebony forend tip, detachable swivels and sling; front sling swivel stud attached to bbl. Weight: 8.5 lbs. Made from 1972 to 1992.

MODEL 70 CLASSIC SM
Similar to Model 70 Classic Sporter except w/checkered black composite stock and matte metal finish. Made from 1994 to 1996.
MODEL 70 CLASSIC SM . . . . . . NiB $765 Ex $595 Gd $355
.375 H&H . . . . NiB $944 Ex $765 Gd $535
w/BOSS, add $150
w/open sights, add $50

MODEL 70 CLASSIC SPORTER
Similar to Model 70 Sporter except w/pre-64-style action w/controlled round feeding, classic-style stock. Optional open sights. Made from 1994 to 2006.
Standard model. . . . . NiB $835 Ex $599 Gd $456
w/BOSS, add. $150
w/open sights, add $50

MODEL 70 CLASSIC SPORTER STAINLESS
Similar to Model 70 Classic Sporter except w/matte stainless steel finish. Weight: 7.5 lbs. No sights. Made from 1994 to 2006.
Standard model. . . . . NiB $875 Ex $679 Gd $369
Magnum model. . . . . NiB $845 Ex $743 Gd $498
w/BOSS, add. $126

MODEL 70 CUSTOM SHARPSHOOTER
Calibers: .22-250, .223, .308 Win., .300 Win. Mag. 24- or 26-inch bbl. 44.5 inches overall (24-inch bbl.). Weight: 11 lbs. Custom-fitted, hand-honed action. McMillan A-2 target-style stock. Matte blue or stainless finish. Made from 1992 to 1996.
Blued model . . . . NiB $2145 Ex $1598 Gd $1195
NiB $2145 Ex $1598 Gd $1195 . . . NiB $2167 Ex $1620 Gd $2125

MODEL 70 CUSTOM SPORTING SHARPSHOOTER
Similar to Custom Sharpshooter Model except w/sporter-style gray composite stock. Stainless 24- or 26-inch bbl. w/blued receiver. Calibers: .270, 7mm STW, .300 Win. Mag. Made 1993 to 2006.
Blued model (disc. 1995) . . NiB $2155 Ex $1635 Gd $1266
Stainless model . . . . NiB $2260 Ex $1723 Gd $1319

**Winchester Model 70
International Army Match (1964)**

**Winchester Model 70
Mannlicher (1964)**

**Winchester Model 70
Standard (1964)**

**Winchester Model 70
Target (1964)**

**MODEL 70 GOLDEN 50TH ANNIVERSARY EDITION
BOLT-ACTION RIFLE. . . . . . NiB $1693 Ex $1279 Gd $1039**
Caliber: .300 Win. Three round magazine. 24-inch bbl. 44.5 inches overall. Weight: 7.75 lbs. Checkered American walnut stock. Hand-engraved American scroll pattern on bbl., receiver, magazine cover, trigger guard and pistol-grip cap. Sights: Adj. rear; hooded front ramp. Inscription on bbl. reads "The Rifleman's Rifle 1937 to 1987." Only 500 made 1986 to 1987. (Value for guns in new condition.)

**MODEL 70 FEATHERWEIGHT
CLASSIC . . . . NiB $735 Ex $520 Gd $449**
Similar to Model 70 XTR Featherweight except w/controlled-round feeding system. Calibers: .270, .280 and .30-06. Made 1992 to 2006.

**MODEL 70 INTERNATIONAL
ARMY MATCH . . . . NiB $1095 Ex $944 Gd $654**
Caliber: .308 Win. (7.62mm NATO). Five round magazine, clip slot in receiver bridge. 24-inch heavy barrel. Weight: 11 lbs. No sights, but drilled and tapped for front and rear iron sights, and/or scope mounts. ISU target stock. Intro. 1973; disc.

MODEL 70 LIGHTWEIGHT . . . NiB $679 Ex $449 Gd $227
Calibers: .22-250 and .223 Rem.; .243, .270 and .308 Win.; .30-06 Springfield. Five round mag. capacity (6-round .223 Rem.). 22-inch barrel. 42 to 42.5 inches overall. Weight: 6 to 6.25 lbs. Checkered classic straight stock. Sling swivel studs. Made from 1986 to 1995.

MODEL 70 MAGNUM
Same as Model 70 except w/3-round magazine, 24-inch bbl., reinforced stock w/recoil pad. Weight: 7.75 lbs. (except 8.5 lbs. in .375 H&H Mag.). Calibers: .264 Win. Mag., 7mm

Rem. Mag., .300 Win. Mag., .338 Win. Mag., .375 H&H Mag. Made from 197 to 1980.
.375 H&H Magnum . . . . NiB $655 Ex $533 Gd $400
Other magnum calibers . . . . . . NiB $554 Ex $495 Gd $388

MODEL 70 STANDARD . . . . . . NiB $677 Ex $439 Gd $331
Same as Model 70A except w/5-round magazine, Monte Carlo stock w/cheekpiece, black forend tip and pistol-grip cap w/ white spacers, checkered pistol grip and forearm, detachable sling swivels. Same calibers plus .227 Win. Made from 1972 to 1980.

**MODEL 70 STANDARD
CARBINE. . . . . NiB $596 Ex $437 Gd $369**
Same general specifications as Standard Model 70 except 19-inch bbl. and weight: 7.25 lbs. Shallow recoil pad. Walnut stock and forend w/traditional Model 70 checkering. Swivel studs. No sights, but drilled and tapped for scope mount.

MODEL 70 SPORTER DBM. . . . NiB $755 Ex $585 Gd $359
Same general specifications as Model 70 Sporter SSM except w/detachable box magazine. Calibers: .22-250 (disc. 1994), .223 (disc. 1994), .243 (disc. 1994), .270, 7mm Rem. Mag., .308 (disc. 1994), .30-06, .300 Win. Mag. Made from 1992 to 1994.
S-model (w/iron sights). . . . . . . NiB $589 Ex $496 Gd $369

**MODEL 70 STAINLESS
SPORTER SSM. . . . . NiB $688 Ex $495 Gd $390**
Same general specifications as Model 70 XTR Sporter except w/checkered black composite stock and matte finished receiver, bbl. and other metal parts. Calibers: .270, 7mm Rem. Mag., .30-06, .300 Win. Mag., .338 Win. Mag. Weight: 7.75 lbs. Made 1992 to 1994.

MODEL 70 CLASSIC
SUPER GRADE. . . . .**NiB $977 Ex $857 Gd $590**
Calibers: .270, 7mm Rem. Mag., .30-06, .300 Win. Mag., .338 Win. Mag. Five round magazine (standard), 3-round (magnum). 24-inch bbl. 44.5 inches overall. Weight: 7.75 lbs. Checkered walnut stock w/sculptured cheekpiece and tapered forend. Scope bases and rings, no sights. Controlled-round feeding system. Made from 1990 to 1995. Improved in 1999. Disc. 2006.

MODEL 70 TARGET
. . . .**NiB $976 Ex $945 Gd $588**
Calibers: .30-06 and .308 Win. (7.62mm NATO). Five round magazine. 26-inch heavy bbl. Weight: 10.5 lbs. No sights, but drilled and tapped for scope mount and open sights. High-comb Marksman-style target stock, aluminum hand stop and swivels. Intro. 1972. Disc.

MODEL 70 ULTRA MATCH
. . **NiB $1099 Ex $976 Gd $569**
Similar to Model 70 Target but custom grade w/26-inch heavy bbl. w/deep counterbore, glass bedding, externally adj. trigger. Intro. 1972. Disc.

MODEL 70 VARMINT (HEAVY BARREL)
Same as Model 70 Standard except w/medium-heavy, counterbored 26-inch bbl., no sights, stock w/less drop. Weight: 9 lbs. Calibers: .22-250 Rem., .223 Rem., .243 Win., .308 Win. Made 1972-93. Model 70 SHB, in .308 Win. only w/black synthetic stock and matte blue receiver/bbl. Made from 1992 to 1993.
Model 70 Varmint . . . .**NiB $699 Ex $633 Gd $390**
Model 70 SHB (synthetic stock,
heavy bbl.) . . . .**NiB $745 Ex $641 Gd $440**

MODEL 70 WIN-CAM RIFLE
. . **NiB $576 Ex $488 Gd $338**
Caliber: .270 Win. and .30-06 Springfield. 24-inch barrel. Camouflage one-piece laminated stock. Recoil pad. Drilled and tapped for scope. Made from 1986 to 1987.

MODEL 70 WINLITE
BOLT-ACTION RIFLE. . . . .**NiB $855 Ex $570 Gd $448**
Calibers: .270 Win., .280 Rem., .30-06 Springfield, 7mm Rem., .300 Win. Mag., and .338 Win. Mag. Five round magazine; 3-round for Magnum calibers. 22-inch bbl.; 24-inch for Magnum calibers. 42.5 inches overall; 44.5, Magnum calibers. Weight: 6.25 to 7 lbs. Fiberglass stock w/rubber recoil pad, sling swivel studs. Made from 1986 to 1990.

MODEL 70 WIN-TUFF BOLT-ACTION RIFLE
Calibers: .22-250, .223, .243, .270, .308 and .30-06 Springfield. 22-inch bbl. Weight: 6.25–7 lbs. Laminated dye-shaded brown wood stock w/recoil pad. Barrel drilled and tapped for scope. Swivel studs. FWT Model made from 1986 to 1994. LW Model intro. 1992.
Featherweight model . . . .**NiB $590 Ex $470 Gd $388**
Lightweight model (Made 1992–93)NiB $590 Ex $470 Gd $388

MODEL 70 XTR
FEATHERWEIGHT. . . . .**NiB $590 Ex $470 Gd $388**
Similar to Standard Win. Model 70 except lightweight American walnut stock w/classic Schnabel forend, checkered. 22-inch bbl., hooded blade front sight, folding leaf rear sight.

Stainless-steel magazine follower. Weight: 6.75 lbs. Made from 1984 to 1994.

MODEL 70 XTR SPORTER
RIFLE. . . . .**NiB $744 Ex $545 Gd $376**
Calibers: .264 Win. Mag., 7mm Rem. Mag., .300 Win. Mag., .200 Weatherby Mag., and .338 Win. Mag. Three round magazine. 24-inch barrel. 44.5 inches overall. Weight: 7.75 lbs. Walnut Monte Carlo stock. Rubber buttpad. Receiver tapped and drilled for scope mounting. Made from 1986 to 1994.

MODEL 70 XTR SPORTER
MAGNUM. . . . .**NiB $598 Ex $482 Gd $369**
Calibers: .264 Win. Mag., 7mm Rem. Mag., .300 Win. Mag., .338 Win. Mag. Three round magazine. 24-inch bbl. 44.5 inches overall. Weight: 7.75 lbs. No sights furnished, optional adj. folding leaf rear; hooded ramp. Receiver drilled and tapped for scope. Checkered American walnut Monte Carlo-style stock w/satin finish. Made from 1986 to 1994.

MODEL 70 XTR SPORTER
VARMINT . . . .**NiB $707 Ex $420 Gd $268**
Same general specifications as Model 70 XTR Sporter, except in calibers .223, .22-250, .243 only. Checkered American walnut Monte Carlo-style stock w/cheekpiece. Made from 1986 to 1994.

MODEL 70A
. . . .**NiB $450 Ex $316 Gd $231**
Calibers: .222 Rem., .22-250, .243 Win., .25-06, .270 Win., .30-06, .308 Win. Four round magazine. 22-inch bbl. (except 24- or 26-inch in 25-06). Weight: 7.5 lbs. Sights: Open rear; hooded ramp front. Monte Carlo stock w/checkered pistol grip and forearm, sling swivels. Made from 1972 to 1978.

MODEL 70A MAGNUM
. . . . . .**NiB $476 Ex $316 Gd $236**
Same as Model 70A except w/3-round magazine, 24-inch bbl., recoil pad. Weight: 7.75 lbs. Calibers: .264 Win. Mag., 7mm Rem. Mag., .300 Win. Mag. Made from 1972 to 1978

MODEL 70 ULTIMATE CLASSIC BOLT-ACTION RIFLE
Calibers: .25-06 Rem., .264 Win., .270 Win., .270 Wby. Mag., .280 Rem., 7mm Rem. Mag., 7mm STW, .30-06, Mag., .300 Win. Mag., .300 Wby. Mag., .300 H&H Mag., .338 Win. Mag., .340 Wby. Mag., .35 Whelen, .375 H&H Mag., .416 Rem. Mag. and .458 Win. Mag. Three, 4- or 5-round magazine. 22-24- 26-inch stainless bbl. in various configurations including: full-fluted tapered round, half round and half octagonal or tapered full octagonal. Weight: 7.75 to 9.25 lbs. Checkered fancy walnut stock. Made in 1995.
Model 70 Ultimate Classic . **NiB $2153 Ex $1999 Gd $1098**
Magnum calibers (.375 H&H, .416 and .458), add. **$250**

MODEL 70 LAMINATED STAINLESS BOLT-ACTION
RIFLE. . . . .**NiB $2150 Ex $1792 Gd $952**
Calibers: .270 Win., .30-06 Spfld., 7mm Rem. Mag., .300 Win. Mag., and .338 Win. Mag. Five round magazine. 24-inch bbl. 44.75 inches overall. Weight: 8 to 8.525 lbs. Gray/Black laminated stock. Made from 1998 to 1999.

MODEL 70 CHARACTERISTICS

MODEL 70 FIRST MODEL (SERIAL NUMBERS 1 – 80,000)
First manufactured in 1936; first sold in 1937. Receiver drilled for Lyman No. 57W or No. 48WJS receiver peep sights. Also drilled and tapped for Lyman or Fecker scope sight block.

Winchester Model 70
Featherweight

Winchester Model 70 Golden
50th Anniversary

Winchester Model 70
Featherweight Classic

Winchester Model 70
Lightweight

Winchester Model 70
Magnum

Winchester Model 70 Carbine

Weight w/24-inch bbl. in all calibers except .375 H&H Mag.: 8.25 lbs. 9 lbs. in H&H Mag. Early type safety located on bolt top. Production of this model ended in 1942 near serial number 80,000 due to World War II.*Cross-sectional view of the pre-1964 Winchester Model 70's speed lock action. This action cocks on the opening movement of the bolt with polished, smooth-functioning cams and guide lug, ensuring fast and smooth operation.*

MODEL 70 SECOND MODEL (SERIAL NUMBERS 80,000–350,000)

All civilian production of Winchester Model 70 rifles halted during World War II. Production resumed in 1947 w/improved safety and integral front-sight ramp. Serial numbers started at around 80,000. This model type was produced until 1954, ending around serial number 350,000.

MODEL 70 THIRD MODEL (SERIAL NUMBERS 350,000 – 400,000)

This variety was manufactured from 1954 to 1960 and retained many features of the Second Model except that a folding rear sight replaced the earlier type and front-sight ramps were brazed onto the bbl. rather than being an integral part of the bbl. The Model 70 Featherweight Rifle was intro. in 1954 in .308 WCF caliber. It was fitted w/light 22-inch bbl. and was also available w/either a Monte Carlo or Standard stock. The

.243 Win. cartridge was added in 1955 in all grades of the Winchester Model 70 except the National Match and Bull Gun models. The .358 Win. cartridge was also intro. in 1955, along w/new Varmint Model chambered in .243 caliber only.

MODEL 70 FOURTH MODEL (SERIAL NUMBERS 400,000 – 500,000)

Different markings were inscribed on the barrels of these models and new magnum calibers were added; that is, .264 Win Mag., .338 Win. Mag. and .458 Win. Mag. All bbls. of this variation were about 0.13 inch shorter than previous ones. The .22 Hornet and .257 Roberts were disc. in 1962; the .358 Win. caliber in 1963.

MODEL 70 FIFTH MODEL (SERIAL NUMBERS 500,000 TO ABOUT 570,000)

These rifles may be recognized by slightly smaller checkering patterns and slightly smaller lightweight stocks. Featherweight bbls. were marked "Featherweight." Webbed recoil pads were furnished on magnum calibers.

POST-1964 MODEL 70 RIFLES

In 1964, the Winchester-Western Division of Olin Industries claimed that they were losing money on every Model 70 they produced. Both labor and material costs had increased to a level that could no longer be ignored. Other models followed suit. Consequently, sweeping changes were made to the entire Winchester line. Many of the older, less popular models

**Winchester Model 70
XTR Sporter**

Winchester Model 70A

were discontinued. Models that were to remain in production were modified for lower production costs.

1964 WINCHESTER MODEL 70 RIFLES SERIAL NUMBERS 570,000 TO ABOUT 707,000)

The first version of the "New Model 70s" utilized a free-floating barrel, swaged rifle bore, new stock and sights, new type of bolt and receiver, and a different finish throughout on both the wood and metal parts. The featherweight grade was dropped, but six other grades were available in this new line:

Standard
Deluxe (Replaced Previous Super Grade)
Magnum
Varmint
Target
African

1966 MODEL 70 RIFLES (SERIAL NUMBERS 707,000-G TO ABOUT 1,005,000)

In general, this group of Model 70s had fancier wood checkering, cross-bolt stock reinforcement, improved wood finish and improved action. One cross-bolt reinforcement was used on standard guns. Magnum calibers, however, used an additional forward cross-bolt and red recoil pad. The free-floating barrel clearance forward of the breech taper was reduced in thickness. Impressed checkering was used on the Deluxe models until 1968. Hand checkering was once again used on Deluxe and Carbine models in 1969; the big, red "W" was removed from all grip caps. A new, red safety-indicator and undercut cheekpiece was introduced in 1971.

1972 MODEL 70 RIFLES
(SERIAL NUMBERS G1,005,000 TO ABOUT G1,360,000)

Both the barrels and receivers for this variety of Model 70s were made from chrome molybdenum (C-M) steel. The barrels were tapered w/spiral rifling, ranging in length from 22 to 24 inches. Calibers .222 Rem., .227 Win. .22-250, .243 Win., .25-06, .270, .308 Win., .30-06 and .458 WM used the 22-inch length, while the following calibers used the 24-inch length: .222 Rem., .22-250, .243 Win., .264 Win. Mag., 7mm Mag., .300 and .375 H&H Mag. The .227 Win caliber was dropped in 1973; Mannlicher stocks were also disc. in 1973. The receiver for this variety of Model 70s was machined from a block of C-M steel. A new improved anti-bind bolt was introduced along with a new type of ejector. Other improvements included hand-cut checkering, pistol-grip stocks with pistol-grip and dark forend caps. An improved satin wood finish was also utilized.

1978 MODEL 70 RIFLES (SERIAL NUMBERS BEGAN AROUND G1,360,000)

This variety of Model 70 was similar to the 1972 version except that a new XTR style was added which featured high-luster

wood and metal finishes, fine-cut checkering, and similar embellishments. All Model 70 rifles made during this period used the XTR style; no standard models were available. In 1981, beginning with serial number G1,440,000 (approximately), a Featherweight version of the Model 70 XTR was introduced. The receiver was identical to the 1978 XTR, but lighter barrels were fitted. Stocks were changed to a lighter design with larger scroll checkering patterns and a Schnabel forend with no Monte Carlo comb. A satin sheen stock finish on the featherweight version replaced the high-luster finish used on the other XTR models. A new-style red buttplate with thick, black rubber liner was used on the Featherweight models. The grip cap was also redesigned for this model. 2006 – U.S. Repeating Arms Model 70 RIFLES

In the early 1980s, negotiations began between Olin Industries and an employee-based corporation. The result of these negotiations ended with Olin selling all tools, machinery, supplies, etc. at the New Haven plant to the newly-formed corporation which was eventually named U.S. Repeating Arms Company. Furthermore, U.S. Repeating Arms Company purchased the right to use the Winchester name and logo. Winchester Model 70s went through very few changes the first two years after the transition. However, in 1984, the Featherweight Model 70 XTR rifles were offered in a new short action for .22-250 Rem., .223 Rem., .243 Win. and .308 Win. calibers, in addition to their standard action which was used for the longer cartridges. A new Model 70 lightweight carbine was also introduced this same year. Two additional models were introduced in 1985 — the Model 70 Lightweight Mini-Carbine Short Action and the Model 70 XTR Sporter Varmint. The Model 70 Winlite appeared in the 1986 "Winchester" catalog, along with two economy versions of the Model 70 — the Winchester Ranger and the Ranger Youth Carbine. Five or six different versions of the Winchester Model 70 had been sufficient for 28 years (1937 to 1964). Now, changes in design and the addition of new models each year seemed to be necessary to keep the rifle alive. New models were added, old models dropped, changed in design, etc., on a regular basis. Still, the Winchester Model 70 Bolt-Action Repeating Rifle — in any of its variations — is the most popular bolt-action rifle ever built.

MODEL 70 BLACK SHADOW . NiB $556 Ex $379 Gd $300
Calibers: .243 Win., .270 Win., .300 Win. Mag., .308 Win., .338 Win. Mag., .30-06 Spfld., 7mm STW., 7mm Rem. Mag. and 7mm-08 Rem. Three, 4- or 5-round magazine. 20- 24- 25- or 26-inch bbls. 39.5 to 46.75 inches overall.Weight: 6.5 to 8.25 lbs. Composite, Walnut or Gray/Black laminated stocks. Made from 1998 to 2006.

**MODEL 70 CLASSIC CAMO BOLT-ACTION
RIFLE. . . . . NiB $990 Ex $887 Gd $554**
Calibers: .270 Win., 30-06 Spfld., 7mm Rem. Mag., .300 Win. Mag. Three or 5-round magazine. 24- or 26-inch bbl. 44.75 to 46.75 inches overall. Weight: 7.25 to 7.5 lbs. Mossy Oak finish and composite stock. Made from 1998 to 2006.

MODEL 70 CLASSIC COMPACT
BOLT-ACTION RIFLE......NiB $3329 Ex $2221 Gd $2069
Calibers: .243 Win., .308 Win., and 7mm-08 Rem. Three round magazine. 20-inch bbl., 39.5 inches overall. Weight: 6.5 lbs. Walnut stock. Made from 1998 to 2006.

MODEL 70 CLASSIC LAREDO RANGE
HUNTER BOLT-ACTION RIFLE
Calibers: 7mm STW, 7mm Rem. mag., .300 Win. Mag. Three round magazine. 26-inch bbl. 46.75 inches overall. Weight: 9.5 lbs. Composite stock. Made from 1996 to 1999.
Classic Laredo.............NiB $788 Ex $675 Gd $500
w/fluted bbl. (intro. 1998) ....NiB $833 Ex $733 Gd $513
Bossa Classic model ....NiB $800 Ex $689 Gd $466

MODEL 70 COYOTE........NiB $875 Ex $612 Gd $432
Calibers: .22-250 Rem., .223 Rem., and .243 Win. Five or 6-round magazine. 24- inch bbl., 44 inches overall. Weight: 9 lbs. Medium-heavy stainless steel barrel w/laminated stock. Reverse taper forend. Made from 1999. Disc.

MODEL 70 RANGER COMPACT
RIFLE...................NiB $555 Ex $369 Gd $257
Calibers: .22-250 Rem., .223 Rem., .243 Win., 7mm-08 Rem., Mag., and .308 Win. Five or 6-round magazine. 20- or 22-inch bbl. 41 inches overall. Weight: 6.5 lbs. Adjustable TRUGLO front and rear fiber optic sights. Push-feed action. Made from 1999 to 2000.

MODEL 70 STEALTH RIFLE....NiB $920 Ex $707 Gd $449
Varminter style bolt-action rifle. Calibers: .22-250 Rem., .223 Rem., and .308 Win. Five or 6-round magazine. 26- inch bbl. 46 inches overall. Weight: 10.75 lbs. Black synthetic stock w/Pillar Plus Accu Block and full-length aluminum bedding block. Matte blue finish. Made from 1999. Disc.

MODEL 71 LEVER-ACTION REPEATER
Solid frame. Caliber: .348 Win. Four round tubular magazine. 20- or 24-inch bbl. Weight: 8 lbs. Sights: Open or peep rear; bead front on ramp w/hood. Walnut stock. Made from 1935 to 1957.
Standard Grade (no checkering, grip cap,
sling or swivels) ....NiB $1370 Ex $1167 Gd $789
Special Grade (checkered pistol grip and forearm, grip cap,
QD swivels and sling) ..NiB $2144 Ex $1798 Gd $1129
Special Grade carbine (w/20-inch bbl.,
disc. 1940) ....NiB $2695 Ex $2155 Gd $1769
Standard Grade carbine
(20-inch bbl., disc. 1940) NiB $2266 Ex $1880 Gd $1249

MODEL 72 BOLT-ACTION
REPEATER ....NiB $525 Ex $266 Gd $189
Tubular magazine. Takedown. Caliber: .22 Short, Long, LR. Magazine holds 20 Short, 16 Long or 15 LR. 25-inch bbl. Weight: 5.75 lbs. Sights: Peep or open rear; bead front. Plain pistol-grip stock. Made from 1938 to 1959.

MODEL 73 LEVER-ACTION REPEATER
See Model 1873 rifles, carbines, "One of One Thousand" and other variations of this model at the beginning of Winchester Rifle Section. Note: The Winchester Model 1873 was the first lever-action repeating rifle bearing the Winchester name.

MODEL 74 SELF-LOADING
RIFLE....................NiB $389 Ex $290 Gd $198
Takedown. Calibers: .22 Short only, .22 LR only. Tubular magazine in buttstock holds 20 Short, 14 LR. 24-inch bbl. Weight:

6.25 lbs. Sights: Open rear; bead front. Plain pistol-grip stock, one-piece. Made from 1939 to 1955.

MODEL 75 SPORTING RIFLE..NiB $600 Ex $299 Gd $210
Same as Model 75 Target except has 24-inch bbl., checkered sporter stock, open rear sight; bead front on hooded ramp, weight: 5.5 lbs.

MODEL 75 TARGET RIFLE ....NiB $600 Ex $299 Gd $210
Caliber: .22 LR. 5- or 10-round box magazine. 28-inch bbl. Weight: 8.75 lbs. Target sights (Lyman, Redfield or Winchester). Target stock w/pistol grip and semi-beavertail forearm, swivels and sling. Made from 1938 to 1959.

MODEL 77 SEMIAUTOMATIC RIFLE,
CLIP TYPE.................NiB $322 Ex $190 Gd $133
Solid frame. Caliber: .22 LR. Eight round clip magazine. 22-inch bbl. Weight: About 5.5 lbs. Sights: Open rear; bead front. Plain, one-piece pistol-grip stock. Made from 1955 to 1963.

MODEL 77, TUBULAR
MAGAZINE ....NiB $379 Ex $269 Gd $200
Same as Model 77. Clip type except has tubular magazine holding 15 rounds. Made from 1955 to 1963.

MODEL 86 CARBINE AND RIFLE
See Model 1886 at beginning of Winchester Rifle section.

MODEL 88 CARBINE
Same as Model 88 Rifle except has 19-inch bbl., plain carbine-style stock and forearm with bbl. band. Weight: 7 lbs. Made 1968 to 1973.
Standard calibers ....NiB $1335 Ex $1098 Gd $866
.284 Win. ....NiB $2095 Ex $1788 Gd $1077

MODEL 88 LEVER-ACTION RIFLE
Hammerless. Calibers: .243 Win., .284 Win., .308 Win., .358 Win. Four round box magazine. Three round in pre-1963 models and in .284. 22-inch bbl. Weight: About 7.25 lbs. One-piece walnut stock with pistol-grip, swivels (1965 and later models have basket-weave ornamentation instead of checkering). Made from 1955 to 1973. Note: .243 and .358 introduced 1956, later discontinued 1964; .284 introduced 1963.
Model 88 (checkered stock) ..NiB $1045 Ex $744 Gd $469
w/basketweave checkering ...NiB $1045 Ex $744 Gd $469
.243 Win...............NiB $1269 Ex $1088 Gd $899
.284 Win. ....NiB $2300 Ex $1969 Gd $1675

MODEL 94 PRE WWII, POST-'64 TO 2006
NOTE: *Post-'64 Model 94 rifles began with serial number 2700000. In 1992 a crossbolt safety was added except for "100th Anniversary" models made in 1994. Manufacturing ceased in New Haven, CT, in 2006.*

MODEL 94 ANTIQUE CARBINE NiB $588 Ex $448 Gd $290
Same as standard Post-64 Model 94 Carbine except has decorative scrollwork and casehardened receiver, brass-plated loading gate, saddle ring; caliber .30-30 only. Made from 1964 to 1984.

MODEL 94 CARBINE
Same as Model 1894 Rifle except 20-inch round bbl., 6-round full-length magazine. Weight: About 6.5 lbs. Originally made in calibers .25-35, .30-30, .32 Special and .38-55. From 1940 to 1964 barrels were rollmarked "Model 94" These models are all considerd "pre-'64" models and demand a premium. Original version discontinued 1964.

Winchester Model 70
Black Shadow

Winchester Model 70
Classic Camo

Winchester Model 72

Winchester Model 74

Pre WWII (under
No. 1,300,000) . . . . NiB $7250 Ex $5988 Gd $3866
Postwar, pre-1964
(under No. 2,707,000) . . . . . NiB $865 Ex $707 Gd $530

MODEL 94 CLASSIC CARBINE . . NiB $655 Ex $443 Gd $400
Same as Canadian Centennial '67 Commemorative Carbine except without commemorative details; has scroll-engraved receiver, gold-plated loading gate. Made from 1967 to 1970.

MODEL 94 CLASSIC RIFLE . . NiB $6744 Ex $5467 Gd $4388
Same as Centennial '67 Commemorative Rifle except without commemorative details; has scroll-engraved receiver, gold-plated loading gate. Made from 1968 to 1970.

MODEL 94 DELUXE CARBINE . . NiB $845 Ex $600 Gd $400
Caliber: .30-30 Win. Six round magazine. 20-inch bbl. 37.75 inches overall. Weight: 6.5 lbs. Semi-fancy American walnut stock with rubber buttpad, long forearm and specially cut checkering. Engraved with "Deluxe" script. Made from 1987 to 2006.

MODEL 94 LONG BARREL
RIFLE. . . . . NiB $707 Ex $449 Gd $370
Caliber: .30-30 Win. Seven round magazine. 24-inch bbl. 41.75 inches overall. Weight: 7 lbs. American walnut stock. Blade front sight. Made from 1987 to 2006.

MODEL 94 TRAPPER
Same as Model 94 Carbine except w/16-inch bbl. and weighs 6 lbs. 2 oz. Angle Eject introduced in 1985 also chambered for .357 Mag., .44 Mag. and .45 LC. Made from 1980 to 2006.
Top eject (disc. 1984) . . . . NiB $755 Ex $573 Gd $388
Angle eject (.30-30) . . . . NiB $445 Ex $306 Gd $200
.357 Mag., .44 mag., .45 LC, add $50

MODEL 94 WIN-TUFF RIFLE . . NiB $556 Ex $400 Gd $297
Caliber: .30-30 Win. Six round magazine. 20-inch bbl. 37.75 inches overall. Weight: 6.5 lbs. Brown laminated wood stock. Made from 198 to -2006.

MODEL 94 WRANGLER CARBINE
Same as standard Model 94 Carbine except has 16-inch bbl., engraved receiver and chambered for .32 Special & .38-55 Win.
Top-eject model (disc. 1984) . . NiB $623 Ex $414 Gd $331
Wranger II, angle-eject model
(disc. 1985) . . . . NiB $544 Ex $387 Gd $244

MODEL 94 XTR BIG BORE
Modified Model 94 action for added strength. Calibers: .307 Win., .356 Win., .375 Win. or .444 Marlin. 20-inch bbl. Six round magazine. Rubber buttpad. Checkered stock and forearm. Weight: 6.5 lbs. Made from 1978 to 2006.
Top eject (disc. 1984) . . . . NiB $755 Ex $577 Gd $488
Angle eject (intro. 1985). . . . . . NiB $441 Ex $379 Gd $255
.356 Win. or .375 Win., add $200

MODEL 94 XTR LEVER-ACTION RIFLE
Same general specifications as standard M94 and Angle Eject M94 except chambered for .30-30 Win. and 7-30 Waters and has 20- or 24-inch bbl. Weight: 6.5 to 7 lbs. Made from 1978 to 1988 by U.S. Repeating Arms.
Top eject (disc. 1984) . . . . NiB $744 Ex $ 533 Gd $445
Angle eject (.30-30) . . . . NiB $744 Ex $533 Gd $445
Deluxe angle eject (.30-30) . . . NiB $744 Ex $533 Gd $445
7-30 Waters, add $100

NOTE: *In 2010 production of Model 94 rifles resumed with manufacturing done by Miroku in Japan and continues to date.*

GRADING: **NiB** = New in Box   **Ex** = Excellent or NRA 95%   **Gd** = Good or NRA 68%

Winchester Model 75
Sporting

Winchester Model 88
Pre-1965

Winchester Model 70
Coyote

Winchester Model 70
Ranger Compact

Winchester Model 70
Stealth

Winchester Model 94
Traditional

Winchester Model 94
Long Barrel

MODEL 94 CARBINE . . . . . .NIB $1199 EX $1000 Gd $930
Similar to Post-'64 Model 94. Calibers: .30-30 and .38-55. 20-inch bbl. 7-rnd. magazine. Top tang safety. Rebounding hammer. Plain walnut stock and forearm. Weight: 6.5 lbs. Made from 2013 to present.
Short Rifle (2012-present) . . . . NiB $1229 Ex $990 Gd $900
Sporter (half round, half octagon bbl., checkered stock,
  2011-present) . . . . NiB $1399 Ex $1280 Gd $955
Trails End Takedown (.30-30, .38-55, .450 Marlin;
  round bbl.; checkered stock;
  2012-present) . . . . NiB $1495 Ex $1379 Gd $1055

MODEL 94 COMMEMORATIVES

MODEL 94 ANTLERED GAME . NiB $775 Ex $639 Gd $482
Standard Model 94 action. Gold-colored medallion inlaid in stock. Antique gold-plated receiver, lever tang and bbl. bands. Medallion and receiver engraved with elk, moose, deer and caribou. 20.5-inch bbl. Curved steel buttplate. In .30-30 caliber. 19,999 made in 1978.

MODEL 94 BICENTENNIAL
'76 CARBINE. . . . . .NiB $944 Ex $812 Gd $654
Same as Standard Model 94 Carbine except caliber .30-30 Win. only; antique silver-finished, engraved receiver; stock and forearm of fancy walnut, checkered, Bicentennial medallion embedded in buttstock, curved buttplate. 20,000 made in 1976.

MODEL 94 BUFFALO BILL COMMEMORATIVE
Same as Centennial '66 Rifle except receiver is black-chromed, scroll-engraved and bears name "Buffalo Bill"; hammer, trigger, loading gate, saddle ring, forearm cap, and buttplate are nickel-plated; Buffalo Bill Memorial Assn. commemorative medallion embedded in buttstock; "Buffalo Bill Commemorative" inscribed on bbl., facsimile signature "W.F. Cody, Chief of Scouts" on tang. Carbine has 20-inch bbl., 6-round magazine, 7-lb. weight. 112,923 made in 1968.
Carbine . . . . .NiB $733 Ex $597 Gd $433
Rifle . . . . .NiB $778 Ex $650 Gd $469
Matched carbine/rifle set . . NiB $1590 Ex $1370 Gd $1007

CANADIAN CENTENNIAL '67 COMMEMORATIVE
Same as Centennial '66 Rifle except receiver engraved with maple leaves and forearm cap is black-chromed, buttplate is blued, commemorative inscription in gold on barrel and top tang: "Canadian Centennial 1867–1967." Carbine has 20-inch bbl., 6-round magazine, weight: 7 lb., 90,398 made in 1967.
Carbine . . . . .NiB $667 Ex $498 Gd $300
Rifle . . . . .NiB $667 Ex $498 Gd $300
Matched carbine/rifle set . . . . .NiB $725 Ex $535 Gd $350

CENTENNIAL '66 COMMEMORATIVE
Commemorates Winchester's 100th anniversary. Standard Model 94 action. Caliber: .30-30. Full-length magazine holds 8 rounds. 26-inch octagon bbl. Weight: 8 lbs. Gold-plated receiver and forearm cap. Sights: Open rear; post front. Saddle ring. Walnut buttstock and forearm with high-gloss finish, solid brass buttplate. Commemorative inscription on bbl. and top tang of receiver. 100,478 made in 1966.
Carbine . . . . .NiB $727 Ex $537 Gd $353
Rifle . . . . .NiB $727 Ex $537 Gd $353
Matched carbine/rifle set . . . NiB $1579 Ex $1355 Gd $954

MODEL 94 CHEYENNE
COMMEMORATIVE . . . . .NiB $976 Ex $755 Gd $642
Available in Canada only. Same as Standard Model 94 Carbine except chambered for .44-40. 11,227 made in 1977.

MODEL 94 CHIEF CRAZY HORSE
COMMEMORATIVE . . . . .NiB $888 Ex $733 Gd $521
Cailber: .38-55, 7-round tubular magazine. 24-inch bbl., 41.75 inches overall. Walnut stock with medallion of the United Sioux Tribes; buttstock and forend also decorated with brass tacks. Engraved receiver. Open rear sights; bead front sight. 19,999 made in 1983.

MODEL 94 COLT COMMEMORATIVE
CARBINE SET . . . . .NiB $2689 Ex $2077 Gd $1370
Standard Model 94 action. Caliber: .44-40 Win. 20-inch bbl. Weight: 6.25 lbs. Features the horse-and-rider trademark and distinctive WC monogram in gold etching on left side of receiver. Sold in set with Colt Single Action Revolver chambered for same caliber.

MODEL 94 COWBOY COMMEMORATIVE CARBINE
Same as Standard Model 94 Carbine except caliber .30-30 only; nickel-plated receiver, tangs, lever, bbl. bands; engraved receiver, "Cowboy Commemorative" on bbl., commemorative medallion embedded in buttstock; curved buttplate. 20,915 made in 1970. Nickel-silver medallion inlaid in stock. Antique silver-plated receiver engraved with scenes of the old frontier. Checkered walnut stock and forearm. 19,999 made in 1970.
Cowboy carbine . . . . .NiB $744 Ex $588 Gd $414
1 of 300 model . . . . .NiB $3278 Ex $2966 Gd $2288

MODEL 94 GOLDEN SPIKE COMMEMORATIVE
CARBINE. . . . . .NiB $855 Ex $670 Gd $495
Same as Standard Model 94 Carbine except caliber .30-30 only; gold-plated receiver, tangs and bbl. bands; engraved receiver, commemorative medallion embedded in stock. 64,758 made in 1969.

MODEL 94 ILLINOIS SESQUICENTENNIAL
COMMEMORATIVE CARBINE. . . NiB $622 Ex $398 Gd $287
Same as Standard Model 94 Carbine except caliber .30-30 only; gold-plated buttplate, trigger, loading gate, and saddle ring; receiver engraved with profile of Lincoln, commemorative inscription on receiver, bbl.; souvenir medallion embedded in stock. 31,124 made in 1968.

MODEL 94 LEGENDARY FRONTIERSMEN
COMMEMORATIVE . . . . .NiB $769 Ex $655 Gd $488
Standard Model 94 action. Caliber: .39-55. 24-inch round bbl. Nickel-silver medallion inlaid in stock. Antique silver-plated receiver engraved with scenes of the old frontier. Checkered walnut stock and forearm. 19,999 made in 1979.

MODEL 94 LEGENDARY LAWMEN
COMMEMORATIVE . . . . .NiB $769 Ex $655 Gd $488
Same as Standard Model 94 Carbine except .30-30 Win. only; antique silver-plated receiver engraved with action law-enforcement scenes. 16-inch Trapper bbl., antique silver-plated bbl. bands. 19,999 made in 1978.

MODEL 94 LONE STAR COMMEMORATIVE
Same as Theodore Roosevelt Rifle except yellow-gold plating; "Lone Star" engraving on receiver and bbl., commemorative medallion embedded in buttstock. 30,669 made in 1970.
Rifle or carbine . . . . .NiB $754 Ex $598 Gd $449
Matched carbine/rifle set . . . NiB $1499 Ex $1288 Gd $955

MODEL 94 NRA CENTENNIAL
MUSKET . . . . .NiB $707 Ex $597 Gd $479
Commemorates 100th anniversary of National Rifle Association of America. Standard Model 94 action. Caliber: .30-30. Seven round magazine. 26-inch bbl. Sights: Military folding

RIFLES

Winchester Model 94
Long Barrel

Winchester Model 94
Win-Tuff

Winchester Model 94
Wrangler II Angle Eject

Winchester Model 94
XTR Big Bore

Winchester Model 94
XTR 7-30 Waters

Winchester Model 66
Commemorative

Winchester Model 94
Chief Crazy Horse Commemorative

rear; blade front. Black chrome-finished receiver engraved "NRA 1871–1971" plus scrollwork. Barrel inscribed "NRA Centennial Musket." Musket-style buttstock and full-length forearm; commemorative medallion embedded in buttstock. Weight: 7.13 lbs. Made in 1971.

MODEL 94 NRA CENTENNIAL
RIFLE . . . . NiB $715 Ex $609 Gd $520
Same as Model 94 Rifle except has commemorative details as in NRA Centennial Musket (barrel inscribed "NRA Centennial Rifle"); caliber .30-30, 24-inch bbl., QD sling swivels. Made in 1971.

MODEL 94 NRA CENTENNIAL
MATCHED SET . . . . NiB $1400 Ex $1266 Gd $1077
Rifle and musket were offered in sets with consecutive serial numbers. Note: Production figures not available. These rifles offered in Winchester's 1972 catalog.

MODEL 94 NEBRASKA CENTENNIAL
COMMEMORATIVE CARBINE NiB $1133 Ex $933 Gd $633
Same as Standard Model 94 Carbine except caliber .30-30 only; gold-plated hammer, loading gate, bbl. band, and butt-plate; souvenir medallion embedded in stock, commemorative inscription on bbl. 2,500 made in 1966.

**Winchester Colt
Commemorative Set**

**Winchester Model 94
NRA Centennial**

MODEL 94 THEODORE ROOSEVELT COMMEMORATIVE RIFLE/CARBINE

Standard Model 94 action. Caliber: .30-30. Rifle has 6-round half-magazine, 26-inch octagon bbl., weight: 7.5-lb. Carbine has 6-round full magazine, 20-inch bbl., weight: 7-lb. White gold-plated receiver, upper tang, and forend cap; receiver engraved with American Eagle, "26th President 1901–1909," and Roosevelt's signature. Commemorative medallion embedded in buttstock. Saddle ring. Half pistol-grip, contoured lever. 49,505 made in 1969.

Carbine . . . . NiB $733 Ex $560 Gd $398
Rifle . . . . NiB $733 Ex $560 Gd $398
Matched set . . . . NiB $1415 Ex $1153 Gd $805

MODEL 94 TEXAS RANGER ASSOCIATION

CARBINE. . . . . NiB $769 Ex $654 Gd $498
Same as Texas Ranger Commemorative Model 94 except special edition of 150 carbines, numbered 1 through 150, with hand-checkered full-fancy walnut stock and forearm. Sold only through Texas Ranger Association. Made in 1973.

MODEL 94 TEXAS RANGER

COMMEMORATIVE CARBINE . NiB $655 Ex $496 Gd $400
Same as Standard Model 94 Carbine except caliber .30-30 Win. only, stock and forearm of semi-fancy walnut, replica of Texas Ranger star embedded in buttstock, curved buttplate. 5,000 made in 1973.

MODEL 94 JOHN WAYNE COMMEMORATIVE

CARBINE. . . . . NiB $1597 Ex $1166 Gd $769
Standard Model 94 action. Caliber: .32-40. 18.5-inch bbl. Receiver is pewter-plated with engraving of Indian attack and cattle drive scenes. Oversized bow on lever. Nickel-silver medallion in buttstock bears a bas-relief portrait of Wayne.

Selected American walnut stock with deep-cut checkering. Introduced by U.S. Repeating Arms in 1981.

MODEL 94 WELLS FARGO & CO. COMMEMORATIVE

CARBINE. . . . . NiB $770 Ex $544 Gd $339
Same as Standard Model 94 Carbine except .30-30 Win. only; antique silver-finished, engraved receiver; stock and forearm of fancy walnut, checkered, curved buttplate. Nickel-silver stagecoach medallion (inscribed "Wells Fargo & Co. —1852–1977—125 Years") embedded in buttstock. 20,000 made in 1977.

MODEL 94 O. F. WINCHESTER COMMEMORATIVE

RIFLE. . . . . NiB $854 Ex $650 Gd $599
Standard Model 94 action. Caliber: .38-55. 24-inch octagonal bbl. Receiver is satin gold-plated with distinctive engravings. Stock and forearm semi-fancy American walnut with high grade checkering.

MODEL 94 WRANGLER CARBINE

Same as standard Model 94 Carbine except w/16-inch bbl., engraved receiver and chambered for .32 Special and .38-55 Win. Angle Eject introduced in 1985 as Wrangler II, also chambered for .30-30 Win., .44 Mag. and .45 LC. Made 1980 to 1986. Re-introduced in 1992.

Top eject (disc. 1984) . . . . NiB $398 Ex $290 Gd $200
Wrangler II, angle eject (.30-30)NiB $390 Ex $285 Gd $195
.44 Mag or .45 LC, add $50

MODEL 94 WYOMING DIAMOND JUBILEE COMMEMORATIVE

CARBINE. . . . . NiB $2166 Ex $1812 Gd $1347
Same as Standard Model 94 Carbine except caliber .30-30 Win. only, receiver engraved and casehardened in colors, brass saddle ring and loading gate, souvenir medallion embedded in buttstock, commemorative inscription on bbl. 1,500 made in 1964.

Winchester Model 100

Winchester Model 250 Deluxe

Winchester Model 270 Deluxe

MODEL 94 ALASKAN PURCHASE CENTENNIAL COMMEMORATIVE
CARBINE. . . . . NiB $2379 Ex $2006 Gd $1339
Same as Wyoming issue except different medallion and inscription. 1,501 made in 1967.

MODEL 94 OLIVER WINCHESTER 200TH ANNIVERSARY
CUSTOM GRADE RIFLE . . . NiB $1959 Ex $1880 Gd $1630
Reintroduction of Model 94, similar as Post-'64 models except .30-30, 8-rnd. magazine. Bbl.: 26-inch half octagon, half round. Weight: 8 lbs. Sights: buckhorn rear; Marbles front. Finish: blued, engraved. High grade walnut stock. Made 2010.
High Grade (silver nitride finish) NiB $1469 Ex $1400 Gd $1055

MODEL 100 AUTOLOADING
RIFLE . . . . .NiB $675 Ex $559 Gd $466
Gas-operated semiautomatic. Calibers: .243, .284, .308 Win. Four round clip magazine (3-round in .284). 22-inch bbl. Weight: 7.25 lbs. Sights: Open rear; hooded ramp front. One-piece stock w/pistol grip, basket-weave checkering, grip cap, sling swivels. Made from 1961 to 1973.

MODEL 100 CARBINE . . . . . . .NiB $800 Ex $622 Gd $482
Same as Model 100 Rifle except has 19-inch bbl., plain carbine-style stock and forearm with bbl. band. Weight: 7 lbs. Made 1967 to 1973.

MODEL 121 DELUXE . . . . .NiB $200 Ex $126 Gd $90
Same as Model 121 Standard except has ramp front sight, stock with fluted comb and sling swivels. Made from 1967 to 1973.

MODEL 121 STANDARD BOLT-ACTION
SINGLE SHOT. . . . . .NiB $167 Ex $100 Gd $80
Caliber: .22 Short, Long, LR. 20.75-inch bbl. Weight: 5 lbs. Sights: Open rear; bead front. Monte Carlo-style stock. Made 1967 to 1973.

MODEL 121 YOUTH . . . . .NiB $200 Ex $126 Gd $90
Same as Model 121 Standard except has 1.25-inch shorter stock. Made from 1967 to 1973.

MODEL 131 BOLT-ACTION
REPEATER . . . . .NiB $269 Ex $227 Gd $178
Caliber: .22 Short, Long or LR. Seven round clip magazine. 20.75-inch bbl. Weight: 5 lbs. Sights: Open rear; ramp front. Plain Monte Carlo stock. Made from 1967 to 1973.

MODEL 135 . . . . .NiB $244 Ex $169 Gd $155
Same as Model 131 except chambered for .22 WMR cartridge. Magazine holds 5 rounds. Made in 1967.

MODEL 141 BOLT-ACTION TUBULAR
REPEATER . . . . .NiB $279 Ex $216 Gd $155
Same as Model 131 except has tubular magazine in buttstock; holds 19 Short, 15 Long, 13 LR. Made from 1967 to 1973.

MODEL 145. . . . . NiB $256 Ex $200 Gd $145
Same as Model 141 except chambered for .22 WMR; magazine holds 9 rounds. Made in 1967.

MODEL 150 LEVER-ACTION
CARBINE. . . . . .NiB $244 Ex $180 Gd $126
Same as Model 250 except has straight loop lever, plain carbine-style straight-grip stock and forearm with bbl. band. Made from 1967 to 1973.

MODEL 190 CARBINE . . . . . . .NiB $255 Ex $195 Gd $135
Same as Model 190 rifle except has carbine-style forearm with bbl. band. Made from 1967 to 1973.

MODEL 190 SEMIAUTOMATIC
RIFLE. . . . . .NiB $265 Ex $210 Gd $145
Same as current Model 290 except has plain stock and forearm. Made from 1966 to 1978.

MODEL 250 DELUXE RIFLE . . . NiB $300 Ex $233 Gd $150
Same as Model 250 Standard Rifle except has fancy walnut Monte Carlo stock and forearm, sling swivels. Made from 1965 to 1971.

MODEL 250 STANDARD LEVER-ACTION
RIFLE. . . . . .NiB $249 Ex $175 Gd $126
Hammerless. Caliber: .22 Short, Long or LR. Tubular magazine holds 21 Short, 17 Long, 15 LR. 20.5-inch bbl. Sights: Open rear; ramp front. Weight: About 5 lbs. Plain stock and forearm on early production; later model has checkering. Made from 1963 to 1973.

Winchester Model 310

Winchester Model 320

Winchester Model 490 Rifle

Winchester Model 670 Bolt-Action Rifle

Winchester Model 670 Magnum

MODEL 255 DELUXE RIFLE . . . NiB $338 Ex $265 Gd $175
Same as Model 250 Deluxe Rifle except chambered for .22 WMR cartridge. Magazine holds 11 rounds. Made 1965 to 1973.

MODEL 255 STANDARD RIFLE . . . NiB $265 Ex $198 Gd $144
Same as Model 250 Standard Rifle except chambered for .22 WMR cartridge. Magazine holds 11 rounds. Made from 1964 to 1970.

MODEL 270 DELUXE RIFLE . . . NiB $288 Ex $149 Gd $145
Same as Model 270 Standard Rifle except has fancy walnut Monte Carlo stock and forearm. Made from 1965 to 1973.

MODEL 270 STANDARD
SLIDE-ACTION RIFLE . . . . NiB $200 Ex $137 Gd $110
Hammerless. Caliber: .22 Short, Long or LR. Tubular magazine holds 21 Short, 17 Long, 15 LR. 20.5-inch bbl. Sights: Open rear; ramp front. Weight: About 5 lbs. Early production had plain walnut stock and forearm (slide handle); latter also furnished in plastic (Cycolac); last model has checkering. Made from 1963 to 1973.

MODEL 278 DELUXE RIFLE . . . NiB $322 Ex $268 Gd $144
Same as Model 270 Deluxe Rifle except chambered for .22 WMR cartridge. Tubular magazine holds 11 rounds. Made 1965–70.

MODEL 278 STANDARD RIFLE . . . NiB $266 Ex $190 Gd $133
Same as Model 270 Standard Rifle except chambered for .22 WMR cartridge. Magazine holds 11 rounds. Made from 1964–70.

MODEL 290 DELUXE RIFLE . . . NiB $325 Ex $278 Gd $175
Same as Model 290 Standard Rifle except has fancy walnut Monte Carlo stock and forearm. Made from 1965 to 1973.

MODEL 290 STANDARD SEMIAUTOMATIC RIFLE
Caliber: .22 Long or LR. Tubular magazine holds 17 Long, 15 LR. 20.5-inch bbl. Sights: Open rear; ramp front. Weight: About 5 lbs. Plain stock and forearm on early production; current model has checkering. Made from 1963 to 1977.
w/plain stock/forearm . . . . NiB $286 Ex $227 Gd $133
w/checkered stock/forearm . . . NiB $300 Ex $255 Gd $156

MODEL 310 BOLT-ACTION
SINGLE SHOT . . . . NiB $370 Ex $300 Gd $210
Caliber: .22 Short, Long, LR. 22-inch bbl. Weight: 5.63 lbs. Sights: Open rear; ramp front. Monte Carlo stock w/checkered pistol-grip and forearm, sling swivels. Made from 1972 to 1975.

MODEL 320 BOLT-ACTION
REPEATER . . . . NiB $370 Ex $300 Gd $210
Same as Model 310 except has 5-round clip magazine. Made from 1972 to 1974.

MODEL 490 SEMIAUTOMATIC
RIFLE . . . . NiB $388 Ex $298 Gd $234
Caliber: .22 LR. Five round clip magazine. 22-inch bbl. Weight: 6 lbs. Sights: Folding leaf rear; hooded ramp front. One-piece walnut stock w/checkered pistol grip and forearm. Made 1975 to 1977.

MODEL 670 BOLT-ACTION
SPORTING RIFLE . . . . NiB $386 Ex $308 Gd $231
Calibers: .227 Win., .243 Win., .270 Win., .30-06, .308 Win. Four round magazine. 22-inch bbl. Weight: 7 lbs. Sights: Open rear; ramp front. Monte Carlo stock w/checkered pistol-grip and forearm. Made from 1967 to 1973.

MODEL 670 CARBINE . . . . NiB $356 Ex $338 Gd $244
Same as Model 670 Rifle except has 19-inch bbl. Weight: 6.75 lbs. Calibers: .243 Win., .270 Win., .30-06. Made from 1967 to 1970.

Winchester Model 9422
Boy Scouts of America Commemorative

Winchester Model 9422
Eagle Scout Limited Edtion

Winchester Model 9422
WinCam

Winchester Model 9422
XTR Classic

MODEL 670 MAGNUM . . . . . . NiB $410 Ex $356 Gd $281
Same as Model 670 Rifle except has 24-inch bbl., reinforced stock with recoil pad with slightly different checkering pattern. Weight: 7.25 lbs. Calibers: .264 Win. Mag., 7mm Rem. Mag., .300 Win. Mag. Open rear sight; ramp front sight with hood. Made from 1967 to 1970.

MODEL 770 BOLT-ACTION
SPORTING RIFLE . . . . NiB $443 Ex $321 Gd $277
Model 70-type action. Calibers: .22-250, .222 Rem., .243, .270 Win., .30-06. Four round box magazine. 22-inch bbl. Sights: Open rear; hooded ramp front. Weight: 7.13 lbs. Monte Carlo stock, checkered pistol-grip and forend; sling swivels. Made from 1969 to 1971.

MODEL 770 MAGNUM . . . . . . NiB $443 Ex $318 Gd $233
Same as Standard Model 770 except 24-inch bbl., weight: 7.25 lbs., recoil pad. Calibers: 7mm Rem. Mag., .264 and .300 Win. Mag. Made from 1969 to 1971.

MODEL 9422 LEVER-ACTION RIMFIRE RIFLES
Similar to the standard Model 94 except chambered for .22 Rimfire. Calibers: .22 Short, Long, LR. (9422) or .22 WMR (9422M). Tubular magazine holds 21 or 15 Short.17 or 12 Long, 15 or 11 LR (9422 or Trapper) or 11 or 8 WRM (9422M or Trapper M). 16.5- or 20.5 inch bbl. 33.125- to 37.125 inches overall. Weight: 5.75 to 6.25 lbs. Open rear sight; hooded ramp front. Carbine-style stock and barrel-band forearm. Stock options: Walnut (Standard), laminated brown (WinTuff), laminated green (WinCam). Made from 1972. Disc.

Standard model.	NiB $655	Ex $368	Gd $265
WinCam model.	NiB $690	Ex $376	Gd $254
WinTuff model	NiB $533	Ex $337	Gd $233
Legacy model	NiB $844	Ex $577	Gd $300
Trapper model (16.5-inch bbl.)	NiB $765	Ex $456	Gd $268

XTR Classic model	NiB $800	Ex $587	Gd $370
High Grade Series I.	NiB $1389	Ex $1085	Gd $770
High Grade Series II.	NiB $1389	Ex $1985	Gd $770

25th Anniversary Edition
Grade (1 of 2,500) . . . . NiB $860 Ex $569 Gd $447
25th Anniversary Edition
High Grade (1 of 250) . . NiB $1688 Ex $1233 Gd $1044
25th Anniversary Edition
High Grade (1 of 250) . . . . . NiB $843 Ex $667 Gd $495
Eagle Scout Commemorative
(1 of 1,000) . . . . NiB $1448 Ex $1177 Gd $988
.22 WRM, add. **10%**

DOUBLE XPRESS RIFLE . . . NiB $4889 Ex $4550 Gd $3000
Over/under double rifle. Calibers: .257 Roberts, .270 Win., .30-06, 7x57mm, 7x57mmR, 7x65mmR or 9.3x74mmR. 23.5-inch bbl. Weight: 8.5 lbs. Manufactured for Olin Corp. by Olin-Kodensha in Japan. Made 1984 to 1985.

RANGER YOUTH BOLT-ACTION
CARBINE . . . . NiB $499 Ex $338 Gd $270
Calibers: .223 (discontinued 1989), .243 Win., and .308 Win. Four and 5-round magazine. Bbl.: 20-inch. Weight: 5.75 lbs. American hardwood stock. Open rear sight. Made 1985 to 2006 by U.S. Repeating Arms.

RANGER LEVER-ACTION
CARBINE . . . . NiB $655 Ex $398 Gd $290
Caliber: .30-30. Five round tubular magazine. Bbl.: 20-inch round. Weight: 6.5 lbs. American hardwood stock. Economy version of Model 94. Made from 1985 to 2006 by U.S. Repeating Arms.

RANGER BOLT-ACTION CARBINE . . NiB $470 Ex $388 Gd $243
Calibers: .223 Rem., .243 Win., .270, .30-06, 7mm Rem. (discontinued 1985), Mag. Three and 4-round magazine. Bbl.:

Winslow Commander Grade

Winslow Crown Grade

Winslow Regent Grade
Bushmaster Stock

24-inch in 7mm; 22-inch in .270 and .30-06. Open sights. American hardwood stock. Made from 1985 to 1999 by U.S. Repeating Arms.

SUPER X (SXR)
Semiautomatic. Caliber: .270 WSM, .30-06, .300 WSM, .300 Win. Mag., 3- or 4-round magazine, 22- or 24-in. bbl., no sights, checkered walnut stock. Blued finish. Made from 2006-09.
Grade I . . . . NiB $790 Ex $600 Gd $450

WILDCAT
Bolt action. Caliber: .22 LR, 5- or 10-round magazine, 21-in. regular or heavy bbl., fixed sights, checkered hardwood stock. Blued finish. 4.5 to 5.5 lbs. Imported from Russia 2007-09.
Standard bbl. . . . . NiB $215 Ex $150 Gd $115
Heavy bbl.. . . . . NiB $255 Ex $200 Gd $165

MODEL 1892 GRADE I LEVER-ACTION RIFLE
Similar to the original Model 1892. Calibers: .357 Mag., .44-40, .44 Mag., .45 LC. 10-round magazine. 24-inch round bbl. Weight: 6.25 lbs. 41.25 inches overall. Bead front sight, adjustable buckhorn rear. Etched receiver and gold trigger. Blue finish. Smooth straight-grip walnut stock and forearm w/ metal grip cap. Made from 1997. Disc.
Standard Rifle . . . . NiB $800   Ex $713   Gd $482
Short Rifle (w/20-inch bbl.,
   .44 Mag. only) . . . . NiB $750   Ex $495   Gd $352

MODEL 1892 GRADE II LEVER-ACTION
RIFLE. . . . . NiB $1388   Ex $1167   Gd $828
Similar to the Grade I Model 1892 except w/gold appointments and receiver game scene. Chambered .45 LC only. Limited production of 1,000 in 1997.

WINSLOW ARMS COMPANY — Camden, South Carolina

BOLT-ACTION SPORTING RIFLE
Action: FN Supreme Mauser, Mark X Mauser, Remington 707 and 788, Sako, Winchester 70. Standard calibers: .17-222, .17-223, .222 Rem., .22-250, .243 Win., 6mm Rem., .25-

06, .257 Roberts, .270 Win., 7x57, .280 Rem., .284 Win., .308 Win., .30-06, .358 Win. Magnum calibers: .17-222 Mag., .257 Wby., .264 Win., .270 Wby., 7mm Rem., 7mm Wby., .300 H&H, .300 Wby., .300 Win., .308 Norma, 8mm Rem., .338 Win., .358 Norma, .375 H&H, .375 Wby., .458 Win. Three-round magazine in standard calibers, 2-round in magnum. 24-inch barrel in standard calibers, 26-inch in magnum. Weight: With 24-inch bbl., 7 to 7.5 lbs.; with 26-inch bbl., 8 to 9 lbs. No sights. Stocks: "Bushmaster" with slender pistol-grip and beavertail forearm, "Plainsmaster" with full curl pistol-grip and flat forearm; both styles have Monte Carlo cheekpiece. Values shown are for basic rifle in each grade; extras such as special fancy wood, more elaborate carving, inlays and engraving can increase these figures considerably. Made from 1962 to 1989.
Commander Grade . . . . . . NiB $1897   Ex $1565   Gd $1177
Regal Grade . . . . NiB $2066   Ex $1590   Gd $1322
Regent Grade . . . . NiB $2175   Ex $1698   Gd $1443
Regimental Grade . . . . NiB $2966   Ex $2490   Gd $1788
Crown Grade . . . . NiB $3228   Ex $2579   Gd $2188
Royal Grade . . . . NiB $3590   Ex $2666   Gd $2077
Imperial Grade . . . . NiB $4100   Ex $3695   Gd $3000
Emperor Grade . . . . NiB $7070   Ex $5266   Gd $4590

ZEPHYR — U.S.
Manufactured by Victor Sarasqueta Company, Eibar, Spain; imported by Stoeger.

DOUBLE RIFLE . . . . . NiB $22,656 Ex $18,622 Gd $12,799
Boxlock. Double barrels. Calibers: Available in practically every caliber from .22 Hornet to .505 Gibbs. Bbls.: 22 to 28 inches standard, but any lengths were available on special order. Weight: 7 lbs. for the smaller calibers up to 12 or more lbs. for the larger calibers. Imported by Stoeger from about 1938 to 1951.

Shotguns

ADAMY, GEBR. JAGDWAFFEN — Suhl, Germany

Custom gunmaker established 1820; currently from 1921. Previously imported by New England Custom Gun service, Claremont, NH. Specializes in custom break-action shotguns (S/S, O/U) drillings, vierlings, single-shot rifles. Models and grades are numerous, contact factory for specific information .

ALDENS — Chicago, Illinois

MODEL 670 CHIEFTAIN SLIDE
ACTION . . . . NiB $331 Ex $239 Gd $190
Hammerless. Gauges: 12, 20 and others. Three round tubular magazine. Bbl.: 26- to 30-inch; various chokes. Weight: 6.25 to 7.5 lbs. depending on bbl. length and ga. Walnut-finished hardwood stock.

AMERICAN ARMS — N. Kansas City, Missouri

See also Franchi Shotguns.

BRISTOL (STERLING) O/U . . . . NiB $853 Ex $621 Gd $500
Boxlock w/Greener crossbolt and engraved sideplates. Single selective trigger. Selective automatic ejectors. Gauges: 12, 20; 3-inch chambers. 26-, 28-, 30-, or 32-inch vent-rib bbls. w/screw-in choke tubes (Improved Cylinder/Modified/Full). Weight: 7 lbs. Antique-silver receiver w/game scene or scroll engraving. Checkered full pistol-grip-style buttstock and forearm w/high-gloss finish. Imported 1986-88 designated Bristol; redesignated Sterling 1989 to 1990.

BRITTANY HAMMERLESS
DOUBLE . . . . NiB $863 Ex $744 Gd $508
Boxlock w/engraved case-colored receiver. Single selective trigger. Selective automatic ejectors. Gauges: 12, 20. 3-inch chambers. Bbls.: 25- or 27-inch w/screw-in choke tubes (IC/M/F). Weight: 6.5 lbs. (20 ga.). Checkered English-style walnut stock w/semi-beavertail forearm or pistol-grip stock w/high-gloss finish. Imported 1989 to 2000.

CAMPER SPECIAL . . . . NiB $217 Ex $166 Gd $90
Similar to the Single Barrel except takedown model w/21-inch bbl., M choke and pistol-grip stock. Made in 1989.

COMBO . . . . NiB $292 Ex $200 Gd $156
Similar to the Single-Barrel model except available w/interchangeable rifle and shotgun bbls. .22 LR/20-ga. shotgun or .22 Hornet/12-ga. shotgun. Rifle bbl. has adj. rear sights; blade-type front sight. Made in 1989.

DERBY HAMMERLESS DOUBLE
Sidelock w/engraved sideplates. Single non-selective or double triggers. Selective automatic ejectors. Gauges: 12, 20, 28 and .410. 3 inch chambers. Bbls.: 26-inch (IC/M) or 28-inch (M/F). Weight: 6 lbs. (20 ga.). Checkered English-style walnut stock and splinter forearm w/hand-rubbed oil finish. Engraved frame/sideplates w/antique silver finish. Imported 1986 to 1994.

12 or 20 ga. . . . . NiB $1254 Ex $907 Gd $677
28 ga. or .410 (disc. 1991) . . . NiB $1377 Ex $979 Gd $855

F.S. SERIES O/U
Greener crossbolt in Trap and Skeet configuration. Single selective trigger. Selective automatic ejectors. 12 gauge only. 26-, 28-, 30-, or 32-inch separated bbls. Weight: 6.5 to 7.25 lbs. Black or chrome receiver. Checkered walnut buttstock and forearm. Imported 1986 to 1987.

Model F.S. 200 Boxlock . . . . . . NiB $867 Ex $677 Gd $490
Model F.S. 300 Boxlock . . . . . . NiB $1099 Ex $827 Gd $568
Model F.S. 400 Sidelock . . . . NiB $1386 Ex $1197 Gd $871
Model F.S. 500 Sidelock . . . . NiB $1386 Ex $1197 Gd $871

GENTRY/YORK HAMMERLESS DOUBLE
Chrome, coin-silver or color casehardened boxlock receiver w/scroll engraving. Double triggers. Extractors. Gauges: 12, 16, 20, 28, .410. 3-inch chambers (16 and 28 have 2.75-inch). Bbls.: 26-inch (IC/M) or 28-inch (M/F, 12, 16 and 20). Weight: 6.75 lbs. (12 ga.). Checkered walnut buttstock w/pistol-grip and beavertail forearm; both w/semi-gloss oil finish. Imported as York from 1986 to 1988, redesignated Gentry 1989 to 2000.
Gentry 12, or 16 or 20 ga. . . . . . . NiB $733 Ex $577 Gd $428
Gentry 28 ga. or .410. . . . . . . NiB $755 Ex $590 Gd $488
York 12, 16 or 20 ga. (disc. 1988). . . . NiB $690 Ex $577 Gd $433
York 20 ga. or .410 . . . . NiB $690 Ex $577 Gd $433

GRULLA #2 HAMMERLESS DOUBLE
True sidelock w/engraved detachable sideplates. Double triggers. Extractors and cocking indicators. Gauges: 12, 20, .410 w/3-inch chambers; 28 w/2.75-inch. 26-inch bbl. Imported 1989 to 2000.

American Arms
Bristol (Sterling) Over/Under

American Arms
Derby Hammerless Double

American Arms
Gentry/York Hammerless Double

American Arms
Silver Over/Under

American Arms
WS/SS Hammerless Double

Standard model. . . . . NiB $3798 Ex $2886 Gd $2166
Two-bbl. set (disc. 1995). . . NiB $3876 Ex $3688 Gd $2544

SILVER I O/U
Boxlock. Single selective trigger. Extractors. Gauges: 12, 20 and .410 w/3-inch chambers; 28 w/2.75 inch. Bbls.: 26-inch (IC/M), 28-inch (M/F, 12 and 20 ga. only). Weight: 6.75 lbs. (12 ga.). Checkered walnut stock and forearm. Antique-silver receiver w/scroll engraving. Imported 1987 to 2000.
12 or 20 ga. . . . . NiB $622 Ex $535 Gd $368
28 ga. or .410. . . . . NiB $663 Ex $590 Gd $477

SILVER II O/U
Similar to Model Silver I except w/selective automatic ejectors and 26-inch bbls. w/screw-in tubes (12 and 20 ga.). Fixed chokes (28 and .410). Made 1987 to 2000.
12 or 20 ga . . . . NiB $735 Ex $600 Gd $489
28 ga or .410 . . . . NiB $730 Ex $652 Gd $464
Upland Lite II . . . . NiB $1254 Ex $1066 Gd $855
Two-bbl. set . . . . NiB $1293 Ex $1088 Gd $867

SILVER LITE O/U
Similar to Model Silver II except w/blued, engraved alloy receiver. Available in 12 and 20 ga. only. Imported from 1990 to 1992.

Standard Model . . . . NiB $922 Ex $655 Gd $477
Two-bbl. Set . . . . NiB $1169 Ex $908 Gd $733

SILVER SKEET/TRAP . . . . NiB $855 Ex $640 Gd $569
Similar to the Silver II Model except has 28-inch (Skeet) or 30-inch (Trap) ported bbls. w/target-style rib and mid-bead sight. Imported 1992 to 1994.

SILVER SPORTING O/U . . . . . NiB $966 Ex $768 Gd $633
Boxlock. Single selective trigger. Selective automatic ejectors. Gauges: 12, 2.75-inch chambers. 28-inch bbls.w/Franchoke tubes (SK, IC, M and F). Weight: 7.5 lbs. Checkered walnut stock and forearm. Special broadway rib and vented side ribs. Engraved receiver w/chrome-nickel finish. Imported from 1990 to 2000.

SINGLE-SHOT SHOTGUN
Break-open action. Gauges: 10 (3.5), 12, 20, .410, 3-inch chamber. Weight: about 6.5 lbs. Bead front sight. Walnut-finished hardwood stock w/checkered grip and forend. Made from 1988 to 1990.
10 ga. (3.5-inch) . . . . NiB $198 Ex $117 Gd $75
12 & 20 ga., .410 . . . . NiB $200 Ex $99 Gd $66
Multi-choke bbl., add $50

SLUGGER SINGLE-SHOT
SHOTGUN . . . . NiB $190 Ex $100 Gd $79
Similar to the Single-Shot model except in 12 and 20 ga. only w/24-inch slug bbl. Rifle-type sights and recoil pad. Made 1989 to 1990.

TS/OU 12 SHOTGUN . . . . NiB $744 Ex $555 Gd $490
Turkey Special. Boxlock. Single selective trigger. Selective automatic ejectors. Gauge: 12, 3.5-inch chambers. Bbls.: 24-inch O/U w/screw-in choke tubes (IC, M, F). Weight: 6 lbs. 15 oz. Checkered European walnut stock and beavertail forearm. Matte blue finish. Imported 1987 to 2000.

TS/SS 10 HAMMERLESS
DOUBLE . . . . NiB $700 Ex $533 Gd $400
Turkey Special. Same general specifications as Model WS/ SS 10, except w/26-inch side-by-side bbls., screw-in choke tubes (F/F) and chambered for 10-ga. 3.5-inch shells. Weight: 10 lbs., 13 oz. Imported 1987 to 1993.

TS/SS 12 HAMMERLESS
DOUBLE . . . . NiB $766 Ex $533 Gd $421
Same general specifications as Model WS/SS 10 except in 12 ga. w/26-inch side-by-side bbls. and 3 screw-in choke tubes (IC/M/F). Weight: 7 lbs., 6 oz. Imported 1987 to 2000.

WS O/U 12 SHOTGUN . . . . . . NiB $644 Ex $538 Gd $377
Waterfowl Special. Boxlock. Single selective trigger. Selective automatic ejectors. Gauge: 12; 3.5-inch chambers. Bbls.: 28-inch O/U w/screw-in tubes (IC/M/F). Weight: 7 lbs. Checkered European walnut stock and beavertail forearm. Matte blue metal finish. Imported 1987-2000.

WS/SS 10 HAMMERLESS
DOUBLE . . . . NiB $883 Ex $671 Gd $428
Waterfowl Special. Boxlock. Double triggers. Extractors. Gauge: 10; 3.5-inch chambers. Bbls.: 32-inch side/side choked F/F. Weight: About 11 lbs. Checkered walnut stock and beavertail forearm w/satin finish. Parkerized metal finish. Imported from 1987 to 1995.

WT O/U SHOTGUN. . . . . NiB $844 Ex $657 Gd $533
Same general specifications as Model WS/OU 12 except chambered for 10-ga. 3.5-inch shells. Extractors. Satin wood finish and matte blue metal. Imported 1987 to 2000.

ARMALITE, INC. — Costa Mesa, California

AR-17 GOLDEN GUN . . . . NiB $863 Ex $643 Gd $559
Recoil-operated semiautomatic. High-test aluminum bbl. and receiver housing. 12 ga. only. Two round capacity. 24-inch bbl. w/interchangeable choke tubes: IC/M/F. Weight: 5.6 lbs. Polycarbonate stock and forearm recoil pad. Gold-anodized finish standard, also made w/black finish. Made 1964 to 1965. Fewer than 2,000 produced.

ARMSCOR (Arms Corp.) — Manila, Philippines
Imported until 1991 by Armscor Precision, San Mateo, CA; 1991–95 by Ruko Products, Inc., Buffalo NY.

MODEL M-30 FIELD PUMP SHOTGUN
Double slide-action bars w/damascened bolt. Gauge: 12 only w/3-inch chamber. Bbl.: 28-inch w/fixed chokes or choke tubes. Weight: 7.6 lbs. Walnut or walnut finished hardwood stock.
Model M-30F (w/hard
  wood stock, fixed choke) . . . NiB $288 Ex $212 Gd $149
Model M-30F (w/hardwood
  stock and choke tubes) . . . . . NiB $288 Ex $212 Gd $149
Model M-30F/IC (w/walnut
  stock and choke tubes) . . . . . NiB $366 Ex $247 Gd $169

MODEL M-30 RIOT PUMP
Double-action slide bar w/damascened bolt. Gauge: 12 only w/3-inch chamber. Bbls: 18.5 and 20-inch w/IC bore. Five- or 7-round magazine. Weight: 7 lbs, 2 ozs. Walnut finished hardwood stock.

Model M-30R6
(W/5-round magazine) . . . . NiB $190 Ex $121 Gd $90
Model M-30R8
(W/7-round magazine) . . . . NiB $219 Ex $135 Gd $100

MODEL M-30 SPECIAL COMBO
Simlar to Special Purpose Model except has detachable synthetic stock that removes to convert to pistol-grip configuration.
Model M-30C (disc. 1995) . . . . NiB $249 Ex $200 Gd $155
Model M-30RP (disc. 1995) . . . NiB $249 Ex $200 Gd $155

MODEL M-30 SPECIAL PURPOSE
Double-action slide bar w/damascened bolt. Seven round magazine.   Gauge: 12 only w/3-inch chamber. 20-inch bbl. w/cylinder choke. Iron sights (DG Model) or venter handguard (SAS Model). Weight: 7.5 lbs. Walnut finished hardwood stock.
Model M-30DG (Deer Gun) . . . NiB $266 Ex $198 Gd $137
Model M-30SAS
(Special Air Services) . . . . NiB $277 Ex $218 Gd $125

Armalite AR-17
Golden Gun

Armsport 1050

Armsport 1125

ARMSPORT, INC. — Miami, Florida

1000 SERIES HAMMERLESS DOUBLES
Side-by-side w/engraved receiver, double triggers and extractors. Gauges: 10 (3.5), 12, 20, .410- 3-inch chambers. Model 1033: 10 ga., 32-inch bbl. Model 1050/51: 12 ga., 28-inch bbl., M/F choke. Model 1052/53: 20 ga., 26-inch bbl., I/M choke. Model 1054/57: .410 ga., 26-inch bbl., I/M. Model 1055: 28 ga., Weight: 5.75 to 7.25 lbs. European walnut buttstock and forend. Made in Italy. Importation disc. 1993.

Model 1033 (10 ga., disc. 1989) . . NiB $844 Ex $690 Gd $497
Model 1050 (12 ga., disc. 1993) . . NiB $766 Ex $692 Gd $477
Model 1051 (12 ga., disc. 1985) . . NiB $503 Ex $412 Gd $326
Model 1052 (20 ga., disc. 1985) . . NiB $477 Ex $390 Gd $288
Model 1053 (20 ga., disc. 1993) . . NiB $790 Ex $666 Gd $459
Model 1054 (.410, disc. 1992) . . . NiB $888 Ex $739 Gd $522
Model 1055 (28 ga., disc. 1992) . . NiB $554 Ex $448 Gd $336
Model 1057 (.410, disc. 1985) . . . NiB $569 Ex $481 Gd $357

MODEL 1125 SINGLE-SHOT
SHOTGUN . . . . NiB $196 Ex $139 Gd $98
Bottom-opening lever. Gauges: 12, 20. 3-inch chambers. Bead front sight. Plain stock and forend. Imported 1987-89.

MODEL 2700 GOOSE GUN
Similar to the 2700 Standard Model except 10 ga. w/3.5-inch chambers. Double triggers w/28-inch bbl. choked IC/M or 32-inch bbl., F/F. 12mm wide vent rib. Weight: 9.5 lbs. Canada geese engraved on receiver. Antiqued silver-finished action. Checkered European walnut stock w/rubber recoil pad. Imported from Italy 1986 to 1993.

W/fixed choke . . . . NiB $1167 Ex $933 Gd $676
W/choke tubes . . . . NiB $1433 Ex $979 Gd $724

MODEL 2700 OVER/UNDER SERIES
Hammerless, takedown shotgun w/engraved receiver. Selective single or double triggers. Gauges: 10, 12, 20, 28 and .410. Bbl.: 26-or 28-inch w/fixed chokes or choke tubes. Weight: 8 lbs. Checkered European walnut buttstock and forend. Made in Italy. Importation disc. 1993.

Model 2701 12 ga. (disc. 1985) . . . NiB $613 Ex $500 Gd $357
Model 2702 12 ga. . . . . NiB $635 Ex $525 Gd $378
Model 2703 20 ga. (disc. 1985) . . . NiB $668 Ex $544 Gd $365
Model 2704 20 ga. . . . . NiB $655 Ex $548 Gd $400
Model 2705 (.410, DT, fixed
   chokes) . . . . NiB $775 Ex $638 Gd $454
Model 2730/31 (BOSS-style
   action, SST Choke tubes) . . . NiB $868 Ex $733 Gd $538
Model 2733/35 (Boss-style
   action, extractors) . . . . NiB $790 Ex $644 Gd $466
Model 2741 (Boss-style
   action, ejectors) . . . . NiB $678 Ex $566 Gd $412
Model 2742 Sporting Clays
   (12 ga./choke tubes) . . . . NiB $835 Ex $679 Gd $555
Model 2744 Sporting Clays
   (20 ga./choke tubes) . . . . NiB $855 Ex $677 Gd $499
Model 2750 Sporting Clays
   (12 ga./sideplates) . . . . NiB $955 Ex $723 Gd $528
Model 2751 Sporting Clays
   (20 ga./sideplates) . . . . NiB $943 Ex $759 Gd $544

MODEL 2755 SLIDE-ACTION SHOTGUN
Gauge: 12 w/3-inch chamber. Tubular magazine. Bbls.: 28- or 30-inch w/fixed choke or choke tubes. Weight: 7 lbs. European walnut stock. Made in Italy 1986 to 1987.

Standard model, fixed choke . . NiB $444 Ex $366 Gd $270
Standard model, choke tubes. . . . NiB $579 Ex $489 Gd $355
Police model, 20-inch bbl. . . . . NiB $390 Ex $333 Gd $244

Armsport 2700

Armsport 2741

MODEL 2900 TRI-BARREL (TRILLING) SHOTGUN

Boxlock. Double triggers w/top-tang bbl. selector. Extractors. Gauge: 12; 3-inch chambers. Bbls.: 28-inch (IC, M and F). Weight: 7.75 lbs. Checkered European walnut stock and forearm. Engraved silver receiver. Imported 1986 to 1987 and 1990 to 1993.

Model 2900 (W/fixed chokes) . . NiB $2288 Ex $1844 Gd $1307
Model 2900 (choke tubes). . . . NiB $2945 Ex $2385 Gd $1669
Deluxe grades, add $600

ARRIETA, S.L. — Elgoibar, Spain.

Imported by New England Arms Corp., Wingshooting Adventures Quality Arms, Griffin & Howe and Orvis. Custom double-barreled shotguns with frames scaled to individual gauges. Standard gauges are 12 and 16. Add: 5% for small gauges (20, 24, 28, 32 and .410 bore) on currently manufactured models; $900 for single trigger (most actions); 5% for matched pairs; 10% for rounded action on standard models; extra bbls., add $1375 to $2000 per set.

MODEL 557 STANDARD . . . . . NiB $4428 Ex $3966 Gd $2044
Gauges: 12, 16 or 20. Demi-Bloc steel barrels, detachable engraved sidelocks, double triggers, ejectors.

MODEL 570 LIEJA . . . . NiB $4949 Ex $4210 Gd $2588
Gauges: 12, 16 or 20. Non-detachable sidelocks.

MODEL 578 VICTORIA . . NiB $6280 Ex $4366 Gd $2290
Gauges: 12, 16 or 20. Similar to Model 570 but with fine English scrollwork.

LIGERA MODEL. . . . . NiB $5634 Ex $4247 Gd $3270
Available in all gauges. Lightweight 12 ga. has 2-inch chambers, lightweight or standard action. Includes unique frame engraving and Turkish wood upgrade. Wt. appox. 6 pounds.

MODEL 590 REGINA. . . . . . NiB $3589 Ex $3177 Gd $2229
Gauges: 12, 16 or 20. Similar to Model 570 but has more elaborate engraving.

MODEL 595 PRINCIPE . . . NiB $5579 Ex $4367 Gd $3410
Available in all gauges, sidelock, engraved hunting scenes, ejectors, double triggers.

MODEL 600 IMPERIAL . . . NiB $9115 Ex $5910 Gd $3588
Gauges: 12, 16 or 20. Self-opening action, very ornate engraving throughout.

MODEL 601 IMPERIAL

TYRO . . . . NiB $9350 Ex $6005 Gd $4337
Available in all gauges, sidelock, nickel plating, ejectors, single selective trigger, border engraving.

MODEL 801. . . . . NiB $12,870 Ex $11,665 Gd $10,644
All gauges, detachable sidelocks, ejectors, coin-wash finish, Churchill-style engraving.

MODEL 802. . . . . NiB $13,669 Ex $11,544 Gd $8534
Gauges: 12, 16 or 20. Similar to Model 801 except with non-detachable sidelocks, finest Holland-style engraving.

BOSS ROUND BODY . . . . NiB $8799 Ex $7733 Gd $6477
Available in all gauges, Boss pattern best quality engraving, wood upgrade.

MODEL 803. . . . . NiB $11,333 Ex $9121 Gd $6344
Available in all gauges. Similar to Model 801 except finest Purdey-style engraving.

MODEL 871. . . . . NiB $7333 Ex $4144 Gd $2608
Available in all gauges. Rounded frame sidelock action with Demi-Bloc barrels, scroll engraving, ejectors, double trigger.

MODEL 871 EXTRA FINISH. . . . . NiB $7555 Ex $4759 Gd $3977
Similar to Model 871 except with standard game scene engraving with woodcock and ruffed grouse.

MODEL 872. . . . . NiB $16,788 Ex $13,690 Gd $11,550
Available in all gauges, rounded frame sidelock action, Demi-Bloc barrels, elaborate scroll engraving with third lever fastener.

AyA Model 53E

MODEL 873 . . . . NiB $17,228 Ex $14,788 Gd $11,766
Available in all gauges. Sidelock, gold line engraved action, ejectors, single selective trigger.

MODEL 874 . . . . NiB $12,980 Ex $11,887 Gd $6,777
Available in all gauges. Sidelock, gold line engraved action, Demi-Bloc barrels.

MODEL 875 . . . . NiB $18,960 Ex $14,449 Gd $11,733
Available in all gauges. Custom model built to individual specifications only, elaborate engraving, gold inlays

MODEL 931 . . . . NiB $26,877 Ex $19,785 Gd $15,860
Available in all gauges. Self-opening action, elaborate engraving, H&H selective ejectors.

ASTRA — Guernica, Spain.
Manufactured by Unceta y Compania.

MODEL 650 O/U SHOTGUN
Hammerless, takedown w/double triggers. 12 ga. w/.75-inch chambers. Bbls.: 28-inch (M/F or SK/SK); 30-inch (M/F). Weight: 6.75 lbs. Checkered European walnut buttstock and forend. Disc. 1987.
W/extractors . . . . NiB $733 Ex $579 Gd $454
W/ejectors . . . . NiB $844 Ex $685 Gd $477

MODEL 750 O/U SHOTGUN
Similar to the Model 650 except w/selective single trigger and ejectors. Made in field, skeet and trap configurations from 1980. Disc. 1987.
Field model w/extractors . . . . . NiB $779 Ex $637 Gd $500
Field model w/ejectors . . . . NiB $888 Ex $755 Gd $566
Trap or Skeet model . . . . NiB $1099 Ex $867 Gd $559

AYA (Aguirre Y Aranzabal) — Eibar, Spain
Previously manufactured by Diarm. Imported by Armes De Chasse, Hertford, NC.

MODEL 1 HAMMERLESS DOUBLE
A Holland & Holland sidelock similar to the Model 2 except in 12 and 20 ga. only, w/special engraving and exhibition-grade wood. Weight: 5-8 lbs., depending on ga. Imported by Diarm until 1987, since 1992 by Armes de Chasse.
Model 1 Standard . . . . NiB $9177 Ex $5448 Gd $3229
Model 1 Deluxe . . . . . . NiB $13,110 Ex $10,077 Gd $7470
W/Extra set of bbls., add $750

MODEL 2 HAMMERLESS DOUBLE
Sidelock action w/selective single or double triggers automatic ejectors and safety. Gauges: 12, 20, 28, (2.75-inch chambers); .410 (3-inch chambers). Bbls.: 26- or 28-inch w/various fixed choke combinations. Weight: 7 lbs. (12 ga.). English-style straight walnut buttstock and splinter forend. Imported by Diarm until 1987, since 1992 by Armes de Chasse.
12 or 20 ga. w/double triggers . . . NiB $4777 Ex $3178 Gd $2090
12 or 20 ga. w/single trigger . . . NiB $4777 Ex $3178 Gd $2090
28 ga. or .410 w/double triggers . . . . NiB $4777 Ex $3178 Gd $2090
28 ga. or .410 w/single trigger . . . NiB $3533 Ex $2970 Gd $2135
W/Extra set of bbls., add $1450

MODEL 4 HAMMERLESS DOUBLE
Lightweight Anson & Deely boxlock, scalloped frame. Gauges: 12, 16, 20, 28, and .410. Bbls.: 25- to 28-inch w/concave rib. Importation disc. 1987 and resumed in 1992 by Armes de Chasse.
12 ga. . . . . NiB $2098 Ex $1376 Gd $1099
16 ga. (early importation) . . . NiB $2098 Ex $1376 Gd $1099
20 ga. . . . . NiB $2098 Ex $1376 Gd $1099
28 ga. . . . . NiB $2098 Ex $1376 Gd $1099
.410 ga. . . . . NiB $2098 Ex $1376 Gd $1099
Deluxe grades, add $700

MODEL 37 SUPER
O/U SHOTGUN . . . . NiB $3266 Ex $2279 Gd $2099
Sidelock. automatic ejectors. Selective single trigger. Made in all gauges, bbl. lengths and chokes. Vent rib bbls. Elaborately engraved. Checkered stock (w/straight or pistol grip) and forend. Disc. 1995.

MODEL 37 SUPER A
O/U SHOTGUN . . . . NiB $14,879 Ex $12,776 Gd $11,340
Similar to the Standard Model 37 Super except has nickel steel frame and is fitted w/detachable sidelocks engraved w/game scenes. Importation disc. 1987 and resumed 1992 by Armes de Chasse. Disc.

MODEL 53E . . . . NiB $6860 Ex $4950 Gd $2910
Same general specifications as Model 117 except more elaborate engraving and select figured wood. Importation disc. 1987 and resumed in 1992 by Armes de Chasse.

MODEL 56 HAMMERLESS DOUBLE
Pigeon weight Holland & Holland sidelock w/Purdey-style third lug and sideclips. Gauges: 12, 16, 20. Receiver has fine-line scroll and rosette engraving; gold-plated locks. Importation disc. 1987 and resumed 1992 by Armes de Chasse.
12 ga. . . . . NiB $10,477 Ex $7880 Gd $4610
16 ga. (early importation), add 20%
20 ga. (early importation), add. 20%

MODEL 76 HAMMERLESS
DOUBLE . . . . NiB $955 Ex $838 Gd $529
Anson & Deeley boxlock. Auto ejectors. Selective single trigger. Gauges: 12, 20 (3-inch). Bbls.: 26-, 28-, 30-inch (latter in 12 ga. only), any standard choke combination. Checkered pistol-grip stock/beavertail forend. Disc.

MODEL 76 .410. . . . . NiB $1099 Ex $877 Gd $669
Same general specifications as 12 and 20 ga. Model 76 except chambered for 3-inch shells in .410, has extractors, double triggers, 26-inch bbls. only, English-style stock w/straight grip and small forend. Disc.

SHOTGUNS

AyA Model 76

AyA Model 117

AyA Matador II

AyA Model XXV Boxlock

MODEL 117 HAMMERLESS
DOUBLE .... **NiB $1887 Ex $1077 Gd $868**
Holland & Holland-type sidelocks, hand-detachable. Engraved action. Automatic ejectors. Selective single trigger. Gauges: 12, 20 (3-inch). Bbls.: 26-, 27-, 28-, 30-inch; 27- and 30-inch in 12 ga. only; any standard choke combination. Checkered pistol-grip stock and beavertail forend of select walnut. Manufactured in 1985.

BOLERO .... **NiB $556 Ex $479 Gd $357**
Same general specifications as Matador except non-selective single trigger and extractors. Gauges: 12 16, 20, 20 Magnum (3-inch), .410 (3-inch). Note: This model, prior to 1956, was designated F. I. Model 400 by the importer. Made from 1955 to 63.

CONTENTO OVER/UNDER SHOTGUN
Boxlock w/Woodward side lugs and double internal bolts. Gauge: 12 (2.75-inch chambers). Bbls.: 26-, 28-inch field; 30-, 32-inch trap; fixed chokes as required or screw-in choke tubes. Hand-checkered European walnut stock and forend. Single selective trigger and automatic ejectors.
M.K.2 .... **NiB $1155 Ex $897 Gd $655**
M.K.3 .... **NiB $1887 Ex $1533 Gd $1095**
W/extra bbl., add **$500**

MATADOR HAMMERLESS
DOUBLE .... **NiB $619 Ex $490 Gd $339**
Anson & Deeley boxlock. Selective automatic ejectors. Selective single trigger. Gauges: 12, 16, 20, 20 Magnum (3-inch). Bbls: 26-, 28-, 30-inches; any standard choke com-

bination. Weight: 6.5 to 7.5 lbs., depending on ga. and bbl. length. Checkered pistol-grip stock and beavertail forend. Note: This model, prior to 1956, was designated F. I. Model 400E by the U.S. importer, Firearms Int'l. Corp. of Washington, D.C. Made from 1955 to 1963.

MATADOR II. .... **NiB $754 Ex $567 Gd $421**
Improved version of Matador w/same general specifications except has vent-rib bbls. Made 1964 to 1969.

MATADOR III .... **NiB $859 Ex $744 Gd $590**
Same general specifications as AyA Matador II. Made 1970 to 1985.

MODEL XXV BOXLOCK
Anson & Deeley boxlock w/double locking lugs. Gauges: 12 and 20. 25-inch chopper lump, satin blued bbls. w/Churchill rib. Weight: 5 to 7 lbs. Double triggers. Automatic safety and ejectors. Color-casehardened receiver w/Continental-style scroll and floral engraving. European walnut stock. Imported 1979 to 1986 and 1991.

12 or 20 ga. . . . . NiB $3190 Ex $2688 Gd $2100
W/extra set of bbls., add $1250

MODEL XXV SIDELOCK

Holland & Holland-type sidelock. Gauges: 12, 20, 28 and
.410; 25-, 26-, 27- 28-, 29-, and 32-inch bbls. Chopper lump,
satin blued bbls. w/Churchill rib. Weight: 5 to 7 lbs. Double
triggers standard or selective or non-selective single trigger
optional. Automatic safety and ejectors. Cocking indicators. Color-casehardened or coin-silver-finished receiver w/
Continental-style scroll and floral engraving. Select European
walnut stock w/hand-cut checkering and oil finish. Imported
1979 to 1986 and 1991.
12 or 20 ga. . . . . NiB $5975 Ex $4220 Gd $3188
28 ga. (disc. 1997) . . . . . . NiB $6177 Ex $5063 Gd $3580
.410 bore (disc. 1997) . . . . NiB $6177 Ex $5063 Gd $3580
W/single trigger, add $100
W/single-selective trigger, add $200
W/extra set of bbls., add $2250

BAIKAL — Izhevsk and Tula, Russia

MODEL IZH-18M SINGLE SHOT . . . NiB $110 Ex $80 Gd $65
Hammerless w/cocking indicator. Automatic ejector. Manual
safety.
Gauges: 12 , 20, 16 w/2.75-inch chamber or .410 w/3-inch
chamber. Bbls.: 26-, 28-inch w/fixed chokes (IC, M, F). Weight:
5.5 to 6 lbs. Made in Russia.

MODEL IZH-27 FIELD O/U . . . NiB $400 Ex $341 Gd $244
Boxlock. Double triggers w/extractors. 12 ga.; 2.75-inch
chambers. Bbls.: 26-inch, IC/M; 28-inch, M/F w/fixed chokes.
Weight: 6.75 lbs. Made in Russia.

MODEL IZH-43 FIELD SIDE-BY-SIDE
Side-by-side; boxlock. Double triggers; extractors. 12 or 20 ga.
w/2.75-inch chambers. Bbls: 20-inch cylinder bbl and 26-or
28-inch modified full bbl. Weight: 6.75 to 7 lbs. Checkered
walnut stock, forend. Blued, engraved receiver. Imported 1994
to 1996.
Field model w/20-inch bbl. . . . NiB $425 Ex $275 Gd $200
Model IJ-43 Field
Field model w/26- or 28-inch bbls. . . NiB $425 Ex $275 Gd $200

IZH-43 SERIES SIDE-BY-SIDE
Boxlock. Gauges: 12, 16, 20 or .410 w/2.75- or 3-inch chambers. Bbls.: 20-, 24-, 26- or 28-inch w/fixed chokes or choke
tubes. Single selective or double triggers. Weight: 6.75 lbs.
Checkered hardwood (standard on Hunter II Model) or walnut
stock and forend (standard on Hunter Model). Blued, engraved
receiver. Imported 1994 to 1996.
Model IZH-43 Hunter model
  w/12 ga. w/walnut stock . . . NiB $544 Ex $335 Gd $260
Model IZH-43 Hunter
  Hunter model (20 & 16 ga.,
  .410) . . . . NiB $457 Ex $366 Gd $255
Model IZH-43 Hunter II
  Hunter II model (12 ga. w/enternal
  hammers) . . . . NiB $477 Ex $366 Gd $257
Model IZH-43 Hunter II
  Hunter II model (12 ga.
  hammerless) . . . . NiB $477 Ex $366 Gd $257
Hunter II model (12, 16
  or 20 ga.) . . . . NiB $477 Ex $366 Gd $257
Hunter II model w/walnut stock, add $60

Hunter II model w/single-selective trigger, add $75

MODEL IZH-27 O/U

Boxlock. Single selective trigger w/automatic ejectors or double
triggers w/extractors. Gauges: 12 or 20 w/2.75-inch chambers.
Bbls.: 26-inch or 28-inch w/fixed chokes. Weight: 7 lbs. Checkered
European hardwood stock and forearm. Made in Russia.

Model IJ-27 (w/double
  triggers and extractors.) . . . NiB $400 Ex $334 Gd $171
Model IJ-27 (single selective
  trigger and ejectors) . . . . NiB $400 Ex $334 Gd $171

MODEL MP94 (IZH-94) . . . . . . NiB $560 Ex $350 Gd $220
O/U combination shotgun over rifle. Boxlock. Gauges/calibers:
12 or 20 ga./.223 Rem., .30-06, .308 Win. or 7.62x39mm.
Double triggers w/extractors. Bbls.: 19.5- or 23.5-in. w/ choke
tubes or fixed choke. Weight: 8.5 lbs. Blued. Checkered walnut
stock and forearm. Made in Russia. Made 2009 to date. Also
sold as Model SPR94.
.410/.22 LR or .22 Mag. . . . . . NiB $562 Ex $300 Gd $170

THE BAKER GUN & FORGING CO. —
Batavia, New York. Made 1903–1933 by
Baker Gun Company

BATAVIA LEADER HAMMERLESS DOUBLE

Sidelock. Plain extractors or automatic ejectors. Double triggers. Gauges: 12, 16, 20. Bbls.: 26- to 32-inch; any standard
boring. Weight: About 7.75 lbs. (12 ga. w/30-inch bbls.).
Checkered pistol-grip stock and forearm.
w/extractors . . . . NiB $1465 Ex $944 Gd $500
w/ejectors . . . . NiB $1600 Ex $1100 Gd $400

BATAVIA EJECTOR . . . . NiB $1258 Ex $1178 Gd $798
Same general specifications as the Batavia Leader except
higher quality and finer finish throughout; has Damascus or
homotensile steel bbls., checkered pistol-grip stock and forearm of select walnut; automatic ejectors standard; 12 and 16
ga. only. Deduct 60% for Damascus bbls.

BATAVIA SPECIAL . . . . NiB $2000 Ex $1230 Gd $500
Same general specifications as the Batavia Leader except 12
and 16 ga. only; extractors, Homotensile steel bbls.

BLACK BEAUTY

Same general specifications as the Batavia Leader except
higher quality and finer finish throughout; has line engraving,
special steel bbls., select walnut stock w/straight, full or half-
pistol-grip.
w/extractors . . . . NiB $2000 Ex $1200 Gd $444
Black Beauty Special
  w/extractors . . . . NiB $2166 Ex $1790 Gd $577
Black Beauty Special
  w/ejectors. . . . . NiB $2208 Ex $1834 Gd $544

GRADE R . . . . NiB $4000 Ex $2833 Gd $1106
High-grade gun w/same general specifications as the Batavia
Leader except has fine Damascus or Krupp fluid steel bbls.,
engraving in line, scroll and game scene designs, checkered
stock and forearm of fancy European walnut; 12 and 16 ga.
only. Deduct 60% for Damascus bbls.

GRADE S

Same general specifications as the Batavia Leader except
higher quality and finer finish throughout; has Flui-tempered
steel bbls., line and scroll engraving, checkered stock w/half-

SHOTGUNS

Benelli Executive Grade I

Benelli Executive Grade II

Benelli Executive Grade III

pistol-grip and forearm of semi-fancy imported walnut; 10, 12 and 16 ga.

Non-ejector. . . . . NiB $3886 Ex $2013 Gd $1077
W/ejectors . . . . NiB $4100 Ex $2315 Gd $1366

PARAGON, EXPERT AND DELUXE GRADES

Made to order only, these are the higher grades of Baker hammerless sidelock double-bbl. shotguns. After 1909, the Paragon Grade, as well as the Expert and Deluxe intro. that year, had a crossbolt in addition to the regular Baker system taper wedge fastening. There are early Paragon guns w/ Damascus bbls. and some are non-ejector, but this grade was also produced w/automatic ejectors and w/the finest fluid steel bbls., in lengths to 34 inches, standard on Expert and Deluxe guns. Differences among the three models are in overall quality, finish, engraving and grade of fancy figured walnut in the stock and forearm; Expert and Deluxe wood may be carved as well as checkered. Choice of straight, full or half-pistol grip was offered. A single trigger was available in the two higher grades. The Paragon was available in 10 ga (Damascus bbls. only), and the other two models were regularly produced in 12, 16 and 20 ga.

Paragon grade, no ejector . . NiB $4277 Ex $2660 Gd $2033
Paragon grade w/auto ejector . . . . NiB $4455 Ex $2978 Gd $2270
Expert grade . . . . NiB $6177 Ex $4588 Gd $2844
Deluxe grade . . . . NiB $11,477 Ex $9968 Gd $7133
W/ejectors, add $350

BELKNAP SHOTGUNS — Louisville, Kentucky

MODEL B-68 SINGLE-SHOT . . . NiB $199 Ex $144 Gd $100
Takedown. Visible hammer. Automatic ejector. Gauges: 12, 16, 20 and .410. Bbls.: 26-inch to 36-inch; F choke. Weight: 6 lbs. Plain pistol-grip stock and forearm.

MODEL B-63 SINGLE-SHOT . . . NiB $229 Ex $135 Gd $105
Takedown. Visible hammer. Automatic ejector. Gauges: 12, 20 and .410. Bbls.: 26- to 36-inch, F choke. Weight: Average 6 lbs. Plain pistol-grip stock and forearm.

MODEL B-63E SINGLE-SHOT . . . NiB $209 Ex $133 Gd $95
Same general specifications as Model B-68 except has side lever opening instead of top lever.

MODEL B-64
SLIDE-ACTION SHOTGUN . . . NiB $339 Ex $244 Gd $225
Hammerless. Gauges: 12, 16, 20 and .410. Three round tubular magazine. Various bbl. lengths and chokes from 26-inch to 30-inch. Weight: 6.25 to 7.5 lbs. Walnut-finished hardwood stock.

MODEL B-65C
AUTOLOADING SHOTGUN . . . NiB $533 Ex $400 Gd $290
Browning-type lightweight alloy receiver. 12 ga. only. Four round tubular magazine. Bbl.: plain, 28-inch. Weight: About 8.25 lbs. Disc. 1949.

BENELLI — Urbino, Italy.

Imported by Benelli USA, Accokeek, MD.

MODEL 121 M1
MILITARY/POLICE . . . . NiB $656 Ex $432 Gd $335
Semi-automatic. Gauge: 12. Seven round magazine. 19.75-inch bbl. 39.75 inches overall. Cylinder choke, 2.75-inch chamber. Weight: 7.4 lbs. Matte black finish and European hardwood stock. Post front sight, fixed buckhorn rear sight. Imported in 1985. Disc.

BLACK EAGLE
Semi-automatic. Two-piece aluminum and steel receiver. Ga: 12; 3-inch chamber. Four round magazine. Screw-in choke tubes (SK, IC, M, IM, F). Bbls.: Ventilated rib; 21, 24, 26 or 28 inches w/bead front sight; 24-inch rifled slug. 42.5 to 49.5 inches overall. Weight: 7.25 lbs. (28-inch bbl.). Matte black lower receiver w/blued upper receiver and bbl. Checkered walnut stock w/high-gloss finish and drop adjustment. Imported from 1989 to 1990 and 1997 to 1998.

Benelli Legacy
Limited Edition (Only 250 Made)

Benelli M1 – Super 90 w/Pistol Grip

Limited edition . . . . NiB $1587 Ex $1090 Gd $965
Competition model . . . . NiB $953 Ex $755 Gd $523
Slug model (disc. 1992) . . . . . . NiB $815 Ex $608 Gd $466
Standard model (disc. 1990) . . NiB $879 Ex $770 Gd $505

BLACK EAGLE EXECUTIVE

Semi-automatic. Custom Black Eagle Series. Montefeltro-style rotating bolt w/three locking lugs. All-steel lower receiver engraved, gold inlay by Bottega Incisione di Cesare Giovanelli. 12 ga. only. 21-, 24-, 26-, or 28-inch vent-rib bbl. w/5 screw-in choke tubes (Type I) or fixed chokes. Custom deluxe walnut stock and forend. Built to customer specifications on special order.
Grade I . . . . NiB $4190 Ex $3295 Gd $2293
Grade II . . . . NiB $4378 Ex $3566 Gd $2500
Grade III. . . . . NiB $5690 Ex $4177 Gd $2960

LEGACY

Semi-automatic. Gauges: 12 and 20 ga. w/3-inch chambers. 24- 26- or 28-inch bbl. 47.63 to 49.62 inches overall. Weight: 5.8 to 7.5 lbs. Four round magazine. Five screw-in choke tubes. Lower alloy receiver and upper steel reciever cover. Features Benelli's inertia recoil operating system. Imported 1998 to date.
Legacy model . . . . NiB $1292 Ex $977 Gd $877
Limited Edition . . . . NiB $1944 Ex $1620 Gd $1010

M1 FIELD . . . . NiB $867 Ex $767 Gd $671
Interia-operated semi-automatic. Gauge: 20. Chambers: 2.75 or 3 inches. Bbl. 24 or 26 inches, stepped ventilated rib and red bar sights. Stock: Synthetic, black or camo. Weight: 5.7 to 5.8 lbs. Includes set of five choke tubes. Imported from Italy.

M1 SUPER 90 . . . . NiB $955 Ex $836 Gd $554
Interia-operated semi-automatic. Gauge: 12. Seven round magazine. Cylinder choke. 19.75-inch bbl. 39.75 inches overall. Weight: 7 lbs., 4 oz. to 7 lbs., 10 oz. Matte black finish. Stock and forend made of fiberglass-reinforced polymer. Sights: Post front, fixed buckhorn rear, drift adj. Introduced 1985; when the model line expanded in 1989, this configuration was discontinued.

M1 SUPER 90 DEFENSE . . . . . NiB $1093 Ex $966 Gd $509
Same general specifications as Model Super 90 except w/pis-

tol-grip stock. Available w/Ghost-Ring sight option. Imported 1986 to 1998.

M1 SUPER 90 FIELD

Inertia-recoil semiautomatic shotgun. Gauge: 12; 3-inch chamber. Three round magazine. Bbl.: 21, 24, 26 or 28 inches. 42.5 to 49.5 inches overall. Choke: SK, IC, M, IM, F. Matte receiver. Standard polymer stock or satin walnut (26- or 28-inch bbl. only). Bead front sight. Imported from 1990 to 2006.
w/Realtree camo stock . . . . . . NiB $1066 Ex $743 Gd $488
w/polymer stock . . . . NiB $766 Ex $563 Gd $447
w/walnut stock . . . . NiB $1031 Ex $660 Gd $458

M1 SUPER 90 SLUG

Same general specifications as M1 Super 90 Field except w/5-round magazine. 18.5-inch bbl. Cylinder bore. 39.75 inches overall. Weight: 6.5 lbs. Polymer standard stock. Rifle or Ghost-Ring sights. Imported 1986 to 1998.
w/rifle sights . . . . NiB $988 Ex $677 Gd $549
w/ghost-ring sights . . . . NiB $1096 Ex $786 Gd $659
w/Realtree camo finish, add $150

M1 SUPER 90 SPECIAL

SPORTING AUTOLOADER . . . . NiB $877 Ex $655 Gd $589
Same general specifications as M1 Super 90 Field except w/18.5-inch bbl. 39.75 inches overall. Weight: 6.5 lbs. Ghost-ring sights. Polymer stock. Imported from 1994 to 1998.

M2

Redesign of M1 w/ new receiver, trigger guard, safety. Interia-operated semi-automatic. Imported 2004 to date.
Three Gun . . . . NiB $2350 Ex $1800 Gd $1000
Practical . . . . NiB $1196 Ex $970 Gd $480
Tacical . . . . NiB $1230 Ex $900 Gd $510

M3 SUPER 90 PUMP/AUTOLOADER

Inertia-recoil semiautomatic and/or pump action. Gauge: 12. Seven round magazine. Cylinder choke. 19.75-inch bbl. 41 inches overall (31 inches folded). Weight: 7 to 7.5 lbs. Matte black finish. Stock:

standard synthetic, pistol-grip or folding tubular steel. Standard

Benelli Montefeltro Realtree Camo

Benelli Montefeltro Super 90 Left-Handed Model

rifle or Ghost-Ring sights. Imported 1989 to date. Caution: Increasing the magazine capacity to more than 5 rounds in M3 shotguns w/pistol-grip stocks violates provisions of the 1994 Crime Bill. This model may be used legally only by the military and law-enforcement agencies.

Standard model..........NiB $1477 Ex $1067 Gd $799
Pistol-grip model ....NiB $1644 Ex $1133 Gd $990
w/folding stock ....NiB $1190 Ex $955 Gd $944
w/laser sight ....NiB $1766 Ex $1388 Gd $1100
w/ghost-ring sights, add $100

M4 TACTICAL ....NiB $1680 Ex $1230 Gd $870
Gas-operated semi-automatic. Civilian version of U.S. military M4, gas regulating system. Gauge: 12; 3-inch chamber. Four round magazine. Bbl.: 18.5 inches. 40 inches overall. Choke: M. Matte receiver. Standard and pistol grip sythetic stock. Ghost ring rear, post front sights. Imported from 2003 to date.
M1040 Limited Edition .....NiB $1380 Ex $960 Gd $660

MONTEFELTRO/SUPER 90
Semi-automatic. Gauges: 12 or 20 gauge w/3-inch chamber. 21- 24- 26- or 28-inch bbl. 43.7 to 49.5 inches overall. Weight: 5.3 to 7.5 lbs. Four round magazine. Five screw-in choke tubes (C, IC, M, IM, F). High gloss or satin walnut or Realtree Camo stock. Blued metal finish. Imported 1987 to 1992.
Standard Hunter model .....NiB $1155 Ex $865 Gd $490
Slug model (disc. 1992) ......NiB $744 Ex $639 Gd $440
Turkey model ....NiB $744 Ex $639 Gd $440
Uplander model ....NiB $744 Ex $639 Gd $440
Limited Edition (1995-96) ...NiB $2077 Ex $1688 Gd $1176
20 ga. w/Realtree camo .....NiB $1269 Ex $988 Gd $775
20 ga. Youth Model w/short stock, add...............$75
Left-hand model, add $50

NOVA...................NiB $466 Ex $368 Gd $256
Pump-action. Gauge: 12 or 20. Chambers: 2.75 or 3 in.; 3.5 in. 12 gauge only. Four-round magazine. Bbl. 24, 26 or 28 inches; red bar sights. Stock: Synthetic,(Xtra Brown in 12 gauge or Timber HD in 20 gauge). Montefeltro rotating bolt, magazine cutoff, synthetic trigger assembly. Introduced 1999. Imported from Italy.

SL 121V (SL-80 SERIES) ......Nib $466 Ex $359 Gd $270
Recoil-operated semiautomatic w/split receiver design. Gauge: 12. Five round capacity. 26-, 28- or 30-inch ventilated rib bbl. (26-inch choked M, IM, IC, 28-inch, F, M, IM; 30-inch, F choke - Mag.). Straight walnut stock w/hand-checkered pistol grip and forend. Importation disc. in 1985.

SL 121V SLUG (SL-80 SERIES) . Nib $578 Ex $376 Gd $305
Same general specifications as Benelli SL 121V except designed for rifled slugs and equipped w/rifle sights. Disc. in 1985.

SL 123V (SL-80 SERIES) ......NiB $500 Ex $378 Gd $297
Semi-automatic. Gauge: 12. 26- and 28-inch bbls. 26-inch choked IM, M, IC; 28-inch choked F, IM, M. Disc. in 1985.

SL 201 (SL-80 SERIES)........NiB $459 Ex $365 Gd $300
Semi-automatic. Gauge: 20. 26-inch bbl. Mod. choke. Weight: 5 lbs., 10 oz. Ventilated rib. Disc. in 1985.

SPORT...................NiB $1266 Ex $999 Gd $654
Similar to the Black Eagle Competition model except has one-piece matte-finished alloy receiver w/inscribed red Benelli logo. 26 or 28 inches bbl. w/2 inchangable carbon fiber vent ribs. Oil-finished checkered walnut stock w/adjustable buttpad and buttstock. Imported 1997 to 2002.

SUPER BLACK EAGLE
Interia-operated semi-automatic. Same general specifications as Black Eagle except w/3.5-inch chamber that accepts 2.75-, 3- and 3.5-inch shells. Two round magazine (3.5-inch), 3-round magazine (2.75- or 3-inch). High-gloss, satin finish or camo stock. Realtree camo, matte black or blued metal finish. Imported 1991 to 2005.
Standard model ....NiB $1096 Ex $933 Gd $766
Realtree camo model ......NiB $1221 Ex $1099 Gd $866
Custom slug model ....NiB $1254 Ex $958 Gd $744
Limited edition ....NiB $1979 Ex $1654 Gd $1177
w/wood stock, add................................$40
Left-hand model, add $100

ULTRA LIGHT ....NiB $1480 Ex $1010 Gd $610
Interia-operated semi-automatic. Gauges: 12, 20 or 28 gauge w/3-inch chamber. 24- or 26-inch bbl. 45.5 to 47.5 inches overall. Weight: 5.0 to 6.1 lbs. Two round magazine. Five screw-in choke tubes (C, IC, M, IM, F). High gloss WeatherCoat stock. Blued metal finish. Imported 2006 to date.

CORDOBA ....NiB $1800 Ex $1230 Gd $760
Interia-operated semi-automatic. Gauges: 12 or 20 gauge w/3-inch chamber. 28- or 30-inch bbl. 49.7 to 51.7 inches overall. Weight: 6.3 to 7.3 lbs. Four round magazine. Five screw-in choke tubes (C, IC, M, IM, F). ComfortTech stock. Matte black finish. Imported 2005 to date.

VINCI ....NiB $1300 Ex $930 Gd $560
Interia-operated semi-automatic. Modular construction. Gauges: 12 gauge w/3-inch chamber. 26- or 28-inch bbl. 45.7 to 49.7 inches overall. Weight: 6.7 to 6.9 lbs. Three round magazine. Five screw-in choke tubes (C, IC, M, IM, F). ComfortTech stock. Matte black finish. Imported 2009 to date.

BERETTA USA CORP. — Accokeek, Maryland.
Manufactured by Fabbrica D'Armi Pietro Beretta S.P.A. in Gardone Val Trompia (Brescia), Italy. Imported by Beretta USA. Previously by Garcia Corp.

MODEL 409PB
HAMMERLESS DOUBLE......NiB $966 Ex $733 Gd $545
Boxlock. Double triggers. Plain extractors. Gauges: 12, 16,

Beretta Model 682 Over/Under Sporting

Beretta Model 682 Over/Under Trap

20, 28. Bbls.: 27.5-, 28.5- and 30-inch, IC/M choke or M/F choke. Weight: from 5.5 to 7.75 lbs., depending on ga. and bbl. length. Straight or pistol-grip stock and beavertail forearm, checkered. Imported 1934 to 1964.

MODEL 410E
Same general specifications as Model 409PB except has automatic ejectors and is of higher quality throughout. Imported 1934 to 1964.

12 ga. . . . . NiB $1367 Ex $1144 Gd $922
20 ga. . . . . NiB $2882 Ex $2096 Gd $1377
28 ga. . . . . NiB $3881 Ex $3036 Gd $2456

MODEL 410 10-GA.
MAGNUM. . . . . NiB $1269 Ex $945 Gd $700
Same as Model 410E except heavier construction. Plain extractors. Double triggers. 10-ga. Magnum, 3.5-inch chambers. 32-inch bbls., both F choke. Weight: about 10 lbs. Checkered pistol-grip stock and forearm, recoil pad. Imported 1934 to 1984.

MODEL 411E
Same general specifications as Model 409PB except has sideplates, automatic ejectors and is of higher quality throughout. Imported 1934 to 1964.

12 ga. . . . . NiB $2077 Ex $1700 Gd $1179
20 ga. . . . . NiB $2866 Ex $2234 Gd $1590
28 ga. . . . . NiB $4339 Ex $3977 Gd $2766

MODEL 424 HAMMERLESS
DOUBLE . . . . NiB $1288 Ex $1292 Gd $957
Boxlock. Light border engraving. Plain extractors. Gauges: 12, 20; chambers 2.75-inch in former, 3-inch in latter. Bbls.: 28-inch M/F choke, 26-inch IC/M choke. Weight: 5 lbs. 14 oz. to 6 lbs. 10 oz., depending on ga. and bbl. length. English-style straight-grip stock and forearm, checkered. Imported 1977 to 1984.

MODEL 426E . . . . NiB $1588 Ex $1233 Gd $1067
Same as Model 424 except action body is finely engraved, silver pigeon inlaid in top lever; has selective automatic ejectors and selective single trigger, stock and forearm of select European walnut. Imported 1977-84.

MODEL 450 SERIES HAMMERLESS DOUBLES
Custom English-style sidelock. Single, non-selective trigger or double triggers. Manual safety. Selective automatic ejectors.

Gauge: 12; 2.75- or 3-inch chambers. Bbls.: 26, 28 or 30 inches choked to customers' specifications. Weight: 6.75 lbs. Checkered high-grade walnut stock. Receiver w/coin-silver finish. Imported 1948. Disc.

Model 450 EL (disc. 1982). . . NiB $8334 Ex $6688 Gd $4731
Model 450 EELL (disc.
  1982) . . . . NiB $10,655 Ex $6798 Gd $4880
Model 451 (disc. 1987). . . . NiB $6443 Ex $5670 Gd $3990
Model 451 E (disc. 1989) . . NiB $7125 Ex $6225 Gd $4350
Model 451 EL (disc.
  1985) . . . . NiB $17,787 Ex $14,866 Gd $11,700
Model 451 EELL (disc.
  1990) . . . . NiB $15,788 Ex $12,877 Gd $10,777
Model 452 (Intro.
  1990) . . . . NiB $29,988 Ex $21,980 Gd $18,799
Model 452 EELL
  (intro. 1992) . . . . . NiB $41,665 Ex $35,000 Gd $27,889
w/extra bbls, add 30%

MODEL 470 SERIES HAMMERLESS DOUBLE
Gauge: 12 and 20 ga. w/3-inch chambers. 26- or 28-inch bbl. Weight: 5.9 to 6.5 lbs. Low profile, improved box lock action w/single selective trigger. Selected walnut, checkered stock and forend. Metal front bead sight. Scroll-engraved receiver w/gold inlay and silver chrome finish. Imported 1999 to date.

Silver Hawk 12 ga. . . . . NiB $9332 Ex $6880 Gd $5440
Silver Hawk 20 ga. . . . . NiB $9566 Ex $6465 Gd $5566
EL Silver Hawk 12 ga. . . . . NiB $8310 Ex $7223 Gd $5600
EL Silver Hawk 20 ga. . . . . NiB $8554 Ex $6133 Gd $5477
EELL (Jubilee II) 12 ga. . . . . NiB $8366 Ex $6328 Gd $4790
EELL (Jubilee II) 20 ga. . . . . NiB $9000 Ex $7231 Gd $4889
w/extra bbls., add. 30%

MODEL 625 S/S HAMMERLESS DOUBLE
Boxlock. Gauges: 12 or 20. Bbls.: 26-, 28- or 30-inch w/ fixed choke combinations. Single selective or double triggers w/extractors. Checkered English-style buttstock and forend. Imported 1984 to 1987.

w/double triggers . . . . NiB $1591 Ex $900 Gd $667
w/single selective trigger . . NiB $1880 Ex $1067 Gd $700
20 ga., add $200

MODEL 626 S/S HAMMERLESS DOUBLE
Field Grade side-by-side. Boxlock action w/single selective trigger, extractors and automatic safety. Gauges: 12 (2.75-inch chambers); 20 (3-inch chambers). Bbls.: 26- or 28-inch w/ Mobilchoke or various fixed-choke combinations. Weight:

Beretta Model 687EL

Beretta Model 687EEL

6.75 lbs. (12 ga.). Bright chrome finish. Checkered European walnut buttstock and forend in straight English style. Imported 1985 to 1994.

Model 626 Field (disc. 1988) . . .NiB $1345 Ex $1190 Gd $700
Model 626 Onyx . . . . .NiB $1779 Ex $1288 Gd $1006
Model 626 Onyx (3.5-inch
    magnum, disc. 1993) . . .NiB $1798 Ex $1388 Gd $1098
20 ga., add 50%

MODEL 627 S/S HAMMERLESS DOUBLE
Same as Model 626 S/S except w/engraved sideplates and pistol-grip or straight English-style stock. Imported 1985 to 1994.

Model 627 EL Field . . . . . . NiB $2370 Ex $2090 Gd $1550
Model 627 EL Sport . . . . . . NiB $2592 Ex $2210 Gd $1776
Model 627 EELL . . . . NiB $4460 Ex $3978 Gd $2666

MODEL 682 O/U SHOTGUN
Hammerless takedown w/single selective trigger. Gauges: 12, 20, 28, .410. Bbls.: 26- to 34-inch w/fixed chokes or Mobilchoke tubes. Checkered European walnut buttstock/forend in various grades and configurations. Imported 1984 to 2000.

Comp Skeet model . . . . NiB $1566 Ex $1160 Gd $1004
Comp Skeet Deluxe model NiB $1789 Ex $1440 Gd $1166
Comp Super Skeet . . . . NiB $2599 Ex $2055 Gd $1490
Comp Skeet model, 2-bbl.
    set (disc. 1989) . . . . NiB $5100 Ex $4256 Gd $2920
Comp Skeet, 4 bbl. set
    (disc. 1996). . . . . NiB $5786 Ex $4670 Gd $3241
Sporting Continental . . . . . . NiB $1589 Ex $1170 Gd $1097
Sporting Combo . . . . NiB $1778 Ex $1566 Gd $1180
Gold Sporting . . . . NiB $1788 Ex $1266 Gd $1011
Super Sporting . . . . NiB $1566 Ex $1365 Gd $1291
Comp Trap Gold X . . . . NiB $2269 Ex $1775 Gd $1231
Comp Trap Top Single
    (1986-95) . . . . NiB $2177 Ex $1688 Gd $1166
Comp Trap Live Pigeon
    (1990-98) . . . . NiB $2769 Ex $2255 Gd $1568
Comp Mono/Combo Trap
    Gold X . . . . NiB $2977 Ex $2510 Gd $1765
Comp Mono Trap (1985-88) . .NiB $1867 Ex $1588 Gd $1100

Super Trap Gold X
    (1991-95) . . . . .NiB $2267 Ex $1880 Gd $1266
Super Trap Combo Gold X
    (1991-97) . . . . .NiB $3166 Ex $2478 Gd $1776
Super Trap Top Single Gold X
    (1991-95) . . . . .NiB $2265 Ex $2099 Gd $1369
Super Trap Unsingle
    (1992-94) . . . . .NiB $2210 Ex $2050 Gd $1319

MODEL 686 O/U SHOTGUN
Low-profile improved boxlock action. Single selective trigger. Selective automatic ejectors. Gauges: 12, 20, 28 w/3.5- 3- or 2.75-inch chambers, depending upon ga. Bbls.: 26-, 28-, 30-inch w/fixed chokes or Mobilchoke tubes. Weight: 5.75 to 7.5 lbs. Checkered American walnut stock and forearm of various qualities, depending upon model. Receiver finishes also vary, but all have blued bbls. Sideplates to simulate sidelock action on EL models. Imported 1988 to 1995.

Field Onyx . . . . .NiB $1335 Ex $1108 Gd $733
(3.5-inch Mag., disc.
    1993 & reintro.1996) . .NiB $4370 Ex $2888 Gd $2280
EL Gold Perdiz (1992-97) . .NiB $2077 Ex $1576 Gd $1200
Essential (1994-96) . . . . .NiB $1009 Ex $808 Gd $635
Silver Essential (1997-98) . . . .NiB $1180 Ex $966 Gd $680
Silver Pigeon Onyx
    (intro. 1996) . . . . .NiB $1566 Ex $1254 Gd $870
Silver Perdiz Onyx
    (disc. 1996) . . . . .NiB $1488 Ex $1155 Gd $866
Silver Pigeon/Perdiz Onyx Combo . .NiB $1133 Ex $866 Gd $633
L Silver Perdiz (disc. 1994) . . NiB $1288 Ex $1007 Gd $766
Skeet Silver Pigeon (1996-98) NiB $1276 Ex $988 Gd $766
Skeet Silver Perdiz
    (1994-96) . . . . .NiB $1570 Ex $1288 Gd $944
Skeet Silver Pigeon/Perdiz
    Combo . . . . .NiB $1570 Ex $1288 Gd $944
Sporting Special (1987-93) NiB $1798 Ex $1369 Gd $1100
Sporting English (1991-92) . NiB $1820 Ex $1400 Gd $1188
Sporting Onyx
    w/fixed chokes (1991-92)NiB $1743 Ex $1388 Gd $1014
Sporting Onyx w/ choke
    tubes (intro. 1992) . . . . . .NiB $1344 Ex $1130 Gd $966
Sporting Onyx Gold
    (disc. 1993) . . . . .NiB $1879 Ex $1577 Gd $1188
Sporting Silver Pigeon
    (intro. 1996) . . . . .NiB $1598 Ex $1266 Gd $1005
Sporting Silver Perdiz
    (1993-96) . . . . .NiB $1612 Ex $1288 Gd $1130
Sporting Collection Sport
    (1996-97) . . . . .NiB $1188 Ex $1033 Gd $892
Sporting Combo . . . . .NiB $2667 Ex $2174 Gd $1545
Trap International (1994-95) . . NiB $1144 Ex $967 Gd $755
Trap Silver Pigeon
    (intro. 1997). . . . . .NiB $1266 Ex $1057 Gd $798

Beretta Model A-303

Trap Top Mono (intro. 1998) . . NiB $1279 Ex $1088 Gd $800
Ultralight Onyx (intro. 1992) . . NiB $1599 Ex $1366 Gd $968
Ultralight Del. Onyx
(intro. 1998). . . . . NiB $2056 Ex $1665 Gd $1156

MODEL 687 O/U SHOTGUN
Same as Model 686 except w/decorative sideplates and varying grades of engraving and game-scene motifs.
L Onyx (disc. 1991) . . . . . . NiB $1460 Ex $1233 Gd $865
L Onyx Gold Field (1988-89) . . . . NiB $1688 Ex $1344 Gd $966
L Onyx Silver Pigeon. . . . . . NiB $1288 Ex $1668 Gd $1208
EL Onyx (disc. 1990) . . . . . NiB $2855 Ex $2344 Gd $1629
EL Gold Pigeon . . . . NiB $3266 Ex $2688 Gd $1863
EL Gold Pigeon small
frame . . . . NiB $3090 Ex $2451 Gd $1761
EL Gold Pigeon Sporting
(intro 1993) . . . . NiB $4388 Ex $3571 Gd $2510
EELL Diamond Pigeon . . . . NiB $4416 Ex $3620 Gd $2560
EELL Diamond Pigeon Skeet . . NiB $4233 Ex $3548 Gd $2480
EELL Diamond Pigeon
Sporting . . . . NiB $4416 Ex $3578 Gd $2560
EELL Diamond Pigeon
X Trap . . . . NiB $3966 Ex $3133 Gd $2190
EELL Diamond Pigeon
Mono Trap . . . . NiB $4088 Ex $3310 Gd $2366
EELL Diamond Pigeon
Trap Combo . . . . NiB $5480 Ex $4766 Gd $3266
EELL Field Combo . . . . NiB $4570 Ex $3775 Gd $2760
EELL Skeet 4-bbl. set . . . . . NiB $7588 Ex $5977 Gd $3554
EELL Gallery Special . . . . . NiB $7233 Ex $5610 Gd $3798
EELL Gallery Special
Combo . . . . NiB $8235 Ex $6799 Gd $4571
EELL Gallery Special
pairs . . . . NiB $17,844 Ex $14,560 Gd $10,134
Sporting English (1991-92) . . . NiB $2247 Ex $1867 Gd $1359
Sporting Silver Pigeon
(intro. 1996) . . . . NiB $2079 Ex $1677 Gd $1261
Sporting Silver Perdiz
(1993-96) . . . . NiB $2255 Ex $1767 Gd $1388

MODEL 1200 SERIES SEMIAUTOLOADING SHOTGUN
Short recoil action. Gauge: 12; 2.75- or 3-inch chamber. Six round magazine. 24-, 26- or 28-inch vent-rib bbl. w/fixed chokes or Mobilchoke tubes. Weight: 7.25 lbs. Matte black finish. Adj. technopolymer stock and forend. Imported 1988 to 1990.
w/fixed choke (disc. 1989) . . . NiB $466 Ex $359 Gd $266
Riot (disc. 1994) . . . . NiB $476 Ex $368 Gd $277
w/Mobilchoke (disc. 1994) . . . . NiB $741 Ex $577 Gd $400
Riot model . . . . NiB $805 Ex $633 Gd $451
w/Pistol-grip stock, add $65
w/Tritium sights, add $100

MODEL A-301
AUTOLOADING SHOTGUN . . NiB $644 Ex $470 Gd $356
Field Gun. Gas-operated. Scroll-decorated receiver. Gauge:

12 or 20; 2.75-inch chamber in former, 3-inch in latter. Three round magazine. Bbl.: Ventilated rib; 28-inch F or M choke, 26-inch IC. Weight: 6 lbs., 5 oz. – 6 lbs., 14 oz., depending on gauge and bbl. length. Checkered pistol-grip stock/forearm. Imported 1977 to 1982.

MODEL A-301 MAGNUM . . . . NiB $455 Ex $277 Gd $200
Same as Model A-301 Field Gun except chambered for 12 ga. Three inch Magnum shells, 30-inch F choke bbl. only, stock w/ recoil pad. Weight: 7.25 lbs.

MODEL A-301 SKEET GUN . . . NiB $466 Ex $300 Gd $210
Same as Model A-301 Field Gun except 26-inch bbl. SK choke only, skeet-style stock, gold-plated trigger.

MODEL A-301 SLUG GUN. . . . NiB $488 Ex $287 Gd $217
Same as Model A-301 Field Gun except has plain 22-inch bbl., slug choke, w/rifle sights. Weight: 6 lbs., 14 oz.

MODEL A-301 TRAP GUN . . . . NiB $466 Ex $287 Gd $233
Same as Model A-301 Field Gun except has 30-inch bbl. in F choke only, checkered Monte Carlo stock w/recoil pad, gold-plated trigger. Blued bbl. and receiver. Weight: 7 lbs., 10 oz. Imported 1978 to 1982.

MODEL A-302 SEMIAUTOLOADING SHOTGUN
Similar to gas-operated Model 301. Hammerless, takedown shotgun w/tubular magazine and Mag-Action that handles both 2.75- and 3-inch Magnum shells. Gauge: 12 or 20; 2.75- or 3-inch Mag. chambers. Bbl.: Vent or plain; 22-inch/Slug (12 ga.); 26-inch/IC (12 or 20) 28-inch/M (20 ga.), 28-inch/Multi-choke (12 or 20 ga.) 30-inch/F (12 ga.). Weight: 6.5 lbs., 20 ga.; 7.25.lbs., 12 ga. Blued/ black finish. Checkered European walnut, pistol-grip stock and forend. Imported from 1983 to c. 1987.
Standard model w/fixed choke . . NiB $466 Ex $338 Gd $254
Standard model w/multi-choke . . NiB $490 Ex $345 Gd $258

MODEL A-302 SUPER
LUSSO . . . . NiB $1844 Ex $1452 Gd $1166
A custom A-302 in presentation grade w/hand-engraved receiver and custom select walnut stock.

MODEL A-303 SEMIAUTOLOADER
Similar to Model 302, except w/target specifications in Trap, Skeet and Youth configurations, and weighs 6.5 to 8 lbs. Imported from 1983 to 1996.
Field and Upland models . . . . . NiB $523 Ex $400 Gd $288
Skeet and Trap (disc. 1994) . . . . NiB $488 Ex $366 Gd $257
Slug model (disc. 1992) . . . . . . NiB $453 Ex $377 Gd $260
Sporting Clays. . . . . NiB $600 Ex $453 Gd $279
Super Skeet. . . . . NiB $500 Ex $433 Gd $318
Super Trap. . . . . NiB $643 Ex $494 Gd $388
Waterfowl/Turkey model
(disc. 1992). . . . . NiB $525 Ex $460 Gd $354
w/Mobil choke, add $75

SHOTGUNS

Beretta Model A-390 Field

Beretta Model AL-2

MODEL A-303 YOUTH GUN . . NiB $498 Ex $376 Gd $277
Locked-breech, gas-operated action. Ga: 12 and 20; 2-round magazine. Bbls.: 24, 26, 28, 30 or 32-inches, vent rib. Weight: 7 lbs. (12 ga.), 6 lbs. (20 ga.). Crossbolt safety. Length of pull shortened to 12.5 inches. Imported 1988-96.

MODEL AL-390 SEMIAUTOMATIC SHOTGUN
Gas-operated, self-regulating action designed to handle any size load. Gauges: 12 or 20 w/ 3-inch chamber. Three round magazine. Bbl.: 24, 26, 28 or 30 inches w/vent rib and Mobilchoke tubes. Weight: 7.5 lbs. Select walnut stock w/ adj. comb. Blued or matte black finish. Imported 1992-96. Superseded by AL-390 series.
Standard/Slug models . . . . NiB $525 Ex $377 Gd $296
Field/Silver Mallard models . . . NiB $525 Ex $377 Gd $296
Deluxe/Gold Mallard models . . NiB $485 Ex $335 Gd $250
Turkey/Waterfowl model
    (w/matte finish) . . . . NiB $577 Ex $366 Gd $300
20 ga., add $75

MODEL AL-390 TARGET
Similar to the Model 390 Field except w/2.75-inch chamber. Skeet: 28-inch ported bbl. w/wide vent rib and fixed choke (SK). Trap: 30- or 32-inch w/Mobilchoke tubes. Weight: 7.5 lbs. Fully adj. buttstock. Imported from 1993 to 1996.
Sport Trap model. . . . . NiB $599 Ex $367 Gd $290
Sport Skeet model. . . . . NiB $479 Ex $345 Gd $266
Sporting Clays model (unported) NiB $700 Ex $579 Gd $421
Super Trap model (ported) . . . . NiB $577 Ex $367 Gd $292
Super Skeet model (ported) . . . NiB $569 Ex $355 Gd $307
w/ported bbl., add $100
20 ga., add $75

MODEL AL-1 FIELD GUN. . . . . NiB $566 Ex $349 Gd $279
Same as Model AL-2 gas-operated Field Gun except has bbl. w/o rib, no engraving on receiver. Imported from 1971 to 1973.

MODEL AL-2 AUTOLOADING SHOTGUN
Field Gun. Gas-operated. Engraved receiver (1968 version, 12 ga. only, had no engraving). Gauge: 12 or 20. 2.75-inch chamber. Three round magazine. Bbls.: Vent rib; 30-inch F choke, 28-inch F or M choke, 26-inch IC. Weight: 6.5 to 7.25 lbs, depending on ga. and bbl. length. Checkered pistol-grip stock and forearm. Imported from 1968 to 1975.
w/Plain receiver . . . . NiB $435 Ex $315 Gd $229
w/Engraved receiver . . . . NiB $633 Ex $500 Gd $378

MODEL AL-2 MAGNUM . . . . . NiB $515 Ex $377 Gd $255
Same as Model AL-2 Field Gun except chambered for 12 ga. 3-inch Magnum shells; 30-inch F or 28-inch M choke bbl. only. Weight: About 8 lbs. Imported from 1973 to 1975.

MODEL AL-2 SKEET GUN . . . . NiB $466 Ex $321 Gd $234
Same as Model AL-2 Field Gun except has wide rib, 26-inch bbl. in SK choke only, checkered pistol-grip stock and beavertail forearm. Imported 1973 to 1975.

MODEL AL-2 TRAP GUN . . . . . NiB $445 Ex $341 Gd $246
Same as Model AL-2 Field Gun except has wide rib, 30 inch bbl. in F choke only, beavertail forearm. Monte Carlo stock w/recoil pad. Weight: About 7.75 lbs. Imported from 1973 to 1975.

MODEL AL-3
Similar to corresponding AL-2 models in design and general specifications. Imported from 1975 to 1976.
Field model. . . . . NiB $466 Ex $331 Gd $244
Magnum model . . . . NiB $475 Ex $350 Gd $266
Skeet model . . . . NiB $486 Ex $351 Gd $264
Trap model . . . . NiB $453 Ex $335 Gd $266

MODEL AL-3 DELUXE
TRAP GUN . . . . NiB $700 Ex $566 Gd $339
Same as standard Model AL-3 Trap Gun except has fully-engraved receiver, gold-plated trigger and safety, stock and forearm of premium-grade European walnut, gold monogram escutcheon inlaid in buttstock. Imported 1975 to 1976.

AL390 FIELD SHOTGUN
Lightweight version of A-390 series. Gauges: 12 or 20 ga. 22- 24-, 26-, 28-, or 30-inch bbl., 41.7 to 47.6 inches overall. Weight: 6.4 to 7.5 lbs. Imported 1992 to 1999.
Field/Silver Mallard model
    (12 or 20 ga.) . . . . NiB $655 Ex $465 Gd $300
Field/Silver Mallard Youth
    model (20 ga.) . . . . NiB $500 Ex $355 Gd $245
Field/Slug (12 ga. only) . . . . NiB $525 Ex $433 Gd $266
Silver Mallard camo model . . . . NiB $533 Ex $379 Gd $295
Silver Mallard model,
    synthetic stock . . . . NiB $566 Ex $430 Gd $349

**Beretta Model AL-391
Urika Gold Sporting**

**Beretta Model AL-391
Urika Gold Trap**

Beretta Model BL-1

Gold Mallard (12 or 20 ga.) . . NiB $800 Ex $656 Gd $445
NWTF Special model, camo . . NiB $645 Ex $355 Gd $339
NTWF Special model, synthetic . . NiB $600 Ex $440 Gd $322
NWTF Special Youth model. . . . NiB $590 Ex $367 Gd $292

AL390 SPORT SPORTING SHOTGUN
Similar to Model AL-390 Sport Skeet. Gauges: 12 or 20 ga., 28- or 30-inch bbls. Weight: 6.8 to 8 lbs. Imported from 1995-1999.
Sport Sporting . . . . NiB $566 Ex $396 Gd $300
Sport Sporting Collection . . . . NiB $590 Ex $433 Gd $335
Sport Sporting
  Youth (20 ga. only) . . . . NiB $590 Ex $454 Gd $397
Sport Gold Sporting . . . . NiB $823 Ex $577 Gd $446
EELL Sport
  Diamond Sporting . . . . . NiB $2166 Ex $1488 Gd $1094
w/Ported bbl., add $100

AL390 SPORT SKEET SHOTGUN
Gauges: 12 ga. only. 26- or 28-inch bbl. w/3-round mqagazine. Weight: 7.6 to 8 lbs. Matte finish wood and metal. Imported 1995 to 1999.
Sport Skeet . . . . NiB $498 Ex $366 Gd $279
Sport Super Skeet . . . . NiB $576 Ex $377 Gd $301
w/ported bbl., add $125

AL390 SPORT TRAP SHOTGUN
Gauges: 12 ga. only. 30- or 32-inch bbl. w/3-round chamber. Weight: 7.8 to 8.25 lbs. Matte finish wood and metal. Black recoil rubber pad. Imported from 1995 to 1999.
Sport Trap . . . . NiB $564 Ex $379 Gd $288
Sport Super Trap . . . . NiB $688 Ex $512 Gd $360
Multi-choke bbl. (30-inch only), add $65
w/Ported bbl., add $125

AL391 URIKA AUTOLOADING SHOTGUN
Gauge: 12 and 20 ga. w/3-inch chambers. 28- 30- or 32-inch bbl. Weight: 6.6 to 7.7 lbs. Self-compensating gas valve. Adjustable synthetic and walnut stocks w/ five interchangeable chokes. Imported from 2001 to 2006.
Urika. . . . . NiB $923 Ex $800 Gd $655
Urika synthetic . . . . NiB $865 Ex $758 Gd $600

Urika camo
  w/Realtree Hardwoods. . . . . NiB $977 Ex $844 Gd $654
Urika Gold w/black receiver . . . NiB $896 Ex $588 Gd $464
Urika Gold w/silver receiver . . . NiB $1196 Ex $974 Gd $799
Urika Youth. . . . . NiB $900 Ex $779 Gd $698
Urika Sporting . . . . NiB $1088 Ex $965 Gd $600
Urika Gold
  Sporting w/black receiver. . . NiB $859 Ex $655 Gd $488
Urika Gold Sporting
  w/silver receiver. . . . . NiB $1256 Ex $1011 Gd $733
Urika Trap. . . . . NiB $1047 Ex $798 Gd $633
Urika Gold Trap . . . . NiB $1066 Ex $881 Gd $700
Parallel Target . . . . NiB $1066 Ex $881 Gd $700

MODEL ASE 90 O/U SHOTGUN
Competition-style receiver w/coin-silver finish and gold inlay featuring drop-out trigger group. Gauge: 12; 2.75-inch chamber. Bbls.: 28- or 30-inch w/fixed or Mobilchoke tubes; vent rib. Weight: 8.5 lbs. (30-inch bbl.). Checkered high-grade walnut stock. Imported 1992 to 1994.
Pigeon, Skeet, Trap models NiB $3719 Ex $2466 Gd $1967
Sporting Clays model . . . . . NiB $8171 Ex $6559 Gd $4577
Trap Combo model . . . . NiB $13,878 Ex $10,798 Gd $8657
Deluxe model (introduced
  1996) . . . . NiB $17,366 Ex $12,988 Gd $9853

MODEL ASE SERIES O/U SHOTGUN
Boxlock. Single non-selective trigger. Selective automatic ejectors. gauges: 12 and 20. Bbls. 26-, 28-, 30-inch; IC and M choke or M and F choke. Weight: about 5.75-7 lbs. Checkered pistol-grip stock and forearm. Receiver w/various grades of engraving. Imported 1947 to 1964.
Model ASE (light scroll
  engraving). . . . . NiB $2366 Ex $1971 Gd $1388
Model ASEL (half coverage
  engraving). . . . . NiB $3341 Ex $2679 Gd $1882
Model ASEELL (full coverage
  engraving). . . . . NiB $4966 Ex $4054 Gd $2866
For 20 ga. models, add 95%

MODEL BL-1/BL-2 O/U
Boxlock. Plain extractors. Double triggers.12 gauge, 2.75-inch chambers only. Bbls.: 30-and 28-inch M/F choke, 26-inch IC/M choke. Weight: 6.75-7 lbs., depending on bbl. length. Checkered pistol-grip stock and forearm. Imported 1968 to 1973.

Beretta Model BL3

Beretta Model BL-6

Beretta FS-1 Folding

Beretta Mark II Trap Gun

Beretta S55B

Beretta S682 Gold E Trap

Model BL-1 . . . . NiB $478 Ex $339 Gd $227
Model BL-2 (single selective trigger) . . NiB $596 Ex $487 Gd $356

MODEL BL-2/S . . . . NiB $554 Ex $451 Gd $307
Similar to Model BL-1, except has selective "Speed-Trigger," vent-rib bbls., 2.75- or 3-inch chambers. Weight: 7-7.5 lbs. Imported 1974 to 1976.

MODEL BL-3 . . . . NiB $690 Ex $579 Gd $491
Same as Model BL-1, except has deluxe engraved receiver, selective single trigger, vent-rib bbls., 12 or 20 ga., 2.75-inch or 3-inch chambers in former, 3-inch in latter. Weight: 6-7.5 lbs. depending on ga. and bbl. length. Imported 1968 to 1976.

MODELS BL-4/BL-6
Higher grade versions of Model BL-3 w/more elaborate engraving and fancier wood; Model BL-6 has sideplates. Selective automatic ejectors standard. Imported 1968-76.

Model BL-4 . . . . NiB $966 Ex $779 Gd $633
Model BL-5 . . . . NiB $996 Ex $800 Gd $671
Model BL-6 (1973-76) . . . . . . NiB $1287 Ex $1108 Gd $977

SERIES BL SKEET GUNS
Models BL-3, BL-4, BL-5 and BL-6 w/standard features of their respective grades plus wider rib and skeet-style stock, 26-inch bbls. SK choked. Weight: 6-7.25 lbs. depending on ga.
Model BL-3 skeet gun . . . . . . NiB $1166 Ex $877 Gd $588
Model BL-4 skeet gun . . . . NiB $822 Ex $658 Gd $433
Model BL-5 skeet gun . . . . NiB $966 Ex $700 Gd $582
Model BL-6 skeet gun . . . . . NiB $1139 Ex $1076 Gd $755

SERIES BL TRAP GUNS
Models BL-3, BL-4, BL-5 and BL-6 w/standard features of their respective grades plus wider rib and Monte Carlo stock w/recoil pad; 30-inch bbls., improved M/F or both F choke. Weight: About 7.5 lbs.

Model BL-3 . . . . NiB $679 Ex $466 Gd $388
Model BL-4 . . . . NiB $733 Ex $566 Gd $452
Model BL-5 . . . . NiB $966 Ex $753 Gd $521
Model BL-6 . . . . NiB $1166 Ex $893 Gd $600

D10 TRIDENT TRAP
GUNS . . . . NiB $7520 Ex $5000 Gd $2510
Removeable trigger group. 12 gauge, 3-inch chambers. Bbls.: 30-and 32-inch Optima choke tubes. Weight: 8.8 lbs., depending on bbl. length. Wlanut stock and forearm. Imported 2000 to 2008.
Top Single . . . . NiB $7520 Ex $5000 Gd $2510
Bottom Single . . . . NiB $7520 Ex $5000 Gd $2510
Combo . . . . NiB $9060 Ex $7200 Gd $4000
Model BL-6 . . . . NiB $1166 Ex $893 Gd $600

MODEL FS-1
FOLDING SINGLE . . . . NiB $238 Ex $167 Gd $95
Formerly "Companion." Folds to length of bbl. Hammerless. Underlever. Gauge: 12, 16, 20, 28 or .410. Bbl.: 30-inch in 12 ga., 28-inch in 16 and 20 ga.; 26-inch in 28 and .410 ga.; all F choke. Checkered semipistol-grip stock/forearm. Weight: 4.5-5.5 lbs. depending on ga. Disc. 1971.

MODEL GR-2 HAMMERLESS
DOUBLE . . . . NiB $956 Ex $788 Gd $641
Boxlock. Plain extractors. Double triggers. Gauges: 12, 20; 2.75-inch chambers in former, 3-inch in latter. Bbls.: Vent rib; 30-inch M/F choke (12 ga. only); 28-inch M/F choke, 26-inch IC/M choke. Weight: 6.5 to 7.5 lbs. depending on ga. and bbl. length. Checkered pistol-grip stock and forearm. Imported 1968 to 1976.

MODEL GR-3 . . . . NiB $1174 Ex $1021 Gd $751
Same as Model GR-2 except has selective single trigger chambered for 12-ga. Three inch or 2.75-inch shells. Magnum model has 30-inch M/F choke bbl., recoil pad. Weight: about 8 lbs. Imported 1968 to 1976.

MODEL GR-4 . . . . NiB $1359 Ex $1165 Gd $943
Same as Model GR-2 except has automatic ejectors and selective single trigger, higher grade engraving and wood. 12 ga., 2.75-inch chambers only. Imported 1968 to 1976.

GRADE 100 O/U
SHOTGUN . . . . NiB $2134 Ex $1741 Gd $1288
Sidelock. Double triggers. Automatic ejectors. 12 ga. only. Bbls.: 26-, 28-, 30-inch, any standard boring. Weight: About 7.5 lbs. Checkered stock and forend, straight or pistol grip. Disc.

GRADE 200 . . . . NiB $2780 Ex $2284 Gd $1633
Same general specifications as Grade 00 except higher quality; bores and action parts hard chrome plated. Disc.

MARK II SINGLE-BARREL
TRAP GUN . . . . NiB $774 Ex $623 Gd $441
Boxlock action similar to that of Series "BL" over-and-unders. Engraved receiver. Automatic ejector. 12 ga. only. 32- or 34-inch bbl. w/wide vent rib. Weight: About 8.5 lbs. Monte Carlo stock w/pistol grip and recoil pad, beavertail forearm. Imported 1972 to 1976.

MODEL S55B O/U
SHOTGUN . . . . NiB $672 Ex $490 Gd $336
Boxlock. Plain extractors. Selective single trigger. Gauges: 12, 20; 2.75- or 3-inch chambers in former, 3-inch in latter. Bbls.

vent rib; 30-inch M/F choke or both F choke in 12-ga. Three inch Magnum only; 28-inch M/F choke; 26 inch IC/M choke. Weight: 6.5 to 7.5 lbs. depending on ga. and bbl. length. Checkered pistol-grip stock and forearm. Introduced in 1977. Disc.

MODEL S56E . . . . NiB $853 Ex $567 Gd $356
Same as Model S55B except has scroll-engraved receiver selective automatic ejectors. Introduced in 1977. Disc.

MODEL S58 SKEET GUN . . . . . NiB $855 Ex $621 Gd $443
Same as Model S56E except has 26-inch bbls. of Boehler Antinit Anticorro steel, SK choked, w/wide vent rib; skeet-style stock and forearm. Weight: 7.5 lbs. Introduced in 1977.

MODEL S58 TRAP GUN . . . . . . NiB $620 Ex $494 Gd $368
Same as Model S58 Skeet Gun except has 30-inch bbls. bored IM/F Trap, Monte Carlo stock w/recoil pad. Weight: 7 lbs. 10 oz. Introduced in 1977. Disc.

SILVER HAWK FEATHERWEIGHT
HAMMERLESS DOUBLE-BARREL SHOTGUN
Boxlock. Double triggers or non-selective single trigger. Plain extractor. Gauges: 12, 16, 20, 28, 12 Mag. Bbls.: 26- to 32-inch w/high matted rib, all standard choke combinations. Weight: 7 lbs. (12 ga. w/26-inch bbls.). Checkered walnut stock w/beavertail forearm. Disc. 1967.
w/double triggers . . . . NiB $1133 Ex $844 Gd $521
w/single trigger, add $200

SILVER SNIPE O/U SHOTGUN
Boxlock. Non-selective or selective single trigger. Plain extractor. Gauges: 12, 20, 12 Mag., 20 Mag. Bbls.: 26-, 28-, 30-inch; plain or vent rib; chokes IC/M, M/F, SK number 1 and number 2, F/F. Weight: From about 6 lbs. in 20 ga. to 8.5 lbs. in 12 ga. (Trap gun). Checkered walnut pistol-grip stock, forearm. Imported 1955 to 1967.
w/plain bbl., non-selective
    trigger . . . . NiB $779 Ex $643 Gd $448
w/vent rib bbl., non-selective
    single trigger . . . . NiB $779 Ex $643 Gd $448
w/selective single trigger, add $100

GOLDEN SNIPE O/U
Same as Silver Snipe (see page 430) except has automatic ejectors, vent rib is standard feature. Imported 1959 to 1967.
w/non-selective single trigger . . .NiB $1256 Ex $1065 Gd $645

MODEL 57E O/U
Same general specifications as Golden Snipe, but higher quality throughout. Imported 1955 to 1967.
w/non-selective single trigger . . . NiB $977 Ex $765 Gd $545
w/selective single trigger . . . . NiB $1165 Ex $996 Gd $703

MODEL SL-2 PIGEON SERIES SHOTGUN
Hammerless. Takedown.12 ga. only. Three round magazine. Bbls.: Vent rib; 30-inch F choke, 28-inch M, 26-inch IC. Weight: 7-7.25 lbs., depending on bbl. length. Receiver w/ various grades of engraving. Checkered pistol-grip stock and forearm. Imported 1968 to 1971.
Pump shotgun . . . . NiB $553 Ex $442 Gd $308
Silver Pigeon . . . . NiB $466 Ex $367 Gd $377
Gold Pigeon . . . . NiB $663 Ex $507 Gd $464
Ruby Pigeon . . . . NiB $863 Ex $638 Gd $477

SHOTGUNS

Beretta S682 Gold E Double Trap

Beretta Model SO-2

Beretta Model SO-3

Beretta Model SO-4

Beretta Model SO-5

Beretta Model SO-7

"SO" SERIES SHOTGUNS

Jubilee Series introduced in 1998. The Beretta Boxlock is made with mechanical works from a single block of hot forged, high- resistance steel. The gun is richly engraved in scroll and game scenes. All engraving is signed by master engravers. High-quality finishing on the inside with high polishing of all internal points. Sidelock. Selective automatic ejectors. Selective single trigger or double triggers. 12 ga. only, 2.75- or 3-inch chambers. Bbls.: Vent rib (wide type on skeet and trap guns); 26-, 27-, 29-, 30-inch; any combination of standard chokes. Weight: 7 to 7.75 lbs., depending on bbl. length, style of stock and density of wood. Stock and forearm of select walnut, finely checkered; straight or pistol-grip, field, skeet and trap guns have appropriate styles of stock and forearm. Models differ chiefly in quality of wood and grade of engraving. Models SO-3EL, SO-3EELL, SO4 and SO-5 have hand-detachable locks. "SO-4" is used to designate skeet and trap models derived from Model SO-3EL, but with less elaborate engraving. Models SO3EL and SO-3EELL are similar to the earlier SO-4 and SO-5, respectively. Imported 1933 to date.

Jubilee O/U (.410, 12, 16,
20, 28 ga.) ...... NiB $18,766 Ex $15,580 Gd $12,654
Jubilee II Side-by-side .. NiB $20,888 Ex $16,876 Gd $13,777
Model SO-2 .... NiB $9121 Ex $4760 Gd $3231
Model SO-3 .... NiB $7786 Ex $6988 Gd $4766
Model SO-3EL......... NiB $10,573 Ex $8227 Gd $5470
Model SO-3EELL...... NiB $12,098 Ex $10,866 Gd $8977
Model SO-4 Field, Skeet
or Trap gun......... NiB $10,677 Ex $9154 Gd $7110
Model SO-5 Sporting,
Skeet or Trap model. NiB $12,779 Ex $10,870 Gd $8965
w/extra bbl. set, add............................. 25%

MODELS SO-6 AND SO-9 PREMIUM GRADE SHOTGUNS

High-grade over/unders in the SO series. Gauges: 12 ga. only (SO-6); 12, 20, 28 and .410 (SO-9). Fixed or Mobilchoke (12 ga. only). Sidelock action. Silver or casehardened receiver (SO-6); English custom hand-engraved scroll or game scenes (SO-9). Supplied w/leather case and accessories. Imported 1990 to date.

SO-6 O/U . . . . NiB $9044 Ex $6987 Gd $4733
Model SO-6 EELL O/U . . . . NiB $8343 Ex $6865 Gd $6577
Model SO-9 O/U . . NiB $50,000 Ex $47,750 Gd $45,000
Model SO-9EELL w/custom
    engraving . . . . . NiB $110,000 Ex $95,000 Gd $80,000
w/extra bbl. set, add. 25%

MODEL SO6/SO-7 S/S SHOTGUNS
Side-by-side shotgun w/same general specifications as SO
Series over/unders except higher grade w/more elaborate
engraving, fancier wood.
Model SO-6 (imported 1948-93)...NiB $7254 Ex $6144 Gd $4988
Model SO-7 (imported 1948-90)...NiB $8977 Ex $7238 Gd $6144

MODEL TR-1 SINGLE-SHOT
TRAP GUN . . . . NiB $355 Ex $279
Gd $125
Hammerless. Underlever action. Engraved frame.12 ga. only.
32-inch bbl. w/vent rib. Weight: About 8.25 lbs. Monte Carlo
stock w/pistol grip and recoil pad, beavertail forearm. Imported
1968 to 1971.

MODEL TR-2. . . . . NiB $364 Ex $231 Gd $156
Same as Model TR-1 except has extended ventilated rib.
Imported 1969-73.

VICTORIA PINTAIL (ES100) SEMIAUTOLOADER
Short Montefeltro-type recoil action. Gauge: 12 w/3-inch
chamber. Bbl.: 24-inch slug, 24-, 26- or 28-inch vent rib w/
Mobilchoke tubes. Weight: 7 lbs. to 7 lbs., 5 oz. Checkered
synthetic or walnut buttstock and forend. Matte finish on both
metal and stock. Imported 1993 and 2005.
Field model w/synthetic
    stock (intro. 1998) . . . . NiB $522 Ex $320 Gd $244
Field model w/walnut
    stock (disc. 1998) . . . . NiB $733 Ex $535 Gd $431
Rifled slug model w/synthetic
    stock (intro. 1998) . . . . NiB $544 Ex $378 Gd $296
Stndard slug model
    w/walnut stock (disc. 1998) NiB $544 Ex $378 Gd $296
Wetland Camo model
    (intro. 2000) . . . . NiB $677 Ex $460 Gd $339

BERNARDELLI, VINCENZO —
Gardone V.T. (Brescia), Italy

*Previously imported by Armsport, Miam, FL (formerly by
Magnum Research, Inc., Quality Arms, Stoeger Industries, Inc.
& Action Arms, LTD).*

115 SERIES O/U SHOTGUNS
Boxlock w/single trigger and ejectors. 12 ga. only. 25.5-,
26.75-, and 29.5-inch bbls. Concave top and vented middle
rib. Anatomical
grip stock. Blued or coin-silver finish w/various grades of
engraving. Imported 1985 to 1997.
Standard Model . . . . NiB $1844 Ex $1532 Gd $1176
Hunting Model 115E
    (disc. 1990). . . . . NiB $2247 Ex $1993 Gd $1612
Hunting Model 115L
    (disc. 1990). . . . . NiB $2788 Ex $2391 Gd $2095
Hunting Model 115S
    (disc. 1990) . . . . NiB $3712 Ex $3122 Gd $2210
Target Model 115
    (disc. 1992). . . . . NiB $1977 Ex $1678 Gd $1440

Target Model 115E
    (disc. 1992). . . . . NiB $6108 Ex $5388 Gd $3789
Target Model 115L
    (disc. 1992). . . . . NiB $3855 Ex $3410 Gd $2377
Target Model 115S
    (disc. 1992). . . . . NiB $6077 Ex $4129 Gd $3755
Trap/Skeet Model 115S
    (imported 1996-97) . . . . NiB $3366 Ex $2581 Gd $1786
Sporting Clays Model 115S
    (imported 1995-97) . . . . NiB $3944 Ex $3216 Gd $2533

BRESCIA
HAMMER DOUBLE . . . . NiB $1564 Ex $1096 Gd $839
Back-action sidelock. Plain extractors. Double triggers. Gauges:
12, 20. Bbls.: 27.5 or 29.5-inch M/F choke in 12 ga. 25.5-inch
IC/M choke in 20 ga.. Weight: From 5.75 to 7 lbs., depending
on ga. and bbl. length. English-style stock and forearm, checkered. No longer imported.

ELIO . . . . NiB $1232 Ex $1006 Gd $781
Lightweight game gun, 12 ga. only, w/same general specifications as Standard Gamecock (S. Uberto 1) except weight:
About 6 to 6.25 lbs.; has automatic ejectors, fine English-
pattern scroll engraving. No longer imported.

GAMECOCK, PREMIER (ROME 3)
Same general specifications as Standard Gamecock (S. Uberto
1) except has sideplates, auto ejectors, single trigger. No longer
imported.
Roma 3 (disc. 1989,
    reintroduced 1993-97) . . NiB $1790 Ex $1435 Gd $1108
Roma 3E (disc. 1950) . . . . . NiB $1956 Ex $1600 Gd $1119
Roma 3M w/single trigger
    (disc. 1997). . . . . NiB $1956 Ex $1600 Gd $1119

GAMECOCK, STANDARD (S. UBERTO 1) HAMMERLESS
DOUBLE-BARREL SHOTGUN. . NiB $900 Ex $766 Gd $563
Boxlock. Plain extractors. Double triggers. Gauges: 12, 16, 20;
2.75-inch chambers in 12 and 16, 3-inch in 20 ga. Bbls. 25.5-
inch IC/M choke; 27.5-inch M/F choke. Weight: 5.75-6.5 lbs.,

Bernardelli Gamecock

Bernardelli Standard Gamecock

SHOTGUNS

depending on ga. and bbl. length. English-style straight-grip stock and forearm, checkered. No longer imported.

GARDONE HAMMER
DOUBLE . . . . **NiB $2766 Ex $2261 Gd $1600**
Same general specifications as Brescia except for higher grade engraving and wood, but not as high as the Italia. Half-cock safety. Disc. 1956.

HEMINGWAY HAMMERLESS DOUBLE
Boxlock. Single or double triggers w/hinged front. Selective automatic ejectors. Gauges: 12 and 20 w/2.75- or 3-inch chambers, 16 and 28 w/2.75-inch. Bbls.: 23.5- to 28-inch w/fixed chokes. Weight: 6.25 lbs. Checkered English-style European walnut stock. Silvered and engraved receiver.
Standard model . . . . **NiB $2288 Ex $1866 Gd $1383**
Deluxe model
   w/sideplates (disc. 1993) NiB $2698 Ex $2210 Gd $1679
w/single trigger, add **$125**

ITALIA . . . . **NiB $1866 Ex $1044 Gd $623**
Same general specifications as Brescia except higher grade engraving and wood. Disc. 1986.

ROMA 4 AND ROMA 6
Same as Premier Gamecock (Rome 3) except higher grade engraving and wood, double triggers. Disc. 1997.
Roma 4 (disc. 1989) . . . . . . **NiB $1847 Ex $1412 Gd $1095**
Roma 4E (disc. 1997) . . . . . **NiB $1796 Ex $1370 Gd $1060**
Roma 6 (disc. 1989) . . . . . . **NiB $1488 Ex $1233 Gd $1000**
Roma 6E (disc. 1997) . . . . . **NiB $2533 Ex $2000 Gd $1277**

ROMA 7, 8, AND 9
Side-by-side. Anson & Deeley boxlock; hammerless. Ejectors; double triggers. 12 ga. Barrels: 27.5-or 29.5-inch. M/F chokes. Fancy hand-checkered European walnut straight or pistol-grip stock, forearm. Elaborately engraved, silver-finished sideplates. Imported 1994 to 1997.
Roma 7 . . . . **NiB $3366 Ex $2160 Gd $1500**
Roma 8 . . . . **NiB $3866 Ex $2571 Gd $1880**
Roma 9 . . . . **NiB $4665 Ex $3748 Gd $2977**

S. UBERTO 2 . . . . **NiB $1460 Ex $1277 Gd $898**
Same as Standard Gamecock (S. Uberto 1) except higher grade engraving and wood. Currently imported.

S. UBERTO F.S.
Same as Standard Gamecock except w/higher grade engraving, wood and has auto-ejectors. Disc. 1989, reintro. 1993 to 1997.
Model FS . . . . **NiB $1746 Ex $1544 Gd $1100**
Model V.B. Incisio . . . . **NiB $2169 Ex $1754 Gd $1239**
w/single trigger, add **$100**

HOLLAND V.B. SERIES SHOTGUNS
Holland & Holland-type sidelock action. Auto-ejectors. Double triggers. 12 ga. only. Bbl. length or choke to custom specification. Silver-finish receiver (Liscio) or engraved coin finish receiver (Incisio). Extra-select wood and game scene engraving (Lusso). Checkered   stock (straight or pistol-grip). Imported 1992 to 1997.
Model V.B. Liscio . . . . . . **NiB $11,650 Ex $10,500 Gd $8675**
Model V.B. Incisio . . . . . . **NiB $12,200 Ex $9779 Gd $6755**
Model V.B. Lusso . . . . **NiB $9465 Ex $8119 Gd $5231**
Model V.B. Extra . . . . . . **NiB $14,766 Ex $10,877 Gd $8669**
Model V.B. Gold . . . . **NiB $49,600 Ex $44,688 Gd $37,789**
w/Engraving Pattern No. 4, add **$1250**
w/Engraving Pattern No. 12, add **$5000**

Bernardelli Gardone

Bernardelli Italia

Bernardelli Roma 6

**Boss Hammerless
Double-Barrel**

w/Engraving Pattern No. 20, add **$9500**
w/Single trigger, add **$700**

BOSS & COMPANY — London, England

HAMMERLESS DOUBLE-BARREL
SHOTGUN . . . . **NiB $64,887 Ex $57,955 Gd $35,898**
Sidelock. Automatic ejectors. Double triggers, non-selective or selective single trigger. Made in all gauges, bbl. lengths and chokes. Checkered stock and forend, straight or pistol-grip.

HAMMERLESS O/U
SHOTGUN . . . . **NiB $117,650 Ex $94,800 Gd $45,000**
Sidelock. Automatic ejectors. Selective single trigger. Made

in all gauges, bbl. lengths and chokes. Checkered stock and forend, straight or pistol-grip. Disc.

BREDA MECCANICA BRESCIANA — Brescia, Italy

Formerly ERNESTO BREDA, Milan, Italy. Previously imported by Tristar (Kansas City, MO), Gryphon International (Kansas City, MO) and Diana Imports Co., (San Francisco, CA).

VEGA SPECIAL O/U SHOTGUN NiB $676 Ex $543 Gd $410
12 or 20 gauge. Box lock action. Bbl. 26 or 28 inches; single trigger; ejectors. Blue only.

VEGA SPECIAL TRAP . . . . NiB $966 Ex $733 Gd $590
12 or 20 gauge. Box lock action. Competition triggers and lock. Bbl. 30 or 32 inches; single trigger; ejectors. Blue only.

VEGA LUSSO . . . . NiB $1765 Ex $1430 Gd $1100
12 gauge only, 3-inch chambers. Scalloped box lock action, single selective trigger, ejectors. Bbl. 26 or 28 inches, ventilated rib. Coin finished receiver with light engraving. Deluxe checkered Circassian walnut stock and forearm. Imported 2001 to 2002.

SIRIO STANDARD . . . . NiB $2176 Ex $1788 Gd $1354
12 or 20 gauge. Engraved box lock action. Bbl. 26 or 28 inches; single trigger; ejectors. Blue only. Also available in skeet model.

ANDROMEDA SPECIAL . . . . . . NiB $755 Ex $665 Gd $525
Side-by-side.12 gauge, single trigger; ejectors, select checkered walnut stock; satin finish on receiver with elaborate engraving.

GOLD SERIES SEMIAUTOMATIC SHOTGUN
12 or (lightweight) 20 gauge, 2.75-inch chamber. Bbl. 25 or 27 inches; ventilated rib standard. Recoil operated
Antares Standard Model . . . . . . NiB $543 Ex $421 Gd $336
Argus Model . . . . NiB $521 Ex $390 Gd $266
Aries Model . . . . NiB $521 Ex $390 Gd $266

STANDARD GRADE
GOLD SERIES . . . . NiB $377 Ex $290 Gd $245
12 gauge, 2-3/4-inch chamber. Recoil operated. Bbl. 25 or 27 inches. Light engraving. Disc.

GRADE 1 . . . . NiB $644 Ex $500 Gd $336
Similar to Standard model but with fancier wood and engraving.

GRADE 2 . . . . NiB $756 Ex $644 Gd $500
Similar to Grade 1 but with more engraving, etc.

GRADE 3 . . . . NiB $966 Ex $771 Gd $654
Same as Grade 1 but with custom-quality embellishments.

MAGNUM MODEL . . . . NiB $546 Ex $400 Gd $297
Similar to Standard Grade but with 3-inch chambers.

ALTAIR SPECIAL . . . . NiB $533 Ex $400 Gd $336
12 gauge, 2.75-inch chamber. Gas-operated. Bbl. 25 or 27 inches, ventilated rib standard. Alloy construction, blue or chrome receiver.

ASTRO . . . . NiB $1126 Ex $853 Gd $700
12 gauge (disc. 2002) or 20 gauge, 3-inch chamber. Inertia action. Bbl. 22 (slug), 24, 26, 28 or 30 inches; ventilated rib.

Black synthetic, Advantage camo, or Circassian walnut stock and forearm. Imported 2001.
Advantage camo model, add $125

ASTROLUX . . . . NiB $1588 Ex $1344 Gd $1033
Similar to Astro model except has two-tone receiver with engraving and deluxe checkered Circassian walnut stock and forearm. Imported 2001 to 2002.

ERMES SERIES . . . . NiB $1044 Ex $788 Gd $648
12 gauge, 3-inch chamber. Semiautomatic. Inertia recoil operating system, aluminum alloy receiver, nickeel plated or blue finish on lower receiver. Bbl. 24, 26, or 28 inches. Deluxe checkered Circassian walnut stock and forearm. Imported 2001.
Ermes Silver . . . . NiB $1287 Ex $1095 Gd $869
Ermes Gold . . . . NiB $1452 Ex $1138 Gd $1009

MIRA. . . . . NiB $880 Ex $622 Gd $500
12 gauge, 3-inch chamber. Semiautomatic, gas-operated. Aluminum alloy receiver; black or Advantage camo finish. Bbl. 22 (slug), 24, 26, 28 or 30 inches, ventilated rib. Circassian walnut or black synthetic stock and forearm. Imported 2001.
Sporting Clays model, add $50
w/black synthetic stock & forearm, deduct 10%

ARIES 2 . . . . NiB $879 Ex $793 Gd $649
12 gauge, 2-3/4-inch chamber. Semiautomatic, gas-operated. Engraved two-tone receiver. Bbl. 20 or 30 inches, ventilated rib. Deluxe checkered Circassian walnut or black synthetic stock and forearm. Imported 2001 only.

BRETTON-GAUCHER — St. Etienne, France

BABY STANDARD
SPRINT O/U . . . . NiB $1088 Ex $855 Gd $687
Inline sliding breech action. 12 or 20 gauge w/2.75-inch chambers. 27.5-inch separated bbls. w/vent rib and choke tubes. Weight: 4.8 to 5 lbs. Engraved alloy receiver. Checkered walnut buttstock and forearm w/satin oil finish. Limited import.

SPRINT DELUXE O/U . . . . NiB $1077 Ex $863 Gd $700
Similar to the Standard Model except w/engraved coin-finished receiver and chambered 12, 16 and 20 ga. Limited import.

FAIR PLAY O/U . . . . NiB $1088 Ex $863 Gd $600
Lightweight action similar to the Sprint Model except w/hinged action that pivots open and is chambered 12 or 20 gauge only. Limited import.

BRNO — Brno and Uherski Brod, Czech Republic (formerly Czechoslovakia)

MODEL 500 O/U SHOTGUN . . NiB $900 Ex $777 Gd $568
Hammerless boxlock w/double triggers and ejectors.12 ga. w/2.75-inch chambers. 27.5-inch bbls.. choked M/F. 44 inches overall. Weight: 7 lbs. Etched receiver. Checkered walnut stock w/classic style cheekplece. Imported from 1987 to 1991.

500 SERIES O/U COMBINATION GUNS
Similar to the 500 Series over/under shotgun above, except w/ lower bbl. chambered in rifle calibers and set trigger option. Imported from 1987 to 1995.
Model 502 12 ga./.222 or .243
(disc. 1991) . . . . NiB $2088 Ex $1256 Gd $1077

SHOTGUNS

American Browning Grade I

American Browning Special

Model 502 12 ga. .308 or .30-06
(disc. 1991). . . . . NiB $1164 Ex $1038 Gd $772
Model 571 12 ga./6x65R
(disc. 1993) . . . . NiB $853 Ex $709 Gd $587
Model 572 12 ga./7x65R
(imported since 1992) . . . . . NiB $881 Ex $733 Gd $600
Model 584 12 ga./7x57R
(imported since 1992) . . . NiB $1264 Ex $1033 Gd $800
Sport Series 4-bbl. set
(disc. 1991). . . . . NiB $3153 Ex $2571 Gd $1863

CZ 581 SOLO O/U SHOTGUN . . . NiB $966 Ex $738 Gd $561
Hammerless boxlock w/double triggers, ejectors and automatic safety. 12 ga. w/2.75- or 3-inch chambers. 28-inch bbls. choked M/F. Weight: 7.5 lbs. Checkered walnut stock. Disc. 1996.

SUPER SERIES O/U SHOTGUN
Hammerless sidelock w/selective single or double triggers and ejectors. 12 ga. w/2.75- or 3-inch chambers. 27.5-inch bbls. choked M/F. 44.5 inches overall. Weight: 7.25 lbs. Etched or engraved side plates. Checkered European walnut stock w/classic-style cheekpiece. Imported from 1987 to 1991.
Super Series Shotgun (disc. 1992) . . . NiB $866 Ex $731 Gd $577
Super Series Combo (disc. 1992). . NiB $2021 Ex $1190 Gd $977
Super Ser. 3-bbl. set (disc. 1990) . NiB $1993 Ex $1578 Gd $1266
Super Series engraving, add $1350

ZH 300 SERIES O/U SHOTGUNS
Hammerless boxlock w/double triggers. Gauge: 12 or 16 w/2.75- or 3-inch chambers. Bbls.: 26, 27.5 or 30 inches; choked M/F. Weight: 7 lbs. Skip-line checkered walnut stock w/classic-style cheekpiece. Imported from 1986-93.
Model 300 (disc. 1993) . . . . . NiB $786 Ex $547 Gd $408
Model 301 Field (disc. 1991) . . NiB $667 Ex $582 Gd $400
Model 302 Skeet (disc. 1992) . NiB $745 Ex $557 Gd $442
Model 303 Trap (disc. 1992) . . NiB $749 Ex $566 Gd $449

ZH 300 SERIES O/U COMBINATION GUNS
Similar to the 300 Series over/under shotgun except lower bbl. chambered in rifle calibers.
Model 300 Combo
8-bbl. Set (disc. 1991) . . NiB $3375 Ex $2977 Gd $2500
Model 304 12 ga./7x57R
(disc. 1995) . . . . NiB $846 Ex $698 Gd $535
Model 305 12 ga./5.6x52R
(disc. 1993). . . . . NiB $921 Ex $769 Gd $544
Model 306 12 ga./5.6x50R
(disc. 1993). . . . . NiB $965 Ex $798 Gd $579
Model 307 12 ga./.22 Hornet
(Imported since 1995) . . . . . NiB $843 Ex $755 Gd $507
Model 324 16 ga./7x57R
(disc. 1987). . . . . NiB $880 Ex $742 Gd $509

ZP 149 HAMMERLESS DOUBLE
Sidelock action w/double triggers, automatic ejectors and automatic safety.12 ga. w/2.75- or 3-inch chambers. 28.5-inch bbls. choked M/F. Weight: 7.25 lbs. Checkered walnut buttstock with cheekpiece.
Standard model . . . . NiB $669 Ex $458 Gd $388
Engraved model . . . . NiB $700 Ex $477 Gd $421

BROLIN ARMS, INC. — Pomona, California

FIELD SERIES PUMP SHOTGUN
Slide-action. Gauge: 12 ga. w/3-inch chamber. 24-, 26-, 28- or 30-inch bbl. 44 and 50 inches overall. Weight: 7.3 to 7.6 lbs. Cross-bolt safety. Vent rib bbl. w/screw-in choke tube and bead sights. Non- reflective metal finish. Synthetic or oil-finished wood stock w/swivel studs. Made from 1997 to 1998.
Synthetic stock model . . . . NiB $254 Ex $188 Gd $95
Wood stock model . . . . NiB $200 Ex $129 Gd $75

COMBO MODEL PUMP SHOTGUN
Similar to the Field Model except w/extra 18.5- or 22-inch bbl. w/bead or rifle sight. Made from 1997 to 1998.
Synthetic stock model . . . . NiB $279 Ex $200 Gd $115
Wood stock model . . . . NiB $331 Ex $240 Gd $193

LAWMAN MODEL PUMP SHOTGUN
Similar to the Field Model except has 18.5-inch bbl. w/cylinder bore fixed choke. Weight: 7 lbs. Dual operating bars. Bead, rifle or ghost ring sights. Black synthetic or wood stock. Matte chrome or satin nickel finish. Made from 1997 to 1999.
Synthetic stock model . . . . NiB $217 Ex $151 Gd $90
Wood stock model . . . . NiB $217 Ex $151 Gd $90
w/rifle sights, add $35
w/ghost ring sights, add $50
w/satin nickel finish (disc. 1997), add $50

SLUG MODEL PUMP SHOTGUN
Similar to the Field Model except has 18.5- or 22-inch bbl. w/IC fixed choke or 4-inch extended rifled choke. Rifle or ghost ring sights or optional cantilevered scope mount. Black synthetic or wood stock. Matte blued finish. Made from 1998 to 1999.
Synthetic stock model . . . . NiB $288 Ex $202 Gd $166
Wood stock model . . . . NiB $300 Ex $221 Gd $180
w/rifled bbl., add $25
w/cantilevered scope mount, add. $50

TURKEY SPECIAL PUMP SHOTGUN
Similar to the Field Model except has 22-inch vent-rib bbl. w/ extended extra-full choke. Rifle or ghost ring sights or optional cantilevered scope mount. Black synthetic or wood stock. Matte blued finish. Made from 1998 to 1999.

**Browning Model 12 Limited
Editon Grade I**

**Browning Model 12
Limited Editon Grade V**

**Browning Model 42
Limited Editon Grade V**

Synthetic stock model ....NiB $266 Ex $190 Gd $125
Wood stock model ....NiB $305 Ex $237 Gd $154
w/cantileveredscope mount, add $50

BROWNING — Morgan, Utah

AMERICAN BROWNING SHOTGUNS

Designated "American" Browning because they were produced in Ilion, New York, the following Remington-made Brownings are almost identical to the Remington Model 11A and Sportsman and the Browning Auto-5. They are the only Browning shotguns manufactured in the U.S. during the 20th century and were made for Browning Arms when production was suspended in Belgium because of WW II.

NOTE: *Fabrique Nationale Herstal (formerly Fabrique Nationale d'Armes de Guerre) of Herstal, Belgium, is the long-time manufacturer of Browning shotguns dating back to 1900. Miroku Firearms Mfg. Co. of Tokyo, Japan, bought into the Browning company and has, since the early 1970s, undertaken some of the production. The following shotguns were manufactured for Browning by these two firms.*

GRADE I AUTOLOADER (AUTO-5)
Recoil-operated autoloader. Similar to the Remington Model 11A except w/different style engraving and identified w/the Browning logo. Gauges: 12, 16 or 20. Plain 26- to 32-inch bbl. w/any standard boring. Two or four shell tubular magazine w/magazine cut-off. Weight: About 6.88 lbs. (20 ga.) to 8 lbs. (12 ga.). Checkered pistol-grip stock and forearm. Made from 1940 to 1949.
American Browning Grade I
 Auto-5, 12 or 16 ga........NiB $856 Ex $744 Gd $400
20 ga., add 20%

SPECIAL 441
Same general specifications as Grade I except supplied w/raised matted rib or vent rib. Disc. 1949.
w/raised matted rib ....NiB $894 Ex $756 Gd $435
w/vent rib.................NiB $925 Ex $790 Gd $466
20 ga., add 20%

SPECIAL SKEET MODEL ......NiB $815 Ex $645 Gd $477
Same general specifications as Grade I except has 26-inch bbl. w/vent rib and Cutts Compensator. Disc. 1949.

UTILITY FIELD GUN ....NiB $608 Ex $458 Gd $339
Same general specifications as Grade I except has 28-inch plain bbl. w/Poly Choke. Disc. 1949.

MODEL 12 PUMP SHOTGUN
Special limited edition Winchester Model 12. Gauge: 20 or 28. Five-round tubular magazine. 26-inch bbl., M choke. 45 inches overall. Weight: about 7 lbs. Grade I has blued receiver, checkered walnut stock w/matte finish. Grade V has engraved receiver, checkered deluxe walnut stock w/high-gloss finish. Made from 1988 to 1992. See illustration next page.
Grade I, 20 ga. 8600 prod.....NiB $866 Ex $569 Gd $449
Grade I, 28 ga.............NiB $1166 Ex $912 Gd $744
Grade V, 20 ga 4000 prod...NiB $1455 Ex $1187 Gd $879
Grade V, 28 ga ....NiB $1768 Ex $1344 Gd $961

MODEL 42 LIMITED Edition SHOTGUN
Special limited edition Winchester Model 42 pump shotgun. Same general specifications as Model 12 except w/smaller frame in .410 ga. and 3-inch chamber. Made from 1991 to 1993.
Grade I (6000 produced) .....NiB $967 Ex $744 Gd $466
Grade V (6000 produced)...NiB $1590 Ex $1156 Gd $863

2000 BUCK SPECIAL ....NiB $588 Ex $467 Gd $355
Same as Field Model except has 24-inch plain bbl. Bored for rifled slug and buckshot, fitted w/rifle sights (open rear, ramp front). 12 ga., 2.75-inch or 3-inch chamber; 20 ga., 2.75-inch

SHOTGUNS

Browning M2000 Vent Rib

Browning Model A-500

Browning Automatic-5 Buck Special

Browning Automatic-5 Classic

Browning Automatic-5
Gold Classic

chamber. Weight: 12 ga., 7 lbs., 8 oz.; 20 ga., 6 lbs., 10 oz. Made from 1974 to 1981 by FN.

2000 GAS AUTOMATIC SHOTGUN, FIELD MODEL

Gas-operated. Gauge: 12 or 20. 2.75-inch chamber. Four-round magazine. Bbl.: 26-, 28-, 30-inch, any standard choke plain matted bbl. (12 ga. only) or vent rib. Weight: 6 lbs. 11 oz.-7 lbs. 12 oz. depending on ga. and bbl. length. Checkered pistol-grip stock/forearm. Made from 1974 to 1981 by FN; assembled in Portugal.
w/plain matted bbl. . . . . NiB $559 Ex $468 Gd $346

2000 MAGNUM MODEL . . . . . NiB $579 Ex $377 Gd $300
Same as Field Model except chambered for 3-inch shells, three-round magazine. Bbl.: 26- (20 ga. only), 28-, 30- or 32-inch (latter two 12 ga. only); any standard choke; vent rib. Weight: 6 lbs., 11 oz.-7 lbs., 13 oz. depending on ga. and bbl. Made from 1974 to 1983 by FN.

2000 SKEET MODEL . . . . NiB $527 Ex $441 Gd $338
Same as Field Model except has skeet-style stock w/recoil pad, 26-inch vent-rib bbl., SK choke. 12 or 20 ga., 2.75-inch chamber. Weight: 8 lbs., 1 oz. (12 ga.); 6 lbs., 12 oz. (20 ga.) Made 1974 to 1981 by FN.

2000 TRAP MODEL . . . . NiB $527 Ex $441 Gd $338
Same as Field Model except has Monte Carlo stock w/recoil pad, 30- or 32-inch bbl. w/high-post vent rib and receiver extension, M/I/F chokes. 12 ga., 2.75-inch chamber. Weight: About 8 lbs., 5 oz. Made 1974 to 1981 by FN.

A-500G GAS-OPERATED SEMIAUTOMATIC
Same general specifications as Browning Model A-500R except gas-operated. Made 1990 to 1993.
Buck Special . . . . NiB $590 Ex $466 Gd $339
Hunting model . . . . NiB $688 Ex $491 Gd $388

A-500G SPORTING CLAYS . . . . NiB $663 Ex $490 Gd $388
Same general specifications as Model A-500G except has matte blued receiver w/"Sporting Clays" logo. 28- or 30-inch bbl. w/Invector choke tubes. Made 1992 to 1993.

A-500R SEMIAUTOMATIC
Recoil-operated. Gauge: 12. 26- to 30-inch vent-rib bbls. 24-inch Buck Special. Invector choke tube system. 2.75- or 3-inch Magnum cartridges. Weight: 7 lbs., 3 oz.-8 lbs., 2 oz. Cross-bolt safety. Gold-plated trigger. Scroll-engraved receiver. Gloss-finished walnut stock
and forend. Made by FN from 1987 to 1993.
Hunting model . . . . NiB $677 Ex $476 Gd $388
Buck Special . . . . NiB $692 Ex $490 Gd $433

A-BOLT SERIES SHOTGUN
Bolt-action repeating single-barrel shotgun. 12 ga. only w/3-inch chambers, 2-round magazine. 22- or 23-inch rifled bbl., w/or w/o a rifled invector tube. Receiver drilled and tapped for scope mounts. Bbl. w/ or w/o open sights. Checkered walnut or graphite/fiberglass composite stock. Matte black metal finish. Imported 1995 to 1998.

Stalker model w/
** composite stock** . . . . **NiB $1365 Ex $1077 Gd $867**
Hunter model w/walnut stock . . . **NiB $1365 Ex $1077 Gd $867**
w/rifled bbl., add **$200**
w/open sights, add **$75**

AUTOLOADING SHOTGUNS, GRADES II, III & IV
These higher grade models differ from the Standard or Grade I in general quality, grade of wood, checkering, engraving, etc., otherwise specifications are the same. Grade IV guns, sometimes called Midas Grade, are inlaid w/yellow and green gold. Disc. in 1940.

Grade II, plain bbl. . . . . **NiB $1698 Ex $1390 Gd $976**
Grade III, plain bbl. . . . . **NiB $1580 Ex $1176 Gd $833**
Grade IV, plain bbl. . . . . **NiB $4469 Ex $3865 Gd $3033**
w/raised, matted rib bbl., add **15%**
w/vent. rib bbl., add **30%**

AUTOMATIC-5, LIGHT 20
Same general specifications as Standard Model except light-weight and 20 ga. Bbl.: 26- or 28-inch; plain or vent rib. Weight: About 6.25-6.5 lbs. depending on bbl. Made 1958 to 1976 by FN, since then by Miroku.

FN manu., plain bbl. . . . . **NiB $844 Ex $633 Gd $429**
FN manu., vent. rib bbl. . . . . . **NiB $1267 Ex $988 Gd $687**
Miroku manu., vent. rib,
** fixed choke** . . . . **NiB $965 Ex $743 Gd $846**
Miroku manu., vent. rib,
** invectors** . . . . **NiB $1065 Ex $844 Gd $600**

AUTOMATIC-5, BUCK SPECIAL MODELS
Same as Light 12, Magnum 12, Light 20, Magnum 20, in respective gauges, except 24-inch plain bbl. bored for rifled slug and buckshot, fitted w/rifle sights (open rear, ramp front). Weight: 6.13-8.25 lbs. depending on ga. Made 1964 to 1976 by FN, since then by Miroku.

FN manu., w/plain bbl. . . . . . . **NiB $1276 Ex $889 Gd $567**
Miroku manu., ... **NiB $966 Ex $843 Gd $544**
w/3-inch mag. rec., add **$10%**

AUTOMATIC-5 CLASSIC . . . . . **NiB $1186 Ex $983 Gd $889**
Gauge: 12. 5-round capacity. 28-inch vent rib bbl./M choke. 2.75-inch chamber. Engraved silver-gray receiver. Gold-plated trigger. Crossbolt safety. High-grade, hand-checkered select American walnut stock w/rounded pistol grip. 5,000 issued; made in Japan in 1984, engraved in Belgium.

AUTOMATIC-5 GOLD
CLASSIC . . . . **NiB $9887 Ex $6690 Gd $4690**
Same general specifications as Automatic-5 Classic except engraved receiver inlaid w/gold. Pearl border on stock and forend plus fine-line hand-checkering. Each gun numbered "One of Five Hundred," etc. 500 issued in 1984; made in Belgium.

AUTOMATIC-5, LIGHT 12
12 ga. only. Same general specifications as Standard Model except lightweight (about 7.25 lbs.), has gold-plated trigger.

Guns w/rib have striped matting on top of bbl. Fixed chokes or Invector tubes. Made 1948 to 1976 by FN, since then by Miroku.

FN manu., plain bbl. . . . . **NiB $889 Ex $655 Gd $498**
FN manu., w/raised matte rib . **NiB $954 Ex $777 Gd $675**
FN manu., vent. rib . . . . **NiB $1098 Ex $966 Gd $676**
Miroku manu., vent. rib,
** fixed choke** . . . . **NiB $889 Ex $667 Gd $487**
Miroku manu., vent. rib,
** Invectors** . . . . **NiB $1099 Ex $776 Gd $566**

AUTOMATIC-5, MAGNUM 12 GAUGE
Same general specifications as Standard Model. Chambered for 3-inch Magnum 12-ga. shells. Bbl.: 28-inch M/F, 30- or 32-inch F/F, plain or vent rib. Weight: 8.5-9 lbs. depending on bbl. Buttstock has recoil pad. Made 1958 to 1976 by FN, since then by Miroku. Fixed chokes or Invector tubes.

FN manu., plain bbl. . . . . **NiB $954 Ex $779 Gd $549**
FN manu., vent. rib bbl. . . . . **NiB $1288 Ex $977 Gd $765**
Miroku manu., vent. rib, fixed
** chokes.** . . . . **NiB $888 Ex $645 Gd $455**
Miroku manu., vent. rib,
** Invectors** . . . . **NiB $1066 Ex $707 Gd $500**

AUTOMATIC-5, MAGNUM 20 GAUGE
Same general specifications as Standard Model except chambered for 3-inch Magnum 20-ga. shell. Bbl.: 26- or 28-inch, plain or vent rib. Weight: 7 lbs., 5 oz.-7 lbs., 7 oz. depending on bbl. Made 1967 to 1976 by FN, since then by Miroku.

FN manu., plain bbl. . . . . **NiB $944 Ex $768 Gd $567**
FN manu., vent. rib bbl. . . . . **NiB $1333 Ex $989 Gd $779**
Miroku manu., vent. rib, Invectors . . **NiB $989 Ex $766 Gd $590**

AUTOMATIC-5, SKEET MODEL
12 ga. only. Same general specifications as Light 12. Bbl.: 26-or 28-inch, plain or vent rib, SK choke. Weight: 7 lbs., 5 oz.-7 lbs., 10 oz. depending on bbl. Made by FN prior to 1976, since then by Miroku.

FN manu., plain bbl. . . . . **NiB $1177 Ex $956 Gd $654**
FN manu., vent. rib bbl. . . . **NiB $1769 Ex $1166 Gd $956**
Miroku manu., vent. rib bbl. . . **NiB $987 Ex $766 Gd $554**

AUTOMATIC-5 STALKER
Same general specifications as Automatic-5 Light and Magnum models except w/matte blue finish and black graphite fiberglass stock and forearm. Made from 1992 to 1997.

Light model . . . . **NiB $966 Ex $831 Gd $664**
Magnum model . . . . **NiB $1031 Ex $977 Gd $689**

AUTOMATIC-5, STANDARD (GRADE I)
Recoil-operated. Gauge: 12 or 16 (16-gauge guns made prior to WW II were chambered for 2-inch shells; standard 16 disc. 1964). Four shell magazine in 5-round model, prewar guns were also available in 3-round model. Bbls.: 26- to 32-inch; plain, raised matted or vent rib; choice of standard chokes. Weight: About 8 lbs., in 12 ga., 7.5 lbs., in 16 ga. Checkered pistol-grip stock and forearm. (Note: Browning Special, disc. about 1940.) Made from 1900 to 1973 by FN.

Grade I, plain bbl. . . . . **NiB $844 Ex $677 Gd $544**
Grade I (or Browning Special),
** w/raised matted rib** . . . . **NiB $977 Ex $778 Gd $580**
Grade I (or Browning Special),
** w/vent. s rib** . . . . **NiB $977 Ex $778 Gd $580**

SHOTGUNS

Browning Auto-5 Sweet Sixteen (New Model)

Browning Model B-80 Upland Special

Browning BPS Hunter

Browning BPS Youth & Ladies Model

AUTOMATIC-5, SWEET 16
16 ga. Same general specifications as Standard Model except lightweight (about 6.75 lbs.), has gold plated trigger. Guns w/o VR have striped matting on top of bbl. Made 1937 to 1976 by FN.
w/plain bbl. . . . . NiB $1189 Ex $793 Gd $555
w/raised matted or vent. rib . . NiB $1769 Ex $1388 Gd $1012

AUTO-5, SWEET SIXTEEN
NEW MODEL. . . . . NiB $1399 Ex $1156 Gd $922
Reissue of popular 16-gauge Hunting Model w/5-round capacity, 2.75-inch chamber, scroll-engraved blued receiver, high-gloss French walnut stock w/rounded pistol grip. 26- or 28-inch vent-rib bbl. F choke tube. Weight: 7 lbs., 5 oz. Reintro. 1987 to 1993.AUTOMATIC-5,

TRAP MODEL. . . . . NiB $1277 Ex $965 Gd $777
12 ga. only. Same general specifications as Standard Model except has trap-style stock, 30-inch vent-rib bbl. F choke. Weight: 8.5 lbs. Disc. 1971.

MODEL B-80 GAS-OPERATED
AUTOMATIC. . . . . NiB $699 Ex $577 Gd $400
Gauge: 12 or 20; 2.75-inch chamber. Four round magazine. Bbl.: 26-, 28- or 30-inch, any standard choke, vent-rib bbl. w/ fixed chokes or Invector tubes. Weight: 6 lbs., 12 oz.-8 lbs., 1 oz. depending on ga. and bbl. Checkered pistol-grip stock and forearm. Made 1981 to 1988.

MODEL B-80 PLUS. . . . . NiB $765 Ex $605 Gd $466
Same general specifications as Browning Model B-80 except chambered for 3-inch shotshells. Made in 1988.

MODEL B-80 SUPERLIGHT . . . NiB $689 Ex $544 Gd $432
Same as Standard Model except weighs 1 lb. less.

MODEL B-80 UPLAND
SPECIAL . . . . NiB $698 Ex $566 Gd $433
Gauge: 12 or 20. 22-inch vent-rib bbl. Invector choke tube system. 2.75-inch chambers. 42 inches overall. Weight: 5 lbs., 7 oz. (20 ga.); 6 lbs., 10 oz. (12 ga.). German nickel silver sight bead. Crossbolt safety. Checkered walnut straight-grip stock and forend. Disc. 1988.

BPS DEER HUNTER SPECIAL . . NiB $735 Ex $510 Gd $375
Same general specifications as Standard BPS model except has 20.5-inch bbl. w/adj. rifle-style sights. Solid scope mounting system. Checkered walnut stock w/sling swivel studs. Made from 1992 to date.

BPS GAME GUN TURKEY
SPECIAL . . . . NiB $498 Ex $380 Gd $295
Same general specifications as Standard BPS model except w/ matte blue metal finish and satin-finished stock. Chambered for 12 ga. 3-inch only. 20.5-inch bbl. w/extra full invector choke system. Receiver drilled and tapped for scope. Made from 1992 to 2001.

Browning BPS
Waterfowl – Mossy Oak Shadow Grass

Browning BPS Stalker

Browning B-SS 20 Gauge Sporter

BPS PIGEON GRADE . . . . NiB $699 Ex $449 Gd $354
Same general specifications as Standard BPS model except w/select grade walnut stock and gold-trimmed receiver. Available in 12 ga. from only w/26- or 28-inch vent-rib bbl. Made 1992 to 1998.

BPS PUMP INVECTOR STALKER
Same general specifications as BPS Pump Shotgun except in 10 and 12 ga. w/Invector choke system, 22-, 26-, 28- or 30-inch bbls.; matte blue metal finish w/matte black stock. Made from 1987 to date.
12 ga. model (3-inch) . . . . NiB $577 Ex $412 Gd $290
10- & 12 ga. model (3.5-inch). . NiB $776 Ex $600 Gd $466

BPS PUMP SHOTGUN
Takedown. Gauges: 10, 12 (3.5-inch chamber); 12, 20 and .410 (3-inch) and 28 ga. chambered 2.75-inch. Bbls.: 22-, 24-, 26-, 28-, 30-, or 32-inch; fixed choke or Invector tubes. Weight: 7.5 lbs. (w/28-inch bbl.). Checkered select walnut pistol-grip stock and semi-beavertail forearm, recoil pad. Introduced in 1977 by Miroku.
Magnum Hunter . . . . NiB $690 Ex $589 Gd $477
Magnum Stalker . . . . NiB $690 Ex $589 Gd $477
Magnum Camo . . . . NiB $779 Ex $644 Gd $546
Hunter . . . . NiB $690 Ex $589 Gd $477
Upland . . . . NiB $595 Ex $490 Gd $395
Stalker (26, 28- or 30-inch bbl.) . . . NiB $566 Ex $477 Gd $375
Stalker 24-inch bbl . . . . NiB $566 Ex $477 Gd $375
Game Gun - Turkey Special . . . NiB $478 Ex $390 Gd $277
Game Gun - fully rifled bbl. . . . NiB $700 Ex $622 Gd $490
Hunter 20 ga. . . . . NiB $600 Ex $497 Gd $400
Upland 20 ga. . . . . NiB $600 Ex $497 Gd $400
Micro . . . . NiB $488 Ex $397 Gd $300
Hunter 28 ga. . . . . NiB $590 Ex $480 Gd $400
Bore Hunter .410 . . . . NiB $644 Ex $564 Gd $433
Buck Spec. (10 or 12 ga., 3.5-inch) NiB $700 Ex $566 Gd $470
Buck Spec. (12 or 20 ga.) . . . . . NiB $455 Ex $330 Gd $229
Waterfowl (10 or 12 ga., 3.5-inch) . . . NiB $700 Ex $566 Gd $470
w/fixed choke, deduct $75

BPS YOUTH AND LADIES' MODEL
Lightweight (6 lbs., 11 oz.) version of BPS Pump Shotgun in 20 ga. w/22-inch bbl. and floating vent rib, F choke (invector) tube. Made 1986 to 2002.

Standard Invector model
(disc. 1994) . . . . NiB $390 Ex $288 Gd $195
Invector Plus model . . . . NiB $444 Ex $300 Gd $244

BSA 10 SEMIAUTOMATIC SHOTGUN
Gas-operated short-stroke action. 10 ga.; 3.5-inch chamber. Five round magazine. Bbls.: 26-, 28-or 30-inches w/ Invector tubes and vent rib. Weight: 10.5 lbs. Checkered select walnut buttstock and forend. Blued finish. Made 1993 to date. Note: Although intro. as the BSA 10, this model is now marketed as the Gold Series. See separate listing for pricing.

B-SS SIDE-BY-SIDE
Boxlock. Automatic ejectors. Non-selective single trigger (early production) or selective-single trigger (late production). Gauges: 12 or 20 w/3-inch chambers. Bbls.: 26-, 28-, or 30-inches; IC/M, M/F, or F/F chokes; matte solid rib. Weight: 7 to 7.5 lbs. Checkered straight-grip stock and beavertail forearm. Made from 1972 to 1988 by Miroku.
Standard model (early/NSST) . NiB $1276 Ex $956 Gd $835
Standard model (late/SST) . . . NiB $1276 Ex $956 Gd $835
Grade II (antique
silver receiver) . . . . NiB $3365 Ex $2990 Gd $2455
20 ga. models, add $650

B-SS SIDE-BY-SIDE SIDELOCK
Same general specifications as B-SS boxlock models except sidelock version available in 26- or 28-inch bbl. lengths. 26-inch choked IC/M; 28-inch, M/F. Double triggers. Satin-grayed receiver engraved w/rosettes and scrolls. German nickel-silver sight bead. Weight: 6.25 lbs. to 6 lbs., 11 oz. 12 ga. made in 1983; 20 ga. Made in 1984. Disc. 1988.
12 ga. model . . . . NiB $3865 Ex $3077 Gd $2027
20 ga. model . . . . NiB $5277 Ex $3388 Gd $2879

B-SS S/S 20 GAUGE
SPORTER. . . . . NiB $3241 Ex $2766 Gd $1547
Same as standard B-SS 20 ga. except has selective single trigger, straight-grip stock. Introduced 1977. Disc. 1987.

SHOTGUNS

Browning BT-99 Competition Trap

Browning BT-100 Monte Carlo Stock

Browning BT-100 Competition Trap

Browning Citori Lightning

Browning Citori Gran Lightning

Browning Citori Skeet Gun

BT-99 GRADE I SINGLE
BBL. TRAP . . . . **NiB $1087 Ex $782 Gd $554**
Boxlock. Automatic ejector. 12 ga. only. 32- or 34-inch vent rib bbl., M, IM or F choke. Weight: About 8 lbs. Checkered pistol-grip stock and beavertail forearm, recoil pad. Made 1971 to 1976 by Miroku.

BT-99 MAX
Boxlock. 12 ga. only w/ejector selector and no safety. 32- or 34-inch ported bbl. w/high post vent rib. Checkered select walnut buttstock and finger-grooved forend w/high luster finish. Engraved receiver w/blued or stainless metal finish. Made 1995 to 1996.
Blued. . . . . **NiB $1398 Ex $1110 Gd $790**

Stainless . . . . **NiB $1941 Ex $1590 Gd $1166**
BT-99 PLUS
Similar to the BT-99 Competition except w/Browning Recoil Reduction System. Made 1989 to 1995.
Grade I . . . . **NiB $1869 Ex $1275 Gd $1013**
Pigeon grade . . . . **NiB $1977 Ex $1276 Gd $912**
Signature grade . . . . **NiB $1877 Ex $1233 Gd $888**
Stainless model . . . . **NiB $2106 Ex $1433 Gd $1133**
Golden Clays. . . . . **NiB $2926 Ex $2474 Gd $2310**

BT-99 PLUS MICRO . . . . **NiB $1277 Ex $1088 Gd $872**
Same general specifications as BT-99 Plus except scaled down for smaller shooters. 30-inch bbl. w/adj. rib and Browning's recoil reducer system. Made 1991 to 1996.

BT-100 COMPETITION TRAP SPECIAL
Same as BT-99 except has super-high wide rib and standard Monte Carlo or fully adj. stock. Available w/adj. choke or Invector Plus tubes w/optional porting. Made 1976 to 2000.

Grade I w/fixed choke (disc. 1992)	NiB $1867	Ex $1233	Gd $994
Grade I w/Invectors	NiB $2077	Ex $1156	Gd $1034
Grade I stainless (disc. 1994)	NiB $2366	Ex $1967	Gd $1256
Grade I Pigeon Grade (disc. 1994)	NiB $1650	Ex $1290	Gd $1072

BT-100 SINGLE-SHOT TRAP
Similar to the BT-99 Max, except w/additional stock options and removable trigger group. Made 1995 to 2002.

Grade I blued	NiB $2044	Ex $1366	Gd $1065
Stainless	NiB $2366	Ex $1998	Gd $1387
Satin finish	NiB $1490	Ex $1266	Gd $853
w/adj. comb, add			$150
w/thumbhole stock, add			$350
w/replacement trigger assembly, add			$550
w/fixed choke, deduct			$100

CITORI O/U HUNTING MODELS
Boxlock. Gauges: 12, 16 (disc. 1989), 20, 28 (disc. 1992) and .410 bore (disc. 1989). Bbl. lengths: 24-, 26-, 28-, or 30-inch w/vent rib. Chambered 2.75-, 3- or 3.5-inch mag. Chokes: IC/M, M/F (Fixed Chokes); Standard Invector, or Invector plus choke systems. Overall length ranges from 41-47 inches. 2.75-, 3- or 3-inch Mag. loads, depending on ga. Weight: 5.75 lbs. to 7 lbs. 13 oz. Single selective, gold-plated trigger. Medium raised German nickel-silver sight bead. Checkered, rounded pistol-grip walnut stock w/beavertail forend. Invector Chokes and Invector Plus became standard in 1988 and 1995, respectively. Made from 1973 to date by Miroku.

Grade I (disc. 1994)	NiB $1076	Ex $792	Gd $566
Grade I - 3.5-inch Mag. (1989 to date)	NiB $1076	Ex $792	Gd $566
Grade II (disc. 1983)	NiB $1288	Ex $1079	Gd $721
Grade III (1985-95)	NiB $2077	Ex $1266	Gd $1091
Grade V (disc. 1984)	NiB $2888	Ex $2069	Gd $1243
Grade VI (1985-95)	NiB $2888	Ex $2069	Gd $1277
Sporting Hunter model (12 and 20 ga., 1998 to date)	NiB $1387	Ex $1176	Gd $700
Satin Hunter model (12 ga. only, 1998 to date)	NiB $1266	Ex $1006	Gd $744
W/o Invector choke system, deduct			$150
For 3.5-inch mag., add			$120
For disc. gauges (16, 28 and .410), add			15%

CITORI LIGHTNING O/U MODELS
Same general specifications as the Citori Hunting models except w/classic Browning rounded pistol-grip stock. Made from 1988 to date by Miroku.

Grade I	NiB $1059	Ex $798	Gd $612
Grade III	NiB $1969	Ex $1154	Gd $834
Grade VI	NiB $3166	Ex $2054	Gd $1152
Gran Lightning model	NiB $1998	Ex $1258	Gd $887
Feather Model (alloy receiver)	NiB $1577	Ex $1159	Gd $1013
Feather Combo model (2-bbl. set)	NiB $3500	Ex $2745	Gd $2388
Privilege model (w/engraved sideplates)	NiB $4855	Ex $3966	Gd $2767
Micro model, add			10%
w/o Invector choke system, deduct			$250
28 ga. and .410, add			$15%

CITORI SKEET GUN
Same as Hunting model except has skeet-style stock and forearm, 26- or 28-inch bbls., both bored SK choke. Available w/ either standard vent rib or special target-type, high-post, wide vent rib. Weight (w/26-inch bbls.): 12 ga., 8 lbs., 20 ga., 7 lbs. Made 1974 to date by Miroku.

Grade I	NiB $1390	Ex $1166	Gd $990
Grade II	NiB $1690	Ex $1345	Gd $1125
Grade III	NiB $1789	Ex $1433	Gd $1093
Grade VI (disc. 1995)	NiB $2345	Ex $1765	Gd $1299
Golden Clays	NiB $2866	Ex $1889	Gd $1465
28 ga. and .410, add			15%
Grade I, 3-bbl. set (disc. 1996)	NiB $2465	Ex $2079	Gd $1500
Grade III, 3-bbl. set (disc. 1996)	NiB $3577	Ex $2260	Gd $1545
Grade VI, 3-bbl. set (disc. 1994)	NiB $3781	Ex $2477	Gd $2053
Golden Clays, 3-bbl. set (disc. 1995)	NiB $4376	Ex $3069	Gd $2210
Grade I, 4-bbl. set	NiB $3588	Ex $3066	Gd $2754
Grade III, 4-bbl. set	NiB $4361	Ex $3276	Gd $2390
Grade VI, 4-bbl. set (disc. 1994)	NiB $4733	Ex $3489	Gd $2466
Golden Clays, 4-bbl. set (disc. 1995)	NiB $5656	Ex $3892	Gd $2721

CITORI SPORTING CLAYS
Similar to the standard Citori Lightning model except Classic-style stock with rounded pistol-grip. 30-inch back-bored bbls. with Invector Plus tubes. Receiver with "Lightning Sporting Clays Edition" logo. Made from 1989 to date.

GTI model (disc. 1995)	NiB $1167	Ex $1058	Gd $821
GTI Golden Clays model (1993-94)	NiB $2455	Ex $1749	Gd $1256
Lightning model (intro. 1989)	NiB $1440	Ex $1102	Gd $866
Lightning Golden Clays (1993-98)	NiB $2736	Ex $1871	Gd $1319
Lightning Pigeon Grade (1993-94)	NiB $1622	Ex $1188	Gd $887
Micro Citori Lightning model (w/low rib)	NiB $1588	Ex $1266	Gd $1006
Special Sporting model (intro. 1989)	NiB $1590	Ex $1268	Gd $1010
Special Sporting Golden Clays (1993-98)	NiB $3231	Ex $3110	Gd $2127
Special Sporting Pigeon Grade (1993-94)	NiB $1454	Ex $1167	Gd $944
Ultra model (intro. 1995)	NiB $1661	Ex $1288	Gd $937
Ultra Golden Clays (intro. 1995)	NiB $2134	Ex $1822	Gd $1645
Model 325 (1993-94)	NiB $1292	Ex $1188	Gd $900
Model 325 Golden Clays (1993-94)	NiB $2545	Ex $1889	Gd $1438
Model 425 Grade I (intro. 1995)	NiB $1761	Ex $1216	Gd $1022
Model 425 Golden Clays (intro. 1995)	NiB $2665	Ex $2144	Gd $1977
Model 425 WSSF (intro. 1995)	NiB $1896	Ex $1459	Gd $1256
Model 802 Sporter (ES) Extended Swing (intro. 1996)	NiB $1488	Ex $1299	Gd $993
w/2 bbl. set, add			$1000
w/adj. stock, add			$250
w/high rib, add			$125
w/ported barrels, add			$100

SHOTGUNS

Browning Citori Superlight Field Shotgun

Browning Citori Trap

Browning Citori White Lightning Over/Under

Browning Citori Sporting Hunter Over/Under

Browning Gold Hunter

Browning Liége Over/Under Shotgun

CITORI SUPERLIGHT O/U FIELD SHOTGUNS
Similar to the Citori Hunting model except w/straight-grip stock and Schnabel forend tip. Made by Miroku 1982 to date.
Grade I . . . . NiB $1067 Ex $843 Gd $625
Grade III . . . . NiB $2066 Ex $1590 Gd $1167
Grade V (disc. 1985) . . . . . . NiB $3132 Ex $2398 Gd $2034
Grade VI . . . . NiB $2876 Ex $2334 Gd $1655
w/o Invectors, deduct $300
28 ga. and .410, add 10%

CITORI TRAP GUN
Same as Hunting model except 12 ga. only, has Monte Carlo or fully adjustable stock and beavertail forend, trap-style recoil pad; 20- or 32-inch bbls.; M/F, IM/F, or F/F. Available with either standard vent rib or special target-type, high-post, wide vent rib. Weight: 8 lbs. Made from 1974 to 2001 by Miroku.
Grade I Trap . . . . NiB $1035 Ex $888 Gd $698
Grade I Trap Pigeon grade
  (disc. 1994) . . . . NiB $1857 Ex $1589 Gd $1134
Grade I Trap Signature grade
  (disc. 1994) . . . . NiB $1756 Ex $1477 Gd $1234

Grade I Plus Trap (disc. 1994) . . . NiB $2878 Ex $2330 Gd $2099
Grade I Plus Trap w/ported bbls.
  (disc. 1994) . . . . NiB $1979 Ex $1488 Gd $1253
Grade I Plus Trap
  Combo (disc. 1994) . . . . NiB $2773 Ex $2078 Gd $1760
Grade I Plus Trap Golden Clays
  (disc. 1994) . . . . NiB $3176 Ex $2465 Gd $2200
Grade II w/HP rib
  (disc. 1984) . . . . NiB $1989 Ex $1423 Gd $1166
Grade III Trap . . . . NiB $1958 Ex $1688 Gd $1290
Grade V Trap (disc. 1984) . . NiB $1890 Ex $1656 Gd $1388
Grade VI Trap (disc. 1994) . NiB $2066 Ex $1879 Gd $1488

GRADE VI TRAP
Golden Clays (disc. 1994) . . . . NiB $3000 Ex $2698
Gd $2365

CITORI UPLAND SPECIAL O/U SHOTGUN
A shortened version of the Hunting model fitted with 24-inch bbls. and straight-grip stock.
12, 20 ga. models . . . . NiB $1277 Ex $1097 Gd $900
16 ga. (disc. 1989) . . . . NiB $1426 Ex $1266 Gd $954
w/o Inv. Chokes, deduct $150

CITORI WHITE LIGHTNING O/U SHOTGUN
Similar to the standard Citori Lightning model except w/silver nitride receiver w/scroll and rosette engraving. Satin wood finish w/round pistol grip. Made 1998 to 2001.
12. 20 ga. models . . . . NiB $1769 Ex $1213 Gd $879
28 ga., .410 models
   (Intro. 2000) . . . . NiB $1887 Ex $1369 Gd $1228

CITORI WHITE UPLAND
SPECIAL . . . . NiB $1389 Ex $1168 Gd $879
Similar to the standard Citori Upland model except w/silver nitride receiver w/scroll and rosette engraving. Satin wood finish w/round pistol grip. Made 2000 to 2001.

CYNERY SERIES
Monolock hinge system. Gauges: 12, 20, 28 or .410 bore. Bbl. lengths: 26-, or 28-inch w/vent rib. Chambered 3-inch. Chokes: Invector Plus choke tubes. Overall length ranges from 43-45 inches. Weight: 5 to 6 lbs. Single selective, gold-plated trigger. Wood or composite stock. Silver nitride finish. Made from 2004 to date.
Field grade . . . . NiB $2430 Ex $1810 Gd $930
Classic Field grade . . . . NiB $2360 Ex $1000 Gd $720
Euro Field grade . . . . NiB $2300 Ex $1500 Gd $760
Feather . . . . NiB $2530 Ex $1655 Gd $960
Sporting (made 2004-2007) . NiB $1900 Ex $1410 Gd $840

DOUBLE AUTOMATIC (STEEL RECEIVER)
Short recoil system. Takedown. 12 ga. only. Two round capacity. Bbls.: 26-, 28-, 30-inches; any standard choke. Checkered pistol-grip stock and forend. Weight: About 7.75 lbs. Made 1955 to 1961.
w/plain bbl. . . . . NiB $889 Ex $679 Gd $453
w/recessed-rib bbl. . . . . NiB $1167 Ex $1090 Gd $756

GOLD DEER HUNTER AUTOLOADING SHOTGUN
Similar to the Standard Gold Hunter model except chambered 12 ga. only. 22-inch bbl. W/rifled bore or smooth bore w/5-inch rifled invector tube. Cantilevered scope mount. Made 1997 to 2005.
w/standard finish . . . . NiB $1000 Ex $766 Gd $591
Field model (w/Mossy Oak finish) . . . NiB $956 Ex $619 Gd $495

GOLD HUNTER SERIES
Self-cleaning, gas-operated, short-stroke action. Gauges: 10 or 12 (3.5-inch chamber); 12 or 20 (3-inch chamber). 26-, 28-, or 30-inch bbl. w/Invector or Invector Plus choke tubes. Checkered walnut stock. Polished or matte black metal finish. Made 1990 to date.
Gold Hunter (Light 10 ga. 3.5-inch
   w/walnut stock) . . . . . . NiB $1499 Ex $1277 Gd $1108
Gold Hunter (12 ga. 3.5-inch) . . . NiB $977 Ex $790 Gd $559
Gold Hunter (12 or 20 ga.
   3-inch) . . . . NiB $1067 Ex $880 Gd $670
Gold Hunter Classic model
   (12 or 20 ga., 3-inch) . . . . . . NiB $921 Ex $787 Gd $600
Gold Hunter High Grade Classic
   (12 or 20 ga., 3-inch) . . . NiB $1690 Ex $1225 Gd $1098
Gold Deer Hunter
   (12 ga. w/22-inch bbl.) . . . . NiB $1078 Ex $884 Gd $643
Gold Turkey Hunter Camo
   (12 ga. /24-inch bbl.) . . . . . . NiB $987 Ex $699 Gd $534
Gold Waterfowl Hunter Camo
   (12 ga. w/24-inch bbl.) . . . . NiB $987 Ex $699 Gd $534

GOLD STALKER SERIES
Self-cleaning, gas-operated, short-stroke action. Gauges: 10 or 12 (3.5-inch chamber); 12 or 20 (3-inch chamber). 26-, 28-, or

30-inch bbl. w/Invector or Invector Plus choke tubes. Graphite/fiberglass composite stock. Polished or matte black finish. Made 1998 to 2007.
Gold Stalker Light (10 ga., 3.5-inch
   w/composite stock) . . . . NiB $1487 Ex $1269 Gd $1109
Gold Stalker (12 ga. 3.5-inch) . . NiB $1048 Ex $911 Gd $500
Gold Stalker (12 or 20 ga.,
   3-inch) . . . . NiB $898 Ex $654 Gd $521
Gold Stalker Classic Model
   (21 or 20 ga., 3-inch) . . . NiB $1754 Ex $1228 Gd $1067
Gold Deer Stalker
   (12 ga. w/22-inch bbl.) . . . . NiB $855 Ex $529 Gd $380
Gold Turkey Stalker Camo
   (12 ga. w/24-inch bbl.) . . . . NiB $799 Ex $482 Gd $355
Gold Waterfowl Stalker Camo
   (12 ga. w/24-inch bbl.) . . . . NiB $943 Ex $667 Gd $543

GOLD SPORTING CLAYS SERIES
Similar to Gold Hunter Series except w/2.75-inch chamber and 28- or 30-inch ported bbl. w/Invector Plus chokes. Made 1996 to 2008.
Standard model. . . . . NiB $1132 Ex $821 Gd $677
Sporting Clays (Youth or
   Ladies) . . . . NiB $1677 Ex $1265 Gd $1071
Sporting Clays w/engraved
   nickel receiver . . . . NiB $1793 Ex $1277 Gd $1056

LIEGE O/U SHOTGUN (B26/27)
Boxlock. Automatic ejectors. Non-selective single trigger. 12 ga. only. Bbls.: 26.5-, 28-, or 30-inch; 2.75-inch chambers in 26.5- and 28-inch, 3-inch in 30-inch, IC/M, M/F, or F/F chokes; vent rib. Weight: 7 lbs., 4 oz.to 7 lbs., 14 oz., depending on bbls. Checkered pistol-grip stock and forearm. Made 1973 to 1975 by FN.
Liège (B-26 BAC production). . . NiB $1488 Ex $1161 Gd $988
Liège (B-27 FN prod.,
   Standard Game model). . . NiB $1488 Ex $1161 Gd $988
Deluxe Game model . . . . . . NiB $1522 Ex $1269 Gd $1043
Grand Delux Game model . NiB $1687 Ex $1438 Gd $1210
Deluxe Skeet model . . . . . . NiB $1488 Ex $1161 Gd $988
Deluxe Trap model . . . . NiB $1488 Ex $1161 Gd $988
NRA Sporting . . . . NiB $1067 Ex $700 Gd $5254

LIGHT SPORTING 802ES . . . NiB $1476 Ex $1211 Gd $989
Over/under. Invector-plus choke tubes. 12 ga. only with 28-inch bbl. Weight: 7 lbs., 5 oz.

LIGHTNING SPORTING CLAYS
Similar to the standard Citori Lightning model except Classic-style stock with rounded pistol grip. 30-inch back-bored bbls. with Invector Plus tubes. Receiver with "Lightning Sporting Clays Edition" logo. Made 1989 to 1994.
Standard model . . . . NiB $1396 Ex $1178 Gd $909
Pigeon grade . . . . NiB $1378 Ex $1161 Gd $882

O/U Classic . . . . NiB $2359 Ex $2091 Gd $1389
Gauge: 20, 2.75-inch chambers. 26-inch blued bbls. choked IC/M. Gold-plated, single selective trigger. Manual, top-tang-mounted safety. Engraved receiver. High grade, select American walnut straight-grip stock with Schnabel forend. Fine-line checkering with pearl borders. High-gloss finish. 5,000 issued in 1986; made in Japan, engraved in Belgium.

O/U GOLD CLASSIC . . . . . NiB $6245 Ex $4890 Gd $3179
Same general specifications as Over/Under Classic except more elaborate engravings, enhanced in gold, including profile of John M. Browning. Fine oil finish. 500 issued; made in 1986 in Belgium.

SHOTGUNS

**Browning Over/Under
Gold Classic**

RECOILLESS TRAP SHOTGUN
The action and bbl. are driven forward when firing to achieve 72 percent less recoil. 12 ga, 2.75-inch chamber. 30-inch bbl. with Invector Plus tubes; adjustable vent rib. 51.63 inches overall. Weight: 9 lbs. Adj. checkered walnut buttstock and forend. Blued finish. Made from 1993 to 1996.

STANDARD MODEL	NiB $1088	Ex $865	Gd $644
Micro model (27-inch bbl.)	NiB $1088	Ex $865	Gd $644
Signature model (27-inch bbl.)	NiB $1088	Ex $865	Gd $644

SUPERPOSED BICENTENNIAL
COMMEMORATIVE ... NiB $13,650 Ex $12,790 Gd $9779
Special limited edition issued to commemorate U.S. Bicentennial. 51 guns, one for each state in the Union plus one for Washington, D.C. Receiver with sideplates has engraved and gold-inlaid hunter and wild turkey on right side, U.S. flag and bald eagle on left side, together with state markings inlaid in gold, on blued background. Checkered straight-grip stock and Schnabel-style forearm of highly- figured American walnut. Velvet-lined wood presentation case. Made in 1976 by FN. Value shown is for gun in new, unfired condition. See illustration next page.

SUPERPOSED
BROADWAY 12 TRAP ..... NiB $2084 Ex $1766 Gd $1460
Same as Standard Trap Gun except has 30- or 32-inch bbls. with wider Broadway rib. Disc. 1976.

SUPERPOSED SHOTGUNS, HUNTING MODELS
Over/under boxlock. Selective automatic ejectors. Selective single trigger; earlier models (worth 25% less) supplied w/ double triggers, twin selective triggers or non-selective single trigger. Gauges: 12, 20 (intro. 1949, 3-inch chambers in later production), 28, .410 (latter two ga. intro. 1960). Bbls.: 26.5-, 28-, 30-, 32-inch, raised matted or vent rib, prewar Lightning Model made w/ribbed bbl., postwar version supplied only w/ vent rib; any combination of standard chokes. Weight (w/26.5-inch vent-rib bbls.): Standard 12, 7 lbs., 11 oz., Lightning 12, 7 lbs., 6 oz.; Standard 20, 6 lbs., 8 oz.; Lightning 20, 6 lbs., 4 oz.; Lightning 28, 6 lbs., 7 oz.; Lightning .410, 6 lbs., 10 oz. Checkered pistol-grip stock/forearm.

Higher grades (Pigeon, Pointer, Diana, Midas, Grade VI) differ from standard Grade I models in overall quality, engraving, wood and checkering; otherwise, specifications are the same. Midas Grade and Grade VI guns are richly gold inlaid. Made by FN 1928-1976. Prewar models may be considered as disc. in 1940 when Belgium was occupied by Germany. Grade VI offered 1955-1960. Pointer Grade disc. in 1966, Grade I Standard in 1973, Pigeon Grade in 1974. Lightning Grade I, Diana and Midas Grades were not offered after 1976.

Grade I standard weight	NiB $2390	Ex $1979	Gd $1749
Grade I Lightning	NiB $2209	Ex $1867	Gd $1428
Grade I Lightning, pre-war, matted bbl., no rib	NiB $2979	Ex $2255	Gd $1217

Grade II - Pigeon	NiB $4400	Ex $2790	Gd $1966
Grade III - Pointer	NiB $5000	Ex $4155	Gd $3860
Grade IV - Diana	NiB $8250	Ex $6300	Gd $3760
Grade V - Midas	NiB $7300	Ex $5012	Gd $3690
Grade VI	NiB $10,000	Ex $8292	Gd $6659
For 20 ga., add			20%
For 28 ga., add			75%
For .410, add			50%

Values shown are for models w/vent. rib.
w/raised matted rib, deduct 10%

SUPERPOSED LIGHTNING AND SUPERLIGHT MODELS (REISSUE B-25)
Reissue of popular 12-and 20-ga. Superposed shotguns. Lightning models available in 26.5- and 28-inch bbl. lengths w/2.75- or 3-inch chambering, full pistol grip. Superlight models available in 26.5-inch bbl. lengths w/2.75-inch chambering only, and straight-grip stock w/Schnabel forend. Both have hand-engraved receivers, fine-line checkering, gold-plated single selective trigger, automatic selective ejectors, manual safety. Weight: 6 to 7.5 lbs. Reintroduced 1985.

Grade I, Standard	NiB $2377	Ex $1898	Gd $1344
Grade II, Pigeon	NiB $5696	Ex $3863	Gd $3000
Grade III, Pointer	NiB $8879	Ex $5770	Gd $3760
Grade IV, Diana	NiB $8009	Ex $5679	Gd $3698
Grade V, Midas	NiB $13,750	Ex $11,299	Gd $10,650
w/extra bbls., add			50%

SUPERPOSED MAGNUM .. NiB $1988 Ex $1572 Gd $1189
Same as Grade I except chambered for 12-ga. 3-inch shells, 30-inch vent-rib bbls., stock w/recoil pad. Weight: About 8.25 lbs. Disc. 1976.

SUPERPOSED BLACK
DUCK LTD. ISSUE ...... NiB $10,390 Ex $8977 Gd $5640
Gauge: 12. Superposed Lightning action. 28-inch vent-rib bbls. Choked M/F. 2.75-inch chambers. Weight: 7 lbs., 6 oz. Gold-inlaid receiver and trigger guard engraved w/black duck scenes. Gold-plated, single selective trigger. Top-tang mounted manual safety. Automatic, selective ejectors. Front and center ivory sights. High-grade, hand-checkered, hand-oiled select walnut stock and forend. 500 issued in 1983.

SUPERPOSED MALLARD
DUCK LTD. ISSUE ...... NiB $10,768 Ex $7322 Gd $5680
Same general specifications as Ltd. Black Duck issue except mallard duck scenes engraved on receiver and trigger guard, dark French walnut stock w/rounded pistol-grip. 500 issued in 1981.

SUPERPOSED PINTAIL
DUCK LTD. ISSUE ...... NiB $10,766 Ex $7298 Gd $5660
Same general specifications as Ltd. Black Duck issue except pintail duck scenes engraved on receiver and trigger guard. Stock is of dark French walnut w/rounded pistol-grip. 500 issued in 1982.

SUPERPOSED, PRESENTATION GRADES
Custom versions of Super-Light, Lightning Hunting, Trap and Skeet Models, w/same general specifications as those of standard guns, but of higher overall quality. The four Presentation grades differ in receiver finish (grayed or blued), engraving gold inlays, wood and checkering. Presentation 4 has sideplates. Made by FN, these models were Intro. in 1977.

Presentation 1	NiB $3475	Ex $2770	Gd $12967
Presentation 1, gold-inlaid	NiB $4889	Ex $3388	Gd $2491
Presentation 2	NiB $4956	Ex $3860	Gd $2709

Browning Superposed Broadway 12 Trap

Browning Superposed Grade I Lightning

**Browning Superposed Ltd.
Pintail Duck Issue**

Presentation 2, gold-inlaid . NiB $7900 Ex $5275 Gd $4100
Presentation 3, gold-inlaid . NiB $9975 Ex $7866 Gd $6077
Presentation 4. . . . . NiB $9106 Ex $7320 Gd $5863
Presentation 4, gold-inlaid . . NiB $13,675 Ex $11,960 Gd $9989

SUPERPOSED SKEET GUNS, GRADE I
Same as standard Lightning 12, 20, 28 and .410 Hunting models, except has skeet-style stock and forearm, 26.5- or 28-inch vent-rib bbls. w/SK choke. Available also in All Gauge Skeet Set: Lightning 12 w/one removable forearm and three extra sets of bbls. in 20, 28 and .410 ga. in fitted luggage case. Disc. 1976. (For higher grades see listings for comparable Hunting models)
12 or 20 ga. . . . . NiB $2170 Ex $1690 Gd $1167
28 ga. or .410 . . . . NiB $2566 Ex $2278 Gd $1489
Combo skeet set (all gauges). . NiB $6549 Ex $6000 Gd $5489

SUPERPOSED SUPER
LIGHT MODEL . . . . NiB $7101 Ex $4877 Gd $4128
Ultralight field gun version of Standard Lightning Model has classic straight-grip stock and slimmer forearm. Available only in 12 and 20 gauges (2.75-inch chambers), w/26.5-inch vent-rib bbls. Weight: 6.5 lbs., (12 ga.); 6 lbs., (20 ga.). Made 1967 to 1976.

SUPERPOSED TRAP GUN. . NiB $5321 Ex $3867 Gd $2998
Same as Grade I except has trap-style stock, beavertail forearm, 30-inch vent-rib bbls., 12 ga. only. Disc. 1976. (For higher grades see listings for comparable hunting models)

TWELVETTE DOUBLE AUTOMATIC
Lightweight version of Double Automatic w/same general specifications except aluminum receiver. Bbl. w/plain matted top or vent rib. Weight: 6.75 to 7 lbs., depending on bbl. Receiver is finished in black w/gold engraving; 1956-1961 receivers were also anodized in gray, brown and green w/silver engraving. Made 1955 to 1971
w/plain bbl. . . . . NiB $900 Ex $600 Gd $380
w/vent. rib bbl. . . . . NiB $1000 Ex $750 Gd $476

CZ (CESKA ZBROJOVKA), INC. — Uhersky Brod, Czech Republic

Imported by CZ-USA, Kansas City, KS.

581 SOLO. . . . . NiB $730 Ex $760 Gd $360
O/U boxlock action with double triggers and ejectors. 12 ga. 2-3/4-inch chambers. Disc. 1995, resumed 1999 to 2005.

Left Side

Right Side

Browning Superposed Bicentennial

Browning Superposed Grade IV Diana (Postwar)

Browning Superposed Grade V Midas (Postwar)

SHOTGUNS

ARMARILLO . . . . NiB $625 Ex $430 Gd $210
Similar to Durago S/S, double triggers. Made 2005 to 2006.

BOBWHITE . . . . NiB $778 Ex $500 Gd $260
S/S hammerless boxlock action with double trigger and extractors. 12, 16 or 20 ga. 3-inch chambers. Bbl.: 26 or 28 in. Finish: case hardened. Stock: straight English grip, walnut. Weight: 6 to 7 lbs. Made 2005 to date.

CANVASBACK (103 D) . . . . NiB $670 Ex $460 Gd $275
O/U boxlock action with single trigger and extractors. 12, 20 28 ga. 3-inch chambers. Bbl.: 26 or 28 inches, vent. rib, 5 choke tubes, black chrome finish, light engraving. Stock: pistol grip, checkered walnut. Weight: 6.3 to 7.5 lbs. Made 2005 to 2013.
Gold (gold inlays). . . . . NiB $830 Ex $480 Gd $300
Gold (28 or .410) . . . . add 20%

DURANGO . . . . NiB $725 Ex $530 Gd $245
S/S hammerless boxlock action with single trigger and extractors. 12 or 20 ga. 3-inch chambers. Bbl.: 20 in. Stock: round knob pistol grip, walnut. Weight: 6 to 6.7 lbs. Made 2005 to 2006.

HAMMER COACH . . . . NiB $778 Ex $500 Gd $260
S/S boxlock action with double trigger, exposed hammers and extractors. 12 ga. 3-inch chambers. Bbl.: 20 in., fixed choke. Finish: case hardened. Stock: pistol grip. Weight: 6.7 lbs. Made 2006 to date.
Classic (12, 30-in. bbl.,
    2010-2014). . . . . NiB $963 Ex $580 Gd $300

LIMITED EDITION . . . . NiB $1980 Ex $1520 Gd $800
O/U w/ engraved boxlock action with single gold trigger and ejectors. 12 ga. 3-inch chambers. Bbl.: 28 in., vent. rib. Stock: Cicassin walnut. 50 mfg. Made 2006 to 2009.

MALLARD . . . . NiB $583 Ex $360 Gd $230
O/U boxlock action with dual triggers and extractors. 12 or 20 ga. 3-inch chambers. Bbl.: 28 inches, vent. rib, 5 choke tubes, coin finish receiver, black chrom bbl. Stock: prince of whales grip, Turkish walnut. Weight: 6.5 to 7.5 lbs. Made 2005 to date.

REDHEAD PREMIER . . . . NiB $959 Ex $630 Gd $400
O/U boxlock action with single trigger and ejectors. 12 or 20 ga. 3-inch chambers. Bbl.: 26 or 28 inches, vent. rib, 5 choke tubes, black chrome bbl. coin finish receiver. Stock: pistol grip, checkered walnut. Weight: 6.7 to 7.9 lbs. Made 2005 to date.
Mini (28 or .410, 2005-2013). . NiB $800 Ex $630 Gd $400
Target (12 ga., 30-in. bbl.) . . . NiB $1389 Ex $830 Gd $440

RINGNECK . . . . NiB $1022 Ex $680 Gd $360
S/S boxlock action w/ engraved sideplates, single trigger and extractors. 12, 16 or 20 ga. 3-inch chambers. Bbl.: 26 or 28 inches, 5 choke tubes. Finish: black chrome bbl., case hardened receiver. Stock: pistol grip, checkered walnut. Weight: 6.3 to 7.1 lbs. Made 2005 to date.
16 ga., add $200
Mini (28 or .410). . . . . NiB $1229 Ex $800 Gd $410
Target (12 ga., 30-in. bbl.) . . . NiB $1298 Ex $810 Gd $430
Deluxe Custom (20 ga., 28-in. bbl.,
    2006-2012) . . . . NiB $1700 Ex $1260 Gd $630
Competition (12 ga., 28-in. ported bbl.,
    2010-2011) . . . . NiB $2730 Ex $1830 Gd $1000

SPORTER STANDARD . . . . . . NiB $3122 Ex $1630 Gd $800
O/U boxlock action with single trigger and ejectors. 12 ga. 3-inch chambers. Bbl.: 30 or 32 inches, vent. rib, 6 extended choke tubes, black chrome bbl., matte black receiver. Stock: pistol grip w/ palm swell, adj. comb, Grade II Turkish walnut. Weight: 8.7 lbs. Made 2008 to date.

WOODCOCK DELUXE . . . . . . NiB $1080 Ex $730 Gd $400
O/U boxlock action with single trigger and ejectors. 12 or 20 ga. 3-inch chambers. Bbl.: 26 or 28 inches, vent. rib, 5 choke tubes, black chrome bbl. case hardened receiver w/ sideplates. Stock: prince of whales pistol grip, schnabel forend, walnut. Weight: 6.8 to 7.8 lbs. Made 2005 to 2010.
Custom (20, 2006-2010). . . . . NiB $1900 Ex $1330 Gd $710
Target (12 ga., 30-in. brl.) . . . . NiB $1389 Ex $830 Gd $440

CENTURY ARMS formerly CENTURY INTERNATIONAL ARMS, INC. — St. Albans, VT, and Boca Raton, FL

ARTHEMIS . . . . NiB $522 Ex $390 Gd $259
O/U boxlock action with double triggers and extractors. 12, 20, 28 ga. or .410 bore. 3-inch chambers. 28-inch bbls. Single set trigger, extractors. Checkered wood stock and forearm. Weight: 5.3 to 7.4 lbs. Mfg. in Turkey by Khan. Disc.

ARTHEMIS O/U . . . . NiB $475 Ex $310 Gd $245
Gauge: 12, 20, 28, .410. Bbl.: 28 inches, vent. rib, 3-inch chamber. Single selective trigger, extractors. Stock: Checkered walnut. Weight: 5.3 to 7.4 lbs. Mfg. by PAR. Imported from 2002 to 2009.

CATAMOUNT FURY I . . . . NiB $675 Ex $430 Gd $275
Gas-operated adj. piston, semi-auto w/ detchable 5- or 10-rnd. magazine. Gauge: 12. Bbl.: 20.1 inches, choke tubes. Stock: standard style checkered synthetic. Mfg. in China. Imported 2013 to date.

CATAMOUNT FURY II . . . . . . NiB $695 Ex $450 Gd $295
Similar specs as Fury I except synthetic thumbhole stock. Mfg. in China. Imported 2013 to date.

COACH MODEL . . . . NiB $325 Ex $200 Gd $140
Side-by-side. Gauge: 12, 20, .410. Bbl.: 20 inches, exposed hammers, double trigger. Stock: Checkered walnut. Sling swivels. Mfg. in China.

MODEL IJ2 . . . . NiB $220 Ex $155 Gd $100
Slide-action. Gauge: 12; 2.75-inch or 3-inch chamber. Bbl.: 19 inches, fixed choke. Ghost ring rear or fiber optic sights. Weight: 7 lbs. Mfg. in China.

PHANTOM . . . . NiB $295 Ex $240 Gd $190
Semi-auto. Gauge: 12. 3-inch chamber. Bbl.: 24, 26 or 28 inches; vent. rib. Three choke tubes. Stock: Black synthetic. Mfg. in Turkey. Disc.

PW87 . . . . NiB $390 Ex $325 Gd $160
Repro. of Winchester 1887 lever-action. Gauge: 12. 2-3/4-in. chamber. Bbl.: 19 inches w/ brass bead M choke. Stock: smooth hardwood. Mfg. in China. Imported from 2013 to date.

Churchill Automatic Shotgun

Churchill Windsor Grade Side-by-Side Shotgun

Churchill Windsor Grade Flyweight Shotgun

SAS-12 . . . . **NiB $250 Ex $185 Gd $100**
Semi-auto. Gauge: 12. 2.75-inch chamber. Bbl.: 22 or 23.5
inches. Detachable 3- or 5-round mag.
Ghost ring rear sight, add **$25**

ULTRA 87 . . . . **NiB $255 Ex $180 Gd $110**
Slide-action. Gauge: 12. Bbl.: 19 inches. Optional heat shield
and pistol grip. Side folding stock. Includes extra 28-inch bbl.
Weight: 8.2 lbs.

CHURCHILL — Italy and Spain.
*Imported by Ellett Brothers, Inc., Chapin, SC; previously by
Kassnar Imports, Inc., Harrisburg, PA*

AUTOMATIC SHOTGUN
Gas-operated. Gauge: 12, 2.75- or 3-inch chambers. Five
round magazine w/cutoff. Bbl.: 24-, 25-, 26-, 28-inch w/ICT
choke tubes. Checkered walnut stock w/satin finish. Imported
from 1990 to 1994.
Standard model . . . . **NiB $657 Ex $571 Gd $455**
Turkey model . . . . **NiB $697 Ex $586 Gd $434**

MONARCH O/U SHOTGUN
Hammerless, takedown w/engraved receiver. Selective single
or double triggers. Gauges: 12, 20, 28, .410; 3-inch chambers.
Bbls.: 25- or 26-inch (IC/M); 28-inch (M/F). Weight: 6.5-7.5
lbs. Checkered European walnut buttstock and forend. Made
in Italy from 1986 to 1993.
w/double triggers . . . . **NiB $490 Ex $378 Gd $225**
w/single trigger . . . . **NiB $588 Ex $466 Gd $321**

REGENT O/U SHOTGUNS
Gauges: 12 or 20; 2.75-inch chambers. 27-inch bbls. w/
interchangeable choke tubes and wide vent rib. Single selective trigger, selective automatic ejectors. Checkered pistol-grip
stock in fancy walnut. Imported from Italy 1984 to 1988 and
1990 to 1994.
Regent V(disc. 1988) . . . . **NiB $987 Ex $680 Gd $590**
Regent VII w/sideplates (disc. 1994) . . . . . **NiB $873 Ex $779
Gd $544**

REGENT SKEET . . . . **NiB $873 Ex $779 Gd $544**
12 or 20 ga. w/2.75-inch chambers. Selective automatic ejectors, single-selective trigger. 26-inch over/under bbls. w/vent
rib. Weight: 7 lbs. Made in Italy from 1984 to 1988.

REGENT TRAP. . . . . **NiB $876 Ex $654 Gd $490**
12-ga. competition shotgun w/2.75-inch chambers. 30-inch
over/under bbls. choked IM/F, vent side ribs. Weight: 8 lbs.
Selective automatic ejectors, single selective trigger. Checkered
Monte Carlo stock w/Supercushion recoil pad. Made in Italy
1984 to 1988.

SPORTING CLAYS O/U . . . . . . **NiB $945 Ex $800 Gd $575**
Same general specifications as Windsor IV except in 12 ga.
only w/28-inch ported bbls. and choke tubes. Selective automatic ejectors. Weight: 7.5 lbs. Made from 1992 to 1994.

WINDSOR O/U SHOTGUNS
Hammerless, boxlock w/engraved receiver, selective single
trigger. Extractors or ejectors. Gauges: 12, 20, 28 or .410;
3-inch chambers. Bbls.: 24 to 30 inches w/fixed chokes or
choke tubes. Weight: 6 lbs., 3 oz. (Flyweight) to 7 lbs., 10 oz.
(12 ga.). Checkered straight (Flyweight) or pistol-grip stock
and forend of European walnut. Imported from Italy 1984 to
1993.
Windsor III w/fixed chokes. . . . **NiB $668 Ex $544 Gd $455**
Windsor III w/choke tubes . . . . **NiB $798 Ex $670 Gd $555**
Windsor IV w/fixed chokes
  (disc. 1993) . . . . **NiB $768 Ex $659 Gd $455**
Windsor IV w/choke tubes . . . . **NiB $833 Ex $754 Gd $500**

WINDSOR SIDE-BY-SIDE SHOTGUNS
Boxlock action w/double triggers, ejectors or extractors and
automatic safety. Gauges: 10, (3.5-inch chambers); 12, 20, 28,
.410 (3-inch chambers), 16 (2.75-inch chambers). Bbls.: 23
to 32 inches w/various fixed choke or choke tube combinations. Weight: 5 lbs., 12 oz. (Flyweight) to 11.5 lbs. (10 ga.).
European walnut buttstock and forend. Imported from Spain
1984 to 1990.

SHOTGUNS

E.J. Churchill Premiere

Windsor I 10 ga.............. NiB $569 Ex $400 Gd $327
Windsor I 12 ga. thru .410. ... NiB $569 Ex $400 Gd $327
Windsor II 12 or 20 ga. ...... NiB $569 Ex $400 Gd $327
Windsor VI 12 or 20 ga....... NiB $569 Ex $400 Gd $327

E.J. CHURCHILL, LTD. —
Surrey (previously London), England

The E.J. Churchill shotguns listed below are no longer imported.

PREMIERE QUALITY HAMMERLESS DOUBLE
Sidelock. Automatic ejectors. Double triggers or selective single trigger. Gauges: 12, 16, 20, 28. Bbls.: 25-, 28- 30-, 32-inch; any degree of boring. Weight: 5-8 lbs. depending on ga. and bbl. length. Checkered stock and forend, straight or pistol-grip.
w/double triggers ... NiB $46,775 Ex $36,950 Gd $30,000
w/single selective trigger, add.................... $10%

FIELD MODEL HAMMERLESS DOUBLE
Sidelock Hammerless ejector gun w/same general specifications as Premiere Model but of lower quality.
w/double triggers ...... NiB $10,667 Ex $9260 Gd $8110
w/single selective trigger, add.................... 10%

PREMIERE QUALITY O/U SHOTGUN
Sidelock. Automatic ejectors. Double triggers or selective single trigger. Gauges: 12, 16, 20, 28. Bbls.: 25-, 28-, 30-, 32-inch, any degree of boring. Weight: 5-8 lbs. depending on ga. and bbl. length. Checkered stock and forend, straight or pistol-grip.
w/double triggers ... NiB $55,000 Ex $38,000 Gd $25,000
w/selective single trigger, add..................... 10%
w/raised vent. rib, add 15%

UTILITY MODEL HAMMERLESS DOUBLE-BARREL
Anson & Deeley boxlock action. Double triggers or single trigger. Gauges: 12, 16, 20, 28, .410. Bbls.: 25-, 28-, 30-, 32-inch, any degree of boring. Weight: 4.5-8 lbs. depending on ga. and bbl. length. Checkered stock and forend, straight or pistol-grip.
w/double triggers .... NiB $7340 Ex $6077 Gd $4340
w/single selective trigger, add..................... 10%

XXV PREMIERE HAMMERLESS
DOUBLE.......... NiB $47,000 Ex $40,000 Gd $35,000
Sidelock. Assisted opening. Automatic ejectors. Double triggers. Gauges: 12, 20. 25-inch bbls. w/narrow, quick-sighting rib; any standard choke combination. English-style straight-grip stock and forearm, checkered.

XXV IMPERIAL .... NiB $14,775 Ex $12,700 Gd $9775
Similar to XXV Premiere but no assisted opening feature.

XXV HERCULES .... NiB $10,750 Ex $9450 Gd $6680
Boxlock, otherwise specifications same as for XXV Premiere.

XXV REGAL............ NiB $6277 Ex $4988 Gd $3500
Similar to XXV Hercules but w/o assisted opening feature. Gauges: 12, 20, 28, .410.

CLASSIC DOUBLES — Tochigi, Japan
Imported by Classic Doubles International, St. Louis, MO, and previously by Olin as Winchester Models 101 and 23.

MODEL 101 O/U SHOTGUN
Boxlock. Engraved receiver w/single selective trigger, auto ejectors and combination bbl. selector and safety. Gauges: 12, 20, 28 or .410, 2.75-, 3-inch chambers, 25.5- 28- or 30-inch vent-rib bbls. Weight: 6.25 – 7.75 lbs. Checkered French walnut stock. Imported from 1987 to 1990.
Classic I Field .... NiB $1590 Ex $1488 Gd $1033
Classic II Field............ NiB $1879 Ex $1540 Gd $1133
Classic Sporter .... NiB $2066 Ex $1788 Gd $1233
Classic Sporter combo .... NiB $3475 Ex $2870 Gd $2035
Classic Trap........... NiB $1380 Ex $1166 Gd $990
Classic Trap Single....... NiB $1435 Ex $1140 Gd $1089
Classic Trap combo....... NiB $2560 Ex $2053 Gd $1498
Classic Skeet........... NiB $1765 Ex $1600 Gd $1179
Classic Skeet 2-bbl. set .... NiB $2867 Ex $2374 Gd $1790
Classic Skeet 4-bbl. set .... NiB $4488 Ex $3972 Gd $2633
ClassicWaterfowler....... NiB $1554 Ex $1266 Gd $1031
For Grade II (28 ga.), add........................ $900
For Grade II (.410), add $300

MODEL 201 SIDE-BY-SIDE SHOTGUN
Boxlock. Single selective trigger, automatic safety, selective ejectors. Gauges: 12 or 20; 3-inch chambers. 26- or 28-inch vent-rib bbl., fixed chokes or internal tubes. Weight: 6 to 7 lbs. Checkered French walnut stock and forearm. Imported 1987 to 1990.
Field model............. NiB $2687 Ex $1490 Gd $1264
Skeet model .... NiB $2687 Ex $1490 Gd $1264
With internal choke tubes, add.................... $100

MODEL 201
SMALL BORE SET .... NiB $4650 Ex $3751 Gd $2975
Same general specifications as the Classic Model 201 except w/smaller frame, in 28 ga. (IC/M) and .410 (F/M). Weight: 6-6.5 lbs. Imported from 1987 to 1990.

COGSWELL & HARRISON, LTD. —
London, England

AMBASSADOR HAMMERLESS DOUBLE-BARREL
SHOTGUN .... NiB $6056 Ex $4533 Gd $3718
Boxlock. Sideplates w/game scene or rose scroll engraving. Automatic ejectors. Double triggers. Gauges: 12, 16, 20. Bbls.: 26-28-, 30-inch; any choke combination. Checkered straight-grip stock and forearm. Disc.

**Cogswell & Harrison
Best Quality
Hammerless Sidelock**

**Colt Auto Shotgun
Ultra Light Standard**

**Colt Custom
Hammerless Double**

AVANT TOUT SERIES HAMMERLESS DOUBLE-BARREL

SHOTGUNS . . . . **NiB $2688 Ex $2133 Gd $1954**
Boxlock. Sideplates (except Avant Tout III Grade). Automatic ejectors. Double triggers or single trigger (selective or non-selective). Gauges: 12, 16, 20. Bbls.: 25-, 27.5-, 30-inch, any choke combination. Checkered stock and forend, straight grip standard. Made in three models (Avant Tout I or Konor, Avant Tout II or Sandhurst. Avant Tout III or Rex) which differ chiefly in overall quality of engraving, grade of wood, checkering, etc. General specifications are the same. Disc.

Avant Tout I. . . . . NiB $3544 Ex $3160 Gd $2477
Avant Tout II . . . . NiB $2983 Ex $2786 Gd $1966
Avant Tout III . . . . NiB $2254 Ex $2090 Gd $1760
w/non-selective single trigger, add $250
w/selective single trigger, add $425

BEST QUALITY HAMMERLESS
SIDELOCK DOUBLE-BARREL SHOTGUN
Hand-detachable locks. Automatic ejectors. Double triggers or single trigger (selective or non-selective). Gauges: 12, 16, 20. Bbls.: 25-, 26-, 28-, 30-inch, any choke combination. Checkered stock and forend, straight grip standard.

Victor model. . . . . NiB $6570 Ex $5461 Gd $4130
Primic model (disc.) . . . . . . NiB $6640 Ex $5521 Gd $4200
w/non-selective single trigger, add $250
w/selective single trigger, add. $450

HUNTIC MODEL HAMMERLESS DOUBLE
Sidelock. Automatic ejectors. Double triggers or single trigger (selective or non-selective). Gauges: 12, 16, 20. Bbls.: 25-, 27.5-, 30-inch; any choke combination. Checkered stock and forend, straight grip standard. Disc.

w/double triggers . . . . NiB $4077 Ex $2986 Gd $1769
w/non-selective single trigger, add $250
w/selective single trigger, add. $400

MARKOR HAMMERLESS DOUBLE
Boxlock. Non-ejector or ejector. Double triggers. Gauges: 12, 16, 20. Bbls.: 27.5 or 30-inch; any choke combination. Checkered stock and forend, straight grip standard. Disc.

Non-ejector . . . . NiB $1784 Ex $1599 Gd $1188
Ejector model, add 20%

REGENCY HAMMERLESS
DOUBLE. . . . . NiB $4395 Ex $3667 Gd $2971
Anson & Deeley boxlock action. Automatic ejectors. Double triggers. Gauges: 12, 16, 20. Bbls.: 26-, 28-, 30-inch, any choke combination. Checkered straight-grip stock and forearm.

Introduced in 1970 to commemorate the firm's bicentennial, this model has deep scroll engraving and the name "Regency" inlaid in gold on the rib. Disc.

COLT'S MFG. CO., INC. — Hartford, Connecticut
Auto Shotguns were made by Franchi and are similar to corresponding models of that manufacturer.

AUTO SHOTGUN — ULTRA LIGHT STANDARD
Recoil-operated. Takedown. Alloy receiver. Gauges: 12, 20. Mag. holds 4 rounds. Bbls.: plain, solid or vent rib, chrome-lined; 26-inch IC or M choke, 28-inch M or F choke, 30-inch F choke, 32-inch F choke. Weight: 12 ga., about 6.25 lbs. Checkered pistol-grip stock and forearm. Made 1964 to 1966.

w/plain bbl. . . . . NiB $400 Ex $297 Gd $200
w/solid rib bbl. . . . . NiB $450 Ex $344 Gd $250
w/vent. rib bbl. . . . . NiB $450 Ex $344 Gd $250

AUTO SHOTGUN — MAGNUM CUSTOM
Same as Magnum except has engraved receiver, select walnut stock and forearm. Made 1964 to 66.

w/Solid-rib bbl. . . . . NiB $544 Ex $422 Gd $300
w/vent. rib bbl. . . . . NiB $600 Ex $470 Gd $351

AUTO SHOTGUN — ULTRA LIGHT CUSTOM
Same as Standard Auto except has engraved receiver, select walnut stock and forearm. Made 1964 to 1966.

w/solid-rib bbl. . . . . NiB $544 Ex $470 Gd $366
w/vent. rib bbl. . . . . NiB $600 Ex $495 Gd $379

AUTO SHOTGUN — MAGNUM
Same as Standard Auto except steel receiver,chambered for 3-inch Magnum shells, 30- and 32-inch bbls. in 12 ga., 28-inch in 20 ga. Weight: 12 ga., about 8.25 lbs. Made 1964 to 1966.

w/plain bbl. . . . . NiB $552 Ex $447 Gd $332
w/solid-rib bbl. . . . . NiB $622 Ex $470 Gd $356
w/vent. rib bbl. . . . . NiB $644 Ex $500 Gd $371

CUSTOM HAMMERLESS
DOUBLE. . . . . NiB $766 Ex $509 Gd $446
Boxlock. Double triggers. Auto ejectors. Gauges: 12 Mag., 16. Bbls.: 26-inch IC/M; 28-inch M/F; 30-inch F/F. Weight: 12 ga., about 7.5 lbs. Checkered pistol-grip stock and beavertail forearm. Made in 1961.

SHOTGUNS

Colt Standard Pump

Colt-Sauer Drilling

COLTSMAN PUMP SHOTGUN . . NiB $489 Ex $355 Gd $269
Takedown. Gauges: 12, 16, 20. Magazine holds 4 rounds. Bbls.: 26-inch IC; 28-inch M or F choke; 30-inch F choke. Weight: About 6 lbs. Plain pistol-grip stock and forearm. Made 1961 to 1965 by Manufrance.

CUSTOM PUMP . . . . NiB $500 Ex $377 Gd $286
Same as Standard Pump shotgun except has checkered stock, vent-rib bbl. Weight: About 6.5 lbs. Made 1961 to 1963 by Manufrance.

SAUER DRILLING . . . . NiB $4466 Ex $3778 Gd $2360
Three-bbl. combination gun. Boxlock. Set rifle trigger. Tang bbl. selector, automatic rear sight positioner. 12 ga. over .30-06 or .243 rifle bbl. 25-inch bbls., F and M choke. Weight: About 8 lbs. Folding leaf rear sight, blade front w/brass bead. Checkered pistol-grip stock and beavertail forearm, recoil pad. Made 1974 to 1985 by J. P. Sauer & Sohn, Eckernförde, Germany.

CONNECTICUT VALLEY CLASSICS —
Westport, Connecticut

SPORTER 101 O/U
Gauge: 12; 3-inch chamber. Bbls.: 28-, 30- or 32-inch w/ screw-in tubes. Weight: 7.75 lbs. Engraved stainless or nitrided receiver; blued bbls.

Checkered American black walnut buttstock and forend w/low-luster satin finish. Made from 1993 to 1998.
Classic Sporter . . . . NiB $1966 Ex $1634 Gd $1388
Stainless Classic Sporter . . NiB $2764 Ex $2259 Gd $1744

FIELD O/U
Similar to the standard Classic Sporter over/under model except w/30-inch bbls. only and non-reflective matte blued finish on both bbls. and receiver for Waterfowler; other grades w/different degrees of embellishment; Grade I the lowest and Grade III the highest. Made 1993 to 1998.
Grade I . . . . NiB $2788 Ex $2308 Gd $1683
Grade II . . . . NiB $3166 Ex $2521 Gd $1790
Grade III . . . . NiB $3767 Ex $2866 Gd $1946
Waterfowler . . . . NiB $2581 Ex $2264 Gd $1598

CONNENTO/VENTUR — Formerly imported by Ventura, Seal Beach, California

Model 51 . . . . NiB $456 Ex $361 Gd $295
Gauge: 12, 16, 20, 28 and .410. Double-barrel, box-lock action. Barrels: 26, 28, 30 and 32 inches; various chokes; extractors; and double triggers. Checkered walnut stock. Introduced in 1980, discontinued 1985.

Model 52 . . . . NiB $610 Ex $433 Gd $329
Same as Model 51 except in 10 gauge.

Model 53 . . . . NiB $538 Ex $449 Gd $300
Same as Model 51 except with scalloped receiver, automatic ejectors and optional single selective trigger. Discontinued in 1985.

W/single trigger, add 25%

Model 62 . . . . NiB $1132 Ex $990 Gd $760
Holland & Holland-design sidelock shotgun with various barrel lengths and chokes; automatic ejectors; cocking indicators. Floral engraved receiver, checkered walnut stock. Discontinued in 1982.

Model 64 . . . . NiB $1388 Ex $1054 Gd $877
Same as Model 62 except deluxe finish. Discontinued.

Grade I . . . . NiB $1259 Ex $988 Gd $844
Gauge: 12. Over/under shotgun. Barrels: 32 inches; screw-in choke tubes; high ventilated rib; automatic ejectors; single selective trigger standard. Checkered Monte Carlo walnut stock.

Mark II . . . . NiB $1569 Ex $1236 Gd $1006
Same as Mark I model but with an extra single barrel and fitted leather case.

Mark III . . . . NiB $1788 Ex $1469 Gd $1100
Same as Mark I model but with finely figured walnut stock and engraved metal.

Mark III Combo . . . . NiB $2877 Ex $2243 Gd $2071
Same as Mark III model above but with extra single barrel and fitted leather case.

CHARLES DALY, INC. — New York, New York

The pre-WWII Charles Daly shotguns, w/the exception of the Commander, were manufactured by various firms in Suhl, Germany. The postwar guns, except for the Novamatic series, were produced by Miroku Firearms Mfg. Co., Tokyo. Miroku ceased production in 1976 and the Daly trademark was acquired by Outdoor Sports Headquarters, in Dayton, Ohio. OSHI continued to market O/U shotguns from both Italy and Spain under the Daly logo. Automatic models were produced in Japan for distribution in the USA. In 1996, KBI, Inc. in Harrisburg, PA acquired the Daly trademark and currently imports firearms under that logo.

COMMANDER O/U SHOTGUN

Daly-pattern Anson & Deeley system boxlock action. Automatic ejectors. Double triggers or Miller selective single trigger. Gauges: 12, 16,20, 28, .410. Bbls.: 26- to 30-inch, IC/M or M/F choke. Weight: 5.25 to 7.25 lbs. depending on ga. and bbl. length. Checkered stock and forend, straight or pistol grip. The two models, 100 and 200, differ in general quality, grade of wood, checkering, engraving, etc.; otherwise specs are the same. Made in Belgium c. 1939.

Model 100 . . . . NiB $665 Ex $500 Gd $397
Model 200 . . . . NiB $866 Ex $703 Gd $511
w/Miller single trigger, add. $150

HAMMERLESS DOUBLE-BARREL SHOTGUN

Daly-pattern Anson & Deeley system boxlock action. Automatic ejectors except "Superior Quality" is non-ejector. Double triggers. Gauges: 10, 12, 16, 20, 28, .410. Bbls.: 26- to 32-inch, any combination of chokes. Weight: from 4 to 8.5 lbs. depending on ga. and bbl. length. Checkered pistol-grip stock and forend. The four grades—Regent Diamond, Diamond, Empire, Superior—differ in general quality, grade of wood, checkering, engraving, etc.; otherwise specifications are the same. Disc. about 1933.

Diamond quality. . . . . NiB $12,677 Ex $10,445 Gd $7869
Empire quality. . . . . NiB $6133 Ex $4632 Gd $3144
Regent Diamond quality . . NiB $14,878 Ex $12,966 Gd $10,077
Superior quality . . . . NiB $1522 Ex $1292 Gd $1000

HAMMERLESS DRILLING

Daly pattern Anson & Deeley system boxlock action. Plain extractors. Double triggers, front single set for rifle bbl. Gauges: 12, 16, 20, .25-20, .25-35, .30-30 rifle bbl. Supplied in various bbl. lengths and weights. Checkered pistol-grip stock and forend. Auto rear sight operated by rifle bbl. selector. The three grades — Regent Diamond, Diamond, Superior—differ in general quality, grade of wood, checkering, engraving, etc.; otherwise, specifications are the same. Disc. 1933.

Diamond quality. . . . . NiB $7235 Ex $5530 Gd $4200
Regent Diamond quality . . NiB $14,866 Ex $11,977 Gd $9977
Superior quality . . . . NiB $3733 Ex $2988 Gd $2036

HAMMERLESS DOUBLE

EMPIRE GRADE . . . . NiB $1887 Ex $1352 Gd $1091
Boxlock. Plain extractors. Non-selective single trigger. Gauges: 12, 16, 20; 3-inch chambers in 12 and 20, 2.75-inch in 16 ga. Bbls.: vent rib; 26-, 28-, 30-inch (latter in 12 ga. only); IC/M, M/F, F/F. Weight: 6 to 7.75 lbs., depending on ga. and bbls. Checkered pistol-grip stock and beavertail forearm. Made 1968 to 1971.

1974 WILDLIFE

COMMEMORATIVE . . . . . . NiB $2466 Ex $2167 Gd $1477
Limited issue of 500 guns. Similar to Diamond Grade over/under. 12-ga. trap and skeet models only. Duck scene engraved on right side of receiver, fine scroll on left side. Made in 1974.

NOVAMATIC LIGHTWEIGHT AUTOLOADER

Same as Breda. Recoil-operated. Takedown. 12 ga., 2.75-inch chamber.

Four-round tubular magazine. Bbls.: Plain vent rib; 26-inch IC or Quick-Choke w/three interchangeable tubes, 28-inch M or F choke. Weight (w/26-inch vent-rib bbl.): 7 lbs., 6 oz. Checkered pistol-grip stock and forearm. Made 1968 by Ernesto Breda, Milan, Italy.

w/plain bbl. . . . . NiB $398 Ex $277 Gd $198
w/vent rib bbl. . . . . NiB $397 Ex $260 Gd $200
w/Quick-Choke, add $50

NOVAMATIC SUPER LIGHTWEIGHT

Lighter version of Novamatic Lightweight. Gauges: 12, 20. Weight (w/26-inch vent-rib bbl.): 12 ga., 6 lbs., 10 oz., 20 ga., 6 lbs. SK choke available in 26-inch vent-rib bbl. 28-inch bbls. in 12 ga. only. Quick-Choke in 20 ga. w/plain bbl. Made 1968 by Ernesto Breda, Milan, Italy.

12 ga., plain bbl. . . . . NiB $387 Ex $288 Gd $198
12 ga., vent. rib bbl. . . . . NiB $387 Ex $288 Gd $198
20 ga., plain bbl. . . . . NiB $543 Ex $433 Gd $315
20 ga., plain bbl. w/Quick-Choke NiB $388 Ex $335 Gd $217
20 ga., vent. rib bbl. . . . . NiB $433 Ex $290 Gd $200

NOVAMATIC SUPER LIGHTWEIGHT

20 GA. MAGNUM . . . . NiB $377 Ex $296 Gd $200
Same as Novamatic Super Lightweight 2, except 3-inch chamber, has 3-round magazine, 28-inch vent-rib bbl., F choke.

NOVAMATIC

12 GA. MAGNUM . . . . NiB $377 Ex $296 Gd $200
Same as Novamatic Lightweight, except chambered for 12-ga. Magnum 3-inch shell. Has 3-round magazine, 30-inch vent rib bbl., F choke, and stock w/recoil pad. Weight: 7.75 lbs.

Post-War Charles Daly shotguns were imported by Sloan's Sporting Goods trading as Charles Daly in New York. In 1976, Outdoor Sports Headquarters acquired the Daly trademark and continued to import European-made shotguns under that logo. In 1996, KBI, Inc., in Harrisburg, PA, acquired the Daly trademark and currently imports firearms under that logo.

NOVAMATIC TRAP GUN . . . . . NiB $643 Ex $500 Gd $355
Same as Novamatic Lightweight except has 30-inch vent rib bbl., F choke and Monte Carlo stock w/recoil pad. Weight: 7.75 lbs.

O/U SHOTGUNS (PRE-WWII)

Daly-pattern Anson & Deeley-system boxlock action. Sideplates. Auto ejectors. Double triggers. Gauges: 12, 16, 20. Supplied in various bbl. lengths and weights. Checkered pistol-grip stock and forend. The two grades — Diamond and Empire — differ in general quality, grade of wood, checkering, engraving, etc.; otherwise specifications are the same. Disc. about 1933.

Diamond Quality . . . . NiB $6133 Ex $4965 Gd $3476
Empire Quality . . . . NiB $4771 Ex $3865 Gd $2700

O/U SHOTGUNS (POST-WWII)

Boxlock. Auto ejectors or selective auto/manual ejection. Selective single trigger. Gauges: 12, 12 Magnum (3-inch chambers), 20 (3-inch chambers), 28, .410. Bbls.: Vent rib; 26-, 28-, 30-inch; standard choke combinations. Weight: 6 to 8 lbs. depending on ga. and bbls. Select walnut stock w/pistol grip, fluted forearm checkered; Monte Carlo comb on trap guns; recoil pad on 12-ga. mag. and trap models. The various grades differ in quality of engraving and wood. Made from 1963 to 1976.

Diamond grade . . . . NiB $1588 Ex $1266 Gd $990
Field grade . . . . NiB $933 Ex $800 Gd $576
Superior grade . . . . NiB $1139 Ex $1008 Gd $853
Venture grade . . . . NiB $900 Ex $773 Gd $525

SEXTUPLE MODEL SINGLE-BARREL TRAP GUN

Daly-pattern Anson & Deeley system boxlock action. Six locking bolts. Auto ejector. 12 ga. only. Bbls.: 30-, 32-, 34-inch, vent-rib. Weight: 7.5 to 8.25 lbs. Checkered pistol-grip stock and forend. The two models made Empire and Regent Diamond differ in general quality, grade of wood, checkering, engraving, etc., otherwise specifications are the same. Disc. about 1933.

SHOTGUNS

Charles Daly Over/Under
Field Grade (Postwar)

Charles Daly
Field Semiauto

Charles Daly Field III
Over/Under

Charles Daly Over/Under
Presentation Grade

**Regent Diamond
  quality (Linder)** . . . . NiB $2788 Ex $2188 Gd $1886
Empire quality (Linder) . . . . NiB $5300 Ex $4260 Gd $3143
**Regent Diamond quality
  (Sauer)** . . . . NiB $3921 Ex $3288 Gd $2876
Empire quality (Sauer) . . . . NiB $2966 Ex $2377 Gd $1677

SINGLE-SHOT TRAP GUN
Daly-pattern Anson & Deeley system boxlock action. Auto ejector. 12 ga. only. Bbls.: 30-, 32-, 34-inch, vent rib. Weight: 7.5 to 8.25 lbs. Checkered pistol-grip stock and forend. This model was made in Empire Quality only. Disc. about 1933.
Empire grade (Linder) . . . . . NiB $4765 Ex $3966 Gd $2960
Empire grade (Sauer) . . . . . NiB $2477 Ex $2099 Gd $1776

SUPERIOR GRADE
SINGLE-SHOT TRAP . . . . NiB $954 Ex $833 Gd $700
Boxlock. Automatic ejector. 12 ga. only. 32- or 34-inch vent-rib bbl., F choke. Weight: About 8 lbs. Monte Carlo stock w/ pistol grip and recoil pad, beavertail forearm, checkered. Made 1968 to 1976.

DIAMOND GRADE O/U
Boxlock. Single selective trigger. Selective automatic ejectors. Gauges: 12 and 20, 3-inch chambers (2.75 target grade). Bbls.: 26, 27- or 30-inch w/fixed chokes or screw-in tubes. Weight: 7 lbs. Checkered European walnut stock and forearm w/oil finish. Engraved antique silver receiver and blued bbls. Made from 1984 to 1990.

Standard model . . . . NiB $1088 Ex $900 Gd $670
Skeet model . . . . NiB $1155 Ex $966 Gd $733
Trap model . . . . NiB $1155 Ex $966 Gd $733

DIAMOND GTX DL HUNTER O/U SERIES
Sidelock. Single selective trigger and selective auto ejectors. Gauges: 12, 20, 28 ga. or .410 bore. 26-, 28- and 30-inch bbls w/3-inch chambers (2.75-inch 28 ga.). Choke tubes (12 and 20 ga.), Fixed chokes (28 and 410). Weight: 5-8 lbs. Checkered European walnut stock w/hand-rubbed oil finish and recoil pad. Made from 1997 to 2001.
Diamond GTX DL Hunter. . . NiB $11,977 Ex $9478 Gd $5800
**Diamond GTX EDL
  Hunter** . . . . NiB $13,778 Ex $10,771 Gd $8987
**Diamond GTX Sporting
  (12 or 20 ga.)** . . . . NiB $5921 Ex $4771 Gd $3380
**Diamond GTX Skeet
  (12 or 20 ga.)** . . . . NiB $5540 Ex $4380 Gd $3100
**Diamond GTX Trap
  (12 ga. only)** . . . . NiB $6144 Ex $4766 Gd $3200

EMPIRE DL HUNTER O/U . . NiB $1456 Ex $1277 Gd $956
Boxlock. Ejectors. Single selective trigger. Gauges:12, 20, 28 ga. and .410 bore. 26- or 28- inch bbls. w/3-inch chambers (2.75-inch 28 ga.). Choke tubes (12 and 20 ga.), Fixed chokes (28 and .410). Engraved coin-silver receiver w/game scene. Imported from 1997 to 1998.

EMPIRE EDL HUNTER SERIES
Similar to Empire DL Hunter except engraved sideplates. Made 1998 to date.

Hunter model . . . . NiB $1477 Ex $1133 Gd $890
Sporting model . . . . NiB $1371 Ex $1108 Gd $870
Skeet model . . . . NiB $1388 Ex $1170 Gd $880
Trap model . . . . NiB $1366 Ex $1109 Gd $853
28 ga., add $110
.410 ga, add $150
Multi-chokes w/Monte
  Carlo stock, add $175

DSS HAMMERLESS DOUBLE . . NiB $885 Ex $744 Gd $561
Boxlock. Single selective trigger. Selective automatic ejectors. Gauges: 12 and 20; 3-inch chambers. 26-inch bbls. w/
screw-in choke tubes. Weight: 6.75 lbs. Checkered walnut
pistol-grip stock and semi-beavertail forearm w/recoil pad.
Engraved antique silver receiver and blued bbls. Made from
1990. Disc.

FIELD GRADE O/U . . . . NiB $675 Ex $570 Gd $449
Boxlock. Single selective trigger. Extractors. Gauges: 12 and 20;
3-inch chambers. Bbls.: 26-inch, IC/M; 28-inch, M/F. Weight:
6.75 lbs. (12 ga.). Checkered walnut stock and forearm w/
semi-gloss finish and recoil pad. Engraved color-casehardened
receiver and blued bbls. Made from 1989. Disc.

FIELD SEMIAUTO SHOTGUN . NiB $622 Ex $476 Gd $377
Recoil-operated. Takedown. 12-ga. and 12-ga. Magnum. Bbls.:
27- and 30-inch; vent rib. Made from 1982 to 1988.

FIELD III O/U SHOTGUN . . . . NiB $679 Ex $580 Gd $445
Boxlock. Plain extractors. Non-selective single trigger. Gauges:
12 or 20. Bbls.: vent rib; 26- and 28-inch; IC/M, M/F. Weight: 6
to 7.75 lbs. depending on ga. and bbls. Chrome-molybdenum
steel bbls. Checkered pistol-grip stock and forearm. Made from
1982. Disc.

LUXIE O/U . . . . NiB $900 Ex $733 Gd $529
Similar to the Field Grade except w/selective automatic ejectors and choke tubes. Gauges: 12, 20, 28 and .410. Receiver
w/antique silver finish and blued bbls. Made from 1989 to
1994.

MULTI-XII SELF-LOADING
SHOTGUN . . . . NiB $656 Ex $490 Gd $387
Similar to the gas-operated field semiauto except w/new Multi-
Action gas system designed to shoot all loads w/o adjustment.
12 ga. w/3-inch chamber. 27-inch bbl. w/Invector choke tubes,
vent rib. Made in Japan from 1987 to 1988.

PRESENTATION GRADE O/U . . . NiB $1254 Ex $1009 Gd $770
Purdey boxlock w/double cross-bolt. Gauges: 12 or 20.
Engraved receiver w/single selective trigger and auto-ejectors.
27-inch chrome-molybdenum steel, rectified, honed and
internally chromed, vent-rib bbls. Hand-checkered deluxe
European walnut stock. Made from 1982 to 1986.

SUPERIOR II SHOTGUN O/U . . . NiB $1064 Ex $880 Gd $602
Boxlock. Plain extractors. Non-selective single trigger. Gauges:
12 or 20. Bbls.: chrome-molybdenum vent rib 26-, 28-,
30-inch, latter in magnum only, assorted chokes. Silver
engraved receiver. Checkered pistol-grip stock and forearm.
Made from 1982 to 1988

SPORTING CLAYS O/U . . . . . . NiB $833 Ex $644 Gd $535
Similar to the Field Grade except in 12 ga. only w/ported bbls.
and internal choke tubes. Made from 1990 to 1996.

CHIAPPA FIREARMS LTD., — DAYTON, OH

*Chiappa owns ARMI SPORT REPLICA FIREARMS MFG. and
manufactures Cimarron, Legacy Sports, Taylor's & Co. Imported
currently, manufactured in Italy.*

MODEL 1887 . . . . NiB $1363 Ex $1295 Gd $400
Lever action. Gauge: 12 ga., 18.5, 22, 24 or 28-inch bbl.,
choke tubes. Color-casehardened or chrome receiver. Weight:
6.6 lbs. Stock:
oil finished smooth walnut. Made from 2009 to date.

DAKOTA ARMS, INC. — Sturgis, South Dakota

CLASSIC FIELD GRADE
S/S SHOTGUN . . . . NiB $7566 Ex $6548 Gd $4456
Boxlock. Gauge: 20 ga. 27-inch bbl. w/fixed chokes. Double
triggers. Selective ejectors. Color-casehardened receiver.
Weight: 6 lbs. Checkered English walnut stock and splinter
forearm w/hand-rubbed oil finish. Made from 1996 to 1998.

PREMIER GRADE
S/S SHOTGUN . . . . NiB $14,765 Ex $11,466 Gd $9224
Similar to Classic Field Grade model except w/50% engraving
coverage. Exhibition grade English walnut stock. Made from
1996 to date.

AMERICAN LEGEND
S/S SHOTGUN . . . . . NiB $16,750 Ex $15,000 Gd $11,550
Limited edition built to customer's specifications. Gauge: 20
ga. 27-inch bbl. Double triggers. Selective ejectors. Fully
engraved, coin-silver finished receiver w/gold inlays. Weight:
6 lbs. Hand checkered special-selection English walnut stock
and forearm. Made from 1996 to 2005.

DARNE S.A. — Saint-Etienne, France

HAMMERLESS DOUBLE-BARREL SHOTGUNS
Sliding-breech action w/fixed bbls. Auto ejectors. Double triggers. Gauges: 12, 16, 20, 28; also 12 and 20 Magnum w/3-inch
chambers. Bbls.: 27.5-inch standard, 25.5- to 31.5-inch lengths
available; any standard choke combination. Weight: 5.5 to 7 lbs.
depending on ga. and bbl. length. Checkered straight-grip or
pistol-grip stock and forearm. The various models differ in grade
of engraving and wood. Manufactured from 1881 to 1979.
Model R11 (Bird Hunter) . . NiB $7044 Ex $4698 Gd $2677
Model R15 (Pheasant
  Hunter) . . . . NiB $14,900 Ex $12,785 Gd $10,000
Model R16 (Magnum) . . . . . NiB $3775 Ex $2730 Gd $2167
Model V19 (Quail
  Hunter) . . . . NiB $22,000 Ex $17,500 Gd $14,275
Model V22 . . . . NiB $31,000 Ex $26,800 Gd $22,975
Model V Hors Série No. 1 . . . . NiB $77,000 Ex $58,650 Gd $46,790

DAVIDSON GUNS — Manufactured by Fabrica de Armas ILJA, Eibar, Spain; distributed by Davidson Firearms Co., Greensboro, North Carolina

MODEL 63B DOUBLE-BARREL
SHOTGUN . . . . NiB $433 Ex $279 Gd $200
Anson & Deeley boxlock action. Frame engraved and nickel

Davidson Model 63B
Double-Barrel Shotgun

plated. Plain extractors. Auto safety. Double triggers. Gauges: 12, 16, 20, 28, .410. Bbl. lengths: 25 (.410 only), 26, 28, 30 inches (latter 12 ga. only). Chokes: IC/ M, M/F, F/F. Weight: 5 lbs., 11 oz. (.410) to 7 lbs. (12 ga.). Checkered pistol-grip stock and forearm of European walnut. Made in 1963. Disc.

MODEL 63B MAGNUM
Similar to standard Model 63B except chambered for 10 ga. 3.5-inch, 12 and 20 ga. 3-inch Magnum shells; 10 ga. has 32-inch bbls., choked F/F. Weight: 10 lb., 10 oz. Made from 1963. Disc.

12-and 20 ga. magnum	NiB $455	Ex $300	Gd $210
10 ga. magnum	NiB $477	Ex $369	Gd $230

MODEL 69SL DOUBLE-BARREL
SHOTGUN . . . . NiB $455 Ex $400 Gd $270
Sidelock action w/detachable sideplates, engraved and nickel plated. Plain extractors. Auto safety. Double triggers. 12 and 20 ga. Bbls.: 26-inch IC/M, 28-inch M/F. Weight: 12 ga., 7 lbs., 20 ga., 6.5 lbs. Pistol-grip stock and forearm of European walnut, checkered. Made from 1963 to 1976.

MODEL 73 STAGECOACH
HAMMER DOUBLE . . . . NiB $331 Ex $229 Gd $130
Sidelock action w/detachable sideplates and exposed hammers. Plain extractors. Double triggers. Gauges: 12, 20, 3-inch chambers. 20-inch bbls, M/F chokes. Weight: 7 lbs., 12 ga.; 6.5 lbs., 20 ga. Checkered pistol-grip stock and forearm. Made from 1976. Disc.

DIAMOND SHOTGUNS
Currently imported by ADCO Sales, Inc, Woburn, MA. Company established circa 1981, all guns manufactured in Turkey.

GOLD SERIES
(SEMIAUTOMATIC) . . . . NiB $354 Ex $280 Gd $175
12 gauge, 3-inch chamber. Gas operated. Bbl. 24 (slug) or 28 inches. Ventilated rib with three choke tubes. Semi-humpback design, anodized alloy frame, gold etching. Rotary bolt. Black synthetic or checkered Turkish walnut forearm and stock with recoil pad. Value $50 less for slug version.

IMPERIAL SERIES . . . . NiB $475 Ex $345 Gd $265
Gauge: 12 (3.5-inch) or 20 (3-inch). Bbl.: 24 (12 ga. slug), 26 (20 ga.) or 28 inches; vent. rib, rotary bi-lateral bolt, deluxe checkered stock and forearm. Imported 2003.

ELITE SERIES . . . . NiB $445 Ex $323 Gd $200
Gauge: 12, 3-inch. Bbl.: 22 (slug), 24, 26 or 28 inches; ventilated rib, deluxe checkered walnut stock and forearm. Imported 2001. Deduct $50 for slug model.

PANTHER SERIES . . . . NiB $415 Ex $338 Gd $200
Gauge: 12, 3-inch. Gas-operated. Black synthetic stock and forearm. Bbl.: 20 (slug or regular) or 28 inches. Imported 2002.
Walnut stock and forearm, add $75
Slug version . . . . deduct $50

MARINER . . . . NiB $338 Ex $198 Gd $110
Gauge: 12, 3-inch. Gas operated. Bbl.: 20 (slug) or 22 inches. Vent. rib. Anodized alloy frame and receiver, satin silver finish. Checkered walnut stock and forearm. Imported 2002.
Slug model, deduct $50

GOLD ELITE SERIES
(SLIDE-ACTION) . . . . NiB $354 Ex $260 Gd $200
12 gauge, 3-inch chamber. Bbl. 24 (slug with open sights), or 28 inches; ventilated rib. Semi-humpback design. Anodized alloy frame, synthetic black or Turkish walnut stock and forearm. Weight: 7 lbs. Imported 2001. Value $40 less for synthetic stock.

EXCEL ARMS OF AMERICA — Gardner, Massachusetts

SERIES 100 O/U SHOTGUN
Gauge: 12. Single selective trigger. Selective auto ejectors. Hand-checkered European walnut stock w/full pistol grip, tulip forend. Black metal finish. Chambered for 2.75-inch shells (Model 103 for 3-inch). Weight: 6. 88 to 7.88 lbs. Disc 1988.

Model 101 w/26-inch bbl., IC/M	NiB $465	Ex $367	Gd $266
Model 102 w/28-inch bbl., IC/M	NiB $465	Ex $367	Gd $266
Model 103 w/30-inch bbl., M/F	NiB $465	Ex $367	Gd $266
Model 104 w/28-inch bbl., IC/M	NiB $465	Ex $367	Gd $266
Model 105, w/28-inch bbl., 5 choke tubes	NiB $645	Ex $480	Gd $387
Model 106, w/28-inch bbl., 5 choke tubes	NiB $776	Ex $689	Gd $558
Model 107 Trap, w/30-inch bbl., Full or 5 tubes	NiB $776	Ex $689	Gd $558

SERIES 200 SIDE-BY-SIDE
SHOTGUN . . . . NiB $667 Ex $496 Gd $368
Gauges: 12, 20, 28 and .410. Bbls.: 26-, 27- and 28-inch; various choke combinations. Weight: 7 lbs. average. American or European-style stock and forend. Made from 1985 to 1987.

SERIES 300 O/U
SHOTGUN . . . . NiB $1328 Ex $1133 Gd $1033
Gauge: 12. Bbls.: 26-, 28- and 29-inch. Non-glare black-chrome matte finish. Weight: 7 lbs. average. Selective auto ejectors, engraved receiver. Hand-checkered European walnut stock and forend. Made from 1985 to 1986.

Fox Model B

FABARM — Brescia, Italy

Currently imported by Heckler & Koch, Inc., of Sterling, VA (previously by Ithaca Acquisition Corp., St. Lawrence Sales, Inc. and Beeman Precision Arms, Inc.)

See Current listings under "Heckler & Koch."

FIAS — Fabrica Italiana Armi Sabatti Gardone Val Trompia, Italy

GRADE I O/U
Boxlock. Single selective trigger. Gauges: 12, 20, 28, .410; 3-inch chambers. Bbls.: 26-inch IC/M; 28-inch M/F; screw-in choke tubes. Weight: 6.5 to 7.5 lbs. Checkered European walnut stock and forearm. Engraved receiver and blued finish.

12 ga. model	NiB $587	Ex $480	Gd $355
20 ga. model	NiB $633	Ex $512	Gd $367
28 ga. and .410	NiB $800	Ex $665	Gd $457

FOX — Made by A. H. Fox Gun Co., Philadelphia, Pennsylvania, 1903 to 1930, and since then by Savage Arms, originally of Utica, New York, now of Westfield, Massachusetts. In 1993, Connecticut Manufacturing Co. of New Britain, Connecticut reintroduced selected models.

Values shown are for 12 and 16 ga. doubles made by A. H. Fox. Twenty gauge guns often are valued up to 75% higher. Savage-made Fox models generally bring prices 25% lower. With the exception of Model B, production of Fox shotguns was discontinued about 1942.

MODEL B HAMMERLESS
DOUBLE . . . . NiB $523 Ex $387 Gd $244
Boxlock. Double triggers. Plain extractor. Gauges: 12, 16, 20, .410. 24- to 30-inch bbls., vent rib on current production; chokes: M/F, C/M, F/F (.410 only). Weight: About 7.5 lbs., 12 ga. Checkered pistol-grip stock and forend. Made about 1940 to 1985.

MODEL B-ST . . . . NiB $644 Ex $475 Gd $350
Same as Model B except has non-selective single trigger. Made from 1955-66.

MODEL B-DE . . . . NiB $645 Ex $476 Gd $351
Same as Model B-ST except frame finished in satin chrome, select walnut buttstock w/checkered pistol grip and beavertail forearm. Made from 1965 to 1966.

MODEL B-DL . . . . NiB $678 Ex $558 Gd $421
Same as Model B-ST except frame finished in satin chrome, select walnut buttstock w/checkered pistol grip side panels, beavertail forearm. Made from 1962 to 1966.

MODEL B-SE . . . . NiB $922 Ex $700 Gd $531
Same as Model B except has selective ejectors and single trigger. Made from 1966 to 1989.

HAMMERLESS DOUBLE-BARREL SHOTGUNS
The higher grades have the same general specifications as the standard Sterlingworth model, w/differences chiefly in workmanship and materials. Higher grade models are stocked in fine select walnut; quantity and quality of engraving increases w/grade and price. Except for Grade A, all other grades have auto ejectors.

Grade A	NiB $3160	Ex $1641	Gd $1895
Grade AE	NiB $3598	Ex $2977	Gd $2110
Grade BE	NiB $4962	Ex $3988	Gd $2860
Grade CE	NiB $6200	Ex $5110	Gd $3628
Grade DE	NiB $12,779	Ex $11,360	Gd $10,475
Grade FE	NiB $22,679	Ex $18,960	Gd $13,000
Grade XE	NiB $8634	Ex $7321	Gd $4208
w/Kautzy selective single trigger, add			$400
w/vent. rib, add			$500
w/beavertail forearm, add			$300
20 ga. model, add			60%

SINGLE-BARREL TRAP GUNS
Boxlock. Auto ejector.12 ga. only. 30- or 32-inch vent-rib bbl. Weight: 7.5 to 8 lbs. Trap-style stock and forearm of select walnut, checkered, recoil pad optional. The four grades differ chiefly in quality of wood and engraving; Grade M guns, built to order, have finest Circassian walnut. Stock and receiver are elaborately engraved and inlaid w/gold. Disc. 1942. Note: In 1932, the Fox Trap Gun was redesigned and those manufactured after that date have a stock w/full pistol grip and Monte Carlo comb; at the same time frame was changed to permit the rib line to extend across it to the rear.

Grade JE	NiB $3990	Ex $2367	Gd $2031
Grade KE	NiB $5366	Ex $4979	Gd $4000
Grade LE	NiB $6778	Ex $4789	Gd $3760
Grade ME	NiB $15,975	Ex $12,880	Gd $9355

"SKEETER" DOUBLE-BARREL
SHOTGUN . . . . NiB $4990 Ex $4078 Gd $2855
Boxlock. Gauge: 12 or 20. Bbls.: 28 inches w/full-length vent rib. Weight: Approx. 7 lbs. Buttstock and beavertail forend of select American walnut, finely checkered. Soft rubber recoil pad and ivory bead sights. Made in early 1930s.

STERLINGWORTH DELUXE
Same general specifications as Sterlingworth except 32-inch bbl. also available, recoil pad, ivory bead sights.

w/extractors	NiB $2187	Ex $1654	Gd $1100
w/ejectors	NiB $2370	Ex $1979	Gd $1466
20 ga., add			$45%

SHOTGUNS

Franchi Model 500
Standard Autoloader

Franchi Model 520 Deluxe

Franchi Model 520
Eldorado Gold

Franchi 612 Variopress Advantage

Franchi 612 Variopress Sporting

Franchi 612 Variopress

Franchi 620 Variopress Advantage

Franchi 620 Variopress

**Franchi Model 2004
Trap Single Barrel**

STERLINGWORTH HAMMERLESS DOUBLE
Boxlock. Double triggers (Fox-Kautzky selective single trigger extra). Plain extractors (auto ejectors extra). Gauges: 12,16, 20. Bbl. lengths: 26-, 28-, 30-inch; chokes F/F, M/F, C/M (any combination of C to F choke borings was available at no extra cost). Weight: 12 ga., 6.88 to 8.25 lbs.; 16 ga., 6 to 7 lbs.; 20 ga., 5.75 to 6.75 lbs. Checkered pistol-grip stock and forearm.

w/extractors . . . . NiB $1800 Ex $1489 Gd $1000
w/ejectors . . . . NiB $2170 Ex $1770 Gd $1254
w/selective single trigger, add 25%

STERLINGWORTH SKEET AND UPLAND GUN
Same general specifications as the standard Sterlingworth except has 26- or 28-inch bbls. w/skeet boring only, straight-grip stock. Weight: 7 lbs. (12 ga.).

w/extractors . . . . NiB $2588 Ex $2066 Gd $1489
w/ejectors . . . . NiB $3000 Ex $2469 Gd $1785
20 ga., add 45%

SUPER HE GRADE . . . . NiB $5863 Ex $4791 Gd $3310
Long-range gun made in 12 ga. only (chambered for 3-inch shells on order), 30- or 32-inch full choke bbls., auto ejectors standard. Weight: 8.75 to 9.75 lbs. General specifications same as standard Sterlingworth.

CMC HAMMERLESS DOUBLE-BARREL SHOTGUNS
High-grade doubles similar to the original Fox models. 20 ga. only. 26- 28- or 30-inch bbls. Double triggers automatic safety and ejectors. Weight: 5.5 to 7 lbs. Custom Circassian walnut stock w/hand-rubbed oil finish. Custom stock configuration: straight, semi- or full pistol-grip stock w/traditional pad, hard rubber plate checkered or skeleton butt; Schnabel, splinter or beavertail forend. Made 1993 to date.

CE grade . . . . NiB $9221 Ex $6855 Gd $4900
XE grade . . . . NiB $9066 Ex $7221 Gd $5054
DE grade . . . . NiB $13,788 Ex $11,650 Gd $7900
FE grade . . . . NiB $18,977 Ex $15,220 Gd $11,760
Exhibition grade . . . . NiB $27,480 Ex $22,760 Gd $14,990

LUIGI FRANCHI S.P.A. — Brescia, Italy

MODEL 48/AL ULTRA LIGHT SHOTGUN
Recoil-operated, takedown, hammerless shotgun w/tubular magazine. Gauges: 12 or 20 (2.75-inch); 12-ga. Magnum (3-inch chamber). Bbls.: 24- to 32-inch w/various choke combinations. Weight: 5 lbs., 2 oz. (20 ga.) to 6.25 lbs. (12 ga.). Checkered pistol-grip walnut stock and forend w/high-gloss finish.

Standard model. . . . . NiB $779 Ex $554 Gd $430
Hunter or magnum models . . . NiB $977 Ex $580 Gd $476

MODEL 500 STANDARD
AUTOLOADER . . . . NiB $400 Ex $288 Gd $190
Gas-operated. 12 gauge. Four round magazine. Bbls.: 26-, 28-inch; vent rib; IC, M, IM, F chokes. Weight: About 7 lbs. Checkered pistol-grip stock and forearm. Made from 1976 to 1980.

MODEL 520 DELUXE . . . . NiB $478 Ex $355 Gd $279
Same as Model 500 except higher grade w/engraved receiver. Made from 1975 to 1979.

MODEL 520 ELDORADO
GOLD . . . . NiB $1088 Ex $877 Gd $743
Same as Model 520 except custom grade w/engraved and gold-inlaid receiver, finer quality wood. Intro. 1977.

MODEL 610VS SEMIAUTOMATIC SHOTGUN
Gas-operated Variopress system adjustable to function w/2.75- or 3- inch shells. 12 gauge. Four round magazine. 26- or 28-inch vent rib bbls. w/Franchoke tubes. Weight: 7 lbs., 2 oz. 47.5 inches overall. Alloy receiver w/four-lug rotating bolt and loaded chamber indicator. Checkered European walnut butt-stock and forearm w/satin finish. Imported from 1997.

Standard model. . . . . NiB $766 Ex $600 Gd $445
Engraved model . . . . NiB $800 Ex $655 Gd $500

MODEL 612 VARIOPRESS AUTOLOADING SHOTGUN
Gauge: 12 ga. Only. 24- to 28-inch bbl. 45 to 49-inches over-all. Weight: 6.8 to 7 lbs. Five round magazine. Bead type sights with C, IC, M chokes. Blued, matte or Advantage camo finish. Imported from 1999 to 2004.

w/satin walnut stock,
   blued finish. . . . . NiB $645 Ex $559 Gd $369
w/synthetic stock, matte finish NiB $665 Ex $590 Gd $400
w/Advantage camo finish . . . . . NiB $800 Ex $645 Gd $449
Defense model . . . . NiB $600 Ex $469 Gd $360
Sporting model . . . . NiB $966 Ex $733 Gd $544

MODEL 620 VARIOPRESS AUTOLOADING SHOTGUN
Gauge: 20 ga. Only. 24- 26- or 28-inch bbl. 45 to 49-inches overall. Weight: 5.9 to 6.1 lbs. Five round magazine. Bead type sights with C, IC, M chokes. Satin walnut or Advantage camo stock. Imported from 1999 to 2004.

w/satin walnut stock, matte finish. . . NiB $655 Ex $498 Gd $367
w/Advantage camo finish . . . . . NiB $790 Ex $554 Gd $421
Youth model w/short stock . . . . NiB $615 Ex $490 Gd $379

MODEL 2003 TRAP O/U . . NiB $1355 Ex $1109 Gd $1005
Boxlock. Auto ejectors. Selective single trigger. 12 ga. Bbls.: 30-, 32-inch IM/F, F/F, high-vent rib. Weight (w/30-inch bbl.): 8.25 lbs. Checkered walnut beavertail forearm and stock w/ straight or Monte Carlo comb, recoil pad. Luggage-type carrying case. Introduced 1976. Disc.

MODEL 2004 TRAP SINGLE
BARREL TRAP . . . . NiB $1366 Ex $1288 Gd $915
Same as Model 2003 except single bbl., 32- or 34-inch. Full choke. Weight (w/32-inch bbl.): 8.25 lbs. Introduced 1976. Disc.

MODEL 2005 COMBINATION
TRAP. . . . . NiB $1977 Ex $1760 Gd $1233
Model 2004/2005 type gun w/two sets of bbls., single and over/under. Introduced 1976. Disc.

MODEL 2005/3 COMBINATION
TRAP. . . . . NiB $2660 Ex $2175 Gd $1648
Model 2004/2005 type gun w/three sets of bbls., any combination of single and over/under. Introduced 1976. Disc.

SHOTGUNS

Franchi Astore 5

MODEL 3000/2 COMBINATION

TRAP . . . . NiB $2876 Ex $2599 Gd $1879
Boxlock. Automatic ejectors. Selective single trigger. 12 ga. only. Bbls.: 32-inch over/under choked F/IM, 34-inch under-barrel M choke; high vent rib. Weight (w/32-inch bbls.): 8 lbs., 6 oz. Choice of six different castoff buttstocks. Introduced 1979. Disc.

ALCIONE HAMMERLESS

DOUBLE . . . . NiB $763 Ex $633 Gd $544
Boxlock. Anson & Deeley system action. Auto ejectors. Double triggers. 12 ga. Various bbl. lengths, chokes, weights. Checkered straight-grip stock and forearm. Made from 1940-50.

ALCIONE O/U SHOTGUN

Hammerless, takedown shotgun w/engraved receiver. Selective single trigger and ejectors. 12 ga. w/3-inch chambers. Bbls.: 26-inch (IC/M, 28-inch (M/F). Weight: 6.75 lbs. Checkered French walnut buttstock and forend. Imported from Italy. 1982 to 1989.
Standard model . . . . NiB $755 Ex $648 Gd $479
SL model (disc. 1986) . . . . . . NiB $1290 Ex $1077 Gd $800

ALCIONE CLASSIC . . . . NiB $763 Ex $633 Gd $544

O/U. Boxlock. Auto ejectors. Single select trigger. 12 ga. only. 26- or 28-in. bbl. lengths, choke tubes, 7.5 lbs. blue non-engraved receiver. Checkered stock and forearm. Made from 2004-2005.

ALCIONE FIELD (97-12 IBS) O/U

Similar to the Standard Alcione model except w/nickel-finished receiver. 26- or 28-inch bbls. w/Franchoke tubes. Imported from 1998 to 2005.
Standard Field model . . . . . . NiB $1263 Ex $1009 Gd $700
SL Field model (w/sideplates, disc.) . . . . NiB $1296 Ex $1007 Gd $865

ALCIONE SPORT

(SL IBS) O/U . . . . NiB $1567 Ex $1380 Gd $1134
Similar to the Alcione Field model except chambered for 2.75 or 3-inch shells. Ported 29-inch bbls. w/target vent rib and Franchoke tubes.

ALCIONE SX O/U . . . . NiB $1540 Ex $1060 Gd $700
Removable engraved sideplates. 12 ga. only. 26- or 28-in. vent rib bbls. w/ choke tubes. Weight: 7.4 lbs. Imported from 2001 to 2005.

ALCIONE TITANIUM O/U . . NiB $1540 Ex $1060 Gd $700
Aluminum alloy receiver w/ titanium inserts. Removable side-plates. 12 or 20 ga. 26- or 28-in. vent rib bbls. w/ choke tubes. Weight: 6.8 lbs. Imported from 2002 to 2005.

ALCIONE 2000 SX O/U

SHOTGUN . . . . NiB $1790 Ex $1388 Gd $1100
Similar to the Standard Alcione model except w/silver finished receiver and gold inlays. 28-inch bbls. w/Franchoke tubes. Weight: 7.25 lbs. Imported from 1996 to 1997.

ARISTOCRAT FIELD

MODEL O/U . . . . NiB $754 Ex $600 Gd $434
Boxlock. Selective auto ejectors. Selective single trigger. 12 ga. Bbls.: 26-inch IC/M; 28- and 30-inch M/F choke, vent rib. Weight (w/26-inch bbls.): 7 lbs. Checkered pistol-grip stock and forearm. Made from 1960 to 1969.

ARISTOCRAT DELUXE AND SUPREME GRADES

Available in Field, Skeet and Trap models w/the same general specifications as standard guns of these types. Deluxe and Supreme Grades are of higher quality, w/stock and forearm of select walnut, elaborate relief engraving on receiver, trigger guard, tang and top lever. Supreme game birds inlaid in gold. Made from 1960 to 1966.
Deluxe grade . . . . NiB $1077 Ex $844 Gd $657
Supreme grade . . . . NiB $1577 Ex $1340 Gd $1098

ARISTOCRAT IMPERIAL AND MONTE CARLO GRADES

Custom guns made in Field, Skeet and Trap models w/the same general specifications as standard for these types. Imperial and Monte Carlo grades are of highest quality w/stock and forearm of select walnut, fine engraving — elaborate on latter grade. Made 1967 to 1969.
Imperial grade . . . . NiB $4134 Ex $2570 Gd $2160
Monte Carlo grade . . . . NiB $3677 Ex $2920 Gd $2100

ARISTOCRAT MAGNUM

MODEL . . . . NiB $765 Ex $557 Gd $469
Same as Field Model except chambered for 3-inch shells, has 32-inch bbls. choked F/F; stock has recoil pad. Weight: About 8 lbs. Made from 1962 to 1965.

ARISTOCRAT SILVER KING . . . NiB $888 Ex $712 Gd $559
Available in Field, Magnum, Meet and Trap models w/the same general specifications as standard guns of these types. Silver King has stock and forearm of select walnut more elaborately engraved silver-finished receiver. Made 1962 to 1969.

ARISTOCRAT SKEET MODEL . . NiB $866 Ex $754 Gd $544
Same general specifications as Field Model except made only w/26-inch vent-rib bbls. w/SK chokes No. 1 and No. 2, skeet-style stock and forearm. Weight: About 7.5 lbs. Later production had wider (10mm) rib. Made from 1960 to 1969.

ARISTOCRAT TRAP MODEL . . . NiB $877 Ex $754 Gd $561
Same general specifications as Field Model except made only w/30-inch vent-rib bbls., M/F choke, trap-style stock w/recoil pad, beavertail forearm. Later production had Monte Carlo comb, 10mm rib. Made from 1960 to 1969.

ASTORE HAMMERLESS

DOUBLE . . . . NiB $1032 Ex $866 Gd $713
Boxlock. Anson & Deeley system action. Plain extractors. Double triggers. 12 ga. Various bbl. lengths, chokes, weights. Checkered straight-grip stock and forearm. Made 1937 to 1960.

ASTORE II . . . . NiB $1389 Ex $1166 Gd $876
Similar to Astore S but not as high grade. Furnished w/either plain extractors or auto ejectors, double triggers, pistol-grip stock. Bbls.: 27-inch IC/IM; 28-inch M/F chokes. Currently manufactured for Franchi in Spain.

Franchi Falconet Over/Under Buckskin

Franchi Crown Grade

Franchi Diamond Grade

Franchi Eldorado

ASTORE 5 . . . . **NiB $2458 Ex $1987 Gd $1466**
Same as Astore except has higher grade wood, fine engraving. automatic ejectors, single trigger, 28-inch bbl. M/F or IM/F chokes are standard on current production. Disc.

DE LUXE MODEL PRITI O/U . . **NiB $400 Ex $320 Gd $210**
Boxlock. 12 or 20 ga. only. 26- or 28-in. vent rib bbls. w/ choke tubes. Single trigger. Weight: 7.4 lbs. Imported from 1988 to 1989.

RENAISSANCE FIELD O/U . . **NiB $1430 Ex $1240 Gd $680**
Boxlock. Blued receiver. 12, 20 or 28 ga. 26- or 28-in. vent rib bbls. w/ choke tubes. Oil finish walnut stock w/ Twin Shock recoil pad. Weight: 5.5 to 6.2 lbs. Imported from 2006 to 2010.
Classic (gold trigger & inlays) . .**NiB $1560 Ex $1230 Gd $800**
Classic Combo (two bbl. set) . **NiB $2330 Ex $1700 Gd $1200**
Elite (engraved w/ gold inlays) . .**NiB $2000 Ex $1500 Gd $830**
Sporting (30-in. ported bbls.) . . .**NiB $1930 Ex $1460 Gd $830**

VELOCE O/U . . . . **NiB $1250 Ex $1000 Gd $740**
Aluminum engraved receiver w/ gold inlays. 20 or 28 ga. 26- or 28-in. vent rib bbls. w/ choke tubes. Pistol or straight deluxe oil finish stock. Weight: 5.5 to 5.8 lbs. Imported from 2001 to 2005.
Grade II (semi pistol grip) . . .**NiB $1760 Ex $1240 Gd $900**
Squire (two bbl. set) . . . . . .**NiB $2070 Ex $1500 Gd $910**

STANDARD MODEL AUTOLOADER
Recoil operated. Light alloy receiver. Gauges: 12, 20. Four round magazine. Bbls.: 26-, 28-, 30-inch; plain, solid or vent rib, IC/ M, F chokes. Weight: 12 ga., about 6.25 lbs. 20 ga., 5.13 lbs. Checkered pistol-grip stock and forearm. Made from 1950. Disc.
w/plain bbl. . . . . **NiB $490 Ex $335 Gd $260**
w/solid rib . . . . **NiB $550 Ex $512 Gd $339**
w/vent rib . . . . **NiB $560 Ex $489 Gd $368**

CROWN, DIAMOND AND IMPERIAL GRADE
Same general specifications as Standard Model except these are custom guns of the highest quality. Crown Grade has hunting scene engraving, Diamond Grade has silver-inlaid scroll engraving; Imperial Grade has elaborately engraved hunting scenes w/figures inlaid in gold. Stock and forearm of fancy walnut. Made from 1954 to 1975.
Crown grade . . . . **NiB $1670 Ex $1496 Gd $1212**
Diamond grade . . . . **NiB $2044 Ex $1760 Gd $1233**
Imperial grade . . . . **NiB $2480 Ex $2239 Gd $1799**

STANDARD MODEL MAGNUM
Same general specifications as Standard model except has 3-inch chamber, 32-inch (12 ga.) or 28-inch (20 ga.) F choke bbl., recoil pad. Weight: 12 ga., 8.25 lbs.; 20 ga., 6 lbs. Formerly designated "Superange Model." Made from 1954 to 1988.
w/plain bbl. . . . . **NiB $500 Ex $412 Gd $286**
w/vent rib . . . . **NiB $577 Ex $468 Gd $360**

DYNAMIC-12
Same general specifications and appearance as Standard Model, except 12 ga. only, has heavier steel receiver. Weight: About 7.25 lbs. Made from 1965 to 1972.
W/plain bbl. . . . . **NiB $522 Ex $430 Gd $331**
W/vent rib . . . . **NiB $550 Ex $433 Gd $330**

DYNAMIC-12 SLUG GUN . . . . **NiB $578 Ex $490 Gd $354**
Same as standard gun except 12 ga. only, has heavier steel receiver. Made 1965 to 1972.

DYNAMIC-12 SKEET GUN . . . . **NiB $677 Ex $549 Gd $456**
Same general specifications and appearance as Standard model except has heavier steel receiver, made only in 12 ga. w/26-inch vent-rib bbl., SK choke, stock and forearm of extra fancy walnut. Made from 1965 to 1972.

ELDORADO MODEL . . . . **NiB $588 Ex $370 Gd $355**
Same general specifications as Standard model except highest grade w/gold-filled engraving, stock and forearm of select walnut, vent-rib bbl. only. Made from 1954 to 1975.

FALCONET INTERNATIONAL
SKEET MODEL . . . . **NiB $1163 Ex $977 Gd $800**
Similar to Standard Skeet model but higher grade. Made 1970 to 1974.

FALCONET INTERNATIONAL
TRAP MODEL . . . . **NiB $1165 Ex $980 Gd $803**
Similar to Standard model but higher grade; w/straight or Monte Carlo comb stock. Made from 1970 to 1974.

SHOTGUNS

Franchi Hunter Model
w/Ventilated Rib

Franchi Black Magic
48/AL Semiautomatic

Franchi LAW-12

Franchi SPAS-12

Franchi Sporting 2000

FALCONET O/U FIELD MODELS
Boxlock. Auto ejectors. Selective single trigger. Gauges: 12, 16, 20, 28, .410. Bbls.: 24-, 26-, 28-, 30-inch; vent rib. Chokes: C/IC, IC/M, M/F. Weight: from about 6 lbs. Engraved lightweight alloy receiver, light-colored in Buckskin model, blued in Ebony model, pickled silver in Silver model. Checkered walnut stock and forearm. Made from 1968 to 1975.
Buckskin or Ebony model .... NiB $655 Ex $460 Gd $449
Silver model .... NiB $655 Ex $460 Gd $449

FALCONET STANDARD SKEET
MODEL .... NiB $1055 Ex $876 Gd $690
Same general specifications as Field models except made only w/26-inch bbls. w/SK chokes No. 1 and No. 2, wide vent rib, color-casehardened receiver skeet-style stock and forearm. Weight: 12 ga., about 7.75 lbs. Made from 1970 to 1974.

FALCONET STANDARD
TRAP MODEL .... NiB $1366 Ex $965 Gd $744
Same general specifications as Field models except made only in 12 ga. w/30-inch bbls., choked M/F, wide vent rib, color-casehardened receiver, Monte Carlo trap style stock and forearm, recoil pad. Weight: About 8 lbs. Made from 1970 to 1974.

GAS-OPERATED SEMIAUTOMATIC SHOTGUN
Gas-operated, takedown, hammerless shotgun w/tubular magazine. 12 ga. w/2.75-inch chamber. Five round magazine. Bbls.: 24 to 30 inches w/vent rib. Weight: 7.5 lbs. Gold-plated trigger. Checkered pistol-grip stock and forend of European walnut. Imported from Italy 1985 to 1990.
Prestige model .... NiB $677 Ex $456 Gd $449
Elite model .... NiB $688 Ex $571 Gd $388

HAMMERLESS SIDELOCK DOUBLES
Hand-detachable locks. Self-opening action. Auto ejectors. Double triggers or single trigger. Gauges: 12,16, 20. Bbl. lengths, chokes, weights according to customer's specifications. Checkered stock and forend, straight or pistol grip. Made in six grades — Condor, Imperiale, Imperiale S, Imperiale Montecarlo No. 5, Imperiale Montecarlo No.11, Imperiale Montecarlo Extra — which differ chiefly in overall quality, engraving, grade of wood, checkering, etc.; general specifications are the same. Only the Imperial Montecarlo Extra Grade is currently manufactured.
Condor grade .... NiB $7897 Ex $6200 Gd $4978
Imperial, Imperiales
   grades............. NiB $11,776 Ex $9899 Gd $7217
Imperial Monte Carlo grades
   No. 5, 11 .... NiB $32,766 Ex $25,777 Gd $21,989
Imperial Monte Carlo
   Extra grade .... Custom only. Prices start at $110,000

HUNTER MODEL
Same general specifications as Standard Model except higher grade w/engraved receiver; w/ribbed bbl. only. Made from 1950 to 1990.
w/solid rib . . . . NiB $500 Ex $390 Gd $322
w/vent rib . . . . NiB $616 Ex $488 Gd $400

HUNTER MODEL MAGNUM . . NiB $544 Ex $454 Gd $330
Same as Standard Model Magnum except higher grade w/ engraved receiver, vent rib bbl. only. Formerly designated "Wildfowler Model." Made from 1954 to 1973.

PEREGRINE MODEL 400 . . . . . NiB $733 Ex $544 Gd $400
Same general specifications as Model 451 except has steel receiver. Weight (w/26.5-inch bbl.): 6 lbs., 15 oz. Made from 1975 to 1978.

PEREGRINE MODEL 451 O/U . NiB $605 Ex $451 Gd $267
Boxlock. Lightweight alloy receiver. Automatic ejectors. Selective single trigger. 12 ga. Bbls.: 26.5-, 28-inch; choked C/IC, IC/M, M/F; vent rib. Weight (w/26.5-inch bbls.): 6 lbs., 1 oz. Checkered pistol-grip stock and forearm. Made from 1975 to 1978.

SKEET GUN . . . . NiB $450 Ex $320 Gd $228
Same general specifications and appearance as Standard Model except made only w/26-inch vent-rib bbl., SK choke. Stock and forearm of extra fancy walnut. Made from 1972 to 1974.

SLUG GUN . . . . NiB $435 Ex $288 Gd $190
Same as Standard Model except has 22-inch plain bbl., Cyl. bore, folding leaf open rear sight, gold bead front sight. Made 1960 to 1990. Disc.

TURKEY GUN . . . . NiB $556 Ex $377 Gd $298
Same as Standard Model Magnum except higher grade w/tur-key scene engraved receiver, 12 ga. only, 36-inch matted-rib bbl., Extra Full choke. Made from 1963 to 1965.

BLACK MAGIC 48/AL SEMIAUTOMATIC
Similar to the Franchi Model 48/AL except w/Franchoke screw-in tubes and matte black receiver w/Black Magic logo. Gauge: 12 or 20, 2.75-inch chamber. Bbls.: 24-, 26-, 28-inch w/vent rib; 24-inch rifled slug w/sights. Weight: 5.2 lbs. (20 ga.). Checkered walnut buttstock and forend. Blued finish.
Standard model. . . . . NiB $657 Ex $543 Gd $466
Trap model . . . . NiB $722 Ex $596 Gd $500

FALCONET 2000 O/U . . . . . NiB $1355 Ex $1121 Gd $967
Boxlock. Single selective trigger. Selective automatic ejectors. Gauge: 12, 2.75-inch chambers. Bbls.: 26-inch w/Franchoke tubes; IC/M/F. Weight: 6 lbs. Checkered walnut stock and forearm. Engraved silver receiver w/gold-plated game scene. Imported from 1992 to 1993.

LAW-12 SHOTGUN . . . . NiB $689 Ex $454 Gd $377
Similar to the SPAS-12 Model except gas-operated semiauto-matic
action only, ambidextrous safety, decocking lever and adj. sights. Made from 1983 to 1994.

SPAS-12 SHOTGUN
Selective operating system functions as a gas-operated semi-automatic or pump action. Gauge: 12, 2.75-inch chamber. Seven round magazine. Bbl.: 21.5 inches w/cylinder bore and muzzle protector or optional screw-in choke tubes, matte fin-ish. 41 inches overall w/fixed stock. Weight: 8.75 lbs. Blade front sight, aperture rear sight. Folding or black nylon buttstock w/pistol grip and forend, non-reflective anodized finish. Made from 1983 to 1994. Limited importation.
Fixed stock model . . . . . . NiB $5000 Ex $4500 Gd $2390
Folding stock model . . . . . . NiB $7000 Ex $6500 Gd $3390
w/choke tubes, add. $150

SPORTING 2000 O/U . . . . . NiB $1376 Ex $1125 Gd $966
Similar to the Franchi Falconet 2000. Boxlock. Single selec-tive trigger. Selective automatic ejectors. Gauge: 12; 2.75-inch chambers. Ported (1992-93) or unported 28-inch bbls., w/ vent rib. Weight: 7.75 lbs. Blued receiver. Bead front sight. Checkered walnut stock and forearm; plastic composition butt-plate. Imported from 1992-93 and 1997 to 1998.

AUGUSTE FRANCOTTE & CIE., S.A. — Liège, Belgium

Francotte shotguns for many years were distributed in the U.S. by Abercrombie & Fitch of New York City. This firm has used a series of model designations for Francotte guns which do not correspond to those of the manufacturer. Because so many Francotte owners refer to their guns by the A & F model names and numbers, the A & F series is included in a listing separate from that of the standard Francotte numbers.

BOXLOCK HAMMERLESS DOUBLES
Anson & Deeley system. Side clips. Greener crossbolt on mod-els 6886, 8446, 4996 and 9261; square crossbolt on Model 6930, Greener-Scott crossbolt on Model 8537, Purdey bolt on Models 11/18E and 10/18E/628. Auto ejectors. Double triggers. Made in all standard gauges, barrel lengths, chokes, weights. Checkered stock and forend, straight or pistol-grip. The eight models listed vary chiefly in fastenings as described above, finish and engraving, etc.; custom options increase value. Disc.
Model 6886 . . . . NiB $14,688 Ex $13,879 Gd $11,776
Model 8446 (Francotte Special),
  6930, 4996 . . . . . . NiB $15,889 Ex $14,799 Gd $14,776
Model 8537, 9261 (Francotte Original),
  11/18E . . . . NiB $17,345 Ex $16,221 Gd $14,998
Model 10/18E/628 . . NiB $17,998 Ex $16,789 Gd $15,900

Francotte Model 8446

Francotte Model 6886

SHOTGUNS

Francotte Model
10/18E628

Francotte Model 9261

Galef Silver Snipe Over/Under Shotgun

BOXLOCK HAMMERLESS DOUBLES – A & F SERIES
Boxlock, Anson & Deeley type. Crossbolt. Sideplate on all except Knockabout Model. Side clips. Auto ejectors. Double triggers. Gauges: 12, 16, 20, 28, .410. Bbls.: 26- to 32-inch in 12 ga., 26- and 28-inch in other ga.; any boring. Weight: 4.75 to 8 lbs. depending on gauge and barrel length. Checkered stock and forend; straight, half or full pistol grip. The seven grades (No. 45 Eagle Grade, No. 30, No. 25, No. 20, No. 14, Jubilee Model, Knockabout Model) differ chiefly in overall quality, engraving, grade of wood, checkering, etc.; general specifications are the same. Disc.

Jubilee model No. 14	NiB $4200	Ex $2633	Gd $1470
Jubilee model No. 18	NiB $4687	Ex $3577	Gd $1890
Jubilee model No. 20	NiB $5670	Ex $4122	Gd $2250
Jubilee model No. 25	NiB $6245	Ex $4738	Gd $2290
Jubilee model No. 30	NiB $7832	Ex $6110	Gd $3580
Eagle grade No. 45	NiB $11,100	Ex $8854	Gd $5220
Knockabout model	NiB $3377	Ex $2688	Gd $1769
20 ga., add			125%
28 ga. or .410, add			300%

BOXLOCK HAMMERLESS DOUBLES (W/SIDEPLATES)
Anson & Deeley system. Reinforced frame w/side clips. Purdey-type bolt except on Model 8535, which has Greener crossbolt. Auto ejectors. Double triggers. Made in all standard gauges, bbl. lengths, chokes, weights. Checkered stock and forend, straight or pistol grip. Models 10594, 8535 and 6982 are of equal quality, differing chiefly in style of engraving; Model 9/40E/38321 is a higher grade gun in all details and has fine English-style engraving. Built to customer specifications.

Models 10594, 8535, 6982 NiB $6044 Ex $4566 Gd $3177
Model 9/40E/3831 . . . . NiB $6588 Ex $5344 Gd $3889

FINE O/U SHOTGUN . . NiB $10,566 Ex $8978 Gd $6450
Model 9/40.SE. Boxlock, Anson & Deeley system. Auto ejectors. Double triggers. Made in all standard gauges; bbl. length, boring to order. Weight: About 6.75 lbs. 12 ga. Checkered stock and forend, straight or pistol grip. Manufactured to customer specifications. Disc 1990.

FINE SIDELOCK HAMMERLESS
DOUBLE . . . . NiB $26,350 Ex $21,789 Gd $15,680
Model 120.HE/328. Automatic ejectors. Double triggers. Made in all standard ga.; bbl. length, boring, weight to order. Checkered stock and forend, straight or pistol-grip. Manufactured to customer specifications. Disc. 1990.

HALF-FINE O/U
SHOTGUN . . . . NiB $11,656 Ex $9377 Gd $6275
Model SOB.E/11082. Boxlock, Anson & Deeley system. Auto ejectors. Double triggers. Made in all standard gauges; barrel length, boring to order. Checkered stock and forend, straight or pistol grip. Note: This model is similar to No. 9/40.SE except general quality lower. Disc. 1990.

GALEF SHOTGUNS — Manufactured for J. L. Galef & Son, Inc., New York, New York; by M. A. V. I., Gardone F. T., Italy; by Zabala Hermanos, Eiquetta, Spain; and by Antonio Zoli, Gardone V. T., Italy

SILVER SNIPE OVER/UNDER
SHOTGUN . . . . NiB $699 Ex $598 Gd $445
Boxlock. Plain extractors. Single trigger. Gauges: 12, 20; 3-inch chambers. Bbls: 26-, 28-, 30-inch (latter in 12 ga. only); IC/M, M/F chokes; vent rib. Weight: 12 ga. w/28-inch bbls., 6.5 lbs. Checkered walnut pistol-grip stock and forearm. Introduced by Antonio Zoli in 1968. Disc. See illustration previous page.

GOLDEN SNIPE . . . . NiB $689 Ex $570 Gd $455
Same as Silver Snipe, except has selective automatic ejectors. Made by Antonio Zoli 1968 to date.

MONTE CARLO TRAP
SINGLE-BARREL SHOTGUN . . . NiB $356 Ex $221 Gd $177
Hammerless. Underlever. Plain extractor. 12 ga. 32-inch bbl., F choke, vent rib.
Weight: About 8.25 lbs. Checkered pistol-grip stock w/Monte Carlo comb and recoil pad, beavertail forearm. Introduced by M. A. V. I. in 1968. Disc.

SILVER HAWK HAMMERLESS
DOUBLE . . . . NiB $565 Ex $455 Gd $300

Galef Companion Folding Single-Barrel Shotgun

Galef Zabala Hammerless Double-Barrel Shotgun

Boxlock. Plain extractors. Double triggers. Gauges: 12, 20; 3-inch chambers. Bbls.: 26-, 28-, 30-inch (latter in 12 ga. only); IC/M, M/F chokes. Weight: 12 ga. w/26-inch bbls., 6 lbs. 6 oz. Checkered walnut pistol-grip stock and beavertail forearm. Made by Angelo Zoli 1968 to 1972.

COMPANION FOLDING SINGLE-BARREL SHOTGUN

Hammerless. Underlever. Gauges: 12 Mag., 16, 20 Mag., 28, .410. Bbls.: 26-inch (.410 only), 28-inch (12, 16, 20, 28), 30-inch (12-ga. only); F choke; plain or vent rib. Weight: 4.5 lbs. for .410 to 5 lbs., 9 oz. for 12 ga. Checkered pistol-grip stock and forearm. Made by M. A. V. I. from 1968-83.

w/plain bbl. . . . . NiB $245 Ex $179 Gd $95
w/ventilated rib . . . . NiB $270 Ex $196 Gd $110

ZABALA HAMMERLESS DOUBLE-BARREL SHOTGUN

Boxlock. Plain extractors. Double triggers. Gauges: 10 Mag., 12 Mag., 16, 20 Mag., 28, .410. Bbls.: 22-, 26-, 28-, 30-, 32-inch; IC/C, IC/M, M/F chokes. Weight: 12 ga. w/28-inch bbls., 7.75 lbs. Checkered walnut pistol-grip stock and beavertail forearm, recoil pad. Made by Zabala from 1972-83.

10 ga. . . . . NiB $355 Ex $270 Gd $200
Other ga. . . . . NiB $244 Ex $179 Gd $115

GAMBA — Gardone V. T. (Brescia), Italy

DAYTONA COMPETITION O/U

Boxlock w/Boss-style locking system. Anatomical single trigger; optional adj., single-selective release trigger. Selective automatic ejectors. Gauge: 12 or 20; 2.75- or 3-inch chambers. Bbls.: 26.75-, 28-, 30- or 32-inch choked SK/SK, IM/F or M/F. Weight: 7.5 to 8.5 lbs. Black or chrome receiver w/blued bbls. Checkered select walnut stock and forearm w/oil finish. Imported by Heckler & Koch until 1992.

American Trap model . . . . . NiB $2240 Ex $1680 Gd $1021
Pigeon, Skeet, Trap models . . NiB $1323 Ex $1078 Gd $877
Sporting model . . . . NiB $5678 Ex $4498 Gd $3123
Sideplate model . . . . NiB $11,789 Ex $9809 Gd $5977
Engraved models . . . . . . NiB $13,788 Ex $10,666 Gd $7477
Sidelock model . . . . . . NiB $28,560 Ex $23,778 Gd $19,580

ARMAS GARBI — Eibar, Spain

MODEL 100
SIDELOCK SHOTGUN . . . . NiB $5700 Ex $3433 Gd $2433

Gauges: 12, 16, 20 and 28. Bbls.: 25-, 28-, 30-inch. Action: Holland & Holland pattern sidelock; automatic ejectors and double trigger. Weight: 5 lbs., 6 oz. to 7 lbs. 7 oz. English-style straight grip stock w/fine-line hand-checkered butt; classic forend. Made from 1985 to date.

MODEL 101
SIDELOCK SHOTGUN . . . . NiB $6788 Ex $4331 Gd $3000
Same general specifications as Model 100 above, except the sidelocks are handcrafted w/hand-engraved receiver; select walnut straight-grip stock.

MODEL 102
SIDELOCK SHOTGUN . . . . NiB $7175 Ex $4576 Gd $3177
Similar to the Model 101 except w/large scroll engraving. Made from 1985 to 1993.

MODEL 103
HAMMERLESS DOUBLE
Similar to Model 100 except w/Purdey-type, higher grade engraving.
Model 103A Standard . . NiB $14,675 Ex $11,650 Gd $9967
Model 103A Royal Deluxe . . . NiB $11,870 Ex $9443 Gd $7655
Model 103B . . . . NiB $21,660 Ex $17,707 Gd $15,990
Model 103B Royal Deluxe . . NiB $25,677 Ex $22,770 Gd $18,989

MODEL 200 HAMMERLESS
DOUBLE . . . . NiB $17,766 Ex $15,221 Gd $11,488
Similar to Model 100 except w/double heavy-duty locks. Continental-style floral and scroll engraving. Checkered deluxe walnut stock and forearm.

GARCIA CORPORATION — Teaneck, New Jersey

BRONCO 22/.410
O/U COMBO . . . . NiB $300 Ex $197 Gd $100
Swing-out action. Takedown. 18.5-inch bbls.; .22 LR over, .410 ga. under. Weight: 4.5 lbs. One-piece stock and receiver, crackle finish. Intro. In 1976. Disc.

BRONCO .410 SINGLE SHOT . . NiB $233 Ex $120 Gd $90
Swing-out action. Takedown. .410 ga. 18.5-inch bbl. Weight: 3.5 lbs. One-piece stock and receiver, crackle finish. Intro. In 1967. Disc.

Golden Eagle
Model 5000 Grade II Field

Gorosabel
Model 504 Shotgun

Greener Empire Model
Hammerless

Greener
Far-Killer

GOLDEN EAGLE FIREARMS INC. — Houston, Texas. Manufactured by Nikko Firearms Ltd., Tochigi, Japan

EAGLE MODEL 5000
GRADE I FIELD O/U .... NiB $989 Ex $844 Gd $659
Receiver engraved and inlaid w/gold eagle head. Boxlock. Auto ejectors. Selective single trigger. 12, 20 ga.; 2.75- or 3-inch chambers, 12 ga., 3-inch, 20 ga. Bbls.: 26-, 28-, 30-inch (latter only in 12-ga. 3-inch Mag.); IC/M, M/F chokes; vent rib. Weight: 6.25 lbs., 20 ga.; 7.25 lbs., 12 ga.; 8 lbs., 12-ga. Mag. Checkered pistol-grip stock and semi-beavertail forearm. Imported 1975-82. Note: Guns marketed 1975 to 1976 under the Nikko brand name have white receivers; guns made since 1976 are blued.

EAGLE MODEL 5000
GRADE I SKEET .... NiB $954 Ex $743 Gd $522
Same as Field model except has 26- or 28-inch bbls. w/wide (11 mm) vent rib, SK choked. Imported from 1975 to 1982.

EAGLE MODEL 5000
GRADE I TRAP .... NiB $954 Ex $755 Gd $569
Same as Field model except has 30-, or 32-inch bbls. w/wide (11 mm) vent rib (M/F, IM/F, F/F chokes), trap-style stock w/ recoil pad. Imported from 1975 to 1982.

EAGLE MODEL 5000
GRADE II FIELD .... NiB $1077 Ex $890 Gd $776
Same as Grade I Field model except higher grade w/fancier wood, more elaborate engraving and "screaming eagle" inlaid in gold. Imported from 1975 to 1982.

EAGLE MODEL 5000
GRADE II SKEET .... NiB $1100 Ex $940 Gd $800
Same as Grade I Skeet model except higher grade w/fancier wood, more elaborate engraving and "screaming eagle" inlaid in gold; inertia trigger, vent side ribs. Imported from 1975-82.

EAGLE MODEL 5000
GRADE II TRAP .... NiB $1100 Ex $940 Gd $800
Same as Grade I Trap model except higher grade w/fancier wood, more elaborate engraving and "screaming eagle" inlaid in gold; inertia trigger, vent side ribs. Imported from 1975 to 1982.

EAGLE MODEL 5000
GRADE III GRANDEE ..... NiB $2760 Ex $2255 Gd $1798
Best grade, available in Field, Skeet and Trap models w/same general specifications as lower grades. Has sideplates w/game scene engraving, scroll on frame and bbls., fancy wood (Monte Carlo comb, full pistol-grip and recoil pad on Trap model). Made from 1976 to 1982.

GOROSABEL — Spain

MODEL 503 SHOTGUN ..... NiB $1088 Ex $866 Gd $735
Gauges: 12, 16, 20 and .410. Action: Anson & Deely-style boxlock. Bbls.: 26-, 27-, and 28-inch. Select European walnut, English or pistol grip, sliver or beavertail forend, hand-checkering. Scalloped frame and scroll engraving. Intro. 1985; disc.

MODEL 504 SHOTGUN ..... NiB $1167 Ex $953 Gd $655
Gauge: 12 or 20. Action: Holland & Holland-style sidelock. Bbl.: 26-, 27-, or 28-inch. Select European walnut, English or pistol grip, sliver or beavertail forend, hand-checkering. Holland-style large scroll engraving. Inro. 1985; disc.

MODEL 505 SHOTGUN .... NiB $1590 Ex $1266 Gd $965
Gauge: 12 or 20. Action: Holland & Holland-style sidelock. Bbls.: 26-, 27-, or 28-inch. Select European walnut, English or pistol grip, silver or beavertail forend, hand-checkering. Purdey-style fine scroll and rose engraving. Intro. 1985; disc.

**Greifelt Grade No. 1
Over-and-Under Shotgun**

Greifelt Model 22

Non-ejector, 12 ga.	NiB $1577	Ex $1122	Gd $909
Ejector, 12 ga.	NiB $3897	Ex $3138	Gd $2217
Non-ejector, 10 or 8 ga.	NiB $2886	Ex $2231	Gd $1977
Ejector, 10 or 8 ga.	NiB $5500	Ex $4230	Gd $3110

G. P. (GENERAL PURPOSE)
SINGLE BARREL . . . . NiB $444 Ex $358 Gd $229
Greener Improved Martini Lever Action. Takedown. Ejector. 12 ga. only. Bbl. lengths: 26-, 30-, 32-inch. M or F choke. Weight: 6.25 to 6.75 lbs. depending on bbl. length. Checkered straight-grip stock and forearm.

HAMMERLESS EJECTOR DOUBLE-BARREL SHOTGUNS
Boxlock. Auto ejectors. Double triggers, non-selective or selective single trigger. Gauges: 12, 16, 20, 28, .410 (two latter gauges not supplied in Grades DH40 and DH35). Bbls.: 26-, 28-, 30-inch; any choke combination. Weight: From 4.75 to 8 lbs. Depending on ga. and bbl. length. Checkered stock and forend, straight- or half-pistol grip. The Royal, Crown, Sovereign and Jubilee models differ in quality, engraving, grade of wood, checkering, etc. General specifications are the same.

Royal Model Grade DH75	NiB $4170	Ex $3008	Gd $2166
Crown Model Grade DH55	NiB $5166	Ex $3188	Gd $2270
Sovereign Model Grade DH40	NiB $5277	Ex $4866	Gd $3900
Jubilee Model Grade DH35	NiB $4197	Ex $3145	Gd $2176

w/selective single trigger, add $400
w/non-selective single trigger, add $300
w/vent. rib, add $425
w/single trigger, add $455

STEPHEN GRANT — Hertfordshire, England

BEST QUALITY SELF-OPENER DOUBLE-BARREL
SHOTGUN . . . . NiB $19,870 Ex $16,920 Gd $12,612
Sidelock, self-opener. Gauges: 12, 16 and 20. Bbls.: 25 to 30 inches standard. Highest-grade English or European walnut straight-grip buttstock and forearm w/Greener type lever. Imported by Stoeger in the 1950s.

BEST QUALITY SIDE-LEVER DOUBLE-BARREL
SHOTGUN . . . . NiB $13,657 Ex $11,770 Gd $9879
Sidelock, self-lever. Gauges: 12, 16 and 20. Bbls.: 25 to 30 inches standard. Highest-grade English or European walnut straight-grip buttstock and forearm w/Greener type lever. Imported by Stoeger in the 1950s.

W. W. GREENER, LTD. — Birmingham, England

EMPIRE MODEL HAMMERLESS DOUBLES
Boxlock. Non-ejector or w/automatic ejectors. Double triggers. 12 ga. only (2.75-inch or 3-inch chamber). Bbls.: 28- to 32-inch; any choke combination. Weight: from 7.25 to 7.75 lbs. depending on bbl. length. Checkered stock and forend, straight- or half-pistol grip. Also furnished in "Empire Deluxe Grade," this model has same general specs, but deluxe finish.
Empire model, non-ejector NiB $1887 Ex $1671 Gd $1388
Empire model, ejector. . . . . NiB $1955 Ex $1771 Gd $1480
Empire Deluxe model,
  non-ejector . . . . NiB $2088 Ex $1933 Gd $1387
Empire Deluxe model,
  ejector . . . . NiB $2677 Ex $2200 Gd $1588

FARKILLER MODEL GRADE F35
HAMMERLESS DOUBLE-BARREL SHOTGUN
Boxlock. Non-ejector or w/automatic ejectors. Double triggers. Gauges: 12 (2.75-inch or 3-inch), 10, 8. Bbls.: 28-, 30- or 32-inch. Weight: 7.5 to 9 lbs. in 12 ga. Checkered stock, forend; straight or half-pistol grip.

GREIFELT & COMPANY — Suhl, German

GRADE NO. 1 O/U SHOTGUN
Anson & Deeley boxlock, Kersten fastening. Auto ejectors. Double triggers or single trigger. Elaborately engraved. Gauges: 12, 16, 20, 28, .410. Bbls.: 26- to 32-inch, any combination of chokes, vent or solid matted rib. Weight: 4.25 to 8.25 lbs. depending on ga. and bbl. length. Straight- or pistol-grip stock, Purdey-type forend, both checkered. Manufactured prior to World War II.
w/solid matted-rib bbl.,
  except .410 & 28 ga. . . . NiB $3797 Ex $3166 Gd $2280
w/solid matted-rib bbl.,
  .410 & 28 ga. . . . . NiB $3844 Ex $3208 Gd $2300
w/ventilated rib, add $125
w/single trigger, add $550

GRADE NO. 3 O/U SHOTGUN
Same general specifications as Grade No. 1 except less fancy engraving. Manufactured prior to World War II.
w/solid matted-rib bbl.,
  except .410 & 28 ga. . . . NiB $2987 Ex $2379 Gd $1979
w/solid matted-rib bbl.,
  .410 & 28 ga. . . . . NiB $5187 Ex $4156 Gd $3110
w/ventilated rib, add $125
w/single trigger, add $450

MODEL 22
HAMMERLESS DOUBLE . . . NiB $2288 Ex $1843 Gd $1244
Anson & Deeley boxlock. Plain extractors. Double triggers. Gauges: 12 and 16. Bbls.: 28- or 30-inch, M/F choke. Checkered stock and forend, pistol grip and cheekpiece standard, English-style stock also supplied. Manufactured since World War II.

SHOTGUNS

Greifelt Model 103E

Greifelt Model 103

MODEL 22E
HAMMERLESS DOUBLE . . . NiB $2866 Ex $2430 Gd $1832
Same as Model 22 except has automatic ejectors.

MODEL 103
HAMMLERLESS DOUBLE . . NiB $2100 Ex $1821 Gd $1292
Anson & Deeley boxlock. Plain extractors. Double triggers. Gauges: 12 and 16. Bbls.: 28- or 30-inch, M and F choke. Checkered stock and forend, pistol grip and cheekpiece standard, English-style stock also supplied. Manufactured since World War II.

MODEL 103E
HAMMERLESS DOUBLE . . . NiB $2200 Ex $1727 Gd $1224
Same as Model 103 except has automatic ejectors.

MODEL 143E O/U SHOTGUN
General specifications same as pre-war Grade No. 1 Over-and-Under, except this model is not supplied in 28 and .410 ga. or w/32-inch bbls. Model 143E is not as high quality as the Grade No. 1 gun. Mfd. Since World War II.
w/raised matted rib,
double triggers . . . . NiB $2571 Ex $2068 Gd $1563
w/vent. rib, single
selective trigger . . . . NiB $2860 Ex $2276 Gd $1865

HAMMERLESS DRILLING (THREE-BARREL
COMBINATION GUN) . . . . NiB $3677 Ex $3220 Gd $2179
Boxlock. Plain extractors. Double triggers, front single set for rifle bbl. Gauges: 12, 16, 20; rifle bbl. in any caliber adapted to this type of gun. 26-inch bbls. Weight: About 7.5 lbs. Auto rear sight operated by rifle bbl. selector. Checkered stock and forearm, pistol-grip and cheekpiece standard. Manufactured prior to WW II. Note: Value shown is for guns chambered for cartridges readily obtainable. If rifle bbl. is an odd foreign caliber, value will be considerably less.

O/U COMBINATION GUN
Similar in design to this maker's over-and-under shotguns. Gauges: 12, 16, 20, 28, .410; rifle bbl. in any caliber adapted to this type of gun. Bbls.: 24- or 26-inch, solid matted rib. Weight: From 4.75 to 7.25 lbs. Folding rear sight. Manufactured prior to WWII. Note: Values shown are for gauges other than .410 w/ rifle bbl. Chambered for a cartridge readily obtainable; if in an odd foreign caliber, value will be considerably less. .410 ga. increases in value by about 50%.
w/non-automatic ejector . . NiB $5477 Ex $4651 Gd $3822
w/automatic ejector . . . . . . NiB $6055 Ex $5310 Gd $4430

HARRINGTON & RICHARDSON ARMS —Gardner, Massachussets now H&R 1871, Inc.

Formerly Harrington & Richardson Arms Co. of Worcester, Mass. One of the oldest and most distinguished manufacturers of handguns, rifles and shotguns, H&R suspended operations on January 24, 1986. In 1987, New England Firearms was established as an independent company producing selected H&R models under the NEF logo. In 1991, H&R 1871, Inc. was formed from the residual of the parent company and then took over the New England Firearms facility. H&R 1871 produced firearms under both their logo and the NEF brand name until 1999, when the Marlin Firearms Company acquired the assets of H&R 1871.

NO. 3 HAMMERLESS
SINGLE-SHOT SHOTGUN . . . . . NiB $230 Ex $115 Gd $85
Takedown. Automatic ejector. Gauges: 12, 16, 20, .410. Bbls.: plain, 26- to 32-inch, F choke. Weight: 6.5 to 7.25 lbs. depending on ga. and bbl. length. Plain pistol-grip stock and forend. Discontinued 1942.

NO. 5 STANDARD LIGHTWEIGHT
HAMMER SINGLE. . . . . NiB $227 Ex $120 Gd $90
Takedown. Auto ejector. Gauges: 24, 28, .410. Bbls.: 26- or 28-inch, F choke. Weight: About 4 to 4.75 lbs. Plain pistol-grip stock/forend. Discontinued 1942.

NO. 6 HEAVY BREECH SINGLE-SHOT
HAMMER SHOTGUN. . . . . NiB $244 Ex $135 Gd $90
Takedown. Automatic ejector. Gauges: 10, 12, 16, 20. Bbls.: Plain, 28- to 36-inch, F choke. Weight: About 7 to 7.25 lbs. Plain stock and forend. Discontinued 1942.

NO. 7 & 9 BAY STATE SINGLE-SHOT
HAMMER SHOTGUN. . . . . NiB $235 Ex $140 Gd $95
Takedown. Automatic ejector. Gauges: 12, 16, 20, .410. Bbls.: Plain 26- to 32-inch, F choke. Weight: 5.5 to 6.5 lbs. depending on ga. and bbl. length. Plain pistol-grip stock and forend. Discontinued 1942.

NO. 8 STANDARD SINGLE-SHOT
HAMMER SHOTGUN. . . . . NiB $255 Ex $145 Gd $98
Takedown. Automatic ejector. Gauges: 12, 16, 20, 24, 28, .410. Bbl.: plain, 26- to 32-inch, F choke. Weight: 5.5 to 6.5 lbs. depending on ga. and bbl. length. Plain pistol-grip stock and forend. Made from 1908 to 1942.

MODEL 348 GAMESTER
BOLT-ACTION SHOTGUN . . . . . NiB $217 Ex $117 Gd $88
Takedown. 12 and 16 ga. Two round tubular magazine,

Harrington & Richardson
Model 400 Pump

Harrington & Richardson
Model 403 Autoloading

Harrington & Richardson
Model 404C

Harrington & Richardson
No. 3, 5, 6, 7 and 8 shotguns (top to bottom)

28-inch bbl, F choke. Plain pistol-grip stock. Weight: About 7.5 lbs. Made from 1949 to 1954.

MODEL 349 GAMESTER
DELUXE . . . . **NiB $220 Ex $115 Gd $85**
Same as Model 348 except has 26-inch bbl. W/adj. choke device, recoil pad. Made from 1953 to 1955.

MODEL 351 HUNTSMAN
BOLT-ACTION SHOTGUN . . . . **NiB $239 Ex $200 Gd $125**
Takedown. 12 and 16 ga. Two round tubular magazine. Pushbutton safety. 26-inch bbl. w/H&R variable choke. Weight: About 6.75 lbs. Monte Carlo stock w/recoil pad. Made from 1956 to 1958.

MODEL 400 PUMP. . . . . NiB $335 Ex $254 Gd $180
Hammerless. Gauges: 12, 16, 20. Tubular magazine holds 4 shells. 28-inch bbl., F choke. Weight: About 7.25 lbs. Plain pistol-grip stock (recoil pad in 12 and 16 ga.), grooved slide handle. Made from 1955 to 1967.

MODEL 401 . . . . NiB $335 Ex $240 Gd $190
Same as Model 400 on previous page, except has H&R variable choke. Made from 1956-63.

MODEL 402 . . . . NiB $315 Ex $220 Gd $170
Similar to Model 400 except .410 ga., weight: About 5.5 lbs. Made from 1959-67.

MODEL 403 AUTOLOADING
SHOTGUN . . . . **NiB $338 Ex $300 Gd $210**
Takedown. .410 ga. Tubular magazine holds four shells. 26-inch bbl., F choke. Weight: About 5.75 lbs. Plain pistol-grip stock and forearm. Made in 1964.

MODEL 404/404C PUMP
SHOTGUN . . . . **NiB $366 Ex $275 Gd $209**
Boxlock. Plain extractors. Double triggers. Gauges: 12, 20, .410. Bbls.: 28-inch in 12 ga. (M/F choke), 26-inch in 20 ga. (IC/M and .410 (F/F). Weight: 5.5 to 7.25 lbs. Plain walnut-finished hardwood stock and forend on Model 404; 404C checkered. Made in Brazil by Amadeo Rossi from 1969-1972.

SHOTGUNS

Harrington & Richardson
Model 440

Harrington & Richardson
Model 1212 Waterfowl

Harrington & Richardson
Golden Squire — Model 159

Harrington & Richardson
Harrich No. 1

Harrington & Richardson
Topper No. 48

Harrington & Richardson
Topper No. 162 — Slug Gun

MODEL 440 PUMP SHOTGUN . . NiB $255 Ex $194 Gd $145
Hammerless. Gauges: 12, 16, 20. 2.75-inch chamber in 16 ga., 3-inch in 12 and 20 ga. Three round magazine. Bbls.: 26-, 28-, 30-inch; IC, M, F choke. Weight: 6.25 lbs. Plain pistol-grip stock and slide handle, recoil pad. Made from 1968-73.

MODEL 442 PUMP SHOTGUN . . NiB $320 Ex $254 Gd $188
Same as Model 440 except has vent rib bbl., checkered stock and forearm, weight: 6.75 lbs. Made from 1969-73.

ULTRA SLUG SERIES. . . . . NiB $287 Ex $220 Gd $175
Singel shot 12 or 20 ga w/3-inch chamber w/heavy-wall 24-inch fully rifled bbl. w/scope . Weight: 9 lbs. Walnut-stained Monte Carlo stock, sling swivels, black nylon sling. Made from 1995 to date.

MODEL 1212 FIELD . . . . NiB $435 Ex $321 Gd $250
Boxlock. Plain extractors. Selective single trigger. 12 ga., 2.75-inch chambers. 28-inch bbls., IC/IM, vent rib. Weight: 7 lbs. Checkered walnut pistol-gip stock and fluted forearm. Made 1976-80 by Lanber Arms S. A., Zaldibar (Vizcaya), Spain.

**Model 1212
WATERFOWL GUN . . . . NiB $544 Ex $368 Gd $277**
Same as Field Gun except chambered for 12-ga, 3-inch mag. shells, has 30-inch bbls., M/F chokes, stock and recoil pad, weight: 7.5 lbs. Made from 1976 to 1980.

MODEL 1908
SINGLE-SHOT SHOTGUN . . . . NiB $244 Ex $177 Gd $100
Takedown. Automatic ejector. Gauges: 12, 16, 24 and 28. Bbls.: 26- to 32-inch, F choke. Weight: 5.25 to 6.5 lbs. depending on ga. and bbl. length. Casehardened receiver. Plain pistol-grip stock. Bead front sight. Made from 1908 to 1934.

MODEL 1908 .410 (12MM)
SINGLE-SHOT SHOTGUN . . . . NiB $233 Ex $177 Gd $120
Same general specifications as standard Model 1908 except chambered for .410 or 12mm shot cartridge w/bbl. milled down at receiver to give a more pleasing contour.

MODEL 1915 SINGLE-SHOT SHOTGUN
Takedown. Both non-auto and auto-ejectors available. Gauges: 24, 28, .410, 14mm and 12mm. Bbls.: 26- or 28-inch, F choke. Weight: 4 to 4.75 lbs. depending on ga. and bbl. length. Plain black walnut stock w/semi pistol-grip.
24 ga. NiB $390 Ex $275 Gd $190
28, .410 ga.. . . . . NiB $390 Ex $275 Gd $190

FOLDING GUN . . . . NiB $320 Ex $210 Gd $165
Single bbl. hammer shotgun hinged at the front of the frame, the bbl. folds down against the stock. Light Frame model: gauges — 28, 14mm, .410; 22-inch bbl.; weighs about 4.5 lbs. Heavy Frame model: gauges — 12, 16, 20, 28, .410; 26-inch bbl.; weighs from 5.75 to 6.5 lbs. Plain pistol-grip stock and forend. Disc. 1942.

GOLDEN SQUIRE MODEL 159 SINGLE-BARREL
HAMMER SHOTGUN. . . . . . . NiB $265 Ex $170 Gd $121
Hammerless. Side lever. Automatic ejection. Gauges: 12, 20. Bbls: 30-inch in 12 ga., 28-inch in 20 ga., both F choke. Weight: About 6.5 lbs. Straight-grip stock w/recoil pad, forearm w/Schnabel. Made from 1964 to 1966.

GOLDEN SQUIRE JR.
MODEL 459 . . . . NiB $255 Ex $170 Gd $125
Same as Model 159 except gauges 20 and .410, 26-inch bbl., youth stock. Made in 1964.

HARRICH NO. 1 SINGLE-BARREL
TRAP GUN . . . . NiB $1733 Ex $1456 Gd $974
Anson & Deeley-type locking system w/Kersten top locks and double underlocking lugs. Sideplates engraved w/hunting scenes. 12 ga. Bbls.: 32-, 34-inch; F choke; high vent rib. Weight: 8.5 lbs. Checkered Monte Carlo stock w/pistol-grip and recoil pad, beavertail forearm, of select walnut. Made in Austria 1971 to 1975.

"TOP RIB"
SINGLE-BARREL SHOTGUN. . . NiB $335 Ex $265 Gd $190
Takedown. Auto ejector. Gauges: 12, 16 and 20. Bbls.: 28- to 30-inch, F choke w/full-length matted top rib. Weight: 6.5 to 7 lbs. depending on ga. and bbl. length. Black walnut pistol-grip stock (capped) and forend; both checkered. Flexible rubber buttplate. Made during 1930s.

TOPPER NO. 48 SINGLE-BARREL
HAMMER SHOTGUN. . . . . . . NiB $280 Ex $195 Gd $145
Similar to old Model 8 Standard. Takedown. Top lever. Auto ejector. Gauges: 12, 16, 20, .410. Bbls.: plain; 26- to 30-inch; M or F choke. Weight: 5.5 to 6.5 lbs. depending on ga. and bbl. length. Plain pistol-grip stock and forend. Made from 1946 to 1957.

TOPPER MODEL 099 DELUXE . . . NiB $244 Ex $155 Gd $110
Same as Model 158 except has matte nickel finish, semipistol grip walnut-finished American hardwood stock; semibeavertail forearm; 12, 16, 20, and .410 ga. Made from 1982 to 1986.

TOPPER MODEL 148 SINGLE-SHOT
HAMMER SHOTGUN. . . . . . . NiB $200 Ex $177 Gd $120
Takedown. Side lever. Auto-ejection. Gauges: 12, 16, 20, .410. Bbls.: 12 ga.,30-, 32- and 36-inch; 16 ga., 28- and 30-inch; 20 and .410 ga., 28-inch; F choke. Weight: 5 to 6.5 lbs. Plain pistol-grip stock and forend, recoil pad. Made from 1958 to 1961.

TOPPER MODEL 158 (058) SINGLE-SHOT
HAMMER SHOTGUN. . . . . . . NiB $245 Ex $165 Gd $120
Takedown. Side lever. Automatic ejection. Gauges: 12, 20, .410 (2.75-inch and 3-inch shells); 16 (2.75-inch). bbl. length and choke combinations: 12 ga., 36-inch/F, 32-inch/F, 30-inch/F, 28-inch/F or M; .410, 28-inch/F. Weight: about 5.5 lbs. Plain pistol-grip stock and forend, recoil pad. Made from 1962 to 1981. Note: Designation changed to 058 in 1974.

TOPPER MODEL 162
SLUG GUN. . . . . NiB $300 Ex $221 Gd $165
Same as Topper Model 158 except has 24-inch bbl., Cyl. bore, w/rifle sights. Made from 1968 to 1986.

TOPPER MODEL 176 10 GA.
MAGNUM. . . . . NiB $280 Ex $185 Gd $145
Similar to Model 158, but has 36-inch heavy bbl. chambered for 3.5-inch 10- ga. Mag. shells, weight: 10 lbs.; stock w/Monte Carlo comb and recoil pad, longer and fuller forearm. Made from 1977 to 1986.

TOPPER MODEL 188 DELUXE . . NiB $265 Ex $200 Gd $145
Same as standard Topper Model 148 except has chromed frame, stock and forend in black, red, yellow, blue, green, pink, or purple colored finish. .410 ga. only. Made from 1958 to 1961.

TOPPER MODEL 198 (098)
DELUXE . . . . NiB $244 Ex $180 Gd $130
Same as Model 158 except has chrome-plated frame, black finished stock and forend; 12, 20 and .410 ga. Made 1962 to 1981. Note: Designation changed to 098 in 1974.

TOPPER JR. MODEL 480 . . . . . NiB $236 Ex $165 Gd $100
Similar to No. 48 Topper except has youth-size stock, 26-inch bbl, .410 ga. only. Made from 1958-61.

TOPPER NO. 488 DELUXE . . . . NiB $254 Ex $179 Gd $115
Same as standard No. 48 Topper except chrome-plated frame, black lacquered stock and forend, recoil pad. Disc. 1957.

TOPPER MODEL 490 . . . . NiB $245 Ex $185 Gd $135
Same as Model 158 except has youth-size stock (3 inches shorter), 26-inch bbl.; 20 and 28 ga. (M choke), .410 (F). Made 1962 to 1986.

TOPPER MODEL 490
GREENWING . . . . NiB $266 Ex $190 Gd $140
Same as the Model 490 except has a special high-polished finish. Made from 1981 to 1986.

SHOTGUNS

Harrington & Richardson
Topper Model 198 (098)

Harrington & Richardson
Topper Model 490 — Greenwing

Harrington & Richardson
Topper — Classic Youth

Harrington & Richardson
Topper — Deluxe

TOPPER JR. MODEL 580 . . . . . NiB $210 Ex $166 Gd $100
Same as Model 480 except has colored stocks as on Model 188. Made from 1958 to 1961.

TOPPER MODEL 590 . . . . NiB $210 Ex $166 Gd $100
Same as Model 490 except has chrome-plated frame, black finished stock and forend. Made from 1962 to 1963.

The following models are manufactured and distributed by the reorganized company of H&R 1871, Inc.

**MODEL 098 TOPPER
CLASSIC YOUTH** . . . . NiB $200 Ex $155 Gd $100
Same as Topper Junior except also available in 28 ga. and has checkered American black walnut stock/forend w/satin finish and recoil pad. Made from 1991 to date.

MODEL 098 TOPPER DELUXE . NiB $200 Ex $155 Gd $100
Same as Model 098 Single Shot Hammer except in 12 ga., 3-inch chamber only. 28-inch bbl.; Mod. choke tube. Made from 1992 to date.

**MODEL 098 TOPPER
DELUXE RIFLED SLUG GUN** . . . NiB $217 Ex $125 Gd $95
Same as Topper Deluxe Shotgun except has compensated 24-inch rifled slug bbl. Nickel plated receiver and blued bbl. Black finished hardwood stock. Made from 1996 to date.

**MODEL 098 TOPPER HAMMER
SINGLE-SHOT SHOTGUN** . . . . . NiB $165 Ex $115 Gd $88
Side lever. Automatic ejector. Gauges: 12, 20 and .410; 3-inch chamber. Bbls.: 28-inch, (12 ga./M); 26-inch, (20 ga./M); 26-inch (.410/F). Weight: 5 to 6 lbs. Satin nickel receiver, blued bbl. Plain pistol-grip stock and semibeavertail forend w/black finish. Re-Intro. 1992.

MODEL 098 TOPPER JUNIOR . . NiB $200 Ex $129 Gd $90
Same as Model 098 except has youth-size stock and 22-inch bbl. 20 or .410 ga. only. Made 1991 to date.

Heckler & Koch Red Lion Mark II

Heckler & Koch Classic Lion Grade I

MODEL .410 TAMER
SHOTGUN . . . . **NiB $200 Ex $145 Gd $100**
Takedown. Topper-style single-shot, side lever action w/auto ejector. Gauge: .410; 3-inch chamber. 19.5-inch bbl. 33 inches overall. Weight: 5.75 lbs. Black polymer thumbhole stock designed to hold 4 extra shotshells. Matte nickel finish. Made from 1994 to date.

MODEL N.W.T.F. TURKEY MAG
Same as Model 098 Single-Shot Hammer except has 24-inch bbl. chambered 10 or 12 ga. w/3.5-inch chamber w/screw-in choke tube. Weight: 6 lbs. American hardwood stock, Mossy Oak camo finish. Made from 1991 to 1996.
NWTF 10 ga. Turkey Mag
(Made 1996) . . . . **NiB $200 Ex $125 Gd $90**
NWTF 12 ga. Turkey Mag
(Made 1991-95) . . . . **NiB $200 Ex $125 Gd $90**

MODEL N. W. T. F.
YOUTH TURKEY GUN. . . . . **NiB $195 Ex $115 Gd $88**
Same as Model N.W.T.F. Turkey Mag except has 22-inch bbl. chambered in 20 ga. w/3-inch chamber and fixed full choke. Realtree camo finish. Made from 1994 to 1995.

MODEL SB1-920
ULTRA SLUG HUNTER. . . . . . . **NiB $275 Ex $198 Gd $155**
Special 12 ga. action w/12 ga. bbl. blank underbored to 20 ga. to form a fully rifled slug bbl. Gauge: 20 w/3 inch chamber. 24-inch bbl. Weight: 8.5 lbs. Satin nickel receiver, blued bbl. Walnut finished hardwood Monte Carlo stock. Made from 1996 to 1998.

MODEL ULTRA SLUG HUNTER . . **NiB $275 Ex $219 Gd $175**
12 or 20 ga. w/3-inch chamber. 22- or 24-inch rifled bbl. Weight: 9 lbs. Matte black receiver and bbl. Walnut finished hardwood Monte Carlo stock. Made from 1997 to date.

MODEL ULTRA SLUG HUNTER
DELUXE . . . . **NiB $335 Ex $210 Gd $155**
Similar to Ultra Slug Hunter model except with compensated bbl. Made from 1997 to date.

HECKLER & KOCH FABARM — Oberndorf am Neckar, Germany, and Sterling, Virginia
CLASSIC LION SIDE-BY-SIDE SHOTGUN
12 ga. only. 28- or 30-inch non-ported Tribor bbl. w/3-inch chamber. 46.5 to 48.5-inches overall. Weight: 7 to 7.2 lbs.

Five choke tubes; C, IC, M, IM, F. Traditional boxlock design. Oil-finished walnut forearms and stocks w/diamond-cut checkering. Imported from 1999 to date.
Classic Lion Grade I . . . . **NiB $1456 Ex $1288 Gd $890**
Classic Lion Grade II. . . . . **NiB $2177 Ex $1766 Gd $1292**

CAMO LION SEMI-AUTO
SHOTGUN . . . . **NiB $988 Ex $853 Gd $679**
12 ga. Only. 24 to 28-inches Tribor bbl. 44.25-48.25-inches overall. Weight: 7-7.2 lbs. 3 inch chamber w/5 choke tubes - C, IC, M, IM, F. Two round mag. Camo covered walnut stock w/rear front bar sights. Imp. 1999 to date.

MAX LION O/U
SHOTGUN . . . . **NiB $1977 Ex $1660 Gd $1000**
12 or 20 ga. 26- 28- or 30-inch TriBore system bbls. 42.5-47.25-inches overall. Weight: 6.8-7.8 lbs. 3-inch chamber w/5 choke tubes - C, IC, M, IM, F. Single selective adj. trigger and auto ejectors. Side plates w/high-grade stock and rubber recoil pad. Made from 1999 to date.

RED LION MARK II SEMI-AUTO
SHOTGUN . . . . **NiB $954 Ex $700 Gd $544**
12 ga. Only. 24- 26- or 28-inch TriBore system bbls. 44.25 to 48.25-inches overall. Weight: 7 to 7.2 lbs. 3-inch chamber w/five choke tubes- C, IC, M, IM, F. Two round magazine. Matte finish w/walnut wood stock. Rubber vented recoil pad w/leather cover. Made from 1999 to date.

SILVER LION O/U
SHOTGUN . . . . **NiB $1388 Ex $1097 Gd $766**
12 or 20 ga. 26- 28- or 30-inch TriBore system bbls. 43.25-47.25 inchesoverall. 3-inch chamber w/5 choke tubes - C, IC, M, IM, F. Single selective trig. and auto ejectors. Wal. stock w/rubber recoil pad. Made from 1999 to date.

SPORTING CLAY LION
SEMI-AUTO SHOTGUN . . . . . **NiB $1087 Ex $944 Gd $644**
12 ga. only. 28- or 30-inch bbl. w/3-inch chamber and ported Tribore system barrel. Matte finish w/gold plated trigger and carrier release button. Made from 1999 to date.

HERCULES SHOTGUNS

See Listings under "W" for Montgomery Ward.

SHOTGUNS

Heym Model 22S
"Safety" Shotgun/Rifle Combination Gun

Heym Model 55
BF Shotgun/Rifle

HEYM — Münnerstadt, Germany

MODEL 22S "SAFETY" SHOTGUN/
RIFLE COMBINATION . . . . **NiB $3798 Ex $2889 Gd $2250**
16 and 20 ga. Cal: .22 Mag., .22 Hornet, .222 Rem., .222 Rem.
Mag., 5.6x50R Mag., 6.5x57R, 7x57R, .243 Win. 24-inch bbls.
40 inches overall. Weight: About 5.5 lbs. Single-set trigger. Left-
side bbl. selector. Integral dovetail base for scope mounting.
Arabesque engraving. Walnut stock. Disc. 1993.

MODEL 55 BF SHOTGUN/
RIFLE COMBO . . . . **NiB $7045 Ex $5370 Gd $4398**
12, 16 and 20 ga. Calibers: 5.6x50R Mag., 6.5x57R, 7x57R,
7x65R, .243 Win., .308 Win., .30-06. 25-inch bbls., 42 inches
overall. Weight: About 6.75 lbs. Black satin-finished, corro-
sion-resistant bbls. of Krupp special steel. Hand-checkered
walnut stock w/long pistol-grip. Hand-engraved leaf scroll.
German cheekpiece. Disc. 1988.

J. C. HIGGINS

See Sears, Roebuck & Company.

HUGLU HUNTING FIREARMS — Huglu,
Turkey. Imported by Turkish Firearms Corp.

MODEL 101 B 12 AT-DT
COMBO O/U TRAP . . . . . . **NiB $2387 Ex $1885 Gd $1444**
Over/Under boxlock. 12 ga. w/3-inch chambers. Combination
30- or 32-inch top single & O/U bbls. w/fixed chokes or choke
tubes. Weight: 8 lbs. Automatic ejectors or extractors. Single
selective trigger. Manual safety. Circassian walnut Monte Carlo
trap stock w/palm-swell grip and recoil pad. Silvered frame w/
engraving. Imported from 1993 to 1997.

MODEL 101 B 12 ST
O/U TRAP . . . . **NiB $1577 Ex $1377 Gd $937**
Same as Model 101 AT-DT except in 32-inch O/U configura-
tion only. Imported from 1994 to 1996.

MODEL 103 B 12 ST O/U
Boxlock. Gauges: 12, 16, 20, 28 or .410. 28-inch bbls. w/fixed
chokes. Engraved action w/inlaid game scene and dummy
sideplates. Double triggers, extractors and manual safety.
Weight: 7.5 lbs. Circassian walnut stock. Imported 1995 to
1996.
Model 103B w/extractors . . . . . **NiB $954 Ex $733 Gd $496**
28 ga. and .410, add **$125**

MODEL 103 C 12 ST O/U
Same general specs as Model 103 B 12 S except w/extractors
or ejectors. 12 or 20 ga. w/3-inch chambers. Black receiver
w/50% engraving coverage. Imported from 1995 to 1097.
Model 103C w/extractors . . . . **NiB $920 Ex $733 Gd $578**
Model 103C w/ejectors . . . . . . **NiB $979 Ex $766 Gd $634**

MODEL 103 D 12 ST O/U
Same gen. specs as Mdl. 103 B 12 ST except stand. boxlock.
Ext. or eject. 12 or 20 ga. w/3-inch chambers. 80% engraving
coverage. Imp. from 1995 to 1997.
Model 103D w/extractors . . . . **NiB $920 Ex $733 Gd $578**
Model 103D w/ejectors . . . . . . **NiB $979 Ex $766 Gd $634**

MODEL 103 F 12 ST O/U
Same as Model 103 B except extractors or ejectors. 12 or 20
ga. only. 100% engraving coverage. Imported from 1996 to
1997.
Model 103F w/extractors . . . . **NiB $1000 Ex $835 Gd $657**
Model 103F w/ejectors . . . . . **NiB $1154 Ex $1010 Gd $745**

MODEL 104 A 12 ST O/U
Boxlock. Gauges: 12, 20, 28 or .410. 28-inch bbls. w/fixed
chokes or choke tubes. Silvered, engraved receiver w/15%

High Standard Flite-King Brush

High Standard Flite-King Deluxe Rib — 12 Gauge

High Standard Flite-King Deluxe Rib — 12 Gauge (Adjustable Choke)

engraving coverage. Double triggers, manual safety and extractors or ejectors. Weight: 7.5 lbs. Circassian walnut stock w/field dimensions. Imported from 1995 to 1997.

Model 104A w/extractors .... NiB $777 Ex $688 Gd $545
Model 104A w/ejectors ...... NiB $790 Ex $700 Gd $600
28 ga. and .410, add $150
w/Choke Tubes, add $75

MODEL 200 SERIES DOUBLE
Boxlock. Gauges: 12, 20, 28, or .410 w/3-inch chambers. 28-inch bbls. w/fixed chokes. Silvered, engraved receiver. Extractors, manual safety, single selective trigger or double triggers. Weight: 7.5 lbs. Circassion walnut stock. Imported from 1995 to 1997.
Model 200 (w/15%
  engraving coverage, SST) .. NiB $1033 Ex $878 Gd $633
Model 201 (w/30%
  engraving coverage, SST) . NiB $1277 Ex $1100 Gd $955
Model 202 (w/Greener
  cross bolt, DT) .... NiB $888 Ex $645 Gd $469
28 ga. and .410, add $125

HIGH STANDARD SPORTING ARMS — East Hartford, Connecticut; formerly High Standard Mfg. Corp. of Hamden, CT

In 1966, High Standard introduced new series of Flite-King Pumps and Supermatic autoloaders, both readily identifiable by the damascened bolt and restyled checkering. To avoid confusion, these models are designated "Series II" in this text. This is not an official factory designation. Operation of this firm was discontinued in 1984.

FLITE-KING FIELD
PUMP—12 GA. .... NiB $256 Ex $180 Gd $110
Hammerless. Magazine holds five rounds. Bbls.: 26-inch IC, 28-inch M or F, 30-inch F choke. Weight: 7.25 lbs. Plain pistol-grip stock and slide handle. Made from 1960 to 1966.

FLITE-KING BRUSH—12 GA.
... NiB $285 Ex $245 Gd $170
Same as Flite-King Field 2 except has 18- or 20-inch bbl. (cylinder bore) w/rifle sights. Made from 1962 to 1964.

FLITE-KING BRUSH DELUXE
.. NiB $275 Ex $190 Gd $120
Same as Flite-King Brush except has adj. peep rear sight, checkered pistol grip, recoil pad, fluted slide handle, swivels and sling. Not available w/18-inch bbl. Made from 1964 to 1966.

FLITE-KING BRUSH (SERIES II)
... NiB $275 Ex $190 Gd $120
Same as Flite-King Deluxe 12 (II) except has 20-inch bbl., cylinder bore, w/rifle sights. Weight: 7 lbs. Made from 1966 to 1975.

FLITE-KING BRUSH
DELUXE (II) .... NiB $290 Ex $200 Gd $135
Same as Flite-King Brush (II) except has adj. peep rear sight, swivels and sling. Made from 1966-75.

FLITE-KING DELUXE 12 GA. (SERIES II)
Hammerless. Five round magazine. 27-inch plain bbls.w/adj. choke. 26-inch IC, 28-inch M or F. 30-inch F choke. Weight: About 7.25 lbs. Checkered pistol-grip stock and forearm, recoil pad. Made from 1966 to 1975.
w/adj. choke .... NiB $245 Ex $170 Gd $110
w/fixed choke .... NiB $245 Ex $170 Gd $110

FLITE-KING DELUXE
20, 28, .410 GA. (SERIES II) ... NiB $255 Ex $178 Gd $120
Same as Flite-King Deluxe 12 (II) except chambered for 20 and .410 ga. 3-inch shell, 28 ga. 2.75-inch shell w/20- or 28-inch plain bbl. Weight: About 6 lbs. Made from 1966 to 1975.

FLITE-KING DELUXE RIB
12 GA. .... NiB $280 Ex $200 Gd $155
Same as Flite-King Field 12 except vent rib bbl. (28-inch M or F. 30-inch F). Checkered stock and forearm. Made from 1961-66.

SHOTGUNS

High Standard Flite-King Field
12 Gauge

High Standard Flite-King Field
20 Gauge

High Standard Flite-King Field Trophy
20 Gauge

High Standard Supermatic Deluxe
12 Gauge (II)

High Standard Supermatic Deluxe
12 Gauge (II) (Adjustable Choke)

High Standard Supermatic Deluxe Deer II

High Standard Supermatic Deluxe Duck Rib

High Standard Supermatic Deluxe Rib

High Standard Supermatic Duck —12 Gauge Magnum

FLITE-KING DELUXE RIB 12 GA. (II)
Same as Flite-King Deluxe 12 (II) except has vent rib bbl., available in 27-inch w/adj. choke, 28-inch M or F, 30-inch F choke. Made from 1966 to 1975.

w/adj. choke . . . . .NiB $292 Ex $217 Gd $175
w/fixed choke. . . . . .NiB $292 Ex $217 Gd $175

FLITE-KING DELUXE RIB 20 GA. . . NiB $265 Ex $198 Gd $125
Same as Flite-King Field 20 except vent-rib bbl. (28 inch M or F), checkered stock and slide handle. Made from 1962 to 1966.

FLITE-KING DELUXE RIB 20, 28, .410 GA. (SERIES II)
Same as Flite-King Deluxe 20, 28, .410 (II) except 20 ga. available w/27-inch adj. choke, 28-inch M or F choke. Weight: about 6.25 lbs. Made from 1966 to 1975.

w/adj. choke. . . . . .NiB $265 Ex $198 Gd $125
w/o adj. choke . . . . .NiB $265 Ex $198 Gd $125

FLITE-KING DELUXE SKEET GUN
12 GA. (SERIES II). . . . . .NiB $544 Ex $423 Gd $318
Same as Flite-King Deluxe Rib 12 (II) except available only w/26-inch vent rib bbl., SK choke, recoil pad optional. Made from 1966 to 1975.

FLITE-KING DELUXE SKEET GUN
20, 28, .410 GA. (SERIES II) . . . .NiB $454 Ex $39 Gd $243
Same as Flite-King Deluxe Rib 20, 28, .410 (II) except available only w/26-inch vent-rib bbl., SK choke. Made 1966 to 1975.

FLITE-KING DELUXE TRAP
GUN (SERIES II)) . . . . .NiB $338 Ex $265 Gd $129
Same as Flite-King Deluxe Rib 12 (II) except available only w/30-inch vent-rib bbl., F choke; trap-style stock. Made 1966 to 1975.

FLITE-KING FIELD PUMP
20 GA. . . . . .NiB $250 Ex $175 Gd $135
Hammerless. Chambered for 3-inch Magnum shells, also handles 2.75-inch. Magazine holds four rounds. Bbls.: 26-inch IC, 28-inch M or F choke. Weight: About 6 lbs. Plain pistol-grip stock and slide handle. Made from 1961 to 1966.

FLITE-KING FIELD PUMP
SHOTGUN 16 GA . . . . .NiB $250 Ex $175 Gd $135
Same general specifications as Flite-King 12 except not available in Brush, Skeet and Trap Models or 30-inch bbl. Values same as for 12-ga. guns. Made from 1961 to 1965.

FLITE-KING PUMP
SHOTGUN (.410). . . . . .NiB $350 Ex $275 Gd $235
Same general specifications as Flite-King 20 except not available in Special and Trophy Models, or w/other than 26-inch choke bbl. Add $100 to 20 gauge price. Made from 1962 to 1966.

FLITE-KING SKEET 12 GA. . . . .NiB $330 Ex $225 Gd $170
Same as Flite-King Deluxe Rib except 26-inch vent rib bbl., w/ SK choke. Made from 1962 to 1966.

FLITE-KING SPECIAL 12 GA. . . NiB $250 Ex $175 Gd $135
Same as Flite-King Field 12 except has 27-inch bbl. w/adj. choke. Made from 1960 to 1966.

FLITE-KING SPECIAL 20 GA. . . NiB $250 Ex $175 Gd $135
Same as Flite-King Field 20 except has 27-inch bbl. w/adj. choke. Made from 1961 to 1966.

FLITE-KING TRAP 12 GA. . . . . .NiB $330 Ex $225 Gd $140
Same as Flite-King Deluxe Rib 12 except 30-inch vent rib bbl., F choke, special trap stock w/recoil pad. Made from 1962 to 1966.

FLITE-KING TROPHY 12 GA. . . NiB $290 Ex $200 Gd $105
Same as Flite-King Deluxe Rib 12 except has 27-inch vent rib bbl. w/adj. choke. Made from 1960 to 1966.

FLITE-KING TROPHY 20 GA. . . NiB $290 Ex $200 Gd $105
Same as Flite-King Deluxe Rib 20 except has 27-inch vent rib bbl. w/adj. choke. Made from 1962 to 1966.

SUPERMATIC DEER GUN. . . . . NiB $345 Ex $165 Gd $100
Same as Supermatic Field 12 except has 22-inch bbl. (cylinder bore) w/rifle sights, checkered stock and forearm, recoil pad. Weight: 7.75 lbs. Made in 1965.

SUPERMATIC DELUXE 12 GA. (SERIES II)
Gas-operated autoloader. Four round magazine. Bbls.: Plain; 27-inch w/adj. choke (disc. about 1970); 26-inch IC, 28-inch M or F. 30-inch F choke. Weight: About 7.5 lbs. Checkered pistol-grip stock and forearm, recoil pad. Made from 1966 to 1975.

w/adj. choke . . . . .NiB $375 Ex $195 Gd $120
w/vent. rib, add $40

SUPERMATIC DELUXE 20 GA. (SERIES II)
Same as Supermatic Deluxe 12 (II) except chambered for 20 ga. Three inch shell; bbls. available in 27-inch w/adj. choke (disc. about 1970), 26-inch IC, 28-inch M or F choke. Weight: About 7 lbs. Made from 1966 to 1975.

w/adj. choke . . . . .NiB $315 Ex $199 Gd $99
Vent Rib, add $20

SUPERMATIC DELUXE DEER GUN
(SERIES II). . . . . NiB $345 Ex $165 Gd $100
Same as Supermatic Deluxe 12 (II) except has 22-inch bbl., cylinder bore, w/rifle sights. Weight: 7.75 lbs. Made from 1966 to 1974.

SUPERMATIC DELUXE DUCK
12 GA. MAGNUM (SERIES II). . NiB $335 Ex $227 Gd $140
Same as Supermatic Deluxe 12 (II) except chambered for 3-inch magnum shells, 3-round magazine, 30-inch plain bbl., F choke. Weight: 8 lbs. Made from 1966 to 1974.

SUPERMATIC DELUXE RIB
12 GA. . . . . .NiB $335 Ex $227 Gd $140
Same as Supermatic Field 12 except vent rib bbl. (28-inch M or F, 30-inch F), checkered stock and forearm. Made from 1961 to 1966.

SUPERMATIC DELUXE RIB 12 GA. (II)
Same as Supermatic Deluxe 12 (II) except has vent rib bbl.; available in 27-inch w/adj. choke, 28-inch M or F, 30-inch F choke. Made from 1966 to 1975.

w/adj. choke . . . . .NiB $335 Ex $227 Gd $140
w/vent. rib, add $50

SUPERMATIC DELUXE RIB
20 GA. . . . . .NiB $377 Ex $265 Gd $180
Same as Supermatic Field 20 except vent rib bbl. (28-inch M or F), checkered stock and forearm. Made from 1963 to 1966.

SUPERMATIC DELUXE RIB 20 GA. (II)
Same as Supermatic Deluxe 20 (II) except has vent rib bbl. Made from 1966 to 1975.

SHOTGUNS

High Standard Supermatic Duck Rib — 12 Gauge

High Standard Supermatic Shadow Automatic

High Standard Supermatic Shadow Indy

High Standard Supermatic Shadow Seven

High Standard Supermatic Special

High Standard Supermatic Trophy

w/adj. choke . . . . NiB $377 Ex $265 Gd $180
w/vent. rib, add $50

SUPERMATIC DELUXE SKEET GUN
12 GA. (SERIES II) . . . . NiB $380 Ex $275 Gd $190
Same as Supermatic Deluxe Rib 12 (II) except available only w/26-inch vent rib bbl., SK choke. Made from 1966 to 1975.

SUPERMATIC DELUXE SKEET GUN
20 GA. (SERIES II) . . . . NiB $370 Ex $285 Gd $200
Same as Supermatic Deluxe Rib 20 (II) except available only w/26-inch vent rib bbl., SK choke. Made from 1966 to 1975.

SUPERMATIC DELUXE
TRAP GUN (SERIES II) . . . . . . NiB $315 Ex $239 Gd $177
Same as Supermatic Deluxe Rib 12 (II) except available only w/30-inch vent rib bbl., full choke; trap-style stock. Made 1966 to 1975.

SUPERMATIC DELUXE DUCK RIB
12 GA. MAG. (SERIES II) . . . . . NiB $375 Ex $265 Gd $180
Same as Supermatic Deluxe Rib 12 (II) except chambered for 3-inch magnum shells, 3-round magazine; 30-inch vent rib bbl., F choke. Weight: 8 lbs. Made from 1966 to 1975.

SUPERMATIC DUCK
12 GA. MAG. . . . . NiB $355 Ex $241 Gd $188
Same as Supermatic Field 12 except chambered for 3-inch Magnum shell, 30-inch F choke bbl., recoil pad. Made from 1961 to 1966.

SUPERMATIC TROPHY 12 GA... NiB $300 Ex $198 Gd $140
Same as Supermatic Deluxe Rib 12 except has 27-inch vent-rib bbl. w/adj. choke. Made from 1961 to 1966.

SUPERMATIC DUCK RIB
12 GA. MAG. .... NiB $355 Ex $241 Gd $188
Same as Supermatic Duck 12 Magnum except has vent rib bbl., checkered stock and forearm. Made from 1961 to 1966.

SUPERMATIC FIELD AUTOLOADING
SHOTGUN 12 GA. .... NiB $270 Ex $197 Gd $110
Gas-operated. Magazine holds four rounds. Bbls.: 26-inch IC, 28-inch M or F choke, 30-inch F choke. Weight: About 7.5 lbs. Plain pistol-grip stock and forearm. Made from 1960 to 1966.

SUPERMATIC FIELD AUTOLOADING
SHOTGUN 20 GA .... NiB $290 Ex $217 Gd $156
Gas-operated. Chambered for 3-inch mag. shells, also handles 2.75-inch. Magazine holds three rounds. Bbls.: 26-inch IC, 28-inch M or F choke. Weight: About 7 lbs. Plain pistol-grip stock and forearm. Made from 1963 to 1966.

SUPERMATIC SHADOW
AUTOMATIC.............. NiB $455 Ex $265 Gd $200
Gas-operated. Ga.: 12, 20, 2.75- or 3-inch chamber in 12 ga., 3-inch in 20 ga. Mag. holds four 2.75-inch shells, three 3-inch. Bbls.: Full-size airflow rib; 26-inch (IC or SK choke), 28-inch (M, IM or F), 30-inch (trap or F choke), 12-ga. 3-inch Mag. available only in 30-inch F choke; 20 ga. not available in 30-inch. Weight: 12 ga., 7 lbs. Checkered walnut stock and forearm. Made 1974 to 1975 by Caspoll Int'l., Inc., Tokyo.

SUPERMATIC SHADOW
INDY O/U................ NiB $935 Ex $770 Gd $500
Boxlock. Fully engraved receiver. Selective auto ejectors. Selective single trigger. 12 ga. 2.75-inch chambers. Bbls.: Full-size airflow rib; 27.5 inch both SK choke, 29.75-inch IM/F or F/F. Weight: W/29.75-inch bbls., 8 lbs. 2 oz. Pistol-grip stock w/recoil pad, ventilated forearm, skip checkering. Made 1974 to 1975 by Caspoll Int'l., Inc., Tokyo.

SUPERMATIC SHADOW SEVEN .. NiB $755 Ex $533 Gd $400
Same general specifications as Shadow Indy except has conventional vent rib, less elaborate engraving, standard checkering forearm is not vented, no recoil pad. 27.5-inch bbls.; also available in IC/M, M/F choke. Made from 1974 to 1975.

SUPERMATIC SKEET 12 GA.... NiB $344 Ex $245 Gd $177
Same as Supermatic Deluxe Rib 12 except 26-inch vent-rib bbl. w/SK choke. Made from 1962 to 1966.

SUPERMATIC SKEET 20 GA.... NiB $390 Ex $277 Gd $217
Same as Supermatic Deluxe Rib 20 except 26-inch vent-rib bbl. w/SK choke. Made from 1964 to 1966.

SUPERMATIC SPECIAL 12 GA. NiB $290 Ex $190 Gd $145
Same as Supermatic Field 12 except has 27-inch bbl. w/adj. choke. Made from 1960 to 1966.

SUPERMATIC SPECIAL 20 GA. NiB $315 Ex $220 Gd $145
Same as Supermatic Field 20 except has 27-inch bbl. w/adj. choke. Made from 1963 to 1966.

SUPERMATIC TRAP 12 GA. ... NiB $330 Ex $245 Gd $170
Same as Supermatic Deluxe Rib 12 except 30-inch vent rib bbl., F choke, special trap stock w/recoil pad. Made from 1962 to 1966.

SUPERMATIC TROPHY 20 GA. NiB $360 Ex $275 Gd $190
Same as Supermatic Deluxe Rib 20 except has 27-inch vent rib bbl. w/adj. choke. Made from 1963 to 1966.

HOLLAND & HOLLAND, LTD. —
London, England

BADMINTON HAMMERLESS DOUBLE-BARREL SHOTGUN, ORIGINAL NO. 2 GRADE
General specifications same as Royal Model except without self-opening action. Made as a game gun or pigeon and wildfowl gun. Introduced in 1902. Disc.
w/double triggers ... NiB $27,875 Ex $22,500 Gd $18,975
w/single trigger..... NiB $28,875 Ex $24,000 Gd $19,600
20 ga., add 25%
28 ga., add 40%
.410, add.. 65%

CENTENARY MODEL HAMMERLESS
DOUBLE-BARREL SHOTGUN
Lightweight (5.5 lbs.). 12 ga. game gun designed for 2-inch shell. Made in four grades — Model Deluxe, Royal, Badminton, Dominion. Values: Add 35% to prices shown for standard guns in those grades. Disc. 1962.

DOMINION MODEL HAMMERLESS
DOUBLE-BBL. SHOTGUN ...NiB $7355 Ex $6121 Gd $3896
Game Gun. Sidelock. Auto ejectors. Double triggers. Gauges: 12, 16, 20. bbls. 25- to 30-inch, any standard boring. Checkered stock and forend, straight grip standard. Disc. 1967.

DELUXE HAMMERLESS DOUBLE
Same as Royal Model except has special engraving and exhibition grade stock and forearm. Currently manufactured.
w/double triggers ... NiB $44,579 Ex $41,960 Gd $34,590
w/single trigger .... NiB $66,800 Ex $53,980 Gd $40,676

NORTHWOOD MODEL HAMMERLESS DOUBLE-BARREL
SHOTGUN .... NiB $6154 Ex $4944 Gd $4000
Anson & Deeley system boxlock. Auto ejectors. Double triggers. Gauges: 12, 16, 20, 28 in Game Model; 28 ga. not offered in Pigeon Model; Wildfowl Model in 12 ga. only (3-inch chambers available). Bbls.: 28-inch standard in Game and Pigeon Models, 30-inch in Wildfowl Model; other lengths, any standard choke combination available. Weight: From 5 to 7.75 lbs. depending on ga. and bbls. Checkered straight-grip or pistol-grip stock and forearm. Disc. 1990.

RIVIERA MODEL
PIGEON GUN ..... NiB $32,877 Ex $25,788 Gd $19,900
Same as Badminton Model but supplied w/two sets of bbls., double triggers. Disc. 1967.

ROYAL MODEL HAMMERLESS DOUBLE
Self-opening. Sidelocks hand-detachable. Auto ejectors. Double triggers or single trigger. Gauges: 12, 16, 20, 28 .410. Built to customer's specifications as to bbl. length, chokes, etc. Made as a Game Gun or Pigeon and Wildfowl Gun, the latter having treble-grip action and side clips. Checkered stock and forend, straight grip standard. Made from 1885, disc. 1951.

SHOTGUNS

Hign Standard Supermatic Special

Holland & Holland Badminton

Holland & Holland Dominion

Holland & Holland
Royal Double-Barrel Shotgun

IGA Coach Gun

w/double triggers ... NiB $39,900 Ex $31,676 Gd $28,800
w/single trigger .... NiB $44,980 Ex $42,600 Gd $36,700

ROYAL MODEL O/U
Sidelocks, hand-detachable. Auto-ejectors. Double triggers or single trigger. 12 ga. Built to customer's specifications as to bbl. length, chokes, etc. Made as a Game Gun or Pigeon and Wildfowl Gun. Checkered stock and forend, straight grip standard. Note: In 1951 Holland & Holland introduced its New Model Under/Over w/an improved, narrower action body. Disc. 1960.
New model
   (double triggers) . NiB $40,770 Ex $32,550 Gd $21,900
New model
   (single trigger) ... NiB $41,800 Ex $33,750 Gd $22,500
Old model
   (double triggers) . NiB $33,970 Ex $27,600 Gd $20,550
Old model
   (single trigger) ... NiB $36,975 Ex $29,500 Gd $21,880

SINGLE-SHOT SUPER TRAP GUN
Anson & Deeley system boxlock. Auto-ejector. No safety. 12 ga. Bbls.: Wide vent rib, 30- or 32-inch, w/Extra Full choke. Weight: About 8.75 lbs. Monte Carlo stock w/pistol grip and recoil pad, full beavertail forearm. Models differ in grade of engraving and wood used. Disc.
Standard grade .... NiB $4890 Ex $2988 Gd $1598
Deluxe grade .... NiB $7355 Ex $6355 Gd $3559
Exhibition grade .... NiB $9677 Ex $7355 Gd $4977

IGA Turkey S/S Shotgun

SPORTING O/U .... NiB $31,750 Ex $24,776 Gd $17,870
Blitz action. Auto ejectors; single selective trigger. Gauges: 12 or 20 w/2.75-inch chambers. Barrels: 28- to 32-inch w/screw-in choke tubes. Hand-checkered European walnut straight-grip or pistol grip stock, forearm. Made from 1993 to 2003 .

SPORTING O/U
DELUXE .... NiB $38,875 Ex $32,669 Gd $23,670
Same general specs as Sporting O/U except better engraving and select wood. Made from 1993 to date.

HUNTER ARMS COMPANY —
Fulton, New York

FULTON HAMMERLESS DOUBLE-BARREL SHOTGUN
Boxlock. Plain extractors. Double triggers or non-selective single trigger. Gauges: 12 16, 20. Bbls.: 26- to 32-inch various choke combinations. Weight: about 7 lbs. Checkered pistol-grip stock and forearm. Disc. 1948.
w/double triggers .... NiB $775 Ex $450 Gd $375
w/single trigger .... NiB $990 Ex $700 Gd $555

SPECIAL HAMMERLESS DOUBLE-BARREL SHOTGUN
Boxlock. Plain extractors. Double triggers or non-selective single trigger. Gauges: 12,16, 20. Bbls.: 26- to 30-inch various choke combinations. Weight: 6.5 to 7.25 lbs. depending on bbl. length and ga. Checkered full pistol-grip stock and forearm. Disc. 1948.
w/double triggers .... NiB $933 Ex $655 Gd $500
w/single trigger .... NiB $1155 Ex $820 Gd $600

IGA — Veranopolis, Brazil
Imported by Stoeger Industries, Inc., Accokeek, Maryland.

STANDARD COACH GUN
Side-by-side double. Gauges: 12, 20 and .410. 20-inch bbls. w/3-inch chambers. Fixed chokes (standard model) or screw-in tubes (deluxe model). Weight: 6.5 lbs. Double triggers. Ejector and automatic safety. Blued or nickel finish. Hand-rubbed oil-finished pistol grip stock and forend w/hand checkering (hardwood on standard model or Brazilian walnut (deluxe). Imported from 1983 to 2000.
blued finish................ NiB $400 Ex $295 Gd $200
nickel finish................ NiB $465 Ex $377 Gd $259
engraved stock .... NiB $445 Ex $335 Gd $225
Deluxe Coach Gun (intro. 1997) NiB $400 Ex $290 Gd $195
w/choke tubes, add........................... $75

CONDOR I
O/U, single trigger; Gauges: 12 or 20. 26- or 28-inch bbls. of chrome-molybdenum steel. Chokes: Fixed — M/F or IC/M; screw-in choke tubes (12 and 20 ga.). Three inch chambers.

Weight: 6.75 to 7 lbs. Sighting rib w/anti-glare surface. Hand-checkered hardwood pistol-grip stock and forend. Imported from 1983 to 1985.
w/fixed choke.............. NiB $420 Ex $377 Gd $210
w/screw-in tubes .... NiB $510 Ex $441 Gd $350

CONDOR II .... NiB $477 Ex $365 Gd $290
Same general specifications as the Condor I O/U except w/double triggers and fixed chokes only; 26-inch bbls., IC/M; 28-inch bbls., M/F.

CONDOR OUTBACK .... NiB $499 Ex $370 Gd $290
Same general specifications as the Condor I O/U except w/ 20-inch bbls., IC/M choke tubes, rifle-style sights. Made 2007 to date.

CONDOR SUPREME......... NiB $655 Ex $545 Gd $477
Same general specifications as Condor I except upgraded w/fine-checkered Brazilian walnut buttstock and forend, a matte-laquered finish, and a massive monoblock that joins the bbls. in a solid one-piece assembly at the breech end. Bbls. w/recessed interchangeable choke tubes formulated for use w/steel shot. Automatic ejectors. Imported from 1995 to 2000.

CONDOR TURKEY MODEL ... NiB $755 Ex $600 Gd $445
12 gauge only. 26-inch vent-rib bbls. w/3-inch chambers fitted w/recessed interchangeable choke tubes. Weight: 8 lbs. Mechanical single trigger. Ejectors and automatic safety. Advantage camouflage on stock and bbls. Made from 1997 to 2000.

CONDOR WATERFOWL
MODEL.................. NiB $770 Ex $605 Gd $475
Similar to Condor Turkey-Advantage camo model except w/30-inch bbls. Made from 1998 to 2000.

DELUXE HUNTER CLAYS ..... NiB $700 Ex $552 Gd $435
Same general specifications and values as IGA Condor Supreme. Imported from 1997 to 1999.

DOUBLE DEFENSE .... NiB $499 Ex $280 Gd $135
Similar to Coach S/S box lock. Gauges: 12 or 20 ga., 20-inch ported bbls. w/ Picatinny rails. Fixed IC choke; 3-inch chambers. Weight: 6.4 to 7.1 lbs. Single trigger. Matte black finish receiver and pistol-grip wood stock. Imported from 2009 to date.
Non-ported bbl. .... NiB $479 Ex $275 Gd $120

ERA MODEL 2000 .... NiB $500 Ex $379 Gd $290
Gauge: 12 w/3-inch chambers. 26- or 28-inch bbls. of chrome-molybdenum steel w/screw-in choke tubes. Extractors. Manual safety. (Mechanical triggers.) Weight: 7 lbs. Checkered Brazilian hardwood stock w/oil finish. Imported from 1992 to 1995.

REUNA SINGLE-SHOT
Visible hammer. Under-lever release. Gauges: 12, 20 and .410; 3-inch chambers. 26- or 28-inch bbls. w/fixed chokes or screw-in choke tubes (12 ga. only). Extractors. Weight: 5.25 to 6.5

SHOTGUNS

IGA Condor Turkey O/U Shotgun

IGA Deluxe Hunter Clay Shotgun

IGA Uplander Side-by-Side Shotgun

lbs. Plain Brazilian hardwood stock and semi-beavertail forend. Imported from 1992 to1998.

w/fixed choke . . . . NiB $210 Ex $155 Gd $90
w/choke tubes. . . . . NiB $275 Ex $190 Gd $145

UPLANDER
S/S box lock; Gauges: 12, 20, 28 and .410. 26- or 28-inch bbls. of chrome-molybdenum steel. Various fixed-choke combinations; screw-in choke tubes (12 and 20 ga.). Three inch chambers (2.75-inch in 28 ga.). Weight: 6.25 to 7 lbs. Double triggers. Automatic safety. Matte-finished solid sighting rib. Hand checkered pistol-grip or straight stock and forend w/hand-rubbed, oil-finish. Imported from 1997 to 2000.

Upland w/fixed chokes. . . . . . . NiB $390 Ex $275 Gd $225
Upland w/screw-in tubes . . . . . NiB $420 Ex $345 Gd $290
English model (straight grip) . . . NiB $500 Ex $395 Gd $290
Ladies model. . . . . NiB $477 Ex $365 Gd $300
Supreme model. . . . . NiB $610 Ex $477 Gd $325
Youth model . . . . NiB $477 Ex $345 Gd $270

UPLANDER TURKEY MODEL . NiB $588 Ex $440 Gd $379
12 gauge only. 24-inch solid rib bbls. w/3-inch chambers choked F&F. Weight: 6.75 lbs. Double triggers. Automatic safety. Advantage camouflage on stock and bbls. Made from 1997 to 2000.

ITHACA GUN COMPANY — King Ferry (formerly Ithaca), New York; Ithaca Acquisition Corp./Ithaca Gun Co.

**MODEL 37 BICENTENNIAL
COMMEMORATIVE** . . . . NiB $645 Ex $553 Gd $445
Limited to issue of 1976. Similar to Model 37 Supreme except has special Bicentennial design etched on receiver, fancy walnut stock and slide handle. Serial numbers U.S.A. 0001 to U.S.A. 1976. Originally issued w/presentation case w/cast-pewter belt buckle. Made in 1976. Best value is for gun in new, unfired condition.

MODEL 37 DEERSLAYER DELUXE
Formerly "Model 87 Deerslayer Deluxe" reintroduced under the original Model 37 designation w/the same specifications. Available w/smooth bore or rifled bbl. Reintroduced 1996. Disc.

Deluxe model (smoothbore) . . . NiB $575 Ex $490 Gd $335
Deluxe model (rifled bbl.). . . . . NiB $608 Ex $522 Gd $370

MODEL 37 DEERSLAYER II . . . . NiB $608 Ex $522 Gd $370
Gauges: 12 or 20 ga. Five round capacity. 20- or 25-inch rifled bbl. Weight: 7 lbs. Monte Carlo checkered walnut stock and forearm. Receiver drilled and tapped for scope mount. Made 1996 to 2000.

**MODEL 37 DEERSLAYER
STANDARD.** . . . . NiB $355 Ex $280 Gd $225
Same as Model 37 Standard except has 20- or 26-inch bbl. bored for rifled slugs, rifle-type open rear sight and ramp front sight. Weight: 5.75 to 6.5 lbs. depending on ga. and bbl. length. Made from 1959-86.

**MODEL 37 DEERSLAYER
SUPER DELUXE** . . . . NiB $465 Ex $344 Gd $220
Formerly "Deluxe Deerslayer." Same as Model 37 Standard Deerslayer except has stock and slide handle of fancy walnut. Made 1962 to 1986.

**MODEL 37 ENGLISH
ULTRALIGHT** . . . . NiB $635 Ex $500 Gd $400
Same general specifications as Model 37 Ultralite except straight buttstock, 25-inch Hot Forged vent-rib bbl. Made 1984 to 1987.

Ithaca Model 37 English Ultra

Ithaca Model 37 Featherlight Standard

Ithaca Model 37 Deerslayer Super Deluxe

Ithaca Model 37 Supreme Grade

MODEL 37 FEATHERLIGHT STANDARD GRADE SLIDE-ACTION REPEATING SHOTGUN

Adaptation of the earlier Remington Model 17, a Browning design patented in 1915. Hammerless. Takedown. Gauges: 12, 16 (disc. 1973), 20. Four round magazine. Bbl. lengths: 26-, 28-, 30-inch (the latter in 12 ga. only); standard chokes. Weight: From 5.75 to 7.5 lbs. depending on ga. and bbl. length. Checkered pistol-grip stock and slide handle. Some guns made in the 1950s and 1960s have grooved slide handle; plain or checkered pistol-grip. Made 1937 to 1984.

Standard model w/checkered

pistol grip	NiB $675	Ex $390	Gd $300
w/plain stock	NiB $325	Ex $229	Gd $190
Model 37D Deluxe (1954-77)	NiB $675	Ex $390	Gd $300
Model 37DV Deluxe vent rib (1962-84)	NiB $675	Ex $390	Gd $300
Model 37R Deluxe solid rib (1955-61)	NiB $675	Ex $390	Gd $300
Model 37V Standard vent rib (1962-84)	NiB $315	Ex $244	Gd $148

MODEL 37 FIELD GRADE

MAG. W/TUBES . . . . NiB $355 Ex $298 Gd $199
Same general specifications as Model 37 Featherlight except 32-inch bbl. and detachable choke tubes. Vent rib bbl. Made 1984 to 1987.

MODEL 37 CLASSIC . . . . NiB $755 Ex $555 Gd $465

Ggs: 12 or 20 ga. 20- or 28-inch vent rib bbl. w/choke tubes. Knuckle-cut receiver and orig. style "ring-tail" forend. Lim. prod. Made from 1998 to 2005.

MODEL 37 $1000 GRADE

Custom built, elaborately engraved and inlaid w/gold, hand-finished working parts, stock and forend of select figured walnut. General specifications same as standard Model 37. Note: Designated The $1000 Grade prior to World War II. Made 1937 to 1967.

$1000 grade	NiB $5988	Ex $4776	Gd $3987
$5000 grade	NiB $5588	Ex $4487	Gd $3960

MODEL 37 SUPREME GRADE . . NiB $955 Ex $588 Gd $535

Available in Skeet or Trap Gun, similar to Model 37T. Made 1967-86 and 1997. Subtract $225 for newer models.

MODEL 37 ULTRALITE

Same general specifications as Model 37 Featherlight except streamlined forend, gold trigger, Sid Bell grip cap and vent rib. Weight: 5 to 5.75 lbs. Made from 1984 to 1987.

Standard	NiB $559	Ex $400	Gd $363
W/choke tubes, add			$150

MODEL 37R SOLID RIB GRADE

Same general specifications as the Model 37 Featherlight except has a raised solid rib, adding about .25 pounds of weight. Made 1937 to 1967.

w/checkered grip and slide handle	NiB $400	Ex $310	Gd $200
w/plain stock	NiB $292	Ex $195	Gd $145

MODEL 37S SKEET GRADE . . . NiB $565 Ex $455 Gd $335

Same general specifications as the Model 37 Featherlight except has vent rib and large extension-type forend; weight: About .5 lb. more. Made from 1937 to 1955.

SHOTGUNS

Ithaca Model 51 Deluxe Trap

Ithaca Model 66RS Buckbuster

MODEL 37T TARGET GRADE . . NiB $545 Ex $376 Gd $255
Same general specifications as Model 37 Featherlight except
has vent-rib bbl., checkered stock and slide handle of fancy
walnut (choice of skeet- or trap-style stock). Note: This model
replaced Model 37S Skeet and Model 37T Trap. Made from
1955- to 191.

MODEL 37T TRAP GRADE . . . . NiB $545 Ex $376 Gd $255
Same gen. specs. as Mdl. 37S except has straighter trap-style
stock of select walnut, recoil pad; weight: About .5 lb. more.
Made from 1937-55.

MODEL 37 TURKEYSLAYER
Gauges: 12 ga. (Standard) or 20 ga. (youth). Slide action.
22-inch bbl. Extended choke tube. Weight: 7 lbs. Advantage
camouflage or Realtree pattern. Made from 1996 to 2005.
Standard model . . . . NiB $425 Ex $260 Gd $190
Youth model (intro. 1998). . . . NiB $555 Ex $456 Gd $345

MODEL 37 WATERFOWLER . . . NiB $490 Ex $375 Gd $260
12 ga. only w/28-inch bbl. Wetlands camouflage. Made 1998
to 2005.

MODEL 51 DEERSLAYER . . . . . NiB $400 Ex $279 Gd $200
Same as Model 51 Standard except has 24-inch plain bbl. w/
slug boring, rifle sights, recoil pad. Weight: About 7.25 lbs.
Made from 1972 to 1984.

MODEL 51 SUPREME SKEET
GRADE . . . . NiB $525 Ex $390 Gd $270
Same as Model 51 Standard except 26-inch vent-rib bbl. only,
SK choke, skeet-style stock, semi-fancy wood. Weight: About 8
lbs. Made from 1970 to 1987.

MODEL 51 SUPREME TRAP
Same as Model 51 Standard except 12 ga. only, 30-inch bbl. w/
broad floating rib, F choke, trap-style stock w/straight or Monte
Carlo comb, semifancy wood, recoil pad. Weight: About 8 lbs.
Made from 1970 to 1987.
w/straight stock . . . . NiB $544 Ex $390 Gd $295
w/Monte Carlo stock, add $75

MODEL 51 FEATHERLITE STANDARD
Gas-operated. Gauges: 12, 20. Three round. Bbls.: Plain or vent
rib, 30-inch F choke (12 ga. only), 28-inch F or M, 26-inch IC.
Weight: 7.25-7.75 lbs. depending on ga. and bbl. Checkered
pistol-grip stock, forearm. Made 1970 to 1980. Avail. in 12 and

20 ga., 28-inch M choke only.
w/plain barrel . . . . NiB $300 Ex $197 Gd $121
w/vent rib, add $65

MODEL 51A STANDARD MAGNUM
Same as Model 51 Standard except has 3-inch chamber,
handles Magnum shells only; 30-inch bbl. in 12 ga., 28-inch
in 20 ga., F or M choke, stock w/recoil pad. Weight: 7.75-8 lbs.
Made 1972 to 1982.
w/plain bbl. (disc. 1976) . . . . . . NiB $375 Ex $290 Gd $200
w/camo finish, add $65

MODEL 51A TURKEY GUN . . . NiB $455 Ex $300 Gd $217
Same general specifications as standard Model 51 Magnum
except 26-inch bbl. and matte finish. Disc. 1986.

MODEL 66 LONG TOM . . . . . . NiB $210 Ex $155 Gd $100
Same as Model 66 Standard except 36-inch F choke bbl.,
12 ga. only, checkered stock and recoil pad standard. Made
1969 to 1974.

MODEL 66 STANDARD SUPER SINGLE LEVER
Single shot. Hand-cocked hammer. Gauges: 12 (disc. 1974),
20, .410, 3-inch chambers. Bbls.: 12 ga., 30-inch F choke,
28-inch F or M; 20 ga., 28-inch F or M; .410, 26-inch F.
Weight: About 7 lbs. Plain or checkered straight-grip stock,
plain forend. Made from 1963 to 1978.
Standard model . . . . NiB $220 Ex $115 Gd $90
Vent. rib model (20 ga., 1969-74) . . . NiB $225 Ex $159 Gd $135
Youth model (1965-78) . . . . NiB $250 Ex $179 Gd $130

MODEL 66RS BUCKBUSTER . . NiB $279 Ex $200 Gd $155
Same as Model 66 Standard except has 22-inch bbl. cylinder
bore w/rifle sights, later version has recoil pad. Originally
offered in 12 and 20 ga.; the former was disc. in 1970. Made
from 1967 to 1978.

*Previously issued as the Ithaca Model 37, the Model 87
guns listed below were made available through the Ithaca
Acquisition Corp. From 1986-95. Production of the Model 37
resumed under the original logo in 1996.*

MODEL 87 DEERLSLAYER SHOTGUN
Gauges: 12 or 20, 3-inch chamber. Bbls.: 18.5-, 20- or 25-inch
(w/special or rifled bore). Weight: 6 to 6.75 lbs. Ramp blade
front sight, adj. rear. Receiver grooved for scope. Checkered
American walnut pistol-grip stock and forearm. Made from
1988 to 1996.

**Ithaca Hammerless
Field Grade**

**Ithaca Hammerless
No. 2**

**Ithaca Hammerless
No. 4**

Basic model . . . . NiB $445 Ex $355 Gd $225
Basic Field Combo
  (w/extra 28-inch bbl.) . . . . . NiB $475 Ex $390 Gd $280
Deluxe model . . . . NiB $480 Ex $395 Gd $290
Deluxe Combo
  (w/extra 28-inch bbl.) . . . . . NiB $635 Ex $460 Gd $339
DSPS (8-round model) . . . . NiB $554 Ex $400 Gd $290
Field model . . . . NiB $433 Ex $330 Gd $287
Monte Carlo model . . . . NiB $448 Ex $356 Gd $255
Ultra model (disc. 1991) . . . . . NiB $500 Ex $398 Gd $325

MODEL 87 DEERSLAYER II
RIFLED SHOTGUN . . . . NiB $600 Ex $433 Gd $310
Similar to Standard Deerslayer except w/solid frame
construction and 25-inch rifled bbl. Monte Carlo stock. Made
1988 to 1996.

MODEL 87 ULTRALITE
FIELD PUMP SHOTGUN . . . . . NiB $490 Ex $387 Gd $260
Gauges: 12 and 20; 2.75-inch chambers. 25-inch bbl. w/choke
tube. Weight: 5 to 6 lbs. Made from 1988 to 1990.

MODEL 87 FIELD GRADE
Gauge: 12 or 20.; 3-inch chamber. Five round magazine. Fixed
chokes or screw-in choke tubes (IC, M, F). Bbls.: 18.5-inch
(M&P); 20- and 25-inch (Combo); 26-, 28-, 30-inch vent rib.
Weight: 5 to 7 lbs. Made from 1988 to 1996.
Basic field model (disc. 1993). . NiB $446 Ex $270 Gd $210
Camo model . . . . NiB $490 Ex $339 Gd $260
Deluxe model . . . . NiB $505 Ex $340 Gd $280
Deluxe Combo model. . . . . NiB $590 Ex $493 Gd $377
English model . . . . NiB $490 Ex $339 Gd $260
Hand grip model
  (w/polymer pistol-grip) . . . . . NiB $533 Ex $425 Gd $315
M&P model (disc. 1995) . . . . . . NiB $466 Ex $380 Gd $279
Supreme model. . . . . NiB $720 Ex $589 Gd $400
Turkey model . . . . NiB $445 Ex $365 Gd $256
Ultra Deluxe model (disc. 1992) NiB $400 Ex $356 Gd $260

HAMMERLESS DOUBLE-BARREL SHOTGUNS
Boxlock. Plain extractors, auto ejectors standard on the "E"
grades. Double triggers, non-selective or selective single
trigger extra. Gauges: Magnum 10, 12; 12, 16, 20, 28, .410.

Bbls.: 26- to 32-inch, any standard boring. Weight: 5.75
(.410) to 10.5 lbs. (Magnum 10). Checkered pistol-grip stock
and forearm standard. Higher grades differ from Field Grade
in quality of workmanship, grade of wood, checkering,
engraving, etc.; general specifications are the same. Ithaca
doubles made before 1925 (serial number 425,000) the rotary
bolt and a stronger frame were adopted. Values shown are
for this latter type; earlier models valued about 50% lower.
Smaller gauge guns may command up to 75% higher. Disc.
1948.
Field grade . . . . NiB $1088 Ex $900 Gd $677
No. 1 grade. . . . . NiB $1377 Ex $1099 Gd $890
No. 2 grade. . . . . NiB $2480 Ex $2077 Gd $1100
No. 3 grade. . . . . NiB $2456 Ex $1866 Gd $1376
No. 4E grade (ejector) . . . . . NiB $6225 Ex $3688 Gd $2977
No. 5E grade (ejector) . . . . . NiB $5235 Ex $3767 Gd $4400

Extras:
Magnum 10 or 12 ga.
  (in other than the four highest grades), add **20%**

**Ithaca Hammerless
Field Grade**

Ithaca Model 5-E

SHOTGUNS

Ithaca-Perazzi
Competition I Skeet

Ithaca-Perazzi
Competition I Trap

Ithaca-Perazzi
Light Game

Ithaca-Perazzi
Mirage Trap

Automatic ejectors (grades No. 1, 2, 3,
  w/ejectors designated No. 1E, 2E, 3E), add 35%
Selective single trigger, add $250
Non-selective single trigger, add $200
Beavertail forend (Field No. 1 or 2), add $200
Beavertail forend (No. 3 or 4), add $200
Beavertail forend (No. 5, 7 or $2000 grade), add $200
Ventilated rib (No. 4, 5, 7 or $2000 grade), add $400
Ventilated rib (lower grades), add $250

LSA-55 TURKEY GUN . . . . NiB $935 Ex $700 Gd $590
Over/under shotgun/rifle combination. Boxlock. Exposed hammer. Plain extractor. Single trigger. 12 ga./222 Rem. 24.5-inch ribbed bbls. (rifle bbl. has muzzle brake). Weight: About 7 lbs. Folding leaf rear sight, bead front sight. Checkered Monte Carlo stock and forearm. Made 1970 to 1977 by Oy Tikkakoski AB, Finland.

MAG-10 AUTOMATIC SHOTGUN
Gas-operated. 10 ga. 3.5-inch Magnum. Three round capacity. 32-inch plain (Standard Grade only) or vent-rib bbl. F choke.

Ithaca Single-Shot Trap
"Dollar Grade"

Weight: 11 lbs., plain bbl.; 11.5 lbs., vent rib. Standard grade has plain stock and forearm. Deluxe and Supreme Grades have checkering, semi-fancy and fancy wood respectively, and stud swivel. All have recoil pad. Deluxe and Supreme grades made 1974 to 191982. Standard Grade intro. in 1977. All grades disc. 1986.

Camo model	NiB $735	Ex $555	Gd $379
Deluxe grade	NiB $890	Ex $774	Gd $522
Roadblocker	NiB $855	Ex $740	Gd $533
Standard grade, plain bbl.	NiB $744	Ex $610	Gd $477
Standard grade w/vent. rib	NiB $844	Ex $633	Gd $530
Standard grade, w/choke tubes	NiB $988	Ex $755	Gd $544
Supreme grade	NiB $1044	Ex $856	Gd $600

SINGLE-SHOT TRAP, FLUES AND KNICK MODELS
Boxlock. Hammerless. Ejector. 12 ga. only. Bbl. lengths: 30-, 32-, 34-inch (32-inch only in Victory grade). Vent rib. Weight: About 8 lbs. Checkered pistol-grip stock and forend. Grades differ only in quality of workmanship, engraving, checkering, wood, etc. Flues Model, serial numbers under 400,000, made 1908 to 1921. Triple-bolted Knick Model, serial numbers above 400,000, made since 1921. Victory Model disc. in 1938, No. 7-E in 1964, No. 4-E in 1976, No. 5-E in 1986, Dollar Grade in 1991. Values shown are for Knick Model; Flues models about 50% lower.

Victory grade	NiB $1379	Ex $1100	Gd $925
No. 4-E	NiB $3766	Ex $3470	Gd $1790
No. 5-E	NiB $5000	Ex $4766	Gd $2128
No. 6-E (rare)	NiB $16,980	Ex $14,700	Gd $10,000
No. 7-E (rare)	NiB $7445	Ex $6000	Gd $4655

$2,000 grade . . . . NiB $9,500 Ex $8500 Gd $6650
Pre-war $1000 grade . . . NiB $10,000 Ex $9577 Gd $6650
Sousa grade (rare) . . .NiB $14,500+ Ex $12,700+ Gd $9000+

NOTE: *The following Ithaca-Perazzi shotguns were manufactured by Manifattura Armi Perazzi, Brescia, Italy. See also separate Perazzi listings.*

**PERAZZI COMPETITION
I SKEET** . . . . NiB $14,877 Ex $13,900 Gd $11,270
Boxlock. Auto ejectors. Single trigger. 12 ga. 26.75-inch vent-rib bbls. SK choke w/integral muzzle brake. Weight: About 7.75 lbs. Checkered skeet-style pistol-grip buttstock and forearm; recoil pad. Made from 1969 to 1974.

**PERAZZI COMPETITION
TRAP I O/U** . . . . NiB $14,889 Ex $13,679 Gd $11,650
Boxlock. Auto ejectors. Single trigger. 12 ga. 30- or 32-inch vent-rib bbls. IM/F choke. Weight: About 8.5 lbs. Checkered pistol-grip stock, forearm; recoil pad. Made from 1969 to 1974.

**PERAZZI COMPETITION I
TRAP SINGLE BARREL** . . NiB $11,770 Ex $9455 Gd $7655
Boxlock. Auto ejection. 12 ga. 32- or 34-inch bbl., vent rib, F choke. Weight: 8.5 lbs. Checkered Monte Carlo stock and beavertail forearm, recoil pad. Made from 1973 to 1978.

**PERAZZI COMPETITION IV
TRAP GUN** . . . . NiB $13,890 Ex $11,870 Gd $10,000
Boxlock. Auto ejection. 12 ga. 32- or 34-inch bbl. With high, wide vent rib, four interchangeable choke tubes (Extra Full, F, IM, M). Weight: About 8.75 lbs. Checkered Monte Carlo stock and beavertail forearm, recoil pad. Fitted case. Made from 1977 to 1978.

**PERAZZI LIGHT GAME
O/U FIELD** . . . . NiB $15,800 Ex $14,790 Gd $13,955
Boxlock. Auto ejectors. Single trigger. 12 ga. 27.5-inch vent rib bbls., M/F or IC/M choke. Weight: 6.75 lbs. Checkered field-style stock and forearm. Made from 1972 to 74.

PERAZZI MIRAGE . . . . . . .NiB $6987 Ex $4677 Gd $2700
Same as Mirage Trap except has 28-inch bbls., M and Extra Full choke, special stock and forearm for live bird shooting. Weight: About 8 lbs. Made from 1973 to 1978.

PERAZZI MIRAGE SKEET . .NiB $4350 Ex $3866 Gd $2789
Same as Mirage Trap except has 28-inch bbls. w/integral muzzle brakes, SK choke, skeet-stype stock and forearm. Weight: About 8 lbs. Made from 1973 to 1978.

PERAZZI MIRAGE TRAP . . .NiB $4365 Ex $3900 Gd $2820
Same general specifications as MX-8 Trap except has tapered rib. Made from 1973 to 1978.

PERAZZI MT-6 SKEET . . . . .NiB $4233 Ex $3380 Gd $2770
Same as MT-6 Trap except has 28-inch bbls. w/two skeet choke tubes instead of Extra Full and F, skeet-style stock and forearm. Weight: About 8 lbs. Made from 1976 to 1978.

**PERAZZI MT-6 TRAP
COMBO** . . . . .NiB $5377 Ex $4260 Gd $3100
MT-6 w/extra single under bbl. w/high-rise aluminum vent rib, 32- or 34-inch; seven interchanageable choke tubes (IC through Extra Full). Fitted case. Made from 1977 to 1978.

PERAZZI MT-6 TRAP O/U . . .NiB $3700 Ex $2566 Gd $2044
Boxlock. Auto selective ejectors. Non-selective single trigger. 12 ga. Barrels separated, wide vent rib, 30-or 32-inch, five interchangeable choke tubes (Extra full, F, IM, M, IC). Weight: About 8.5 lbs. Checkered pistol-grip stock/forearm, recoil pad. Fitted case. Made from 1976 to 1978.

**PERAZZI MX
8 TRAP COMBO** . . . . .NiB $5688 Ex $4355 Gd $2460
MX-8 w/extra single bbl., vent rib, 32- or 34-inch, F choke, forearm; two trigger groups included. Made from 1973 to 1978.

PERAZZI MX-8 TRAP O/U . . . NiB $4356 Ex $3879 Gd $2889
Boxlock. Auto selective ejectors. Non-selective single trigger. 12 ga. Bbls.: High vent rib; 30- or 32-inch, IM/F choke. Weight: 8.25 to 8.5 lbs. Checkered Monte Carlo stock and forearm, recoil pad. Made from 1969 to 1978.

**PERAZZI SINGLE-BARREL
TRAP GUN** . . . . NiB $3350 Ex $2459 Gd $2000
Boxlock. Auto ejection. 12 ga. 34-inch vent rib bbl., F choke. Weight: Abaout 8.5 lbs. Checkered pistol-grip stock, forearm; recoil pad. Made from 1971 to 1972.

The following Ithaca-SKB shotguns, manufactured by SKB Arms Company, Tokyo, Japan, were distributed in the U.S. by Ithaca Gun Company from 1966-1976. See also listings under SKB.

SKB MODEL 100 SIDE-BY-SIDE . . .NiB $779 Ex $580 Gd $490
Boxlock. Plain extractors. Selective single trigger. Auto safety. Gauges: 12 and 20; 2.75-inch and 3-inch chambers respectively. Bbls.: 30-inch, F/F (12 ga. only); 28-inch, F/M; 26-inch, IC/M (12 ga. only); 25-inch, IC/M (20 ga. only). Weight: 12 ga., about 7 lbs.; 20 ga., about 6 lbs. Checkered stock and forend. Made 1966 to 1976.

SKB MODEL 150 FIELD GRADE . . . NiB $770 Ex $600 Gd $488
Same as Model 100 except has fancier scroll engraving, beavertail forearm. Made from 1972 to 1974.

SKB 200E FIELD GRADE S/S . . . NiB $1077 Ex $767 Gd $580
Same as Model 100 except auto selective ejectors, engraved and silver-plated frame, gold-plated nameplate and trigger, beavertail forearm. Made from 1966 to 1976.

**Ithaca-SKB
Model 100**

GRADING: **NiB** = New in Box   **Ex** = Excellent or NRA 95%   **Gd** = Good or NRA 68%

Ithaca-SKB
Model 280 English

Ithaca-SKB
Model 700 Skeet Grade

Ithaca-SKB
Model 900 Deluxe

Ithaca-SKB
Century Trap

Ithaca-SKB
Century II Trap

Ithaca-SKB
Model XL300

SKB MODEL 200E SKEET GUN.... NiB $995 Ex $687 Gd $485
Same as Model 200E Field Grade except 26-inch (12 ga.) and
25-inch (20 ga./2.75-inch chambers) bbls., SK choke; nonauto-
matic safety and recoil pad. Made from 1966 to 1976.

SKB MODEL 200 ENGLISH ..NiB $1154 Ex $990 Gd $759
Same as Model 200E except has scrolled game scene engraving on frame, English-style straight-grip stock; 30-inch bbls. not
available; special quail gun in 20 ga. has 25-inch bbls., both
bored IC. Made from 1971 to 1976.

SKB MODEL 300 STANDARD AUTOMATIC SHOTGUN
Recoil-operated. Gauges: 12, 20 (3-inch). Five round capacity.
Bbls.: plain or vent rib; 30-inch F choke (12 ga. only), 28-inch
F or M, 26-inch IC. Weight: about 7 lbs. Checkered pistol-grip
stock and forearm. Made from 1968 to 1972.
w/plain barrel.............NiB $1088 Ex $765 Gd $490
20 ga, add...................................30%

SKB MODEL 500
FIELD GRADE O/U.........NiB $665 Ex $455 Gd $323
Boxlock. Auto selective ejectors. Selective single trigger. Non-
automatic safety. Gauges: 12 and 20; 2.75-inch and 3-inch
chambers respectively. Vent-rib bbls.: 30-inch M/F (12 ga.
only); 28-inch M/F; 26-inch IC/M. Weight: 12 ga., about 7.5
lbs; 20 ga., about 6.5 lbs. Checkered stock and forearm. Made
from 1966 to 1976.

SKB MODEL 500 MAGNUM.... NiB $639 Ex $455 Gd $344
Same as Model 500 Field Grade except chambered for 3-inch
12 ga. shells, has 30-inch bbls., IM/F choke. Weight: About 8
lbs. Made 1973 to 1976.

SKB MODEL 600 DOUBLES
GUN....................NiB $1096 Ex $766 Gd $500
Same as Model 600 Trap Grade except specially choked
for 21-yard first target, 30-yard second. Made from 1973 to
1975.

SKB MODEL 600 FIELD

GRADE . . . . NiB $1100 Ex $775 Gd $525
Same as Model 500 except has silver-plated frame, higher grade wood. Made from 1969 to 1976.

SKB MODEL 600 MAGNUM . . . NiB $1125 Ex $800 Gd $550

Same as Model 600 Field Grade except chambered for 3-inch 12 ga. shells; has 30-inch bbls., IM/F choke. Weight: 8.5 lbs. Made from 1969 to 1972.

SKB MODEL 600 SKEET GRADE

Same as Model 500 except also available in 28 and .410 ga., has silver-plated frame, higher grade wood, recoil pad, 26- or 28-inch bbls. (28-inch only in 28 and .410), SK choke. Weight: 7 to 7.75 lbs. depending on ga. and bbl. length. Made from 1966 to 1976.
12 or 20 ga. . . . . NiB $1155 Ex $830 Gd $575
28 ga. or .410. . . . . NiB $1500 Ex $1266 Gd $1077

SKB MODEL 600 SKEET SET. . . NiB $2866 Ex $2249 Gd $1545

Model 600 Skeet Grade w/matched set of 20, 28 and .410 ga. bbls., 28-inch, fitted case. Made from 1970-76.

SKB MODEL 600

TRAP GRADE O/U . . . . NiB $1055 Ex $700 Gd $533
Same as Model 500 except 12 ga. only, has silver-plated frame, 30- or 32-inch bbls. choked F/F or F/IM, choice of Monte Carlo or straight stock of higher grade wood, recoil pad. Weight: About 8 lbs. Made from 1966 to 1976.

SKB MODEL 680 ENGLISH. . . . NiB $1388 Ex $1055 Gd $775

Same as Model 600 Field Grade except has intricate scroll engraving, English-style straight-grip stock and forearm of extra-fine walnut; 30-inch bbls. not available. Made from 1973 to 1976.

SKB MODEL 700

SKEET COMBO SET . . . . . . NiB $3988 Ex $2970 Gd $2175
Model 700 Skeet Grade w/matched set of 20, 28 and .410 ga. bbls., 28-inch fitted case. Made from 1970 to 1971.

SKB MODEL 700 SKEET

GRADE . . . . NiB $955 Ex $779 Gd $575
Same as Model 600 Skeet Grade except not available in 28 and .410 ga., has more elaborate scroll engraving, extra-wide rib, higher grade wood. Made from 1969 to 1975.

SKB MODEL 700 TRAP GRADE . . . NiB $945 Ex $665 Gd $544

Same as Model 600 Trap Grade except has more elaborate scroll engraving, extra-wide rib, higher grade wood. Made 1969 to 1975.

SKB MODEL 700

DOUBLES GUN . . . . NiB $866 Ex $744 Gd $559
Same as Model 700 Trap Grade except choked for 21-yard first target, 30-yard second target. Made from 1973 to 1975.

SKB MODEL 900

DELUXE AUTOMATIC. . . . . . . NiB $475 Ex $359 Gd $255
Same as Model 30 except has game scene etched and gold-filled on receiver, vent rib standard. Made 1968 to 1972.

SKB MODEL 900 SLUG GUN. . NiB $350 Ex $264 Gd $190

Same as Model 900 Deluxe except has 24-inch plain bbl. w/ slug boring, rifle sights. Weight: About 6.5 lbs. Made 1970 to 1972.

SKB CENTURY SINGLE-SHOT

TRAP GUN . . . . NiB $689 Ex $500 Gd $356
Boxlock. Auto ejector. 12 ga. Bbls.: 32- or 34-inch, vent rib, F choke. Weight: About 8 lbs. Checkered walnut stock w/pistol grip, straight or Monte Carlo comb, recoil pad, beavertail forearm. Made 1973 to 1974.

SKB CENTURY II TRAP . . . . . . NiB $700 Ex $495 Gd $400

Boxlock. Auto ejector. 12 ga. Bbls.: 32- or 34-inch, vent rib, F choke. Weight: 8.25 lbs. Improved version of Century. Same general specifications except has higher comb on checkered stock stock, reverse-taper beavertail forearm w/redesigned locking iron. Made from 1975 to 1976.

SKB MODEL XL300 STANDARD AUTOMATIC

Gas-operated. Gauges: 12, 20 (3-inch). Five round capacity. Bbls.: Plain or vent rib; 30-inch F choke (12 ga. only), 28-inch F or M, 26-inch IC. Weight: 6 to 7.5 lbs. depending on ga. and bbl. Checkered pistol-grip stock, forearm. Made from 1972 to 1976.
w/plain barrel . . . . NiB $389 Ex $296 Gd $210
w/ventilated rib . . . . NiB $365 Ex $283 Gd $205

SKB MODEL XL900

DELUXE AUTOMATIC. . . . . . . NiB $379 Ex $335 Gd $260
Same as Model XL300 except has game scene finished in silver on receiver, vent rib standard. Made from 1972 to 1976.

SKB MODEL XL

900 SKEET GRADE . . . . NiB $490 Ex $377 Gd $315
Gas-operated. Gauges: 12, 20 (3-inch). Five round tubular magazine. Same as Model XL900 Deluxe except has scrolled receiver finished in black chrome, 26-inch bbl. only, SK choke, skeet-style stock. Weight: 7 or 7.5 lbs. depending on ga. Made from 1972 to 1976.

SKB MODEL XL

900 SLUG GUN . . . . NiB $445 Ex $377 Gd $290
Same as Model XL900 Deluxe except has 24-inch plain bbl. w/ slug boring, rifle sights. Weight: 6.5 or 7 lbs. depending on ga. Made from 1972 to 1976.

SKB MODEL

XL900 TRAP GRADE. . . . . NiB $488 Ex $358 Gd $290
Same as Model XL900 Deluxe except 12 ga. only, has scrolled receiver finished in black chrome, 30-inch bbl. only, IM or F choke, trap style w/straight or Monte Carlo comb, recoil pad. Weight: About 7.75 lbs. Made from 1972 to 1976.

IVER JOHNSON ARMS & CYCLE WORKS — Fitchburg, Massachusetts; currently a division of the American Military Arms Corp., Jacksonville, Arkansas

CHAMPION GRADE TOP SNAP

Auto ejector. Gauges: 12,16, 20, 28 and .410. Bbls.: 26- to 36-inch, F choke. Weight: 5.75 to 7.5 lbs. depending on ga. and bbl.length. Plain pistol-grip stock and forend. Extras include checkered stock and forend, pistol-grip cap and knob forend. Known as Model 36. Also made in a Semi-Octagon Breech, Top Matted and Jacketed Breech (extra heavy) models. Made in Champion Lightweight as Model 39 in gauges 24, 28, 32 and .410, .44 and .45 caliber, 12 and 14mm w/ same extras. $200; add $100 in the smaller and obsolete gauges. Made from 1909 to 1973.

SHOTGUNS

Standard model. . . . . NiB $377 Ex $290 Gd $100
Semi-octagon breech . . . . NiB $466 Ex $351 Gd $229
Top matted rib (disc. 1948). . . . NiB $398 Ex $297 Gd $195

HERCULES GRADE HAMMERLESS DOUBLE
Boxlock. (Some made w/false sideplates.) Plain extractors and auto ejectors. Double or Miller single triggers (both selective or non-selective). Gauges: 12, 16, 20 and .410. Bbl. lengths: 26- to 32-inch, all chokes. Weight: 5.75 to 7.75 lbs. depending on ga. and bbl. length. Checkered stock and forend. Straight grip in .410 ga. w/both 2.5- and 3-inch chambers. Extras include Miller single trigger, Jostam Anti-Flinch recoil pad and Lyman ivory sights at extra cost. Disc. 1946.

w/double triggers, extractors . . . .NiB $1166 Ex $955 Gd $760
w/double triggers, ejectors, add. 30%
w/non-selective single trigger, add $50
w/selective single trigger, add. $50
.410 ga., add 100%

MATTED RIB SINGLE-SHOT HAMMER SHOTGUN
IN SMALLER GAUGES. . . . . . . NiB $400 Ex $355 Gd $210
Same general specifications as Champion Grade except has solid matted top rib, checkered stock and forend. Weight: 6 to 6.75 lbs. Disc. 1948.

MODEL 412/422 SILVER SHADOW O/U SHOTGUN
Boxlock. Plain extractors. Double triggers or non-selective single trigger. 12 ga., 3-inch chambers. Bbls.: 26-inch IC/M; 28-inch IC/M, 28-inch M/F; 30-inch both F choke; vent rib. Weight: w/28-inch bbls., 7.5 lbs. Checkered pistol-grip stock/forearm. Made by F. Marocchi, Brescia, Italy from 1973 to 1977.
Model 412 w/double triggers . NiB $590 Ex $455 Gd $387
Model 422 w/single trigger . . . NiB $754 Ex $600 Gd $445
SKEETER MODEL HAMMERLESS DOUBLE
Boxlock. Plain extractors or selective auto ejectors. Double triggers or Miller single trigger (selective or non-selective). Gauges: 12, 16, 20, 28 and .410. 26- or 28-inch bbls., skeet boring standard. Weight: About 7.5 lbs.; less in smaller gauges. Pistol- or straight-grip stock and beavertail forend, both checkered, of select fancy-figured black walnut. Extras include Miller single trigger, selective or non-selective, Jostam Anti-Flinch recoil pad and Lyman ivory rear sight at additional cost. Disc. 1942.
w/double triggers,
    plain extractors. . . . . . . NiB $2298 Ex $1987 Gd $1133
w/double triggers, automatic ejectors, add 20%
w/non-selective single trigger, add 20%
w/selective single trigger, add. 50%
20 ga,add 30%
28 ga., add 90%
.410 ga., add 100%

SPECIAL TRAP SINGLE-SHOT
HAMMER SHOTGUN . . . . . . NiB $500 Ex $365 Gd $298
Auto ejector. 12 ga. only. 32-inch bbl. w/vent rib, F choke. Checkered pistol-grip stock and forend. Weight: about 7.5 lbs. Disc. 1942.

SUPER TRAP HAMMERLESS DOUBLE
Boxlock. Plain extractors. Double trigger or Miller single trigger (selective or non-selective), 12 ga. only, F choke 32-inch bbl., vent rib. Weight: 8.5 lbs. Checkered pistol-grip stock and beavertail forend, recoil pad, Disc. 1942.
w/double triggers . . . . NiB $1756 Ex $1170 Gd $990
w/non-selective single trigger, add $150
w/selective single trigger, add. $150

KBI INC.

See listings under Armscor, Baikal, Charles Daly, Fias, & Omega.

KESSLER ARMS CORP. — Deggendorf, Germany

LEVER-MATIC REPEATING
SHOTGUN . . . . .NiB $335 Ex $227 Gd $179
Lever action. Takedown. Gauges: 12, 16, 20; three-round magazine. Bbls.: 26-, 28-, 30-inch; F choke. Plain pistol-grip stock, recoil pad. Weight: 7 to 7.75 lbs. Disc. 1953.

Three Shot Bolt-Action Repeater . . .NiB $200 Ex $138 Gd $90
Takedown. Gauges: 12, 16, 20. Two-round detachable box magazine. Bbls.: 28-inch in 12 and 16 ga.; 26-inch in 20 ga.; F choke. Weight: 6.25 to 7.25 lbs. depending on ga. and bbl. length. Plain one-piece pistol-grip stock recoil pad. Made from 1951 to 1953.

H. KRIEGHOFF JAGD UND SPORTWAFFENFABRIK — Ulm (Donau), Germany

MODEL 32 FOUR-BARREL SKEET SET
Over/under w/four sets of matched bbls.: 12, 20, 28 and .410 ga., in fitted case. Available in six grades that differ in quality of engraving and wood. Disc. 1979.
Standard grade . . . . .NiB $9344 Ex $7120 Gd $4688
München grade. . . . . NiB $10,077 Ex $8767 Gd $6233
San Remo grade . . . . NiB $13,876 Ex $11,990 Gd $10,550
Monte Carlo grade . . NiB $20,000 Ex $17,890 Gd $14,650
Crown grade. . . . . . . NiB $27,700 Ex $22,800 Gd $15,660
Super Crown grade. . NiB $29,000 Ex $24,770 Gd $17,600
Exhibition grade . . . . NiB $32,000 Ex $28,900 Gd $23,750

MODEL 32 STANDARD GRADE O/U
Similar to prewar Remington Model 23. Boxlock. Auto ejector. Single trigger. Gauges: 12, 20, 28, .410. Bbls.: Vent rib, 26.5- to 32-inch, any chokes. Weight: 12 ga. Field gun w/28-inch bbls., about 7.5 lbs. Checkered pistol-grip stock and forearm of select walnut; available in field, skeet and trap styles. Made from 1958 to 1981.
w/one set of bbls. . . . . .NiB $3125 Ex $2460 Gd $2099
Low-rib two-bbl. trap combo. . .NiB $4166 Ex $3550 Gd $2779
Vandalia (high-rib) two- bbl.
    trap combo. . . . . .NiB $5355 Ex $4288 Gd $3150

MODEL 32 STANDARD GRADE
SINGLE-SHOT TRAP GUN . NiB $4160 Ex $3277 Gd $3080
Same action as over/under. 28 ga.or .410 bore w/low vent rib on bbl.; M, IM, or F choke. Checkered Monte Carlo buttstock w/thick cushioned recoil pad, beavertail forearm. Disc. 1979.

MODEL K-80
Refined and enhanced version of the Mdl. 32. Single selective mech. trig., adj. for position; release trigger optional. Fixed chokes or screw-in choke tubes. Interchangeable front bbl. Hangers to adjust point of impact. Quick-removable stock. Color casehardened or satin grey fin. rec.; alum. alloy rec. on lightweight models. Avail. in stand. plus 5 engraved grades. Made from 1980 to date. Standard grade shown except where noted.

Krieghoff Model 32 Standard Field Gun

Krieghoff Model 32 Single-Shot Trap

Krieghoff K-80 w/Screw-in Choke Tubes

Krieghoff K-80 Trap Unsingle

SKEET MODELS

Skeet International . . . . NiB $9160 Ex $5375 Gd $3853
Skeet Special. . . . . NiB $9277 Ex $6659 Gd $4390
Skeet standard model . . . . . NiB $9000 Ex $4788 Gd $3360
Skeet w/choke tubes. . . .NiB $12,776 Ex $9879 Gd $5780
SKEET SETS - Disc. 1999. Standard grade
    2-bbl. set. . . . . NiB $12,769 Ex $10,000 Gd $6690
Standard grade
    4-bbl. set. . . . . NiB $14,879 Ex $11,890 Gd $9877
Bavaria grade 4-bbl. set . . . NiB $11,900 Ex $9388 Gd $7710
Danube grade
    4-bbl. set. . . . . NiB $23,998 Ex $20,600 Gd $17,000
Gold Target grade
    4-bbl. set. . . . . NiB $31,800 Ex $24,800 Gd $17,955

SPORTING MODELS

Pigeon. . . . . NiB $9980 Ex $6654 Gd $4135
Sporting Clays. . . . . NiB $9566 Ex $5760 Gd $4400

TRAP MODELS

Trap Combo, add 30%
Trap Single, add $600
Trap Standard . . . . NiB $10,550 Ex $7677 Gd $4612
Trap Unsingle . . . . NiB $11,880 Ex $9678 Gd $6389
RT models (removable trigger), add $1500

KRIEGHOFF MODEL KS-5 SINGLE-BARREL TRAP

Boxlock w/no sliding top-latch. Adjustable or optional release trigger. Gauge: 12; 2.75-inch chamber. Bbl.: 32-, 34-inch w/ fixed choke or screw-in tubes. Weight: 8.5 lbs. Adjustable or Monte Carlo European walnut stock. Blued or nickel receiver. Made from 1985 to 1999. Redesigned and streamlined in 1993.
Standard model
    w/fixed chokes . . . . NiB $2650 Ex $1887 Gd $1109
Standard model w/tubes, add. $250
Special model w/adj.
    rib & stock, add $250

Special model w/adj. rib
    & stock, choke tubes, add. $500

TRUMPF DRILLING. . . NiB $14,987 Ex $13,677 Gd $10,880
Boxlock. Steel or Dural receiver. Split extractor or ejector for shotgun bbls. Double triggers. Gauges: 12, 16, 20; latter w/ either 2.75- or 3-inch chambers. Calibers: .243, 6.5x57r5, 7x57r5, 7x65r5, .30-06; other calibers available. 25-inch bbls. w/solid rib, folding leaf rear sight, post or bead front sight; rifle bbl. soldered or free floating. Weight: 6.6 to 7.5 lbs. depending on type of receiver, ga. and caliber. Checkered pistol-grip stock w/cheekpiece and forearm of figured walnut, sling swivels. Made from 1953 to 2003.

NEPTUN DRILLING . . . NiB $14,988 Ex $11,987 Gd $9000
Same general specifications as Trumpf model except has side-locks w/hunting scene engraving. Disc. 2003.

NEPTUN-PRIMUS
DRILLING. . . . . NiB $19,800 Ex $16,779 Gd $13,980
Deluxe version of Neptun model; has detachable sidelocks, higher grade engraving and fancier wood. Disc. 2003.

Krieghoff Neptun Drilling

SHOTGUNS

**Krieghoff ULM
Over/Under**

TECK O/U
RIFLE-SHOTGUN . . . . NiB $9788 Ex $5780 Gd $4466
Boxlock. Kersten dble. crossbolt system. Steel or Dural receiver. Split extractor or eject. for shotgun bbl. Single or double triggers. Gauges: 12, 16, 20; latter w/either 2.75- or 3-inch chamber. Cal: .22 Hornet, .222 Rem., .222 Rem. Mag., 7x57r5, 7x64, 7x65r5, .30-30, .300 Win. Mag., .30-06, .308, 9.3x74R. 25-inch bbls. With solid rib, folding leaf rear sight, post or bead front sight; over bbl. is shotgun, under bbl. rifle (later fixed or interchangeable; ext. rifle bbl., $175). Wt: 7.9-9.5 lbs. depending on type of rec. and caliber. Checkered pistol-grip stock w/ cheekpiece and semi-beavertail forearm of fig. walnut, sling swivels. Made from 1967 to 2004. Note: This comb. gun is similar in appearance to the same model shotgun.

TECK O/U SHOTGUN . . . . NiB $7354 Ex $5678 Gd $4000
Boxlock. Kersten double crossbolt system. Auto ejector. Single or double triggers. Gauges: 12, 16, 20; latter w/either 2.75- or 3-inch chambers. 28-inch vent-rib bbl., M/F choke. Weight: About 7 lbs. Checkered walnut pistol-grip stock and forearm. Made 1967 to 1989.

ULM O/U
RIFLE-SHOTGUN . . . NiB $16,228 Ex $12,876 Gd $10,336
Same general specifications as Teck model except has sidelocks w/leaf Arabesque engraving. Made from 1963-2004. Note: This combination gun is similar in appearance to the same model shotgun.

ULM O/U SHOTGUN . NiB $13,899 Ex $11,679 Gd $8445
Same general specifications as Teck model except has sidelocks w/leaf Arabesque engraving. Made from 1958 to 2004.

ULM-P LIVE PIGEON GUN
Sidelock. Gauge: 12. 28- and 30-inch bbls. Chokes: F/IM. Weight: 8 lbs. Oil-finished, fancy English walnut stock w/semi-beavertail forearm. Light scrollwork engraving. Tapered, vent rib. Made from 1983 to 2004.
Standard . . . . NiB $19,577 Ex $15,890 Gd $11,088
Dural. . . . . NiB $13,776 Ex $11,087 Gd $9459

ULM-PRIMUS O/U . . NiB $19,779 Ex $17,888 Gd $13,090
Deluxe version of Ulm model; detachable sidelocks, higher grade engraving and fancier wood. Made from 1958 to 2004.

ULM-PRIMUS O/U
RIFLE-SHOTGUN . . . NiB $21,870 Ex $18,744 Gd $15,877
Deluxe version of Ulm model; has detachable sidelocks, higher grade engraving and fancier wood. Made 1963 to 2004. Note: This combination gun is similar in appearance to the same model shotgun.

ULM-S SKEET GUN
Sidelock. Gauge: 12. Bbl.: 28-inch. Chokes: Skeet/skeet. Other specifications similar to the Model ULM-P. Made from 1983-86.
Bavaria . . . . NiB $13,789 Ex $11,132 Gd $9000
Standard . . . . NiB $1188 Ex $9131 Gd $7330

ULM-P O/U LIVE TRAP GUN
Over/under sidelock. Gauge: 12. 30-inch bbl. Tapered vent rib. Chokes: IM/F; optional screw-in choke. Custom grade versions command a higher price. Disc. 1986.
Bavaria . . . . NiB $18,966 Ex $15,980 Gd $12,776
Standard . . . . NiB $15,660 Ex $13,000 Gd $10,100

ULTRA TS RIFLE-SHOTGUN
Deluxe Over/Under combination w/25-inch vent-rib bbls. Chambered 12 ga. only and various rifle calibers for lower bbl. Kickspanner design permits cocking w/thumb safety. Satin receiver. Weight: 6 lbs. Made from 1985 to 1995 Disc.
Ultra O/U combination . . . NiB $4220 Ex $3670 Gd $2800
Ultra B w/selective front trigger NiB $5589 Ex $4498 Gd $4000

LANBER — Zaldibar, Spain

MODEL 82 O/U SHOTGUN. . . NiB $577 Ex $459 Gd $390
Boxlock. Gauge: 12 or 20; 3-inch chambers. 26- or 28-inch vent-rib bbls. w/ejectors and fixed chokes. Weight: 7 lbs., 2 oz. Double or single-selective trigger. Engraved silvered receiver. Checkered European walnut stock and forearm. Imported 1994.

MODEL 87 DELUXE . . . . NiB $875 Ex $760 Gd $555
Over/Under; boxlock. Single selective trigger. 12 or 20 gauge w/3-inch chambers. Barrels: 26- or 28-inch w/choke tubes. Silvered engraved receiver. Imported 1994 only.

MODEL 97 SPORTING CLAYS . NiB $998 Ex $790 Gd $566
Over/Under; boxlock. Single selective trigger. 12 ga. w/2.75-inch chambers. Bbls: 28-inch w/choke tubes. European walnut stock, forend. Engraved receiver. Imported 1994 only.

MODEL 844 MST
MAGNUM O/U . . . . NiB $533 Ex $448 Gd $360
Field grade. Gauge: 12. 3-inch Mag. chambers. 30-inch flat vent-rib bbls. Chokes: M/F. Weight: 7 lbs., 7 oz. Single selective trigger. Blued bbls. and engraved receiver. European walnut stock w/hand-checkered pistol grip and forend. Imported from 1984 to 1986.

MODEL 2004 LCH O/U . . . . . . NiB $669 Ex $490 Gd $370
Field grade. Gauge: 12. 2.75-inch chambers. 28-inch flat vent-rib bbls. 5 interchangeable choke tubes: Cyl, IC, M, IM, F. Weight: About 7 lbs. Single selective trigger. Engraved silver receiver w/fine-line scroll. Walnut stock w/checkered pistol-grip and forend. Rubber recoil pad. Imported from 1984 to 1986.

MODEL 2004 LCH O/U SKEET . . . NiB $855 Ex $659 Gd $544
Same as Model 2004 LCH except 28-inch bbls. w/5 interchangeable choke tubes. Imported from 1984 to 1986.

MODEL 2004 LCH O/U TRAP . . . NiB $764 Ex $520 Gd $413
Gauge: 12. 30-inch vent-rib bbls. Three interchangeable choke tubes: M, IM, F. Manual safety. Other specifications same as Model 2004 LCH O/U. Imported from 1984 to 1986.

Lanber Model 82
Field Grade

Laurona Grand
Trap — GTO

CHARLES LANCASTER — London, England

**"TWELVE-TWENTY" DOUBLE-BARREL
SHOTGUN** . . . . **NiB $16,788 Ex $14,990 Gd $10,880**
Sidelock, self-opener. Gauge: 12. Bbls.: 24 to 30 inches
standard. Weight: About 5.75 lbs. Elaborate metal engraving.
Highest quality English or French walnut buttstock and fore-
arm. Imported by Stoeger in the 1950s.

JOSEPH LANG & SONS — London, England

**HIGHEST QUALITY
O/U SHOTGUN** . . . . **NiB $31,900 Ex $27,678 Gd $20,980**
Sidelock. Gauges: 12, 16, 20, 28 and .410. Bbls.: 25 to 30
inches standard. Highest grade English or French walnut buttstock and forearm. Selective single trigger. Imported by Stoeger
in 1950s.

LAURONA — Eibar, Spain

MODEL 300 SERIES
Same general specifications as Model 300 Super Series except
supplied w/29-inch over/under bbls. and beavertail forearms.
Disc. 1992.
Trap model . . . . **NiB $1377 Ex $1190 Gd $921**
Sporting Clays model . . . . . **NiB $1389 Ex $1440 Gd $1000**

SILHOUETTE 300 O/U
Boxlock. Single selective trigger. Selective automatic ejectors.
Gauge: 12; 2.75-, 3- or 3.5-inch chambers. 28- or 29-inch
vent-rib bbls. w/flush or knurled choke tubes. Weight: 7.75 to
8 lbs. Checkered pistol-grip European walnut stock and bea-
vertail forend. Engraved receiver w/silvered finish and black
chrome bbls. Made from 1988 to 1992.
Model 300 Sporting Clays . . . **NiB $1498 Ex $1277 Gd $900**
Model 300 Trap, single . . . . . **NiB $1577 Ex $1264 Gd $900**
Model 300 Ultra-Magnum . **NiB $1599 Ex $1300 Gd $1055**

SUPER MODEL O/U SHOTGUNS
Boxlock. Single selective or twin single triggers. Selective automatic ejectors. Gauges: 12 or 20; 2.75- or 3-inch chambers.
26-, 28- or 29-inch vent-rib bbls. w/fixed chokes or screw-in
choke tubes. Weight: 7 to 7.25 lbs. Checkered pistol-grip
European walnut stock. Engraved receiver w/silvered finish and
black chrome bbls. Made from 1985 to 1989.

Model 82 Super Game (disc.) . . **NiB $688 Ex $500 Gd $395**
Model 83 MG Super Game . . . **NiB $1090 Ex $800 Gd $707**
Model 84 S Super Trap . . . . . **NiB $1366 Ex $1150 Gd $986**
Model 85 MS Super Game . . . **NiB $1098 Ex $833 Gd $727**
Model 85 MS 2-bbl. set. . . . . **NiB $2200 Ex $1789 Gd $1340**
**Model 85 MS Special Sporting
  (disc.)** . . . . **NiB $1390 Ex $1173 Gd $999**
Model 85 MS Super Trap. . . . **NiB $1386 Ex $1160 Gd $974**
Model 85 MS Pigeon. . . . . . . **NiB $1409 Ex $1190 Gd $1034**
Model 85 MS Super Skeet. . **NiB $1409 Ex $1190 Gd $1034**

LEBEAU-COURALLY — Liege, Belgium

**BOXLOCK SIDE
BY-SIDE SHOTGUNS.** . . **NiB $19,000 Ex $15,870 Gd $10,477**
Gauges: 12, 16, 20 and 28. 26- to 30-inch bbls. Weight: 6.5
lbs. average. Checkered, hand-rubbed, oil-finished, straight-
grip stock of French walnut. Classic forend. Made from 1986
to 1988 and 1993.

LEFEVER ARMS COMPANY —
Syracuse and Ithaca, New York

*Lefever sidelock hammerless double-barrel shotguns were
made by Lefever Arms Company of Syracuse, New York from
about 1885-1915 (serial numbers 1 to 70,000) when the
firm was sold to Ithaca Gun Company of Ithaca, New York.
Production of these models was continued at the Ithaca plant
until 1919 (serial numbers 70,001 to 72,000). Grades listed
are those that appear in the last catalog of the Lefever Gun
Company, Syracuse. In 1921, Ithaca introduced the boxlock
Lefever Nitro Special double, followed in 1934 by the Lefever
Grade A; there also were two single-barrel Lefevers made from
1927-42. Manufacture of Lefever brand shotguns was disc. in
1948. Note: "New Lefever" boxlock shotguns made circa 1904
to 1906 by D. M. Lefever Company, Bowling Green, Ohio, are
included in a separate listing.*

GRADE A HAMMERLESS DOUBLE-BARREL SHOTGUN
Boxlock. Plain extractors or auto ejector. Single or double triggers. Gauges: 12, 16, 20, .410. Bbls.: 26-32 inches, standard
chokes. Weight: About 7 lbs. in 12 ga. Checkered pistol-grip
stock and forearm. Made from 1934 to 1942.

SHOTGUNS

**Lefever A Grade
Hammerless Double-Barrel Shotgun**

w/plain extractors,
double triggers . . . . NiB $1198 Ex $955 Gd $773
w/automatic ejector, add 33%
w/single trigger, add. 10%
w/Beavertail Forearm, add $100
16 ga., add 25%
20 ga., add 80%
.410 ga., add 200%

GRADE A SKEET MODEL
Same as A Grade except standard features include auto ejector, single trigger, beavertail forearm; 26-inch bbls., skeet boring. Disc. 1942.
A Grade Skeet model, 12 ga . . . NiB $1699 Ex $1188 Gd $880
16 ga., add 40%
20 ga., add 80%
.410 ga., add 200%

HAMMERLESS SINGLE-SHOT
TRAP GUN . . . . NiB $766 Ex $600 Gd $477
Boxlock. Ejector. 12 ga. only. 26- or 32-inch bbl.; Full choke. Weight: About 8 lbs. Checkered pistol-grip stock. Auto ejector; boxlock. Made from 1904 to 1906. Rare.

LONG RANGE HAMMERLESS
SINGLE-BARREL FIELD GUN . . NiB $500 Ex $394 Gd $277
Boxlock. Plain extractor. Gauges: 12, 16, 20, .410. Bbl. lengths: 26-32 inches. Weight: 5.5 to 7 lbs. depending on ga. and bbl. length. Checkered pistol-grip stock and forend. Made from 1927 to 1942.

NITRO SPECIAL HAMMERLESS DOUBLE
Boxlock. Plain extractors. Single or double triggers. Gauges: 12, 16, 20, .410. Bbls.: 26- to 32-inch, standard chokes. Weight: about 7 lbs. in 12 ga. Checkered pistol-grip stock and forend. Made 1921 to 1948.
Nitro Special w/double triggers . . . NiB $855 Ex $522 Gd $377
Nitro Special W/single trigger . NiB $933 Ex $654 Gd $433
16 ga., add 25%
20 ga., add 50%
.410 ga., add 200%

SIDELOCK HAMMERLESS DOUBLES
Plain extractors or auto ejectors. Boxlock. Double triggers or selective single trigger. Gauges: 10, 12, 16, 20. Bbls.: 26-32 inches; standard choke combinations. Weight: 5.75 to 10.5 lbs. depending on ga. and bbl. length. Checkered walnut straight-grip or pistol-grip stock and forearm. Grades differ chiefly in quality of workmanship, engraving, wood, checkering, etc.; general specifications are the same. DS and DSE Grade guns lack the cocking indicators found on all other models. Suffix "E" means model has auto ejector; also standard on A, AA, Optimus, and Thousand Dollar Grade guns.
H grade. . . . . NiB $2266 Ex $1770 Gd $1480
HE grade . . . . NiB $3270 Ex $2266 Gd $1780
G grade . . . . NiB $2288 Ex $1998 Gd $1440
GE grade . . . . NiB $3388 Ex $2771 Gd $1880
F grade . . . . NiB $2566 Ex $1966 Gd $1276
FE grade . . . . NiB $3360 Ex $2770 Gd $1866
E grade . . . . NiB $3790 Ex $2690 Gd $2210
EE grade . . . . NiB $5750 Ex $3880 Gd $2547
D grade. . . . . NiB $4980 Ex $3777 Gd $2869
DE grade. . . . . NiB $7132 Ex $4971 Gd $4111
DS grade. . . . . NiB $1754 Ex $1530 Gd $1129
DSE grade . . . . NiB $2184 Ex $1788 Gd $1290
C grade . . . . NiB $7443 Ex $4270 Gd $2988
CE grade . . . . NiB $9112 Ex $8445 Gd $6110
B grade . . . . NiB $10,500 Ex $8667 Gd $6330
BE grade . . . . NiB $10,580 Ex $8777 Gd $6580
A grade . . . . NiB $19,880 Ex $17,900 Gd $16,888
AA grade. . . . . NiB $28,566 Ex $23,667 Gd $21,876
Optimus grade . . . . . NiB $47,900 Ex $42,870 Gd $37,980
Thousand Dollar gradeNiB $78,980 Ex $46,888 Gd $36,890
w/single trigger, add. 10%
10 ga., add 15%
16 ga., add 45%
20 ga., add 90%

D. M. LEFEVER COMPANY —
Bowling Green, Ohio

In 1901, D. M. "Uncle Dan" Lefever, founder of the Lefever Arms Company, withdrew from that firm to organize D. M. Lefever, Sons & Company (later D. M. Lefever Company) to manufacture the "New Lefever" boxlock double- and single-barrel shotguns. These were produced at Bowling Green, Ohio, from about 1904-1906, when Dan Lefever died and the factory closed permanently. Grades listed are those that appear in the last catalog of D. M. Lefever Co.

HAMMERLESS DOUBLE-BARREL SHOTGUNS
"New Lefever." Boxlock. Auto ejector standard on all grades except O Excelsior, which was regularly supplied w/plain extractors (auto ejector offered as an extra). Double triggers or selective single trigger (latter standard on Uncle Dan Grade, extra on all others). Gauges: 12, 16, 20. Bbls.: Any length and choke combination. Weight: 5.5 to 8 lbs. depending on ga. and bbl. length. Checkered walnut straight-grip or pistol-grip stock and forearm. Grades differ chiefly in quality of workmanship, engraving, wood, checkering, etc. General specifications are the same.
O Excelsior grade w/plain
extractors . . . . NiB $2889 Ex $2255 Gd $1989
O Excelsior grade w/automatic
ejectors. . . . . NiB $3244 Ex $2990 Gd $2469
No. 9, F grade. . . . . NiB $3277 Ex $2929 Gd $2240
No. 8, E grade. . . . . NiB $4240 Ex $3888 Gd $2377
No. 7, D grade . . . . NiB $5277 Ex $4766 Gd $3698
No. 6, C grade . . . . NiB $7000 Ex $4590 Gd $3667
No. 5, B grade . . . . NiB $6722 Ex $4588 Gd $3292
No. 4, AA grade . . . . NiB $10,770 Ex $8857 Gd $5497
Uncle Dan grade. . . . . Very rare: $165,000+
w/single trigger, add. 10%
16 ga., add 45%
20 ga., add 15%

D. M. LEFEVER SINGLE-BARREL TRAP GUN
Boxlock. Auto ejector. 12 ga. only. Bbls.: 26- to 32 inches, F choke. Weight: 6.5 to 8 lbs. depending on bbl. length. Checkered walnut pistol-grip stock and forearm. Made 1904 to 1906. Extremely rare.

Lefever Sidelock DE Grade

Lefever Sidelock AA Grade

Lefever Sidelock Sideplate BE Grade

Lefever Sidelock
Thousand Dollar Grade

Lefever Sidelock Sideplate CE Grade

Lefever Sidelock Optimus Grade

Magtech Model 586.2
Slide-Action

MAGTECH — San Antonio, Texas.

Manufactured by CBC in Brazil.

MODEL 586-2 SLIDE-ACTION SHOTGUN
Gauge: 12; 3-inch chamber. 19-, 26- or 28-inch bbl.; fixed chokes or integral tubes. 46.5 inches overall. Weight: 8.5 lbs. Double-action slide bars. Brazilian hardwood stock. Polished blued finish. Imported 1992 to 1995.

Model 586.2F (28-inch bbl.,
   fixed choke) . . . . NiB $288 Ex $147 Gd $100
Model 586.2P (19-inch plain
   bbl., cyl. bore) . . . . NiB $244 Ex $165 Gd $99
Model 586.2 S (24-inch bbl.,
   rifle sights, cyl. bore) . . . . NiB $290 Ex $155 Gd $125
Model 586.2 VR (vent rib w/tubes) . . NiB $275 Ex $198 Gd $135

MARLIN FIREARMS CO. — North Haven
(formerly New Haven), Connecticut

MODEL 16 VISIBLE HAMMER SLIDE-ACTION REPEATER
Takedown. 16 ga. Five round tubular magazine. Bbls.: 26- or 28-inch, standard chokes. Weight: About 6.25 lbs. Pistol-grip stock, grooved slide handle; checkering on higher grades. Difference among grades is in quality of wood, engraving on Grades C and D. Made from 1904 to 1910.

Grade A . . . . NiB $400 Ex $322 Gd $297
Grade B . . . . NiB $590 Ex $477 Gd $388
Grade C . . . . NiB $722 Ex $466 Gd $388
Grade D . . . . NiB $1496 Ex $1377 Gd $947

MODEL 17 BRUSH GUN . . . . . NiB $389 Ex $297 Gd $190
Same as Model 17 Standard except has 26-inch bbl., cylinder bore. Weight: About 7 lbs. Made from 1906 to 1908.

Marlin Model 17
Standard

Marlin Model 28B
Hammerless Slide-Action Repeater

Marlin Model 30
Visible Hammer Slide-Action Repeater

Marlin Model 43A
Hammerless Slide-Action Repeater

Marlin Model 43T
Hammerless Slide-Action Repeater

Marlin Model 53
Hammerless Slide-Action

Marlin Model 55
Goose Gun

Marlin Model 55
Hunter Bolt-Action Repeater

MODEL 17 RIOT GUN . . . . . . NiB $480 Ex $308 Gd $200
Same as Model 17 Standard except has 20-inch bbl., cylinder bore. Weight: About 6.88 lbs. Made from 1906 to 1908.

MODEL 17 STANDARD VISIBLE HAMMER
SLIDE-ACTION REPEATER . . . . NiB $422 Ex $290 Gd $188
Solid frame.12 ga. Five round tubular magazine. Bbls.: 30- or 32-inch, F choke. Weight: About 7.5 lbs. Straight-grip stock, grooved slide handle. Made from 1906 to 1908.

MODEL 19 VISIBLE HAMMER SLIDE-ACTION REPEATER
Similar to Model 1898 but improved, lighter weight, w/two extractors, matted sighting groove on receiver top. Weight: About 7 lbs. Made from 1906-07.
Grade A . . . . NiB $466 Ex $390 Gd $277
Grade B . . . . NiB $566 Ex $448 Gd $339
Grade C . . . . NiB $744 Ex $390 Gd $244
Grade D . . . . NiB $1396 Ex $1087 Gd $944

MODEL 21 TRAP VISIBLE HAMMER
SLIDE-ACTION REPEATER
Similar to Model 19 w/same general specifications except has straight-grip stock. Made from 1907 to 1909.
Grade A . . . . NiB $433 Ex $290 Gd $197
Grade B . . . . NiB $580 Ex $450 Gd $344
Grade C . . . . NiB $788 Ex $590 Gd $445
Grade D . . . . NiB $1488 Ex $1116 Gd $977

MODEL 24 VISIBLE HAMMER SLIDE-ACTION REPEATER
Similar to Model 19 but has improved takedown system and auto recoil safety lock, solid matted rib on frame. Weight: About 7.5 lbs. Made from 1908 to 1915.
Grade A . . . . NiB $376 Ex $190 Gd $112
Grade B . . . . NiB $448 Ex $277 Gd $156
Grade C . . . . NiB $766 Ex $500 Gd $410
Grade D . . . . NiB $1500 Ex $1399 Gd $1177

MODEL 26
BRUSH GUN . . . . NiB $388 Ex $270 Gd $135
Same as Model 26 Standard except has 26-inch bbl., cylinder bore. Weight: About 7 lbs. Made from 1909 to 1915.

MODEL 26 RIOT GUN . . . . NiB $360 Ex $266 Gd $131
Same as Model 26 Standard except has 20-inch bbl., cylinder bore. Weight: About 6.88 lbs. Made from 1909 to 1915.

MODEL 26 STANDARD VISIBLE HAMMER
SLIDE-ACTION REPEATER . . . . NiB $366 Ex $298 Gd $199
Similar to Model 24 Grade A except solid frame and straight-grip stock. 30- or 32-inch full choke bbl. Weight: About 7.13 lbs. Made from 1909-15.

MODEL 28 HAMMERLESS SLIDE-ACTION REPEATER
Takedown. 12 ga. Five round tubular magazine. Bbls.: 26-, 28-, 30-, 32-inch, standard chokes; matted-top bbl. except on Model 28D, which has solid matted rib. Weight: About 8 lbs. Pistol-grip stock, grooved slide handle; checkering on higher grades. Grades differ in quality of wood, engraving on Models 28C and 28D. Made 1913 to 1922; all but Model 28A disc. in 1915.
Model 28A . . . . NiB $433 Ex $288 Gd $165
Model 28B . . . . NiB $577 Ex $458 Gd $313
Model 28C . . . . NiB $755 Ex $544 Gd $340
Model 28D . . . . NiB $1480 Ex $1198 Gd $955

MODEL 28T TRAP GUN . . . . . . NiB $789 Ex $566 Gd $449
Same as Model 28 except has 30-inch matted-rib bbl., Full choke, straight-grip stock w/high-fluted comb of fancy walnut, checkered. Made in 1915.

MODEL 28TS TRAP GUN . . . . . NiB $588 Ex $400 Gd $378
Same as Model 28T except has matted-top bbl., plainer stock. Made in 1915.

MODEL 30 FIELD GUN . . . . . . NiB $466 Ex $355 Gd $245
Same as Model 30 Grade B except has 25-inch bbl., Mod. choke, straight-grip stock. Made from 1913 to 1914.

MODEL 30 VISIBLE HAMMER SLIDE-ACTION REPEATER
Similar to Model 16 but w/Model 24 improvements. Made from 1910-14. See illustration previous page.
Grade A . . . . NiB $460 Ex $388 Gd $210
Grade B . . . . NiB $660 Ex $433 Gd $309
Grade C . . . . NiB $777 Ex $566 Gd $363
Grade D . . . . NiB $1488 Ex $1177 Gd $1065

MODELS 30A, 30B, 30C, 30D
Same as Model 30; designations were changed in 1915. Also available in 20 ga. w/25- or 28-inch bbl., matted-top bbl. on all grades. Suffixes "A," "B," "C" and "D" correspond to former grades. Made in 1915.
Model 30A . . . . NiB $412 Ex $290 Gd $188
Model 30B . . . . NiB $576 Ex $445 Gd $310
Model 30C . . . . NiB $756 Ex $554 Gd $39
Model 30D . . . . NiB $1421 Ex $1131 Gd $1070

MODEL 31 STANDARD VISIBLE HAMMER
SLIDE-ACTION REPEATER . . . . NiB $366 Ex $298 Gd $199
Similar to Model 24 Grade A except solid frame and straight-grip stock. 30- or 32-inch full choke bbl. Weight: About 7.13 lbs. Made from 1909-15.
Model 31A . . . . NiB $476 Ex $355 Gd $254
Model 31B . . . . NiB $598 Ex $455 Gd $389
Model 31C . . . . NiB $766 Ex $644 Gd $490
Model 31D . . . . NiB $1498 Ex $1154 Gd $990

MODEL 31F FIELD GUN . . . . . NiB $488 Ex $366 Gd $271
Same as Model 31B except has 25-inch bbl., M choke, straight- or pistol-grip stock. Made from 1915 to 1917.

MODEL 42A VISIBLE HAMMER
SLIDE-ACTION REPEATER . . . . NiB $498 Ex $366 Gd $288
Similar to pre-World War I Model 24 Grade A w/same general specifications but not as high quality. Made from 1922-34.

MODEL 43 HAMMERLESS SLIDE-ACTION REPEATER
Similar to pre-World War I Models 28A, 28T and 28TS, w/ same general specifications but not as high quality. Made from 1923 to 1930.
Model 43A . . . . NiB $355 Ex $200 Gd $144
Model 43TS . . . . NiB $665 Ex $400 Gd $228

MODEL 44 HAMMERLESS SLIDE-ACTION REPEATER
Similar to pre-World War I Model 31A w/same general specifications but not as high quality. 20 ga. only. Model 44A is a standardgrade field gun. Model 44S Special Grade has checkered stock and slide handle of fancy walnut. Made from 1923 to 1935.
Model 44A . . . . NiB $466 Ex $381 Gd $222
Model 44S . . . . NiB $622 Ex $476 Gd $338

SHOTGUNS

Marlin Model 55
Swap Gun

Marlin Model 59
Bolt-Action Single

Marlin Model 60
Single Shot

MODEL 49 VISIBLE HAMMER SLIDE-ACTION REPEATING

SHOTGUN . . . . NiB $566 Ex $449 Gd $367
Economy version of Model 42A, offered as a bonus on the
purchase of four shares of Marlin stock. About 3000 made
1925 to 1928.

MODEL 50DL BOLT

ACTION SHOTGUN . . . . NiB $388 Ex $229 Gd $131
Gauge: 12 w/3-inch chamber. Two round magazine. 28-inch
bbl. w/modified choke. 48.75 inches overall. Weight: 7.5 lbs.
Checkered black synthetic stocks w/ventilated rubber recoil
pad. Made 1997 to 1999.

MODEL 53 HAMMERLESS

SLIDE-ACTION REPEATER . . . . NiB $480 Ex $200 Gd $144
Similar to Model 43A w/same general specifications. Made
1929 to 1930.

MODEL 55 GOOSE GUN

Same as Model 55 Hunter except chambered for 12-ga. 3-inch
Magnum shell, has 36-inch bbl., F choke, swivels and sling.
Weight: About 8 lbs. Walnut stock (standard model) or check-
ered black synthetic stock w/ventilated rubber recoil pad (GDL
model). Made from 1962 to 1996.
Model 55 Goose Gun . . . . NiB $335 Ex $266 Gd $195
Model 55GDL Goose Gun
   (intro. 1997) . . . . NiB $398 Ex $297 Gd $239

MODEL 55 HUNTER BOLT-ACTION REPEATER

Takedown. Gauges: 12, 16, 20. Two round clip magazine.
28-inch bbl. (26-inch in 20 ga.), F or adj. choke. Plain pistol-
grip stock; 12 ga. has recoil pad. Weight: About 7.25 lbs.; 20
ga., 6.5 lbs. Made 1954 to 1965.
w/plain bbl. . . . . NiB $120 Ex $70 Gd $50
w/adj. choke . . . . NiB $155 Ex $99 Gd $75

MODEL 55 SWAMP GUN . . . . . NiB $225 Ex $179 Gd $90
Same as Model 55 Hunter except chambered for 12-ga. 3-inch
Magnum shell, has shorter 20.5-inch bbl. w/adj. choke, sling
swivels and slightly better-quality stock. Weight: About 6.5 lbs.
Made from 1963 to 1965.

MODEL 55S SLUG GUN . . . . NiB $200 Ex $99 Gd $75
Same as Model 55 Goose Gun except has 24-inch bbl., cylinder bore, rifle sights. Weight: About 7.5 lbs. Made from 1974
to 1979.

MODEL 59 AUTO-SAFE

BOLT-ACTION SINGLE . . . . NiB $244 Ex $176 Gd $95
Takedown. Auto thumb safety, .410 ga. 24-inch bbl., F choke.
Weight: About 5 lbs. Plain pistol-grip stock. Made 1959 to
1961.

MODEL 60 SINGLE-SHOT

SHOTGUN . . . . NiB $210 Ex $145 Gd $95
Visible hammer. Takedown. Boxlock. Automatic ejector. 12
ga. 30- or 32-inch bbl., F choke. Weight: About 6.5 lbs. Pistol-
grip stock, beavertail forearm. Note: Only about 600 were
produced in 1923.

MODEL 63 HAMMERLESS SLIDE-ACTION REPEATER

Similar to Models 43A and 43T w/same general specifica-
tions. Model 63TS Trap Special is same as Model 63T Trap
Gun except stock style and dimensions to order. Made from
1931-35.
Model 63A . . . . NiB $466 Ex $355 Gd $200
Model 63T or 63TS . . . . NiB $484 Ex $355 Gd $241

MODEL 90 STANDARD O/U SHOTGUN

Hammerless. Boxlock. Double triggers; non-selective single
trigger was available as an extra on pre-war guns except .410.
Gauges: 12, 16, 20, .410. Bbls.: Plain; 26-, 28- or 30-inch;
chokes IC/M or M/F; bbl. designchanged in 1949, eliminating
full-length rib between bbls. Weight: 12 ga., about 7.5 lbs.; 16

**Marlin Model 90
Standard Over-and-Under**

**Marlin Model 120
Magnum Slide-Action Repeater**

**Marlin Model 410
Lever-Action Repeater**

**Marlin Model 512
Slugmaster**

and 20 ga., about 6.25 lbs. Checkered pistol-grip stock and forearm, recoil pad standard on prewar guns. Postwar production: Model 90-DT (double trigger), Model 90-ST (single trigger). Made from 1937 to 1958.

w/double triggers	NiB $566	Ex $400	Gd $245
w/single trigger	NiB $670	Ex $555	Gd $435
Combination model	NiB $2879	Ex $1976	Gd $1777
16 ga., deduct			10%
20 ga., add			15%
.410, add			30%

MODEL 120 MAGNUM

SLIDE-ACTION REPEATER .... NiB $354 Ex $230 Gd $155
Hammerless. Takedown. 12 ga. (3-inch). Four round tubular magazine. Bbls.: 26-inch vent rib, IC; 28-inch vent rib M choke; 30-inch vent rib, F choke; 38-inch plain, F choke; 40-inch plain, F choke; 26-inch slug bbl. w/rifle sights, IC. Weight: About 7.75 lbs. Checkered pistol-grip stock and forearm, recoil pad. Made from 1971 to 1985.

MODEL 120 SLUG GUN ..... NiB $344 Ex $265 Gd $175
Same general specifications as Model 120 Magnum except w/20-inch bbl. and about .5 lb. lighter in weight. No vent rib. Adj. rear rifle sights; hooded front sight. Disc. 1990.

MODEL 410 LEVER-ACTION REPEATER
Action similar to that of Marlin Model 93 rifle. Visible hammer. Solid frame. .410 ga. (2.5-inch shell). Five round tubular magazine. 22- or 26-inch bbl., F choke. Weight: About 6 lbs. Plain pistol-grip stock and grooved beavertail forearm. Made from 1929-32.

Model 410 w/22-inch bbl.	NiB $1546	Ex $1463	Gd $1320
Model 410 w/26-inch bbl.	NiB $1470	Ex $1355	Gd $1110
Deluxe model, add			30%

MODEL 512 SLUGMASTER SHOTGUN
Bolt-action repeater. Gauge: 12; 3-inch chamber, 2-round magazine. 21-inch rifled bbl. w/adj. open sight. Weight: 8 lbs. Walnut-finished birch stock (standard model) or checkered black synthetic stock w/ventilated rubber recoil pad (GDL model). Made from 1994 to 1999.

Model 512 Slugmaster	NiB $466	Ex $338	Gd $243
Model 512DL Slugmaster (intro. 1998)	NiB $390	Ex $278	Gd $176
Model 512P Slugmaster w/ported bbl. (intro. 1999)	NiB $447	Ex $366	Gd $260

MODEL 1898 VISIBLE HAMMER SLIDE-ACTION REPEATER
Takedown. 12 ga. Five shell tubular magazine. Bbls.: 26-, 28-, 30-, 32-inch; standard chokes. Weight: About 7.25 lbs. Pistol-grip stock, grooved slide handle; checkering on higher grades. Difference among grades is in quality of wood, engraving on Grades C and D. Made 1898 to 1905. Note: This was the first Marlin shotgun.

Grade A (Field)	NiB $387	Ex $270	Gd $190
Grade B	NiB $558	Ex $400	Gd $294
Grade C	NiB $700	Ex $554	Gd $449
Grade D	NiB $2170	Ex $1799	Gd $954

MODEL 55-10 SUPER
GOOSE .... NiB $292 Ex $225 Gd $179
Similar to Model 55 Goose Gun except chambered for 10 ga. 3.5-inch Magnum shell, has 34-inch heavy bbl., F choke. Weight: About 10.5 lbs. Made from 1976 to 1985.

SHOTGUNS

Marlin Model 55-10
Super Goose 10

Marlin Premier Mark I
Slide-Action Repeater

Marlin Premier Mark IV

Marlin-Glenfield
Model 50 Bolt-Action Repeater

Marocchi Conquista
Sporting Clays

PREMIER MARK I
SLIDE-ACTION REPEATER .... **NiB $255 Ex $198 Gd $110**
Hammerless. Takedown. 12 ga. Magazine holds 3 shells. Bbls.: 30-inch F choke, 28-inch M, 26-inch IC or SK choke. Weight: About 6 lbs. Plain pistol-grip stock and forearm. Made in France from 1960-63.

PREMIER MARK II & IV
Same action and mechanism as Premier Mark except engraved receiver (Mark IV is more elaborate), checkered stock and forearm, fancier wood, vent rib and similar refinements. Made 1960 to 1963.
Premier Mark II .... **NiB $356 Ex $265 Gd $200**
Premier Mark IV (plain barrel) **NiB $389 Ex $339 Gd $233**
Premier Mark IV (vent rib barrel) ... **NiB $400 Ex $370 Gd $280**

GLENFIELD MODEL 50
BOLT-ACTION REPEATER ..... **NiB $320 Ex $255 Gd $175**
Similar to Model 55 Hunter except chambered for 12-or 20-ga., 3-inch Magnum shell; has 28-inch bbl. in 12 ga., 26-inch in 20 ga., F choke. Made from 1966 to 1974.

GLENFIELD 778 SLIDE-ACTION
REPEATER .... **NiB $325 Ex $255 Gd $180**
Hammerless. 12 ga. 2.75-inch or 3-inch. Four round tubular magazine. Bbls.: 26-inch IC, 28-inch M, 30-inch F, 38-inch MXR, 20-inch slug bbl. Weight: 7.75 lbs. Checkered pistol-grip. Made from 1979 to 1984.

MAROCCHI — Brescia, Italy
Imported by Precision Sales International of Westfield, MA.

CONQUISTA MODEL O/U SHOTGUN
Boxlock. Gauge: 12; 2.75-inch chambers. 28-, 30- or 32-inch vent rib bbl. Fixed choke or internal tubes. 44.38 to 48 inches overall. Weight: 7.5 to 8.25 lbs. Adj. single-selective trigger. Checkered American walnut stock w/recoil pad. Imported 1994 to 2003.
Lady Sport Grade I .... **NiB $1978 Ex $1754 Gd $1288**
Lady Sport Grade II ...... **NiB $2144 Ex $1788 Gd $1488**
Lady Sport Grade III...... **NiB $3577 Ex $2875 Gd $2290**
Skeet Model Grade I...... **NiB $1895 Ex $1544 Gd $1154**
Skeet Model Grade II..... **NiB $2250 Ex $1863 Gd $1455**
Skeet Model Grade III..... **NiB $3598 Ex $3210 Gd $2240**
Sporting Clays Grade I .... **NiB $1890 Ex $1669 Gd $1275**

**Maverick Model 88
Pump Shotgun (Vent Rib)**

Sporting Clays Grade II. . . . NiB $2200 Ex $1790 Gd $1376
Sporting Clays Grade III . . . NiB $3550 Ex $2977 Gd $2169
Trap Model Grade I . . . . . . NiB $1890 Ex $1588 Gd $1300
Trap Model Grade II . . . . . . NiB $2170 Ex $1877 Gd $1470
Trap Model Grade III . . . . . NiB $3588 Ex $3120 Gd $2260
Left-handed model, add 10%

MAVERICK ARMS, INC. — Eagle Pass, Texas
Ditrubuted by O.F. Mossberg.

MODEL 88 BULLPUP . . . . NiB $265 Ex $190 Gd $110
Gauge: 12; 3-inch chamber. Bbl.: 18.5-inch w/fixed choke, blued. Weight: 9.5 lbs. Dual safeties: Grip style and crossbolt. Fixed sights in carrying handle. High-impact black synthetic stock; trigger-forward bullpup configuration w/twin pistol-grip design. Made 1990 to 1995.

MODEL 88 DEER GUN . . . . NiB $377 Ex $241 Gd $176
Crossbolt safety and dual slide bars. Cylinder bore choke. Gauge: 12 only w/3-inch chamber. Bbl.: 24-inch. Weight: 7 lbs. Synthetic stock and forearm. Disc. 1995.

MODEL 88 PUMP SHOTGUN
Gauge: 12; 2.75- or 3-inch chamber. Bbl.: 28 inches/M or 30 inches/F w/fixed choke or screw-in integral tubes; plain or vent rib, blued. Weight: 7.25 lbs. Bead front sight. Black synthetic or wood buttstock and forend; forend grooved. Made from 1989 to date.
Synthetic stock w/plain bbl. . . . NiB $287 Ex $228 Gd $175
Synthetic stock w/vent-rib bbl. NiB $300 Ex $238 Gd $195
Synthetic Combo w/18.5-in. bbl. NiB $321 Ex $220 Gd $184
Wood stock w/vent-rib bbl./tubes . . NiB $300 Ex $225 Gd $179
Wood Combo w/vent-rib bbl./tubes . . NiB $255 Ex $200 Gd $162

MODEL 88 SECURITY . . . . NiB $275 Ex $190 Gd $145
Crossbolt safety and dual slide bars. Optional heat shield. Cylinder bore choke. Gauge: 12 only w/3-inch chamber. Bbl.: 18.5-inches. Weight: 6 lbs., 8 ozs. Synthetic stock and forearm.
Made from 1993 to date.

MODEL 91 PUMP SHOTGUN
Same as Model 88, except w/2.75-, 3- or 3.5-inch chamber, 28-inch bbl. W/ACCU-F choke, crossbolt safety and synthetic stock only. Made from 1991 to 1995.
Synthetic stock w/plain bbl. . . . NiB $330 Ex $256 Gd $180
Synthetic stock w/vent-rib bbl. NiB $335 Ex $270 Gd $195

MODEL 95 BOLT-ACTION . . . . NiB $255 Ex $190 Gd $140
Modified, fixed choke. Built-in two round magazine. Gauge: 12 only. Bbl.: 25-inch. Weight: 6.75 lbs. Bead sight. Synthetic stock and rubber recoil pad. Made from 1995 to 1997.

MODEL HS12 TACTICAL . . . . . NiB $582 Ex $350 Gd $150
O/U boxlock. C or IM choke. Single trigger w/ extractors. Gauge: 12 only. Bbl.: 18.5-in. Weight: 6.25 lbs. Fiber optic sight. Synthetic stock w/ rubber recoil pad. Picatinny rails. Made from 2011 to date.
Thunder Ranch . . . . NiB $583 Ex $360 Gd $160

MODEL HUNTER FIELD . . . . . . NiB $518 Ex $275 Gd $130
O/U boxlock. C or IM choke. Single trigger w/ extractors. Gauge: 12 only. Bbl.: 28-in. Weight: 7 lbs. Front bead sight. Synthetic stock w/ rubber recoil pad. Made from 2010 to date.

GEBRÜDER MERKEL — Suhl, Germany
Manufactured by Suhler Jagd-und Sportwaffen GmbH. Imported by GSI, Inc., Trussville, AL, previously by Ames de Chasse.

**MODEL 8 HAMMERLESS
DOUBLE** . . . . NiB $1522 Ex $1190 Gd $955
Anson & Deeley boxlock action w/Greener double-bbl. hook lock. Double triggers. Extractors. Automatic safety. Gauges: 12, 16, 20; 2.75- or 3-inch chambers. 26-or 28-inch bbls. w/fixed standard chokes. Checkered European walnut stock, pistol-grip or English-style w/or w/o cheekpiece. Scroll-engraved receiver w/tinted marble finish.

MODEL 47E SIDE-BY-SIDE . . . NiB $4000 Ex $3200 Gd $1890
Hammerless boxlock similar to Model 8 except w/automatic ejectors and cocking indicators. Double hook bolting. Single selective or double triggers. 12, 16 or 20 ga. w/2.75-inch chambers. Standard bbl lengths, choke combos. Hand-checkered European walnut stock, forearm; pistol-grip and cheekpiece or straight English style; sling swivels.

**MODEL 47LSC
SPORTING CLAYS S/S** . . . . NiB $3100 Ex $2500 Gd $1789
Anson & Deeley boxlock action w/single-selective adj. trigger, cocking indicators and manual safety. Gauge: 12; 3-inch chambers. 28-inch bbls.w/Briley choke tubes and H&H-style ejectors. Weight: 7.25 lbs. Color case-hardened receiver w/ Arabesque engraving. Checkered select-grade walnut stock, beavertail forearm. Imported from 1993 to 1994.

**MODELS 47SL, 147SL, 247SL, 347SL, 447SL
HAMMERLESS SIDELOCKS**
Same general specifications as Model 147E except has sidelocks engraved w/Arabesques, borders, scrolls or game scenes in varying degrees of elaborateness.
Model 47SL . . . . NiB $8350 Ex $5780 Gd $4200
Model 147SL . . . . NiB $10,099 Ex $7988 Gd $6754
Model 147SSL . . . . NiB $9655 Ex $6130 Gd $4200
Model 247SL . . . . NiB $8360 Ex $5110 Gd $3966
Model 347SL . . . . NiB $7229 Ex $5263 Gd $3800
Model 447SL . . . . NiB $10,450 Ex $8550 Gd $5110
28 ga. .410, add 20%

SHOTGUNS

GRADING: **NiB =** New in Box **Ex =** Excellent or NRA 95% **Gd =** Good or NRA 68%

**Merkel Model
47E Side-by-Side**

**Merkel Model 247S
Hammerless Sidelock**

**Merkel Model 347S
Hammerless Sidelock**

**Merkel Model 122
Hammerless Double**

NOTE: *Merkel over/under guns were often supplied with accessory barrels, interchangeable to convert the gun into an arm of another type; for example, a set might consist of one pair each of shotgun, rifle and combination gun barrels. Each pair of interchangeable barrels has a value of approximately one-third that of the gun with which they are supplied.*

MODEL 100 O/U SHOTGUN
Hammerless. Boxlock. Greener crossbolt. Plain extractor. Double triggers. Gauges: 12, 16, 20. Made w/plain or ribbed bbls. in various lengths and chokes. Plain finish, no engraving. Checkered forend and stock w/pistol grip and cheekpiece or English-style. Made prior to WWII.
w/plain bbl. . . . . NiB $1964 Ex $1771 Gd $1333
w/ribbed bbl. . . . . NiB $2175 Ex $1890 Gd $1377

MODELS 101 AND 101E O/U
Same as Model 100 except ribbed bbl. standard, has separate extractors (ejectors on Model 101E), English engraving. Made prior to World War II.
Model 101 . . . . NiB $2210 Ex $1879 Gd $1360
Model 101E . . . . NiB $2330 Ex $1968 Gd $1466

MODEL 122
HAMMERLESS DOUBLE . . . NiB $3965 Ex $3177 Gd $2300
Similar to the Model 147S except w/nonremovable sidelocks in gauges 12, 16 or 20. Imported since 1993.

MODEL 122E HAMMERLESS
SIDELOCK. . . . . NiB $4865 Ex $3850 Gd $2700
Similar to the Model 122 except w/removable sidelocks and cocking indicators. Importation disc. 1992.

MODEL 126E HAMMERLESS
SIDELOCK. . . . . NiB $25,788 Ex $22,650 Gd $18,700
Holland & Holland system, hand-detachable locks. Auto ejectors. Double triggers. 12, 16 or 20 gauge w/standard bbl. lengths and chokes. Checkered forend and pistol-grip stock; available w/cheekpiece or English-style buttstock. Elaborate game scenes and engraving. Made prior to WW II.

MODEL 127E HAMMERLESS
SIDELOCK. . . . . NiB $24,849 Ex $21,939 Gd $16,374
Similar to the Model 126E except w/elaborate scroll engraving on removable sidelocks w/cocking indicators. Made prior to WW II.

MODEL 128E HAMMERLESS
BOXLOCK DOUBLE . NiB $28,679 Ex $22,167 Gd $16,954
Scalloped Anson & Deeley action w/hinged floorplate and removable sideplates. Auto-ejectors. Double triggers. Elaborate hunting scene or Arabesque engraving. 12, 16 or 20 gauge w/ various bbl. lengths and chokes. Checkered forend and stock w/pistol grip and cheekpiece or English-style. Made prior to WW II.

MODEL 130 HAMMERLESS
BOXLOCK DOUBLE . . . NiB $21,400 Ex $18,560 Gd $16,450
Similar to Model 128E except w/fixed sideplates. Auto ejectors. Double triggers. Elaborate hunting scene or Arabesque engraving. Made prior to WW II.

MODELSL 147 & 147E HAMMERLESS
BOXLOCK DOUBLE-BARREL
Anson & Deeley system w/extractors or auto ejectors. Single selective or double triggers. Gauges: 12, 16, 20 or 28 ga.

**Merkel Model 147E
Hammerless Boxlock Double-Barrel Shotgun**

**Merkel Model 200E
O/U Shotgun**

**Merkel Model 203E
Sidelock O/U Shotgun**

(Three-inch chambers available in 12 and 20 ga.). Bbls.: 26-inch standard, other lengths available w/any standard choke combination. Weight: 6.5 lbs. Checkered straight-grip stock and forearm. Disc. 1998.

Model 147 w/extractors . . . NiB $2588 Ex $2254 Gd $1899
Model 147E w/ejectors . . . . NiB $5540 Ex $3770 Gd $2840

MODELS 200, 200E, 201, 201E, 202, 202E & 202EL O/U SHOTGUNS

Hammerless. Boxlock. Kersten double crossbolt. Scalloped frame. Sideplates on Models 202 and 202E. Arabesque or hunting engraving supplied on all except Models 200 and 200E. "E" models have ejectors, others have separate extractors, signal pins, double triggers. Gauges: 12, 16, 20, 24, 28, 32 (last three not available in postwar guns). Ribbed bbls. in various lengths and chokes. Weight: 5.75 to 7.5 lbs. depending on bbl. length and gauge. Checkered forend and stock w/pistol grip and cheekpiece or English-style. The 200, 201, and 202 differ in overall quality, engraving, wood, checkering, etc.; aside from the faux sideplates on Models 202 and 202E, general specifications are the same. Models 200, 201, 202, and 202E, all made before WW II, are disc. Models 201E &202E in production w/ revised 2000 series nomenclature.

Model 200 . . . . NiB $2920 Ex $2255 Gd $1730
Model 200E. . . . . NiB $3688 Ex $2987 Gd $2116
Model 200 ES Skeet . . . . . . NiB $4760 Ex $4200 Gd $2977
Model 200ET Trap. . . . . NiB $4660 Ex $4189 Gd $3255
Model 200 SC Sporting Clays. . . NiB $6930 Ex $4599 Gd $3238
Model 201 (disc.) . . . . NiB $3400 Ex $2566 Gd $1888
Model 201E (Pre-WW II) . NiB $7335 Ex $4990 Gd $3288
Model 201E (Post-WW II). . NiB $5100 Ex $3991 Gd $2977
Model 201 ES Skeet . . . . . . NiB $8100 Ex $6655 Gd $5133
Model 201 ET Trap . . . . NiB $7661 Ex $6255 Gd $4409
Model 202 (disc.) . . . . NiB $8255 Ex $5588 Gd $3577
Model 202E (Pre-WW II). . NiB $8255 Ex $4967 Gd $3886
Model 202E (Post-WWII &
  202EL). . . . . NiB $7091 Ex $5897 Gd $3994

MODEL 203E SIDELOCK O/U SHOTGUNS

Hammerless action w/hand-detachable sidelocks. Kersten double cross bolt, auto ejectors and double triggers. Gauges: 12 or 20 (16, 24, 28 and 32 disc.). 26.75- or 28-inch vent rib bbls. Arabesque engraving standard or hunting engraving optional on coin-finished receiver. Checkered English or pistol-grip stock and forend.

Model 203E sidelock
  (disc. 1998). . . . . NiB $10,335 Ex $8556 Gd $5830
Model 203ES skeet (imported
  1993-97). . . . . NiB $12,450 Ex $12,330 Gd $10,245
Model 203ET trap
  (disc. 1997). . . . . . NiB $13,770 Ex $12,560 Gd $10,665

MODEL 204E O/U . . . . NiB $8843 Ex $6751 Gd $4766
Similar to Model 203E; has Merkel sidelocks, fine English engraving. Made prior to World War II.

MODEL 210E SIDE-LOCK

O/U . . . . NiB $7239 Ex $5340 Gd $3882
Kersten double cross-bolt, scroll-engraved, casehardened receiver. 12, 16 or 20 ga. Double-triggers; pistol-grip stock w/ cheekpiece.

MODEL 211E SIDE-LOCK

O/U . . . . NiB $6865 Ex $5388 Gd $4488
Same specifications as Model 210E except w/engraved hunting scenes on silver-gray receiver.

SHOTGUNS

**Merkel Model 303E
O/U Shotgun**

MODELS 300, 300E, 301, 301E AND 302 O/U
Merkel-Anson system boxlock. Kersten double crossbolt, two underlugs, scalloped frame, sideplates on Model 302. Arabesque or hunting engraving. "E" models and Model 302 have auto ejectors, others have separate extractors. Signal pins. Double triggers. Gauges: 12, 16, 20, 24, 28, 32. Ribbed bbls. in various lengths and chokes. Checkered forend and stock w/pistol grip and cheekpiece or English-style. Grades 300, 301 and 302 differ in overall quality, engraving, wood, checkering, etc.; aside from the dummy sideplates on Model 302, general specifications are the same. Manufactured prior to World War II.

Model 300 . . . . NiB $5865 Ex $3579 Gd $2988
Model 300E . . . . NiB $8155 Ex $6888 Gd $5224
Model 301 . . . . NiB $6960 Ex $4977 Gd $3200
Model 301E . . . . NiB $8235 Ex $6276 Gd $5004
Model 302 . . . . NiB $14,998 Ex $12,688 Gd $10,097

MODEL 303E SIDELOCK O/U
Hammerless action w/hand-detachable sidelocks. Kersten double cross bolt, auto ejectors and double triggers. Gauges: 12 or 20 (16, 24, 28 and 32 disc.). 26.75- or 28-inch vent rib bbls. Arabesque engraving standard or hunting engraving optional on coin-finished receiver. Checkered English or pistol-grip stock and forend.

Model 203E sidelock (disc.
  1998) . . . . NiB $10,335 Ex $8556 Gd $5830

MODEL 304E O/U . . NiB $24,770 Ex $19,760 Gd $13,010
Special version of the Model 303E-type, but higher quality throughout. This is the top grade Merkel over/under. Currently manufactured. Special order items.

MODELS 400, 400E, 401, 401E O/U
Similar to Model 101 except have Kersten double crossbolt, Arabesque engraving on Models 400 and 400E, hunting engraving on Models 401 and 401E, finer general quality. "E" models have Merkel ejectors, others have separate extractors. Made prior to World War II.

Model 400 . . . . NiB $2190 Ex $1993 Gd $1465
Model 400E . . . . NiB $2433 Ex $2254 Gd $1934
Model 401 . . . . NiB $2798 Ex $2170 Gd $1588
Model 401E . . . . NiB $4366 Ex $3757 Gd $2486

O/U COMBINATION GUNS ("BOCKBÜCHSFLINTEN")
Shotgun bbl. over, rifle bbl. under. Gauges: 12, 16, 20; calibers: 5.6x35 Vierling, 7x57r5, 8x57JR, 8x60R Mag., 9.3x53r5, 9.3x72r5, 9.3x74R and others including domestic calibers from .22 Hornet to .375 H&H. Various bbl. lengths, chokes and weights. Other specifications and values correspond to those of Merkel over/under shotguns listed below. Currently

manufactured. Model 210 & 211 series disc. 1992.
Models 410, 410E, 411E (see shotgun models 400, 400E, 401, 401E)
Models 210, 210E, 211, 211E, 212, 212E (see shotgun models 200, 200E, 201, 201E, 202, 202E)

MODEL 2000EL O/U
Kersten double cross-bolt. Gauges: 12 and 20. 26.75- or 28-inch bbls. Weight: 6.4 to 7.28 lbs. Scroll engraved silver-gray receiver. Automatic ejectors and single selective or double triggers. Checkered forend and stock w/pistol grip and cheekpiece or English-style stock w/luxury grade wood. Imported from 1998 to 2005.

Model 2000EL Standard . . NiB $5733 Ex $4560 Gd $3288
Model 2000EL Sporter . . . . NiB $5980 Ex $4677 Gd $3455

MODEL 2001EL O/U
Gauges: 12, 16, 20 and 28; Kersten double cross-bolt lock receiver. 26.75- or 28-inch IC/mod, mod/full bbls. Weight: 6.4 to 7.28 lbs. Three-piece forearm, automatic ejectors and single selective or double triggers. Imported from 1993 to 2005.

Model 2001EL 12 ga. . . . . . NiB $6566 Ex $5270 Gd $3880
Model 2001EL 16 ga.
  (disc. 1997). . . . . NiB $6400 Ex $5277 Gd $3760
Model 2001EL 20 ga. . . . . . NiB $6400 Ex $5277 Gd $3760
Model 2001EL 28 ga.
  (made 1995) . . . . NiB $7200 Ex $5933 Gd $4200

MODEL 2002EL . . . . NiB $11,990 Ex $8530 Gd $6177
Same specifications as Model 2000EL except hunting scenes w/Arabesque engraving.

ANSON DRILLINGS
Three-bbl. combination guns; usually made w/double shotgun bbls., over rifle bbl., although "Doppelbüchsdrillingen" were made w/two rifle bbls. over and shotgun bbl. under. Hammerless.Boxlock. Anson & Deeley system. Side clips. Plain extractors. Double triggers. Gauges: 12, 16, 20; rifle calibers: 7x57r5, 8x57JR and 9.3x74R are most common, but other calibers from 5.6mm to 10.75mm available. Bbls.: standard drilling 25.6 inches; short drilling, 21.6 inches. Checkered pistol-grip stock and forend. The three models listed differ chiefly in overall quality, grade of wood, etc.; general specifications are the same. Made prior to WW II.

Model 142 Engraved . . . . . . NiB $5698 Ex $4887 Gd $3366
Model 142 Standard . . . . . NiB $4880 Ex $3688 Gd $2588
Model 145 Field . . . . NiB $3865 Ex $3200 Gd $2365

MIIDA — Manufactured for Marubeni America Corp., New York, by Olin-Kodensha Co., Tochigi, Japan

MODEL 612 FIELD
GRADE O/U . . . . NiB $863 Ex $665 Gd $400
Boxlock. Auto ejectors. Selective single trigger. 12 ga. Bbls.: Vent rib; 26-inch, IC/M; 28-inch, M/F choke. Weight: W/26-inch bbl., 6 lbs., 11 oz. Checkered pistol-grip stock and forearm. Made 1972 to 1974.

MODEL 2100 SKEET GUN . . . . NiB $954 Ex $749 Gd $488
Similar to Model 612 except has more elaborate engraving on frame (50 percent coverage), skeet-style stock and forearm of select grade wood; 27-inch vent-rib bbls., SK choke. Weight: 7 lbs., 11 oz. Made from 1972 to 1974.

Miida Model 612
Field Grade O/U

Mossberg Model 83D

MODEL 2200T TRAP GUN,
MODEL 2200S SKEET GUN . . . NiB $925 Ex $691 Gd $541
Similar to Model 612 except more elaborate engraving on
frame (60 percent coverage), trap- or skeet-style stock and
semi-beavertail forearm of fancy walnut, recoil pad on trap
stock. Bbls.: Wide vent rib; 29.75-inch, IM/F choke on Trap
Gun; 27-inch, SK choke on Skeet Gun. Weight: Trap, 7 lbs., 14
oz.; Skeet, 7 lbs., 11 oz. Made 1972 to 1974.

MODEL 2200 TRAP
& SKEET MODELS . . . . NiB $1088 Ex $766 Gd $594
Same as models 2200T and 2200S except more elaborate
engraving on frame (70% coverage). Made from 1972 to 1974.

GRANDEE MODEL GRT/IRS
TRAP/SKEET GUN . . . . NiB $2655 Ex $2390 Gd $1866
Boxlock w/sideplates. Frame, breech ends of bbls., trigger
guard and locking lever fully engraved and gold inlaid. Auto
ejectors. Selective single trigger. 12 ga. Bbls.: Wide vent rib;
29-inch, F choke on Trap Gun; 27-inch, SK choke on Skeet
Gun. Weight: Trap, 7 lbs., 14 oz.; Skeet, 7 lbs., 11 oz. Trap- or
skeet-style stock and semi-beavertail forearm of extra fancy
wood, recoil pad on trap stock. Made 1972 to 1974.

MITCHELL ARMS — Santa Ana, California

MODEL 9104/9105 PUMP SHOTGUNS
Slide action in Field/Riot configuration. Gauge: 12; 5-round
tubular magazine. 20-inch bbl.; fixed choke or screw-in tubes.
Weight: 6.5 lbs. Plain walnut stock. Made from 1994 to 1996.
Model 9104 (w/plain bbl.) . . . . NiB $299 Ex $288 Gd $188
Model 9105 (w/rifle sight) . . . . NiB $299 Ex $288 Gd $188
w/choke tubes, add $40

MODEL 9108/9109 PUMP SHOTGUN
Slide action in Military/Police/Riot configuration. Gauge: 12,
7-round tubular magazine. 20-inch bbl.; fixed choke or screw-
in tubes. Weight: 6.5 lbs. Plain walnut stock and grooved slide
handle w/brown, green or black finish. Blued metal. Made
from 1994 to 1996.
Model 9108 (w/plain bbl.) . . . . NiB $292 Ex $225 Gd $196
Model 9109 (w/rifle sights) . . . . NiB $292 Ex $225 Gd $196
w/choke tubes, add $40

MODEL 9111/9113 PUMP SHOTGUN
Slide action in Military/Police/Riot configuration. Gauge:
12; 6-round tubular magazine. 18.5-inch bbl.; fixed choke
or screw-in tubes. Weight: 6.5 lbs. Synthetic or plain walnut
stock and grooved slide handle w/brown, green or black finish.
Blued metal. Made from 1994 to 1996.
Model 9111 (w/plain bbl.) . . . . NiB $292 Ex $225 Gd $196
Model 9113 (w/rifle sights) . . . . NiB $292 Ex $225 Gd $196
w/choke tubes, add $40

MODEL 9114/9114FS
Slide action in Military/Police/Riot configuration. Gauge: 12;
7-round tubular magazine. 20-inch bbl.; fixed choke or screw-
in tubes. Weight: 6.5-7 lbs. Synthetic pistol-grip or folding
stock. Blued metal. Made from 1994 to 1996.
Model 9114 . . . . NiB $345 Ex $245 Gd $169
Model 9114FS . . . . NiB $345 Ex $245 Gd $169

MODEL 9115/9115FS
PUMP SHOTGUN . . . . NiB $366 Ex $240 Gd $159
Slide action in Military/Police/Riot configuration. Gauge: 12;
6-round tubular magazine. 18.5-inch bbl. w/heat-shield hand-
guard. Weight: 7 lbs. Gray synthetic stock and slide handle.
Parkerized metal. Made from 1994 to 1996.

MONTGOMERY WARD

See shotgun listings under "W".

MORRONE SHOTGUN — Manufactured by Rhode Island Arms Company, Hope Valley, Rhode Island

STANDARD MODEL 46 O/U . NiB $1366 Ex $890 Gd $677
Boxlock. Plain extractors. Non-selective single trigger. Gauges:
12, 20. Bbls.: Plain, vent rib; 26-inch IC/M; 28-inch M/F choke.
Weight: About 7 lbs., 12 ga.; 6 lbs., 20 ga. Checkered straight-
or pistol-grip stock and forearm. Made 1949-53. Note: Fewer
than 500 of these guns were produced, about 50 in 20 ga.. A
few had vent-rib bbls. Value shown is for 12 ga. w/plain bbls..
The rare 20 ga. and vent-rib types should bring considerably
more.

O.F. MOSSBERG & SONS, INC. — North Haven, Connecticut;

Formerly New Haven, Connecticut.

MODEL G4, 70, 73 & 73B . . . . . . NiB $150 Ex $85 Gd $50
Single shot. .410 ga. only. Made from 1932 to 1940.

MODEL 83D & 183D . . . . NiB $217 Ex $121 Gd $95
Bolt action, 3-round. Takedown. .410 ga. only. Two shell fixed
top-loading magazine. 23-inch bbl. w/two interchangeable
choke tubes (M/F). Later production had 24-inch bbl. Plain
one-piece pistol-grip stock. Weight: about 5.5 lbs. Originally
designated Model 83D, changed in 1947 to Model 183D.
Made from 1940 to 1971.

GRADING: **NiB** = New in Box   **Ex** = Excellent or NRA 95%   **Gd** = Good or NRA 68%   **519**

Mossberg Model 85D
Bolt-Action Repeating Shotgun

Mossberg Model 183K

Mossberg Model 185K

Mossberg Model 200K
Slide-Action Repeater

Mossberg Model 395K
Bolt-Action Repeater

MODEL 85D & 185D BOLT-ACTION
REPEATING SHOTGUN . . . . NiB $217 Ex $121 Gd $95
Bolt action. Takedown. 3-round. 20 ga. only. Two-shell detachable box magazine. 25-inch bbl., three interchangeable choke tubes (F, M, IC). Later production had 26-inch bbl. w/F/IC choke tubes. Weight: About 6.25 lbs. Plain one-piece, pistol-grip stock. Originally designated Model 85D, changed in 1947 to Model 185D. Made from 1940 to 1971.

MODEL 183K . . . . NiB $240 Ex $131 Gd $100
Same as Model 183D except has 25-inch bbl. w/variable C-Lect-Choke instead of interchangeable choke tubes. Made 1953 to 1986.

MODEL 185K . . . . NiB $240 Ex $131 Gd $100
Same as Model 185D except has variable C-Lect-Choke instead of interchangeable choke tubes. Made from 1950 to 1963.

MODEL 190D . . . . NiB $240 Ex $131 Gd $100
Same as Model 185D except in 16 ga. Weight: About 6 lbs. Made from 1955 to 1971.

MODEL 190K . . . . NiB $240 Ex $131 Gd $100
Same as Model 185K except in 16 ga. Takedown. Three round capacity; 2-round magazine. Weight: About 6.75 lbs. Made 1956 to 1963.

MODEL 195D . . . . NiB $240 Ex $131 Gd $100
Same as Model 185D except in 12 ga. Takedown. Three round capacity; 2-round magazine. Weight: About 6.75 lbs. Made 1955 to 1971.

MODEL 195K . . . . NiB $240 Ex $131 Gd $100
Same as Model 185K except in 12 ga. Takedown. Three round capacity; 2-round magazine. Weight: About 7.5 lbs. Made 1956 to 1963.

MODEL 200D . . . . NiB $355 Ex $240 Gd $125
Same as Model 200K except w/two interchangeable choke tubes instead of C-Lect choke. Made from 1955 to 1959.

MODEL 200K
SLIDE-ACTION REPEATER . . . . NiB $355 Ex $190 Gd $120
12 ga. 3-round detachable box magazine. 28-inch bbl. C-Lect choke. Plain pistol-grip stock. Black nylon slide handle. Weight: About 7.5 lbs. Made from 1955 to 1959.

MODEL 395K BOLT-ACTION
REPEATER . . . . NiB $255 Ex $155 Gd $120
Takedown. Three round (detachable-clip magazine holds two rounds).12 ga. (3-inch chamber). 28-inch bbl. w/C-Lect-Choke. Weight: About 7.5 lbs. Monte Carlo stock w/recoil pad. Made 1963 to 1983.

Mossberg Mode 500
Accu-Choke

Mossberg Model 500
Camo Pump

Mossberg Model 500
Bullpup Shotgun

MODEL 385K . . . . **NiB $240 Ex $131 Gd $100**
Same as Model 395K except 20 ga. (3-inch), 26-inch bbl. w/C-Lect-Choke. Weight: About 6.25 lbs.

MODEL 390K . . . . **NiB $240 Ex $131 Gd $100**
Same as Model 395K except 16 ga. (2.75-inch). Made 1963 to 1974.

MODEL 395S SLUGSTER . . . . . **NiB $240 Ex $131 Gd $100**
Same as Model 395K except has 24-inch bbl., cylinder bore, rifle sights, swivels and web sling. Weight: About 7 lbs. Made from 1968 to 1981.

MODEL 500 ACCU-CHOKE
SHOTGUN . . . . **NiB $290 Ex $231 Gd $125**
Pump-action. Gauge: 12. 24- or 28-inch bbl. Weight: 7.25 lbs. Checkered walnut-finished wood stock w/ventilated recoil pad. Available w/synthetic field or Speed-Feed stocks. Drilled and tapped receivers, swivels and camo sling on camo models. Made from 1987 to date.

MODEL 500 BANTAM SHOTGUN
Same as Model 500 Sporting Pump except 20 or .410 ga. only. 22-inch w/ACCU-Choke tubes or 24-inch w/F choke; vent rib. Scaled-down checkered hardwood or synthetic stock w/ standard or Realtree camo finish. Made from 1990 to 1996 and 1998 to 1999.
Bantam Model (hardwood stock). . . NiB $255 Ex $198 Gd $130
Bantam Model (synthetic stock) . . . NiB $330 Ex $229 Gd $165
Bantam Model (Realtree camo), add $75

MODEL 500 BULLPUP
SHOTGUN . . . . **NiB $722 Ex $486 Gd $344**
Pump. Gauge: 12. Six or 8-round capacity. Bbl.: 18.5 to 20 inches. 26.5 and 28.5 inches overall. Weight: About 9.5 lbs.

Multiple independent safety systems. Dual pistol grips, rubber recoil pad. Fully enclosed rifle-type sights. Synthetic stock. Ventilated bbl. heat shield. Made from 1987 to 1990.

MODEL 500 CAMO PUMP
Same as Model 500 Sporting Pump except 12 ga. only. Receiver drilled and tapped. QD swivels and camo sling. Special camouflage finish.
Standard model . . . . NiB $390 Ex $255 Gd $200
Combo model (w/ext. Slugster bbl.) . . . NiB $409 Ex $270 Gd $220

MODEL 500 CAMPER . . . . **NiB $290 Ex $210 Gd $175**
Same general specifications as Model 500 Field Grade except .410 bore, 6-round magazine, 18.5-inch plain cylinder bore bbl. Synthetic pistol grip and camo carrying case. Made 1986 to 1990.

Mossberg Model 500
Camper

Mossberg Model 500 Persuader
Law Enforcement

Mossberg Model 500
Mariner

MODEL 500 FIELD GRADE HAMMERLESS SLIDE-ACTION REPEATER

Pre-1977 type. Takedown. Gauges: 12, 16, 20, .410. Three inch chamber (2.75-inch in 16 ga.). Tubular magazine holds five 2.75-inch rounds or four three-inch. Bbls.: Plain- 30-inch regular or heavy Magnum, F choke (12 ga. only); 28-inch, M or F; 26-inch, IC or adj. C-Lect-Choke; 24-inch Slugster, cylinder bore, w/rifle sights. Weight: 5.75 to lbs. Plain pistol-grip stock w/recoil pad, grooved slide handle. After 1973, these guns have checkered stock and slide handles; Models 500AM and 500AS have receivers etched w/game scenes. The latter has swivels and sling. Made from 1962 to 1976.

Model 500A, 12 ga.,	NiB $310	Ex $225	Gd $170
Model 500AM, 12 ga., hvy.			
Mag. bbl.	NiB $310	Ex $225	Gd $170
Model 500AK, 12 ga.,			
C-Lect-Choke	NiB $335	Ex $250	Gd $190
Model 500AS, 12 ga.,			
Slugster	NiB $359	Ex $250	Gd $195
Model 500B 16 ga.,	NiB $369	Ex $275	Gd $205
Model 500BK, 16 ga.,			
C-Lect-Choke	NiB $300	Ex $220	Gd $145
Model 500BS, 16 ga., Slugster	NiB $359	Ex $250	Gd $195
Model 500C 20 ga.,	NiB $360	Ex $275	Gd $160
Model 500CK, 20 ga.,			
C-Lect-Choke	NiB $335	Ex $250	Gd $190
Model 500CS, 20 ga., Slugster	NiB $330	Ex $239	Gd $180
Model 500E, .410 ga.,	NiB $300	Ex $220	Gd $140
Model 500EK, .410 ga.,			
C-Lect-Choke	NiB $350	Ex $275	Gd $165

MODEL 500 "L" SERIES

"L" in model designation. Same as pre-1977 Model 500 Field Grade except not available in 16 ga., has receiver etched w/ different game scenes; Accu-Choke w/three interchangeable tubes (IC, M, F) standard, restyled stock and slide handle. Bbls.: plain or vent rib; 30- or 32-inch, heavy, F choke (12 ga. Magnum and vent rib only); 28-inch, Accu-Choke (12 and 20 ga.); 26-inch F choke (.410 bore only); 18.5-inch (12 ga. only), 24-inch (12 and 20 ga.) Slugster w/rifle sights, cylinder bore. Weight: 6 to 8.5 lbs. Intro. 1977.

Model 500ALD, 12 ga.,			
plain bbl. (disc. 1980)	NiB $275	Ex $195	Gd $110
Model 500ALDR, 12 ga.,			
vent rib	NiB $300	Ex $220	Gd $131
Model 500ALMR, 12 ga., Heavy Duck			
Gun (disc. 1980)	NiB $325	Ex $240	Gd $165
Model 500CLD, 20 ga.,			
plain bbl. (disc. 1980)	NiB $355	Ex $265	Gd $185
Model 500CLDR, 20 ga.,			
vent rib	NiB $310	Ex $235	Gd $135
Model 500CLS, 20 ga.,			
Slugster (disc. 1980)	NiB $355	Ex $265	Gd $185
Model 500EL, .410 ga.,			
plain bbl. (disc. 1980)	NiB $295	Ex $200	Gd $125

Model 500ELR, .410 ga.,			
vent rib	NiB $325	Ex $240	Gd $135

MODEL 500 MARINER

SHOTGUN	NiB $500	Ex $390	Gd $277

Slide action. Gauge: 12. 18.5 or 20-inch bbl. Six round and 8-round respectively. Weight: 7.25 lbs. High-strength synthetic buttstock and forend. Available in extra round-carrying Speed Feed synthetic buttstock. All metal treated for protection against saltwater corrosion. Intro. 1987.

MODEL 500 MUZZLELOADER

COMBO.	NiB $390	Ex $275	Gd $190

Same as Model 500 Sporting Pump except w/extra 24-inch rifled .50-caliber muzzleloading bbl. w/ramrod. Made 1991 to 1996.

MODEL 500 PERSUADER LAW ENFORCEMENT

Similar to pre-1977 Model 500 Field Grade except 12 ga. only, 6- or 8-round capacity, has 18.5- or 20-inch plain bbl., cylinder bore, either shotgun or rifle sights, plain pistol-grip stock and grooved slide handle, sling swivels. Special Model 500ATP8-SP has bayonet lug, Parkerized finish. Intro. 1995.

Model 500ATP6, 6-round, 18.5-inch			
bbl., shotgun sights	NiB $410	Ex $275	Gd $190
Model 500ATP6CN, 6-round, nickle finish			
"Cruiser" pistol-grip.	NiB $440	Ex $300	Gd $225
Model 500ATP6N, 6-round, nickel finish, 2.75-			
or 3-inch Mag. shells	NiB $410	Ex $275	Gd $190
Model 500ATP6S, 6-round,			
18.5-inch bbl., rifle sights	NiB $410	Ex $275	Gd $190
Model 500ATP8, 8-round,			
20-inch bbl., shotgun sights	NiB $440	Ex $300	Gd $225
Model 500ATP8S, 8-round,			
20-inch bbl., rifle sights	NiB $450	Ex $315	Gd $240
Model 500ATP8-SP Spec.			
Enforcement	NiB $391	Ex $313	Gd $226
Model 500 Bullpup	NiB $690	Ex $500	Gd $345
Model 500 Intimidator w/laser			
sight, blued	NiB $644	Ex $470	Gd $329
Model 500 Intimidator w/laser sight,			
parkerized	NiB $425	Ex $320	Gd $190
Model 500 Security			
combo pack	NiB $345	Ex $270	Gd $185
Model 500 Cruiser w/pistol			
grip	NiB $440	Ex $325	Gd $220

MODEL 500 PIGEON GRADE

Same as Model 500 Super Grade except higher quality w/fancy wood, floating vent rib; field gun hunting dog etching, trap and skeet guns have scroll etching. Bbls.: 30-inch, F choke (12 ga. only); 28-inch, M choke; 26-inch, SK choke or C-Lect-Choke. Made from 1971 to 1975.

Model 500APR, 12 ga., field,			
trap or skeet	NiB $510	Ex $409	Gd $320

Mossberg Model 500
Turkey/Deer Combo

Model 500APKR, 12 ga.
field gun, C-Lect-Choke . . . . NiB $455 Ex $279 Gd $144
Model 500 APTR, 12 ga., Trap gun,
Monte Carlo stock . . . . NiB $475 Ex $300 Gd $165
Model 500CPR, 20 ga., field
or skeet gun . . . . NiB $365 Ex $279 Gd $180
Model 500EPR, .410 ga.
field or skeet gun . . . . NiB $345 Ex $292 Gd $190

MODEL 500 CAMO COMBO
SHOTGUN . . . . NiB $440 Ex $335 Gd $255
Gauges: 12 and 20. 24- and 28-inch bbl. w/adj. rifle sights.
Weight: 7 to 7.25 lbs. Available w/blued or camo finish. Drilled
and tapped receiver w/sling swivels and camo web sling. Made
from 1987 to 1998.

MODEL 500 PUMP SLUGSTER SHOTGUN
Gauges: 12 or 20 w/3-inch chamber. 24-inch smoothbore
or rifled bbl. w/adj. rifle sights or intregral scope mount and
optional muzzle break (1997 porting became standard).
Weight: 7 to 7.25 lbs. Wood or synthetic stock w/standard
or Woodland Camo finish. Blued, matte black or Marinecote
metal finish. Drilled and tapped receiver w/camo sling and
swivels. Made 1987 to date.
Slugster (w/cyl. bore, rifle sights) . . . NiB $335 Ex $245 Gd $190
Slugster (w/rifled bore, ported) . . . NiB $415 Ex $335 Gd $240
Slugster (w/rifled bore, unported) . . . . NiB $320 Ex $219 Gd $190
Slugster (w/rifled bore, ported,
integral scope mount) . . . . . NiB $320 Ex $219 Gd $190
Slugster (w/Marinecote and synthetic stock), add $100
Slugster (w/Truglo fiber optics), add $50

MODEL 500 REGAL SLIDE-ACTION REPEATER
Similar to regular Model 500 except higher quality workman-
ship throughout. Gauges: 12 and 20. Bbls.: 26- and 28-inch
w/various chokes, or Accu-Choke. Weight: 6.75 to 7.5 lbs.
Checkered walnut stock and forearm. Made from 1985 to
1987.
Model 500 w/Accu-Choke . . . . NiB $320 Ex $219 Gd $190
Model 500 w/fixed choke . . . . NiB $300 Ex $200 Gd $165

MODEL 500 SPORTING PUMP
Gauges: 12, 20 or .410, 2.75- or 3-inch chamber. Bbls.: 22 to
28 inches w/fixed choke or screw-in tubes; plain or vent rib.
Weight: 6.25 to 7.25 lbs. White bead front sight, brass mid-
bead. Checkered hardwood buttstock and forend w/walnut
finish.
Standard model . . . . NiB $345 Ex $275 Gd $190
Field combo (w/extra Slugster bbl.) . . NiB $440 Ex $325 Gd $240

MODEL 500 SUPER GRADE
Same as pre-1977 Model 500 Field Grade except not made in
16 ga., has vent rib bbl., checkered pistol grip and slide handle.
Made from 1965- to 1976.
Model 500AR, 12 ga. . . . . NiB $400 Ex $299 Gd $221

Model 500AMR, 12 ga.,
heavy magnum bbl. . . . . NiB $400 Ex $299 Gd $221
Model 500AKR, 12 ga.,
C-Lect-Choke . . . . NiB $425 Ex $315 Gd $235
Model 500CR 20 ga. . . . . NiB $400 Ex $299 Gd $221
Model 500CKk, 20 ga.,
C-Lect-Choke . . . . NiB $425 Ex $315 Gd $235
Model 500ER, .410 ga. . . . . NiB $400 Ex $299 Gd $221
Model 500EKR, .410 ga.,
C-Lect-Choke . . . . NiB $425 Ex $315 Gd $235

MODEL 500 TURKEY/DEER
COMBO . . . . NiB $425 Ex $315 Gd $235
Pump (slide action). Gauge: 12. 20- and 24-inch bbls. Weight:
7.25 lbs. Drilled and tapped receiver, camo sling and swivels. Adj.
rifle sights and camo finish. Vent rib. Made from 1987 to 1997.

MODEL 500 TURKEY GUN . . . NiB $465 Ex $325 Gd $254
Same as Model 500 Camo Pump except w/24-inch ACCU-
Choke bbl. w/extra full choke tube and ghost ring sights. Made
1992 to 1997.

MODEL 500 VIKING PUMP SHOTGUN
Gauges: 12 or 20 w/3-inch chamber. 24-, 26- or 28-inch bbls.
available in smoothbore w/Accu-Choke and vent rib or rifled
bore w/iron sights and optional muzzle brake (1997 porting
became standard). Optional optics: Slug Shooting System (SSS).
Weight: 6.9 to 7.2 lbs. Moss-green synthetic stock. Matte black
metal finish. Made from 1996 to 1998.
Mdl. 500 Viking (w/VR &
choke tubes, unported) . . . . . NiB $300 Ex $225 Gd $144
Mdl. 500 Viking (w/rifled
bore, ported) . . . . NiB $390 Ex $295 Gd $240
Mdl. 500 Viking (w/rifled
bore, SSS & ported) . . . . NiB $390 Ex $295 Gd $240
Mdl. 500 Viking
(w/rifled bore, unported) . . . NiB $300 Ex $225 Gd $144
Mdl. 500 Viking Turkey
(w/VR, tubes, ported) . . . . . . NiB $300 Ex $225 Gd $144

MODEL 500 WATERFOWL/DEER
COMBO . . . . NiB $455 Ex $350 Gd $285
Same general specifications as the Turkey/Deer combo except
w/either 28- or 30-inch bbl. along w/the 24-inch bbl. Made
from 1987 to date.

MODEL 500 ATR SUPER
GRADE TRAP . . . . NiB $400 Ex $310 Gd $225
Same as pre-1977 Model 500 Field Grade except 12 ga. only
w/vent-rib bbl.; 30-inch F choke, checkered Monte Carlo stock
w/recoil pad, beavertail slide handle. Made from 1968 to 1971.

MODEL 500 DSPR DUCK STAMP
COMMEMORATIVE . . . . NiB $600 Ex $465 Gd $300
Limited edition of 1000 to commemorate the Migratory Bird
Hunting Stamp program. Same as Model 500DSPR Pigeon

SHOTGUNS

Mossberg Model 590 Military

Mossberg Model 595 Bolt-Action Repeater

Grade 12-Gauge Magnum Heavy Duck Gun w/heavy 30-inch vent-rib bbl., F choke; receiver has special wood duck etching. Gun accompanied by a special wall plaque. Made in 1975.

MODEL 590 BULLPUP . . . . **NiB $745 Ex $449 Gd $335**
Same general specifications as the Model 500 Bullpup except 20-inch bbl. and 9-round magazine. Made from 1989 to 1990.

MODEL 590 MARINER PUMP
Same general specifications as the Model 590 Military Security except has Marinecote metal finish and field configuration synthetic stock w/pistiol-grip conversion included. Made 1989 to 1999.
Model 590 Mariner (w/18.5-inch
  bbl.) . . . . **NiB $645 Ex $554 Gd $470**
Model 590 Mariner (w/20-inch bbl.) NiB $645 Ex$554 Gd$470
Model 590 Mariner (w/grip conversion), add **$40**
Model 590 Mariner (w/ghost ring sight), add **$75**

MODEL 590 MILITARY
SECURITY . . . . **NiB $544 Ex $389 Gd $290**
Same general specifications as the Model 590 Military except there is no heat shield and gun has short pistol-grip style instead of buttstock. Weight: About 6.75 lbs. Made from 1987 to 1993.

MODEL 590 MILITARY SHOTGUN
Slide-action. Gauge: 12. 9-round capacity. 20-inch bbl. Weight: About 7 lbs. Synthetic or hardwood buttstock and forend. Ventilated bbl. heat shields. Equipped w/bayonet lug. Blued or Parkerized finish. Made from 1987 to date.
Synthetic model, blued . . . . . . **NiB $465 Ex $377 Gd $260**
Synthetic model Parkerized . . **NiB $490 Ex $400 Gd $280**
Speedfeed model, blued . . . . . **NiB $475 Ex $380 Gd $285**
Speedfeed model, Parkerized . **NiB $475 Ex $ 380 Gd $285**
Intimidator model
  w/laser sight, blued . . . . **NiB $640 Ex $500 Gd $365**
Intimidator model
  w/laser sight, Parkerized . . . **NiB $665 Ex $515 Gd $380**
For ghost ring sight, add **$100**

MODEL 595/595K
BOLT-ACTION REPEATER . . . . . **NiB $425 Ex $260 Gd $159**
12 ga. only. Four round detachable magazine. 18.5-inch bbl. Weight: About 7 lbs. Walnut finished stock w/recoil pad and sling swivels. Made 1985 to 1986.

MODEL 695 BOLT-ACTION SLUGSTER
Gauge: 12 w/3-inch chamber. Two round detachable magazine. 22-inch fully rifled and ported bbl. w/blade front and folding leaf rear sights. Receiver drilled and tapped for Weaver style scope bases. Available w/1.5x-4.5x scope or fiber optics installed. Weight: 7.5 lbs. Black synthetic stock w/swivel studs and recoil pad. Made 1996 to 2002.
Model 695 (w/ACCU-choke
  bbl.) . . . . **NiB $300 Ex $220 Gd $175**
Model 695 (w/open sights) . . . . **NiB $380 Ex $296 Gd $207**
Model 695 (w/1.5x-4.5x
  Bushnell scope) . . . . **NiB $390 Ex $310 Gd $219**
Model 695 (w/Truglo
  fiber optics) . . . . **NiB $385 Ex $305 Gd $210**
Model 695 OFM Camo . . . . **NiB $355 Ex $280 Gd $196**

MODEL 695 BOLT-ACTION
TURKEY GUN . . . . **NiB $375 Ex $265 Gd $195**
Similar to 695 Slugster Model except has smoothbore 22-inch bbl. w/extra-full turkey Accu-choke tube. Bead front and U-notch rear sights. Full OFM camo finish. Made from 1996 to 2002.

MODEL 712 AUTOLOADING SHOTGUN
Gas-operated, takedown, hammerless shotgun w/5-round (4-round w/3-inch chamber) tubular magazine. 12 ga. Bbls.: 28-inch vent rib or 24-inch plain bbl. Slugster w/rifle sights. Fixed choke or ACCU-choke tube system. Weight: 7.5 lbs. Plain alloy receiver w/top-mounted ambidextrous safety. Checkered. stained hardwood stock w/recoil pad. Imported from Japan 1986 to 1990.
Mdl. 712 w/fixed chokes . . . . . **NiB $369 Ex $237 Gd $185**
Mdl. 712 w/ACCU-Choke
  tube system . . . . **NiB $390 Ex $275 Gd $219**
Mdl. 712 Regal w/ACCU-Choke
  tube system . . . . **NiB $390 Ex $275 Gd $219**
Mdl. 712 Regal w/ACCU-Choke II
  tube sys . . **NiB $390 Ex $275 Gd $219**

MODEL 835 FIELD PUMP SHOTGUN
Similar to the Model 9600 Regal except has walnut-stained hardwood stock and one ACCU-Choke tube only.
Standard model . . . . **NiB $365 Ex $220 Gd $154**
Turkey model . . . . **NiB $365 Ex $220 Gd $154**
Combo model (24- & 28-inch bbls.) . . **NiB $390 Ex $250 Gd $180**

**Mossberg Model 1000
Junior Autoloading**

**Mossberg Model 5500
Guardian**

MODEL 835 "NWTF" ULTI-MA SHOTGUN
National Wild Turkey Federation pump-action. Gauge: 12, 3.5-inch chamber. 24-inch vent-rib bbl. w/four ACCU-MAG chokes. Realtree camo finish. QD swivel and post. Made from 1989 to 1993.
Limited Edition model . . . . **NiB $470 Ex $366 Gd $239**
Special Edition model . . . . **NiB $400 Ex $325 Gd $225**

MODEL 835 REGAL ULTI-MAG PUMP
Gauge: 12, 3.5-inch chamber. Bbls.: 24- or 28-inch vent-rib w/ACCU-Choke screw-in tubes. Weight: 7.75 lbs. White bead front, brass mid-bead. Checkered hardwood or synthetic stock w/camo finish. Made 1991 to 1996.
Special model . . . . **NiB $400 Ex $350 Gd $235**
Standard model . . . . **NiB $509 Ex $377 Gd $295**
Camo Synthetic model . . . . **NiB $490 Ex $375 Gd $299**
Combo model . . . . **NiB $528 Ex $420 Gd $310**

MODEL 835 VIKING PUMP SHOTGUN
Gauge: 12 w/3-inch chamber. 28-inch smoothbore bbl. w/ Accu-Choke, vent rib and optional muzzle brake (in 1997 porting became standard). Weight: 7.7 lbs. Green synthetic stock. Matte black metal finish. Made from 1996 to 1998.
**Model 835 Viking (w/VR and
   choke tubes, ported)**. . . . . . . **NiB $300 Ex $217 Gd $175**
**Model 835 Viking (w/VR
   and choke tubes, unported)** . **NiB $445 Ex $270 Gd $210**

MODEL 1000 AUTOLOADING SHOTGUN
Gas-operated, takedown, hammerless shotgun w/tubular magazine. Gauges: 12, 20; 2.75- or 3-inch chamber. Bbls.: 22- to 30-inch vent rib w/fixed choke or ACCU-Choke tubes; or 22-inch plain bbl, Slugster w/rifle sights. Weight: 6.5 to 7.5 lbs. Scroll-engraved alloy receiver, crossbolt-type safety. Checkered walnut buttstock and forend. Imported from Japan 1986 to 1987.
Junior model, 20 ga., 22-inch bbl.. . . **NiB $555 Ex $435 Gd $320**
Standard model w/fixed choke . . . **NiB $555 Ex $435 Gd $320**
Standard model w/choke tubes . . . **NiB $555 Ex $435 Gd $320**

MODEL 1000 SUPER AUTOLOADING SHOTGUN
Similar to Model 1000, but in 12 ga. only w/3-inch chamber and new gas metering system. Bbls.: 26-, 28- or 30-inch vent rib w/ACCU-Choke tubes.
Standard model w/choke tubes . . **NiB $555 Ex $435 Gd $320**
Waterfowler model (Parkerized) . . **NiB $590 Ex $466 Gd $380**

MODEL 1000S SUPER SKEET . . **NiB $655 Ex $500 Gd $422**
Similar to Model 1000 in 12 or 20 ga., except w/all-steel receiver and vented jug-type choke for reduced muzzle jump. Bright-point front sight and brass mid-bead. 1 and 2 oz. forend cap weights.

MODEL 5500 AUTOLOADING SHOTGUN
Gas-operated. Takedown. 12 ga. only. Four round magazine (3-round w/3-inch shells). Bbls.: 18.5- to 30-inch; various chokes. Checkered walnut finished hardwood. Made from 1985 to 1986.
Model 5500 w/ACCU-Choke . . **NiB $300 Ex $210 Gd $148**
Model 5500 modified junior . . **NiB $300 Ex $210 Gd $148**
Model 5500 Slugster. . . . . **NiB $355 Ex $209 Gd $155**
Model 5500 12 ga. Mag . . . . . . **NiB $335 Ex $254 Gd $190**
Model 5500 Guardian . . . . **NiB $330 Ex $250 Gd $180**

MODEL 5500 MKII AUTOLOADING SHOTGUN
Same as Model 5500 except equipped w/two Accu-Choke bbls.: 26-inch ported for non-Magnum 2.75-inch shells; 28-inch for magnum loads. Made from 1988 to 1993.
Standard model . . . . **NiB $330 Ex $209 Gd $135**
Camo model . . . . **NiB $366 Ex $270 Gd $198**
NWTF Mossy Oak model . . . . . **NiB $415 Ex $330 Gd $225**
USST model (1991-92) . . . . **NiB $370 Ex $292 Gd $217**

MODEL 6000 AUTO
SHOTGUN . . . . **NiB $320 Ex $231 Gd $198**
Similar to the Model 9200 Regal except has 28-inch vent-rib bbl. w/mod. ACCU-Choke tube only. Made 1993 only.

MODEL 9200 CAMO SHOTGUN
Similar to the Model 9200 Regal except has synthetic stock and forend and is completely finished in camouflage pattern (incl. bbl.). Made from 1993 to date.
Standard model (OFM camo) . . **NiB $500 Ex $415 Gd $306**
Turkey model (Mossy Oak camo) . . . **NiB $475 Ex $429 Gd $360**
**Turkey model (Shadow Branch
   camo)** . . . . **NiB $615 Ex $490 Gd $376**
**Comb. model (24 & 28-inch bbls.
   w/OFM camo)** . . . . **NiB $635 Ex $515 Gd $390**

MODEL 9200 CROWN (REGAL) AUTOLOADER
Gauge: 12; 3-inch chamber. Bbls.: 18.5- to 28-inch w/ ACCU-Choke tubes; plain or vent rib. Weight: 7.25 to 7.5 lbs. Checkered hardwood buttstock and forend w/walnut finish. Made from 1992 to 2001.

Navy Arms Model 83
Bird Hunter O/U

Navy Arms Model 100
Field Hunter Double-Barrel Shotgun

Model 9200 Bantam (w/1-inch
shorter stock) . . . . NiB $500 Ex $433 Gd $329
Model 9200 w/ACCU-Choke . . . NiB $500 Ex $433 Gd $329
Model 9200 w/rifled bbl. . . . . NiB $500 Ex $433 Gd $329
Model 9200 Combo (w/extra
Slugster bbl.). . . . . NiB $550 Ex $493 Gd $379
Model 9200 SP (w/matte blue finish,
18.5-inch bbl.) . . . . NiB $500 Ex $433 Gd $329

MODEL 9200 PERSUADER. . . . NiB $500 Ex $443 Gd $329
Similar to the Model 9200 Regal except has 18.5-inch plain bbl. w/fixed mod. choke. Parkerized finish. Black synthetic stock w/sling swivels. Made from 1996 to 2001.

MODEL 9200 A1
JUNGLE GUN . . NiB $665 Ex $533 Gd $347
Similar to the Model 9200 Persuader except has mil-spec heavy wall 18.5-inch plain bbl. w/cyl. bore designed for 00 Buck shot. 12 ga. w/2.75-inch chamber. Five round magazine. 38.5 inches overall. Weight: 7 lbs. Black synthetic stock. Parkerized finish. Made from 1998 to 2001.

MODEL 9200
SPECIAL HUNTER . . NiB $555 Ex $435 Gd $365
Similar to the Model 9200 Regal except has 28-inch vent-rib bbl. w/ACCU-Choke tubes. Parkerized finish. Black synthetic stock. Made from 1998 to 2001.

MODEL 9200 TROPHY
Similar to the Model 9200 Regal except w/24-inch rifled bbl. or 24- or 28-inch vent-rib bbl. w/ACCU-Choke tubes. Checkered walnut stock w/sling swivels. Made from 1992 to 1998.
Trophy (w/vent rib bbl.) . . . . . . NiB $650 Ex $583 Gd $479
Trophy (w/rifled bbl. & cantilever
scope mount) . . . . NiB $675 Ex $609 Gd $495
Trophy (w/rifled bbl. & rifle sights) . . . NiB $635 Ex $570 Gd $460

MODEL 9200 USST
AUTOLOADER . . NiB $525 Ex $390 Gd $295
Similar to the Model 9200 Regal except has 26-inch vent-rib bbl. w/ACCU-Choke tubes. "United States Shooting Team" engraved on receiver. Made from 1993 to date.

MODEL 9200
VIKING AUTOLOADER . . . . . . NiB $425 Ex $330 Gd $290
Gauge: 12 w/3-inch chamber. 28-inch smoothbore bbl. W/ Accu-Choke and vent rib. Weight: 7.7 lbs. Green synthetic stock. Matte black metal finish. Made from 1996 to 1998.

MODEL HS410
HOME SECURITY PUMP SHOTGUN
Gauge: .410; 3-inch chamber. Bbl.: 18.5-inch w/muzzle brake; blued. Weight: 6.25 lbs. Synthetic stock and pistol-grip slide.

Optional laser sight. Made from 1990 to date. A similar version of this gun is marketed by Maverick Arms under the same model designation.
Standard model . . . . NiB $345 Ex $270 Gd $195
Laser model . . . . NiB $544 Ex $396 Gd $277

LINE LAUNCHER . . . . NiB $1066 Ex $833 Gd $545
Gauge: 12 w/blank cartridge. Projectile travels from 250 to 275 feet.

"NEW HAVEN BRAND" SHOTGUNS
Promotional models, similar to their standard guns but plainer in finish, are marketed by Mossberg under the "New Haven" brand name. Values generally are about 20 percent lower than for corresponding standard models.

ONYX RESERVE SPORTING . . . NiB $760 Ex $580 Gd $370
O/U boxlock, blued engraved receiver. Gauges: 12 only; 3-inch chambers. Bbls.: 28-inch ported vent-rib. Checkered walnut stock and forearm. Made 2010 to 2012.

SILVER RESERVE FIELD . . . . . . NiB $600 Ex $460 Gd $340
O/U boxlock, gold inlay silver receiver. Gauges: 12, 20, 28 or .410. Bbls.: 26- or 28-in. vent-rib. Checkered walnut stock and forearm. Extractors. Mfg. in Turkey. Imported from 2005 to 2012.
Sporting . . . . NiB $755 Ex $585 Gd $400

SILVER RESERVE II FIELD . . . . . NiB $736 Ex $470 Gd $300
O/U boxlock, silver receiver w/ engraving. Gauges: 12, 20, 28 or .410. Bbls.: 26- or 28-in. vent-rib. Checkered black walnut stock and forearm. Extractors or ejectors. Imported from 2012 to date.
Sporting (ported 28-in. bbl.) . . NiB $1253 Ex $580 Gd $350
Super Sport (ported 30- or
32-in. bbl.) . . . . NiB $1253 Ex $580 Gd $350

SILVER RESERVE FIELD . . . . . . NiB $860 Ex $640 Gd $370
S/S boxlock, blued or silver w/ scroll engrved receiver, extractors. Gauges: 12, 20, 28 or .410. Bbls.: 26- or 28-in. Checkered black walnut stock and forearm. Extractors. Made from 2008 to 2012.
Onyx (12 ga., onyx finish) . . . . NiB $860 Ex $640 Gd $380

SILVER RESERVE II FIELD . . . . NiB $1100 Ex $690 Gd $420
S/S boxlock, blued or silver w/ scroll engrved receiver. Gauges: 12, 20 or 28. Bbls.: 26- or 28-in. Checkered black walnut stock and forearm. Weight: 6.5 to 7.5 lbs. Made from 2012 to date.

NAVY ARMS —Ridgefield, New Jersey

MODEL 83/93 BIRD HUNTER O/U
Hammerless. Boxlock, engraved receiver. Gauges: 12 and 20; 3-inch chambers. Bbls.: 28-inch chrome lined w/double

vent-rib construction. Checkered European walnut stock and forearm. Gold plated triggers. Imported 1984 to 1990.

Model 83 w/extractors ......NiB $355 Ex $285 Gd $200
Model 93 w/ejectors ....NiB $379 Ex $339 Gd $255

MODEL 95/96 O/U SHOTGUN
Same as the Model 83/93 except w/five interchangeable choke tubes. Imported 1984 to 1990.

Model 95 w/extractors ......NiB $448 Ex $355 Gd $210
Model 96 w/ejectors ....NiB $555 Ex $376 Gd $280

MODEL 100/150 FIELD HUNTER DOUBLE-BARREL SHOTGUN
Boxlock. Gauges: 12 and 20. Bbls.: 28-inch chrome lined. Checkered European walnut stock and forearm. Imported 1984 to 1990.

Model 100 ....NiB $460 Ex $390 Gd $288
Model 150 (auto ejectors) ....NiB $510 Ex $355 Gd $290

MODEL 100 O/U SHOTGUN. . NiB $277 Ex $169 Gd $109
Hammerless, takedown shotgun w/engraved chrome receiver. Single trigger. 12, 20, 28, or .410 ga. w/3-inch chambers. Bbls.: 26-inch (F/F or SK/SK); vent rib. Weight: 6.25 lbs. Checkered European walnut buttstock and forend. Imported 1986 to 1990.

NEW ENGLAND FIREARMS —

Gardner, Massachusetts

In 1987, New England Firearms was established as an independent company producing selected H&R models under the NEF logo after Harrington & Richardson suspended operations on January 24, 1986. In 1991, H&R 1871, Inc. was formed from the residual of the parent H&R company and then took over the New England Firearms facility. H&R 1871 produced firearms under both their logo and the NEF brand name until 1999, when the Marlin Firearms Company acquired the assets of H&R 1871.

NEW ENGLAND FIREARMS NWTF TURKEY SPECIAL
Similar to Turkey and Goose models except 10 or 20 gauge w/22- or 24-inch plain bbl. w/screw-in full-choke tube. Mossy Oak camo finish on entire gun. Made from 1992 to 1996.

Turkey Special 10 ga. ....NiB $265 Ex $177 Gd $98
Turkey Special 20 ga. ....NiB $335 Ex $219 Gd $189

NRA FOUNDATION YOUTH . . NiB $190 Ex $155 Gd $100
Smaller scale version of Pardner Model chambered for 20, 28 or .410 w/22- inch plain bbl. High luster blue finish. NRA Foundation logo laser etched on stock. Made from 1999 to 2002.

PARDNER SHOTGUN
Takedown. Side lever. Single bbl. Gauges: 12, 20 and .410 w/3-inch chamber; 16 and 28 w/2.75-inch chamber. 26-, 28- or 32-inch, plain bbl. w/fixed choke. Weight: 5-6 lbs. Bead front sight. Pistol grip-style hardwood stock w/walnut finish. Made from 1988 to date.

Standard model ....NiB $255 Ex $185 Gd $99
Youth model ....NiB $255 Ex $185 Gd $99
Turkey model ....NiB $323 Ex $217 Gd $110
w/32-inch bbl., add $40

PARDNER SPECIAL PURPOSE 10-GA SHOTGUN
Similar to the standard Pardner model except chambered 10 ga. only w/3.5-inch chamber. 24- or 28-inch, plain bbl. w/full choke tube or fixed choke. Weight: 9.5 lbs. Bead front sight.

Pistol-grip-style hardwood stock w/camo or matte black finish. Made from 1989 to date.

Special Purpose model w/fixed
    choke ....NiB $315 Ex $220 Gd $125
w/camo finish, add $40
w/choke tube, add $25
w/24-inch bbl. turkey option, add $50

PARDNER SPECIAL PURPOSE
WATERFOWL SINGLE-SHOT . . NiB $255 Ex $190 Gd $129
Similar to Special Purpose 10 Ga. model except w/32-inch bbl. Mossy Oak camo stock w/swivel and sling. Made from 1988 to date.

PARDNER TURKEY GUN
Similar to Pardner model except chambered in 12 ga. w/3.0- or 3.5-inch chamber. 24-inch plain bbl. W/turkey full-choke tube or fixed choke. Weight: 9.5 lbs. American hardwood stock w/ camo or matte black finish. Made from 1999 to date.

Standard Turkey model ......NiB $200 Ex $110 Gd $85
Camo Turkey model ....NiB $200 Ex $110 Gd $85

SURVIVOR SERIES
Takedown single bbl. shotgun w/side lever release, Automatic ejector and patented transfer-bar safety. Gauges: 12, 20, and .410/.45 ACP w/3-inch chamber. 22-inch bbl. w/modified choke and bead sight. Weight: 6 lbs. Polymer stock and forend w/hollow cavity for storage. Made 1992 to 1993 and 1995 to date.

12 or 20 ga. w/blued finish.....NiB $220 Ex $144 Gd $98
12 or 20 ga. w/nickel finish .. NiB $260 Ex $177 Gd $120
.410/.45 LC add $75

TRACKER SLUG GUN
Similar to Pardner model except in 10, 12 or 20 ga. w/24-inch w/cylinder choke or rifled slug bbl. (Tracker II). Weight: 6 lbs. American hardwood stock w/walnut or camo finish, Schnabel forend, sling swivel studs. Made from 1992 to 2001.

Tracker Slug (10 ga.) ....NiB $180 Ex $110 Gd $79
Tracker Slug (12 or 20 ga.) ....NiB $219 Ex $120 Gd $85
Tracker II (rifled bore) ....NiB $219 Ex $120 Gd $85

NIKKO FIREARMS LTD. — Tochigi, Japan

See listings under Golden Eagle Firearms, Inc.

NOBLE MANUFACTURING COMPANY —
Haydenville, Massachusetts

Series 602 and 70 are similar in appearance to the corresponding Model 66 guns.

MODEL 40 HAMMERLESS SLIDE-ACTION
REPEATING SHOTGUN ......NiB $255 Ex $190 Gd $130
Solid frame. 12 ga. only. Five round tubular magazine. 28-inch bbl. w/ventilated Multi-Choke. Weight: About 7.5 lbs. Plain pistol-grip stock, grooved slide handle. Made from 1950 to 1955.

MODEL 50 SLIDE-ACTION ...NiB $266 Ex $190 Gd $125
Same as Model 40 except w/o Multi-Choke. M or F choke bbl. Made from 1953 to 1955.

MODEL 60 HAMMERLESS SLIDE-ACTION
REPEATING SHOTGUN ......NiB $325 Ex $255 Gd $159
Solid frame. 12 and 16 ga. Five round tubular magazine. 28-inch bbl. w/adj. choke. Plain pistol-grip stock w/recoil pad,

SHOTGUNS

Noble Model 65

Noble Key Lock Fire
Control Mechanism
Supplied with models
66, 166L and 602

Noble Model 66RCLP
Hammerless Slide-Action Repeating Shotgun

grooved slide handle. Weight: About 7.5 lbs. Made from 1955 to 1966.

MODEL 65 . . . . NiB $300 Ex $225 Gd $165
Same as Model 60 except without adj. choke and recoil pad. M or F choke bbl. Made from 1955 to 1966.

MODEL 66CLP . . . . NiB $235 Ex $185 Gd $135
Same as Model 66RCLP except has plain bbl. Introduced in 1967. Disc.

**MODEL 66RCLP HAMMERLESS SLIDE-ACTION
REPEATING SHOTGUN** . . . . . . NiB $339 Ex $235 Gd $176
Solid frame. Key lock fire control mechanism. Gauges: 12, 16. 3-inch chamber in 12 ga. Five round tubular magazine. 28-inch bbl., vent rib, adj. choke. Weight: About 7.5 lbs. Checkered pistol-grip stock and slide handle, recoil pad. Made from 1967 to 1970.

MODEL 66RLP . . . . NiB $329 Ex $225 Gd $165
Same as Model 66RCLP except w/F or M choke. Made 1967 to 1970.

MODEL 66XL . . . . NiB $245 Ex $185 Gd $129
Same as Model 66RCL except has plain bbl., F or M choke, slide handle only checkered, no recoil pad. Made from 1967 to 1970.

**MODEL 70CLP HAMMERLESS SLIDE-ACTION
REPEATING SHOTGUN** . . . . . . NiB $277 Ex $198 Gd $145
Solid frame. .410 gauge. Magazine holds 5 rounds. 26-inch bbl. w/adj. choke. Weight: About 6 lbs. Checkered buttstock and forearm, recoil pad. Made from 1958 to 1970.

MODEL 70RCLP . . . . NiB $280 Ex $199 Gd $149
Same as Model 70CLP except has vent rib. Made 1967 to 1970.

MODEL 70RLP . . . . NiB $278 Ex $199 Gd $145
Same as Model 70CLP except has vent rib and no adj. choke. Made from 1967 to 1970.

MODEL 70XL . . . . NiB $255 Ex $160 Gd $110
Same as Model 70CLP except without adj. choke and checkering on buttstock. Made from 1958 to 1970.

**MODEL 80
AUTOLOADING SHOTGUN** . . NiB $344 Ex $265 Gd $196
Recoil-operated. .410 ga. Magazine holds three 3-inch shells, four 2.5-inch shells. 26-inch bbl., full choke. Weight: About 6 lbs. Plain pistol-grip stock and fluted forearm. Made from 1964 to 1966.

MODEL 166L DEER GUN . . . . . NiB $355 Ex $270 Gd $199
Solid frame. Key lock fire control mechanism. 12 ga. 2.75-inch chamber. Five round tubular magazine. 24-inch plain bbl., specially bored for rifled slug. Lyman peep rear sight, post ramp front sight. Receiver dovetailed for scope mounting. Weight: About 7.25 lbs. Checkered pistol-grip stock and slide handle, swivels and carrying strap. Made from 1967 to 1970.

**MODEL 420
HAMMERLESS DOUBLE** . . . . . NiB $466 Ex $361 Gd $255
Boxlock. Plain extractors. Double triggers. Gauges: 12 ga. 3-inch mag.; 16 ga.; 20 ga. 3-inch mag.; .410 ga. Bbls.: 28-inch, except .410 in 26-inch, M/F choke. Weight: About 6.75 lbs. Engraved frame. Checkered walnut stock and forearm. Made from 1958 to 1970.

**MODEL 450E
HAMMERLESS DOUBLE** . . . . . NiB $490 Ex $376 Gd $290
Boxlock. Engraved frame. Selective auto ejectors. Double triggers. Gauges: 12, 16, 20. 3-inch chambers in 12 and 20 ga. 28-inch bbls., M/F choke. Weight: About 6 lbs., 14 oz., 12 ga. Checkered pistol-grip stock and beavertail forearm, recoil pad. Made from 1967 to 1970.

MODEL 602CLP . . . . NiB $366 Ex $255 Gd $235
Same as Model 602RCLP except has plain barrel. Made from 1958 to 1970.

**MODEL 602RCLP HAMMERLESS SLIDE-ACTION
REPEATING SHOTGUN** . . . . . . NiB $355 Ex $255 Gd $190
Solid frame. Key lock fire control mechanism. 20 ga. 3-inch chamber. Five round tubular magazine. 28-inch bbl., vent rib,

Noble Model 450E
Hammerless Double

Noble Model 66XL

Noble Model 80
Autoloading Shotgun

Noble Model 166L
Deer Gun

Noble Model 420
Hammerless Double

Omega Deluxe Side-by-Side Shotgun

adj. choke. Weight: About 6.5 lbs. Checkered pistol-grip stock/ slide handle, recoil pad. Made from 1967 to 1970.

MODEL 602RLP . . . . **NiB $315 Ex $233 Gd $157**
Same as Model 602RCLP except without adj. choke, bored F or M choke. Made from 1967 to 1970.

MODEL 602XL . . . . **NiB $285 Ex $177 Gd $145**
Same as Model 602RCL except has plain bbl., F or M choke, slide handle only checkered, no recoil pad. Made from 1958 to 1970.

MODEL 662 . . . . **NiB $308 Ex $244 Gd $165**
Same as Model 602CLP except has aluminum receiver and bbl. Weight: About 4.5 lbs. Made from 1966 to 1970.

OMEGA — Brescia, Italy, and Korea

FOLDING OVER/UNDER STANDARD SHOTGUN
Hammerless Boxlock. Gauges: 12, 20, 28 w/2.75-inch chambers or .410 w/3-inch chambers. Bbls.: 26- or 28-inch vent-rib w/fixed chokes (IC/M, M/F or F/F (.410). Automatic safety. Single trigger. 40.5 inches overall (42.5 inches, 20 ga., 28-inch bbl.). Weight: 6 to 7.5 lbs. Checkered European walnut stock and forearm. Imported from 1984 to 1994.
Standard model (12 ga.) . . . . . . **NiB $475 Ex $355 Gd $298**
Standard model (20 ga.) . . . . . . **NiB $475 Ex $355 Gd $298**

Standard model (28 ga. & .410) NiB $475 Ex $355 Gd $298
O/U DELUXE SHOTGUN . . . . . **NiB $390 Ex $287 Gd $200**
Gauges: 20, 28 and .410. 26- or 28-inch vent-rib bbls. 40.5 inches overall (42.5 inches, 20 ga., 28-inch bbl.). Chokes: IC/M, M/F or F/F (.410). Weight: About 5.5-6 lbs. Single trigger. Automatic safety. European walnut stock w/checkered pistol grip and tulip forend. Imported from Italy 1984 to 1990.

DELUXE SIDE-BY-SIDE . . . . **NiB $290 Ex $225 Gd $165**
Same general specifications as the Standard Side-by-Side except has checkered European walnut stock and low bbl. rib. Made in Italy from 1984 to 1989.

STANDARD SIDE-BY-SIDE . . . . . **NiB $245 Ex $135 Gd $90**
Gauge: .410. 26-inch bbl. 40.5 inches overall. Choked F/F. Weight: 5.5 lbs. Double trigger. Manual safety. Checkered beechwood stock and semi-pistol grip. Imported from Italy 1984 to 1989.

STANDARD SINGLE-SHOT SHOTGUN
Gauges: 12, 16, 20, 28 and .410. Bbl. lengths: 26-, 28- or 30-inches. Weight: 5 lbs., 4 oz. to 5 lbs., 11 oz. Indonesian walnut stock. Matte-chromed receiver and top lever break. Imported from 1984 to 1987.
Standard fixed . . . . **NiB $155 Ex $90 Gd $65**
Standard folding . . . . **NiB $175 Ex $110 Gd $75**
Deluxe folding . . . . **NiB $255 Ex $185 Gd $95**

GRADING: **NiB** = New in Box **Ex** = Excellent or NRA 95% **Gd** = Good or NRA 68% **529**

Parker B.H. Grade

Parker C.H. Grade

Parker A-1 Special Grade

Parker A.H. Grade

Parker S.C. Grade

Parker D.H. Grade

Parker G.H. Grade

DELUXE SINGLE-SHOT . . . . NiB $229 Ex $145 Gd $99
Same general specifications as the Standard single bbl. except has checkered walnut stock, top lever break, fully-blued receiver, vent rib. Imported from Korea 1984 to 1987.

PARKER BROTHERS — Meriden, Connecticut

This firm was taken over by Remington Arms Company in 1934 and its production facilities moved to Remington's Ilion, New York, plant. In 1984, Winchester took over production until 1999.

HAMMERLESS DOUBLE-BARREL SHOTGUNS

Grades V.H. through A-1 Special. Boxlock. Auto ejectors. Double triggers or selective single trigger. Gauges: 10, 12, 16, 20, 28, .410. Bbls.: 26- to 32-inch, any standard boring. Weight: 6.88-8.5 lbs.,12 ga. Stock and forearm of select walnut, checkered; straight, half-or full-pistol grip.
Grades differ only in quality of workmanship, grade of wood, engraving, checkering, etc. General specifications are the same for all. Disc. about 1940.

V.H. grade, 12 or 16 ga. . . . NiB $5733 Ex $4187 Gd $2266
V.H. grade, 20 ga. . . . . NiB $9455 Ex $6077 Gd $3145
V.H. grade, 28 ga. . . . NiB $28,998 Ex $27,966 Gd $26,778
V.H. grade, .410 . . . . NiB $34,669 Ex $25,766 Gd $21,560
G.H. grade, 12 ga. . . . . NiB $7566 Ex $3998 Gd $2779
G.H. grade, 16 ga. . . . . NiB $8120 Ex $4233 Gd $2988
G.H. grade, 20 ga. . . . . NiB $12,960 Ex $10,679 Gd $7789
G.H. grade, 28 ga. . . NiB $33,790 Ex $29,645 Gd $27,889
G.H. grade, .410. . . . NiB $45,890 Ex $39,955 Gd $27,987
D.H. grade, 12 or 16 ga. . . NiB $10,440 Ex $7866 Gd $4350
D.H. grade, 20 ga. . . NiB $16,777 Ex $13,790 Gd $11,556
D.H. grade, 28 ga. . . NiB $43,088 Ex $39,655 Gd $32,200
D.H. grade, .410. . . . NiB $72,799 Ex $48,950 Gd $37,788
C.H. grade, 12 or 16 ga. . . . . NiB $17,300 Ex $13,988 Gd $10,996
C.H. grade, 20 ga. . . NiB $25,779 Ex $20,099 Gd $17,376
C.H. grade, 28 ga. . . NiB $73,588 Ex $60,977 Gd $52,411
B.H. grade, 12 or 16 ga. . . . NiB $21,689 Ex $18,933 Gd $16,900
B.H. grade, 20 ga. . . . . NiB $31,889 Ex $22,765 Gd $17,766

Parker-Hale Model 545A

B.H. grade, 28 ga.. . . NiB $40,550 Ex $33,980 Gd $24,665
A.H. grade, 12 or 16 ga.. . . NiB $92,778 Ex $80,000 Gd $66,789
A.H. grade, 20 ga. . . NiB $57,778 Ex $40,099 Gd $30,277
A.H. grade, 28 ga. . . NiB $104,000 Ex $88,987 Gd $67,033
A.A.H. grade, 12 or 16 ga. . . NiB $57,980 Ex $52,077 Gd $37,773
A.A.H. grade, 20 ga. . . . . NiB $83,672 Ex $62,955 Gd $43,900
A.A.H. grade, 28 ga.. . . . NiB $200,000 Ex $175,000 Gd $155,000
A-1 Special grade,
   12 or 16 ga. . . . . NiB $100,000 Ex $80,000 Gd $60,000
A-1 Special grade, 20 ga. . . NiB $82,000 Ex $65,000 Gd $45,000
A-1 Special grade,
   28 ga. . . . . . . NiB $200,000 Ex $165,000 Gd $110,000
w/selective-single trigger, add 20%
w/vent. rib, add 35%
Non-ejector models, deduct 30%

SINGLE-SHOT TRAP GUNS
Hammerless. Boxlock. Ejector. 12 ga. only. Bbl. lengths: 30-, 32-, 34-inch, any boring, vent rib. Weight: 7.5-8.5 lbs. Stock and forearm of select walnut, checkered; straight, half-or full-pistol grip. The five grades differ only in quality of workmanship, grade of wood, checkering, engraving, etc. General specifications same for all. Disc. about 1940.
S.C. grade . . . . NiB $9355 Ex $7088 Gd $5167
S.B. grade . . . . NiB $11,870 Ex $7279 Gd $6344
S.A. grade . . . . NiB $17,500 Ex $14,223 Gd $11,989
S.A.1 Special (rare) . . NiB $42,000 Ex $31,000 Gd $27,000

SKEET GUN
Same as other Parker doubles from Grade V.H.E. up except selective single trigger and beavertail forearm are standard on this model, as are 26-inch bbls., SK choke. Discontinued about 1940. Values are 35 percent higher.

TROJAN HAMMERLESS DOUBLE-BARREL SHOTGUN
Boxlock. Plain extractors. Double trigger or single trigger. Gauges: 12, 16, 20. Bbls.: 30-inch both F choke (12 ga. only), 26- or 28-inch M and F choke. Weight: 6.25-7.75 lbs. Checkered pistol-grip stock and forearm. Disc. 1939.
12 ga. . . . . NiB $5444 Ex $4249 Gd $2677
16 ga. . . . . NiB $6077 Ex $4488 Gd $3210
20 ga. . . . . NiB $6898 Ex $4539 Gd $3556

**Parker Trojan Hammerless
Double-Barrel Shotgun**

PARKER REPRODUCTIONS — Middlesex, New Jersey

HAMMERLESS DOUBLE-BARREL SHOTGUNS
Reproduction of the original Parker boxlock. Single selective trigger or double triggers. Selective automatic ejectors. Automatic safety. Gauges: 12, 16, 20, 28 or .410 w/2.75- or 3-inch chambers. Bbls.: 26- or 28-inch w/fixed or internal screw choke tubes SK/SK, IC/M, M/F. Weight: 5.5-7 lbs. Checkered English-style or pistol-grip American walnut stock w/beavertail or splinter forend and checkered skeleton buttplate. Color casehardened receiver with game scenes and scroll engraving. Produced in Japan by Olin Kodensha from 1984-88.
DHE grade, 12 ga. . . . . NiB $4250 Ex $3288 Gd $1366
DHE grade, 12 ga Sporting
   Clays . . . . NiB $4466 Ex $3890 Gd $2877
DHE grade, 20 ga . . . . NiB $4866 Ex $3989 Gd $2977
DHE grade, 28 ga . . . . NiB $5433 Ex $3200 Gd $2366
DHE grade 2-barrel set
   (16 & 20 ga.) . . . . NiB $6590 Ex $4880 Gd $3588
DHE grade 2-barrel set
   (28 & .410) . . . . NiB $7377 Ex $5433 Gd $3980
DHE grade 3-barrel set . . . NiB $10,000 Ex $6566 Gd $5080
B grade Bank Note Lim. Ed.,
   12 ga. . . . . NiB $5799 Ex $4765 Gd $3499
B grade Bank Note Lim. Ed.,
   20 ga. . . . . NiB $7352 Ex $6088 Gd $4139
B grade Bank Note Lim. Ed.,
   28 ga. . . . . NiB $12,000 Ex $9898 Gd $7455
B grade Bank Note Lim. Ed.,
   .410 ga.. . . . . NiB $13,900 Ex $10,000 Gd $8894
A-1 Special grade, 12 ga.. . . . NiB $10,877 Ex $8871 Gd $6000
A-1 Special grade, 16 ga. . . NiB $12,433 Ex $10,770 Gd $7379
A-1 Special grade, 20 ga.. . . NiB $10,665 Ex $8932 Gd $6281
A-1 Special grade, 28 ga. . . NiB $14,933 Ex $12,966 Gd $9855
A-1 Special gr. 2-barrel set . . . NiB $13,770 Ex $10,433 Gd $7791
A-1 Special gr. 3-barrel set . . . NiB $29,650 Ex $23,991 Gd $17,498
A-1 Special gr. custom
   engraved . . . . NiB $17,888 Ex $14,699 Gd $10,000
A-1 Special gr. custom 2-barrel
   set . . . . NiB $14,600 Ex $10,553 Gd $7699
w/extra bbl. set, add $500

PARKER-HALE LIMITED — Manufactured by Ignacio Ugartechea, Spain

MODEL 645A (AMERICAN)
SIDE-BY-SIDE SHOTGUN . . . NiB $1344 Ex $1116 Gd $844
Gauges: 12, 16 and 20. Boxlock action. 26- and 28-inch bbls. Chokes: IC/M, M/F. Weight: 6 lbs. average. Single non-selective trigger. Automatic safety. Hand-checkered pistol grip walnut stock w/beavertail forend. Raised matted rib. English scroll-design engraved receiver. Discontinued 1990.

SHOTGUNS

Parker-Hale Model 645E

Pedersen Model 1000 Grade I

Pedersen Model 1000 Grade II

MODEL 645E (ENGLISH) SIDE-BY-SIDE SHOTGUN

Same general specifications as the Model 645A except double triggers, straight grip, splinter forend, checkered butt and concave rib. Disc. 1990.

12, 16, 20 ga. with 26- or 28-inch
bbl. . . . . NiB $1388 Ex $1166 Gd $898
28, .410 ga. with 27-inch
bbl. . . . . NiB $1800 Ex $1490 Gd $1128

MODEL 645E-XXV

12, 16, 20 ga. with 25-inch bbl. NiB $1288 Ex $1189 Gd $900
28, .410 ga. with 25-inch bbl. . . . . NiB $1698 Ex $1377 Gd $1110

PEDERSEN CUSTOM GUNS — North Haven, Connecticut; div. of O.F. Mossberg & Sons, Inc.

MODEL 1000 O/U HUNTING SHOTGUN

Boxlock. Auto ejectors. Selective single trigger. Gauges: 12, 20. 2.75-inch chambers in 12 ga., 3-inch in 20 ga. Bbls.: Vent rib; 30-inch M/F (12 ga. only); 28-inch IC/M (12 ga. only), M/F; 26-inch IC/M. Checkered pistol-grip stock and forearm. Grade I is the higher quality gun with custom stock dimensions, fancier wood, more elaborate engraving, silver inlays. Made from 1973 to 1975.

Grade I . . . . NiB $2366 Ex $1969 Gd $1449
Grade II . . . . NiB $2210 Ex $1781 Gd $1290

MODEL 1000 MAGNUM

Same as Model 1000 Hunting Gun except chambered for 12-ga. Magnum 3-inch shells, 30-inch bbls., IM/F choke. Made 1973 to 1975.

Grade I . . . . NiB $2809 Ex $2277 Gd $1677
Grade II . . . . NiB $2400 Ex $1900 Gd $1378

MODEL 1000 SKEET GUN

Same as Model 1000 Hunting Gun except has skeet-style stock; 26- and 28-inch bbls. (12 ga. only), SK choke. Made from 1973 to 1975.

Grade I . . . . NiB $2433 Ex $1977 Gd $1698
Grade II . . . . NiB $1998 Ex $1569 Gd $1062

MODEL 1000 TRAP GUN

Same as Model 1000 Hunting Gun except 12 ga. only, has Monte Carlo trap-style stock, 30- or 32-inch bbls., M/F or IM/F choke. Made from 1973 to 1975.

Grade I . . . . NiB $2287 Ex $1862 Gd $1300
Grade II . . . . NiB $1844 Ex $1477 Gd $1106

MODEL 1500 O/U

HUNTING SHOTGUN . . . . NiB $790 Ex $676 Gd $478
Boxlock. Auto ejectors. Selective single trigger. 12 ga. 2.75- or 3-inch chambers. Bbls.: vent rib; 26-inch IC/M; 28- and 30-inch M/F; Magnum has 30-inch, IM/F choke. Weight: 7-7.5 lbs., depending on bbl. length. Checkered pistol-grip stock and forearm. Made from 1973 to 1975.

MODEL 1500 SKEET GUN . . . . NiB $833 Ex $690 Gd $569

Same as Model 1500 Hunting Gun except has skeet-style stock, 27-inch bbls., SK choke. Made from 1973 to 1975.

MODEL 1500 TRAP GUN. . . . . NiB $788 Ex $648 Gd $520

Same as Model 1500 Hunting Gun except has Monte Carlo trap-style stock, 30- or 32-inch bbls., M/F or IM/F chokes. Made 1973 to 1975.

MODEL 2000 HAMMERLESS DOUBLE

Boxlock. Auto ejectors. Selective single trigger. Gauges: 12, 20. 2.75-inch chambers in 12 ga., 3-inch in 20 ga. Bbls.: Vent rib; 30-inch M/F (12 ga. only); 28-inch M/F, 26-inch IC/M choke. Checkered pistol-grip stock and forearm. Grade I is the higher quality gun w/custom dimensions, fancier wood, more elaborate engraving, silver inlays. Made from 1973 to 1974.

Grade I . . . . NiB $2887 Ex $2260 Gd $1740
Grade II . . . . NiB $2389 Ex $2276 Gd $1578

MODEL 2500

HAMMERLESS DOUBLE . . . . . . NiB $780 Ex $655 Gd $356
Boxlock. Auto ejectors. Selective single trigger. Gauges: 12, 20. 2.75-inch chambers in 12 ga., 3-inch in 20 ga. Bbls.: Vent rib;

Perazzi DB81 Over/Under Trap

Perazzi Mirage Over/Under Shotgun

28-inch M/F; 26-inch IC/M choke. Checkered pistol-grip stock and forearm. Made 1973 to 1974.

MODEL 4000 HAMMERLESS SLIDE-ACTION REPEATING SHOTGUN . . . . . . NiB $597 Ex $440 Gd $375
Custom version of Mossberg Model 500. Full-coverage floral engraving on receiver. Gauges: 12, 20, .410. Three-inch chamber. Bbls.: Vent rib; 26-inch IC or SK choke; 28-inch F or M; 30-inch F. Weight: 6-8 lbs. depending on ga. and bbl. Checkered stock and slide handle of select wood. Made in 1975.

MODEL 4000 TRAP GUN . . . . . NiB $590 Ex $466 Gd $265
Same as standard Model 4000 except 12 ga. only, has 30-inch F choke bbl., Monte Carlo trap-style stock w/recoil pad. Made in 1975.

MODEL 4500 . . . . NiB $500 Ex $390 Gd $335
Same as Model 4000 except has simpler scroll engraving. Made in 1975.

MODEL 4500 TRAP GUN . . . . . NiB $525 Ex $420 Gd $366
Same as Model 4000 Trap Gun except has simpler scroll engraving. Made in 1975.

J. C. PENNEY CO., INC. — Dallas, Texas

MODEL 4011
AUTOLOADING SHOTGUN . . NiB $377 Ex $290 Gd $197
Hammerless. Five round magazine. Bbls.: 26-inch IC; 28-inch M or F; 30-inch F choke. Weight: 7.25 lbs. Plain pistol-grip stock and slide handle.

MODEL 6610
SINGLE-SHOT SHOTGUN . . . . . NiB $205 Ex $100 Gd $75
Hammerless. Takedown. Auto ejector. Gauges: 12, 16, 20 and .410. Bbl. length: 28-36 inches. Weight: About 6 lbs. Plain pistol-grip stock and forearm.

MODEL 6630
BOLT-ACTION SHOTGUN . . . . NiB $254 Ex $179 Gd $115
Takedown. Gauges: 12, 16, 20. Two round clip magazine. 26- and 28-inch bbl. lengths; with or without adj. choke. Plain pistol-grip stock. Weight: About 7.25 lbs.

MODEL 6670
SLIDE-ACTION SHOTGUN . . NiB $260 Ex $188 Gd $140
Hammerless. Gauges: 12, 16, 20, and .410. Three round tubular magazine. Bbls.: 26- to 30-inch; various chokes. Weight: 6.25-7.25 lbs. Walnut finished hardwood stock.

MODEL 6870 SLIDE-ACTION SHOTGUN . . . . NiB $315 Ex $225 Gd $178
Hammerless. Gauges: 12, 16, 20, .410. Four round magazine. Bbls.: Vent rib; 26- to 30-inch, various chokes. Weight: Average 6.5 lbs. Plain pistol-grip stock.

PERAZZI — Manufactured by Manifattura Armi Perazzi, Brescia, Italy

See also listings under Ithaca-Perazzi.

DB81 O/U TRAP. . . . . NiB $5266 Ex $4300 Gd $3450
Gauge: 12; 2.75-inch chambers. 29.5- or 31.5-inch bbls. w/ wide vent rib; M/F chokes. Weight: 8 lbs., 6 oz. Detachable and interchangeable trigger with flat V-springs. Bead front sight. Interchangeable and custom-made checkered stock; beavertail forend. Imported 1988 to 1994.

DB81 SINGLE-SHOT TRAP . . . NiB $5300 Ex $4277 Gd $3389
Same general specifications as the DB81 over/under except in single bbl. version w/32- or 34-inch wide vent-rib bbl., F choke. Imported 1988 to 1994.

GRAND AMERICAN 88 SPECIAL SINGLE TRAP
Same general specifications as MX8 Special Single Trap except w/high ramped rib. Fixed choke or screw-in choke tubes.
Model 88 standard . . . . . . NiB $4988 Ex $3988 Gd $2777
Model 88 w/interchangeable
  choke tubes . . . . NiB $4990 Ex $4100 Gd $3099

MIRAGE O/U SHOTGUN
Gauge: 12; 2.75-inch chambers. Bbls.: 27.63-, 29.5- or 31.5-inch vent-rib w/fixed chokes or screw-in choke tubes. Single selective trigger. Weight: 7 to 7.75 lbs. Interchangeable and custom-made checkered buttstock and forend.
Competition Trap,
  Skeet, Pigeon, Sporting . . . NiB $6400 Ex $5440 Gd $3200
Skeet 4-barrel sets   . . . NiB $14,680 Ex $12,890 Gd $9800
Competition Special (w/adj. 4-position
  trigger) add. $500

MX-1 O/U SHOTGUN
Similar to Model MX8 except w/ramp-style, tapered rib and modified stock configuration.
Competition Trap, Skeet,
  Pigeon & Sporting . . . . . NiB $6799 Ex $5240 Gd $3390
MXIC (w/choke tubes) . . . . NiB $3698 Ex $3288 Gd $2298
MXIB (w/flat low rib) . . . . . NiB $3467 Ex $2980 Gd $2098

SHOTGUNS

Perazzi MX3 Over/Under Shotgun

Perazzi MX8 Over/Under Shotgun

Perazzi MX20 Over/Under Game Gun

Perazzi TMX Single Shot Trap

MX-2 O/U SHOTGUN
Similar to Model MX8 except w/broad high-ramped competition rib.
Competition-Trap, Skeet,
  Pigeon & Sporting . . . . . NiB $6780 Ex $3544 Gd $3589
MX2C (w/choke tubes) . . . NiB $4988 Ex $3998 Gd $2766

MX-3 O/U SHOTGUN
Similar to Model MX8 except w/ramp-style, tapered rib and modified stock configuration.
Competition Trap, Skeet,
  Pigeon & Sporting. NiB $48,988 Ex $42,998 Gd $35,999
Competition Special (w/adj. 4-position trigger) add . . . $400
Game models . . . . NiB $4478 Ex $3659 Gd $2699
Combo O/U plus SB . . . . . NiB $5563 Ex $4478 Gd $3380
SB Trap 32- or 34-inch . . . . NiB $3987 Ex $3166 Gd $2267
Skeet 4-bbl. sets . . . . . . NiB $12,888 Ex $10,099 Gd $7789
Skeet Special 4-bbl. sets . . . NiB $13,066 Ex $11,288 Gd $8,996

MX-3 SPECIAL PIGEON
SHOTGUN . . . . NiB $5344 Ex $4276 Gd $3110
Gauge: 12; 2.75-inch chambers. 29.5- or 31.5-inch vent rib bbl.; IC/M and extra full chokes. Weight: 8 lbs., 6 oz. Detachable and interchangeable trigger group w/flat V-springs. Bead front sight. Interchangeable and custom-made checkered stock for live pigeon shoots; splinter forend. Imported 1991 to 1992.

MX-4 O/U SHOTGUN
Similar to Model MX3 in appearance and shares the MX8 locking system. Detachable, adj. 4-position trigger standard. Interchangeable choke tubes optional.
Competition Trap,
  Skeet, Pigeon & Sporting NiB $4487 Ex $4089 Gd $3124
MX4C (w/choke tubes) . . . NiB $5388 Ex $4500 Gd $3787

MX-5 O/U GAME GUN
Similar to Model MX8 except in hunting configuration, chambered in 12 or 20 ga. Non-detachable single selective trigger.

MX5 Standard . . . . NiB $3977 Ex $2886 Gd $2066
MX5C (w/choke tubes) . . . NiB $4264 Ex $3188 Gd $2200

MX-6 AMER.
TRAP SINGLE-BARREL . . . . NiB $4302 Ex $2677 Gd $1988
Single shot. Removable trigger group. 12 ga. Barrels: 32- or 34-inch with fixed or choke tubes. Raised vent rib. Checkered European walnut Monte Carlo stock, beavertail forend. Imported 1995 to 1998.

MX-6 SKEET O/U . . . . NiB $4277 Ex $3100 Gd $2250
Same general specs as MX6 American Trap single barrel except over/under; boxlock. Barrels: 26.75- or 27.50-inch. Imported 1995 to 1998.

MX-6 SPORTING O/U . . . . NiB $4277 Ex $3100 Gd $2250
Same specs as MX6 American Trap single barrel except over/under; boxlock. Single selective trigger; external selector. Barrels: 28.38-, 29.50-, or 31.50-inch. Imported 1995 to 1998.

MX-6 TRAP O/U . . . . NiB $4350 Ex $2929 Gd $1877
Same general specs as MX6 American Trap single barrel except over/under; boxlock. Barrels: 29.50-, 30.75-, or 31.50-inch. Imported 1995 to 1998.

MX-7 O/U SHOTGUN . . . . NiB $4188 Ex $3755 Gd $2690
Similar to Model MX12 except w/MX3-style receiver and top-mounted trigger selector. Bbls.: 28.73-, 2.5-, 31.5-inch w/vent rib; screw-in choke tubes. Imported 1992 to 1998.

MX-8 O/U SHOTGUN
Gauge: 12, 2.75-inch chambers. Bbls.: 27.63-, 29.5- or 31.5-inch vent-rib w/fixed chokes or screw-in choke tubes. Weight: 7 to 8.5 lbs. Interchangeable and custom-made checkered stock; beavertail forend. Special models have detachable and interchangeable 4-position trigger group w/flat V-springs. Imported 1968 to date.
MX-8 Standard . . . . NiB $8099 Ex $4133 Gd $2377

**MX-8 Special (adj. 4-pos.
trigger)** . . . . **NiB $4229 Ex $3378 Gd $2490**
**MX-8 Special single
(32-or 34-inch bbl.)** . . . **NiB $8380 Ex $7121 Gd $4365**
MX-8 Special combo . . . . . **NiB $8009 Ex $6355 Gd $4682**

MX-8/20 O/U SHOTGUN NiB $4155 Ex $3370 Gd $2499
Similar to the Model MX8 except w/smaller frame and custom
stock. Available in sporting or game configurations with fixed
chokes or screw-in tubes. Imported 1993 to date.

MX-9 O/U SHOTGUN . . . . **NiB $6880 Ex $5672 Gd $4200**
Gauge: 12; 2.75-inch chambers. Bbls.: 29.5- or 30.5-inch w/
choke tubes and vent side rib. Selective trigger. Checkered walnut stock w/adj. cheekpiece. Available in single bbl., combo,
O/U trap, skeet, pigeon and sporting models. Imported 1993
to 1994.

MX-10 O/U SHOTGUN . **NiB $8293 Ex $5760 Gd $34,105**
Similar to the Model MX9 except w/fixed chokes and different
rib configuration. Imported 1993.

**MX-10 PIGEON-ELECTROCIBLES
O/U** . . . . **NiB $8996 Ex $6133 Gd $4400**
Over/Under; boxlock.   Removable trigger group; external
selector. 12 gauge. Barrels: 27.50- or 29.50-inch. Checkered
European walnut adjustable stock, beavertail forend. Imported
1995 to date.

**MX–11 AMERICAN
TRAP COMBO** . . . . **NiB $5440 Ex $4688 Gd $3277**
Over/Under; boxlock. External selector. Removable trigger
group; single selective trigger. 12 ga. Bbls: 29-1/2- to 34-inch
with fixed or choke tubes; vent rib. European walnut Monte
Carlo adjustable stock, beavertail forend. Imported 1995 to
date.

**MX-11 AMERICAN TRAP
SINGLE BARREL** . . . . **NiB $5155 Ex $4309 Gd $2879**
Same general specs as MX11 American Trap combo except 32-
or 34-inch single bbl. Imported 1995 to 1996.

**MX-11 PIGEON-ELECTROCIBLES
O/U** . . . . **NiB $5331 Ex $4277 Gd $3100**
Same specs as MX11 American Trap combo except 27.50 O/U
bbls. Checkered European walnut pistol grip adjustable stock,
beavertail forend. Imported 1995 to 1996.

MX-11 SKEET O/U . . . . **NiB $5390 Ex $4369 Gd $3122**
Same general specs as MX11 American Trap combo except
26.75 or 27.50-inch O/U bbls. Checkered European walnut
pistol-grip adjustable stock, beavertail forend. Imported 1995
to 1996.

MX-11 SPORTING O/U . . . **NiB $5344 Ex $4766 Gd $3409**
Same general specs as MX11 American Trap combo except
28.38, 29.50-, or 31.50-inch O/U bbls. Checkered European
walnut pistol-grip adjustable stock, beavertail forend. Imported
1995 to 1996.

MX-11 TRAP O/U . . . . **NiB $5293 Ex $4266 Gd $3109**
Same general specs as MX11 American Trap combo except
29.50,- 30.75, or 31.50-inch O/U bbls. Checkered European
walnut pistol-grip adjustable stock, beavertail forend. Imported
1995 to 1996.

MX-12 O/U GAME GUN

Gauge: 12, 2.75-inch chambers. Bbls.: 26-, 27.63-, 28.38- or
29.5-inch, vent rib, fixed chokes or screw-in choke tubes.
Non-detachable single selective trigger group w/coil springs.
Weight: 7.25 lbs. Interchangeable and custom-made check-
ered stock; Schnabel forend.
MX12 Standard . . . . **NiB $7966 Ex $4312 Gd $3100**
MX12C (w/choke tubes) . . **NiB $7994 Ex $4366 Gd $3180**

**MX-14 AMERICAN TRAP
SINGLE-BARREL** . . . . **NiB $6892 Ex $3677 Gd $2573**
Single shot. Removable trigger group; unsingle configura-
tion. 12 ga. Bbl: 34-inch with fixed or choke tubes; vent rib.
Checkered European walnut Monte Carlo adjustable stock,
beavertail forend. Imported 1995 to 1996.

**MX-15 AMERICAN TRAP
SINGLE-BARREL** . . . . **NiB $6654 Ex $4138 Gd $2998**
Full choke. Detachable trigger group. Gauge: 12 only with
2.75-inch chamber. Bbls: 32 and 34-inch. Weight: 8 lbs., 6 oz.

MX-20 O/U GAME GUN
Gauges: 20, 28 and .410; 2.75- or 3-inch chambers. 26-inch
vent-rib bbls., M/F chokes or screw-in chokes. Auto selective
ejectors. Selective single trigger. Weight: 6 lbs., 6 oz. Non-
detachable coil-spring trigger. Bead front sight. Interchangeable
and custom-made checkered stock w/Schnabel forend.
Imported from 1988 to date.
Standard grade . . . . **NiB $5311 Ex $4255 Gd $2987**
Standard grade w/gold outline . . . **NiB $8991 Ex $7200 Gd $5102**
MX20C w/choke tubes . . . . **NiB $5886 Ex $4480 Gd $3171**
SC3 grade . . . . **NiB $9766 Ex $7764 Gd $5433**
SCO grade . . . . **NiB $13,978 Ex $11,888 Gd $9166**

MX-28 O/U GAME GUN . . . **NiB $15,660 Ex $12,987 Gd $9821**
Similar to the Model MX12 except chambered in 28 ga. w/26-
inch bbls. fitted to smaller frame. Imported from 1993 to date.

**MX-410 O/U GAME
GUN** . . . . **NiB $15,890 Ex $13,298 Gd $10,350**
Similar to the Model MX12 except in .410 bore w/3-inch
chambers, 26-inch bbls. fitted to smaller frame. Imported from
1993 to date.

**TM1 SPECIAL
SINGLE-SHOT TRAP** . . . . . . **NiB $3150 Ex $2770 Gd $2000**
Gauge: 12- 2.75-inch chambers. 32- or 34-inch bbl. w/wide
vent rib; full choke. Weight: 8 lbs., 6 oz. Detachable and interchangeable trigger group with coil springs. Bead front sight.
Interchangeable and custom-made stock w/checkered pistol
grip and beavertail forend. Imported from 1988 to 1995.

**TMX SPECIAL
SINGLE-SHOT TRAP** . . . . . . **NiB $3890 Ex $2553 Gd $1966**
Same general specifications as Model TM1 Special except w/
ultra-high rib. Interchangeable choke tubes optional.

PIOTTI — Brescia, Italy

BOSS O/U . . . . **NiB $58,998 Ex $50,000 Gd $35,965**
Over/Under; sidelock. Gauges: 12 or 20. Barrels: 26- to
32-inch. Standard chokes. Best quality walnut. Custom-made
to customer's specifications. Imported from 1993 to date.

KING NO. 1 SIDELOCK . . . **NiB $35,866 Ex $29,821 Gd $19,670**
Gauges: 10, 12, 16, 20, 28 and .410. 25- to 30-inch bbls. (12
ga.), 25- to 28-inch (other ga.). Weight: About 5 lbs. (.410) to 8

SHOTGUNS

Piotti
Piuma Boxlock Side-by-Side Shotgun

Powell No. 7
Aristocrat Grade Double

lbs. (12 ga.) Holland & Holland pattern sidelock. Double triggers standard. Coin finish or color casehardened. Level file-cut rib. Full-coverage scroll engraving, gold inlays. Hand-rubbed, oil-finished, straight-grip stock with checkered butt, splinter forend.

KING EXTRA SIDE-BY-SIDE
SHOTGUN . . . . NiB $77,850 Ex $52,290 Gd $42,777
Same general specifications as the Piotti King No. 1 except has choice of engraving, gold inlays, plus stock is of exhibition-grade wood.

LUNIK SIDE-LOCK
SHOTGUN . . . . NiB $35,660 Ex $31,299 Gd $26,000
Same general specifications as the Monte Carlo model except has level, file-cut rib. Renaissance-style, large scroll engraving in relief, gold crown in top lever, gold name, and gold crest in forearm, finely figured wood.

MONTE CARLO
SIDE-LOCK SHOTGUN . NiB $11,488 Ex $9889 Gd $7577
Gauges: 10, 12, 16, 20, 28 or .410. Bbls.: 25- to 30-inch. Holland & Holland pattern sidelock. Weight: 5-8 lbs. Automatic ejectors. Double triggers. Hand-rubbed oil-finished straight-grip stock with checkered butt. Choice of Purdey-style scroll and rosette or Holland & Holland-style large scroll engraving.

PIUMA BOXLOCK SIDE-BY-SIDE
SHOTGUN . . . . NiB $18,667 Ex $12,933 Gd $10,011
Same general specifications as the Monte Carlo model except has Anson & Deeley boxlock action w/demi-bloc bbls., scalloped frame. Standard scroll and rosette engraving. Hand-rubbed, oil-finished straight-grip stock.

WILLIAM POWELL & SON, LTD. — Birmingham, England

NO. 1 BEST GRADE DOUBLE-BARREL
SHOTGUN . . . . NiB $42,777 Ex $38,698 Gd $31,033
Sidelock. Gauges: Made to order with 12, 16 and 20 the most common. Bbls.: Made to order in any length but 28 inches was recommended. Highest grade French walnut buttstock and forearm with fine checkering. Metal elaborately engraved. Imported by Stoeger from about 1938 to 1951.

NO. 2 BEST GRADE
DOUBLE-BARREL . . NiB $29,766 Ex $24,761 Gd $16,888
Same general specifications as the Powell No. 1 except plain finish without engraving. Imported by Stoeger from about 1938 to 1951.

NO. 6 CROWN GRADE
DOUBLE-BARREL . . NiB $15,999 Ex $12,733 Gd $10,111
Boxlock. Gauges: Made to order with 12, 16 and 20 the most common. Bbls.: Made to order, but 28 inches was recom-

mended. Highest grade French walnut buttstock and forearm with fine checkering. Metal elaborately engraved. Uses Anson & Deeley locks. Imported by Stoeger from about 1938 to 1951.

NO. 7 ARISTOCRAT GRADE DOUBLE-BARREL
SHOTGUN . . . . NiB $9022 Ex $6988 Gd $4766
Same general specifications as the Powell No. 6 Crown Grade Double-Barrel above, except with lower quality wood and metal engraving.

PRECISION SPORTS SHOTGUNS — Cortland, New York; manufactured by Ignacio Ugartechea, Spain

600 SERIES AMERICAN HAMMERLESS DOUBLES
Boxlock. Single selective trigger. Selective automatic ejectors. Automatic safety. Gauges: 12, 16, 20, 28, .410; 2.75- or 3-inch chambers. Bbls.: 26-,27- or 28-inch w/raised matte rib; choked IC/M or M/F. Weight: 5.75-7 lbs. Checkered pistol-grip walnut buttstock with beavertail forend. Engraved silvered receiver with blued bbls. Imported from 1986 to 1994.

640A (12, 16, 20 ga. w/extractors) . . . NiB $1177	Ex $909	Gd $677
640A (28 ga., .410 w/extractors) . . . NiB $1288	Ex $1067	Gd $779
640 Slug Gun (12 ga. w/extractors) . . . . NiB $1277	Ex $1059	Gd $723
645A (12, 16, 20 ga. w/ejectors) . . . NiB $1177	Ex $909	Gd $677
645A (28 ga., .410, two-bbl. set) . . . NiB $1488	Ex $1176	Gd $877
645A (20/28 ga. two-bbl. set) . . . NiB $1563	Ex $1253	Gd $919
650A (12 ga. w/extractors, choke tubes) . . . . NiB $1165	Ex $977	Gd $710
655A (12 ga. w/ejectors, choke tubes) . . . . NiB $1288	Ex $1022	Gd $766

600 SERIES ENGLISH HAMMERLESS DOUBLES
Boxlock. Same general specifications as American 600 series except w/double triggers and concave rib. Checkered English-style walnut stock w/splinter forend, straight grip and oil finish.

640E (12, 16, 20 ga. w/extractors) . . . NiB $956	Ex $790	Gd $622
640E (28 ga., .410 w/extractors) . . . . NiB $1088	Ex $900	Gd $644
640 Slug Gun (12 ga. w/extractors) NiB $1297	Ex $1044	Gd $780
645E (12, 16, 20 ga. w/ejectors) . . . NiB $1300	Ex $1066	Gd $800
645E (28 ga., .410 w/ejectors) . . . . . NiB $1266	Ex $1022	Gd $776
645E (20/28 ga. two-bbl. set) . . . . . NiB $1545	Ex $1296	Gd $1000
650E (12 ga. w/extractors, choke tubes) . . . . NiB $1178	Ex $938	Gd $715
655E (12 ga. w/ejectors, choke tubes) . . . . NiB $1190	Ex $980	Gd $750

MODEL 640M MAGNUM 10 HAMMERLESS DOUBLE
Similar to Model 640E except in 10 ga. w/3.5-inch Mag. chambers. Bbls.: 26-, 30-, 32-inch choked F/F.

Premier Ambassador
Field Grade

Premier Continental
Field Grade

Purdey Hammerless
Double-Barrel Shotgun

Model 640M Big Ten, Turkey   NiB $1106 Ex $933 Gd $700
Model 640M Goose Gun . . . . NiB $1133 Ex $955 Gd $735

MODEL 645E-XXV HAMMERLESS DOUBLE
Similar to Model 645E except w/25-inch bbl. and Churchill-style rib.

645E-XXV (12, 16, 20 ga.
w/ejectors) . . . . **NiB $1160 Ex $982 Gd $755**
645E-XXV (28, .410 ga.
w/ejectors) . . . . **NiB $1366 Ex $1093 Gd $835**

PREMIER SHOTGUNS
Premier shotguns have been produced by various gunmakers in Europe.

AMBASSADOR MODEL FIELD GRADE HAMMERLESS
DOUBLE-BARREL SHOTGUN. . NiB $544 Ex $466 Gd $377
Sidelock. Plain extractors. Double triggers. Gauges: 12, 16, 20, .410. 3-inch chambers in 20 and .410 ga., 2.75- inch in 12 and 16 ga. Bbls.: 26-inch in .410 ga., 28 inch in other ga.; choked M/F. Weight: 6 lbs., 3 oz.-7 lbs., 3 oz. depending on gauge. Checkered pistol-grip stock and beavertail forearm. Intro. in 1957; disc.

BRUSH KING . . . . **NiB $440 Ex $330 Gd $255**
Same as standard Regent model except chambered for 12 (2.75-inch) and 20 ga. (3-inch) only; has 22-inch bbls., IC/M choke, straight-grip stock. Weight: 6 lbs., 3 oz. in 12 ga.; 5 lbs., 12 oz. in 20 ga. Introduced in 1959; disc.

CONTINENTAL MODEL FIELD GRADE HAMMER
DOUBLE-BARREL SHOTGUN. . NiB $577 Ex $426 Gd $300
Sidelock. Exposed hammers. Plain extractors. Double triggers. Gauges: 12, 16, 20, .410. Three inch chambers in 20 and .410 ga., 2.75-inch in 12 and 16 ga. Bbls.: 26-inch in .410 ga.; 28-inch in other ga.; choked M/F. Weight: 6 lbs., 3 oz.-7 lbs., 3 oz. depending on gauge. Checkered pistol-grip stock and English-style forearm. Introduced in 1957; disc.

MONARCH SUPREME GRADE HAMMERLESS
DOUBLE-BARREL SHOTGUN. . NiB $667 Ex $487 Gd $367
Boxlock. Auto ejectors. Double triggers. Gauges: 12, 20. 2.75-inch chambers in 12 ga., 3-inch in 20 ga. Bbls.: 28-inch M/F; 26-inch IC/M choke. Weight: 6 lbs., 6 oz., 7 lbs., 2 oz.

depending on gauge and bbl. Checkered pistol-grip stock and beavertail forearm of fancy walnut. Introduced in 1959; disc.

PRESENTATION
CUSTOM GRADE . . . . **NiB $1488 Ex $1109 Gd $856**
Similar to Monarch model but made to order of higher quality with hunting scene engraving, gold and silver inlay, fancier wood. Introduced in 1959; disc.

REGENT 10 GA.
MAGNUM EXPRESS . . . . **NiB $665 Ex $431 Gd $345**
Same as standard Regent model except chambered for 10-ga. Magnum 3.5-inch shells, has heavier construction, 32-inch bbls. choked F/F, stock with recoil pad. Weight: 11.25 lbs. Introduced in 1957; disc.

REGENT 12 GA.
MAGNUM EXPRESS . . . . **NiB $465 Ex $388 Gd $290**
Same as standard Regent model except chambered for 12-ga. Magnum 3-inch shells, has 30-inch bbls. choked F and F, stock with recoil pad. Weight: 7.25 lbs. Introduced in 1957; disc.

REGENT FIELD GRADE HAMMERLESS
DOUBLE-BARREL SHOTGUN. . NiB $477 Ex $355 Gd $271
Boxlock. Plain extractors. Double triggers. Gauges: 12,16, 20, 28, .410. Three inch chambers in 20 and .410 ga., 2.75-inch in other gauges. Bbls.: 26-inch IC/M, M/F (28 and .410 ga. only); 28-inch M/F; 30-inch M/F (12 ga. only). Weight: 6 lbs., 2 oz.-7 lbs., 4 oz. depending on gauge and bbl. Checkered pistol-grip stock and beavertail forearm. Introduced in 1955; disc.

JAMES PURDEY & SONS, LTD. —
London, England

HAMMERLESS DOUBLE-BARREL SHOTGUN
Sidelock. Auto ejectors. Single or double triggers. Gauges: 12, 16, 20. Bbls.: 26-, 27-, 28-, 30-inch (latter in 12 ga. only);any boring, any shape or style of rib. Weight: 5.25-5.5 lbs. depending on model, gauge and bbl length. Checkered stock and forearm, straight grip standard, pistol-grip also available. Purdey guns of this type have been made from about 1880 to

SHOTGUNS

Purdey Over and Under

Purdey Single-Shot Trap

Remington Model 11-87
Premier Autoloader

date. Models include: Game Gun, Featherweight Game Gun, Two-Inch Gun (chambered for 12 ga. 2-inch shells), Pigeon Gun (w/3rd fastening and side clips), values of all models are the same.

With double triggers .. NiB $62,700 Ex $54,890 Gd $44,782
With single trigger, add. $1000

OVER/UNDER SHOTGUN
Sidelock. Auto ejectors. Single or double triggers. Gauges: 12 16, 20. Bbls.: 26-, 27-, 28-, 30-inch (latter in 12 ga. only); any boring, any style rib. Weight: 6-7.5 pounds depending on gauge and bbl. length. Checkered stock and forend, straight or pistol grip. Prior to WW II, the Purdey Over/Under Gun was made with a Purdey action; since the war James Purdey & Sons have acquired the busi-ness of James Woodward & Sons and all Purdey over/under guns are now built on the Woodward principle. General specifications of both types are the same.

With Purdey action,
double triggers . . . NiB $78,880 Ex $52,609 Gd $24,655
With Woodward action, double triggers, add. $3000
w/single trigger, add 10%

SINGLE-BARREL
TRAP GUN . . . . NiB $12,775 Ex $10,560 Gd $8,300
Sidelock. Mechanical features similar to those of the over/under model with Purdey action. 12 ga. only. Built to customer's specifications. Made prior to World War II.

REMINGTON ARMS CO. — Ilion, New York

Eliphalet Remington Jr. began making long arms with his father in 1816. In 1828 they moved their facility to Ilion, N.Y., where it remained a family-run business for decades. As the family began to diminish, other people bought controlling interests and today, still a successful gunmaking company, it is a subsidiary of the DuPont Corporation. Currently owned by the Freedom Group.

MODEL 10A STANDARD GRADE SLIDE-ACTION
REPEATING SHOTGUN . . . . . . NiB $420 Ex $335 Gd $255
Hammerless. Takedown. Six-round capacity. 12 ga. only. Five shell tubular magazine. Bbls.: Plain; 26- to 32-inch; choked F, M or Cyl. Weight: About 7.5 lbs. Plain pistol-grip stock, grooved slide handle. Made from 1907 to 1929.

MODEL 11 SPECIAL, TOURNAMENT, EXPERT AND PREMIER GRADE GUNS
These higher grade models differ from the Model 11A in general quality, grade of wood, checkering, engraving, etc. General specifications are the same.

11B Special grade . . . . NiB $788 Ex $609 Gd $466
11D Tournament grade . . . . . NiB $1388 Ex $1122 Gd $866
11E Expert grade . . . . NiB $1880 Ex $1455 Gd $1090
11F Premier grade . . . . NiB $2998 Ex $2356 Gd $1800

MODEL 11A STANDARD GRADE AUTOLOADER
Hammerless Browning type. Five round capacity. Takedown. Gauges: 12, 16, 20. Tubular magazine holds four rounds. Bbls.: Plain, solid or vent rib, lengths from 26-32 inches, F, M, IC, Cyl., SK chokes. Weight: About 8 lbs., 12 ga.; 7.5 lbs., 16 ga.; 7.25 lbs., 20 ga. Checkered pistol grip and forend. Made from 1905 to 1949.

w/plain barrel . . . . NiB $355 Ex $260 Gd $229
w/solid-rib barrel . . . . NiB $477 Ex $339 Gd $366
w/ventilated-rib barrel . . . . . . .NiB $544 Ex $420 Gd $367

MODEL 11R RIOT GUN . . . . . . NiB $445 Ex $300 Gd $195
Same as Model 11A Standard grade except has 20-inch plain barrel, 12 ga. only. Remington Model 11-48. (See Remington Sportsman-48 Series.)

NOTE: *Model 11-87 bbls. are not interchangable w/ Model 1100 bbls.*

MODEL 11-87 PREMIER AUTOLOADER
Gas-operated. Gauge: 12; 3-in. chamber. Bbl.: 26-, 28- or 30-in. with REMChoke. Weight: 8.13- 8.38 lbs., depending on bbl. length. Checkered walnut w/ satin finish. Made from 1987 to 2006.

Deer Gun w/cant. scope mt. . . . . NiB $855 Ex $654 Gd $477
Premier Skeet (1987-1999) . . . NiB $740 Ex $535 Gd $420
Premier Standard . . . . NiB $766 Ex $598 Gd $455
Premier Trap (1987-1999) . . . . . NiB $844 Ex $707 Gd $510
Left-hand models, add $125

Remington Model 11-87 SPS

Remington Model 11-87 SPS Camo

Remington Model 11-87 SP Walnut Stock

Remington Model SP-10 Magnum Camo

MODEL 11-87 PREMIER SUPER MAGNUM
Gas-operated. Gauge: 12 only, 3-1/2-in. chamber. Bbl.: 28-in. only with extended REMChoke. Weight: 8.4 lbs. Checkered gloss finish walnut stock and forend. Made from 2001 to 2006.

standard . . . . NiB $760 Ex $622 Gd $479
Camo (disc. 2004). . . . . NiB $836 Ex $684 Gd $489

MODEL 11-87 SP (SPECIAL PURPOSE)
Same general specifications as Model 11-87 Premier except with non-reflective wood finish and Parkerized metal. 26-, 28- or 30-in. vent-rib bbl. with REMChoke tubes. Made from 1987 to 1993.

standard . . . . NiB $600 Ex $400 Gd $280
Deer Gun (21-in. bbl., rifle sights)NiB $690 Ex $445 Gd $295
Magnum (3-1/2-in. chamber) . . NiB $730 Ex $450 Gd $300

MODEL 11-87 SPS (SPECIAL PURPOSE SYNTHETIC)
Same general specifications as Model 11-87 SP except with synthetic buttstock and forend. 21-, 26- or 28-inch vent-rib bbl. with REMChoke tubes. Matte black or Mossy Oak camo finish (except NWTF turkey gun). Made from 1990 to 2007.

Deer Gun (21-in. bbl., rifle
  sights) . . . . NiB $696 Ex $494 Gd $358
Magnum (3-in., matte black,
  disc. 2004) . . . . NiB $733 Ex $643 Gd $471
Camo (Mossy Oak camo) . . . . NiB $760 Ex $622 Gd $479
Deer Gun w/cant. scope mt.
  (1987-2005) . . . . NiB $859 Ex $633 Gd $490
NWTF Turkey Gun
  (Brown Trebark, disc. 1993) NiB $775 Ex $690 Gd $510
NWTF Turkey Gun
  (Greenleaf, disc. 1996). . . . . NiB $725 Ex $650 Gd $479
NWTF Turkey
  Gun (Mossy Oak, disc. 1996)NiB $730 Ex $655 Gd $485

NWTF Turkey Gun (Mossy Oak Breakup,
introduced 1999) . . . . NiB $730 Ex $655 Gd $485
NWTF 20 ga. Turkey Gun (Mossy Oak
  Breakup, 1998 only) . . . . NiB $730 Ex $655 Gd $485
Thumbhole Deer Gun
  (2006-2007) . . . . NiB $730 Ex $655 Gd $485
SPST Turkey Gun (matte bl.) . . NiB $730 Ex $655 Gd $485
Super Magnum (3-1/2-in.,
  matte black, disc. 2007) . . . . NiB $950 Ex $730 Gd $300
Super Magnum Turkey Camo (3-1/2-in., Mossy
  Oak Breakup, disc. 2007) . . . NiB $950 Ex $730 Gd $300
Waterfowl (Mossy Oak Shadow
  Grass) . . . . NiB $1010 Ex $780 Gd $530

MODEL 11-87 SPORTING
CLAYS . . . . . NiB $866 Ex $700 Gd $509
Gas-operated. Gauge: 12 only. Bbl.: 26-in. only with extended REMChoke. Weight: 7.5 lbs. Checkered satin finish walnut stock and forend. Made from 1929 to 1999.

NP (nickel plated receiver) . . . . NiB $890 Ex $735 Gd $533

MODEL 11-87 SPORTSMAN
Same general specifications as Model 11-87 Premier except with matte metal finish. 12 or 20 ga. Bbl.: 20- or 21-in. rifled or 26- or 28-in. w/ REMChoke. Weight: 7.3-8.3 lbs. Made from 2005 to date.

Camo (Mossy Oak New Breakup) . . . NiB $915 Ex $570 Gd $370
Field (wood stock). . . . . NiB $845 Ex $470 Gd $270
ShurShot (synthetic thumbhole stock, cantilever
  scope mount) . . . . NiB $1012 Ex $680 Gd $430
Synthetic (synthetic stock) . . . NiB $804 Ex $460 Gd $260
Synthetic Deer (synthetic stock,
  cantilever. scope mount) . . NiB $929 Ex $585 Gd $385

SHOTGUNS

Remington Model 870
Competition Trap

Remington Model 870
Brushmaster

Remington Model 870
Express Super Magnum

MODEL 11-96 EURO LIGHTWEIGHT
AUTOLOADING SHOTGUN . . NiB $800 Ex $644 Gd $500
Lightweight version of Model 11-87 w/reprofiled receiver. 12 ga. only w/3-inch chamber. 26- or 28-inch bbl. w/6mm vent rib and REM Choke tubes. Semi-fancy Monte Carlo walnut buttstock and forearm. Weight: 6.8 lbs. w/26-inch bbl. Made in 1996 only.

MODEL 17A STANDARD GRADE SLIDE-ACTION
REPEATING SHOTGUN
Hammerless. Takedown. Five round capacity. 20 ga. only. Four round tubular magazine. Bbls.: plain; 26- to 32-inch; choked F, M or Cyl. Weight: About 5.75 lbs. Plain pistol-grip stock, grooved slide handle. Made 1921-33. Note: The present Ithaca Model 37 is an adaptation of this Browning design.
Plain barrel . . . . NiB $422 Ex $292 Gd $190
Solid rib . . . . NiB $490 Ex $400 Gd $290

MODEL 29A STANDARD GRADE SLIDE-ACTION
REPEATING SHOTGUN . . . . . . NiB $390 Ex $300 Gd $287
Hammerless. Takedown. Six round capacity. 12 ga. only. Five round tubular magazine. Bbls.: plain- 26- to 32-inch, choked F, M or Cyl. Weight: About 7.5 lbs. Checkered pistol-grip stock and slide handle. Made from 1929 to 1933.

MODEL 29T TARGET GRADE . . NiB $600 Ex $490 Gd $377
Same general specifications as Model 29A except has trap-style stock with straight grip, extension slide handle, vent rib bbl. Disc. 1933.

MODEL 31/31L SKEET GRADE
Same general specifications as Model 31A except has 26-inch bbl. with raised solid or vent rib, SK choke, checkered pistol-grip stock and beavertail forend. Weight: About 8 lbs., 12 ga. Made from 1932 to 1939.
Model 31 Standard w/raised
solid rib . . . . NiB $477 Ex $290 Gd $200
Model 31 Standard w/ventilated
rib . . . . NiB $566 Ex $408 Gd $335
Model 31L Lightweight w/raised
solid rib . . . . NiB $455 Ex $330 Gd $245
Model 31L Lightweight w/ventilated
rib . . . . NiB $555 Ex $350 Gd $287

MODEL 31D SPECIAL, TOURNAMENT,
EXPERT AND PREMIER GRADE GUNS
These higher grade models differ from the Model 31A in general quality, grade of wood, checkering, engraving, etc. General specifications are the same.
Model 31B Special grade . . . . . NiB $745 Ex $600 Gd $477
Model 31D Tournament grade . . . NiB $1688 Ex $1099 Gd $722
Model 31E Expert grade . . . . NiB $1890 Ex $1266 Gd $977
Model 31F Premier grade . NiB $3100 Ex $2013 Gd $1544

MODEL 31A SLIDE-ACTION REPEATER
Hammerless. Takedown. 3- or 5-round capacity. Gauges: 12, 16, 20. Tubular magazine. Bbls.: Plain, solid or vent rib; lengths from 26 -32 inches; F, M, IC, C or SK choke. Weight: About 7.5 lbs., 12 ga.; 6.75 lbs., 16 ga.; 6.5 lbs., 20 ga. Earlier models have checkered pistol-grip stock and slide handle; later models have plain stock and grooved slide handle. Made from 1931 to 1949.
Model 31A with plain barrel . . NiB $479 Ex $366 Gd $244
Model 31A with solid rib barrel . . . NiB $565 Ex $443 Gd $300
Model 31A with vent rib barrel . . . NiB $580 Ex $465 Gd $335
Model 31H Hunter
w/sporting-style stock . . . . . NiB $440 Ex $292 Gd $222
Model 31R Riot Gun w/20-inch
plain bbl., 12 ga. . . . . NiB $509 Ex $388 Gd $287

MODEL 31S TRAP SPECIAL/31TC TRAP GRADE
Same general specifications as Model 31A except 12 ga. only, has 30- or 32-inch vent-rib bbl., F choke, checkered trap stock with full pistol grip and recoil pad, checkered extension beavertail forend. Weight: About 8 lbs. (Trap Special has solid-rib bbl., half pistol-grip stock with standard walnut forend).
Model 31S Trap Special . . . . . . NiB $655 Ex $490 Gd $423
Model 31TC Trap grade . . . . . NiB $955 Ex $677 Gd $590
MODEL 32A STANDARD GRADE O/U
Hammerless. Takedown. Auto ejectors. Early model had double triggers, later built with selective single trigger only. 12 ga. only. Bbls.: Plain, raised matted solid or vent rib; 26-, 28-, 30-, 32-inch; F/M choke standard, option
of any combination of F, M, IC, C, SK choke. Weight: About 7.75 lbs. Checkered pistol-grip stock and forend. Made from 1932 to 1942.
w/double triggers . . . . NiB $2165 Ex $1800 Gd $1287

w/selective single trigger . . **NiB $2466 Ex $2100 Gd $1533**
w/raised solid rib, add **10%**
w/ventilated rib, add **20%**

MODEL 32 TOURNAMENT, EXPERT AND PREMIER GRADE GUNS
These higher-grade models differ from the Model 32A in general quality, grade of wood, checkering, engraving, etc. General specifications are the same. Made from 1932 to 1942.
Model 32D Tournament grade . . . NiB $4377 Ex $3310 Gd $2560
Model 32E Expert grade . . . NiB $4598 Ex $4166 Gd $3000
Model 32F Premier grade   NiB $6986 Ex $5809 Gd $3976

MODEL 32 SKEET GRADE . . **NiB $2200 Ex $1798 Gd $1433**
Same general specifications as Model 32A except 26- or 28-inch bbl., SK choke, beavertail forend, selective single trigger only. Weight: About 7.5 lbs. Made from 1932 to 1942.

MODEL 32TC
TARGET (TRAP) GRADE . . NiB $3233 Ex $2866 Gd $1974
Same general specifications as Model 32A except 30- or 32-inch vent-rib bbl., F choke, trap-style stock with checkered pistol-grip and beavertail forend. Weight: About 8 lbs. Made from l932 to 1942.

MODEL 89 (1889) . . . . **NiB $2133 Ex $1788 Gd $1141**
Hammers. Circular action. Gauges: 10, 12, 16, 28- to 32-inch bls.; steel or Damascus twist. Weight 7-10 lbs. Made from 1889 to 1908.

MODEL 90-T SINGLE-SHOT
TRAP . . . . NiB $1988 Ex $1790 Gd $1377
Gauge: 12; 2.75-inch chambers. 30-, 32- or 34-inch vent-rib bbl. with fixed chokes or screw-in REMChokes; ported or non-ported. Weight: 8.25 lbs. Checkered American walnut standard or Monte Carlo stock with low-luster finish. Engraved sideplates and drop-out trigger group optional. Made from 1990 to 1997.

MODEL 105 CTI . . . . **NiB $1230 Ex $880 Gd $600**
Gas-operated, semi-automatic. Titanium and carbon fiber receiver. Gauge: 12; 3-inch chamber. Bbl.: 26- or 28-inch with REMChoke. Weight: 7 lbs., depending on bbl. length. Checkered walnut stock and forend in satin finish. Made from 2006 to 2008.
105 CTi-II (2009 only) . . . . . . NiB $1230 Ex $880 Gd $600

MODEL 396 O/U
Boxlock. 12 ga. only w/2.75-inch chamber. 28- and 30-inch blued bbls. w/Rem chokes. Weight: 7.50 lbs. Nitride-grayed, engraved receiver, trigger guard, tang, hinge pins and forend metal. Engraved sideplates. Checkered satin-finished American walnut stock w/target style forend. Made from 1996 to 1998.
Sporting Clays . . . . NiB $1933 Ex $1658 Gd $1277
396 Skeet . . . . NiB $1855 Ex $1544 Gd $1153

MODEL 870 "ALL AMERICAN"
TRAP GUN . . . . NiB $1277 Ex $1073 Gd $777
Same as Model 870TB except custom grade with engraved receiver, trigger guard and bbl.; Monte Carlo or straight-comb stock and forend of fancy walnut; available only with 30-inch F choke bbl. Made from 1972 to 1977.

MODEL 870 COMPETITION
TRAP . . . . NiB $766 Ex $555 Gd $439
Based on standard Model 870 receiver except is single-shot with gas-assisted recoil-reducing system, new choke design, a high step-up vent rib and redesigned stock, forend with cut checkering and satin finish. Weight: 8.5 lbs. Made from 1981 to 1987.

MODEL 870 STANDARD . . . . . **NiB $566 Ex $444 Gd $339**
Same as Model 870 Wingmaster Riot Gun except has rifle-type sights.

MODEL 870 BRUSHMASTER DELUXE
Same as Model 870 Standard except available in 20 ga. as well as 12, has cut-checkered, satin-finished American walnut stock and forend, recoil pad.
Right-hand model . . . . NiB $559 Ex $477 Gd $366
Left-hand model . . . . NiB $659 Ex $490 Gd $380

MODEL 870 EXPRESS
Same general specifications Model 870 Wingmaster except has low-luster walnut-finished hardwood stock with pressed checkering and black recoil pad. Gauges: 12, 20 or .410, 3-inch chambers. Bbls.: 26- or 28-inch vent-rib with REMChoke; 25-inch vent-rib with fixed   choke (.410 only). Black oxide metal finish. Made from 1987 to date.
12 or 20 ga. . . . . NiB $355 Ex $290 Gd $200
.410 (w/fixed choke) . . . . NiB $455 Ex $300 Gd $225
Combo (w/extra 20-inch deer
bbl.) . . . . NiB $465 Ex $387 Gd $290

MODEL 870 EXPRESS DEER GUN
Same general specifications as Model 870 Express except in 12 ga. only, 20-inch bbl. with fixed IC choke, adj. rifle sights and Monte Carlo stock. Made from 1991 to date.
w/standard barrel . . . . NiB $433 Ex $297 Gd $200
w/rifled barrel . . . . NiB $450 Ex $310 Gd $220

MODEL 870 ESM (EXPRESS MAGNUM)
Similar to Model 870 Express except chambered for 12 ga. mag. w/3.5-inch chamber. Bbls.: 23-, 26- or 28-inch vent rib w/REM Choke. Checkered low-luster walnut-finished hardwood, black synthetic or camo buttstock and forearm. Matte black oxide metal finish or full camo finish. Made from 1998 to date.
Model 870 ESM
(w/hardwood stock) . . . . . . NiB $455 Ex $310 Gd $225
Model 870 ESM
(w/black synthetic stock) . . . NiB $455 Ex $310 Gd $225
Model 870 ESM
(w/camo synthetic stock) . . . NiB $488 Ex $395 Gd $259
Model 870 ESM Synthetic
Turkey (w/synthetic stock) . . NiB $488 Ex $395 Gd $259
Model 870 ESM camo
Turkey (w/full camo) . . . . . . NiB $488 Ex $395 Gd $259
Model 870 ESM combo
(w/full camo, extra bbl.) . . . NiB $509 Ex $400 Gd $323

MODEL 870 EXPRESS
SYNTHETIC HOME DEFENSE . . NiB $422 Ex $300 Gd $200
Slide action, hammerless, takedown. 12 ga. only. 18-inch bbl. w/cylinder choke and bead front sight. Positive checkered synthetic stock and forend with non-reflective black finish. Made from 1995 to date.

MODEL 870 EXPRESS
TURKEY GUN . . . . NiB $448 Ex $290 Gd $210
Same general specifications as Model 870 Express except has 21-inch vent-rib bbl. and Turkey Extra-Full REMChoke. Made from 1991 to date.

Remington Model 870
Marine Magnum

Remington Model 870
Special Field

Remington Model 870
Special Purpose Deer Gun

Remington Model 870
Wingmaster Field Gun

MODEL 870 EXPRESS
YOUTH GUN . . . . NiB $391 Ex $248 Gd $181
Same general specifications as Model 870 Express except has scaled-down stock with 12.5-inch pull and 21-inch vent rib bbl. with REMChoke. Made from 1991 to date.

MODEL 870 LIGHTWEIGHT
Same as standard Model 870 but with scaled-down receiver and lightweight mahogany stock; 20 ga. only. 2.75-inch chamber. Bbls.: plain or vent rib; 26-inch, IC; 28-inch, M or F choke. REMChoke available from 1987. Weight 5.75 lbs. w/26-inch plain bbl. American walnut stock and forend with satin or Hi-gloss finish. Made from 1972 to 1994.
w/plain barrel . . . . NiB $477 Ex $366 Gd $290
w/ventilated rib barrel . . . . NiB $490 Ex $380 Gd $315
w/REMChoke barrel . . . . NiB $566 Ex $435 Gd $335

MODEL 870 LIGHTWEIGHT MAGNUM
Same as Model 870 Lightweight but chambered for 20 ga. Magnum 3-inch shell; 28-inch bbl., plain or vent rib, F choke. Weight: 6 lbs. with plain bbl. Made from 1972 to 1994.
w/plain barrel . . . . NiB $477 Ex $377 Gd $292
w/ventilated rib barrel . . . . NiB $580 Ex $455 Gd $422

MODEL 870 MAGNUM DUCK GUN
Same as Model 870 Field Gun except has 3-inch chamber 12 and 20 gauge Magnum only. 28- or 30-inch bbl., plain or vent rib, M or F choke, recoil pad. Weight: About 7 or 6.75 lbs. Made from 1964 to date.
w/plain barrel . . . . NiB $310 Ex $225 Gd $179
w/ventilated rib barrel . . . . NiB $655 Ex $430 Gd $335

MODEL 870
MARINE MAGNUM . . . . NiB $735 Ex $496 Gd $359
Same general specifications as Model 870 Wingmaster except with 7-round magazine, 18-inch plain bbl. with fixed IC choke, bead front sight and nickel finish. Made from 1992 to date.

MODEL 870
SA SKEET GUN, SMALL GAUGE . . . NiB $875 Ex $677 Gd 529
Similar to Wingmaster Model 870SA except chambered for 28 and .410 ga. (2.5-inch chamber for latter); 25-inch vent rib bbl., SK choke. Weight: 6 lbs., 28 ga.; 6.5 lbs., .410. Made from 1969 to 1982.

MODEL 870 MISSISSIPPI
MAGNUM DUCK GUN . . . . . . NiB $865 Ex $667 Gd $520
Same as Remington Model 870 Magnum duck gun except has 32-inch bbl. "Ducks Unlimited" engraved receiver, Made in 1983.

MODEL 870
SPECIAL FIELD SHOTGUN. . . . NiB $466 Ex $322 Gd $245
Pump action. Hammerless. Gauge: 12 or 20. 21-inch vent-rib bbl. with REMChoke. 41.5 inches overall. Weight: 6-7 lbs. Straight-grip checkered walnut stock and forend. Made from 1987 to 1995.

MODEL 870 SPECIAL PURPOSE DEER GUN
Similar to Special Purpose Magnum except with 20-inch IC choke, rifle sights. Matte black oxide and Parkerized finish. Oil-finished, checkered buttstock and forend with recoil pad. Made from 1986 to date.
Model 870 SP Deer Gun . . . . . NiB $744 Ex $488 Gd $333

**Remington Model 870TC
Wingmaster Trap**

**Model 870 SP Deer Gun,
cant. scope mt.** . . . . **NiB $800 Ex $523 Gd $366**

MODEL 870 SPECIAL
PURPOSE MAGNUM . . . . **NiB $735 Ex $555 Gd $467**
Similar to the 870 Magnum duck gun except with 26-, 28- or 30-inch vent rib REMChoke bbl.12 ga. only; 3-inch chamber. Oil-finished field-grade stock with recoil pad, QD swivels and Cordura sling. Made from 1985 to date.

MODEL 870SPS MAGNUM
Same general specifications Model 870 Special Purpose Magnum except with synthetic stock and forend. 26- or 28-inch vent-rib bbl. with REMChoke tubes. Matte black or Mossy Oak camo finish. Made from 1991 to date.
70 SPS Mag. (black syn. stock) . **NiB $688 Ex $455 Gd $325**
870 SPS-T Camo (Mossy Oak camo). . **NiB $866 Ex $533 Gd $400**

MODEL 870 WINGMASTER FIELD GUN
Same general specifications as Model 870AP except checkered stock and forend. Later models have REMChoke systems in 12 ga. Made from 1964 to date.
w/plain barrel . . . . **NiB $366 Ex $264 Gd $155**
w/ventilated rib barrel . . . . **NiB $665 Ex $439 Gd $266**

MODEL 870 WINGMASTER FIELD GUN, SMALL BORE
Same as standard Model 870 except w/scaled-down lightweight receivers. Gauges: 28 and .410. Plain or vent rib 25-inch bbl. choked IC, M or F. Weight: 5.5-6.25 lbs. depending on gauge and bbl. Made 1969 to 1994.
w/plain barrel . . . . **NiB $775 Ex $600 Gd $445**
w/ventilated-rib barrel . . . . **NiB $808 Ex $625 Gd $465**

MODEL 870 WINGMASTER
MAGNUM DELUXE GRADE . . . **NiB $667 Ex $559 Gd $400**
Same as Model 870 Magnum standard grade except has checkered stock and extension beavertail forearm, bbl. with matted top surface. Disc. in 1963.

MODEL 870 WINGMASTER
MAGNUM STANDARD GRADE NiB $633 Ex $479 Gd $365
Same as Model 870AP except chambered for 12 ga. 3-inch Magnum, 30-inch F choke bbl., recoil pad. Weight: About 8.25 lbs. Made 1955 to 1963.

MODEL 870 WINGMASTER REMCHOKE SERIES
Slide action, hammerless, takedown with blued all-steel receiver. Gauges: 12, 20; 3-inch chamber. Tubular magazine. Bbls.: 21-, 26-, 28-inch vent-rib with REM Choke. Weight: 7.5 lbs. (12 ga.). Satin-finished, checkered walnut buttstock and forend with recoil pad. Right- or left-hand models. Made from 1986 to date.
Standard model, 12 ga. . . . . . . **NiB $500 Ex $377 Gd $266**
Standard model, 20 ga. . . . . . . **NiB $535 Ex $400 Gd $288**
Youth model, 21-inch barrel . . . **NiB $500 Ex $377 Gd $321**

MODEL 870ADL WINGMASTER DELUXE GRADE
Same general specifications as Wingmaster Model 870AP except has pistol-grip stock and extension beavertail forend,

both finely checkered; matted top surface or vent-rib bbl. Made 1950 to 1963.
w/matted top-surface barrel . . . **NiB $488 Ex $365 Gd $288**
w/ventilated-rib barrel . . . . **NiB $509 Ex $412 Gd $300**

MODEL 870AP WINGMASTER STANDARD GRADE
Hammerless. Takedown. Gauges: 12, 16, 20. Tubular magazine holds four rounds. Bbls.: Plain, matted top surface or vent rib; 26-inch IC, 28-inch M or F choke, 30-inch F choke (12 ga. only). Weight: About 7 lbs., 12 ga.; 6.75 lbs., 16 ga.; 6.5 lbs., 20 ga. Plain pistol-grip stock, grooved forend. Made 1950 to 1963.
w/plain barrel . . . . **NiB $359 Ex $300 Gd $209**
w/matted surface barrel . . . . . . **NiB $435 Ex $335 Gd $225**
w/ventilated rib barrel . . . . **NiB $466 Ex $372 Gd $260**
Left-hand model . . . . **NiB $489 Ex $400 Gd $265**

MODEL 870BDL WINGMASTER DELUXE SPECIAL
Same as Model 870ADL except select American walnut stock and forend. Made from 1950 to 1963.
w/matted surface barrel . . . . . . **NiB $665 Ex $445 Gd $310**
w/ventilated-rib barrel . . . . **NiB $715 Ex $477 Gd $349**

MODEL 870D, 870F WINGMASTER
TOURNAMENT AND PREMIER GRADE GUNS
These higher-grade models differ from the Model 870AP in general quality, grade of wood, checkering, engraving, etc. General operating specifications are essentially the same. Made from 1950 to date.
Model 870D Tournament grade NiB $3139 Ex $2288 Gd $1660
Model 870F Premier grade NiB $6445 Ex $4753 Gd $3465
Model 870F Premier gr.
     w/gold inlay . . . . **NiB $10,098 Ex $7517 Gd $5237**

MODEL 870R
WINGMASTER RIOT GUN . . . **NiB $375 Ex $280 Gd $210**
Same as Model 870AP except 20-inch bbl., IC choke, 12 ga. only.

MODEL 870 SA WINGMASTER SKEET GUN
Same general specifications as Model 870AP except has 26-inch vent-rib bbl., SK choke, ivory bead front sight, metal bead rear sight, pistol-grip stock and extension beavertail forend. Weight: 6.75 to 7.5 lbs. depending on gauge. Made 1950 to 1982.
Model 870SA Skeet grade
     (disc. 1982) . . . . **NiB $677 Ex $395 Gd $288**
Model 870SC Skeet Target
     grade (disc. 1980) . . . . **NiB $795 Ex $549 Gd $400**

MODEL 870TB WINGMASTER
TRAP SPECIAL . . . . **NiB $633 Ex $500 Gd $388**
Same general specifications as Model 870AP Wingmaster except has 28- or 30-inch vent rib bbl., F choke, metal bead front sight, no rear sight. "Special" grade trap-style stock and forend, both checkered, recoil pad. Weight: About 8 lbs. Made from 1950 to 1981.

SHOTGUNS

**Remington Model 1100
Field w/Ventilated Rib**

**Remington Model 1100
Deer Gun**

**Remington Model 1100
SA Skeet Gun**

REMINGTON MODEL
870TC TRAP GRADE . . . . NiB $795 Ex $554 Gd $400
Same as Model 870 Wingmaster TC except has tournament-grade walnut in stock and forend w/satin finish. Over-bored 30-inch vent rib bbl. w/ 2.75-inch chamber and RemChoke tubes. Reissued in 1996. See separate listing for earlier model.

MODEL 870TC WINGMASTER TRAP GRADE
Same as Model 870TB except higher-grade walnut in stock and forend, has both front and rear sights. Made 1950-79. Model 870 TC reissued in 1996. See separate listing for later model.
Model 870 TC Trap (Standard) . NiB $515 Ex $466 Gd $325
Model 870 TC Trap (Monte Carlo) NiB $545 Ex $480 Gd $366

MODEL 878A AUTOMASTER . . NiB $376 Ex $266 Gd $195
Gas-operated Autoloader. 12 ga., 3-round magazine. Bbls.: 26-inch IC, 28-inch M choke, 30-inch F choke. Weight: About 7 lbs. Plain pistol-grip stock and forearm. Made from 1959-62.

MODEL 887 NITRO MAG . . . NiB $445 Ex $285 Gd $200
Based on Model 870 except has Armorlokt overmolding on metal. 26- or 28-inch bbl. Finish: matte black. Stock: black synthetic. Made from 2009 to date.
Camo Combo . . . . NiB $728 Ex $700 Gd $300
Tactical (extended magazine, Picatinny rail, ported extended choke tube) . . . . NiB $534 Ex $340 Gd $230
Waterfowl Camo (Real Tree
   Advantage Max-4 finish . . . . NiB $594 Ex $370 Gd $270

NOTE: *New stock checkering patterns and receiver scroll markings were incorporated on all standard Model 1100 field, magnum, skeet and trap models in 1979.*

MODEL 1100 FIELD
Gas-operated. Hammerless. Takedown. Gauges: 12, 16, 20. Bbls.: plain or vent. rib; 30-inch F, 28-inch M or F, 26-inch IC; or REMChoke tubes. Weight: Average 7.25-7.5 lbs. depending on ga. and bbl. length. Checkered walnut pistol-grip stock and forearm in high-gloss finish. Made 1963 to 1988. 16 ga. discontinued 1980.

w/plain barrel . . . . NiB $380 Ex $291 Gd $200
w/ventilated-rib barrel . . . . NiB $422 Ex $356 Gd $239
REMChoke model . . . . NiB $466 Ex $390 Gd $292
REMChoke, Left-hand action . . . . NiB $744 Ex $544 Gd $356

MODEL 1100 CLASSIC FIELD . NiB $675 Ex $480 Gd $310
Similar to Model 1100 Field except 12, 16, 20 or .410 w/ light contoured REMchoke bbl. Non-engraved receiver. Made from 2003 to 2006.

MODEL 1100 DEER GUN . . . . . NiB $515 Ex $386 Gd $265
Same as Model 1100 Field Gun except has 22-inch barrel, IC, with rifle-type sights; 12 and 20 ga. only; recoil pad. Weight: About 7.25 lbs. Made from 1963 to 1998.

MODEL 1100 DUCKS UNLIMITED ATLANTIC
COMMEMORATIVE . . . . NiB $1188 Ex $987 Gd $766
Limited production for one year. Similar specifications to Model 1100 Field except with 32-inch F choke, vent rib bbl. 12-ga. Magnum only. Made in 1982.

MODEL 1100 DUCKS UNLIMITED "THE CHESAPEAKE"
COMMEMORATIVE . . . . NiB $878 Ex $753 Gd $555
Limited edition 1 to 2400. Same general specifications as Model 1100 Field except sequentially numbered with markings "The Chesapeake." 12 ga. Magnum with 30-inch F choke, vent rib bbl. Made in 1981.

MODEL 1100 FIELD GRADE, SMALL BORE
Same as standard Model 1100 but scaled down. Gauges: 28, .410. 25-inch bbl., plain or vent rib; IC, M or F choke. Weight: 6.25-7 lbs. depending on gauge and bbl. Made from 1969 to 1994.
w/plain barrel . . . . NiB $669 Ex $533 Gd $435
w/ventilated rib . . . . NiB $866 Ex $677 Gd $480

MODEL 1100 G3 . . . . NiB $1050 Ex $800 Gd $500
Similar to Model 1100 Field except satin finish steel receiver with titanium PVD coating. 12 or 20 ga.; 3-in. chamber. Bbls.: 26- or 28-in. vent rib w/ ProBore choke tubes. Weight: 6.7-7.6 lbs. depending on bbl. length. Stock: RealWood fiber laminate w/ high gloss finish and checkering. Made from 2006 to 2008.

**Remington Model 1100
Special Field**

MODEL 1100 LIGHTWEIGHT
Same as standard Model 1100 but scaled-down receiver and lightweight mahogany stock; 20 ga. only, 2.75-inch chamber. Bbls.: Plain or vent rib; 26-inch IC; 28-inch M and F choke. Weight: 6.25 lbs. Made from 1970 to 1976.
w/plain barrel . . . . NiB $654 Ex $500 Gd $390
w/ventilated rib . . . . NiB $735 Ex $566 Gd $408

MODEL 1100 LIGHTWEIGHT MAGNUM
Same as Model 1100 Lightweight but chambered for 20 gauge Magnum 3-inch shell; 28-inch bbl., plain or vent rib, F choke. Weight: 6.5 lbs. Made from 1977 to 1998.
w/plain barrel . . . . NiB $688 Ex $544 Gd $422
w/ventilated rib . . . . NiB $788 Ex $590 Gd $466
w/choke tubes . . . . NiB $855 Ex $598 Gd $466

MODEL 1100 LT-20 DUCKS UNLIMITED SPECIAL
COMMEMORATIVE . . . . NiB $1486 Ex $1156 Gd $844
Limited edition 1 to 2400. Same general specifications as Model 1100 Field except sequentially numbered with markings, "The Chesapeake." 20 ga. only. 26-inch IC, vent-rib bbl. Made in 1981.

MODEL 1100 LT-20 SERIES
Same as Model 1100 Field Gun except in 20 ga. with shorter 23-inch vent rib bbl., straight-grip stock. REMChoke series has 21-inch vent rib bbl., choke tubes. Weight: 6.25 lbs. Checkered grip and forearm. Made from 1977 to 1995.
LT-20 Special . . . . NiB $588 Ex $498 Gd $377
LT-20 Deer Gun . . . . NiB $490 Ex $399 Gd $295
LT-20 Youth . . . . NiB $585 Ex $444 Gd $300

MODEL 1100 MAGNUM . . . . . NiB $598 Ex $499 Gd $378
Limited production. Similar to the Model 1100 Field except with 26-inch F choke, vent rib bbl. and 3-inch chamber. Made in 1981.

MODEL 1100 MAGNUM DUCK GUN
Same as Model 1100 Field Gun except has 3-inch chamber,12 and 20 ga. Mag. only. 30-inch plain or vent rib bbl. in 12 ga., 28-inch in 20 ga.; M or F choke. Recoil pad. Weight: About 7.75 lbs. Made from 1963 to 1988.
w/plain barrel . . . . NiB $555 Ex $399 Gd $324
w/ventilated rib barrel . . . . NiB $575 Ex $435 Gd $355

MODEL 1100
ONE OF 3000 FIELD . . . . NiB $1210 Ex $966 Gd $790
Limited edition, numbered 1 to 3000. Similar to Model 1100 Field except with fancy wood and gold-trimmed etched hunting scenes on receiver. 12 gauge with 28-inch Mod., vent rib bbl. Made in 1980.

MODEL 1100 SA SKEET GUN
Same as Model 1100 Field Gun, 12 and 20 ga. except has 26-inch vent-rib bbl., SK choke or with Cutts Compensator. Weight: 7.25-7.5 lbs. Made from 1963 to 1994.
w/skeet-choked barrel . . . . NiB $977 Ex $644 Gd $388
w/Cutts Comp, add. $200
Left-hand action, add $75

MODEL 1100 SA
LIGHTWEIGHT SKEET . . . . NiB $655 Ex $497 Gd $366
Same as Model 1100 Lightweight except has skeet-style stock and forearm, 26-inch vent-rib bbl., SK choke. Made from 1971 to 1997.

MODEL 1100 SA
SKEET SMALL BORE . . . . NiB $625 Ex $443 Gd $311
Similar to standard Model 1100SA except chambered for 28 and .410 ga. (2.5-inch chamber for latter); 25-inch vent-rib bbl., SK choke. Weight: 6.75 lbs., 28 ga.; 7.25 lbs., .410. Made from 1969 to 1994.

MODEL 1100 SB
LIGHTWEIGHT SKEET . . . . NiB $644 Ex $433 Gd $310
Same as Model 1100SA Lightweight except has select wood. Introduced in 1977.

MODEL 1100 SB SKEET GUN. . NiB $654 Ex $443 Gd $319
Same specifications as Model 1100SA except has select wood. Made from 1963 to 1997.

MODEL 1100
SPECIAL FIELD SHOTGUN. . . . NiB $600 Ex $492 Gd $388
Gas-operated. Five round capacity. Hammerless. Gauges: 12, 20 or .410. 21- or 23-in. vent-rib bbl. with REMChoke. Weight: 6.5-7.25 lbs. Straight-grip checkered walnut stock and forend. Note: .410 Made from 1983 to 1999.

MODEL 1100 SP MAGNUM
Same as Model 1100 Field except 12 ga. only with 3-inch chambers. Bbls.: 26- or 30-inch F choke; or 26-inch with REM Choke tubes; vent rib. Non-reflective matte black, Parkerized bbl. and receiver. Satin-finished stock and forend. Made 1986.
w/fixed choke . . . . NiB $475 Ex $397 Gd $321
w/REMchoke . . . . NiB $490 Ex $417 Gd $344

MODEL 1100 SPECIAL FIELD
Similar to Model 1100 Field except 12, 20 or .410. Bbls.: 21- and 23-in. vent rib w/ REMChoke tubes (intro. 1987). Weight: Average 7.25-7.5 lbs. depending on ga. and bbl. length. High gloss checkered walnut straight-grip stock and forearm. Made 1983 to 1999.
12 ga. . . . . NiB $525 Ex $350 Gd $200
20 ga. . . . . NiB $690 Ex $540 Gd $400
.410 . . . . NiB $840 Ex $710 Gd $480

MODEL 1100 SYNTHETIC . . . . NiB $435 Ex $280 Gd $170
Similar to Model 1100 Field except 12, 16 or 20 ga. Bbls.: 26- or 28-in. vent rib w/ REMChoke tubes. Weight: Average 7-7.5 lbs. depending on ga. and bbl. length. Sythentic stock and forearm. Made 1996 to 2004.
Deer . . . . NiB $500 Ex $280 Gd $170
LT 20 Youth . . . . NiB $440 Ex $270 Gd $160

SHOTGUNS

**Remington Model 1100
Tournament Trap**

**Remington Model 3200
"One of 1000" Skeet**

MODEL 1100 TAC-2 . . . . NiB $800 Ex $580 Gd $400
Similar to Model 1100 Field except 12 ga. only; 2-3/4-in. chamber. Bbls.: 18- or 22-in. vent rib w/ REMChoke tubes, HiViz sights. Weight: 7.5 lbs. depending on bbl. length. Stock: black sythentic SFIV. 6- or 8-rnd. capacity. Made 2006 to date.
Tac-4 (pistol grip) . . . . NiB $870 Ex $650 Gd $240

MODEL 1100 TACTICAL. . . . . . NiB $435 Ex $280 Gd $170
Similar to Model 1100 Field except 12 ga. only; 3-in. chamber. Bbls.: 18- or 22-in. vent rib w/ REMChoke tubes, HiViz sights. Weight: 7.5 lbs. depending on bbl. length. Sythentic pistol grip or standard stock and forearm. 6- or 8-rnd. capacity. Disc 2006.

MODEL 1100 TOURNAMENT/PREMIER
These higher grade guns differ from standard models in overall quality, grade of wood, checkering, engraving, gold inlays, etc. General specs are the same. Made 1963 to 1994; 1997 to 1999; 2003.
1100D Tournament . . . . NiB $966 Ex $633 Gd $577
1100F Premier . . . . NiB $1266 Ex $1059 Gd $833
1100F Premier w/ gold inlay NiB $10,332 Ex $7833 Gd $4460

**MODEL 1100
TOURNAMENT SKEET . . . . NiB $977 Ex $738 Gd $490**
Similar to Model 1100 Field except with 26-inch bbl. SK choke. Gauges: 12, LT-20, 28, and .410. Features select walnut stocks and new cut-checkering patterns. Made from 1979- to 1999.

MODEL 1100TA TRAP GUN. . . NiB $529 Ex $417 Gd $330
Similar to Model 1100TB Trap Gun except with regular-grade stocks. Available in both left- and right-hand versions. Made 1979 to 1986.

MODEL 1100TB TRAP GUN
Same as Model 1100 Field Gun except has special trap stock, straight or Monte Carlo comb, recoil pad; 30-inch vent-rib bbl., F or M trap choke; 12 ga. only. Weight: 8.25 lbs. Made 1963 to 1979.
Straight stock . . . . NiB $588 Ex $460 Gd $339
Monte Carlo stock . . . . NiB $599 Ex $443 Gd $360

**MODEL 1900
HAMMERLESS DOUBLE. . . NiB $1889 Ex $1366 Gd $1177**
Improved version of Model 1894. Boxlock. Auto ejector. Double triggers. Gauges: 10, 12, 16. Bbls.: 28 to 32 inches. Value shown is for standard grade with ordnance steel bbls. Made 1900 to 1910.

MODEL 3200 FIELD GRADE . . .NiB $1388 Ex $1178 Gd $900
O/U, boxlock. Auto ejectors. Selective single trigger. 12 ga. 2.75-inch chambers. Bbls.: Vent rib, 26- and 28-inch M/F; 30-inch IC/M. Weight: About 7.75 lbs. with 26-inch bbls. Checkered pistol-grip stock/forearm. Made from 1973 to 1978.

**MODEL 3200 COMPETITION
SKEET GUN . . . . NiB $1799 Ex $1588 Gd $1165**
Same as Model 3200 Skeet Gun except has gilded scrollwork on frame, engraved forend, latch plate and trigger guard, select fancy wood. Made from 1973 to 1984.

**MODEL 3200
COMPETITION SKEET SET . NiB $5733 Ex $4790 Gd $3300**
Similar specifications to Model 3200 Field. 12-ga. O/U with additional, interchangeable bbls. in 20, 28, and .410 ga. Cased. Made from 1980 to 1984.

**MODEL 3200
COMPETITION TRAP GUN NiB $1598 Ex $1266 Gd $1177**
Same as Model 3200 Trap Gun except has gilded scrollwork on frame, engraved forend, latch plate and trigger guard, select fancy wood. Made from 1973 to 1984.

**MODEL 3200
FIELD GRADE MAGNUM. . NiB $1766 Ex $1588 Gd $1177**
Same as Model 3200 Field except chambered for 12 ga. mag. 3-inch shells 30-inch bbls., M and F or both F choke. Made 1975 to 1984.

**MODEL 3200
"ONE OF 1000" SKEET. . . . NiB $2088 Ex $1577 Gd $1288**
Same as Model 3200 "One of 1000" Trap except has 26- or 28-inch bbls., SK choke, skeet-style stock and forearm. Made in 1974.

**MODEL 3200
"ONE OF 1000" TRAP . . . . NiB $2170 Ex $1660 Gd $1375**
Limited edition numbered 1 to 1000. Same general specifications as Model 3200 Trap Gun but has frame, trigger guard and forend latch elaborately engraved (designation "One of 1,000" on frame side), stock and forearm of high grade walnut. Supplied in carrying case. Made in 1973.

MODEL 3200 SKEET GUN . . NiB $1779 Ex $1398 Gd $1055
Same as Model 3200 Field Grade except skeet-style stock and full beavertail forearm, 26- or 28-inch bbls., SK choke. Made from 1973-80.

546

Remington Rider No. 9 Single-Shot Shotgun

Remington Sportsman Autoloader

Remington Sportsman — 48A

MODEL 3200

SPECIAL TRAP GUN . . . . NiB $1598 Ex $1366 Gd $988
Same as Model 3200 Trap Gun except has select fancy-grade wood and other minor refinements. Made from 1973 to 1984.

MODEL 3200 TRAP GUN . . NiB $1499 Ex $1262 Gd $1077
Same as Model 3200 Field Grade except trap-style stock w/ Monte Carlo or straight comb, select wood, beavertail forearm, 30- or 32-inch bbls. w/ventilated rib, IM/F or F/F chokes. Made 1973 to 1977.

RIDER NO. 9 SINGLE-SHOT . . NiB $555 Ex $433 Gd $335
Improved version of No. 3 Single Barrel Shotgun made in the late 1800s. Semi-hammerless. Gauges 10, 12, 16, 20, 24, 28. 30- to 32-inch plain bbl. Weight: About 6 lbs. Plain pistol-grip stock and forearm. Auto ejector. Made from 1902 to 1910.

SP-10. . . . . NiB $1480 Ex $1050 Gd $730
Autoloader. Takedown. Gas-operated with stainless steel piston. 10 ga., 3.5-inch chamber. Bbls.: 30-inch vent-rib with REMChoke screw-in tubes. Weight: 11 lbs. Metal bead front. Checkered walnut stock with satin finish. QD swivels and camo sling. Made from 1989 to 2010.

SP-10 MAGNUM CAMO . . NiB $1560 Ex $1000 Gd $710
Same general specifications as Model SP-10 except has 23- or 26-inch bbl. Finish: Mossy Oak, Mossy Oak BreakUp, Mossy Oak Obession, Bottomland or Duck Blind. Stock: standard or thumbhole. Made from 1993 to 2010.
Synthetic (matte finish). . . . . . . NiB $990 Ex $800 Gd $560
Turkey (Mossy Oak Obession) . . NiB $1660 Ex $1100 Gd $810
Turkey Combo (turkey bbl.
and deer bbl.) . . . . NiB $1300 Ex $930 Gd $660
Waterfowl (Mossy Oak
Duck Blind) . . . . NiB $1570 Ex $1010 Gd $350

SP-10 TURKEY CAMO

NWTF 25TH ANNIVERSARY NiB $1050 Ex $775 Gd $710
Same general specifications as Model SP-10 except limited manufacture for NWTF 25th Anniversary in 1998. Made 1998 only.

PEERLESS O/U . . . . NiB $1165 Ex $966 Gd $788
Boxlock action and removable, engraved sideplates. Gauge: 12 only with 3-inch chambers. Barrels: 26-, 28-, or 30-inch with vent rib and REMChoke system. Automatic safety and single selective trigger. Weight: 7.25 lbs. to 7.5 lbs. Blued receiver and bbls. Checkered American walnut stock. Made from 1993 to 1998.

SPORTSMAN A STANDARD GRADE AUTOLOADER

Same general specifications as Model 11A except magazine holds two shells. Also available in "B" Special Grade, "D" Tournament Grade, "E" Expert Grade, "F" Premier Grade. Made from 1931 to 1948. Same values as for Model 11A.
48D . . . . NiB $445 Ex $321 Gd $226

VERSA MAX

Gas operated semi-auto. 12 ga., 3-1/2-in. chambers only. Bbls.: 26- or 28-in. w/ vent rib, HiViz bead, and Pro Bore choke tubes. Finish: matte black. Stock: black synthetic w/ gray checkered insert panels. Made from 2010 to date.
Synthetic . . . . NiB $1427 Ex $900 Gd $530
Synthetic Left Hand . . . . NiB $1497 Ex $970 Gd $600
Waterfowl Camo . . . . NiB $1630 Ex $1100 Gd $660
Waterfowl Pro . . . . NiB $1730 Ex $1120 Gd $670
Wood Tech . . . . NiB $1630 Ex $1100 Gd $660

VERSA MAX COMPETITION

TACTICAL . . . . NiB $1699 Ex $1100 Gd $660
Same general specs as Versa Max except has 22-in. bbl. and 8-round capacity. Finish: green cerakote. Made from 2014 to date.

VERSA MAX SPORTSMAN . . NiB $1045 Ex $700 Gd $500
Same general specs as Versa Max except w/ 26- or 28-in. bbl. w/ one choke tube, black synthetic stock, matte blue finish. Made from 2013 to date.
Camo . . . . NiB $1199 Ex $730 Gd $500
Turkey Model . . . . NiB $1199 Ex $730 Gd $500

VERSA MAX TACTICAL . . . . NiB $1699 Ex $1100 Gd $660
Same general specs as Versa Max except has 22-in. vent rib bbl. w/ HiViz sights, magazine extension, and Picatinny rail. Finish: black. Made from 2012 to date.
Zombie Gargoyle Green finish. . . NiB $1627 Ex $1100 Gd $730
Zombie Pink Explosion finish
(2013 only) . . . . NiB $1627 Ex $1100 Gd $730

SHOTGUNS

**Remington Sportsman
48SC Skeet Target Grade**

**Remington Sportsman
48A Standard**

**Remington Sportsman
48A Small Gauge**

SPORTSMAN SKEET GUN
Same general specifications as the Sportsman A except has 26-inch bbl. (plain, solid or vent rib), SK choke, beavertail forend. Disc. in 1949.

Plain barrel	NiB $408	Ex $320	Gd $255
Solid-rib barrel	NiB $408	Ex $320	Gd $255
Ventilated rib barrel	NiB $475	Ex $355	Gd $290

MODEL 48 MOHAWK AUTO
Streamlined receiver. Hammerless. Takedown. Gauges: 12, 16, 20. Tubular magazine holds two rounds. Bbls.: Plain, matted top surface or vent rib; 26-inch IC, 28-inch M or F choke, 30-inch F choke (12 ga. only). Weight: About 7.5 lbs., 12 ga.; 6.25 lbs., 16 ga.; 6.5 lbs., 20 ga. Pistol-grip stock, grooved forend, both checkered. Made from 1949 to 1959.

Plain bbl..	NiB $376	Ex $270	Gd $198
Matted top-surface bbl.	NiB $466	Ex $355	Gd $290
Ventilated rib bbl.	NiB $566	Ex $477	Gd $379

MODEL 48 B, D, F SPORTSMAN
SELECT, TOURNAMENT & PREMIER GRADE GUNS
These higher grade models differ from the Sportsman-48A in general quality, grade of wood, checkering, engraving, etc. General specifications are the same. Made from 1949 to 1959.

Sportsman-48B Select grade	NiB $490	Ex $330	Gd $225
Sportsman-48D Tournament grade	NiB $1688	Ex $1178	Gd $988
Sportsman-48F Premier grade	NiB $6355	Ex $3988	Gd $2500

MODEL 48SA SPORTSMAN SKEET GUN
Same general specifications as Sportsman-48A except has 26-inch bbl. with matted top surface or vent rib, SK choke, ivory bead front sight, metal bead rear sight. Made from 1949 to 1960.

plain barrel	NiB $377	Ex $279	Gd $200
ventilated rib barrel	NiB $466	Ex $344	Gd $229
Sportsman-48SC Skeet	NiB $577	Ex $466	Gd $355
Tournament grade.	NiB $1688	Ex $1299	Gd $1100
Sportsman-48SF Skeet Premier grade	NiB $6220	Ex $4014	Gd $2444

MODEL 11-48A RIOT GUN . . . NiB $420 Ex $322 Gd $276
Same as Model 11-48A except 20-inch plain barrel and 12 ga. only. Disc. in 1969.

MODEL 11-48A STANDARD
GRADE 4-ROUND AUTOLOADER .410 & 28 GAUGE
Same general specifications as Sportsman-48A except gauge, 3-round magazine, 25-inch bbl. Weight: About 6.25 lbs. 28 ga. introduced 1952, .410 in 1954. Disc. in 1969. Values same as shown for Sportsman-48A.

MODEL 11-48A STANDARD GRADE AUTOLOADER
Same general specifications as Sportsman-48A except magazine holds four rounds, forend not grooved. Also available in Special Grade (11-48B), Tournament Grade (11-48D) and Premier Grade (11-48F). Made 1949 to 1969. Values same as for Sportsman-48A.

MODEL 11-48SA SKEET
28 GA. AND .410 . . . . NiB $398 Ex $300 Gd $233
Same general specifications as Model 11-48A 28 gauge except has 25-inch vent rib bbl., SK choke. 28 ga. introduced 1952, .410 in 1954.

MODEL 58 SKEET, TARGET, TOURNAMENT
AND PREMIER GRADES
These higher grade models differ from the Sportsman-58SA in general quality, grade of wood, checkering, engraving, and other refinements. General operating and physical specifications are the same.

Sportsman-58C Skeet Gun	NiB $544	Ex $397	Gd $322
Sportsman-58D Tournament	NiB $1656	Ex $1267	Gd $1100
Sportsman-58SF Premier	NiB $6222	Ex $3566	Gd $2924

SPORTSMAN-58 TOURNAMENT AND PREMIER
These higher grade models differ from the Sportsman-58ADL with vent-rib bbl. in general quality, grade of wood, checkering, engraving, etc. General specifications are the same.

Sportsman-58D Tournament	NiB $1099	Ex $824	Gd $590
Sportsman-58F Premier	NiB $1889	Ex $1488	Gd $1051

MODEL 58ADL AUTOLOADER
Deluxe grade. Gas-operated. 12 ga. Three round magazine. Bbls.: plain or vent rib, 26-, 28- or 30-inch; IC, M or F choke, or Remington Special Skeet choke. Weight: About 7 lbs. Checkered pistol-grip stock and forearm. Made from 1956 to 1964.

plain barrel	NiB $366	Ex $267	Gd $188
ventilated rib barrel	NiB $433	Ex $320	Gd $221

Richland Model 200

Richland Model 202

Richland Model 707 Deluxe

Richland Model 711
Long Range Waterfowl Magnum

MODEL 58BDL DELUXE SPECIAL GRADE
Same as Model 58ADL except select grade wood.
plain barrel . . . . NiB $544 Ex $422 Gd $338
ventilated rib barrel . . . . NiB $577 Ex $476 Gd $390

MODEL 58SADL
SKEET GRADE . . . . NiB $588 Ex $432 Gd $338
Same general specifications as Model 58ADL with vent-rib bbl.
except special skeet stock and forearm.

REVELATION SHOTGUNS

See Western Auto listings.

RICHLAND ARMS COMPANY — Blissfield, Michigan; manufactured in Italy and Spain

MODEL 200
FIELD GRADE DOUBLE . . . . . . NiB $400 Ex $294 Gd $179
Hammerless, boxlock, Anson & Deeley-type. Plain extractors. Double triggers. Gauges: 12, 16, 20, 28, .410 (3-inch chambers in 20 and .410; others have 2.75-inch). Bbls.: 28-inch M/F choke, 26-inch IC/M; .410 with 26-inch M/F only; 22-inch IC/M in 20 ga. only. Weight: 6 lbs., 2 oz. to 7 lbs., 4 oz. Checkered walnut stock with cheekpiece, pistol grip, recoil pad; beavertail forend. Made in Spain from 1963 to 1985.

MODEL 202
ALL-PURPOSE FIELD GUN . . . . NiB $554 Ex $348 Gd $245
Hammerless, boxlock, Anson & Deeley-type. Same as Model

200 except has two sets of barrels same gauge. 12 ga.: 30-inch bbls. F/F, 3-inch chambers; 26-inch bbls. IC/M, 2.75-inch chambers. 20 gauge: 28-inch bbls. M/F; 22-inch bbls. IC/M, 3-inch chambers. Made from 1963. Disc.

MODEL 707
DELUXE FIELD GUN . . . . NiB $433 Ex $266 Gd $180
Hammerless, boxlock, triple bolting system. Plain extractors. Double triggers. Gauges: 12, 2.75-inch chambers; 20, 3-inch chambers. Bbls.: 12 ga., 28-inch M/F, 26-inch IC/M; 20 ga., 30-inch F/F, 28-inch M/F, 26-inch IC/M. Weight: 6 lbs., 4 oz. to 6 lbs., 15 oz. Checkered walnut stock and forend, recoil pad. Made from 1963 to 1972.

MODEL 711 LONG-RANGE WATERFOWL MAGNUM DOUBLE-BARREL SHOTGUN
Hammerless, boxlock, Anson & Deeley-type, Purdey triple lock. Plain extractors. Double triggers. Auto safety. Gauges: 10, 3.5-inch chambers; 12, 3-inch chambers. Bbls.: 10 ga., 32-inch; 12 ga., 30-inch; F/F. Weight: 10 ga., 11 pounds; 12 ga., 7.75 lbs. Checkered walnut stock and beavertail forend; recoil pad. Made in Spain from 1963 to 1985.
10 ga. magnum . . . . NiB $545 Ex $356 Gd $280
12 ga. magnum . . . . NiB $566 Ex $377 Gd $300

MODEL 808
O/U SHOTGUN . . . . NiB $559 Ex $394 Gd $290
Boxlock. Plain extractors. Non-selective single trigger. 12 ga. only. Bbls. (Vickers steel): 30-inch F/F; 28-inch M/F; 26-inch IC/M. Weight: 6 lbs., 12 oz. to 7 lbs., 3 oz. Checkered walnut stock/forend. Made in Italy from 1963 to 1968.
Premier grade . . . . NiB $6220 Ex $4014 Gd $2444

SHOTGUNS

**Rigby Regal
Side Lock**

JOHN RIGBY & CO. — London, England

HAMMERLESS BOXLOCK DOUBLE-BARREL SHOTGUN
Auto ejectors. Double triggers. Made in all gauges, barrel lengths and chokes. Checkered stock and forend, straight grip standard. Made in two grades: Sackville and Chatsworth. These guns differ in general quality, engraving, etc.; specifications are the same.

Sackville grade . . . . NiB $6450 Ex $4255 Gd $3790
Chatsworth grade . . . . NiB $4779 Ex $4109 Gd $3200

HAMMERLESS SIDELOCK DOUBLE-BARREL SHOTGUN
Auto ejectors. Double triggers. Made in all gauges, barrel lengths and chokes. Checkered stock and forend, straight grip standard. Made in two grades: Regal (best quality) and Sandringham; these guns differ in general quality, engraving, etc., specifications are the same.

Regal grade . . . . NiB $13,677 Ex $11,773 Gd $9892
Sandringham grade . . . . . NiB $11,088 Ex $9000 Gd $5698

RIZZINI, BATTISTA — Marcheno, Italy

Rizzini was purchased by San Swiss AG IN 2002. Imported in the U. S. by SIB Arms, Exeter, New Hampshire; William Larkin Moore & Co., Scottsdale, Arizona; and New England Arms Co., Kittery, Maine.

AURUM O/U . . . . NiB $2770 Ex $2243 Gd $2016
Gauge: 12, 16 and 20. Boxlock action, light engraving. Case included. Introduced 1996.

AURUM LIGHT . . . . NiB $4088 Ex $2867 Gd $2390
Similaar to Aurum but 16 gauge only. Imported beginning in 2000.

ARTEMIS . . . . NiB $2733 Ex $2270 Gd $1966
Similarf to Aurum but with improved engraving and gold inlays.

ARTEMIS DELUXE . . . . NiB $6777 Ex $3861 Gd $3223
Similar to Artemis but with detailed game scene engraving. Available in all gauges

ARTEMIS EL . . . . NiB $17,776 Ex $14,600 Gd $12,980
Same as Artemis Deluxe. Custom gun with superior quality wood and detailed hand engraving. Disc. 2000.

MODEL 780 FIELD . . . . NiB $2140 Ex $1088 Gd $977
Gauge: 10, 12 or 16. Boxlock action, double triggers, extractors, walnut stock and forearm. Disc. 2000.
10 gauge, add $625
Ejector model (S780EL), add $200
Single selective trigger with ejectors, add $250
SST, ejectors and upgraded stock, add $425

MODEL S780 EMEL . NiB $14,900 Ex $13,655 Gd $11,330
Same as Model 780 Field but with special engraving and hand finished.

MODEL 780 COMPETITION . . . NiB $1488 Ex $1276 Gd $1099
Same as Model 780 Field but with skeet, trap or sporting clays features. Disc.1998.

**MODEL 780
SMALL GAUGE SERIES** . . . . NiB $1388 Ex $1164 Gd $889
Same as Model 780 Field but in 20, 28, or 36 gauge. Double triggers, ejectors. Disc. 1998.

MODEL 782 EM FIELD . . . NiB $1566 Ex $1275 Gd $1074
Gauge: 12 or 16. Boxlock action with sideplates, single selective trigger, ejectors and extractors, walnut stock and forearm. Disc. 1998.
Model 782 EM Slug, add $550
Model 782 EML, add $450

MODEL S782 EMEL . NiB $14,990 Ex $11,860 Gd $10,066
Same as Model 782 EM Field but specially engraved and hand finished.

**MODEL S782 EMEL
DELUXE** . . . . NiB $13,899 Ex $11,776 Gd $10,066
Gauge: 10, 12, 16, 20, 28, 36 and .410. Barrel:28-inch ventilated rib with choke tubes (except .410); coin-finish engraving; gold inlaids; fine scroll borders; Deluxe English walnut stock. Imported 1994.

**MODEL 790
COMPETITION** . . . . NiB $1877 Ex $1687 Gd $1261
Gauge: 12 or 20. Available in trap, skeet or sporting clays models. Black frame outlined with gold line engraving. Disc. 1999.
20 ga. Sporting (sideplates and QD stock), add $1200
Trap model, 20 gauge, subtract $200

**MODEL 790 SMALL
GAUGE** . . . . NiB $1499 Ex $1179 Gd $1088
Similar to Model 790 Competition but in 20, 29, or 36 guages. Single selective trigger, ejectors. Disc. 2000.

MODEL 790 EL . . . . NiB $7088 Ex $4977 Gd $3766
Same as Model 790 but hand finished with 18k gold inlays, hand engraving.

**MODEL S790 EMEL
DELUXE** . . . . NiB $12,970 Ex $10,088 Gd $8990
Guages: All. Custom gun with 27.5-inch ventilated-rib bbls. choke tubes (except .410); color case-hardened or coin-finished receiver; ornate engraving with Rizzini crest. Stock is deluxe English walnut; leather case included.

**MODEL 792 SMALL GAUGE
MAGNUM**   NiB $1791 Ex $1476 Gd $1199
Gauge: 20, 28, or 36. Magnum chambers. Single selective trigger; ejectors; engraved sideplates. Disc. 1998.

**MODEL 792 EMEL
DELUXE** . . . . NiB $9133 Ex $8093 Gd $6166
Same as Model 793 but hand finished with 18k gold inlays and hand engraving.

Rossi Hammerless Double-Barrel Shotgun

Rossi Overland Hammer Double

Rottweil American Skeet

MODEL S792 EMEL.... NiB $14,000 Ex $11,980 Gd $10,760
Guages: All. Custom gun with 27.5-inch ventilated-rib bbls. choke tubes (except .410); coin-finished receiver; sideplates with fine game scene engraving and scroll borders; deluxe English walnut stock; leather case included. Imported 1994.

MODEL 2000 TRAP ......NiB $1798 Ex $1448 Gd $1190
Guage: 12 only. Nickel-finished receiver; sideplates; gold trigger; ventilated-rib bbls.. Disc 1998.

MODEL 2000
TRAP EL ....NiB $5477 Ex $4100 Gd $3110
Same as Model 2000 Trap but hand finished with 18k gold inlays and ornate hand engraving.

MODEL 2000-SP ....NiB $3210 Ex $2976 Gd $2241
Guage: 12 only. Bbls.: 26, 29.5, or 32 inches. Over-bored barrels with choke tubes. Engraved sideplates, semi-fancy select QD stock. Case included. Imported 1994 to 1998.

PREMIER SPORTING .....NiB $2669 Ex $2280 Gd $1881
Guages: 12 or 20. Bbls.: 28, 29.5 or 32 inches five chokes per bbl.. Custom built on request. Imported 1994

SPORTING EL ....NiB $3126 Ex $2390 Gd $2177
Same as Premier model but includes multiple chokes and fitted case. Disc. 2000.

**UPLAND EL .... NiB $2793 Ex $2277
Gd $1965**
Guages: All. Custom gun with 27.5-inch ventilated-rib bbls. choke tubes (except .410); case-hardened receiver; deluxe walnut stock. Hard case included. Imported 1994.

ROSSI — Sao Leopoldo, Brazil

SQUIRE HAMMERLESS DOUBLE-
BARREL SHOTGUN ....NiB $435 Ex $333 Gd $245
Boxlock. Plain extractors. Double triggers. 12 and 20 ga., .410. Three-inch chambers. Bbls.: 20-, 26-inch IC/M; 28-inch M/F

choke. Weight: 7 to 7.5 lbs. Pistol-grip hardwood stock and beavertail forearm, uncheckered. Made 1985 to 1990.

OVERLUND
HAMMER DOUBLE ....NiB $380 Ex $244 Gd $179
Sidelock. Plain extractors. Double triggers. Gauges: 12, .410; 3-inch chambers. Bbls.: 20-inch, IC/M in 12 g.; 26-inch, F/F choke in .410. Weight: 7 lbs. (12 ga.); 6 lbs. (.410). Pistol-grip stock and beavertail forearm, uncheckered. Note: Because of its resemblance to the short-barreled doubles carried by guards riding shotgun on 19th-century stagecoaches, the 12 ga. version originally was called the "Coach Gun." Made 1968 to 1989.

ROTTWEIL SHOTGUNS — Germany

MODEL 72 O/U SHOTGUN... NiB $1988 Ex $1687 Gd $1277
Hammerless, takedown with engraved receiver. 12 ga.; 2.75-inch chambers. 26.75-inch bbls. with SK/SK chokes. Weight: 7.5 lbs. Interchangeable trigger groups and buttstocks. Checkered French walnut buttstock and forend. Imported from Germany.

MODEL 650 FIELD
O/U SHOTGUN ....NiB $888 Ex $675 Gd $544
Breech action. Gauge: 12. 28-inch bbls. Six screw-in choke tubes. Automatic ejectors. Engraved receiver. Checkered pistol grip stock. Made from 1984 to 1986.

AMERICAN SKEET.......NiB $2010 Ex $1798 Gd $1288
Boxlock action. Gauge: 12. 27-inch vent-rib bbls. 44.5 inches overall. SK chokes. Weight: 7.5 lbs. Designed for tube sets. Hand-checkered European walnut stock with modified forend. Made from 1984 to 1987.

INTERNATIONAL
TRAP SHOTGUN ....NiB $2066 Ex $1799 Gd $1263
Box lock action. Gauge: 12. 30-inch bbls. 48.5 inches overall. Weight: 8 lbs. Choked IM/F. Selective single trigger. Metal bead front sight. Checkered European walnut stock w/pistol grip. Engraved action. Made from 1984 to 1987.

SHOTGUNS

Ruger Red Label — 20 Gauge (1982)

Ruger Red Label Over and Under (Stainless)

RUGER — Southport, Connecticut

RED LABEL STANDARD GRADE
O/U boxlock. Auto ejectors. Selective single trigger. 12, 20 or 28 ga. w/2.75- or 3-inch chambers. 26-inch vent-rib bbl., IC/M or SK choke. Single selective trigger. Selective automatic ejectors. Automatic top safety. Standard gold bead front sight. Pistol-grip or English-style American walnut stock and forearm w/hand-cut checkering. The 20 ga. Model was introduced in 1977; 12 ga. version in 1982 and the stainless receiver became standard in 1985. Choke tubes were optional in 1988 and standard in 1990. Weight: 7.0 to 7.5 lbs.

Fixed chokes	NiB $1733	Ex $1388	Gd $1077
Screw-in tube	NiB $1760	Ex $1410	Gd $1100
Grade 1 engraving	NiB $1893	Ex $1421	Gd $1107
Grade 2 engraving	NiB $2298	Ex $2100	Gd $1733
Grade 3 engraving	NiB $2798	Ex $2255	Gd $2100

RED LABEL O/U ALL-WEATHER STAINLESS
Gauges: 12 ga. Only. Bbls.: 26- 28- or 30-inch w/various chokes, fixed or screw-in tubes. Stainless receiver and barrel. Checkered black synthetic stock and forearm. Weight: 7.5 lbs. Made 1999 to 2006.

All-weather stainless model	NiB $1387	Ex $1189	Gd $900
w/30-inch bbl., add			$200

RED LABEL WOODSIDE
Similar to the Red Label O/U Stainless except in 12 ga. only with wood sideplate extensions. Made from 1995 to 2002. Disc.

Standard	NiB $1687	Ex $1445	Gd $1110
Engraved	NiB $2389	Ex $1955	Gd $1533

RED LABEL SPORTING CLAYS
Similar to the standard Red Label model except chambered 12 or 20 ga. only w/30-inch vent-rib bbls., no side ribs; backbored w/screw-in choke tubes (not interchangeable w/other Red Label O/U models). Brass front and mid-rib beads. Made from 1992 to 2011.

Standard	NiB $1766	Ex $1288	Gd $998
Engraved	NiB $2680	Ex $2110	Gd $1590

RED LABEL "WILDLIFE FOREVER" SPECIAL EDITION
Limited edition commemorating the 50th Wildlife Forever anniversary. Similar to the standard Red Label model except chambered 12 ga. only w/engraved receiver enhanced w/gold mallard and pheasant inlays. 300 produced in 1993.

Special edition	NiB $1690	Ex $1655	Gd $1299
Special edition w/hard case, add			$200

GOLD LABEL
GOLD LABEL	NiB $3650 EX $2288 GD $1060

S/S boxlock. Auto ejectors. Selective single trigger. 12 ga. w/ 3-inch chambers. 28-inch solid-rib bbl., choke tubes. Top safety. Pistol-grip or English-style American walnut stock and forearm w/hand-cut checkering. Stainless receiver. Made from 2002 to 2008.

SAIGA — Mfg. by Izhmash in Izhevsk, Russia; last imported by RWC Group in Tullytown, PA

SAIGA-12
AK-style action, gas-operated piston, semi-auto w/ detachable 5-rnd. magazine. 12 or 20 ga. w/ 3-in. chamber. Bbl.: 19- or 22-in. w/ choke tubes (12 ga. only). Stock: black synthetic. Finish: matte black. Weight: 6.7 to 10 lbs. Imported 2002 to 2004, reintroduced 2006 to 2014. Importation banned since 2014 dues US sanctions.

12 or 20 ga.	NiB $780	Ex $500	Gd $300
.410	NiB $646	Ex $415	Gd $250
Hunting Model (monte carlo style stock in wood or synthetic)	NiB $885	Ex $580	Gd $360
Skeletonized Stock	NiB $994	Ex $660	Gd $400
Tactical (AR15 style stock, 10-rnd. magazine)	NiB $1239	Ex $1115	Gd $734

VICTOR SARASQUETA, S.A. — Eibar, Spain

MODEL 3 HAMMERLESS
BOXLOCK DOUBLE-BARREL SHOTGUN
Plain extractors or auto ejectors. Double triggers. Gauges: 12, 16, 20. Made in various bbl. lengths, chokes and weights. Checkered stock and forend, straight grip standard. Imported from 1985-87.

Model 3, plain extractors	NiB $599	Ex $445	Gd $329
Model 3E, automatic ejectors	NiB $655	Ex $500	Gd $435

HAMMERLESS SIDELOCK DOUBLES
Automatic ejectors (except on Models 4 and 203 which have plain extractors). Double triggers. Gauges: 12, 16, 20. Barrel lengths, chokes and weights made to order. Checkered stock and forend, straight grip standard. Models differ chiefly in overall quality, engraving, grade of wood, checkering, etc.; general specifications are the same. Imported from 1985 to 1987.

Model 4	NiB $779	Ex $643	Gd $441
Model 4E	NiB $879	Ex $754	Gd $570
Model 203	NiB $744	Ex $600	Gd $435

Sarasqueta Model 3 Hammerless Boxlock

Sauer Model 66 Field Grade II

Sauer Model 66 Field Grade III

Sarasqueta Models 6E, 11E and 12E

Model 203E	NiB $800	Ex $632	Gd $544
Model 6E	NiB $1388	Ex $1108	Gd $700
Model 7E	NiB $1443	Ex $1156	Gd $965
Model 10E	NiB $2588	Ex $2188	Gd $1966
Model 11E	NiB $2800	Ex $2577	Gd $2234
Model 12E	NiB $3110	Ex $2770	Gd $2369

J. P. SAUER & SOHN — Eckernförde, Germany; formerly Suhl, Germany

MODEL 66 O/U FIELD GUN

Purdey-system action with Holland & Holland-type sidelocks. Selective single trigger. Selective auto ejectors. Automatic safety. Available in three grades of engraving. 12 ga. only. Krupp special steel bbls. w/vent rib 28-inch, M/F choke. Weight: About 7.25 lbs. Checkered walnut stock and forend; recoil pad. Made from 1966 to 1975.

Grade I	NiB $2377	Ex $2120	Gd $1798
Grade II	NiB $3256	Ex $2460	Gd $2190
Grade III	NiB $4100	Ex $3712	Gd $2644

MODEL 66 O/U SKEET GUN

Same as Model 66 Field Gun except 26-inch bbls. with wide vent rib, SK choked- skeet-style stock and ventilated beavertail forearm; non-automatic safety. Made from 1966 to 1975.

Grade I	NiB $2312	Ex $2198	Gd $1655
Grade II	NiB $3270	Ex $2980	Gd $2110
Grade III	NiB $3988	Ex $3655	Gd $2980

MODEL 66 O/U TRAP GUN

Same as Model 66 Skeet Gun except has 30-inch bbls. choked F/F or M/F; trap-style stock. Values same as for Skeet model. Made from 1966 to 1975.

MODEL 3000E DRILLING

Combination rifle and double barrel shotgun. Blitz action with Greener crossbolt, double underlugs, separate rifle cartridge extractor, front set trigger, firing pin indicators, Greener side safety, sear slide selector locks right shotgun bbl. for firing rifle bbl. Gauge/calibers12 ga. (2.75-inch chambers); .222, .243,

Sauer Model 3000E Drilling

SHOTGUNS

Sauer BBF 54 Combination Rifle/ Shotgun

Sauer Royal Double-Barrel Shotgun

.30-06, 7x65R. 25-inch Krupp-Special steel bbls.; M/F choke automatic folding leaf rear rifle sight. Weight: 6.5 to 7.25 lbs. depending on rifle caliber. Checkered walnut stock and forend; pistol grip, Monte Carlo comb and cheekpiece, sling swivels. Standard model with Arabesque engraving; Deluxe model with hunting scenes engraved on action. Currently manufactured. Note: Also see listing under Colt.

Standard model . . . . NiB $4490 Ex $3891 Gd $2776
Deluxe model . . . . NiB $5782 Ex $4669 Gd $3533

ARTEMIS DOUBLE-BARREL SHOTGUN
Holland & Holland-type sidelock with Greener crossbolt double underlugs, double sear safeties, selective single trigger, selective auto ejectors. Grade I with fine-line engraving, Grade II with full English Arabesque engraving. 12 ga. (2.75-inch chambers). Krupp special steel bbls., 28-inch, M/F choke. Weight: About 6.5 lbs. Checkered walnut pistol-grip stock and beavertail forend; recoil pad. Made from1966 to 1977.

Grade I . . . . NiB $5698 Ex $4766 Gd $4133
Grade II . . . . NiB $6880 Ex $5744 Gd $4500

BBF 54 O/U COMBINATION RIFLE/SHOTGUN
Blitz action with Kersten lock, front set trigger fires rifle bbl., slide-operated sear safety. Gauge/calibers: 16 ga.; .30-30, .30-06, 7x65R, 25-inch Krupp special steel bbls.; shotgun bbl. F choke, folding-leaf rear sight. Weight: About 6 lbs. Checkered walnut stock and forend; pistol grip, mod. Monte Carlo comb and cheekpiece, sling swivels. Standard model with Arabesque engraving; Deluxe model with hunting scenes engraved on action. Currently manufactured.

Standard model . . . . NiB $2977 Ex $2455 Gd $1766
Deluxe model . . . . NiB $3566 Ex $3088 Gd $2655

ROYAL DOUBLE-BARREL SHOTGUNS
Anson & Deeley action (boxlock) with Greener crossbolt, double underlugs, signal pins, selective single trigger, selective auto ejectors, auto safety. Scalloped frame with Arabesque engraving. Krupp special steel bbls. Gauges: 12, 2.75-inch chambers, 20, 3-inch chambers. Bbls.: 30-inch (12 ga. only) and 28-inch, M/F- 26-inch (20 ga. only), IC/M. Weight: 12 ga., about 6.5 lbs.; 20 ga., 6 lbs. Checkered walnut pistol-grip stock and beavertail forend; recoil pad. Made from 1955 to 1977.

Standard model . . . . NiB $1790 Ex $1533 Gd $1206
20 ga. add 20%

SAVAGE ARMS — Westfield, Massachusetts.
Formerly located in Utica, New York. Currently owned by ATK.

MODEL 24C .22/.410 O/U
COMBINATION . . . . NiB $570 Ex $388 Gd $245
Same as Stevens No. 22-.410 with walnut stock and forearm. Made from 1950 to 1965.

MODEL 24C
CAMPER'S COMPANION . . . . . NiB $675 Ex $466 Gd $290
Same as Model 24FG except made in .22 Magnum/20 ga. only; has 20-inch bbls., shotgun tube Cyl. bore. Weight: 5.75 lbs. Trap in butt provides ammunition storage; comes with carrying case. Made 1972 to 1989.

MODEL 24 FIELD . . . . NiB $498 Ex $277 Gd $190
Same as Models 24DL and 24MDL except frame has black or casehardened finish. Game scene decoration of frame eliminated in 1974; forearm uncheckered after 1976. Made from 1970 to 1989.

MODEL 24DL . . . . NiB $400 Ex $366 Gd $243
Same general specifications as Model 24S except top-lever opening; satin-chrome-finished frame decorated with game scenes, checkered Monte Carlo stock and forearm. Made from 1962 to 1965.

MODEL 24F-12T TURKEY GUN . . . NiB $700 Ex $488 Gd $337
12- or 20-ga. shotgun bbl./.22 Hornet, .223 or .30-30 caliber rifle. 24-inch blued bbls., 3-inch chambers, extra removable F choke tube. Hammer block safety. Color casehardened frame. DuPont Rynite camo stock. Swivel studs. Made from 1989 to 2007.

MODEL 24FG FIELD GRADE . . . NiB $525 Ex $433 Gd $276
Same general specifications as Model 24S except top lever opening. Made 1972. Disc.

MODEL 24MDL . . . . NiB $577 Ex $400 Gd $229
Same as Model 24DL except rifle bbl. chambered for 22 WMR. Made from 1962 to 1969.

MODEL 24MS . . . . NiB $690 Ex $535 Gd $389
Same as Model 24S except rifle bbl. chambered for 22 WMR. Made from 1964 to 1971.

MODEL 24S O/U
COMBINATION . . . . NiB $477 Ex $339 Gd $225
Boxlock. Visible hammer. Side lever opening. Plain extractors. Single trigger. 20 ga. or .410 bore shotgun bbl. under 22 LR bbl., 24-inch. Open rear sight, ramp front, dovetail for scope mounting. Weight: About 6.75 lbs. Plain pistol-grip stock and forearm. Made from 1964 to 1971.

Savage Model 24
.22-/.410 O/U Combination

Savage Model 24-VS
Camper/Survival/Centerfire Rifle/Shotgun

Savage 24-C

Savage 24-D

Savage Model 24-F -12T

Savage Model 24-V

MODEL 24V . . . . NiB $588 Ex $379 Gd $298
Similar to Model 24D except 20 ga. under .222 Rem., .22 Rem., .357 Mag., .22 Hornet or .30-30 rifle bbl. Made 1967 to 1989.

MODEL 24-CS CAMPER'S COMPANION
CENTERFIRE RIFLE/SHOTGUN . . . NiB $680 Ex $389 Gd $319
Caliber: .22 LR over 20 ga. Nickel finish full-length stock and accessory pistol-grip stock. Overall length: 36 inches with full stock; 26 inches w/pistol grip. Weight: About 5.75 lbs. Made 1972 to 1988.
.357 Mag./20 ga., add $50

MODEL 28A STANDARD GRADE SLIDE-ACTION
REPEATING SHOTGUN . . . . . . NiB $445 Ex $398 Gd $300
Hammerless. Takedown. 12 ga. Five round tubular magazine. Plain bbl., lengths: 26-,28-, 30-, 32-inches, choked C/M/F.

Weight: About 7.5 lbs. with 30-inch bbl. Plain pistol-grip stock, grooved slide handle. Made from 1928 to 1931.

MODEL 28B . . . . NiB $366 Ex $287 Gd $245
Raised matted rib; otherwise the same as Model 28A.

MODEL 28D TRAP GRADE. . . . NiB $366 Ex $287 Gd $245
Same general specifications as Model 28A except has 30-inch F choke bbl. w/matted rib, trap-style stock w/checkered pistol grip, checkered slide handle of select walnut.

MODEL 30 SOLID FRAME HAMMERLESS
SLIDE-ACTION SHOTGUN . . . NiB $290 Ex $221 Gd $175
Gauges: 12, 16, 20, .410. 2.75-inch chamber in 16 ga., 3- inch in other ga. Magazine holds four 2.75-inch shells or three 3-inch shells. Bbls.: Vent rib; 26-, 28-, 30-inch; IC, M, F choke. Weight: Average 6.25 to 6.75 lbs. depending on ga. Plain pistol-grip stock (checkered on later production), grooved slide handle. Made from 1958 to 1970.

Savage Model 30

Savage Model 30 Slug Gun

Savage Model 30-FG

Savage Model 69-RXL

Savage Model 220

Savage Model 242

**MODEL 30 TAKEDOWN
SLUG GUN**................**NiB $255 Ex $175 Gd $125**
Same as Model 30FG except 21-inch cyl. bore bbl. with rifle
sights. Made from 1971 to 1979.

MODEL 30AC SOLID FRAME..**NiB $379 Ex $288 Gd $179**
Same as Model 30 Solid Frame except has 26-inch bbl. with
adj. choke; 12 ga. only. Made from 1959 to 1970.

MODEL 30AC TAKEDOWN...**NiB $366 Ex $265 Gd $160**
Same as Model 30FG except has 26-inch bbl. with adj. choke;
12 and 20 ga. only. Made from 1971 to 1972.

MODEL 30D TAKEDOWN....**NiB $277 Ex $200 Gd $167**
Deluxe Grade. Same as Model 30FG except has receiver
engraved with game scene, vent rib bbl., recoil pad. Made
from 1971. Disc.

**MODEL 30FG TAKEDOWN HAMMERLESS
SLIDE-ACTION SHOTGUN**....**NiB $265 Ex $180 Gd $95**
Field Grade. Gauges: 12, 20, .410. Three-inch chamber.
Magazine holds four 2.75-inch shells or three 3-inch shells.
Bbls.: plain; 26-inch F choke (.410 ga. only); 28-inch M/F
choke; 30-inch F choke (12 ga. only). Weight: Average 7 to
7.75 lbs. depending on gauge. Checkered pistol-grip stock,
fluted slide handle. Made 1970 to 1979.

MODEL 30L SOLID FRAME...**NiB $300 Ex $241 Gd $176**
Same as Model 30 Solid Frame except left-handed model with ejection port and safety on left side; 12 ga. only. Made 1959 to 1970.

**MODEL 30T SOLID FRAME
TRAP AND DUCK**..........**NiB $377 Ex $288 Gd $190**
Same as Model 30 Solid Frame except only in 12 ga. w/30-inch
F choke bbl.; has Monte Carlo stock with recoil pad, weight:
About 8 lbs. Made from 1963 to 1970.

Savage Model 312
Field Grade O/U

Savage Model 312
Trap O/U

Savage Model 330

MODEL 30T TAKE DOWN

TRAP GUN . . . . **NiB $335 Ex $292 Gd $197**
Same as Model 30D except only in 12 ga. w/30-inch F choke bbl. Monte Carlo stock with recoil pad. Made from 1970 to 1973.

MODEL 69-RXL SLIDE-ACTION

SHOTGUN . . . . **NiB $366 Ex $256 Gd $190**
Similar to Model 67 (law enforcement configuration). Hammerless, side ejection top tang safe for left- or right-hand use. 12 ga. chambered for 2.75- and 3-inch magnum shells. 18.25-inch bbl. Tubular magazine holds 6 rounds (one less for 3-inch mag). Walnut finish hardwood stock with recoil pad and grooved operating handle. Weight: About 6.5 lbs. Made from 1982 to 1989.

MODEL 210F BOLT-ACTION

SLUG GUN. . . . . **NiB $490 Ex $377 Gd $290**
Built on Savage 110 action. Gauge: 12 w/3-inch chamber. Two round detachable magazine. 24-inch fully rifled bbl. Receiver drilled and tapped for scope mounts w/no sights. Weight: 7.5 lbs. Checkered black synthetic stock w/swivel studs and recoil pad. Made from 1997 to 2000.

MODEL 210FT BOLT-ACTION

SHOTGUN . . . . **NiB $599 Ex $459 Gd $335**
Similar to Model 210F except has smoothbore 24-inch bbl. w/ choke tubes. Bead front and U-notch rear sights. Advantage Camo finish. Made from 1997 to 2000.

MODEL 220 SINGLE-BARREL

SHOTGUN . . . . **NiB $590 Ex $386 Gd $265**
Hammerless. Takedown. Auto ejector. Gauges: 12,16, 20 .410. Single shot. Bbl. lengths: 12 ga., 28- to 36-inch, 16 ga., 28- to 32-inch; 20 ga., 26- to 32-inch; .410 bore, 26-and 28-inch. F choke. Weight: about 6 lbs. Plain pistol-grip stock and wide forearm. Made 1938 to 1965.

MODEL 220AC

. . . . **NiB $490 Ex $255 Gd $190**
Same as Model 220 except has Savage adj. choke.

MODEL 220L

. . . . **NiB $490 Ex $388 Gd $229**
Same general specifications as Model 220 except has side lever opening instead of top lever. Made from 1965 to 1972.

MODEL 220P

. . . . **NiB $490 Ex $388 Gd $229**
Same as Model 220 except has PolyChoke bbl., made in 12 ga. with 30-inch bbl., 16 and 20 ga. with 28-inch bbl., no .410 bore; recoil pad.

MODEL 242 O/U SHOTGUN.

. . **NiB $498 Ex $376 Gd $292**
Similar to Model 24D except both bbls. .410 bore, F choke. Weight: About 7 lbs. Made from 1977 to 1980.

MODEL 312 FIELD GRADE

. . . **NiB $688 Ex $554 Gd $400**
Gauge: 12; 2.75- or 3-inch chambers. 26- or 28-inch bbls. w/ vent rib; F/M/IC chokes. 43 or 45 inches overall. Weight: 7 lbs. Internal hammers. Top tang safety. American walnut stock with checkered pistol grip and recoil pad. Made from 1990 to 1993.

MODEL 312 SPORTING

CLAYS O/U. . . . . **NiB $688 Ex $578 Gd $445**
Same as Model 312 Field Grade except furnished with number 1 and number 2 Skeet tubes and 28-inch bbls. only. Made 1990 to 1993.

MODEL 312 TRAP O/U

. . . . . . **NiB $756 Ex $600 Gd $477**
Same as Model 312 Field Grade except with 30-inch bbls. only, Monte Carlo buttstock, weight: 7.5 lbs. Made from 1990 to 1993.

MODEL 330 O/U SHOTGUN.

. **NiB $589 Ex $477 Gd $398**
Boxlock. Plain extractors. Selective single trigger. Gauges: 12, 20. 2.75-inch chambers in 12 ga., 3-inch in 20 gauge. Bbls.: 26-inch IC/M; 28-inch M/F; 30-inch M/F choke (12 ga. only). Weight: 6.25 to 7.25 lbs., depending on gauge. Checkered pistol-grip stock and forearm. Made from 1969 to 1978.

SHOTGUNS

Savage Model 333Y

Savage Model 333
20 Gauge

Savage Model 440

Savage Model 440T

Savage Model 550

Savage Model 750

Savage Model 775

Savage Model 775-SC

Savage Model 2400
O/U Combination Gun

MODEL 333 O/U SHOTGUN
Boxlock. Auto ejectors. Selective single trigger. Gauges: 12, 20. 2.75-inch chambers in 12 ga., 3-inch in 20 ga. Bbls.: vent rib; 26-inch SK choke, IC/M; 28-inch M/F; 30-inch M/F choke (12 ga. only). Weight: Average 6.25 to 7.25 lbs. Checkered pistol-grip stock and forearm. Made from 1973 to 1979.
Model 333 12 ga. . . . . **NiB $598 Ex $467 Gd $366**
Model 333 20 ga., add **30%**

MODEL 333T TRAP GUN . . . . . **NiB $654 Ex $498 Gd $396**
Similar to Model 330 except only in 12 ga. with 30-inch vent-rib bbls., IM/F choke; Monte Carlo stock w/recoil pad. Weight: 7.75 lbs. Made from 1972 to 1979.

MODEL 420 O/U SHOTGUN
Boxlock. Hammerless. Takedown. Automatic safety. Double triggers or non-selective single trigger. Gauges: 12, 16, 20. Bbls.: Plain, 26- to 30-inch (the latter in 12 ga. only); choked M/F, C/IC. Weight with 28-inch bbls.: 12 ga., 7.75 lbs.; 16 ga., 7.5 lbs.; 20 ga., 6.75 lbs. Plain pistol-grip stock and forearm. Made from 1938 to 1942.
With double triggers . . . . **NiB $589 Ex $477 Gd $300**
With single trigger . . . . **NiB $633 Ex $498 Gd $376**

MODEL 430
Same as Model 420 except has matted top bbl., checkered stock of select walnut with recoil pad, checkered forearm. Made from 1938 to 1942.
With double triggers . . . . **NiB $677 Ex $544 Gd $390**
With single trigger . . . . **NiB $677 Ex $559 Gd $443**

MODEL 440 O/U SHOTGUN . . **NiB $635 Ex $490 Gd $387**
Boxlock. Plain extractors. Selective single trigger. Gauges: 12, 20. 2.75-inch chambers in 12 ga., 3-inch in 20 ga. Bbls.: Vent rib; 26-inch SK choke, IC/M; 28-inch M/F; 30-inch M/F choke (12 ga. only). Weight: Average 6 to 6.5 lbs. depending on ga. Made from 1968 to 1972.

MODEL 440T TRAP GUN . . . . . **NiB $598 Ex $488 Gd $392**
Similar to Model 440 except only in 12 ga. with 30-inch bbls., extra-wide vent rib, IM/F choke. Trap-style Monte Carlo stock and semibeavertail forearm of select walnut, recoil pad. Weight: 7.5 lbs. Made from 1969 to 1972.

MODEL 444 DELUXE
O/U SHOTGUN . . . . **NiB $687 Ex $500 Gd $369**
Similar to Model 440 except has auto ejectors, select walnut stock and semi-beavertail forearm. Made from 1969 to 1972.

MODEL 550
HAMMERLESS DOUBLE . . . . . **NiB $355 Ex $290 Gd $200**
Boxlock. Auto ejectors. Non-selective single trigger. Gauges: 12, 20. 2.75-inch chamber in 12 ga., 3-inch in 20 ga. Bbls.: Vent rib; 26-inch IC/M; 28-inch M/F; 30-inch M/F choke (12 ga. only). Weight: 7 to 8 lbs. Checkered pistol-grip stock and semi-beavertail forearm. Made 1971 to 1973.

MODEL 720 STANDARD GRADE 5 SHOT AUTOLOADING
SHOTGUN . . . . **NiB $335 Ex $269 Gd $200**
Browning type. Takedown. 12 and 16 ga. Four round tubular magazine. Bbl.: plain; 26- to 32-inch (the latter in 12 ga. only); choked IC, M, F. Weight: About 8.25 lbs., 12 ga. with 30-inch bbl.; 16 ga., about .5 lb. lighter. Checkered pistol-grip stock and forearm. Made from 1930 to 1949.

MODEL 726 UPLAND SPORTER AUTO
SHOTGUN . . . . **NiB $377 Ex $292 Gd $233**
Same as Model 720 except has 2-round magazine capacity. Made from 1931 to 1949.

MODEL 740C SKEET GUN . . . . **NiB $410 Ex $300 Gd $237**
Same as Model 726 except has special skeet stock and full beavertail forearm, equipped with Cutts Compensator. Bbl. length overall with spreader tube is about 24.5 inches. Made from 1936 to 1949.

MODEL 745 LIGHTWEIGHT
AUTOLOADER . . . . **NiB $377 Ex $266 Gd $198**
Three- or five-round models. Same general specifications as Model 720 except has lightweight alloy receiver, 12 ga. only, 28-inch plain bbl. Weight: About 6.75 lbs. Made from 1940 to 1949.

MODEL 750 AUTO SHOTGUN . . . **NiB $355 Ex $287 Gd $239**
Browning-type autoloader. Takedown. 12 ga. Four round tubular magazine. Bbls.: 28-inch F or M choke; 26-inch IC. Weight: About 7.25 lbs. Checkered walnut pistol-grip stock and grooved forearm. Made from 1960 to 1967.

MODEL 750-AC . . . . **NiB $377 Ex $280 Gd $210**
Same as Model 750 except has 26-inch bbl. with adj. choke. Made from 1964 to 1967.

MODEL 750-SC . . . . **NiB $368 Ex $267 Gd $198**
Same as Model 750 except has 26-inch bbl. with Savage Super Choke. Made from 1962 to 1963.

MODEL 755 STANDARD
GRADE AUTOLOADER . . . . **NiB $389 Ex $297 Gd $245**
Streamlined receiver. Takedown.12 and 16 ga. Four round tubular magazine (a three-round model with magazine capacity of two rounds was also produced until 1951). Bbl.: Plain, 30-inch F choke (12 ga. only), 28-inch F or M, 26-inch IC. Weight: About 8.25 lbs., 12 ga. Checkered pistol-grip stock and forearm. Made from 1949 to 1958.

MODEL 755-SC . . . . **NiB $389 Ex $297 Gd $245**
Same as Model 755 except has 26-inch bbl. w/recoil-reducing, adj. Savage Super Choke.

MODEL 775 LIGHTWEIGHT . . **NiB $389 Ex $297 Gd $245**
Same general specifications as Model 755 except has lightweight alloy receiver, weight: About 6.73 lbs. Made from 1950 to 1965.

MODEL 775-SC . . . . **NiB $410 Ex $300 Gd $255**
Same as Model 775 except has 26-inch bbl. with Savage Super Choke.

MODEL 2400 O/U COMBINATION . . . **NiB $775 Ex $577 Gd $450**
Boxlock action similar to that of Model 330. Plain extractors. Selective single trigger. 12-ga. (2.75-inch chamber) shotgun bbl., F choke over .308 Win. or .222 Rem. rifle bbl.; 23.5-inch; solid matted rib with blade front sight and folding leaf rear, dovetail for scope mounting. Weight: About 7.5 lbs. Monte Carlo stock w/pistol grip and recoil pad, semibeavertail forearm, checkered. Made 1975 to 1979 by Valmet.

SEARS, ROEBUCK & COMPANY — Chicago, Illinois (J. C. Higgins and Ted Williams Models)

Although they do not correspond to specific models below, the names Ted Williams and J. C. Higgins have been used to designate various Sears shotguns at various times.

MODEL 18
BOLT-ACTION REPEATER . . . . . . NiB $200 Ex $125 Gd $90
Takedown. Three round top-loading magazine. Gauge: .410 only. Bbl.: 25-inch w/variable choke. Weight: About 5.75 lbs.

MODEL 20 SLIDE-ACTION
REPEATER . . . . NiB $300 Ex $210 Gd $155
Hammerless. Five round magazine. Bbls.: 26- to 30-inch w/ various chokes. Weight: 7.25 lbs. Plain pistol-grip stock and slide handle.

MODEL 21 SLIDE-ACTION
REPEATER . . . . NiB $320 Ex $235 Gd $190
Same general specifications as the Model 20 except vent rib and adustable choke.

MODEL 30 SLIDE-ACTION
REPEATER . . . . NiB $305 Ex $220 Gd $175
Hammerless. Gauges: 12, 16, 20 and .410. Four round magazine. Bbls.: 26- to 30-inch, various chokes. Weight: 6.5 lbs. Plain pistol-grip stock, grooved slide handle.

MODEL 97 SINGLE-SHOT
SHOTGUN . . . . NiB $165 Ex $100 Gd $79
Takedown. Visible hammer. Automatic ejector. Gauges: 12, 16, 20 and .410. Bbls.: 26- to 36-inch, F choke. Weight: Average 6 lbs. Plain pistol-grip stock and forearm.

MODEL 97-AC SINGLE-SHOT
SHOTGUN . . . . NiB $190 Ex $121 Gd $89
Same general specifications as Model 97 except fancier stock and forearm.

MODEL 101.7 DOUBLE-BARREL
SHOTGUN . . . . NiB $335 Ex $229 Gd $175
Boxlock. Double triggers. Gauges: 12, 16, 20, .410. Bbls.: 26- to 32-inch, choked M and F. Weight: From 6 to 7.5 lbs. Plain stock and forend.

MODEL 101.7C DOUBLE-BARREL
SHOTGUN . . . . NiB $345 Ex $239 Gd $185
Same general specifications as Model 101.7 except checkered stock and forearm.

MODEL 101.25 BOLT-ACTION
SHOTGUN . . . . NiB $220 Ex $125 Gd $90
Takedown. .410 gauge. Five round tubular magazine. 24-inch bbl., F choke. Weight: About 6 lbs. Plain, one-piece pistol-grip stock.

MODEL 101.40 SINGLE-SHOT
SHOTGUN . . . . NiB $175 Ex $105 Gd $80
Takedown. Visible hammer. Automatic ejector. Gauges: 12, 16, 20 and .410. Bbls.: 26- to 36-inch, F choke. Weight: Average 6 lbs. Plain pistol-grip stock and forearm.

MODEL 101.1120 BOLT-ACTION
REPEATER . . . . NiB $170 Ex $119 Gd $88

Takedown. .410 ga. 24-inch bbl., F choke. Weight: About 5 lbs. Plain one-piece pistol-grip stock.

MODEL 101.1380
BOLT-ACTION REPEATER . . . . . . NiB $195 Ex $130 Gd $95
Takedown. Gauges: 12, 16, 20. Two round detachable box magazine. 26-inch bbl., F choke. Weight: About 7 lbs. Plain one-piece pistol-grip stock.

MODEL 101.1610 DOUBLE-BARREL
SHOTGUN . . . . NiB $495 Ex $322 Gd $275
Boxlock. Double triggers. Plain extractors. Gauges: 12, 16, 20 and .410. Bbls.: 24- to 30-inch. Various chokes, but mostly M and F. Weight: About 7.5 lbs, 12 ga. Checkered pistol-grip stock and forearm.

MODEL 101.1701 DOUBLE-BARREL
SHOTGUN . . . . NiB $420 Ex $335 Gd $240
Same general specifications as Model 101.1610 except satin chrome frame and select walnut stock and forearm.

MODEL 101.5350-D
BOLT-ACTION REPEATER . . . . . . NiB $229 Ex $120 Gd $89
Takedown. Gauges: 12, 16, 20. Two round detachable box magazine. 26-inch bbl., F choke. Weight: About 7.25 lbs. Plain one piece pistol-grip stock.

MODEL 101.5410
BOLT-ACTION REPEATER . . . . . . NiB $200 Ex $115 Gd $90
Same general specifications as Model 101.5350-D.

SKB ARMS COMPANY — Tokyo, Japan
Imported by G.U. Inc., Omaha, Nebraska

MODEL 385 SIDE-BY-SIDE . . . NiB $2200 Ex $1790 Gd $1176
Boxlock action w/double locking lugs. Gauges: 12, 20 and 28 w/2.75- and 3-inch chambers. 26- or 28-inch bbls. w/ Inter-Choke tube system. Single selective trigger. Selective automatic ejectors and automatic safety. Weight: 6 lbs., 10 oz. Silver nitride receiver w/engraved scroll and game scene. Solid rib w/flat matte finish and metal front bead sight. Checkered American walnut English or pistol-grip stock. Imported from 1992.

MODELS 300 AND 400 SIDE-BY-SIDE SHOTGUNS
Similar to Model 200E except higher grade. Models 300 and 400 differ in that the latter has more elaborate engraving and fancier wood.
Model 300 . . . . NiB $1077 Ex $900 Gd $635
Model 400 . . . . NiB $1566 Ex $1309 Gd $1187

MODEL 400 SKEET . . . . NiB $1566 Ex $1309 Gd $1187
Similar to Model 200E Skeet except higher grade with more elaborate engraving and full fancy wood.

MODEL 480 ENGLISH . . . . NiB $1766 Ex $1510 Gd $1377
Similar to Model 280 English except higher grade with more elaborate engraving and full fancy wood.

MODEL 500 SERIES O/U SHOTGUN
Boxlock. Gauges: 12 and 20 w/2.75-or 3-inch chambers. Bbls.: 26-, 28- or 30-inch with vent rib; fixed chokes. Weight: 7.5 to 8.5 lbs. Single selective trigger. Selective automatic ejectors. Manual safety. Checkered walnut stock. Blue finish with scroll engraving. Imported 1967 to 1980.
500 Field, 12 ga. . . . . NiB $1000 Ex $750 Gd $415

SKB Model 585 Field

SKB Model 605 Trap

SKB Model 885 Trap

500 Field, 20 ga, add. 20%
500 Magnum, 12 ga, add. 25%

MODEL 500 SMALL

GAUGE O/U SHOTGUN . . . . . NiB $884 Ex $652 Gd $466
Similar to Model 500 except gauges 28 and .410; has 28-inch vent-rib bbls., M/F chokes. Weight: About 6.5 lbs.

MODEL 505 O/U SHOTGUN

Blued boxlock action. Gauge: 12, 20, 28 and .410. Bbls.: 26-, 28, 30-inch; IC/M, M/F or inner choke tubes. 45.19 inches overall. Weight: 6.6 to 7.4 lbs. Hand checkered walnut stock. Metal bead front sight, ejectors, single selective trigger and ejectors. Introduced 1988.
Standard Field, Skeet or
  Trap grade. . . . . NiB $1365 Ex $1188 Gd $765
Standard Two-bbl. Field set . . . NiB $1590 Ex $1277 Gd $1006
Skeet grade, three-bbl. set . . . NiB $1904 Ex $1888 Gd $1301
Sporting Clays . . . . NiB $1189 Ex $977 Gd $668
Trap grade two-bbl. set . . . . . . NiB $965 Ex $800 Gd $652

MODEL 585 O/U SHOTGUN

Boxlock. Gauges: 12, 20, 28 and .410; 2.75-or 3-inch chambers. Bbls.: 26-, 28-, 30-, 32- or 34-inch with vent rib; fixed chokes or Inter-choke tubes. Weight: 6.5 to 8.5 lbs. Single selective trigger. Selective automatic ejectors. Manual safety. Checkered walnut stock in standard or Monte Carlo style. Silver nitride finish with engraved game scenes. Made from 1992 to 2008.
Field, Skeet, Trap grades . . . NiB $1477 Ex $1211 Gd $933
Field grade, two-bbl. set . . NiB $2376 Ex $1969 Gd $1387
Skeet set (20, 28, .410 ga.) . . . NiB $2933 Ex $2460 Gd $1977
Sporting Clays . . . . NiB $1700 Ex $1390 Gd $1054
Trap Combo (two-bbl. set) NiB $2433 Ex $1976 Gd $1366

MODEL 600 SERIES O/U SHOTGUN

Similar to 500 Series except w/silver nitride receiver. Checkered deluxe walnut stock in both Field and Target Grade configurations . Imported from 1969 to 1980.
600 Field, 12 ga. . . . . NiB $1093 Ex $773 Gd $540
600 Field, 20 ga. . . . . NiB $1100 Ex $977 Gd $650
600 Magnum, 12 ga.
  3-inch chambers . . . . NiB $1100 Ex $977 Gd $650

600 Skeet or Trap grade . . . . NiB $1154 Ex $1008 Gd $690
600 Trap Doubles model . . . . NiB $1154 Ex $1008 Gd $690

MODEL 600 SMALL GAUGE. . . NiB $1210 Ex $945 Gd $650

Same as Model 500 Small Gauge except higher grade with more elaborate engraving and fancier wood.

MODEL 605 SERIES O/U SHOTGUN

Similar to the Model 505 except w/engraved silver nitride receiver and deluxe wood. Introduced 1988.
Field, Skeet, Trap grade . . . . NiB $1233 Ex $1026 Gd $779
Skeet three-bbl. set . . . . . . NiB $2290 Ex $2003 Gd $1544
Sporting Clays . . . . NiB $1266 Ex $1033 Gd $780

MODEL 680 ENGLISH O/U SHOTGUN

Similar to 600 Series except w/English style select walnut stock and fine scroll engraving. Imported from 1973 to 1977.
680 English, 12 ga. . . . . NiB $1477 Ex $1179 Gd $993
680 English, 20 ga. . . . . NiB $1788 Ex $1165 Gd $1055

MODEL 685 DELUXE O/U

Similar to the 585 Deluxe except with semi-fancy American walnut stock. Gold trigger and jeweled barrel block. Silvered receiver with fine engraving.
Field, Skeet, Trap grade . . . NiB $1477 Ex $1319 Gd $1066
Field grade, two-bbl. set . . NiB $1977 Ex $1819 Gd $1566
Skeet set . . . . NiB $1977 Ex $1819 Gd $1566
Sporting Clays . . . . NiB $1477 Ex $1319 Gd $1066
Trap Combo, two-bbl. set. NiB $2189 Ex $1844 Gd $1360

MODEL 800 SKEET/TRAP O/U

Similar to Model 700 Skeet and Trap except higher grade with more elaborate engraving and fancier wood.
Skeet model . . . . NiB $1329 Ex $1166 Gd $973
Trap model . . . . NiB $1266 Ex $1090 Gd $945

MODEL 880 SKEET/TRAP

Similar to Model 800 Skeet except has sideplates.
Skeet model . . . . NiB $1688 Ex $1470 Gd $1137
Trap model . . . . NiB $1859 Ex $1466 Gd $1123

SHOTGUNS

Sile Field Master II

MODEL 885 DELUXE O/U
Similar to the 685 Deluxe except with engraved sideplates.
Field, Skeet, Trap grade ...NiB $1779 Ex $1456 Gd $1160
Field grade, two-bbl. set ..NiB $2665 Ex $2167 Gd $1800
Skeet Set...............NiB $1782 Ex $1693 Gd $1366
Sporting Clays..........NiB $1834 Ex $1500 Gd $1220
Trap Combo ....NiB $2591 Ex $2277 Gd $1989

The following SKB shotguns were distributed by Ithaca Gun Co. from 1966-76. For specific data, see corresponding listings under Ithaca.

CENTURY SINGLE-BARREL TRAP GUN
The SKB catalog does not differentiate between Century and Century II; however, specifications of current Century are those of Ithaca-SKB Century II.
Century (505)..............NiB $966 Ex $831 Gd $634
Century II (605).........NiB $1190 Ex $1006 Gd $798

GAS-OPERATED AUTOMATIC SHOTGUNS
Model XL300 with plain barrel ...NiB $365 Ex $247 Gd $180
Model XL300 with vent rib....NiB $400 Ex $365 Gd $217
Model XL900 ....NiB $449 Ex $300 Gd $198
Model XL900 Trap...........NiB $487 Ex $376 Gd $221
Model XL900 Skeet..........NiB $510 Ex $375 Gd $266
Model XL900 Slug...........NiB $488 Ex $370 Gd $259
Model 1300 Upland, Slug.....NiB $598 Ex $455 Gd $290
Model 1900 Field, Trap, Slug ..NiB $588 Ex $443 Gd $376

SKB OVER/UNDER SHOTGUNS
Model 500 Field ....NiB $677 Ex $489 Gd $389
Model 500 Magnum ....NiB $690 Ex $500 Gd $421
Model 600 Field ....NiB $1070 Ex $883 Gd $600
Model 600 Magnum ....NiB $1165 Ex $955 Gd $690
Model 600 Trap ....NiB $1190 Ex $975 Gd $710
Model 600 Doubles ....NiB $1190 Ex $975 Gd $710
Model 600 Skeet—12 or 20 ga.... NiB $1190 Ex $975 Gd $710
Model 600 Skeet—28 or .410NiB $1595 Ex $1266 Gd $1065
Model 600 Skeet Combo ..NiB $2651 Ex $2210 Gd $2085
Model 600 English ....NiB $1190 Ex $975 Gd $710
Model 700 Trap.............NiB $950 Ex $844 Gd $630
Model 700 Doubles ....NiB $877 Ex $600 Gd $490
Model 700 Skeet............NiB $988 Ex $765 Gd $633
Model 700 Skeet Combo ..NiB $2690 Ex $2166 Gd $1650

SKB RECOIL-OPERATED AUTOMATIC SHOTGUNS
Model 300—with plain barrel ...NiB $477 Ex $370 Gd $269
Model 300—with vent rib ....NiB $554 Ex $425 Gd $335
Model 900 ....NiB $559 Ex $400 Gd $298
Model 900 Slug ....NiB $573 Ex $455 Gd $360

SKB SIDE-BY-SIDE DOUBLE-BARREL SHOTGUNS
Model 100 ....NiB $795 Ex $650 Gd $425
Model 150 ....NiB $795 Ex $650 Gd $425
Model 200E...............NiB $1179 Ex $900 Gd $808
Model 200E Skeet ....NiB $1179 Ex $900 Gd $808
Model 280 English ....NiB $1280 Ex $1006 Gd $922

SIG SAUER — (SIG) Schweizerische Industrie-Gesellschaft, Neuhausen, Switzerland
MODEL SA3 O/U SHOTGUN
Monobloc boxlock action. Single selective trigger. Automatic ejectors. Gauges: 12 or 20 w/3- inch chambers. 26-, 28- or 30-inch vent rib bbls. w/choke tubes. Weight: 6.8 to 7.1 lbs. Checkered select walnut stock and forearm. Satin nickel-finished receiver w/game scene and blued bbls. Imported from 1997-98.
Field model ....NiB $1294 Ex $1126 Gd $966
Sporting Clays model .....NiB $1500 Ex $1398 Gd $1225

MODEL SA5 O/U SHOTGUN
Similar to SA3 Model except w/detachable sideplates. Gauges: 12 or 20 w/3- inch chambers. 26.5-, 28- or 30-inch vent rib bbls. w/choke tubes. Imported from 1997 to 1999.
Field model ....NiB $2288 Ex $2055 Gd $1530
Sporting Clays model .....NiB $2455 Ex $2160 Gd $1880

SILE DISTRIBUTORS — New York, New York

FIELD MASTER II O/U
SHOTGUN ....NiB $735 Ex $615 Gd $479
Gauge: 12, 3-inch chambers. 28-inch bbl., IC, M, IM, F choke tubes. 45.25 inches overall. Weight: 7.25 lbs. Satin-finished walnut, checkered stock and forend. Introduced 1989.

L.C. SMITH — Made 1890–1945 by Hunter Arms Company, Fulton, New York 1946–51 and 1968–73 and 2004 by Marlin Firearms Company, New Haven, Connecticut

L. C. SMITH DOUBLE-BARREL SHOTGUNS
Values shown are for L. C. Smith doubles made by Hunter. Those of 1946-51 Marlin manufacture generally bring prices about 1/3 lower. Smaller gauge models, especially in the higher grades, command premium prices: Up to 50 percent more for 20 gauge, up to 400 percent for .410.

Crown grade, double triggers,
  automatic ejectors ... NiB $11,650 Ex $9000 Gd $7750
Crown grade, selective single trigger,
  automatic ejectors ..NiB $12,275 Ex $10,200 Gd $9976
Deluxe grade, selective single trigger,
  automatic ejectors NiB $80,000 Ex $65,000 Gd $44,000
Eagle grade, double triggers,
  automatic ejectors .....NiB $7450 Ex $6600 Gd $3540
Eagle grade, selective
  single trigger.........NiB $8433 Ex $7210 Gd $4450
Field grade, double trigger
  plain extractors ....NiB $1877 Ex $1659 Gd $1200

L.C. Smith Crown

L.C. Smith Field

L.C. Smith 1968 Field Grade

L.C. Smith 1968 Deluxe

L.C. Smith Single-Shot Trap Gun

Field grade, double triggers
    auto. ej. . . . . .NiB $2400 Ex $2175 Gd $1765
Field grade, non-selective single trigger,
    plain extractors . . . . . . .NiB $1788 Ex $1489 Gd $1016
Field grade, selective single trigger,
    automatic ejectors. . . . .NiB $2276 Ex $1998 Gd $1688
Ideal grade, double triggers,
    plain extractors . . . . . . .NiB $2698 Ex $2100 Gd $1933
Ideal grade, double triggers,
    auto. ej. . . . . .NiB $3355 Ex $2288 Gd $1987
Ideal grade, selective single trigger,
    automatic ejectors . . . . .NiB $2979 Ex $2466 Gd $2132
Monogram grade, selective single trigger,
    automatic ejectors NiB $17,800 Ex $15,888 Gd $11,880
Olympic grade, selective single trigger,
    automatic ejectors . . . .NiB $7225 Ex $5179 Gd $3889
Premier grade, selective single trigger
    automatic ejectors NiB $42,975 Ex $33,670 Gd $25,000
Skeet Special, non-selective single trigger,
    automatic ejectors . . . .NiB $4055 Ex $3329 Gd $2165
Skeet Special, selective single trigger,
    auto ejectors. . . . . .NiB $4070 Ex $3360 Gd $2185
.410 ga. . . . . .NiB $14,887 Ex $11,965 Gd $9865
Specialty grade, double triggers,
    auto ejectors . . . . .NiB $4177 Ex $3688 Gd $3245
Specialty grade, selective single trigger,
    automatic ejectors . . . . .NiB $3866 Ex $3390 Gd $2788
Trap grade, sel. single trigger,
    auto ej. . . . . .NiB $3687 Ex $3255 Gd $2877

L. C. SMITH HAMMERLESS DOUBLE-BARREL SHOTGUNS

Sidelock. Auto ejectors standard on higher grades, extra on Field and Ideal Grades. Double triggers or Hunter single trigger (non-selective or selective). Gauges: 12, 16, 20, .410. Bbls.: 26- to 32-inch, any standard boring. Weight: 6.5 to 8.25 lbs., 12 ga. Checkered stock and forend; choice of straight, half or full pistol grip, beavertail or standard-type forend. Grades differ only in quality of workmanship, wood, checkering, engraving, etc. Same general specifications apply to all. Manufacture of these L. C. Smith guns was discontinued in 1951. Production of Field Grade 12 ga. was resumed 1968-73. Note: L. C. Smith Shotguns manufactured by the Hunter Arms Co. 1890-13 were designated by numerals to indicate grade with the exception of Pigeon and Monogram.

00 grade . . . . .NiB $1577 Ex $1369 Gd $1100
0 grade . . . . .NiB $1735 Ex $1575 Gd $1244
1 grade . . . . .NiB $2170 Ex $1876 Gd $1390
2 grade . . . . .NiB $3533 Ex $2177 Gd $1566
3 grade . . . . .NiB $4480 Ex $3066 Gd $2200
Pigeon . . . . .NiB $5250 Ex $3688 Gd $2531
4 grade . . . . .NiB $6244 Ex $5187 Gd $4966
5 grade . . . . NiB $10,300 Ex $8879 Gd $6610
Monogram . . . . NiB $13,975 Ex $11,755 Gd $10,000
A1 . . . . .NiB $7225 Ex $4488 Gd $3240
A2. . . . . NiB $14,779 Ex $11,960 Gd $10,066
A3 . . . . NiB $42,600 Ex $37,988 Gd $32,776

HAMMERLESS DOUBLE
MODEL 1968 FIELD GRADE . NiB $1165 Ex $980 Gd $644
Re-creation of the original L. C. Smith double. Sidelock. Plain extractors. Double triggers. 12 ga. 28-inch vent-rib bbls., M/F choke. Weight: About 6.75 lbs. Checkered pistol-grip stock and forearm. Made from 1968 to 1973.

HAMMERLESS DOUBLE
MODEL 1968 DELUXE . . . . .NiB $1688 Ex $1076 Gd $884
Same as 1968 Field Grade except has Simmons floating vent rib, beavertail forearm. Made from 1971 to 1973.

SINGLE-SHOT TRAP GUNS
Boxlock. Hammerless. Auto ejector.12 gauge only. Bbl. lengths: 32- or 34-inch. Vent rib. Weight: 8 to 8.25 lbs. Checkered pistol-grip stock and forend, recoil pad. Grades vary in quality of workmanship, wood, engraving, etc.; general specifications

Smith & Wesson Model 1000 Magnum

Smith & Wesson Model 3000 Slide Action

are the same. Disc. 1951. Note: Values shown are for L. C. Smith single-barrel trap guns made by Hunter. Those of Marlin manufacture generally bring prices about one-third lower.

Olympic grade	NiB $3188	Ex $2677	Gd $2190
Specialty grade	NiB $3598	Ex $3200	Gd $2560
Crown grade	NiB $4488	Ex $3900	Gd $2677
Monogram grade	NiB $8865	Ex $6231	Gd $4997
Premier grade	Very rare (Three or fewer manufactured)		
Deluxe grade	Very rare (Four or fewer manufactured)		

NOTE: Marlin resurrected the L.C. Smith brand from 2005 to 2009 importing O/U and S/S models from manufacturers in Italy and Spain.

MODEL LC12 . . . . **NiB $860 Ex $800 Gd $560**
O/U boxlock. Ejectors. !2 ga. only; 28-in. bbl., vent rib, choke tubes. Stock: fluer-de-lis checkered walnut w/ pistol grip.
LC20 (20 ga.) . . . . **NiB $1000 Ex $875 Gd $580**

MODEL LC12 DB . . . . **NiB $1400 Ex $1280 Gd $900**
S/S boxlock. Ejectors. Detachable side plates. !2 ga. only; 28-in. bbl., vent rib, choke tubes. Stock: fluer-de-lis checkered walnut w/ pistol grip, beavertail forend.
LC20 DB (20 ga.) . . . . **NiB $1600 Ex $1480 Gd $1200**
LC28 DB (28 ga.) . . . . **NiB $1900 Ex $1695 Gd $1395**
LC410 DB (.410) . . . . **NiB $1900 Ex $1695 Gd $1395**

SMITH & WESSON — Springfield, Massachusetts

Howa manufactured, disc. 1984.

MDEL 916 SLIDE-ACTION REPEATER
Hammerless. Solid frame. Gauges: 12, 16, 20. Three inch chamber in 12 and 20 ga. Five round tubular magazine. Bbls.: plain or vent rib; 20-inch C (12 ga., plain only); 26-inch IC- 28-inch M or F; 30-inch F choke (12 ga. only). Weight: With 28-inch plain bbl., 7.25 lbs. Plain pistol-grip stock, fluted slide handle. Made 1972 to 1981.
Plain bbl. . . . . **NiB $225 Ex $170 Gd $110**
Ventilated rib bbl. . . . . **NiB $255 Ex $185 Gd $120**

MODEL 916T
Same as Model 916 except takedown, 12 ga. only. Not available with 20-inch bbl. Made from 1976 to 1981.
Plain bbl. . . . . **NiB $250 Ex $180 Gd $115**
Ventilated rib bbl. . . . . **NiB $275 Ex $200 Gd $140**

MODEL 1000 AUTOLOADER . . **NiB $433 Ex $355 Gd $240**
Gas-operated. Takedown. Gauges: 12, 20. 2.75-inch chamber in 12 ga., 3-inch in 20 ga. Four round magazine. Bbls.: Vent rib, 26-inch SK choke, IC; 28-inch M or F; 30-inch F choke (12 ga.

only). Weight: With 28-inch bbl., 6.5 lbs. in 20 ga.,7.5 lbs. in 12 ga. Checkered pistol-grip stock and forearm. Made from 1972. Disc.

MODEL 3000
SLIDE ACTION . . . . **NiB $425 Ex $295 Gd $190**
Hammerless. 20-ga. Bbls.: 26-inch IC; 28-inch M or F. Chambered for 3-inch magnum and 2.75-inch loads. American walnut stock and forearm. Checkered pistol grip and forearm. Introduced 1982.

MODEL 1000 . . . . **NiB $425 Ex $295 Gd $190**
Same as Model 3000 but an earlier version.

MODEL 1000 MAGNUM . . . . . **NiB $595 Ex $445 Gd $398**
Same as standard Model 1000 except chambered for 12 ga. magnum, 3-inch shells; 30-inch bbl. only, M or F choke; stock with recoil pad. Weight: About 8 lbs. Introduced in 1977.

SPRINGFIELD ARMS — Built by Savage Arms Company, Utica, New York

SPRINGFIELD DOUBLE-BARREL
HAMMER SHOTGUN . . . . **NiB $588 Ex $439 Gd $366**
Gauges: 12 and 16. Bbls.: 28 to 32 inches. In 12 ga., 32-inch model, both bbls. have F choke. All other gauges and barrel lengths are left barrel, Full; right barrel, Mod. Weight: 7.25 to 8.25 lbs., depending on gauge and bar rel length. Black walnut checkered buttstock and forend. Disc. 1934.

SQUIRES BINGHAM CO., INC. — Makati, Rizal, Philippines

MODEL 30 PUMP . . . . **NiB $366 Ex $255 Gd $175**
Hammerless. 12 ga. Five round magazine. Bbl.: 20-inch Cyl.; 28-inch M; 30-inch F choke. Weight: About 7 lbs. Pulong Dalaga stock and slide handle. Currently manufactured.

J. STEVENS ARMS COMPANY — Chicopee Falls, Massachusetts; division of Savage Arms Corporation

NO. 20 "FAVORITE"
SHOTGUN . . . . **NiB $325 Ex $217 Gd $140**
Calibers: .22 and .32 shot. Smoothbore bbl. Blade front sight; no rear. Made from 1893 to 1939.

Squires Bingham Model 30 Pump Shotgun

Stevens Model 51

Stevens Model 58

Stevens Model 58-410

Stevens Model 67 Pump Shotgun

NO. 39 NEW MODEL
POCKET SHOTGUN . . . . **NiB $800 Ex $605 Gd $490**
Gauge: .410. Calibers: .38-40 shot, .44-40 shot. Bbls.: 10, 12, 15 or 18 inches, half-octagonal smoothbore. Shotgun sights. Made 1895 to 1906.

NO. 22-.410 O/U COMBINATION GUN
.22 caliber rifle barrel over .410 ga. shotgun barrel. Visible hammer. Takedown. Single trigger. 24-inch bbls., shotgun bbl. F choke. Weight: About 6 lbs. Open rear sight and ramp front sight of sporting rifle type. Plain pistol-grip stock and forearm; originally supplied with walnut stock and forearm. "Tenite" (plastic) was used in later production. Made 1939 to 1950. Note: This gun is now manufactured as the Savage Model 24.
Wood stock and forearm . . . . . **NiB $545 Ex $435 Gd $300**
Tenite stock and forearm . . . . . **NiB $525 Ex $460 Gd $345**

MODEL 51 BOLT-ACTION
SHOTGUN . . . . **NiB $235 Ex $154 Gd $95**
Single shot. Takedown. .410 ga. 24-inch bbl., F choke. Weight: About 4.75 lbs. Plain one-piece pistol-grip stock. checkered on later models. Made from 1962 to 1971.

MODEL 58 BOLT-ACTION
REPEATER . . . . **NiB $254 Ex $165 Gd $120**
Takedown. Gauges: 12, 16, 20. Two round detachable box magazine. 26-inch bbl., F choke. Weight: About 7.25 lbs. Plain one piece pistol-grip stock on early models w/takedown screw on bottom of forend. Made 1933-81. Note: Later production

models have 3-inch chamber in 20 ga., checkered stock with recoil pad.

MODEL 58-.410 BOLT-ACTION
REPEATER . . . . **NiB $225 Ex $130 Gd $95**
Takedown. .410 ga. Three round detachable box magazine. 24-inch bbl., F choke. Weight: About 5.5 lbs. Plain one piece pistol-grip stock, checkered on later production. Made from 1937 to 1981.

MODEL 59 BOLT-ACTION
REPEATER . . . . **NiB $255 Ex $190 Gd $135**
Takedown. .410 ga. Five round tubular magazine. 24-inch bbl., F choke. Weight: About 6 lbs. Plain, one piece pistol-grip stock, checkered on later production. Made from 1934 to 1973.

MODEL 67 PUMP SHOTGUN
Hammerless, side-ejection solid-steel receiver. Gauges: 12, 20 and .410, 2.75- or 3-inch shells. Bbls.: 21-, 26-, 28- 30-inch with fixed chokes or interchangeable choke tubes, plain or vent rib. Weight: 6.25 to 7.5 lbs. Optional rifle sights. Walnut-finished hardwood stock with corncob-style forend.
Standard model, plain bbl. . . . . **NiB $245 Ex $195 Gd $120**
Standard model, vent rib   . . . . **NiB $255 Ex $205 Gd $125**
Standard model, w/choke tubes . . . **NiB $275 Ex $220 Gd $155**
Slug model w/rifle sights . . . . . **NiB $255 Ex $205 Gd $125**
Lobo model, matte finish   . . . . **NiB $255 Ex $205 Gd $125**
Youth model, 20 ga. . . . . **NiB $260 Ex $210 Gd $130**
Camo model. w/choke tubes . . **NiB $275 Ex $220 Gd $155**

SHOTGUNS

Stevens Model 67 Waterfowl Shotgun

Stevens Model 77

Stevens Model 94C

Stevens Model 95

Stevens Model 94 Youth

Stevens Model 124
Cross-Bolt Repeater

Stevens Model 258

Stevens Model 311

Stevens Model 620

MODEL 67 WATERFOWL

SHOTGUN . . . . NiB $335 Ex $200 Gd $135
Hammerless. Gauge: 12. Three round tubular magazine. Walnut finished hardwood stock. Weight: About 7.5 lbs. Made 1972 to 1989.

MODEL 77 SLIDE-ACTION

REPEATER . . . . NiB $225 Ex $130 Gd $95
Solid frame. Gauges: 12, 16, 20. Five round tubular magazine. Bbls.: 26-inch IC, 28-inch M or F choke. Weight: About 7.5 lbs. Plain pistol-grip stock with recoil pad, grooved slide handle. Made from 1954 to 1971.

MODEL 77-AC . . . . NiB $217 Ex $125 Gd $95
Same as Model 77 except has Savage Super Choke.

MODEL 79-VR SUPER VALUE. . . . NiB $355 Ex $265 Gd $190
Hammerless, side ejection. Bbl.: Chambered for 2.75-inch and 3-inch mag. shells. 12, 20, and .410 ga. vent rib. Walnut finished hardwood stock with checkering on grip. Weight: 6.75-7 lbs. Made 1979 to 1990.

MODEL 94 SINGLE-SHOT

SHOTGUN . . . . NiB $165 Ex $95 Gd $70
Takedown. Visible hammer. Auto ejector. Gauges: 12, 16, 20, 28, .410. Bbls.: 26-, 28-, 30-, 32-, 36-inch, F choke. Weight: About 6 lbs. depending on gauge and barrel. Plain pistol-grip stock and forearm. Made from 1939 to 1961.

MODEL 94C . . . . NiB $165 Ex $95 Gd $70
Same as Model 94 except has checkered stock, fluted forearm on late production. Made from 1965 to 1990.

MODEL 94Y YOUTH GUN. . . . . . NiB $165 Ex $95 Gd $70
Same as Model 94 except made in 20 and .410 ga. only; has 26-inch F choke bbl., 12.5-inch buttstock with recoil pad; checkered pistol grip and fluted forend on late production. Made from 1959 to 1990.

MODEL 95 SINGLE-SHOT

SHOTGUN . . . . NiB $200 Ex $140 Gd $95
Solid frame. Visible hammer. Plain extractor. 12 ga. Three-inch chamber. Bbls.: 28-inch M- 30-inch F choke. Weight: About 7.25 lbs. Plain pistol-grip stock, grooved forearm. Made 1965 to 1969.

MODEL 107 SINGLE-SHOT

HAMMER SHOTGUN. . . . . NiB $217 Ex $129 Gd $95
Takedown. Auto ejector. Gauges: 12, 16, 20, .410. Bbl. lengths: 28- and 30-inch (12 and 16 ga.), 28-inch (20 ga.), 26-inch (.410); F choke only. Weight: About 6 lbs., 12 bore ga. Plain pistol-grip stock and forearm. Made from about 1937 to 1953.

MODEL 124

BOLT-ACTION REPEATER . . . . . NiB $265 Ex $198 Gd $155
Hammerless. Solid frame. 12 ga. only. Two round tubular magazine. 28-inch bbl.; IC, M or F choke. Weight: About 7 lbs. Tenite stock and forearm. Made from 1947 to 1952.

MODEL 240 O/U SHOTGUN. . . NiB $448 Ex $375 Gd $270
Visible hammer. Takedown. Double triggers. .410 ga. 26-inch bbls., F choke. Weight: 6 lbs. Tenite (plastic) pistol-grip stock and forearm. Made from 1940 to 1949.

MODEL 258 BOLT-ACTION

REPEATER . . . . NiB $290 Ex $174 Gd $100
Takedown. 20-gauge. Two round detachable box magazine. 26-inch barrel, Full choke. Weight: About 6.25 lbs. Plain, one piece pistol-grip stock. Made from 1937 to 1965.

MODEL 311 SPRINGFIELD HAMMERLESS DOUBLE
Same general specifications as Stevens Model 530 except earlier production has plain stock and forearm; checkered on current guns. Originally produced as a "Springfield" gun, this model became a part of the Stevens line in 1948 when the Springfield brand name was discontinued. Made from 1931 to 1989.
Pre-WWII . . . . NiB $675 Ex $450 Gd $325
Post-WWII . . . . NiB $335 Ex $200 Gd $125

MODEL 311-R

HAMMERLESS DOUBLE. . . . . . NiB $300 Ex $225 Gd $145
Same general specifications as Stevens Model 311 except compact design for law enforcement use. Bbls.: 18.25-inch 12 gauge with solid rib, chambered for 2.75 and 3-inch Mag. shells. Double triggers and auto top tang safety. Walnut finished hardwood stock with recoil pad and semi-beavertail forend. Weight: About 6.75 lbs. Made from 1982 to 1989.

MODEL 530

HAMMERLESS DOUBLE . . . . . NiB $335 Ex $245 Gd $200
Boxlock. Double triggers. Gauges: 12, 16, 20, .410. Bbl. lengths: 26- to 32-inch; choked M/F, C/M, F/F. Weight: 6 to 7.5 pounds depending on gauge and barrel length. Checkered pistol-grip stock and forearm; some early models with recoil pad. Made from 1936 to 1954.

MODEL 530M. . . . . NiB $339 Ex $255 Gd $210
Same as Model 530 except has Tenite (plastic) stock and forearm. Disc. about 1947.

MODEL 530ST DOUBLE GUN NiB $339 Ex $255 Gd $210
Same as Model 530 except has non-selective single trigger. Disc.

MODEL 620 HAMMERLESS SLIDE-ACTION

REPEATING SHOTGUN . . . . . . NiB $400 Ex $255 Gd $180
Takedown. Gauges: 12, 16, 20. Five round tubular magazine. Bbl. lengths: 26-, 28-, 30-, 32-inch; choked F, M IC, C. Weight: About 7.75 lbs., 12 ga.; 7.25 lbs., 16 ga.- 6 lbs., 20 ga. Checkered pistol-grip stock and slide handle. Made from 1927 to 1953.

MODEL 620-C . . . . NiB $365 Ex $255 Gd $160
Same specifications as Model 620 except equipped with Cutts Compensator and two choke tubes.

Stevens Model 620-P

Stevens Model 820

MODEL 620-P. . . . . NiB $288 Ex $200 Gd $155
Same specifications as Model 620 equipped with Aero-Dyne PolyChoke and 27-inch bbl.

MODEL 620-PV . . . . NiB $280 Ex $190 Gd $155
Same specifications as Model 620 except equipped with ventilated PolyChoke and 27-inch bbl.

MODEL 621 . . . . NiB $359 Ex $210 Gd $155
Same as Model 620 except has raised solid matted-rib barrel. Disc.

**MODEL 820 HAMMERLESS
REPEATING SHOTGUN** . . . . . . NiB $388 Ex $266 Gd $190
Solid frame. 12 gauge only. Five round tubular magazine. 28-inch barrel; IC, M or F choke. Weight: About 7.5 lbs. Plain pistol-grip stock, grooved slide handle. Early models furnished w/Tenite buttstock and forend. Made from 1949 to 1954.

MODEL 820-SC . . . . NiB $400 Ex $330 Gd $217
Same as Model 820 except has Savage Super Choke.

**MODEL 940 SINGLE-SHOT
SHOTGUN** . . . . NiB $256 Ex $138 Gd $110
Same general specifications as Model 94 except has side lever opening instead of top lever. Made from 1961 to 1970.

**MODEL 940Y
YOUTH GUN** . . . . NiB $265 Ex $155 Gd $115
Same general specifications as Model 94Y except has side lever opening instead of top lever. Made from 1961 to 1970.

MODEL 9478 . . . . NiB $145 Ex $90 Gd $65
Takedown. Visible hammer. Automatic ejector. Gauges: 12, 20, .410. Bbls.: 26-, 28-, 30-, 36-inch; Full choke. Weight: Average 6 pounds depending on gauge and barrel. Plain pistol-grip stock and forearm. Made from 1978 to 1985.

MODEL 5151 SPRINGFIELD. . . NiB $556 Ex $435 Gd $300
Same specifications as the Stevens Model 311 except with checkered grip and forend; equipped with recoil pad and two ivory sights.

STOEGER
See IGA and Tikka shotguns.

TAR-HUNT CUSTOM RIFLES, INC. — Bloomsburg, Pennsylvania

**MODEL RSG-12 MATCHLESS BOLT-ACTION
SLUG GUN.** . . . . NiB $2366 Ex $2165 Gd $1590
Similar to Professional model except has McMillan Fibergrain stock and deluxe blue finish. Made from 1995 to 2004.

**MODEL RSG-12 PEERLESS BOLT-ACTION
SLUG GUN.** . . . . NiB $2944 Ex $2577 Gd $2320
Similar to Professional model except has McMillan Fibergrain stock and deluxe NP-3 (Nickel/Teflon) metal finish. Made from 1995 to 2004.

**MODEL RSG-12 PROFESSIONAL
BOLT-ACTION SLUG GUN**
Bolt action 12 ga. w/2.75-inch chamber, 2-round detachable magazine, 21.5-inch fully rifled bbl. w/ or w/o muzzle brake. Receiver drilled and tapped for scope mounts w/ no sights. Weight: 7.75 lbs. 41.5 inches overall. Checkered black McMillan fiberglass stock w/swivel studs and Pachmayr Deacelerator pad. Made from 1991 to 2004.
**RSG-12 model w/o muzzle
brake (disc. 1993)**. . . . . . NiB $2688 Ex $2320 Gd $1997
**RSG-12 model w/muzzle
brake** . . . . NiB $2700 Ex $2375 Gd $2044

**MODEL RSG-20 MOUNTAINEER BOLT ACTION
SLUG GUN.** . . . . NiB $2276 Ex $1966 Gd $1433
Similar to Professional model except 20 ga. w/2.75 inch chamber. Black McMillan synthetic stock w/blind magazine. Weight: 6.5 lbs. Made from 1997 to 2004.

TECNI-MEC SHOTGUNS — Italy. Imported by RAHN Gun Work, Inc., Hastings, MI

MODEL SPL 640 FOLDING SHOTGUN
Gauges: 12, 16, 20, 24, 28, 32 and .410 bore. 26-inch bbl. Chokes: IC/IM. Weight: 6.5 lbs. Checkered walnut pistol-grip stock and forend. Engraved receiver. Available with single or double triggers. Imported from 1988 to 1994.
w/single trigger. . . . . NiB $596 Ex $477 Gd $369
w/double trigger. . . . . NiB $655 Ex $498 Gd $388

THOMPSON/CENTER ARMS — Rochester, New Hampshire, and Springfield, Massachusetts

Purchased by Smith & Wesson in 2006.

CONTENDER

.410 CARBINE..............NiB **$500** Ex **$387** Gd **$279**
Gauge: .410 smoothbore. 21-inch vent rib bbl. 34.75 inches overall. Weight: About 5.25 lbs. Bead front sight. Rynite stock and forend. Made 1991 to date.

ENCORE 20 GA. SHOTGUN

Gauge: 20 smoothbore w/rifled slug bbl. or 26-inch vent-rib bbl. w/three internal screw choke tubes, 38 to 40.5 inches overall. Weight: About 5.25 to 6 lbs. Bead or fiber optic sights. Walnut stock and forend. Made from 1998 to date.
Encore 20 ga.
w/vent rib.................NiB **$485** Ex **$390** Gd **$275**
Encore 20 ga.
w/rifled slug bbl.............NiB **$522** Ex **$421** Gd **$300**
w/extra bbl., add $325

HUNTER SHOTGUN MODEL.. NiB **$580** Ex **$466** Gd **$355**
Single shot. Gauge: 10 or 12, 3.5-inch chamber, 25-inch field bbl. with F choke. Weight: 8 lbs. Bead front sight. American black walnut stock with recoil pad. Made from 1987 to 1992.

HUNTER SLUG MODEL......NiB **$580** Ex **$466** Gd **$355**
Gauge: 10 (3.5-inch chamber) or 12 (3-inch chamber). Same general specifications as Model '87 Hunter Shotgun except with 22-inch slug (rifled) bbl. and rifle sights. Made from 1987 to 1992.

TIKKA — Manufactured by Sako, Ltd. in Armi Marocchi, Italy

M 07 SHOTGUN/

RIFLE COMBINATION .....NiB **$1287** Ex **$1009** Gd **$766**
Gauge/caliber: 12/.222 Rem. Shotgun bbl.: About 25 inches; rifled bbl.: About 22.75 inches. 40.66 inches overall. Weight: About 7 lbs. Dovetailed for telescopic sight mounts Single trigger with selector between the bbls. Vent rib. Monte Carlo-style walnut stock with checkered pistol grip and forend. Made from 1965 to 1987.

M 77 O/U SHOTGUN .....NiB **$1345** Ex **$1265** Gd **$950**
Gauge: 12. 27-inch vent-rib bbls., approx. 44 inches overall, weight: About 7.25 lbs. Bbl. selector. Ejectors. Monte Carlo-style walnut stock with checkered pistol grip and forend; roll-over cheekpiece. Made from 1977 to 1987.

M 77K SHOTGUN/ RIFLE

COMBINATION ....NiB **$1733** Ex **$1388** Gd **$1009**
Gauge: 12/70. Calibers: .222 Rem., 5.6x52r5, 6.5x55, 7x57r5, 7x65r5, .308 Win. Vent-rib bbls.: About 25 inches (shotgun); 23 inches (rifle), 42.3 inches overall. Weight: About 7.5 lbs. Double triggers. Monte Carlo-style walnut stock with checkered pistol grip and forend; rollover cheekpiece. Made from 1977 to 1986.

412S/512S SHOOTING SYSTEM

Boxlock action with both under lug and sliding top latch locking mechanism designed to accept interchangeable monobloc barrels, including O/U shotgun, combination and double rifle configurations. Blued or satin nickel receiver w/cocking indicators. Selective single trigger design w/barrel selector incorporated into the trigger (double triggers available). Blued barrels assemblies w/extractors or auto ejectors as required. Select American walnut stock with checkered pistol grip and forend. Previously produced in Finland (same as the former Valmet Model 412) but currently manufactured in Italy by joint venture arrangement with Armi Marocchi. From 1990-93, Stoeger Industries imported this model as the 412/S. In 1993 the nomenclature of this shooting system was changed to 512/S. Disc. 1997. Note: For double rifle values, see Tikka Rifles.

MODEL 412S/512S O/U SHOTGUN

Gauge: 12 w/3-inch chambers. 24-, 26-, 28- or 30-inch chrome-lined bbls. w/blued finish and integral stainless steel choke tubes. Weight: 7.25 to 7.5 lbs. Blue or matte nickel receiver. Select American walnut from stock with checkered pistol grip and forend. Imported 1990 to 1997.

Standard Field model ......NiB **$1145**	Ex **$989**	Gd **$766**
Standard Trap model ......NiB **$1277**	Ex **$1050**	Gd **$766**
Premium Field model .....NiB **$1688**	Ex **$1279**	Gd **$1100**
Premium Trap model .....NiB **$1688**	Ex **$1279**	Gd **$1100**
Sporting Clays model ......NiB **$1233**	Ex **$1054**	Gd **$866**

w/extra O/U shotgun bbl., add....................$700
w/extra O/U combo bbl., add $800
w/extra O/U rifle bbl., add.....................$1025

MODEL 412S/512S OVER/UNDER COMBINATION

Gauge: 12 w/3-inch chamber. Calibers: .222 Rem., .30-06 or .308 Win. Blue or matte nickel receiver, 24-inch chrome-lined bbls. w/extractors and blued finish. Weight: 7.25 to 7.5 lbs. Select American walnut stock with checkered pistol grip and forend. Imported from 1990 to 1997.
Standard Combination model NiB **$1598** Ex **$1335** Gd **$1109**
Premium Combination model NiB **$1622** Ex **$1365** Gd **$1135**
Extra barrel options, add........................$800

TRADITIONS PERFORMANCE FIREARMS — Importers of shotguns produced by Fausti Stefano of Brescia, Italy, and ATA Firearms, Turkey

FIELD HUNTER MODEL......NiB **$825** Ex **$630** Gd **$535**
Same as Field I except 12 and 20 gauge, 3-inch chambers, screw-in chokes and extractors.

CLASSIC SERIES, FIELD I O/U . NiB **$853** Ex **$677** Gd **$545**
Available in 12, 20, 28 (2 3/4-inch chamber) and .410 gauge, 26- or 28-inch vent rib bbls. W/fixed chokes and extractors. Weight: 6 3/4 to 7 1/4 lbs. Blued finish, silver receiver engraved with game birds. Single, selective trigger. Brass bead front sight. European walnut stock. Overall length 43 to 45 inches. Intro. 2000.

FIELD II MODEL............NiB **$945** Ex **$679** Gd **$555**
Same as Field I except with screw-in chokes and automatic ejectors.

FIELD III GOLD MODEL ...NiB **$1217** Ex **$1109** Gd **$998**
Same as Field I model except 12 gauge only, high-grade, oil-finish walnut, coin-finish receiver with engraved pheasants and woodcock, deep blue finish on barrels, automatic ejectors and non-slip recoil pad.

SHOTGUNS

SPORTING CLAY II MODEL . . NiB $1165 Ex $977 Gd $620
Same as Sporting Clay III model but with European walnut stocks, cut checkering and extended choke tubes. Overall length: 47 inches. Weight: 7 3/4 lbs.

CLASSIC SERIES O/U
SPORTING CLAY III . . . . NiB $1200 Ex $1095 Gd $985
Available in 12 and 20 gauge, 3-inch chambers, high grade walnut stock, oil-satin finish, palm swell Schnabel forend. 28- and 30-inch bbls. with 3/8-inch top and middle vent rib, red target front bead sight. Automatic ejectors, extended choke tubes. Weight: 8 1/4 lbs. Intro. 2000.

UPLAND II MODEL . . . . NiB $1065 Ex $775 Gd $546
Same as Upland III model except with English walnut straight-grip stock and Schnabel forend, 24- and 26-inch vent rib bbls., floral engraving on blued receiver, automatic ejectors.

UPLAND III MODEL . . . . NiB $1187 Ex $977 Gd $755
Same as Sporting Clay III model but round pistol grip and Schnabel forend, blued receiver with engraved upland scene, weight: 7 1/2 lbs.

MAG 350 SERIES
TURKEY II O/U . . . . NiB $1144 Ex $942 Gd $700
Magnum 3 1/2-inch chambers in 12 gauge only, 24- and 26-inch bbls., screw-in flush fitting chokes: F and XF. Matte finish, engraved receiver, Mossy Oak or Realtree camo. Intro. 2000.

WATERFOWL II MODEL . . . . . NiB $1159 Ex $910 Gd $715
Same as Turkey II model except with Advantage Wetlands camo stock and barrels, weight: 8 lbs., overall length 45 inches. Waterfowl model has 28-inch bbls.

MAG HUNTER II . . . . NiB $1159 Ex $910 Gd $715
Same as Turkey II model except blued engraved receiver and matte finish walnut stocks, 3 1/2-inch chambers, 28-inch bbls. with screw-in chokes.

ELITE HUNTER . . . . NiB $1256 Ex $1044 Gd $770
Same as Elite Field model except 12 and 20 gauge, European walnut stock, beavertail forend, screw-in choke tubes, extractors, three-inch chambers. Blued finish. Vent-rib, tang safety. Weight: 6 1/2 pounds.

ELITE FIELD I DT . . . . NiB $1006 Ex $853 Gd $600
Same as Elite Field I except with double triggers, fixed chokes, extractors. Available in 12, 20, 28 (2 3/4-inch chambers) and .410. Bbls: 26 inches, fixed IC/M chokes. Weight: 5 1/2 to 6 1/4 lbs

ELITE FIELD I ST . . . . NiB $1118 Ex $1065 Gd $790
Same as Elite Field III except single trigger, fixed chokes, extractors; European walnut stock. Available in 12, 20, 28 (2 3/4-inch chambers) and .410 gauge; fixed IC/M chokes. Weight: 5 3/4 to 6 1/2 lbs.

ELITE FIELD III ST . . . . NiB $1967 Ex $1689 Gd $1333
Checkered English walnut straight stock, splinter forend, fixed chokes. Available in 28 and .410 gauge, 26-inch chrome-lined bbls., Cylinder and Modified chokes. Silver trigger guard and receiver with hand-finished engraving of upland game scenes with gold inlays. Automatic ejectors. Brass front sight bead. Weight: About 6 1/2 lbs. Intro. 2000.

AL 2100 SEMI-AUTO FIELD SERIES,
WALNUT MODEL . . . . NiB $366 Ex $245 Gd $190
Gas-operated, 12 and 20 gauge, 3-inch chambers, cut-checkered Turkish walnut stock and forend, blued 26- and 28-inch vent rib bbls., multi-choke system, chrome bore lining. Weight: About 6 lbs. Rifled barrel with cantilever mount available Intro. 2001.

SYNTHETIC STOCK MODEL . . . NiB $350 Ex $290 Gd $225
Same as the ALS 2100 Walnut model except with synthetic stock, matted finish on receiver and bbl., weight: About 6 lbs.

YOUTH MODEL . . . . NiB $344 Ex $229 Gd $175
Same as ALS 2100 Walnut model except with a shorter walnut stock (length of pull: 13 1/2 inches). Available in 12 or 20 gauge with 24-inch vent rib barrel, weight: 5 1/2 to 6 lbs.

HUNTER COMBO MODEL
Same as ALS 2100 Walnut model except comes with two bbls. (28-inch vent rib and 24-inch slug), TruGlo adjustable sights and cantilever mount. Available with Turkish walnut or synthetic stock with matte barrel finish. Weight: 6 1/2 lbs.
Walnut stock . . . . NiB $500 Ex $377 Gd $210
Synthetic stock . . . . NiB $475 Ex $339 Gd $220

SLUG HUNTER MODEL . . . . . . NiB $355 Ex $245 Gd $190
Same as ALS 2100 Walnut except with fully-rifled barrel, choice of walnut or synthetic stocks, matte or blue finish; rifle or TruGlo adjustable sights. Weight: About 6 1/4 lbs.

TURKEY HUNTER/
WATERFOWL MODEL . . . . NiB $375 Ex $265 Gd $220
Same as ALS 2100 Walnut except with synthetic stock, 3-inch chambers, 26-inch vent rib bbl., screw-in chokes, Mossy Oak or Realtree camo stocks.

HOME SECURITY MODEL . . . . NiB $335 Ex $260 Gd $190
Same as ALS 2100 Walnut but with 20-inch cylinder-bore bbl., synthetic stock, 3-inch chambers, six-round capacity with 2 3/4-inch shells. Weight: About 6 lbs.

TRISTAR SPORTING ARMS —
North Kansas City, Missouri

MODEL 1887 LEVER-ACTION
REPEATER . . . . NiB $765 Ex $580 Gd $445
Copy of John Browning's Winchester Model 1887 lever-action shotgun. 12 ga. only. 30-inch bbl. which may be cut down to any desired length of 18 inches or more. Version shown has 20-inch bbl. Imported from 1997 to 1999.

MODEL 300 O/U SHOTGUN . . NiB $465 Ex $335 Gd $199
Similar to the Model 333 except 12 ga. only w/3-inch chambers, 26- or 28-inch vent rib bbls. w/extractors and fixed chokes. Etched receiver w/double triggers and standard walnut stock. Imported 1994 to 1998.

MODEL 311 SIDE-BY-SIDE SHOTGUN
Boxlock action w/underlug and Greener cross bolt. 12 or 20 ga. w/3-inch chambers, 20, 28- or 30-inch bbls. w/choke tubes or fixed chokes (311R). Double triggers. Extractors. Black chrome finish. Checkered Turkish walnut buttstock and forend. Weight: 6.9 to 7.2 lbs. Imported from 1994 to 1997.
**311 Model (w/extractors and
choke tubes) . . . . NiB $575 Ex $476 Gd $390**

**Valmet Model 412 K
O/U Field Shotgun**

**311R Model (w/20-inch bbls.
and fixed chokes)** . . . . NiB $445 Ex $355 Gd $235

MODEL 330 O/U SHOTGUN
Similar to the Model 333 except 12 ga. only w/3-inch chambers. 26-, 28- or 30-inch vent rib bbls w/extractors or ejectors and fixed chokes or choke tubes. Etched receiver and standard walnut stock. Imported from 1994 to 1999.
**330 model (w/ extractor and
fixed chokes)**. . . . . NiB $545 Ex $420 Gd $300
**330 D model (w/ejectors and
choke tubes)** . . . . NiB $733 Ex $567 Gd $488

MODEL 333 O/U SHOTGUN
Boxlock action. 12 or 20 ga. w/3-inch chambers. 26-, 28- or 30-inch vent rib bbls. w/choke tubes. Single selective trigger. Selective automatic ejectors. Engraved receiver w/satin nickel finish. Checkered Turkish fancy walnut buttstock and forend. Weight: 7.5 to 7.75 lbs. Imported from 1994 to 1998.
Field model. . . . . NiB $844 Ex $700 Gd $545
Sporting Clays model (1994-97) . . NiB $900 Ex $755 Gd $580
TRL Ladies Field model. . . . . . . NiB $800 Ex $675 Gd $550
**SCL Ladies Sporting Clays model
(1994-97)** . . . . NiB $900 Ex $755 Gd $580

SHOTGUNS OF ULM — Ulm, Germany
See listings under Krieghoff.

U.S. REPEATING ARMS CO. — New Haven, Connecticut
See also Winchester shotgun listings.

VALMET — Jyväskylä, Finland

NOTE: *In 1987, Valmet and Sako merged and the Valmet production facilities were moved to Riihimaki, Finland. In 1989 a joint venture agreement was made with Armi Marocchi, and when production began in Italy, the Valmet name was changed to Tikka (Oy Tikkakoski Ab).*

See also Savage Models 330, 333T, 333 and 2400, which were produced by Valmet.

LION O/U SHOTGUN. . . . . NiB $475 Ex $388 Gd $293
Boxlock. Selective single trigger. Plain extractors. 12 ga. only. Bbls.: 26-inch IC/M; 28-inch M/F, 30-inch M/F, F/F. Weight: About 7 lbs. Checkered pistol-grip stock and forearm. Imported 1947 to 1968.

**MODEL 412 S O/U FIELD
SHOTGUN** . . . . NiB $955 Ex $744 Gd $535
Hammerless. 12-ga., 3-inch chamber, 36-inch bbl., F/F chokes. American walnut Monte Carlo stock. Disc 1989.

MODEL 412 S SHOTGUN RIFLE
COMBINATION . . . . NiB $1135 Ex $956 Gd $745
Similar to model 412 K except bottom bbl. chambered for .222 Rem., .223 Rem., .243 Win., .308 Win. or .30-06. 12-ga. shotgun bbl. with IM choke. Monte Carlo American walnut stock, recoil pad.

MODEL 412 O/U
FIELD SHOTGUN . . . . NiB $866 Ex $723 Gd $587
12-ga. chambered for 2.75-inch shells. 26-inch bbl., IC/M chokes; 28-inch bbl., M/F chokes; 12-ga. chambered for 3-inch shells, 30-inch bbl., M/F chokes. 20-ga. (3-inch shells); 26-inch bbl., IC/M chokes; 28-inch bbl., M/ F chokes. American walnut Monte Carlo stock.

MODEL 412 ST SKEET . . . . . . NiB $1176 Ex $922 Gd $766
Similar to Model 412 K except skeet stock and chokes. 12 and 20 ga. Disc. 1989.

MODEL 412 SE TRAP . . . . NiB $1176 Ex $922 Gd $766
Similar to Model 412 K Field except trap stock, recoil pad. 30-inch bbls., IM/F chokes. Disc.1989.
w/extra bbl., add. $500

MONTGOMERY WARD — Chicago, Illinois; Western Field and Hercules Models

Although they do not correspond to specific models below, the names Western Field and Hercules have been used to designate various Montgomery Ward shotguns at various times.

MODEL 25 SLIDE-ACTION
REPEATER . . . . NiB $337 Ex $228 Gd $178
Solid frame. 12 ga. only. Two- or 5-round tubular magazine. 28-inch bbl., various chokes. Weight: About 7.5 lbs. Plain pistol-grip stock, grooved slide handle.

MODEL 40 O/U SHOTGUN. . . NiB $866 Ex $700 Gd $522
Hammerless. Boxlock. Double triggers. Gauges: 12, l6, 20, .410. Bbls.: Plain; 26- to 30-inch, various chokes. Checkered pistol-grip stock and forearm.

MODEL 40N
SLIDE-ACTION REPEATER . . . . NiB $329 Ex $233 Gd $179
Same general specifications as Model 25.

(WESTERN FIELD) MODEL 50
PUMPGUN. . . . . NiB $300 Ex $244 Gd $178
Solid frame. Gauges: 12 and 16. Two- and 5-round magazine. 26-, 28- or 30-inch bbl., 48 inches overall w/28-inch bbl. Weight: 7.25 - 7.75 lbs. Metal bead front sight. Walnut stock and grooved forend.

(WESTERN FIELD) MODEL 52
DOUBLE-BARREL SHOTGUN. . NiB $388 Ex $277 Gd $191
Hammerless coil-spring action. Gauges: 12, 16, 20 and .410. 26-, 28-, or 30-inch bbls., 42 to 46 inches overall, depending upon bbl. length. Weight: 6 (.410 ga. w/26-inch bbl.) to 7.25

SHOTGUNS

Ward Western Field Model 50

Ward Western Field Model 52

Weatherby Model 82
Autoloading Shotgun

lbs. (12 ga. w/30-inch bbls.), depending upon gauge and bbl. length. Casehardened receiver; blued bbls. Plain buttstock and forend. Made circa 1954.

MODEL 172 BOLT-ACTION
SHOTGUN . . . . .NiB $217 Ex $139 Gd $95
Takedown. Two-round detachable clip magazine.12 ga. 28-inch bbl. with variable choke. Weight: About 7.5 lbs. Monte Carlo stock with recoil pad.

MODEL 550A SLIDE-ACTION
REPEATER . . . . .NiB $367 Ex $265 Gd $190
Takedown. Gauges: 12, 16, 20, .410. Five-round tubular magazine. Bbls.: Plain, 26- to 30-inch, various chokes. Weight: 6 (.410 ga. w/26-inch bbl.) to 8 lbs. (12 ga. w/30-inch bbls.). Plain pistol-grip stock and grooved slide handle.

MODEL SB300 DOUBLE-BARREL
SHOTGUN . . . . .NiB $376 Ex $298 Gd $220
Same general specifications as Model SD52A.

MODEL SB312 DOUBLE-BARREL
SHOTGUN . . . . .NiB $421 Ex $337 Gd $244
Boxlock. Double triggers. Plain extractors. Gauges: 12, 16, 20, .410. Bbls.: 24- to 30-inch. Various chokes. Weight: About 7.5 lbs. in 12 ga.; 6.5 lbs in .410 ga. Checkered pistol-grip stock and forearm.

MODEL SD52A DOUBLE-BARREL
SHOTGUN . . . . .NiB $344 Ex $255 Gd $200
Boxlock. Double triggers. Plain extractors. Gauges: 12, 16, 20, .410. Bbls.: 26- to 32-inch, various chokes. Plain forend and pistol-grip buttstock. Weight: 6 (.410 ga., 26-inch bbls.) to 7.5 lbs. (12 ga., 32-inch bbls.).

WEATHERBY, INC. — Pasa Robles, CA

MODEL 82 AUTOLOADING
SHOTGUN . . . . .NiB $556 Ex $435 Gd $332
Hammerless, gas-operated. 12 ga. only. Bbls.: 22- to 30-inch, various integral or fixed chokes. Weight: 7.5 lbs. Checkered walnut stock and forearm. Imported from 1982 to 1989.
BuckMaster Auto Slug
   w/rifle sights (1986-90) . . . .NiB $570 Ex $455 Gd $355
w/fixed choke, deduct $50

MODEL 92 SLIDE-ACTION
SHOTGUN . . . . .NiB $390 Ex $288 Gd $217
Hammerless, short-stroke action. 12 ga.; 3-inch chamber. Tubular magazine. Bbls.: 22-, 26-, 28-, 30-inch with fixed choke or IMC choke tubes; plain or vent rib with rifle sights. Weight: 7.5 lbs. Engraved, matte black receiver and blued barrel. Checkered high-gloss buttstock and forend. Imported from Japan 1982 to 1989.
Standard Model 92 . . . . .NiB $330 Ex $261 Gd $195
BuckMaster Pump Slug
   w/rifle sights, (intro. 1986). .NiB $420 Ex $315 Gd $235

ATHENA O/U SHOTGUN
Engraved boxlock action with Greener crossbolt and sideplates. Gauges: 12, 20, 28 and .410; 2.75- or 3.5-inch chambers. Bbls.: 26-, 28-, 30- or 32-inch with fixed or IMC Multi-choke tubes. Weight: 6.75 to 7.38 lbs. Single selective trigger. Selective auto ejectors. Top tang safety. Checkered Claro walnut stock and forearm with high-luster finish. Imported from 1982 to 2002.
Field Model w/IMC multi-chokes,
   12 or 20 ga. . . . . .NiB $2177 Ex $1898 Gd $1635

Weatherby Model 92
Slide-Action Shotgun

Weatherby Athena
O/U Shotgun

Weatherby Centurion
Automatic Shotgun

Weatherby Olympian Trap
O/U Shotgun

Weatherby Orion
O/U Shotgun

Field Model W/fixed chokes,
   28 ga. or .410 . . . . NiB $1976 Ex $1645 Gd $1389
Skeet Model w/fixed chokes,
   12 or 20 ga. . . . . NiB $1766 Ex $1432 Gd $1255
Skeet Model w/fixed chokes,
   28 ga. or .410 . . . . NiB $3320 Ex $2888 Gd $2366
Master Skeet tube set . . . . . NiB $3155 Ex $2776 Gd $2388
Trap Model w/IC tubes . . . . NiB $2388 Ex $1977 Gd $1677
Grade V (1993 to date) . . . . NiB $3566 Ex $3100 Gd $2665

CENTURION AUTOMATIC SHOTGUN
Gas-operated. Takedown. 12 ga. 2.75-inch chamber. Three round magazine. Bbls.: Vent ribs; 26-inch SK, IC or M 28-inch M or F; 30-inch Full choke. Weight: With 28-inch bbl., 7 lbs. 10.5 oz. Checkered pistol-grip stock and forearm, recoil pad. Made in Japan from 1972 to 1981.
Field Grade . . . . NiB $398 Ex $288 Gd $219
Trap Gun (30-inch full-choke
   bbl.) . . . . NiB $435 Ex $377 Gd $235
Deluxe model (etched receiver,
   fancy wood stock) . . . . NiB $525 Ex $425 Gd $265

OLYMPIAN O/U SHOTGUN
Gauges: 12 and 20. 2.75- (12 ga.) and 3-inch (20 ga.) chambers. Bbls.: 26-, 28-, 30, and 32-inch. Weight: 6.75 - 8.75 lbs. American walnut stock and forend. Disc. 1980.
Field Model . . . . NiB $988 Ex $700 Gd $577

Skeet Model . . . . NiB $1033 Ex $800 Gd $690
Trap Model . . . . NiB $995 Ex $745 Gd $650

ORION O/U SHOTGUN
Boxlock with Greener crossbolt. Gauges: 12, 20, 28 and .410; 2.75- or 3-inch chambers. Bbls.: 26-, 28, 30-, 32- or 34-inch with fixed or IMC Multi-Choke tubes. Weight: 6.5 to 9 lbs. Single selective trigger. Selective auto ejectors. Top tang safety. Checkered, high-gloss pistol-grip Claro walnut stock and forearm. Finish: Grade I, plain blued receive; Grade II, engraved blued receiver; Grade III, silver gray receiver. Imported from 1982 and 2002.
Orion I Field w/IC (12 or 20 ga.) . . . NiB $1456 Ex $1188 Gd $975
Orion II Field w/IC (12 or 20 ga.) . . . NiB $1155 Ex $965 Gd $743
Orion II Classic w/IC
   (12, 20 or 28 ga.) . . . . . . NiB $1644 Ex $1388 Gd $1166
Orion II Sporting Clays w/IC
   (12 ga.) . . . . NiB $1997 Ex $1688 Gd $1388
Orion III Field w/IC
   (12 or 20 ga.) . . . . NiB $1688 Ex $1397 Gd $1188
Orion III Classic w/IC
   (12 or 20 ga.) . . . . NiB $1988 Ex $1669 Gd $1367
Orion III English Field w/IC
   (12 or 20 ga.) . . . . NiB $1733 Ex $1448 Gd $1244
Orion Upland w/IC
   (12 or 20 ga.) . . . . NiB $1376 Ex $1133 Gd $976

GRADING: **NiB** = New in Box   **Ex** = Excellent or NRA 95%   **Gd** = Good or NRA 68%

**Weatherby Patrician
Deluxe Grade**

**Weatherby Regency
Trap Gun**

Skeet II w/fixed chokes ....NiB $1355 Ex $1125 Gd $950
Super Sporting Clays .....NiB $1988 Ex $1743 Gd $1129

PATRICIAN SLIDE-ACTION SHOTGUN
Hammerless. Takedown. 12 ga. 2.75-inch chamber. Four round tubular magazine. Bbls.: Vent rib; 26-inch, SK, IC M; 28-inch, M F; 30-inch, F choke. Weight: With 28-inch bbl., 7 lbs., 7 oz. Checkered pistol-grip stock and slide handle, recoil pad. Made in Japan from 1972 to 1982.
Field Grade................NiB $369 Ex $248 Gd $125
Deluxe model (etched receiver,
  fancy grade stock).........NiB $455 Ex $329 Gd $260
Trap Gun (w/30-inch
  full-choke bbl.)...........NiB $399 Ex $255 Gd $190

REGENCY FIELD GRADE O/U
SHOTGUN ....NiB $1387 Ex $1266 Gd $885
Boxlock with sideplates, elaborately engraved. Auto ejectors. Selective single trigger. Gauges: 12, 20. 2.75-inch chamber in 12 ga., 3-inch in 20 ga. Bbls.: Vent rib; 26-inch SK, IC/M, M/F (20 ga. only); 28-inch SK, IC/M, M/F; 30-inch M/F (12 ga only). Weight with 28-inch bbls.: 7 lbs., 6 oz., 12 ga.; 6 lbs., 14 oz., 20 ga. Checkered pistol-grip stock and forearm of fancy walnut. Made in Italy from 1965 to 1982.

REGENCY TRAP GUN........NiB $990 Ex $823 Gd $688
Similar to Regency Field Grade except has trap-style stock with straight or Monte Carlo comb. Bbls. have vent side ribs and high, wide vent top rib; 30- or 32-inch, M/F, IM/F or F/F chokes. Weight: With 32-inch bbls., 8 lbs. Made in Italy from 1965 to 1982.

WESTERN ARMS CORP. — Ithaca, New York

A division of Ithaca Gun Company

LONG RANGE HAMMERLESS DOUBLE
Boxlock. Plain extractors. Single or double triggers. Gauges: 12, 16, 20, .410. Bbls.: 26- to 32-inch, M/F choke standard. Weight: 7.5 lbs., 12 ga. Plain pistol-grip stock and forend. Made 1929 to 1946.
Double triggers ....NiB $398 Ex $244 Gd $165
Single trigger ....NiB $400 Ex $295 Gd $188

WESTERN AUTO — Kansas City, Missouri

MODEL 300H SLIDE-ACTION
REPEATER ....NiB $435 Ex $300 Gd $255
Gauges: 12,16, 20, .410. Four round tubular magazine. Bbls.: 26- to 30-inch, various chokes. Weight: About 7 lbs. Plain pistol-grip stock, grooved slide handle.

MODEL 310A SLIDE-ACTION
REPEATER ....NiB $366 Ex $270 Gd $200
Takedown. 12 ga. Five round tubular magazine. Bbls.: 28- and 30-inch. Weight: About 7.5 lbs. Plain pistol-grip stock.

MODEL 310B SLIDE-ACTION
REPEATER ....NiB $377 Ex $245 Gd $190
Same general specifications as Model 310A except chambered for 16 ga.

MODEL 310C SLIDE-ACTION
REPEATER ....NiB $365 Ex $269 Gd $180
Same general specifications as Model 310A except chambered for 20 ga.

MODEL 310E SLIDE-ACTION
REPEATER ....NiB $425 Ex $366 Gd $229
Same general specifications as Model 310A except chambered for .410 bore.

MODEL 325BK BOLT-ACTION
REPEATER ....NiB $276 Ex $190 Gd $125
Takedown. Two round detachable clip magazine. 20 ga. 26-inch bbl. with variable choke. Weight: 6.25 lbs.

WESTERN FIELD

See "W" for listings under Montgomery Ward.

WESTLEY RICHARDS & CO., LTD. — Birmingham, England

The Pigeon and Wildfowl gun, available in all of the Westley Richards models except the Ovundo, has the same general specifications as the corresponding standard field gun except has magnum action of extra strength and treble bolting, chambered for 12 gauge only (2.75- or 3-inch); 30-inch full choke barrels standard. Weight: About 8 lbs. The manufacturer warns that 12-gauge magnum shells should not be used in their standard weight double-barrel shotguns.

**Westley Richards
Deluxe Sidelock**

BEST QUALITY BOXLOCK HAMMERLESS DOUBLE-BARRELSHOTGUN

Boxlock. Hand-detachable locks and hinged cover plate. Selective ejectors. Double triggers or selective single trigger. Gauges: 12, 16, 20. Barrel lengths and boring to order. Weight: 5.5 to 6.25 lbs. depending on ga. and bbl. length. Checkered stock and forend, straight or half-pistol grip. Also supplied in Pigeon and Wildfowl models with same values. Made from 1899 to date.

Double triggers ..... NiB $22,975 Ex $18,990 Gd $14,270
Selective single trigger NiB $26,790 Ex $21,998 Gd $14,880

BEST QUALITY SIDELOCK HAMMERLESS DOUBLE-BARREL SHOTGUN

Hand-detachable sidelocks. Selective ejectors. Double triggers or selective single trigger. Gauges: 12, 16, 20, 28, .410. Bbl. lengths and boring to order. Weight: 4.75 to 6.75 lbs., depending on ga. and bbl. length. Checkered stock and forend, straight or half-pistol grip. Also supplied in Pigeon and Wildfowl models with same values. Currently manufactured.

Double triggers ..... NiB $29,669 Ex $26,766 Gd $22,880
Selective single trigger.... NiB $30,000 Ex $27,898 Gd $24,550

DELUXE MODEL BOXLOCK HAMMERLESS DOUBLE-BARREL SHOTGUN

Same general specifications as standard Best Quality gun except higher quality throughout. Has Westley Richards top-projection and treble-bite lever-work, hand-detachable locks.

Also supplied in Pigeon and Wildfowl models with same values. Currently manufactured.

w/double trigger ..... NiB $12,767 Ex $10,433 Gd $8998
**w/selective single
    trigger ....** NiB $32,880 Ex $30,880 Gd $13,990

DELUXE MODEL SIDELOCK

Same as Best Quality Sidelock except higher grade engraving and wood. Currently manufactured.

w/double triggers ... NiB $27,889 Ex $22,999 Gd $14,887
w/single trigger ..... NiB $31,998 Ex $26,999 Gd $18,998

MODEL E HAMMERLESS DOUBLE

Anson & Deeley-type boxlock action. Selective ejector or non-ejector. Double triggers. Gauges: 12, 16, 20. Barrel lengths and boring to order. Weight: 5.5 to 7.25 lbs. depending on type, ga. and bbl. length. Checkered stock and forend, straight or half-pistol grip. Also supplied in Pigeon and Wildfowl models with same values. Currently manufactured.

Ejector model .... NiB $5388 Ex $4378 Gd $2990
Non-ejector model .... NiB $4998 Ex $3788 Gd $3277

OVUNDO (O/U) ... NiB $19,677 Ex $16,999 Gd $12,998
Hammerless. Boxlock. Hand-detachable locks. Dummy sideplates. Selective ejectors. Selective single trigger. 12 ga. Barrel lengths and boring to order. Checkered stock/forend, straight or half-pistol grip. Mfd. before WW II.

TED WILLIAMS

See Sears shotguns.

WINCHESTER —New Haven, Connecticut

Formerly Winchester Repeating Arms Co., and then mfd. by Winchester-Western Div., Olin Corp., later by U.S. Repeating Arms Company. In 1999, production rights were acquired by Browning Arms Company.

**Westley Richards
Best Quality Sidelock**

**Westley Richards
Deluxe Boxlock**

**Westley Richards
Model E**

SHOTGUNS

Winchester Model 12 Classic
Limited Edition Grade I

Winchester Model 12
Field Gun (1972 Type)

Winchester Model 12
Pigeon Grade

Winchester Model 12 Standard

Winchester Model 12
Trap w/Monte Carlo Stock

MODEL 12 CLASSIC LIMITED Edition
Gauge: 20; 2.75-inch chamber. Bbl.: 26-inch vent rib; IC. Weight: 7 lbs. Checkered walnut buttstock and forend. Polished blue finish (Grade I) or engraved with gold inlays (Grade IV). Made from 1993 to 1995.

Grade I (4000) . . . . NiB $1100   Ex $889   Gd $656
Grade IV (1000) . . . . NiB $1700   Ex $1308   Gd $998

MODEL 12 FEATHERWEIGHT. . . NiB $688   Ex $577   Gd $555
Same as Model 12 Standard w/plain barrel except has alloy trigger guard. Modified takedown w/redesigned magazine tube, cap and slide handle. 12 ga. only. Bbls.: 26-inch IC; 28-inch M or F; 30-inch F choke. Serial numbers with "F" prefix. Weight: About 6.75 lbs. Made from 1959 to 1962.

MODEL 12 FIELD GUN, 1972 TYPE. . . NiB $800   Ex $685   Gd $522
Same general specifications as Standard Model 12 but 12 ga. only, 26- 28- or 30-inch vent rib bbl., standard chokes. Engine-turned bolt and carrier. Hand-checkered stock/slide handle of semifancy walnut. Made from 1972 to 1975.

MODEL 12 HEAVY DUCK GUN
Same general specifications as Standard Grade except 12 ga. only chambered for 3-inch shells. 30- or 32-inch plain, solid or vent rib bbl. w/full choke only. Three round magazine. Checkered slide handle and pistol-grip walnut buttstock w/recoil pad. Weight: 8.5 to 8.75 lbs. Made from 1935 to 1963.

Plain bbl. ` . . . . NiB $1366   Ex $890   Gd $644
Solid rib (disc. 1959) . . . . . . NiB $1977   Ex $1288   Gd $876
Vent. rib . . . . NiB $3288   Ex $2810   Gd $2466

MODEL 12 PIGEON GRADE
Deluxe versions of the regular Model 12 Standard or Field Gun, Duck Gun, Skeet Gun and Trap Gun made on special order. This grade has finer finish throughout, hand-smoothed action, engine-turned breech bolt and carrier, stock and extension slide handle of high grade walnut, fancy checkering, stock dimensions to individual specifications. Engraving and carving available at extra cost ranging from about $135 to over $1000. Disc. 1965.

Field Gun, plain bbl. . . . . . NiB $4233   Ex $3698   Gd $3166
Field Gun, vent rib . . . . NiB $2255   Ex $1987   Gd $1459
Skeet Gun, matted rib. . . . . NiB $2255   Ex $1987   Gd $1459
Skeet Gun, vent rib. . . . . . . NiB $3889   Ex $3350   Gd $3180
Skeet Gun, Cutts Compensator . . . NiB $1755   Ex $1398   Gd $1100
Trap Gun, matted rib . . . . . NiB $2233   Ex $1966   Gd $1399
Trap Gun, vent rib . . . . NiB $2288   Ex $2190   Gd $2008
16 ga. (Field), add 100%
16 ga. (Skeet), add 100%

**Winchester Model 12
12-4 Engraving**

20 ga. (Field), add 175%
20 ga. (Skeet), add 175%
28 ga. (Skeet), add 550%

MODEL 12 RIOT GUN . . . . . . NiB $977 Ex $844 Gd $600
Same general specifications as plain barrel Model 12 Standard
except has 20-inch cylinder bore bbl., 12 gauge only. Made
from 1918 to 1963.

MODEL 12 SKEET GUN . . . NiB $2200 Ex $1977 Gd $1488
Gauges: 12, 16, 20, 28. Five round tubular magazine. 26-inch
matted rib bbl., SK choke. Weight: About 7.75 lbs., 12 ga.;
6.75 lbs., other gauges. Bradley red or ivory bead front sight.
Winchester 94B middle sight. Checkered pistol-grip stock and
extension slide handle. Disc. after WWII.

**MODEL 12 SKEET GUN,
CUTTS COMPENSATOR** . . . . NiB $1233 Ex $1000 Gd $766
Same general specifications as standard Model 12 Skeet Gun
except has plain bbl. fitted with Cutts Compensator, 26 inches
overall. Disc. 1954.

**MODEL 12 SKEET GUN,
PLAIN-BARREL** . . . . NiB $2099 Ex $1887 Gd $1650
Same general specifications as standard Model 12 Skeet except
w/no rib.

**MODEL 12 SKEET GUN,
VENT RIB** . . . . NiB $4288 Ex $3760 Gd $3290
Same general specifications as standard Model 12 Skeet Gun
except has 26-inch bbl. with vent rib, 12 and 20 ga. Disc. in 1965.

**MODEL 12 SKEET GUN,
1972 TYPE** . . . . NiB $1288 Ex $909 Gd $663
Same gen. specifications as Standard Model 12 but 12 ga. only.
26-inch vent rib bbl., SK choke. Engine-turned bolt and carrier.
Hand-checkered skeet-style stock and slide handle of choice
walnut, recoil pad. Made from 1972 to 1975.

**MODEL 12 STANDARD GR.,
MATTED RIB** . . . . NiB $835 Ex $579 Gd $443
Same general specifications as plain bbl. Model 12 Standard
except has solid raised matted rib. Disc. after World War II.

**MODEL 12 STANDARD GR.,
VENT RIB** . . . . NiB $866 Ex $571 Gd $400
Same general specifications as plain barrel Model 12 Standard
except has vent rib. 26.75- or 30-inch bbl., 12 ga. only. Disc.
after World War II.

MODEL 12 STANDARD SLIDE-ACTION REPEATER
Hammerless. Takedown. Gauges: 12, 16, 20, 28. Six round
tubular magazine. Plain bbl. Lengths: 26- to 32-inches; choked
F to Cyl. Weight: About 7.5 lbs., 12 ga. 30-inch, 6.5 lbs. in
other ga. with 28-inch bbl. Plain pistol-grip stock, grooved
slide handle. Made from 1912 to 1964.
12 ga., 28-inch bbl., Full choke . . . . NiB $870 Ex $733 Gd $534
16 ga. . . . . NiB $966 Ex $881 Gd $533
20 ga. . . . . NiB $1277 Ex $855 Gd $633
28 ga. NiB $5767 Ex $3488 Gd $2499

**MODEL 12 SUPER PIGEON
GRADE** . . . . NiB $4329 Ex $3887 Gd $3176
Custom version of Model 12 with same general specifications
as standard models. 12 ga. only. 26-, 28- or 30-inch vent-rib
bbl., any standard choke. Engraved receiver. Hand-smoothed
and fitted action. Full fancy walnut stock and forearm made to
individual order. Made from 1965 to 1972.

MODEL 12 TRAP GUN
Same general specifications as Standard Model 12 except has
straighter stock, checkered pistol grip and extension slide han-
dle, recoil pad, 30-inch matted-rib bbl., F choke, 12 ga. only.
Disc. after World War II; vent rib model disc. 1965.
Matted rib bbl. . . . . NiB $2210 Ex $1966 Gd $1544
Straight stock, vent rib . . . . NiB $2299 Ex $2178 Gd $1933
Monte Carlo stock, vent rib . . . NiB $2175 Ex $2000 Gd $1865

**MODEL 12 TRAP GUN, 1972
TYPE** . . . . NiB $1299 Ex $1077 Gd $669
Same general specifications as Standard Model 12 but 12
gauge only. 30-inch vent-rib bbl., F choke. Engine-turned bolt
and carrier. Hand-checkered trap-style stock (straight or Monte
Carlo comb) and slide handle of select walnut, recoil pad.
Intro. in 1972. Disc.

**MODEL 20 SINGLE-SHOT HAMMER
GUN** . . . . NiB $1577 Ex $1266 Gd $1008
Takedown. .410 bore. 2.5-inch chamber. 26-inch bbl., F
choke. Checkered pistol-grip stock and forearm. Weight: About
6 lbs. Made from 1919 to 1924.

**ORIGINAL MODEL 21 DOUBLE-BARREL SHOTGUNS
(ORIGINAL PRODUCTION SERIES - 1930 to 1959)**
Hammerless. Boxlock. Automatic safety. Double triggers or
selective single trigger, selective or non-selective ejection (all
postwar Model 21 shotguns have selective single trigger and
selective ejection). Gauges: 12, 16, 20, 28 and .410 bore.
Bbls.: Raised matted rib or vent rib; 26-, 28-, 30-, 32-inch, the
latter in 12 ga. only; F, IM, M, IC, SK chokes. Weight: 7.5 lbs.,
12 ga. w/30-inch bbl.; about 6.5 lbs. 16 or 20 ga. w/28-inch
bbl. Checkered pistol- or straight-grip stock, regular or beavertail forend. Made from 1930 to 1959.
Standard Grade, 12 ga. . . . NiB $7344 Ex $6100 Gd $4350
Standard Grade, 16. Ga. . . NiB $9000 Ex $5466 Gd $4000
Standard Grade, 20 ga. . NiB $10,008 Ex $6355 Gd $3988
Tournament Grade, 12 ga.
   (1933-34) . . . . NiB $5733 Ex $5000 Gd $3889
Tournament Grade, 16 ga.
   (1933-34) . . . . NiB $6893 Ex $6324 Gd $4388

Winchester Model 21
Custom Grade

Winchester Model 21
Pigeon Grade

Winchester Model 23

Winchester Model 24

Winchester Model 25

Winchester Model 36

Winchester Model 37

Tournament Grade, 20 ga.
(1933-34) . . . . NiB $8244 Ex $6887 Gd $4632
Trap Grade, 12 ga.
(1940-59) . . . . NiB $5689 Ex $5000 Gd $4277
Trap Grade, 16 ga.
(1940-59) . . . . NiB $6044 Ex $4988 Gd $3776
Trap Grade, 20 ga.
(1940-59) . . . . NiB $7768 Ex $6322 Gd $3200
Skeet Grade, 12 ga.
(1936-59) . . . . NiB $5463 Ex $4465 Gd $3100
Skeet Grade, 16 ga.
(1936-59) . . . . NiB $6200 Ex $4988 Gd $3677
Skeet Grade, 20 ga.
(1936-59) . . . . NiB $7100 Ex $5998 Gd $4325
Duck Gun, 12 ga., 3-inch
(1940-52) . . . . NiB $5980 Ex $4966 Gd $3544

Magnum, 12 ga., 3-inch)
(1953-59) . . . . NiB $5688 Ex $4765 Gd $3300
Magnum, 20 ga., 3-inch
(1953-59) . . . . NiB $6900 Ex $5779 Gd $4200
Cust. Deluxe grade,
12 ga. (1993-59). . . . . . NiB $8634 Ex $6892 Gd $4855
Cust. Deluxe grade,
16 ga., (1933-59) . . . . NiB $10,339 Ex $8833 Gd $6450
Cust. Deluxe grade,
20 ga. (1933-59). . . . . NiB $11,880 Ex $9893 Gd $6588
Cust. Deluxe grade, 28 ga.
(1933-59) Very Rare . . . . NiB $30,000+
Cust. Deluxe grade, .410 (1933-59)
Very Rare . . . . NiB $35,000+
*Fewer than 100 sm. bore models (28 ga. and .410) were built,
which precludes accurate pricing, but projected values could*

exceed $30,000. Such rare specimens should be authenticated by factory letter and/or independent appraisals.

w/vent. rib,12 ga. models, add $900
w/vent. rib, 16 ga. models, add $1825
w/vent. rib, 20 ga. models, add $1375
w/double triggers & extractors, deduct 30%
w/double triggers, selective ejection, deduct 20%

With Custom Engraving:
No.1 pattern, add 25%
No. 2 pattern, add 35%
No. 3 pattern, add 50%
No. 4 pattern, add 35%
No. 5 pattern, add 65%
No. 6 pattern, add 75%

MODEL 21 CUSTOM, PIGEON, GRAND AMERICAN (CUSTOM SHOP SERIES - PRODUCTION 1959 TO 1981)

Since 1959 the Model 21 has been offered through the Custom Shop in deluxe models. (Custom, Pigeon, Grand American) on special order. General specifications same as for Model 21 standard models except these custom guns have full fancy American walnut stock and forearm with fancy checkering, finely polished and hand-smoothed working parts, etc.; engraving inlays, carved stocks and other extras are available at additional cost. Made 1959 to 1981.

Custom grade, 12 ga. . . . NiB $11,980 Ex $9876 Gd $6759
Custom grade, 16 ga. . . NiB $17,544 Ex $13,977 Gd $10,655
Custom grade, 20 ga. . . NiB $14,677 Ex $11,877 Gd $8321

Pigeon grade, 12 ga. NiB $17,889 Ex $14,670 Gd $10,300
Pigeon grade, 16 ga. NiB $22,889 Ex $18,987 Gd $13,770
Pigeon grade, 20 ga. NiB $21,800 Ex $19,880 Gd $14,800
Grand American, 12 ga. NiB $25,700 Ex $19,900 Gd $14,600
Grand American, 16 ga. NiB $39,600 Ex $31,877 Gd $22,955
Grand American, 20 ga. NiB $30,888 Ex $27,888 Gd $20,556
Grand American 3-barrel Set . . NiB $42,750 Ex $35,799 Gd $25,799
Small Bore Models
   28 ga. and .410 (fewer than 20 made), ... $35,000+
Fewer than 20 Small Bore models (28 ga. and .410) were built during this period, which precludes accurate pricing, but projected values could exceed $35,000. Such rare specimens should be authenticated by factory letter and/or independent appraisals.

For Custom Shop Engraving from this period:
#1 Pattern, add 10%
#2 Pattern, add 15%
#3 Pattern, add 25%
#4 Pattern, add 35%
#5 Pattern, add 45%
#6 Pattern, add 50%

MODEL 21 U.S.R.A. CUSTOM SERIES (CUSTOM SHOP PRODUCTION 1982 TO DATE*)

Individual model designations for the Model 21 (made from 1931 to 1982) were changed when U. S. Repeating Arms Company assumed production. The new model nomenclature for the Custom/Built catagory, includes: Standard Custom, Special Custom and Grand American — all of which are available on special order through the Custom Shop. General specifications remained the same on these consolidated model variations and included the addition of a Small Bore 2-Barrel Set (28/.410) and a 3-Barrel Set (20/28/.410). Made 1982 to date *Winchester stopped cataloging the Model 21 after 1987. Current manufacture is by Connecticut Shotgun Manufacturing Company with guns marked Model 21.

Standard custom model . . . NiB $6988 Ex $5570 Gd $4000
Special Custom model . . . . NiB $8000 Ex $6500 Gd $4666
Grand American model NiB $14,880 Ex $12,980 Gd $9660
Grand American model,
   2-bb. set . . . . NiB $48,900 Ex $38,790 Gd $26,998
Grand American, 3-bbl.
   set . . . . NiB $72,877 Ex $59,988 Gd $26,800

The values shown above represent the basic model in each catagory. Since many customers took advantage of the custom built options, individual gun appointments vary and values will need to be adjusted accordingly. For this reason, individual appraisals should be obtained on all subject firearms.

MODEL 23 SIDE-BY-SIDE SHOTGUN

Boxlock. Single trigger. Automatic safety. Gauges: 12, 20, 28, .410. Bbls.: 25.5-, 26-, 28-inch with fixed chokes or Winchoke tubes. Weight: 5.88 to 7 lbs. Checkered American walnut buttstock and forend. Made in 1979 for Olin at its Olin-Kodensha facility, Japan.
Classic 23 (gold inlay,
   engraved) . . . . NiB $2779 Ex $2466 Gd $2365
Custom 23 (plain receiver,
   Winchoke) . . . . NiB $1477 Ex $1155 Gd $966
Heavy Duck 23, Standard . NiB $2768 Ex $2398 Gd $2077
Lightweight 23, Classic . . . . NiB $2188 Ex $1808 Gd $1266
Light Duck 23, Standard . . . NiB $2987 Ex $2665 Gd $2240
Light Duck 23, 12 ga. Golden
   Quail. . . . . NiB $2877 Ex $2549 Gd $2266
Light Duck 23, .410 Golden
   Quail. . . . . NiB $4577 Ex $4328 Gd $3972
Custom Set 23, 20 & 28 ga. . . . NiB $6988 Ex $5100 Gd $3766

MODEL 24 HAMMERLESS DOUBLE

Boxlock. Double triggers. Plain extractors. Auto safety. Gauges: 12, 16, 20. Bbls.: 26-inch IC/M; 28-inch M/F (also IC/M in 12 ga. only); 30-inch M and F in 12 ga. only. Weight: About 7.5 lbs., 12 ga. Metal bead front sight. Plain pistol-grip stock, semi-beavertail forearm. Made from 1939 to 1957.
12 ga. model . . . . NiB $966 Ex $733 Gd $544
16 ga. model . . . . NiB $1088 Ex $800 Gd $623
20 ga. model . . . . NiB $1221 Ex $945 Gd $711

MODEL 25 RIOT GUN . . . . NiB $677 Ex $455 Gd $390

Same as Model 25 Standard except has 20-inch cylinder bore bbl., 12 ga. only. Made from 1949 to 1955.

MODEL 25 7550 . . . . Ex $404 Gd $358

Hammerless. Solid frame. 12 ga. only. Four round tubular magazine. 28-in. Plain bbl.; IC, M or F choke. Weight: About 7.5 lbs. Metal bead front sight. Plain pistol-grip stock, grooved slide handle. Made from 1949 to 1955.

MODEL 36 SINGLE-SHOT

BOLT ACTION . . . . NiB $1893 Ex $1688 Gd $1477
Takedown. Uses 9mm Short or Long shot or ball cartridges interchangeably. 18-inch bbl. Plain stock. Weight: About 3 lbs. Made from 1920 to 1927.

MODEL 37 SINGLE-SHOT SHOTGUN

Semi-hammerless. Auto ejection. Takedown. Gauges: 12, 16, 20, 28, .410. Bbl. lengths: 28-, 30-, 32-inch in all gauges except .410; 26- or 28-inch in .410; all barrels plain with F choke. Weight: About 6.5 pounds, 12 ga. Made from 1937 to 1963.
12, 16, 20 ga. models . . . . NiB $559 Ex $438 Gd $315
Youth model (20 ga.
   w/red dot indicator) . . . . NiB $559 Ex $438 Gd $315

SHOTGUNS

Winchester Model 37A

Winchester Model 37A Youth

Winchester
Model 40 Skeet

Winchester
Model 41 Deluxe

Winchester Model 42
Classic Limited Edition

Winchester Model 42
Standard

.410 model . . . . NiB $769 Ex $588 Gd $437
28 ga. model ("Red Letter"
   version) . . . . NiB $2687 Ex $2531 Gd $2033
Other "Red Letter" models, add 20%
W/32-inch bbl., add 15%

MODEL 37A SINGLE-SHOT SHOTGUN
Similar to Model 370 except has engraved receiver and gold trigger, checkered pistol-grip stock, fluted forearm; 16 ga. available with 30-inch bbl. only. Made from 1973 to 1980.

12, 16 or 20 ga. models	NiB $579	Ex $300	Gd $219
28 ga. model	NiB $2590	Ex $2331	Gd $2268
.410 model	NiB $754	Ex $559	Gd $366
w/32-inch bbl., add $50			

MODEL 37A YOUTH . . . . NiB $566 Ex $397 Gd $244
Similar to Model 370 Youth except has engraved receiver and gold trigger, checkered pistol-grip stock, fluted forearm. Made 1973 to 1980.

MODEL 40 STANDARD
AUTOLOADER . . . . NiB $977 Ex $721 Gd $533
Streamlined receiver. Hammerless. Takedown. 12 ga. only. Four round tubular magazine. 28- or 30-inch bbl.; M or F choke. Weight: About 8 lbs. Bead sight on ramp. Plain pistol-grip stock, semi-beavertail forearm. Made from 1940 to 1941.

MODEL 40 SKEET GUN . . . . . NiB $1188 Ex $966 Gd $700
Same general specifications as Model 40 Standard except has 24-inch plain bbl. w/Cutts Compensator and screw-in choke tube, checkered forearm and pistol grip, grip cap. Made 1940 to 1941.

MODEL 41 SINGLE-SHOT BOLT ACTION
Takedown. .410 bore. 2.5-inch chamber (chambered for 3-inch shells after 1932). 24-inch bbl., F choke. Plain straight stock standard. Also made in deluxe version. Made from 1920 to 1934.

Standard model.	NiB $800	Ex $618	Gd $509
Deluxe model	NiB $954	Ex $732	Gd $600

Winchester Model 50 Skeet

MODEL 42 STANDARD GRADE

Hammerless. Takedown. .410 bore (3- or 2.5-inch shell). Tubular magazine holds five 3-inch or six 2.5-inch shells. 26- or 28-inch plain or solid-rib bbl.; cylinder bore, M or F choke. Weight: 5.8 to 6.5 lbs. Plain pistol-grip stock; grooved slide handle. Made from 1933 to 1963.

w/plain bbl. . . . . NiB $2675 Ex $2143 Gd $1609
Model 42 Standard w/solid rib. . . . NiB $3750 Ex $3396 Gd $3184

MODEL 42

CLASSIC LTD. EDITION . . . NiB $1886 Ex $1599 Gd $1179
Gauge: .410 with 2.75-inch chamber. Bbl.: 26-inch vent rib; F choke. Weight: 7 lbs. Checkered walnut buttstock and forend. Engraved blue with gold inlays. Limited production of 850. Made from 1993.

MODEL 42 DELUXE . NiB $22,700 Ex $19,745 Gd $17,998
Same general specifications as the Model 42 Trap Grade except available w/vent rib after 1955. Finer finish throughout w/hand-smoothed action, engine-turned breech bolt and carrier, stock and extension slide handle of high grade walnut, fancy checkering, stock dimensions to individual specifications. Engraving and carving were offered at extra cost. Made 1940-63.

Note: *Exercise caution on VR models not marked "DELUXE" on the bottom of the receiver. A factory letter will insure that the rib was installed during the initial manufacturing process. Unfortunately, factory authentication is not always possible due to missing or destroyed records. To further complicate this matter, not all VR ribs were installed by Winchester. From 1955-63, both Deluxe and Skeet Grade models were available with Simmons style ribs. After-market rib installations are common.*

MODEL 42 PIGEON GRADE

This higher-grade designation is similar to the Deluxe grade and is available in all configurations. May be identified by engraved Pigeon located at the base of the magazine tube. Most production occurred in the late 1940's. **NOTE:** *To determine the value of any Model 42 Pigeon Grade, add 50% to value listed under the specified Model 42 configuration.*

MODEL 42 SKEET GUN

Same general specifications as Model 42 Standard except has checkered straight or pistol-grip stock and extension slide handle, 26- or 28-inch plain, solid-rib or vent-rib bbl. May be choked F., Mod., Imp. Cyl. or Skeet. Note: Some Model 42 Skeet Guns are chambered for 2.5-inch shells only. Made from 1933 to 1963.

w/plain bbl. . . . . NiB $6277 Ex $4500 Gd $3769
w/solid rib . . . . NiB $6277 Ex $4500 Gd $3769
w/vent. rib . . . . NiB $6833 Ex $5971 Gd $4948
w/ 2.5-inch chamber, add. 35%

MODEL 42 TRAP GRADE

This higher grade designation was available in both field and skeet configurations and is fitted w/deluxe wood w/trap grade checkering pattern and marked "TRAP" on bottom of receiver. Made 1934 to 1939. Superseded by the Deluxe model in 1940.

w/plain bbl. . . . . NiB $27,977 Ex $24,770 Gd $22,665
w/solid rib . . . . NiB $27,977 Ex $24,770 Gd $22,665
w/vent. rib . . . . NiB $27,855 Ex $25,693 Gd $23,449

MODEL 50 FIELD GUN,

VENT RIB . . . . NiB $766 Ex $541 Gd $396
Same as Model 50 Standard except has vent rib.

MODEL 50 SKEET GUN . . . NiB $1422 Ex $1269 Gd $1031
Same as Model 50 Standard except has 26-inch vent-rib bbl. with SK choke, skeet-style stock of select walnut.

MODEL 50 STANDARD GRADE . . NiB $779 Ex $500 Gd $388
Non-recoiling bbl. and independent chamber. Gauges: 12 and 20. Two round tubular magazine. Bbl.: 12 ga. — 26-, 28-, 30-inch; 20 ga. — 26-, 28-inch; IC, SK, M, F choke. Checkered pistol-grip stock and forearm. Weight: About 7.75 lbs. Made from 1954 to 1961.

MODEL 50 TRAP GUN . . . . NiB $1466 Ex $1284 Gd $1066
Same as Model 50 Standard except 12 ga. only, has 30-inch vent-rib bbl. with F choke, Monte Carlo stock of select walnut.

MODEL 59 SEMI-AUTOMATIC . . . NiB $878 Ex $655 Gd $555
Gauge: 12. Magazine holds two rounds. Alloy receiver. Win-Lite steel and fiberglass bbl.: 26-inch IC, 28-inch M or F choke, 30-inch F choke; also furnished with 26-inch bbl. with Versalite choke (interchangeable F, M, IC tubes; one supplied with gun). Weight: About 6.5 lbs. Checkered pistol-grip stock and forearm. Made 1959 to 1965.

MODEL 1893 . . . . NiB $1100 Ex $930 Gd $600
First pump-action shotgun manufactured by Winchester. Standard Grade. Solid frame. Gauges: 12 black powder shells only. Five-round tubular magazine. Bbl.: Plain; 30 or 32 inches, F choked. Plain pistol-grip stock, grooved slide handle. Appox. 34,000 mfg. Made from 1893 to 1897.

MODEL 1897 BUSH GUN

Takedown or solid frame. Same general specifications as standard Model 1897 except w/ 26-in. cylinder bore bbl. Made 1897 to 1931.
w/solid frame . . . . NiB $995 Ex $700 Gd $554
Takedown model. . . . . NiB $1299 Ex $1056 Gd $800

MODEL 1897 RIOT GUN

Takedown or solid frame. Same general specifications as standard Model 1897 except 12 ga. only, 20-inch cylinder bore bbl. Made from 1898 to 1935.
w/solid frame . . . . NiB $1544 Ex $1187 Gd $900
Takedown model. . . . . NiB $1390 Ex $1055 Gd $773

SHOTGUNS

Winchester Model 1897 Riot Gun

Winchester Model 101

MODEL 1897 TRAP, TOURNAMENT & PIGEON GRADES
These higher grade models offer higher overall quality than the standard grade. Made from 1897 to 1939.

Standard Trap grade	NiB $2600	Ex $2208	Gd $1188
Special Trap grade	NiB $1794	Ex $1566	Gd $1180
Tournament grade (Black Diamond)	NiB $2971	Ex $2387	Gd $1698
Pigeon grade	NiB $11,000	Ex $9533	Gd $3000

MODEL 1897 TRENCH GUN .. NiB $4800 Ex $3693 Gd $2138
Solid frame. Same as Model 1897 Riot Gun except has handguard and is equipped with a bayonet. World War I government issue, from 1917 to 1918.
w/military markings, add 20%

MODEL 1897 SLIDE-ACTION REPEATER
Standard Grade. Takedown or solid frame. Gauges: 12 and 16. Five-round tubular magazine. Bbl.: Plain; 26 to 32 inches, the latter in 12 ga. only; choked F to Cyl. Weight: About 7.75 lbs. (12 ga. w/28-inch barrel). Plain pistol-grip stock, grooved slide handle. Made from 1897 to 1957.

12 ga. w/solid frame	NiB $1110	Ex $855	Gd $675
16 ga. w/solid frame	NiB $1110	Ex $855	Gd $675
12 ga., takedown model	NiB $1356	Ex $1108	Gd $888
16 ga., takedown model	NiB $1356	Ex $1108	Gd $888

NOTE: *All Winchester Model 101s are mfd. for Olin Corp. at its Olin-Kodensha facility in Tochigi, Japan. Production for Olin Corp. stopped in Nov. 1987. Importation of Model 101s was continued by Classic Doubles under that logo until 1990. See separate heading for additional data.*

MODEL 101
COMBINATION GUN .... NiB $2983 Ex $2777 Gd $2369
12-ga. Winchoke bbl. on top and rifle bbl. chambered for .30-06 on bottom (over/under). 25-inch bbls. Engraved receiver. Hand checkered walnut stock and forend. Weight: 8.5 lbs. Mfd. for Olin Corp. in Japan.

MODEL 101 DIAMOND
GRADE TARGET .... NiB $1978 Ex $1596 Gd $1180
Similar to Model 101 Standard except silvered frame and Winchoke interchangeable choke tubes. Made from 1981 to 1990.

MODEL 101 O/U FIELD GUN
Boxlock. Engraved receiver. Auto ejectors. Single selective trigger. Combination bbl. selector and safety. Gauges: 12 and 28, 2.75-inch chambers; 20 and .410, 3-inch chambers. Vent rib bbls.: 30- (12 ga. only) and 26.5-inch, IC/M. Weight: 6.25 to 7.75 lbs. depending on gauge and bbl. length. Hand-checkered French walnut and forearm. Made from 1963 to 1981. Gauges other than 12 introduced 1966.

12 and 20 ga.	NiB $1099	Ex $882	Gd $723
28 and .410 ga.	NiB $1622	Ex $1244	Gd $977
12 and 20 ga. mag.	NiB $1288	Ex $1077	Gd $766

MODEL 101 MAGNUM. .... NiB $1300 Ex $1000 Gd $520
Same specifications as Model 101 Field except w/ 30-in. bbl., 12 or 20 ga. with 3-inch chambers. 25.5-inch bbls. with F/M or F/F choke. Made 1966 to 1981.

MODEL 101 PIGEON GRADE
Similar to Model 101 Standard except engraved silvered frame and select wood. Winchoke tubes. Made from 1974 to 1987.

12 ga. model	NiB $2200	Ex $1820	Gd $1150
20 ga. model	NiB $2700	Ex $2000	Gd $1500
28 ga. model	NiB $3760	Ex $2920	Gd $1700
.410 model	NiB $3530	Ex $2925	Gd $1700

MODEL 101 PIGEON GRADE LIGHTWEIGHT
Similar to Model 101 Standard except 20 ga. only w/ 27-in. bbl. Receiver engraved w/ gold. Limited production. Made 1995 to 1996.
Two Bbl. Set .... NiB $3600 Ex $2960 Gd $1900

MODEL 101 PIGEON GRADE
SPORTING .... NiB $2275 Ex $1630 Gd $900
Similar to Model 101 Standard except 12 ga. only w/ 30- or 32-in. ported, wide rib bbl. Silver nitride receiver. Stock: adj. comb, high grade walnut. Made 2009 to 2010.

MODEL 101 QUAIL SPECIAL
Same specifications as small-frame Model 101 except in 28 and .410 ga. with 3-inch chambers. 25.5-inch bbls. with choke tubes (28 ga.) or M/F chokes (.410). Imported from Japan in 1984 to 1987.

12 ga. model	NiB $3155	Ex $2926	Gd $2554
20 ga.	NiB $3599	Ex $3466	Gd $3200
28 ga. model	NiB $5799	Ex $4933	Gd $4200
.410 model	NiB $4733	Ex $4122	Gd $3888

Winchester Model 370

Winchester Model 1001
Sporting Clays

Winchester Model 1200
Field Gun

Winchester Model 1200
Field Gun w/Vent Rib

MODEL 101 SKEET . . . . NiB $1200 Ex $830 Gd $600
Same specifications as Model 101 Field except w/ 26.5-in. bbl., 12 or 20 ga. oe 28-in. bbl., 28 ga. or .410. Made 1966 to 1984.

Three Gauge Set
1974 to 1984) . . . . NiB $3800 Ex $3100 Gd $2000

MODEL 101 TRAP . . . . NiB $1330 Ex $950 Gd $620
Same specifications as Model 101 Field except w/ 30 or 32-in. bbl., 12 ga. only. Standard or wide vent rib. Made 1966 to 1984.

MODEL 370
SINGLE-SHOT SHOTGUN . . . . . NiB $245 Ex $200 Gd $99
Visible hammer. Auto ejector. Takedown. Gauges: 12, 16, 20, 28, .410. 2.75-inch chambers in 16 and 28 ga., 3-inch in other ga. Bbls.: 12 ga., 30-, 32- or 36-inch,16 ga; 30- or 32-inch; 20 and 28 ga., 28-inch; .410 bore, 26-inch, all F choke. Weight: 5.5-6.25 lbs. Plain pistol-grip stock and forearm. Made from 1968 to 1973.

MODEL 370 YOUTH MODEL
Same as standard Model 370 except has 26-inch bbl. and 12.5-inch stock with recoil pad; 20 gauge with IM choke, .410 bore with F choke. Made from 1968 to 1973.
12, 16 or 20 ga. models . . . . . . NiB $244 Ex $190 Gd $121
20 ga. model . . . . NiB $300 Ex $221 Gd $165
.410 model . . . . NiB $355 Ex $220 Gd $175

MODEL 1001 O/U SHOTGUN
Boxlock. 12 ga., 2.75- or 3-inch chambers. Bbls.: 28- or 30-inch vent rib; WinPlus choke tubes. Weight: 7-7.75 lbs. Checkered walnut buttstock and forend. Blued finish with scroll engraved receiver. Made from 1993 to 1998.
Field model (28-inch bbl., 3-inch) . . . NiB $1133 Ex $978 Gd $726
Sporting Clays model . . . . . . NiB $1166 Ex $1044 Gd $863
Sporting Clays Lite model . . . . NiB $1187 Ex $990 Gd $734

MODEL 1200 DEER GUN . . . . . NiB $398 Ex $221 Gd $155
Same as standard Model 1200, except has special 22-inch bbl. with rifle-type sights, for rifled slug or buckshot; 12 ga. only. Weight: 6.5 lbs. Made from 1965 to 1974.

MODEL 1200 DEFENDER SERIES
SLIDE-ACTION SECURITY SHOTGUNS
Hammerless. 12 ga. w/3-inch chamber. 18-inch bbl. w/cylinder bore and metal front bead or rifle sights. Four- or 7-round magazine. Weight: 5.5 to 6.75 lbs. 25.6 inches (PG Model) or 38.6 inches overall. Matte blue finish. Synthetic pistol grip or walnut finished hardwood buttstock w/grooved synthetic or hardwood slide handle. NOTE: Even though the 1200 series was introduced in 1964 and was supplanted by the Model 1300 in 1978, the Security series (including the Defender model) was marketed under 1200 series alpha-numeric product codes (G1200DM2R) until 1989. In 1990, the same Defender model was marketed under a 4-digit code (7715) and was then advertised in the 1300 series.
Defender w/hardwood
stock,bead sight . . . . NiB $325 Ex $233 Gd $188
Defender w/hardwood
stock, rifle sights. . . . . NiB $325 Ex $233 Gd $188
Defender model w/pistol-grip
stock . . . . NiB $325 Ex $233 Gd $188
Defender Combo model
w/extra 28-inch plain bbl. . . NiB $345 Ex $290 Gd $239
Defender Combo model
w/extra 28-inch vent rib bbl. NiB $425 Ex $344 Gd $239

MODEL 1200 MAGNUM FIELD GUN
Same as standard Model 1200 except chambered for 3-inch 12 and 20 ga. magnum shells; plain or vent-rib bbl., 28- or 30-inch, F choke. Weight: 7.38 to 7.88 lbs. Made from 1964 to 1983.
w/plain bbl. . . . . NiB $325 Ex $240 Gd $179
w/vent. rib bbl. . . . . NiB $350 Ex $265 Gd $190
w/recoil reduction system, add $100

SHOTGUNS

Winchester Model 1300
Deer Series — Black Shadow
Synthetic Stock

Winchester Model 1300
Deer Series — Advantage
Full Camo Pattern

Winchester Model 1300
Defender Series — Stainless
Marine Synthetic Stock

Winchester Model 1300
Lady Defender — Synthetic Full Stock

Winchester Model 1300
Lady Defender — Synthetic Pistol Grip Stock

Winchester Model 1300
Defender 5-Shot Combo

MODEL 1200 RANGER
SLIDE-ACTION SHOTGUN . . . NiB $400 Ex $285 Gd $195
Hammerless. 12 and 20 ga.; 3-inch chambers. Walnut finished hardwood stock, ribbed forearm. 28-inch vent-rib bbl.; Winchoke system. Weight: 7.25 lbs. Made from 1982 to 1990 by U. S. Repeating Arms.

MODEL 1200 RANGER YOUTH
SLIDE-ACTION SHOTGUN . . . NiB $400 Ex $285 Gd $195
Same general specifications as standard Ranger Slide-Action except chambered for 20 ga. only, has Four round magazine, recoil pad on buttstock, weight: 6.5 lbs. Mfd. by U. S. Repeating Arms.

MODEL 1200 RANGER SLIDE-ACTION FIELD GUN
Front-locking rotary bolt. Takedown. Four round magazine. Gauges: 12, 16, 20 (2.75-inch chamber). Bbl.: Plain or vent

rib; 26-, 28-, 30-inch; IC, M, F choke or with Winchoke (interchangeable tubes IC-M-F). Weight: 6.5 to 7.25 lbs. Checkered pistol-grip stock and fore

arm (slide handle), recoil pad; also avail. 1966 to 1970 w/ Winchester recoil reduction system (Cycolac stock). Made from 1964 to 1983.

w/plain bbl.	NiB $400	Ex $285	Gd $195
w/vent. rib bbl.	NiB $420	Ex $305	Gd $217
w/recoil reduction system, add			$100
w/Winchoke, add			$50

MODEL 1200 STAINLESS MARINE SERIES SLIDE-ACTION SECURITY SHOTGUN

Similar to Model 1200 Defender except w/6-round magazine. 18-inch bbl. of ordnance stainless steel w/cylinder bore and rifle sights. Weight: 7 lbs. Bright chrome finish. Synthetic pistol grip or walnut finished hardwood buttstock w/grooved synthetic or hardwood slide handle.Made from 1984 to 1990.

w/hardwood stock	NiB $325	Ex $235	Gd $175
w/pistol-grip stock	NiB $325	Ex $235	Gd $175

MODEL 1200 STAINLESS POLICE SERIES SLIDE-ACTION SECURITY SHOTGUN

Similar to Model 1200 Defender except w/6-round magazine. 18-inch bbl. of ordnance stainless steel w/cylinder bore and rifle sights. Weight: 7 lbs. Matte chrome finish. Synthetic pistol grip or walnut- finished hardwood buttstock w/grooved synthetic or hardwood slide handle.Made from 1984-90.

Police model w/hardwood stock	NiB $255	Ex $202	Gd $125
Police model w/pistol grip stock	NiB $255	Ex $202	Gd $125

MODEL 1200 TRAP GUN

Same as standard Model 1200 except 12 gauge only. Has 2-round magazine, 30-inch vent-rib bbl., Full choke or 28-inch with Winchoke. Semi-fancy walnut stock, straight Made from 1965-73. Also available 1966 to 1970 w/Winchester recoil reduction system.

w/straight trap stock	NiB $425	Ex $260	Gd $180
w/Monte Carlo stock	NiB $425	Ex $260	Gd $180
w/Recoil reduction system, add			$100
w/Winchoke, add			$50

MODEL 1200 RANGER

COMBINATION SHOTGUN. . . NiB $440 Ex $300 Gd $217
Same as Ranger Deer combination except has one 28-inch vent-rib bbl. with M choke and one 18-inch Police Cyl. bore bbl. Made 1987 to 1990.

MODEL 1200 SKEET GUN . . . . NiB $450 Ex $310 Gd $225

Same as standard Model 1200 except 12 and 20 ga. only; has 2-round magazine, specially tuned trigger, 26-inch vent-rib bbl. SK choke, semi-fancy walnut stock and forearm. Weight: 7.25 to 7.5 lbs. Made 1965 to 1973. Also avail. 1966 to 1970 with Winchester recoil reduction system (add $50 to value).

MODEL 1300 CAMOPACK. . . . NiB $465 Ex $390 Gd $279

Gauge: 12.3-inch Magnum. Four round magazine. Bbls.: 30-and 22-inch with Winchoke system. Weight: 7 lbs. Laminated stock with Win-Cam camouflage green, cut checkering, recoil pad, swivels and sling. Made from 1987-88.

MODEL 1300 DEER SERIES

Similar to standard Model 1300 except 12 or 20 ga. only w/ special 22-inch cyl. bore or rifled bbl. and rifle-type sights. Weight: 6.5 lbs. Checkered walnut or synthetic stock w/satin walnut, black or Advantage Full Camo Pattern finish. Matte blue or full-camo metal finish. Made from 1994 to 2006.

w/walnut stock (intro. 1994)	NiB $425	Ex $360	Gd $265
Black Shadow Deer model w/synthetic stock (intro. 1994)	NiB $400	Ex $298	Gd $220
Advantage Camo model (1995-98)	NiB $445	Ex $377	Gd $280
Deer Combo			
Deer Combo w/22- and 28-inch bbls. (1994-98)	NiB $515	Ex $455	Gd $390
W/rifled bbl. (intro. 1996), add			$75

MODEL 1300 DEFENDER SERIES

Gauges: 12 or 20 ga. 18- 24- 28-inch vent rib bbl. w/3-inch chamber. Four-, 7- or 8- round magazine. Weight: 5.6 to 7.4 lbs. Blued, chrome or matte stainless finish. Wood or synthetic stock. Made from 1985 to 2006.

Combo model	NiB $490	Ex $375	Gd $277
Hardwood stock model	NiB $365	Ex $299	Gd $200
Synthetic pistol-grip model	NiB $270	Ex $283	Gd $203
Synthetic stock model	NiB $335	Ex $279	Gd $225
Lady Defender synthetic stock (made 1996)	NiB $320	Ex $255	Gd $210
Lady Defender synthetic Pistol-grip (made 1996)	NiB $320	Ex $255	Gd $210
Stainless marine model w/synthetic stock	NiB $555	Ex $435	Gd $290

MODEL 1300 DELUXE SLIDE-ACTION

Gauges: 12 and 20 w/3-inch chamber. Four round magazine. Bbl.:22, 26 or 28 inch vent rib bbl. w/Winchoke tubes. Weight: 6.5 lbs. Checkered walnut buttstock and forend w/high luster finish. Polished blue metal finish with roll-engraved receiver. Made from 1984 to 2006.

Model 1300 Deluxe w/high gloss finish	NiB $500	Ex $390	Gd $292
Model 1300 Ladies/Youth model w/22-inch bbl., (disc. 1992)	NiB $455	Ex $360	Gd $258

MODEL 1300 FEATHERWEIGHT SLIDE-ACTION SHOTGUN

Hammerless. Takedown. Four round magazine. Gauges: 12 and 20 (3-inch chambers). Bbls.: 22, 26 or 28 inches w/plain or vent rib w/Winchoke tubes. Weight: 6.38 to 7 lbs. Checkered walnut buttstock, grooved slide handle. Made from 1978 to 1994.

w/plain bbl.	NiB $400	Ex $365	Gd $290
w/vent. rib	NiB $400	Ex $365	Gd $290
XTR model	NiB $400	Ex $365	Gd $290

MODEL 1300 RANGER SERIES

Gauges: 12 or 20 ga. w/3-inch chamber. Five round magazine. 22- (Rifled), 26- or 28-inch vent-rib bbl. w/Winchoke tubes. Weight: 7.25 lbs. Blued finish. Walnut-finished hardwood buttstock and forend. Made from 1984 to 2006.

Standard model	NiB $377	Ex $366	Gd $270
Combo model	NiB $465	Ex $399	Gd $280
Ranger Deer combo (D&T w/rings & bases)	NiB $455	Ex $380	Gd $265
Ranger Ladies/Youth	NiB $366	Ex $255	Gd $190

MODEL 1300 SLIDE-ACTION FIELD GUN

Takedown w/front-locking rotary bolt. Gauges: 12, 20 w/3-inch chamber. Four round magazine. Bbl.: Vent rib; 26-, 28-, 30-inch w/ Win-choke tubes IC-M-F). Weight: 7.25 lbs. Checkered walnut or synthetic stock w/standard, black or Advantage Full Camo Pattern finish. Matte blue or full-camo metal finish. Made from 1994 to 2006.

SHOTGUNS

Winchester Model 1300
Turkey Gun

Winchester Model 1300
XTR w/Winchoke

Winchester Model 1300
Magnum Waterfowl

Standard Field w/walnut stock . NiB $445 Ex $320 Gd $266
Black Shadow w/black
　synthetic stock . . . . NiB $365 Ex $275 Gd $200
Advantage Camo model . . . . . . NiB $455 Ex $375 Gd $290

MODEL 1300 SLUG HUNTER SERIES
Similar to standard Model 1300 except chambered 12 ga. only w/special 22-inch smoothbore w/sabot-rifled choke tube or fully rifled bbl. w/rifle-type sights. Weight: 6.5 lbs. Checkered walnut, hardwood or laminated stock w/satin walnut or WinTuff finish. Matte blue metal finish. Made from 1988 to 1994.
w/hardwood stock . . . . NiB $465 Ex $365 Gd $250
w/laminated stock. . . . . NiB $515 Ex $400 Gd $290
w/walnut stock . . . . NiB $500 Ex $380 Gd $265
Whitetails Unlimited model
　w/beavertail forend . . . . NiB $475 Ex $396 Gd $300
w/sabot-rifled choke tubes, add $50

MODEL 1300 TURKEY SERIES
Gauges: 12 or 20 ga. 22-inch bbl. w/3-inch chamber. Four round magazine. 43 inches overall. Weight: 6.4 to 6.75 lbs. Buttstock and magazine cap, sling studs w/Cordura sling. Drilled and tapped to accept scope base. Checkered walnut, synthetic or laminated wood stock w/low luster finish. Matte blue or full camo finish. Made from 1985 to 2006.
w/Advantage camo . . . . NiB $390 Ex $285 Gd $216
w/Realtree All-Purpose camo . . NiB $488 Ex $369 Gd $275
w/Realtre Gray All-Purpose
　camo. . . . . NiB $500 Ex $405 Gd $325
w/Realtree All-Purpose
　camo (matte finish). . . . . NiB $525 Ex $420 Gd $355
w/Black Shadow synthetic stockNiB $355 Ex $285 Gd $190
w/Win-Cam green
　laminate stock . . . . NiB $445 Ex $365 Gd $225

Win-Cam combo
　(22- or 30-inch bbl.) . . . . NiB $465 Ex $420 Gd $350
Win-Cam NWTF model
　(22- or 30-inch bbl.) . . . . NiB $525 Ex $375 Gd $285
Win-Cam Youth/Ladies
　model (20 ga.) . . . . NiB $565 Ex $435 Gd $310
Win-Tuf model w/brown
　laminated wood stock. . . . . . . NiB $490 Ex $388 Gd $265

MODEL 1300 WATERFOWL SLIDE-ACTION SHOTGUN
Similar to 1300 Standard model except has 28- or 30-inch vent rib bbl. w/Winchoke tubes. Weight: 7 lbs. Matte blue metal finish. Checkered walnut finished hardwood or brown laminated Win-Tuffwood stock w/camo sling, swivels and recoil pad. Made from 1984 to 1992.
w/hardwood stock . . . . NiB $435 Ex $300 Gd $220
w/laminated stock. . . . . NiB $435 Ex $300 Gd $220

MODEL 1300 XTR
SLIDE-ACTION . . . . NiB $550 Ex $455 Gd $3209
Hammerless. Takedown. Four shot magazine. Gauges: 12 and 20 (3-inch chambers). Bbl.: Plain or vent rib; 28-inch bbls.; Winchoke (interchangeable tubes IC-M-F). Weight: About 7 lbs. Disc. 2006.

MODEL 1400 AUTOMATIC FIELD GUN
Gas-operated. Front-locking rotary bolt. Takedown. Two round magazine. Gauges: 12, 16, 20 (2.75-inch chamber). Bbl.: Plain or vent rib; 26-, 28-, 30-inch; IC, M, F choke, or with Winchoke (interchangeable tubes IC-M-F). Weight: 6.5 to 7.25 lbs. Checkered pistol-grip stock and forearm, recoil pad, also available with Winchester recoil reduction system (Cycolac stock). Made from 1964 to 1968.
w/plain bbl. . . . . NiB $355 Ex $244 Gd $190
w/vent. rib bbl. . . . . NiB $390 Ex $244 Gd $196

Winchester Model 1400 Field

Winchester Model 1500 w/Plain Barrel

Winchester Model 1500
w/Vent Rib Barrel

w/recoil reduction system, add $125
w/Winchoke, add $50

MODEL 1400 DEER GUN. . . . . NiB $369 Ex $255 Gd $190
Same as standard Model 1400 except has special 22-inch bbl.
with rifle-type sights, for rifle slug or buckshot; 12 ga. only.
Weight: 6.25 lbs. Made from 1965 to 1968.

MODEL 1400
MARK II DEER GUN. . . . . NiB $460 Ex $345 Gd $290
Same general specifications as Model 1400 Deer Gun. Made
from 1968-73.

MODEL 1400 MARK II FIELD GUN
Same general specifications as Model 1400 Field Gun, except
not chambered for 16 gauge; Winchester Recoil Reduction
System not available after 1970. Only 28-inch barrels w/
Winchoke offered after 1973. Made from 1968 to 1978.
w/plain bbl. . . . . NiB $450 Ex $365 Gd $287
w/plain bbl. and Winchoke. . . . NiB $475 Ex $388 Gd $315
w/ vent. rib bbl. . . . . NiB $544 Ex $390 Gd $290
w/vent. rib bbl. and Winchoke NiB $566 Ex $445 Gd $390

Add for Winchester recoil reduction system $150

MODEL 1400 MARK II
SKEET GUN . . . . NiB $535 Ex $423 Gd $356
Same general specifications as Model 1400 Skeet Gun. Made
from 1968 to 1973.

MODEL 1400 MARK II TRAP GUN
Same general specifications as Model 1400 Trap Gun except
also furnished with 28-inch bbl. and Winchoke. Winchester
recoil reduction system not available after 1970. Made from
1968 to 1973.
w/straight stock . . . . NiB $655 Ex $475 Gd $353
w/Monte Carlo stock . . . . NiB $657 Ex $525 Gd $400
w/recoil reduction system, add $150
w/Winchoke, add $50

MODEL 1400 MARK II
UTILITY SKEET . . . . NiB $590 Ex $445 Gd $355
Same general specifications as Model 1400 Mark II Skeet Gun
except has stock and forearm of field grade walnut. Made 1970
to 1973.

MODEL 1400 MARK II
UTILITY TRAP. . . . . NiB $590 Ex $445 Gd $355
Same as Model 1400 Mark II Trap Gun except has Monte Carlo
stock/forearm of field grade walnut. Made from 1970 to 1973.

MODEL 1400 RANGER SEMIAUTOMATIC
SHOTGUN. . . . . NiB $566 Ex $365 Gd $255
Gauges: 12, 20. Two round magazine. 28-inch vent rib bbl.
with F choke. Overall length: 48.63 inches. Weight: 7 to
7.25 lbs. Walnut finish, hardwood stock and forearm with cut
checkering. Made from 1984 to 1990 by U. S. Repeating Arms.

MODEL 1400 RANGER SEMIAUTOMATIC
DEER SHOTGUN . . . . NiB $500 Ex $369 Gd $255
Same general specifications as Ranger Semiautomatic except
24.13-inch plain bbl. with rifle sights. Mfd. by U.S. Repeating Arms.

MODEL 1400 SKEET GUN . . . . NiB $525 Ex $420 Gd $375
Same as standard Model 1400 except 12 and 20 ga. only,
26-inch vent-rib bbl., SK choke, semi-fancy walnut stock and
forearm. Weight: 7.25 to 7.5 lbs. Made from 1965 to 1968.
Also available with Winchester recoil reduction system (add
$50 to value).

MODEL 1400 TRAP GUN
Same as standard Model 1400 except 12 ga. only with 30-inch
vent-rib bbl., F choke. Semi-fancy walnut stock, straight or
Monte Carlo trap style. Also available with Winchester recoil
reduction system. Weight: About 8.25 lbs. Made from 1965
to 1968.
w/straight stock . . . . NiB $435 Ex $320 Gd $220
w/Monte Carlo stock . . . . NiB $455 Ex $340 Gd $245
w/recoil reduction system, add. $150

MODEL 1500 XTR
SEMIAUTOMATIC. . . . . NiB $465 Ex $300 Gd $290
Gas-operated. Gauges: 12 and 20 (2.75-inch chambers). Bbl.:
Plain or vent rib; 28-inch; WinChoke (interchangeable tubes
IC-M-F). American walnut stock and forend; checkered grip
and forend. Weight: 7.25 lbs. Made from 1978 to 1982.

MODEL 1885 SINGLE-SHOT
SHOTGUN . . . . NiB $4377 Ex $3554 Gd $2566
Falling-block action, same as Model 1885 Rifle. Highwall
receiver. Solid frame or takedown. 20 ga. 3-inch chamber.

SHOTGUNS

Winchester Ranger Deer

Winchester Ranger Slide-Action

Winchester Model 1885
Single-Shot

Winchester Model 1
Field Super-X

Winchester Xpert
96 Field

Winchester Xpert
96 Trap

26-inch bbl.; plain, matted or matted rib; Cyl. bore, M or F choke. Weight: About 5.5 lbs. Straight-grip stock and forearm. Made from 1914 to 1916.

MODEL 1887 LEVER-ACTION SHOTGUN
First of John Browning's patent shotgun designs produced by Winchester. 10 or 12 ga. on casehardened frame fitted w/20-inch blued, cylinder bore or full choke 30- or 32-inch bbl. Plain or checkered walnut stock and forend. Made from 1887 to 1901.

10 or 12 ga. Standard
model . . . . NiB $4188 Ex $3765 Gd $3287
10 or 12 ga. Deluxe model . . . NiB $9233 Ex $8977 Gd $6450
10 or 12 ga. Riot Gun . . . . NiB $2770 Ex $2256 Gd $1656
w/.70-150 Ratchet rifled bbl.
.70 cal. rifle/87 produced). . . NiB $4350 Ex $3000 Gd $2275
w/3 or 4 blade Del. Damascus bbl., add 20%

MODEL 1901 LEVER-ACTION SHOTGUN
Same general specifications as Model 1887, of which this is a redesigned version. 10 ga. only. Made from 1901 to 1920.
Standard model . . . . NiB $4379 Ex $3988 Gd $3500
Deluxe model . . . . NiB $6100 Ex $4988 Gd $3360

MODEL 1911 AUTO-
LOADING SHOTGUN . . . . NiB $755 Ex $655 Gd $500
Hammerless. Takedown. 12 gauge only. Four round tubular magazine. Bbl.: plain, 26- to 32-inch, standard borings. Weight: About 8.5 lbs. Plain or checkered pistol-grip stock and forearm. Made from 1911 to 1925.

RANGER DEER COMBINATION . . . NiB $455 Ex $365 Gd $245
Gauge: 12, 3-inch Magnum. Three round magazine. Bbl.: 24-inch Cyl. bore deer bbl. and 28-inch vent rib bbl. with WinChoke system. Weight: 7.25 lbs. Made from 1987 to 1990.

SUPER-X MODEL I
AUTO FIELD GUN . . . . NiB $390 Ex $280 Gd $245
Gas-operated. Takedown.12 ga. 2.75-inch chamber Four round magazine. Bbl.: Vent rib 26-inch IC; 28-inch M or F; 30-inch F choke. Weight: About 7 lbs. Checkered pistol-grip stock. Made 1974 to 1984.

SUPER-X MODEL I SKEET GUN . . . NiB $977 Ex $755 Gd $590
Same as Super-X Field Gun except has 26-inch bbl., SK choke, skeet-style stock and forearm of select walnut. Made 1974 to 1984.

Woodward
Single-Shot Trap

Woodward O/U
Special Trap Grade

SUPER-X MODEL I TRAP GUN
Same as Super-X Field Gun except has 30-inch bbl., IM or F choke, trap-style stock (straight or Monte Carlo comb) and forearm of select walnut, recoil pad. Made from 1974 to 1984.
w/straight stock . . . . NiB $790 Ex $588 Gd $425
w/Monte Carlo stock . . . . NiB $875 Ex $655 Gd $470

XPERT MODEL 96 O/U
FIELD GUN. . . . . NiB $975 Ex $770 Gd $677
Boxlock action similar to Model 101. Plain receiver. Auto ejectors. Selective single trigger. Gauges: 12, 20. 3-inch chambers. Bbl.: Vent rib; 26-inch IC/M; 28-inch M/F, 30-inch F/F choke (12 ga. only). Weight: 6.25 to 8.25 lbs. depending on ga. and bbls. Checkered pistol-grip stock and forearm. Made from 1976-81 for Olin Corp. at its Olin-Kodensha facility in Japan.

XPERT MODEL 96 SKEET GUN . . . NiB $975 Ex $770 Gd $677
Same as Xpert Field Gun except has 2.75-inch chambers, 27-inch bbls., SK choke, skeet-style stock and forearm. Made 1976 to 1981.

XPERT MODEL 96 TRAP GUN
Same as Xpert Field Gun except 12 ga. only, 2.75-inch chambers, has 30-inch bbls., IM/F or F/F choke, trap-style stock (straight or Monte Carlo comb) with recoil pad. Made from 1976 to 1981.
w/straight stock . . . . NiB $975 Ex $770 Gd $677
w/Monte Carlo stock . . . . . . NiB $1133 Ex $990 Gd $697

JAMES WOODWARD & SONS —
London, England

James Woodward & Sons was acquired by James Purdey & Sons after World War II.

BEST QUALITY HAMMERLESS DOUBLE
Sidelock. Automatic ejectors. Double triggers or single trigger. Built to order in all standard gauges, bbl. lengths, boring and other specifications. Made as a field gun, pigeon and wildfowl gun, skeet gun or trap gun. Manufactured prior to World War II.
12 ga. w/double triggers . . . . NiB $30,000 Ex $22,700 Gd $18,900
20 ga. w/double triggers . . . . NiB $33,000 Ex $26,890 Gd $18,700
28 ga. w/double triggers . . . . NiB $40,600 Ex $33,560 Gd $25,000
.410 ga. w/double triggers . . . NiB $45,000 Ex $36,900 Gd $25,000
w/selective single trigger, add 10%

BEST QUALITY O/U SHOTGUN
Sidelock. Automatic ejectors. Double triggers or single trigger. Built to order in all standard gauges, bbl. lengths, boring and other specifications, including Special Trap Grade with vent rib. Woodward introduced this type of gun in 1908. Made until World War II.
12 ga. w/double triggers . . . . NiB $31,660 Ex $25,850 Gd $20,000
20 ga. w/double triggers . . . . NiB $42,500 Ex $35,980 Gd $25,500
28 ga. w/double triggers . . . . NiB $55,000 Ex $44,900 Gd $32,000
.410 ga. .410 w/double triggers . . . NiB $63,000 Ex $49,800 Gd $35,000
w/single trigger, add 10%

BEST QUALITY
SINGLE-SHOT TRAP . NiB $14,860 Ex $12,790 Gd $10,000
Sidelock. Mechanical features of the O/U gun. Vent rib bbl. 12 ga. only. Built to customer's specifications and measurements, including type and amount of checkering, carving and engraving. Made prior to World War II.

ZEPHYR — Manufactured by Victor Sarasqueta Company, Eibar, Spain

MODEL 1
O/U SHOTGUN . . . . NiB $1341 Ex $1083 Gd $778
Same general specifications as Field Model O/U except with more elaborate engraving, finer wood and checkering. Imported by Stoeger 1930s- to 1951.

MODEL 2
O/U SHOTGUN . . . . NiB $1746 Ex $1393 Gd $994
Sidelock. Auto ejectors. Gauges: 12, 16, 20, 28 and .410. Bbls.: 25 to 30 inches most common. Modest scroll engraving on receiver and sideplates. Checkered, straight-grain select walnut buttstock and forend. Imported by Stoeger 1930s to 1951.

MODEL 3
O/U SHOTGUN . . . . NiB $2369 Ex $1888 Gd $1337
Same general specifications as Zephyr Model 2 O/U except with more elaborate engraving, finer wood and checkering. Imported by Stoeger 1930s to 1951.

MODEL 400E FIELD GRADE DOUBLE-BARREL SHOTGUN
Anson & Deeley boxlock system. Gauges: 12 16, 20, 28 and .410. Bbls.: 25 to 30 inches. Weight: 4.5 lbs. (.410) to 6.25 lbs. (12 ga.). Checkered French walnut buttstock and forearm. Modest scroll engraving on bbls., receiver and trigger guard. Imported by Stoeger 1930s to 1950s.
12, 16 or 20 ga. . . . . NiB $2166 Ex $1388 Gd $1000
28 ga. or .410 . . . . NiB $1877 Ex $1497 Gd $1000
w/selective single trigger, add $250

SHOTGUNS

Zephyr Crown, Premier and Royal Grades (top to bottom)

MODEL 401 E SKEET GRADE DOUBLE-BARREL SHOTGUN
Same general specifications as Field Grade except with beavertail forearm. Bbls.: 25 to 28 inches. Imported by Stoeger
1930s to 1950s.
12, 16 or 20 ga. . . . . NiB $1954 Ex $1600 Gd $1216
28 ga., or .410 . . . . NiB $2144 Ex $1698 Gd $1277
w/selective single trigger, add $450
w/non-selective single trigger, add $300

MODEL 402E DELUXE DOUBLE-BARREL
SHOTGUN . . . . NiB $2455 Ex $2089 Gd $1466
Same general specifications as Model 400E Field Grade except
for custom refinements. The action was carefully hand-honed
for smoother operation; finer, elaborate engraving throughout,
plus higher quality wood in stock and forearm. Imported by
Stoeger 1930s to 1950s.

CROWN GRADE. . . . . NiB $1800 Ex $1498 Gd $1056
Boxlock. Gauges: 12, 16, 20, 28 and .410. Bbls.: 25 to 30
inches standard but any lengths could be ordered. Weight: 6
lbs., 4 oz. (.410) to 7 lbs., 4 oz. (12 ga.). Checkered Spanish
walnut stock and beavertail forearm. Receiver engraved with
scroll patterns. Imported by Stoeger 1938 to 1951.

FIELD MODEL O/U SHOTGUN . . NiB $988 Ex $745 Gd $566
Anson & Deeley boxlock. Auto ejectors. Gauges: 12, 16 and
20. Bbls.: 25 to 30 inches standard- full-length matt rib. Double
triggers. Checkered buttstock and forend. Light scroll engraving
on receiver. Imported by Stoeger 1930s to 1951.

HONKER SINGLE-SHOT
SHOTGUN . . . . NiB $676 Ex $580 Gd $390
Sidelock. Gauge: 10; 3.5-inch magnum. 36-inch vent rib barrel w/F choke. Weight: 10.5 lbs. Checkered select Spanish
walnut buttstock and beavertail forend; recoil pad. Imported
by Stoeger 1950s to 1972.

PINEHURST DOUBLE-BARREL
SHOTGUN . . . . NiB $1388 Ex $1190 Gd $800
Boxlock. Gauges: 12, 16, 20, 28 and .410. Bbls.: 25 to 28
inches most common. Checkered, select walnut buttstock and
forend. Selective single trigger and auto ejectors. Imported by
Stoeger 1950s to 1972.

PREMIER GRADE DOUBLE-BARREL
SHOTGUN . . . . NiB $2870 Ex $2300 Gd $1560
Sidelock. Gauges: 12, 16, 20, 28 and .410. Bbls.: Any length,
but 25 to 30 inches most popular. Weight: 4.5 lbs. (.410) to 7
lbs. (12 ga.). Checkered high-grade French walnut buttstock
and forend. Imported by Stoeger 1930s to 1951.

ROYAL GRADE DOUBLE-BARREL
SHOTGUN . . . . NiB $4388 Ex $2287 Gd $2077
Same general specifications as the Premier Grade except
with more elaborate engraving, finer checkering and wood.
Imported by Stoeger 1930s to 1951.

STERLINGWORTH II DOUBLE-BARREL
SHOTGUN . . . . NiB $1000 Ex $790 Gd $678
Genuine sidelocks with color-casehardened sideplates.
Gauges: 12, 16, 20 and .410. Bbls.: 25 to 30 inches. Weight:
6 lbs., 4 oz. (.410) to 7 lbs., 4 oz. (12 ga.). Select Spanish
walnut buttstock and beavertail forearm. Light scroll engrav-
ing on receiver and sideplates. Automatic, sliding-tang safety.
Imported by Stoeger 1950s to 1972.

THUNDERBIRD DOUBLE-BARREL
SHOTGUN . . . . NiB $1221 Ex $900 Gd $755
Sidelock. Gauges: 12 and 10 Magnum. Bbls.: 32-inch, both F
choke. Weight: 8 lbs., 8 oz. (12 ga.), 12 lbs. (10 ga.). Receiver
elaborately engraved with waterfowl scenes. Checkered select
Spanish walnut buttstock and beavertail forend. Plain extractors, double triggers. Imported by Stoeger 1950 to 1972.

UPLAND KING DOUBLE-BARREL
SHOTGUN . . . . NiB $1290 Ex $1066 Gd $886
Sidelock. Gauges: 12, 16, 20, 28 and .410. Bbls.: 25 to 28
inches most popular. Checkered buttstock and forend of select
walnut. Selective single trigger and auto ejectors. Imported by
Stoeger 1950 to 1972.

UPLANDER 4E DOUBLE-BARREL
SHOTGUN . . . . NiB $900 Ex $688 Gd $525
Same general specifications as the Zephyr Sterlingworth II
except with selective auto ejectors and highly polished sideplates. Imported by Stoeger 1951 to 1972.

WOODLANDER II DOUBLE-BARREL
SHOTGUN . . . . NiB $645 Ex $465 Gd $377
Boxlock. Gauges: 12, 20 and .410. Bbls.: 25 to 30 inches.
Weight: 6 lbs., 4 oz. (.410) to 7 lbs., 4 oz. (12 ga.). Checkered
Spanish walnut stock and beavertail forearm. Engraved receiv-
er. Imported by Stoeger 1950 to 1972.

Index

INDEX

INDEX

INDEX

INDEX